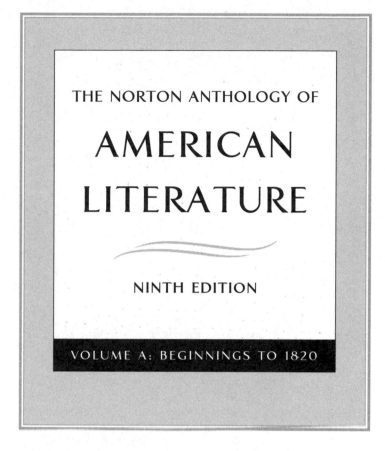

THE NORTON ANTHOLOGY OF

AMERICAN

LITERATURE

NINTH EDITION

VOLUME A: BEGINNINGS TO 1820

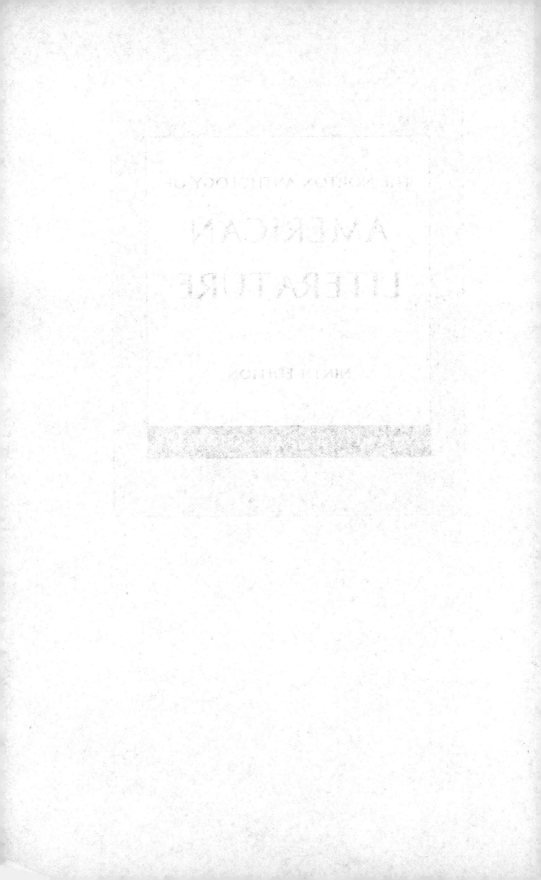

Michael A. Elliott
ASA GRIGGS CANDLER PROFESSOR OF ENGLISH AND AMERICAN STUDIES
EMORY UNIVERSITY

Sandra M. Gustafson
PROFESSOR OF ENGLISH AND AMERICAN STUDIES
UNIVERSITY OF NOTRE DAME

Amy Hungerford
BIRD WHITE HOUSUM PROFESSOR OF ENGLISH AND AMERICAN STUDIES
AND DIRECTOR OF THE DIVISION OF THE HUMANITIES
YALE UNIVERSITY

Mary Loeffelholz
PROFESSOR OF ENGLISH
NORTHEASTERN UNIVERSITY

THE NORTON ANTHOLOGY OF

AMERICAN LITERATURE

NINTH EDITION

Robert S. Levine, *General Editor*
PROFESSOR OF ENGLISH AND
DISTINGUISHED UNIVERSITY PROFESSOR AND
DISTINGUISHED SCHOLAR TEACHER
University of Maryland, College Park

VOLUME A: BEGINNINGS TO 1820

W · W · NORTON & COMPANY
NEW YORK · LONDON

W. W. Norton & Company has been independent since its founding in 1923, when William Warder Norton and Mary D. Herter Norton first published lectures delivered at the People's Institute, the adult education division of New York City's Cooper Union. The firm soon expanded its program beyond the Institute, publishing books by celebrated academics from America and abroad. By midcentury, the two major pillars of Norton's publishing program—trade books and college texts—were firmly established. In the 1950s, the Norton family transferred control of the company to its employees, and today—with a staff of four hundred and a comparable number of trade, college, and professional titles published each year—W. W. Norton & Company stands as the largest and oldest publishing house owned wholly by its employees.

Editor: Julia Reidhead
Managing Editor, College: Marian Johnson
Manuscript Editors: Kurt Wildermuth, Harry Haskell, Michael Fleming, Candace Levy
Assistant Editor: Rachel Taylor
Managing Editor, College Digital Media: Kim Yi
Media Editor: Carly Fraser Doria
Media Project Editor: Kristin Sheerin
Marketing Manager, Literature: Kimberly Bowers
Production Manager: Sean Mintus
Cover Design: Tiani Kennedy
Photo Editor: Cat Abelman
Permissions Manager: Megan Jackson Schindel
Permissions Clearing: Margaret Gorenstein
Composition: Westchester Book Group

Since this page cannot legibly accommodate all the copyright notices,
the Permissions Acknowledgments constitute an extension of the copyright page.

Library of Congress Cataloging-in-Publication Data

Names: Levine, Robert S. (Robert Steven), 1953–editor.
Title: The Norton anthology of American literature / Robert S. Levine, general editor ;
 Michael A. Elliott, Sandra M. Gustafson, Amy Hungerford, Mary Loeffelholz.
Description: Ninth edition. | New York : W. W. Norton & Company, 2017. |
 Includes bibliographical references and index.
Identifiers: LCCN 2016043347 | **ISBN 9780393935714** (pbk., v. a : alk. paper) |
 ISBN 9780393264470 (pbk., v. b : alk. paper) | ISBN 9780393264487
 (pbk., v. c : alk. paper) | ISBN 9780393264494 (pbk., v. d : alk. paper) |
 ISBN 9780393264500 (pbk., v. e : alk. paper)
Subjects: LCSH: American literature. | United States—Literary collections.
Classification: LCC PS507 .N65 2016 | DDC 810.8—dc23
 LC record available at https://lccn.loc.gov/2016043347

W. W. Norton & Company, Inc., 500 Fifth Avenue, New York, NY 10110
wwnorton.com

W. W. Norton & Company Ltd., 15 Carlisle Street, London W1D 3BS

4 5 6 7 8 9 0

Contents

Preface to the Ninth Edition

The Ninth Edition of *The Norton Anthology of American Literature* is the first for me as General Editor; for the Eighth Edition, I served as Associate General Editor under longstanding General Editor Nina Baym. On the occasion of a new general editorship, we have undertaken one of the most extensive revisions in our long publishing history. Three new section editors have joined the team: Sandra M. Gustafson, Professor of English and Concurrent Professor of American Studies at the University of Notre Dame, who succeeds Wayne Franklin and Philip Gura as editor of "American Literature, Beginnings to 1820"; Michael A. Elliott, Professor of English at Emory University, who succeeds Nina Baym, Robert S. Levine, and Jeanne Campbell Reesman as editor of "American Literature, 1865–1914"; and Amy Hungerford, Professor of English and American Studies at Yale University, who succeeds Jerome Klinkowitz and Patricia B. Wallace as editor of "American Literature since 1945." These editors join Robert S. Levine, editor of "American Literature, 1820–1865," and Mary Loeffelholz, editor of "American Literature, 1914–1945." Each editor, new or continuing, is a well-known expert in the relevant field or period and has ultimate responsibility for his or her section of the anthology, but we have worked closely from first to last to rethink all aspects of this new edition. Volume introductions, author headnotes, thematic clusters, annotations, illustrations, and bibliographies have all been updated and revised. We have also added a number of new authors, selections, and thematic clusters. We are excited about the outcome of our collaboration and anticipate that, like the previous eight editions, this edition of *The Norton Anthology of American Literature* will continue to lead the field.

From the anthology's inception in 1979, the editors have had three main aims: first, to present a rich and substantial enough variety of works to enable teachers to build courses according to their own vision of American literary history (thus, teachers are offered more authors and more selections than they will probably use in any one course); second, to make the anthology self-sufficient by featuring many works in their entirety along with extensive selections for individual authors; third, to balance traditional interests with developing critical concerns in a way that allows for the complex, rigorous, and capacious study of American literary traditions. As early as 1979, we anthologized work by Anne Bradstreet, Mary Rowlandson, Sarah Kemble Knight, Phillis Wheatley, Margaret Fuller, Harriet Beecher Stowe, Frederick Douglass, Sarah Orne Jewett, Kate Chopin, Mary E. Wilkins Freeman, Booker T. Washington, Charles W. Chesnutt, Edith Wharton,

W. E. B. Du Bois, and other writers who were not yet part of a standard canon. Yet we never shortchanged writers—such as Franklin, Emerson, Whitman, Hawthorne, Melville, Dickinson, Hemingway, Fitzgerald, and Faulkner—whose work many students expected to read in their American literature courses, and whom most teachers then and now would not think of doing without.

The so-called canon wars of the 1980s and 1990s usefully initiated a review of our understanding of American literature, a review that has enlarged the number and diversity of authors now recognized as contributors to the totality of American literature. The traditional writers look different in this expanded context, and they also appear different according to which of their works are selected. Teachers and students remain committed to the idea of the literary—that writers strive to produce artifacts that are both intellectually serious and formally skillful—but believe more than ever that writers should be understood in relation to their cultural and historical situations. We address the complex interrelationships between literature and history in the volume introductions, author headnotes, chronologies, and some of the footnotes. As in previous editions, we have worked with detailed suggestions from many teachers on how best to present the authors and selections. We have gained insights as well from the students who use the anthology. Thanks to questionnaires, face-to-face and phone discussions, letters, and email, we have been able to listen to those for whom this book is intended. For the Ninth Edition, we have drawn on the careful commentary of over 240 reviewers and reworked aspects of the anthology accordingly.

Our new materials continue the work of broadening the canon by representing thirteen new writers in depth, without sacrificing widely assigned writers, many of whose selections have been reconsidered, reselected, and expanded. Our aim is always to provide extensive enough selections to do the writers justice, including complete works wherever possible. Our Ninth Edition offers complete longer works, including Hawthorne's *The Scarlet Letter* and Kate Chopin's *The Awakening*, and such new and recently added works as Margaret Fuller's *The Great Lawsuit*, Abraham Cahan's *Yekl: A Tale of the New York Ghetto*, Nella Larsen's *Passing*, Katherine Anne Porter's *Pale Horse, Pale Rider*, Nathanael West's *The Day of the Locust*, and August Wilson's *Fences*. Two complete works—Eugene O'Neill's *Long Day's Journey into Night* and Tennessee Williams's *A Streetcar Named Desire*—are exclusive to *The Norton Anthology of American Literature*. Charles Brockden Brown, Louisa May Alcott, Upton Sinclair, and Junot Díaz are among the writers added to the prior edition, and to this edition we have introduced John Rollin Ridge, Constance Fenimore Woolson, George Saunders, and Natasha Trethewey, among others. We have also expanded and in some cases reconfigured such central figures as Franklin, Hawthorne, Dickinson, Twain, and Hemingway, offering new approaches in the headnotes, along with some new selections. In fact, the headnotes and, in many cases, selections for such frequently assigned authors as William Bradford, Washington Irving, James Fenimore Cooper, William Cullen Bryant, Lydia Maria Child, Henry Wadsworth Longfellow, Ralph Waldo Emerson, Harriet Beecher Stowe, Mark Twain, William Dean Howells, Henry James, Kate

Chopin, W. E. B. Du Bois, Edith Wharton, Willa Cather, and William Faulkner have been revised, updated, and in some cases entirely rewritten in light of recent scholarship. The Ninth Edition further expands its selections of women writers and writers from diverse ethnic, racial, and regional backgrounds—always with attention to the critical acclaim that recognizes their contributions to the American literary record. New and recently added writers such as Samson Occom, Jane Johnston Schoolcraft, John Rollin Ridge, and Sarah Winnemucca, along with the figures represented in "Voices from Native America," enable teachers to bring early Native American writing and oratory into their syllabi, or should they prefer, to focus on these selections as a freestanding unit leading toward the moment after 1945 when Native writers fully entered the mainstream of literary activity.

We are pleased to continue our popular innovation of topical gatherings of short texts that illuminate the cultural, historical, intellectual, and literary concerns of their respective periods. Designed to be taught in a class period or two, or used as background, each of the sixteen clusters consists of brief, carefully excerpted primary and (in one case) secondary texts, about six to ten per cluster, and an introduction. Diverse voices—many new to the anthology—highlight a range of views current when writers of a particular time period were active, and thus allow students better to understand some of the large issues that were being debated at particular historical moments. For example, in "Slavery, Race, and the Making of American Literature," texts by David Walker, William Lloyd Garrison, Angelina Grimké, Sojourner Truth, James M. Whitfield, and Martin R. Delany speak to the great paradox of pre–Civil War America: the contradictory rupture between the realities of slavery and the nation's ideals of freedom.

The Ninth Edition strengthens this feature with eight new and revised clusters attuned to the requests of teachers. To help students address the controversy over race and aesthetics in *Adventures of Huckleberry Finn*, we have revised a cluster in Volume C that shows what some of the leading critics of the past few decades thought was at stake in reading and interpreting slavery and race in Twain's canonical novel. New to Volume A is "American Literature and the Varieties of Religious Expression," which includes selections by Elizabeth Ashbridge, John Woolman, and John Marrant, while Volume B offers "Science and Technology in the Pre–Civil War Nation." Volume C newly features "Becoming American in the Gilded Age," and we continue to include the useful "Modernist Manifestos" in Volume D. We have added to the popular "Creative Nonfiction" in Volume E new selections by David Foster Wallace and Hunter S. Thompson, who join such writers as Jamaica Kincaid and Joan Didion.

The Ninth Edition features an expanded illustration program, both of the black-and-white images, 145 of which are placed throughout the volumes, and of the color plates so popular in the last two editions. In selecting color plates—from Elizabeth Graham's embroidered map of Washington, D.C., at the start of the nineteenth century to Jeff Wall's "After 'Invisible Man'" at the beginning of the twenty-first—the editors aim to provide images relevant to literary works in the anthology while depicting arts and artifacts representative of each era. In addition, graphic works—segments from the colonial

children's classic *The New-England Primer* and from Art Spiegelman's canonical graphic novel, *Maus*, and a facsimile page of Emily Dickinson manuscript, along with the many new illustrations—open possibilities for teaching visual texts.

Period-by-Period Revisions

Volume A, Beginnings to 1820. Sandra M. Gustafson, the new editor of Volume A, has substantially revised the volume. Prior editions of Volume A were broken into two historical sections, with two introductions and a dividing line at the year 1700; Gustafson has dropped that artificial divide to tell a more coherent and fluid story (in her new introduction) about the variety of American literatures during this long period. The volume continues to feature narratives by early European explorers of the North American continent as they encountered and attempted to make sense of the diverse cultures they met, and as they sought to justify their aim of claiming the territory for Europeans. These are precisely the issues foregrounded by the revised cluster "First Encounters: Early European Accounts of Native America," which gathers writings by Hernán Cortés, Samuel de Champlain, Robert Juet, and others, including the newly added Thomas Harriot. In addition to the standing material from *The Bay Psalm Book*, we include new material by Roger Williams; additional poems by Annis Boudinot Stockton; Abigail Adams's famous letter urging her husband to "Remember the Ladies"; an additional selection from Olaudah Equiano on his post-emancipation travels; and Charles Brockden Brown's "Memoirs of Carwin the Biloquist" (the complete "prequel" to his first novel, *Wieland*). We continue to offer the complete texts of Rowlandson's enormously influential *A Narrative of the Captivity and Restoration of Mrs. Mary Rowlandson*, Benjamin Franklin's *Autobiography* (which remains one of the most compelling works on the emergence of an "American" self), Royall Tyler's popular play *The Contrast*, and Hannah Foster's novel *The Coquette*, which uses a real-life tragedy to meditate on the proper role of well-bred women in the new republic and testifies to the existence of a female audience for the popular novels of the period. New to this volume is Washington Irving, a writer who looks back to colonial history and forward to Jacksonian America. The inclusion of Irving in both Volumes A and B, with one key overlapping selection, points to continuities and changes between the two volumes.

Five new and revised thematic clusters of texts highlight themes central to Volume A. In addition to "First Encounters," we have included "Native American Oral Literature," "American Literature and the Varieties of Religious Expression," "Ethnographic and Naturalist Writings," and "Native American Eloquence: Negotiation and Resistance." "Native American Oral Literature" features creation stories, trickster tales, oratory, and poetry from a spectrum of traditions, while "Native American Eloquence" collects speeches and accounts by Canassatego and Native American women (both new to the volume), Pontiac, Chief Logan (as cited by Thomas Jefferson), and Tecumseh, which, as a group, illustrate the centuries-long pattern of initial peaceful contact between Native Americans and whites mutating into bitter and violent conflict. This cluster, which focuses on Native Americans' points of view, complements "First Encounters," which focuses on European

colonizers' points of view. The Native American presence in the volume is further expanded with increased representation of Samson Occom, which includes an excerpt from his sermon at the execution of Moses Paul, and the inclusion of Sagoyewatha in "American Literature and the Varieties of Religious Expression." Strategically located between the Congregationalist Protestant (or late-Puritan) Jonathan Edwards and the Enlightenment figure Franklin, this cluster brings together works from the perspectives of the major religious groups of the early Americas, including Quakerism (poems by Francis Daniel Pastorius, selections from autographical narratives of Elizabeth Ashbridge and John Woolman), Roman Catholicism (poems by Sor Juana, two Jesuit Relations, with biographical accounts of Father Isaac Jogues and Kateri Tekakwitha), dissenting Protestantism (Marrant), Judaism (Rebecca Samuel), and indigenous beliefs (Sagoyewatha). The new cluster "Ethnographic and Naturalist Writings" includes writings by Sarah Kemble Knight and William Byrd, along with new selections by Alexander Hamilton, William Bartram, and Hendrick Aupaumut. With this cluster, the new cluster on science and technology in Volume B, and a number of new selections and revisions in Volumes C, D, and E, the Ninth Edition pays greater attention to the impact of science on American literary traditions.

Volume B, American Literature, 1820–1865. Under the editorship of Robert S. Levine, this volume over the past several editions has become more diverse. Included here are the complete texts of Emerson's *Nature*, Hawthorne's *Scarlet Letter*, Thoreau's *Walden*, Douglass's *Narrative*, Whitman's *Song of Myself*, Melville's *Benito Cereno* and *Billy Budd*, Rebecca Harding Davis's *Life in the Iron Mills*, and Margaret Fuller's *The Great Lawsuit*. At the same time, aware of the important role of African American writers in the period, and the omnipresence of race and slavery as literary and political themes, we have recently added two major African American writers, William Wells Brown and Frances E. W. Harper, along with Douglass's novella *The Heroic Slave*. Thoreau's "Plea for Captain John Brown," a generous selection from Stowe's *Uncle Tom's Cabin*, and the cluster "Slavery, Race, and the Making of American Literature" also help remind students of how central slavery was to the literary and political life of the nation during this period. "Native Americans: Resistance and Removal" gathers oratory and writings—by Native Americans such as Black Hawk and whites such as Ralph Waldo Emerson—protesting Andrew Jackson's ruthless national policy of Indian removal. Newly added is a selection from *The Life and Adventures of Joaquín Murieta*, by the Native American writer John Rollin Ridge. This potboiler of a novel, set in the new state of California, emerged from the debates that began during the Indian removal period. Through the figure of the legendary Mexican bandit Murieta, who fights back against white expansionists, Ridge responds to the violence encouraged by Jackson and subsequent white leaders as they laid claim to the continent. Political themes, far from diluting the literary imagination of American authors, served to inspire some of the most memorable writing of the pre-Civil War period.

Women writers recently added to Volume B include Lydia Huntley Sigourney, the Native American writer Jane Johnston Schoolcraft, and

Louisa May Alcott. Recently added prose fiction includes chapters from Cooper's *The Last of the Mohicans*, Sedgwick's *Hope Leslie*, and Melville's *Moby-Dick*, along with Poe's "The Black Cat" and Hawthorne's "Wakefield." For the first time, we print Melville's "Hawthorne and His Mosses" as it appeared in the 1850 *Literary World*. Poetry by Emily Dickinson is now presented in the texts established by R. W. Franklin and includes a facsimile page from Fascicle 10. For this edition we have added several poems by Dickinson that were inspired by the Civil War. Other selections added to this edition include Fanny Fern's amusing sketch "Writing 'Compositions,'" the chapter in Frederick Douglass's *My Bondage and My Freedom* on his resistance to the slave-breaker Covey, three poems by Melville ("Dupont's Round Fight," "A Utilitarian View of the Monitor's Fight," and "Art"), and Whitman's "The Sleepers."

Perhaps the most significant addition to Volume B is the cluster "Science and Technology in the Pre–Civil War Nation," with selections by the canonical writers Charles Dickens, Edgar Allan Poe, and Frederick Douglass, by the scientists Jacob Bigelow and Alexander Humboldt, and by the editor-writer Harriet Farley. The cluster calls attention to the strong interest in science and technology throughout this period and should provide a rich context for reconsidering works such as Thoreau's *Walden* and Melville's "The Paradise of Bachelors and the Tartarus of Maids." In an effort to underscore the importance of science and technology to Poe and Hawthorne in particular, we have added two stories that directly address these topics: Poe's "The Facts in the Case of M. Valdemar" and Hawthorne's "The Artist of the Beautiful" (which reads nicely in relation to his "The Birth-Mark" and "Rappaccini's Daughter"). Emerson, Whitman, and Dickinson are among the many other authors in Volume B who had considerable interest in science.

Volume C, American Literature, 1865–1914. Newly edited by Michael A. Elliott, the volume includes expanded selections of key works, as well as new ones that illustrate how many of the struggles of this period prefigure our own. In addition to complete longer works such as Twain's *Adventures of Huckleberry Finn*, Chopin's *The Awakening*, James's *Daisy Miller*, and Stephen Crane's *Maggie: A Girl of the Streets*, the Ninth Edition now includes the complete text of *Yekl: A Tale of the New York Ghetto*, a highly influential novella of immigrant life that depicts the pressures facing newly arrived Jews in the nation's largest metropolis. Also new is a substantial selection from Sarah Orne Jewett's *The Country of the Pointed Firs*, a masterpiece of literary regionalism that portrays a remote seaside community facing change.

Americans are still reflecting on the legacy of the Civil War, and we have added two works approaching that subject from different angles. Constance Fenimore Woolson's "Rodman the Keeper" tells the story of a Union veteran who maintains a cemetery in the South. In "The Private History of a Campaign That Failed," Mark Twain reflects with wit and insight on his own brief experience in the war. In the Eighth Edition, we introduced a section on the critical controversy surrounding race and the conclusion of *Adventures of Huckleberry Finn*. That section remains as important as ever, and new additions incorporate a recent debate about the value of an expurgated edition of the novel.

We have substantially revised clusters designed to give students a sense of the cultural context of the period. New selections in "Realism and Naturalism" demonstrate what was at stake in the debate over realism, among them a feminist response from Charlotte Perkins Gilman. "Becoming American in the Gilded Age," a new cluster, introduces students to writing about wealth and citizenship at a time when the nation was undergoing transformation. Selections from one of Horatio Alger's popular novels of economic uplift, Andrew Carnegie's "Gospel of Wealth," and Charles W. Chesnutt's "The Future American" together reveal how questions about the composition of the nation both influenced the literature of this period and prefigured contemporary debates on immigration, cultural diversity, and the concentration of wealth.

The turn of the twentieth century was a time of immense literary diversity. "Voices from Native America" brings together a variety of expressive forms—oratory, memoir, ethnography—through which Native Americans sought to represent themselves. It includes new selections by Francis LaFlesche, Zitkala Ša, and Chief Joseph. For the first time, we include the complete text of José Martí's "Our America," in a new translation by Martí biographer Alfred J. López. By instructor request, we have added fiction and nonfiction by African American authors: Charles W. Chesnutt's "Po' Sandy," Pauline Hopkins's "Talma Gordon," and expanded selections from W. E. B. Du Bois's *Souls of Black Folk* and James Weldon Johnson's *Autobiography of an Ex-Colored Man*.

Volume D, American Literature 1914–1945. Edited by Mary Loeffelholz, Volume D offers a number of complete longer works—Eugene O'Neill's *Long Day's Journey into Night* (exclusive to the Norton Anthology), William Faulkner's *As I Lay Dying*, and Willa Cather's *My Ántonia*. To these we have added Nella Larsen's *Passing*, which replaces *Quicksand*, and Nathanael West's *The Day of the Locust*. We added *Passing* in response to numerous requests from instructors and students who regard it as one of the most compelling treatments of racial passing in American literature. The novel also offers rich descriptions of the social and racial geographies of Chicago and New York City. West's darkly comic *The Day of the Locust* similarly offers rich descriptions of the social and racial geography of Los Angeles. West's novel can at times seem bleak and not "politically correct," but in many ways it is the first great American novel about the film industry, and it also has much to say about the growth of California in the early decades of the twentieth century. New selections by Zora Neale Hurston ("Sweat") and John Steinbeck ("The Chrysanthemums") further contribute to the volume's exploration of issues connected with racial and social geographies.

Selections by Ezra Pound, T. S. Eliot, Marianne Moore, Hart Crane, and Langston Hughes encourage students and teachers to contemplate the interrelation of modernist aesthetics with ethnic, regional, and popular writing. In "Modernist Manifestos," F. T. Marinetti, Mina Loy, Ezra Pound, Willa Cather, William Carlos Williams, and Langston Hughes show how the manifesto as a form exerted a powerful influence on international modernism in all the arts. Another illuminating cluster addresses central events of the modern period. In "World War I and Its Aftermath," writings by Ernest Hemingway, Gertrude Stein, Jessie Redmon Fauset, and others explore sharply

divided views on the U.S. role in World War I, as well as the radicalizing effect of modern warfare—with 365,000 American casualties—on contemporary writing. We have added to this edition a chapter from Hemingway's first novel, *The Sun Also Rises*, which speaks to the impact of the war on sexuality and gender. Other recent and new additions to Volume D include Faulkner's popular "A Rose for Emily," Katherine Anne Porter's novella *Pale Horse, Pale Rider*, Gertrude Stein's "Objects," Marianne Moore's ambitious longer poem "Marriage," poems by Edgar Lee Masters and Edwin Arlington Robinson, and Jean Toomer's "Blood Burning Moon."

Volume E, American Literature, 1945 to the Present. Amy Hungerford, the new editor of Volume E, has revised the volume to present a wider range of writing in poetry, prose, drama, and nonfiction. As before, the volume offers the complete texts of Tennessee Williams's *A Streetcar Named Desire* (exclusive to this anthology), Arthur Miller's *Death of a Salesman*, Allen Ginsberg's *Howl*, Sam Shepard's *True West*, August Wilson's *Fences*, David Mamet's *Glengarry Glen Ross*, and Louise Glück's long poem *October*. A selection from Art Spiegelman's prize-winning *Maus* opens possibilities for teaching the graphic novel. We also include teachable stand-alone segments from influential novels by Saul Bellow (*The Adventures of Augie March*) and Kurt Vonnegut (*Slaughterhouse-Five*), and, new to this edition, Jack Kerouac (*On the Road*) and Don DeLillo (*White Noise*). The selection from one of DeLillo's most celebrated novels tells what feels like a contemporary story about a nontraditional family navigating an environmental disaster in a climate saturated by mass media. Three newly added stories— Patricia Highsmith's "The Quest for *Blank Claveringi*," Philip K. Dick's "Precious Artifact," and George Saunders's "CivilWarLand in Bad Decline"— reveal the impact of science fiction, fantasy, horror, and (especially in the case of Saunders) mass media on literary fiction. Also appearing for the first time are Edward P. Jones and Lydia Davis, contemporary masters of the short story, who join such short fiction writers as Ann Beattie and Junot Díaz. Recognized literary figures in all genres, ranging from Robert Penn Warren and Elizabeth Bishop to Leslie Marmon Silko and Toni Morrison, continue to be richly represented. In response to instructors' requests, we now include Flannery O'Connor's "A Good Man Is Hard to Find" and James Baldwin's "Sonny's Blues."

One of the most distinctive features of twentieth- and twenty-first-century American literature is a rich vein of African American poetry. This edition adds two contemporary poets from this living tradition: Natasha Trethewey and Tracy K. Smith. Trethewey's selections include personal and historical elegies; Smith draws on cultural materials as diverse as David Bowie's music and the history of the Hubble Space Telescope. These writers join African American poets whose work has long helped define the anthology— Rita Dove, Gwendolyn Brooks, Robert Hayden, Audre Lorde, and others.

This edition gives even greater exposure to literary and social experimentation during the 1960s, 1970s, and beyond. The work of two avant-garde playwrights joins "Postmodern Manifestos" (which pairs nicely with "Modernist Manifestos" in Volume D). Introduced to the anthology through their short, challenging pieces, Charles Ludlam and Richard Foreman cast the mechanics of performance in a new light. Reading their thought pieces in

relation to the volume's complete plays helps raise new questions about how the seemingly more traditional dramatic works engage structures of time, plot, feeling, and spectatorship. To our popular cluster "Creative Nonfiction" we have added a new selection by Joan Didion, from "Slouching Towards Bethlehem," which showcases her revolutionary style of journalism as she comments on experiments with public performance and communal living during the 1960s. A new selection from David Foster Wallace in the same cluster pushes reportage on the Maine Lobster Festival into philosophical inquiry: how can we fairly assess the pain of other creatures? This edition also introduces poet Frank Bidart through his most famous work—*Ellen West*—in which the poet uses experimental forms of verse he pioneered during the 1970s to speak in the voice of a woman battling anorexia. Standing authors in the anthology, notably John Ashbery and Amiri Baraka, fill out the volume's survey of radical change in the forms, and social uses, of literary art.

We are delighted to offer this revised Ninth Edition to teachers and students, and we welcome your comments.

Additional Resources from the Publisher

The Ninth Edition retains the paperback splits format, popular for its flexibility and portability. This format accommodates the many instructors who use the anthology in a two-semester survey, but allows for mixing and matching the five volumes in a variety of courses organized by period or topic, at levels from introductory to advanced. We are also pleased to offer the Ninth Edition in an ebook format. The Digital Anthologies include all the content of the print volumes, with print-corresponding page and line numbers for seamless integration into the print-digital mixed classroom. Annotations are accessible with a click or a tap, encouraging students to use them with minimal interruption to their reading of the text. The e-reading platform facilitates active reading with a powerful annotation tool and allows students to do a full-text search of the anthology and read online or off. The Digital Editions can be accessed from any computer or device with an Internet browser and are available to students at a fraction of the print price at digital.wwnorton.com/americanlit9pre1865 and digital.wwnorton.com/americanlit9post1865. For exam copy access to the Digital Editions and for information on making the Digital Editions available through the campus bookstore or packaging the Digital Editions with the print anthology, instructors should contact their Norton representative.

To give instructors even more flexibility, Norton is making available the full list of 254 Norton Critical Editions. A Norton Critical Edition can be included at a discounted price with either package (Volumes A and B; Volumes C, D, E) or any individual split volume. Each Norton Critical Edition gives students an authoritative, carefully annotated text accompanied by rich contextual and critical materials prepared by an expert in the subject. The publisher also offers the much-praised guide *Writing about American Literature*, by Karen Gocsik (University of California–San Diego) and Coleman Hutchison (University of Texas–Austin), free with either package or any individual split volume.

In addition to the Digital Editions, for students using *The Norton Anthology of American Literature*, the publisher provides a wealth of free

resources at digital.wwnorton.com/americanlit9pre1865 and digital.wwnorton .com/americanlit9post1865. There students will find more than seventy reading-comprehension quizzes on the period introductions and widely taught works with extensive feedback that points them back to the text. Ideal for self-study or homework assignments, Norton's sophisticated quizzing engine allows instructors to track student results and improvement. For over thirty works in the anthology, the sites also offer Close Reading Workshops that walk students step-by-step through analysis of a literary work. Each workshop prompts students to read, reread, consider contexts, and answer questions along the way, making these perfect assignments to build close-reading skills.

The publisher also provides extensive instructor-support materials. New to the Ninth Edition is an online Interactive Instructor's Guide at iig.wwnorton.com/americanlit9/full. Invaluable for course preparation, this resource provides hundreds of teaching notes, discussion questions, and suggested resources from the much-praised *Teaching with* The Norton Anthology of American Literature: *A Guide for Instructors* by Edward Whitley (Lehigh University). Also at this searchable and sortable site are quizzes, images, and lecture PowerPoints for each introduction, topic cluster, and twenty-five widely taught works. A PDF of *Teaching with NAAL* is available for download at wwnorton.com/instructors.

Finally, Norton Coursepacks bring high-quality digital media into a new or existing online course. The coursepack includes all the reading comprehension quizzes (customizable within the coursepack), the Writing about Literature video series, a bank of essay and exam questions, bulleted summaries of the period introductions, and "Making Connections" discussion or essay prompts to encourage students to draw connections across the anthology's authors and works. Coursepacks are available in a variety of formats, including Blackboard, Canvas, Desire2Learn, and Moodle, at no cost to instructors or students.

Editorial Procedures

As in past editions, editorial features—period introductions, headnotes, annotations, and bibliographies—are designed to be concise yet full and to give students necessary information without imposing a single interpretation. The editors have updated all apparatus in response to new scholarship: period introductions have been entirely or substantially rewritten, as have many headnotes. All selected bibliographies and each period's general-resources bibliographies, categorized by Reference Works, Histories, and Literary Criticism, have been thoroughly updated. The Ninth Edition retains three editorial features that help students place their reading in historical and cultural context—a Texts/Contexts timeline following each period introduction, a map on the front endpaper of each volume, and a chronological chart, on the back endpaper, showing the lifespans of many of the writers anthologized.

Whenever possible, our policy has been to reprint texts as they appeared in their historical moment. There is one exception: we have modernized most spellings and (very sparingly) the punctuation in Volume A on the principle that archaic spellings and typography pose unnecessary problems

for beginning students. We have used square brackets to indicate titles supplied by the editors for the convenience of students. Whenever a portion of a text has been omitted, we have indicated that omission with three asterisks. If the omitted portion is important for following the plot or argument, we give a brief summary within the text or in a footnote. After each work, we cite the date of first publication on the right; in some instances, the latter is followed by the date of a revised edition for which the author was responsible. When the date of composition is known and differs from the date of publication, we cite it on the left.

The editors have benefited from commentary offered by hundreds of teachers throughout the country. Those teachers who prepared detailed critiques, or who offered special help in preparing texts, are listed under Acknowledgments, on a separate page. We also thank the many people at Norton who contributed to the Ninth Edition: Julia Reidhead, who supervised the Ninth Edition; Marian Johnson, managing editor, college; Carly Fraser Doria, media editor; manuscript editors Kurt Wildermuth, Michael Fleming, Harry Haskell, and Candace Levy; Rachel Taylor and Ava Bramson, assistant editors; Sean Mintus, production manager; Cat Abelman, photo editor; Julie Tesser, photo researcher; Debra Morton Hoyt, art director; Tiani Kennedy, cover designer; Megan Jackson Schindel, permissions manager; and Margaret Gorenstein, who cleared permissions. We also wish to acknowledge our debt to the late George P. Brockway, former president and chairman at Norton, who invented this anthology, and to the late M. H. Abrams, Norton's advisor on English texts. All have helped us create an anthology that, more than ever, testifies to the continuing richness of American literary traditions.

ROBERT S. LEVINE, General Editor

Acknowledgments

Among our many critics, advisors, and friends, the following were of especial help toward the preparation of the Ninth Edition, either with advice or by providing critiques of particular periods of the anthology: Melissa Adams-Campbell (Northern Illinois University); Rolena Adorno (Yale University); Heidi Ajrami (Victoria College); Simone A. James Alexander (Seton Hall University); Brian Anderson (Central Piedmont Community College); Lena Andersson (Fulton-Montgomery Community College); Marilyn Judith Atlas (Ohio University); Sylvia Baer (Gloucester County College); George H. Bailey (Northern Essex Community College); Margarita T. Barceló (MSU Denver); Peter Bellis (University of Alabama–Birmingham); Randall Blankenship (Valencia College); Susanne Bloomfield (University of Nebraska–Kearney); David Bordelon (Ocean County College); Patricia Bostian (Central Piedmont Community College); Maria Brandt (Monroe Community College); Tamara Ponzo Brattoli (Joliet Junior College); Joanna Brooks (San Diego State University); David Brottman (Iowa State University); Arthur Brown (University of Evansville); Martin Brückner (University of Delaware); Judith Budz (Fitchburg State University); Dan Butcher (University of Alabama–Birmingham); Maria J. Cahill (Edison State College); Ann Cameron (Indiana University–Kokomo); Brad Campbell (Cal Poly); Mark Canada (University of North Carolina–Pembroke); Gerry Canavan (Marquette University); Ann Capel (Gadsden State Community College, Ayers Campus); Elisabeth Ceppi (Portland State University); Tom Cerasulo (Elms College); Mark Cirino (University of Evansville); Josh Cohen (Emory University); Matt Cohen (University of Texas–Austin); William Corley (Cal Poly Pomona and U.S. Naval Academy); David Cowart (University of South Carolina); Paul Crumbley (Utah State University); Ryan Cull (New Mexico State University); Sue Currell (University of Sussex); Kathleen Danker (South Dakota State University); Clark Davis (University of Denver); Eve Davis (Virginia Union University); Matthew R. Davis (University of Wisconsin–Stevens Point); Laura Dawkins (Murray State University); Bruce J. Degi (Metropolitan State University of Denver); Jerry DeNuccio (Graceland University); Lisa DeVries (Victoria College); Lorraine C. DiCicco (King's University College); Joshua A. Dickson (SUNY Jefferson); Rick Diguette (Georgia Perimeter College); Raymond F. Dolle (Indiana State University); James Donelan (UC Santa Barbara); Clark Draney (College of Southern Idaho); John Dudley (University of South Dakota); Sara Eaton (North Central College); Julia Eichelberger (College of Charleston); Marilyn Elkins (California State University–Los Angeles); Sharyn Emery (Indiana

University Southeast); Hilary Emmett (University of East Anglia); Terry Engebresten (Idaho State University); Patrick Erben (University of West Georgia); Timothy J. Evans (College of William & Mary); Duncan Faherty (CUNY); Laura Fine (Meredith College); Daniel Fineman (Occidental College); Pat Gantt (Utah State University); Xiongya Gao (Southern University at New Orleans); Becky Jo Gesteland (Weber State University); Paul Gilmore (Rutgers University); Len Gougeon (University of Scranton); Carey Goyette (Clinton Community College); Sarah Graham (University of Leicester); Alan Gravano (Marshall University); James N. Green (Library Company of Philadelphia); Laura Morgan Green (Northeastern University); John Gruesser (Kean University); Bernabe G. Gutierrez (Laredo Community College); Julia Hans (Fitchburg State University); Stephanie Hawkins (University of North Texas); Catherine F. Heath (Victoria College); Roger Hechy (SUNY Oneonta); Terry Heller (Coe College); Carl Herzig (St. Ambrose University); Eric Heyne (University of Alaska–Fairbanks); Thomas Alan Holmes (East Tennessee State University); Greg Horn (Southwest Virginia Community College); Ruth Y. Hsu (University of Hawaii–Manoa); Kate Huber (Temple University); Zach Hutchins (Colorado State University); Thomas Irwin (University of Missouri–St. Louis); Elizabeth Janoski (Lackawanna College); Andrew Jenkins (College of Central Florida); Luke Johnson (Mesabi Range College); Mark Johnson (San Jacinto College); Paul Jones (Ohio University); Roger Walton Jones (Ranger College); Jennifer Jordan-Henley (Roane State Community College); Mark Kamrath (University of Central Florida); Rachel Key (El Centro College); Julie H. Kim (Northeastern Illinois University); Vincent King (Black Hills State University); Denis Kohn (Baldwin Wallace University); Gary Konas (University of Wisconsin–La Crosse); Michael Kowalewski (Carleton College); Michael Lackey (University of Minnesota–Morris); Jennifer Ladino (University of Idaho); Thomas W. LaFleur (Laredo Community College); Andrew Lanham (Yale University); Christopher Leise (Whitman College); Beth Leishman (Northwest MS Community College); Jennifer Levi (Cecil College); Alfred J. López (Purdue University); Paul Madachy (Prince George's Community College); Etta Madden (Missouri State University); Marc Malandra (Biola University); David Malone (Union University); Matt Martin (Wesleyan College); Stephen Mathewson (Central New Mexico Community College); Liz Thompson Mayo (Jackson State Community College); David McCracken (Coker College); Kathleen McDonald (Norwich University); John McGreevy (University of Notre Dame); Dana McMichael (Abilene Christian University); Sandra Measels (Holmes Community College); Eric Mein (Normandale Community College); Christine Mihelich (Marywood University); Deborah M. Mix (Ball State University); Aaron Moe (Washington State University); Joelle Moen (Brigham Young University–Idaho); Lisa Muir (Wilkes Community College); Lori Muntz (Iowa Wesleyan College); Justine Murison (University of Illinois); Jillmarie Murphy (Union College); Harold Nelson (Minot State University); Howard Nelson (Cayuga Community College); Lance Newman (Westminster College); Taryn Okuma (The Catholic University of America); Stanley Orr (University of Hawai'i–West O'ahu); Samuel Otter (University of California–Berkeley); Susan Scott Parrish (University of Michigan); Martha H. Patterson (McKendree University); Michelle Paulsen (Victoria College); Daniel G. Payne (SUNY Oneonta); Ian Peddie (Georgia

Gwinnett College); Aaron Matthew Percich (West Virginia University); Tom Perrin (Huntingdon College); Sandra Petrulionis (Penn State–Altoona); Christopher Phillips (Lafayette College); Kenneth M. Price (University of Nebraska); Maria Pollack (Hudson Valley Community College); Marty G. Price (Mississippi State University); Kieran Quinlan (University of Alabama–Birmingham); Wesley Raabe (Kent State University); Maria Ramos (J. Sargeant Reynolds Community College); Palmer Rampell (Yale University); Rick Randolph (Kauai Community College); Kimberly Reed (Lipscomb University); Joan Reeves (Northeast Alabama Community College); Elizabeth Renker (The Ohio State University); Joseph Rezek (Boston University); Anne Boyd Rioux (University of New Orleans); Marc Robinson (Yale University); Jane Rosecrans (J. Sargeant Reynolds Community College); Phillip Round (University of Iowa); Jeffrey Rubinstein (Hillborough Community College); Maureen Ryan (University of Southern Mississippi); Jamie Sadler (Richmond Community College); Gordon Sayre (University of Oregon); Jennifer Schell (University of Alaska–Fairbanks); Jim Schrantz (Tarrant County College); Joshua Schuster (University of Western Ontario); Marc Seals (University of Wisconsin–Baraboo/Sauk County); Carl Sederholm (Brigham Young University); Larry Severeid (Utah State University–Eastern); Anna Shectman (Yale University); Deborah Sims (USC and UCR); Claudia Slate (Florida Southern College); Brenda R. Smith (Kent State University–Stark); Martha Nell Smith (University of Maryland); Eric Sterling (Auburn University Montgomery); Julia Stern (Northwestern University); Billy J. Stratton (University of Denver); Steve Surryhne (California State University–San Francisco); Timothy Sweet (West Virginia University); David Taylor (University of North Texas); Jan Thompson (University of Nebraska–Kearney); Robin Thompson (Governors State University); Marjory Thrash (Pearl River Community College); Nicole Tonkovich (UC San Diego); Steve Tracy (University of Massachusetts–Amherst); Alan Trusky (Forence-Darlington Tech College); April Van Camp (Indian River State College); Joanne van der Woude (University of Groningen); Abram van Engen (Washington University); Laura Veltman (California Baptist University); Eliza Waggoner (Miami University–Middletown); Catherine Waitinas (Cal Poly State University); Laura Dassow Walls (University of Notre Dame); Raquel Wanzo (Laney College); Bryan Waterman (New York University); Stephanie Wells (Orange Coast College); Jeff Westover (Boise State University); Belinda Wheeler (Paine College); Chris Wheeler (Horry-Georgetown Technical College); Steven J. Whitton (Jacksonville State University); Elizabeth Wiet (Yale University); Jason Williams (Brigham Young University–Idaho); Barbara Williamson (Spokane Falls Community College); Gaye Winter (Mississippi Gulf Coast Community College); Kelly Wisecup (University of North Texas); Aiping Zhang (California State University–Chico).

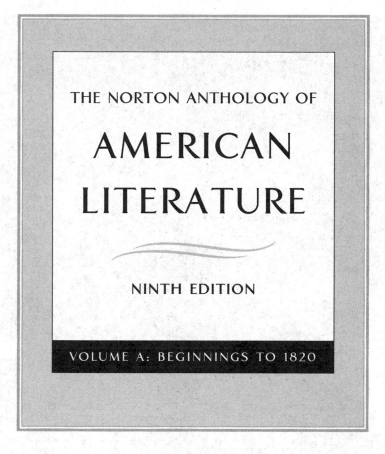

THE NORTON ANTHOLOGY OF

AMERICAN

LITERATURE

NINTH EDITION

VOLUME A: BEGINNINGS TO 1820

Beginnings
to 1820

QUESTIONS OF IDENTITY

In 1631, the English captain John Smith published *Advertisements for the Unexperienced Planters of New England, or Any Where: Or, the Path-way to Experience to Erect a Plantation*, the last and most polished of his works. Smith had been instrumental in the 1607 founding of Jamestown in Virginia, England's first long-lived American settlement, and he later provided guidance for both the Pilgrims who established Plymouth in 1620 and the Puritans who founded the Massachusetts Bay Colony 10 years later. Reading *Advertisements for the Unexperienced Planters* now, when anticolonial and independence movements have made colonization justly suspect, Smith's endorsement of English plantations in North America strikes a discordant note. Smith anticipated such objections, for he heard them from his contemporaries. "Many good religious devout men have made it a great question, as a matter in conscience, by what warrant they might goe to possesse those Countries, which are none of theirs, but the poore Salvages [i.e., savages']," he wrote. He considered the answer to this objection self-evident: "for God did make the world to be inhabited with mankind, and to have his name knowne to all Nations, and from generation to generation." Although hardly a pious man, Smith saw God's hand at work in England's seizing of the Americas.

On a more mundane level, the dense population and soil depletion in England seemed to Smith sufficient reason to take advantage of the fact that "here in Florida, Virginia, New-England, and Cannada, is more land than all the people in Christendome can

John White, **Indian Village of Secoton** (detail), 1585. For more information about this image, see the color insert in this volume.

3

manure [i.e., cultivate], and yet more to spare than all the natives of those Countries can use and culturate." The continent's native inhabitants, he enthused, would "sell you a whole Countrey" in exchange "for a copper kettle and a few toyes, as beads and hatchets." In his text, Smith did not consider that these "sales" might have been based on different concepts of property, nor did he dwell on the deadly epidemics that decimated Native societies following the arrival of Europeans. He based his arguments for colonization on the precedents available in sacred and secular history. Adam and Eve established a plantation, Smith argued, as did Noah and his family after the flood, and so on through "the Hebrewes, Lacedemonians, the Goths, Grecians, Romans, and the rest." Moreover Portugal and Spain had a one-hundred-and-forty-year lead on England in terms of colony formation, and they were wresting great wealth from the people of the Americas, who once had possessed the natural resources. It would be "neglect of our duty and religion" as well as "want of charity to those poore Salvages" to fail to challenge these Roman Catholic countries for control of the hemisphere, Smith concluded. The difficulty today of seeing European settlement as an expression of "charity" to the "Salvages" means that the "great question" raised by the "good religious devout men" opposed to colonization remains fresh and vital.

In 1805, the Seneca orator Sagoyewatha, or Red Jacket, offered a Native perspective on colonization in an address to the missionary Jacob Cram that can serve as a rebuttal of Smith. "There was a time when our forefathers owned this great island," Sagoyewatha told Cram. "Their seats extended from the rising to the setting sun. The Great Spirit had made it for the use of Indians." When "your forefathers" arrived, he continued, "they found friends and not enemies. They told us they had fled from their own country for fear of wicked men, and had come here to enjoy their religion. They asked us for a small seat. We took pity on them, granted their request; and they sat down amongst us." Sagoyewatha went on to describe the devastating impact on Native Americans of the strong alcohol introduced by Europeans and to relate how the once small colonial populations had grown and spilled over onto lands that the Natives had not meant to relinquish. He also challenged Cram on the relevance of Christianity to Native communities, which, he stressed, had their own religious traditions. In addition, Christianity hardly seemed a unifying force for good. "If there is but one religion," Sagoyewatha asked, "why do you white people differ so much about it? Why [are you] not all agreed, as you can all read the book [i.e., the Bible]?"

In his 1782 book *Letters from an American Farmer*, the French-born writer J. Hector St. John de Crèvecœur posed another resonant question: "What is an American?" Crèvecœur offered his most explicit answer to this question in Letter III, where he described "the American" as a "new man, who acts upon new principles; he must therefore entertain new ideas, and form new opinions." The American people were "a mixture of English, Scotch, Irish, French, Dutch, Germans and Swedes," he wrote, emphasizing that they farmed their own land and peacefully practiced various faiths, including Roman Catholicism, Quakerism, and several forms of Protestantism. Crèvecœur's description captured important aspects of late colonial society. In its early years, the American colonies were shaped by competing empires: the large ones—New Spain, New France, and the English colonies, including Virginia and New England—and more modest efforts, such as New Netherland and New

Sweden. In the eighteenth century, even as Britain consolidated its empire in North America, an influx of immigrants from Northern Europe produced in the mid-Atlantic colonies the particular mixture that Crèvecœur described. He contrasted this American "melting" of peoples with life in Europe, where national and religious divisions fueled chronic wars while lingering feudal systems and powerful states oppressed the common people.

Elsewhere in *Letters*, Crèvecœur complicated his idealized vision of America as a place where Europeans could liberate themselves from the constraints of the Old World. He noted the attractions of the frontier, a borderland where hunting surpassed agriculture as the dominant mode of life. In that contact zone, European Americans adopted the customs and habits of Native Americans even as they sought to supplant them. He also reported on the hierarchical plantation-based societies of the southern colonies, and the horrors inflicted there on enslaved African Americans. His description of a caged slave is one of the most unforgettable passages in the book. In these selections, the liberating potential of the New World is shown to have sharp limits, and the process of nation-formation to have negative ramifications as well as positive consequences.

Letters from an American Farmer proved an immediate sensation, for it offered insights into what the emerging nation might become, and how the result might affect Europe. Though Crèvecœur was probably a Loyalist supporter of British rule, his work was greeted enthusiastically by political radicals in England and Enlightenment philosophes in France, as well as by the American statesman Thomas Jefferson, who echoed Crèvecœur's enthusiasm for the yeoman farmer in his *Notes on the State of Virginia* (1787). After a period of relative neglect in the nineteenth century, Crèvecœur's vision of America was revived in 1908, when Israel Zangwill's "The Melting Pot," a play focused on recent waves of European immigration, became a smash hit. Readers embraced *Letters* as a classic of American literature presenting an archetype of American identity. Unfortunately, the resulting view of *Letters* highlighted the formation of white American identity while marginalizing nonwhites. In recent years, a more comprehensive approach to Crèvecœur's work has emphasized the sections on slavery and white/ Native interactions on the frontier. *Letters from an American Farmer* offers today's readers vivid accounts of assumptions and contradictions that helped shape the early United States and its literature.

Nearly four decades after *Letters from an American Farmer* became one of the literary hits of the age of revolution, Washington Irving cast a backward look at this founding era in his tale "Rip Van Winkle." Irving was born in 1783, the year that the Treaty of Paris brought a formal close to the Revolutionary War, and he was named for the Virginia planter and slave owner who led the Continental Army to victory and later became the first president of the United States. Irving was one of the earliest American-born authors to win international literary celebrity, which he achieved as an expatriate writer living in England. The work that first made him famous was *The Sketch Book* (1819–20), a volume of stories and essays that includes his best-known tales, "Rip Van Winkle" and "The Legend of Sleepy Hollow." While these stories take place in the Catskill region of New York and there are two essays on Native American life and history, the bulk of the volume concerns English customs. This fact suggests the limits to revolutionary change in the

literary world of Irving's day. Despite the ambition of many writers to create distinctly "American" works, the literature of the United States remained oriented toward England for decades after independence.

"Rip Van Winkle" emphasizes continuity more than transformation, and it highlights the checkered quality of human nature rather than its potential for radical new beginnings. Based on a German folktale and set in a sleepy Dutch village on the Hudson River shortly before the Revolution, the story features Rip, a slacker who embarks on a hunting expedition to evade his wife's demands. In the mountains, he mysteriously finds himself in the company of the English explorer Henry Hudson, who in 1609 traveled from New York Harbor as far as Albany, sailing up the river that now bears his name. Hudson and his men silently invite Rip to drink with them, and he soon falls into a deep and unnaturally prolonged sleep. When he returns to his village after a 20-year interval, the Revolution has passed, and Rip finds much that is unfamiliar, as well as things that are uncannily familiar yet somehow different. Frustrated, he bursts out, "Does nobody here know Rip Van Winkle?"—and a version of his younger self is pointed out to him. This person turns out to be the son he left at home two decades earlier, now grown up to be a man much like his father.

Irving invites his readers to consider the disorienting nature of social transformation. He particularly contrasts the quieter, slower colonial world with the bustle and clamor of the newly democratizing political culture. The story suggests that despite some obvious superficial differences, not very much has changed, and that some of the circumstances that have changed have not necessarily improved. These central themes are captured in Irving's description of how the image of King George III on the sign of the local inn has been repainted as George Washington. The sign offers a compelling symbol of how things can remain the same underneath even as external appearances transform. The excitement of radical change and the appeal of tradition and continuity that Irving explores in this story have been fertile themes for many American writers. Questions about the competing values and historical narratives that shape American identities were as relevant for Irving's readers as they had been two hundred years earlier for John Smith.

EXPLORING ORIGINS

The question of identity is often tied to the nature of origins. Most of the earliest surviving writings about the Americas are narratives of discovery, a vast and frequently fascinating category of works that includes Samuel de Champlain's chronicles of New France; Thomas Harriot's descriptions of Native customs and natural resources in the Chesapeake Bay region; and— of great interest to Washington Irving—the account of Henry Hudson's explorations written by Robert Juet, the sailor who later mutinied and set Hudson adrift in the bay that bears his name, never to be seen again. Irving's retelling of the Hudson story in his *History of New-York* (1809) greatly mutes the brutality in Juet's narrative to present a colonial history that is notably relaxed and genial, while explicitly marginalizing Native Americans. Virtually all colonization narratives tell a story that is closer to Juet's than to Irving's. These works show that while some elements of influence

Columbus Landing in the Indies, from *La Lettera dell'isole che ha trovata nouovamenta il re di'spagna,* 1493. This woodcut was created to accompany a metrical version, by the Florentine poet Giuliano Dati, of the letter Columbus wrote describing his first voyage. The image is interesting for its symbolic presentation of European authority (in the person of Ferdinand of Spain) and its early conceptualization of what the Taino Indians looked like.

and exchange were peaceful, conflict and violence were major forces shaping this new world. Individually and collectively, these writings demonstrate that "discovery" entailed a many-sided process of confrontation and exchange among heterogeneous European, American, and, eventually, African peoples. It was out of encounters such as the ones described in these narratives that the hybrid cultural universe of the Atlantic world began to emerge.

In 1828, Irving published a biography of Christopher Columbus, the Genoese explorer who sailed across the Atlantic four times on behalf of the Spanish Empire. Columbus's own writings provide a remarkable view into the radical changes that his voyage of 1492 set in motion. His *Letter to Luis de Santangel Regarding the First Voyage* (1493)—better known as the Letter of Discovery—was the first printed account of the territory that Europeans later came to call America. This riveting description of the unexpected marvels that Columbus and his crew encountered in the West Indies circulated widely throughout Europe. Columbus lavished praise on the stunning island mountains, the many different types of trees and beautiful forms of vegetation, the rivers that appeared to be full of gold, and the fertile soil promising agricultural riches. He described the indigenous population as welcoming, loosely organized, and largely defenseless. And in a harbinger of

things to come, he told how "in the first island that I came to, I took some of them by force." He captured these Natives—and took some of them with him on the return voyage to Europe—with the idea that Europeans and Natives could learn to communicate through gestures and, eventually, language. Before long, however, captivity in the service of potentially peaceful exchange yielded to other types of coercion, including enslavement.

Perhaps it was one of Columbus's original captives who in 1494 returned home to relate tales of a new world full of "marvels"—that is, the marvels of Spain, which were as unfamiliar to his Native audience as the marvels of the West Indies were to Columbus's European readers. The man in question was a Taino Indian from the Bahamas, who had been baptized and renamed Diego Colón, after Columbus's son. (Colón is the Spanish version of the family's name.) Diego Colón and another captive served as translators for a large party of Spaniards, around fifteen hundred, who arrived in the Caribbean early in November 1493. In the words of the Spanish historian Andrés Bernáldez, who knew Columbus well and edited his papers, Colón regaled the other Natives with tales of "the things which he had seen in Castile and the marvels of Spain, . . . the great cities and fortresses and churches, . . . the people and horses and animals, . . . the great nobility and wealth of the sovereigns and great lords, . . . the kinds of food, . . . the festivals and tournaments [and] bull-fighting." Colón's story catches in miniature the extraordinary changes that began to occur as natives of Europe encountered natives of the Americas in a sustained way for the first time in recorded history.

Each group of peoples was of course the product and agent of its own history and brought a unique sense of "reality" to the encounter. For example, the year of Columbus's first voyage was also the year of the Spanish *Reconquista*, that is, the final defeat of the Islamic Moors of North Africa who had conquered Spain more than 700 years earlier. The *Reconquista* was just one phase of the centuries-long wars between Christian and Muslim empires that shaped European perceptions of, and actions in, the Americas. Captain John Smith had earned his military title fighting in southeastern Europe against the imperial forces of the Ottoman Turks, then at the height of their power. There were recognizably imperial states in the Americas as well. In the two centuries before Columbus's voyage, the Aztecs had consolidated an empire in present-day Mexico, and over the course of the fourteenth century the Inca Empire had expanded to encompass territory from what is now southern Colombia to Chile. Because of the Aztec and Inca presences, the view of European conquest as a contest of empires is particularly strong in Spanish accounts. The conquistador Hernán Cortés described the sophistication and wealth that existed in the Aztec capital, Tenochtitlán, before he ordered his forces to destroy it. In a more muted way, Smith portrayed English interactions with the Powhatan Indians as the product of their competing imperial projects, with Chief Powhatan undertaking to absorb the English newcomers within his expanding area of influence while Smith struggled to establish dominance.

When the Europeans arrived in the Americas, the indigenous people numbered between fifty million and one hundred million. Mass deaths among the indigenous communities facilitated European expansion. Almost literally from 1492, Native peoples started to die in large numbers. Whole pop-

ulations plummeted as diseases such as smallpox, measles, and typhus spread throughout the Caribbean and then on the mainland of Central and South America. These diseases became even more lethal as a consequence of war, enslavement, brutal mistreatment, and despair. The rapid introduction of slavery of Native Americans by Europeans, which Columbus helped initiate, reflects both historical practices and contemporary developments. The word "slave" derives from "Slav," which refers to speakers of Slavic languages, in central and eastern Europe; many Slavs were taken as property by Spanish Muslims in the ninth century. Race-based slavery emerged shortly before Columbus's first voyage: the European slave trade in Africa began in 1441, and in 1452 Pope Nicholas V authorized the enslaving of non-Christians. In 1500 slavery was a common form of labor, with variants around the globe, including in Africa and the Americas. Columbus had intended to create a market in enslaved Americans, and a substantial number of Natives were taken as slaves, but ultimately this project failed because too many Native people died. Europeans began transporting small numbers of enslaved Africans to the Americas shortly after arriving there. Those numbers soon multiplied, and the social and cultural features of this new world became even more complex as the slaves introduced the arts and traditions of various African societies.

The impacts in the Americas of disease and of slavery can be seen in miniature in the history of the Caribbean island Hispaniola. The population of Hispaniola (estimated at between one hundred thousand and eight million in 1492) plunged following the Spanish occupation, partly through disease

New World Natives, from an anonymous German woodcut, c. 1505. The text accompanying this detailed early illustration comments on Native Americans and their customs, praising their physical appearance and healthfulness as well as their distaste for both private property and public government. Only in passing does it assert that they kill and eat their enemies, smoking the dead bodies above their fires, as on closer inspection the woodcut indicates.

and partly through abuses of the *encomienda* system, which gave individual Spaniards claims to Native labor and wealth. Faced with this sudden decline in Native workers, Spain introduced African slavery there as early as 1501. In 1522, the first major slave rebellion in the Americas took place on the island, when enslaved African Muslims killed nine Spaniards. From this point forward, slave resistance became commonplace. Nevertheless, by the mid-sixteenth century the Native population had been so completely displaced by African slaves that the Spanish historian Antonio de Herrera called the island "an effigy or an image of Ethiopia itself." Hispaniola was the leading edge of broader devastations and transformations; colonization, disease, and slavery had similarly sweeping effects in many parts of the Americas.

It would be inaccurate to picture indigenous Americans as merely victims suffering an inexorable decline. The motif of the "vanishing Indian" that became prominent in the early nineteenth century misrepresents historical realities, which involved unevenly textured cultural developments. Some indigenous Americans made shrewd use of the European presence to forward their own aims. In 1519, the disaffected Natives in the Aztec Empire threw in their lot with Cortés because they saw a chance to settle the score with their overlord, Montezuma. In New England, the Pequot War of 1637 involved a similar alignment on the English side of such tribes as the Narragansetts and the Mohegans, who had grievances with the militarily aggressive Pequots. The Powhatans of the Chesapeake Bay region and the Iroquois in the Northeast seized on European technology and the European market, adopting novel weaponry (the gun) and incorporating new trade goods into their networks as a means of consolidating advantages gained before the arrival of the colonists. Beginning in the eighteenth century, the Comanches built an empire that dominated other Native groups and contested European (and later United States and Mexican) power in the southern plains and southwestern regions of North America. Above all, Native societies were not static. Even as their populations shrank, indigenous Americans resisted, transformed, and exploited the cultural and social practices that Europeans and Africans brought to the Americas. Eventually, these resilient, resourceful peoples embraced writing and print to protect their communities, advance their interests, and convey their vital place in the world.

Meanwhile, the African population in the Americas was expanding. Although free blacks were a growing presence, most of the Africans were slaves who were often forced into heterogeneous groups that brought together members of various cultures speaking distinct languages. Under the harsh conditions of European domination, they created new forms of expression that retained ties to their cultures of origin. One notable instance of this dynamic process involves the West African figure of Esu Elegbara, the guardian of the crossroads and interpreter of the gods, who appears in works of verbal art created in African communities throughout the Americas. Esu features in narrative praise poems, divination verses, lyrical songs, and prose narratives and is particularly connected with matters of heightened (that is, "literary") language and interpretation. By the eighteenth century, many African Americans practiced Christianity, and the Bible provided a stock of characters and rhetorical postures that they used to articulate their experiences and worldviews and to advocate for their freedom.

LITERARY BACKGROUNDS AND
CONSEQUENCES OF 1492

Apart from the literatures of ancient Greece and Rome, few of the works now regarded as classics of European literature had been produced when Columbus sailed in 1492. Those that did exist can be grouped into a few genres. There were epic poems, such as *Beowulf* (English), *The Song of Roland* (French), and Dante's *Divine Comedy* (Italian); chivalric romances, including *Sir Gawain and the Green Knight* (English); shorter romances, such as the lais of Marie de France; story sequences, including the Italian writer Boccaccio's *Decameron* and the English poet Chaucer's *Canterbury Tales*; sacred lyric poems, such as by Hildegard of Bingen; and sonnets, notably those by the Italian poet Petrarch, who honed the form into a major genre that, during the Renaissance, Shakespeare made important to English literature. Aristotle's and Cicero's works were already widely known, and the revival of Greco-Roman classics that characterized the Renaissance was on the horizon. Augustine's *Confessions* was among the broadly influential works of sacred prose, while secular chronicles and histories attracted many readers. In 1300, Marco Polo's account of his travels to China began to circulate; *The Travels of Sir John Mandeville*, a fabulous account of a journey through the Middle East and beyond, appeared five or six decades later. Published in manuscript before the Gutenberg printing press was invented around 1440, both works are thought to have influenced Christopher Columbus's writings about his "new world."

Beginning with the publication in 1493 of Columbus's Letter of Discovery, the printing press became part of the engine driving European expansion in the Americas. Explorers and adventurers produced a large and intriguing body of literature that communicated the wonders of the new world, described Native societies with varying degrees of accuracy and appreciation, and offered explanations and justifications for numerous colonial projects. In some cases, notably that of the Spanish friar Bartolomé de las Casas, writers also testified about the atrocities being committed against Native peoples. Print increasingly made possible the dissemination of texts rich with imagery and practical knowledge, helping to stir individual imaginations and national ambitions with regard to the West Indies and the Americas and, in a few instances, seeking to limit the negative impact of colonization on indigenous Americans.

Cataclysms such as the devastation of the Indies and the Conquest of Mexico produced not only the Spanish narratives of Columbus, Cortés, and Las Casas but also Native responses. For example, in 1528 anonymous Native writers, working in the Nahuatl language of the Aztecs but using the Roman alphabet introduced by the Spanish, lamented the fall of their capital to Cortés:

> Broken spears lie in the roads;
> we have torn our hair in our grief.
> The houses are roofless now, and their walls
> are red with blood.

No one reading these four lines will easily glorify the conquest of Mexico or of the Americas more generally. Such testimonies offer an essential outlook

on this painful history. The selections in this volume grouped under "First Encounters: Early European Accounts of Native America" offer both European and indigenous perspectives. So, for instance, the excerpt from Robert Juet's narrative of Hudson's third voyage, published in 1625, relates the same events as the Delaware narrative that John Heckewelder recorded from his Native sources in the early nineteenth century—which in turn also provides an important perspective on the narrative of these events offered, later in the volume, by Heckewelder's contemporary Washington Irving.

At the time of conquest Native Americans had rich oral cultures that valued memory over material means of preserving texts. There were some important exceptions. The Aztecs and a few other groups produced written works in their own languages, though Spanish conquerors destroyed many of the *amoxtli* and other types of Native "books." Many indigenous communities used visual records in subtle and sophisticated ways, with a notable example being the Andean quipu, a type of knotted string. North American recording devices included shellwork belts, known as *wampum*, and painted animal hides, tepees, and shields. The histories and rituals encoded in these devices were translated into spoken language in ways that had significant parallels in what is sometimes called print culture. Scripture was regularly interpreted and delivered in a sermon in much the same manner as a *wampum* belt might be "read" at a treaty conference. Again, a printed narrative might be read aloud, similar to the way that Native tales were recounted; while hymns and ballads were designed for singing and provided an early contact point between European and Native verbal artists.

In addition to taking diverse forms, early American literature reflects the linguistic and cultural range of the colonial world. Spanish, French, German and its variants, and other European languages are prominent in the written archive about North America, as exemplified here in works by writers such as Álvar Núñez Cabeza de Vaca, Samuel de Champlain, Sor Juana Inés de la Cruz, and Francis Daniel Pastorius. Dozens of Native languages left traces, which include evidence of at least eight creation narratives, with notable examples being the Iroquois and Navajo creation stories included in this volume. Although English eventually became the main language in the United States, and thus the dominant medium of classic American literature, it was a late arrival in the Americas. Likewise, although the New England colonies, founded in the early seventeenth century, have conventionally been regarded as the central source of early American literature, the first North American settlements were established elsewhere many years earlier. The Spanish founded colonies at present-day St. Augustine, Florida (1565), and Santa Fe, New Mexico (1610), and Dutch settlers established New Netherland (1614), which came to include New York City and Albany (1614). All of these cities, which started as colonial outposts, are older than Boston (1630), which was not even the first permanent English settlement in North America. That distinction goes to the Jamestown colony, in Virginia (1607).

The writings of Thomas Harriot and John Smith about Virginia's Chesapeake Bay region are crucial to a full understanding of the English-language literature of the Americas. Harriot produced the first account of England's new world in *A Brief and True Report of the New Found Land of Virginia* (1588), which combines descriptions of marketable commodities, a detailed and often accurate description of Native beliefs and practices, and a narration

of how Wingina, the Algonquian headman on Roanoke Island, interacted with the English colonizers and sought to understand the devastating effects of the illnesses that followed in their wake. As noted earlier, John Smith was an enthusiastic and prolific proselytizer for English colonization, instrumental in the establishment of Virginia and influential as well in the founding of New England. Smith epitomized those proponents of colonization who came from the underclasses in their native countries, and he made a powerful case for the opportunities that America offered them. Energetic and confident, Smith could be subversive, even mutinous, in his writings as in his life. His works present a vision of America as a place where much that was genuinely new might be learned and created. This vision came to maturity in his writings about New England, and helped to shape what many regard as the most influential body of writings from the early period.

LITERARY NEW ENGLAND

The founding of Plymouth Plantation, in 1620, marks a new phase in the literary history of colonial North America. The first months of the Plymouth colony were inauspicious. After landing on the raw Massachusetts shore in November 1620, the Pilgrims braced for winter. They survived this "starving time" with the essential aid of the nearby Wampanoag Indians and their leader, Massasoit. From these "small beginnings," as the colony's leader, William Bradford, refers to them in *Of Plymouth Plantation* (c. 1630), grew a community that later came to be invested with a symbolic significance that far exceeded its size and remote location. The Pilgrims' religious motivation for leaving England is only part of the story. Backed by English investors, the seafaring migration was commercial as well as spiritual. Among the hundred people on the group's ship, the *Mayflower*, almost three times as many were secular settlers as were Separatist Puritans. The persistent tension between the material and spiritual goals of the Plymouth colonists appears in many early writings about the region. For instance, Thomas Morton portrays this conflict in values in *New English Canaan* (1637), where the Plymouth leaders appear not as holy men but as domineering and repressive antagonists of Morton's colony at Ma-re Mount. Morton also conveys a different sensibility about relations with the Natives, expressing little desire to convert them to Christianity and focusing instead on joining with them in May Day festivities. Although Morton probably overstated the ideological differences and minimized the economic rivalry with Plymouth, the contrast suggests a spectrum of colonial responses to their new environment. In addition, Morton's language reflects a major strand in English Renaissance writing, a playful style that contrasts with the plain style of Bradford and other Puritan authors.

Much larger than either Plymouth or Ma-re Mount was the Massachusetts Bay Colony, founded in 1630 by Puritans under John Winthrop. The Massachusetts Bay colonists initially wanted to retain their ties with the Church of England, leading to their designation as non-Separating Congregationalists, which distinguished them from the more radical Separatists at Plymouth. On other issues, they shared basic beliefs with the Pilgrims: both agreed with the Protestant Reformation leader Martin Luther that no pope

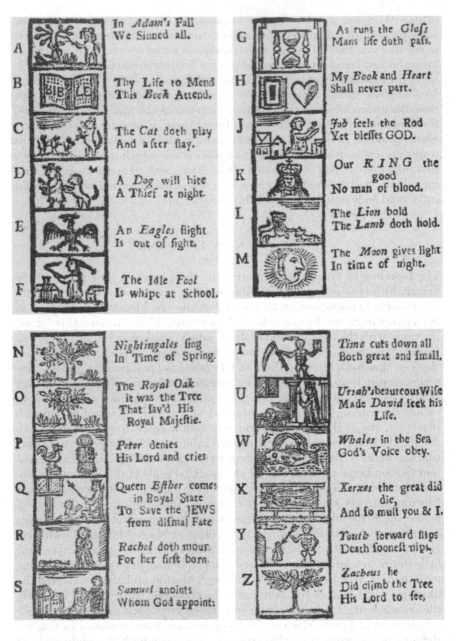

A		In *Adam's* Fall / We Sinned all.
B		Thy Life to Mend / This *Book* Attend.
C		The *Cat* doth play / And after flay.
D		A *Dog* will bite / A Thief at night.
E		An *Eagles* flight / Is out of fight.
F		The Idle *Fool* / Is whipt at School.
G		As runs the *Glafs* / Mans life doth pafs.
H		My *Book* and *Heart* / Shall never part.
J		*Job* feels the Rod / Yet blefles GOD.
K		Our *KING* the good / No man of blood.
L		The *Lion* bold / The *Lamb* doth hold.
M		The *Moon* gives light / In time of night.
N		*Nightingales* fing / In Time of Spring.
O		The *Royal Oak* / it was the Tree / That fav'd His / Royal Majeftie.
P		*Peter* denies / His Lord and cries
Q		Queen *Efther* comes / in Royal State / To Save the JEWS / from difmal Fate
R		*Rachel* doth mour, / For her firft born.
S		*Samuel* anoints / Whom God appoint:
T		*Time* cuts down all / Both great and fmall.
U		*Uriah's* beauteous Wife / Made *David* feek his / Life.
W		*Whales* in the Sea / God's Voice obey.
X		*Xerxes* the great did / die, / And fo muft you & I.
Y		*Youth* forward flips / Death fooneft nips,
Z		*Zacheus* he / Did climb the Tree / His Lord to fee,

The New-England Primer (1690). Like other Protestants, Puritans believed that the Bible should be accessible to all believers, and to that end *The New-England Primer* was designed for children learning to read. Benjamin Harris printed the first edition in Boston; a London edition appeared in 1701. Many more editions followed—though very few copies survived.

In the mid-eighteenth century, Benjamin Franklin's Philadelphia print shop sold nearly forty thousand copies of its own later version. This page is from *The New-England Primer, a Reprint of the Earliest Known Edition* (1899), edited by Paul Leicester Ford, which reproduces the one surviving, incomplete copy of the 1727 edition.

or bishop had the right to impose any law on a Christian without consent, and both accepted the Reformation theologian John Calvin's view that God freely chose (or "elected") those he would save and those he would damn eternally.

Puritans have a grim reputation as religious zealots, prudes, and killjoys. These conceptions stem from the Calvinist doctrine of election. However, counter to the stereotype, Puritans did not necessarily consider most people damned before birth. Instead, they argued that Adam broke the "Covenant of Works"—the promise God made to Adam that he was immortal and could live in Paradise forever as long as he obeyed God's commandments—when he disobeyed and ate of the tree of knowledge of good and evil, thereby bringing sin and death into the world. Their central doctrine was the new "Covenant of Grace," a binding agreement that Jesus Christ made with all people who believed in him and that he sealed with his Crucifixion, promising them eternal life. The New England churches aspired to be more rigorous than others, and this idea of the covenant contributed to the feeling that they were a special few. When John Winthrop in *A Model of Christian Charity* (written 1630) expressed the ideals that he wanted the colonists to embrace, he wrote that the eyes of the world were on them and that they should strive to be an example for all, a "city upon a hill."

In their respective histories of Plymouth and Massachusetts Bay, Bradford and Winthrop wished to record the actualization of the founding dream, which was first and foremost a dream of a purified community of mutually supporting Protestant Christians.

In keeping with the doctrine of election, Puritan ministers typically addressed themselves not to the hopelessly unregenerate but to the spiritually indifferent—that is, to the potentially "elect." They spoke to the heart more often than the mind, always distinguishing between heartfelt "saving faith" and "historical," or rational, understanding. While preachers sometimes sought to evoke fear by focusing on the terrors of hell, as the latter-day Puritan Jonathan Edwards famously did in his sermon "Sinners in the Hands of an Angry God" (1741), this method did not reflect the exclusive—or even the main—tenor of Puritan religious life. The considerable joy and love in Puritanism resulted directly from meditation on Christ's redeeming power. The

The Tenth Muse. Anne Bradstreet's first book appeared in London in 1650, with the title *The Tenth Muse, Lately Sprung up in America.* There were nine muses in the classical world. In 1678, this second edition of Bradstreet's poems was published in Boston.

minister-poet Edward Taylor conveys this element of Puritan experience in his rapturous litany of Christ's attributes: "He is altogether lovely in everything, lovely in His person, lovely in His natures, lovely in His properties, lovely in His offices, lovely in His titles, lovely in His practice, lovely in His purchases and lovely in His relations." All of Taylor's art considers the miraculous gift of the Incarnation, reflecting his typically Puritan sensibility. Similar qualities are evident in the works of Anne Bradstreet, a Puritan and the first British North American writer to publish a volume of poetry. Bradstreet confessed her religious doubts to her children, but she emphasized that it was "upon this rock Christ Jesus" that she built her faith. The Puritan minister Michael Wigglesworth titled a poem *The Day of Doom* (1662), but concluded it with God joyfully embracing the saints in heaven.

A comparable emphasis on sacred feeling inhabits the poetry of the Mexican Catholic nun Sor Juana Inés de la Cruz and the narratives of the North American Quaker writers Elizabeth Ashbridge and John Woolman. Indeed, religious emotion provided a unifying factor for diverse denominations, leading to the kind of melding that Crèvecœur would later find characteristic of American life. The closest thing in New England to Crèvecœur's ideal was in the Providence colony, which the Puritan theologian Roger Williams helped guide toward a more capacious understanding of religious freedom than was accepted in Plymouth or Massachusetts Bay. Williams insisted that "christenings make not Christians." In other words, as he interpreted the doctrine of election, rituals and displays meant less than inner faith. Accordingly, he helped make Providence a refuge for religious dissenters and outsiders, including Antinomians, Quakers, and Jews. He also worked hard—and for a time, successfully—to establish good relations with the region's Narragansett Indians. However, harmonious relations were shattered in 1675, when King Philip led the Wampanoags and their Narragansett allies to war against the colonies, with devastating effects on both sides. In her captivity narrative, the Puritan settler Mary Rowlandson movingly describes the mutual betrayal experienced by the indigenous people and the colonists.

Just over a decade after Rowland's captivity, King William's War became the first in a series of conflicts between New England and New France that culminated in 1763 with Britain's victory in the French and Indian War. During the intervening decades, colonists regularly fought alongside European troops and Native allies. European state politics informed the fighting, as did religious differences between Protestant Britain and Catholic France. The *Jesuit Relations*, vast chronicles of life in the borderlands of New France, reflect the imperial and religious tensions. A 1647 narrative included in this anthology focuses on Isaac Jogues, one of the eight Jesuit missionaries killed by Natives, canonized (i.e., sainted) by the Roman Catholic Church, and sometimes referred to as the North American Martyrs. A 1744 narrative included here tells the life story of Kateri Tekakwitha, a Mohawk woman from central New York who in 2012 became the first indigenous American to be canonized by the Church.

Conflicts between Protestant England and Catholic France infused events that roiled Puritan communities as well, notably including the Salem witchcraft crisis of 1692. That famous and, in a certain sense, defining crisis reflected complex transformations of colonial authority and identity.

Though small in comparison to the witch trials that took place in Europe and the British Isles in roughly the same period, the tragic events at Salem, which culminated in the execution of twenty people, loom large in part because of their distinctive features and overdetermined meaning. The trials unfolded as the new royal charter transformed Massachusetts Bay from a colony to a province, shifting power to the metropolis. Meanwhile, rivals to Puritanism were becoming more visible, not only in New France, but also in other British colonies with different religious identities and competing understandings of the relationship between church and state. Maryland, established in 1634, had a strong association with both Catholicism and religious toleration, while Rhode Island, which had grown from Roger Williams's settlement at Providence, was granted a royal charter in 1663. The founding of the Quaker colony of Pennsylvania in 1681 posed an especially strong challenge to the Bay Colony, both because of the rapid growth of Philadelphia into a major hub and because of Quakerism's competing approach to Christian reform.

One of the most controversial features of Quakerism was its embrace of women's religious leadership. This issue resonated in the colony that had banished Anne Hutchinson in 1638 and, some two decades later, went on to execute Mary Dyer, a follower of Hutchinson who later embraced Quaker beliefs and returned to Massachusetts to challenge its authorities. In 1661, shortly after the end of the Commonwealth and the restoration of the monarchy, King Charles II rebuked the Bay Colony for executing Dyer and three male Quakers. Concerns about Puritan intolerance contributed to the new regime's approach to the Massachusetts charter, which unfolded over three decades even as the monarchy underwent a sustained period of instability that culminated in the Glorious Revolution of 1688, when the Catholic King James II was replaced by the Protestant monarchs William and Mary. All these developments contributed in important though indirect ways to the Salem proceedings.

Several men were executed during the Salem crisis, but the majority of the condemned were women. What's more, the first person to be accused was the enslaved woman Tituba, who was practicing folk rituals with a group of Puritan girls when the "afflictions" began. Probably an Indian from the South American mainland, Tituba had arrived in Salem by way of Barbados. In 1656, that island had been the immediate point of origin of the first Quaker evangelists to Massachusetts, who were accused of witchcraft and imprisoned. Though the Puritans understood what was happening to their community in different terms than those suggested here, focusing their fears on the presence of the devil in Massachusetts rather than on social, political, and religious pressures, their writings did at times reflect an awareness that many forces inflamed the crisis. Two selections in this volume give some insight into this symbolically important moment in early American literary history: the diary of Samuel Sewall, who had served as a judge in the Salem trials and went on to take an early stand against slavery, and the excerpt from Cotton Mather's Wonders of the Invisible World (1693), which shows how an internationally renowned Puritan intellectual who was attuned to the new science sought to understand the nature of witchcraft.

ENLIGHTENMENT IDEALS

The Salem witch trials proved to be a watershed moment, tied to dramatic social and economic changes during the late colonial period. These shifts were gradually matched by transformations in intellectual life. By the early eighteenth century, scientists and philosophers in Europe and the Americas had posed great challenges to seventeenth-century beliefs. Many intellectuals now embraced the power of the human mind to comprehend the universe as never before. What is sometimes called the "modern era"— characterized principally by the gradual supplanting of religious worldviews by scientific and philosophical ideas anchored in experiential knowledge— emerged from efforts to conceive of human existence in new terms. These developments in science and philosophy, known generally as the Enlightenment, did not necessarily lead to secularization. For example, Isaac Newton and John Locke—respectively, the leading English scientist and philosopher of the age—both sought to resolve implicit conflicts between their work and Christian tradition. Newton's study of the laws of motion and gravity had the potential to undermine religious beliefs insofar as it revealed a natural order that was perhaps independent of divine power. Locke's theory of the human mind as a tabula rasa, or blank slate, endowed with powers of perception but without innate content, posed a direct challenge to established forms of Christianity by calling into question the idea of original sin. Arguing that God worked in reasonable, not necessarily mysterious ways, these thinkers saw nothing heretical in contending that the universe was an orderly system whose laws humanity could comprehend through the application of reason.

Many Enlightenment scientists and philosophers deduced the existence of a supreme being from the construction of the universe rather than from the Bible, a view often called Deism. For many Deists, a harmonious universe could represent the beneficence of God, and this positivity extended to an optimistic view of human nature. Locke said that "our business" here on earth "is not to know all things, but those which concern our conduct," prompting his followers to consider human actions and motives as worthy objects of study. The philosophers of the Scottish Common Sense school built on Locke's insights about human faculties to propose that sympathy and sociability functioned as a kind of emotional glue that could unite communities no longer held together by shared beliefs and traditional structures of authority. Indeed, they claimed that one's supreme moral obligation was to relate to one's fellows through a natural power of sympathy. Adam Smith's *Theory of Moral Sentiments* (1759) was a notably influential contributor to this vein of social analysis. Meanwhile, earlier modes of thought—for instance, Bradford's and Winthrop's penchants for the allegorical and emblematic, with every natural and human event seen as a direct message from God—came to seem anachronistic and quaint.

Interest in ordinary individuals as part of nature and society led to developments in literature. While religiously themed works such as John Milton's *Paradise Lost* (1667) and John Bunyan's *Pilgrim's Progress* (1678) remained popular, the novel began to take a recognizably modern shape in the early eighteenth century. English novelists such as Aphra Behn, Daniel Defoe,

Samuel Richardson, Henry Fielding, and Laurence Sterne portrayed emotions and experiences with increasing directness. In the colonies, the influences that were giving birth to the Anglophone novel also engendered new forms of descriptive naturalist and ethnographic writing, exemplified here in selections from Sarah Kemble Knight, William Byrd, Alexander Hamilton, Hendrick Aupaumut, and William Bartram. The same confluence of intellectual and social developments also gave rise to nonfiction works such as Benjamin Franklin's *Autobiography* (written between 1771 and 1790).

George Whitefield, c. 1741, by John Wollaston. Transatlantic revivalist George Whitefield preaching to a crowded meeting during the Great Awakening.

Modernity has often been characterized as a radical break from faith-based forms of thought. Consider, however, that both the religious Bunyan and the more secular Defoe were among Franklin's literary influences. From the old to the new there were substantial continuities, as well as shifts that were more gradual than immediate. In the first half of the eighteenth century, a number of religious revivals occurred in England and America, but they were fueled by the new emphasis on emotion as a defining component of human experience. For example, the religious fires that burned from 1734 until about 1750 in what became known as the Great Awakening were directly produced by the Locke-inspired cult of feeling that was reshaping narrative prose. Now ministers, echoing the Enlightenment philosophers, argued that humanity's greatest pleasure—indeed, its purpose—was to do good for others and that sympathetic emotions might guarantee future glory. These ideas, a small part of earlier religious thought, acquired a new salience in connection with revivalism.

The most significant figure in transatlantic revivalism was Jonathan Edwards, a leading minister and theologian who helped form this new culture with a series of "awakenings" in and around Northampton, Massachusetts. Edwards's description of these events in *A Faithful Narrative of the Surprising Work of God* (1737) was hugely influential on the movement. Having read Locke, Edwards believed that if his parishioners were to be awakened from their spiritual slumbers they had to experience religion viscerally, not just comprehend it intellectually. In a series of sermons and treatises, Edwards worked to rejuvenate the basic tenets of Calvinism, including that of unconditional election, the sixteenth-century doctrine most difficult for eighteenth-century minds to accept.

Edwards insisted that such doctrines made sense in terms of Enlightenment science, and he developed what one literary historian has called a "rhetoric of sensation" to persuade his listeners that God's sovereignty was not only the most reasonable doctrine but also the most "delightful" and that it revealed itself to him, in an almost sensuous way, as "exceeding pleasant, bright, and sweet." In carefully reasoned, calmly argued prose, Edwards brought many in his audience to accept that "if the great things of religion are rightly understood, they will affect the heart." This "heart religion," as it later came to be known, involved both the terrors of hell, which Edwards describes in the sermon "Sinners in the Hands of an Angry God," and the joy that his faith brought him, as he expresses it in his "Personal Narrative" (c. 1740) and his apostrophe to his future wife, Sarah Pierpont (written in 1723). In Edwards's work, the pietist strains of Puritan writing—the embrace of emotion and its verbal expression—were amplified and brought close to similar developments in secular literature. For example, the English writer Samuel Richardson's novel *Pamela; or, Virtue Rewarded* (1740) was a favorite in the Edwards household.

The revivalists' styles of worship proved more welcoming to Native American and African American Christians than the Puritans' styles had been. Nonwhites had greater opportunities for literacy and training for the ministry, and mixed-race and nonwhite congregations were formed in increasing numbers. As a result, the Great Awakening fostered greater mingling of white, red, and black expressive styles in sacred song and speech—including hymnody, whose flourishing during the period also contributed to the growth of secular poetry—and led to the writing of some of the earliest English-language literature by Native Americans and African Americans. The writers John Marrant, Samson Occom, Hendrick Aupamut, Olaudah Equiano, and Phillis Wheatley emerged from this evangelical melding of cultures. At the same time, a parallel "Indians Great Awakening" revived indigenous spiritual practices and helped catalyze the resistance of leaders such as Sagoyewatha, Pontiac, and Tecumseh to colonial military and cultural power.

PURSUING HAPPINESS

In the second half of the eighteenth century, religion continued to play a major role in many colonists' lives even as politics took on a new importance. After winning the French and Indian War in 1763, Britain consolidated its empire in North America. To help pay for its war debt, the monarchy heavily taxed the colonies. Colonial resentments about increasingly heavy-handed tax policies escalated until April 1775, when the Battles of Lexington and Concord, both in Massachusetts, began the American Revolutionary War against Britain. That summer, representatives from the thirteen British North American colonies convened a Second Continental Congress to take charge of the war effort. In the June 7, 1776, session of this Congress, Richard Henry Lee of Virginia brought a decade of colonial agitation to the boiling point by moving that "these united colonies are, and of a right ought to be, free and independent states." Another Virginian, Thomas Jefferson, led a committee—including John Adams of Massachusetts and Benjamin Franklin of Pennsylvania—that drafted a Declaration of Independence, which was

The Destruction of Tea at Boston Harbor, lithograph by Nathaniel Currier. The Boston Tea Party of 1763, when colonists, some disguised as Native Americans, protested a new British tax on tea and other commodities.

issued on July 4. The heart of this document was the statement that "certain truths are self-evident, that all men are created equal, that they are endowed by their Creator with certain unalienable Rights, that among these are Life, Liberty and the pursuit of Happiness." These words reflect Jefferson's reading of the Scottish Common Sense philosophers, particularly Francis Hutcheson and Lord Kames (Henry Home), who built on Locke's work to argue that a moral sense is common to all humans. This universal sense of right and wrong justified the overthrow of tyrants, the restoration of political order, and the establishment of new covenants—not, as Bradford and Winthrop would have argued, for the glory of God, but, as the Declaration argued, for the individual's right to happiness on earth.

In January 1776 the young journalist Thomas Paine published his pamphlet *Common Sense,* which proved hugely influential in tipping the scales toward revolution. Though Paine probably did not choose his title to allude to the Scottish philosophers who were so important for Jefferson and other patriot leaders, his manifesto invoked similar ideas. In arguing that separation from England was the colonists' only reasonable course and that "the Almighty" had planted these feelings in us "for good and wise purposes," Paine appealed to basic tenets of the Enlightenment. He had emigrated from England to America in 1774 with a letter of recommendation from Benjamin Franklin. Franklin was, among many other things, a successful newspaper editor and printer, and Paine was quickly hired to edit the *Pennsylvania Magazine,* one of the new periodicals transforming the literary scene. The first newspaper in the colonies had appeared in 1704, and by the time of the Revolution there were almost fifty papers and forty magazines. Paine's magazine work helped shape a plain style that proved effective in catalyzing revolution. He was the most prominent of a number of writers who took

Syllabus of lectures from the Young Ladies' Academy, in Philadelphia, 1787. Educational opportunities for girls expanded after the American Revolution. The Young Ladies' Academy opened in 1787, attracting great interest from leaders in what was then the nation's capital.

advantage of the transformation in print culture that was to make modern authorship possible.

After the former colonists' victory over the British in 1783, people from greatly different backgrounds and of varied nationalities now found reasons to call themselves "Americans." America, as Washington Irving would later note, was a "logocracy," a polity based in and governed by words, and the political events of the 1770s presented a distinctive opportunity for writers. The most significant works of the period are political writings, and among the most notable of these are the essays that the statesmen Alexander Hamilton, John Jay, and James Madison wrote for New York newspapers in 1787–88

in support of the new federal Constitution, which are collectively known as *The Federalist* or *The Federalist Papers*. The impact of the revolution on the rise of early national literature can also be seen in the career of Philip Freneau, who aspired to be a full-time writer, combining journalism with belles lettres. Though he failed to sustain himself with his pen, Freneau made numerous contributions to the literature of the Revolution. His volume *Poems Written Chiefly during the Late War* (1786) contains notable patriotic works, and his later political poetry includes a tribute to Thomas Paine.

Women writers, too, expressed a revolutionary political sensibility. In the most famous letter of her lively and informative correspondence with her husband, John, Abigail Adams exhorted the Second Continental Congress to "remember the Ladies" in the new code of laws they were then framing. John and his fellows largely failed to heed Abigail's call. However, inspired by Enlightenment ideals of reason and equality, women such as Annis Boudinot Stockton, Judith Sargent Murray, Susanna Rowson, and Hannah Webster Foster wrote works exploring women's rights as citizens. Murray tackled the subject in her essays on the intellectual capacities of women, whereas Stockton's poems, as well as the writings of Rowson and Foster, explored the social and legal constraints on women and considered their right to be equal partners in the new nation's democratic experiment. Like such self-consciously "American" productions as Royall Tyler's play *The Contrast* (first performed 1787) and Franklin's *Autobiography*, these works mark the beginning of a new sense of national identity.

Not all the responses to the new order were enthusiastic or uncritical. For example, fiction offered an avenue for biting social critique. Often considered the first American novel, William Hill Brown's *The Power of Sympathy* was published in 1789, the year that the first government under the new Constitution was established. It tells an anti-utopian tale of incest and suicide. Charles Brockden Brown adapted the conventions of Gothic fiction to explore the dangers and limits of democratic republicanism in works such as his novella *Memoirs of Carwin, the Biloquist* (1803–05), a prequel to his better-known novel *Wieland; or The Transformation: An American Tale* (1798), which develops Carwin's story in tragic ways. Rowson's *Charlotte Temple* (1791) and Foster's *The Coquette* (1797) were important precursors of the many popular sentimental novels of the nineteenth century—most famously, Harriet Beecher Stowe's antislavery novel *Uncle Tom's Cabin* (1852)—that carried powerful social messages.

Perhaps the most hopeful aspects of the Revolution were represented by Benjamin Franklin, whose reputation continued to grow after his death, in 1790. As parts of his *Autobiography* appeared in print in 1791 and 1818— the full text finally became available in 1868—Franklin increasingly came to represent the promise of the Enlightenment in America. He was self-educated, social, assured, a man of the world, ambitious, public-spirited, speculative about the nature of the universe, and in matters of religion content "to observe the actual conduct of humanity rather than to debate supernatural matters that are unprovable"—a stance that John Locke had earlier endorsed. Franklin always presented himself as depending on first-hand experience, too worldly-wise to be caught off guard, and minding "the main chance" (i.e., for personal gain), as a Franklinian character in Tyler's

The Contrast counsels. These aspects of Franklin's persona, however, belie another side of him and of the eighteenth century: an idealistic assumption about the common good. He absorbed this sense partly from the works of Cotton Mather, which he encountered during his Boston youth, and it forms the basis of the American Revolution's great public documents, especially the Declaration of Independence.

The Revolution established the United States as an independent nation with ideals such as freedom and equality that were both ambitious and deeply ambiguous. The only people who consistently possessed the right to vote in the new government were white men who owned property. Most African Americans were enslaved, and many Native communities were being pushed off their lands. Yet Revolutionary principles appealed to some writers who suffered from their limited application. In 1774, the year she was manumitted, the poet Phillis Wheatley wrote a letter to the Mohegan leader and Presbyterian minister Samson Occom that was later printed in a dozen colonial newspapers. Here Wheatley posited that "in every human Breast, God has implanted a Principle, which we call Love of Freedom; it is impatient of Oppression, and pants for Deliverance." Though they sometimes used language similar to Wheatley's, Revolutionary leaders held conflicting views about slavery. George Washington, the first U.S. president, freed his slaves in his will. Thomas Jefferson, the third president, liberated just five slaves, leaving the vast majority in bondage at his death. Benjamin Franklin owned slaves for many years. He embraced the antislavery cause late in life, and in 1787 became the president of the first abolitionist organization in the United States. John Adams, the second U.S. president, never owned slaves and sought to gradually end the system through legislation, an effort that succeeded in some places. Even Adams, however, was uneasy with the Quaker-led abolitionist movement, whose at times confrontational strategies he believed counterproductive. The rising urgency of the abolitionists reflected changing realities. After the inventor Eli Whitney patented the cotton gin in 1794, the slave system gained a new lease on its brutal life. The end of the Atlantic slave trade in 1807 led, not to slavery's eventual demise as Adams and many others in the founding generation had hoped, but to forms of enslavement that in some ways were even crueler than before.

The conditions for many Native Americans also worsened in the nineteenth century. Various eastern tribes had sided with the British during the Revolution, driven by their vulnerability to colonial expansion. After the British defeat, they were exposed to the vengeance and greed of white Americans. Entire tribes were systematically displaced from their traditional territories, pushed ever farther west, or forced onto reservations. In an effort to resist the United States' encroachments on Native territory, the confederacy headed by Shawnee leader Tecumseh sided with the British in the War of 1812, a two-and-a-half-year conflict that resolved issues left from the Revolution with a U.S. victory. Meanwhile, Tecumseh's confederation collapsed after American forces killed him in 1813. "Indian Removal" was vigorously debated in the 1820s, with anti-Removal activism emerging as a major social movement. Eventually the movement failed, and Removal became the policy of the federal government.

In 1820, freedom and equality remained future prospects for multitudes of Americans. Many white men still could not vote unless they owned prop-

erty, though restrictions lessened more quickly over the next decade as universal white manhood suffrage became a reality. Women could not vote, and while the educational opportunities for white women were expanding, their legal status remained sharply limited. They were wards of their fathers until marriage, at which point their legal identities were merged with their husbands', so that they could not own property or keep any wages they earned. Yet many people embraced the idea that with the application of intelligence the principles of liberty could be extended and the human lot improved. This "progressive" or "perfectibilist" spirit was fostered in some places by newer liberal Churches such as the Unitarians and Universalists, as well as the more established Quakers. Imaginative energy flowed into extending the principles of liberty codified by the Revolutionary generation and correcting a variety of institutional and social injustices. In addition to the causes previously mentioned, post-Revolutionary social movements targeted the misuse of prisons, the use of capital punishment, the existence of war, and the treatment of the blind and disabled. Many works of literature reflected on this progressive sensibility, whether to foster it or to question its premises.

*

While at the start of the period covered in this volume "America" was merely notional—and its literature even more so—by 1820 "American literature" had come to mean something fairly specific: the poems, short stories, novels, essays, orations, plays, and other works produced by authors who hailed from, or resided in, the United States of America. As this list of genres suggests, "literature" itself had come to resemble its contemporary meaning more closely than it did in 1492. Printed works had become far more accessible, giving rise to an increasingly robust literary marketplace that featured both locally produced works and influential writings from across the Atlantic. Technological innovations such as the cylinder press created sweeping transformations in the book market, and new kinds of writers (women, African Americans, Native Americans, laborers) were finding outlets for their creations. All the while American literature continued to be shaped by its formation in the Atlantic world's crucible of cultures, its distinctive configuration of the sacred and the secular, the influence of the American Revolution, and the intertwined histories of empire and nation.

BEGINNINGS TO 1820

TEXTS	CONTEXTS
Peoples indigenous to the Americas orally perform and transmit various "literary" genres, including speeches, songs, and stories	
	1000–1300 Anasazi communities inhabit southwestern regions
	1492 Christopher Columbus arrives in the Bahamas • An estimated 4–7 million Native Americans in what is now the United States, including Alaska
1493 Columbus, **"Letter to Luis de Santangel Regarding the First Voyage"**	
	1500 Native American populations begin to be ravaged by European diseases • Enslaved Africans begin arriving in small numbers
	1514 Bartolomé de las Casas petitions Spanish Crown to treat Native American peoples as humanely as other subject populations
	1519–21 Cortés conquers Aztecs in Mexico
	1526 Spanish explorers bring first African slaves to South Carolina
	1539 First printing press in the Americas set up in Mexico City • Hernando de Soto invades Florida
1542 Álvar Núñez Cabeza de Vaca, *The Relation of Álvar Núñez Cabeza de Vaca*	
1552 Bartolomé de las Casas, *The Very Brief Relation of the Devastation of the Indies*	
	1558–1603 Reign of Elizabeth I
	1584 Walter Raleigh lands on "island" of Roanoke; names it "Virginia" for Queen Elizabeth (sometimes called the Virgin Queen)
	1603–13 Samuel de Champlain explores the Saint Lawrence River; founds Québec
	1607 Jamestown is established in Virginia • Powhatan confederacy saves colonists from starving; teaches them to plant tobacco
	1619 Twenty Africans arrive in Jamestown on a Dutch vessel as indentured servants; they are the first known Africans in a British colony
	1620 *Mayflower* drops anchor in Plymouth Harbor
	1621 First Thanksgiving, at Plymouth

Boldface titles indicate works in the anthology.

TEXTS	CONTEXTS
1624 John Smith, *The General History of Virginia, New England, and the Summer Isles*	
1630 John Winthrop, "A Model of Christian Charity" (pub. 1838)	1630–43 Immigration of English Puritans to Massachusetts Bay
1630–50 William Bradford writes *Of Plymouth Plantation* (pub. 1856)	1634 The first English settlers arrive in Maryland aboard *The Ark* and *The Dove*
1637 Thomas Morton, *New English Canaan*	1637 Pequot War
	1638 Anne Hutchinson banished from Bay Colony for challenging Puritan beliefs
1640 **Bay Psalm Book**	
1643 Roger Williams, *A Key into the Language of America*	1642–51 English Civil War
1650 Anne Bradstreet, *The Tenth Muse*	1649 Execution of Charles I
1662 Michael Wigglesworth, *The Day of Doom*	1660 Restoration of British monarchy
	1663 Royal Charter granted to Rhode Island (and Providence Plantation)
1673–1729 Samuel Sewall keeps his *Diary* (pub. 1878–82)	
	1675–76 King Philip's War destroys power of Native American tribes in New England
	1681 William Penn founds Pennsylvania
1682 Mary Rowlandson's *Narrative of the Captivity and Restoration*	
1682–1725 Edward Taylor writing his *Preparatory Meditations* (pub. 1939, 1960)	1689–97 King William's War (first of four colonial wars involving France, Britain, and Spain)
	1691 New royal charter creates the Province of Massachusetts Bay, which includes Plymouth
	1692 Salem witchcraft trials
1702 Cotton Mather, *Magnalia Christi Americana*	
	1718 French found New Orleans
	1726–56 The Great Awakening
1741 Jonathan Edwards, *Sinners in the Hands of an Angry God*	1741 Vitus Bering discovers Alaska
	1755–63 French and Indian Wars
1768 Samson Occom, *A Short Narrative of My Life* (pub. 1982)	
1771–90 Benjamin Franklin continues his *Autobiography* (Part I pub. 1818)	
1773 Phillis Wheatley, *Poems on Various Subjects*	1773 Boston Tea Party
1774–83 John and Abigail Adams exchange **letters** (pub. 1840, 1875)	
	1775–83 American Revolutionary War

TEXTS	CONTEXTS
1776 Thomas Paine, *Common Sense*	1776 Declaration of Independence
1780s Annis Boudinot Stockton publishes **poems** in magazines and newspapers	
1782 J. Hector St. John de Crèvecoeur, *Letters from an American Farmer*	
	1783 Britain opens "Old Northwest" (region south of Great Lakes) to United States after Treaty of Paris ends American Revolution
1786 Philip Freneau, *Poems*	
1787 Thomas Jefferson, *Notes on the State of Virginia* • Royall Tyler, *The Contrast*	1787 U.S. Constitution adopted
1787–88 *The Federalist* papers	
1789 Olaudah Equiano, *The Interesting Narrative of the Life of Olaudah Equiano*	1789 George Washington elected first president
1790 Judith Sargent Murray, *On the Equality of the Sexes*	
	1791 Washington, D.C., established as U.S. capital
1797 Hannah Foster, *The Coquette*	
1803–05 Charles Brockden Brown, *Memoirs of Carwin*	1803 United States buys Louisiana Territory from France
	1812–14 War of 1812 (against England)
1819 Washington Irving, *Rip Van Winkle*	1819 Spain exchanges the Florida Territory for U.S. assumption of $5 million in debts • Missouri asks to be admitted as a slave state, sparking a crisis resolved the next year through the Missouri Compromise

Native American Oral Literature

The languages, political economies, and religious beliefs of Native American peoples are extremely diverse, and so are their tales, orations, songs, chants, and other oral genres. Examples of oral works include the trickster tale cycles of the Winnebago Indians (or Ho-Chunks), Apache jokes, Hopi personal naming and grievance chants, Yaqui deer songs, and Yuman dream songs. Many genres have a religious or spiritual dimension, including Piman shamanic chants, Iroquois condolence rituals, Navajo curing and blessing chants, and Chippewa songs of the Great Medicine Society. Most of the works were not translated into alphabetic forms until long after the arrival of Europeans, and the circumstances of their initial creation and development are largely unknown. The use of written records in the precontact Americas was relatively circumscribed, and European conquerors systematically destroyed the bodies of writing in places such as Tenochtitlán (present-day Mexico City), leaving just a handful of the pictograph codices known as *amoxtli* to carry forward pre-Columbian practices. Other indigenous American recording devices include Andean *quipu*, which are colored, knotted strings used to represent a numeric system. In North America, painted hides or bark and wampum belts made of shell could serve as prompts for the recitation of tales or in treaty negotiations and other ceremonies. These nonalphabetic texts share some of the mnemonic and narrative functions of literature.

Although the term "literature" comes from the Latin *littera*, "letter," and so has been linked to alphabetic writing, all literature has roots in the oral arts. In keeping with Aristotle's *Poetics* (c. 335 B.C.E.), the earliest surviving work of literary theory, forms of Western literature have traditionally been grouped into lyric, which takes its name from the lyre, a stringed instrument used by the ancient Greeks to accompany a song or recitation; drama, which originated in the religious cultures of ancient Greece and the medieval Christian Church; and epic (more broadly, narrative), developed in and for oral performance. (The first works of Euro-American literature, the *Vinland Sagas* of the thirteenth century, are epics.) Rhetoric and oratory, which Aristotle treated separately from the other forms because of their prominent and distinctive place in ancient Greek culture, also involve the spoken word. There are parallels as well as differences between these Aristotelian genres and the types of oral literature created by the earliest American societies.

From first contact, Europeans were intrigued by indigenous oral performances and sought to translate them into alphabetic written forms. Christopher Columbus and the explorers who came after him described the formal speeches of Native leaders, even though they often did not understand their meaning. Over time, Native artists taught Europeans and European Americans to recognize other kinds of verbal art, such as creation tales and poetic songs. Eventually collaboration and indigenous authorship became more common. Today scholars are actively studying pre-Columbian history and art, and the sources and traditions of the most ancient texts from the American hemisphere are gradually coming to be better understood.

The archive of Native American oral genres continues to expand as new instances are identified in the written record or transcribed in a modern form. The selections in this cluster represent some genres that were common in the repertoires of many North American indigenous societies before 1820: creation and trickster tales,

orations, and songs (here rendered as poems). Native American creation stories serve Native cultures much as the Book of Genesis serves the Judeo-Christian world: they posit a general outlook and offer perspectives on what life is and how to understand it. All Native peoples have stories of the earliest times; reprinted here are two, one from the Iroquois of the Northeast and one from the Navajo of the Southwest. Like creation stories, trickster tales are among the most ancient elements of Native American cultures, and they have survived because they provide both pleasure and instruction. The term "trickster" is often used to describe a wandering, bawdy, gluttonous, and obscene figure, a threat to order everywhere. Yet a trickster can also be a culture hero, one who long ago helped establish the order of the world that we know today, and in this way as well trickster tales resemble creation stories. The qualities of this paradoxical figure—both creator and destroyer of order—are on display in the selection from the Winnebago trickster cycle included in this section.

Oratory was the first Native American genre that Europeans recognized as a verbal art. Formalized speech is a common feature of human cultures, notably in diplomatic settings, whether a reception at a European court or a performance of an Iroquois condolence ritual. The formalized modes of address that Native Americans used in their early encounters with Europeans were often lavishly described in narratives, such as the account of Sir Francis Drake's voyage excerpted here. One reason such scenes were central in Renaissance-era accounts is that the writers were imitating classical historiography, with its emphasis on oratory. As set pieces in their narratives, the writers included moving and aesthetically pleasing speeches based more or less loosely on memory and other sources. "Powhatan's Discourse of Peace and War," by John Smith, and "King Philip's Speech," by William Apess, are reconstructed works that provide narrative drama in their original contexts and stand alone as effective examples of Native eloquence.

The poems included here were transcribed by Euro-Americans in the eighteenth and early nineteenth centuries, reflecting an evolving approach to Native American oral genres. While the three recorders of these works served as diplomats and, in one case, as a missionary, they took an active interest in indigenous verbal arts. At the time, a ballad revival in Britain had awakened a curiosity about oral traditions and popular culture, a curiosity that fed into literary Romanticism. Transcriber-authors took indigenous forms from their ritual or other performance contexts and brought them in written form to non-Native audiences. These transcribers often collaborated with the artists to present something of the larger contexts and significances of the works to readers.

The selections in this cluster illustrate the variety of ways that Native American oral literature has been experienced historically, and suggest some of the pleasures and complexities involved in its reception today. Whether reconstructed from memory, recorded with the aid of a translator, or produced by Native authors, they provide insight into the verbal arts of pre-Columbian America as they have survived to the present. The more modern works included here were created with the involvement of indigenous verbal artists, and their sources can be traced to the period before 1820 covered by this volume.

STORIES OF THE BEGINNING
OF THE WORLD

THE IROQUOIS CREATION STORY

The people known collectively as the Iroquois (as the French called them), or the Five Nations (as the English called them), were made up of the Mohawk, Seneca, Oneida, Onondaga, and Cayuga nations. This confederacy may have formed in the thirteenth or fourteenth century. In the eighteenth century, the Tuscarora of North Carolina joined the confederacy, which became the Six Nations. The heart of Iroquois country lies in what is now upstate New York, west of the Hudson River. At different times in its long history "the ambiguous Iroquois Empire," as one scholar has termed it, extended around Lake Ontario, including parts of what is now Canada, and south into present-day Pennsylvania. The Six Nations called themselves People of the Longhouse (*Haudenosaunee* in Seneca, *Kanosoni* in Mohawk), in reference to their primary type of dwelling. Their longhouses were about twenty feet wide and from forty to two hundred feet long, accommodating several families who shared cooking fires. The largest Iroquois towns included as many as two thousand people.

The Iroquois creation story exists in some twenty-five written or printed versions, making it one of the best-known instances of Native American oral literature. The Frenchman Gabriel Sagard first translated and transcribed the tale in 1623. Two centuries later, David Cusick became the first Native person to write it down. Cusick published the version included here on the eve of Andrew Jackson's election to the presidency, and he was well aware of Jackson's stated intention of "removing"

Atotarho. This is one of four engravings that David Cusick included in the second edition (1828) of *Sketches of the Ancient History of the Six Nations*. It shows the war chief of the Onondagas, Atotarho, said to be a sorcerer, with a twisted body and snakes in his hair. Several times Atotarho rejected pleas from the Great Peacemaker, Deganawidah, and his follower, Hiawatha, that he join them in uniting the Iroquois. Finally, after they healed him and combed the tangles from his hair, he agreed and became the traditional "firekeeper"—tender of the sacred fire—of the Iroquois Confederacy.

eastern Indians to lands west of the Mississippi. Perhaps because the Iroquois were under intensifying pressure from white settlement, Cusick's version emphasizes the conflict between the twins Enigorio, the good mind, and Enigonhahetgea, the bad mind. Although the story involves monsters and supernatural events, Cusick calls the work a history, because it tells the history of the Iroquois Confederacy.

David Cusick was born around 1780 on the Oneida Reservation in central New York, in Madison County, to a Tuscorora family. His father, Nicholas, an important leader among his people, was a Christian who had served on the American side during the Revolution. Educated by the missionary Samuel Kirkland, David Cusick became a physician and an artist. The woodcuts at the front of the second edition (1828) of his *Sketches of the Ancient History of the Six Nations* are his work. Cusick's *Sketches* was well known in its time and served as an important source for Henry Rowe Schoolcraft's influential *Notes on the Iroquois* (1847), which shaped the literary culture of the day. In his preface to that work, Schoolcraft wrote that "no nation of the widely spread red race of America, has displayed so high and heroic a love of liberty, united with the true art of government, and personal energy and stamina of character, as the Iroquois."

Part I of Cusick's *Sketches*, excerpted here, deals with the foundation and establishment of the Iroquois world. Parts II and III present the ancient Iroquois as defending themselves against both monsters and other tribes by means that may have resonated with the Iroquois defense against expansionist Americans.

The Iroquois Creation Story[1]

A Tale of the Foundation of the Great Island, Now North America;— the Two Infants Born, and the Creation of the Universe

Among the ancients there were two worlds in existence. The lower world was in great darkness;—the possession of the great monster; but the upper world was inhabited by mankind; and there was a woman conceived[2] and would have the twin born. When her travail drew near, and her situation seemed to produce a great distress on her mind, and she was induced by some of her relations to lay herself on a mattress which was prepared, so as to gain refreshments to her wearied body; but while she was asleep the very place sunk down towards the dark world.[3] The monsters of the great water were alarmed at her appearance of descending to the lower world; in consequence all the species of the creatures were immediately collected into where it was expected she would fall. When the monsters were assembled, and they made consultation, one of them was appointed in haste to search the great deep, in order to procure some earth, if it could be obtained; accordingly the monster descends, which succeeds, and returns to the place. Another requisition was presented, who would be capable to secure the woman from the terrors of the great water, but none was able to comply except a large turtle

1. The text is from the first edition of *Sketches of the Ancient History of the Six Nations* (1827).
2. I.e., a woman, known as Sky Woman, who became pregnant without sexual activity. "Mankind": humans, although they have different powers than those of humans as we understand them. "The great monster": or monsters, undefined

creatures. In other versions, the "monsters" are some type of familiar animal; here, Cusick conveys the mystery and danger in the unformed universe.
3. Other versions have Sky Woman either being pushed out of the upper world or accidentally falling.

came forward and made proposal to them to endure her lasting weight, which was accepted. The woman was yet descending from a great distance. The turtle executes upon the spot, and a small quantity of earth was varnished on the back part of the turtle. The woman alights on the seat prepared, and she receives a satisfaction.[4] While holding her, the turtle increased every moment and became a considerable island of earth, and apparently covered with small bushes. The woman remained in a state of unlimited darkness, and she was overtaken by her travail to which she was subject. While she was in the limits of distress one of the infants in her womb was moved by an evil opinion and he was determined to pass out under the side of the parent's arm, and the other infant in vain endeavoured to prevent his design.[5] The woman was in a painful condition during the time of their disputes, and the infants entered the dark world by compulsion, and their parent expired in a few moments. They had the power of sustenance without a nurse, and remained in the dark regions. After a time the turtle increased to a great Island and the infants were grown up, and one of them possessed with a gentle disposition, and named ENIGORIO, i.e. the good mind. The other youth possessed an insolence of character, and was named ENIGONHAHET-GEA, i.e. the bad mind.[6] The good mind was not contented to remain in a dark situation, and he was anxious to create a great light in the dark world; but the bad mind was desirous that the world should remain in a natural state. The good mind determines to prosecute his designs, and therefore commences the work of creation. At first he took the parent's head, (the deceased) of which he created an orb, and established it in the centre of the firmament, and it became of a very superior nature to bestow light to the new world, (now the sun) and again he took the remnant of the body and formed another orb, which was inferior to the light (now moon). In the orb a cloud of legs appeared to prove it was the body of the good mind, (parent). The former was to give light to the day and the latter to the night; and he also created numerous spots of light, (now stars); these were to regulate the days, nights, seasons, years, etc. Whenever the light extended to the dark world the monsters were displeased and immediately concealed themselves in the deep places, lest they should be discovered by some human beings. The good mind continued the works of creation, and he formed numerous creeks and rivers on the Great Island, and then created numerous species of animals of the smallest and the greatest, to inhabit the forests, and fishes of all kinds to inhabit the waters. When he had made the universe he was in doubt respecting some being to possess the Great Island; and he formed two images of the dust of the ground in his own likeness, male and female,

4. I.e., she lands safely, without harm.

5. Other versions of the story have Sky Woman give birth to a daughter, who again becomes supernaturally pregnant (perhaps by the spirit of the turtle), and it is *she* who conceives the twins. The twins argue even in the womb, the Evil Twin deciding not to be born in the normal way but to burst through his mother's side, which leads to her death. The theme of rival twins is widespread in the Americas.

6. More commonly, the Good Twin is called Tharonhiawagon (Sky-Grasper, Creator, or Upholder of the Heavens), and the Evil Twin is

named Tawiscaron (Evil-Minded, Flint, Ice, Patron of Winter, or various disasters). Cusick's Enigorio is a rough translation of the Tuscarora word for "good-minded" into Mohawk, and his Enigonhahetgea is an equally rough translation into Seneca, Onondaga, or Cayuga of the Tuscarora word for "bad-minded." Cusick has probably changed the Tuscarora words best known to him into these other Iroquois languages because they were considered to be more prestigious than Tuscarora, the Tuscaroras having only recently joined the Iroquois Confederacy.

and by his breathing into their nostrils he gave them the living souls, and named them EA-GWE-HOWE, i.e., a real people;[7] and he gave the Great Island all the animals of game for their maintenance and he appointed thunder to water the earth by frequent rains, agreeable of the nature of the system; after this the Island became fruitful and vegetation afforded the animals subsistence. The bad mind, while his brother was making the universe, went throughout the Island and made numerous high mountains and falls of water, and great steeps, and also creates various reptiles which would be injurious to mankind; but the good mind restored the Island to its former condition. The bad mind proceeded further in his motives and he made two images of clay in the form of mankind; but while he was giving them existence they became apes;[8] and when he had not the power to create mankind he was envious against his brother; and again he made two of clay. The good mind discovered his brother's contrivances, and aided in giving them living souls, (it is said these had the most knowledge of good and evil). The good mind now accomplishes the works of creation, notwithstanding the imaginations of the bad mind were continually evil; and he attempted to enclose all the animals of game in the earth, so as to deprive them from mankind; but the good mind released them from confinement, (the animals were dispersed, and traces of them were made on the rocks near the cave where it was closed). The good mind experiences that his brother was at variance with the works of creation, and feels not disposed to favor any of his proceedings, but gives admonitions of his future state. Afterwards the good mind requested his brother to accompany him, as he was proposed to inspect the game, etc., but when a short distance from their moninal residence,[9] the bad mind became so unmanly that he could not conduct his brother any more.[1] The bad mind offered a challenge to his brother and resolved that who gains the victory should govern the universe; and appointed a day to meet the contest. The good mind was willing to submit to the offer, and he enters the reconciliation with his brother; which he falsely mentions that by whipping with flags would destroy his temporal life;[2] and he earnestly solicits his brother also to notice the instrument of death, which he manifestly relates by the use of deer horns, beating his body he would expire. On the day appointed the engagement commenced, which lasted for two days: after pulling up the trees and mountains as the track of a terrible whirlwind, at last the good mind gained the victory by using the horns, as mentioned the instrument of death, which he succeeded in deceiving his brother and he crushed him in the earth; and the last words uttered from the bad mind were, that he would have equal power over the souls of mankind after death; and

7. Humans. "EA-GWE-HOWE": Tuscarora term used by speakers of all the languages of the Six Nations; today, it simply means Indian or Indians.

8. Cusick may have seen an ape or a depiction of apes (there are no apes native to the New World) and decided to name them as the creatures made by the Evil Twin in contrast to the humans made by the Good Twin. Some later renditions of the Iroquois creation story also refer to apes at this point in the narrative.

9. Cusick perhaps means their nominal (named or designated) residence.

1. I.e., the Evil Twin became so rude and obnoxious that the Good Twin could not lead ("conduct") his brother to the appointed place any longer.

2. The Good Twin tells his brother that he can be killed by being beaten with corn stalks, rushes, reeds, or cattails. Cusick calls this a deception; other accounts treat it as a confession of weakness. Next, the Evil Twin admits that he would die if beaten with the antlers of deer.

he sinks down to eternal doom, and became the Evil Spirit.[3] After this tumult the good mind repaired to the battle ground, and then visited the people and retires from the earth.[4]

3. This event may reflect an awareness of the Christian belief in the devil as the ultimate evil spirit, ruler over the lower depths.

4. Other versions go on to say that the Good Twin teaches the people how to grow corn and how to avoid harm by means of prayer and ritual.

THE NAVAJO CREATION STORY

The Navajo language is closely related to that of some Canadian and Alaskan tribes, reflecting the history of its speakers. The Navajo Nation, or Din'e— "the People," migrated to the Southwest from more northerly points somewhere between six hundred and a thousand years ago. There they learned farming and weaving from long-settled Pueblo peoples and silverworking skills from Mexicans. They were first called Navajo—from *Apachu de Nabajo*, or Apaches Who Cultivate Fields—by Spanish invaders in the sixteenth century. The Navajo Nation today is the second-largest indigenous group in the United States, outnumbered only by the Cherokees. It occupies an area in Arizona, New Mexico, and Utah larger than the combined area of Massachusetts, New Hampshire, and Vermont.

The Navajo story of the "emergence" of the People and their establishment of a world is ancient and complex. It describes a progressive creation that occurs in four or five stages, depending on the version, and culminates in the emergence of the "glittering world," that is, the world we now inhabit. The tale highlights the constant work involved to develop and sustain relations of harmony and balance among the gods, the People, and all other sentient beings. Especially central is the cultivation of a relationship of harmony and balance between husband and wife, reflected in the relationship between First Man and First Woman. The presence of the *Nádleeh*, that is, "those who have the spirit of both male and female," is important to this balance. The Nádleeh are the first of five pairs of twins born to First Man and First Woman. They are either hermaphrodites or men performing what was regarded as women's work, for which they are in no way stigmatized. Indeed, they are credited with creating pottery and basketry, two arts of great significance in Navajo culture.

Other important relationships in the tale include the ties between the Din'e and the *Hashch'ééh Dine'é*, the Holy People, who are instrumental in creating humankind and provide instruction in matters of life and death, teaching the Din'e about evil as well as good; and with the *Kiis'áanii*, that is, the Pueblo peoples. Animals and other nonhuman creatures play significant roles in the tale, as when the trickster Coyote (*Mai'i*) produces a flood that threatens to wipe out the People.

The Navajo have produced a rich body of oral literature—narrative and poetry—including several written versions of the Navajo creation story. The earliest written version is from the late nineteenth century. Printed here is a contemporary retelling by the Navajo teacher and writer Irvin Morris. Born in 1958, Morris is a member of the Tobaahi, or Water's Edge clan of the Navajo Nation. The recipient of an MFA in creative writing from Cornell University and a doctorate in American Indian Studies from the State University of New York at Buffalo, he teaches at Din'e College in Tsaile, Arizona. Morris begins his book *From the Glittering World*—a blend of history, fictionalized memoir, and Navajo stories—with this version of the creation story to situate the non-Navajo reader.

Hajíínéí[1]

(The Emergence)

Alk'idáá' jinni.[2] It happened a long time ago, they say. In the beginning there was only darkness, with sky above and water below. Then by some mysterious and holy means, sky and water came together. When they touched, that's when everything began. That was the First World, which was like an island floating in a sea of mist. It was red in color and it was an ancient place. There were no people living there, only *Nílch'i Dine'é*,[3] who existed in spiritual form. They could travel like the wind. There were also *Hashch'ééh Dine'é*, the Holy People, whose form and beauty we have inherited. There was no sun or moon, and there were no stars. The only source of light was the sky, which comprised four sacred colors and glowed with a different hue and lit the world from a different direction according to the time of day. When the eastern sky glowed white, it was considered dawn, and the *Nílch'i Dine'é* would awaken and began to stir in preparation for the day. When the southern sky glowed blue, it was considered day, and the *Nílch'i Dine'é* went about their daily activities. When the western sky was yellow, it was considered evening, and the *Nílch'i Dine'é* put away their work and amusements. When the northern sky turned black, it was considered night, and the *Nílch'i Dine'é* lay down and went to sleep. At the center of that First World, there was a place called *Tóbilhaask'id*[4] where water welled up out of the ground in a great fountain, which was the source of three rivers flowing toward the east, south, and west. No river flowed toward the north, the direction of death and darkness. There were twelve groups of *Nílch'i Dine'é* dwelling in twelve places in that First World, with four groups living in each of the three directions. No one lived to the north. These *Nílch'i Dine'é* had lived there from the very beginning. They were called ants, dragonflies, beetles, bats, and locusts, but they were spiritual beings, not insects or animals. The waters surrounding their world were inhabited by four powerful guardians, *Tééholtsódii* (the Water Monster) to the east, *Dééhtsoh dootl'izh* (Blue Heron) to the south, *Ch'al* (Frog) to the west, and *Ii'ni'dzil ligai* (White Mountain Thunder) to the north. These spiritual beings had lived peacefully and amicably in that world for a long time; but after a while trouble arose, and it was because of adultery.[5] The First World was a holy place, and the immoral behavior of the *Nílch'i Dine'é* angered the water guardians, who did not like what they saw. They did not like the deceit, jealousy, and turmoil that resulted from the debauchery. "Do you not like living here?" the guardians scolded. "Do you not value this place? If you cannot behave properly, then you must leave." Three times they were warned by the guardians, but the *Nílch'i Dine'é* did not listen. When they

1. The text is from chapter 1 of Irvin Morris, *From the Glittering World* (1997).
2. A long time ago, they say, or it is said. Morris begins his written performance of the creation story with this traditional opening to remind his readers that he is telling a story told many times before. The editor is indebted to Irvin Morris for help with the annotations to this text.
3. Supernatural or spiritual beings associated with wind or air.
4. Place where Streams Come Together; an elevated place such as a hill or mound, perhaps suggesting a raised fountain.
5. Even for spiritual beings, adultery destroys the harmony between husbands and wives.

corrupted themselves a fourth time,[6] *Ii'ni'dzil ligaii*, the guardian being from the north, who hadn't spoken before, said, "Because you do not listen, you must depart at once!" But the *Nílch'i Dine'é* were lost in their wickedness and did not heed. Seeing this, the guardians were outraged and turned their backs on them; they refused to listen to excuses or pleas for forgiveness. The *Nílch'i Dine'é* had to be punished. One morning they saw something on the horizon. It looked like a ring of snowy mountains surrounding them, an unbroken wall of white higher and wider than they could fly across. When it came closer, they saw what it was. The water guardians had sent a great flood. Frightened, the *Nílch'i Dine'é* soared into the air and flew in circles until they reached the sky, but then they discovered that it was smooth and solid. They tried to break through the rigid surface, but they could not even make a scratch. Just as they were ready to give up in despair, a strange blue head emerged from the sky. "Go to the east," it said. The *Nílch'i Dine'é* went to the east and flew through the narrow opening into a blue world, the Second World. There they looked around and saw that the land was barren and flat. They did not see anyone living nearby. Scouts were sent out to see if there were others like themselves further out, but after two days they returned saying they could find no one. But then, one morning, a small group of blue beings appeared. The *Nílch'i Dine'é* saw that these blue beings were like themselves—with legs, feet, bodies, and wings like theirs—and they realized that they could understand their language. The blue beings, who were Swallows,[7] welcomed the newcomers and addressed them as kinsmen. They promised to be friends and allies forever, but before long one of the *Nílch'i Dine'é* took liberties with the head Swallow's wife. That treachery was quickly discovered, and bad feelings immediately arose. "Traitors!" the Swallows cried. "We took you in as friends and relatives, and this is how you repay us? Could this be why you were asked to leave the lower world?" The Swallows demanded that they leave immediately, and once again the *Nílch'i Dine'é* took flight. Once again they encountered a solid sky and could not find an entrance. Just when they were about to give up, a white head mysteriously appeared. "Go to the south," it said. There the locusts led them into the Third World, which was white, through a crooked opening. Again scouts were sent out, and again they found nothing. But in time they discovered that this world was inhabited by Grasshoppers.[8] The *Nílch'i Dine'é* begged the Grasshoppers to let them stay. As before, the hosts addressed the *Nílch'i Dine'é* as friends and kin and mingled with them. All went well for a while, but then one of the *Nílch'i Dine'é* grew weak and committed adultery with the wife of a Grasshopper. The Grasshoppers were incensed and told the *Nílch'i Dine'é* to leave. This time, when they encountered the impenetrable sky, a red head materialized. "Go to the west," it said. When they entered into the Fourth World through a winding entrance hole in the west, they saw that it was black and white. No one greeted them. The land appeared empty. But they saw four great snow-capped mountains in the distance: one to the east, another to the south, a third to the west, and the fourth to the north. The scouts were dispatched to see if anyone

6. Four, sometimes as two pairs of two, is an important pattern number for the Navajos, signifying completion or wholeness.
7. Supernaturals of the earliest times, who were precursors of today's swallows.
8. Supernaturals who were the precursors of today's grasshoppers.

lived on those mountains, but they failed to reach the first three. When they went to the northern mountain, however, they returned with fascinating news. A strange group of beings lived there, dwelling in holes in the ground. These were *Kiis'áanii*, the Pueblo peoples, who were living in pit-houses.[9] The *Nílch'i Dine'é* immediately set out to greet the inhabitants of this new land, who welcomed them and prepared a feast of corn, squash, pumpkins, and beans. This time, the *Nílch'i Dine'é* resolved to behave themselves. And true to their word, they conducted themselves well, and their days passed uneventfully. Then one day a voice was heard calling from the east. Three times the voice called, each time coming closer. Upon the fourth call, four mysterious beings appeared. They were Holy People: White Body, who is called *Hashch'éélti'í* (Talking God); Blue Body, known as *Tóneinilii* (Water Sprinkler); Yellow Body, called *Hasch'éélitsoi* (Calling God); and Black Body, referred to as *Hashch'é lizhin* (Fire God). These Holy People did not speak, but they tried to communicate with motions and gestures. However, the *Nílch'i Dine'é* did not understand them. Thus the Holy People appeared, four times over four days. On the fourth day, when the *Nílch'i Dine'é* still could not understand the signs, Black Body finally spoke: "We want to make more people, but in forms that are more pleasing to us," he said. "You have bodies like us, but you also have the teeth, feet, and claws of insects and four-leggeds. And you smell bad. But first, you must purify yourselves before we return." And so the *Nílch'i Dine'é* washed themselves and dried their limbs with sacred cornmeal, white for men and yellow for women. On the twelfth day the deities returned, bringing with them two buckskins and two ears of corn. Blue Body and Black Body carried two buckskins, one of which they laid on the ground. Yellow Body carried two perfect ears of corn, white and yellow, and laid them on the buckskin. The second buckskin was placed over the corn and the *Nílch'i Dine'é* were told to stand back, and the sacred wind entered between the buckskins. As the wind blew, Mirage People appeared and walked around the buckskins. On the fourth turn, the ears of corn moved. When the buckskin was lifted, a man and woman lay where the ears of corn had been. The white ear had been turned into a man and the yellow ear had been turned into a woman. These were *Áltsé Hastiin* and *Áltsé Asdzáán*, First Man and First Woman. These were the first real people, five-fingered beings, and they were made in the image of the Holy People.[1] The Holy People then instructed these new people to build a shelter. First Man and First Woman entered the shelter and thus became husband and wife. First Man was given a rock crystal—the symbol of clear thought—to burn for fire, and First Woman was given turquoise—which represents the power of speech—to burn. In four days a pair of twins were born to them, and these first children were *Nádleeh*, those who have the spirit of both male and female. Only the first pair were like that. In four days another pair of twins were born, and so on. In all, five pairs of twins were born to them. Four days after the birth of the pair of twins, the Holy People took First Man and First Woman away to the east, to the sacred mountains where they dwelt. There, First Man and First Woman remained for four days. When they returned, the Holy People then took all their children to the east and kept them for

9. *Kiis'áanii* means "People Who Live in Upright Houses." The ancient Pueblo peoples lived in various structures, including pit-houses with roofs supported by upright timbers.

1. The Hashch'ééh Dine'é, mentioned in the opening lines of the tale.

four days too. It is during this time that they all received instructions from the Holy People. They learned how to live a good life and to conduct themselves in a manner befitting their divine origins. But because the Holy People were capable of good and evil, they also learned about the terrible secrets of witchcraft as well. After they returned, First Man and First Woman were occasionally seen wearing masks resembling *Hashch'éhooghan* and *Hashch'éélti'í*.[2] While thus attired they were holy and they prayed for good things for the people: long life, ample rain, and abundant harvests. Those ceremonies were passed on to bless and protect future generations; the prayers, songs, and rituals have not changed from that time. When it came time to marry, the children of First Man and First Woman joined with the *Kiis'áanii* and the children of the Mirage People[3] and others. In four days, children were born to these couples, and in four days those descendants bore offspring also. Soon the land was populated with the growing progeny of First Man and First Woman. They planted great fields of corn and other crops. They also built an earthen dam, and the *Nádleeh* were appointed to be its guardians; while they watched over the dam they created beautiful and useful things, pottery and basketry, and the people praised these inventions. For eight years they lived in comfort and peace. Their days passed uneventfully. Then one day, they saw a strange thing: they saw the sky reach down, while at the same time the earth rose up to meet it. From the point of their union sprang two beings now known as Coyote and Badger,[4] the children of the sky. Their arrival portended both good and bad things for the people. The people prospered for many years, but one day First Woman and First Man had an argument. First Man was a great hunter and provided much food, but First Woman made an ungrateful remark that insulted and greatly angered First Man.[5] He left her and went to the other side of the fire and remained there all night. In the morning First Man called together all the men and told them about First Woman's insult. "Let's teach the women a lesson," he said. "We shall gather our tools and belongings and move away. They'll learn they can't get along without us after all." The men agreed and gathered up their tools and all the things they had made. First Man, recalling the industriousness of the *Nádleeh*, invited them to come along, and they brought their grinding stones, baskets, cooking utensils, and other useful implements. The men crossed the river and quickly set up a new camp. They cut brush and built new shelters and hunted. When they were hungry, the *Nádleeh* cooked for them. Across the river, the planted fields they had left behind were ripening. Soon the women harvested corn and other crops and made ready for the winter. Their harvest was abundant and they ate well. They pitied the men, who had to do without fresh corn, squash, and beans. In the evenings, they came down to the river and called to the men and taunted them. "How are you getting along over there? Do you remember the taste of roasted corn?" The men had brought seeds with them, but since it was so late in the season, they had not planted. That winter they ate mostly cakes and mush made from the cornmeal that the *Nádleeh* had brought

2. House God and Talking God, respectively, although these gods also have other names.
3. Like the Holy People, supernatural beings.
4. Powerful godlike creatures.
5. In other versions of the story, First Woman's remark is a very bawdy suggestion that not First Man but *joosh* (the vagina) is, by her indirect reasoning, responsible for successful hunting and the provision of food. First Man's response represents an excessive loss of self-control.

along. The following spring, however, the men planted fields larger than those planted by the women. And this time, without the men's help in the fields, the women's harvest was not as plentiful as before. That winter they did not taunt the men. By the fourth year, the men could not eat all the food they grew, and most of it was left in the fields. The women, however, began to run short of food and soon were facing starvation. They had also begun to miss the company of men. The more brazen used objects such as cacti and smooth stones to satisfy themselves, and some say the monsters that later plagued the people were the result of that practice. In time, First Man realized that they could not live apart forever. He realized that the people were in danger of dying out if they did not reproduce. One evening he called to First Woman and they talked about this. They decided that unless they became one people again they would disappear. So the women crossed the river on rafts and joined the men again, and there was great rejoicing and feasting. However, it was soon discovered that three women were missing, a woman and her two daughters. The people thought they had drowned, but they had been captured instead by the Water Monster, *Tééholtsódii*. The people called to the Holy People for help, and White Body and Blue Body appeared with two shells. They set these shells on the water and caused them to spin, and the water underneath the spinning shell opened up to reveal the four-chambered dwelling where the monster lived. Accompanied by Coyote a man and woman descended to the dwelling and searched the chambers—first the one to the east, which was a room of dark waters, then the one to the south, which was made of blue waters; then the one to the west, which was made of yellow waters—and found nothing. Then they entered the north chamber, which was the one made of waters of all colors, and saw the women in there with *Tééholtsódii*. They also saw the children of Water Monster scampering about. The rescue party reclaimed the women and left, but unbeknownst to them Coyote stole one of the Water Monster's children and tucked it under his robe. When they returned, they were greeted joyously and the people feasted again. The following morning, however, the people noticed something disturbing. They saw many animals running past as if fleeing something. All day this went on, and by the third day the commotion had greatly increased. On the morning of the fourth day, they noticed a white light shining up from the horizon. They sent Locust to investigate and he returned with startling news. The strange light was coming from a wall of water that was converging on them from all sides.[6] The people fled to a nearby hill and thought about what they should do. They cried and proclaimed that this was surely their doom. Then one of the people suggested they plant the seed of a tree so they might climb on it and escape the danger. Squirrel produced two seeds, juniper and piñon, and planted them.[7] The seeds sprouted and grew quickly, but the trees soon began to branch out and flattened into squat shapes. Then Weasel produced two seeds also, pine and spruce, and planted them. The seeds grew into tall trees, but they soon tapered into points and stopped growing. The people wailed in despair. But then someone called out that two people were approaching, an old man and a young man. These men went directly to the summit and did

6. The threat to the world by flood appears in many Native American creation stories and precedes awareness of the account in the biblical Book of Genesis.
7. Other versions of the story have Squirrel and his wife providing help.

not speak but sat down facing east, the young man first and the old man behind him. The old man then produced seven buckskin bags and spoke: "I have gathered soil from the seven sacred mountains in these bundles and I shall give them to you, but I cannot help you further." The people turned to the young man and he said, "I will help you, but you must not watch what I do." So the people left him and waited at a distance. When the young man finally called them, they saw that he had spread out the contents of the bags of soil and planted in it thirty-two reeds with thirty-two joints. He began to sing, and as he did the reeds began to grow, sending roots deep into the earth. The thirty-two reeds fused into one great reed, which soon towered into the sky. The young man told them to enter a hole that appeared on the east side of the reed. As the floodwaters crashed together outside, the hole closed up and sealed tightly. The reed commenced to grow quickly, lifting the people above the rising water. The Holy People accompanied them. When the reed had reached the sky, Black Body secured the reed against the sky with a plume from his headdress. This sky was solid and there was no opening in its surface, so Locust, who was good at making holes, began to scratch and dig. Eventually he broke through, and the people rejoiced. Turkey was the last to climb out, and his white-tipped tail feathers remain to this day as a reminder of their escape. One by one, the people climbed out of the giant reed into this, the Fifth World, the Glittering World.

The flood immediately receded after Coyote's mischief was discovered and *Tééholtsódii's* baby was returned. Again, the people sent out scouts. Finding the land to their liking, they proceeded to dwell upon it, planting fields and making their homes just as in the lower worlds. There were many people by this time and they nearly filled the land. The Holy People performed a test to determine their future. A magic shell was tossed onto a body of water; if it floated, the people would live forever; if it sank, each person would eventually die. The object floated and the people rejoiced, but then Coyote tossed a second stone into the water. It sank, and the people wailed. Then Coyote said, "If we do not die, we shall soon overrun the world. There will be no room for us all."[8] The people saw the wisdom of his words and reluctantly agreed. One morning not long afterward, they noticed that one of the *Nádleeh* had stopped breathing. This was the first death. With instructions from the Holy People, they prepared the body and placed it in a rocky crevice. At about the same time, there was a dispute with the *Kiis'áanii*[9] over the seed corn that had been brought from the lower world, and the groups separated because of it. First Man and First Woman, with the help of the Holy People, marked the boundaries of this new homeland with four sacred mountains made of the soil brought from the lower worlds. Three other mountains were set inside the boundaries. In an elaborate ceremony, the mountains were named and dressed. *Sisnaajiní*[1] was set to the east; it was fastened to the earth with a bolt of lightning and decorated with white shell, white lightning, white corn, dark clouds, and male rain. A cover of sheet lightning was placed over the mountain to protect and adorn it, and Rock Crystal Boy and Rock Crystal Girl were made to dwell there. *Tsoodzil*[2] was set to the south; it was fastened to the earth with a great stone knife, adorned with turquoise,

8. Coyote's responsibility for the fact that humans will eventually die is stated in many Native American stories.

9. The Pueblo peoples, introduced earlier.
1. Sierra Blanca Peak.
2. Mount Taylor.

dark mist, and female rain, and over it all was placed a covering of evening sky. One Turquoise Boy and One Corn Kernel Girl were given a home there. *Dook'o'oosłííd*[3] was set to the west; it was fastened to the earth with a sun-beam, ornamented with abalone shell, black clouds, and yellow corn, and the whole was covered with yellow clouds. White Corn Boy and Yellow Corn Boy were settled there. *Dibé ntsaa*[4] was set to the north; it was fastened to the earth with a rainbow and decorated with jet and dark mist, and it was covered with a sheet of darkness. Pollen Boy and Grasshopper Girl were made to live there. The inner mountains were also named and sanctified. *Dzilná'oodilii*[5] was fastened to the earth with a sunbeam, adorned with dark clouds and male rain, and Soft Goods Boy and Soft Goods Girl were given a home there. *Ch'óol'í'íi*[6] was fastened to the earth with a streamer of rain and decorated with pollen, dark mist, and female rain. Boy Who Produces Jewels and Girl Who Produces Jewels were made to dwell there. *Ak'idahnást'ání*[7] was fastened to the earth with a Mirage Stone, ornamented with black clouds and male rain, and guarded by Mirage Stone Boy and Red Coral Girl. In the Fifth World, as in the lower world, the people lived in accordance with the daily cycles of the four changing colors of the sky. But now more light was needed, so the sun and the moon were created. The old man who had helped them escape from the flood in the lower world was given the honor of bearing the sun across the sky, and the young man who had also helped them escape was given the privilege of carrying the moon at night. In return for their sacrifice and labor, they were given immortality and powerful sacred names. In the Fifth World, the people began filling the land and many places were named. The land was rich and the people prospered upon it, but the land soon grew dangerous. *Naayéé'*, monsters, were roaming the land, and they were hunting and eating the people. In time there were only a few people left. These monsters were the offspring of stones and cacti, the result of some women's conduct during the separation of the sexes: *Deelgééd*, the horned monster; *Tsélkáá'adah hwídziiltaal'ii*, who kicked people off cliffs; *Bináá' yee 'aghánii*, who killed with his eyes; and *Tsénináhilééh*, the flying monster who lived atop *Tsébit'a'ii*. In time there were only four people left in the world. These people took refuge near *Tsélgai*, White Rock. First Man went out to pray every day at dawn. One morning he heard a strange sound like the cries of a baby coming from atop *Ch'óol'í'íi*. For three mornings when he went out to pray he heard the sounds coming from atop the cloud-shrouded peak. On the fourth morning, Talking God appeared and instructed him to ascend the mountain. Atop the highest peak First Man found an infant who was *Asdzáán Nádleehí*, Changing Woman, the most beloved of all the deities. He took her home, and because she was holy, she reached maturity in four days. After a time, Changing Woman left to live on *Dzilná'oodilii*. While she was living there she bathed in a waterfall and basked in the Sun. In four days, she gave birth to twin boys, who were the sons of the waterfall and the Sun. They were *Tóbágíshchíní* (Born-for-Water), and *Naayéé'neizghání* (Monster

3. Never Has Thawed on Top, or San Francisco Peak.
4. Big Mountain Sheep, or the La Plata Mountains.
5. Mountain Around Which Things Happen[ed], or Travelers Circle, with suggestions of the continuity of life.

6. The English meaning is not entirely clear. *Ch'o* means "spruce," but it can also refer to directionality or looking outward. According to Morris, it refers to a vantage point from which one can look out and see everything.
7. Butte Piled on a Butte.

Slayer). They quickly grew to maturity also. With the help of the Spider Woman, *Jóhonaa'éí*, and other helpers, the Twins rid the land of the monsters. *Naayéé'neizghání* went out and slew the monsters, while *Tóbágíshchíní* remained home and conducted protection ceremonies to ensure victory. One of the last monsters to perish was *Yéi'iitsoh*, the Giant. He was also a son of the Sun; however, because he was killing people the Sun decided to help the Twins to stop him. *Jóhonaa'éí* gave the Twins weapons made of lightning, and he taught them magic that enabled them to travel high over the land on the arching rainbow, which is the road used by the Holy People. After the defeat of the Giant only four monsters remained, Old Age, Poverty, Hunger, and Cold, but the Twins spared these creatures so the people would not grow complacent as immortals. When the land was safe, the Sun asked Changing Woman to become his wife. She did not consent at first, but after the Sun made promises that she would not be leaving her people forever, she agreed. He built a beautiful house for her to dwell in, on an island in the western sea. Before she left, she made more people by rubbing skin from under her arms and from under her breasts. These were the four original clans: *Honágháahnii*, *Bit'ahnii*, *Hashtl'ishnii*, and *Tódích'ii'nii*.[8] Changing Woman took some of these people to live with her, but they soon grew lonesome and they left her home in the western sea to return to *Dinétah*. The Twins left this world to dwell with the Holy People when their work was finished. They left this world from a place where two great rivers meet. They promised that they would always keep watch over the people; it is said that they can still be seen sometimes, floating in the mist above the spot where the waters converge. The Holy People also returned to their home, but they are always within reach through the songs and prayers they gave us. Lastly, a sacred rainbow was placed around *Diné bikéyah*, our homeland, for protection and as a blessing and a reminder of the sacredness of this land. It is said that so long as *Diné* remain within this boundary, we will have the blessings and protection of the Holy People. So long as we remain within these boundaries we will be living in the manner that the Holy People prescribed for us.

8. There are a great many Navajo clans, but these four are the original clans created from Changing Woman's body. "*Honágháahnii*": the One Walks Around You clan. "*Bit'ahnii*": the Folded Arms People, the Leaf clan, or the Under His Cover clan. "*Hashtl'ishnii*": the Mud clan. "*Tódích'ili'nii*": the Bitter Water People.

TRICKSTER TALES

FROM THE WINNEBAGO TRICKSTER CYCLE

The Winnebagos, or Ho-Chunks, came to their homelands—at the western end of what is now Green Bay, Wisconsin—from some more southeasterly location perhaps a thousand years ago. They lived by hunting and fishing; by planting corn, squash, and beans; and by gathering wild rice and berries. The French explorer Jean Nicolet is credited as their first European contact, in 1634. The English name "Winnebago" comes from the Algonquian people's name for the tribe, "people of

the dirty water," which may simply refer to the strong smell of Wisconsin's Lake Winnebago and Fox River in the summer. The Ho-Chunks' name for themselves, "Ho-chungra," means "people of the parent speech," or "people of the Big Voice." Now geographically divided—mainly between Wisconsin and Nebraska—as a consequence of colonization and the provisions of nineteenth-century treaties, the Ho-Chunks claim that their ancestors played an important role in the creation and preservation of the large, mysterious earthen mounds that exist along the Mississippi River and throughout the Midwest.

Winnebago culture is rich in trickster tales. The story reprinted here comes from *The Trickster: A Study in American Indian Mythology* (1956), a collection of forty-nine Winnebago trickster stories edited by the American cultural anthropologist and folklorist Paul Radin. A student of the eminent anthropologist Franz Boas, Radin had begun collecting Winnebago stories in the early 1900s. He did not hear the tales narrated, nor did he know the identity of the narrator. Rather, as he notes, "an older individual" told the stories in Ho-Chunk to a Winnebago consultant, Sam Blowsnake, who wrote them down. Then Radin, Blowsnake, and another Winnebago man, Oliver LaMere, collaborated on the translation into English, which Radin, following Boas's methods, published in literate prose.

The tale of the trickster and the talking "laxative bulb" is widespread throughout Native American cultures. The trickster (or "the old man," as he is twice called here) interacts with plants and trees, sometimes defying them and at other times relying on them to get oriented. He also engages with humans, who foolishly listen to him and then suffer the consequences. The trickster plays the fool with the greatest vigor. His efforts to escape the consequences of his actions—and to recover from those consequences once his efforts fail—propel the narrative. To cleanse and restore himself, the trickster performs some hard and extremely unpleasant work that involves a reorientation toward the natural world. Apart from the entertainment value of its scatological humor and farcical elements, this story teaches numerous lessons, such as do not be gullible and do not think of yourself as superior to natural forces.

[Trickster and the Talking Bulb]

23

As he went wandering around aimlessly he suddenly heard someone speaking. He listened very carefully and it seemed to say, "He who chews me will defecate; he will defecate!" That was what it was saying. "Well, why is this person talking in this manner?" said Trickster. So he walked in the direction from which he had heard the speaking and again he heard, quite near him, someone saying: "He who chews me, he will defecate; he will defecate!" This is what was said. "Well, why does this person talk in such fashion?" said Trickster. Then he walked to the other side. So he continued walking along. Then right at his very side, a voice seemed to say, "He who chews me, he will defecate; he will defecate!" "Well, I wonder who it is who is speaking. I know very well that if I chew it, I will not defecate." But he kept looking around for the speaker and finally discovered, much to his astonishment, that it was a bulb on a bush. The bulb it was that was speaking. So he seized it, put it in his mouth, chewed it, and then swallowed it. He did just this and then went on.

"Well, where is the bulb gone that talked so much? Why, indeed, should I defecate? When I feel like defecating, then I shall defecate, no sooner. How could such an object make me defecate!" Thus spoke Trickster. Even as he

spoke, however, he began to break wind. "Well this, I suppose, is what it meant. Yet the bulb said I would defecate, and I am merely expelling gas. In any case I am a great man even if I do expel a little gas!" Thus he spoke. As he was talking he again broke wind. This time it was really quite strong. "Well, what a foolish one I am. This is why I am called Foolish One, Trickster." Now he began to break wind again and again. "So this is why the bulb spoke as it did, I suppose." Once more he broke wind. This time it was very loud and his rectum began to smart. "Well, it surely is a great thing!" Then he broke wind again, this time with so much force, that he was propelled forward. "Well, well, it may even make me give another push, but it won't make me defecate," so he exclaimed defiantly. The next time he broke wind, the hind part of his body was raised up by the force of the explosion and he landed on his knees and hands. "Well, go ahead and do it again! Go ahead and do it again!" Then, again, he broke wind. This time the force of the expulsion sent him far up in the air and he landed on the ground, on his stomach. The next time he broke wind, he had to hang on to a log, so high was he thrown. However, he raised himself up and, after a while, landed on the ground, the log on top of him. He was almost killed by the fall. The next time he broke wind, he had to hold on to a tree that stood near by. It was a poplar and he held on with all his might yet, nevertheless, even then, his feet flopped up in the air. Again, and for the second time, he held on to it when he broke wind and yet he pulled the tree up by the roots. To protect himself, the next time, he went on until he came to a large tree, a large oak tree. Around this he put both his arms. Yet, when he broke wind, he was swung up and his toes struck against the tree. However, he held on.

After that he ran to a place where people were living. When he got there, he shouted, "Say, hurry up and take your lodge down, for a big warparty is upon you and you will surely be killed! Come let us get away!" He scared them all so much that they quickly took down their lodge, piled it on Trickster, and then got on him themselves. They likewise placed all the little dogs they had on top of Trickster.[1] Just then he began to break wind again and the force of the expulsion scattered the things on top of him in all directions. They fell far apart from one another. Separated, the people were standing about and shouting to one another; and the dogs, scattered here and there, howled at one another. There stood Trickster laughing at them till he ached.

Now he proceeded onward. He seemed to have gotten over his troubles. "Well, this bulb did a lot of talking," he said to himself, "yet it could not make me defecate." But even as he spoke he began to have the desire to defecate, just a very little. "Well, I suppose this is what it meant. It certainly bragged a good deal, however." As he spoke he defecated again. "Well, what a braggart it was! I suppose this is why it said this." As he spoke these last words, he began to defecate a good deal. After a while, as he was sitting down, his body would touch the excrement. Thereupon he got on top of a log and sat down there but, even then, he touched the excrement. Finally, he climbed up a log that was leaning against a tree. However, his body still touched the excrement, so he went up higher. Even then, however, he touched it so he climbed still higher up. Higher and higher he had to go. Nor was he able to stop defecating. Now he was on top of the tree. It was small and quite uncomfortable. Moreover, the excrement began to come up to him.

1. These actions are inappropriate responses to the supposed danger.

24

Even on the limb on which he was sitting he began to defecate. So he tried a different position. Since the limb, however, was very slippery he fell right down into the excrement. Down he fell, down into the dung. In fact he disappeared in it, and it was only with very great difficulty that he was able to get out of it. His raccoon-skin blanket was covered with filth, and he came out dragging it after him. The pack he was carrying on his back was covered with dung, as was also the box containing his penis.[2] The box he emptied and then placed it on his back again.

25

Then, still blinded by the filth, he started to run. He could not see anything. As he ran he knocked against a tree. The old man cried out in pain. He reached out and felt the tree and sang:

"Tree, what kind of a tree are you? Tell me something about yourself!"

And the tree answered, "What kind of a tree do you think I am? I am an oak tree. I am the forked oak tree that used to stand in the middle of the valley. I am that one," it said. "Oh, my, is it possible that there might be some water around here?" Trickster asked. The tree answered, "Go straight on." This is what it told him. As he went along he bumped up against another tree. He was knocked backwards by the collision. Again he sang:

"Tree, what kind of a tree are you? Tell me something about yourself!"

"What kind of a tree do you think I am? The red oak tree that used to stand at the edge of the valley, I am that one." "Oh, my, is it possible that there is water around here?" asked Trickster. Then the tree answered and said, "Keep straight on," and so he went again. Soon he knocked against another tree. He spoke to the tree and sang:

"Tree, what kind of a tree are you? Tell me something about yourself!"

"What kind of a tree do you think I am? The slippery elm tree that used to stand in the midst of the others, I am that one." Then Trickster asked, "Oh, my, is it possible that there would be some water near here?" And the tree answered and said, "Keep right on." On he went and soon he bumped into another tree and he touched it and sang:

"Tree, what kind of a tree are you? Tell me something about yourself!"

"What kind of a tree do you think I am? I am the basswood tree that used to stand on the edge of the water. That is the one I am." "Oh, my, it is good," said Trickster. So there in the water he jumped and lay. He washed himself thoroughly.

It is said that the old man almost died that time, for it was only with the greatest difficulty that he found the water. If the trees had not spoken to him he certainly would have died. Finally, after a long time and only after great exertions, did he clean himself, for the dung had been on him a long time and had dried. After he had cleansed himself he washed his raccoon-skin blanket and his box.

2. That the trickster carries his penis in a box was established in earlier stories. It is this box that he washes at the end of the next section of the story.

ORATORY

FROM THE WORLD ENCOMPASSED BY SIR FRANCIS DRAKE

I n 1577–80, the English explorer Sir Francis Drake (c. 1542–1596) circumnavigated the world in his ship the *Golden Hind*, landing in 1579 on what is now the California coast. The notes of the ship chaplain, Francis Fletcher, were compiled and published in 1628 as *The World Encompassed by Sir Francis Drake*, and the following excerpt from that volume is Fletcher's account of the landing. The Coast Miwok people who figure in the selection inhabited the areas north of present-day San Francisco, including Marin and southern Sonoma counties. They lived in villages of up to several hundred people that were located in sheltered places near fresh water. In the late sixteenth century, Spanish galleons began making trips between Mexico and the Philippines, traveling along this stretch of coast. The Miwoks' reception of Drake's company may have been informed by earlier meetings with groups of Spaniards.

This account illustrates the period's conventions for representing early encounters between Natives and Europeans. Some elements of the narrative resemble descriptions of formal diplomacy in European courts, as when the king and his entourage move in a procession to the English fort. Other features of the account are strikingly unfamiliar, such as the self-mutilating dance that ensues. The narrative concludes with an abrupt shift as the orations that puzzle Drake ("our General") and his men are suddenly revealed to contain "supplications, that he would take the province and kingdom into his hand, and become their king and patron." Drake did, in fact, claim the area for Queen Elizabeth I, naming it Nova Albion ("New Great Britain").

There is ample reason to think that the Miwoks' request that the English rule them did not happen but is instead a mistranslation designed to encourage support for the colonial enterprise among the narrative's readers. Exploration narratives generally were written to achieve particular goals, such as advancing the career of the author or the expedition leader or shaping an approach to colonization. But while this scene includes a suspicious appeal and spontaneous conversation that call the credibility of the whole account into question, the narrative remains valuable for its texture and details. The process of teasing out the plausible from the implausible is one of the interesting challenges of reading exploration narratives.

From The World Encompassed by Sir Francis Drake[1]

* * *

Against the end of three days more (the news having the while spread itself farther, and as it seemed a great way up into the country), were assembled the greatest number of people which we could reasonably imagine to dwell within any convenient distance round about. Amongst the rest the king himself, a man of a goodly stature and comely personage, attended with his

1. The text is from *The World Encompassed by Sir Francis Drake, Being His Next Voyage to That to Nombre de Dios* (reprint, 1854).

guard of about 100 tall and warlike men, this day, *viz.*,[2] June 26, came down to see us.

Before his coming, were sent two ambassadors or messengers to our General, to signify that their *Hióh*, that is, their king, was coming and at hand. They in the delivery of their message, the one spoke with a soft and low voice, prompting his fellow; the other pronounced the same, word by word, after him with a voice more audible, continuing their proclamation (for such it was) about half an hour. Which being ended, they by signs made request to our General, to send something by their hands to their *Hióh* or king, as a token that his coming might be in peace. Our General willingly satisfied their desire; and they, glad men, made speedy return to their *Hióh*. Neither was it long before their king (making as princely a show as possibly he could) with all his train came forward.

In their coming forwards they cried continually after a singing manner, with a lusty courage. And as they drew nearer and nearer towards us, so did they more and more strive to behave themselves with a certain comeliness and gravity in all their actions.

In the forefront came a man of a large body and goodly aspect, bearing the scepter or royal mace (made of a certain kind of black wood, and in length about a yard and a half) before the king. Whereupon hanged two crowns, a bigger and a less, with three chains of a marvellous length, and often doubled, besides a bag of the herb *Tabáh*.[3] The crowns were made of knitwork, wrought upon most curiously with feathers of divers[4] colours, very artificially placed, and of a formal fashion. The chains seemed of a bony substance, every link or part thereof being very little, thin, most finely burnished, with a hole pierced through the midst. The number of links going to make one chain, is in a manner infinite; but of such estimation it is amongst them, that few be the persons that are admitted to wear the same; and even they to whom its lawful to use them, yet are stinted[5] what number they shall use, as some ten, some twelve, some twenty, and as they exceed in number of chains, so thereby are they known to be the more honorable personages.

Next unto him that bore this scepter, was the king himself with his guard about him; his attire upon his head was a caul of knitworke,[6] wrought upon somewhat like the crowns, but differing much both in fashion and perfectness of work; upon his shoulders he had on a coat of the skins of conies,[7] reaching to his waist; his guard also had each coats of the same shape, but of other skins; some having cauls likewise stuck with feathers, or covered over with a certaine down, which groweth up in the country upon an herb much like our lettuce, which exceeds any other down in the world for fineness, and being layed upon their cauls, by no winds can be removed. Of such estimation is this herb amongst them, that the down thereof is not lawful to be worn, but of such persons as are about the king (to whom also it is permitted to wear a plume of feathers on their heads, in sign of honour), and the seeds are not used but only in sacrifice to their gods. After these, in their order, did follow the naked sort of common people, whose hair being long, was gathered into a

2. Abbreviation for *videlicet*: that is to say, namely (Latin).
3. Tobacco.
4. Various.

5. Restricted in.
6. A knitted headdress, resembling a hairnet.
7. Rabbits.

bunch behind, in which stuck plumes of feathers; but in the forepart only single feathers like horns, every one pleasing himself in his own device.

This one thing was observed to be general amongst them all, that every one had his face painted, some with white, some black, and some with other colours, every man also bringing in his hand one thing or other for a gift or present. Their train or last part of their company consisted of women and children, each woman bearing against her breast a round basket or two, having within them divers things, as bags of *Tobâh*,[8] a root which they call *Petáh*, whereof they make a kind of meal, and either bake it into bread, or eat it raw; broiled fishes, like a pilchard; the seed and down aforenamed, with such like.

Their baskets were made in fashion like a deep bowl, and though the matter were rushes, or such other kind of stuffe, yet was it so cunningly handled, that the most part of them would hold water: about the brims they were hanged with pieces of the shells of pearls, and in some places with two or three links at a place, of the chains forenamed: thereby signifying that they were vessels wholly dedicated to the only use of the gods they worshipped; and besides this, they were wrought upon with the matted down of red feathers, distinguished into divers works and forms.

In the mean time, our General having assembled his men together (as forecasting the danger and worst that might fall out) prepared himself to stand upon sure ground, that we might at all times be ready in our own defence, if any thing should chance otherwise than was looked for or expected.

Wherefore every man being in a warlike readiness, he marched within his fenced place, making against their approach a most warlike show (as he did also at all other times of their resort), whereby if they had been desperate enemies, they could not have chosen but have conceived terror and fear, with discouragement to attempt anything against us, in beholding of the same.

When they were come somewhat near unto us, trooping together, they gave us a common or general salutation, observing in the mean time a general silence. Whereupon, he who bore the scepter before the king, being prompted by another whom the king assigned to that office, pronounced with an audible and manly voice what the other spoke to him in secret, continuing, whether it were his oration or proclamation, at the least half an hour. At the close whereof there was a common *Amen*, in sign of approbation, given by every person: and the king himself, with the whole number of men and women (the little children only remaining behind) came further down the hill, and as they came set themselves again in their former order.

And being now come to the foot of the hill and near our fort, the scepter bearer, with a composed countenance and stately carriage began a song, and answerable thereunto observed a kind of measures in a dance: whom the king with his guard and every other sort of person following, did in like manner sing and dance, saving only the women, who danced but kept silence. As they danced they still came on: and our General perceiving their plain and simple meaning, gave order that they might freely enter without interruption within our bulwark. Where, after they had entered, they yet continued their song and dance a reasonable time, their women also following them with their wassail bowls[9] in their hands, their bodies bruised, their faces torn, their duges,

8. I.e., *Tabáh*: tobacco.
9. The rush bowls mentioned previously, here compared to punchbowls used at Christmas.

breasts, and other parts bespotted with blood, trickling down from the wounds, which with their nails they had made before their coming.

After that they had satisfied, or rather tired themselves in this manner, they made signs to our General to have him sit down; unto whom both the king and divers others made several orations, or rather, indeed, if we had understood them, supplications, that he would take the province and kingdom into his hand, and become their king and patron: making signs that they would resign unto him their right and title in the whole land, and become his vassals in themselves and their posterities: which that they might make us indeed believe that it was their true meaning and intent, the king himself, with all the rest, with one consent and with great reverence, joyfully singing a song, set the crown upon his head, enriched his neck with all their chains, and offering unto him many other things, honoured him by the name of *Hyóh*. Adding thereunto (as it might seem) a song and dance of triumph; because they were not only visited of the gods (for so they still judged us to be), but the great and chief God was now become their God, their king and patron, and themselves were become the only happy and blessed people in the world.

These things being so freely offered, our General thought not meet to reject or refuse the same, both for that he would not give them any cause of mistrust or disliking of him (that being the only place, wherein at this present, we were of necessity enforced to seek relief of many things), and chiefly for that he knew not to what good end God had brought this to pass, or what honour and profit it might bring to our country in time to come.

Wherefore, in the name and to the use of her most excellent majesty, he took the scepter, crown, and dignity of the said country into his hand; wishing nothing more than that it had lain so fitly for her majesty to enjoy, as it was now her proper own, and that the riches and treasures thereof (wherewith in the upland countries it abounds) might with as great conveniency be transported, to the enriching of her kingdom here at home, as it is in plenty to be attained there; and especially that so tractable and loving a people as they showed themselves to be, might have means to have manifested their most willing obedience the more unto her, and by her means, as a mother and nurse of the Church of Christ, might by the preaching of the Gospel, be brought to the right knowledge and obedience of the true and everliving God.

The ceremonies of this resigning and receiving of the kingdom being thus performed, the common sort, both of men and women leaving the king and his guard about him, with our General, dispersed themselves among our people, taking a diligent view or survey of every man; and finding such as pleased their fancies (which commonly were the youngest of us), they presently enclosing them about offered their sacrifices unto them, crying out with lamentable shriekes and moans, weeping and scratching and tearing their very flesh off their faces with their nails; neither were it the women alone which did this, but even old men, roaring and crying out, were as violent as the women were.

We groaned in spirit to see the power of Satan so far prevail in seducing these so harmless souls, and laboured by all means, both by showing our great dislike, and when that served not, by violent withholding of their hands from that madness, directing them (by our eyes and hands lift up towards heaven) to the living God whom they ought to serve; but so mad were they upon their idolatry, that forcibly withholding them would not prevail (for as

soon as they could get liberty to their hands again, they would be as violent as they were before) till such time, as they whom they worshipped were conveyed from them unto the tents, whom yet as men besides themselves, they would with fury and outrage seek to have again.

After that time had a little qualified their madness, they then began to show and make known unto us their griefs and diseases which they carried about them; some of them having old aches, some shrunk sinews, some old sores and chancred ulcers, some wounds more lately received, and the like; in most lamentable manner craving help and cure thereof from us; making signs, that if we did but blow upon their griefs, or but touched the diseased places, they would be whole.

Their griefs we could not but take pity on them, and to our power desire to help them: but that (if it pleased God to open their eyes) they might understand we were but men and no gods, we used ordinary means, as lotions, emplasters,[1] and unguents, most fitly (as far as our skills could guess) agreeing to the natures of their griefs, beseeching God, if it made for his glory, to give cure to their diseases by these means. The like we did from time to time as they resorted to us.[2]

Few were the days, wherein they were absent from us, during the whole time of our abode in that place; and ordinarily every third day they brought their sacrifices, till such time as they certainly understood our meaning, that we took no pleasure, but were displeased with them; whereupon their zeal abated, and their sacrificing, for a season, to our good liking ceased; notwithstanding they continued still to make their resort unto us in great abundance, and in such sort, that they oft-times forgot to provide meat for their own sustenance; so that our General (of whom they made account as of[3] a father) was fain to perform the office of a father to them, relieving them with such victuals as we had provided for our selves, as mussels, seals, and such like, wherein they took exceeding much content; and seeing that their sacrifices were displeasing to us, yet (hating ingratitude) they sought to recompence us with such things as they had, which they willingly enforced upon us, though it were never so necessary or needful for themselves to keep.

They are a people of a tractable, free, and loving nature, without guile or treachery; their bows and arrows (their only weapons, and almost all their wealth) they use very skillfully, but yet not to do any great harm with them, being by reason of their weakeness more fit for children than for men, sending the arrows neither far off nor with any great force: and yet are the men commonly so strong of body, that that which 2 or 3 of our men could hardly bear, one of them would take upon his back, and without grudging carry it easily away, up hill and down hill an English mile together: they are also exceeding swift in running, and of long continuance, the use whereof is so familiar with them, that they seldom go, but for the most part run. One thing we observed in them with admiration, that if at any time they chanced to see a fish so near the shore that they might reach the place without swimming, they would never, or very seldom, miss to take it.

* * *

1. Plasters, i.e., preparations with medicinal properties that were spread on the skin, where they hardened.

2. Came to us for aid.
3. I.e., they regarded as.

POWHATAN'S DISCOURSE
OF PEACE AND WAR

P owhatan was a powerful confederation of Indian tribes in the Chesapeake Bay
region of present-day Virginia. In the early 1600s, the Powhatan confederacy
occupied an area that was roughly one hundred miles on each side. They called the
area Tsenacommacah, and it had a precontact population of roughly twenty-five
thousand. By 1607, when Captain John Smith arrived with the expedition sent by
the Virginia Company of London to establish Jamestown, the population had
shrunk by some ten thousand people, largely from diseases borne to Tsenacom-
macah by previous Europeans. These colonists included a Spanish mission that had
been briefly established there in 1571 and the English "lost colony" at Roanoke,
which had vanished by 1590. Despite its diminished population, the Powhatan con-
federacy remained a regional power involved in far-flung trade networks. It included
more than thirty tribes, each with its own chief, or werowance. The tribal alliance
was held together mainly by marriage and in some cases by coercion.

Powhatan was the adopted name of the paramount chief, or mamanatowick, of
the Powhatans at the time of Jamestown's settlement. His given name was Wahun-
sunacock, and he was the father of Pocohantas. Chief Powhatan was probably in his
mid sixties when, in late 1607, he captured Smith and held him for under a month,
which was long enough for Smith to learn a great deal about the Powhatans and
their leader. (For more on Smith, see the selection of his writings later in this
volume.) Smith and Chief Powhatan struck an alliance, and the English and the
Powhatans became trading partners. The food and other assistance that the Pow-
hatans supplied to Jamestown allowed the English colony to survive through its
first winter, though more than half the men and boys in the small colony died even
with their aid, leaving only thirty-eight of the original hundred and forty-four colo-
nists. The metal tools, copper kettles, and glass beads provided by the English
enabled the Powhatans to establish trade dominance over inland tribes.

"Powhatan's Discourse of Peace and War" appears in Smith's *General History of
Virginia, New England, and the Summer Isles* (1624), as the opening speech in his
account of the tense negotiations that led to this trade agreement. In the full text,
Smith describes the speech as a "subtle discourse" intended to deceive and manipulate
the English, to which he responded with considerable bluster and thinly veiled threats.
Probably based at least in part on Smith's memories of these events, the discourse and
the entire scene are informed by the conventions of classical historiography, which
often features set speeches that distill key elements and add drama to the narrative. As
reconstructed by Smith, Powhatan's speech makes a compelling case for peaceful rela-
tions, even as questions of its authenticity and sincerity add layers of complexity.

Powhatan's Discourse of Peace and War[1]

**Captain Smith, you may understand that I having seen the death of all my
people thrice, and not any one living of those three generations but my self;[2]**

1. The text is from John Smith, *The Generall
Historie of Virginia, New-England, and the Sum-
mer Isles: With the Names of the Adventurers,
Planters, and Governors from Their First Begin-*
ning, Ano: 1584. To This present 1624 (1624).
2. Powhatan refers to deaths from both disease
and warfare.

I know the difference of peace and war better than any in my country. But now I am old and ere long must die, my brethren, namely Opitchapam, Opechancanough, and Kekataugh, my two sisters, and their two daughters, are distinctly each others successors. I wish their experience no less than mine, and your love to them no less than mine to you. But this bruit from Nandsamund,[3] that you are come to destroy my country, so much affrighteth all my people as they dare not visit you. What will it avail you to take that by force you may quickly have by love, or to destroy them that provide you food? What can you get by war, when we can hide our provisions and fly to the woods? whereby you must famish by wronging us your friends. And why are you thus jealous of our loves seeing us unarmed, and both do, and are willing still to feed you, with that you cannot get but by our labours? Think you I am so simple, not to know it is better to eat good meat, lie well, and sleep quietly with my women and children, laugh and be merry with you, have copper, hatchets, or what I want being your friend: than be forced to fly from all, to lie cold in the woods, feed upon acorns, roots, and such trash, and be so hunted by you, that I can neither rest, eat, nor sleep; but my tired men must watch, and if a twig but break, every one crieth there commeth Captain Smith: then must I fly I know not whither: and thus with miserable fear, end my miserable life, leaving my pleasures to such youths as you, which through your rash unadvisedness may quickly as miserably end, for want of that, you never know where to find. Let this therefore assure you of our loves, and every year our friendly trade shall furnish you with corn, and now also, if you would come in friendly manner to see us, and not thus with your guns and swords as to invade your foes.

3. Noise or rumor from Nansemond, another tribe of the Chesapeake region.

KING PHILIP'S SPEECH

King Philip was the English name adopted by the Wampanoag leader Metacom (c. 1638–1676), who led an alliance against the English colonies in Massachusetts, Rhode Island, and Connecticut in what became known as King Philip's War (1675–76). Philip was the son of Massassoit, who had maintained peaceful relations with the Plymouth colonists since their arrival in 1620. In 1662, when Philip became the leader of the Wampanoag alliance, longstanding grievances over land and regional governance had transformed the region into a powder keg. War erupted in 1675, after the Plymouth colony executed three Wampanoags. Philip's alliance exacted great costs on the English but was defeated after Philip was killed in the Great Swamp Fight of August 1676.

After the war, there was an outpouring of printed works giving English perspectives on the conflict, most famously the popular captivity narrative of Mary Rowlandson (reprinted later in this volume), which first appeared in 1682 and was republished many times. Rowlandson's descriptions of her interactions with Philip show him to have been in some measure generous and sympathetic toward her, even as he held her prisoner. Other reports on the war were less respectful toward the defeated leader, notably the account of Captain Benjamin Church, whose celebrity as

a military hero arose partly from his role in Philip's death. In *Entertaining Passages Relating to Philip's War* (1716), Church described Philip's dead body as looking like that of "a doleful, great, naked, dirty beast" and told how he had ordered the corpse drawn and quartered. Philip's head was staked on a pole in Plymouth, where it remained for years.

It was the kind of dehumanization of Philip found in *Entertaining Passages* that the Pequot leader and Methodist minister William Apess set out to correct in 1836, when he delivered his "Eulogy on King Philip" at the Odeon in Boston. "King Philip's Speech" is from that eulogy. Speeches offering a Native American perspective on America's colonial wars had become a popular genre after Thomas Jefferson published "Chief Logan's Speech" (included in this volume). Claiming descent from Philip, Apess described him as a leading American, the equal of George Washington and Alexander the Great, a "hero of the wilderness" and martyr to a lost cause who deserved universal respect. By way of introduction, Apess explained that "this famous speech of Philip was calculated to arouse them to arms, to do the best they could in protecting and defending their rights."

King Philip's Speech[1]

BROTHERS,—You see this vast country before us, which the great Spirit gave to our fathers and us; you see the buffalo and deer that now are our support.— Brothers, you see these little ones, our wives and children, who are looking to us for food and raiment; and you now see the foe before you, that they have grown insolent and bold; that all our ancient customs are disregarded; the treaties made by our fathers and us are broken, and all of us insulted; our council fires disregarded, and all the ancient customs of our fathers; our brothers murdered before our eyes, and their spirits cry to us for revenge. Brothers, these people from the unknown world will cut down our groves, spoil our hunting and planting grounds, and drive us and our children from the graves of our fathers, and our council fires, and enslave our women and children.

1. The text is from *Eulogy on King Philip, as Pronounced at the Odeon, in Federal Street, Boston, by the Rev. William Apes[s], An Indian* (1836).

POETRY

These three selections of early Native American poetry have been excerpted from prose accounts published between 1765 and 1820. They were chosen to illustrate various styles and sources. Interest in oral literatures was strong on both sides of the Atlantic in the eighteenth century, with works such as Thomas Percy's *Reliques of Ancient English Poetry* (1765) and Sir Walter Scott's *Minstrelsy of the Scottish Border* (1802) representing British traditions. In North America, the appeal of indigenous chants and songs for non-Native readers arose in part from a desire to establish a Native equivalent to the ancient poetry of the British isles that Percy and Scott had collected in their volumes. After the American Revolution, a new nationalism in search of local origins provided an additional motive for collecting and enjoying Native poetry.

The Cherokee war song included here appears as "A Translation of the War-Song. *Caw waw noo dee, &c.*" in *The Memoirs of Lieut. Henry Timberlake* (1765). Historically, the Cherokees occupied a broad territory in the Southeast, including areas of what are now the Carolinas, Georgia, and Tennessee. Timberlake had served in the Second Virginia Regiment under Colonel William Byrd, whose ethnographic and naturalist writings are excerpted elsewhere in this volume. Timberlake's *Memoirs* are a rich source of information about mid-eighteenth-century Cherokee culture and society. He had traveled to Tennessee to conduct peace negotiations in 1761, and he later accompanied Ostenaco and two other Cherokee chiefs to London. Of the songs printed in his volume, Timberlake wrote: "Both the ideas and verse are very loose in the original, and they are set to as loose a music, many composing both tunes and song off hand, according to the occasion; tho' some tunes, especially those taken from the northern Indians, are extremely pretty, and very like the Scotch."

The Reverend John Heckewelder, a Moravian missionary, printed the Lenape war song included here as "The Song of the Lenape Warriors Going Against the Enemy" in his *History, Manners, and Customs of the Indian Nations Who Once Inhabited Pennsylvania and the Neighbouring States* (1818). The Lenapes (also known as the Lenni Lenapes or Delaware Indians) were ancient inhabitants of the Middle Atlantic region, occupying parts of what later became several states, including New Jersey, Pennsylvania, and New York. Their diplomatic and mediation skills were widely admired. Heckewelder spent more than a decade as a missionary to the Lenape in Pennsylvania and Ohio, and he later worked for the United States Senate as a treaty negotiator. The novelist James Fenimore Cooper drew heavily on Heckewelder's *History* in his *Leatherstocking Tales*. Heckewelder's introduction to the song included here emphasizes the impossibility of capturing the vocal tones and musical accompaniment of the performance, which he compares to the difficulties of describing "the melodies of the ancient Greeks." He nevertheless reports how the performers sang the words "in short lines . . . most generally in detached parts, as time permits and as the occasion or their feelings prompt them. Their accent is very pathetic [i.e., sad], and the whole, in their language, produces considerable effect."

The two Cherokee songs of friendship included here are drawn from a letter written by Dr. Samuel L. Mitchill in 1817 to the secretary of the American Antiquarian Society (AAS), which was published three years later in *Archaeologia Americana*, a volume of the society's *Transactions*. In his letter, Mitchill describes how his interactions with the Osages and Cherokees during his service as the chairman of the U.S. Senate Committee on Indian Affairs led to the transcription of several songs and poems. Of the performance of the Cherokee songs of friendship he notes, "They repeat the song and chorus until they are tired." The words of these songs were written down for him by "Mr. Hicks, a Cherokee of the half blood, with his own hand," while they were in the company of several military officers and Double Head, a Cherokee warrior. Mitchill sent the songs to the AAS as part of an ongoing effort by that organization to record indigenous American history and culture.

Cherokee War Song[1]

Where'er the earth's enlighten'd by the sun,
Moon shines by night, grass grows, or waters run,
Be't known that we are going, like men, afar,

1. The text is from *The Memoirs of Lieut. Henry Timberlake (Who Accompanied Three Cherokee Indians to England in the Year 1762)* (1765).

In hostile fields to wage destructive war;
Like men we go, to meet our country's foes, 5
Who, woman-like, shall fly our dreaded blows;
Yes, as a woman, who beholds a snake,
In gaudy horror, glisten thro' the brake,
Starts trembling back, and stares with wild surprize,
Or pale thro' fear, unconscious, panting, flies.[2] 10
Just so these foes, more tim'rous than the hind,
Shall leave their arms and only clothes behind;
Pinch'd by each blast, by ev'ry thicket torn,
Run back to their own nation, now its scorn:
Or in the winter, when the barren wood 15
Denies their gnawing entrails nature's food,
Let them sit down, from friends and country far,
And wish, with tears, they ne'er had come to war.
We'll leave our clubs,[3] dew'd with their country show'rs,
And, if they dare to bring them back to ours, 20
Their painted scalps shall be a step to fame,
And grace our own and glorious country's name.
Or if we warriors spare the yielding foe,
Torments at home the wretch must undergo.[4]
But when we go, who knows which shall return, 25
When growing dangers rise with each new morn?
Farewell, ye little ones, ye tender wives,
For you alone we would conserve our lives!
But cease to mourn, 'tis unavailing pain,
If not fore-doom'd, we soon shall meet again. 30
But, O ye friends! in case your comrades fall,
Think that on you our deaths for vengeance call;
With uprais'd tomahawks pursue our blood,
And stain, with hostile streams, the conscious wood,
That pointing enemies may never tell 35
The boasted place where we, their victims, fell.[5]

2. "As the Indians fight naked, the vanquished are constrained to endure the rigours of the weather in their flight, and live upon roots and fruit, as they throw down their arms to accelerate their flight thro' the woods" [Timberlake's note].
3. "It is the custom of the Indians, to leave a club something of the form of a cricket-bat, but with their warlike exploits engraved on it, in their enemy's country, and the enemy accepts the defiance, by bringing this back to their country" [Timberlake's note].
4. "The prisoners of war are generally tortured by the women, at the party's return, to revenge the death of those that have perished by the wretch's countrymen. This savage custom has been so much mitigated of late, that the prisoners were only compelled to marry, and then generally allowed all the privileges of the natives. This lenity, however, has been a detriment to the nation; for many of these returning to their countrymen, have made them acquainted with the country-passes, weaknesses, and haunts of the Cherokees; besides that it gave the enemy greater courage to fight against them" [Timberlake's note].
5. "Their custom is generally to engrave their victory on some neighbouring tree, or set up some token of it near the field of battle; to this their enemies are here supposed to point to, as boasting their victory over them, and the slaughter that they made" [Timberlake's note].

Lenape War Song[1]

O poor me!
Who[2] am going out to fight the enemy,
And know not whether I shall return again,
To enjoy the embraces of my children
And my wife. 5
O poor creature!
Whose life is not in his own hands,
Who has no power over his own body,
But tries to do his duty
For the welfare of his nation. 10
O! thou Great Spirit above!
Take pity on my children
And on my wife!
Prevent their mourning on my account!
Grant that I may be successful in this attempt— 15
That I may slay my enemy,
And bring home the trophies of war
To my dear family and friends,
That we may rejoice together.
O! take pity on me! 20
Give me strength and courage to meet my enemy,
Suffer me to return again to my children,
To my wife
And to my relations!
Take pity on me and preserve my life 25
And I will make to thee a sacrifice.

Two Cherokee Songs of Friendship[1]

Song the First

Can, nal, li, èh, ne-was-tu.
A friend you resemble.
Chorus. Yai, ne, noo, way. E,noo,way,hā.

Song the Second

Ti, nai, tau, nā, cla, ne-was-tu.
Brothers I think we are.
Chorus. Yai, ne, noo, way. E,noo,way,hā.

1. The text is from *History, Manners, and Customs of The Indian Nations Who Once Inhabited Pennsylvania and the Neighbouring States* (1818; rev. ed. 1876).
2. Heckewelder wrote "Whom."
1. The texts are from "Letter from Dr. Samuel L. Mitchill," *Transactions and Collections of the American Antiquarian Society* (1820).

CHRISTOPHER COLUMBUS
1451–1506

I n Washington Irving's widely read biography of Christopher Columbus, first published in 1828, the acclaimed American writer described the European adventurer as possessing an "ardent and enthusiastic imagination which threw a magnificence over his whole course of thought." "In his letters and journals," Irving observed, "instead of detailing circumstances with the technical precision of a mere navigator, he notices the beauties of nature with the enthusiasm of a poet or a painter." Popular travel narratives by Marco Polo and Sir John Mandeville probably influenced Columbus's plans for his historic first voyage and shaped his prose style, Irving remarked, and he described as well a "visionary" cast of mind that was evident in everything Columbus did. Summing up the meaning of the adventurer's dramatic life, Irving wrestled with the fact that the consequences of this visionary quality were often destructive to himself and those around him—not least due to his role in making slavery a central part of the encounter between Europe and the Americas.

Born into a family of wool workers near the Mediterranean port of Genoa, Columbus turned to the sea as a young man, developed a plan to find a commercially viable Atlantic route to Asia, and in 1492 won the support of the Spanish monarchs, Ferdinand and Isabella, for this "enterprise of the Indies." His unexpected discoveries led to three later voyages intended to establish Spanish power in the West Indies and in South America. What seemed an auspicious beginning was followed by a long series of disasters and disappointments. His willingness to enslave the natives, and his lack of interest in indigenous social and cultural forms, had devastating consequences. What had appeared to him to be friendly relations with the Taino Indians on the island of Hispaniola in 1492 turned sour as the settlers demanded gold and sexual partners from their hosts. On Columbus's return to the island in 1494, none of the Europeans remained alive. A new settlement fell into disorder while he was away in Cuba and Jamaica. In 1496, he was forced to return to Spain to clear his name of politically motivated charges made against him by European rivals involved in the colonies. A third voyage, begun in 1498, took him for the first time to the South American mainland. The lushness of nature there made him believe he was near paradise, but when he returned to Hispaniola, he discovered the Spanish settlers on that island in open rebellion against his authority. Able to reach a truce only at the expense of the Taino Indians, who were virtually enslaved by the rebels, Columbus soon found himself under arrest. He was sent in chains to Spain in 1500 to answer yet more charges. His last voyage, intended to restore his tarnished reputation, resulted in a long period of suffering in Panama and shipwreck in Jamaica. During this time, Columbus underwent a virtual breakdown, even suffering delusional periods. Rescued at last, he returned to Europe and died not long afterward. His discoveries in the West Indies were left in a state of violent disorder.

The supposed *Journal* of Columbus's first voyage is actually a summary prepared by the cleric and reformer Bartolomé de las Casas (also present in this volume). However, several documents regarding the four voyages survive from Columbus's hand. His letter to Luis de Santangel, a court official who helped secure financing for the first voyage, provides a more authentic account. This so-called Letter of Discovery served as the basis for the first printed description of America, initially issued in 1493 and widely translated and reprinted across Europe. Here, Columbus writes of marvels in a manner that becomes entwined with the language of posses-

sion. A memorandum regarding the second voyage, intended by Columbus for the Spanish monarchs (whose responses to each point also survive), offers useful insights into the emerging ambiguities and problems of the Hispaniola colony. For the third and fourth voyages, three letters from Columbus, two sent to the Crown and one to a woman of the Spanish court, detail his deepening worldly and spiritual troubles. His emotional fragility and spiritual despair are effectively conveyed in the excerpt from his letter to Ferdinand and Isabella regarding his fourth voyage that is included here along with the letter to Santangel.

The following texts are from *Select Documents Illustrating the Four Voyages of Columbus* (1930–33), translated and edited by Cecil Jane.

Letter of Discovery

[At sea, February 15, 1493]

Sir,

As I know that you will be pleased at the great victory with which Our Lord has crowned my voyage, I write this to you, from which you will learn how in thirty-three days, I passed from the Canary Islands to the Indies with the fleet which the most illustrious king and queen our sovereigns gave to me. And there I found very many islands filled with people innumerable, and of them all I have taken possession for their highnesses, by proclamation made and with the royal standard unfurled, and no opposition was offered to me. To the first island which I found I gave the name *San Salvador*,[1] in remembrance of the Divine Majesty, Who has marvelously bestowed all this; the Indians call it "Guanahani." To the second I gave the name *Isla de Santa María de Concepción*; to the third, *Fernandina*; to the fourth, *Isabella*; to the fifth, *Isla Juana*,[2] and so to each one I gave a new name.

When I reached Juana I followed its coast to the westward, and I found it to be so extensive that I thought that it must be the mainland, the province of Catayo.[3] And since there were neither towns nor villages on the seashore, but only small hamlets, with the people of which I could not have speech because they all fled immediately, I went forward on the same course, thinking that I should not fail to find great cities and towns. And at the end of many leagues,[4] seeing that there was no change and that the coast was bearing me northwards, which I wished to avoid since winter was already beginning and I proposed to make from it to the south, and as moreover the wind was carrying me forward, I determined not to wait for a change in the weather and retraced my path as far as a certain harbor known to me. And from that point I sent two men inland to learn if there were a king or great cities. They traveled three days' journey and found an infinity of small hamlets and people without number, but nothing of importance. For this reason they returned.

I understood sufficiently from other Indians, whom I had already taken, that this land was nothing but an island. And therefore I followed its coast eastwards for one hundred and seven leagues to the point where it ended.

1. The precise identity of the Bahamian island Columbus named San Salvador is not known today, although many theories have been put forward, most positing that Watling Island is the likeliest site.
2. Of these four islands, only the identity of Juana (Cuba) is today certain.
3. I.e., China (or "Cathay").
4. Renaissance units of measurement were inexact. Columbus's "league" was probably about four miles.

And from that cape I saw another island distant eighteen leagues from the former, to the east, to which I at once gave the name "Española."[5] And I went there and followed its northern coast, as I had in the case of Juana, to the eastward for one hundred and eighty-eight great leagues in a straight line. This island and all the others are very fertile to a limitless degree, and this island is extremely so. In it there are many harbors on the coast of the sea, beyond comparison with others which I know in Christendom, and many rivers, good and large, which is marvelous. Its lands are high, and there are in it very many sierras and very lofty mountains, beyond comparison with the island of Tenerife.[6] All are most beautiful, of a thousand shapes, and all are accessible and filled with trees of a thousand kinds and tall, and they seem to touch the sky. And I am told that they never lose their foliage, as I can understand, for I saw them as green and as lovely as they are in Spain in May, and some of them were flowering, some bearing fruit, and some in another stage, according to their nature. And the nightingale[7] was singing and other birds of a thousand kinds in the month of November there where I went. There are six or eight kinds of palm, which are a wonder to behold on account of their beautiful variety, but so are the other trees and fruits and plants. In it are marvelous pine groves, and there are very large tracts of cultivatable lands, and there is honey, and there are birds of many kinds and fruits in great diversity. In the interior are mines of metals, and the population is without number. Española is a marvel.

The sierras and mountains, the plains and arable lands and pastures, are so lovely and rich for planting and sowing, for breeding cattle of every kind, for building towns and villages. The harbours of the sea here are such as cannot be believed to exist unless they have been seen, and so with the rivers, many and great, and good waters, the majority of which contain gold. In the trees and fruits and plants, there is a great difference from those of Juana. In this island, there are many spices and great mines of gold and of other metals.

The people of this island, and of all the other islands which I have found and of which I have information, all go naked, men and women, as their mothers bore them, although some women cover a single place with the leaf of a plant or with a net of cotton which they make for the purpose. They have no iron or steel or weapons, nor are they fitted to use them, not because they are not well built men and of handsome stature, but because they are very marvellously timorous. They have no other arms than weapons made of canes, cut in seeding time, to the ends of which they fix a small sharpened stick. And they do not dare to make use of these, for many times it has happened that I have sent ashore two or three men to some town to have speech, and countless people have come out to them, and as soon as they have seen my men approaching they have fled, even a father not waiting for his son. And this, not because ill has been done to anyone; on the contrary, at every point where I have been and have been able to have speech, I have given to them of all that I had, such as cloth and many other things, without receiving anything for it; but so they are, incurably timid. It is true that, after they have been reassured

5. I.e., Hispaniola, where the countries of Haiti and the Dominican Republic are located.
6. The largest of the Canary Islands.
7. Not native to the Western Hemisphere. Nor is the honeybee, presumably the source of the honey mentioned below. The existence of gold in the rivers, also mentioned below, was purely conjectural.

and have lost their fear, they are so guileless and so generous with all they possess, that no one would believe it who has not seen it. They never refuse anything which they possess, if it be asked of them; on the contrary, they invite anyone to share it, and display as much love as if they would give their hearts, and whether the thing be of value or whether it be of small price, at once with whatever trifle of whatever kind it may be that is given to them, with that they are content. I forbade that they should be given things so worthless as fragments of broken crockery and scraps of broken glass, and ends of straps, although when they were able to get them, they fancied that they possessed the best jewel in the world. So it was found that a sailor for a strap received gold to the weight of two and a half *castellanos*,[8] and others much more for other things which were worth much less. As for new *blancas*, for them they would give everything which they had, although it might be two or three *castellanos'* weight of gold or an *arroba*[9] or two of spun cotton. . . . They took even the pieces of the broken hoops of the wine barrels and, like savages, gave what they had, so that it seemed to me to be wrong and I forbade it. And I gave a thousand handsome good things, which I had brought, in order that they might conceive affection, and more than that, might become Christians and be inclined to the love and service of their highnesses and of the whole Castilian nation, and strive to aid us and to give us of the things which they have in abundance and which are necessary to us. And they do not know any creed and are not idolaters; only they all believe that power and good are in the heavens, and they are very firmly convinced that I, with these ships and men, came from the heavens, and in this belief they everywhere received me, after they had overcome their fear. And this does not come because they are ignorant; on the contrary, they are of a very acute intelligence and are men who navigate all those seas, so that it is amazing how good an account they give of everything, but it is because they have never seen people clothed or ships of such a kind.

And as soon as I arrived in the Indies, in the first island which I found, I took by force some of them, in order that they might learn and give me information of that which there is in those parts, and so it was that they soon understood us, and we them, either by speech or signs, and they have been very serviceable.[1] I still take them with me, and they are always assured that I come from Heaven, for all the intercourse[2] which they have had with me; and they were the first to announce this wherever I went, and the others went running from house to house and to the neighbouring towns, with loud cries of, "Come! Come to see the people from Heaven!" So all, men and women alike, when their minds were set at rest concerning us, came, so that not one, great or small, remained behind, and all brought something to eat and drink, which they gave with extraordinary affection. In all the island, they have very many canoes, like rowing *fustas*,[3] some larger, some smaller, and some are larger than a *fusta* of eighteen benches. They are not so broad, because they are made of a single log of wood, but a *fusta* would not keep up with them in rowing, since their speed is a thing incredible. And in these they navigate among all those islands, which are

8. A *castellano* was a gold coin.
9. A *blanca* was a copper coin. An *arroba* was equal to twenty-five pounds.
1. No record exists of how many indigenous people Columbus took captive, but only seven

survived the voyage to Spain. On the second voyage, one of these seven acted as interpreter.
2. Communication, exchange.
3. A *fusta* was a moderate-sized ship, smaller than a galley, with banks of oars and a single mast.

innumerable, and carry their goods. One of these canoes I have seen with seventy and eighty men in her, and each one with his oar.

In all these islands, I saw no great diversity in the appearance of the people or in their manners and language.[4] On the contrary, they all understand one another, which is a very curious thing, on account of which I hope that their highnesses will determine upon their conversion to our holy faith, towards which they are very inclined.

I have already said how I have gone one hundred and seven leagues in a straight line from west to east along the seashore of the island Juana, and as a result of that voyage, I can say that this island is larger than England and Scotland together,[5] for, beyond these one hundred and seven leagues, there remain to the westward two provinces to which I have not gone. One of these provinces they call "Avan,"[6] and there the people are born with tails; and these provinces cannot have a length of less than fifty or sixty leagues, as I could understand from those Indians whom I have and who know all the islands.

The other, Española, has a circumference greater than all Spain, from Colibre, by the sea-coast, to Fuenterabia in Vizcaya, since I voyaged along one side one hundred and eighty-eight great leagues in a straight line from west to east.[7] It is a land to be desired and, seen, it is never to be left. And in it, although of all I have taken possession for their highnesses and all are more richly endowed than I know how, or am able, to say, and I hold them all for their highnesses, so that they may dispose of them as, and as absolutely as, of the kingdoms of Castile, in this Española, in the situation most convenient and in the best position for the mines of gold and for all intercourse as well with the mainland here as with that there, belonging to the Grand Khan, where will be great trade and gain, I have taken possession of a large town, to which I gave the name *Villa de Navidad*,[8] and in it I have made fortifications and a fort, which now will by this time be entirely finished, and I have left in it sufficient men[9] for such a purpose with arms and artillery and provisions for more than a year, and a *fusta*, and one, a master of all seacraft, to build others, and great friendship with the king of that land, so much so, that he was proud to call me, and to treat me as, a brother. And even if he were to change his attitude to one of hostility towards these men, he and his do not know what arms are and they go naked, as I have already said, and are the most timorous people that there are in the world, so that the men whom I have left there alone would suffice to destroy all that land, and the island is without danger for their persons, if they know how to govern themselves.

In all these islands, it seems to me that all men are content with one woman, and to their chief or king they give as many as twenty. It appears to me that the women work more than the men. And I have not been able to learn if they hold private property; what seemed to me to appear was that, in that which one had, all took a share, especially of eatable things.

4. Columbus was mistaken about the single language, as he later discovered. In fact, there was considerable linguistic diversity.
5. Actually, Cuba occupies roughly forty-three thousand square miles, whereas England alone is more than fifty thousand square miles in area.
6. The Natives called one region of the island "Havana," and "Avan" may be Columbus's rendering of that name.
7. Again, Columbus overstates his comparison.

The coastline of Spain and Portugal measures roughly nineteen hundred miles, whereas that of Española is about fifteen hundred miles. "Colibre": Collioure, in the Pyrenees; "Fuenterabia:" Hondarribia, a coastal town in northwestern Spain.
8. A site on the modern bay of Caracol, in Haiti. "Grand Khan": the Chinese emperor.
9. Columbus left approximately forty men at La Navidad.

In these islands I have so far found no human monstrosities, as many expected,[1] but on the contrary the whole population is very well-formed, nor are they negroes as in Guinea, but their hair is flowing, and they are not born where there is intense force in the rays of the sun; it is true that the sun has there great power, although it is distant from the equinoctial line twenty-six degrees. In these islands, where there are high mountains, the cold was severe this winter, but they endure it, being used to it and with the help of meats which they eat with many and extremely hot spices. As I have found no monsters, so I have had no report of any, except in an island "Quaris,"[2] the second at the coming into the Indies, which is inhabited by a people who are regarded in all the islands as very fierce and who eat human flesh. They have many canoes with which they range through all the islands of India and pillage and take as much as they can. They are no more malformed than the others, except that they have the custom of wearing their hair long like women, and they use bows and arrows of the same cane stems, with a small piece of wood at the end, owing to lack of iron which they do not possess. They are ferocious among these other people who are cowardly to an excessive degree, but I make no more account of them than of the rest. These are those who have intercourse with the women of "Matinino,"[3] which is the first island met on the way from Spain to the Indies, in which there is not a man. These women engage in no feminine occupation, but use bows and arrows of cane, like those already mentioned, and they arm and protect themselves with plates of copper, of which they have much.

In another island, which they assure me is larger than Española, the people have no hair. In it, there is gold incalculable, and from it and from the other islands, I bring with me Indians as evidence.

In conclusion, to speak only of that which has been accomplished on this voyage, which was so hasty, their highnesses can see that I will give them as much gold as they may need, if their highnesses will render me very slight assistance; moreover, spice and cotton, as much as their highnesses shall command; and mastic, as much as they shall order to be shipped and which, up to now, has been found only in Greece, in the island of Chios, and the Seignory[4] sells it for what it pleases; and aloe wood, as much as they shall order to be shipped, and slaves, as many as they shall order to be shipped and who will be from the idolaters.[5] And I believe that I have found rhubarb and cinnamon, and I shall find a thousand other things of value, which the people whom I have left there will have discovered, for I have not delayed at any point, so far as the wind allowed me to sail, except in the town of Navi-

1. Among those who expected to find human monstrosities was Pierre d'Ailly, a French theologian, philosopher, and cardinal. Columbus annotated his own copy of d'Ailly's cosmographic and astronomical writings, the *Imago Mundi* (written between 1410 and 1419 and printed sometime between 1480 and 1490).
2. Either Dominica or Maria Galante.
3. Now Martinique. "Intercourse": here, in the sexual sense.
4. The Genoese government. "Chios": an island, now part of Greece, that had been claimed by Genoa since 1346; Columbus may have visited there in 1474–75. "Mastic": a natural resin produced from the mastic tree, sometimes known as "the tears of Chios." The trade in mastic was controlled by a company that became a tributary to the Ottomans in 1453.
5. In 1452, Pope Nicholas V authorized the Portuguese to reduce any non-Christians to the status of slaves; two years later, he granted Portugal a monopoly of the slave trade with Africa. Spain ignored the monopoly status that Nicholas had granted to Portugal and began trading in African slaves. On arriving in the West Indies, Columbus almost immediately began to take captives, and a bit later he participated in the enslavement of Native people. He eventually developed a plan for a slave trade in indigenous Americans.

dad, in order to leave it secured and well established, and in truth, I should have done much more, if the ships had served me, as reason demanded.

This is enough . . . [6] and the eternal God, our Lord, Who gives to all those who walk in His way triumph over things which appear to be impossible, and this was notably one; for, although men have talked or have written of these lands, all was conjectural, without suggestion of ocular evidence, but amounted only to this, that those who heard for the most part listened and judged it to be rather a fable than as having any vestige of truth. So that, since Our Redeemer has given this victory to our most illustrious king and queen, and to their renowned kingdoms, in so great a matter, for this all Christendom ought to feel delight and make great feasts and give solemn thanks to the Holy Trinity with many solemn prayers for the great exaltation which they shall have, in the turning of so many peoples to our holy faith, and afterwards for temporal benefits, for not only Spain but all Christians will have hence refreshment and gain.

This, in accordance with that which has been accomplished, thus briefly.

Done in the caravel, off the Canary Islands,[7] on the fifteenth of February, in the year one thousand four hundred and ninety-three.

At your orders. El Almirante.[8]

[Postscript]

After having written this, and being in the sea of Castile, there came on me so great a south-south-west wind, that I was obliged to lighten ship. But I ran here to-day into this port of Lisbon,[9] which was the greatest marvel in the world, whence I decided to write to their highnesses. In all the Indies, I have always found weather like May; where I went in thirty-three days and I had returned in twenty-eight, save for these storms which have detained me for fourteen days, beating about in this sea. Here all the sailors say that never has there been so bad a winter nor so many ships lost.

Done on the fourth day of March.

1493

From Letter to Ferdinand and Isabella Regarding the Fourth Voyage[1]

[Jamaica, July 7, 1503]

* * *

Of Española, Paria,[2] and the other lands, I never think without weeping. I believed that their example would have been to the profit of others; on the

6. There is a gap here in the original manuscript.
7. Columbus was in fact off Santa Maria, one of the islands in the Azores. "Caravel": a fast, light sailing ship, much used by the Portuguese for exploring the African coast. Two of the three ships on Columbus's first voyage, the *Niña* and the *Pinta*, were caravels.
8. The Admiral.
9. Columbus's decision to go to Lisbon, Portugal, aroused suspicions in Spain, where Portugal was regarded as a major rival.
1. Written on Jamaica in 1503, this letter was hand carried from there to Hispaniola by Diego Mendez.
2. Paria was the mainland region of what is now Venezuela, near the island of Trinidad. Columbus, who had first landed in South America ("Terra Firma," as he terms it later) in 1498, argued that the terrestrial paradise lay nearby.

contrary, they are in an exhausted state; although they are not dead, the infirmity is incurable or very extensive; let him who brought them to this state come now with the remedy if he can or if he knows it; in destruction, everyone is an adept. It was always the custom to give thanks and promotion to him who imperiled his person. It is not just that he who has been so hostile to this undertaking should enjoy its fruits or that his children should. Those who left the Indies, flying from toils and speaking evil of the matter and of me, have returned with official employment.[3] So it has now been ordained in the case of Veragua.[4] It is an ill example and without profit for the business and for justice in the world.

The fear of this, with other sufficient reasons, which I saw clearly, led me to pray your highnesses before I went to discover these islands and Terra Firma, that you would leave them to me to govern in your royal name. It pleased you; it was a privilege and agreement, and under seal and oath, and you granted me the title of viceroy and admiral and governor general of all. And you fixed the boundary, a hundred leagues beyond the Azores and the Cape Verde Islands, by a line passing from pole to pole, and you gave me wide power over this and over all that I might further discover. The document states this very fully.

The other most important matter, which calls aloud for redress, remains inexplicable to this moment. Seven years I was at your royal court, where all to whom this undertaking was mentioned, unanimously declared it to be a delusion. Now all, down to the very tailors, seek permission to make discoveries. It can be believed that they go forth to plunder, and it is granted to them to do so, so that they greatly prejudice my honor and do very great damage to the enterprise. It is well to give to God that which is His due and to Caesar that which belongs to him.[5] This is a just sentiment and based on justice.

The lands which here obey Your Highnesses are more extensive and richer than all other Christian lands. After I, by the divine will, had placed them under your royal and exalted lordship, and was on the point of securing a very great revenue, suddenly, while I was waiting for ships to come to your high presence with victory and with great news of gold, being very secure and joyful, I was made a prisoner and with my two brothers was thrown into a ship, laden with fetters, stripped to the skin, very ill-treated, and without being tried or condemned. Who will believe that a poor foreigner could in such a place rise against Your Highnesses, without cause, and without the support of some other prince, and being alone among your vassals and natural subjects, and having all my children at your royal court?

I came to serve at the age of twenty-eight years, and now I have not a hair on my body that is not gray, and my body is infirm, and whatever remained to me from those years of service has been spent and taken away from me and sold, and from my brothers, down to my very coat, without my being heard or seen, to my great dishonor. It must be believed that this was not done by your royal command. The restitution of my honor, the reparation of

3. Although it appears that Columbus has specific personal enemies in mind, it is not clear whom he means.
4. I.e., Panama, where Columbus was shipwrecked earlier in this voyage.

5. Cf. "Render therefore unto Caesar the things which are Caesar's, and unto God the things that are God's" (Matthew 22.21).

my losses, and the punishment of him who did this, will spread abroad the fame of your royal nobility. The same punishment is due to him who robbed me of the pearls, and to him who infringed my rights as admiral.[6] Very great will be your merit, fame without parallel will be yours, if you do this, and there will remain in Spain a glorious memory of Your Highnesses, as grateful and just princes.

The pure devotion which I have ever borne to the service of Your Highnesses, and the unmerited wrong that I have suffered, will not permit me to remain silent, although I would fain do so; I pray Your Highnesses to pardon me. I am so ruined as I have said; hitherto I have wept for others; now, Heaven have mercy upon me, and may the earth weep for me. Of worldly goods, I have not even a *blanca*[7] for an offering in spiritual things. Here in the Indies I have become careless of the prescribed forms of religion. Alone in my trouble, sick, in daily expectation of death, and encompassed about by a million savages, full of cruelty and our foes, and so separated from the holy Sacraments of Holy Church, my soul will be forgotten if it here leaves my body. Weep for me, whoever has charity, truth, and justice.

I did not sail upon this voyage to gain honor or wealth; this is certain, for already all hope of that was dead. I came to Your Highnesses with true devotion and with ready zeal, and I do not lie. I humbly pray Your Highnesses that if it please God to bring me forth from this place, that you will be pleased to permit me to go to Rome and to other places of pilgrimage. May the Holy Trinity preserve your life and high estate, and grant you increase of prosperity.

Done in the Indies in the island of Jamaica, on the seventh of July, in the year one thousand five hundred and three.

1505

6. The reference is to Alonso de Ojeda (1468–c. 1516), who had taken pearls—part of what was reserved to Columbus under his agreement with the Spanish Crown—from Paria to Española.
7. See n. 9, p. 61.

BARTOLOMÉ DE LAS CASAS
1474–1566

"I saw all these things I have described, and countless others." So wrote Bartolomé de las Casas, the Spanish "Apostle of the Indians," who is best known as early modern Europe's most eloquent advocate for Native American rights. During Las Casas's early career as a soldier, he observed and, to some extent, participated in the atrocities that were being perpetrated on the Native inhabitants of the Americas, often in the name of Christianity. Increasingly troubled by these events, and provoked by the gaps between Christian ideals and the brutality committed in its name, Las Casas gradually sought in his religious faith a means to challenge the violence that was decimating indigenous communities. In a famous sermon of 1514,

delivered shortly after he entered the Roman Catholic priesthood, Las Casas repudiated the institution of forced labor known as the *encomienda* system and returned the Indian serfs he had been awarded.

From this time until his death, Las Casas engaged in a vigorous campaign to institute a more just relationship between America's European colonizers and its indigenous inhabitants. Las Casas spoke, wrote, and published against existing practices, often in excoriating terms, to audiences on both sides of the Atlantic. He proposed alternatives to the existing system, including, to his later regret, the introduction of Africans as slaves to replace the forced labor of indigenous Americans. He engaged in practical efforts to establish more-benign colonial relations, notably in Venezuela in 1520, and again in Chiapas, Mexico, during the mid-1540s after his appointment as bishop there, but these projects largely failed.

Las Casas's arguments had their greatest successes in 1537, when Pope Paul III forbade all further Native enslavements, and in 1542, when the Spanish emperor Charles V followed suit in the New Laws of the Indies, which gave Native Americans full protection of the courts, forbidding their enslavement on any grounds. "We order and command that henceforth," ran one clause in the New Laws, "for no cause whatsoever, whether of war, rebellion, ransom, or in any other manner, can any Indian be made a slave." Not long afterward, Las Casas was once again disappointed, when Charles V revoked key features of the New Laws in the face of pressure from settlers. The reformer spent the last twenty years of his life writing about his long crusade in the West Indies.

Las Casas had family ties to Christopher Columbus as well as personal memories of the excitement surrounding the "discoveries." He helped shape Columbus's legacy by transcribing the logbook from the first voyage in what is the only surviving copy of that document; he also transcribed and annotated Columbus's diaries. Of Las Casas's own writings, the most important in his own era was *Brevísima relación de la destrucción de las Indias*. (There are minor variations in English translations of the title, rendered in the following text as *An Account, Much Abbreviated, of the Destruction of the Indies*.) First published in 1552, *Destruction of the Indies* was based on oral arguments that Las Casas had used a decade earlier to persuade a special royal commission to frame the legal code of 1542. The emphasis in the printed text on personal witness, like the biting irony of his descriptions of "Christians," stems from the rhetorical context of the original setting.

Destruction of the Indies details with chilling effect the devastation visited on Native Americans by conquistadors and colonizers in pursuit of wealth. Las Casas was widely accused of treason and endured charges of heresy, partly because the quick translation of this work into several other languages provided Spain's enemies with ample evidence of his country's sins in America—a point that Protestant nations such as the Netherlands and England especially wished to highlight, at least partly in the interest of their own colonial projects. Ironically, the later Protestant "Black Legend" of Spanish devastations in the West Indies derives in important ways from the polemical exposé that the Catholic priest Bartolomé de las Casas intended less as a denunciation of Spain's past behavior than as a call to its future reform.

From An Account, Much Abbreviated, of the Destruction of the Indies[1]

On the Island Hispaniola

On the island Hispaniola, which was the first, as we said, wherein the Christians entered and began the devastations and perditions of these nations, and first destroyed them and wiped the land clean of inhabitants, these Christians began to take the women and children of the Indians to serve them and use them ill, and they would eat their victuals that issued from the sweat of their brow and their hard work, and yet still were not content with what the Indians gave them willingly, according to the ability that each one had, which is not ever much, for they seldom have more than that which they have most immediate need of and can produce with little labour. And in truth, what suffices for three houses of ten persons each for a month, a Christian will eat and destroy in one day, and these Christians did them many other acts of compulsion and violence and vexation.

The Indians, at this treatment, began to see that those men must not have come down from the sky, or heaven,[2] and some hid their victuals, others their women and children, while others fled into the wilderness to remove themselves from men of such hard and terrible conversation.[3] The Christians would smite them with their hands and strike them with their fists and beat them with sticks and cudgels, until they finally laid hands upon the lords of the villages. And this practice came to such great temerity and shamelessness and ignominy that a Christian captain did violate the wife of the greatest king, the lord of all the island.[4] And at that, the Indians began to seek ways to cast the Christians from their lands; they took up arms, which are but weak and petty things, of little offence and resistance and even less defence (for which reason, all their wars are little more than what would be games with wooden swords here in this land, or even children's games), and at that, the Christians with their horses and swords and pikes and lances began to wreak slaughters and singular cruelties upon them.

They would enter into the villages and spare not children, or old people, or pregnant women, or women with suckling babes, but would open the woman's belly and hack the babe to pieces, as though they were butchering lambs shut up in their pen. They would lay wagers who might slice open the belly of a man with one stroke of their blade, or cut off a man's head with one swift motion of their pike, or spill out his entrails. They would snatch babes from their mothers' breasts and take them by their feet and dash their heads against the rocks. Others would fling them over their shoulders into the rivers, laughing and jeering, and as they fell into the water they would call out: "Thrash, you little bugger!"; other babes, they would run their swords

1. The text is from *An Account, Much Abbreviated, of the Destruction of the Indies* (2003), ed. Franklin W. Knight, trans. Andrew Hurley.
2. Christopher Columbus, Thomas Harriot, and other early European arrivals in the Americas reported that Native peoples took them to be gods who had come from the heavens.
3. Social interaction.
4. Francisco de Valenzuela raped the wife of the Taino cacique (chief) Enriquillo (c. 1498–?),

who had been raised in a Franciscan monastery on Santo Domingo. Angered by this treatment, Enriquillo led revolts against the Spanish from 1519 to 1538 from a base in the mountains that attracted Natives and escaped African slaves. Charles V eventually ordered that a peace treaty be signed, the first such treaty between Europeans and indigenous Americans. Las Casas was involved in the reconciliation with Enriquillo that followed.

through mother and child at once, and all that they came across. They would erect long gibbets,[5] but no higher than that a man's feet might dangle just above the ground, and bind thirteen of the Indians at one time, in honour and reverence, they said, of Our Redeemer and the twelve Apostles, and put firewood around it and burn the Indians alive. Others, they would tie or bind their bodies all about with dry straw, and set fire to the straw and burn them that way. Others, and all those that they desired to let live, they would cut off both their hands but leave them hanging by the skin, and they would say to them: "Go, and take these letters," which was to say, carry the news to the people who have hidden themselves in the mountains and the wilderness. They would often slay the lords and nobles in this way: They would weave together twigs and branches, like unto a gridiron,[6] but made of twigs, and raise it on forked poles or limbs of trees set into the ground, and tether the lords and nobles to that grate and set a slow fire below it, so that little by little, crying out and screaming from those torments, and in desperation, they would give up their souls.

I myself saw that once, four or five lords and men of high rank were being burned on grates in this way (and I even think that there may have been two or three pairs of grates on which others were also being burned), and on account of their loud cries and clamours, the captain seemed to take pity on them, or perhaps they disturbed his sleep, and he ordered them hanged; but the executioner that was burning them, who was worse than any hangman (and I know what his name is and even met certain kinsmen of his in Seville),[7] was not content to hang them, and so with his hands he sewed their mouths shut with sticks, so that they could make no sounds, and then poked up the fire and roasted them as long as he had first desired. I vouchsafe that I did see all the things I have writ above, and infinite numbers of others. And because all those who were able to flee, did hide themselves in the wilderness and go up into the mountains to escape those men who were so inhumane, so pitiless, and so savage, and such abominable destroyers and foremost enemies of the human lineage, the Spaniards taught and trained hunting hounds, fierce and savage dogs that would no sooner see an Indian than they would tear him to pieces, and would rather set upon a man and eat him than if he were a pig. These dogs wrought dreadful havoc and butcheries. And because sometimes, though seldom, the Indians would slay a Christian, though for good and just reason and in holy justice, the Spaniards made a law amongst themselves that for every one Christian that the Indians slew, the Christians would slay an hundred Indians.

* * *

From all that coast, which was once filled with people, they have brought to the island of Hispaniola and that of San Juan[8] two million or more souls whom they have taken in their raids, and all of those, too, they have slain on those islands and sent to the mines or to other hard labour, over and above the multitudes who lived on them, as we have said above. And it is a great pity and it breaks one's heart to see that coast of fertile, blessed land, now desert and bare of people.

5. Gallows.
6. A frame of parallel metal bars used for grilling.
7. A city in southern Spain.
8. Puerto Rico was called San Juan until 1521.

And this is a truth that may easily be confirmed: That they never bring a ship filled with Indians, stolen and assaulted in this manner, as I have said, that they do not cast into the sea, dead, the third part of those who are upon it, having left that many more dead in taking them from their lands. The reason is that, in order to accomplish their ends they must have many people, to obtain more money for more slaves, and they carry but little food or water (so that the tyrants who style themselves "shipowners" may save a little money), hardly enough store, or a little more, for the Spaniards who go in the ship to carry out their raids, and so there is not enough for the poor, sad Indians, and so they die of hunger and thirst, and the answer is to throw them into the sea. And in truth one man who was with them told me that from one island of the Lucayos,[9] where they cause great devastation in this wise, to the Island of Hispaniola, which is sixty or seventy leagues, a ship might sail without compass and without map, taking its course by the trail of Indians floating on the surface of the sea, thrown dead from a ship that went before.

Then, from the moment they remove them from the ship onto the island where they have carried the Indians to be sold as slaves, it would break the heart of any man in whom any jot of mercy were remaining, to see children and old persons, men and women, naked and starving, and falling in a faint from hunger. Then, as though they were lambs, fathers are separated from their sons and wives from their husbands, making herds of ten or twenty persons, and lots are cast for them, so that the groups of them may be carried off by the wretched "shipowners," who are those who put in their part of the money to fit out the armada of two or three ships, and the tyrannical raiders who go out to lay hold of them and set upon them in their homes. And when it happens that within such a lot there is some Indian that is old or sick, the tyrant calls out to the one who is apportioning the lots: "This old man, to the devil with him. What are you giving him to me for, to bury him? This sick one, why should I take him, to cure him?" And one may see here in what great esteem the Spaniards hold the Indians, and may judge whether they obey the divine commandment from which the Law and the Prophets all derive, that men should love one another.

The tyranny that the Spaniards exercise against the Indians in finding or diving for pearls is one of the most cruel and shameful things in the world. There is no hellish and hopeless life on this earth that may be compared with it, however hard and terrible taking out the gold in the mines may be. They throw them into the sea in three and four and five yards' depth from early morning until the sun has set. They are always underwater swimming, without respite, tearing from the seabed the oysters in which the pearls are found. Bearing little nets and gasping for air, they come to the surface, where a Spanish torturer awaits them in a canoe or little rowboat, and if they dally too long in resting, they are beaten and water is poured upon their head to make them dive again. Their food is fish, and also the fish that contains the pearls, and bread made of cassava and sometimes of maize, which are the common breads in those parts, the first of very little substance and the other toilsome to make, and with which they never fill themselves. The beds that

9. The Bahamas.

they are given of a night is that they are cast into stocks[1] set into the ground, so that they cannot run away. Often they dive into the sea in their fishing or search for pearls and never come up again, because two species of most bloodthirsty and vicious sea beasts,[2] which can swallow a man down whole, do eat them and kill them. And one can see here whether the Spaniards who in their search for pearls act in this wise have obeyed the divine precepts of love for God and man by putting these poor creatures in the way of danger both temporal and of the soul as well, because they die outside the faith and without sacraments, and all for their own infinite greed. And another thing, giving them such a miserable life until they wear them away and consume them in the space of but a few and easily numbered days. Because for men, living under the water without respite is a thing impossible for very long, most especially when the constant coldness of the water penetrates them to their very innards, and so all of them generally die spitting blood from out their mouths, by reason of the tightness of chest that seizes them from being so long and so constantly without respite, and with the diarrhea caused by the cold. Their hair, which is by nature black, becomes burned like the hair of sailors, and salt trails run down their backs, so that they appear to be monsters in the form of men, or another species entirely. In this incomparable labour, or to say the truth, this hellish enterprise, the Spaniards have spent[3] and consumed all the Indians of the Lucayos that once lived on that island when the Spaniards descended into this species of farming. And each one of them was worth fifty or one hundred *castellanos*,[4] and they sold them publicly, even though such treatment was forbidden by their own justices (unjust enough, if truth be told), although the Lucayos were fine swimmers. And in these parts there have died countless others from other provinces and parts.

1542–46 1552

1. Wooden structures for securing a person's hands and feet.
2. Sharks and barracuda.

3. Worn out, used up.
4. Spanish gold coins.

ÁLVAR NÚÑEZ CABEZA DE VACA
c. 1490–1558

One of the most common forms of writing to emerge from the European encounter with the Americas was travel or exploration narratives. These narratives, in Spanish frequently called *relaciónes*, combined adventure and captivity tales with descriptions of the manners and customs of local inhabitants. While the descriptive passages sometimes resemble the modern scholarly genre of ethnography, they were written with different aims from those of academic anthropologists. In the dedication to his *relación*, Álvar Núñez Cabeza de Vaca asserts that his account "is of no trivial value" because it will help adventurers who seek to "subdue those countries and bring them to a knowledge of the true faith and true Lord and bring them under the imperial dominion" of Spain's Emperor Charles V, grandson

and successor of Ferdinand and Isabella. This frank statement captures the stance and tone of many such narratives.

A soldier of modest noble background who had fought in Italy and Spain, Cabeza de Vaca sailed in the 1527 expedition to Florida led by Panfilo de Narváez. Impetuous, self-centered, and a poor leader, Narváez first took his six hundred men to Hispaniola, where a quarter of them deserted, and then to Cuba, where two of the six ships were lost in a hurricane. Ten months after leaving Spain, the expedition became stranded near what is now Sarasota Bay, on Florida's west coast. Narváez asserted possession of Florida even as the inhabitants of Sarasota Bay (probably Calusa Indians) made, in Cabeza de Vaca's words, "many signs and threats [that] left little doubt that they were bidding us to go." Soon the expedition, reduced to eating its horses, sought to escape other groups of Florida Indians, from the Timucuan of the Suwannee River area to the Apalachees of the Panhandle. They built clumsy "barges" and retreated to the sea, traveling west along the edge of the Gulf of Mexico. Narváez took the best oarsmen in his own craft and left the other barges behind him as they neared what is now Mobile Bay, in Alabama. As he pulled away from the others he told them, with false magnanimity, that (again, in Cabeza de Vaca's word's) "it was no longer a time when one should command another"—in short, every man for himself! With that, Narváez and his crew disappeared, apparently lost at sea.

The other rafts passed the mouth of what seems to have been the Mississippi River and, in November 1528, wrecked on an island, which they called Malhado (Misfortune, or Doom; present-day Galveston Island or San Luis Island, Texas). Cabeza de Vaca survived and was initially accompanied by three fellow survivors: the Spaniards Andrés Dorantes and Alonso del Castillo Maldonado and Dorantes's black slave, Estevánico, who was from the Moroccan town of Azemmor. During the subsequent decade, alone or with drifting groups of other survivors, Cabeza de Vaca underwent a North American odyssey. He spent his first two years on the Texas coast as a prisoner and slave of the Capoque and Han clans of the Karankawa Indians. He then gradually progressed north and west, gaining status and power among the Caddos, Atakapas, Coahuiltecans, and other Native communities from his activities as a merchant and, especially, his skill as a healer. By 1535, he reached present-day New Mexico, where he encountered the Jumanos and Conchos, then headed southwest into Mexico as the leader of a vast crowd of Pimas and Opatas who reverently followed him from village to village.

The heady mood of the journey dissipated the following March, however, when the wanderers encountered a party of Spanish slave hunters under Diego de Alcaraz in western Mexico. Seeing the terror exhibited by his Indian escorts at the men he described as "Christian slavers," Cabeza de Vaca became openly critical of Alcaraz, who arrested him, sent him south, and seized as slaves the six hundred Natives in his company. From Mexico City, where he agitated against the cruel (and technically illegal) activities of the likes of Alcaraz, Cabeza de Vaca went to Spain in 1537. After making similar protestations to Charles V, he was allowed to lead an expedition to South America in 1540. As governor of the Río de la Plata region, Cabeza de Vaca hoped to enact enlightened policies toward the Natives, but his colonists, profiting from slavery, removed him forcibly from office and sent him in chains back to Spain in 1545. After long delays in settling the dispute, in 1551 he was exiled to what is now Algeria and forbidden to return to America.

Cabeza de Vaca composed his first narrative of the Narváez expedition during the three years he spent in Spain before his departure for Río de la Plata. It was published in 1542; a corrected and expanded version, which includes the story of his later American experience, appeared in 1555. Addressed to Charles V, the 1542 account sought to justify his conclusions regarding Spanish policy and behavior in America as well as to argue for renewed explorations and settlement in the regions he had crossed. Several later Spanish expeditions, including those of Coronado and de Soto, clearly drew on Cabeza de Vaca's arguments and knowledge. More important, however, *The Rela-*

tion of Álvar Núñez Cabeza de Vaca sought to recount (with remarkable understatement) his sufferings and many brushes with death and to explore his complex feelings regarding the Native Americans and his countrymen's dealings with them. The selections included here demonstrate the range and complexity of his rhetorical modes, from dedicatory prose to ethnographic-style writing to dramatic recounting.

From The Relation of Álvar Núñez Cabeza de Vaca[1]

[Dedication]

Sacred Caesarian Catholic Majesty:

Among all the princes who have reigned, I know of none who has enjoyed the universal esteem of Your Majesty at this day, when strangers vie in approbation with those motivated by religion and loyalty.

Although everyone wants what advantage may be gained from ambition and action, we see everywhere great inequalities of fortune, brought about not by conduct but by accident, and not through anybody's fault but as the will of God. Thus the deeds of one far exceed his expectation, while another can show no higher proof of purpose than his fruitless effort, and even the effort may go unnoticed.

I can say for myself that I undertook the march abroad, on royal authorization, with a firm trust that my service would be as evident and distinguished as my ancestors', and that I would not need to speak to be counted among those Your Majesty honors for diligence and fidelity in affairs of state. But my counsel and constancy availed nothing toward those objectives we set out to gain, in your interests, for our sins. In fact, no other of the many armed expeditions into those parts has found itself in such dire straits as ours, or come to so futile and fatal a conclusion.

My only remaining duty is to transmit what I saw and heard in the nine years I wandered lost and miserable over many remote lands. I hope in some measure to convey to Your Majesty not merely a report of positions and distances, flora and fauna, but of the customs of the numerous, barbarous people I talked with and dwelt among, as well as any other matters I could hear of or observe. My hope of going out from among those nations was always small; nevertheless, I made a point of remembering all the particulars, so that should God our Lord eventually please to bring me where I am now, I might testify to my exertion in the royal behalf.

Since this narrative, in my opinion, is of no trivial value for those who go in your name to subdue those countries and bring them to a knowledge of the true faith and true Lord and bring them under the imperial dominion, I have written very exactly. Novel or, for some persons, difficult to believe though the things narrated may be, I assure you they can be accepted without hesitation as strictly factual. Better than to exaggerate, I have minimized all things; it is enough to say that the relation is offered Your Majesty for truth.

I beg that it may be received as homage, since it is the most one could bring who returned thence naked.

1. The text is from *Adventures in the Unknown Interior of America* (1961), edited and translated by Cyclone Covey.

* * *

[The Malhado Way of Life]

The people[2] we came to know there are tall and well built. Their only weapons are bows and arrows, which they use with great dexterity. The men bore through one of their nipples, some both, and insert a joint of cane two and a half palms long by two fingers thick. They also bore their lower lip and wear a piece of cane in it half a finger in diameter.

Their women toil incessantly.

From October to the end of February every year, which is the season these Indians live on the island, they subsist on the roots I have mentioned,[3] which the women get from under water in November and December. Only in these two months, too, do they take fish in their cane weirs. When the fish is consumed, the roots furnish the one staple. At the end of February the islanders go into other parts to seek sustenance, for then the root is beginning to grow and is not edible.

These people love their offspring more than any in the world and treat them very mildly.

If a son dies, the whole village joins the parents and kindred in weeping. The parents set off the wails each day before dawn, again at noon, and at sunset, for one year. The funeral rites occur when the year of mourning is up. Following these rites, the survivors wash off the smoke stain of the ceremony in a symbolic purgation. All the dead are lamented this way except the aged, who merit no regrets. The dead are buried, except medicine-men, who are cremated. Everybody in the village dances and makes merry while the pyre of a medicine-man kindles, and until his bones become powder. A year later, when his rites are celebrated, the entire village again participating, this powder is presented in water for the relatives to drink.

Each man has an acknowledged wife, except the medicine-men, who may have two or three wives apiece. The several wives live together in perfect amity.

When a daughter marries, she must take everything her husband kills in hunting or catches in fishing to the house of her father, without daring to eat or to withhold any part of it, and the husband gets provided by female carrier from his father-in-law's house. Neither the bride's father nor mother may enter the son-in-law's house after the marriage, nor he theirs; and this holds for the children of the respective couples. If a man and his in-laws should chance to be walking so they would meet, they turn silently aside from each other and go a crossbow-shot out of their way, averting their glance to the ground. The woman, however, is free to fraternize with the parents and relatives of her husband. These marriage customs prevail for more than fifty leagues inland from the island.

At a house where a son or brother may die, no one goes out for food for three months, the neighbors and other relatives providing what is eaten. Because of this custom, which the Indians literally would not break to save their lives, great hunger reigned in most houses while we resided there, it being a time of repeated deaths. Those who sought food worked hard, but they could get little in that severe season. That is why Indians who kept me left the island by canoe for oyster bays on the main.

2. The Capoques and Hans of coastal Texas.
3. I.e., "certain roots which taste like nuts, mostly grubbed from [under] the water with great labor."

Three months out of every year they eat nothing but oysters and drink very bad water. Wood is scarce; mosquitoes, plentiful. The houses are made of mats; their floors consist of masses of oyster shells. The natives sleep on these shells—in animal skins, those who happen to own such.

Many a time I would have to go three days without eating, as would the natives. I thought it impossible that life could be so prolonged in such protracted hunger; though afterwards I found myself in yet greater want, as shall be seen.

The Indians who had Alonso del Castillo, Andrés Dorantes, and the others of their barge who remained alive, spoke a different dialect and claimed a different descent from these I lived among. They frequented the opposite shore of the main to eat oysters, staying till the first of April, then returning.

The distance to the main is two leagues at the widest part of the channel.[4] The island itself, which supports the two tribes commodiously, is half a league wide by five long.

The inhabitants of all these parts go naked, except that the women cover some part of their persons with a wool that grows on trees,[5] and damsels dress in deerskin.

The people are generous to each other with what little they have. There is no chief. All belonging to the same lineage keep together. They speak two languages: Capoque and Han.

They have a strange custom when acquaintances meet or occasionally visit, of weeping for half an hour before they speak. This over, the one who is visited rises and gives his visitor all he has. The latter accepts it and, after a while, carries it away, often without a word. They have other strange customs, but I have told the principal and most remarkable of them.

In April [1529] we went to the seashore and ate blackberries all month, a time of [dance ceremonies] and fiestas among the Indians.

* * *

[Our Life among the Avavares and Arbadaos]

All the Indians of this region[6] are ignorant of time, either by the sun or moon; nor do they reckon by the month or year. They understand the seasons in terms of the ripening of fruits, the dying of fish, and the position of stars, in which dating they are adept.

The Avavares always treated us well. We lived as free agents, dug our own food, and lugged our loads of wood and water. The houses and our diet were like those of the nation we had just come from, but the Avavares suffer yet greater want, having no corn, acorns, or pecans. We always went naked like them and covered ourselves at night with deerskins.

Six of the eight months we dwelled with these people we endured acute hunger; for fish are not found where they are either. At the end of the eight months, when the prickly pears were just beginning to ripen again [mid-June 1535], I traveled with the Negro—unknown to our hosts—to others a day's

4. Renaissance units of measurement were inexact. Cabeza de Vaca's "league" was probably about four miles.

5. I.e., Spanish moss.

6. Having escaped from the Capoques and Hans, Cabeza de Vaca is now among the Avavares and Arbadaos in inland Texas.

journey farther on: the Maliacones.[7] When three days had passed, I sent Estevánico to fetch Castillo and Dorantes.

When they got there, the four of us set out with the Maliacones, who were going to find the small fruit of certain trees which they subsist on for ten or twelve days while the prickly pears are maturing. They joined another tribe, the Arbadaos, who astonished us by their weak, emaciated, swollen condition.

We told the Maliacones with whom we had come that we wanted to stop with these Arbadaos. The Maliacones despondently returned the way they came, leaving us alone in the brushland near the Arbadao houses. The observing Arbadaos talked among themselves and came up to us in a body. Four of them took each of us by the hand and led us to their dwellings.

Among them we underwent fiercer hunger than among the Avavares. We ate not more than two handfuls of prickly pears a day, and they were still so green and milky they burned our mouths. In our lack of water, eating brought great thirst. At nearly the end of our endurance we bought two dogs for some nets, with other things, and a skin I used for cover.

I have already said that we went naked through all this country; not being accustomed to going so, we shed our skins twice a year like snakes. The sun and air raised great, painful sores on our chests and shoulders, and our heavy loads caused the cords to cut our arms. The region is so broken and so overgrown that often, when we gathered wood, blood flowed from us in many places where the thorns and shrubs tore our flesh. At times, when my turn came to get wood and I had collected it at heavy cost in blood, I could neither drag nor bear it out. My only solace in these labors was to think of the sufferings of our Redeemer, Jesus Christ, and the blood He shed for me. How much worse must have been his torment from the thorns than mine here!

I bartered with these Indians in combs I made for them and in bows, arrows, and nets. We made mats, which are what their houses consist of and for which they feel a keen necessity. Although they know how to make them, they prefer to devote their full time to finding food; when they do not, they get too pinched with hunger.

Some days the Indians would set me to scraping and softening skins. These were my days of greatest prosperity in that place. I would scrape thoroughly enough to sustain myself two or three days on the scraps. When it happened that these or any people we had left behind gave us a piece of meat, we ate it raw. Had we put it to roast, the first native who came along would have filched it. Not only did we think it better not to risk this, we were in such a condition that roasted meat would have given us pain. We could digest it more easily raw.

Such was our life there, where we earned our meager subsistence by trade in items which were the work of our own hands.

[Pushing On]

Eating the dogs seemed to give us strength enough to go forward; so commending ourselves to the guidance of God our Lord, we took leave of our hosts, who pointed out the way to others nearby who spoke their language.

7. Neighbors of the Avavares and Arbadaos. "The Negro": Estevánico.

Rain caught us. We traveled the day in the wet and got lost. At last, we made for an extensive scrub wood stretch, where we stopped and pulled prickly pear pads, which we cooked overnight in a hot oven we made. By morning they were ready.

After eating, we put ourselves again in the hands of God and set forth. We located the path we had lost and, after passing another scrub wood stretch, saw houses. Two women who were walking in the "forest" with some boys fled deep into it in fright to call their men, when they noticed us heading for the houses. The men arrived and hid behind trees to look at us. We called to them, and they came up very timidly. After some conversation, they told us their food was very scarce and that many houses of their people stood close by, to which they would conduct us.

At nightfall we came to a village of fifty dwellings. The residents looked at us in astonishment and fear. When they grew somewhat accustomed to our appearance, they felt our faces and bodies and then their own, comparing.

We stayed in that place overnight. In the morning the Indians brought us their sick, beseeching our blessing. They shared with us what they had to eat—prickly pear pads and the green fruit roasted. Because they did this with kindness and good will, gladly foregoing food to give us some, we tarried here several days.

Other Indians came from beyond in that interval and, when they were about to depart, we told our hosts we wanted to go with them. Our hosts felt quite uneasy at this and pressed us warmly to stay. In the midst of their weeping we left them.

[Customs of That Region]

From the Island of Doom to this land, all the Indians we saw have the custom of not sleeping with their wives from the time they are discovered pregnant to two years after giving birth. Children are suckled until they are twelve, when they are old enough to find their own support. We asked why they thus prolonged the nursing period, and they said that the poverty of the land frequently meant—as we witnessed—going two or three days without eating, sometimes four; if children were not allowed to suckle in seasons of scarcity, those who did not famish would be weaklings.

Anyone who chances to fall sick on a foraging trip and cannot keep up with the rest is left to die, unless he be a son or brother; him they will help, even to carrying on their back.

It is common among them all to leave their wives when there is disagreement, and directly reconnect with whomever they please. This is the course of men who are childless. Those who have children never abandon their wives.

When Indian men get into an argument in their villages, they fist-fight until exhausted, then separate. Sometimes the women will go between and part them, but men never interfere. No matter what the disaffection, they do not resort to bows and arrows. After a fight, the disputants take their houses (and families) and go live apart from each other in the scrub wood until they have cooled off; then they return and from that moment are friends as if nothing had happened. No intermediary is needed to mend their friendship.

In case the quarrelers are single men, they repair to some neighboring people (instead of the scrub wood), who, even if enemies, welcome them

warmly and give so largely of what they have that when the quarrelers' animosity subsides, they return to their home village rich.

* * *

[The First Confrontation]

When we saw for certain that we were drawing near the Christians, we gave thanks to God our Lord for choosing to bring us out of such a melancholy and wretched captivity. The joy we felt can only be conjectured in terms of the time, the suffering, and the peril we had endured in that land.

The evening of the day we reached the recent campsite, I tried hard to get Castillo or Dorantes to hurry on three days, unencumbered, after the Christians who were now circling back into the area we had assured protection. They both reacted negatively, excusing themselves for weariness, though younger and more athletic than I; but they being unwilling, I took the Negro and eleven Indians next morning to track the Christians. We went ten leagues, past three villages where they had slept.

The day after that, I overtook four of them on their horses. They were dumbfounded at the sight of me, strangely undressed and in company with Indians. They just stood staring for a long time, not thinking to hail me or come closer to ask questions.

"Take me to your captain," I at last requested; and we went together half a league to a place where we found their captain, Diego de Alcaraz.

When we had talked awhile, he confessed to me that he was completely undone, having been unable to catch any Indians in a long time; he did not know which way to turn; his men were getting too hungry and exhausted. I told him of Castillo and Dorantes ten leagues away with an escorting multitude. He immediately dispatched three of his horsemen to them, along with fifty of his Indian allies. The Negro went, too, as a guide; I stayed behind.

I asked the Christians to furnish me a certificate of the year, month, and day I arrived here, and the manner of my coming; which they did.[8] From this river to the Christian town, Sant Miguel[9] within the government of the recently created province of New Galicia, is a distance of thirty leagues.

[The Falling-Out with Our Countrymen]

After five days, Andrés Dorantes and Alonso del Castillo arrived with those who had gone for them; and they brought more than 600 natives of the vicinity whom the Indians who had been escorting us drew out of the woods and took to the mounted Christians, who thereupon dismissed their own escort.

When they arrived, Alcaraz begged us to order the villagers of this river out of the woods in the same way to get us food. It would be unnecessary to command them to bring food, if they came at all; for the Indians were always diligent to bring us all they could.

We sent our heralds to call them, and presently there came 600 Indians with all the corn they possessed. They brought it in clay-sealed earthen pots which had been buried. They also brought whatever else they had; but we wished only a meal, so gave the rest to the Christians to divide among themselves.

8. It was probably March 1536.
9. I.e., Culiacán, the northernmost Spanish set-
tlement in Mexico at that time, located in Sinaloa near the mouth of the Gulf of California.

After this we had a hot argument with them, for they meant to make slaves of the Indians in our train. We got so angry that we went off forgetting the many Turkish-shaped bows, the many pouches, and the five emerald arrowheads, etc., which we thus lost. And to think we had given these Christians a supply of cowhides and other things that our retainers had carried a long distance!

It proved difficult to persuade our escorting Indians to go back to their homes, to feel apprehensive no longer, and to plant their corn. But they did not want to do anything until they had first delivered us into the hands of other Indians, as custom bound them. They feared they would die if they returned without fulfiling this obligation whereas, with us, they said they feared neither Christians nor lances.

This sentiment roused our countrymen's jealousy. Alcaraz bade his interpreter tell the Indians that we were members of his race who had been long lost; that his group were the lords of the land who must be obeyed and served, while we were inconsequential. The Indians paid no attention to this. Conferring among themselves, they replied that the Christians lied: We had come from the sunrise, they from the sunset; we healed the sick, they killed the sound; we came naked and barefoot, they clothed, horsed, and lanced; we coveted nothing but gave whatever we were given, while they robbed whomever they found and bestowed nothing on anyone.

<p style="text-align:center">✳ ✳ ✳</p>

To the last I could not convince the Indians that we were of the same people as the Christian slavers. Only with the greatest effort were we able to induce them to go back home. We ordered them to fear no more, reestablish their towns, and farm.

Already the countryside had grown rank from neglect. This is, no doubt, the most prolific land in all these Indies. It produces three crops a year; the trees bear a great variety of fruit; and beautiful rivers and brimming springs abound throughout. There are gold- and silver-bearing ores. The people are well disposed, serving such Christians as are their friends with great good will. They are comely, much more so than the Mexicans. This land, in short, lacks nothing to be regarded as blest.

When the Indians took their leave of us they said they would do as we commanded and rebuild their towns, if the Christians let them. And I solemnly swear that if they have not done so it is the fault of the Christians.

After we had dismissed the Indians in peace and thanked them for their toil in our behalf, the Christians subtly sent us on our way in the charge of an alcalde named Cebreros, attended by two horsemen.[1] They took us through forests and wastes so we would not communicate with the natives and would neither see nor learn of their crafty scheme afoot. Thus we often misjudge the motives of men; we thought we had effected the Indians' liberty, when the Christians were but poising to pounce.

<p style="text-align:center">✳ ✳ ✳</p>

c. 1536–40 1542

1. I.e., they were, in effect, under arrest.

First Encounters: Early European Accounts of Native America

C hristopher Columbus's voyage of 1492 unleashed a torrent of words from innumerable mouths and pens, words designed to describe, promote, dispute, or defend accounts of events that took place in the contact zone between Europeans and Native Americans. "First encounter" is how the Pilgrim leaders William Bradford and Edward Winslow, among others, labeled such an initial contact. The phrase suggests the drama of what was, in reality, a series of moments that unfolded over many decades. Often, what seemed to be a "first" encounter turned out to involve Natives who had previously interacted with Europeans or had even been to Europe. Before he rescued the settlers at Plymouth, for example, the Pawtuxet man Tisquantum, or Squanto as he is more familiarly known, had been taken captive to Europe, where he remained for over a decade before returning to find his native village decimated by European-borne illnesses.

Though there was travel in both directions, most of the written and printed accounts that survive offer a European perspective on these encounters. In describing the greatly varied inhabitants of the Western Hemisphere for European eyes and minds, these writers crafted something like a notion of culture. Although from a certain perspective Europeans, with their primitive firearms and disease-wracked bodies, were not all that different from the inhabitants of the Western Hemisphere, the contrasts were evident to both sides from the beginning, and the sense of difference often deepened over time. European descriptions of the habits and attitudes of Native Americans caused widespread reflection on the question of what key traits defined human nature globally.

Along with providing such descriptive passages, many of them richly informative about Native customs and practices, the literature of the contact zone pulses with incident, sensation, and turmoil. Tragedy is often near the surface. Many narratives subtly indicate an expanding European footprint that is visible in accounts of Natives killed by infectious diseases that were new to the Western Hemisphere. One such disease, smallpox, could wipe out an entire village and spread rapidly throughout a region. "Virgin soil" epidemics were the largest single cause of Native deaths, and mortality rates were often made worse by European actions.

Consider the catastrophic eruption of smallpox in Tenochtitlán (located where Mexico City is today). This plague occurred in 1520, the year after the arrival of the Spanish conquistador Hernán Cortés and his army. Thirty years later, survivors of the plague described its effects to Bernardino de Sahagún, a Franciscan friar, who then produced a chilling account in his *General History of Things of New Spain*, also known as *The Florentine Codex*:

> There was indeed perishing; many indeed died of it. No longer could they walk; they only lay in their abodes, in their beds. No longer could they move, no longer could they bestir themselves, no longer could they raise themselves, no longer could they stretch themselves out face down, no longer could they stretch themselves out on their backs. And when they bestirred themselves, much did they cry out. There was much perishing. . . . Indeed many people died of them [i.e., smallpox pustules], and many just died of hunger. There was death from hunger; there was no one to take care of another; there was no one to attend to another.

This painfully vivid description captures the essence of innumerable similar scenes that unfolded in indigenous communities across two continents over some four hundred years, until inoculation against smallpox became widely available in the twentieth century.

For Cortés, the epidemic mainly made it possible to seize the city. In 1519, Tenochtitlán had been the thriving center of the Aztec Empire at the height of its power. In his correspondence with King Charles V of Spain, Cortés portrayed the Aztecs as a serious challenge to Spanish domination of the region. His lavishly beautiful account of the Aztec capital—with its amply stocked markets, large temples, and expansive public squares—presents a major civilization previously unknown to Europeans. In describing an urban center the equal of most European cities, Cortés was tempting the king to support the colonization effort. Otherwise, Charles might have focused on opportunities closer to home, particularly since he had recently been elected to the office of Holy Roman Emperor.

In *A Brief and True Report of the New Found Land of Virginia* (1588), the first printed English-language account of America, Thomas Harriot highlights the possibilities for trade and settlement, as well as providing a richly detailed ethnographic description of the Indians in the Outer Banks area of present-day North Carolina and the Chesapeake Bay region. Harriot's admiration for the abundance there is closely linked to his sense that the opportunities for profit are rich, at least in part because of the relatively unthreatening presence of the native Algonquians. Harriot also offers a poignant and troubling account of how the Natives in the region suffered from the "invisible bullets" of disease brought by the English—and how Native leaders aspired to enlist the English in their cause and to use these "bullets" against their enemies.

Other features of the literature of encounter dominate the selection from *The Voyages of the Sieur de Champlain* (1613). Samuel de Champlain's description of the battle that he and his Algonquin allies fought against their Iroquois opponents highlights the complex rivalries between indigenous groups that Europeans often exploited. Champlain shows himself drawing on his allies' wartime practices, such as dream interpretation, and he provides an action-filled description of the fight. The gruesome torture scene is an early written representation of Iroquois war customs. Champlain's self-righteous condemnation of Iroquois practices should be read with the knowledge that similar forms of torture and execution (such as drawing and quartering or burning at the stake) were then widely used in Europe.

In *History, Manners, and Customs of the Indian Nations* (1818), John Heckewelder renders a Delaware Indian version of a 1609 encounter with Henry Hudson's expedition, giving the tale a mythic frame signaled by the opening phrase, "A great many years ago." Probably derived from an oral narrative that had been passed down over generations, Heckewelder's rendition offers a striking counterpoint to Robert Juet's contemporary journal-style account of these events, which was published in his *Third Voyage of Master Henry Hudson* (1625). Both versions describe the ritual elements of the encounter and highlight Native experience with what was to them a novel intoxicant, alcohol. While Heckewelder's version of this "first encounter" is not an "authentic" rendition of Delaware experience, it tells the story from the distinctive perspective of the local people. But whereas Heckewelder's narrative is both portentous and vaguely droll, Juet's account of the same events emphasizes the mutual fearfulness, distrust, and brutality that undermined Europeans' early attempts to establish trade at "Manna-hata" (Manhattan).

A different kind of counterpoint emerges between the description of the landing of the Pilgrims at Plymouth Rock in *Mourt's Relation* (1622), by Bradford and Winslow, excerpted here, and the grand narrative of the legendary landing that Bradford presented in *Of Plymouth Plantation*, which appears later in this anthology. The contemporary account that Bradford coauthored with his good friend Winslow portrays the days and weeks after the landing as a narrative of confused

movements and puzzling discoveries: a "black thing" seen on the beach along with buried caches of corn, large burying grounds, and deserted clusters of Indian wigwams, probably emptied by a smallpox epidemic such as the one that Bradford describes in *Of Plymouth Plantation*. Bradford and Winslow emphasize the confusion between wolves and men, an episode that conveys the larger ambiguity of the colonizing efforts in which all these writers took part. Bradford's later version of these events reveals how colonial actors subsequently sought to dispel at least some of the fuzziness of earlier reports, sometimes imbuing them with clearer moral lessons.

Representing the colonial projects of Spain, France, Holland, and England, the following selections describe a range of locales spanning the first century and a half of the European presence in the Americas. They illuminate various elements that shaped the "first encounters"—from fear, disease, and violence to wonder, curiosity, ambition, and even, at times, respect.

HERNÁN CORTÉS

Typical in some ways of the class of colonial agents that quickly developed in Spain and its American possessions after 1492, Hernán Cortés (1485–1543) was from a noble family in Extremadura, Spain. He spent two years at the great university at Salamanca, in the Spanish region of Castile, where he studied law and later worked as a notary. He also acquired familiarity with the histories, chronicles, and romances of chivalry that formed the literary culture of the Castilian nobility. Cortés already had much experience as a magistrate and military leader in Hispaniola and Cuba when in 1519 the governor of Cuba, Diego Velázquez, gave him command of an expedition to round up stranded Spaniards on the mainland of Yucatán. Ambitious to make a name for himself, Cortés took advantage of an ambiguity in his orders and pursued a bold course of exploration. Once on the Mexican coast, he destroyed his ships so his men could not back out. He then plunged inland, gathering Native allies for what proved a remarkable and remarkably bloody conquest of the Aztec Empire. The five letters that Cortés wrote to Charles V were intended to create a rationale for his technically illegal actions. The following selection derives from the second letter, written after the Spaniards had arrived in Tenochtitlán (here called Temixtitan) but before they began their fight against the Aztec forces, which were led by the emperor Moctezuma II (here, Mutezuma).

From Second Letter to the Spanish Crown[1]

[Description of Tenochtitlán]

This great city of Temixtitan * * * is as big as Seville or Córdoba.[2] The main streets are very wide and very straight; some of these are on the land, but the rest and all the smaller ones are half on land, half canals where they paddle their canoes. All the streets have openings in places so that the water

1. The text is from *Hernán Cortés: Letters from Mexico* (1971), edited and translated by A. R. Pagden.
2. Prominent cities in Spain.

Tenochtitlán, or Mexico City, from *Praeclara Ferdinandi Cortesii de Nova maris Oceani Hyspania Narratio,* 1524. This German map of the Aztec capital, based on a sketch reportedly made for Cortés, accompanied a translation of his second and third letters to Charles V. It displays the material complexity documented in his prose.

may pass from one canal to another. Over all these openings, and some of them are very wide, there are bridges made of long and wide beams joined together very firmly and so well made that on some of them ten horsemen may ride abreast.

Seeing that if the inhabitants of this city wished to betray us they were very well equipped for it by the design of the city, for once the bridges had been removed they could starve us to death without our being able to reach the mainland, as soon as I entered the city I made great haste to build four brigantines, and completed them in a very short time. They were such as could carry three hundred men to the land and transport the horses whenever we might need them.

This city has many squares where trading is done and markets are held continuously. There is also one square twice as big as that of Salamanca, with arcades all around, where more than sixty thousand people come each day to buy and sell, and where every kind of merchandise produced in these

lands is found; provisions as well as ornaments of gold and silver, lead, brass, copper, tin, stones, shells, bones, and feathers. They also sell lime, hewn and unhewn stone, adobe bricks, tiles, and cut and uncut woods of various kinds. There is a street where they sell game and birds of every species found in this land: chickens, partridges and quails, wild ducks, flycatchers, widgeons, turtledoves, pigeons, cane birds, parrots, eagles and eagle owls, falcons, sparrow hawks and kestrels, and they sell the skins of some of these birds of prey with their feathers, heads and claws. They sell rabbits and hares, and stags and small gelded dogs which they breed for eating.

There are streets of herbalists where all the medicinal herbs and roots found in the land are sold. There are shops like apothecaries', where they sell ready-made medicines as well as liquid ointments and plasters. There are shops like barbers' where they have their hair washed and shaved, and shops where they sell food and drink. There are also men like porters to carry loads. There is much firewood and charcoal, earthenware braziers and mats of various kinds like mattresses for beds, and other, finer ones, for seats and for covering rooms and hallways. There is every sort of vegetable, especially onions, leeks, garlic, common cress and watercress, borage, sorrel, teasels and artichokes; and there are many sorts of fruit, among which are cherries and plums like those in Spain.

They sell honey, wax, and a syrup made from maize canes, which is as sweet and syrupy as that made from the sugar cane. They also make syrup from a plant which in the islands is called maguey,[3] which is much better than most syrups, and from this plant they also make sugar and wine, which they likewise sell. There are many sorts of spun cotton, in hanks of every color, and it seems like the silk market at Granada,[4] except here there is a much greater quantity. They sell as many colors for painters as may be found in Spain and all of excellent hues. They sell deerskins, with and without the hair, and some are dyed white or in various colors. They sell much earthenware, which for the most part is very good; there are both large and small pitchers, jugs, pots, tiles, and many other sorts of vessel, all of good clay and most of them glazed and painted. They sell maize both as grain and as bread and it is better both in appearance and in taste than any found in the islands or on the mainland. They sell chicken and fish pies, and much fresh and salted fish, as well as raw and cooked fish. They sell hen and goose eggs, and eggs of all the other birds I have mentioned, in great number, and they sell tortillas made from eggs.

Finally, besides those things which I have already mentioned, they sell in the market everything else to be found in this land, but they are so many and so varied that because of their great number and because I cannot remember many of them nor do I know what they are called I shall not mention them. Each kind of merchandise is sold in its own street without any mixture whatever; they are very particular in this. Everything is sold by number and size, and until now I have seen nothing sold by weight. There is in this great square a very large building like a courthouse, where ten or twelve persons sit as judges. They preside over all that happens in the markets, and sentence criminals. There are in this square other persons who walk among

3. A large, spiked plant (also called aloe) from which both a sweet syrup and a strong liquor (pulque) are still produced today.
4. Another prominent Spanish city.

the people to see what they are selling and the measures they are using; and they have been seen to break some that were false.

There are, in all districts of this great city, many temples or houses for their idols. They are all very beautiful buildings, and in the important ones there are priests of their sect who live there permanently; and, in addition to the houses for the idols, they also have very good lodgings. All these priests dress in black and never comb their hair from the time they enter the priesthood until they leave; and all the sons of the persons of high rank, both the lords and honored citizens also, enter the priesthood and wear the habit from the age of seven or eight years until they are taken away to be married; this occurs more among the first-born sons, who are to inherit, than among the others. They abstain from eating things, and more at some times of the year than at others; and no woman is granted entry nor permitted inside these places of worship.

Amongst these temples there is one, the principal one, whose great size and magnificence no human tongue could describe, for it is so large that within the precincts, which are surrounded by a very high wall, a town of some five hundred inhabitants could easily be built. All round inside this wall there are very elegant quarters with very large rooms and corridors where their priests live. There are as many as forty towers, all of which are so high that in the case of the largest there are fifty steps leading up to the main part of it; and the most important of these towers is higher than that of the cathedral of Seville. They are so well constructed in both their stone and woodwork that there can be none better in any place, for all the stonework inside the chapels where they keep their idols is in high relief, with figures and little houses, and the woodwork is likewise of relief and painted with monsters and other figures and designs. All these towers are burial places of chiefs, and the chapels therein are each dedicated to the idol which he venerated.

There are three rooms within this great temple for the principal idols, which are of remarkable size and stature and decorated with many designs and sculptures, both in stone and in wood. Within these rooms are other chapels, and the doors to them are very small. Inside there is no light whatsoever; there only some of the priests may enter, for inside are the sculptured figures of the idols, although, as I have said, there are also many outside.

The most important of these idols, and the ones in whom they have most faith, I had taken from their places and thrown down the steps; and I had those chapels where they were cleaned, for they were full of the blood of sacrifices; and I had images of Our Lady and of other saints put there, which caused Mutezuma and the other natives some sorrow. First they asked me not to do it, for when the communities learnt of it they would rise against me, for they believed that those idols gave them all their worldly goods, and that if they were allowed to be ill treated, they would become angry and give them nothing and take the fruit from the earth leaving the people to die of hunger. I made them understand through the interpreters how deceived they were in placing their trust in those idols which they had made with their hands from unclean things. They must know that there was only one God, Lord of all things, who had created heaven and earth and all else and who made all of us; and He was without beginning or end, and they must adore

and worship only Him, not any other creature or thing. And I told them all I knew about this to dissuade them from their idolatry and bring them to the knowledge of God our Saviour. All of them, especially Mutezuma, replied that they had already told me how they were not natives of this land, and that as it was many years since their forefathers had come here, they well knew that they might have erred somewhat in what they believed, for they had left their native land so long ago; and as I had only recently arrived from there, I would better know the things they should believe, and should explain to them and make them understand, for they would do as I said was best. Mutezuma and many of the chieftains of the city were with me until the idols were removed, the chapel cleaned and the images set up, and I urged them not to sacrifice living creatures to the idols, as they were accustomed, for, as well as being most abhorrent to God, Your Sacred Majesty's laws forbade it and ordered that he who kills shall be killed. And from then on they ceased to do it, and in all the time I stayed in that city I did not see a living creature killed or sacrificed.

The figures of the idols in which these people believe are very much larger than the body of a big man. They are made of dough from all the seeds and vegetables which they eat, ground and mixed together, and bound with the blood of human hearts which those priests tear out while still beating. And also after they are made they offer them more hearts and anoint their faces with the blood. Everything has an idol dedicated to it, in the same manner as the pagans who in antiquity honored their gods. So they have an idol whose favor they ask in war and another for agriculture; and likewise for each thing they wish to be done well they have an idol which they honor and serve.

There are in the city many large and beautiful houses, and the reason for this is that all the chiefs of the land, who are Mutezuma's vassals, have houses in the city and live there for part of the year; and in addition there are many rich citizens who likewise have very good houses. All these houses have very large and very good rooms and also very pleasant gardens of various sorts of flowers both on the upper and lower floors.

Along one of the causeways to this great city run two aqueducts made of mortar. Each one is two paces wide and some six feet deep, and along one of them a stream of very good fresh water, as wide as a man's body, flows into the heart of the city and from this they all drink. The other, which is empty, is used when they wish to clean the first channel. Where the aqueducts cross the bridges, the water passes along some channels which are as wide as an ox; and so they serve the whole city.

Canoes paddle through all the streets selling the water; they take it from the aqueduct by placing the canoes beneath the bridges where those channels are, and on top there are men who fill the canoes and are paid for their work. At all the gateways to the city and at the places where these canoes are unloaded, which is where the greater part of the provisions enter the city, there are guards in huts who receive a *certum quid*[5] of all that enters. I have not yet discovered whether this goes to the chief or to the city, but I think to the chief, because in other markets in other parts I have seen this tax paid to the ruler of the place. Every day, in all the markets and public

5. A certain part (Latin).

places there are many workmen and craftsmen of every sort, waiting to be employed by the day. The people of this city are dressed with more elegance and are more courtly in their bearing than those of the other cities and provinces, and because Mutezuma and all those chieftains, his vassals, are always coming to the city, the people have more manners and politeness in all matters. Yet so as not to tire Your Highness with the description of the things of this city (although I would not complete it so briefly), I will say only that these people live almost like those in Spain, and in as much harmony and order as there, and considering that they are barbarous and so far from the knowledge of God and cut off from all civilized nations, it is truly remarkable to see what they have achieved in all things.

* * *

1522

THOMAS HARRIOT

T homas Harriot (1560–1621) was an important English scientist and mathematician, but he remained for many years an obscure figure, and little is known about his early life. Born in Oxfordshire, he enrolled at the University at Oxford seventeen years later, earning a reputation for brilliance and befriending the geographer Richard Hakluyt. Soon after graduating, he went to work for Sir Walter Raleigh, who became his patron. A year after Raleigh's first voyage to the Americas in 1584, Harriot sailed with Sir Richard Grenville, making astronomical observations along the way. Anchored at Roanoke Island, off the Outer Banks of what is now North Carolina, Grenville's expedition explored the mainland. In his capacity as a kind of staff scientist, Harriot observed the topography and the flora and fauna, as well as taking note of the customs and language of the local people. He made drawings and maps and developed a phonetic system for recording and learning the native Algonquian language. When Sir Francis Drake (see p. 47) arrived, warning of an imminent Spanish attack on the settlement at Roanoke, Harriot and his party sailed with Drake for England. *A Brief and True Report of the New Found Land of Virginia* (1588) became Harriot's only work to appear in print during his lifetime, and it was reprinted twice by Richard Hakluyt. This abstract of a lost longer work offered a compendium of useful information for prospective planters and colonists. In 1590, Theodor de Bry produced a Latin edition that had engravings based on the watercolors made by John White, a member of Harriot's party. De Bry's volume was enormously popular, going through seventeen editions between 1590 and 1620. In later years, Harriot achieved considerable fame as a religious freethinker as well as a scholar and explorer.

From A Brief and True Report of the New Found Land of Virginia[1]

Of the Nature and Manners of the People

It resteth[2] I speak a word or two of the natural inhabitants, their natures and manners, leaving large discourse thereof until time more convenient hereafter: now only so far forth, as that you may know, how that they in respect of troubling our inhabiting and planting, are not to be feared; but that they shall have cause both to fear and love us, that shall inhabit with them.

They are a people clothed with loose mantles made of deer skins, & aprons of the same round about their middles; all else naked; of such a difference of statures only as we in England;[3] having no edge tools or weapons of iron or steel to offend us withal, neither know they how to make any: those weapons they have, are only bows made of witch hazel, & arrows of reeds; flat edged truncheons also of wood about a yard long, neither have they any thing to defend themselves but targets made of barks; and some armours made of sticks wickered together with thread.

Their towns are but small, & near the sea coast but few, some containing but 10 or 12 houses: some 20: the greatest that we have seen have been but of 30 houses: if they be walled it is only done with barks of trees made fast to stakes, or else with poles only fixed upright and close one by another.

Their houses are made of small poles made fast at the tops in round form after the manner as is used in many arbories[4] in our gardens of England, in most towns covered with barks, and in some with artificial mats made of long rushes; from the tops of the houses down to the ground. The length of them is commonly double to the breadth, in some places they are but 12 and 16 yards long, and in other some we have seen of four and twenty.

In some places of the country one only town belongeth to the government of a _wiróans_ or chief lord; in other some two or three, in some six, eight, & more; the greatest _wiróans_ that yet we had dealing with had but eighteen towns in his government, and able to make not above seven or eight hundred fighting men at the most: The language of every government is different from any other, and the farther they are distant the greater is the difference.

Their manner of wars amongst themselves is either by sudden surprising one another most commonly about the dawning of the day, or moon light; or else by ambushes, or some subtle devices: Set battles are very rare, except it fall out where there are many trees, where either part may have some hope of defence, after the delivery of every arrow, in leaping behind some or other.

If there fall out any wars between us & them, what their fight is likely to be, we having advantages against them so many manner of ways, as by our discipline, our strange weapons and devices else; especially by ordnance[5] great and small, it may be easily imagined; by the experience we have had in some places, the turning up of their heels against us in running away was their best defence.

In respect of us they are a people poor, and for want[6] of skill and judgement in the knowledge and use of our things, do esteem our trifles before

1. The text is from A Briefe and True Report of the New Found Land of Virginia (1588; rpt. 1903).
2. I.e., it seems appropriate that.
3. Ranging in size as English people do.

4. Archaism for "places where trees are grown."
5. Mounted guns; artillery.
6. Lack.

things of greater value: Notwithstanding in their proper manner considering the want of such means as we have, they seem very ingenious; for although they have no such tools, nor any such crafts, sciences and arts as we; yet in those things they do, they show excellence of wit. And by how much they upon due consideration shall find our manner of knowledges and crafts to exceed theirs in perfection, and speed for doing or execution, by so much the more is it probable that they should desire our friendships & love, and have the greater respect for pleasing and obeying us. Whereby may be hoped if means of good government be used, that they may in short time be brought to civility, and the embracing of true religion.

Some religion they have already, which although it be far from the truth, yet being as it is, there is hope it may be the easier and sooner reformed.

They believe that there are many gods which they call *montóac*, but of different sorts and degrees; one only chiefe and great God, which hath been from all eternity. Who as they affirm when he purposed to make the world, made first other gods of a principal order to be as means and instruments to be used in the creation and government to follow; and after the sun, moon, and stars, as petty gods and the instruments of the other order more principal. First they say were made waters, out of which by the gods was made all diversity of creatures that are visible or invisible.

For mankind they say a woman was made first, which by the working of one of the gods, concieved and brought forth children: And in such sort they say they had their beginning.

But how many years or ages have passed since, they say they can make no relation having no letters nor other such means as we to keep records of the particularities of times past, but only tradition from father to son.

They think that all the gods are of human shape, & therfore they represent them by images in the forms of men, which they call *kewasówok*; one alone is called *kewás*; them they place in houses appropriate or temples which they call *machicómuck*; where they worship, praise, sing, and make many times offerings unto them. In some *machicómuck* we have seen but one *kewás*, in some two, and in other some three; the common sort think them to be also gods.

They believe also the immortality of the soul, that after this life as soon as the soul is departed from the body according to the works it hath done, it is either carried to heaven the habitacle[7] of gods, there to enjoy perpetual bliss and happiness, or else to a great pit or hole, which they think to be in the furthest parts of their part of the world toward the sun set, there to burn continually: the place they call *popogusso*.

For the confirmation of this opinion, they told me two stories of two men that had been lately dead and revived again; the one happened but few years before our coming into the country, of a wicked man which having been dead and buried, the next day the earth of the grave being seen to move, was taken up again; who made declaration where his soul had been, that is to say very near entering into *popogusso*, had not one of the gods saved him & gave him leave to return again, and teach his friends what they should do to avoid that terrible place of torment.

7. Dwelling place.

The other happened in the same year we were there, but in a town that was threescore miles from us, and it was told me for strange news that one being dead, buried and taken up again as the first, showed that although his body had lain dead in the grave, yet his soul was alive, and had traveled far in a long broad way, on both sides whereof grew most delicate and pleasant trees, bearing more rare and excellent fruits than ever he had seen before or was able to express, and at length came to most brave and fair houses, near which he met his father, that had been dead before, who gave him great charge to go back again and show his friends what good they were to do to enjoy the pleasures of that place, which when he had done he should after come again.

What subtlety soever be in the *wiroances* and priests, this opinion worketh so much in many of the common and simple sort of people that it maketh them have great respect to their governours, and also great care what they do, to avoid torment after death, and to enjoy bliss; although notwithstanding there is punishment ordained for malefactors, as stealers, whoremongers, and other sorts of wicked doers; some punished with death, some with forfeitures, some with beating, according to the greatness of the facts.

And this is the sum of their religion, which I learned by having special familiarity with some of their priests. Wherein they were not so sure grounded, nor gave such credit to their traditions and stories but through conversing with us they were brought into great doubts of their own, and no small admiration of ours, with earnest desire in many, to learn more than we had means for want of perfect utterance in their language to express.

Most things they saw with us, as mathematical instruments, sea compasses, the virtue of the loadstone in drawing iron, a perspective glass whereby was showed many strange sights, burning glasses, wildfire works,[8] guns, books, writing and reading, spring clocks that seem to go off themselves, and many other things that we had, were so strange unto them, and so far exceeded their capacities to comprehend the reason and means how they should be made and done, that they thought they were rather the works of gods than of men, or at the leastwise they had been given and taught us of the gods. Which made many of them to have such opinion of us, as that if they knew not the truth of God and religion already, it was rather to be had from us, whom God so specially loved, than from a people that were so simple, as they found themselves to be in comparison of us. Whereupon greater credit was given unto that we spoke of concerning such matters.

Many times and in every town where I came, according as I was able, I made declaration of the contents of the Bible; that therein was set forth the true and only God, and his mighty works, that therein was contained the true doctrine of salvation through Christ, with many particularities of miracles and chief points of religion, as I was able then to utter, and thought fit for the time. And although I told them the book materially & of it self was not of any such virtue, as I thought they did concieve, but only the doctrine therein contained; yet would many be glad to touch it, to embrace it, to kiss it, to hold it to their breasts and heads, and stroke over all their body with it to show their hungry desire of that knowledge which was spoken of.

8. An incendiary weapon, like Greek fire. "Burning glasses": large convex lenses used to concentrate the sun's rays, potentially causing ignition.

The *wiroans* with whom we dwelt, called Wingina, and many of his people would be glad many times to be with us at our prayers, and many times call upon us both in his own town, as also in others whither he sometimes accompanied us, to pray and sing psalms; hoping thereby to be partaker of the same effects which we by that meanes also expected.[9]

Twice this *wiroans* was so grievously sick that he was like to die, and as he lay languishing, doubting of any help by his owne priests, and thinking he was in such danger for offending us and thereby our God, sent for some of us to pray and be a means to our God that it would please him either that he might live or after death dwell with him in bliss; so likewise were the requests of many others in the like case.

On a time also when their corn began to wither by reason of a drought which happened extraordinarily, fearing that it had come to pass by reason that in some thing they had displeased us, many would come to us & desire us to pray to our God of England, that he would preserve their corn, promising that when it was ripe we also should be partakers of the fruit.

There could at no time happen any strange sickness, losses, hurts, or any other cross[1] unto them, but that they would impute to us the cause or means therof for offending or not pleasing us.

One other rare and strange accident, leaving others, will I mention before I end, which moved the whole country that either knew or heard of us, to have us in wonderful admiration.

There was no town where we had any subtle device practiced against us, we leaving it unpunished or not revenged (because we sought by all means possible to win them by gentleness) but that within a few days after our departure from every such town, the people began to die very fast, and many in short space; in some towns about twenty, in some fourty, in some sixty, & in one six score, which in truth was very many in respect of their numbers.[2] This happened in no place that we could learn but where we had been, where they used some practise against us, and after such time; The disease also so strange, that they neither knew what it was, nor how to cure it; the like by report of the oldest men in the country never happened before, time out of mind. A thing specially observed by us as also by the natural inhabitants themselves.

Insomuch that when some of the inhabitants which were our friends & especially the *wiroans* Wingina had observed such effects in four or five towns to follow their wicked practises, they were persuaded that it was the work of our God through our means, and that we by him might kill and slay whom we would without weapons and nor come near them.

And thereupon when it had happened that they had understanding that any of their enemies had abused us in our journeys, hearing that we had wrought no revenge with our weapons, & fearing upon some cause the matter should so rest: did come and entreat us that we would be a means to our God that they as others that had dealt ill with us might in like sort die; alleging

9. Many indigenous religions in the Americas readily incorporate new practices, an approach sometimes called syncretism.
1. Trouble, as in cross to bear.
2. Harriot and his contemporaries did not understand how disease was spread; germ theory was not developed until the nineteenth century. In this section, Harriot describes how Wingina and the colonists offered competing interpretations for the devastating illnesses that swept through the region after the arrival of the English.

how much it would be for our credit and profit, as also theirs; and hoping furthermore that we would do so much at their requests in respect of the friendship we professe them.

Whose entreaties although we showed that they were ungodlie, affirming that our God would not subject him selfe to any such prayers and requests of men: that indeed all thinges have been and were to be done according to his good pleasure as he had ordained: and that we to show our selves his true servants ought rather to make petition for the contrary, that they with them might live together with us, be made partakers of his truth & serve him in righteousness; but notwithstanding in such sort, that we refer that as all other things, to be done according to his divine will & pleasure, and as by his wisdom he had ordained to be best.

Yet because the effect fell out so suddenly and shortly after according to their desires, they thought neverthelesse it came to pass by our means, and that we in using such speeches unto them did but dissemble the matter, and therefore came unto us to give us thanks in their manner that although we satisfied them not in promise, yet in deeds and effect we had fulfilled their desires.

This marvelous accident in all the country wrought so strange opinions of us, that some people could not tell whether to think us gods or men, and the rather because that all the space of their sicknesse, there was no man of ours known to die, or that was specially sick: they noted also that we had no women amongst us, neither that we did care for any of theirs.

Some therefore were of opinion that we were not born of women, and therefore not mortal, but that we were men of an old generation many years past then risen again to immortality.

Some would likewise seem to prophesy that there were more of our generation yet to come, to kill theirs and take their places, as some thought the purpose was by that which was already done.

Those that were immediatly to come after us they imagined to be in the air, yet invisible & without bodies, & that they by our entreaty & for the love of us did make the people to die in that sort as they did by shooting invisible bullets into them.

To confirm this opinion their physicians to excuse their ignorance in curing the disease, would not be ashamed to say, but earnestly make the simple people believe, that the strings of blood that they sucked out of the sick bodies, were the strings wherewithal the invisible bullets were tied and cast.

Some also thought that we shot them ourselves out of our pieces from the place where we dwelt, and killed the people in any such town that had offended us as we listed,[3] how far distant from us soever it were.

And other some said that it was the special work of God for our sakes, as we our selves have cause in some sort to think no less, whatsoever some do or may imagine to the contrary, specially some astrologers knowing of the eclipse of the sun which we saw the same year before in our voyage thitherward, which unto them appeared very terrible. And also of a comet which began to appear but a few days before the beginning of the said sickness. But to conclude them from being the special causes of so special an accident, there are farther reasons than I think fit at this present to be alleged.

3. Archaism for "pleased" or "chose."

These their opinions I have set down the more at large that it may appear unto you that there is good hope they may be brought through discreet dealing and government to the embracing of the truth, and consequently to honour, obey, feare and love us.

And although some of our company towards the end of the year, showed themselves too fierce, in slaying some of the people, in some towns, upon causes that on our part, might easily enough have been borne withal: yet notwithstanding because it was on their part justly deserved, the alteration of their opinions generally & for the most part concerning us is the less to be doubted. And whatsoever else they may be, by carefulness of ourselves need nothing at all to be feared.

The best nevertheless in this as in all actions besides is to be endeavored and hoped, & of the worst that may happen notice to be taken with consideration, and as much as may be eschewed.

* * *

1588

SAMUEL DE CHAMPLAIN

B orn into a seafaring family near La Rochelle, a city on France's Atlantic coast, Samuel de Champlain (c. 1570–1635) did more than any other Frenchman of his time to deepen his country's interest in North America. He had already crossed the ocean six times by 1603, when (as royal geographer under the command of the explorer François Pont-Gravé) he sailed up the Saint Lawrence River as far as the future site of Montreal. The expedition traded with the Natives there for valuable furs before returning to France. Early in 1604, Champlain published his official report, *Des Sauvages*, or *Of the Indians*, illustrated with his own maps, and in April he returned to North America under the command of the Sieur de Monts, a Protestant merchant who was a native of Champlain's own region. (*Sieur*, meaning "Sir," was an honorific title in old French.) In 1608, Champlain made another voyage, during which he founded Quebec City. The next year he gathered Indian allies from several tribes in the Saint Lawrence valley and the mountains to the north, then journeyed up the Richelieu River into the long, narrow lake to the south that today bears his name. While on this trip, which he wrote about in his next book, *Les Voyages de Sieur de Champlain* (1613), he and his allies met and defeated a party of Mohawk Indians from what is now central New York. This violent encounter, related in the following selection, helped turn most Mohawk and their kin in the Iroquois Confederacy against the French for the next 150 years.

From The Voyages of the Sieur de Champlain[1]

[The Iroquois]

We departed on the following day, pursuing our way up the river[2] as far as the entrance to the lake. * * *

On the following day we entered the lake * * * in which I saw four beautiful islands[3] * * * which, like the Iroquois river, were formerly inhabited by Indians: but have been abandoned, since they have been at war with one another. There are also several rivers flowing into the lake, on whose banks are many fine trees of the same varieties we have in France, with many of the finest vines I had seen anywhere. * * *

Continuing our way along this lake in a westerly direction and viewing the country, I saw towards the east very high mountains on the tops of which there was snow. I enquired of the natives whether these parts were inhabited. They said they were, and by the Iroquois, and that in those parts there were beautiful valleys and fields rich in corn such as I have eaten in that country, along with other products in abundance. And they said that the lake went close to the mountains, which, as I judged, might be some twenty-five leagues[4] away from us. Towards the south I saw others which were not less lofty than the first-mentioned, but there was no snow on these. The Indians told me that it was there that we were to meet their enemies, that the mountains were thickly populated, and that we had to pass a rapid which I saw afterwards. Thence they said we had to enter another lake.[5] * * *

Now as we began to get within two or three days' journey of the home of their enemy, we proceeded only by night, and during the day we rested. Nevertheless, they kept up their usual superstitious ceremonies in order to know what was to happen to them in their undertakings, and often would come and ask me whether I had had dreams and had seen their enemies. I would tell them that I had not, but nevertheless continued to inspire them with courage and good hope. When night came on, we set off on our way until the next morning. Then we retired into the thick woods where we spent the rest of the day. Towards ten or eleven o'clock, after walking around our camp, I went to take a rest, and while asleep I dreamed that I saw in the lake near a mountain our enemies, the Iroquois, drowning before our eyes. I wanted to succour them, but our Indian allies said to me that we should let them all perish; for they were bad men. When I awoke they did not fail to ask me as usual whether I had dreamed anything. I told them what I had seen in my dream. This gave them such confidence that they no longer had any doubt as to the good fortune awaiting them.

Evening having come, we embarked in our canoes in order to proceed on our way, and as we were paddling along very quietly, and without making any noise, about ten o'clock at night on the twenty-ninth of [July], at the

1. The text is from *The Works of Samuel de Champlain in Six Volumes* (1925), vol. 2, edited by H. P. Biggar and translated by John Squair.
2. Now known as the Richelieu; called by Champlain "the Iroquois river" and "the river of the Iroquois."
3. Lake Champlain contains a number of large islands near where the Richelieu flows out of its north end.
4. This length could have been from fifty to seventy-five miles.
5. Now known as Lake George; connected to Lake Champlain through the short La Chute River, site of the rapids mentioned in the previous sentence.

extremity of a cape[6] which projects into the lake on the west side, we met the Iroquois on the war-path. Both they and we began to utter loud shouts and each got his arms ready. We drew out into the lake and the Iroquois landed and arranged all their canoes near one another. Then they began to fell trees with the poor axes which they sometimes win in war, or with stone axes; and they barricaded themselves well.

Our Indians all night long also kept their canoes close to one another and tied to poles in order not to get separated, but to fight all together in case of need. We were on the water within bowshot of their barricades. And when they were armed, and everything in order, they sent two canoes which they had separated from the rest, to learn from their enemies whether they wished to fight, and these replied that they had no other desire, but that for the moment nothing could be seen and that it was necessary to wait for daylight in order to distinguish one another. They said that as soon as the sun should rise, they would attack us, and to this our Indians agreed. Meanwhile the whole night was spent in dances and songs on both sides, with many insults and other remarks, such as the lack of courage of our side, how little we could resist or do against them, and that when daylight came our people would learn all this to their ruin. Our side too was not lacking in retort, telling the enemy that they would see such deeds of arms as they had never seen, and a great deal of other talk, such as is usual at the siege of a city. Having sung, danced, and flung words at one another for some time, when daylight came, my companions and I were still hidden, lest the enemy should see us, getting our fire-arms ready as best we could, being however still separated, each in a canoe of the Montagnais Indians.[7] After we were armed with light weapons, we took, each of us, an arquebus[8] and went ashore. I saw the enemy come out of their barricade to the number of two hundred, in appearance strong, robust men. They came slowly to meet us with a gravity and calm which I admired; and at their head were three chiefs. Our Indians likewise advanced in similar order, and told me that those who had the three big plumes were the chiefs, and that there were only these three, whom you could recognize by these plumes, which were larger than those of their companions; and I was to do what I could to kill them. I promised them to do all in my power, and told them that I was very sorry they could not understand me, so that I might direct their method of attacking the enemy, all of whom undoubtedly we should thus defeat; but that there was no help for it, and that I was very glad to show them, as soon as the engagement began, the courage and readiness which were in me.

As soon as we landed, our Indians began to run some two hundred yards towards their enemies, who stood firm and had not yet noticed my companions who went off into the woods with some Indians. Our Indians began to call to me with loud cries; and to make way for me they divided into two groups, and put me ahead some twenty yards, and I marched on until I was within some thirty yards of the enemy, who as soon as they caught sight of me halted and gazed at me and I at them. When I saw them make a move to

6. Now known as Crown Point; in the southern part of Lake Champlain.
7. Members of this group of peoples, from the mountainous region north of the Saint Law-

rence River, accompanied Champlain on his expedition into the territory of their ancient enemies, the Iroquois.
8. An early, relatively heavy kind of gun.

draw their bows upon us, I took aim with my arquebus and shot straight at one of the three chiefs, and with this shot two fell to the ground and one of their companions was wounded who died thereof a little later. I had put four bullets into my arquebus. As soon as our people saw this shot so favorable for them, they began to shout so loudly that one could not have heard it thunder, and meanwhile the arrows flew thick on both sides. The Iroquois were much astonished that two men should have been killed so quickly, although they were provided with shields made of cotton thread woven together and wood, which were proof against their arrows. This frightened them greatly. As I was reloading my arquebus, one of my companions fired a shot from within the woods, which astonished them again so much that, seeing their chiefs dead, they lost courage and took to flight, abandoning the field and their fort, and fleeing into the depth of the forest, whither I pursued them and laid low still more of them. Our Indians also killed several and took ten or twelve prisoners. The remainder fled with the wounded. Of our Indians fifteen or sixteen were wounded with arrows, but these were quickly healed.

After we had gained the victory, our Indians wasted time in taking a large quantity of Indian corn and meal belonging to the enemy, as well as their shields, which they had left behind, the better to run. Having feasted, danced, and sung, we three hours later set off for home with the prisoners. The place where this attack took place is in 43° and some minutes of latitude, and was named Lake Champlain.

<p style="text-align:center">* * *</p>

Having gone about eight leagues, the Indians, towards evening, took one of the prisoners to whom they made a harangue on the cruelties which he and his friends without any restraint had practiced upon them, and that similarly he should resign himself to receive as much, and they ordered him to sing, if he had the heart. He did so, but it was a very sad song to hear.

Meanwhile our Indians kindled a fire, and when it was well lighted, each took a brand and burned this poor wretch a little at a time in order to make him suffer the greater torment. Sometimes they would leave off, throwing water on his back. Then they tore out his nails and applied fire to the ends of his fingers and to his membrum virile.[9] Afterwards they scalped him and caused a certain kind of gum to drip very hot upon the crown of his head. Then they pierced his arms near the wrists and with sticks pulled and tore out his sinews by main force, and when they saw they could not get them out, they cut them off. This poor wretch uttered strange cries, and I felt pity at seeing him treated in this way. Still he bore it so firmly that sometimes one would have said he felt scarcely any pain. They begged me repeatedly to take fire and do like them. I pointed out to them that we did not commit such cruelties, but that we killed people outright, and that if they wished me to shoot him with the arquebus, I should be glad to do so. They said no; for he would not feel any pain. I went away from them as if angry at seeing them practice so much cruelty on his body. When they saw that I was not pleased, they called me back and told me to give him a shot with the arquebus. I did so, without his perceiving anything, and with one shot caused him to escape all the tortures he would have suffered rather than see him brutally

9. Virile member (Latin); i.e., penis.

Fort des Yroquois, from *Les Voyages du Sieur de Champlain* (1613). This woodcut depicts a French attack on an Iroquois fort during a second expedition undertaken in 1610. The fort (A) was a typical palisade constructed of horizontal and vertical logs but could not adequately protect the Iroquois, who (B) threw themselves into the river to escape the French (D, F) and what Champlain called "all our Indian allies" (E). The attackers also cut down high trees (H) "in order to demolish the Iroquois Fort."

treated. When he was dead, they were not satisfied; they opened his body and threw his bowels into the lake. Afterwards they cut off his head, arms and legs, which they scattered about; but they kept the scalp, which they had flayed, as they did with those of all the others whom they had killed in their attack. They did another awful thing, which was to cut his heart into several pieces and to give it to a brother of the dead man to eat and to others of his companions who were prisoners. These took it and put it into their mouths, but would not swallow it. Some of the Algonquin Indians who were guarding the prisoners made them spit it out and threw it into the water. That is how these people act with regard to those whom they capture in war. And it would be better for them to die fighting, and be killed at once, as many do, rather than to fall into the hands of their enemies. When this execution was over, we set out upon our return with the rest of the prisoners, who went along continually singing, without other expectation than to be tortured like him of whom we have spoken. When we arrived at the rapids of the river of the Iroquois, the Algonquins returned into their own country and the Ochategu's[1] also with some of the prisoners, all much pleased at what had taken place in the war, and because I had gone with them willingly. So we all separated with great protestations of mutual friendship, and they asked me if I would not go to their country, and aid them continually like a brother. I promised them I would.

<p style="text-align:center">✻ ✻ ✻</p>

<p style="text-align:right">1613</p>

1. Actually, the Yendots, a tribe allied with the Algonquins against the Iroquois. Champlain mistook their chief's name, Ochateguin, for the tribe's name.

ROBERT JUET

In 1609, the same year that Samuel de Champlain journeyed south into Iroquois territory, the English navigator Henry Hudson (c. 1570–1611) abandoned his orders from the powerful Dutch East Indies Company. Instead of seeking out a Northeast Passage leading around Russia to the Americas, Hudson sailed west toward the coast of what is now the northeastern United States. Upon arrival, he entered the large bay at the lower end of the river that later came to bear his name and set out to explore the bay's islands, including "Manna-hata" (Manhattan). Hudson then sailed up the river for 150 miles or so, to the vicinity of present-day Albany. During his exploration of this river, Hudson and his crew encountered Native peoples (such as the Lenni Lenape, or Delaware; and the Mahicanni, or River Indians), with whom they traded in an atmosphere fraught with suspicion and punctuated by acts of open hostility and violence. As recounted in the following selection, the explorers also entertained one Indian with brandy, a tragicomic episode that blends elements of the convivial and the brutal. Then, continuing to manifest the odd mixture of curiosity, mercantile savvy, and armed intransigence that had marked their travels upstream, they went back downriver. Robert Juet (d. 1611), who kept the best contemporary record of the

voyage but about whom little else is known, apparently was an English sailor with a penchant for violence. While traveling again with Hudson in June 1611, Juet helped foment a mutiny among his discontented fellow sailors. They overpowered Hudson and set him adrift, with his son and a handful of supporters, in a small boat and with few provisions. The abandoned group disappeared in what thereafter was known as Hudson's Bay. Juet, acting as navigator, died a few days before the starving mutineers reached the coast of Ireland that September.

Hudson set adrift. This painting, *The Last Voyage of Henry Hudson* (1881), is by the British artist John Collier (1850–1934). It shows Hudson with his son and a crew member after they were set adrift in June 1611 by a mutinous crew that included Robert Juet. Hudson was attempting to find the Northwest Passage. He and his companions were never seen again.

From The Third Voyage of Master Henry Hudson[1]

[September 4, 1609]

* * * At night the wind blew hard at the north-west, and our anchor came home and we drove on shore, but took no hurt, thanked be God, for the ground is soft sand and ooze. This day the people of the country came aboard of us, seeming very glad of our coming, and brought green tobacco, and gave us of it for knives and beads. They go in deer skins loose, well dressed. They have yellow copper. They desire clothes, and are very civil. They have great store of maize or Indian wheat, whereof they make good bread. The country is full of great and tall oaks.

The *fifth*, in the morning, as soon as the day was light, the wind ceased and the flood came. So we heaved off our ship again into five fathoms water, and sent our boat to sound the bay,[2] and we found that there was three fathoms hard by the southern shore. Our men went on land there, and saw great store of men, women, and children, who gave them tobacco at their coming on land. So they went up into the woods, and saw great store of very goodly oaks and some currants. For one of them came aboard and brought some dried, and gave me some, which were sweet and good. This day many of the people came aboard, some in mantles of feathers, and some in skins of divers[3] sorts of good furs. Some women also came to us with hemp. They had red copper tobacco pipes, and other things of copper they did wear about their necks. At night they went on land again, so we rode very quiet, but durst not trust them.

The *sixth*, in the morning, was fair weather, and our master sent John Colman, with four other men in our boat, over to the north-side to sound the other river, being four leagues[4] from us. They found by the way shoal water, two fathoms; but at the north of the river eighteen, and twenty fathoms, and very good riding for ships; and a narrow river to the westward, between two islands. The lands, they told us, were as pleasant with grass and flowers and goodly trees as ever they had seen, and very sweet smells came from them. So they went in two leagues and saw an open sea, and returned; and as they came back, they were set upon by two canoes, the one having twelve, the other fourteen men. The night came on, and it began to rain, so that their match[5] went out; and they had one man slain in the fight, which was an Englishman, named John Colman, with an arrow shot into his throat, and two more hurt. It grew so dark that they could not find the ship that night, but labored to and fro on their oars. They had so great a stream, that their grapnel[6] would not hold them.

The *seventh*, was fair, and by ten of the clock they returned aboard the ship, and brought our dead man with them, whom we carried on land and

1. The text is from *Henry Hudson the Navigator* (1860), edited and translated by G. M. Asher.
2. New York Bay.
3. Various.
4. This distance would have been about twelve miles.
5. A wax-coated fuse kept burning to ignite the

matchlock guns that soldiers carried before the invention of the flintlock mechanism. Whereas in the latter device gunpowder is lighted by sparks struck from a piece of flint stone, matchlock weapons had to be lighted by hand.
6. Small, claw-tipped anchor.

buried, and named the point after his name, Colmans Point. Then we hoisted in our boat, and raised her side with waist boards[7] for defence of our men. So we rode still all night, having good regard to our watch.

The *eighth*, was very fair weather, we rode still very quietly. The people came aboard us, and brought tobacco and Indian wheat to exchange for knives and beads, and offered us no violence. So we fitting up our boat did mark[8] them, to see if they would make any show of the death of our man; which they did not.

The *ninth*, fair weather. In the morning, two great canoes came aboard full of men; the one with their bows and arrows, and the other in show of buying of knives to betray us; but we perceived their intent. We took two of them to have kept them, and put red coats on them, and would not suffer the other to come near us. So they went on land, and two other came aboard in a canoe; we took the one and let the other go; but he which we had taken, got up and leapt over-board. Then we weighed and went off into the channel of the river, and anchored there all night.

* * *

The *fifteenth*, in the morning, was misty, until the sun arose: then it cleared. So we weighed with the wind at south, and ran up into the river twenty leagues, passing by high mountains. We had a very good depth, as six, seven, eight, nine, ten, twelve, and thirteen fathoms, and great store of salmons in the river. This morning our two savages got out of a port[9] and swam away. After we were under sail, they called to us in scorn. At night we came to other mountains, which lie from[1] the river's side. There we found very loving people, and very old men: where we were well used. Our boat went to fish, and caught great store of very good fish.

* * *

The *one and twentieth* was fair weather, and the wind all southerly: we determined yet once more to go farther up into the river. * * * Our master and his mate determined to try some of the chief men of the country, whether they had any treachery in them. So they took them down into the cabin, and gave them so much wine and *aqua vitae*[2] that they were all merry: and one of them had his wife with them, which sat so modestly, as any of our country women would do in a strange place. In the end one of them was drunk, which had been aboard of our ship all the time that we had been there: and that was strange to them; for they could not tell how to take it. The canoes and folk went all on shore: but some of them came again, and brought stropes of beads: some had six, seven, eight, nine, ten; and gave him.[3] So he slept all night quietly.

The *two and twentieth* was fair weather: in the morning our master's mate and four more of the company went up with our boat to sound the river higher up. The people of the country came not aboard till noon: but when they came, and saw the savages well, they were glad. So at three of the clock in the afternoon they came aboard, and brought tobacco, and more beads,

7. Boards inserted atop the low sides, or waist, of a ship.
8. Watch.
9. Hole for a gun.
1. I.e., away from.

2. Brandy.
3. I.e., gave him the "stropes of beads": belts of wampum, which was made from marine shells and used as a kind of money.

and gave them to our master, and made an oration, and showed him all the country round about. Then they sent one of their company on land, who presently returned, and brought a great platter full of venison dressed by themselves; and they caused him to eat with them: then they made him reverence[4] and departed, all save the old man that lay aboard.

<p style="text-align:center">* * *</p>

The *first of October*, fair weather, the wind variable between the west and the north. In the morning we weighed at seven of the clock with the ebb, and got down below the mountains, which was seven leagues. Then it fell calm and the flood was come, and we anchored at twelve of the clock. The people of the mountains came aboard us, wondering at our ship and weapons. We bought some small skins of them for trifles. This afternoon, one canoe kept hanging under our stern with one man in it, which we could not keep from thence, who got up by our rudder to the cabin window, and stole out my pillow, and two shirts, and two bandoliers.[5] Our master's mate shot at him, and struck him on the breast, and killed him. Whereupon all the rest fled away, some in their canoes, and so leapt out of them into the water. We manned our boat, and got our things again. Then one of them that swam got hold of our boat, thinking to overthrow it.[6] But our cook took a sword, and cut off one of his hands, and he was drowned. By this time the ebb was come, and we weighed and got down two leagues: by that time it was dark. So we anchored in four fathoms water, and rode well.

The *second*, fair weather. At break of day we weighed, the wind being at north-west, and got down seven leagues; then the flood was come strong, so we anchored. Then came one of the savages that swam away from us at our going up the river with many others, thinking to betray us. But we perceived their intent, and suffered none of them to enter our ship. Whereupon two canoes full of men, with their bows and arrows shot at us after our stern: in recompense whereof we discharged six muskets, and killed two or three of them. Then above an hundred of them came to a point of land to shoot at us. There I shot a falcon[7] at them, and killed two of them: whereupon the rest fled into the woods. Yet they manned off another canoe with nine or ten men, which came to meet us. So I shot at it also a falcon, and shot it through, and killed one of them. Then our men with their muskets killed three or four more of them. So they went their way; within a while after we got down two leagues beyond that place, and anchored in a bay, clear from all danger of them on the other side of the river, where we saw a very good piece of ground: and hard by it there was a cliff, that looked of the color of a white[8] green, as though it were either copper or silver mine: and I think it to be one of them, by the trees that grow upon it. For they be all burned, and the other places are green as grass; it is on that side of the river that is called Manna-hata. There we saw no people to trouble us: and rode quietly all night; but had much wind and rain.

<p style="text-align:center">* * *</p>

<p style="text-align:right">1625</p>

4. Paid him their respects.
5. Ammunition belts.
6. Tip it over.

7. Light cannon.
8. Whitish.

JOHN HECKEWELDER

A missionary to Native Americans and a member of the pietist Moravian Church in Pennsylvania, John Heckewelder (1743–1823) was born in England to German parents who were refugees from religious persecution in Germany. He emigrated with them to America in 1754 and first traveled to Native territory in 1762. For the rest of his long life, he was intimately associated with the Lenni Lenape, or Delaware, and their allies and neighbors in Ohio. Although Heckewelder cared deeply for the Natives, he sought to convert them to the faith of the European invaders, whose interests at various points he directly served—as an agent of the American rebels during the Revolution and as an agent of the U.S. government in the period when settlers began moving into Native lands. After retiring to Bethlehem, Pennsylvania, in 1810, Heckewelder spent his last years writing accounts of his travels as well as descriptions of the manners and customs of Native communities. James Fenimore Cooper drew on these ethnographic writings in his Leatherstocking Tales (1827–41). One of Heckewelder's best-known works, An Account of the History, Manners, and Customs of the Indian Nations Who Once Inhabited Pennsylvania and the Neighbouring States (1819), includes a brief Native story he had picked up years before. That story, the following selection, has both striking parallels to and suggestive differences from the previous selection, by Robert Juet. Heckewelder's version provides a fascinating glimpse of the Native side of the narrative divide in descriptions of "first encounters."

From History, Manners, and Customs of the Indian Nations[1]

[Delaware Legend of Hudson's Arrival]

The Lenni Lenape claim the honor of having received and welcomed the Europeans on their first arrival in the country, situated between New England and Virginia. It is probable, however, that the Mahicanni or Mohicans, who then inhabited the banks of the Hudson, concurred in the hospitable act. The relation I am going to make was taken down many years since from the mouth of an intelligent Delaware Indian, and may be considered as a correct account of the tradition existing among them of this momentous event. I give it as much as possible in their own language.

A great many years ago, when men with a white skin had never yet been seen in this land, some Indians who were out a fishing, at a place where the sea widens, espied at a great distance something remarkably large floating on the water, and such as they had never seen before. These Indians immediately returning to the shore, apprised their countrymen of what they had observed, and pressed them to go out with them and discover what it might be. They hurried out together, and saw with astonishment the phenomenon which now appeared to their sight, but could not agree upon what it was; some believed it to be an uncommonly large fish or animal, while others

1. The text is from John Heckewelder, History, Manners, and Customs of the Indian Nations Who Once Inhabited Pennsylvania and the Neighbouring States (1876), edited by William C. Reichel.

were of opinion it must be a very big house floating on the sea. At length the spectators concluded that this wonderful object was moving towards the land, and that it must be an animal or something else that had life in it; it would therefore be proper to inform all the Indians on the inhabited islands of what they had seen, and put them on their guard. Accordingly they sent off a number of runners and watermen to carry the news to their scattered chiefs, that they might send off in every direction for the warriors, with a message that they should come on immediately. These arriving in numbers, and having themselves viewed the strange appearance, and observing that it was actually moving towards the entrance of the river or bay; concluded it to be a remarkably large house in which the Mannitto (the Great or Supreme Being) himself was present, and that he probably was coming to visit them. By this time the chiefs were assembled at [New] York island, and deliberating in what manner * * * they should receive their Mannitto on his arrival. Every measure was taken to be well provided with plenty of meat for a sacrifice. The women were desired to prepare the best victuals. All the idols or images were examined and put in order, and a grand dance was supposed not only to be an agreeable entertainment for the Great Being, but it was believed that it might, with the addition of a sacrifice, contribute to appease him if he was angry with them. The conjurers were also set to work, to determine what this phenomenon portended, and what the possible result of it might be. To these and to the chiefs and wise men of the nations, men, women, and children were looking up for advice and protection. Distracted between hope and fear, they were at a loss what to do; a dance, however, commenced in great confusion. While in this situation, fresh runners arrive declaring it to be a large house of various colours, and crowded with living creatures. It appears now to be certain, that it is the great Mannitto, bringing them some kind of game, such as he had not given them before, but other runners soon after arriving declare that it is positively a house full of human beings, of quite a different colour from that of the Indians, and dressed differently from them; that in particular one of them was dressed entirely in red, who must be the Mannitto himself. They are hailed from the vessel in a language they do not understand, yet they shout or yell in return by way of answer, according to the custom of their country; many are for running off to the woods, but are pressed by others to stay, in order not to give offence to their visitor, who might find them out and destroy them. The house, some say, large canoe, at last stops, and a canoe of a smaller size comes on shore with the red man, and some others in it; some stay with his canoe to guard it. The chiefs and wise men, assembled in council, form themselves into a large circle, towards which the man in red clothes approaches with two others. He salutes them with a friendly countenance, and they return the salute after their manner. They are lost in admiration; the dress, the manners, the whole appearance of the unknown strangers is to them a subject of wonder; but they are particularly struck with him who wore the red coat all glittering with gold lace, which they could in no manner account for. He, surely, must be the great Mannitto, but why should he have a white skin? Meanwhile, a large *Hackhack*[2]

2. Drinking vessel.

is brought by one of his servants, from which an unknown substance is poured out into a small cup or glass, and handed to the supposed Mannitto. He drinks—has the glass filled again, and hands it to the chief standing next to him. The chief receives it, but only smells the contents and passes it on to the next chief, who does the same. The glass or cup thus passes through the circle, without the liquor being tasted by any one, and is upon the point of being returned to the red clothed Mannitto, when one of the Indians, a brave man and a great warrior, suddenly jumps up and harangues the assembly on the impropriety of returning the cup with its contents. It was handed to them, says he, by the Mannitto, that they should drink out of it, as he himself had done. To follow his example would be pleasing to him; but to return what he had given them might provoke his wrath, and bring destruction on them. And since the orator believed it for the good of the nation that the contents offered them should be drunk, and as no one else would do it, he would drink it himself, let the consequence be what it might; it was better for one man to die, than that a whole nation should be destroyed. He then took the glass, and bidding the assembly a solemn fare-well, at once drank up its whole contents. Every eye was fixed on the reso-lute chief, to see what effect the unknown liquor would produce. He soon began to stagger, and at last fell prostrate on the ground. His companions now bemoan his fate, he falls into a sound sleep, and they think he has expired. He wakes again, jumps up and declares, that he has enjoyed the most delicious sensations, and that he never before felt himself so happy as after he had drunk the cup. He asks for more, his wish is granted; the whole assembly then imitate him, and all become intoxicated.

After this general intoxication had ceased, for they say that while it lasted the whites had confined themselves to their vessel, the man with the red clothes returned again, and distributed presents among them, consisting of beads, axes, hoes, and stockings such as the white people wear. They soon became familiar with each other, and began to converse by signs. The Dutch made them understand that they would not stay here, that they would return home again, but would pay them another visit the next year, when they would bring them more presents, and stay with them awhile; but as they could not live without eating, they should want a little land of them to sow seeds, in order to raise herbs and vegetables to put into their broth. They went away as they had said, and returned in the following season, when both parties were much rejoiced to see each other; but the whites laughed at the Indians, seeing that they knew not the use of the axes and hoes they had given them the year before; for they had these hanging to their breasts as ornaments, and the stockings were made use of as tobacco pouches. The whites now put handles to the former for them, and cut trees down before their eyes, hoed up the ground, and put the stockings on their legs. Here, they say, a general laughter ensued among the Indians, that they had remained ignorant of the use of such valuable implements, and had borne the weight of such heavy metal hanging to their necks, for such a length of time. They took every white man they saw for an inferior Man-nitto attendant upon the supreme Deity who shone superior in the red and laced clothes. As the whites became daily more familiar with the Indians, they at last proposed to stay with them, and asked only for so much ground for a garden spot as, they said, the hide of a bullock would

cover or encompass, which hide was spread before them. The Indians readily granted this apparently reasonable request; but the whites then took a knife, and beginning at one end of the hide, cut it up to a long rope, not thicker than a child's finger, so that by the time the whole was cut up, it made a great heap; they then took the rope at one end, and drew it gently along, carefully avoiding its breaking. It was drawn out into a circular form, and being closed at its ends, encompassed a large piece of ground. The Indians were surprised at the superior wit[3] of the whites, but did not wish to contend with them about a little land, as they had still enough themselves. The white and red men lived contentedly together for a long time, though the former from time to time asked for more land, which was readily obtained, and thus they gradually proceeded higher up the Mahicannittuck,[4] until the Indians began to believe that they would soon want all their country, which in the end proved true.

1819

3. In the sense of canniness. The trick probably was modeled on the one employed in the ancient world by Dido, queen of Carthage, when she struck a bargain for the site where that city was founded on the north African coast.
4. Now the Hudson River.

WILLIAM BRADFORD EDWARD WINSLOW

Growing up among radical nonconforming Protestants in rural northern England, William Bradford (1590–1657) embraced their cause at a young age. Early in the seventeenth century, he accompanied them on their exile in the Netherlands, where they settled in Leiden (or Leyden). Edward Winslow (1595–1655) was brought up in relative ease in Worcestershire, closer to London, largely untouched by spiritual concerns. He encountered Bradford and the other exiles while traveling in Leiden and, embracing the new sense of purpose that he found in their spiritual life, in 1620 he joined them on their voyage to America. Once the colonists had established themselves at Plymouth, Massachusetts, Bradford and Winslow became important public figures: each, for instance, served several terms as governor. The book they wrote together during their first months in New England, *Mourt's Relation* (1622), suggests their common objectives and shared viewpoint. In later decades, the two went their separate ways. After returning to England on public business in 1646, Winslow became involved in Oliver Cromwell's Puritan government. He died of yellow fever in the West Indies after jointly commanding an unsuccessful military campaign against the Spanish colony of Santo Domingo. Bradford remained at Plymouth, serving as its governor for more than three decades, and writing the main account of its history, *Of Plymouth Plantation*. Bradford retells the Cape Cod story included here in the tenth chapter of the first book of *Of Plymouth Plantation*, which appears later in this volume.

From Mourt's Relation[1]

[Cape Cod Forays]

Wednesday the sixth of December [1620] we set out, being very cold and hard weather, we were a long while after we launched from the ship, before we could get clear of a sandy point, which lay within less than a furlong of the same. In which time, two were very sick, and Edward Tilley had like to have sounded with cold; the gunner was also sick unto death, (but hope of trucking[2] made him to go) and so remained all that day, and the next night; at length we got clear of the sandy point, and got up our sails, and within an hour or two we got under the weather shore,[3] and then had smoother water and better sailing, but it was very cold, for the water froze on our clothes, and made them many times like coats of iron: we sailed six or seven leagues[4] by the shore, but saw neither river nor creek, at length we met with a tongue of land, being flat off from the shore, with a sandy point, we bore up to gain the point, and found there a fair income or road,[5] of a bay, being a league over at the narrowest, and some two or three in length, but we made right over to the land before us, and left the discovery of this income till the next day: as we drew near to the shore, we espied some ten or twelve Indians, very busy about a black thing, what it was we could not tell, til afterwards they saw us, and ran to and fro, as if they had been carrying some thing away, we landed a league or two from them, and had much ado to put ashore anywhere, it lay so full of flat sands, when we came to shore, we made us a baricado,[6] and got firewood, and set out our sentinels, and betook us to our lodging, such as it was; we saw the smoke of the fire which the savages made that night, about four or five miles from us, in the morning we divided our company, some eight in the shallop,[7] and the rest on the shore went to discover this place, but we found it only to be a bay, without either river or creek coming into it, yet we deemed it to be as good an harbor as Cape Cod, for they that sounded it, found a ship might ride in five fathom water, we on the land found it to be a level soil, but none of the fruitfulest; we saw two becks[8] of fresh water, which were the first running streams that we saw in the country, but one might stride over them: we found also a great fish, called a *grampus* dead on the sands, they in the shallop found two of them also in the bottom of the bay, dead in like sort, they were cast up at high water, and could not get off for the frost and ice; they were some five or six paces long, and about two inches thick of fat, and fleshed like a swine, they would have yielded a great deal of oil, if there had been time and means to have taken it, so we finding nothing for our turn, both we and our shallop returned. We then directed our course along the sea sands, to the place where we first saw the Indians, when we were there,

1. The text is from William Bradford and Edward Winslow, *Mourt's Relation, or Journal of the Plantation at Plymouth* (1622; rpt., 1865), edited by Henry Martyn Dexter. *Mourt's Relation* was first published in London by Bradford's brother-in-law, George Mourt.
2. Trading. "Sounded": fainted.
3. The shore from which the wind was blowing.
4. This distance might have been about eighteen to twenty-one miles.
5. Protected inlet or roadstead.
6. Barricade.
7. Small sailing vessel often used in coastal exploration.
8. Brooks.

we saw it was also a *grampus* which they were cutting up, they cut it into long rands[9] or pieces, about an ell long, and two handfuls broad, we found here and there a piece scattered by the way, as it seemed, for haste: this place the most were minded[1] we should call, the *Grampus Bay*, because we found so many of them there: we followed the track of the Indians' bare feet a good way on the sands, at length we saw where they struck into the woods by the side of a pond, as we went to view the place, one said, he thought he saw an Indian house among the trees, so went up to see: and here we and the shallop lost sight one of another till night, it being now about nine or ten o'clock, so we light on a path, but saw no house, and followed a great way into the woods, at length we found where corn had been set,[2] but not that year, anon we found a great burying place, one part whereof was encompassed with a large palazado, like a churchyard, with young spires[3] four or five yards long, set as close one by another as they could two or three foot in the ground within it was full of graves, some bigger, and some less, some were also paled about, and others had like an Indian house made over them, but not matted: those graves were more sumptuous than those at Corne-hill,[4] yet we digged none of them up, but only viewed them, and went our way; without[5] the palazado were graves also, but not so costly: from this place we went and found more corn ground, but not of this year. As we ranged we light on four or five Indian houses, which had been lately dwelt in, but they were uncovered and had no mats about them, else they were like those we found at Corne-hill, but had not been so lately dwelt in, there was nothing left but two or three pieces of old matts, a little sedge,[6] also a little further we found two baskets full of parched acorns hid in the ground, which we supposed had been corn when we began to dig the same, we cast earth thereon again and went our way. All this while we saw no people, we went ranging up and down till the sun began to draw low, and then we hasted out of the woods, that we might come to our shallop, which when we were out of the woods, we espied a great way off, and called them to come unto us, the which they did as soon as they could, for it was not yet high water, they were exceeding glad to see us, (for they feared because they had not seen us in so long a time) thinking we would have kept by the shoreside, so being both weary and faint, for we had eaten nothing all that day, we fell to make our rendezvous[7] and get firewood, which always cost us a great deal of labor, by [the] time we had done, and our shallop come to us, it was within night, and we fed upon such victuals as we had, and betook us to our rest, after we had set out our watch. About midnight we heard a great and hideous cry, and our sentinel called, *Arm, arm.* So we bestirred ourselves and shot off a couple of muskets, and noise ceased; we concluded, that it was a company of wolves or foxes, for one told us, he had heard such a noise in New-found-land. About five o'clock in the morning we began to be stirring, and two or three which doubted whether their Pieces would go off or no made trial of them, and shot them off, but thought nothing at all,

9. Strips.
1. Most people thought.
2. Planted.
3. Saplings. "Palazado": palisade; fence of thin posts or pales.
4. A spot on Cape Cod where they had unearthed buried stores of grain. Corn Hill was also an ancient ward in London. "Indian house": Native American wigwams were constructed of timber frames and covered with woven mats.
5. Outside.
6. Reed used for roofing.
7. Camp.

after prayer we prepared ourselves for breakfast, and for a journey, and it being now the twilight in the morning, it was thought meet to carry the things down to the shallop: some said, it was not best to carry the armor down, others said, they would be readier, two or three said, they would not carry theirs, till they went themselves, but mistrusting nothing at all: as it fell out, the water not being high enough, they laid the things down upon the shore, and came up to breakfast. Anon, all upon a sudden, we heard a great and strange cry, which we knew to be the same voices, though they varied their notes, one of our company being abroad came running in, and cried, *They are men, Indians, Indians,*[8] and withal, their arrows came flying amongst us, our men ran out with all speed to recover their arms, as by the good Providence of God they did. In the meantime, Captain *Miles Standish,* having a snaphance[9] ready, made a shot, and after him another, after they two had shot, other two of us were ready, but he wished us not to shoot, till we could take aim, for we knew not what need we should have, and there were four only of us, which had their arms there ready, and stood before the open side of our Baricado, which was first assaulted, they thought it best to defend it, lest the enemy should take it and our stuff, and so have the more vantage against us, our care was no less for the Shallop, but we hoped all the rest would defend it; we called unto them to know how it was with them, and they answered, Well, Well, every one, and be of good courage: we heard three of their Pieces go off, and the rest called for a fire-brand to light their matches,[1] one took a log out of the fire on his shoulder and went and carried it unto them, which was thought did not a little discourage our enemies. The cry of our enemies was dreadful, especially, when our men ran out to recover their Arms, their note was after this manner, *Woath woach ha ha hach woach:* our men were no sooner come to their Arms, but the enemy was ready to assault them.

There was a lusty man and no wit less valiant, who was thought to be their Captain, stood behind a tree within half a musket shot of us, and there let his arrows fly at us; he was seen to shoot three arrows, which were all avoided, for he at whom the first arrow was aimed, saw it, and stooped down and it flew over him, the rest were avoided also: he stood three shots of a Musket, at length one took full aim at him, after which he gave an extraordinary cry and away they went all, we followed them about a quarter of a mile, but we left six to keep our shallop, for we were careful of our business: then we shouted all together two several[2] times, and shot off a couple of muskets and so returned: this we did that they might see we were not afraid of them nor discouraged. Thus it pleased God to vanquish our Enemies and give us deliverance, by their noise we could not guess that they were less than thirty or forty, though some thought that they were many more yet in the dark of the morning, we could not so well discern them among the trees, as they could see us by our fireside, we took up eighteen of their arrows which we have sent to England by Master Jones, some whereof were headed with brass, others with Harts horn,[3] and others with Eagles' claws many more no doubt were shot, for these we found, were almost covered with leaves: yet by the

8. As opposed to the wolves or foxes that the Englishmen had earlier thought the men to be.
9. An early version of a flintlock gun.
1. Wax-coated fuses used with guns lacking snaphance devices.
2. Separate.
3. I.e., points made from deer antlers.

especial providence of God, none of them either hit or hurt us, though many came close by us, and on every side of us, and some coats which hung up in our baricado, were shot through and through. So after we had given God thanks for our deliverance, we took our shallop and went on our journey, and called this place, *The first encounter.* * * *

1622

JOHN SMITH
1580–1631

One of the most vivid episodes in the literature of colonial British North America is a scene from the writings of Captain John Smith that takes place at the "court" of Powhatan, the mamanatowick (or paramount chief) of the Algonquians in the Chesapeake Bay region. (For more on Powhatan, see the excerpt from "Powhatan's Discourse" earlier in this volume.) Smith was a leading member of the English company that had established the colony of Jamestown, in what is now Virginia. While on an expedition to discover the source of the Chickahominy River, he was taken captive by some of Powhatan's men. Arriving at Powhatan's residence at Werowocomoco—on the York River, north of Jamestown—Smith was greeted with an elaborate welcoming ceremony and feast. Soon afterward, however, he was suddenly dragged before Powhatan and threatened with execution. The mamanatowick's preteen daughter Mataoka, better known as Pocahontas (c. 1596–1617), pleaded with her father not to kill Smith. When her appeal appeared to be failing, she shielded Smith's head with her arms and saved his life—or so Smith claimed. Historians and anthropologists have speculated that what Smith describes as a rescue from execution was instead a ceremony designed to make Smith subordinate to Powhatan, thereby transforming Jamestown into a tributary of the Algonquian leader.

The romantic narrative about how Pocahontas rescued John Smith forms one of the central myths of English colonization. It emerges from a short passage in *The General History of Virginia, New England, and the Summer Isles* (1624), a historical compilation that Smith produced jointly with several other writers. In the years between Smith's return from Virginia in 1609 and the appearance of the *General History,* Smith had published other accounts of his Virginia adventures that mention Pocahontas. But the lines devoted to her "rescue" of him appear exclusively in the *General History.* That volume appeared seven years after she died on board a ship while returning from England with her husband—the white colonist John Rolfe—and their son, Thomas. By the time the *General History* was published in London, no one was available to corroborate Smith's account of his dramatic rescue or clarify its significance. The mythology that has grown out of these few brief lines, sometimes conflating the rescue of Smith with Pocahontas's subsequent marriage to Rolfe, is a striking example of how some colonial-era texts have accrued layers of meaning that extend well beyond the words on the page.

This scene is not the only romancelike feature of Smith's writings. The English adventurer deliberately cultivated an aura resembling that of a knight in a chivalric romance—but with important differences. Like Sir Walter Raleigh, the aristocratic English explorer and champion of colonization, Smith pursued adventure

and glory. Unlike Raleigh, he was not an aristocrat but a farmer's son. This difference in status forms a major element in Smith's writings. He hailed from the east of England, where his father had a farm on the edge of the Lincolnshire Wolds, an area of considerable natural beauty. The young Smith found the countryside too quiet for his taste. Shortly after his father died in 1596, the restless sixteen-year-old went to the Netherlands to fight for Dutch independence from Philip II of Spain. The fight was part of the European wars of religion, which pitted Protestants against Roman Catholics and, on the eastern front, Christians against Muslims. Smith was one of many planters whose involvement in the colonization of the Americas was colored by experience in these often brutal conflicts. Following his tour of duty in the Netherlands, he fought in the Mediterranean, and he later joined the Austrian imperial army in its war against the Ottoman Empire, which at that time encompassed large swathes of southeastern Europe and the Middle East, as well as parts of North Africa. While fighting the Ottomans in Hungary, Smith earned promotion to the captain's rank that became an enduring part of his public persona. He claimed, apparently with at least some degree of truth, that he had defeated and beheaded a succession of three Turkish officers in single combat. The coat of arms that he was later awarded showed the three severed heads.

Eventually, Smith was wounded in battle, taken prisoner, and sold as a slave to a Turkish noblewoman. Smith described his developing attachment to this noblewoman in his semiautobiographical work, *The True Travels, Adventures, and Observations of Captaine John Smith, in Europe, Asia, Affrica, and America* (1630). The romance might have ended in marriage, with Smith converting to Islam and serving as an Ottoman bureaucrat. Instead, the Englishman killed the noblewoman's brother in ambiguous circumstances—Smith may have mistaken a form of training for mistreatment—and escaped. Smith later gave place names drawn from his Turkish adventures to areas in New England, such as Three Turks' Heads (near Cape Ann in Massachusetts), which John Winthrop mentioned in his journal account of the Puritans' arrival in 1630.

After returning to England in the winter of 1604–05, Smith began looking for his next adventure. The twenty-six-year-old veteran had an assertive personality and military experience that were attractive qualities to the members of the Virginia Company of London as they organized their 1606 expedition to establish what they hoped would be England's first permanent plantation in North America. But those qualities also carried liabilities. Smith sometimes used force unnecessarily, and his hard-to-control temper and stubborn self-reliance could make him a troublesome companion. He ran afoul of the people in charge of the expedition on the voyage to America in 1607, when he was placed under arrest and threatened with execution. Then, in a remarkable turn of events, his name was found on the list of council members that the company had designated to run the colony, which had been kept secret until the group's arrival. The company had recognized qualities in Smith that they believed would be useful to the group, and so despite his comparatively modest status and his propensity for challenging authority, they gave him a role in the Jamestown colony's leadership.

Smith set out to organize the men and explore and map the region. Many of the other colonists were from elite backgrounds, and they were often unwilling or unable to perform the hard and dangerous work that settlement demanded. The colonists who survived rampant illness, famine, warfare, and other mishaps increasingly came to value Smith's leadership, and in 1608 he was elected to the colony's highest office, becoming the equivalent of its governor. But official status offered little protection in the volatile colonial setting. When Smith returned to Jamestown after being held captive by Powhatan—the episode where he was "rescued" by Pocahontas—he was charged with the deaths of the two soldiers who had accompanied him on the expedition that ended in his capture. Smith was saved from hanging

when the colonists were distracted by the fortuitous arrival of a fleet with much-needed supplies from England. Not long afterward, however, Smith's gunpowder bag mysteriously exploded in his lap while he napped on the deck of an exploring vessel—possibly because a disgruntled member of the company had thrown a match into the powder. Smith left Virginia in 1609, never to return.

Smith is most closely associated with the Virginia enterprise, but he also took an active interest in New England, and his works form an important bridge between these first two permanent English colonies in North America. In 1614 he voyaged to New England, and he, not the Puritans, gave the region its name. He offered the Pilgrims his services as a guide for their voyage in 1620, but they chose instead to put Smith's helpful books and maps in the hands of a more temperate military leader, Myles Standish. If not for this rejection and some unfortunate setbacks that prevented future voyages, Smith might have become more famous for this second aspect of his American career than for the first: he published more works on New England than on Virginia, seeing in the northern region great potential for "middling" English settlers. Smith's New England works have a strong ideological caste, in that they focus more on the idea of America and less on the many challenges of establishing plantations there, doubtless a reflection of his indirect involvement.

Smith published some nine books between 1608 and 1631, including his works on Virginia and New England, books for aspiring seamen, and *The True Travels*. Many of his writings have a distinctly Elizabethan caste to them, though with a difference. In his works, the heroic ideal of the elite adventurer, typified by Sir Walter Raleigh, gives way to the prototype of the independent self-made man. Tales of exploration, piracy, and military adventure had stirred Smith's youthful imagination, and he longed to create his own heroic narratives. Rather than simply reproduce heroic literary conventions, Smith actively transformed them. In contrast to Raleigh, who was associated with the high literary ideals embodied in Edmund Spenser's epic poem *The Faerie Queen* (1590), Smith wrote prose accounts addressed to the expanding market for popular printed works, which was driven in part by the public appetite for writings about the colonization effort. Though largely untutored in the finer points of style, he had an ear for a good story and a capacity for striking metaphors. Sprinkled with classical allusions and references to the popular theater, his writings also demonstrate his mastery of the humanistic genres of oratory, history, and descriptive travel writing.

The most lasting and influential contribution of his writings was a vision of England's colonies as places where people of all economic backgrounds could support themselves as small farmers, in healthful and pleasant circumstances, with greater liberty than might be possible elsewhere. The outlines of the yeoman farmer ideal that would be so important for Virginia's Thomas Jefferson emerge clearly in Smith's works. The negative aspects of this vision emerge as well in passages revealing how this figure comes to overshadow and dominate those who pursued other modes of life, notably America's indigenous inhabitants. Perhaps Smith's most salient quality as a writer is his special knack for illustrating the connections between the often sordid or brutal details of the colonization enterprise and the imaginative work that propelled it.

The following texts are from *Travels and Works of Captain John Smith* (1910), edited by Edward Arber and A. G. Bradley.

From The General History of Virginia, New England, and the Summer Isles[1]

From *The Third Book*[2]

FROM CHAPTER 2. WHAT HAPPENED TILL THE FIRST SUPPLY[3]

Being thus left to our fortunes, it fortuned that within ten days[4] scarce ten amongst us could either go, or well stand, such extreme weakness and sickness oppressed us. And thereat none need marvel, if they consider the cause and reason, which was this:

Whilst the ships stayed, our allowance was somewhat bettered, by a daily proportion of biscuit, which the sailors would pilfer to sell, give, or exchange with us, for money, Sassafras,[5] furs, or love. But when they departed, there remained neither tavern, beer house, nor place of relief, but the common kettle.[6] Had we been as free from all sins as [from] gluttony, and drunkenness, we might have been canonized for Saints; but our President would never have been admitted, for engrossing to his private [use], oatmeal, sack, oil, aqua vitae, beef, eggs, or what not, but the kettle;[7] that indeed he allowed equally to be distributed, and that was half a pint of wheat, and as much barley boiled with water for a man a day, and this having fried some twenty-six weeks in the ship's hold, contained as many worms as grains, so that we might truly call it rather so much bran then corn; our drink[8] was water, our lodgings castles in the air.

With this lodging and diet, our extreme toil in bearing and planting palisades, so strained and bruised us, and our continual labor in the extremity of the heat had so weakened us, as were cause sufficient to have made us as miserable in our native country, or any other place in the world.

From May, to September [1607], those that escaped, lived upon sturgeon, and sea crabs. Fifty in this time we buried, the rest seeing the President's[9] projects to escape these miseries in our pinnace by flight (who all this time had neither felt want nor sickness) so moved our dead spirits, as we deposed him and established Ratcliffe in his place, (Gosnold being dead, Kendall deposed). Smith newly recovered, Martin[1] and Ratcliffe were by his care preserved and relieved, and the most of the soldiers recovered with the skillful diligence of Master Thomas Wotton our general surgeon.

1. The Bermuda Islands.
2. The Third Book is titled "The Proceedings and Accidents of the English Colony in Virginia" and is derived from Smith's Virginia book of 1612.
3. The bulk of this chapter may have been written by Smith, although at its publication in 1612 it was credited solely to Thomas Studley, chief storekeeper of the colony. In 1624, Smith added to Studley's signature at the end of this section of the text not only his own initials but also the names of Robert Fenton and Edward Harrington as part authors. Studley died early in the first year, on August 28, 1607, four days after Harrington, so neither could have written much of what is partly attributed to them. Of Robert Fenton nothing is known.
4. By the end of June 1607, after Captain Christopher Newport (d. 1617) left to fetch new supplies from England. "Fortuned": happened.
5. The bark of the sassafras tree, sold for its supposed medicinal qualities, was a valuable commodity in London.
6. I.e., the communal resources.

7. I.e., President Edward Maria Wingfield (c. 1560–1613), a man of high connections in England, would not have been canonized because he diverted many supplies (everything except the contents of the common kettle) for his own use, including sack (wine) and aqua vitae (brandy).
8. "Drink," here used ironically, customarily referred to wine or beer. "Corn": grain.
9. I.e., Wingfield's.
1. Captain John Martin (c. 1567–1632?) was a colonist best known for his contentiousness. "Captain John Ratcliffe" was an alias of John Sicklemore, master of one of the vessels on the voyage over and a member of the local council. The most enigmatic figure in Jamestown, he was elected president of the council in September 1607, but later fell out with Smith. Captain Bartholomew Gosnold (ca. 1572–1607), who had explored New England before the first Jamestown voyage, probably had been responsible for Smith's recruitment to the venture. Captain George Kendall was executed for mutiny later in the year.

But now was all our provision spent, the sturgeon gone, all helps abandoned, each hour expecting the fury of the savages, when God the patron of all good endeavors, in that desperate extremity so changed the hearts of the savages, that they brought such plenty of their fruits, and provision, as no man wanted.[2]

And now where some affirmed it was ill done of the Council to send forth men so badly provided, this incontradictable reason will show them plainly they are too ill advised to nourish such ill conceits: first, the fault of our going was our own; what could be thought fitting or necessary we had; but what we should find, or want, or where we should be, we were all ignorant, and supposing to make our passage in two months, with victual to live, and the advantage of the spring to work; we were at sea five months, where we both spent our victual and lost the opportunity of the time and season to plant, by the unskilfull presumption of our ignorant transporters, that understood not at all, what they undertook.

Such actions have ever since the world's beginning been subject to such accidents, and everything of worth is found full of difficulties: but nothing so difficult as to establish a commonwealth so far remote from men and means, and where men's minds are so untoward[3] as neither do well themselves, nor suffer others. But to proceed.

The new President and Martin, being little beloved, of weak judgment in dangers, and less industry in peace, committed the managing of all things abroad[4] to Captain Smith: who by his own example, good words, and fair promises, set some to mow, others to bind thatch, some to build houses, others to thatch them, himself always bearing the greatest task for his own share, so that in short time, he provided most of them lodgings, neglecting any for himself.

This done, seeing the savages' superfluity begin to decrease [Smith] (with some of his workmen) shipped himself in the shallop[5] to search the country for trade. The want of[6] the language, knowledge to manage his boat without sails, the want of a sufficient power (knowing the multitude of the savages), apparel for his men, and other necessaries, were infinite impediments yet no discouragement.

Being but six or seven in company he went down the river to Kecoughtan[7] where at first they scorned him as a famished man, and would in derision offer him a handful of corn, a piece of bread, for their swords and muskets, and such like proportions also for their apparel. But seeing by trade and courtesy there was nothing to be had, he made bold to try such conclusions as necessity enforced; though contrary to his commission, [he] let fly[8] his muskets, ran his boat on shore, whereat they all fled into the woods.

So marching towards their houses, they might see great heaps of corn: much ado he had to restrain his hungry soldiers from present taking of it, expecting as it happened that the savages would assault them, as not long after they did with a most hideous noise. Sixty or seventy of them, some black, some

2. I.e., was in want.
3. Intractable.
4. I.e., outside the colony's palisade.
5. An open boat.
6. Inability to speak.

7. A village near the mouth of the James River whose inhabitants, the Kecoughtans, were members of the Powhatan Confederacy.
8. Fired.

red, some white, some particoloured, came in a square order,[9] singing and dancing out of the woods, with their Okee (which was an Idol made of skins, stuffed with moss, all painted and hung with chains and copper) borne before them, and in this manner, being well armed with clubs, targets, bows and arrow, they charged the English that so kindly received them with their muskets loaded with pistol shot, that down fell their God, and divers[1] lay sprawling on the ground; the rest fled again to the woods, and ere long sent one of their Quiyoughkasoucks[2] to offer peace, and redeem their Okee.

Smith told them, if only six of them would come unarmed and load his boat, he would not only be their friend, but restore them their Okee, and give them beads, copper, and hatchets besides, which on both sides was to their contents[3] performed, and then they brought him venison, turkeys, wild fowl, bread, and what they had, singing and dancing in sign of friendship till they departed.

In his return he discovered the town and country of Warraskoyack.[4]

> Thus God unboundless by His power,
> Made them thus kind, would us devour.

Smith perceiving (notwithstanding their late misery) not any regarded but from hand to mouth[5] (the company being well recovered) caused the pinnace to be provided with things fitting to get provision for the year following, but in the interim he made three or four journeys and discovered the people of Chickahominy.[6] Yet what he carefully provided the rest carelessly spent.

Wingfield and Kendall living in disgrace * * * strengthened themselves with the sailors and other confederates, to regain their former credit and authority, or at least such means aboard the pinnace, (being fitted to sail as Smith had appointed for trade) to alter her course and to go for England.

Smith, unexpectedly returning, had the plot discovered to him, much trouble he had to prevent it, till with store of saker[7] and musket shot he forced them stay or sink in the river: which action cost the life of Captain Kendall.

These brawls are so disgustful, as some will say they were better forgotten, yet all men of good judgment will conclude, it were better their baseness should be manifest to the world, than the business bear the scorn and shame of their excused disorders.[8]

The President and Captain Archer[9] not long after intended also to have abandoned the country, which project also was curbed, and suppressed by Smith.

9. "Square order": formation. "Particoloured": i.e., painted for battle.
1. Several. "Targets": small shields. "So kindly": in such a way.
2. Smith elsewhere defines this term as referring to the "petty gods" of the Algonquian-speaking peoples, but here it may mean priests.
3. I.e., in mutual contentment.
4. A village on the south side of the James River.
5. I.e., none of the settlers, despite their recent sufferings, gave any thought to gathering a store of provision for the future.
6. The region along the Chickahominy River, which empties into the James River a short distance west of Jamestown.

7. Shot for a small cannon used in sieges and on shipboard. "Discovered": revealed.
8. I.e., it is necessary to recount these troubles and lay the blame on the responsible individuals (Wingfield and Kendall), rather than let the whole "business" of the colony suffer ill repute.
9. Gabriel Archer (c. 1575–1609?) had been an associate of Bartholomew Gosnold before the Jamestown voyage. Having gone back to England in 1608 as a confirmed opponent of Smith, he returned to Virginia the following year to head an anti-Smith faction but died during the starving time the next winter. Ratcliffe (Sicklemore) was still president.

The Spaniard never more greedily desired gold then he victual,[1] nor his soldiers more to abandon the country, than he to keep it. But [he found] plenty of corn in the river of Chickahominy, where hundreds of savages in divers places stood with baskets expecting his coming.

And now the winter approaching, the rivers became so covered with swans, geese, ducks, and cranes that we daily feasted with good bread, Virginia peas, pumpkins, and putchamins, fish, fowl, and divers sorts of wild beasts as fat as we could eat them, so that none of our Tuftaffety humorists[2] desired to go for England.

But our comedies never endured long without a tragedy, some idle exceptions[3] being muttered against Captain Smith, for not discovering the head of Chickahominy river, and [he being] taxed by the council to be too slow in so worthy an attempt. The next voyage he proceeded so far that with much labor by cutting of trees asunder he made his passage, but when his barge could pass no farther, he left her in a broad bay out of danger of shot, commanding none should go ashore till his return; himself with two English and two savages went up higher in a canoe, but he was not long absent but his men went ashore, whose want of government gave both occasion and opportunity to the savages to surprise one George Cassen, whom they slew and much failed not to have cut off the boat and all the rest.[4]

Smith little dreaming of that accident, being got to the marshes at the river's head twenty miles in the desert,[5] had his two men slain (as is supposed) sleeping by the canoe, whilst himself by fowling sought them victual, who finding he was beset with 200 savages, two of them he slew, still defending himself with the aid of a savage his guide, whom he bound to his arm with his garters, and used him as a buckler,[6] yet he was shot in his thigh a little, and had many arrows that stuck in his clothes but no great hurt, till at last they took him prisoner.

When this news came to Jamestown, much was their sorrow for his loss, few expecting what ensued.

Six or seven weeks those barbarians kept him prisoner, many strange triumphs and conjurations they made of him, yet he so demeaned[7] himself amongst them, as he not only diverted them from surprising the fort, but procured his own liberty, and got himself and his company such estimation amongst them, that those savages admired him more than their owne Quiyoughkasoucks.

The manner how they used and delivered him, is as followeth:

The savages having drawn from George Cassen whither Captain Smith was gone, prosecuting that opportunity they followed him with 300 bowmen, conducted by the King of Pamunkey, who in divisions searching the turnings of the river, found Robinson and Emry by the fireside; those they shot full of arrows and slew.[8] Then finding the Captain, as is said, that used the savage

1. I.e., Smith wanted to find food for the colonists as much as Spanish conquistadors wanted to find gold.
2. Self-indulgent persons who might be given to wearing lace. "Putchamins": persimmons.
3. Objections.
4. I.e., only through fault of their own did they fail to wipe out Cassen's whole party. "Government": discipline.
5. Wilderness.
6. Shield. "Garters": laces used for tying clothing.
7. Behaved.
8. I.e., these are the two men mentioned above as having been killed while they slept by the canoe (the fireside being by the canoe). John Robinson was a "gentleman"; Thomas Emry was a carpenter. "King of Pamunkey": Opechancanough, Powhatan's younger half-brother (d. 1644) and Smith's captor, who led the Powhatan Confederacy's attack on the colonists in 1622 and as late as 1644 attempted one last time to expel them from the country.

that was his guide as his shield (three of them being slain and divers other so galled)[9] all the rest would not come near him. Thinking thus to have returned to his boat, regarding them, as he marched, more than his way, [he] slipped up to the middle in an oozy creek and his savage with him, yet dared they not come to him till being near dead with cold, he threw away his arms. Then according to their composition[1] they drew him forth and led him to the fire, where his men were slain. Diligently they chafed his benumbed limbs.

He demanding for their captain, they showed him Opechancanough, King of Pamunkey, to whom he gave a round ivory double compass dial. Much they marveled at the playing of the fly[2] and needle, which they could see so plainly and yet not touch it because of the glass that covered them. But when he demonstrated by that globe-like jewell, the roundness of the earth, and skies, the sphere of the sun, moon, and stars, and how the sun did chase the night round about the world continually, the greatness of the land and sea, the diversity of nations, variety of complexions, and how we were to them antipodes,[3] and many other such like matters, they all stood as amazed with admiration.

Notwithstanding, within an hour after, they tied him to a tree, and as many as could stand about him prepared to shoot him, but the King holding up the compass in his hand, they all laid down their bows and arrows, and in a triumphant manner led him to Orapaks, where he was after their manner kindly feasted, and well used.[4]

Their order in conducting him was thus: Drawing themselves all in file, the King in the midst had all their pieces[5] and swords borne before him. Captain Smith was led after him by three great savages holding him fast by each arm, and on each side six went in file with their arrows nocked.[6] But arriving at the town (which was but only thirty or forty hunting houses made of mats, which they remove as they please, as we our tents), all the women and children staring to behold him, the soldiers first all in file performed the form of a Bissom[7] so well as could be, and on each flank, officers as sergeants to see them keep their orders. A good time they continued this exercise and then cast themselves in a ring, dancing in such several postures and singing and yelling out such hellish notes and screeches; being strangely painted, every one [had] his quiver of arrows and at his back a club, on his arm a fox or an otter's skin or some such matter for his vambrace, their heads and shoulders painted red, with oil and pocones mingled together, which scarlet-like color made an exceeding handsome show, his bow in his hand, and the skin of a bird with her wings abroad[8] dryed, tied on his head, a piece of copper, a white shell, a long feather with a small rattle growing at the tails of their snakes tied to it, or some such like toy. All this while, Smith and the King stood in the midst, guarded as before is said, and after three dances they all departed. Smith they conducted to a long house where thirty or forty tall fellows did guard him, and ere long more bread and venison was brought him than would have served twenty men. I think his stomach at that

9. Wounded.
1. Agreement for surrender.
2. Compass card.
3. On the opposite side of the globe.
4. Treated. "Orapaks": a village located farther inland, later the residence of Powhatan.
5. Guns.

6. Notched; i.e., with their arrows fitted on the bowstring ready for use.
7. From an Italian term denoting a snakelike formation.
8. Outspread. "Vambrace": forearm protection. "Pocones": a vegetable dye.

time was not very good; what he left they put in baskets and tied over his head. About midnight they set the meat again before him; all this time not one of them would eat a bit with him, till the next morning they brought him as much more, and then did they eat all the old, and reserved the new as they had done the other, which made him think they would fat him to eat him. Yet in this desperate estate, to defend him from the cold, one Maocassater brought him his gown, in requital[9] of some beads and toys Smith had given him at his first arrival in Virginia.

Two days after, a man would have slain him (but that the guard prevented it) for the death of his son, to whom they conducted him to recover the poor man then breathing his last. Smith told them that at Jamestown he had a water would do it, if they would let him fetch it, but they would not permit that, but made all the preparations they could to assault Jamestown, craving his advice, and for recompence he should have life, liberty, land, and women. In part of a table book[1] he wrote his mind to them at the fort, what was intended, how they should follow that direction to affright the messengers, and without fail send him such things as he wrote for. And an inventory with them. The difficulty and danger, he told the savages, of the mines, great guns, and other engines[2] exceedingly affrighted them, yet according to his request they went to Jamestown in as bitter weather as could be of frost and snow, and within three days returned with an answer.

But when they came to Jamestown, seeing men sally out as he had told them they would, they fled, yet in the night they came again to the same place where he had told them they should receive an answer and such things as he had promised them, which they found accordingly, and with which they returned with no small expedition to the wonder of them all that heard it, that he could either divine[3] or the paper could speak.

Then they led him to the Youghtanunds, the Mattapanients, the Piankatanks, the Nantaughtacunds, and Onawmanients upon the rivers of Rappahannock and Potomac, over all those rivers, and back again by divers other several nations,[4] to the King's habitation at Pamunkey where they entertained him with most strange and fearful conjurations:[5]

> As if near led to hell,
> Amongst the devils to dwell.

Not long after, early in a morning, a great fire was made in a long house, and a mat spread on the one side as on the other; on the one they caused him to sit, and all the guard went out of the house, and presently came skipping in a great grim fellow all painted over with coal[6] mingled with oil, and many snakes' and weasels' skins stuffed with moss, and all their tails tied together so as they met on the crown of his head in a tassel, and round about the tassel was as a coronet of feathers, the skins hanging round about his head, back, and shoulders and in a manner covered his face, with a hellish

9. Payment.
1. A notebook.
2. Weaponry.
3. Perform magic. "Expedition": speed.
4. Other Algonquian-speaking groups. The named groups were part of the Powhatan Confederacy.

5. Incantations. However, Smith derived the following couplet from a translation of the ancient Roman writer Seneca published by Martin Fotherby in his philosophical treatise *Atheomastix* (1622).
6. I.e., charcoal.

voice, and a rattle in his hand. With most strange gestures and passions he began his invocation and environed[7] the fire with a circle of meal; which done, three more such like devils came rushing in with the like antic tricks, painted half black, half red, but all their eyes were painted white and some red strokes like mustaches along their cheeks. Round about him those fiends danced a pretty while, and then came in three more as ugly as the rest, with red eyes and white strokes over their black faces. At last they all sat down right against him, three of them on the one hand of the chief priest, and three on the other. Then all with their rattles began a song; which ended, the chief priest laid down five wheat corns; then straining his arms and hands with such violence that he sweat and his veins swelled, he began a short oration;[8] at the conclusion they all gave a short groan and then laid down three grains more. After that, began their song again, and then another oration, ever laying down so many corns as before till they had twice encircled the fire; that done, they took a bunch of little sticks prepared for that purpose, continuing still their devotion, and at the end of every song and oration they laid down a stick betwixt the divisions of corn. Till night, neither he nor they did either eat or drink, and then they feasted merrily with the best provisions they could make. Three days they used this ceremony; the meaning whereof, they told him, was to know if he intended them well or no. The circle of meal signified their country, the circles of corn the bounds of the sea, and the sticks his country. They imagined the world to be flat and round, like a trencher,[9] and they in the midst.

After this they brought him a bag of gunpowder, which they carefully preserved till the next spring, to plant as they did their corn, because they would be acquainted with the nature of that seed.

Opitchapam, the King's brother,[1] invited him to his house, where, with as many platters of bread, fowl, and wild beasts as did environ him, he bid him welcome, but not any of them would eat a bit with him but put up all the remainder in baskets.

At his return to Opechancanough's, all the King's women and their children, flocked about him for their parts,[2] as a due by custom, to be merry with such fragments:

But his waking mind in hideous dreams did oft see wondrous shapes,
Of bodies strange, and huge in growth, and of stupendous makes.[3]

At last they brought him to Werowocomoco,[4] where was Powhatan, their Emperor. Here more than two hundred of those grim courtiers stood wondering at him, as [if] he had been a monster, till Powhatan and his train had put themselves in their greatest braveries.[5] Before a fire upon a seat like a bedstead, he sat covered with a great robe made of raccoon skins and all the tails hanging by. On either hand did sit a young wench of sixteen or eighteen years and along on each side [of] the house, two rows of men and behind them as many women, with all their heads and shoulders painted

7. Encircled.
8. Prayer. "Wheat corns": i.e., five kernels of Indian corn.
9. A flat, wooden dish.
1. Actually the chief's half-brother; he succeeded Powhatan in 1618.

2. Gifts.
3. From a translation of the ancient Roman writer Lucretius by Fotherby.
4. Powhatan's village on the north shore of the York River, almost due north of Jamestown.
5. Finery; i.e., costumes.

"Map of the old Virginia," by Robert Vaughan, from John Smith, *The General History of Virginia, New England, and the Summer Isles* (1624). This map of Old Virginia, the part of coastal North Carolina where the first English explorations and settlements took place in the 1580s, is surrounded by images portraying John Smith's warlike encounters around Jamestown some twenty years later. The panel in the lower right corner shows the intervention of Pocahontas in the supposed execution of Smith.

red, many of their heads bedecked with the white down of birds, but every one with something, and a great chain of white beads about their necks.

At his entrance before the King, all the people gave a great shout. The Queen of Appomattoc[6] was appointed to bring him water to wash his hands, and another brought him a bunch of feathers, instead of a towel to dry them; having feasted him after their best barbarous manner they could, a long consultation was held, but the conclusion was, two great stones were brought before Powhatan; then as many as could, laid hands on him, dragged him to them, and thereon laid his head and being ready with their clubs to beat out his brains, Pocahontas, the King's dearest daughter, when no entreaty could prevail, got his head in her arms and laid her own upon his to save him from death, whereat the Emperor was contented he should live to make him hatchets, and her bells, beads, and copper, for they thought him as well of all occupations as themselves.[7] For the King himself will make his own robes, shoes, bows, arrows, pots; plant, hunt, or do any thing so well as the rest.

6. Opossunoquonuske was the weroansqua, or leader, of a small village (Appamatuck) near the future site of Petersburg, Virginia. In 1610, she was killed by the English in retaliation for the deaths of fourteen settlers.

7. I.e., they thought him as variously skilled as themselves.

> They say he bore a pleasant show,
> But sure his heart was sad.
> For who can pleasant be, and rest,
> That lives in fear and dread:
> And having life suspected, doth
> It still suspected lead.[8]

Two days after, Powhatan having disguised himself in the most fearfulest manner he could, caused Captain Smith to be brought forth to a great house in the woods and there upon a mat by the fire to be left alone. Not long after, from behind a mat that divided the house, was made the most dolefulest noise he ever heard; then Powhatan more like a devil than a man, with some two hundred more as black as himself, came unto him and told him now they were friends, and presently he should go to Jamestown, to send him two great guns and a grindstone for which he would give him the Country of Capahowasic and for ever esteem him as his son Nantaquoud.[9]

So to Jamestown with twelve guides Powhatan sent him. That night they quartered in the woods, he still expecting (as he had done all this long time of his imprisonment) every hour to be put to one death or other, for all their feasting. But almighty God (by His divine providence) had mollified the hearts of those stern barbarians with compassion. The next morning betimes they came to the fort, where Smith having used the savages with what kindness he could, he showed Rawhunt, Powhatan's trusty servant, two demi-culverins[1] and a millstone to carry [to] Powhatan; they found them somewhat too heavy, but when they did see him discharge them, being loaded with stones, among the boughs of a great tree loaded with icickles, the ice and branches came so tumbling down that the poor savages ran away half dead with fear. But at last we regained some conference with them and gave them such toys and sent to Powhatan, his women, and children such presents as gave them in general full content.

Now in Jamestown they were all in combustion, the strongest preparing once more to run away with the pinnace; which with the hazard of his life, with saker falcon[2] and musket shot, Smith forced now the third time to stay or sink.

Some no better than they should be, had plotted with the President the next day to have put him to death by the Levitical[3] law, for the lives of Robinson and Emry; pretending the fault was his that had led them to their ends: but he quickly took such order with such lawyers that he laid them by the heels till he sent some of them prisoners for England.

Now ever once in four or five days, Pocahontas with her attendants brought him so much provision that saved many of their lives, that else for all this had starved with hunger.

> Thus from numb death our good God sent relief,
> The sweet assuager of all other grief.[4]

8. Derived from a translation of the ancient Greek playwright Euripides by Fotherby.
9. I.e., Powhatan would esteem him as highly as his own son Nantaquoud. Capahowasic was along the York River, near where Smith was held prisoner.
1. Large cannons.

2. Small artillery piece.
3. "And he that killeth any man shall surely be put to death" (Leviticus 24.17).
4. The first line appears to be Smith's, inspired by Fotherby. The second comes from Fotherby's translation of a quotation from Euripides in a text by the ancient Greek writer Plutarch.

His relation of the plenty he had seen, especially at Werowocomoco, and of the state and bounty of Powhatan (which till that time was unknown), so revived their dead spirits (especially the love of Pocahontas)[5] as all men's fear was abandoned.

Thus you may see what difficulties still crossed any good endeavor; and the good success of the business being thus oft brought to the very period of destruction; yet you see by what strange means God hath still delivered it.

* * *

From *The Fourth Book*

[SMITH'S FAREWELL TO VIRGINIA]

Thus far I have traveled in this Wilderness of Virginia, not being ignorant for all my pains this discourse will be wrested, tossed and turned as many ways as there is leaves;[6] that I have written too much of some, too little of others, and many such like objections. To such I must answer, in the Company's name I was requested to do it,[7] if any have concealed their approved experiences from my knowledge, they must excuse me: as for every fatherless or stolen relation,[8] or whole volumes of sophisticated rehearsals, I leave them to the charge of them that desire them. I thank God I never undertook anything yet [for which] any could tax me of carelessness or dishonesty, and what is he to whom I am indebted or troublesome?[9] Ah! were these my accusers but to change cases and places with me [for] but two years, or till they had done but so much as I, it may be they would judge more charitably of my imperfections. But here I must leave all to the trial of time, both myself, Virginia's preparations, proceedings and good events, praying to that great God the protector of all goodness to send them as good success as the goodness of the action[1] and country deserveth, and my heart desireth.

1624

From A Description of New England

Who can desire more content, that hath small means; or but only his merit to advance his fortune, than to tread, and plant that ground he hath purchased by the hazard of his life? If he have but the taste of virtue and magnanimity, what to such a mind can be more pleasant, than planting and building a foundation for his posterity, got from the rude earth, by God's blessing and his own industry, without prejudice[1] to any? If he have any grain of faith or zeal in religion, what can he do less hurtful to any; or more agreeable to God,

5. I.e., the evident affection of Pocahontas for Smith and the English was instrumental in reviving the colonists' spirits.
6. Pages.
7. Smith was not requested to write the whole *General History* by the Virginia Company, so it is not clear what he means here. Possibly the discourse to which he refers is the brief summary of recommendations for the "reformation" of

Virginia that ends the Fourth Book and that he drew up at the request of the royal commissioners charged with effecting that reformation.
8. I.e., anonymous or "fugitive" narratives. "Approved": proven.
9. I.e., and who is it that I have been a burden to?
1. Venture. "Events": results.
1. Harm. "Magnanimity": greatness of spirit.

than to seek to convert those poor savages to know Christ, and humanity, whose labors with discretion will triple requite thy charge and pains? What so truly suits with honor and honesty, as the discovering things unknown? erecting towns, peopling countries, informing the ignorant, reforming things unjust, teaching virtue; and gaining to our native mother country a kingdom to attend her, finding employment for those that are idle, because they know not what to do: so far from wronging any, as to cause posterity to remember thee; and remembering thee, ever honor that remembrance with praise?

* * *

Then, who would live at home idly (or think in himself any worth to live) only to eat, drink, and sleep, and so die? Or by consuming that carelessly, [which] his friends got worthily? Or by using that miserably, that maintained virtue honestly? Or for being descended nobly, pine with the vain vaunt of great kindred, in penury?[2] Or (to maintain a silly show of bravery) toil out thy heart, soul, and time, basely, by shifts,[3] tricks, cards, and dice? Or by relating news of others' actions, shark[4] here or there for a dinner, or supper; deceive thy friends, by fair promises, and dissimulation, in borrowing where thou never intendest to pay; offend the laws, surfeit with excess, burden thy country, abuse thyself, despair in want, and then cozen[5] thy kindred, yea even thine own brother, and wish thy parents' death (I will not say damnation) to have their estates? though thou seest what honors, and rewards, the world yet hath for them will seek them and worthily deserve them.

* * *

Let this move you to embrace employment, for those whose educations, spirits, and judgments want but your purses; not only to prevent such accustomed dangers, but also to gain more thereby than you have. And you fathers that are either so foolishly fond, or so miserably covetous, or so wilfully ignorant, or so negligently careless, as that you will rather maintain your children in idle wantonness, till they grow your masters; or become so basely unkind, as they wish nothing but your deaths; so that both sorts grow dissolute: and although you would wish them anywhere to escape the gallows, and ease your cares; though they spend you here one, two, or three hundred pound a year; you would grudge to give half so much in adventure with them, to obtain an estate, which in a small time but with a little assistance of your providence,[6] might be better than your own. But if an angel should tell you, that any place yet unknown can afford such fortunes; you would not believe him, no more than Columbus was believed there was any such land as is now the well-known abounding America; much less such large regions as are yet unknown, as well in America, as in Africa, and Asia, and Terra Incognita; where were courses for gentlemen (and them that would be so reputed) more suiting their qualities, than begging from their Prince's generous disposition, the labors of his subjects, and the very marrow of his maintenance.

I have not been so ill bred, but I have tasted of plenty and pleasure, as well as want and misery: nor doth necessity yet, or occasion of discontent, force

2. I.e., live in poverty while claiming great ancestors.
3. Expedients. "Bravery": fine appearances.

4. Sponge.
5. Deceive. "Excess": overindulgence.
6. Provision.

me to these endeavors: nor am I ignorant what small thank I shall have for my pains; or that many would have the World imagine them to be of great judgment, that can but blemish these my designs, by their witty objections and detractions: yet (I hope) my reasons with my deeds, will so prevail with some, that I shall not want[7] employment in these affairs, to make the most blind see his own senselessness, and incredulity; hoping that gain will make them affect that, which religion, charity, and the common good cannot. It were but a poor device in me, to deceive myself; much more the king, state, my friends and country, with these inducements: which, seeing his Majesty hath given permission, I wish all sorts of worthy, honest, industrious spirits, would understand: and if they desire any further satisfaction, I will do my best to give it: Not to persuade them to go only;[8] but go with them: Not leave them there; but live with them there.

I will not say, but by ill providing and undue managing, such courses may be taken, [that] may make us miserable enough:[9] But if I may have the execution of what I have projected; if they want to eat, let them eat or never digest me.[1] If I perform what I say, I desire but that reward out of the gains [which] may suit my pains, quality, and condition. And if I abuse you with my tongue, take my head for satisfaction. If any dislike at the year's end, defraying their charge,[2] by my consent they should freely return. I fear not want of company sufficient, were it but known what I know of those countries; and by the proof of that wealth I hope yearly to return, if God please to bless me from such accidents, as are beyond my power in reason to prevent: For, I am not so simple to think, that ever any other motive than wealth, will ever erect there a commonwealth; or draw company from their ease and humors at home, to stay in New England to effect my purposes.

And lest any should think the toil might be insupportable, though these things may be had by labor, and diligence: I assure myself there are who delight extremely in vain pleasure, that take much more pains in England, to enjoy it, than I should do here to gain wealth sufficient: and yet I think they should not have half such sweet content: for, our pleasure here is still gains; in England charges and loss. Here nature and liberty affords us that freely, which in England we want, or it costeth us dearly. What pleasure can be more, than (being tired with any occasion[3] a-shore, in planting vines, fruits, or herbs, in contriving their own grounds, to the pleasure of their own minds, their fields, gardens, orchards, buildings, ships, and other works, &c.) to recreate themselves before their own doors, in their own boats upon the sea; where man, woman and child, with a small hook and line, by angling, may take diverse sorts of excellent fish, at their pleasures? And is it not pretty sport, to pull up two pence, six pence, and twelve pence, as fast as you can haul and veer a line?[4] He is a very bad fisher [that] cannot kill in one day with his hook and line, one, two, or three hundred cods: which dressed and dried, if they be sold there for ten shillings the hundred (though in England they will give more than twenty) may not both the servant, the master, and merchant, be well content with this gain? If a man work but

7. Lack.
8. Alone.
9. I.e., he won't promise that even with bad management they'll succeed.
1. I.e., or never read Smith's works.

2. I.e., once they have paid the cost of their support for the year.
3. Task.
4. I.e., fish.

three days in seven, he may get more than he can spend, unless he will be excessive. Now that carpenter, mason, gardener, tailor, smith, sailor, forgers,[5] or what other, may they not make this a pretty recreation though they fish but an hour in a day, to take more than they eat in a week? or if they will not eat it, because there is so much better choice; yet sell it, or change it, with the fishermen, or merchants, for anything they want. And what sport doth yield a more pleasing content, and less hurt or charge than angling with a hook; and crossing the sweet air from isle to isle, over the silent streams of a calm sea? Wherein the most curious may find pleasure, profit, and content.

Thus, though all men be not fishers: yet all men, whatsoever, may in other matters do as well. For necessity doth in these cases so rule a commonwealth, and each in their several functions, as their labors in their qualities may be as profitable, because there is a necessary mutual use of all.

For Gentlemen, what exercise should more delight them, than ranging daily those unknown parts, using fowling and fishing, for hunting and hawking?[8] and yet you shall see the wild hawks give you some pleasure, in seeing them stoop (six or seven after one another) an hour or two together, at the schools of fish in the fair harbors, as those ashore at a fowl; and never trouble nor torment yourselves, with watching, mewing,[6] feeding, and attending them: nor kill horse and man with running and crying, See you not a hawk?[7] For hunting also: the woods, lakes, and rivers afford not only chase sufficient, for any that delights in that kind of toil, or pleasure; but such beasts to hunt, that besides the delicacy of their bodies for food, their skins are so rich, as may well recompence thy daily labor, with a captains pay.

For laborers, if those that sow hemp, rape,[8] turnips, parsnips, carrots, cabbage, and such like; give twenty, thirty, forty, fifty shillings yearly for an acre of ground, and meat, drink, and wages to use it, and yet grow rich; when better, or at least as good ground, may be had, and cost nothing but labor; it seems strange to me, any such should there grow poor.

My purpose is not to persuade children [to go] from their parents; men from their wives; nor servants from their masters: only, such as with free consent may be spared: But that each parish, or village, in city, or country, that will but apparell their fatherless children, of thirteen or fourteen years of age, or young married people, that have small wealth to live on; here by their labor may live exceedingly well: provided always that first there be a sufficient power to command them, houses to receive them, means to defend them, and meet provisions for them; for, any place may be overlain:[9] and it is most necessary to have a fortress (ere this grow to practice) and sufficient masters (as, carpenters, masons, fishers, fowlers, gardeners, husbandman, sawyers, smiths, spinsters, tailors, weavers, and such like) to take ten, twelve, or twenty, or as there is occasion, for apprentices. The masters by this may quickly grow rich; these may learn their trades themselves, to do the like; to a general and an incredible benefit, for king, and country, master, and servant.

1616

5. I.e., ironworkers.
6. Keeping in a cage. "Stoop": swoop down.
7. Smith contrasts the delight of watching wild hawks hunt their prey in America with the tedious care that keepers of trained hawks in England must give their birds—as when such birds fly away and must be hunted for all over the countryside.
8. The rape plant.
9. Overcome.

From New England's Trials[1]

Here I must entreat a little your favors to digress. They[2] did not kill the English because they were Christians, but for their weapons and commodities, that were rare novelties; but now they fear we may beat them out of their dens, which lions and tigers would not admit[3] but by force. But must this be an argument for an Englishman,[4] or discourage any either in Virginia or New England? No: for I have tried them both.

For Virginia, I kept that country with thirty-eight, and had not[5] to eat but what we had from the savages. When I had ten men able to go abroad, our commonwealth was very strong: with such a number I ranged that unknown country fourteen weeks; I had but eighteen to subdue them all, with which great army I stayed six weeks before their greatest king's habitations, till they had gathered together all the power they could; and yet the Dutchmen sent at a needless excessive charge did help Powhatan how to betray me.[6]

* * *

For wronging a soldier but the value of a penny, I have caused Powhatan [to] send his own men to Jamestown to receive their punishment at my discretion. It is true in our greatest extremity they shot me, slew three of my men, and by the folly of them that fled took me prisoner: yet God made Pocahontas the king's daughter the means to deliver me: and thereby taught me to know their treacheries to preserve the rest.

It was also my chance in single combat to take the king of Paspahegh[7] prisoner: and by keeping him, [I] forced his subjects to work in chains till I made all the country pay contribution; having little else whereon to live.

Twice in this time I was their president, and none can say in all that time I had a man slain: but for keeping them in that fear I was much blamed both there and here: yet I left five hundred behind me that, through their confidence, in six months came most to confusion, as you may reade at large in the description of Virginia.[8]

1. Tests or experiments, not sufferings.
2. The Powhatans. Smith is here speaking of the massacre of three hundred forty-seven settlers in Jamestown, Virginia—one-quarter of that colony's English population—in March 1622. News of the massacre reached New England in May of that year. In mustering support for settlement in New England, he obviously had to take into account the dampening effect of events in Virginia.
3. Allow.
4. I.e., such events are not strong enough to dissuade an Englishman.
5. Nothing. "With thirty-eight": i.e., he protected or secured Virginia by means of a very modest force.
6. Several "Dutch" (probably German) skilled workers had been shipped to Virginia in 1608. Sent to build a house for Powhatan, they hinted to him that they would take his side against the English and soon were plotting against Smith and the colony. Arrested by the English and brought back to Jamestown for execution, they were saved when a new ship arrived from England, bringing fresh supplies and important new instructions for President Smith and Virginia's governing council.
7. The Algonquian name for the region around Jamestown. Smith took its werowance, or chief, Wowinchopunck, prisoner in 1609, an episode shown in an engraving in the *General History* (p. 120; see the lower left panel).
8. I.e., Smith's first book, which contains a section so titled. "President": Smith was president of the Virginia council for only a single term; he probably means "twice during the time I was their president these things happened," although the passage may have been garbled. "Confidence": i.e., overconfidence.

When I went first to these desperate designs, it cost me many a forgotten pound to hire men to go; and procrastination caused more [to] run away than went. But after the ice was broken, came many brave voluntaries: notwithstanding since I came from thence, the honorable company have been humble suitors to his Majesty to get vagabonds and condemned men to go thither; nay so much scorned was the name of Virginia, some did choose to be hanged ere they would go thither, and were: yet for all the worst of spite, detraction, and discouragement, and this lamentable massacre, there is more honest men now suitors to go, then ever hath been constrained knaves; and it is not unknown to most men of understanding, how happy many of those calumniators do think themselves, that they might be admitted, and yet pay for their passage to go now to Virginia: and had I but means to transport as many as would go, I might have choice of 10,000 that would gladly be in any of those new places, which were so basely condemned by ungrateful base minds.

To range this country of New England in like manner I had but eight, as is said, and amongst their brute conditions I met many of their silly encounters, and without any hurt, God be thanked; when your West country men[9] were many of them wounded and much tormented with the savages that assaulted their ship, as they did say themselves, in the first year I was there, 1614; and though Master Hunt, then master with me, did most basely in stealing some savages from that coast to sell, when he was directed to have gone for Spain.[1] * * * I speak not this out of vainglory, as it may be some gleaners,[2] or some [that] was never there may censure me: but to let all men be assured by those examples, what those savages are, that thus strangely do murder and betray our countrymen. But to the purpose.

What is already writ of the healthfulness of the air, the richness of the soil, the goodness of the woods, the abundance of fruits, fish, and fowl in their season, they still affirm that have been there now near two years, and at one draught they have taken 1000 basses, and in one night twelve hogsheads[3] of herring. They are building a strong fort, they hope shortly to finish, in the interim they are well provided: their number is about a hundred persons, all in health, and well near sixty acres of ground well planted with corn, besides their gardens well replenished with useful fruits; and if their adventurers would but furnish them with necessaries for fishing, their wants would quickly be supplied.[4]

To supply them this sixteenth of October is going the *Paragon* with sixty-seven persons, and all this is done by private men's purses. And to conclude in their own words, should they write of all plenties they have found, they think they should not be believed.

* * *

9. I.e., men from Southwest England. "Brute": tough.
1. Smith here refers to the tough going among earlier English voyagers to New England, especially Sir Ferdinando Gorges (1568–1647), a backer of Smith, and Thomas Hunt, who had been with Smith on the latter's 1614 voyage to the region. Hunt had stirred up much trouble with the local American Indians by kidnapping more than twenty of them, including the Native American Tisquantum (called Squanto by the Pilgrims) to sell into slavery in Spain.
2. Those who pick through events in search of bits of scandal.
3. Large casks. "Draught": haul of the fish net.
4. Here Smith speaks of the Plymouth settlers. "Adventurers": the investors who backed the Pilgrim venture.

Thus you may see plainly the yearly success from New England (by Virginia)[5] which has been so costly to this kingdom and so dear to me, which either to see perish or but bleed, pardon me though it passionate[6] me beyond the bounds of modesty, to have been sufficiently able to foresee it, and had neither power nor means how to prevent it. By that acquaintance I have with them, I may call them my children; for they have been my wife, my hawks, my hounds, my cards, my dice, and in total my best content, as indifferent to my heart as my left hand to my right:[7] and notwithstanding all those miracles of disasters [that] have crossed both them and me, yet were there not one Englishman remaining (as God be thanked there is some thousands) I would yet begin again with as small means as I did at the first. Not for that I have any secret encouragement from any I protest, more than lamentable experiences: for all their discoveries I can yet hear of, are but pigs of my own sow;[8] nor more strange to me than to hear one tell me he hath gone from Billingsgate and discovered Greenwich, Gravesend, Tilbury, Queenborough, Leigh, and Margate;[9] which to those [who] did never hear of them, though they dwell in England, might be made seem some rare secrets and great countries unknown: except the relations of Master Dirmer.[1]

* * *

What here I have writ by relation, if it be not right, I humbly entreat your pardons; but I have not spared any diligence to learn the truth of them that have been actors or sharers in those voyages: in some particulars they might deceive me, but in the substances they could not, for few could tell me anything, except where they fished. But seeing all those [that] have lived there, do confirm more than I have written, I doubt not but all those testimonies with these new-begun examples of plantation, will move both city and country freely to adventure with me and my partners more than promises, seeing I have from his Majesty letters patent,[2] such honest, free, and large conditions assured me from his commissioners, as I hope will satisfy any honest understanding.

1622

5. I.e., by Virginia's example; Plymouth had barely been settled, but the longer experience of the English in Virginia (with all its faults) could be used to suggest the probable course of events in New England.
6. Excite; imbue with passion.
7. I.e., as equally dear to me as one hand or the other.
8. The offspring of Smith's deeds; i.e., the accomplishments of others would not have been possible had he not gone before.
9. Well-known places in England.
1. Smith means that once he led the way into America, the English who followed him accomplished nothing truly bold. The exception was Captain Thomas Dermer (d. 1621), who had accompanied Smith to New England in 1614, had spent two years in Newfoundland (1616–18), and had returned to New England in 1619, in the process acquiring more knowledge about the region than Smith. (For more on Dermer, see references in Bradford's *Of Plymouth Plantation*, on p. 151 ff.)
2. I.e., official documents sealed with the king's signet.

WILLIAM BRADFORD
1590–1657

William Bradford's *Of Plymouth Plantation* offered the first sustained treatment of New England's early history, and it helped shape enduring cultural narratives about the small settlement that a group of religious dissenters known as the Pilgrims established on the Massachusetts coast in 1620. Written between roughly 1630 and 1650, *Of Plymouth Plantation* casts a backward look on the Plymouth colony's early history and seeks meaning in its major episodes. As he composed his retrospective account, Bradford revised more immediate, journalistic-style narratives such as *Mourt's Relation* (1622), which Bradford coauthored with Edward Winslow, another Plymouth leader. (See the excerpt in the "First Encounters" cluster, earlier in this volume.) He also incorporated and reworked his own notes. In the resulting narrative, Bradford portrays the uncertain and ambiguous emergence of providential meaning.

Bradford's life, with its many losses and dislocations as well as its strong if sometimes muted sense of purpose, provides a model of the Plymouth community. He was born in Yorkshire, in the northeast of England, a region still retaining marks of Viking invasions from centuries past. Bradford's father died when he was an infant, and he was passed among relatives and taught the arts of farming. His life changed at age twelve or thirteen, when he heard the sermons of Richard Clyfton. Clyfton was the Nonconformist minister of a small community in Scrooby, Nottinghamshire, a neighboring parish. Despite opposition from his uncles and grandparents, in 1606 Bradford left home and joined the community.

The members of the Scrooby church were known as "Separatists" because they were not sympathetic to the idea of a national Church, such as the one that King Henry VIII established in England after he broke with the pope. Separating from the Church of England was, however, by English law an act of treason, and many believers paid a high price for their dreams of purity. Other Puritan critics of the established Church, such as the non-Separating Congregationalists who eventually settled Boston, struck a middle path, retaining ties to the Church of England even as they developed a different organizational structure. Despite these differences, the churches at both Plymouth and the neighboring Massachusetts Bay Colony embraced John Calvin's Congregationalist model. Calvin (1509–1564), a French theologian, called upon Protestant reformers to set up "particular," independent churches, each founded on a formal covenant that would be sworn to by its members. In Congregational churches, God offered himself as a contractual partner to each believer in a contract freely initiated but perpetually binding. The model was twofold: the Old Testament covenant that God made with Adam and renewed through Jesus Christ, as well as the tight-knit communities of the early Christian churches.

Wishing to pursue their beliefs about church government more freely, the Scrooby community took up residence in the Netherlands, in Leiden (or Leyden), where Bradford joined them in 1609. But they suffered from continued government harassment, and with the Netherlands on the brink of war with Catholic Spain, the community took counsel from Captain John Smith and petitioned the English government for a grant of land in North America. In mid-September 1620, a portion of the congregation and a group of entrepreneurs sailed from Plymouth, England, for America. The rest of the congregation was expected to follow at some future time. The voyage on the *Mayflower* went relatively smoothly, though one person died, and there was

some friction with the often less-than-godly mariners. The colonists' original grant was for land in the Virginia territory, but high seas prevented them from reaching that area and, after an initial foray at Cape Cod, they settled just north of the Cape at an area they named Plymouth, adapting the name that Smith gave to the region in his 1614 expedition. Soon after the *Mayflower*'s arrival on the coast, Bradford's wife, Dorothy, fell overboard and drowned. However, little is known about this tragedy; strikingly, Bradford does not mention Dorothy's death in his journal or other writings.

In the second book of Bradford's history he describes the signing of the Mayflower Compact, a civil covenant designed to allow the temporal state to serve the devout citizen. It was the first of numerous "plantation covenants" intended both to protect the rights of citizens from the reach of established governments and to assert the community's authority to create its own "civil body politic" and make its own laws. The sense of communal purpose bolstered by the Compact helped sustain the Plymouth settlement through its difficult first months. Having arrived in winter and being inadequately provisioned, the company was decimated in the "Starving Time" that followed, losing half its members to disease and undernourishment. The colony's first governor, John Carver, was one of the fatalities, and Bradford was elected in Carver's place. As governor, Bradford was chief judge and jury, oversaw agriculture and trade, and made allotments of land. He also conferred with John Winthrop, a leader of neighboring Massachusetts Bay Colony, about matters of regional interest. Bradford served as governor for most of his remaining years.

Bradford was the first person to use the word "Pilgrims," from Hebrews 11.13 in the Geneva Bible, to describe the community of believers who sailed on the *Mayflower*. (The Geneva Bible, also known as the English Bible, was translated by Reformed English Protestants living in Switzerland; this version, used by Puritans, was outlawed by the Church of England.) For Bradford, as for the other members of this community, the decision to settle at Plymouth was the last step in their long journey to escape religious oppression in England. *Of Plymouth Plantation* situates their self-exile in the arc of Christian history as well as in the more recent events surrounding the Protestant Reformation, which sparked wars of religion that plagued England and the rest of Europe for generations. In the opening pages of his Plymouth history, Bradford invokes John Foxe's *Acts and Monuments* (1563), which relates the sufferings of Protestants under Mary Tudor, who as queen of England (1553–58) briefly reinstated Roman Catholicism and oversaw the execution by burning of some three hundred Protestants. Foxe's account, also known as *Foxe's Book of Martyrs*, was an iconic portrayal of Protestant oppression at the hands of Catholic authorities. The continued oppression of dissenters under Anglican rulers had driven the Plymouth colonists first to the Netherlands and then to America, where they hoped to find greater autonomy and opportunity.

This remote settlement was hardly isolated. Bradford locates Plymouth in an expanding network of relations with indigenous communities; with other English settlements, which had a mixture of commercial and religious imperatives; and with numerous European colonies. The latter included the neighboring Dutch colonies, which were Protestant; the more distant yet, ideologically speaking, more threatening French and Spanish colonies, which were Catholic; and the European colonies in the West Indies. Amid European colonization of the Americas, imperial rivalries, and religious conflicts, the Puritans sought to re-create the primitive simplicity of early Christianity.

Cotton Mather, in *Magnalia Christi America* (1702), his ecclesiastical history of New England, describes the self-educated Bradford as

> a person for study as well as action; and hence notwithstanding the difficulties which he passed in his youth, he attained unto a notable skill in languages. . . . But the Hebrew he most of all studied, because, he said, he would see with his

own eyes the ancient oracles of God in their native beauty. . . . The crown of all
his life was his holy, prayerful, watchful and fruitful walk with God, wherein he
was exemplary.

The primitivist impulse animating Bradford and his companions made the success
or failure of the Plymouth colony more than a worldly venture—it was a measure of
their ability to interpret God's will as they found it in Scripture and to remake the
world in its image.

However, the sense of unified purpose in the opening pages of Bradford's chron-
icle splinters as his account proceeds. Contributing to this fracture was the diffi-
culty that the Plymouth community had in finding a suitable minister. The group's
beloved pastor, John Robinson, died before he could cross the Atlantic. Several sub-
stitutes were inadequate or worse. Bradford relates the story of the Reverend John
Lyford, who served the colony for years. A secret Anglican sympathizer, Lyford betrayed
the colonists and was later implicated in misadventures and crimes, including
a rape. The Reverend Roger Williams briefly served the Plymouth church but left
after a few years for ideological reasons. Some of the other major episodes that tested
Bradford and the community, represented in the following selections, include the
conflict with Thomas Morton (whose competing version of these events is presented
later); tensions involving other colonies; the war with the Pequot Indians; an episode
of bestiality; and, perhaps most challenging for Bradford, the drift of people away from
Plymouth, drawn by economic opportunities, and the resulting divisions in the
church. Finding that his lifelong search for a stable, like-minded community had once
again been thwarted, the aging Bradford compared Plymouth to "an ancient mother,
grown old and forsaken of her children."

Bradford composed his history at the height of the English Civil War, and it
remained unpublished for over two centuries. The manuscript mysteriously dis-
appeared around the time of the American Revolution. The first book (through chap-
ter IX) had been copied into the Plymouth church records and was thus preserved, but
the second book was believed lost. In 1855 the manuscript was located in the palace
of the bishop of London, probably having been removed from Boston's Old South
Church by British soldiers or the departing Tory governor, Thomas Hutchinson. After
several decades of negotiations, the manuscript was returned to the United States in
1897 and deposited in the Massachusetts State Library.

Though not available in a printed edition until 1856, Bradford's manuscript was
a major source for other historians and interpreters of the New England experience,
such as Cotton Mather and Samuel Sewall. The incidents reported in Bradford's
history continued to guide interpretations of the New England past even when the
manuscript's location was unknown. In the early nineteenth century, the leading
political thinker and orator Daniel Webster traced the origins of the U.S. Constitu-
tion to the Mayflower Compact, contributing to the formation of a narrative about
the Puritan sources of American democracy that influenced the French writer Alexis
de Tocqueville's landmark study *Democracy in America* (1835, 1840). These develop-
ments in turn helped catalyze a literary reconsideration of the Puritan past. Some of
the major events that Bradford describes in *Of Plymouth Plantation* were cast into
fictional form by writers such as Nathaniel Hawthorne, whose story "The May-Pole
of Merry Mount" (written 1835–36) portrays the conflict between the Plymouth colo-
nists and Thomas Morton's settlement at Ma-re Mount, and Herman Melville, who
gave the name of the Pequot Indians to his ill-fated ship in *Moby-Dick* (1851).

Perhaps the main reason for Plymouth's continued place in American memory
today is its association with the Thanksgiving holiday. Thanksgiving feasts were
common practices in early modern Europe, where they were held on special occasions
to celebrate harvests and other important communal events, and this remained the
practice in the colonies and United States well into the nineteenth century. Presi-
dent Abraham Lincoln initiated Thanksgiving Day as a national holiday in 1863,

intending it as a unifying gesture in the midst of the Civil War. Seventy-six years later, President Franklin Delano Roosevelt moved the holiday from the last week of November to the previous week to help bolster retail sales during the Great Depression.

One striking thing about Bradford's narrative is how little his account of the "First Thanksgiving," in 1621, matches the popular image of that event, which features Puritans and Native Americans sharing the fruits of the land together. The vision of friendly cohabitation derives more directly from a passage in Bradford and Winslow's *Mourt's Relation*, which highlights the presence of the Wampanoag sachem (paramount chief) Massasoit and some ninety of his men, describes how "three days we entertained and feasted" them, and links the celebration to the "Covenant of Peace" between the colonists and the natives. In recounting the same event decades later, Bradford does not mention the Natives, the peace covenant, or a feast. Instead, he stresses the natural bounty that the community enjoyed and insists on the truthfulness of his earlier reports regarding the land's potential. Though elsewhere Bradford mentions the peace agreement with Massasoit, far more memorable is his account of the burning of Mystic Fort, one of the worst colonial atrocities, where the Puritans slaughtered some four hundred Pequot men, women, and children, backed up by their Narragansett allies.

The differences between the two firsthand descriptions of the Plymouth colonists' first thanksgiving suggest Bradford's shifting priorities and audiences. Once the leading edge of radical Protestant colonization, the small plantation at Plymouth came, after 1630, to be overshadowed by Boston and the Massachusetts Bay Colony, and then by rapidly evolving events in England: civil war, the execution of King Charles I, and the establishment of the Commonwealth of England. Toward the end of the period when he revised his history, the future of New England was in doubt. The overthrow of the British monarchy made some Puritan colonists, notably including Winslow, decide to cast their fortunes with the new regime. Bradford oriented the events that he chronicled toward the changing scenes in England, New England, and the larger Atlantic world.

When Bradford wrote in his opening paragraph that his goal was to relate the main events of the Plymouth colony's short history, making them "manifest in a plain style, with singular regard unto the simple truth in all things," he knew that his work would include matter that he elsewhere described as "tedious and uncomfortable." The full history oscillates between passages of crisp, descriptive prose, sometimes embellished with claims of providential significance, and murky, drawn-out accounts of uncertain financial and political dealings. The uneven texture of the narrative registers the challenges that Bradford faced in both relating the flow of events during a volatile historical moment and trying to discern the signs of God's will in those events.

Of Plymouth Plantation[1]

From *Book I*

FROM CHAPTER I. [THE ENGLISH REFORMATION]

* * * When as by the travail and diligence of some godly and zealous preachers, and God's blessing on their labors, as in other places of the land, so in the North parts,[2] many became enlightened by the word of God, and had

1. The text is adapted from William Bradford, *Bradford's History "Of Plimoth Plantation." From* *the Original Manuscript* (1897).
2. I.e., of England and Scotland.

their ignorance and sins discovered[3] unto them, and began by His grace to reform their lives, and make conscience of their ways, the work of God was no sooner manifest in them, but presently they were both scoffed and scorned by the profane[4] multitude, and the ministers urged with the yoke of subscription,[5] or else must be silenced; and the poor people were so vexed with apparitors, and the pursuivants, and the commissary courts,[6] as truly their affliction was not small; which, notwithstanding, they bore sundry years with much patience, till they were occasioned (by the continuance and increase of these troubles, and other means which the Lord raised up in those days) to see further into things by the light of the word of God. How not only these base and beggarly ceremonies were unlawful, but also that the lordly and tyranous power of the prelates ought not to be submitted unto; which thus, contrary to the freedom of the gospel, would load and burden men's consciences, and by their compulsive power make a profane mixture of persons and things in the worship of God. And that their offices and callings, courts and canons, etc. were unlawful and anti-Christian; being such as have no warrant in the word of God; but the same that were used in popery, and still retained. Of which a famous author thus writeth in his Dutch commentaries: At the coming of King James into England,

> The new king (saith he) found there established the reformed religion, according to the reformed religion of King Edward VI. Retaining, or keeping still the spiritual state of the bishops, etc. after the old manner, much varying and differing from the reformed churches in Scotland, France, and the Netherlands, Embden, Geneva, etc. whose reformation is cut, or shaped much nearer the first Christian churches, as it was used in the Apostles' times.[7]

So many therefore of these professors[8] as saw the evil of these things, in these parts, and whose hearts the Lord had touched with heavenly zeal for his truth, they shook off this yoke of anti-Christian bondage, and as the Lord's free people, joined themselves (by a covenant of the Lord) into a church estate, in the fellowship of the gospel, to walk in all his ways, made known, or to be made known unto them, according to their best endeavors, whatsoever it should cost them, the Lord assisting them. And that it cost them something this ensuing history will declare.

These people became two distinct bodies or churches, and in regard of distance of place did congregate severally; for they were of sundry towns and villages, some in Nottinghamshire, some of Lincolnshire, and some of Yorkshire, where they border nearest together. In one of these churches (besides others of note) was Mr. John Smith,[9] a man of able gifts, and a good preacher, who afterwards was chosen their pastor. But these afterwards falling into

3. Revealed.
4. Worldly.
5. I.e., threatened with forced compliance with the tenets of the Church of England.
6. "Apparitors . . . courts": the ecclesiastical courts and their officers.
7. Bradford quotes the Dutch historian Emanuel van Meteren's *General History of the Netherlands* (1608). King Edward VI reigned from 1547 to 1553. King James I reigned from 1603 to

1625. Most Puritans preferred the Calvinist system in Geneva or the Church of Scotland, which replaced a hierarchy of archbishops, bishops, and priests with a national assembly and a parish presbytery consisting of the ministers and elders.
8. Believers.
9. Not the soldier and explorer; a Cambridge University graduate who seceded from the Church of England in 1605.

some errors in the Low Countries,[1] there (for the most part) buried themselves, and their names.

But in this other church (which must be the subject of our discourse) besides other worthy men, was Mr. Richard Clyfton, a grave and revered preacher, who by his pains and diligence had done much good, and under God had been a means of the conversion of many. And also that famous and worthy man Mr. John Robinson,[2] who afterwards was their pastor for many years, till the Lord took him away by death. Also Mr. William Brewster[3] a reverent man, who afterwards was chosen an elder of the church and lived with them till old age.

But after these things they could not long continue in any peaceable condition, but were hunted and persecuted on every side, so as their former afflictions were but as flea-bitings in comparison of these which now came upon them. For some were taken and clapped up in prison, others had their houses beset and watched night and day, and hardly escaped their hands;[4] and the most were fain to fly and leave their houses and habitations, and the means of their livelihood. Yet these and many other sharper things which afterward befell them, were no other than they looked for, and therefore were the better prepared to bear them by the assistance of God's grace and spirit. Yet seeing themselves thus molested, and that there was no hope of their continuance there, by a joint consent they resolved to go into the Low Countries, where they heard was freedom of religion for all men; as also how sundry from London, and other parts of the land, had been exiled and persecuted for the same cause, and were gone thither, and lived at Amsterdam, and in other places of the land. So after they had continued together about a year, and kept their meetings every Sabbath in one place or other, exercising the worship of God amongst themselves, notwithstanding all the diligence and malice of their adversaries, they seeing they could no longer continue in that condition, they resolved to get over into Holland as they could; which was in the year 1607 and 1608.

* * *

CHAPTER IV. SHOWING THE REASONS AND CAUSES OF THEIR REMOVAL

After they had lived in this city about some eleven or twelve years (which is the more observable being the whole time of that famous truce between that state and the Spaniards)[5] and sundry of them were taken away by death, and many others began to be well stricken in years, the grave mistress Experience having taught them many things, those prudent governors with sundry of the sagest members began both deeply to apprehend their present dangers, and wisely to foresee the future, and think of timely remedy. In the agitation of their thoughts, and much discourse of things hereabout, at length they began to incline to this conclusion, of removal to some other place. Not out of any newfangledness, or other such like giddy humor, by which men are oftentimes transported to their great hurt and danger, but

1. The Netherlands.
2. Like John Smith and Richard Clyfton, a Cambridge graduate and a Separatist.
3. A church leader of the Pilgrims in both Leyden and Plymouth.
4. I.e., were nearly captured by the authorities.

5. The struggle for independence by provinces of the Netherlands, a Protestant country, against Spain, a Catholic country, was interrupted by a twelve-year truce that began on March 30, 1609; this truce was now coming to a close. "This city": Leyden.

for sundry weighty and solid reasons; some of the chief of which I will here briefly touch. And first, they saw and found by experience the hardness of the place and country to be such, as few in comparison would come to them, and fewer that would bide it out, and continue with them. For many that came to them, and many more that desired to be with them, could not endure that great labor and hard fare, with other inconveniences which they underwent and were contented with. But though they loved their persons, approved their cause, and honored their sufferings, yet they left them as it were weeping, as Orpah did her mother-in-law Naomi, or as those Romans did Cato[6] in Utica, who desired to be excused and borne with, though they could not all be Catos. For many, though they desired to enjoy the ordinances of God in their purity, and the liberty of the gospel with them, yet, alas, they admitted of bondage, with danger of conscience, rather than to endure these hardships; yea, some preferred and chose the prisons in England, rather than this liberty in Holland, with these afflictions. But it was thought that if a better and easier place of living could be had, it would draw many, and take away these discouragements. Yea, their pastor would often say, that many of those who both wrote and preached now against them, if they were in a place where they might have liberty and live comfortably, they would then practice as they did.

Secondly. They saw that though the people generally bore all these difficulties very cheerfully, and with a resolute courage, being in the best and strength of their years, yet old age began to steal on many of them (and their great and continual labors, with other crosses and sorrows, hastened it before the time), so as it was not only probably thought, but apparently seen, that within a few years more they would be in danger to scatter, by necessities pressing them, or sink under their burdens, or both. And therefore according to the divine proverb, that a wise man seeth the plague when it cometh, and hideth himself, Proverbs 22:3, so they like skillful and beaten soldiers were fearful either to be entrapped or surrounded by their enemies, so as they should neither be able to fight nor fly; and therefore thought it better to dislodge betimes to some place of better advantage and less danger, if any such could be found.

Thirdly; as necessity was a taskmaster over them, so they were forced to be such, not only to their servants, but in a sort, to their dearest children; the which as it did not a little wound the tender hearts of many a loving father and mother, so it produced likewise sundry sad and sorrowful effects. For many of their children, that were of best dispositions and gracious inclinations, having learned to bear the yoke in their youth,[7] and [being] willing to bear part of their parents' burden, were, oftentimes, so oppressed with their heavy labors, that though their minds were free and willing, yet their bodies bowed under the weight of the same, and became decrepit in their early youth; the vigor of nature being consumed in the very bud as it were. But that which was more lamentable, and of all sorrows most heavy to be borne, was that many of their children, by these occasions, and the great licentiousness of

6. Ancient Roman statesman of unbending integrity who committed suicide after being defeated in battle by the future emperor Julius Caesar. Orpah was the sister-in-law of Ruth, who did not leave their mother-in-law: "And they lifted up their voice, and wept again: and Orpah kissed her mother-in-law; but Ruth clave unto her" (Ruth 1.14).
7. "It is good for a man that he bear the yoke in his youth" (Lamentations 3.27).

youth in that country, and the manifold temptations of the place, were drawn away by evil examples into extravagant and dangerous courses, getting the reins off their necks, and departing from their parents. Some became soldiers, others took upon them far voyages by sea, and other some worse courses, tending to dissoluteness and the danger of their souls, to the great grief of their parents and dishonor of God. So that they saw their posterity would be in danger to degenerate and be corrupted.

Lastly (and which was not least), a great hope and inward zeal they had of laying some good foundation, or at least to make some way thereunto, for the propagating and advancing the gospel of the kingdom of Christ in those remote parts of the world; yea, though they should be but even as stepping-stones unto others for the performing of so great a work.

These, and some other like reasons, moved them to undertake this resolution of their removal; the which they afterward prosecuted with so great difficulties, as by the sequel will appear.

The place they had thoughts on was some of those vast and unpeopled countries of America, which are fruitful and fit for habitation, being devoid of all civil inhabitants, where there are only savage and brutish men, which range up and down, little otherwise than the wild beasts of the same. This proposition being made public and coming to the scanning of all, it raised many variable opinions amongst men, and caused many fears and doubts amongst themselves. Some, from their reasons and hopes conceived, labored to stir up and encourage the rest to undertake and prosecute the same; others, again, out of their fears, objected against it, and sought to divert from it, alleging many things, and those neither unreasonable nor unprobable; as that it was a great design, and subject to many unconceivable perils and dangers; as, besides the casualties of the seas (which none can be freed from) the length of the voyage was such, as the weak bodies of women and other persons worn out with age and travail (as many of them were) could never be able to endure. And yet if they should, the miseries of the land which they should be exposed unto, would be too hard to be borne; and likely, some or all of them together, to consume and utterly to ruinate them. For there they should be liable to famine, and nakedness, and the want, in a manner, of all things. The change of air, diet, and drinking of water, would infect their bodies with sore sicknesses, and grievous diseases. And also those which should escape or overcome these difficulties, should yet be in continual danger of the savage people, who are cruel, barbarous, and most treacherous, being most furious in their rage, and merciless where they overcome; not being content only to kill, and take away life, but delight to torment men in the most bloody manner that may be; flaying some alive with the shells of fishes, cutting off the members and joints of others by piecemeal, and broiling on the coals, eat the collops[8] of their flesh in their sight whilst they live; with other cruelties horrible to be related. And surely it could not be thought but the very hearing of these things could not but move the very bowels of men to grate within them, and make the weak to quake and tremble. It was further objected, that it would require greater sums of money to furnish such a voyage, and to fit them with necessaries, than their consumed estates would amount to; and yet they must as well look to be seconded

8. Slices, portions.

with supplies, as presently to be transported. Also many precedents of ill success, and lamentable miseries befallen others in the like designs, were easy to be found, and not forgotten to be alleged; besides their own experience, in their former troubles and hardships in their removal into Holland, and how hard a thing it was for them to live in that strange place, though it was a neighbor country, and a civil and rich commonwealth.

It was answered, that all great and honorable actions are accompanied with great difficulties, and must be both enterprised and overcome with answerable courages. It was granted the dangers were great, but not desperate; the difficulties were many, but not invincible. For though there were many of them likely, yet they were not certain; it might be sundry of the things feared might never befall; others by provident care and the use of good means, might in a great measure be prevented; and all of them, through the help of God, by fortitude and patience, might either be borne, or overcome. True it was, that such attempts were not to be made and undertaken without good ground and reason; not rashly or lightly as many have done for curiosity or hope of gain, etc. But their condition was not ordinary; their ends were good and honorable; their calling lawful, and urgent; and therefore they might expect the blessing of God in their proceeding. Yea, though they should lose their lives in this action, yet might they have comfort in the same, and their endeavors would be honorable. They lived here but as men in exile, and in a poor condition; and as great miseries might possibly befall them in this place, for the twelve years of truce were now out, and there was nothing but beating of drums, and preparing for war, the events whereof are always uncertain. The Spaniard might prove as cruel as the savages of America, and the famine and pestilence as sore here as there, and their liberty less to look out for remedy. After many other particular things answered and alleged on both sides, it was fully concluded by the major part, to put this design in execution, and to prosecute it by the best means they could.

*　　*　　*

FROM CHAPTER VII. OF THEIR DEPARTURE FROM LEYDEN, AND OTHER
THINGS THEREABOUT, WITH THEIR ARRIVAL AT SOUTHAMPTON,
WHERE THEY ALL MET TOGETHER, AND TOOK IN THEIR PROVISIONS

At length, after much travail and these debates, all things were got ready and provided. A small ship[9] was bought, and fitted in Holland, which was intended as to serve to help to transport them, so to stay in the country and attend upon fishing and such other affairs as might be for the good and benefit of the colony when they came there. Another was hired at London, of burden about nine score;[1] and all other things got in readiness. So being ready to depart, they had a day of solemn humiliation, their pastor taking his text from Ezra 8.21: "And there at the river, by Ahava, I proclaimed a fast, that we might humble ourselves before our God, and seek of Him a right way for us, and for our children, and for all our substance." Upon which he spent a good part of the day very profitably, and suitable to their present occasion. The rest of the time was spent in pouring out prayers to the Lord with great fervency, mixed with abundance of tears. And the time being come that they must

9. The *Speedwell*, with a capacity of sixty tons.
1. The *Mayflower* had a capacity of one hundred eighty tons.

depart, they were accompanied with most of their brethren out of the city, unto a town sundry miles off called Delfshaven, where the ship lay ready to receive them. So they left that goodly and pleasant city, which had been their resting place near twelve years; but they knew they were pilgrims,[2] and looked not much on those things, but lifted up their eyes to the heavens, their dearest country, and quieted their spirits. When they came to the place they found the ship and all things ready; and such of their friends as could not come with them followed after them, and sundry also came from Amsterdam to see them shipped and to take their leave of them. That night was spent with little sleep by the most, but with friendly entertainment and Christian discourse and other real expressions of true Christian love. The next day, the wind being fair, they went aboard, and their friends with them, where truly doleful was the sight of that sad and mournful parting; to see what sighs and sobs and prayers did sound amongst them, what tears did gush from every eye, and pithy speeches pierced each heart; that sundry of the Dutch strangers that stood on the quay as spectators, could not refrain from tears. Yet comfortable and sweet it was to see such lively and true expressions of dear and unfeigned love. But the tide (which stays for no man) calling them away that were thus loath to depart, their reverend pastor falling down on his knees, and they all with him, with watery cheeks commended them with most fervent prayers to the Lord and His blessing. And then with mutual embraces and many tears, they took their leaves one of another, which proved to be the last leave to many of them.

* * *

At their parting Mr. Robinson writ a letter to the whole company, which, though it hath already been printed,[3] yet I thought good here likewise to insert it, as also a brief letter writ at the same time to Mr. Carver,[4] in which the tender love and godly care of a true pastor appears:

My dear Brother, I received enclosed in your last letter the note of information, which I shall carefully keep and make use of as there shall be occasion. I have a true feeling of your perplexity of mind and toil of body, but I hope that you who have always been able so plentifully to administer comfort unto others in their trials, are so well furnished for yourself as that far greater difficulties than you have yet undergone (though I conceive them to have been great enough) cannot oppress you, though they press you, as the Apostle speaks.[5] The spirit of a man (sustained by the spirit of God) will sustain his infirmity;[6] I doubt not so will yours. And the better much when you shall enjoy the presence and help of so many godly and wise brethren, for the bearing of part of your burthen, who also will not admit into their hearts the least thought of suspicion of any the least negligence, at least presumption, to have been in you, whatsoever they think in others. Now what shall I say or write unto you and your good wife, my loving sister?[7]

2. "They were strangers and pilgrims on the earth" (Hebrews 11.13).
3. In *Mourt's Relation*.
4. John Carver (c. 1576–1621), the colony's first governor.
5. See 2 Corinthians 1.8 and Acts 18.5.
6. Proverbs 18.14.
7. Carver's wife was Robinson's sister.

Even only this, I desire (and always shall) unto you from the Lord, as unto my own soul; and assure yourself that my heart is with you, and that I will not forslow[8] my bodily coming at the first opportunity. I have written a large letter to the whole, and am sorry I shall not rather speak than write to them; and the more, considering the want of a preacher, which I shall also make some spur to my hastening after you. I do ever commend my best affection unto you, which if I thought you made any doubt of, I would express in more, and the same more ample and full words. And the Lord in whom you trust and whom you serve ever in this business and journey, guide you with His hand, protect you with His wing, and show you and us His salvation in the end, and bring us in the meanwhile together in the place desired, if such be His good will, for His Christ's sake.
Amen. Yours, etc.

July 27, 1620 John Robinson

This was the last letter that Mr. Carver lived to see from him. The other follows:

Loving and Christian friends, I do heartily and in the Lord salute you all, as being they with whom I am present in my best affection, and most earnest longings after you, though I be constrained for a while to be bodily absent from you. I say constrained, God knowing how willingly, and much rather than otherwise, I would have borne my part with you in this first brunt, were I not by strong necessity held back for the present. Make account of me in the meanwhile, as of a man divided in myself with great pain, and as (natural bonds set aside) having my better part with you. And though I doubt not but in your godly wisdoms, you both foresee and resolve upon that which concerneth your present state and condition, both severally and jointly, yet have I thought it but my duty to add some further spur of provocation unto them, who run already, if not because you need it, yet because I owe it in love and duty. And first, as we are daily to renew our repentance with our God, especially for our sins known, and generally for our unknown trespasses, so doth the Lord call us in a singular manner upon occasions of such difficulty and danger as lieth upon you, to a both more narrow search and careful reformation of your ways in his sight; lest He, calling to remembrance our sins forgotten by us or unrepented of, take advantage against us, and in judgment leave us for the same to be swallowed up in one danger or other; whereas, on the contrary, sin being taken away by earnest repentance and the pardon thereof from the Lord sealed up unto a man's conscience by His spirit, great shall be his security and peace in all dangers, sweet his comforts in all distresses, with happy deliverance from all evil, whether in life or in death.
 Now next after this heavenly peace with God and our own consciences, we are carefully to provide for peace with all men what in us lieth, especially with our associates; and for that watchfulness must be had, that we neither at all in ourselves do give, no, nor easily take offense being given by others. Woe be unto the world for offenses, for though it be necessary (considering the malice of Satan and man's corruption) that offenses come, yet

8. Delay.

woe unto the man or woman either by whom the offense cometh, saith Christ, Matthew 18.7. And if offenses in the unseasonable use of things in themselves indifferent, be more to be feared than death itself, as the Apostle teacheth, 1 Corinthians 9.15, how much more in things simply evil, in which neither honor of God nor love of man is thought worthy to be regarded. Neither yet is it sufficient that we keep ourselves by the grace of God from giving offense, except withal we be armed against the taking of them when they be given by others. For how unperfect and lame is the work of grace in that person, who wants charity to cover a multitude of offenses, as the scriptures speak.[9] Neither are you to be exhorted to this grace only upon the common grounds of Christianity, which are, that persons ready to take offense, either want[1] charity, to cover offenses, or wisdom duly to weigh human frailty; or lastly, are gross, though close hypocrites, as Christ our Lord teacheth, Matthew 7.1, 2, 3, as indeed in my own experience, few or none have been found which sooner give offense, than such as easily take it; neither have they ever proved sound and profitable members in societies, which have nourished this touchy humor. But besides these, there are diverse motives provoking you above others to great care and conscience this way: As first, you are many of you strangers, as to the persons, so to the infirmities one of another, and so stand in need of more watchfulness this way, lest when such things fall out in men and women as you suspected not, you be inordinately affected with them; which doth require at your hands much wisdom and charity for the covering and preventing of incident offenses that way. And, lastly, your intended course of civil community will minister continual occasion of offense, and will be as fuel for that fire, except you diligently quench it with brotherly forebearance. And if taking of offense causelessly or easily at men's doings be so carefully to be avoided, how much more heed is to be taken that we take not offense at God himself, which yet we certainly do so often as we do murmur at His providence in our crosses, or bear impatiently such afflictions as wherewith He pleaseth to visit us. Store up therefore patience against the evil day, without which we take offense at the Lord himself in His holy and just works.

A fourth thing there is carefully to be provided for, to wit, that with your common employments you join common affections truly bent upon the general good, avoiding as a deadly plague of your both common and special comfort all retiredness of mind for proper advantage, and all singularly affected any manner of way; let every man repress in himself and the whole body in each person, as so many rebels against the common good, all private respects of men's selves, not sorting with the general conveniency. And as men are careful not to have a new house shaken with any violence before it be well settled and the parts firmly knit, so be you, I beseech you, brethren, much more careful, that the house of God which you are, and are to be, be not shaken with unnecessary novelties or other oppositions at the first settling thereof.

Lastly, whereas you are become a body politic, using amongst yourselves civil government, and are not furnished with any persons of special eminency above the rest, to be chosen by you into office of government, let your wisdom and godliness appear, not only in choosing such persons as do

9. See 1 Peter 4.8. 1. Lack.

entirely love and will promote the common good, but also in yielding unto them all due honor and obedience in their lawful administrations; not beholding in them the ordinariness of their persons, but God's ordinance for your good, not being like the foolish multitude who more honor the gay coat, than either the virtuous mind of the man, or glorious ordinance of the Lord. But you know better things, and that the image of the Lord's power and authority which the magistrate beareth,[2] is honorable, in how mean persons soever. And this duty you both may the more willingly and ought the more conscionably to perform, because you are at least for the present to have only them for your ordinary governors, which yourselves shall make choice of for that work.

Sundry other things of importance I could put you in mind of, and of those before mentioned, in more words, but I will not so far wrong your godly minds as to think you heedless of these things, there being also divers[3] among you so well able to admonish both themselves and others of what concerneth them. These few things therefore, and the same in few words, I do earnestly commend unto your care and conscience, joining therewith my daily incessant prayers unto the Lord, that He who hath made the heavens and the earth, the sea and all rivers of waters, and whose providence is over all His works, especially over all His dear children for good, would so guide and guard you in your ways, as inwardly by His Spirit, so outwardly by the hand of His power, as that both you and we also, for and with you, may have after matter of praising His name all the days of your and our lives. Fare you well in Him in whom you trust, and in whom I rest.

<div style="text-align: right">

An unfeigned wellwiller of your happy
success in this hopeful voyage,

JOHN ROBINSON

</div>

This letter, though large, yet being so fruitful in itself, and suitable to their occasion, I thought meet to insert in this place.

All things being now ready, and every business dispatched, the company was called together, and this letter read amongst them, which had good acceptation with all, and after fruit with many. Then they ordered and distributed their company for either ship, as they conceived for the best. And chose a Governor and two or three assistants for each ship, to order the people by the way, and see to the disposing of their provisions, and such like affairs. All which was not only with the liking of the masters of the ships, but according to their desires. Which being done, they set sail from thence about the fifth of August.

<div style="text-align: center">

* * *

</div>

CHAPTER IX. OF THEIR VOYAGE, AND HOW THEY PASSED THE SEA;
AND OF THEIR SAFE ARRIVAL AT CAPE COD

September 6. These troubles being blown over,[4] and now all being compact together in one ship, they put to sea again with a prosperous wind, which continued divers days together, which was some encouragement unto them;

2. See Romans 13.4.
3. Several.
4. Some of Bradford's community sailed on the *Speedwell* from Delftshaven early in August 1620, but that ship's unseaworthiness forced their transfer to the *Mayflower*.

yet, according to the usual manner, many were afflicted with seasickness. And I may not omit here a special work of God's providence. There was a proud and very profane young man, one of the seamen, of a lusty,[5] able body, which made him the more haughty; he would always be contemning the poor people in their sickness, and cursing them daily with grievous execrations, and did not let[6] to tell them, that he hoped to help to cast half of them overboard before they came to their journey's end, and to make merry with what they had; and if he were by any gently reproved, he would curse and swear most bitterly. But it pleased God before they came half seas over, to smite this young man with a grievous disease, of which he died in a desperate manner, and so was himself the first that was thrown overboard. Thus his curses lighted on his own head; and it was an astonishment to all his fellows, for they noted it to be the just hand of God upon him.

After they had enjoyed fair winds and weather for a season, they were encountered many times with cross winds, and met with many fierce storms, with which the ship was shroudly[7] shaken, and her upper works made very leaky; and one of the main beams in the midships was bowed and cracked, which put them in some fear that the ship could not be able to perform the voyage. So some of the chief of the company, perceiving the mariners to fear the sufficiency of the ship, as appeared by their mutterings, they entered into serious consultation with the master and other officers of the ship, to consider in time of the danger; and rather to return than to cast themselves into a desperate and inevitable peril. And truly there was great distraction and difference of opinion amongst the mariners themselves; fain would they do what could be done for their wages' sake (being now half the seas over) and on the other hand they were loath to hazard their lives too desperately. But in examining of all opinions, the master and others affirmed they knew the ship to be strong and firm underwater; and [as] for the buckling of the main beam, there was a great iron screw the passengers brought out of Holland, which would raise the beam into his place; the which being done, the carpenter and master affirmed that with a post put under it, set firm in the lower deck, and otherways bound, he would make it sufficient. And as for the decks and upper works they would caulk them as well as they could, and though with the working of the ship they would not long keep staunch,[8] yet there would otherwise be no great danger, if they did not overpress[9] her with sails. So they committed themselves to the will of God, and resolved to proceed. In sundry of these storms the winds were so fierce, and the seas so high, as they could not bear a knot of sail, but were forced to hull,[1] for divers days together. And in one of them, as they thus lay at hull, in a mighty storm, a lusty young man (called John Howland) coming upon some occasion above the gratings, was, with a seele[2] of the ship thrown into [the] sea; but it pleased God that he caught hold of the topsail halyards, which hung overboard, and ran out at length; yet he held his hold (though he was sundry fathoms under water) till he was hauled up by the same rope to the brim of the water, and then with a boat hook and other means got into the ship again, and his life saved; and though he was something ill with it, yet he lived many years after,

5. Strong, energetic.
6. Hesitate.
7. Shrewdly, in its original sense of badly or dangerously.
8. Watertight.
9. Overburden.
1. Drift before the weather under very little sail.
2. Roll.

and became a profitable member both in church and commonwealth. In all this voyage there died but one of the passengers, which was William Butten, a youth, servant to Samuel Fuller, when they drew near the coast. But to omit other things (that I may be brief) after long beating at sea they fell with that land which is called Cape Cod; the which being made and certainly known to be it, they were not a little joyful. After some deliberation had amongst themselves and with the master of the ship, they tacked about and resolved to stand for the southward (the wind and weather being fair) to find some place about Hudson's River[3] for their habitation. But after they had sailed that course about half the day, they fell amongst dangerous shoals and roaring breakers, and they were so far entangled therewith as they conceived themselves in great danger; and the wind shrinking upon them withal, they resolved to bear up again for the Cape, and thought themselves happy to get out of those dangers before night overtook them, as by God's providence they did. And the next day they got into the Cape Harbor,[4] where they rid in safety. A word or two by the way of this cape; it was thus first named by Captain Gosnold and his company, Anno[5] 1602, and after by Captain Smith was called Cape James, but it retains the former name amongst seamen. Also that point which first showed those dangerous shoals unto them, they called Point Care, and Tucker's Terror, but the French and Dutch to this day call it Malabarr, by reason of those perilous shoals,[6] and the losses they have suffered there.

Being thus arrived in a good harbor and brought safe to land, they fell upon their knees and blessed the God of heaven, who had brought them over the vast and furious ocean, and delivered them from all the perils and miseries thereof, again to set their feet on the firm and stable earth, their proper element. And no marvel if they were thus joyful, seeing wise Seneca was so affected with sailing a few miles on the coast of his own Italy; as he affirmed, that he had rather remain twenty years on his way by land, than pass by sea to any place in a short time, so tedious and dreadful was the same unto him.[7]

But here I cannot but stay and make a pause, and stand half amazed at this poor people's present condition, and so I think will the reader, too, when he well considers the same. Being thus passed the vast ocean, and a sea of troubles before in their preparation (as may be remembered by that which went before), they had now no friends to welcome them, nor inns to entertain or refresh their weatherbeaten bodies, no houses or much less towns to repair to, to seek for succor. It is recorded in scripture as a mercy to the apostle and his shipwrecked company, that the barbarians showed them no small kindness in refreshing them,[8] but these savage barbarians, when they met with them (as after will appear) were readier to fill their sides full of arrows than otherwise. And for the season it was winter, and they that know the winters of that country know them to be sharp and violent, and subject to cruel and fierce storms, dangerous to travel to known places, much more to search an unknown coast. Besides, what could they see but a hideous and

3. The Hudson River, in New York.
4. They arrived at present-day Provincetown Harbor on November 11, 1620, after sixty-five days at sea.
5. In the year (Latin).
6. The prefix *mal* means "bad," a reference to

the dangerous sandbars.
7. Bradford cites *Moral Epistles to Lucilius*, by the Roman Stoic philosopher Seneca (4? B.C.E.–65 C.E.).
8. See Acts 28.1–2.

desolate wilderness, full of wild beasts and wild men? And what multitudes there might be of them they knew not. Neither could they, as it were, go up to the top of Pisgah,[9] to view from this wilderness a more goodly country to feed their hopes; for which way soever they turned their eyes (save upward to the heavens) they could have little solace or content in respect of any outward objects. For summer being done, all things stand upon them with a weatherbeaten face, and the whole country, full of woods and thickets, represented a wild and savage hue. If they looked behind them, there was the mighty ocean which they had passed, and was now as a main bar and gulf to separate them from all the civil parts of the world. If it be said they had a ship to succor them, it is true; but what heard they daily from the master and company? but that with speed they should look out a place with their shallop,[1] where they would be at some near distance; for the season was such as he would not stir from thence till a safe harbor was discovered by them where they would be, and he might go without danger; and that victuals consumed apace, but he must and would keep sufficient for themselves and their return. Yea, it was muttered by some, that if they got not a place in time, they would turn them and their goods ashore and leave them. Let it also be considered what weak hopes of supply and succor they left behind them, that might bear up their minds in this sad condition and trials they were under; and they could not but be very small. It is true, indeed, the affections and love of their brethren at Leyden was cordial and entire towards them, but they had little power to help them, or themselves; and how the case stood between them and the merchants at their coming away, hath already been declared. What could now sustain them but the spirit of God and His grace? May not and ought not the children of these fathers rightly say: "Our fathers were Englishmen which came over this great ocean, and were ready to perish in this wilderness; but they cried unto the Lord, and He heard their voice, and looked on their adversity,"[2] "Let them therefore praise the Lord, because He is good, and His mercies endure forever." "Yea, let them which have been redeemed of the Lord, show how He hath delivered them from the hand of the oppressor. When they wandered in the desert wilderness out of the way, and found no city to dwell in, both hungry, and thirsty, their soul was overwhelmed in them. Let them confess before the Lord His loving kindness, and His wonderful works before the sons of men."[3]

CHAPTER X. SHOWING HOW THEY SOUGHT OUT A PLACE OF HABITATION; AND WHAT BEFELL THEM THEREABOUT

Being thus arrived at Cape Cod the 11th of November, and necessity calling them to look out a place for habitation (as well as the master's and mariners' importunity), they having brought a large shallop with them out of England, stowed in quarters in the ship, they now got her out and set their carpenters to work to trim her up; but [she] being much bruised and shattered in the ship with foul weather, they saw she would be long in mending. Whereupon a few of them tendered themselves to go by land and discover those nearest

9. Mountain from which Moses saw the Promised Land (Deuteronomy 34.1–4).
1. Small vessel fitted with one or more masts.

2. Deuteronomy 26.6–8 [Bradford's note].
3. Psalm 107.1, 2, 4, 5, 8 [Bradford's note].

places, whilst the shallop was in mending, and the rather because as they went into that harbor there seemed to be an opening some two or three leagues off,[4] which the master judged to be a river. It was conceived there might be some danger in the attempt, yet seeing them resolute, they were permitted to go, being sixteen of them, well armed, under the conduct of Captain Standish,[5] having such instructions given them as was thought meet. They set forth the 15th of November, and when they had marched about the space of a mile by the seaside, they espied five or six persons with a dog coming towards them, who were savages, but they fled from them, and ran up into the woods, and the English followed them, partly to see if they could speak with them, and partly to discover if there might not be more of them lying in ambush. But the Indians seeing themselves thus followed, they again forsook the woods, and ran away on the sands as hard[6] as they could, so as they could not come near them, but followed them by the track of their feet sundry miles, and saw that they had come the same way. So, night coming on, they made their rendezvous and set out their sentinels, and rested in quiet that night, and the next morning followed their track till they had headed a great creek, and so left the sands, and turned another way into the woods. But they still followed them by guess, hoping to find their dwellings, but they soon lost both them and themselves, falling into such thickets as were ready to tear their clothes and armor in pieces, but were most distressed for want of drink. But at length they found water and refreshed themselves, [it] being the first New England water they drunk of, and was now in their great thirst as pleasant unto them as wine or beer had been in foretimes. Afterwards they directed their course to come to the other shore, for they knew it was a neck of land they were to cross over, and so at length got to the seaside, and marched to this supposed river, and by the way found a pond of clear fresh water, and shortly after a good quantity of clear ground where the Indians had formerly set corn, and some of their graves. And proceeding further they saw new stubble where corn had been set the same year, also they found where lately a house had been, where some planks and a great kettle was remaining, and heaps of sand newly paddled with their hands, which they, digging up, found in them divers fair Indian baskets filled with corn, and some in ears, fair and good, of divers colors, which seemed to them a very goodly sight (having never seen any such before). This was near the place of that supposed river they came to seek, unto which they went and found it to open itself into two arms with a high cliff of sand in the entrance, but more like to be creeks of salt water than any fresh, for aught they saw, and that there was good harborage for their shallop, leaving it further to be discovered by their shallop when she was ready. So their time limited them being expired, they returned to the ship, lest they should be in fear of their safety, and took with them part of the corn, and buried up the rest, and so like the men from Eshcol[7] carried with them of the fruits of the land, and showed their brethren, of which, and their return, they were marvelously glad, and their hearts encouraged.

4. This distance might have been six to nine miles.
5. Myles Standish (1584?–1656), a professional soldier who had fought in the Netherlands, was employed by the Pilgrims.

6. Fast.
7. In Numbers 13.23–26, scouts sent out by Moses to search the wilderness return after forty days with clusters of grapes picked near a brook they call Eschol.

After this, the shallop being got ready, they set out again for the better discovery of this place, and the master of the ship desired to go himself, so there went some thirty men, but found it to be no harbor for ships but only for boats. There was also found two of their houses covered with mats, and sundry of their implements in them, but the people were run away and could not be seen.[8] Also there was found more of their corn, and of their beans of various colors. The corn and beans they brought away, purposing to give them full satisfaction when they should meet with any of them (as about some six months afterward they did, to their good content). And here is to be noted a special providence of God, and a great mercy to this poor people, that here they got seed to plant them corn the next year, or else they might have starved, for they had none, nor any likelihood to get any till the season had been past (as the sequel did manifest). Neither is it likely they had had this, if the first voyage had not been made, for the ground was now all covered with snow, and hard frozen. But the Lord is never wanting unto his in their greatest needs; let his holy name have all the praise.

The month of November being spent in these affairs, and much foul weather falling in, the 6th of December they sent out their shallop again with ten of their principal men, and some seamen, upon further discovery, intending to circulate that deep bay of Cape Cod. The weather was very cold, and it froze so hard as the spray of the sea lighting on their coats, they were as if they had been glazed; yet that night betimes they got down into the bottom of the bay, and as they drew near the shore[9] they saw some ten or twelve Indians very busy about something. They landed about a league or two from them, and had much ado to put ashore anywhere, it lay so full of flats. [After their] being landed, it grew late, and they made themselves a barricade with logs and boughs as well as they could in the time, and set out their sentinel and betook them to rest, and saw the smoke of the fire the savages made that night. When morning was come they divided their company, some to coast along the shore in the boat, and the rest marched through the woods to see the land, if any fit place might be for their dwelling. They came also to the place where they saw the Indians the night before, and found they had been cutting up a great fish like a grampus,[1] being some two inches thick of fat like a hog, some pieces whereof they had left by the way; and the shallop found two more of these fishes dead on the sands, a thing usual after storms in that place, by reason of the great flats of sand that lie off. So they ranged up and down all that day, but found no people, nor any place they liked. When the sun grew low, they hasted out of the woods to meet with their shallop, to whom they made signs to come to them into a creek hard by, the which they did at high water, of which they were very glad, for they had not seen each other all that day, since the morning. So they made them a barricado (as usually they did every night) with logs, stakes, and thick pine boughs, the height of a man, leaving it open to leeward, partly to shelter them from the cold and wind (making their fire in the middle, and lying round about it), and partly to defend them from any sudden assaults of the savages, if they should surround them.

8. Descendants of these Nauset Indians, the Wampanoag, today live on the reservation in Mashpee, Cape Cod.

9. Near present-day Eastham.
1. Probably a pilot whale.

So being very weary, they betook them to rest. But about midnight, they heard a hideous and great cry, and their sentinel called, "Arm! arm," so they bestirred them and stood to their arms, and shot off a couple of muskets, and then the noise ceased. They concluded it was a company of wolves, or such like wild beasts, for one of the seamen told them he had often heard such a noise in Newfoundland. So they rested till about five of the clock in the morning, for the tide, and their purpose to go from thence, made them be stirring betimes. So after prayer they prepared for breakfast, and it being day dawning, it was thought best to be carrying things down to the boat. But some said it was not best to carry the arms down, others said they would be the readier, for they had lapped them up in their coats from the dew. But some three or four would not carry theirs till they went themselves, yet as it fell out, the water being not high enough, they laid them down on the bankside, and came up to breakfast. But presently, all on the sudden, they heard a great and strange cry, which they knew to be the same voices they heard in the night, though they varied their notes, and one of their company being abroad came running in, and cried, "Men, Indians, Indians," and withal, their arrows came flying amongst them. Their men ran with all speed to recover their arms, as by the good providence of God they did. In the meantime, of those that were there ready, two muskets were discharged at them, and two more stood ready in the entrance of their rendezvous, but were commanded not to shoot till they could take full aim at them, and the other two charged again with all speed, for there were only four had arms there, and defended the barricado, which was first assaulted. The cry of the Indians was dreadful, especially when they saw their men run out of the rendezvous toward the shallop, to recover their arms, the Indians wheeling about upon them. But some running out with coats of mail on, and cutlasses in their hands, they soon got their arms, and let fly amongst them, and quickly stopped their violence. Yet there was a lusty man, and no less valiant, stood behind a tree within half a musket shot, and let his arrows fly at them. He was seen [to] shoot three arrows, which were all avoided. He stood three shots of a musket, till one taking full aim at him, made the bark or splinters of the tree fly about his ears, after which he gave an extraordinary shriek, and away they went all of them. They[2] left some to keep the shallop, and followed them about a quarter of a mile, and shouted once or twice, and shot off two or three pieces, and so returned. This they did, that they might conceive that they were not afraid of them or any way discouraged. Thus it pleased God to vanquish their enemies, and give them deliverance; and by His special providence so to dispose that not any one of them were either hurt, or hit, though their arrows came close by them, and on every side them, and sundry of their coats, which hung up in the barricado, were shot through and through. Afterwards they gave God solemn thanks and praise for their deliverance, and gathered up a bundle of their arrows, and sent them into England afterward by the master of the ship, and called that place the "First Encounter." From hence they departed, and coasted all along, but discerned no place likely for harbor, and therefore hasted to a place that their pilot (one Mr. Coppin, who had been in the country before) did assure them was a good harbor, which he had been in, and they might fetch it before night, of which they were glad, for it began to

2. The English.

be foul weather. After some hours' sailing, it began to snow and rain, and about the middle of the afternoon, the wind increased, and the sea became very rough, and they broke their rudder, and it was as much as two men could do to steer her with a couple of oars. But their pilot bade them be of good cheer, for he saw the harbor; but the storm increasing, and night drawing on, they bore what sail they could to get in, while they could see. But herewith they broke their mast in three pieces, and their sail fell overboard, in a very grown sea, so as they had like to have been cast away; yet by God's mercy they recovered themselves, and having the flood[3] with them, struck into the harbor. But when it came to, the pilot was deceived in the place, and said, the Lord be merciful unto them, for his eyes never saw that place before, and he and the master's mate would have run her ashore, in a cove full of breakers, before the wind. But a lusty seaman which steered, bade those which rowed, if they were men, about with her, or else they were all cast away, the which they did with speed. So he bid them be of good cheer and row lustily, for there was a fair sound before them, and he doubted not but they should find one place or other where they might ride in safety. And though it was very dark, and rained sore,[4] yet in the end they got under the lee of a small island, and remained there all that night in safety. But they knew not this to be an island till morning, but were divided in their minds: some would keep the boat for fear they might be amongst the Indians; others were so weak and cold, they could not endure, but got ashore, and with much ado got fire (all things being so wet) and the rest were glad to come to them, for after midnight the wind shifted to the northwest, and it froze hard. But though this had been a day and night of much trouble and danger unto them, yet God gave them a morning of comfort and refreshing (as usually He doth to His children), for the next day was a fair sunshining day, and they found themselves to be on an island secure from the Indians, where they might dry their stuff, fix their pieces,[5] and rest themselves, and gave God thanks for His mercies, in their manifold deliverances. And this being the last day of the week, they prepared there to keep the Sabbath. On Monday they sounded[6] the harbor, and found it fit for shipping, and marched into the land, and found divers cornfields, and little running brooks, a place (as they supposed) fit for situation. At least it was the best they could find, and the season, and their present necessity, made them glad to accept of it. So they returned to their ship again with this news to the rest of their people, which did much comfort their hearts.

On the 15th of December they weighed anchor to go to the place they had discovered, and came within two leagues of it, but were fain to bear up again, but the 16th day the wind came fair, and they arrived safe in this harbor, and afterwards took better view of the place, and resolved where to pitch their dwelling,[7] and the 25th day began to erect the first house for common use to receive them and their goods.

3. Flood tide.
4. Heavily.
5. Weapons.

6. Measured the depth of.
7. The landing, at Plymouth, occurred on December 21.

From *Book II*

* * *

FROM CHAPTER XI.[1] THE REMAINDER OF ANNO 1620

I shall a little return back and begin with a combination[2] made by them before they came ashore, being the first foundation of their government in this place, occasioned partly by the discontented and mutinous speeches that some of the strangers[3] amongst them had let fall from them in the ship (that when they came ashore they would use their own liberty; for none had power to command them, the patent[4] they had being for Virginia, and not for New England, which belonged to another Government, with which the Virginia Company had nothing to do), and partly that such an act by them done (this their condition considered) might be as firm as any patent, and in some respects more sure.

The form was as followeth.

In the name of God, Amen. We whose names are underwritten, the loyal subjects of our dread sovereign Lord, King James, by the grace of God, of Great Britain, France, and Ireland king, defender of the faith, etc., having undertaken, for the glory of God, and advancement of the Christian faith, and honor of our king and country, a voyage to plant the first colony in the northern parts of Virginia, do by these presents solemnly and mutually in the presence of God, and one of another, covenant and combine ourselves together into a civil body politic, for our better ordering and preservation and furtherance of the ends aforesaid; and by virtue hereof to enact, constitute, and frame such just and equal laws, ordinances, acts, constitutions, and offices, from time to time, as shall be thought most meet and convenient for the general good of the Colony, unto which we promise all due submission and obedience. In witness whereof we have hereunder subscribed our names at Cape Cod the 11th of November, in the year of the reign of our sovereign lord, King James, of England, France, and Ireland the eighteenth, and of Scotland the fifty-fourth. Anno Domini[5] 1620.

After this they chose, or rather confirmed, Mr. John Carver[6] (a man godly and well approved amongst them) their governor for that year. And after they had provided a place for their goods, or common store, (which were long in unlading for want of boats, foulness of the winter weather, and sickness of divers)[7] and begun some small cottages for their habitation, as time would admit, they met and consulted of laws and orders, both for their civil and military government, as the necessity of their condition did require, still adding thereunto as urgent occasion in several times, and as cases did require.

1. Bradford did not number the chapters in Book II.
2. A form of union.
3. Bradford's term for the voyagers who were not members of the Separatist church.
4. A document signed by a sovereign granting privileges to those named in it.
5. In the year of the Lord (Latin).
6. A tradesman, like Bradford, and an original member of the group that went to Holland.
7. Several people. "Unlading": unloading.

[DIFFICULT BEGINNINGS]

In these hard and difficult beginnings they found some discontents and murmurings arise amongst some, and mutinous speeches and carriages[8] in other; but they were soon quelled and overcome by the wisdom, patience, and just and equal carriage of things by the governor and better part, which clave[9] faithfully together in the main. But that which was most sad and lamentable was, that in two or three months' time half of their company died, especially in January and February, being the depth of winter, and wanting houses and other comforts; being infected with the scurvy and other diseases, which this long voyage and their inaccommodate condition had brought upon them; so as there died sometimes two or three of a day, in the foresaid time; that of one hundred and odd persons, scarce fifty remained. And of these in the time of most distress, there was but six or seven sound persons, who, to their great commendations be it spoken, spared no pains, night nor day, but with abundance of toil and hazard of their own health, fetched them wood, made them fires, dressed them meat, made their beds, washed their loathsome clothes, clothed and unclothed them; in a word, did all the homely[1] and necessary offices for them which dainty and queasy stomachs cannot endure to hear named; and all this willingly and cheerfully, without any grudging in the least, showing herein their true love unto their friends and brethren, a rare example and worthy to be remembered. Two of these seven were Mr. William Brewster, their reverend elder, and Myles Standish, their captain and military commander, unto whom myself and many others were much beholden in our low and sick condition. And yet the Lord so upheld these persons, as in this general calamity they were not at all infected either with sickness or lameness. And what I have said of these, I may say of many others who died in this general visitation, and others yet living, that whilst they had health, yea, or any strength continuing, they were not wanting[2] to any that had need of them. And I doubt not but their recompense is with the Lord.

But I may not here pass by another remarkable passage not to be forgotten. As this calamity fell among the passengers that were to be left here to plant, and were hasted ashore and made to drink water, that the seamen might have the more beer, and one[3] in his sickness, desiring but a small can of beer, it was answered, that if he were their own father he should have none. The disease began to fall amongst them also, so as almost half of their company died before they went away, and many of their officers and lustiest men, as the boatswain, gunner, three quartermasters, the cook, and others. At which the master was something stricken and sent to the sick ashore and told the governor he should send for beer for them that had need of it, though he drunk water homeward bound. But now amongst his company there was far another kind of carriage in this misery than amongst the passengers: for they that before had been boon companions in drinking and jollity in the time of their health and welfare, began now to desert one another in this calamity, saying they would not hazard their lives for them, they should be

8. Attitudes.
9. Past tense of *cleave*: stuck closely. "Carriage": handling.
1. Intimate, domestic.

2. Lacking in attention.
3. Which was this author himself [Bradford's note].

infected by coming to help them in their cabins, and so, after they came to die by it, would do little or nothing for them, but if they died let them die. But such of the passengers as were yet aboard showed them what mercy they could, which made some of their hearts relent, as the boatswain (and some others), who was a proud young man, and would often curse and scoff at the passengers. But when he grew weak, they had compassion on him and helped him; then he confessed he did not deserve it at their hands, he had abused them in word and deed. "O!" saith he, "you, I now see, show your love like Christians indeed one to another, but we let one another lie and die like dogs." Another lay cursing his wife, saying if it had not been for her he had never come [on] this unlucky voyage, and anon cursing his fellows, saying he had done this and that, for some of them, he had spent so much, and so much, amongst them, and they were now weary of him, and did not help him, having need. Another gave his companion all he had, if he died, to help him in his weakness; he went and got a little spice and made him a mess of meat once or twice, and because he died not so soon as he expected, he went amongst his fellows, and swore the rogue would cozen[4] him, he would see him choked before he made him any more meat; and yet the poor fellow died before morning.

[DEALINGS WITH THE NATIVES]

All this while the Indians came skulking about them, and would sometimes show themselves aloof off, but when any approached near them, they would run away. And once they stole away their tools where they had been at work, and were gone to dinner. But about the 16th of March a certain Indian came boldly amongst them, and spoke to them in broken English, which they could well understand, but marveled at it. At length they understood by discourse with him, that he was not of these parts, but belonged to the eastern parts, where some English ships came to fish, with whom he was acquainted, and could name sundry of them by their names, amongst whom he had got his language.[5] He became profitable to them in acquainting them with many things concerning the state of the country in the east parts where he lived, which was afterwards profitable unto them; as also of the people here, of their names, number, and strength; of their situation and distance from this place, and who was chief amongst them. His name was Samoset; he told them also of another Indian whose name was Squanto, a native of this place, who had been in England and could speak better English than himself. Being, after some time of entertainment and gifts, dismissed, a while after he came again, and five more with him, and they brought again all the tools that were stolen away before, and made way for the coming of their great sachem,[6] called Massasoit, who, about four or five days after, came with the chief of his friends and other attendance, with the aforesaid Squanto. With whom, after friendly entertainment, and some gifts given him, they made a peace with him (which hath now continued this twenty-four years)[7] in these terms:

4. Cheat. "Mess": meal.
5. The Abnaki chief Samoset had encountered English fishing vessels in southern Maine; he picked up his English there and may have come south with Captain Thomas Dermer (see n. 1, p. 128; and see the reference to him below).
6. Chief.
7. Bradford's aside indicates that, having begun his history in 1630, he was writing this part in 1644.

1. That neither he nor any of his, should injure or do hurt to any of their people.
2. That if any of his did any hurt to any of theirs, he should send the offender, that they might punish him.
3. That if anything were taken away from any of theirs, he should cause it to be restored, and they should do the like to his.
4. If any did unjustly war against him, they would aid him; if any did war against them, he should aid them.
5. He should send to his neighbors confederates, to certify them of this, that they might not wrong them, but might be likewise comprised in the conditions of peace.
6. That when their men came to them, they should leave their bows and arrows behind them.

After these things he returned to his place called Sowams, some forty mile from this place, but Squanto continued with them, and was their interpreter, and was a special instrument sent of God for their good beyond their expectation. He directed them how to set their corn, where to take fish, and to procure other commodities, and was also their pilot to bring them to unknown places for their profit, and never left them till he died. He was a native of this place, and scarce any left alive besides himself. He was carried away with divers others by one Hunt, a master of a ship, who thought to sell them for slaves in Spain; but he got away for England, and was entertained by a merchant in London, and employed to Newfoundland and other parts, and lastly brought hither into these parts by one Mr. Dermer, a gentleman employed by Sir Ferdinando Gorges and others, for discovery, and other designs in these parts. Of whom I shall say something, because it is mentioned in a book set forth Anno 1622 by the President and Council for New England,[8] that he made the peace between the savages of these parts and the English, of which this plantation, as it is intimated, had the benefit. But what a peace it was, may appear by what befell him and his men.

This Mr. Dermer was here the same year that these people came, as appears by a relation written by him, and given me by a friend, bearing date June 30, Anno 1620. And they came in November following, so there was but four months difference. In which relation to his honored friend, he hath these passages of this very place:

> I will first begin (saith he) with that place from whence Squanto, or Tisquantum, was taken away, which in Capt. Smith's map is called Plymouth (and I would that Plymouth[9] had the like commodities). I would that the first plantation might here be seated, if there come to the number of fifty persons, or upward. Otherwise at Charlton,[1] because there the savages are less to be feared. The Pokanokets, which live to the west of Plymouth, bear an inveterate malice to the English, and are of more strength than all the savages from thence to Penobscot.[2] Their

8. I.e., *A Brief Relation of the Discovery and Plantation of New England* (1622), by Gorges (c. 1566–1647), an English colonial entrepreneur. Gorges had a patent for settling in northern New England, but he hired explorers and did not travel to America.
9. Here, Dermer means Plymouth, England. John

Smith published his *Description of New England* two years after his 1614 voyage. Tisquantum was Squanto's Indian name.
1. Near the mouth of the Charles River, in present-day Boston and Charlestown.
2. A large bay on Maine's central coast. "Pokanokets": the Wampanoags, the tribe of Massasoit.

desire of revenge was occasioned by an Englishman, who having many of them on board, made a great slaughter with their murderers[3] and small shot, when as (they say) they offered no injury on their parts. Whether they were English or no, it may be doubted; yet they believe they were, for the French have so possessed them; for which cause Squanto cannot deny but they would have killed me when I was at Namasket, had he not entreated hard for me. The soil of the borders of this great bay, may be compared to most of the plantations which I have seen in Virginia. The land is of diverse sorts, for Patuxet is a hardy but strong soil, Nauset and Satucket are for the most part a blackish and deep mould, much like that where groweth the best tobacco in Virginia.[4] In the bottom of that great bay is store of cod and bass, or mullet, etc.

But above all he commends Pokanoket for the richest soil, and much open ground fit for English grain, etc.

Massachusetts is about nine leagues from Plymouth, and situate in the midst between both, is full of islands and peninsulas, very fertile for the most part.

(With sundry such relations which I forbear to transcribe, being now better known than they were to him.)

He was taken prisoner by the Indians at Monomoit[5] (a place not far from hence, now well known). He gave them what they demanded for his liberty, but when they had got what they desired, they kept him still and endeavored to kill his men, but he was freed by seizing on some of them, and kept them bound till they gave him a canoe's load of corn. Of which, see Purchas, lib. 9, fol. 1778.[6] But this was Anno 1619.

After the writing of the former relation he came to the Isle of Capawack[7] (which lies south of this place in the way to Virginia), and the foresaid Squanto with him, where he going ashore amongst the Indians to trade, as he used to do, was betrayed and assaulted by them, and all his men slain, but one that kept the boat; but himself got aboard very sore wounded, and they had cut off his head upon the cuddy of the boat, had not the man rescued him with a sword. And so they got away, and made shift to get into Virginia, where he died, whether of his wounds or the diseases of the country, or both together, is uncertain. By all which it may appear how far these people were from peace, and with what danger this plantation was begun, save as the powerful hand of the Lord did protect them. These things were partly the reason why they[8] kept aloof and were so long before they came to the English. Another reason (as after themselves made known) was how about three years before, a French ship was cast away at Cape Cod, but the men got ashore, and saved their lives, and much of their victuals, and other

3. Small cannons.
4. If Dermer was not lying about the soil, it has been much degraded since his visit. Patuxet ("at the little falls") was the Indian name for Plymouth. Nauset, named for the local Indian tribe, was near present-day Eastham. Satucket ("near the mouth of the stream") was a Nauset village close to the town of Brewster.
5. Once a harbor near Orleans and Harwich.
6. Samuel Purchas (1577–1626) was an English

clergyman and collector of travel writings, famous for compiling the four-volume work to which Bradford refers: *Purchas His Pilgrimes* (1625). "Lib.": abbreviation for *liber*: book (Latin). "Fol.": abbreviation for *folio*: sheet, or page (Latin). This reference is to p. 1778 in book 9 of vol. 4.
7. Martha's Vineyard.
8. The Indians.

goods. But after the Indians heard of it, they gathered together from these parts, and never left watching and dogging them till they got advantage, and killed them all but three or four which they kept, and sent from one sachem to another, to make sport with, and used them worse than slaves (of which the foresaid Mr. Dermer redeemed two of them) and they conceived this ship[9] was now come to revenge it.

Also, as after was made known, before they came to the English to make friendship, they got all the powachs[1] of the country, for three days together, in a horrid and devilish manner to curse and execrate them with their conjurations, which assembly and service they held in a dark and dismal swamp.

But to return. The spring now approaching, it pleased God the mortality began to cease amongst them, and the sick and lame recovered apace, which put as it were new life into them, though they had borne their sad affliction with much patience and contentedness, as I think any people could do. But it was the Lord which upheld them, and had beforehand prepared them; many having long borne the yoke, yea from their youth. Many other smaller matters I omit, sundry of them having been already published in a journal made by one of the company,[2] and some other passages of journeys and relations already published, to which I refer those that are willing to know them more particularly. And being now come to the 25th of March, I shall begin the year 1621.

FROM CHAPTER XII. ANNO 1621
* * *
[THE FIRST THANKSGIVING]

They began now to gather in the small harvest they had, and to fit up their houses and dwellings against winter, being all well recovered in health and strength, and had all things in good plenty; for as some were thus employed in affairs abroad, others were exercised in fishing, about cod, and bass, and other fish, of which they took good store, of which every family had their portion. All the summer there was no want.[3] And now began to come in store of fowl, as winter approached, of which this place did abound when they came first (but afterward decreased by degrees). And besides waterfowl, there was great store of wild turkeys, of which they took many, besides venison, etc. Besides they had about a peck of meal a week to a person, or now since harvest, Indian corn to that proportion. Which made many afterwards write so largely of their plenty here to their friends in England, which were not feigned, but true reports.

* * *

FROM CHAPTER XIX. ANNO 1628
* * *
[MR. MORTON OF MERRYMOUNT]

About some three or four years before this time, there came over one Captain Wollaston, a man of pretty parts,[4] and with him three or four more of some eminency, who brought with them a great many servants, with provisions

9. The *Mayflower.*
1. Medicine men.
2. *Mourt's Relation.*

3. Lack.
4. I.e., of a clever nature.

and other implements for to begin a plantation, and pitched themselves in a place within the Massachusetts [Bay Colony] which they called, after their Captain's name, Mount Wollaston.[5] Amongst whom was one Mr. Morton,[6] who, it should seem, had some small adventure of his own or other men's amongst them, but had little respect amongst them, and was slighted by the meanest servants. Having continued there some time, and not finding things to answer their expectations, nor profit to arise as they looked for, Captain Wollaston takes a great part of the servants, and transports them to Virginia, where he puts them off at good rates, selling their time to other men;[7] and writes back to one Mr. Rasdall, one of his chief partners, and accounted their merchant, to bring another part of them to Virginia likewise, intending to put them off there as he had done the rest. And he, with the consent of the said Rasdall, appointed one Fitcher to be his lieutenant, and govern the remains of the plantation, till he or Rasdall returned to take further order thereabout. But this Morton abovesaid, having more craft than honesty (who had been a kind of pettifogger, of Furnivals Inn) in the other's absence, watches an opportunity (commons being but hard amongst them) and got some strong drink and other junkets, and made them a feast;[8] and after they were merry, he began to tell them, he would give them good counsel. "You see," saith he, "that many of your fellows are carried to Virginia; and if you stay till this Rasdall return, you will also be carried away and sold for slaves with the rest. Therefore I would advise you to thrust out this Lieutenant Fitcher; and I, having a part in the Plantation, will receive you as my partners and consociates; so may you be free from service, and we will converse, trade, plant, and live together as equals, and support and protect one another," or to like effect. This counsel was easily received; so they took opportunity, and thrust Lieutenant Fitcher out [of] doors, and would suffer him to come no more amongst them, but forced him to seek bread to eat, and other relief from his neighbors, till he could get passage for England. After this they fell to great licentiousness, and led a dissolute life, pouring out themselves into all profaneness. And Morton became lord of misrule,[9] and maintained (as it were) a school of Atheism. And after they had got some good into their hands, and got much by trading with the Indians, they spent it as vainly, in quaffing and drinking both wine and strong waters in great excess, and, as some reported, £10 worth in a morning. They also set up a maypole, drinking and dancing about it many days together, inviting the Indian women, for their consorts, dancing and frisking together, like so many fairies, or furies rather, and worse practices. As if they had anew revived

5. Now Quincy, Massachusetts.

6. Very little is known of Captain Wollaston or Thomas Morton other than what Bradford tells. Wollaston may have been Richard Wollaston, a ship's captain and sometime pirate. Morton (c. 1579–1647) trained as a lawyer in London, moved to New England in the 1620s. He tangled with Bradford, partly because of his anti-Puritanism and more liberal version of colonialism, presented in his *New English Canaan* (1637), excerpted below. Morton named his settlement Ma-Re Mount, or "Hill by the Sea." The Puritans sarcastically called it Merrymount.

7. A servant was someone employed in agricultural or domestic labor; the servants in this case

were indentured, meaning that their time had been purchased by their original employers (or masters) in exchange for their transportation to the colonies, and hence the remainder of their time could be sold to others.

8. The shifty lawyer ("pettifogger") Morton (who studied law at Furnivals Inn, one of London's Inns of Court), knowing that the settlers' ordinary food ("commons") was in short supply, threw a feast of alcohol and delicacies ("junkets") to win over the hearts and minds of the remaining servants.

9. The master of the carnival-like atmosphere of old English holidays, especially at Christmas.

and celebrated the feasts of the Roman Goddess Flora, or the beastly prac-
tices of the mad Bacchinalians.[1] Morton likewise (to show his poetry) com-
posed sundry rhymes and verses, some tending to lasciviousness, and others
to the detraction and scandal of some persons, which he affixed to this idle
or idol maypole. They changed also the name of their place, and instead of
calling it Mount Wollaston, they call it Merrymount, as if this jollity would
have lasted ever. But this continued not long, for after Morton was sent for
England (as follows to be declared) shortly after came over that worthy gen-
tleman, Mr. John Endicott, who brought over a patent under the broad seal,
for the government of the Massachusetts, who visiting those parts caused
that maypole to be cut down, and rebuked them for their profaneness, and
admonished them to look there should be better walking; so they now, or
others, changed the name of their place again, and called it Mount Dagon.[2]

Now to maintain this riotous prodigality and profuse excess, Morton,
thinking himself lawless, and hearing what gain the French and fishermen
made by trading of pieces,[3] powder, and shot to the Indians, he, as the head
of this consortship, began the practise of the same in these parts; and first
he taught them how to use them, to charge and discharge, and what pro-
portion of powder to give the piece, according to the size or bigness of the
same; and what shot to use for fowl, and what for deer. And having thus
instructed them, he employed some of them to hunt and fowl for him, so as
they became far more active in that employment than any of the English, by
reason of their swiftness of foot, and nimbleness of body, being also quick-
sighted, and by continual exercise well knowing the haunts of all sorts of
game. So as when they saw the execution that a piece would do, and the
benefit that might come by the same, they became mad, as it were, after
them, and would not stick to give any price they could attain to for them,
accounting their bows and arrows but baubles in comparison of them.

* * *

This Morton having thus taught them the use of pieces, he sold them all he
could spare, and he and his consorts determined to send for many out of
England, and had by some of the ships sent for above a score. The which
being known, and his neighbors meeting the Indians in the woods armed
with guns in this sort, it was a terror unto them, who lived stragglingly,[4] and
were of no strength in any place. And other places (though more remote)
saw this mischief would quickly spread over all, if not prevented. Besides,
they saw they should keep no servants, for Morton would entertain any, how
vile soever, and all the scum of the country, or any discontents, would flock
to him from all places, if this nest was not broken; and they should stand in
more fear of their lives and goods (in short time) from this wicked and
debauched crew, than from the savages themselves.

So sundry of the chief of the straggling plantations, meeting together,
agreed by mutual consent to solicit those of Plymouth (who were then of
more strength than them all) to join with them, to prevent the further growth

1. At the ancient revels in honor of Bacchus,
Roman god of wine, frenzied worshipers drank,
danced, and even tore apart wild animals and
devoured them. Flora, the Roman goddess of
flowers and vegetation, was the center of a cult
that put on risqué farces.

2. According to Judges 16.23–31, the Philistines
captured and tortured Samson, who brought
down the temple of the Philistine god Dagon.
3. Guns.
4. In a scattered fashion.

of this mischief, and suppress Morton and his consorts before they grew to further head and strength. Those that joined in this action (and after contributed to the charge of sending him for England) were from Piscataqua, Naumkeag, Winnisimmett, Wessaguset, Nantasket, and other places where any English were seated. Those of Plymouth being thus sought to by their messengers and letters, and weighing both their reasons, and the common danger, were willing to afford them their help, though themselves had least cause of fear or hurt. So, to be short, they first resolved jointly to write to him, and in a friendly and neighborly way to admonish him to forbear these courses, and sent a messenger with their letters to bring his answer. But he was so high as he scorned all advice, and asked who had to do with him; he had and would trade pieces with the Indians in despite of all, with many other scurillous terms full of disdain. They sent to him a second time, and bade him be better advised, and more temperate in his terms, for the country could not bear the injury he did; it was against their common safety, and against the King's proclamation. He answered in high terms as before, and that the King's proclamation was no law, demanding what penalty was upon it. It was answered, more than he could bear, His Majesty's displeasure. But insolently he persisted, and said the King was dead and his displeasure with him, and many the like things; and threatened withal that if any came to molest him, let them look to themselves, for he would prepare for them. Upon which they saw there was no way but to take him by force, and having so far proceeded, now to give over would make him far more haughty and insolent. So they mutually resolved to proceed, and obtained of the governor of Plymouth to send Captain Standish, and some other aid with him, to take Morton by force. The which accordingly was done. But they found him to stand stiffly in his defense, having made fast his doors, armed his consorts, set divers dishes of powder and bullets ready on the table; and if they had not been over-armed with drink, more hurt might have been done. They summoned him to yield, but he kept his house, and they could get nothing but scoffs and scorns from him; but at length, fearing they would do some violence to the house, he and some of his crew came out, but not to yield, but to shoot; but they were so steeled[5] with drink as their pieces were too heavy for them; himself with a carbine (over-charged and almost half filled with powder and shot, as was after found) had thought to have shot Captain Standish, but he stepped to him, and put by his piece, and took him. Neither was there any hurt done to any of either side, save that one was so drunk that he ran his own nose upon the point of a sword that one held before him as he entered the house, but he lost but a little of his hot blood.[6] Morton they brought away to Plymouth, where he was kept, till a ship went from the Isle of Shoals for England, with which he was sent to the Council of New England;[7] and letters written to give them information of his course and carriage; and also one was sent at their common charge to inform their

5. Insensible.
6. In his own book, Morton refers to Standish as "Captain Shrimp" and says it would have been easy for him to destroy these "nine worthies" like "a flock of wild geese," but that he loathed violence and asked for his freedom to leave. He suggests that he was treated brutally because the Pilgrims wished to shame him before the Indian

revelers.
7. The Council of New England was a joint stock company established by the British Crown in 1620. Its role was to colonize and govern New England. "Isle of Shoals": i.e., the Isles of Shoals, a group of small Atlantic islands straddling the borders of Maine and New Hampshire.

Honors more particularly, and to prosecute against him. But he fooled of the messenger, after he was gone from hence, and though he went for England, yet nothing was done to him, not so much as rebuked, for aught was heard; but returned the next year. Some of the worst of the company were dispersed, and some of the more modest kept the house till he should be heard from. But I have been too long about so unworthy a person, and bad a cause.

* * *

FROM CHAPTER XXIII. ANNO 1632

* * *

[PROSPERITY WEAKENS COMMUNITY]

Also the people of the plantation began to grow in their outward estates, by reason of the flowing of many people into the country, especially into the Bay of the Massachusetts, by which means corn and cattle rose to a great price, by which many were much enriched, and commodities grew plentiful; and yet in other regards this benefit turned to their hurt, and this accession of strength to their weakness. For now as their stocks increased, and the increase vendible,[8] there was no longer any holding them together, but now they must of necessity go to their great lots; they could not otherwise keep their cattle; and having oxen grown, they must have land for plowing and tillage. And no man now thought he could live, except he had cattle and a great deal of ground to keep them, all striving to increase their stocks. By which means they were scattered all over the bay, quickly, and the town, in which they lived compactly till now, was left very thin, and in a short time almost desolate. And if this had been all, it had been less, though too much; but the church must also be divided, and those that had lived so long together in Christian and comfortable fellowship must now part and suffer many divisions. First, those that lived on their lots on the other side of the bay (called Duxbury) they could not long bring their wives and children to the public worship and church meetings here, but with such burthen, as, growing to some competent number, they sued[9] to be dismissed and become a body of themselves; and so they were dismissed (about this time), though very unwillingly. But to touch this sad matter, and handle things together that fell out afterward: to prevent any further scattering from this place, and weakening of the same, it was thought best to give out some good farms to special persons, that would promise to live at Plymouth, and likely to be helpful to the church or commonwealth, and so tie the lands to Plymouth as farms for the same; and there they might keep their cattle and tillage by some servants, and retain their dwellings here. And so some special lands were granted at a place general, called Green's Harbor, where no allotments had been in the former division, a place very well meadowed, and fit to keep and rear cattle, good store. But alas! this remedy proved worse than the disease; for within a few years those that had thus got footing there rent themselves away, partly by force, and partly wearing the rest with importunity and pleas of necessity, so as they must either suffer them to go, or live in continual opposition and contention. And others still, as they conceived themselves straitened,[1] or to want accommodation, break away under one pretense or other, thinking

8. Salable.
9. Petitioned, requested.

1. Financially hampered.

their own conceived necessity, and the example of others, a warrant suffi-
cient for them. And this, I fear, will be the ruin of New England, at least of
the churches of God there, and will provoke the Lord's displeasure against
them.

* * *

FROM CHAPTER XXV. ANNO 1634

* * *

[TROUBLES TO THE WEST]

This year (in the forepart of the same) they sent forth a bark to trade at the
Dutch plantation, and they met there with one Captain Stone, that had lived
in Christopher's, one of the West Indies islands, and now had been some
time in Virginia, and came from thence into these parts.[2] He kept company
with the Dutch governor,[3] and, I know not in what drunken fit, he got leave
of the governor to seize on their[4] bark, when they were ready to come away,
and had done their market, having the value of £500 worth of goods aboard
her; having no occasion at all, or any color of ground for such a thing, but
having made the governor drunk, so as he could scarce speak a right word;
and when he urged him here about, he answered him, *Als 't u beleeft.*[5] So he
got aboard (the chief of their men and merchant being ashore) and with some
of his own men, made the rest of theirs weigh anchor, set sail, and carry her
away towards Virginia. But divers of the Dutch seamen, which had been
often at Plymouth, and kindly entertained there, said one to another, "Shall
we suffer our friends to be thus abused, and have their goods carried away,
before our faces, whilst our governor is drunk?" They vowed they would never
suffer it; and so got a vessel or two and pursued him, and brought him in
again, and delivered them their bark and goods again.

Afterwards Stone came into the Massachusetts, and they sent and com-
menced suit against him for this fact; but by mediation of friends it was taken
up, and the suit let fall. And in the company of some other gentlemen Stone
came afterwards to Plymouth, and had friendly and civil entertainment
amongst them, with the rest; but revenge boiled within his breast (though
concealed) for some conceived he had a purpose (at one time) to have stabbed
the governor, and put his hand to his dagger for that end, but by God's prov-
idence and the vigilance of some, was prevented. He afterward returned to
Virginia, in a pinnace, with one Captain Norton and some others; and, I
know not for what occasion, they would needs go up Connecticut River; and
how they carried themselves I know not, but the Indians knocked him in
the head, as he lay in his cabin, and had thrown the covering over his face
(whether out of fear or desperation is uncertain); this was his end. They like-
wise killed all the rest, but Captain Norton defended himself a long time
against them all in the cook room, till by accident the gunpowder took fire,
which (for readiness) he had set in an open thing before him, which did so
burn, and scald him, and blind his eyes, as he could make no longer resis-
tance, but was slain also by them, though they much commended his valor.

2. Captain John Stone, with a cargo of cattle
bound for Boston, had put into New Amsterdam
to replenish his water supply. "Bark": ship.
3. Wouter van Twiller, director-general of New
Netherland from 1633 to 1638.
4. I.e., Plymouth Plantation's.
5. As you please (Dutch).

And having killed the men, they made a prey of what they had, and chaffered away some of their things to the Dutch that lived there. But it was not long before a quarrel fell between the Dutch and them, and they would have cut off their bark, but they slew the chief sachem with the shot of a murderer.

I am now to relate some strange and remarkable passages. There was a company of people lived in the country, up above in the river of Connecticut, a great way from their trading house there, and were enemies to those Indians which lived about them, and of whom they stood in some fear (being a stout people). About a thousand of them had enclosed themselves in a fort, which they had strongly palisadoed about. Three or four Dutchmen went up in the beginning of winter to live with them, to get their trade, and prevent them [from] bringing it to the English, or to fall into amity with them, but at spring to bring all down to their place. But their enterprise failed, for it pleased God to visit these Indians with a great sickness, and such a mortality that of a thousand above nine hundred and a half of them died, and many of them did rot above ground for want of burial, and the Dutchmen almost starved before they could get away, for ice and snow. But about February they got with much difficulty to their trading house, whom they kindly relieved, being almost spent with hunger and cold. Being thus refreshed by them divers days, they got to their own place, and the Dutch were very thankful for this kindness.

This spring, also, those Indians that lived about their trading house[6] there fell sick of the smallpox, and died most miserably, for a sorer disease cannot befall them. They fear it more than the plague, for usually they that have this disease have them[7] in abundance, and for want of bedding and linen and other helps, they fall into a lamentable condition, as they lie on their hard mats, the pox breaking and mattering, and running one into another, their skin cleaving (by reason thereof) to the mats they lie on. When they turn them, a whole side will flay off at once, as it were, and they will be all of a gore blood, most fearful to behold; and then being very sore, what with cold and other distempers, they die like rotten sheep. The condition of this people was so lamentable, and they fell down so generally of this disease, as they were in the end not able to help one another; no, not to make a fire, nor to fetch a little water to drink, nor any to bury the dead; but would strive as long as they could, and when they could procure no other means to make fire, they would burn the wooden trays and dishes they ate their meat in, and their very bows and arrows; and some would crawl out on all four to get a little water, and sometimes die by the way, and not be able to get in again. But those of the English house, though at first they were afraid of the infection, yet seeing their woeful and sad condition and hearing their pitiful cries and lamentations, they had compassion of them, and daily fetched them wood and water, and made them fires, got them victuals whilst they lived, and buried them when they died. For very few of them escaped, notwithstanding they did what they could for them, to the hazard of themselves. The chief sachem himself now died, and almost all his friends and kindred. But by the marvelous goodness and providence of God not one of the English

6. The Plymouth outpost at present-day Windsor.

7. I.e., the skin eruptions characteristic of smallpox.

was so much as sick, or in the least measure tainted with this disease, though they daily did these offices for them for many weeks together. And this mercy which they showed them was kindly taken, and thankfully acknowledged of all the Indians that knew or heard of the same; and their masters here did much commend and reward them for the same.

* * *

FROM CHAPTER XXVII. ANNO 1636

* * *

[WAR THREATS]

In the year 1634, the Pequots (a stout and warlike people), who had made wars with sundry of their neighbors, and puffed up with many victories, grew now at variance with the Narragansetts, a great people bordering upon them. These Narragansetts held correspondence and terms of friendship with the English of the Massachusetts. Now the Pequots, being conscious of the guilt of Captain Stone's death, whom they knew to be an Englishman, as also those that were with him, and being fallen out with the Dutch, lest they should have over many enemies at once, sought to make friendship with the English of the Massachusetts, and for that end sent both messengers and gifts unto them, as appears by some letters sent from the governor hither:

> Dear and worthy Sir: etc. To let you know somewhat of our affairs, you may understand that the Pequots have sent some of theirs to us, to desire our friendship, and offered much wampum[8] and beaver, etc. The first messengers were dismissed without answer; with the next we had divers days conference, and taking the advice of some of our ministers, and seeking the Lord in it, we concluded a peace and friendship with them, upon these conditions: that they should deliver up to us those men who were guilty of Stone's death, etc. And if we desired to plant in Connecticut, they should give up their right to us, and so we would send to trade with them as our friends (which was the chief thing we aimed at, being now in war with the Dutch and the rest of their neighbors). To this they readily agreed, and that we should mediate a peace between them and the Narragansetts, for which end they were content we should give the Narragansetts part of that present they would bestow on us (for they stood so much on their honor, as they would not be seen to give anything of themselves). As for Captain Stone, they told us there were but two left of those who had any hand in his death, and that they killed him in a just quarrel, for (say they) he surprised two of our men, and bound them, to make them by force to show him the way up the river,[9] and he with two other coming on shore, nine Indians watched him, and when they were asleep in the night, they killed them, to deliver their own men; and some of them going afterwards to the pinnace, it was suddenly blown up. We are now preparing to send a pinnace unto them, etc.

In another of his, dated the 12th of the first month, he hath this:

8. Beads of polished shells, used as money.
9. There is little trust to be given to their rela- tions in these things [Bradford's note].

Our pinnace is lately returned from the Pequots; they put off but little commodity, and found them a very false people, so as they mean to have no more to do with them. I have divers other things to write unto you, etc.

Yours ever assured,
JOHN WINTHROP

Boston, 12th of the 1st month, 1634

After these things, and, as I take, this year, John Oldham (of whom much is spoken before), being now an inhabitant of the Massachusetts, went with a small vessel and slenderly manned, a-trading into these south parts, and upon a quarrel between him and the Indians was cut off by them (as hath been before noted) at an island called by the Indians Munisses, but since by the English Block Island. This, with the former about the death of Stone, and the baffling[1] of the Pequots with the English of the Massachusetts, moved them to set out some to take revenge, and require satisfaction for these wrongs; but it was done so superficially, and without their acquainting of those of Connecticut and other neighbors with the same, as they did little good. But their neighbors had more hurt done, for some of the murderers of Oldham fled to the Pequots, and though the English went to the Pequots, and had some parley with them, yet they did but delude them, and the English returned without doing anything to purpose, being frustrate of their opportunity by the others' deceit.[2] After the English were returned, the Pequots took their time and opportunity to cut off some of the English as they passed in boats, and went on fowling, and assaulted them the next spring at their habitations, as will appear in its place. I do but touch these things, because I make no question they will be more fully and distinctly handled by themselves, who had more exact knowledge of them, and whom they did more properly concern.

* * *

FROM CHAPTER XXVIII. ANNO 1637

* * *

[WAR WITH THE PEQUOTS]

In the fore part of this year, the Pequots fell openly upon the English at Connecticut, in the lower parts of the river, and slew sundry of them as they were at work in the fields, both men and women, to the great terror of the rest, and went away in great pride and triumph, with many high threats. They also assaulted a fort at the river's mouth, though strong and well defended; and though they did not there prevail, yet it struck them with much fear and astonishment to see their bold attempts in the face of danger, which made them in all places to stand upon their guard, and to prepare for resistance, and earnestly to solicit their friends and confederates in the Bay of Massachusetts to send them speedy aid, for they looked for more forcible assaults. Mr. Vane, being then governor, writ from their General Court to them here, to join with them in this war, to which they were cordially willing, but took

1. Frustration.
2. Under orders from Massachusetts Bay, John Endicott led an expedition into Pequot country in late August 1637 that served only to stir up the anger of the Indians.

opportunity to write to them about some former things, as well as present, considerable hereabout.

<center>* * *</center>

In the meantime, the Pequots, especially in the winter before, sought to make peace with the Narragansetts, and used very pernicious arguments to move them thereunto: as that the English were strangers and began to overspread their country, and would deprive them thereof in time, if they were suffered to grow and increase; and if the Narragansetts did assist the English to subdue them, they did but make way for their own overthrow, for if they were rooted out, the English would soon take occasion to subjugate them. And if they would harken to them, they should not need to fear the strength of the English, for they would not come to open battle with them, but fire their houses, kill their cattle, and lie in ambush for them as they went abroad upon their occasions, and all this they might easily do without any or little danger to themselves. The which course being held, they well saw the English could not long subsist, but they would either be starved with hunger, or be forced to forsake the country; with many the like things, insomuch that the Narragansetts were once wavering, and were half minded to have made peace with them, and joined against the English. But again when they considered, how much wrong they had received from the Pequots, and what an opportunity they now had by the help of the English to right themselves, revenge was so sweet unto them, as it prevailed above all the rest, so as they resolved to join with the English against them, and did. The Court here agreed forthwith to send fifty men at their own charge, and with as much speed as possibly they could, got them armed, and had made them ready under sufficient leaders, and provided a bark to carry them provisions and tend upon them for all occasions. But when they were ready to march (with a supply from the Bay) they had word to stay, for the enemy was as good as vanquished, and there would be no need.

I shall not take upon me exactly to describe their proceedings in these things, because I expect it will be fully done by themselves, who best know the carriage and circumstances of things; I shall therefore but touch them in general. From Connecticut (who were most sensible of the hurt sustained, and the present danger), they set out a party of men, and another party met them from the Bay, at the Narragansetts, who were to join with them. The Narragansetts were earnest to be gone before the English were well rested and refreshed, especially some of them which came last. It should seem their desire was to come upon the enemy suddenly, and undiscovered. There was a bark of this place, newly put in there, which was come from Connecticut, who did encourage them to lay hold of the Indians' forwardness, and to show as great forwardness as they, for it would encourage them, and expedition[3] might prove to their great advantage. So they went on, and so ordered their march, as the Indians brought them to a fort of the enemy's[4] (in which most of their chief men were) before day. They approached the same with great silence, and surrounded it both with English and Indians, that they might not break out, and so assaulted them with great courage, shooting amongst

3. Speed.
4. A fortified Pequot village near the Mystic River.

them, and entered the fort with all speed; and those that first entered found sharp resistance from the enemy, who both shot at and grappled with them. Others ran into their houses, and brought out fire, and set them on fire, which soon took in their mats, and, standing close together, with the wind, all was quickly on a flame, and thereby more were burnt to death than was otherwise slain. It burnt their bowstrings, and made them unserviceable. Those that escaped the fire were slain with the sword; some hewed to pieces, others run through with their rapiers, so as they were quickly dispatched, and very few escaped. It was conceived they thus destroyed about four hundred at this time. It was a fearful sight to see them thus frying in the fire, and the streams of blood quenching the same, and horrible was the stink and scent thereof; but the victory seemed a sweet sacrifice,[5] and they gave the praise thereof to God, who had wrought so wonderfully for them, thus to enclose their enemies in their hands, and give them so speedy a victory over so proud and insulting an enemy. The Narragansett Indians, all this while, stood round about, but aloof from all danger, and left the whole execution to the English, except it were the stopping of any that broke away, insulting over their enemies in this their ruin and misery, when they saw them dancing in the flames, calling them by a word in their own language, signifying, "O brave Pequots!" which they used familiarly among themselves in their own praise, in songs of triumph after their victories. After this service was thus happily accomplished, they marched to the waterside, where they met with some of their vessels, by which they had refreshing with victuals and other necessaries. But in their march the rest of the Pequots drew into a body, and accosted them, thinking to have some advantage against them by reason of a neck of land, but when they saw the English prepare for them, they kept aloof, so as they neither did hurt, nor could receive any. After their refreshing and repair together for further counsel and directions, they resolved to pursue their victory, and follow the war against the rest, but the Narragansett Indians most of them forsook them, and such of them as they had with them for guides, or otherwise, they found them very cold and backward in the business, either out of envy, or that they saw the English would make more profit of the victory than they were willing they should, or else deprive them of such advantage as themselves desired by having them become tributaries unto them, or the like.

* * *

That I may make an end of this matter: this Sassacus (the Pequots' chief sachem)[6] being fled to the Mohawks, they cut off his head, with some other of the chief of them, whether to satisfy the English, or rather the Narragansetts (who, as I have since heard, hired them to do it) or for their own advantage, I well know not; but thus this war took end. The rest of the Pequots were wholly driven from their place, and some of them submitted themselves to the Narragansetts, and lived under them; others of them betook themselves to the Mohegans, under Uncas, their sachem, with the approbation of the English of Connecticut, under whose protection Uncas lived, and he and his men had been faithful to them in this war, and done them very good service. But this did so vex the Narragansetts, that they had not the whole

5. See Leviticus 2.2.
6. Reportedly seventy-seven years old at the time, Sassacus held sway over much of southern New England before the war.

sway over them, as they have never ceased plotting and contriving how to bring them under, and because they cannot attain their ends, because of the English who have protected them, they have sought to raise a general conspiracy against the English.

* * *

FROM CHAPTER XXXII. ANNO 1642

* * *

[A HORRIBLE TRUTH]

There was a youth whose name was Thomas Granger; he was servant to an honest man of Duxbury, being about sixteen or seventeen years of age. (His father and mother lived at the same time at Scituate.) He was this year detected of buggery, and indicted for the same, with a mare, a cow, two goats, five sheep, two calves, and a turkey. Horrible it is to mention, but the truth of the history requires it. He was first discovered by one that accidentally saw his lewd practice towards the mare. (I forbear particulars.) Being upon it examined and committed, in the end he not only confessed the fact with that beast at that time, but sundry times before, and at several times with all the rest of the forenamed in his indictment; and this his free confession was not only in private to the magistrates, though at first he strived to deny it, but to sundry, both ministers and others, and afterwards, upon his indictment, to the whole court and jury, and confirmed it at his execution. And whereas some of the sheep could not so well be known by his description of them, others with them were brought before him, and he declared which were they, and which were not. And accordingly he was cast by the jury, and condemned, and after executed about the 8th of September, 1642. A very sad spectacle it was; for first the mare, and then the cow, and the rest of the lesser cattle, were killed before his face, according to the law, Leviticus 20.15,[7] and then he himself was executed. The cattle were all cast into a great and large pit that was digged of purpose for them, and no use made of any part of them.

Upon the examination of this person, and also of a former that had made some sodomitical attempts upon another, it being demanded of them how they came first to the knowledge and practice of such wickedness, the one confessed he had long used it in old England; and this youth last spoken of said he was taught it by another that had heard of such things from some in England when he was there, and they kept cattle together. By which it appears how one wicked person may infect many, and what care all ought to have what servants they bring into their families.

But it may be demanded how came it to pass that so many wicked persons and profane people should so quickly come over into this land, and mix themselves amongst them, seeing it was religious men that began the work, and they came for religion's sake. I confess this may be marveled at, at least in time to come, when the reasons thereof should not be known; and the more because here was so many hardships and wants met withal. I shall therefore endeavor to give some answer hereunto. And first, according to that in the gospel, it is ever to be remembered that where the Lord begins to sow

7. "And if a man lie with a beast, he shall surely be put to death: and ye shall slay the beast."

good seed, there the envious man will endeavor to sow tares.[8] Secondly, men being to come over into a wilderness, in which much labor and service was to be done about building and planting, etc., such as wanted help in that respect, when they could not have such as they would, were glad to take such as they could; and so, many untoward servants, sundry of them proved, that were thus brought over, both men and women kind; who, when their times were expired, became families of themselves, which gave increase hereunto. Thirdly, another and a main reason hereof was, that men, finding so many godly disposed persons willing to come into these parts, some began to make a trade of it, to transport passengers and their goods, and hired ships for that end; and then, to make up their freight and advance their profit, cared not who the persons were, so they had money to pay them. And by this means the country became pestered with many unworthy persons, who, being come over, crept into one place or other. Fourthly, again, the Lord's blessing usually following his people, as well in outward as spiritual things (though afflictions be mixed withal) do make many to adhere to the people of God, as many followed Christ, for the loaves' sake, John 6.26, and a mixed multitude came into the wilderness with the people of God out of Egypt of old, Exodus 12.38. So also there were sent by their friends some under hope that they would be made better; others that they might be eased of such burthens, and they kept from shame at home that would necessarily follow their dissolute courses. And thus, by one means or other, in twenty years' time, it is a question whether the greater part be not grown the worser.

* * *

FROM CHAPTER XXXIV. ANNO 1644

* * *

[PROPOSED REMOVAL TO NAUSET]

Mr. Edward Winslow was chosen governor this year.

Many having left this place,[9] as is before noted, by reason of the straitness and barrenness of the same, and their finding of better accommodations elsewhere, more suitable to their ends and minds; and sundry others still upon every occasion desiring their dismissions, the church began seriously to think whether it were not better jointly to remove to some other place, than to be thus weakened, and as it were insensibly dissolved. Many meetings and much consultation was held hereabout, and divers[1] were men's minds and opinions. Some were still for staying together in this place, alleging men might here live, if they would be content with their condition, and that it was not for want or necessity so much that they removed, as for the enriching of themselves. Others were resolute upon removal, and so signified that here they could not stay, but if the church did not remove, they must; insomuch as many were swayed, rather than there should be a dissolution, to condescend[2] to a removal, if a fit place could be found, that might more conveniently and comfortably receive the whole, with such accession of others as might come to them, for their better strength and subsistence,

8. Weeds common in grain fields. See Matthew 13.25.
9. I.e., Plymouth.

1. Varied, divided.
2. In the old sense of "agree."

and some such like cautions and limitations. So as, with the aforesaid pro-
visos, the greater part consented to a removal to a place called Nauset, which
had been superficially viewed and the good will of the purchasers (to whom
it belonged) obtained, with some addition thereto from the Court. But now
they began to see their error, that they had given away already the best and
most commodious places to others, and now wanted themselves: for this place
was about fifty miles from hence, and at an outside of the country, remote
from all society; also, that it would prove so strait, as it would not be compe-
tent to receive the whole body, much less be capable of any addition or
increase, so as (at least in a short time) they should be worse there than they
are now here. The which, with sundry other like considerations and inconve-
niences, made them change their resolutions. But such as were before resolved
upon removal took advantage of this agreement, and went on notwithstand-
ing, neither could the rest hinder them, they having made some beginning.
And thus was this poor church left, like an ancient mother, grown old and
forsaken of her children, though not in their affections, yet in regard of their
bodily presence and personal helpfulness. Her ancient members being most of
them worn away by death, and these of later time being like children trans-
lated into other families, and she like a widow left only to trust in God. Thus
she that had made many rich became herself poor.[3]

1630–50 1856

3. See 2 Corinthians 6.10 and 1 Timothy 5.5.

THOMAS MORTON
c. 1579–1647

Thomas Morton's amusing and irreverent history, *New English Canaan* (pub-
lished in Amsterdam in 1637), deals with some of the same episodes as the previ-
ous selection, William Bradford's *Of Plymouth Plantation.* However, Morton, an
Anglican, tells a very different version of the conflict between the devout colonists at
Plymouth and Boston and Morton's mixed community of Native Americans, sailors,
and traders at Ma-re Mount, which his Puritan neighbors sarcastically called "Merry
Mount." Deftly deploying mock-epic conventions, Morton celebrated the qualities—
sensuality, worldliness, and embrace of the region's indigenous peoples—that made
him an economic rival and potent enemy of the Puritans. The religious exiles did not
celebrate Christmas, let alone the old pagan festival of May Day, and they were less
intimate with their Native neighbors. When Morton erected a maypole at Ma-re
Mount and invited the "Lasses in beaver coats" to join him and his men in dancing
around it and drinking "good liquor," he was defiantly demonstrating his closeness
to American Natives and violating Puritan norms of decorum. More to the point,
he was unequivocally stating his ideological differences with what he humorously
portrayed as the straitlaced and self-important Pilgrims. A long line of literary treat-
ments of Morton and his colony, most famously Nathaniel Hawthorne's story "The

May-Pole of Merry Mount" (written 1835–36), makes him of continuing fascination today.

Raised in the West Country of England, Morton studied law at the Inns of Court in London. He later came to serve as an attorney for the Council for New England, which had been established in 1620 to promote the colonization of the lands north of modern-day New York. Morton enjoyed many contacts with the court of King Charles I. He was also the sort of figure around whom rumors and tales tended to circulate: by the time he left England for Massachusetts Bay in 1624, the gossip about him included rumors that he had mistreated his wife and murdered an associate.

The most persistent tales about Morton date from his brief career in New England. He joined with a Captain Wollaston (perhaps Richard Wollaston, a ship's captain and sometime pirate) to settle a site in what is now Quincy, Massachusetts, which they named Mount Wollaston. After Wollaston departed for Virginia, Morton renamed the settlement Ma-re Mount (from the Latin for "Hill by the Sea"). As a base for the New England fur trade, the outpost enjoyed very good relations with Native traders. The rumors about Morton, including the charge that he began the sale of guns to New England Indians, may have stemmed from the Pilgrims' desire to monopolize the lucrative market in furs. In any case, the threat from such sales was probably exaggerated, for the type of gun available at the time—the matchlock—was unwieldy, inaccurate, and time-consuming to load. In some ways, it was much less effective than Indian bows and arrows.

In 1627 the Pilgrim authorities seized Morton, and he was deported for trial in England the following year, but there was insufficient proof to sustain the charges against him. He returned to New England a year later, only to be taken into custody once more by the indignant Pilgrims, who burned his house and deported him again for trial. While in exile in England, Morton began a lawsuit against the Massachusetts Bay Colony, the Puritans' sponsor. In 1635, as a prosecutor for the Council of New England, he successfully petitioned to have the colony's charter repealed. When he returned one last time to New England in 1643, he proceeded to tangle yet again with the authorities in the colony. The Puritans' "professed old adversary," as John Winthrop termed him, was again ordered to leave. After a brief exile in Rhode Island, a colony that was friendly to those who opposed the Puritan authorities, Morton made the mistake of going back to Massachusetts, where he was arrested for conspiracy and jailed for a year. The aged rebel emerged from confinement in poor health in 1645. He died two years later in York, Maine.

Morton's witty, sometimes puzzling, always lighthearted narrative of the maypole episode features exuberant wordplay and mirthful performances of song and dance, which the comically staid and sober Pilgrims fail to understand, no less to appreciate. Pitting "Captain Shrimp" (i.e., Captain Myles Standish, the military leader of the Plymouth Colony) against "mine host" (himself), the account makes use of Morton's considerable learning. Its references to ancient and modern literature include a mention of Don Quixote battling the windmill, which shows Morton's familiarity with recent developments in European literature. (The first volume of Miguel de Cervantes's novel Don Quixote was published in Madrid in 1605 and rapidly spread across Europe; an English translation appeared in 1612.) In Morton's vibrant worldview, language proliferated meanings that could not be controlled by a single group. Responding to the Puritans' desire to restore the Church to biblical purity, Morton articulated a competing approach to a complicated era, leading his opponents to consider him, as he put it, "the very hydra," or many-headed monster, "of the time."

From New English Canaan[1]

From *The Third Book* [*The Incident at Merry Mount*][2]

CHAPTER XIV. OF THE REVELS OF NEW CANAAN

The inhabitants of Passonagessit[3] (having translated the name of their habitation from that ancient savage name to Ma-re Mount, and being resolved to have the new name confirmed for a memorial to after ages) did devise amongst themselves to have it performed in a solemn manner, with revels and merriment after the old English custom; [they] prepared to set up a Maypole upon the festival day of Philip and Jacob,[4] and therefore brewed a barrel of excellent beer and provided a case of bottles to be spent, with other good cheer, for all comers of that day. And because they would have it in a complete form, they had prepared a song fitting to the time and present occasion. And upon May Day they brought the Maypole to the place appointed, with drums, guns, pistols, and other fitting instruments for that purpose, and there erected it with the help of savages that came thither of purpose to see the manner of our revels. A goodly pine tree of 80 foot long was reared up, with a pair of buckhorns nailed on somewhat near unto the top of it, where it stood as a fair sea-mark for directions how to find out the way to mine host of Ma-re Mount.

And because it should more fully appear to what end it was placed there, they had a poem in readiness made, which was fixed to the Maypole, to show the new name confirmed upon that plantation, which, although it were made according to the occurrence of the time, it being enigmatically composed, puzzled the Separatists[5] most pitifully to expound it, which (for the better information of the reader) I have here inserted.

THE POEM

Rise Oedipus,[6] and, if thou canst, unfold
What means Charybdis underneath the mold,
When Scylla[7] solitary on the ground
(Sitting in form of Niobe[8]) was found,
Till Amphitrite's darling did acquaint

1. The text was edited by Charles Francis Adams Jr. for the Prince Society (1883). "Canaan": in the Bible, the Israelites' promised land.
2. *New English Canaan* consists of three parts. The first book describes "the natives, their manners and customs, with their tractable nature and love towards the English." The second book is titled "Containing a Description of the Beauty of the Country with Her Natural Endowments, Both in the Land and Sea; with the Great Lake of Iroquois" (Lake Champlain, New York). The third book is titled "Containing a Description of the People That Are Planted There, What Remarkable Accidents Have Happened There Since They Were Settled, What Tenents [religious doctrines] They Hold, Together with the Practice of Their Church."
3. At [a place] near the little point (Algonquian, literal trans.).
4. May 1 is the feast day of Saints Philip and James (Jacob being the Latin form of James), but why they are joined together on this day is not known. The raising of a maypole was a secular tradition harking back to the Roman festivals in honor of the renewal of vegetative life.
5. The colonists at Plymouth, who distinguished themselves from other Puritans by separating from the Church of England, which they regarded as incapable of reform.
6. In Greek mythology, he solved the riddle of the Sphinx.
7. In Greek mythology, a monster who lived in a cave opposite the monster Charybdis and devoured sailors.
8. In Greek mythology, the gods slew her fourteen children; she is usually depicted weeping for them.

Grim Neptune with the tenor of her plaint,[9]
And caused him send forth Triton[1] with the sound
Of trumpet loud, at which the seas were found
So full of protean[2] forms that the bold shore
Presented Scylla a new paramour
So strong as Samson and so patient
As Job[3] himself, directed thus, by fate,
To comfort Scylla so unfortunate.
I do profess, by Cupid's beauteous mother,[4]
Here's Scogan's choice[5] for Scylla, and none other;
Though Scylla's sick with grief, because no sign
Can there be found of virtue masculine.
Asclepius[6] come; I know right well
His labor's lost when you may ring her knell.
The fatal sisters'[7] doom none can withstand,
Nor Cytherea's[8] power, who points to land
With proclamation that the first of May
At Ma-re Mount shall be kept holiday.

The setting up of this Maypole was a lamentable spectacle to the precise Separatists that lived at New Plymouth.[9] They termed it an idol; yea, they called it the Calf of Horeb[1] and stood at defiance with the place, naming it Mount Dagon, threatening to make it a woeful mount and not a merry mount.

The riddle, for want of Oedipus,[2] they could not expound, only they made some explication of part of it and said it was meant by Samson Job, the carpenter of the ship that brought over a woman to her husband that had been there long before and thrived so well that he sent for her and her children to come to him, where shortly after he died; having no reason but because of the sound of those two words, when as (the truth is) the man they applied it to was altogether unknown to the author.

There was likewise a merry song made which (to make their revels more fashionable) was sung with a chorus, every man bearing his part, which they performed in a dance, hand in hand about the Maypole, while one of the company sang and filled out the good liquor, like Ganymede and Jupiter.[3]

9. Complaint, lament. "Amphitrite's darling": a sarcastic reference to Scylla, whom Amphitrite, Neptune's wife, turned into a hideous monster because Neptune loved her.
1. The son of Poseidon, god of the sea, he is usually depicted with a conch shell as his horn.
2. Changing.
3. The long-suffering Old Testament patriarch. Samson was the Israelite who brought down with his own hands the temple of the Philistines as they honored their god Dagon.
4. Venus, the Roman goddess of love.
5. When John Scogan (1442–1483), jester to King Edward IV, was condemned to be hanged, he was given an opportunity to choose the tree and escaped hanging because he could find none to suit him. "Scogan's choice" became a popular expression in Morton's time and suggested that any choice, even between undesirable alternatives, is better than no choice at all.
6. The Greek god of healing.
7. In Greek and Roman mythology, the three women who determine human destiny.
8. Also called Aphrodite, goddess of love and beauty (known as "Venus" to the Romans).
9. I.e., Plymouth Plantation, not Plymouth in England. "Precise": strict, inflexible.
1. The idol that the Israelites worshiped as their deliverer from Egypt (Exodus 32; Deuteronomy 9.16).
2. I.e., lacking Oedipus's insight.
3. Just as the cupbearer Ganymede brought wine to the most powerful Roman god.

THE SONG

Chorus.

Drink and be merry, merry, merry boys;
Let all your delight be in the Hymen's[4] joys;
Io[5] to Hymen, now the day is come,
About the merry Maypole take a room.
 Make green garlands, bring bottles out
 And fill sweet nectar freely about.
 Uncover thy head and fear no harm,
 For here's good liquor to keep it warm.
Then drink and be merry, &c.
Io to Hymen, &c.
 Nectar is a thing assigned
 By the Deity's own mind
 To cure the heart oppressed with grief,
 And of good liquors is the chief.
Then drink, &c.
Io to Hymen, &c.
 Give to the melancholy man
 A cup or two of't now and then;
 This physic[6] will soon revive his blood,
 And make him be of a merrier mood.
Then drink, &c.
Io to Hymen, &c.
 Give to the nymph that's free from scorn
 No Irish stuff nor Scotch over worn.[7]
 Lasses in beaver coats[8] come away,
 Ye shall be welcome to us night and day.
To drink and be merry, &c.
Io to Hymen, &c.

This harmless mirth made by young men (that lived in hope to have wives brought over to them, that would save them a labor to make a voyage to fetch any over) was much distasted of the precise Separatists that keep much ado about the tithe of mint and cummin,[9] troubling their brains more than reason would require about things that are indifferent,[1] and from that time [they] sought occasion against my honest host of Ma-re Mount, to overthrow his undertakings and to destroy his plantation quite and clean. But because they presumed [that] with their imaginary gifts (which they have out of Phaon's[2] box) they could expound hidden mysteries, to convince them of blindness as well in this as in other matters of more consequence, I will illustrate the poem according to the true intent of the authors of these revels, so much distasted by those moles.

4. In Roman mythology, the god of marriage.
5. Hail (Latin).
6. Medicine.
7. No worn-out Irish or Scottish cloth.
8. Native American women.
9. "Woe unto you, scribes and Pharisees, hypocrites! for ye pay tithe of mint and anise and cummin, and have omitted the weightier matters of the law, judgment, mercy, and faith" (Matthew 23.23).
1. Insignificant.
2. An aged boatman whom Aphrodite rewarded with a chest that contained an elixir that made him young.

Oedipus is generally received for[3] the absolute reader of riddles, who is invoked; Scylla and Charybdis are two dangerous places for seamen to encounter, near unto Venice, and have been by poets formerly resembled to man and wife. The like license the author challenged for a pair of his nomination, the one lamenting for the loss of the other as Niobe for her children. Amphitrite is an arm of the sea, by which the news was carried up and down of a rich widow, now to be taken up or laid down. By Triton is the fame spread that caused the suitors to muster (as it had been to Penelope[4] of Greece), and, the coast lying circular, all our passage to and fro is made more convenient by sea than land. Many aimed at this mark, but he that played Proteus[5] best and could comply with her humor must be the man that would carry her; and he had need have Samson's strength to deal with a Delilah,[6] and as much patience as Job that should come there, for a thing that I did observe in the lifetime of the former.

But marriage and hanging (they say) come by destiny, and Scogan's choice is better [than] none at all. He that played Proteus (with the help of Priapus)[7] put their noses out of joint, as the proverb is.

And this the whole company of the revelers at Ma-re Mount knew to be the true sense and exposition of the riddle that was fixed to the Maypole which the Separatists were at defiance with. Some of them affirmed that the first institution thereof was in memory of a whore, not knowing that it was a trophy erected at first in honor of Maia.[8] The Lady of Learning which [sic] they despise, vilifying the two universities with uncivil terms,[9] accounting what is there obtained by study is but unnecessary learning, not considering that learning does enable men's minds to converse with elements of a higher nature than is to be found within the habitation of the mole.

CHAPTER XV. OF A GREAT MONSTER SUPPOSED TO BE AT MA-RE MOUNT; AND THE PREPARATION MADE TO DESTROY IT

The Separatists, envying the prosperity and hope of the plantation at Ma-re Mount (which they perceived began to come forward and to be in a good way for gain in the beaver trade), conspired together against mine host especially (who was the owner of that plantation) and made up a party against him and mustered up what aid they could, accounting of him as of a great monster.

Many threatening speeches were given out both against his person and his habitation, which[1] they divulged should be consumed with fire. And taking advantage of the time when his company (which seemed little to regard their threats) were gone up unto the inlands to trade with the savages for beaver, they set upon my honest host at a place called Wessaguscus,[2] where, by accident, they found him. The inhabitants there were in good hope of

3. Understood as.
4. The wife of Odysseus, who refused many suitors during his twenty-year absence.
5. In Greek mythology, the sea god, who assumed many shapes.
6. The woman who betrayed Samson (Judges 16).
7. In Greek and Roman mythology, the god of fertility, whose symbol was the phallus.
8. Morton argues that the Separatists accused the revelers at Merry Mount of honoring the licentious Roman goddess Flora rather than Maia, the goddess of the spring.
9. I.e., in their confusion of Flora and Maia the Separatists reveal their contempt for the wisdom of Athena or Minerva, and in their hatred for the classical studies at Oxford and Cambridge they reveal their, for Morton, unsophisticated minds.
1. I.e., his habitation (not his person).
2. Now Weymouth, Massachusetts.

the subversion of the plantation at Ma-re Mount (which they principally aimed at) and the rather because mine host was a man that endeavored to advance the dignity of the Church of England, which they (on the contrary part) would labor to vilify with uncivil terms, inveighing against the sacred Book of Common Prayer[3] and mine host that used it in a laudable manner amongst his family as a practice of piety.

There he would be a means to bring sacks to their mill (such is the thirst after beaver) and [it] helped the conspirators to surprise mine host (who was there all alone), and they charged him (because they would [want to] seem to have some reasonable cause against him, to set a gloss upon[4] their malice) with criminal things, which indeed had been done by such a person, but was of their conspiracy. Mine host demanded of the conspirators who it was that was author of that information that seemed to be their ground for what they now intended. And because they answered they would not tell him, he as peremptorily replied that he would not say whether he had or he had not done as they had been informed.

The answer made no matter (as it seemed) whether it had been negatively or affirmatively made, for they had resolved what he would suffer because (as they boasted) they were now become the greater number; they had shaken off their shackles of servitude and were become masters and masterless people.

It appears they were like bears' whelps in former time when mine host's plantation was of as much strength as theirs, but now (theirs being stronger) they (like overgrown bears) seemed monstrous. In brief, mine host must endure to be their prisoner until they could contrive it so that they might send him for England (as they said), there to suffer according to the merit of the fact which they intended to father upon him, supposing (belike) it would prove a heinous crime.

Much rejoicing was made that they had gotten their capital enemy (as they concluded him) whom they purposed to hamper in such sort that he should not be able to uphold his plantation at Ma-re Mount.

The conspirators sported themselves at my honest host, that meant them no hurt, and were so jocund that they feasted their bodies and fell to tippling as if they had obtained a great prize, like the Trojans when they had the custody of Epeios' pinetree horse.[5]

Mine host feigned grief and could not be persuaded either to eat or drink, because he knew emptiness would be a means to make him as watchful as the geese kept in the Roman Capital,[6] whereon, the contrary part, the conspirators would be so drowsy that he might have an opportunity to give them a slip instead of a tester.[7]

Six persons of the conspiracy were set to watch him at Wessaguscus. But he kept waking, and in the dead of the night (one lying on the bed for further surety), up gets mine host and got to the second door that he was to pass, which, notwithstanding the lock, he got open and shut it after him with such violence that it affrighted some of the conspirators.

3. Containing the prayers adopted by the Church of England; rejected by the Separatists.
4. Explain, rationalize.
5. The wooden horse used by the Greeks to conquer Troy was built by Epeios.

6. When the Gauls attempted to invade Rome in 390 B.C.E. the geese on the Capitoline Hill spoiled the surprise attack by hissing.
7. A counterfeit coin rather than a true sixpence.

The word which was given with an alarm was, "O he's gone, he's gone, what shall we do, he's gone!" The rest (half asleep) start up in amaze[8] and like rams, ran their heads one at another full butt in the dark.

Their grand leader, Captain Shrimp,[9] took on most furiously and tore his clothes for anger, to see the empty nest and their bird gone.

The rest were eager to have torn their hair from their heads, but it was so short that it would give them no hold.[1] Now Captain Shrimp thought in the loss of this prize (which he accounted his masterpiece) all his honor would be lost forever.

In the meantime mine host was got home to Ma-re Mount through the woods, eight miles round about the head of the river Monatoquit that parted the two plantations, finding his way by the help of the lightning (for it thundered as he went terribly), and there he prepared powder, three pounds dried, for his present employment, and four good guns for him and the two assistants left at his house, with bullets of several sizes, three hundred or thereabouts, to be used if the conspirators should pursue him thither; and these two persons promised their aids in the quarrel and confirmed that promise with health in good *rosa solis*.[2]

Now Captain Shrimp, the first captain in the land (as he supposed) must do some new act to repair this loss and to vindicate his reputation, who had sustained blemish by this oversight, begins now to study how to repair or survive his honor; in this manner, calling of council, they conclude.

He takes eight persons more to him, and (like the nine worthies[3] of New Canaan) they embark with preparation against Ma-re Mount where this monster of a man, as their phrase was, had his den; the whole number, had the rest not been from home, being but seven, would have given Captain Shrimp (a *quondam* drummer)[4] such a welcome as would have made him wish for a drum as big as Diogenes' tub,[5] that he might have crept into it out of sight.

Now the nine worthies are approached, and mine host prepared, having intelligence by a savage that hastened in love from Wessaguscus to give him notice of their intent.

One of mine host's men proved a craven; the other had proved his wits to purchase a little valor,[6] before mine host had observed his posture.

The nine worthies coming before the den of this supposed monster (this seven-headed hydra,[7] as they termed him) and began, like Don Quixote against the windmill, to beat a parley and to offer quarter if mine host would yield, for they resolved to send him to England and bade him lay by[8] his arms.

But he (who was the son of a soldier), having taken up arms in his just defense, replied that he would not lay by those arms because they were so needful at sea, if he should be sent over. Yet, to save the effusion of so much worthy blood as would have issued out of the veins of these nine worthies of New Canaan if mine host should have played upon them out at his portholes

8. I.e., in astonishment.
9. Morton's favorite epithet for Captain Myles Standish, who had a ruddy complexion and was short.
1. Puritans objected to fashionably long hair as a vanity.
2. A liquor red like the sun.
3. A group of heroes and kings who, to the medieval mind, represented an ideal of human conduct.

4. A one-time drummer and thus a man of low rank.
5. The Greek philosopher Diogenes (c. 412–323 B.C.E.) was indifferent to status and lived in a tub.
6. I.e., by drinking. "Craven": coward.
7. In Greek mythology, a monster.
8. Put down. "Beat a parley": suggest a conference. "Quarter": clemency.

(for they came within danger like a flock of wild geese, as if they had been tailed[9] one to another, as colts to be sold at a fair), mine host was content to yield upon quarter and did capitulate with them in what manner it should be for more certainty, because he knew what Captain Shrimp was.

He expressed that no violence should be offered to his person, none to his goods, nor any of his household but that he should have his arms and what else was requisite for the voyage, which their herald returns;[1] it was agreed upon and should be performed.

But mine host no sooner had set open the door and issued out, but instantly Captain Shrimp and the rest of the worthies stepped to him, laid hold of his arms, and had him down; and so eagerly was every man bent against him (not regarding any agreement made with such a carnal man), that they fell upon him as if they would have eaten him; some of them were so violent that they would have a slice with scabbard, and all for haste, until an old soldier (of the Queen's, as the proverb is) that was there by accident, clapped his gun under the weapons and sharply rebuked these worthies for their unworthy practices. So the matter was taken into more deliberate consideration.

Captain Shrimp and the rest of the nine worthies made themselves (by this outrageous riot) masters of mine host of Ma-re Mount and disposed of what he had at his plantation.

This they knew (in the eye of the savages) would add to their glory and diminish the reputation of mine honest host, whom they practiced to be rid of upon any terms, as willingly as if he had been the very hydra of the time.

CHAPTER XVI. HOW THE NINE WORTHIES PUT MINE HOST OF MA-RE
MOUNT INTO THE ENCHANTED CASTLE AT PLYMOUTH AND TERRIFIED
HIM WITH THE MONSTER BRIAREUS[2]

The nine worthies of New Canaan having now the law in their own hands (there being no general governor in the land, nor none of the separation that regarded the duty they owe their sovereign, whose natural born subjects they were, though translated out of[3] Holland from whence they had learned to work all to their own ends and make a great show of religion but no humanity), for [sic] they were now to sit in council on the cause.

And much it stood mine honest host upon to be very circumspect and to take Eacus[4] to task for that his voice was more allowed of than both the other; and had not mine host confounded all the arguments that Eacus could make in their defense and confuted him that swayed the rest, they would have made him unable to drink in such manner of merriment any more. So that following this private counsel, given him by one that knew who ruled the roost, the hurricane ceased that else would split his pinnace.[5]

A conclusion was made and sentence given that mine host should be sent to England a prisoner. But when he was brought to the ships for that purpose, no man dared be so foolhardly as to undertake to carry him. So these

9. Tied.
1. Reports.
2. In Greek mythology, a giant who fought the gods. Morton does not identify his tormentor.
3. Removed from.

4. In Greek mythology, a judge in the infernal regions. Morton later identifies him as Samuel Fuller of Plymouth and names William Bradford and Myles Standish as his other two judges.
5. A small sailboat.

worthies set mine host upon an island, without gun, powder, or shot, or dog, or so much as a knife to get anything to feed upon, or any other clothes to shelter him with at winter than a thin suit which he had on at that time. Home he could not get to Ma-re Mount. Upon this island he stayed a month at least and was relieved by savages that took notice that mine host was a sachem[6] of Passonagessit, and would bring bottles of strong liquor to him and unite themselves into a league of brotherhood with mine host, so full of humanity are these infidels before those Christians.

From this place for England sailed mine host in a Plymouth ship[7] (that came into the land to fish upon the coast) that landed him safe in England at Plymouth; and he stayed in England until the ordinary time for shipping to set forth for these parts, and then returned, no man being able to tax[8] him of anything.

But the worthies (in the meantime) hoped they had been rid of him.

* * *

c. 1635 1637

6. Ruling chief. 8. Charge.
7. I.e., from Plymouth, England.

JOHN WINTHROP
1588–1649

When Cotton Mather looked back on the founding years of the Massachusetts Bay Colony in *Magnalia Christi Americana* (1702)—the first attempt at a comprehensive history of the Puritan experiment, excerpted later in this volume— he identified John Winthrop as his model of the ideal earthly ruler. Mather came from a family of prominent Bay Colony ministers, and he was well placed to shape Winthrop's legacy. He did so using a number of sacred and secular analogies, label- ing Winthrop "Nehemias Americanus" after Nehemiah, the biblical governor of Judea who rebuilt the wall of Jerusalem; describing him as a new Moses; and com- paring him favorably to the Greek lawgiver Lycurgus and the devout Roman king Numa. Mather's praise for the man who led the Bay Colony in its early years reflects his era's approach to historical writing, which was strongly influenced by the work of the Greek historian Plutarch, supplemented with Roman and biblical texts. Mather's biography of the Puritan leader also underlines the status and skills that Winthrop brought to his position.

John Winthrop was the son of Adam Winthrop, a lawyer, and Anne Browne, the daughter of a tradesman. He was born in Groton, England, on an estate his father had purchased from King Henry VIII. It was a prosperous farm, and Winthrop had all the advantages of his father's social and economic position. He went to Cam- bridge University for two years—it is likely that he was first exposed to Puritan ideas there—and married at age seventeen. Unlike William Bradford and the Pilgrims, Winthrop was not a Separatist; that is, he wished to reform the Church of England

from within rather than breaking with it and starting fresh. For Puritans like Winthrop, reform involved purging the national Church of the residual presence of Roman Catholicism, especially the hierarchy of the clergy and traditional practices such as kneeling at communion. For a time Winthrop thought of becoming a clergyman, but instead he turned to the practice of law.

In the 1620s, severe economic depression in England made Winthrop realize that he could not depend on the income from his father's estate and would need to find new means of support. The ascension to the throne of Charles I, who was known to be sympathetic to Roman Catholicism and impatient with Puritan reformers, also seemed an ominous sign. Winthrop was not alone in predicting that "God will bring some heavy affliction upon the land, and that speedily." He came to realize that if he antagonized the king by openly espousing the Puritan cause, he would lose everything. The only recourse seemed to be to obtain Charles's permission to emigrate. In March 1629, a group of enterprising merchants, all ardent Puritans, was able to get a charter for land in America from a Crown-approved joint stock company called the Council for New England. They called themselves "The Company of Massachusetts Bay in New England."

Winthrop was chosen governor in October 1629, and for the next twenty years most of the responsibility for the colony rested in his hands. An initial group of some seven hundred emigrants sailed from England with Winthrop on April 8, 1630, aboard the *Arbella*. It has long been believed that Winthrop delivered his sermon *A Model of Christian Charity* either just before departing from England or during the voyage. A review of the historical record suggests a far more ambiguous origin. There is no contemporary account of Winthrop delivering *A Model*, and there exists little evidence of its composition. The manuscript that survives is a copy made during Winthrop's lifetime, possibly incomplete, and of unknown provenance.

A Model of Christian Charity remains an iconic text despite its uncertain past. It sets out clearly and eloquently the ideals of a harmonious Christian community and reminds its audience members that they stand as an example to the world of the triumph or the failure of the Puritan enterprise. And in fact, events at the Massachusetts Bay Colony soon suggested that Winthrop's ideal of a selfless community was impossible to realize. In its first decade, the colony confronted basic differences over religious and civil liberties, social organization, and political structure. The colony also engaged in a brutal war with its Pequot neighbors.

Winthrop was governor for much of this decade, and he was closely involved with all of these conflicts. The frictions in the colony took a personal turn in 1645, when a group of leaders from the town of Hingham challenged Winthrop, then serving as deputy governor, over issues of local autonomy and representative government. Winthrop withstood the resulting impeachment threat and responded in the General Court with a trenchant speech distinguishing between natural liberty and civil or federal liberty, a distinction that remains a classic formulation. These and other disputes are detailed in the journal that he kept from 1630 until his death. Once the Winthrop family made the manuscript available to the colony's historians, including Cotton Mather and William Hubbard, the journal joined William Bradford's manuscript history, *Of Plymouth Plantation*, as a semiofficial history of New England.

Mather's account of Winthrop helped keep his memory alive. Beginning in 1790, when Noah Webster of dictionary fame published the first two volumes of Winthrop's journal, several New England intellectuals affiliated with the Massachusetts Historical Society (founded in 1791) worked to recover his words for future generations. James Savage published the first complete edition of the journal in 1825–26, though the achievement was marred when a fire at Savage's office destroyed the second volume of the manuscript. The first printed edition of *A Model of Christian Charity* appeared in the *Collections of the Massachusetts Historical Society*

in 1838. Eventually, this little-known sermon acquired the status it has today, as an expression of the ideal suggested by its most resonant phrase, "a city upon a hill."

A Model of Christian Charity[1]

I

A MODEL HEREOF

God Almighty in His most holy and wise providence, hath so disposed of the condition of mankind, as in all times some must be rich, some poor, some high and eminent in power and dignity; others mean and in subjection.

THE REASON HEREOF

First, to hold conformity with the rest of His works, being delighted to show forth the glory of His wisdom in the variety and difference of the creatures; and the glory of His power, in ordering all these differences for the preservation and good of the whole; and the glory of His greatness, that as it is the glory of princes to have many officers, so this great King will have many stewards, counting Himself more honored in dispensing His gifts to man by man, than if He did it by His own immediate hands.

Secondly, that He might have the more occasion to manifest the work of His Spirit: first upon the wicked in moderating and restraining them, so that the rich and mighty should not eat up the poor, nor the poor and despised rise up against their superiors and shake off their yoke; secondly in the regenerate,[2] in exercising His graces, in them, as in the great ones, their love, mercy, gentleness, temperance, etc., in the poor and inferior sort, their faith, patience, obedience, etc.

Thirdly, that every man might have need of other, and from hence they might be all knit more nearly together in the bonds of brotherly affection. From hence it appears plainly that no man is made more honorable than another or more wealthy, etc., out of any particular and singular respect to himself, but for the glory of his Creator and the common good of the creature, man. Therefore God still reserves the property of these gifts to Himself as [in] Ezekiel: 16.17. He there calls wealth His gold and His silver.[3] [In] Proverbs: 3.9, he claims their service as His due: honor the Lord with thy riches, etc.[4] All men being thus (by divine providence) ranked into two sorts, rich and poor; under the first are comprehended all such as are able to live comfortably by their own means duly improved; and all others are poor according to the former distribution.

1. The text is from Old South Leaflets, Old South Association, Old South Meetinghouse, Boston, Massachusetts, No. 207 (n.d.), edited by Samuel Eliot Morison.
2. Humanity lost its natural innocence when Adam and Eve fell; that state is called unregenerate. When Jesus Christ came to ransom humankind from Adam and Eve's sin, he offered salvation for those who believed in him and who thus became regenerate, or saved.
3. "Thou hast also taken thy fair jewels made of my gold and of my silver, which I had given thee, and madest to thyself images of men, and didst commit whoredom with them." Textual evidence shows that Winthrop used the Geneva Bible, with occasional variants from the text of the 1599 edition. (The Geneva Bible, also known as the English Bible, was translated by Reformed English Protestants living in Switzerland; this version, used by the Puritans, was outlawed by the Church of England.)
4. "Honor the Lord with thy riches, and with the first fruits of all thine increase. So shall thy barns be filled with abundance, and thy presses shall burst with new wine" (Proverbs 3.9–10).

There are two rules whereby we are to walk one towards another: justice and mercy. These are always distinguished in their act and in their object, yet may they both concur in the same subject in each respect; as sometimes there may be an occasion of showing mercy to a rich man in some sudden danger of distress, and also doing of mere justice to a poor man in regard of some particular contract, etc.

There is likewise a double law by which we are regulated in our conversation one towards another in both the former respects: the law of nature and the law of grace, or the moral law or the law of the Gospel, to omit the rule of justice as not properly belonging to this purpose otherwise than it may fall into consideration in some particular cases. By the first of these laws man as he was enabled so withal [is] commanded to love his neighbor as himself.[5] Upon this ground stands all the precepts of the moral law, which concerns our dealings with men. To apply this to the works of mercy, this law requires two things: first, that every man afford his help to another in every want or distress; secondly, that he performed this out of the same affection which makes him careful of his own goods, according to that of our Savior. Matthew: "Whatsoever ye would that men should do to you."[6] This was practiced by Abraham and Lot in entertaining the Angels and the old man of Gibeah.[7]

The law of grace or the Gospel hath some difference from the former, as in these respects: First, the law of nature was given to man in the estate of innocency; this of the Gospel in the estate of regeneracy. Secondly, the former propounds one man to another, as the same flesh and image of God; this as a brother in Christ also, and in the communion of the same spirit and so teacheth us to put a difference between Christians and others. *Do good to all, especially to the household of faith*: Upon this ground the Israelites were to put a difference between the brethren of such as were strangers though not of Canaanites.[8] Thirdly, the law of nature could give no rules for dealing with enemies, for all are to be considered as friends in the state of innocency, but the Gospel commands love to an enemy. Proof. If thine Enemy hunger, feed him; Love your Enemies, do good to them that hate you. Matthew: 5.44.

This law of the Gospel propounds likewise a difference of seasons and occasions. There is a time when a Christian must sell all and give to the poor, as they did in the Apostles' times.[9] There is a time also when a Christian (though they give not all yet) must give beyond their ability, as they of Macedonia, Corinthians: 2.8.[1] Likewise community of perils calls for

5. Matthew 5.43, 19.19.
6. "Therefore whatsoever ye would that men should do to you: even so do ye to them: for this is the Law and the Prophets" (Matthew 7.12).
7. In Judges 19.16–21, an old citizen of Gibeah offered shelter to a traveling priest or Levite and defended him from enemies from a neighboring city. Abraham entertains the angels in Genesis 18: "Again the Lord appeared unto him in the plain of Mamre, as he sat in his tent door about the heat of the day. And he lifted up his eyes, and looked: and lo, three men stood by him, and when he saw them, he ran to meet them from the tent door, and bowed himself to the ground" (Genesis 18.1–2). Lot was Abraham's nephew, and he escaped the destruction of the city of Sodom because he defended from a mob two angels who were his guests (Genesis 19.1–14).
8. People who lived in Canaan, the biblical promised land for the Israelites.
9. "And they sold their possessions, and goods, and parted them to all men, as everyone had need" (Acts 2.45).
1. "We do you also to wit, brethren, of the grace of God bestowed upon the Churches of Macedonia. Because in great trial of affliction their joy abounded, and their most extreme poverty abounded unto their rich liberality. For to their power (I bear record) yea, and beyond their power they were willing. And prayed us with great instance that we would receive the grace, and fellowship of the ministering which is toward the Saints" (2 Corinthians 8.1–4).

extraordinary liberality, and so doth community in some special service for the Church. Lastly, when there is no other means whereby our Christian brother may be relieved in his distress, we must help him beyond our ability, rather than tempt God in putting him upon help by miraculous or extraordinary means.

This duty of mercy is exercised in the kinds, *giving, lending* and *forgiving*.—

Quest. What rule shall a man observe in giving in respect of the measure?

Ans. If the time and occasion be ordinary, he is to give out of his abundance. Let him lay aside as God hath blessed him. If the time and occasion be extraordinary, he must be ruled by them; taking this withal, that then a man cannot likely do too much, especially if he may leave himself and his family under probable means of comfortable subsistence.

Objection. A man must lay up for posterity, the fathers lay up for posterity and children and he "is worse than an infidel" that "provideth not for his own."

Ans. For the first, it is plain that it being spoken by way of comparison, it must be meant of the ordinary and usual course of fathers and cannot extend to times and occasions extraordinary. For the other place, the Apostle speaks against such as walked inordinately, and it is without question, that he is worse than an infidel who through his own sloth and voluptuousness shall neglect to provide for his family.

Objection. "The wise man's eyes are in his head" saith Solomon, "and foreseeth the plague,"[2] therefore we must forecast and lay up against evil times when he or his may stand in need of all he can gather.

Ans. This very argument Solomon useth to persuade to liberality, Ecclesiastes: "Cast thy bread upon the waters," and "for thou knowest not what evil may come upon the land."[3] Luke: 16.9. "Make you friends of the riches of iniquity." [4] You will ask how this shall be? very well. For first he that gives to the poor, lends to the Lord and He will repay him even in this life an hundred fold to him or his—The righteous is ever merciful and lendeth and his seed enjoyeth the blessing; and besides we know what advantage it will be to us in the day of account when many such witnesses shall stand forth for us to witness the improvement of our talent.[5] And I would know of those who plead so much for laying up for time to come, whether they hold that to be Gospel, Matthew: 6.19: "Lay not up for yourselves treasures upon earth," [6] etc. If they acknowledge it, what extent will they allow it? if only to those primitive times, let them consider the reason whereupon our Savior grounds it. The first is that they are subject to the moth, the rust, the thief. Secondly, they will steal away the heart; where the treasure is there will the heart be also. The reasons are of like force at all times. Therefore the exhortation must be general and perpetual, with always in respect of the love and affection

2. Ecclesiastes 2.14. Solomon was the son of David and successor to David as king of Israel.
3. "Cast thy bread upon the waters: for after many days thou shalt find it. Give a portion to seven, and also to eight: for thou knowest not what evil shall be upon the earth" (Ecclesiastes 11.1–2).
4. The passage in Luke refers to a servant who is about to lose his job managing his boss's accounts. To guarantee that he will be welcome in the houses of his master's debtors, he cuts their bills in half. Jesus explains: "And I say unto you, Make you friends with the riches of iniquity, that when ye shall want, they may receive you into everlasting habitations" (Luke 16.9).
5. Originally a measure of money (as in the weight of gold).
6. "Lay not up treasures for yourselves upon the earth, where the moth and canker corrupt, and where thieves dig through and steal. But lay up treasures for yourselves in heaven, where neither the moth nor canker corrupteth, and where thieves neither dig through nor steal" (Matthew 6.19–20).

to riches and in regard of the things themselves when any special service for the church or particular distress of our brother do call for the use of them; otherwise it is not only lawful but necessary to lay up as Joseph[7] did to have ready upon such occasions, as the Lord (whose stewards we are of them) shall call for them from us. Christ gives us an instance of the first, when He sent his disciples for the ass, and bids them answer the owner thus, the Lord hath need of him.[8] So when the tabernacle was to be built He sends to His people to call for their silver and gold, etc.; and yields them no other reason but that it was for His work. When Elisha comes to the widow of Sareptah and finds her preparing to make ready her pittance for herself and family, He bids her first provide for Him; he challengeth first God's part which she must first give before she must serve her own family.[9] All these teach us that the Lord looks that when He is pleased to call for His right in anything we have, our own interest we have must stand aside till His turn be served. For the other, we need look no further than to that of John: 1: "He who hath this world's goods and seeth his brother to need and shuts up his compassion from him, how dwelleth the love of God in him," which comes punctually to this conclusion: if thy brother be in want and thou canst help him, thou needst not make doubt, what thou shouldst do, if thou lovest God thou must help him.

Quest. What rule must we observe in lending?

Ans. Thou must observe whether thy brother hath present or probable, or possible means of repaying thee, if there be none of these, thou must give him according to his necessity, rather than lend him as he requires. If he hath present means of repaying thee, thou art to look at him not as an act of mercy, but by way of commerce, wherein thou art to walk by the rule of justice; but if his means of repaying thee be only probable or possible, then is he an object of thy mercy, thou must lend him, though there be danger of losing it, Deuteronomy: 15.7: "If any of thy brethren be poor," etc., "thou shalt lend him sufficient."[1] That men might not shift off this duty by the apparent hazard, He tells them that though the year of Jubilee[2] were at hand (when he must remit it, if he were not able to repay it before) yet he must lend him and that cheerfully: "It may not grieve thee to give him" saith He; and because some might object; "why so I should soon impoverish myself and my family," He adds "with all thy work,"[3] etc.; for our Savior, Matthew: 5.42: "From him that would borrow of thee turn not away."

Quest. What rule must we observe in forgiving?

Ans. Whether thou didst lend by way of commerce or in mercy, if he have nothing to pay thee, [you] must forgive, (except in cause where thou hast a

7. The son of Jacob and Rachel, who stored up the harvest in the seven good years before the famine (Genesis 41).
8. Matthew 21.5–7.
9. 1 Kings 17.8–24.
1. "If one of thy brethren with thee be poor within any of thy gates in thy land, which the Lord thy God giveth thee, thou shalt not harden thine heart, nor shut thine hand from thy poor brother: But thou shalt open thine hand unto him, and shalt lend him sufficient for his need which he hath" (Deuteronomy 15.7–8).
2. According to Mosaic law (Leviticus 25.8–13), the Jubilee year followed a cycle of seven sab-batical years. In the fiftieth year, the lands would lie fallow, all work would cease, and all debts would be canceled.
3. "Beware that there be not a wicked thought in thine heart, to say, The seventh year, the year of freedom is at hand: therefore it grieveth thee to look on thy poor brother, and thou givest him nought, and he cry unto the Lord against thee, so that sin be in thee: Thou shalt give him, and let it not grieve thine heart to give unto him: for because of this the Lord thy God shall bless thee in all thy works, and in all that thou puttest thine hand to" (Deuteronomy 15.9–10).

surety or a lawful pledge) Deuteronomy: 15.2. Every seventh year the creditor was to quit that which he lent to his brother if he were poor as appears—verse 8: "Save when there shall be no poor with thee." In all these and like cases, Christ was a general rule, Matthew: 7.12: "Whatsoever ye would that men should do to you, do ye the same to them also."

Quest. What rule must we observe and walk by in cause of community of peril?

Ans. The same as before, but with more enlargement towards others and less respect towards ourselves and our own right. Hence it was that in the primitive church they sold all, had all things in common, neither did any man say that which he possessed was his own. Likewise in their return out of the captivity, because the work was great for the restoring of the church and the danger of enemies was common to all, Nehemiah exhorts the Jews to liberality and readiness in remitting their debts to their brethren, and disposing liberally of his own to such as wanted, and stand not upon his own due, which he might have demanded of them.[4] Thus did some of our forefathers in times of persecution in England, and so did many of the faithful of other churches, whereof we keep an honorable remembrance of them; and it is to be observed that both in Scriptures and later stories of the churches that such as have been most bountiful to the poor saints, especially in these extraordinary times and occasions, God hath left them highly commended to posterity, as Zacheus, Cornelius, Dorcas, Bishop Hooper, the Cuttler of Brussells and divers[5] others. Observe again that the Scripture gives no caution to restrain any from being over liberal this way; but all men to the liberal and cheerful practice hereof by the sweetest promises; as to instance one for many, Isaiah: 58.6: "Is not this the fast I have chosen to loose the bonds of wickedness, to take off the heavy burdens, to let the oppressed go free and to break every yoke, to deal thy bread to the hungry and to bring the poor that wander into thy house, when thou seest the naked to cover them. And then shall thy light break forth as the morning, and thy health shall grow speedily, thy righteousness shall go before God, and the glory of the Lord shall embrace thee; then thou shalt call and the Lord shall answer thee" etc. [Verse] 10: "If thou pour out thy soul to the hungry, then shall thy light spring out in darkness, and the Lord shall guide thee continually, and satisfy thy soul in drought, and make fat thy bones; thou shalt be like a watered garden, and they shalt be of thee that shall build the old waste places" etc. On the contrary, most heavy curses are laid upon such as are straightened towards the Lord and His people, Judges: 5.[23]: "Curse ye Meroshe because ye came not to help the Lord," etc. Proverbs: [21.13]: "He who shutteth his ears from hearing the cry of the poor, he shall cry and shall not be heard." Matthew: 25: "Go ye cursed into everlasting fire" etc. "I was hungry and ye fed me not." 2 Corinthians: 9.6: "He that soweth sparingly shall reap sparingly."

Having already set forth the practice of mercy according to the rule of God's law, it will be useful to lay open the grounds of it also, being the other part of the commandment, and that is the affection from which this exercise

4. Nehemiah was sent by King Artaxerxes to repair the walls of the city of Jerusalem; he saved the city as governor when he persuaded those lending money to charge no interest and to think first of the common good (see Nehemiah 3).
5. Various. The names are of Christian martyrs.

of mercy must arise. The apostle[6] tells us that this love is the fulfilling of the law, not that it is enough to love our brother and so no further; but in regard of the excellency of his parts giving any motion to the other as the soul to the body and the power it hath to set all the faculties on work in the outward exercise of this duty. As when we bid one make the clock strike, he doth not lay hand on the hammer, which is the immediate instrument of the sound, but sets on work the first mover or main wheel, knowing that will certainly produce the sound which he intends. So the way to draw men to works of mercy, is not by force of argument from the goodness or necessity of the work; for though this course may enforce a rational mind to some present act of mercy, as is frequent in experience, yet it cannot work such a habit in a soul, as shall make it prompt upon all occasions to produce the same effect, but by framing these affections of love in the heart which will as natively bring forth the other, as any cause doth produce effect.

The definition which the Scripture gives us of love is this: "Love is the bond of perfection." First, it is a bond or ligament. Secondly it makes the work perfect. There is no body but consists of parts and that which knits these parts together gives the body its perfection, because it makes each part so contiguous to others as thereby they do mutually participate with each other, both in strength and infirmity, in pleasure and pain. To instance in the most perfect of all bodies: Christ and His church make one body. The several parts of this body, considered apart before they were united, were as disproportionate and as much disordering as so many contrary qualities or elements, but when Christ comes and by His spirit and love knits all these parts to Himself and each to other, it is become the most perfect and best proportioned body in the world. Ephesians: 4.16: "Christ, by whom all the body being knit together by every joint for the furniture thereof, according to the effectual power which is the measure of every perfection of parts," "a glorious body without spot or wrinkle," the ligaments hereof being Christ, or His love, for Christ is love (1 John: 4.8). So this definition is right: "Love is the bond of perfection."

From hence we may frame these conclusions. 1. First of all, true Christians are of one body in Christ, 1 Corinthians: 12.12, 27: "Ye are the body of Christ and members of their part." Secondly: The ligaments of this body which knit together are love. Thirdly: No body can be perfect which wants its proper ligament. Fourthly: All the parts of this body being thus united are made so contiguous in a special relation as they must needs partake of each other's strength and infirmity; joy and sorrow, weal and woe. 1 Corinthians: 12.26: "If one member suffers, all suffer with it, if one be in honor, all rejoice with it." Fifthly: This sensibleness and sympathy of each other's conditions will necessarily infuse into each part a native desire and endeavor to strengthen, defend, preserve and comfort the other.

To insist a little on this conclusion being the product of all the former, the truth hereof will appear both by precept and pattern. 1 John: 3.10: "Ye ought to lay down your lives for the brethren." Galatians: 6.2: "bear ye one another's burthens and so fulfill the law of Christ." For patterns we have that first of our Savior who out of His good will in obedience to His father,

6. Saint Paul in his Epistle to the Romans 13.8.

becoming a part of this body, and being knit with it in the bond of love, found such a native sensibleness of our infirmities and sorrows as He willingly yielded Himself to death to ease the infirmities of the rest of His body, and so healed their sorrows. From the like sympathy of parts did the apostles and many thousands of the saints lay down their lives for Christ. Again, the like we may see in the members of this body among themselves. Romans: 9. Paul could have been contented to have been separated from Christ, that the Jews might not be cut off from the body. It is very observable what he professeth of his affectionate partaking with every member: "who is weak" saith he "and I am not weak? who is offended and I burn not;"[7] and again, 2 Corinthians: 7.13. "therefore we are comforted because ye were comforted." Of Epaphroditus he speaketh,[8] Philippians: 2.30. that he regarded not his own life to do him service. So Phoebe[9] and others are called the servants of the church. Now it is apparent that they served not for wages, or by constraint, but out of love. The like we shall find in the histories of the church in all ages, the sweet sympathy of affections which was in the members of this body one towards another, their cheerfulness in serving and suffering together, how liberal they were without repining, harborers without grudging and helpful without reproaching; and all from hence, because they had fervent love amongst them, which only make the practice of mercy constant and easy.

The next consideration is how this love comes to be wrought. Adam in his first estate[1] was a perfect model of mankind in all their generations, and in him this love was perfected in regard of the habit. But Adam rent himself from his creator, rent all his posterity also one from another; whence it comes that every man is born with this principle in him, to love and seek himself only, and thus a man continueth till Christ comes and takes possession of the soul and infuseth another principle, love to God and our brother. And this latter having continual supply from Christ, as the head and root by which he is united, gets the predomining[2] in the soul, so by little and little expels the former. 1 John: 4.7. "love cometh of God and every one that loveth is born of God," so that this love is the fruit of the new birth, and none can have it but the new creature. Now when this quality is thus formed in the souls of men, it works like the spirit upon the dry bones. Ezekiel: 37: "bone came to bone." It gathers together the scattered bones, of perfect old man Adam,[3] and knits them into one body again in Christ, whereby a man is become again a living soul.

The third consideration is concerning the exercise of this love which is twofold, inward or outward. The outward hath been handled in the former preface of this discourse. For unfolding the other we must take in our way that maxim of philosophy *simile simili gaudet*, or like will to like [Latin]; for as it is things which are turned with disaffection to each other, the ground of it is from a dissimilitude arising from the contrary or different nature of

7. 2 Corinthians 11.29.
8. Saint Paul tells the Philippians he will send them a spiritual guide: "But I supposed it necessary to send my brother Epaphroditus unto you my companion in labor, and fellow soldier, even your messenger, and he that ministered unto me such things as I wanted" (Philippians 2.25).

9. A Christian woman praised by Saint Paul in Romans 16.1.
1. I.e., in his innocence.
2. Predominance.
3. Jesus Christ has traditionally been called the New Adam to signify the redemption of humankind from the original sin of Old Adam.

the things themselves; for the ground of love is an apprehension of some resemblance in things loved to that which affects it. This is the cause why the Lord loves the creature, so far as it hath any of His image in it; He loves His elect because they are like Himself, He beholds them in His beloved son. So a mother loves her child, because she thoroughly conceives a resemblance of herself in it. Thus it is between the members of Christ. Each discerns, by the work of the spirit, his own image and resemblance in another, and therefore cannot but love him as he loves himself. Now when the soul, which is of a sociable nature, finds anything like to itself, it is like Adam when Eve was brought to him. She must have it one with herself. This is flesh of my flesh (saith the soul) and bone of my bone. She conceives a great delight in it, therefore she desires nearness and familiarity with it. She hath a great propensity to do it good and receives such content in it, as fearing the miscarriage of her beloved she bestows it in the inmost closet of her heart. She will not endure that it shall want any good which she can give it. If by occasion she be withdrawn from the company of it, she is still looking towards the place where she left her beloved. If she heard it groan, she is with it presently. If she find it sad and disconsolate, she sighs and moans with it. She hath no such joy as to see her beloved merry and thriving. If she see it wronged, she cannot bear it without passion. She sets no bounds to her affections, nor hath any thought of reward. She finds recompense enough in the exercise of her love towards it. We may see this acted to life in Jonathan and David.[4] Jonathan, a valiant man endowed with the spirit of Christ, so soon as he discovers the same spirit in David, had presently his heart knit to him by this lineament of love, so that it is said he loved him as his own soul. He takes so great pleasure in him, that he strips himself to adorn his beloved. His father's kingdom was not so precious to him as his beloved David. David shall have it with all his heart, himself desires no more but that he may be near to him to rejoice in his good. He chooseth to converse with him in the wilderness even to the hazard of his own life, rather than with the great courtiers in his father's palace. When he sees danger towards him, he spares neither rare pains nor peril to direct it. When injury was offered his beloved David, he would not bear it, though from his own father; and when they must part for a season only, they thought their hearts would have broke for sorrow, had not their affections found vent by abundance of tears. Other instances might be brought to show the nature of this affection, as of Ruth and Naomi,[5] and many others; but this truth is cleared enough.

If any shall object that it is not possible that love should be bred or upheld without hope of requital, it is granted; but that is not our cause; for this love is always under reward. It never gives, but it always receives with advantage; first, in regard that among the members of the same body, love and affection are reciprocal in a most equal and sweet kind of commerce. Secondly, in regard of the pleasure and content that the exercise of love carries with it, as we may see in the natural body. The mouth is at all the pains to receive and mince the food which serves for the nourishment of all the other parts of the body, yet it hath no cause to complain; for first the other parts send

4. The story of Jonathan and David is told in 1 Samuel 19 ff.
5. Naomi was Ruth's mother-in-law; when Ruth's husband died, she refused to leave Naomi (Ruth 1.16).

back by several passages a due proportion of the same nourishment, in a better form for the strengthening and comforting the mouth. Secondly, the labor of the mouth is accompanied with such pleasure and content as far exceeds the pains it takes. So is it in all the labor of love among Christians. The party loving, reaps love again, as was showed before, which the soul covets more than all the wealth in the world. Thirdly: Nothing yields more pleasure and content to the soul than when it finds that which it may love fervently, for to love and live beloved is the soul's paradise, both here and in heaven. In the state of wedlock there be many comforts to bear out the troubles of that condition; but let such as have tried the most, say if there be any sweetness in that condition comparable to the exercise of mutual love.

From former considerations arise these conclusions.

First: This love among Christians is a real thing, not imaginary.

Secondly: This love is as absolutely necessary to the being of the body of Christ, as the sinews and other ligaments of a natural body are to the being of that body.

Thirdly: This love is a divine, spiritual nature free, active, strong, courageous, permanent; undervaluing all things beneath its proper object; and of all the graces, this makes us nearer to resemble the virtues of our Heavenly Father.

Fourthly: It rests in the love and welfare of its beloved. For the full and certain knowledge of these truths concerning the nature, use, and excellency of this grace, that which the Holy Ghost hath left recorded, 1 Corinthians: 13, may give full satisfaction, which is needful for every true member of this lovely body of the Lord Jesus, to work upon their hearts by prayer, meditation, continual exercise at least of the special [influence] of His grace, till Christ be formed in them and they in Him, all in each other, knit together by this bond of love.

II

It rests now to make some application of this discourse by the present design, which gave the occasion of writing of it. Herein are four things to be propounded: first the persons, secondly the work, thirdly the end, fourthly the means.

First, For the persons. We are a company professing ourselves fellow members of Christ, in which respect only though we were absent from each other many miles, and had our employments as far distant, yet we ought to account ourselves knit together by this bond of love, and live in the exercise of it, if we would have comfort of our being in Christ. This was notorious in the practice of the Christians in former times; as is testified of the Waldenses,[6] from the mouth of one of the adversaries *Æneas Sylvius* "mutuo [ament][7] penè antequam norunt," they used to love any of their own religion even before they were acquainted with them.

Secondly, for the work we have in hand. It is by a mutual consent, through a special overvaluing providence and a more than an ordinary approbation

6. The Waldenses took their name from Pater Valdes, an early French reformer of the Church. They still survive as a religious community.
7. *Solent amare* is closer to the Latin than is *ament*, the suggestion of the original editor, Samuel Eliot Morison. Aeneas Sylvius Piccolomini (1405–1464), historian and scholar, became Pope Pius II.

of the Churches of Christ, to seek out a place of cohabitation and consort-ship under a due form of government both civil and ecclesiastical. In such cases as this, the care of the public must oversway all private respects, by which, not only conscience, but mere civil policy, doth bind us. For it is a true rule that particular estates cannot subsist in the ruin of the public.

Thirdly. The end is to improve our lives to do more service to the Lord; the comfort and increase of the body of Christ whereof we are members; that ourselves and posterity may be the better preserved from the common corruptions of this evil world, to serve the Lord and work out our salvation under the power and purity of His holy ordinances.

Fourthly, for the means whereby this must be effected. They are twofold, a conformity with the work and end we aim at. These we see are extraordi-nary, therefore we must not content ourselves with usual ordinary means. Whatsoever we did or ought to have done when we lived in England, the same must we do, and more also, where we go. That which the most in their churches maintain as a truth in profession only, we must bring into familiar and constant practice, as in this duty of love. We must love brotherly with-out dissimulation; we must love one another with a pure heart fervently. We must bear one another's burthens. We must not look only on our own things, but also on the things of our brethren, neither must we think that the Lord will bear with such failings at our hands as he doth from those among whom we have lived; and that for three reasons.

First, In regard of the more near bond of marriage between Him and us, where-in He hath taken us to be His after a most strict and peculiar man-ner, which will make Him the more jealous of our love and obedience. So He tells the people of Israel, you only have I known of all the families of the earth, therefore will I punish you for your transgressions. Secondly, because the Lord will be sanctified in them that come near Him. We know that there were many that corrupted the service of the Lord, some setting up altars before His own, others offering both strange fire and strange sacrifices also; yet there came no fire from heaven or other sudden judgment upon them, as did upon Nadab and Abihu,[8] who yet we may think did not sin presump-tuously. Thirdly. When God gives a special commission He looks to have it strictly observed in every article. When He gave Saul a commission to destroy Amaleck, He indented with him upon certain articles,[9] and because he failed in one of the least, and that upon a fair pretense, it lost him the kingdom which should have been his reward if he had observed his commission.

Thus stands the cause between God and us. We are entered into cove-nant[1] with Him for this work. We have taken out a commission, the Lord hath given us leave to draw our own articles. We have professed to enter-prise these actions, upon these and those ends, we have hereupon besought Him of favor and blessing. Now if the Lord shall please to hear us, and bring

8. "But Nadab and Abihu, the sons of Aaron, took either of them his censor, and put fire therein, and put incense thereupon, and offered strange fire before the Lord, which he had not commanded them. Therefore a fire went out from the Lord, and devoured them: so they died before the Lord" (Leviticus 10.1–2). Winthrop's point is that the chosen people are often pun-ished more severely than unbelievers.
9. I.e., made an agreement with him on parts of

a contract. Saul was instructed to destroy the Amalekites and all they possessed, but he spared their sheep and oxen, and in doing so disobeyed God's commandment and was rejected as king (1 Samuel 15.1–34).
1. A legal contract. The Israelites entered into a covenant with God in which he promised to pro-tect them if they kept his word and were faithful to him.

us in peace to the place we desire, then hath He ratified this covenant and sealed our commission, [and] will expect a strict performance of the articles contained in it; but if we shall neglect the observation of these articles which are the ends we have propounded, and, dissembling with our God, shall fall to embrace this present world and prosecute our carnal intentions, seeking great things for ourselves and our posterity, the Lord will surely break out in wrath against us; be revenged of such a perjured people and make us know the price of the breach of such a covenant.

Now the only way to avoid this shipwreck, and to provide for our posterity, is to follow the counsel of Micah,[2] to do justly, to love mercy, to walk humbly with our God. For this end, we must be knit together in this work as one man. We must entertain each other in brotherly affection, we must be willing to abridge ourselves of our superfluities, for the supply of other's necessities. We must uphold a familiar commerce together in all meekness, gentleness, patience and liberality. We must delight in each other, make other's conditions our own, rejoice together, mourn together, labor and suffer together, always having before our eyes our commission and community in the work, our community as members of the same body. So shall we keep the unity of the spirit in the bond of peace. The Lord will be our God, and delight to dwell among us as His own people, and will command a blessing upon us in all our ways, so that we shall see much more of His wisdom, power, goodness and truth, than formerly we have been acquainted with. We shall find that the God of Israel is among us, when ten of us shall be able to resist a thousand of our enemies; when He shall make us a praise and glory that men shall say of succeeding plantations, "the Lord make it like that of NEW ENGLAND." For we must consider that we shall be as a city upon a hill.[3] The eyes of all people are upon us, so that if we shall deal falsely with our God in this work we have undertaken, and so cause Him to withdraw His present help from us, we shall be made a story and a by-word through the world. We shall open the mouths of enemies to speak evil of the ways of God, and all professors for God's sake. We shall shame the faces of many of God's worthy servants, and cause their prayers to be turned into curses upon us till we be consumed out of the good land whither we are agoing.

And to shut up this discourse with that exhortation of Moses, that faithful servant of the Lord, in his last farewell to Israel, Deuteronomy 30.[4] Beloved, there is now set before us life and good, death and evil, in that we

2. An eighth-century-B.C.E. prophet who, in the Book of Micah, speaks continually of God's judgment and the need to hope for salvation: "He hath showed thee, O man, what is good, and what the Lord requireth of thee: surely to do justly, and to love mercy, and to humble thyself, to walk with thy God" (Micah 6.8).
3. "Ye are the light of the world. A city that is set on an hill, cannot be hid. Neither do men light a candle, and put it under a bushel, but on a candlestick, and it giveth light unto all that are in the house" (Matthew 5.14–15).
4. "Behold, I have set before thee this day life and good, death and evil, In that I command thee this day, to love the Lord thy God, to walk in his ways, and to keep his commandment, and his ordinances, and his laws, that thou mayest live, and be

multiplied, and that the Lord thy God may bless thee in the land, whither thou goest to possess it. But if thine heart turn away, so that thou wilt not obey, but shalt be seduced and worship other gods, and serve them, I pronounce unto you this day, that ye shall surely perish, ye shall not prolong your days in the land, whither thou passest over Jordan to possess it. I call heaven and earth to record this day against you, that I have set before you life and death, blessing and cursing: therefore choose life, that both thou and thy seed may live, By loving the Lord thy God, by obeying his voice, and by cleaving unto him: for he is thy life, and the length of thy days, that thou mayest dwell in the land which the Lord sware unto thy fathers, Abraham, Isaac, and Jacob, to give them" (Deuteronomy 30.15–20).

are commanded this day to love the Lord our God, and to love one another, to walk in His ways and to keep His commandments and His ordinance and His laws, and the articles of our covenant with Him, that we may live and be multiplied, and that our Lord our God may bless us in the land whither we go to possess it. But if our hearts shall turn away, so that we will not obey, but shall be seduced, and worship other gods, our pleasures and profits, and serve them; it is propounded unto us this day, we shall surely perish out of the good land whither we pass over this vast sea to possess it.

> Therefore let us choose life,
> that we and our seed
> may live by obeying His
> voice and cleaving to Him,
> for He is our life and
> our prosperity.

1630 1838

From The Journal of John Winthrop[1]

[Sighting Mount Desert Island, Maine]

[June 8, 1630] About 3 in the afternoon we had sight of land to the NW about 15 leagues, which we supposed was the Isles of Monhegen, but it proved Mount Mansell.[2] Then we tacked and stood WSW. We had now fair sunshine weather and so pleasant a sweet ether[3] as did much refresh us, and there came a smell off the shore like the smell of a garden. There came a wild pigeon into our ship and another small land bird.

[Overcoming Satan]

[July 5, 1632] At Watertown there was (in the view of divers[4] witnesses) a great combat between a mouse and a snake, and after a long fight the mouse prevailed and killed the snake. The pastor of Boston, Mr. Wilson,[5] a very sincere, holy man, hearing of it gave this interpretation: that the snake was the devil, the mouse was a poor contemptible people which God had brought hither, which should overcome Satan here and dispossess him of his kingdom. Upon the same occasion he told the governor[6] that before he was resolved to come into this country he dreamed he was here, and that he saw a church arise out of the earth, which grew up and became a marvelous goodly church.

1. The text is from *The Journal of John Winthrop, 1630–1649* (1996), abridged ed., edited by Richard S. Dunn and Laetitia Yeandle.
2. Winthrop saw Mount Desert Island, Maine. The English named it after a British admiral, Sir Robert Mansell (1573–1656); the French explorer Samuel de Champlain (see the "First Encounters" cluster, above) named it Île des Monts Déserts.
3. Air.
4. Several.
5. The Reverend John Wilson (1588–1667), then beginning a pastorate that lasted thirty-seven years.
6. Winthrop.

[Charges Made against Roger Williams]

[December 27, 1633] The governor and assistants met at Boston and took into consideration a treatise which Mr. Williams[7] (then of Salem) had sent to them, and which he had formerly written to the governor[8] and Council of Plymouth, wherein among other things he disputes their right to the lands they possessed here, and concluded that claiming by the King's grant they could have no title, nor otherwise except they compounded[9] with the natives. For this, taking advice with some of the most judicious ministers (who much condemned Mr. Williams's error and presumption), they gave order that he should be convented[1] at the next Court to be censured, etc. There were 3 passages chiefly whereat they were much offended: 1. For that he chargeth King James to have told a solemn public lie, because in his patent he blessed God that he was the first Christian prince that had discovered this land; 2. For that he chargeth him and others with blasphemy for calling Europe Christendom or the Christian world; 3. For that he did personally apply to our present King Charles these 3 places in the Revelation, viz.[2]

Mr. Endecott[3] being absent, the governor wrote to him to let him know what was done, and withal added divers arguments to confute the said errors, wishing him to deal with Mr. Williams to retract the same, etc. Whereunto he returned a very modest and discreet answer. Mr. Williams also wrote very submissively, professing his intent to have been only to have written for the private satisfaction of the governor, etc., of Plymouth without any purpose to have stirred any further in it if the governor here had not required a copy of him; withal offering his book or any part of it to be burnt, etc. So it was left and nothing done in it.

[A Smallpox Epidemic]

[January 20, 1634] Hall and the 2 others[4] who went to Connecticut November 3 came now home, having lost themselves and endured much misery. They informed us that the smallpox was gone as far as any Indian plantation was known to the W[est], and much people dead of it, by reason whereof they could have no trade. At Narragansett by the Indians' report there died 700, but beyond Pascataquack none to the E[ast].

[A Warrant for Roger Williams]

[January 11, 1636] The governor[5] and assistants met at Boston to consult about Mr. Williams, for that they were credibly informed that notwithstanding the injunction laid upon him (upon the liberty granted him to stay till the spring) not to go about to draw others to his opinions, he did use to entertain company in his house and to preach to them, even of such points as he

7. Roger Williams, a Puritan theologian who had emigrated to New England in 1630 and expressed radical views on Church reform and colonialism (his writing is excerpted later in this volume).
8. In 1633, Edward Winslow was governor in Plymouth (see the "First Encounters" cluster).
9. Arranged to make a financial settlement.
1. Summoned to appear.

2. Abbreviation for *videlicet*: namely (Latin).
3. John Endecott (c. 1588–1665): governor to the Massachusetts Bay Colony's advance settlement in Salem from 1628 until Winthrop arrived.
4. Not further identified.
5. John Hays (1594–1654). Winthrop was elected governor again in 1637.

had been censured for; and it was agreed to send him into England by a ship then ready to depart. The reason was because he had drawn above 20 persons to his opinion and they were intended to erect a plantation about the Narragansett Bay, from whence the infection[6] would easily spread into these churches (the people being many of them much taken with the apprehension of his godliness). Whereupon a warrant was sent to him to come presently to Boston to be shipped,[7] etc. He returned answer (and divers of Salem came with it) that he could not come without hazard of his life, etc., whereupon a pinnace was sent with commission to Captain Underhill,[8] etc., to apprehend him and carry him aboard the ship (which then rode at Nantasket), but when they came at his house they found he had been gone 3 days before, but whither they could not learn.

[The Case of Anne Hutchinson]

[October 21, 1636] * * * One Mrs. Hutchinson, a member of the church of Boston, a woman of a ready wit and bold spirit, brought over with her two dangerous errors: 1. That the person of the Holy Ghost dwells in a justified person.[9] 2. That no sanctification can help to evidence to us our justification.[1]—From these two grew many branches; as, 1, Our union with the Holy Ghost, so as a Christian remains dead to every spiritual action, and hath no gifts nor graces, other than such as are in hypocrites, nor any other sanctification but the Holy Ghost Himself.[2]

There joined with her in these opinions a brother of hers, one Mr. Wheelwright, a silenced minister sometimes in England.[3]

[Rev. John Cotton Explains His Position]

[October 25, 1636] The other ministers in the bay, hearing of these things, came to Boston at the time of a general court, and entered conference in private with them, to the end they might know the certainty of these things; that if need were, they might write to the church of Boston about them, to prevent (if it were possible) the dangers which seemed hereby to hang over that and the rest of the churches. At this conference, Mr. Cotton was present, and gave satisfaction[4] to them, so as he agreed with them all in the point of sanctification, and so did Mr. Wheelwright; so as they all did hold that sanctification did help to evidence justification. The same he had delivered plainly in public, divers times; but, for the indwelling of the person of the

6. Misguided teachings. Providence Plantation, the colony Williams started in Rhode Island, received its patent in 1644.
7. I.e., returned to Boston by ship.
8. John Underhill (c. 1597–1672), soldier who organized the Massachusetts Bay Colony militia. "Pinnace": a small, light vessel, usually with two masts.
9. Anne Hutchinson (1591–1643) held the radical view that the "justified"—those elected or chosen for salvation by God—were joined in personal union with God and superior to those lacking such inspiration.
1. I.e., that proper moral conduct is no sign of justification.

2. I.e., that good works are not a sign of God's favor; justification is by faith alone and has nothing to do with either piety or worldly success.
3. John Wheelwright (c. 1592–1679) had been a vicar near Alford, England, where Anne Hutchinson and her husband, William, lived before emigrating to America. Wheelwright was removed from his ministry, probably because he refused to sign an oath of loyalty to the Church of England, and went to Boston in 1636.
4. Satisfied their doubts about him. The sermons of the Reverend John Cotton (1584–1652), a prominent Boston theologian, were admired by the Hutchinsons, which worried his fellow ministers.

Holy Ghost, he held that still, but not union with the person of the Holy Ghost, so as to amount to a personal union.

[Charges Brought against Mrs. Hutchinson and Others]

[November 1, 1637] * * * There was great hope that the late general assembly would have had some good effect in pacifying the troubles and dissensions about matters of religion; but it fell out otherwise. For though Mr. Wheelwright and those of his party had been clearly confuted and confounded in the assembly, yet they persisted in their opinions, and were as busy in nourishing contentions (the principal of them) as before. * * *

The court also sent for Mrs. Hutchinson, and charged her with divers matters, as her keeping two public lectures every week in her house, whereto sixty or eighty persons did usually resort, and for reproaching most of the ministers (viz., all except Mr. Cotton) for not preaching a covenant of free grace, and that they had not the seal of the spirit, nor were able ministers of the New Testament; which were clearly proved against her, though she sought to shift it off.[5] And after many speeches to and fro, at last she was so full as she could not contain, but vented her revelations; amongst which this was one, that she had it revealed to her that she should come into New England, and she should here be persecuted, and that God would ruin us and our posterity and the whole state for the same. So the court proceeded and banished her; but because it was winter, they committed her to a private house where she was well provided, and her own friends and the elders permitted to go to her, but none else.

The court called also Capt. Underhill and some five or six more of the principal, whose hands were to the said petition; and because they stood to justify it they were disfranchised, and such as had public places were put from them.

The court also ordered, that the rest, who had subscribed the petition, (and would not acknowledge their fault, and which near twenty of them did,) and some others, who had been chief stirrers in these contentions, etc., should be disarmed.[6] This troubled some of them very much, especially because they were to bring them in themselves; but at last, when they saw no remedy, they obeyed.

All the proceedings of this court against these persons were set down at large, with the reasons and other observations, and were sent into England to be published there, to the end that our godly friends might not be discouraged from coming to us, etc. * * *

[Mrs. Hutchinson Admonished Further]

[March 1638] While Mrs. Hutchinson continued at Roxbury,[7] divers of the elders and others resorted to her, and finding her to persist in maintaining those gross errors beforementioned and many others to the number of thirty or thereabout, some of them wrote to the church at Boston, offering to make proof of the same before the church, etc., [March] 15; whereupon she was

5. To qualify her statements.
6. Seventy-five people were disarmed, a severe
punishment for this time and place.
7. Near Boston.

called, (the magistrates being desired to give her license to come,) and the lecture was appointed to begin at ten. (The general court being then at Newtown, the governor[8] and the treasurer, being members of Boston, were permitted to come down, but the rest of the court continued at Newtown.) When she appeared, the errors were read to her. The first was that the souls of men are mortal by generation,[9] but after made immortal by Christ's purchase. This she maintained a long time; but at length she was so clearly convinced by reason and scripture, and the whole church agreeing that sufficient had been delivered for her conviction, that she yielded she had been in an error. Then they proceeded to three other errors: That there was no resurrection of these bodies, and that these bodies were not united to Christ, but every person united hath a new body, etc. These were also clearly confuted, but yet she held her own; so as the church (all but two of her sons)[1] agreed she should be admonished, and because her sons would not agree to it, they were admonished also.

Mr. Cotton pronounced the sentence of admonition with great solemnity, and with much zeal and detestation of her errors and pride of spirit. The assembly continued till eight at night, and all did acknowledge the special presence of God's spirit therein; and she was appointed to appear again the next lecture day. * * *

[Mrs. Hutchinson Banished]

[March 22, 1638] Mrs. Hutchinson appeared again; (she had been licensed by the court, in regard she had given hope of her repentance, to be at Mr. Cotton's house that both he and Mr. Davenport[2] might have the more opportunity to deal with her;) and the articles being again read to her, and her answer required, she delivered it in writing, wherein she made a retractation of near all, but with such explanations and circumstances as gave no satisfaction to the church; so as she was required to speak further to them. Then she declared that it was just with God to leave her to herself, as He had done, for her slighting His ordinances, both magistracy and ministry;[3] and confessed that what she had spoken against the magistrates at the court (by way of revelation) was rash and ungrounded; and desired the church to pray for her. This gave the church good hope of her repentance; but when she was examined about some particulars, as that she had denied inherent righteousness, etc., she affirmed that it was never her judgment; and though it was proved by many testimonies that she had been of that judgment, and so had persisted and maintained it by argument against divers, yet she impudently persisted in her affirmation, to the astonishment of all the assembly. So that after much time and many arguments had been spent to bring her to see her sin, but all in vain, the church with one consent cast her out. Some moved to have her admonished[4] once more; but, it being for manifest evil in matter of conversation, it was agreed otherwise; and for that reason also the

8. Winthrop. Newtown was soon thereafter renamed Cambridge.
9. I.e., from the beginning. Orthodox believers hold that the soul is always immortal.
1. Her son Edward Hutchinson and her son-in-law Thomas Savage, both of whom moved to

Rhode Island.
2. John Davenport (1597–1670), a minister.
3. Because Anne Hutchinson's beliefs threatened both civil and ecclesiastical law.
4. Warned.

sentence was denounced by the pastor,[5] matter of manners belonging properly to his place.

After she was excommunicated,[6] her spirits which seemed before to be somewhat dejected revived again, and she gloried in her sufferings, saying that it was the greatest happiness next to Christ that ever befell her. Indeed it was a happy day to the churches of Christ here, and to many poor souls who had been seduced by her, who by what they heard and saw that day were (through the grace of God) brought off quite from her errors, and settled again in the truth.

At this time the good providence of God so disposed, divers of the congregation (being the chief men of the party, her husband being one) were gone to Narragansett to seek out a new place for plantation, and taking liking of one in Plymouth patent, they went thither to have it granted them; but the magistrates there, knowing their spirit, gave them a denial, but consented they might buy of the Indians an island in the Narragansett Bay.[7]

After two or three days the governor sent a warrant to Mrs. Hutchinson to depart this jurisdiction before the last of this month, according to the order of court, and for that end set her at liberty from her former constraint, so as she was not to go forth of her own house till her departure; and upon the 28th she went by water to her farm at the Mount, where she was to take water with Mr. Wheelwright's wife and family to go to Pascataquack; but she changed her mind, and went by land to Providence, and so to the island in the Narragansett Bay which her husband and the rest of that sect had purchased of the Indians, and prepared with all speed to remove unto. For the court had ordered, that except they were gone with their families by such a time they should be summoned to the general court, etc.

[Mrs. Hutchinson Delivers a Child]

[September 1638] * * * Mrs. Hutchinson, being removed to the Isle of Aquiday[8] in the Narragansett Bay, after her time was fulfilled that she expected deliverance of a child, was delivered of a monstrous birth. Hereupon the governor wrote to Mr. Clarke,[9] a physician and a preacher to those of the island, to know the certainty thereof, who returned him this answer: Mrs. Hutchinson, six weeks before her delivery, perceived her body to be greatly distempered and her spirits failing and in that regard doubtful of life, she sent to me etc., and not long after (in *immoderato fluore uterino*)[1] it was brought to light, and I was called to see it, where I beheld innumerable distinct bodies in the form of a globe, not much unlike the swims[2] of some fish, so confusedly knit together by so many several strings (which I conceive were the beginning of veins and nerves) so that it was impossible either to number the small round pieces in every lump, much less to discern from whence every string did fetch its original, they were so snarled one within another. The small globes I likewise opened, and perceived the matter of them (setting

5. I.e., read in public by John Wilson.
6. Cast out of the congregation.
7. William Hutchinson and several others laid out plans for the town of Portsmouth, Rhode Island.
8. Aquidneck Island, Rhode Island.

9. Dr. John Clarke came to Boston in 1637 and was disarmed, having been declared an antinomian (believer that faith alone, not morality, is necessary for salvation).
1. In a heavy discharge from the womb (Latin).
2. Swim bladders.

aside the membrane in which it was involved) to be partly wind and partly water. The governor, not satisfied with this relation, spake after with the said Mr. Clarke, who thus cleared all the doubts: The lumps were twenty-six or twenty-seven, distinct and not joined together; there came no secundine[3] after them; six of them were as great as his fist, and the smallest about the bigness of the top of his thumb. The globes were round things, included in the lumps, about the bigness of a small Indian bean, and like the pearl in a man's eye. The two lumps which differed from the rest were like liver or congealed blood, and had no small globes in them, as the rest had.

[An Earthquake at Aquiday]

[March 16, 1639] * * * At Aquiday also Mrs. Hutchinson exercised[4] publicly, and she and her party (some three or four families) would have no magistracy. She sent also an admonition to the church of Boston; but the elders would not read it publicly because she was excommunicated. By these examples we may see how dangerous it is to slight the censures of the church; for it was apparent that God had given them up to strange delusions. . . . Mrs. Hutchinson and some of her adherents happened to be at prayer when the earthquake was at Aquiday, etc., and the house being shaken thereby, they were persuaded (and boasted of it) that the Holy Ghost did shake it in coming down upon them, as He did upon the apostles.

[The Death of Mrs. Hutchinson and Others]

[September 1643] The Indians near the Dutch, having killed 15 men, began to set upon the English who dwelt under the Dutch. They came to Mrs. Hutchinson's[5] in way of friendly neighborhood, as they had been accustomed, and taking their opportunity, killed her and Mr. Collins, her son-in-law (who had been kept prisoner in Boston, as is before related), and all her family, and such [other] families as were at home; in all sixteen, and put their cattle into their houses and there burnt them. These people had cast off ordinances and churches, and now at last their own people, and for larger accommodation had subjected themselves to the Dutch and dwelt scatteringly near a mile asunder. * * *

[Winthrop's Speech to the General Court]

[July 3, 1645] * * * Then was the deputy governor[6] desired by the Court to go up and take his place again upon the bench, which he did accordingly. And the Court being about to rise, he desired leave for a little speech which was to this effect.

3. Afterbirth.
4. Lectured.
5. After the death of her husband in 1642, Anne Hutchinson moved to Dutch territory: Pelham Bay, now a part of the Bronx in New York City.
6. Winthrop. The governor in 1645 was Thomas Dudley (1576–1653). The "little speech" that follows is one of Winthrop's most important meditations on Christian liberty. Several residents of the town of Hingham argued that "words spoken against the General Court" had been unfairly used and hoped that Winthrop would be impeached for misusing his power as deputy. Winthrop was fully acquitted.

I suppose something may be expected from me upon this charge that is befallen me, which moves me to speak now to you. Yet I intend not to intermeddle in the proceedings of the Court, or with any of the persons concerned therein. Only I bless God that I see an issue[7] of this troublesome business. I also acknowledge the justice of the Court, and for mine own part I am well satisfied. I was publicly charged, and I am publicly and legally acquitted, which is all I did expect or desire. And though this be sufficient for my justification before men, yet not so before the Lord, who hath seen so much amiss in any dispensations (and even in this affair) as calls me to be humbled. For to be publicly and criminally charged in this Court is matter of humiliation (and I desire to make a right use of it), notwithstanding I be thus acquitted. If her father had spit in her face (saith the Lord concerning Miriam), should she not have been ashamed 7 days?[8] Shame had lain upon her whatever the occasion had been. I am unwilling to stay you from your urgent affairs, yet give me leave (upon this special occasion) to speak a little more to this assembly. It may be of some good use to inform and rectify the judgments of some of the people, and may prevent such distempers as have arisen amongst us. The great questions that have troubled the country are about the authority of the magistrates and the liberty of the people. It is yourselves who have called us to this office, and being called by you we have our authority from God in way of an ordinance, such as hath the image of God eminently stamped upon it, the contempt and violation whereof hath been vindicated with examples of divine vengeance. I entreat you to consider that when you choose magistrates you take them from among yourselves, men subject to like passions as you are. Therefore, when you see infirmities in us, you should reflect upon your own, and that would make you bear the more with us, and not be severe censurers of the failings of your magistrates when you have continual experience of the like infirmities in yourselves and others. We account him a good servant who breaks not his covenant.[9] The covenant between you and us is the oath you have taken of us, which is to this purpose, that we shall govern you and judge your causes by the rules of God's laws and our own, according to our best skill. When you agree with a workman to build you a ship or house, etc., he undertakes as well for his skill as for his faithfulness, for it is his profession, and you pay him for both. But when you call one to be a magistrate, he doth not profess nor undertake to have sufficient skill for that office, nor can you furnish him with gifts, etc. Therefore you must run the hazard of his skill and ability. But if he fail in faithfulness, which by his oath he is bound unto, that he must answer for. If it fall out that the case be clear to common apprehension and the rule clear also, if he transgress here the error is not in the skill but in the evil of the will; it must be required of him. But if the case be doubtful, or the rule doubtful, to men of such understanding and parts as your magistrates are, if your magistrates should err here yourselves must bear it.

For the other point concerning liberty, I observe a great mistake in the country about that. There is a twofold liberty: natural (I mean as our nature

7. Termination.
8. Miriam was the sister of Moses and Aaron. "And the Lord said unto Moses, If her father had but spit in her face, should she not be ashamed seven days? let her be shut out from the camp seven days, and after that let her be received in again" (Numbers 12.14).
9. Format agreement.

is now corrupt),[1] and civil or federal. The first is common to man with beasts and other creatures. By this, man as he stands in relation to man simply, hath liberty to do what he list. It is a liberty to evil as well as to good. This liberty is incompatible and inconsistent with authority, and cannot endure the least restraint of the most just authority. The exercise and maintaining of this liberty makes men grow more evil, and in time to be worse than brute beasts, *omnes sumus licentia deteriores*.[2] This is that great enemy of truth and peace, that wild beast which all the ordinances of God are bent against, to restrain and subdue it.

The other kind of liberty I call civil or federal. It may also be termed moral, in reference to the covenant between God and man in the moral law, and the politic covenants and constitutions amongst men themselves. This liberty is the proper end and object of authority and cannot subsist without it, and it is a liberty to that only which is good, just, and honest. This liberty you are to stand for, with the hazard not only of your goods but of your lives, if need be. Whatsoever crosseth this is not authority, but a distemper thereof. This liberty is maintained and exercised in a way of subjection to authority. It is of the same kind of liberty wherewith Christ hath made us free.[3] The woman's own choice makes such a man her husband, yet being so chosen he is her lord and she is to be subject to him, yet in a way of liberty, not of bondage, and a true wife accounts her subjection her honor and freedom, and would not think her condition safe and free but in her subjection to her husband's authority. Such is the liberty of the church under the authority of Christ her King and husband. His yoke is so easy and sweet to her as a bride's ornaments,[4] and if through frowardness or wantonness, etc., she shake it off at any time, she is at no rest in her spirit until she take it up again. And whether her Lord smiles upon her and embraceth her in His arms, or whether He frowns, or rebukes, or smites her, she apprehends the sweetness of His love in all and is refreshed, supported, and instructed by every such dispensation of His authority over her. On the other side, you know who they are that complain of this yoke and say: let us break their bands, etc.; we will not have this man to rule over us. Even so, brethren, it will be between you and your magistrates. If you stand for your natural corrupt liberties, and will do what is good in your own eyes, you will not endure the least weight of authority, but will murmur and oppose and be always striving to shake off that yoke. But if you will be satisfied to enjoy such civil and lawful liberties, such as Christ allows you, then will you quietly and cheerfully submit unto that authority which is set over you in all the administrations of it for your good; wherein if we fail at any time, we hope we shall be willing (by God's assistance) to hearken to good advice from any of you, or in any other way of God. So shall your liberties be preserved in upholding the honor and power of authority amongst you.

The deputy governor having ended his speech, the Court arose, and the magistrates and deputies retired to attend their other affairs. * * *

1. Because we are fallen and subject to death.
2. We are all the worse for license (Latin). From the ancient Roman dramatist Terence, *Heauton Timorumenos* (*The Self-Tormentor*) 3.1.74.
3. "Stand fast therefore in the liberty wherewith Christ hath made us free, and be not entangled again with the yoke of bondage" (Galatians 5.1).
4. "For my yoke is easy, and my burden is light" (Matthew 11.30). "And I John saw the holy city, new Jerusalem, coming down out of heaven from God, prepared as a bride adorned for her husband" (Revelation 21.2).

[A Daughter Returned]

[July 1646] * * * A daughter of Mrs. Hutchinson was carried away by the Indians near the Dutch, when her mother and others were killed by them; and upon the peace concluded between the Dutch and the same Indians, she was returned to the Dutch governor, who restored her to her friends here. She was about 8 years old when she was taken, and continued with them about 4 years, and she had forgot her own language, and all her friends, and was loath to have come from the Indians.

1630–49 1825–26

THE BAY PSALM BOOK

The Protestant Reformation sparked a revival of psalm- and hymn-singing that held important consequences for English-language poetry. Church music had previously been reserved for choirs and other selective ensembles, rather than practiced by the full congregation. The shift in the language of worship from Latin to the vernacular allowed for a more democratic participation in the singing of sacred songs. Protestant denominations differed as to who should be allowed to sing—everyone all the time, or smaller groups in specific contexts—and what kinds of works should be performed in religious settings. This second question hinged on issues of source and of translation. Many of the leading New England ministers believed that only psalms, which were drawn directly from the Bible, and not hymns on religious themes with no specific scriptural source, should be permitted in worship services. They also wanted the psalms to reflect the original Hebrew as closely as possible.

When the first printing press arrived in Cambridge, Massachusetts, in 1638, the ministers in the area took the opportunity to produce their own psalm book. Two years later they issued what has been famous ever since as the first book printed in the English colonies: *The Whole Book of Psalms Faithfully Translated into English Meter* (1640), familiarly known today as the *Bay Psalm Book*. The translators, whose individual efforts have never been fully identified, struggled with some knotty issues. The Reverend John Cotton, a leading theologian, stressed in his preface to the 1640 volume that the translators had not "taken liberty or poetical license to depart from the true and proper sense of David's word." (David, the second king of ancient Israel, was traditionally considered the author of the biblical Book of Psalms.) At the same time, Cotton reassured the public that "as it can be no just offence to any good conscience to sing David's Hebrew songs in English words," it ought to be equally unobjectionable to employ English metrical forms in translations of the psalms. Purity was desirable, but so were comprehensibility and tunefulness. The psalms were performed a capella, often using a system called "lining out," where a leader sang a phrase and the congregation repeated it. This method enabled church members who could not read, or who could not afford a psalter, to participate in the song. The tunes sometimes used to accompany the words were mostly of common origin and simple form, enhancing the earnest, self-restrained beauty of the performance.

A comparison of one of the most familiar psalms as it appears in the *Bay Psalm Book* and in the King James Bible shows how the rough Puritan translation lends itself to vocal performance in a way that its Anglican counterpart does not. Here is part of Psalm 23 from the *Bay Psalm Book*:

> For me a table thou hast spread,
> In presence of my foes;
> Thou dost anoint my head with oil,
> My cup it overflows.

Here is that same part of Psalm 23, from the King James Bible:

> Thou preparest a table before me in the presence of mine enemies: thou anointest my head with oil; my cup runneth over.

Worshipers in the New England colonies and abroad embraced the *Bay Psalm Book*, which was revised several times and widely reprinted. However, the book has always had detractors. In 1829, in the first important anthology of American poetry, the editor Samuel Kettell called the versification of the Bay volume "harsh and unmusical to the last degree." But the simple lines in the sturdy English of the Puritan preachers, whether read aloud or sung, evince an energy that is missing in more polished versions. The rough lines were designed to connect the reader to God, and their awkwardness was a means to an end.

Both versions of the psalms influenced American poetry. Echoes of the King James Bible translations of the psalms occur in, for example, Walt Whitman's free verse. The more metrical versions of the *Bay Psalm Book* influenced the writings of Anne Bradstreet and resonate in Emily Dickinson's poems about God and belief.

From The Bay Psalm Book[1]

Psalm 2

1	Why rage the Heathen furiously?
	Muse[2] vain things people do;
2	Kings of the earth do set themselves,
	Princes consult also:
	With one consent against the Lord, 5
	And his anointed one.
3	Let us asunder break their bands,
	Their cords be from us thrown.
4	Who sits in heav'n shall laugh; the Lord
	Will mock them; then will he 10
5	Speak to them in his ire, and wrath;
	And vex them suddenly.
6	But I anointed have my King
	Upon the holy hill
7	Of Zion: The established 15
	Counsel declare I will.
	God spoke to me, thou art my Son:

1. The texts are from *The Bay Psalm Book: A Facsimile Reprint of the First Edition of 1640* (1956). The numbers in the left margin correspond to the Bible verses.
2. Think (of).

This day I thee begot.
8 Ask thou of me, and I will give
 The Heathen for thy lot:[3] 20
 And of the earth thou shalt possess
 The utmost coasts abroad.
9 Thou shalt them break as potter's sherds[4]
 And crush with iron rod.
10 And now ye Kings be wise, be learn'd 25
 Ye judges of th'earth (Hear!).
11 Serve ye the Lord with reverence,
 Rejoice in him with fear.
12 Kiss ye the Son, lest he be wroth,[5]
 And ye fall in the way.[6] 30
 When his wrath quickly burns, oh blest
 Are all that on him stay.[7]

Psalm 19

TO THE CHIEF MUSICIAN, A PSALM OF DAVID

1 The heavens do declare
 The majesty of God:
 Also the firmament[1] shows forth
 His handiwork abroad.
2 Day speaks to day, knowledge 5
 Night hath to night declar'd.
3 There neither speech nor language is,
 Where their voice is not heard.
4 Through all the earth their line
 Is gone forth, and unto 10
 The utmost end of all the world,
 Their speeches reach also:
 A Tabernacle[2] he
 In them pitched[3] for the Sun,
5 Who bridegroom-like from's[4] chamber goes 15
 Glad giants-race to run.
6 From heaven's utmost end,
 His course and compassing;[5]
 To ends of it, and from the heat
 Thereof is hid nothing. 20

(2)

7 The Lord's law perfect is,
 The soul converting back:
 God's testimony faithful is,

3. Inheritance.
4. Shards, fragments.
5. Wrathful.
6. I.e., fail to be saved.
7. Trust.

1. Sky.
2. Temporary place of worship.
3. Established.
4. From his.
5. Range.

	Makes wise who wisdom lack.	
8	The statutes of the Lord,	25
	Are right, and glad the heart:	
	The Lord's commandment is pure,	
	Light doth to eyes impart.	
9	Jehovah's fear is clean,	
	And doth endure forever:	30
	The judgments of the Lord are true,	
	And righteous altogether.	
10	Than gold, than much fine gold,	
	More to be prized are,	
	Than honey, and the honeycomb,	35
	Sweeter they are by far.	
11	Also thy servant is	
	Admonished from hence:	
	And in the keeping of the same[6]	
	Is a full recompense.	40
12	Who can his errors know?	
	From secret faults cleanse me.	
13	And from presumptuous sins, let thou	
	Kept back thy servant be:[7]	
	Let them not bear the rule	45
	In me,[8] and then shall I	
	Be perfect and shall cleansed be	
	From much iniquity.	
14	Let the words of my mouth,	
	And the thoughts of my heart,	50
	Be pleasing with thee, Lord, my rock,	
	Who my redeemer art.	

Psalm 23

A PSALM OF DAVID

1	The Lord to me a shepherd is,	
	Want therefore shall not I,	
2	He in the folds of tender grass,	
	Doth cause me down to lie:	
	To waters calm me gently leads	5
3	Restore my soul doth He:	
	He doth in paths of righteousness:	
	For His name's sake lead me.	
4	Yea, though in valley of death's shade	
	I walk, none ill I'll fear:	10
	Because Thou art with me, Thy rod	
	And staff my comfort are.	
5	For me a table thou hast spread,	

6. The Lord's judgments (verse 9).
7. An instance in which sense is interrupted by poor proofreading and the need to force rhymes (know/thou). The revised edition of 1651 has

"And from presumptuous sins also / Keep thou thy servant free."
8. I.e., do not let those presumptuous sins (or sins of pride) have power over me.

In presence of my foes:
Thou dost anoint my head with oil, 15
 My cup it overflows.
6 Goodness and mercy surely shall
 All my days follow me:
And in the Lord's house I shall dwell
 So long as days shall be. 20

Psalm 100

A PSALM OF PRAISE

1 Make ye a joyful sounding noise
 Unto Jehovah, all the earth:
2 Serve ye Jehovah with gladness:
 Before His presence come with mirth.
3 Know, that Jehovah He is God, 5
 Who hath us formed, it is He,
 And not ourselves: His own people
 And sheep of His pasture are we.
4 Enter into His gates with praise,
 Into His courts with thankfulness 10
 Make ye confession unto Him
 And His name reverently bless.
5 Because Jehovah He is good,
 For evermore is His mercy:
 And unto generations all 15
 Continue doth His verity.

ANOTHER [VERSION] OF THE SAME

1 Make ye a joyful noise unto
 Jehovah all the earth:
2 Serve ye Jehovah with gladness:
 Before Him come with mirth.
3 Know, that Jehovah He is God, 5
 Not we ourselves, but He
 Hath made us: His people, and sheep
 Of His pasture are we.
4 O enter ye into His gates
 With praise, and thankfulness 10
 Into His courts: confess to Him,
 And His name do ye bless.
5 Because Jehovah He is good,
 His bounteous mercy
 Is everlasting: and His truth 15
 Is to eternity.

 1640

ROGER WILLIAMS
c. 1603–1683

Roger Williams is the preeminent figure associated with freedom of conscience and religious liberty in early New England. Banished from the Massachusetts Bay Colony in 1636 for spreading opinions that the colony's leadership considered dangerous, Williams went on to build Rhode Island into a model of inclusive self-government and a haven for religious minorities, opening it to dissenting refugees from the Puritan colonies and to the first Jewish and Quaker settlers in British North America. Williams also developed close relationships with indigenous leaders in the region, living at times in Native communities and mediating conflicts with other English colonies. In 1643, Williams produced *A Key into the Language of America*, a dictionary and cultural guide to the Algonquian peoples of New England that offers comparative social commentary, including reflections on the moral shortcomings of the English.

Williams was also a brilliant polemicist. A prominent genre in Williams's day, polemic involves a vigorous attack on an individual or an idea. Polemical writings on colonization and on religion contributed importantly to the rise of popular print culture in England. In controversial pamphlets such as "The Bloody Tenet of Persecution" (1644) and "The Hireling Ministry None of Christ's" (1652), Williams took strongly worded positions challenging many of the foundational assumptions of his Puritan neighbors. And in "Christenings Make Not Christians" (1645), Williams theorized about the formation of a truly consent-based religious community, which would not be restricted by race or cultural heritage, compelled by physical violence, or shaped by intellectual and emotional coercion. This work reveals a mind preoccupied with fundamental questions about human consciousness and will. In his life as in his writings, Williams pursued his understanding of liberty of conscience with striking integrity.

The son of a London merchant, Williams took an unexpected turn in 1617 when he met Sir Edward Coke, a leading legal thinker whose advocacy for the common law tradition and challenge to the authority of the king fundamentally shaped the era and transformed English law. Probably impressed by Williams's sharp intellect, Coke helped the young man get a first-rate education. After graduating from Cambridge University in 1627 and taking holy orders, Williams became involved in Church reform. Years later, he said that Archbishop William Laud, the preeminent clergyman in the Church of England under King Charles I, "pursued" him "out of this land." Laud required all clerics to pledge an oath of loyalty to the Church of England, sparking a crisis for dissenting clergy and contributing to the "Great Migration" of Puritans to New England.

In 1631 Williams arrived in Boston with his wife, Mary. He was at first a valued addition to the new colony at Massachusetts Bay, which badly needed men of his intellectual capabilities and educational attainments. Soon, however, Williams refused to minister at the prestigious First Church of Boston because he "durst not officiate to an unseparated people"—that is, a church that retained affiliations with the Anglican orthodoxy. This episode gave Massachusetts authorities their first taste of Williams's deep resistance to the established Church and his enormous confidence in matters of belief. Over the next four years, he ministered to the communities at Plymouth and then Salem. In 1635, while he was at Salem, the Bay

Colony leaders accused him of holding "new and dangerous opinions against the authority of magistrates."

Williams had infuriated and threatened the leaders of Massachusetts by taking four positions, any one of which seriously undermined the theocracy that was at the heart of the Bay Colony government. He denied, first, that Massachusetts had a proper title to its land, arguing that King Charles I could not bestow a title to something that belonged to the Natives. Second, he argued that no unregenerate person (that is, anyone who had not been "born again") could be required either to pray or to swear a legal oath; third, that Massachusetts Bay Colony ministers, who had persuaded the king of England that they wished to remain part of the Church of England, should not only separate from the Church but repent that they had ever served it; and last, that civil authority was limited to civil matters and that magistrates had no jurisdiction over the soul. Williams wanted to create a barrier between Church and state to prevent Christianity from being contaminated by worldly interests. The position was disturbing to Separatist and non-Separatist alike, and it made Williams unwelcome in both Plymouth and Boston.

In his journal for January 1636, John Winthrop notes that when the governor of Massachusetts and his assistants met to reconsider the charge of divisiveness against Williams, they agreed that they could not wait until spring to banish him from the commonwealth. His opinions were dangerous and spreading, so they needed to send him back to England immediately. When they went to Salem to "carry him aboard the ship," however, they found he "had been gone 3 days before, but whither they could not learn." Williams had fled Massachusetts for Rhode Island— reportedly with Winthrop's aid. He found shelter there with the Narragansett Indians and, from that time until his death almost fifty years later, Williams and Providence Plantation were synonymous with the spirit of religious liberty. In 1663, Rhode Island received a royal charter from King Charles II in which freedom of conscience was guaranteed, giving the colony an exceptional status in the English-speaking world.

The Massachusetts authorities did not cite Williams's attitude toward the American Indians in their charges against him, but in this regard as well, his position was antithetical to their own. From the beginning, he wrote, his "soul's desire was to do the natives good, and to that end to have their language." Although he was not interested in assimilating into their culture, Williams presented American Indians as no better or worse than the English "rogues" who dealt with them, and stressed that they possessed complex cultures with their own forms of civility. Williams knew that *A Key into the Language of America* would prove useful to those who wished to convert Native Americans to Christianity. He was not primarily interested in such efforts, and in "Christenings Make Not Christians" he argued against a line of thinking that promoted missionary work, which was ostensibly a central reason for the foundation of the Puritan colonies. *Anyone* not regenerate, Williams argued, was outside the people of God, and to refer to the American Indians as "heathen" was "improperly sinful" and "unchristianly."

He was greatly disappointed when, despite his efforts to befriend the Narragansetts, they burned the settlements at both Warwick and Providence during King Philip's War. By the time Williams died, the future looked grave for the Narragansetts. The great tribe would never recover from the losses incurred during that war. Despite this failure, Williams's efforts to separate religious and civil life, and to promote peaceful interactions among different groups, produced a lasting legacy. The Rhode Island charter offered a model that would be taken up in the U.S. Bill of Rights, which mandates the separation of Church and state and guarantees freedom of speech, of the press, and of assembly.

From A Key into the Language of America[1]

To My Dear and Well-Beloved Friends and Countrymen, in Old and New England

I present you with a key; I have not heard of the like, yet framed,[2] since it pleased God to bring that mighty continent of America to light. Others of my countrymen have often, and excellently, and lately written of the country (and none that I know beyond the goodness and worth of it).

This key, respects the native language of it, and happily may unlock some rarities concerning the natives themselves, not yet discovered.

I drew the materials in a rude lump at sea, as a private help to my own memory, that I might not, by my present absence, lightly lose what I had so dearly bought in some few years hardship, and charges among the barbarians. Yet being reminded by some, what pity it were to bury those materials in my grave at land or sea; and withal, remembering how oft I have been importuned by worthy friends of all sorts, to afford them some helps this way. I resolved (by the assistance of The Most High) to cast those materials into this key, pleasant and profitable for all, but especially for my friends residing in those parts.

A little key may open a box, where lies a bunch of keys.

With this I have entered into the secrets of those countries, wherever English dwell about two hundred miles, between the French and Dutch plantations; for want of this, I know what gross mistakes myself and others have run into.

There is a mixture of this language north and south, from the place of my abode, about six hundred miles; yet within the two hundred miles (aforementioned) their dialects do exceedingly differ; yet not so, but (within that compass) a man may, by this help, converse with thousands of natives all over the country: and by such converse it may please the Father of Mercies to spread civility, (and in His own most holy season) Christianity. For one candle will light ten thousand, and it may please God to bless a little leaven to season the mighty lump of those peoples and territories.

It is expected, that having had so much converse with these natives, I should write some little of them.

Concerning them (a little to gratify expectation) I shall touch upon four heads:

First, by what names they are distinguished.

Secondly, their original[3] and descent.

Thirdly, their religion, manners, customs, etc.

Fourthly, that great point of their conversion.

To the first, their names are of two sorts:

First, those of the English giving: as natives, savages, Indians, wildmen (so the Dutch call them *wilden*), Abergeny[4] men, pagans, barbarians, heathen.

Secondly, their names which they give themselves.

1. The text is from the first edition (1643), reprinted by the Rhode Island and Providence Tercentenary Committee (1936).

2. Shaped.
3. Place of origin.
4. Aboriginal.

I cannot observe that they ever had (before the coming of the English, French or Dutch amongst them) any names to difference themselves from strangers, for they knew none; but two sorts of names they had, and have amongst themselves:

First, general, belonging to all natives, as Nínnuock, Ninnimissinnûwock, Eniskeetomparwog, which signifies Men, Folk, or People.

Secondly, particular names, peculiar to several nations, of them amongst themselves, as Nanhigganġuck, Massachusêuck, Cawasumsêuck, Cowwesġuck, Quintikóock, Qunnipiġuck, Pequttóog, etc.

They have often asked me, why we call them Indians, natives, etc. And understanding the reason, they will call themselves Indians, in opposition to English, etc.

For the second head proposed, their original and descent:

From Adam and Noah[5] that they spring, it is granted on all hands.

But for their later descent, and whence they came into those parts, it seems as hard to find, as to find the wellhead of some fresh stream, which running many miles out of the country to the salt ocean, hath met with many mixing streams by the way. They say themselves, that they have sprung and grown up in that very place, like the very trees of the wilderness.

They say that their great god Kautántowwìt created those parts, as I observed in the chapter of their religion.[6] They have no clothes, books, nor letters, and conceive their fathers never had; and therefore they are easily persuaded that the God that made Englishmen is a greater God, because He hath so richly endowed the English above themselves. But when they hear that about sixteen hundred years ago, England and the inhabitants thereof were like unto themselves, and since have received from God, clothes, books, etc. they are greatly affected with a secret hope concerning themselves.

Wise and judicious men, with whom I have discoursed, maintain their original to be northward from Tartaria:[7] and at my now taking ship, at the Dutch plantation, it pleased the Dutch Governor, (in some discourse with me about the natives), to draw their line from Iceland, because the name Sackmakan (the name for an Indian prince, about the Dutch) is the name for a prince in Iceland.

Other opinions I could number up: under favor I shall present (not mine opinion, but) my observations to the judgment of the wise.

First, others (and myself) have conceived some of their words to hold affinity with the Hebrew.

Secondly, they constantly anoint their heads as the Jews did.

Thirdly, they give dowries for their wives, as the Jews did.

Fourthly (and which I have not so observed amongst other nations as amongst the Jews, and these:) they constantly separate their women (during the time of their monthly sickness) in a little house alone by themselves four or five days, and hold it an irreligious thing for either father or husband or any male to come near them.

They have often asked me if it be so with women of other nations, and whether they are so separated: and for their practice they plead nature and

5. After the great flood described in the Bible, only Noah and his family remained.
6. I.e., in Chapter XXI of Williams's *Key*, which has thirty-two chapters.
7. Mongolia.

tradition. Yet again I have found a greater affinity of their language with the Greek tongue.

2. As the Greeks and other nations, and ourselves call the seven stars (or Charles' Wain, the Bear,)[8] so do they Mosk or Paukunnawaw, the Bear.

3. They have many strange relations of one Wétucks, a man that wrought great miracles amongst them, and walking upon the waters, etc., with some kind of broken resemblance to the Son of God.

Lastly, it is famous that the Sowwest (Sowaniu) is the great subject of their discourse. From thence their traditions. There they say (at the southwest) is the court of their great god Kautántowwìt: at the southwest are their forefathers' souls: to the southwest they go themselves when they die; from the southwest came their corn, and beans out of their great god Kautántow-wìt's field: and indeed the further northward and westward from us their corn will not grow, but to the southward better and better. I dare not conjecture in these uncertainties. I believe they are lost, and yet hope (in the Lord's holy season) some of the wildest of them shall be found to share in the blood of the Son of God. To the third head, concerning their religion, customs, manners etc. I shall here say nothing, because in those 32 chapters of the whole book, I have briefly touched those of all sorts, from their birth to their burials, and have endeavored (as the nature of the work would give way) to bring some short observations and applications home to Europe from America.

Therefore fourthly, to that great point of their conversion, so much to be longed for, and by all New-English so much pretended,[9] and I hope in truth.

For myself I have uprightly labored to suit my endeavors to my pretenses: and of later times (out of desire to attain their language) I have run through varieties of intercourses[1] with them day and night, summer and winter, by land and sea, particular passages tending to this, I have related divers, in the chapter of their religion.

Many solemn discourses I have had with all sorts of nations of them, from one end of the country to another (so far as opportunity, and the little language I have could reach).

I know there is no small preparation in the hearts of multitudes of them. I know their many solemn confessions to myself, and one to another of their lost wandering conditions.

I know strong convictions upon the consciences of many of them, and their desires uttered that way.

I know not with how little knowledge and grace of Christ the Lord may save, and therefore, neither will despair, nor report much.

But since it hath pleased some of my worthy countrymen to mention (of late in print) Wequash, the Péquot captain, I shall be bold so far to second their relations, as to relate mine own hopes of him (though I dare not be so confident as others).

Two days before his death, as I passed up to Qunníhticut[2] River, it pleased my worthy friend Mr. Fenwick, (whom I visited at his house in Saybrook Fort

8. I.e., the constellation known as Ursa Major (Great Bear), the Big Dipper, or Charlemagne's wagon ("wain").
9. Asserted, proffered (with none of the modern connotations of deceit).
1. Conversations.
2. Connecticut.

at the mouth of that river) to tell me that my old friend Wequash lay very sick. I desired to see him, and himself was pleased to be my guide two miles where Wequash lay.

Amongst other discourse concerning his sickness and death (in which he freely bequeathed his son to Mr. Fenwick) I closed[3] with him concerning his soul: he told me that some two or three years before he had lodged at my house, where I acquainted him with the condition of all mankind, & his own in particular; how God created man and all things; how man fell from God, and of his present enmity against God, and the wrath of God against him until repentance. Said he, "your words were never out of my heart to this present;" and said he "me much pray to Jesus Christ." I told him so did many English, French, and Dutch, who had never turned to God, nor loved Him. He replied in broken English: "Me so big naughty heart, me heart all one stone!" Savory expressions using to breathe from compunct and broken hearts, and a sense of inward hardness and unbrokenness [sic]. I had many discourses with him in his life, but this was the sum of our last parting until our General Meeting.[4]

Now, because this is the great inquiry of all men: what Indians have been converted? what have the English done in those parts? what hopes of the Indians receiving the knowledge of Christ?

And because to this question, some put an edge from the boast of the Jesuits in Canada and Maryland, and especially from the wonderful conversions made by the Spaniards and Portugals in the West-Indies, besides what I have here written, as also, beside what I have observed in the chapter of their religion, I shall further present you with a brief additional discourse concerning this great point, being comfortably persuaded that that Father of Spirits, who was graciously pleased to persuade Japhet (the Gentiles) to dwell in the tents of Shem (the Jews),[5] will, in His holy season (I hope approaching), persuade these Gentiles of America to partake of the mercies of Europe, and then shall be fulfilled what is written by the prophet Malachi,[6] from the rising of the sun (in Europe) to the going down of the same (in America), My name shall be great among the Gentiles. So I desire to hope and pray,

Your unworthy countryman,
ROGER WILLIAMS

Directions for the Use of the Language

1. A dictionary or grammar way I had consideration of, but purposely avoided, as not so accommodate to the benefit of all, as I hope this form is.

2. A dialogue also I had thoughts of, but avoided for brevity's sake, and yet (with no small pains) I have so framed every chapter and the matter of it, as I may call it an implicit dialogue.

3. It is framed chiefly after the *Narragansett* dialect, because most spoken in the country, and yet (with attending to the variation of peoples and dialects) it will be of great use in all parts of the country.

3. Came to the end of my talk.
4. I.e., until Judgment Day.
5. Japhet was the third son of Noah and, in some traditions, the progenitor of the Indo-European race (see Genesis 9.18).
6. "For from the rising of the sun even unto the going down of the same my name shall be great among the Gentiles" (Malachi 1.11).

4. Whatever your occasion be, either of travel, discourse, trading etc. turn to the table which will direct you to the proper chapter.

5. Because the life of all language is in the pronunciation, I have been at the pains and charges to cause the accents, tones or sounds to be affixed, (which some understand, according to the Greek language, acutes, graves, circumflexes) for example, in the second leaf[7] in the word *Ewò He*: the sound or tone must not be put on *E*, but *wò* where the grave accent is.

In the same leaf, in the word *Ascowequássin*, the sound must not be on any of the syllables, but on *quáss*, where the acute or sharp sound is.

In the same leaf in the word *Anspaumpmaûntam*, the sound must not be on any other syllable but *maûn*, where the circumflex or long sounding accent is.

6. The English for every Indian word or phrase stands in a straight line directly against the Indian: yet sometimes there are two words for the same thing (for their language is exceeding copious, and they have five or six words sometimes for one thing) and then the English stands against them both: for example in the second leaf:

Cowáunckamish & Cuckquénamish | I pray your favor.

From *An Help to the Native Language of that Part of America Called New England*

FROM CHAPTER I. OF SALUTATION

1. The courteous pagan shall condemn
 Uncourteous Englishmen,
 Who live like foxes, bears and wolves,
 Or lion in his den.
2. Let none sing blessings to their souls, 5
 For that they courteous are:
 The wild barbarians with no more
 Than nature, go so far.
3. If nature's sons both wild and tame,
 Humane and courteous be: 10
 How ill becomes it Sons of God
 To want humanity?

FROM CHAPTER II. OF EATING AND ENTERTAINMENT

1. Coarse bread and water's most,[8] their fare,
 O England's diet fine;
 Thy cup runs ore[9] with plenteous store
 Of wholesome beer and wine.
2. Sometimes God gives them Fish or Flesh, 5
 Yet they're content without;
 And what comes in, they part to[1] friends
 And strangers round about.

7. Page.
8. Mostly.

9. Over.
1. Divide among.

3. God's providence is rich to his,
Let none distrustful be; 10
In wilderness, in great distress,
These ravens have fed me.

FROM CHAPTER VI. OF THE FAMILY AND BUSINESS OF THE HOUSE

1. How busy are the sons of men?
How full their heads and hands?
What noise and tumults in our own,
And eke[2] in Pagan lands?
2. Yet I have found less noise, more peace 5
In wild America,
Where women quickly build the house,
And quickly move away.
[3] English and Indians busy are,
In parts of their abode: 10
Yet both stand idle, till God's call
Set them to work for God. Mat. 20.7.[3]

FROM CHAPTER XI. OF TRAVEL

1. God makes a path, provides a guide,
And feeds in wilderness!
His glorious name while breath remains,
O that I may confess.
2. Lost many a time, I have had no guide, 5
No house, but hollow tree!
In stormy winter night no fire,
No food, no company:
3. In him I have found a house, a bed,
A table, company: 10
No cup so bitter, but's made sweet,
When God shall sweet'ning be.

FROM CHAPTER XVIII. OF THE SEA

[1] They see God's wonders that are call'ed
Through dreadful seas to pass,
In tearing winds and roaring seas,
And calms as smooth as glass.
[2] I have in Europe's ships, oft been 5
In King of terror's hand;
When all have cried, "Now, now we sink,"
Yet God brought safe to land.
[3] Alone 'mongst Indians in canoes,
Sometime o'er-turn'd, I have been 10
Half inch from death, in ocean deep,
God's wonders I have seen.

2. Also (archaic).
3. "And about the eleventh hour he [Christ] went out, and found others standing idle, and said unto them, 'Why stand ye here all the day idle?' They said unto him, 'Because no man hath hired us.' He said unto them, 'Go ye also into the vineyard; and whatsoever is right, that shall ye receive'" (Matthew 20.6–7).

FROM CHAPTER XXI. OF RELIGION, THE SOUL, ETC.

Manìt-manittó, wock. | God, Gods.

Obs. He that questions whether God made the world, the Indians will teach him. I must acknowledge I have received in my converse[4] with them many confirmations of those two great points, Hebrews II. 6. viz:

1. That God is.

2. That He is a rewarder of all them that diligently seek Him.

They will generally confess that God made all, but them in special, although they deny not that Englishman's God made Englishmen, and the heavens and earth there! yet their Gods made them and the heaven, and earth where they dwell.

Nummusquauna-múckqun manìt. | God is angry with me?

Obs. I have heard a poor Indian lamenting the loss of a child at break of day, call up his wife and children, and all about him to lamentation, and with abundance of tears cry out! "O God thou hast taken away my child! thou art angry with me: O turn Thine anger from me, and spare the rest of my children."

If they receive any good in hunting, fishing, harvest etc. they acknowledge God in it.

Yea, if it be but an ordinary accident, a fall, etc. they will say God was angry and did it, *musquàntum manit* God is angry. But herein is their misery:

First, they branch their God-head into many gods.

Secondly, attribute it to creatures.

First, many gods: they have given me the names of thirty seven which I have, all which in their solemn worships they invocate, as:

Kautántowwìt the great Southwest God, to whose house all souls go, and from whom came their corn, beans, as they say.

Wompanand.	The Eastern God.
Chekesuwànd.	The Western God.
Wunnanaméanit.	The Northern God.
Sowwanànd.	The Southern God.
Wetuómanit.	The House God.

Even as the papists have their he and she saint protectors as St. George, St. Patrick, St. Denis, Virgin Mary, etc.

Squáuanit.	The Woman's God.
Muckquachuckquànd.	The Children's God.

Obs. I was once with a native dying of a wound, given him by some murderous English who robbed him and ran him through with a rapier, from whom in the heat of his wound, he at present escaped from them, but dying of his wound, they suffered death at New Plymouth, in New England, this native dying called much upon *Muckquachuckquànd,* which of other natives I understood (as they believed) had appeared to the dying young man, many years before, and bid him whenever he was in distress call upon him.

Secondly, as they have many of these fained deities; so worship they the creatures in whom they conceive doth rest some deity:

4. Conversation.

Keesuckquànd.	The Sun God.
Nanepaûshat.	The Moon God.
Paumpágussit.	The Sea.
Yotáanit.	The Fire God.

Supposing that deities be in these, etc.

<center>* * *</center>

They have a modest religious persuasion not to disturb any man, either themselves English, Dutch, or any in their conscience, and worship, and therefore say:

Aquiewopwaûwash.	Peace, hold your peace.
Aquiewopwaûwock.	
Peeyàuntam.	He is at prayer.
Peeyaúntamwock.	They are praying.
Cowwéwonck.	The soul.

Derived from *cowwene* to sleep, because say they, it works and operates when the body sleeps. *Míchachunck,* the soul, in a higher notion which is of affinity, with a word signifying a looking glass, or clear resemblance, so that it hath its name from a clear sight or discerning, which indeed seems very well to suit with the nature of it.

Wuhóck.	The body
Nohòck: cohòck	My body, your body
Awaunkeesitteoúwincohòck:	
Tunna-awwa commítchichunck-	Whether goes your soul when you
kitonckquèan?	die?
An. Sowánakitaúwaw.	It goes to the southwest.

Obs. They believe that the souls of men and women go to the southwest, their great and good men and women to Kautántowwìt, his house, where they have hopes (as the Turks have of carnal joys). Murderers, thieves and liars, their souls (say they) wander restless abroad.

Now because this book (by God's good providence) may come into the hand of many fearing God, who may also have many an opportunity of occasional discourse with some of these, their wild brethren and sisters, and may speak a word for their and our glorious Maker, which may also prove some preparatory mercy to their souls: I shall propose some proper expressions concerning the creation of the world, and man's estate, and in particular theirs also, which from myself many hundreds of times, great numbers of them have heard with great delight, and great convictions; which, who knows (in God's holy season), may rise to the exalting of the Lord Jesus Christ in their conversion, and salvation?

Nétop Kunnatótemous.	Friend, I will ask you a question.
Natótema:	Speak on.
Tocketunnântum?	What think you?
Awaun Keesiteoûwin	Who made the heavens?
Kéesuck?	
Aûke Wechêkom?	The earth, the sea?
Míttauke.	The world.

Some will answer *Tattá*, I cannot tell, some will answer *Manittôwock*, the gods.

Tà suóg Maníttôwock	How many gods be there?
Maunaŭog Mishaúnawock.	Many, great many.
Nétop machàge.	Friend, not so.
Paûsuck naŭnt manìt.	There is only one God.
Cuppíssittone.	You are mistaken.
Cowauwaúnemun.	You are out of the way.

A phrase which much pleaseth them, being proper for their wandering in the woods, and similitudes greatly please them.

Kukkakótemous, wâchitquáshouwe.	I will tell you, presently.
Kuttaunchemókous.	I will tell you news.
Paûsuck naŭnt manit kéesittin keesuck, etc.	One only God made the heavens etc.
Napannetashèmittan naugecautúmmonab nshque.	Five thousand years ago and upwards.
Naŭgom naŭnt wukkesittínneswâme teâgun.	He alone made all things.
Wuche mateâg.	Out of nothing.
Quttatashuchuckqún-nacauskeesitínnes wâme.	In six days He made all things.
Nquittaqúnne.	The first day He made the light.
Wuckéesitin wequâi.	
Néesqunne.	The second day He made the firmament
Wuckéesitin Keésuck.	
Shúckqunnewuckéesitin Aŭke kà wechêkom	The third day He made the earth and sea.
Yóqunne wuckkéesitin Nippauus kà Nanepaŭshat.	The fourth day He made the sun and the moon.
Neenash-mamockíuwash wêquanantíganash.	Two great lights.
Kà wáme anócksuck.	And all the stars.
Napannetashúckqunne Wuckéesit tin pussuckseésuck wâme.	The fifth day He made all the fowl.
Keesuckquíuke.	In the air, or heavens.
Ka wáme namaŭsuck. Wechekommíuke.	And all the fish in the sea.
Quttatashúkqunne wuckkeésittin penashímwock wamè.	The sixth day He made all the beasts of the field.
Wuttàke wuchè wuckeesittin pausuck Enìn, or, Eneskéetomp.	Last of all he made one man.
Wuche mishquòck.	Of red earth,
Ka wesuonckgonnakaŭnes Adam, túppautea mishquòck.	And called him Adam, or red earth.
Wuttàke wuchè, Câwit míshquock,	Then afterward, while Adam, or red earth, slept,
Wuckaudnúmmenes manìt peetaŭ-gon wuche Adam.	God took a rib from Adam, or red earth.
Kà wuchè peteaúgon. Wukkeesitínnes pausuck squàw.	And of that rib he made one woman.
Kà pawtouwúnnes Adâmuck	And brought her to Adam.

Nawônt Adam wuttúnnawaun	When Adam saw her, he said,
nup-peteâgon ewò.	"This is my bone."
Enadatashúckqunne, aquêi,	The seventh day He rested,
Nagaû wuchè quttatashúckqune	And, therefore, Englishmen work
anacaûsuock Englishmánuck.	six days.
Enadatashuckqunnóckat tauba-	On the seventh day they praise
taûmvock.	God.

Obs. At this relation they are much satisfied, with a reason why (as they observe) the English and Dutch, etc., labor six days, and rest and worship the seventh.

Besides, they will say, we never heard of this before: and then will relate how they have it from their fathers, that Kautántowwìt made one man and woman of a stone, which disliking, he broke them in pieces, and made another man and woman of a tree, which were the fountains of all mankind.

* * *

[1.] Two sorts of men shall naked stand
 Before the burning ire 2 Thes. 1.8[5]
 Of him that shortly shall appear,
 In dreadful flaming fire.
[2.] First, millions know not God, nor for
 His knowledge care to seek:
 Millions have knowledge store, but in
 Obedience are not meek.
[3.] If woe to Indians, where shall Turk,
 Where shall appear the Jew?
 O, where shall stand the Christian false?
 O blessed then the true.

* * *

FROM CHAPTER XXX. OF THEIR PAINTINGS

[1.] Truth is a native, naked beauty; but
 Lying inventions are but Indian paints;
 Dissembling hearts their beauty's but a lie.
 Truth is the proper beauty of God's saints.
2. Foul are the Indians' hair and painted faces, 5
 More foul such hair, such face in Israel.
 England so calls herself, yet there's
 Absalom's foul hair and face of Jezebel.[6]
[3.] Paints will not bide Christ's washing flames of fire,
 Feigned inventions will not bide such storms: 10
 O that we may prevent him, that betimes,
 Repentance tears may wash off all such forms.

1643

5. "And to you who are troubled rest with us, when the Lord Jesus shall be revealed from heaven with his mighty angels, in flaming fire taking vengeance on them that know not God, and that obey not the gospel of our Lord Jesus Christ" (2 Thessalonians 1.7–8).

6. See 2 Samuel 14.26 and 2 Kings 9.30.

From Christenings Make Not Christians

Or a Brief Discourse Concerning That Name Heathen,
Commonly Given to the Indians[1]

AS ALSO CONCERNING THAT GREAT POINT OF THEIR CONVERSION

I shall first be humbly bold to inquire into the name *heathen*, which the English give them, & the Dutch approve and practise in their name *heydenen*, signifying heathen or nations.

How oft have I heard both the English and Dutch (not only the civil, but the most debauched and profane) say, These heathen dogs, better kill a thousand of them than that we Christians should be endangered or troubled with them; better they were all cut off, & then we shall be no more troubled with them: They have spilt our Christian blood, the best way to make riddance of them, cut them all off, and so make way for Christians.

I shall therefore humbly entreat my country-men of all sorts to consider, that although men have used to apply this word *heathen* to the Indians that go naked, and have not heard of that one God, yet this word *heathen* is most improperly, sinfully, and unchristianly so used in this sence. The word *heathen* signifieth no more than *nations* or *gentiles*; so do our translations from the Hebrew כרים and the Greek ἔθνη in the Old and New Testaments promiscuously render these words *gentiles, nations, heathens*.

Why nations? Because the Jews being the only people and nation of God, esteemed (and that rightly) all other people, not only those that went naked, but the famous Babylonians, Caldeans, Medes, and Persians, Greeks and Romans, their stately cities and citizens, inferior [to] themselves, and not partakers of their glorious privileges, but ethnick,[2] gentiles, heathen, or the nations of the world.

Now then we must inquire who are the people of God, his holy nation, since the coming of the Lord Jesus, and the rejection of his first typical holy nation, the Jews.[3]

It is confessed by all, that the Christians, the followers of Jesus, are now the only people of God, his holy nation, &c. ἔθνος ἅγιον; 1. Pet. 2. 9.[4]

Who are then the nations, heathen, or gentiles, in opposition to this people of God? I answer, All people, civilized as well as uncivilized, even the most famous states, cities, and kingdoms of the world: For all must come within that distinction; 1. Cor. 5; within or without.[5]

* * *

Now * * * for the hopes of conversion, and turning the people of America unto God: There is no respect of persons with him, for we are all the work of his hands; from the rising of the sun to the going down thereof, his

1. The text used here was originally published in London in 1645 and was reprinted as no. 14 in the series *Rhode Island Historical Tracts* (1881).
2. In the archaic sense of not being Christian or Jewish.
3. "Typical" in the sense of symbolizing a "holy nation."
4. 1 Peter 2.9 concerns the idea of a holy nation. "&c": i.e., et cetera.

5. Williams says that all peoples have some members who are saved (i.e., "Christians") and some who are not (i.e., "heathens"). He refers specifically to 1 Corinthians 5:12: "For what have I to do to judge them also that are without? do not ye judge them that are within? But them that are without God judgeth. Therefore put away from among yourselves that wicked person."

name shall be great among the nations from the east and from the west, &c. If we respect their sins, they are far short of European sinners: They neither abuse such corporal mercies,[6] for they have them not; nor sin they against the Gospel light (which shines not amongst them), as the men of Europe do: And yet if they were greater sinners than they are, or greater sinners than the Europeans, they are not the further from the great ocean of mercy in that respect.

Lastly, they are intelligent, many very ingenuous, plain-hearted, inquisitive, and (as I said before) prepared with many convictions, &c.

Now * * * for the Catholics' conversion, although I believe I may safely hope that God hath his in Rome, in Spain, yet if Antichrist be their false head (as most true it is) the body, faith, baptism, hope (opposite to the true; Ephes. 4.)[7] are all false also; yea, consequently their preachings, conversions, salvations (leaving secret things to God) must all be of the same false nature likewise.

If the reports (yea, some of their own historians) be true, what monstrous and most inhumane conversions have they made; baptizing thousands, yea, ten thousands of the poor Natives, sometimes by wiles and subtle devices, sometimes by force compelling them to submit to that which they understood not, neither before nor after such their monstrous Christening of them.[8] * * * For our New England parts, I can speak uprightly and confidently, I know it to have been easy for my self long ere this, to have brought many thousands of these Natives, yea, the whole country, to a far greater Antichristian conversion than ever was yet heard of in America. I have reported something in the chapter of their religion, how readily I could have brought the whole country to have observed one day in seven;[9] I add to have received a baptisme (or washing), though it were in Rivers (as the first Christians and the Lord Jesus himself did), to have come to stated church meeting,[1] maintained priests and forms of prayer, and a whole form of Antichristian worship in life and death. Let none wonder at this, for plausible persuasions in the mouths of those whom natural men esteem and love: for the power of prevailing forces and armies hath done this in all the nations (as men speak) of Christendom. Yea, what lamentable experience have we of the turnings and turnings of the body of this land in point of religion in [a] few years?

When England was all popish under Henry the seventh, how easy is conversion wrought to half-papish half-Protestant under Henry the eighth?

From half-Protestanism half-popery under Henry the eighth, to absolute Protestanism under Edward the sixth: from absolute Protestation under Edward the sixth to absolute popery under Queen Mary, and from absolute popery under Queen Mary (just like the weathercock, with the breath of every prince), to absolute Protestanism under Queen Elizabeth &c.[2]

For all this, yet some may ask, why hath there been such a price in my hand not improved?[3] Why have I not brought them to such a conversion as I speak of? I answer, Woe be to me if I call light darkness, or darkness light;

6. I.e., physical resources such as churches and Bibles. "Respect": consider.
7. Ephesians 4.
8. Williams condemns the Catholic practice of mass conversion of Natives in the Americas.
9. I.e., the Christian sabbath. "The chapter . . . religion": i.e., Chapter XXI of Williams's *Key*.
1. Religious service.

2. Williams traces the shifting religious establishments under a series of English monarchs, from King Henry VII (1457–1509; reigned 1485–1509) to Queen Elizabeth I (1533–1603; reigned 1558–1603).
3. Williams alludes to the Parable of the Talents (Matthew 25.14–30).

sweet bitter, or bitter sweet; woe be to me if I call that conversion unto God which is indeed subversion of the souls of millions in Christendom, from one false worship to another, and the profanation of the holy name of God, his holy Son and blessed ordinances. America (as Europe and all nations) lies dead in sin and trespasses: It is not a suit of crimson satin will make a dead man live; take off and change his crimson into white he is dead still; off with that, and shift him into cloth of gold, and from that to cloth of diamonds, he is but a dead man still: For it is not a form, nor the change of one form into another, a finer, and a finer, and yet more fine, that makes a man a convert; I meane such a convert as is acceptable to God in Jesus Christ, according to the visible rule of his last will and testament. * * *

 * * *

* * * It must not be (it is not possible it should be in truth) a conversion of people to the worship of the Lord Jesus by force of arms and swords of steel: So indeed did Nebuchadnezzer deal with all the world; Dan. 3. So doth his antitype and successor the beast deal with all the Earth; Rev. 13. &c.

But so did never the Lord Jesus bring any unto his most pure worship, for he abhors (as all men, yea, the very Indians do) an unwilling spouse, and to enter into a forced bed: The will in worship, if true, is like a free vote, *nec cogit, nec cogitur*:[4] Jesus Christ compels by the mighty persuasions of his messengers to come in, but otherwise with earthly weapons he never did compel nor can be compelled.

The not discerning of this truth hath let out the blood of thousands in civil combustions in all ages; and made the whore[5] drunk & the Earth drunk with the blood of the saints, and witnesses of Jesus.

 1645

4. Neither does he compel, nor is he compelled (Latin).

5. The biblical whore of Babylon; here, the Roman Catholic Church.

ANNE BRADSTREET
c. 1612–1672

Anne Bradstreet produced the first sustained body of poetry in British North America. In Bradstreet's day, many people wrote and read poetry for pleasure, and poems were often included in prose works. (Consider John Smith's writings, Thomas Morton's *New English Canaan* [1637], and Roger Williams's *A Key into the Language of America* [1643], which are excerpted above.) When Bradstreet's *The Tenth Muse* appeared in London in 1650, it became the first published volume of poems in English written by a resident of America. It was widely read in England and the colonies, notably by the New England minister-poet Edward Taylor, who had a copy of the second edition of Bradstreet's poems (1678) in his library.

Bradstreet's work continues to resonate with readers and writers. In the twentieth century, the American poets John Berryman, Susan Howe, and Adrienne Rich all wrote about Bradstreet and her work, inspired by her achievement. In her preface to the 1967 edition of Bradstreet's writings, Rich captured the drama of Bradstreet's life as a woman and a poet in the new British colonies: "To have written poems, the first good poems in America, while rearing eight children, lying frequently sick, keeping house at the edge of wilderness, was to have managed a poet's range and extension within confines as strict as any American poet has confronted." These circumstances, Rich continued, "forced into concentration and permanence a gifted energy that might, in another context, have spent itself in other, less enduring, directions."

Bradstreet's social position helped mitigate the "confines" that Rich described, and her English education provided intellectual resources that fueled her achievement. Her father, Thomas Dudley, manager of the country estate of the Puritan earl of Lincoln, enabled his daughter to receive an education superior to that of most young women of the time, including training in the classics. As a young girl, Bradstreet wrote poems to please her father. Her earliest surviving poems engage with such major literary works as Sir Walter Raleigh's *History of the World* (1614), as well as the writings of the leading English poets Sir Philip Sidney and Edmund Spenser and the French Protestant poet Guillaume de Salluste Du Bartas.

At sixteen she married Simon Bradstreet, a recent graduate of Cambridge University, who worked with Thomas Dudley. She continued to write poetry after their marriage. Simon assisted in preparing the Massachusetts Bay Company for its departure for America, and in 1630 the Bradstreets and the Dudleys sailed with John Winthrop's fleet. Bradstreet writes that when she first "came into this country" she "found a new world and new manners," at which her "heart rose" in resistance. "But after I was convinced it was the way of God, I submitted to it and joined the church at Boston."

Bradstreet's new circumstances posed many challenges and physical trials. As a child, she had endured a bout of rheumatic fever, which led to recurrent periods of severe fatigue. Even so, she eventually bore eight children. Simon's travels and her family's prominence doubtless placed demands on her as well. Her father served several terms as the Bay colony's governor and held other public offices. Her husband, who was secretary to the company and later governor of the colony, was involved in numerous diplomatic missions that took him away from home, including an extended trip to England in 1661. The frequent absence of her husband was one challenge among many. In 1666, she lost most of her worldly possessions when her house burned. She may also have lost manuscripts in the fire.

Like any good Puritan, Bradstreet routinely examined her conscience and wrestled to make sense of events, such as the house fire, in relation to a divine plan. According to one of the "Meditations" Bradstreet wrote for her children, she was troubled many times about the truth of the Scriptures, she never saw any convincing miracles, and she always wondered if the miracles she read about "were feigned." Eventually she came to believe that her eyes gave her the best evidence of God's existence. She is the first in a long line of American poets who took their consolation not from theology but from, as she wrote, the "wondrous works, that I see, the vast frame of the heaven and the earth, the order of all things, night and day, summer and winter, spring and autumn, the daily providing for this great household upon the earth, the preserving and directing of all to its proper end."

Bradstreet's poems circulated in manuscript until, without her knowledge, her brother-in-law John Woodbridge had them printed in London as *The Tenth Muse, Lately Sprung Up in America* (1650). Bradstreet expressed her ambivalence about the print publication of her work in the poem "The Author to Her Book," which she seems to have written in connection with a proposed second edition of *The Tenth Muse*. That volume was published posthumously, in Boston, as *Several Poems Com-*

piled with Great Wit and Learning (1678). This edition shows the growing influence of the *Bay Psalm Book* on Bradstreet's prosody and diction, and it includes a number of new poems in a more lyrical or elegiac vein that contrasts with her early works on public and philosophical themes. The more intimate poems highlight her concern for her family and home and reveal the pleasures that she took in everyday life.

The following texts are from *The Works of Anne Bradstreet* (1967), edited by Jeannine Hensley.

The Prologue

1

To sing of wars, of captains, and of kings,
Of cities founded, commonwealths begun,
For my mean[1] pen are too superior things:
Or how they all, or each their dates have run
Let poets and historians set these forth, 5
My obscure lines shall not so dim their worth.

2

But when my wond'ring eyes and envious heart
Great Bartas'[2] sugared lines do but read o'er,
Fool I do grudge the Muses[3] did not part
'Twixt him and me that overfluent store; 10
A Bartas can do what a Bartas will
But simple I according to my skill.

3

From schoolboy's tongue no rhet'ric we expect,
Nor yet a sweet consort[4] from broken strings,
Nor perfect beauty where's a main defect: 15
My foolish, broken, blemished Muse so sings,
And this to mend, alas, no art is able,
'Cause nature made it so irreparable.

4

Nor can I, like that fluent sweet tongued Greek,
Who lisped at first, in future times speak plain.[5] 20
By art he gladly found what he did seek,
A full requital of his striving pain.
Art can do much, but this maxim's most sure:
A weak or wounded brain admits no cure.

1. Humble.
2. Guillaume de Salluste Du Bartas (1544–1590), a French Protestant writer much admired by the Puritans. He was most famous as the author of *The Divine Weeks,* an epic poem recounting great moments in Christian history.
3. In Greek mythology, the nine goddesses of the arts and sciences. "Fool": i.e., like a fool.
4. Accord, harmony of sound.
5. The ancient Greek orator Demosthenes conquered a speech defect.

5

I am obnoxious to each carping tongue 25
Who says my hand a needle better fits,
A poet's pen all scorn I should thus wrong,
For such despite they cast on female wits:
If what I do prove well, it won't advance,
They'll say it's stol'n, or else it was by chance. 30

6

But sure the antique Greeks were far more mild
Else of our sex, why feigned they those nine
And poesy made Calliope's[6] own child;
So 'mongst the rest they placed the arts divine:
But this weak knot they will full soon untie. 35
The Greeks did nought, but play the fools and lie.

7

Let Greeks be Greeks, and women what they are;
Men have precedency and still excel,
It is but vain unjustly to wage war;
Men can do best, and women know it well 40
Preeminence in all and each is yours;
Yet grant some small acknowledgment of ours.

8

And oh ye high flown quills[7] that soar the skies,
And ever with your prey still catch your praise,
If e'er you deign these lowly lines your eyes 45
Give thyme or parsley wreath, I ask no bays;[8]
This mean and unrefined ore of mine
Will make your glist'ring gold but more to shine.

1650

In Honor of That High and Mighty Princess Queen Elizabeth[1] of Happy Memory

The Proem[2]

Although, great Queen, thou now in silence lie,
Yet thy loud herald Fame doth to the sky

6. The muse of epic poetry.
7. Pens.
8. Garlands of laurel, used to crown a poet.

1. Elizabeth I (1533–1603), queen of England, ascended to the throne in 1558.
2. Prelude.

Thy wondrous worth proclaim in every clime,
And so hath vowed while there is world or time.
So great's thy glory and thine excellence,　　　　　　　5
The sound thereof rapts[3] every human sense,
That men account it no impiety,
To say thou wert a fleshly deity.
Thousands bring offerings (though out of date)
Thy world of honors to accumulate;　　　　　　　10
'Mongst hundred hecatombs of roaring[4] verse,
Mine bleating stands before thy royal hearse.[5]
Thou never didst nor canst thou now disdain
T' accept the tribute of a loyal brain.
Thy clemency did erst esteem as much　　　　　　　15
The acclamations of the poor as rich,
Which makes me deem my rudeness is no wrong,
Though I resound thy praises 'mongst the throng.

The Poem

No Phoenix pen, nor Spenser's poetry,
No Speed's nor Camden's learned history,[6]　　　　20
Eliza's works, wars, praise, can e'er compact;[7]
The world's the theatre where she did act.
No memories nor volumes can contain
The 'leven Olympiads of her happy reign.[8]
Who was so good, so just, so learn'd, so wise,　　25
From all the kings on earth she won the prize.
Nor say I more than duly is her due,
Millions will testify that this is true.
She hath wiped off th' aspersion of her sex,
That women wisdom lack to play the rex.[9]　　　　30
Spain's monarch, says not so, nor yet his host;
She taught them better manners, to their cost.[1]
The Salic law,[2] in force now had not been,
If France had ever hoped for such a queen.
But can you, doctors,[3] now this point dispute,　　35
She's argument enough to make you mute.
Since first the Sun did run his ne'er run race,[4]
And earth had, once a year, a new old face,[5]

3. Enraptures.
4. Loud. "Hecatombs": sacrificial offerings of one hundred beasts, made in ancient Greece.
5. An elaborate framework erected over a royal tomb, to which verses or epitaphs were attached.
6. William Camden (1551–1623) wrote *Annales*, translated in 1630 as *The History of the Most Renowned and Victorious Princess Elizabeth*. "No Phoenix pen": perhaps a reference to the English poet Sir Philip Sidney (1554–1586), the subject of one of Bradstreet's poems, but she may also be referring to any immortal poet's work. (The phoenix is a mythological bird that dies in flames and rises from its ashes.) "Spenser's": Edmund Spenser (c. 1552–1599), author of *The Faerie Queen* (1590, 1596), whose title honors

Elizabeth. "Speed's": John Speed (1552?–1629), author of *Historie of Great Britain* (1611).
7. Reduce to manageable space.
8. Elizabeth I reigned for forty-four years. "Olympiads": four-year intervals between Olympic games; in ancient Greece, dates were calculated by them.
9. King (Latin).
1. Philip II (1527–1598) was Spain's monarch when Queen Elizabeth's navy defeated his "host" (the many ships of the Spanish Armada) in 1588.
2. A law of the Salian Franks that excluded women from succession to the French Crown.
3. Learned men.
4. I.e., never-finished course.
5. I.e., Earth has a new face each spring.

Since time was time, and man unmanly man,
Come show me such a Phoenix if you can. 40
Was ever people better ruled than hers?
Was ever land more happy freed from stirs?[6]
Did ever wealth in England more abound?
Her victories in foreign coasts resound;
Ships more invincible than Spain's, her foe, 45
She wracked, she sacked, she sunk his Armado;
Her stately troops advanced to Lisbon's wall,
Don Anthony[7] in's right there to install.
She frankly helped Frank's brave distressed king;[8]
The states united[9] now her fame do sing. 50
She their protectrix was; they well do know
Unto our dread virago,[1] what they owe.
Her nobles sacrificed their noble blood,
Nor men nor coin she spared to do them good.
The rude untamed Irish, she did quell, 55
Before her picture the proud Tyrone fell.[2]
Had ever prince such counsellors as she?
Herself Minerva[3] caused them so to be.
Such captains and such soldiers never seen,
As were the subjects of our Pallas queen. 60
Her seamen through all straits the world did round;
Terra incognita[4] might know the sound.
Her Drake came laden home with Spanish gold;
Her Essex took Cadiz, their Herculean hold.[5]
But time would fail me, so my tongue would too, 65
To tell of half she did, or she could do.
Semiramis[6] to her is but obscure,
More infamy than fame she did procure.
She built her glory but on Babel's walls,[7]
World's wonder for a while, but yet it falls. 70
Fierce Tomris (Cyrus' headsman) Scythians' queen,[8]
Had put her harness off, had she but seen
Our Amazon in th' Camp of Tilbury,[9]
Judging all valor and all majesty

6. Disturbances.
7. Don Antonio of Crato (1531–1595), who laid claim to the Portuguese throne.
8. Henri IV (1553–1610), Protestant king of France.
9. A reference to the Netherlands, whose national assembly was called the States General. Elizabeth I came to their aid in the wars against Spain.
1. Female warrior.
2. The Irish chieftain Hugh O'Neill (c. 1540–1616), second earl of Tyrone, was defeated by English forces in 1601.
3. The Roman goddess of war, wisdom, chastity, the arts, and justice; in Greece, known as Pallas Athena.
4. Unknown land (Latin).
5. Robert Devereux (1566–1601), second earl of Essex, captured the Spanish port Cadiz, near the legendary Pillars of Hercules at Gibraltar, in 1596. Essex was the patron of the poet Edmund Spenser, who famously declared that the con-

queror's name "through all Spain did thunder, / And Hercules' two pillars, standing hear, / Did make to quake and fear." "Drake": the explorer Sir Francis Drake (1540?–1596) brought back to England Spanish gold from Chile and Peru.
6. Late-ninth-century queen of Assyria, said to have built Babylon.
7. The tower of Babel was built to win fame for its builders (Genesis 11).
8. Tomyris was queen of the Massagetae, a Scythian tribe, whose armies defeated Cyrus the Great of Persia in 529 B.C.E. According to some accounts, Tomyris had Cyrus beheaded and his head thrown into a pot of blood because it was a fitting end to a bloodthirsty man.
9. In 1588, anticipating a Spanish invasion, Elizabeth I reportedly addressed the English troops at Tilbury, on the north bank of the Thames River, dressed like the mythological female warriors known as Amazons and wearing a silver breastplate.

Within that princess to have residence, 75
And prostrate yielded to her excellence.
Dido, first foundress of proud Carthage walls[1]
(Who living consummates her funerals),
A great Eliza, but compared with ours,
How vanisheth her glory, wealth, and powers. 80
Profuse, proud Cleopatra, whose wrong name,[2]
Instead of glory, proved her country's shame,
Of her what worth in stories to be seen,
But that she was a rich Egyptian queen.
Zenobya,[3] potent empress of the East, 85
And of all these without compare the best,
Whom none but great Aurelius could quell;
Yet for our Queen is no fit parallel.
She was a Phoenix queen, so shall she be,
Her ashes not revived, more Phoenix she. 90
Her personal perfections, who would tell
Must dip his pen in th' Heleconian well,[4]
Which I may not, my pride doth but aspire
To read what others write and so admire.
Now say, have women worth? or have they none? 95
Or had they some, but with our Queen is't gone?
Nay masculines, you have thus taxed us long,
But she, though dead, will vindicate our wrong.
Let such as say our sex is void of reason,
Know 'tis a slander now but once was treason. 100
But happy England which had such a queen;
Yea happy, happy, had those days still been.
But happiness lies in a higher sphere,
Then wonder not Eliza moves not here.
Full fraught with honor, riches and with days 105
She set, she set, like Titan[5] in his rays.
No more shall rise or set so glorious sun
Until the heaven's great revolution;[6]
If then new things their old forms shall retain,
Eliza shall rule Albion[7] once again. 110

Her Epitaph

Here sleeps the queen, this is the royal bed
Of th' damask rose, sprung from the white and red,[8]

1. The Latin poet Virgil (70–19 B.C.E.), in book 4 of his *Aeneid*, tells the tale of the fabled queen of Carthage and her self-immolation after she was abandoned by Aeneas.
2. In Greek, Cleopatra—the name of the famous, licentious Egyptian queen (69–30 B.C.E.)—means "glory to the father." Bradstreet extends the meaning to "fatherland."
3. Queen of Palmyra, Syria, famous for her wars of expansion and defeated by the Roman emperor Aurelian in 273.
4. The Hippocrene spring—on Mount Helicon, home of the Muses—was the source of poetic inspiration.

5. The Latin poets' name for the sun god.
6. "And I saw a new heaven and a new earth: for the first heaven and the first earth were passed away; and there was no more sea" (Revelation 21.1).
7. England.
8. Queen Elizabeth's father, Henry VIII (1491–1547), descended from the House of Lancaster, identified with the symbol of the red rose; her mother, Anne Boleyn (1507?–1536), was from the House of York, identified with a white rose. The two houses were at war with each other for many years. Bradstreet suggests that the damask rose of Elizabeth is formed by the intermingling of these two colors.

Whose sweet perfume fills the all-filling air.
This rose is withered, once so lovely fair.
On neither tree did grow such rose before, 115
The greater was our gain, our loss the more.

Another

Here lies the pride of queens, pattern of kings,
So blaze it, Fame, here's feathers for thy wings.
Here lies the envied, yet unparalleled prince,
Whose living virtues speak (though dead long since). 120
If many worlds, as that fantastic framed,
In every one be her great glory famed.

1643 1650

To the Memory of My Dear and Ever Honored Father Thomas Dudley Esq. Who Deceased, July 31, 1653, and of His Age 77

By duty bound and not by custom led
To celebrate the praises of the dead,
My mournful mind, sore pressed, in trembling verse
Presents my lamentations at his hearse,
Who was my father, guide, instructor too, 5
To whom I ought whatever I could do.
Nor is't relation near my hand shall tie;
For who more cause to boast his worth than I?
Who heard or saw, observed or knew him better?
Or who alive than I a greater debtor? 10
Let malice bite and envy gnaw its fill,
He was my father, and I'll praise him still.
Nor was his name or life led so obscure
That pity might some trumpeters procure
Who after death might make him falsely seem 15
Such as in life no man could justly deem.
Well known and loved, where e'er he lived, by most
Both in his native and in foreign coast,
These to the world his merits could make known,
So needs no testimonial from his own; 20
But now or never I must pay my sum;
While others tell his worth, I'll not be dumb.
One of Founders, thy[1] him New England know,
Who stayed thy feeble sides when thou wast low,
Who spent his state,[2] his strength and years with care 25
That after-comers in them might have share.
True patriot of this little commonweal,
Who is't can tax thee aught, but for thy zeal?
Truth's friend thou wert, to errors still a foe,

1. I.e., a founder of the Massachusetts Bay Colony. 2. I.e., estate; position in life.

Which caused apostates to malign so. 30
Thy love to true religion e'er shall shine;
My father's God, be God of me and mine.
Upon the earth he did not build his nest,
But as a pilgrim, what he had, possessed.
High thoughts he gave no harbor in his heart, 35
Nor honors puffed him up when he had part;
Those titles loathed, which some too much do love,
For truly his ambition lay above.
His humble mind so loved humility,
He left it to his race for legacy; 40
And oft and oft with speeches mild and wise
Gave his in charge that jewel rich to prize.
No ostentation seen in all his ways,
An³ in the mean ones of our foolish days,
Which all they have and more still set to view, 45
Their greatness may be judged by what they shew.
His thoughts were more sublime, his actions wise,
Such vanities he justly did despise.
Nor wonder 'twas, low things ne'er much did move
For he a mansion had, prepared above, 50
For which he sighed and prayed and longed full sore
He might be clothed upon for evermore.
Oft spake of death, and with a smiling cheer
He did exult his end was drawing near;
Now fully ripe, as shock of wheat that's grown, 55
Death as a sickle hath him timely mown,
And in celestial barn hath housed him high,
Where storms, nor show'rs, nor aught can damnify.
His generation served, his labors cease;
And to his fathers gathered is in peace. 60
Ah happy soul, 'mongst saints and angels blest,
Who after all his toil is now at rest.
His hoary⁴ head in righteousness was found;
As joy in heaven, on earth let praise resound.
Forgotten never be his memory, 65
His blessing rest on his posterity;
His pious footsteps, followed by his race,
At last will bring us to that happy place
Where we with joy each other's face shall see,
And parted more by death shall never be. 70

His Epitaph

Within this tomb a patriot lies
That was both pious, just, and wise,
To truth a shield, to right a wall,
To sectaries a whip and maul,⁵
A magazine⁶ of history, 75

3. Though.
4. Gray-haired.

5. Hammer or club. "Sectaries": opposing believers.
6. Storehouse.

A prizer of good company,
In manners pleasant and severe;
The good him loved, the bad did fear,
And when his time with years was spent,
If some rejoiced, more did lament. 80

1867

To Her Father with Some Verses

Most truly honored, and as truly dear,
If worth in me or aught I do appear,
Who can of right better demand the same
Than may your worthy self from whom it came?
The principal[1] might yield a greater sum, 5
Yet handled ill, amounts but to this crumb;
My stock's so small I know not how to pay,
My bond[2] remains in force unto this day;
Yet for part payment take this simple mite,[3]
Where nothing's to be had, kings lose their right. 10
Such is my debt I may not say forgive,
But as I can, I'll pay it while I live;
Such is my bond, none can discharge but I,
Yet paying is not paid until I die.

1678

Contemplations

1

Some time now past in the autumnal tide,
When Phoebus[1] wanted but one hour to bed,
The trees all richly clad, yet void of pride,
Were gilded o'er by his rich golden head.
Their leaves and fruits seemed painted, but was true, 5
Of green, of red, of yellow, mixed hue;
Rapt were my senses at this delectable view.

2

I wist[2] not what to wish, yet sure thought I,
If so much excellence abide below,
How excellent is He that dwells on high, 10
Whose power and beauty by His works we know?

1. The capital that yields interest.
2. "Stock" and "bond" include puns on "worth" and "contract," respectively, in their emotional and financial senses.

3. The smallest possible denomination.
1. Apollo, the Greek and Roman sun god.
2. Knew.

Sure He is goodness, wisdom, glory, light,
That hath this under world so richly dight;[3]
More heaven than earth was here, no winter and no night.

3

Then on a stately oak I cast mine eye, 15
Whose ruffling top the clouds seemed to aspire;
How long since thou wast in thine infancy?
Thy strength, and stature, more thy years admire,
Hath hundred winters past since thou wast born?
Or thousand since thou brakest thy shell of horn? 20
If so, all these as nought, eternity doth scorn.

4

Then higher on the glistering Sun I gazed,
Whose beams was shaded by the leafy tree;
The more I looked, the more I grew amazed,
And softly said, "What glory's like to thee?" 25
Soul of this world, this universe's eye,
No wonder some made thee a deity;
Had I not better known, alas, the same had I.

5

Thou as a bridegroom from thy chamber rushes,
And as a strong man, joys to run a race;[4] 30
The morn doth usher thee with smiles and blushes;
The Earth reflects her glances in thy face.
Birds, insects, animals with vegative,[5]
Thy heat from death and dullness doth revive,
And in the darksome womb of fruitful nature dive. 35

6

Thy swift annual and diurnal course,
Thy daily straight and yearly oblique path,
Thy pleasing fervor and thy scorching force,
All mortals here the feeling knowledge hath.[6]
Thy presence makes it day, thy absence night, 40
Quaternal seasons causéd by thy might:
Hail creature, full of sweetness, beauty, and delight.

7

Art thou so full of glory that no eye
Hath strength thy shining rays once to behold?

3. Furnished, adorned.
4. The sun "is as a bridegroom coming out of his chamber, and rejoiceth as a strong man to run a race" (Psalm 19.5).
5. I.e., as well as plant life.
6. I.e., I know the feeling of (the sun).

And is thy splendid throne erect so high, 45
As to approach it, can no earthly mold?
How full of glory then must thy Creator be,
Who gave this bright light luster unto thee?
Admired, adored for ever, be that Majesty.

8

Silent alone, where none or[7] saw, or heard, 50
In pathless paths I lead my wand'ring feet,
My humble eyes to lofty skies I reared
To sing some song, my mazéd[8] Muse thought meet.
My great Creator I would magnify,
That nature had thus decked liberally; 55
But Ah, and Ah, again, my imbecility!

9

I heard the merry grasshopper then sing.
The black-clad cricket bear a second part;
They kept one tune and played on the same string,
Seeming to glory in their little art. 60
Shall creatures abject thus their voices raise
And in their kind resound their Maker's praise
Whilst I, as mute, can warble forth no higher lays?[9]

10

When present times look back to ages past,
And men in being fancy those[1] are dead, 65
It makes things gone perpetually to last,
And calls back months and years that long since fled.
It makes a man more aged in conceit[2]
Than was Methuselah,[3] or's grandsire great,
While of their persons and their acts his mind doth treat. 70

11

Sometimes in Eden fair he seems to be,
Sees glorious Adam there made lord of all,
Fancies the apple, dangle on the tree,
That turned his sovereign to a naked thrall.[4]
Who like a miscreant's driven from that place, 75
To get his bread with pain and sweat of face,
A penalty imposed on his backsliding race.

7. Either.
8. Amazed.
9. Short lyric or narrative poems intended to be sung.
1. I.e., those who.

2. Apprehension, the processes of thought.
3. Thought to have lived 969 years (Genesis 5.27).
4. Slave. For the story of Adam and Eve in Eden, where they ate the apple from the tree of the knowledge of good and evil, see Genesis 1–3.

12

Here sits our grandame in retired place,
And in her lap her bloody Cain new-born;
The weeping imp oft looks her in the face, 80
Bewails his unknown hap[5] and fate forlorn;
His mother sighs to think of Paradise,
And how she lost her bliss to be more wise,
Believing him that was, and is, father of lies.[6]

13

Here Cain and Abel come to sacrifice, 85
Fruits of the earth and fatlings[7] each do bring.
On Abel's gift the fire descends from skies,
But no such sign on false Cain's offering;
With sullen hateful looks he goes his ways,
Hath thousand thoughts to end his brother's days, 90
Upon whose blood his future good he hopes to raise.

14

There Abel keeps his sheep, no ill he thinks;
His brother comes, then acts his fratricide:
The virgin Earth of blood her first draught drinks,
But since that time she often hath been cloyed. 95
The wretch with ghastly face and dreadful mind
Thinks each he sees will serve him in his kind,
Though none on earth but kindred near then could he find.

15

Who fancies not his looks now at the bar,[8]
His face like death, his heart with horror fraught, 100
Nor malefactor ever felt like war,
When deep despair with wish of life hath fought,
Branded with guilt and crushed with treble woes,
A vagabond to Land of Nod[9] he goes.
A city builds, that walls might him secure from foes. 105

16

Who thinks not oft upon the father's ages,
Their long descent, how nephew's sons they saw,
The starry observations of those sages,
And how their precepts to their sons were law,
How Adam sighed to see his progeny, 110

5. Fortune, circumstances. As an adult, Eve's elder
son, Cain, slew his brother, Abel (Genesis 4.8).
6. Satan.
7. Animals fattened for slaughter.

8. I.e., at a (holy) tribunal; facing God's judgment.
9. An unidentified region east of Eden where Cain dwelled after slaying Abel (Genesis 4.16).

Clothed all in his black sinful livery,
Who neither guilt nor yet the punishment could fly.

17

Our life compare we with their length of days
Who to the tenth of theirs doth now arrive?
And though thus short, we shorten many ways, 115
Living so little while we are alive;
In eating, drinking, sleeping, vain delight
So unawares comes on perpetual night,
And puts all pleasures vain unto eternal flight.

18

When I behold the heavens as in their prime, 120
And then the earth (though old) still clad in green,
The stones and trees, insensible of time,
Nor[1] age nor wrinkle on their front are seen;
If winter come and greenness then do fade,
A spring returns, and they more youthful made; 125
But man grows old, lies down, remains where once he's laid.

19

By birth more noble than those creatures all,
Yet seems by nature and by custom cursed,
No sooner born, but grief and care makes fall
That state obliterate he had at first; 130
Nor youth, nor strength, nor wisdom spring again,
Nor habitations long their names retain,
But in oblivion to the final day remain.

20

Shall I then praise the heavens, the trees, the earth
Because their beauty and their strength last longer? 135
Shall I wish there, or never to had birth,
Because they're bigger, and their bodies stronger?
Nay, they shall darken, perish, fade, and die,
And when unmade, so ever shall they lie,
But man was made for endless immortality. 140

21

Under the cooling shadow of a stately elm
Close sat I by a goodly river's side,
Where gliding streams the rocks did overwhelm,
A lonely place, with pleasures dignified.

1. Neither.

I once that loved the shady woods so well, 145
Now thought the rivers did the trees excel,
And if the sun would ever shine, there would I dwell.

22

While on the stealing stream I fixt mine eye,
Which to the longed-for ocean held its course,
I marked, nor crooks, nor rubs,[2] that there did lie 150
Could hinder aught,[3] but still augment its force.
"O happy flood," quoth I, "that holds thy race
Till thou arrive at thy beloved place,
Nor is it rocks or shoals that can obstruct thy pace,

23

Nor is't enough, that thou alone mayst slide 155
But hundred brooks in thy clear waves do meet,
So hand in hand along with thee they glide
To Thetis' house,[4] where all embrace and greet.
Thou emblem true of what I count the best,
O could I lead my rivulets to rest, 160
So may we press to that vast mansion, ever blest."

24

Ye fish, which in this liquid region 'bide,
That for each season have your habitation,
Now salt, now fresh where you think best to glide
To unknown coasts to give a visitation, 165
In lakes and ponds you leave your numerous fry;
So nature taught, and yet you know not why,
You wat'ry folk that know not your felicity.

25

Look how the wantons frisk to taste the air,
Then to the colder bottom straight they dive; 170
Eftsoon to Neptune's[5] glassy hall repair
To see what trade they great ones there do drive,
Who forage o'er the spacious sea-green field,
And take the trembling prey before it yield,
Whose armor is their scales, their spreading fins their shield. 175

26

While musing thus with contemplation fed,
And thousand fancies buzzing in my brain,

2. Difficulties.
3. Anything.
4. I.e., the sea, home of the sea nymph Thetis.

5. Roman god of the ocean. "Eftsoon": soon after-
ward.

The sweet-tongued Philomel[6] perched o'er my head
And chanted forth a most melodious strain
Which rapt me so with wonder and delight, 180
I judged my hearing better than my sight,
And wished me wings with her a while to take my flight.

27

"O merry Bird," said I, "that fears no snares,
That neither toils nor hoards up in thy barn,
Feels no sad thoughts nor cruciating[7] cares 185
To gain more good or shun what might thee harm.
Thy clothes ne'er wear, thy meat is everywhere,
Thy bed a bough, thy drink the water clear,
Reminds not what is past, nor what's to come dost fear."

28

"The dawning morn with songs thou dost prevent,[8] 190
Sets hundred notes unto thy feathered crew,
So each one tunes his pretty instrument,
And warbling out the old, begin anew,
And thus they pass their youth in summer season,
Then follow thee into a better region, 195
Where winter's never felt by that sweet airy legion."

29

Man at the best a creature frail and vain,
In knowledge ignorant, in strength but weak,
Subject to sorrows, losses, sickness, pain,
Each storm his state, his mind, his body break, 200
From some of these he never finds cessation,
But day or night, within, without, vexation,
Troubles from foes, from friends, from dearest, near'st relation.

30

And yet this sinful creature, frail and vain,
This lump of wretchedness, of sin and sorrow, 205
This weatherbeaten vessel wracked with pain,
Joys not in hope of an eternal morrow;
Nor all his losses, crosses, and vexation,
In weight, in frequency and long duration
Can make him deeply groan for that divine translation.[9] 210

6. I.e., the nightingale. In Greek mythology, Philomela, the daughter of King Attica, was transformed into a nightingale after her brother-in-law raped her and tore out her tongue.

7. I.e., excruciating, painful.
8. Anticipate.
9. Transformation.

31

The mariner that on smooth waves doth glide
Sings merrily and steers his bark with ease,
As if he had command of wind and tide,
And now become great master of the seas:
But suddenly a storm spoils all the sport, 215
And makes him long for a more quiet port,
Which 'gainst all adverse winds may serve for fort.

32

So he that saileth in this world of pleasure,
Feeding on sweets, that never bit of th' sour,
That's full of friends, of honor, and of treasure, 220
Fond fool, he takes this earth ev'n for heav'n's bower.
But sad affliction comes and makes him see
Here's neither honor, wealth, nor safety;
Only above is found all with security.

33

O Time the fatal wrack[1] of mortal things, 225
That draws oblivion's curtains over kings;
Their sumptuous monuments, men know them not,
Their names without a record are forgot,
Their parts, their ports, their pomp's[2] all laid in th' dust
Nor wit nor gold, nor buildings scape time's rust; 230
But he whose name is graved in the white stone[3]
Shall last and shine when all of these are gone.

1678

The Flesh and the Spirit

In secret place where once I stood
Close by the banks of Lacrim[1] flood,
I heard two sisters reason on
Things that are past and things to come;
One Flesh was called, who had her eye 5
On worldly wealth and vanity;
The other Spirit, who did rear
Her thoughts unto a higher sphere:
Sister, quoth Flesh, what liv'st thou on,
Nothing but meditation? 10

1. Destroyer.
2. Vanity. "Parts": features. "Ports": places of refuge.
3. "To him that overcometh will I give to eat of the hidden manna and will give him a white stone, and in the stone a new name written, which no man knoweth saving he that receiveth it" (Revelation 2.17). "Scape": escape.
1. In Latin, *lacrima* means "tear."

Doth contemplation feed thee so
Regardlessly to let earth go?
Can speculation satisfy
Notion[2] without reality?
Dost dream of things beyond the moon, 15
And dost thou hope to dwell there soon?
Hast treasures there laid up in store
That all in th' world thou count'st but poor?
Art fancy sick, or turned a sot[3]
To catch at shadows which are not? 20
Come, come, I'll show unto thy sense,
Industry hath its recompense.
What canst desire, but thou may'st see
True substance in variety?
Dost honor like? Acquire the same, 25
As some to their immortal fame,
And trophies[4] to thy name erect
Which wearing time shall ne'er deject.
For riches doth thou long full sore?
Behold enough of precious store. 30
Earth hath more silver, pearls, and gold,
Than eyes can see or hands can hold.
Affect's thou pleasure? Take thy fill,
Earth hath enough of what you will.
Then let not go, what thou may'st find 35
For things unknown, only in mind.

Spirit: Be still thou unregenerate[5] part,
Disturb no more my settled heart,
For I have vowed (and so will do)
Thee as a foe still to pursue. 40
And combat with thee will and must,
Until I see thee laid in th' dust.
Sisters we are, yea, twins we be,
Yet deadly feud 'twixt thee and me;
For from one father are we not, 45
Thou by old Adam[6] wast begot.
But my arise is from above,
Whence my dear Father I do love.
Thou speak'st me fair, but hat'st me sore,
Thy flatt'ring shows[7] I'll trust no more. 50
How oft thy slave, hast thou me made,
When I believed what thou hast said,
And never had more cause of woe
Than when I did what thou bad'st do.
I'll stop mine ears at these thy charms, 55
And count them for my deadly harms.

2. Thought.
3. Fool. "Art fancy sick": i.e., do you have hallu-
cinations?
4. Monuments.
5. Unrepentant, unsaved.

6. In Puritan theology, humankind was lost to
sin after the fall of "old Adam," but was redeemed
by the sacrifice of the "new Adam," Jesus Christ.
7. Exhibitions, displays.

Thy sinful pleasures I do hate,
Thy riches are to me no bait,
Thine honors do, nor will I love;
For my ambition lies above. 60
My greatest honor it shall be
When I am victor over thee,
And triumph shall with laurel head,[8]
When thou my captive shalt be led,
How I do live, thou need'st not scoff, 65
For I have meat thou know'st not of;
The hidden manna[9] I do eat,
The word of life it is my meat.
My thoughts do yield me more content
Than can thy hours in pleasure spent. 70
Nor are they shadows which I catch,
Nor fancies vain at which I snatch,
But reach at things that are so high,
Beyond thy dull capacity:
Eternal substance I do see, 75
With which enrichéd I would be.
Mine eye doth pierce the heavens and see
What is invisible to thee.
My garments are not silk nor gold,
Nor such like trash which earth doth hold, 80
But royal robes I shall have on,
More glorious than the glist'ring sun;
My crown not diamonds, pearls, and gold,
But such as angels' heads enfold.
The city[1] where I hope to dwell, 85
There's none on earth can parallel;
The stately walls both high and strong,
Are made of precious jasper stone;
The gates of pearl, both rich and clear,
And angels are for porters there; 90
The streets thereof transparent gold,
Such as no eye did e'er behold;
A crystal river there doth run,
Which doth proceed from the Lamb's throne.
Of life, there are the waters sure, 95
Which shall remain forever pure,
Nor sun, nor moon, they have no need,
For glory doth from God proceed.
No candle there, nor yet torchlight,
For there shall be no darksome night. 100
From sickness and infirmity
For evermore they shall be free;
Nor withering age shall e'er come there,

8. In classical times, a crown of laurel was a sign of victory for poets, heroes, and athletes.
9. The food sent by God to the Israelites in the wilderness (Exodus 16.15).

1. Lines 85 to 106 follow the description of the heavenly city of the New Jerusalem in Revelation 21–22.

But beauty shall be bright and clear;
This city pure is not for thee, 105
For things unclean there shall not be.
If I of heaven may have my fill,
Take thou the world and all that will.

1678

The Author to Her Book[1]

Thou ill-formed offspring of my feeble brain,
Who after birth didst by my side remain,
Till snatched from thence by friends, less wise than true,
Who thee abroad, exposed to public view,
Made thee in rags, halting to th' press to trudge, 5
Where errors were not lessened (all may judge).
At thy return my blushing was not small,
My rambling brat (in print) should mother call,
I cast thee by as one unfit for light,
Thy visage was so irksome in my sight; 10
Yet being mine own, at length affection would
Thy blemishes amend, if so I could:
I washed thy face, but more defects I saw,
And rubbing off a spot still made a flaw.
I stretched thy joints to make thee even feet,[2] 15
Yet still thou run'st more hobbling than is meet;
In better dress to trim thee was my mind,
But nought save homespun cloth i' th' house I find.
In this array 'mongst vulgars[3] may'st thou roam.
In critic's hands beware thou dost not come, 20
And take thy way where yet thou art not known;
If for thy father asked, say thou hadst none;
And for thy mother, she alas is poor,
Which caused her thus to send thee out of door.

1678

Before the Birth of One of Her Children

All things within this fading world hath end,
Adversity doth still our joys attend;
No ties so strong, no friends so dear and sweet,
But with death's parting blow is sure to meet.
The sentence past is most irrevocable, 5

1. Bradstreet is thought to have written this poem in 1666, when the second edition of *The Tenth Muse* was contemplated.
2. I.e., metrical feet; thus to smooth out the lines.
3. The common people.

A common thing, yet oh, inevitable.
How soon, my Dear, death may my steps attend,
How soon't may be thy lot to lose thy friend,
We both are ignorant, yet love bids me
These farewell lines to recommend to thee, 10
That when that knot's untied that made us one,
I may seem thine, who in effect am none.
And if I see not half my days that's due,
What nature would, God grant to yours and you;
The many faults that well you know I have 15
Let be interred in my oblivious grave;
If any worth or virtue were in me,
Let that live freshly in thy memory
And when thou feel'st no grief, as I no harms,
Yet love thy dead, who long lay in thine arms, 20
And when thy loss shall be repaid with gains
Look to my little babes, my dear remains.
And if thou love thyself, or loved'st me,
These O protect from stepdame's¹ injury.
And if chance to thine eyes shall bring this verse, 25
With some sad sighs honor my absent hearse;
And kiss this paper for thy love's dear sake,
Who with salt tears this last farewell did take.

 1678

To My Dear and Loving Husband

If ever two were one, then surely we.
If ever man were loved by wife, then thee;
If ever wife was happy in a man,
Compare with me, ye women, if you can.
I prize thy love more than whole mines of gold 5
Or all the riches that the East doth hold.
My love is such that rivers cannot quench,
Nor ought but love from thee, give recompense.
Thy love is such I can no way repay,
The heavens reward thee manifold, I pray. 10
Then while we live, in love let's so persevere
That when we live no more, we may live ever.

 1678

1. I.e., stepmother's.

A Letter to Her Husband, Absent upon Public Employment

My head, my heart, mine eyes, my life, nay, more,
My joy, my magazine[1] of earthly store,
If two be one, as surely thou and I,
How stayest thou there, whilst I at Ipswich lie?[2]
So many steps, head from the heart to sever, 5
If but a neck, soon should we be together.
I, like the Earth this season, mourn in black,
My Sun is gone so far in's zodiac,
Whom whilst I 'joyed, nor storms, nor frost I felt,
His warmth such frigid colds did cause to melt. 10
My chilled limbs now numbed lie forlorn;
Return, return, sweet Sol, from Capricorn;[3]
In this dead time, alas, what can I more
Than view those fruits which through thy heat I bore?
Which sweet contentment yield me for a space, 15
True living pictures of their father's face.
O strange effect! now thou art southward gone,
I weary grow the tedious day so long;
But when thou northward to me shalt return,
I wish my Sun may never set, but burn 20
Within the Cancer[4] of my glowing breast,
The welcome house of him my dearest guest.
Where ever, ever stay, and go not thence,
Till nature's sad decree shall call thee hence;
Flesh of thy flesh, bone of thy bone, 25
I here, thou there, yet both but one.

1678

Another [Letter to Her Husband, Absent upon Public Employment]

As loving hind that (hartless) wants[1] her deer,
Scuds through the woods and fern with hark'ning ear,
Perplext, in every bush and nook doth pry,
Her dearest deer, might answer ear or eye;
So doth my anxious soul, which now doth miss 5
A dearer dear (far dearer heart) than this,
Still wait with doubts, and hopes, and failing eye,
His voice to hear or person to descry.
Or as the pensive dove doth all alone

1. Warehouse.
2. Ipswich, Massachusetts. Her husband may have been in England when she wrote this poem.
3. Capricorn, the tenth of the twelve signs of the zodiac, represents winter. "Sol": sun.

4. Cancer, the fourth sign of the zodiac, represents summer.
1. Lacks. "Hind": female deer. "Hartless" puns on *hart* (male deer) and *heart*.

(On withered bough) most uncouthly bemoan 10
The absence of her love and loving mate,
Whose loss hath made her so unfortunate,
Ev'n thus do I, with many a deep sad groan,
Bewail my turtle[2] true, who now is gone,
His presence and his safe return still woos, 15
With thousand doleful sighs and mournful coos.
Or as the loving mullet,[3] that true fish,
Her fellow lost, nor joy nor life do wish,
But launches on that shore, there for to die,
Where she her captive husband doth espy. 20
Mine being gone, I lead a joyless life,
I have a loving peer, yet seem no wife;
But worst of all, to him can't steer my course,
I here, he there, alas, both kept by force.
Return my dear, my joy, my only love, 25
Unto thy hind, thy mullet, and thy dove,
Who neither joys in pasture, house, nor streams,
The substance gone, O me, these are but dreams.
Together at one tree, oh let us browse,
And like two turtles roost within one house, 30
And like the mullets in one river glide,
Let's still remain but one, till death divide.
Thy loving love and dearest dear,
At home, abroad, and everywhere.

1678

In Reference to Her Children, 23 June 1659

I had eight birds hatched in one nest,
Four cocks there were, and hens the rest.
I nursed them up with pain and care,
Nor cost, nor labor did I spare,
Till at the last they felt their wing, 5
Mounted the trees, and learned to sing;
Chief of the brood then took his flight
To regions far and left me quite.
My mournful chirps I after send,
Till he return, or I do end: 10
Leave not thy nest, thy dam and sire,
Fly back and sing amidst this choir.
My second bird did take her flight,
And with her mate flew out of sight;
Southward they both their course did bend, 15
And seasons twain they there did spend,
Till after blown by southern gales,
They norward steered with filled sails.
A prettier bird was nowhere seen,

2. I.e., turtledove. 3. A common species of fish.

Along the beach among the treen.[1] 20
I have a third of color white,
On whom I placed no small delight;
Coupled with mate loving and true,
Hath also bid her dam adieu;
And where Aurora[2] first appears, 25
She now hath perched to spend her years.
One to the academy flew
To chat among that learned crew;
Ambition moves still in his breast
That he might chant above the rest, 30
Striving for more than to do well,
That nightingales he might excel.
My fifth, whose down is yet scarce gone,
Is 'mongst the shrubs and bushes flown,
And as his wings increase in strength, 35
On higher boughs he'll perch at length.
My other three still with me nest,
Until they're grown, then as the rest,
Or[3] here or there they'll take their flight,
As is ordained, so shall they light. 40
If birds could weep, then would my tears
Let others know what are my fears
Lest this my brood some harm should catch,
And be surprised for want of watch,
Whilst pecking corn and void of care, 45
They fall un'wares in fowler's[4] snare,
Or whilst on trees they sit and sing,
Some untoward[5] boy at them do fling,
Or whilst allured with bell and glass,
The net be spread, and caught, alas. 50
Or lest by lime-twigs they be foiled,[6]
Or by some greedy hawks be spoiled.
O would my young, ye saw my breast,
And knew what thoughts there sadly rest,
Great was my pain when I you bred, 55
Great was my care when I you fed,
Long did I keep you soft and warm,
And with my wings kept off all harm,
My cares are more and fears than ever,
My throbs such now as 'fore were never. 60
Alas, my birds, you wisdom want,
Of perils you are ignorant;
Oft times in grass, on trees, in flight,
Sore accidents on you may light.
O to your safety have an eye, 65
So happy may you live and die.
Meanwhile my days in tunes I'll spend,

1. Trees.
2. The Roman goddess of the dawn.
3. Either.
4. Bird catcher's.

5. Unruly, fractious.
6. I.e., caught by means of birdlime (a sticky substance) spread on twigs.

Till my weak lays[7] with me shall end.
In shady woods I'll sit and sing,
And things that passed to mind I'll bring. 70
Once young and pleasant, as are you,
But former toys (no joys) adieu.
My age I will not once lament,
But sing, my time so near is spent.
And from the top bough take my flight 75
Into a country beyond sight,
Where old ones instantly grow young,
And there with seraphims[8] set song;
No seasons cold, nor storms they see;
But spring lasts to eternity. 80
When each of you shall in your nest
Among your young ones take your rest,
In chirping language, oft them tell,
You had a dam that loved you well,
That did what could be done for young, 85
And nursed you up till you were strong,
And 'fore she once would let you fly,
She showed you joy and misery;
Taught what was good, and what was ill,
What would save life, and what would kill. 90
Thus gone, amongst you I may live,
And dead, yet speak, and counsel give:
Farewell, my birds, farewell adieu,
I happy am, if well with you.

1678

In Memory of My Dear Grandchild Elizabeth Bradstreet, Who Deceased August, 1665, Being a Year and a Half Old

1

Farewell dear babe, my heart's too much content,
Farewell sweet babe, the pleasure of mine eye,
Farewell fair flower that for a space was lent,
Then ta'en away unto eternity.
Blest babe, why should I once bewail thy fate, 5
Or sigh thy days so soon were terminate,
Sith[1] thou art settled in an everlasting state.

2

By nature trees do rot when they are grown,
And plums and apples thoroughly ripe do fall,
And corn and grass are in their season mown, 10

7. Ballads, poems. 1. Since.
8. Winged angels.

And time brings down what is both strong and tall.
But plants new set to be eradicate,
And buds new blown to have so short a date,
Is by His hand alone that guides nature and fate.

1678

In Memory of My Dear Grandchild Anne Bradstreet, Who Deceased June 20, 1669, Being Three Years and Seven Months Old

With troubled heart and trembling hand I write,
The heavens have changed to sorrow my delight.
How oft with disappointment have I met,
When I on fading things my hopes have set.
Experience might 'fore this have made me wise, 5
To value things according to their price.
Was ever stable joy yet found below?
Or perfect bliss without mixture of woe?
I knew she was but as a withering flower,
That's here today, perhaps gone in an hour; 10
Like as a bubble, or the brittle glass,
Or like a shadow turning as it was.
More fool then I to look on that was lent
As if mine own, when thus impermanent.
Farewell dear child, thou ne'er shall come to me, 15
But yet a while, and I shall go to thee;
Meantime my throbbing heart's cheered up with this:
Thou with thy Savior art in endless bliss.

1678

On My Dear Grandchild Simon Bradstreet, Who Died on 16 November, 1669, Being But a Month, and One Day Old

No sooner came, but gone, and fall'n asleep.
Acquaintance short, yet parting caused us weep;
Three flowers, two scarcely blown, the last i' th' bud,
Cropped by th' Almighty's hand; yet is He good.
With dreadful awe before Him let's be mute, 5
Such was His will, but why, let's not dispute,
With humble hearts and mouths put in the dust,
Let's say He's merciful as well as just.
He will return and make up all our losses,
And smile again after our bitter crosses. 10
Go pretty babe, go rest with sisters twain;
Among the blest in endless joys remain.

1678

For Deliverance from a Fever

When sorrows had begirt me round,
And pains within and out,
When in my flesh no part was found,[1]
Then didst Thou rid[2] me out.
My burning flesh in sweat did boil, 5
My aching head did break,
From side to side for ease I toil,
So faint I could not speak.
Beclouded was my soul with fear
Of Thy displeasure sore, 10
Nor could I read my evidence
Which oft I read before.
"Hide not Thy face from me!" I cried,
"From burnings keep my soul.
Thou know'st my heart, and hast me tried; 15
I on Thy mercies roll."
"O heal my soul," Thou know'st I said,
"Though flesh consume to nought,
What though in dust it shall be laid,
To glory 't shall be brought." 20
Thou heard'st, Thy rod Thou didst remove
And spared my body frail,
Thou show'st to me Thy tender love,
My heart no more might quail.
O, praises to my mighty God, 25
Praise to my Lord, I say,
Who hath redeemed my soul from pit,[3]
Praises to Him for aye.[4]

1867

Here Follows Some Verses upon the Burning of Our House, July 10th, 1666

Copied Out of a Loose Paper

In silent night when rest I took
For sorrow near I did not look
I wakened was with thund'ring noise
And piteous shrieks of dreadful voice.
That fearful sound of "Fire!" and "Fire!" 5
Let no man know is my desire.
I, starting up, the light did spy,

1. I.e., when nothing was spared.
2. Cleanse. "Thou": God.
3. Hell.
4. Ever.

And to my God my heart did cry
To strengthen me in my distress
And not to leave me succorless. 10
Then, coming out, beheld a space
The flame consume my dwelling place.
And when I could no longer look,
I blest His name that gave and took,[1]
That laid my goods now in the dust. 15
Yea, so it was, and so 'twas just.
It was His own, it was not mine,
Far be it that I should repine;
He might of all justly bereft
But yet sufficient for us left. 20
When by the ruins oft I past
My sorrowing eyes aside did cast,
And here and there the places spy
Where oft I sat and long did lie:
Here stood that trunk, and there that chest, 25
There lay that store I counted best.
My pleasant things in ashes lie,
And them behold no more shall I.
Under thy roof no guest shall sit,
Nor at thy table eat a bit. 30
No pleasant tale shall e'er be told,
Nor things recounted done of old.
No candle e'er shall shine in thee,
Nor bridegroom's voice e'er heard shall be.
In silence ever shall thou lie, 35
Adieu, Adieu, all's vanity.[2]
Then straight I 'gin my heart to chide,
And did thy wealth on earth abide?
Didst fix thy hope on mold'ring dust?
The arm of flesh didst make thy trust? 40
Raise up thy thoughts above the sky
That dunghill mists away may fly.
Thou hast an house on high erect,
Framed by that mighty Architect,
With glory richly furnished, 45
Stands permanent though this be fled.
It's purchaséd and paid for too
By Him who hath enough to do.
A price so vast as is unknown
Yet by His gift is made thine own; 50
There's wealth enough, I need no more,
Farewell, my pelf,[3] farewell my store.
The world no longer let me love,
My hope and treasure lies above.

1867

1. "The Lord gave, and the Lord hath taken away;
blessed be the name of the Lord" (Job 1.21).
2. Empty, worthless. Cf. Ecclesiastes 1.2.

3. Possessions, usually in the sense of being
falsely gained.

As Weary Pilgrim

As weary pilgrim, now at rest,
 Hugs with delight his silent nest,
His wasted limbs now lie full soft
 That mirey steps have trodden oft,
Blesses himself to think upon 5
 His dangers past, and travails done.
The burning sun no more shall heat,
 Nor stormy rains on him shall beat.
The briars and thorns no more shall scratch.
 Nor hungry wolves at him shall catch. 10
He erring paths no more shall tread,
 Nor wild fruits eat instead of bread.
For waters cold he doth not long
 For thirst no more shall parch his tongue.
No rugged stones his feet shall gall, 15
 Nor stumps nor rocks cause him to fall.
All cares and fears he bids farewell
 And means in safety now to dwell.
A pilgrim I, on earth perplexed
 With sins, with cares and sorrows vext, 20
By age and pains brought to decay,
 And my clay house[1] mold'ring away.
Oh, how I long to be at rest
 And soar on high among the blest.
This body shall in silence sleep, 25
 Mine eyes no more shall ever weep,
No fainting fits shall me assail,
 Nor grinding pains my body frail,
With cares and fears ne'er cumb'red be
 Nor losses know, nor sorrows see. 30
What though my flesh shall there consume,
 It is the bed Christ did perfume,
And when a few years shall be gone,
 This mortal shall be clothed upon.
A corrupt carcass down it lies, 35
 A glorious body it shall rise.
In weakness and dishonor sown,
 In power 'tis raised by Christ alone.
Then soul and body shall unite
 And of their Maker have the sight. 40
Such lasting joys shall there behold
 As ear ne'er heard nor tongue e'er told.
Lord make me ready for that day,
 Then come, dear Bridegroom,[2] come away.

August 31, 1669 1867

1. I.e., my body.
2. Christ is the bridegroom, and the soul is married to him. "And Jesus said unto them, Can the children of the bridechamber fast, while the bridegroom is with them? As long as they have the bridegroom with them, they cannot fast" (Mark 2.19).

To My Dear Children

This book by any yet unread,
I leave for you when I am dead,
That being gone, here you may find
What was your living mother's mind.
Make use of what I leave in love,
And God shall bless you from above.
 A. B.

My dear children,

I, knowing by experience that the exhortations of parents take most effect when the speakers leave to speak,[1] and those especially sink deepest which are spoke latest, and being ignorant whether on my death bed I shall have opportunity to speak to any of you, much less to all, thought it the best, whilst I was able, to compose some short matters (for what else to call them I know not) and bequeath to you, that when I am no more with you, yet I may be daily in your remembrance (although that is the least in my aim in what I now do), but that you may gain some spiritual advantage by my experience. I have not studied in this you read to show my skill, but to declare the truth, not to set forth myself, but the glory of God. If I had minded the former, it had been perhaps better pleasing to you, but seeing the last is the best, let it be best pleasing to you.

The method I will observe shall be this: I will begin with God's dealing with me from my childhood to this day.

In my young years, about 6 or 7 as I take it, I began to make conscience of my ways, and what I knew was sinful, as lying, disobedience to parents, etc., I avoided it. If at any time I was overtaken with the like evils, it was as a great trouble, and I could not be at rest till by prayer I had confessed it unto God. I was also troubled at the neglect of private duties though too often tardy that way. I also found much comfort in reading the Scriptures, especially those places I thought most concerned my condition, and as I grew to have more understanding, so the more solace I took in them.

In a long fit of sickness which I had on my bed I often communed with my heart and made my supplication to the most High who set me free from that affliction.

But as I grew up to be about 14 or 15, I found my heart more carnal,[2] and sitting loose from God, vanity and the follies of youth take hold of me.

About 16, the Lord laid His hand sore upon me and smote me with the smallpox. When I was in my affliction, I besought the Lord and confessed my pride and vanity, and He was entreated of me and again restored me. But I rendered not to Him according to the benefit received.

After a short time I changed my condition and was married, and came into this country, where I found a new world and new manners, at which my heart rose. But after I was convinced it was the way of God, I submitted to it and joined to the church at Boston.

After some time I fell into a lingering sickness like a consumption together with a lameness, which correction I saw the Lord sent to humble and try me and do me good, and it was not altogether ineffectual.

1. I.e., stop speaking. 2. I.e., worldly.

It pleased God to keep me a long time without a child, which was a great grief to me and cost me many prayers and tears before I obtained one, and after him gave me many more of whom I now take the care, that as I have brought you into the world, and with great pains, weakness, cares, and fears brought you to this, I now travail[3] in birth again of you till Christ be formed in you.

Among all my experiences of God's gracious dealings with me, I have constantly observed this, that He hath never suffered me long to sit loose from Him, but by one affliction or other hath made me look home, and search what was amiss; so usually thus it hath been with me that I have no sooner felt my heart out of order, but I have expected correction for it, which most commonly hath been upon my own person in sickness, weakness, pains, sometimes on my soul, in doubts and fears of God's displeasure and my sincerity towards Him; sometimes He hath smote a child with a sickness, sometimes chastened by losses in estate,[4] and these times (through His great mercy) have been the times of my greatest getting and advantage; yea, I have found them the times when the Lord hath manifested the most love to me. Then have I gone to searching and have said with David, "Lord, search me and try me, see what ways of wickedness are in me, and lead me in the way everlasting,"[5] and seldom or never but I have found either some sin I lay under which God would have reformed, or some duty neglected which He would have performed, and by His help I have laid vows and bonds upon my soul to perform His righteous commands.

If at any time you are chastened of God, take it as thankfully and joyfully as in greatest mercies, for if ye be His, ye shall reap the greatest benefit by it. It hath been no small support to me in times of darkness when the Almighty hath hid His face from me that yet I have had abundance of sweetness and refreshment after affliction and more circumspection in my walking after I have been afflicted. I have been with God like an untoward[6] child, that no longer than the rod has been on my back (or at least in sight) but I have been apt to forget Him and myself, too. Before I was afflicted, I went astray, but now I keep Thy statutes.[7]

I have had great experience of God's hearing my prayers and returning comfortable answers to me, either in granting the thing I prayed for, or else in satisfying my mind without it, and I have been confident it hath been from Him, because I have found my heart through His goodness enlarged in thankfulness to Him.

I have often been perplexed that I have not found that constant joy in my pilgrimage and refreshing which I supposed most of the servants of God have, although He hath not left me altogether without the witness of His holy spirit, who hath oft given me His word and set to His seal that it shall be well with me. I have sometimes tasted of that hidden manna that the world knows not, and have set up my Ebenezer,[8] and have resolved with myself that against such a promise, such tastes of sweetness, the gates of hell shall never prevail; yet have I many times sinkings and droopings, and

3. Toil, labor.
4. Financial losses.
5. Cf. Psalm 139.23–24.
6. Unruly. "Circumspection": Prudence.
7. Cf. Psalm 119.8.

8. In 1 Samuel 7.12, a stone monument to commemorate a victory over the Philistines. "Manna": the "bread from heaven" (Exodus 16.4) that fed the Israelites in the wilderness.

not enjoyed that felicity that sometimes I have done. But when I have been in darkness and seen no light, yet have I desired to stay myself upon the Lord, and when I have been in sickness and pain, I have thought if the Lord would but lift up the light of His countenance upon me, although He ground me to powder, it would be but light to me; yea, oft have I thought were I in hell itself and could there find the love of God toward me, it would be a heaven. And could I have been in heaven without the love of God, it would have been a hell to me, for in truth it is the absence and presence of God that makes heaven or hell.

Many times hath Satan troubled me concerning the verity of the Scriptures, many times by atheism how I could know whether there was a God; I never saw any miracles to confirm me, and those which I read of, how did I know but they were feigned? That there is a God my reason would soon tell me by the wondrous works that I see, the vast frame of the heaven and the earth, the order of all things, night and day, summer and winter, spring and autumn, the daily providing for this great household upon the earth, the preserving and directing of all to its proper end. The consideration of these things would with amazement certainly resolve me that there is an Eternal Being. But how should I know He is such a God as I worship in Trinity, and such a Savior as I rely upon? Though this hath thousands of times been suggested to me, yet God hath helped me over. I have argued thus with myself. That there is a God, I see. If ever this God hath revealed himself, it must be in His word, and this must be it or none. Have I not found that operation by it that no human invention can work upon the soul, hath not judgments befallen divers who have scorned and contemned it, hath it not been preserved through all ages maugre[9] all the heathen tyrants and all of the enemies who have opposed it? Is there any story but that which shows the beginnings of times, and how the world came to be as we see? Do we not know the prophecies in it fulfilled which could not have been so long foretold by any but God Himself?

When I have got over this block, then have I another put in my way, that admit this be the true God whom we worship, and that be his word, yet why may not the Popish religion be the right? They have the same God, the same Christ, the same word. They only interpret it one way, we another.

This hath sometimes stuck with me, and more it would, but the vain fooleries that are in their religion together with their lying miracles and cruel persecutions of the saints, which admit were they as they term them, yet not so to be dealt withal.

The consideration of these things and many the like would soon turn me to my own religion again.

But some new troubles I have had since the world has been filled with blasphemy and sectaries,[1] and some who have been accounted sincere Christians have been carried away with them, that sometimes I have said, "Is there faith upon the earth?" and I have not known what to think; but then I have remembered the works of Christ that so it must be, and if it were possible, the very elect should be deceived. "Behold," saith our Savior, "I have told you before."[2] That hath stayed my heart, and I can now say,

9. In spite of. "Divers": various (people). "Contemned": despised.

1. Unbelievers, heretics.
2. Cf. John 13.19 and 14.29, Matthew 24.25.

"Return, O my Soul, to thy rest, upon this rock Christ Jesus will I build my faith, and if I perish, I perish"; but I know all the Powers of Hell shall never prevail against it. I know whom I have trusted, and whom I have believed, and that He is able to keep that I have committed to His charge.

Now to the King, immortal, eternal and invisible, the only wise God, be honor, and glory for ever and ever, Amen.

This was written in much sickness and weakness, and is very weakly and imperfectly done, but if you can pick any benefit out of it, it is the mark which I aimed at.

1867

MICHAEL WIGGLESWORTH
1631–1705

I n 1662, twenty-two years after the Boston-area publication of the *Bay Psalm Book* and twelve years after the London publication of Anne Bradstreet's *The Tenth Muse*, an obscure minister from Malden, Massachusetts, created a sensation with *The Day of Doom*, a poem about Judgment Day. Michael Wigglesworth's volume has been called the first American best seller. The initial edition of eighteen hundred copies quickly sold out. Roughly one colonist out of twenty in New England seems to have purchased a copy at that time, and many more read the poem or heard it read aloud. No complete copies of the first edition survive, for it was literally read to pieces. New editions began to appear on both sides of the Atlantic in 1666—the year of the Great Fire of London, a cataclysm that suggested an earthly day of judgment—and *The Day of Doom* continued to be reprinted for over a century.

Brought up in New Haven, Connecticut, Wigglesworth entered Harvard College at sixteen with the plan of becoming a physician, but his introspective, bookish, and didactic nature drew him to the ministry. In 1655 he accepted a call to minister at the Malden church, and he remained there for the next fifty years. On the day Wigglesworth died, the Boston merchant Samuel Sewall noted in his diary that the minister "was very useful as a physician" and described him as "the author of the poem entitled The Day of Doom, which has been so often printed." Wigglesworth's poem was so popular at least partly because it marked a new development in Puritan poetry. The poem dramatizes the final days of humanity, interweaving passages and phrases from the Bible to create an integrated vision of Christian end-times. Like the English poet John Milton in his great epic *Paradise Lost* (1667) and the English prose writer John Bunyan in his allegory *The Pilgrim's Progress* (1678), Wigglesworth let his imagination range far beyond the scriptural words transformed in his work.

Wigglesworth's dramatic imagination is evident in the diary that he kept in his early twenties, where he recorded a number of psychological and emotional crises. At times he was almost paralyzed with anxiety and self-doubt. He was also troubled by erotic feelings, including an attraction to men that he recorded in a special shorthand in his diary but otherwise felt compelled to suppress. Never physically

strong, he fretted over numerous illnesses, including syphilis. Some of his afflictions were real, but others were imaginary. The diary also reveals that Judgment Day was never far from Wigglesworth's mind, a preoccupation that emerges most clearly in his response to his father's death, in 1653. Shortly after hearing the news, which he acknowledged had made him "secretly glad," Wigglesworth "dreamed of the approach of the great and dreadful Day of Judgment." When he awoke, he wept and determined to "follow God with tears and cries until He gave me some hopes of His gracious good will toward me." But two months later, he despaired of his "senselessness" toward this loss and bewailed his "secure, hard heart." "The death of the righteous unlamented," he notes, "is a forerunner of evil to come." Wigglesworth's struggle to maintain a suitable level of attention toward God's will was a challenge familiar to many Puritans, and his vivid imagining of Judgment Day captured their attention.

The Day of Doom so captivated colonial-era readers that many people learned its verses by heart. The minister and poet Edward Taylor said that one of the reasons he loved his wife was that "the Doomsday verses much perfumed her breath." Committing the poem to memory was a formidable task, made easier by Wigglesworth's use of common hymn meter ("fourteeners"—alternating rhymed lines of eight and six syllables) and because the subject of his poem was familiar to Puritans from sermons. Although Wigglesworth published other poems, notably Meat Out of the Eater (1670), nothing he wrote achieved the popularity of these "Doomsday verses." The poem's great appeal to this generation of Puritans is sometimes attributed to its vivid picture of hellfire; but its popularity also derived from its assurance that heaven is a "glorious place! where face to face / Jehovah may be seen," and where the regenerate will reign with Christ eternally, embraced by God "in arms of love." At the end, the poem is as comforting as it is frightening.

From The Day of Doom[1]

1

The security	Still was the night, serene and bright,
of the world	when all men sleeping lay;
before Christ's	Calm was the season, and carnal reason[2]
coming to	thought so 'twould last for ay.[3]
judgment	Soul, take thine ease, let sorrow cease,
Luk. 12.19	much good thou hast in store:
	This was their song, their cups among,
	the evening before.

5

2

Wallowing in all kind of sin,
 vile wretches lay secure:
The best of men had scarcely then

10

1. The text is from The Day of Doom or a Poetical Description of the Great and Last Judgment with Other Poems (1929), edited by Kenneth B. Murdock, which reprints the only complete American edition (1701). The marginal glosses are part of the original text.
2. The rationalizations of the flesh as opposed to spiritual "right reason."
3. Ever.

their lamps kept in good ure.[4]
Mat 25.5 Virgins unwise, who through disguise
 amongst the best were number'd,
Had closed their eyes: yea, and the wise 15
 through sloth and frailty slumber'd.

3

Like as of old, when men grow bold
Mat. 24.37– God's threat'nings to contemn,[5]
38 Who stopped their ear, and would not hear,
 when Mercy warned them: 20
But took their course, without remorse,
 till God began to pour
Destruction the world upon
 in a tempestuous shower.

4

They put away the evil day, 25
 and drowned their care and fears,
Till drowned were they, and swept away
 by vengeance unawares:
1 Thes. 5.3 So at the last, whilst men sleep fast
 in their security, 30
Surprised they are in such a snare
 as cometh suddenly.

5

The sudden- For at midnight brake[6] forth a light,
ness, majesty, which turned the night to day,
& terror of And speedily an hideous cry 35
Christ's did all the world dismay.
appearing. Sinners awake, their hearts do ache,
Mat. 25.6 trembling their loins surpriseth;[7]
2 Pet. 3.10 Amazed with fear, by what they hear,
 each one of them ariseth. 40

6

They rush from beds with giddy heads,
 and to their windows run,
Viewing this light, which shines more bright
Mat. 24.29– then doth the noon-day sun.
30 Straightway appears (they see't with tears) 45
 the Son of God most dread;
Who with His train comes on amain[8]
 to judge both quick[9] and dead.

4. Use, condition.
5. Despise.
6. Broke.

7. I.e., their lower bodies trembled.
8. In full force. "Train": retinue.
9. Living.

7

Before his face the Heav'ns gave place,
 and skies are rent asunder, 50
With mighty voice, and hideous noise,
 more terrible than thunder.
His brightness damps Heav'n's glorious lamps
 and makes them hide their heads,
As if afraid and quite dismayed, 55
 they quit their wonted steads.[1]

2 Pet. 3.10

8

Ye sons of men that durst contemn
 the threat'nings of God's word,
How cheer you now? your hearts, I trow,[2]
 are thrilled[3] as with a sword. 60
Now atheist blind, whose brutish mind
 a God could never see,
Dost thou perceive, dost now believe,
 that Christ thy Judge shall be?

9

Stout courages[4] (whose hardiness 65
 could death and hell out-face)
Are you as bold now you behold
 your Judge draw near apace?
They cry, no, no: alas! and woe!
 our courage all is gone: 70
Our hardiness (fool hardiness)
 hath us undone, undone.

10

No heart so bold, but now grows cold
 and almost dead with fear:
No eye so dry, but now can cry, 75
 and pour out many a tear.
Earth's potentates and powerful states,
 captains and men of might
Are quite abashed, their courage dashed
 at this most dreadful sight. 80

Rev. 6.16

11

Mean[5] men lament, great men do rent
 their robes, and tear their hair:

1. Their accustomed places. 4. Haughty and defiant souls.
2. Trust, believe. 5. Ordinary.
3. Pierced.

Mat. 24.30 They do not spare their flesh to tear
 through horrible despair.
All kindreds wail: all hearts do fail: 85
 horror the world doth fill
With weeping eyes, and loud out-cries,
 yet knows not how to kill.

12

Rev. 6.15–16 Some hide themselves in caves and delves,
 in places under ground: 90
Some rashly leap into the deep,
 to scape by being drowned:
Some to the rocks (O senseless blocks!)[6]
 and woody mountains run,
That there they might this fearful sight, 95
 and dreaded presence shun.

13

In vain do they to mountains say,
 "Fall on us, and us hide
From Judge's ire, more hot than fire,
 for who may it abide?" 100
No hiding place can from His face,
 sinners at all conceal,
Whose flaming eyes hid things doth 'spy,[7]
 and darkest things reveal.

14

The Judge draws nigh, exalted high 105
Mat. 25.31 upon a lofty throne,
Amidst the throng of angels strong,
 lo, Israel's Holy One!
The excellence of Whose presence
 and awful Majesty, 110
Amazeth Nature, and every creature,
 doth more than terrify.

15

The mountains smoke, the hills are shook,
 the earth is rent and torn,
As if she should be clean dissolved, 115
 or from the center borne.
The sea doth roar, forsakes the shore,
 and shrinks away for fear;

6. I.e., stupid people (who think they can escape 7. I.e., whose flaming eyes do espy hidden things.
God's judgment).

The wild beasts flee into the sea,

Rev. 6.14 so soon as He draws near. 120

16

Whose glory bright, whose wondrous might,
 whose power imperial,
So far surpass whatever was
 in realms terrestrial;
That tongues of men (nor Angel's pen) 125
 cannot the same express,
And therefore I must pass it by,
 lest speaking should transgress.

17

1 Thes. 4.16 Before His throne a trump[8] is blown,
Resurrection proclaiming the Day of Doom: 130
of the dead. Forthwith He cries, *"Ye dead arise,*
Joh. 5.28–29 *and unto Judgment come."*
No sooner said, but 'tis obeyed;
 sepulchers opened are:
Dead bodies all rise at His call, 135
 and's mighty power declare.

18

Both sea and land, at His command,
 their dead at once surrender:
The fire and air constrainéd are
 also their dead to tender.[9] 140
The mighty word of this great Lord
 links body and soul together
Both of the just, and the unjust,
 to part no more forever.

 * * *

21

2 Cor. 5.10 Thus everyone before the throne
The sheep of Christ the Judge is brought,
separated Both righteous and impious
from the that good or ill had wrought.
goats. Mat. A separation, and differing station[1] 165
25 by Christ appointed is
(To sinners sad) 'twixt good and bad,
 'twixt heirs of woe and bliss.

8. Trumpet. 1. Standing, place.
9. Offer.

22

Who are
Christ's sheep.
Mat. 5.10–11

At Christ's right hand the sheep do stand,
 His holy martyrs, who 170
For His dear name suffering shame,
 calamity and woe,
Like champions stood, and with their blood
 their testimony sealed;
Whose innocence without offense, 175
 to Christ their Judge appealed.

23

Heb. 12.5–7

Next unto whom there find a room
 all Christ's afflicted ones,
Who being chastised, neither despised
 nor sank amidst their groans: 180
Who by the rod were turned to God,
 and lovéd Him the more,
Not murmuring nor quarreling
 when they were chastened sore.

24

Luk. 7.41,47

Moreover, such as lovéd much, 185
 that had not such a trial,
As might constrain to so great pain,
 and such deep self-denial:
Yet ready were the cross to bear,
 when Christ them called thereto, 190
And did rejoice to hear His voice,
 they're counted sheep also.

25

Joh. 21.15
Mat. 19.14
Joh. 3.3

Christ's flock of lambs there also stands,
 whose faith was weak, yet true;
All sound believers (Gospel receivers) 195
 whose grace was small, but grew:
And them among an infant throng
 of babes, for whom Christ died;
Whom for His own, by ways unknown
 to men, He sanctified. 200

26

Rev. 6.11
Phil. 3.21

All stand before their Savior
 in long white robes yclad,[2]
Their countenance full of pleasance,

2. Dressed.

appearing wondrous glad.
O glorious sight! Behold how bright 205
dust heaps are made to shine,
Conforméd so their Lord unto,
whose glory is divine.

27

The goats At Christ's left hand the goats do stand,
described or all whining hypocrites, 210
the several Who for self-ends did seem Christ's friends,
sorts of repro- but fostered guileful sprites;[3]
bates on the Who sheep resembled, but they dissembled
left hand. (their hearts were not sincere);
Mat. 24.51 Who once did throng Christ's lambs among, 215
 but now must not come near.

28

Luk. 11.24,26 Apostates[4] and run-aways,
Heb. 6.4–6 such as have Christ forsaken,
Heb. 10.29 Of whom the devil, with seven more evil,[5]
 hath fresh possession taken: 220
Sinners ingrain,[6] reserved to pain
 and torments most severe:
Because 'gainst light they sinned with spite,
 are also placéd there.

29

There also stand a num'rous band, 225
Luk. 12.47 that no profession made
Prov. 1.24,26 Of godliness, nor to redress
Joh. 3.19 their ways at all essayed:[7]
Who better knew, but (sinful crew)
 Gospel and law despised; 230
Who all Christ's knocks[8] withstood like blocks
 and would not be advised.

30

Moreover, there with them appear
 a number, numberless
Gal. 3.10 Of great and small, vile wretches all, 235
1 Cor. 6.9 that did God's Law transgress;
Rev. 21.8 Idolaters, false worshipers,
 profaners of God's name,

3. Spirits.
4. Turncoats.
5. I.e., with seven accomplices more evil than he.
6. Inveterate.

7. I.e., tried.
8. Attempts to gain admittance to their souls. "Behold, I stand at the door and knock" (Revelation 3.20).

Who not at all thereon did call,
 or took in vain the same. 240

* * *

38

All silence keep, both goats and sheep,
 before the Judge's throne;

The saints
cleared &
justified.

With mild aspect to His elect[9]
 then spake the Holy One: 300
"My sheep draw near, your sentence hear,
 which is to you no dread,
Who clearly now discern, and know
 your sins are pardonéd.

39

2 Cor. 5.10
Eccles. 3.17
Joh. 3.18

" 'Twas meet[1] that ye should judgéd be, 305
 that so the world may spy
No cause of grudge, when as I judge
 and deal impartially.
Know therefore all, both great and small,
 the ground and reason why 310
These men do stand at My right hand,
 and look so cheerfully.

40

Joh. 17.6
Eph. 1.4

"These men be those My Father chose
 before the world's foundation,
And to Me gave, that I should save 315
 from death and condemnation.
For whose dear sake I flesh did take,
 was of a woman born,
And did inure[2] Myself t'endure,
 unjust reproach and scorn. 320

41

"For them it was that I did pass
 through sorrows many one:
That I drank up that bitter cup,

Rev. 1.5

 which made Me sigh and groan.
The cross his pain[3] I did sustain; 325
 yea more, My Father's ire
I underwent, My blood I spent
 to save them from hell fire.

* * *

9. Those chosen by God for eternal life.
1. I.e., appropriate.
2. Accustom.
3. I.e., the pain of being crucified.

107

Those that
pretend want
of opportunity
to repent.
Prov. 27.1
Jam. 4.13

A wond'rous crowd then 'gan aloud,
 thus for themselves to say, 850
"We did intend, Lord to amend,
 and to reform our way:
Our true intent was to repent,
 and make our peace with Thee;
But sudden death stopping our breath, 855
 left us no liberty.

108

"Short was our time, for in his prime
 our youthful flower was cropped:
We died in youth, before full growth,
 so was our purpose stopped. 860
Let our good will to turn from ill,
 and sin to have forsaken,
Accepted be, O Lord, by Thee,
 and in good part be taken."

109

Are confuted
and convinced.

Eccles. 12.1
Rev. 2.21

To whom the Judge: "Where you allege 865
 the shortness of the space,
That from your birth you lived on earth,
 to compass[4] saving grace:
It was free grace that any space
 was given you at all 870
To turn from evil, defy the devil,
 and upon God to call.

110

Luk. 13.24
2 Cor. 6.2
Heb. 3.7–9

"One day, one week, wherein to seek
 God's face with all your hearts,
A favor was that far did pass 875
 the best of your deserts.[5]
You had a season, what was your reason
 such precious hours to waste?
What could you find, what could you mind
 that was of greater haste? 880

* * *

4. Encompass. 5. Good deeds; merits.

113

Luk. 13.24–
25 etc.
Phil. 2.12

"Had your intent been to repent,
 and had you it desired, 900
There would have been endeavors seen,
 before your time expired.
God makes no treasure, nor hath he pleasure,
 in idle purposes:
Such fair pretenses are foul offenses, 905
 and cloaks for wickedness."

* * *

130

Others plead
for pardon
both from
God's mercy
and justice
Psal. 78.38

Others argue, and not a few,
 "Is not God gracious?
His equity and clemency 1035
 are they not marvelous?
Thus we believed; are we deceived?
 cannot His mercy great,
(As hath been told to us of old)
 assuage His anger's heat? 1040

* * *

132

"Can God delight in such a sight
 as sinners' misery? 1050
Or what great good can this our blood
 bring unto The Most High?

Psal. 30.9
Mic. 7.18

Oh, Thou that dost Thy glory most
 in pard'ning sin display!
Lord, might it please Thee to release, 1055
 and pardon us this day?"

* * *

134

But all too late, grief's out of date, 1065
 when life is at an end.
The glorious King thus answering,
 all to His voice attend:

They
answered.

"God gracious is," quoth He, "like His
 no mercy can be found; 1070
His equity and clemency
 to sinners do abound.

135

Mercy that
now shines
forth in the
vessels of
mercy.
Mic. 7.18
Rom. 9.23
"As may appear by those that here
 are placed at My right hand;
Whose stripes[6] I bore, and cleared the score, 1075
 that they might quitted[7] stand.
For surely none, but God alone,
 whose grace transcends men's thought,
For such as those that were His foes
 like[8] wonders would have wrought. 1080

* * *

137

Luk. 13.34
The day of
grace now
past.
"With cords of love God often strove
 your stubborn hearts to tame: 1090
Nevertheless your wickedness,
 did still resist the same.
If now at last mercy be past
 from you forevermore,
And justice come in mercy's room, 1095
 yet grudge you not therefore.

138

"If into wrath God turnéd hath
 His long long-suffering,
Luk. 19.42–
43
Jud. 4
And now for love you vengeance prove,
 it is an equal thing. 1100
Your waxing[9] worse, hath stopped the course
 of wonted[1] clemency:
Mercy refused, and grace misused,
 call for severity."

* * *

156

These words appall and daunt them all;
 dismayed, and all amort,[2]
Like stocks[3] they stand at Christ's left hand,
 and dare no more retort.

* * *

6. Lashes.
7. Acquitted.
8. Similar.
9. Growing.

1. Familiar, usual.
2. Spiritless, inanimate.
3. Blocks of wood; speechless persons.

182

Behold the
formidable
estate of all
the ungodly,
as they stand
hopeless &
helpless
before an
impartial
Judge, expect-
ing their final
sentence.
Rev. 6.16–17

Thus all men's pleas the Judge with ease
 doth answer and confute, 1450
Until that all, both great and small,
 are silencéd and mute.
Vain hopes are cropped, all mouths are stopped,
 sinners have naught to say,
But that 'tis just, and equal most 1455
 they should be damned for ay.

183

Now what remains, but that to pains
 and everlasting smart,[4]
Christ should condemn the sons of men,
 which is their just desert; 1460
Oh, rueful plights of sinful wights![5]
 oh wretches all forlorn:
'T had happy been they ne're[6] had seen
 the sun, or not been born.

184

Yea, now it would be good they could 1465
 themselves annihilate,
And cease to be, themselves to free
 from such a fearful state.
Oh happy dogs, and swine, and frogs:
 yea serpent's generation, 1470
Who do not fear this doom to hear,
 and sentence of damnation![7]

185

Psal. 139.2–4
Eccles. 12.14

This is their state so desperate:
 their sins are fully known;
Their vanities and villanies 1475
 before the world are shown.
As they are gross and impious,
 so are their numbers more
Than motes i'th' air, or than their hair,
 or sands upon the shore. 1480

186

Divine justice offended is
 and satisfaction claimeth:

4. Hurt.
5. Souls, persons.
6. Never. "'T": that.

7. Animals were not believed to possess souls
and thus could not be damned.

God's wrathful ire kindled like fire,
 against them fiercely flameth.
Their Judge severe doth quite cashier[8] 1485
Mat. 25.45 and all their pleas off take,
That never a man, or[9] dare, or can
 a further answer make.

187

Mat. 22.12 Their mouths are shut, each man is put
Rom. 2.5–6 to silence and to shame: 1490
Luk. 19.42 Nor have they aught within their thought,
 Christ's justice for to blame.
The Judge is just, and plague[1] them must,
 nor will He mercy show
(For mercy's day is past away) 1495
 to any of this crew.

* * *

195

Unto the saints[2] with sad complaints
 should they themselves apply?
Psal. 58.10 They're not dejected, nor ought affected 1555
 with all their misery.
Friends stand aloof, and make no proof
 what prayers or tears can do:
Rev. 21.4 Your godly friends are now more friends
 to Christ than unto you. 1560

196

Where tender love men's hearts did move
 unto a sympathy,
And bearing part of other's smart
 in their anxiety;
1 Cor. 6.2 Now such compassion is out of fashion 1565
 and wholly laid aside:
No friends so near, but saints to hear
 their sentence can abide.

197

One natural brother beholds another
 in this astonied[3] fit, 1570
Compare Yet sorrows not thereat a jot,
Prov. 1.26 with nor pities him a whit.

8. Dismiss from fellowship
9. Either.
1. Punish.
2. Those who experienced saving grace and in this life felt assurance of salvation; not to be confused with the canonized saints of the Catholic Church.
3. Dazed.

1 Joh. 3.2 & The godly wife conceives no grief,
 nor can she shed a tear
2 Cor. 5.16 For the sad state of her dear mate, 1575
 When she his doom doth hear.

198

He that was erst[4] a husband pierced
 with sense of wife's distress,
Whose tender heart did bear a part
 of all her grievances, 1580
Shall mourn no more as heretofore
 because of her ill plight;
Although he see her now to be
 a damned forsaken wight.

199

The tender mother will own no other 1585
 of all her num'rous brood,
But such as stand at Christ's right hand
 acquitted through His blood.
Luk. 16.25 The pious father had now much rather
 his graceless son should lie 1590
In hell with devils, for all his evils
 burning eternally,

200

Than God most high should injury,
Psal. 58.10 by sparing him sustain;[5]
And doth rejoice to hear Christ's voice 1595
 adjudging him to pain;
Who having all, both great and small,
 convinc'd and silencéd,
Did then proceed their doom to read,
 and thus it utteréd: 1600

201

The Judge "*Ye sinful wights, and cursed sprights,*[6]
pronounceth *that work iniquity,*
the sentence *Depart together from me forever*
of condemna- *to endless misery;*
tion. *Your portion take in yonder lake,* 1605
Mat. 25.41 *where fire and brimstone flameth:*
Suffer the smart, which your desert
 as its due wages claimeth."

＊ ＊ ＊

4. At one time. the graceless son.
5. I.e., that God should sustain injury by sparing 6. Spirits.

205

Luk. 13.28

They wring their hands, their caitiff[7] hands
　　and gnash their teeth for terror;
They cry, they roar for anguish sore,　　　　　　1635
　　and gnaw their tongues for horror.
But get away without delay,
　　Christ pities not your cry:
Depart to hell, there may you yell,

Prov. 1.26
　　and roar eternally.　　　　　　　　　　　　1640

206

*It is put in
execution.*

That word, *Depart,* maugre their heart,[8]
　　drives every wicked one,
With mighty power, the selfsame hour,
　　far from the Judge's throne.

Mat. 25.46

Away they're chased by the strong blast　　　　1645
　　of His death-threat'ning mouth:
They flee full fast, as if in haste,
　　although they be full loath.[9]

207

As chaff that's dry, and dust doth fly
　　before the northern wind:　　　　　　　　1650
Right so are they chaséd away,
　　and can no refuge find.
They hasten to the pit of woe,

Mat. 13.41–42
　　guarded by angels stout;[1]
Who to fulfill Christ's holy will,　　　　　　1655
　　attend this wicked rout.[2]

208

HELL.
Mat. 25.30
Mar. 9.43
Isa. 30.33
Rev. 21.8

Whom having brought, as they are taught,
　　unto the brink of hell
(That dismal place far from Christ's face,
　　where death and darkness dwell:　　　　　1660
Where God's fierce ire kindleth the fire,
　　and vengeance feeds the flame
With piles of wood, and brimstone flood,
　　that one can quench the same),

209

*Wicked
men and devils*

With iron bands they bind their hands,　　　　1665
　　and curséd feet together,

7. Wretched.
8. Despite their wishes.
9. Reluctant to do so.

1. Resolute, brave.
2. This wicked fleeing mob.

*cast into it
forever.
Mat. 22.13 &
25.46*

And cast them all, both great and small,
 into that lake forever.
Where day and night, without respite,
 they wail, and cry, and howl 1670
For tort'ring pain, which they sustain
 in body and in soul.

210

Rev. 14.10–11

For day and night, in their despite,
 their torment's smoke ascendeth.
Their pain and grief have no relief, 1675
 their anguish never endeth.
There must they lie, and never die,
 though dying every day:
There must they dying ever lie,
 and not consume away. 1680

* * *

218

*Mar. 9.44
Rom. 2.15*

Thus shall they lie, and wail, and cry,
 tormented, and tormenting
Their gallèd hearts with poisoned darts
 but now too late repenting. 1740
There let them dwell i'th' flames of hell;
 there leave we them to burn,
And back again unto the men
 whom Christ acquits, return.

219

*The saints
rejoice to see
judgment
executed upon
the wicked
world.
Psal. 58.10
Rev. 19.1–3*

The saints behold with courage bold, 1745
 and thankful wonderment,
To see all those that were their foes
 thus sent to punishment:
Then do they sing unto their King
 a song of endless praise: 1750
They praise His name, and do proclaim
 that just are all His ways.

220

*They ascend
with Christ
into heaven
triumphing.
Mat. 25.46
1 Joh. 3.2*

Thus with great joy and melody
 to heav'n they all ascend,
Him there to praise with sweetest lays,[3]
 and hymns that never end, 1755
Where with long rest they shall be blest,
 and nought shall them annoy:

3. Songs.

1 Cor. 13.12 Where they shall see as seen they be,
and whom they love enjoy. 1760

221

Their eternal O glorious place! where face to face
happiness and Jehovah may be seen,
incomparable By such as were sinners whilere[4]
glory there. and no dark veil between.
Where the sun shine, and light divine, 1765
of God's bright countenance,
Doth rest upon them every one,
with sweetest influence.

222

O blessed state of the renate![5]
O wondrous happiness, 1770
To which they're brought, beyond what thought
can reach, or words express!
Rev. 21.4 Grief's water-course,[6] and sorrow's source,
are turned to joyful streams.
Their old distress and heaviness 1775
are vanishéd like dreams.

223

For God above in arms of love
doth dearly them embrace,
Psal. 16.11 And fills their sprights with such delights,
and pleasures in His grace; 1780
As shall not fail, nor yet grow stale
through frequency of use:
Nor do they fear God's favor there,
to forfeit by abuse.

224

Heb. 12.23 For there the saints are perfect saints, 1785
and holy ones indeed,
From all the sin that dwelt within
their mortal bodies freed:
Made kings and priests to God through Christ's
Rev. 1.6 & dear love's transcendency, 1790
22.5 There to remain, and there to reign
with Him eternally.

 1662

4. Once, earlier. 6. Channel bed.
5. Reborn.

MARY ROWLANDSON
c. 1637–1711

On June 20, 1675, the Wampanoag leader Metacom, who was sometimes called King Philip, organized the first of a series of attacks on New England settlements. These attacks, which lasted for more than a year, have become known as "King Philip's War." They were occasioned by the execution in Plymouth of three Wampanoag tribesmen, but the grievances behind them had been growing for decades. Crowded off their lands by the English colonists, the region's Algonquian communities, including the Wampanoag, had begun to experience severe food shortages. Metacom and his allies wanted to regain sovereignty over their territory and to stop further colonial expansion. By the end of the war, in August 1676, three thousand Native Americans were dead, including Metacom, who was killed by a Native ally of the English. Colonial leaders had sold Metacom's wife and children into slavery in the West Indies, along with many other prisoners of the war. The English had suffered major losses as well. More than twelve hundred houses had been burned, and about six hundred colonials were dead. The war to restore Native sovereignty in New England had instead sharply diminished it, though Metacom and his forces had posed an existential challenge to the colonies.

The most famous account of these attacks is *A Narrative of the Captivity and Restoration of Mrs. Mary Rowlandson*, written by the wife of the minister of the town of Lancaster, Massachusetts, fifty miles west of Boston. Rowlandson spent eleven weeks as the Wampanoag's captive. Born in Somersetshire, in the south of England, she moved to New England with her family in 1639. Her father, John White, became a wealthy landholder in the Massachusetts Bay Colony, and in 1653 he settled in Lancaster. Around 1656, she married the Reverend Joseph Rowlandson. The attack on Lancaster occurred on February 20, 1676, while Joseph was away from home. Several members of Rowlandson's family were killed in the attack, and she and three of

A
NARRATIVE
OF THE
CAPTIVITY, SUFFERINGS AND REMOVES
OF
Mrs. *Mary Rowlandson*,

Who was taken Prisoner by the INDIANS with several others, and treated in the most barbarous and cruel Manner by those vile Savages : With many other remarkable Events during her TRAVELS.

Written by her own Hand, for her private Use, and now made public at the earnest Defire of some Friends, and for the Benefit of the afflicted.

BOSTON :

Printed and Sold at JOHN BOYLE's Printing-Office, next Door to the Three Doves in Marlborough-Street.

1773.

A Narrative. Mary Rowlandson, whose narrative first appeared in 1682, had refused to resist—or even try to escape from—her Native American captors. But in this illustration from around 1773, shortly before the beginning of the American Revolution, she has been given a gun and thus elevated into a defender of her realm —like the male patriots who at that time were opposing British policy.

her children were taken captive; her daughter Sarah was badly wounded and died a few days later. During her captivity, Rowlandson was separated from her older children and saw them only occasionally. She was ransomed and released on the second of May, and after several weeks her surviving children were returned. In 1677 she and Joseph moved to Wethersfield, Connecticut, where he died the next year. The town voted to pay her an annuity as their minister's widow. She married Captain Samuel Talcott in Wethersfield on August 6, 1679, and died in that Connecticut Valley town, thirty five years after her famous ordeal.

Shortly after her release by the Wampanoags, Rowlandson began writing about her captivity, prompted by leading members of the clergy, including one who wrote a preface designed to find meaning for the colony in Rowlandson's experiences. (That anonymous author was probably Increase Mather, who is discussed in the headnote for his son, Cotton Mather, below.) Published in 1682, *A Narrative of the Captivity and Restoration of Mrs. Mary Rowlandson* became one of the most popular prose works of the seventeenth century in both British North America and England. The narrative combines high adventure with tragedy and exemplary piety, while also revealing complex psychological and social dynamics. Using "removes" (i.e., departures, movings from place to place) to structure her account, Rowlandson shows how she adjusted to the shock of the attack, the death of her daughter, and her own situation. As Rowlandson recovers and acclimates, she takes more interest in the unfamiliar people and activities around her, recognizing that some actions that initially seemed to reflect the "savagery" of her captors were instead necessitated by their desperate circumstances. She includes striking portrayals of Metacom, who treats her graciously; her master, Quinnapin, who becomes something of a protector for her; and Quinnapin's wife Weetamoo, the "squaw sachem," who treats her more harshly. She also vividly describes a "powwow" and other rituals and practices that were unfamiliar to her and many of her readers. She has some harsh words for "Praying Indians," that is, Native Christians who sided with Metacom against the English. Her closing reflections suggest her lingering trauma and her effort to make sense of her experiences as part of a divine plan. They offer some of the most moving passages about grief and acceptance in American literature.

Several editions of the narrative appeared around the time of the American Revolution, suggesting that part of the work's appeal is its connecting of an individual's experience to a group identity. Its continued popularity contributed to a revival of the genre of the captivity narrative in the early nineteenth century, as Indian Removal and westward expansion created new pressures on Native communities. One of the major descendants in the genre is *A Narrative of the Life of Mrs. Mary Jemison* (1824), the story of a captive white woman who made a life with the Iroquois. Rowlandson's narrative also exerted a lasting influence on American fiction, through works such as James Fenimore Cooper's *The Last of the Mohicans* (1826) and Catharine Maria Sedgwick's *Hope Leslie: Or, Early Times in the Massachusetts* (1827), which were inspired in part by the genre that Rowlandson so powerfully brought to life.

A Narrative of the Captivity and Restoration of
Mrs. Mary Rowlandson[1]

On the tenth of February 1675,[2] came the Indians with great numbers upon Lancaster:[3] their first coming was about sunrising; hearing the noise of some guns, we looked out; several houses were burning, and the smoke ascending to heaven. There were five persons taken in one house; the father, and the mother and a sucking child, they knocked on the head; the other two they took and carried away alive. There were two others, who being out of their garrison[4] upon some occasion were set upon; one was knocked on the head, the other escaped; another there was who running along was shot and wounded, and fell down; he begged of them his life, promising them money (as they told me) but they would not hearken to him but knocked him in head, and stripped him naked, and split open his bowels.[5] Another, seeing many of the Indians about his barn, ventured and went out, but was quickly shot down. There were three others belonging to the same garrison who were killed; the Indians getting up upon the roof of the barn, had advantage to shoot down upon them over their fortification. Thus these murderous wretches went on, burning, and destroying before them.

At length they came and beset our own house, and quickly it was the dolefulest day that ever mine eyes saw. The house stood upon the edge of a hill; some of the Indians got behind the hill, others into the barn, and others behind anything that could shelter them; from all which places they shot against the house, so that the bullets seemed to fly like hail; and quickly they wounded one man among us, then another, and then a third. About two hours (according to my observation, in that amazing time) they had been about the house before they prevailed to fire it (which they did with flax and hemp, which they brought out of the barn, and there being no defense about the house, only two flankers[6] at two opposite corners and one of them not finished); they fired it once and one ventured out and quenched it, but they quickly fired it again, and that took. Now is the dreadful hour come, that I have often heard of (in time of war, as it was the case of others), but now mine eyes see it. Some in our house were fighting for their lives, others wallowing in their blood, the house on fire over our heads, and the bloody heathen ready to knock us on the head, if we stirred out. Now might we hear mothers and children crying out for themselves, and one another, "Lord, what shall we do?" Then I took my children (and one of my sisters', hers) to

1. The text is from *Original Narratives of Early American History, Narratives of Indian Wars 1675–1699* (1952), vol. 14, edited by C. H. Lincoln. All copies of Rowlandson's original edition have been lost. Like most modern editors, Lincoln reprints the second "Addition," first printed in Cambridge, Massachusetts, in 1682. The full title is *The sovereignty and goodness of GOD, together with the faithfulness of his promises displayed; being a narrative of the captivity and restoration of Mrs. Mary Rowlandson, commended by her, to all that desires to know the Lord's doings to, and dealings with her. Especially to her dear children and relations. The second Addition Corrected and amended. Written by her own hand for*

her private use, and now made public at the earnest desire of some friends, and for the benefit of the afflicted. Deut. 32.39. See now that I, even I am he, and there is no god with me; I kill and I make alive, I wound and I heal, neither is there any can deliver out of my hand.
2. Thursday, February 20, 1676, according to the Gregorian calendar, which was adopted in 1752.
3. Then a frontier town of about fifty families.
4. I.e., houses in the town where people gathered for defense.
5. Belly.
6. Projecting fortifications.

go forth and leave the house: but as soon as we came to the door and appeared, the Indians shot so thick that the bullets rattled against the house, as if one had taken an handful of stones and threw them, so that we were fain to give back.[7] We had six stout dogs belonging to our garrison, but none of them would stir, though another time, if any Indian had come to the door, they were ready to fly upon him and tear him down. The Lord hereby would make us the more acknowledge His hand, and to see that our help is always in Him. But out we must go, the fire increasing, and coming along behind us, roaring, and the Indians gaping before us with their guns, spears, and hatchets to devour us. No sooner were we out of the house, but my brother-in-law (being before wounded, in defending the house, in or near the throat) fell down dead, whereat the Indians scornfully shouted, and hallowed,[8] and were presently upon him, stripping off his clothes, the bullets flying thick, one went through my side, and the same (as would seem) through the bowels and hand of my dear child in my arms. One of my elder sisters' children, named William, had then his leg broken, which the Indians perceiving, they knocked him on [his] head. Thus were we butchered by those merciless heathen, standing amazed, with the blood running down to our heels. My eldest sister being yet in the house, and seeing those woeful sights, the infidels hauling mothers one way, and children another, and some wallowing in their blood: and her elder son telling her that her son William was dead, and myself was wounded, she said, "And Lord, let me die with them," which was no sooner said, but she was struck with a bullet, and fell down dead over the threshold. I hope she is reaping the fruit of her good labors, being faithful to the service of God in her place. In her younger years she lay under much trouble upon spiritual accounts, till it pleased God to make that precious scripture take hold of her heart, "And he said unto me, my Grace is sufficient for thee" (2 Corinthians 12.9). More than twenty years after, I have heard her tell how sweet and comfortable that place was to her. But to return: the Indians laid hold of us, pulling me one way, and the children another, and said, "Come go along with us"; I told them they would kill me: they answered, if I were willing to go along with them, they would not hurt me.

Oh the doleful sight that now was to behold at this house! "Come, behold the works of the Lord, what desolations he has made in the earth."[9] Of thirty-seven persons who were in this one house, none escaped either present death, or a bitter captivity, save only one, who might say as he, "And I only am escaped alone to tell the News" (Job 1.15). There were twelve killed, some shot, some stabbed with their spears, some knocked down with their hatchets. When we are in prosperity, Oh the little that we think of such dreadful sights, and to see our dear friends, and relations lie bleeding out their heart-blood upon the ground. There was one who was chopped into the head with a hatchet, and stripped naked, and yet was crawling up and down. It is a solemn sight to see so many Christians lying in their blood, some here, and some there, like a company of sheep torn by wolves, all of them stripped naked by a company of hell-hounds, roaring, singing, ranting, and insulting, as if they would have torn our very hearts out; yet the Lord by His almighty power preserved a number of us from death, for there were twenty-four of us taken alive and carried captive.

7. I.e., eager to return the gunfire. 9. Psalm 46.8.
8. Hollered, yelled.

I had often before this said that if the Indians should come, I should choose rather to be killed by them than taken alive, but when it came to the trial my mind changed; their glittering weapons so daunted my spirit, that I chose rather to go along with those (as I may say) ravenous beasts, than that moment to end my days; and that I may the better declare what happened to me during that grievous captivity, I shall particularly speak of the several removes we had up and down the wilderness.

The First Remove

Now away we must go with those barbarous creatures, with our bodies wounded and bleeding, and our hearts no less than our bodies. About a mile we went that night, up upon a hill within sight of the town, where they intended to lodge. There was hard[1] by a vacant house (deserted by the English before, for fear of the Indians). I asked them whether I might not lodge in the house that night, to which they answered, "What, will you love English men still?" This was the dolefulest night that ever my eyes saw. Oh the roaring, and singing and dancing, and yelling of those black creatures in the night, which made the place a lively resemblance of hell. And as miserable was the waste that was there made of horses, cattle, sheep, swine, calves, lambs, roasting pigs, and fowl (which they had plundered in the town), some roasting, some lying and burning, and some boiling to feed our merciless enemies; who were joyful enough, though we were disconsolate. To add to the dolefulness of the former day, and the dismalness of the present night, my thoughts ran upon my losses and sad bereaved condition. All was gone, my husband gone (at least separated from me, he being in the Bay;[2] and to add to my grief, the Indians told me they would kill him as he came homeward), my children gone, my relations and friends gone, our house and home and all our comforts—within door and without—all was gone (except my life), and I knew not but the next moment that might go too. There remained nothing to me but one poor wounded babe, and it seemed at present worse than death that it was in such a pitiful condition, bespeaking compassion, and I had no refreshing for it, nor suitable things to revive it. Little do many think what is the savageness and brutishness of this barbarous enemy, Ay, even those that seem to profess more than others among them, when the English have fallen into their hands.

Those seven that were killed at Lancaster the summer before upon a Sabbath day, and the one that was afterward killed upon a weekday, were slain and mangled in a barbarous manner, by one-eyed John, and Marlborough's Praying Indians, which Capt. Mosely brought to Boston, as the Indians told me.[3]

1. Close.
2. I.e., Massachusetts Bay, or Boston.
3. On August 30, 1675, Captain Samuel Mosely, encouraged by a number of people who were skeptical of converted American Indians, brought to Boston by force fifteen Christianized American Indians who lived on their own lands in Marlborough, Massachusetts, and accused them (probably unjustly) of an attack on the town of Lancaster on August 22.

The Second Remove[4]

But now, the next morning, I must turn my back upon the town, and travel with them into the vast and desolate wilderness, I knew not whither. It is not my tongue, or pen, can express the sorrows of my heart, and bitterness of my spirit that I had at this departure: but God was with me in a wonderful manner, carrying me along, and bearing up my spirit, that it did not quite fail. One of the Indians carried my poor wounded babe upon a horse; it went moaning all along, "I shall die, I shall die." I went on foot after it, with sorrow that cannot be expressed. At length I took it off the horse, and carried it in my arms till my strength failed, and I fell down with it. Then they set me upon a horse with my wounded child in my lap, and there being no furniture upon the horse's back, as we were going down a steep hill we both fell over the horse's head, at which they, like inhumane creatures, laughed, and rejoiced to see it, though I thought we should there have ended our days, as overcome with so many difficulties. But the Lord renewed my strength still, and carried me along, that I might see more of His power; yea, so much that I could never have thought of, had I not experienced it.

After this it quickly began to snow, and when night came on, they stopped, and now down I must sit in the snow, by a little fire, and a few boughs behind me, with my sick child in my lap; and calling much for water, being now (through the wound) fallen into a violent fever. My own wound also growing so stiff that I could scarce sit down or rise up; yet so it must be, that I must sit all this cold winter night upon the cold snowy ground, with my sick child in my arms, looking that every hour would be the last of its life; and having no Christian friend near me, either to comfort or help me. Oh, I may see the wonderful power of God, that my Spirit did not utterly sink under my affliction: still the Lord upheld me with His gracious and merciful spirit, and we were both alive to see the light of the next morning.

The Third Remove[5]

The morning being come, they prepared to go on their way. One of the Indians got up upon a horse, and they set me up behind him, with my poor sick babe in my lap. A very wearisome and tedious day I had of it; what with my own wound, and my child's being so exceeding sick, and in a lamentable condition with her wound. It may be easily judged what a poor feeble condition we were in, there being not the least crumb of refreshing that came within either of our mouths from Wednesday night to Saturday night, except only a little cold water. This day in the afternoon, about an hour by sun, we came to the place where they intended, *viz.*[6] an Indian town, called Wenimesset, northward of Quabaug. When we were come, Oh the number of pagans (now merciless enemies) that there came about me, that I may say as David, "I had fainted, unless I had believed, etc." (Psalm 27.13). The next day was the Sabbath. I then remembered how careless I had been of God's holy time; how many Sabbaths I had lost and misspent, and how evilly I had walked in

4. West to Princeton, Massachusetts, near Mount Wachusett.
5. February 12–27; they stopped at a Native American village on the Ware River, near New Braintree.
6. Abbreviation for *videlicet*: that is to say, namely (Latin).

God's sight; which lay so close unto my spirit, that it was easy for me to see how righteous it was with God to cut off the thread of my life and cast me out of His presence forever. Yet the Lord still showed mercy to me, and upheld me; and as He wounded me with one hand, so he healed me with the other. This day there came to me one Robert Pepper (a man belonging to Roxbury)[7] who was taken in Captain Beers's fight, and had been now a considerable time with the Indians; and up with them almost as far as Albany, to see King Philip, as he told me, and was now very lately come into these parts.[8] Hearing, I say, that I was in this Indian town, he obtained leave to come and see me. He told me he himself was wounded in the leg at Captain Beers's fight; and was not able some time to go, but as they carried him, and as he took oaken leaves and laid to his wound, and through the blessing of God he was able to travel again. Then I took oaken leaves and laid to my side, and with the blessing of God it cured me also; yet before the cure was wrought, I may say, as it is in Psalm 38.5–6, "My wounds stink and are corrupt, I am troubled, I am bowed down greatly, I go mourning all the day long." I sat much alone with a poor wounded child in my lap, which moaned night and day, having nothing to revive the body, or cheer the spirits of her, but instead of that, sometimes one Indian would come and tell me one hour that "your master will knock your child in the head," and then a second, and then a third, "your master will quickly knock your child in the head."

This was the comfort I had from them, miserable comforters are ye all, as he said.[9] Thus nine days I sat upon my knees, with my babe in my lap, till my flesh was raw again; my child being even ready to depart this sorrowful world, they bade me carry it out to another wigwam (I suppose because they would not be troubled with such spectacles) whither I went with a very heavy heart, and down I sat with the picture of death in my lap. About two hours in the night, my sweet babe like a lamb departed this life on Feb. 18, 1675. It being about six years, and five months old. It was nine days from the first wounding, in this miserable condition, without any refreshing of one nature or other, except a little cold water. I cannot but take notice how at another time I could not bear to be in the room where any dead person was, but now the case is changed; I must and could lie down by my dead babe, side by side all the night after. I have thought since of the wonderful goodness of God to me in preserving me in the use of my reason and senses in that distressed time, that I did not use wicked and violent means to end my own miserable life. In the morning, when they understood that my child was dead they sent for me home to my master's wigwam (by my master in this writing, must be understood Quinnapin, who was a Sagamore,[1] and married King Philip's wife's sister; not that he first took me, but I was sold to him by another Narragansett Indian, who took me when first I came out of the garrison). I went to take up my dead child in my arms to carry it with me, but they bid me let it alone; there was no resisting, but go I must and leave it. When I had been at my master's wigwam, I took the first opportunity I could get to go look after my dead child. When I came I asked them what they had done with it; then they told me it was upon the hill. Then they went and

7. A colonial town.
8. Captain Beers had attempted to save the garrison of Northfield, Massachusetts, on September 4, 1675. "Albany": then a colony in New York.

9. In Job 16.2, Job says: "I have heard many such things: miserable comforters are ye all."
1. A subordinate chief.

showed me where it was, where I saw the ground was newly digged, and there they told me they had buried it. There I left that child in the wilderness, and must commit it, and myself also in this wilderness condition, to Him who is above all. God having taken away this dear child, I went to see my daughter Mary, who was at this same Indian town, at a wigwam not very far off, though we had little liberty or opportunity to see one another. She was about ten years old, and taken from the door at first by a Praying Ind. and afterward sold for a gun. When I came in sight, she would fall aweeping; at which they were provoked, and would not let me come near her, but bade me be gone; which was a heart-cutting word to me. I had one child dead, another in the wilderness, I knew not where, the third they would not let me come near to: "Me (as he said) have ye bereaved of my Children, Joseph is not, and Simeon is not, and ye will take Benjamin also, all these things are against me."[2] I could not sit still in this condition, but kept walking from one place to another. And as I was going along, my heart was even overwhelmed with the thoughts of my condition, and that I should have children, and a nation which I knew not, ruled over them. Whereupon I earnestly entreated the Lord, that He would consider my low estate, and show me a token for good, and if it were His blessed will, some sign and hope of some relief. And indeed quickly the Lord answered, in some measure, my poor prayers; for as I was going up and down mourning and lamenting my condition, my son came to me, and asked me how I did. I had not seen him before, since the destruction of the town, and I knew not where he was, till I was informed by himself, that he was amongst a smaller parcel of Indians, whose place was about six miles off. With tears in his eyes, he asked me whether his sister Sarah was dead; and told me he had seen his sister Mary; and prayed me, that I would not be troubled in reference to himself. The occasion of his coming to see me at this time, was this: there was, as I said, about six miles from us, a small plantation of Indians, where it seems he had been during his captivity; and at this time, there were some forces of the Ind. gathered out of our company, and some also from them (among whom was my son's master) to go to assault and burn Medfield.[3] In this time of the absence of his master, his dame brought him to see me. I took this to be some gracious answer to my earnest and unfeigned desire. The next day, *viz.* to this, the Indians returned from Medfield, all the company, for those that belonged to the other small company, came through the town that now we were at. But before they came to us, Oh! the outrageous roaring and hooping[4] that there was. They began their din about a mile before they came to us. By their noise and hooping they signified how many they had destroyed (which was at that time twenty-three). Those that were with us at home were gathered together as soon as they heard the hooping, and every time that the other went over their number, these at home gave a shout, that the very earth rung again. And thus they continued till those that had been upon the expedition were come up to the Sagamore's wigwam; and then, Oh, the hideous insulting and triumphing that there was over some Englishmen's scalps that they had taken (as their manner is) and brought with them. I cannot but take notice of the wonderful mercy of God to me in those afflictions, in sending

2. Jacob's lamentation in Genesis 42.36.
3. This colonial town in Massachusetts was

attacked on February 21.
4. Whooping.

me a Bible. One of the Indians that came from [the] Medfield fight, had brought some plunder, came to me, and asked me, if I would have a Bible, he had got one in his basket. I was glad of it, and asked him, whether he thought the Indians would let me read? He answered, yes. So I took the Bible, and in that melancholy time, it came into my mind to read first the 28th chapter of Deuteronomy,[5] which I did, and when I had read it, my dark heart wrought on this manner: that there was no mercy for me, that the blessings were gone, and the curses come in their room,[6] and that I had lost my opportunity. But the Lord helped me still to go on reading till I came to Chap. 30, the seven first verses, where I found, there was mercy promised again, if we would return to Him by repentance;[7] and though we were scattered from one end of the earth to the other, yet the Lord would gather us together, and turn all those curses upon our enemies. I do not desire to live to forget this Scripture, and what comfort it was to me.

Now the Ind. began to talk of removing from this place, some one way, and some another. There were now besides myself nine English captives in this place (all of them children, except one woman). I got an opportunity to go and take my leave of them. They being to go one way, and I another, I asked them whether they were earnest with God for deliverance. They told me they did as they were able, and it was some comfort to me, that the Lord stirred up children to look to Him. The woman, *viz.* goodwife[8] Joslin, told me she should never see me again, and that she could find in her heart to run away. I wished her not to run away by any means, for we were near thirty miles from any English town, and she very big with child, and had but one week to reckon, and another child in her arms, two years old, and bad rivers there were to go over, and we were feeble, with our poor and coarse entertainment.[9] I had my Bible with me, I pulled it out, and asked her whether she would read. We opened the Bible and lighted on Psalm 27, in which Psalm we especially took notice of that, *ver. ult.,* "Wait on the Lord, Be of good courage, and he shall strengthen thine Heart, wait I say on the Lord."[1]

The Fourth Remove[2]

And now I must part with that little company I had. Here I parted from my daughter Mary (whom I never saw again till I saw her in Dorchester, returned from captivity), and from four little cousins and neighbors, some of which I never saw afterward: the Lord only knows the end of them. Amongst them also was that poor woman before mentioned, who came to a sad end, as some of the company told me in my travel: she having much grief upon her spirit about her miserable condition, being so near her time,[3] she would be often asking the Indians to let her go home; they not being willing to that, and yet vexed with her importunity, gathered a great company together about her and stripped her naked, and set her in the midst of them, and when they had sung

5. A chapter concerned with blessings for obedience to God and curses for disobedience.
6. I.e., in place of the blessings.
7. "That then the Lord thy God will turn thy captivity, and have compassion upon thee, and will return and gather thee from all the nations" (Deuteronomy 30.3), referring to the Israelites' Babylonian captivity, or exile.

8. I.e., the mistress of a house.
9. Food. "One . . . reckon": i.e., before she was expected to give birth.
1. Verse 14. "*Ver. ult.*": last verse (Latin abbrev.)
2. February 28 to March 3. The camp was between Ware River and Miller's River, in present-day Petersham, Massachusetts.
3. I.e., so soon after giving birth.

and danced about her (in their hellish manner) as long as they pleased they knocked her on [the] head, and the child in her arms with her. When they had done that they made a fire and put them both into it, and told the other children that were with them that if they attempted to go home, they would serve them in like manner. The children said she did not shed one tear, but prayed all the while. But to return to my own journey, we traveled about half a day or little more, and came to a desolate place in the wilderness, where there were no wigwams or inhabitants before; we came about the middle of the afternoon to this place, cold and wet, and snowy, and hungry, and weary, and no refreshing for man but the cold ground to sit on, and our poor Indian cheer.

Heart-aching thoughts here I had about my poor children, who were scattered up and down among the wild beasts of the forest. My head was light and dizzy (either through hunger or hard lodging, or trouble or all together), my knees feeble, my body raw by sitting double night and day, that I cannot express to man the affliction that lay upon my spirit, but the Lord helped me at that time to express it to Himself. I opened my Bible to read, and the Lord brought that precious Scripture to me. "Thus saith the Lord, refrain thy voice from weeping, and thine eyes from tears, for thy work shall be rewarded, and they shall come again from the land of the enemy" (Jeremiah 31.16). This was a sweet cordial to me when I was ready to faint; many and many a time have I sat down and wept sweetly over this Scripture. At this place we continued about four days.

The Fifth Remove[4]

The occasion (as I thought) of their moving at this time was the English army,[5] it being near and following them. For they went as if they had gone for their lives, for some considerable way, and then they made a stop, and chose some of their stoutest men, and sent them back to hold the English army in play whilst the rest escaped. And then, like Jehu,[6] they marched on furiously, with their old and with their young: some carried their old decrepit mothers, some carried one, and some another. Four of them carried a great Indian upon a bier; but going through a thick wood with him, they were hindered, and could make no haste, whereupon they took him upon their backs, and carried him, one at a time, till they came to Banquaug river.[7] Upon a Friday, a little after noon, we came to this river. When all the company was come up, and were gathered together, I thought to count the number of them, but they were so many, and being somewhat in motion, it was beyond my skill. In this travel, because of my wound, I was somewhat favored in my load; I carried only my knitting work and two quarts of parched meal. Being very faint I asked my mistress[8] to give me one spoonful of the meal, but she would not give me a taste. They quickly fell to cutting dry trees, to make rafts to carry them over the river: and soon my turn came to go over. By the advantage of some brush which they had laid upon the raft to sit upon, I did not wet my foot (which many of themselves at the other end were mid-

4. March 3 to March 5.
5. Massachusetts and Connecticut forces.
6. King of Israel (c. 843–816 B.C.E.) who killed the kings Jehoram and Ahaziah (cf. 2 Kings

9.20).
7. Present-day Miller's River, in Orange, Massachusetts.
8. Weetamoo.

leg deep) which cannot but be acknowledged as a favor of God to my weakened body, it being a very cold time. I was not before acquainted with such kind of doings or dangers. "When thou passeth through the waters I will be with thee, and through the rivers they shall not overflow thee" (Isaiah 43.2). A certain number of us got over the river that night, but it was the night after the Sabbath before all the company was got over. On the Saturday they boiled an old horse's leg which they had got, and so we drank of the broth, as soon as they thought it was ready, and when it was almost all gone, they filled it up again.

The first week of my being among them I hardly ate anything; the second week I found my stomach grow very faint for want of something; and yet it was very hard to get down their filthy trash; but the third week, though I could think how formerly my stomach would turn against this or that, and I could starve and die before I could eat such things, yet they were sweet and savory to my taste. I was at this time knitting a pair of white cotton stockings for my mistress; and had not yet wrought upon a Sabbath day. When the Sabbath came they bade me go to work. I told them it was the Sabbath day, and desired them to let me rest, and told them I would do as much more tomorrow; to which they answered me they would break my face. And here I cannot but take notice of the strange providence of God in preserving the heathen. They were many hundreds, old and young, some sick, and some lame; many had papooses at their backs. The greatest number at this time with us were squaws, and they traveled with all they had, bag and baggage, and yet they got over this river aforesaid; and on Monday they set their wigwams on fire, and away they went. On that very day came the English army after them to this river, and saw the smoke of their wigwams, and yet this river put a stop to them. God did not give them courage or activity to go over after us. We were not ready for so great a mercy as victory and deliverance. If we had been God would have found out a way for the English to have passed this river, as well as for the Indians with their squaws and children, and all their luggage. "Oh that my people had hearkened to me, and Israel had walked in my ways, I should soon have subdued their enemies, and turned my hand against their adversaries" (Psalm 81.13–14).

The Sixth Remove[9]

On Monday (as I said) they set their wigwams on fire and went away. It was a cold morning, and before us there was a great brook with ice on it; some waded through it, up to the knees and higher, but others went till they came to a beaver dam, and I amongst them, where through the good providence of God, I did not wet my foot. I went along that day mourning and lamenting, leaving farther my own country, and traveling into a vast and howling wilderness, and I understood something of Lot's wife's temptation, when she looked back.[1] We came that day to a great swamp, by the side of which we took up our lodging that night. When I came to the brow of the hill, that looked toward the swamp, I thought we had been come to a great Indian

9. Monday, March 6, ending near Northfield, Massachusetts.
1. Lot's wife looked back on the wicked city of Sodom and was turned into a pillar of salt (Genesis 19.24).

town (though there were none but our own company). The Indians were as thick as the trees: it seemed as if there had been a thousand hatchets going at once. If one looked before one there was nothing but Indians, and behind one, nothing but Indians, and so on either hand, I myself in the midst, and no Christian soul near me, and yet how hath the Lord preserved me in safety? Oh the experience that I have had of the goodness of God, to me and mine!

The Seventh Remove

After a restless and hungry night there, we had a wearisome time of it the next day. The swamp by which we lay was, as it were, a deep dungeon, and an exceeding high and steep hill before it. Before I got to the top of the hill, I thought my heart and legs, and all would have broken, and failed me. What, through faintness and soreness of body, it was a grievous day of travel to me. As we went along, I saw a place where English cattle had been. That was comfort to me, such as it was. Quickly after that we came to an English path, which so took with me, that I thought I could have freely lyen down and died. That day, a little after noon, we came to Squakeag,[2] where the Indians quickly spread themselves over the deserted English fields, gleaning what they could find. Some picked up ears of wheat that were crickled[3] down; some found ears of Indian corn; some found ground nuts, and others sheaves of wheat that were frozen together in the shock, and went to threshing of them out. Myself got two ears of Indian corn, and whilst I did but turn my back, one of them was stolen from me, which much troubled me. There came an Indian to them at that time with a basket of horse liver. I asked him to give me a piece. "What," says he, "can you eat horse liver?" I told him, I would try, if he would give a piece, which he did, and I laid it on the coals to roast. But before it was half ready they got half of it away from me, so that I was fain to take the rest and eat it as it was, with the blood about my mouth, and yet a savory bit it was to me: "For to the hungry soul every bitter thing is sweet."[4] A solemn sight methought it was, to see fields of wheat and Indian corn forsaken and spoiled and the remainders of them to be food for our merciless enemies. That night we had a mess of wheat for our supper.

The Eighth Remove[5]

On the morrow morning we must go over the river, *i.e.* Connecticut, to meet with King Philip. Two canoes full they had carried over; the next turn I myself was to go. But as my foot was upon the canoe to step in there was a sudden outcry among them, and I must step back, and instead of going over the river, I must go four or five miles up the river farther northward. Some of the Indians ran one way, and some another. The cause of this rout was, as I thought, their espying some English scouts, who were thereabout. In this travel up the river about noon the company made a stop, and sat down; some to eat, and others to rest them. As I sat amongst them, musing of things

2. Near Beers Plain, in Northfield, Massachusetts.
3. I.e., bent (with a crackling sound).

4. Proverbs 27.7.
5. To Coasset, in South Vernon, Vermont.

past, my son Joseph unexpectedly came to me. We asked of each other's welfare, bemoaning our doleful condition, and the change that had come upon us. We had husband and father, and children, and sisters, and friends, and relations, and house, and home, and many comforts of this life: but now we may say, as Job, "Naked came I out of my mother's womb, and naked shall I return: the Lord gave, the Lord hath taken away, blessed be the name of the Lord."[6] I asked him whether he would read. He told me he earnestly desired it, I gave him my Bible, and he lighted upon that comfortable Scripture "I shall not die but live, and declare the works of the Lord: the Lord hath chastened me sore, yet he hath not given me over to death" (Psalm 118.17–18). "Look here, mother," says he, "did you read this?" And here I may take occasion to mention one principal ground of my setting forth these lines: even as the psalmist says, to declare the works of the Lord, and His wonderful power in carrying us along, preserving us in the wilderness, while under the enemy's hand, and returning of us in safety again. And His goodness in bringing to my hand so many comfortable and suitable scriptures in my distress.[7] But to return, we traveled on till night; and in the morning, we must go over the river to Philip's crew. When I was in the canoe I could not but be amazed at the numerous crew of pagans that were on the bank on the other side. When I came ashore, they gathered all about me, I sitting alone in the midst. I observed they asked one another questions, and laughed, and rejoiced over their gains and victories. Then my heart began to fail: and I fell aweeping, which was the first time to my remembrance, that I wept before them. Although I had met with so much affliction, and my heart was many times ready to break, yet could I not shed one tear in their sight; but rather had been all this while in a maze, and like one astonished. But now I may say as Psalm 137.1, "By the Rivers of Babylon, there we sate down: yea, we wept when we remembered Zion." There one of them asked me why I wept. I could hardly tell what to say: Yet I answered, they would kill me. "No," said he, "none will hurt you." Then came one of them and gave me two spoonfuls of meal to comfort me, and another gave me half a pint of peas; which was more worth than many bushels at another time. Then I went to see King Philip. He bade me come in and sit down, and asked me whether I would smoke it (a usual compliment nowadays amongst saints and sinners)[8] but this no way suited me. For though I had formerly used tobacco, yet I had left it ever since I was first taken. It seems to be a bait the devil lays to make men lose their precious time. I remember with shame how formerly, when I had taken two or three pipes, I was presently ready for another, such a bewitching thing it is. But I thank God, He has now given me power over it; surely there are many who may be better employed than to lie sucking a stinking tobacco-pipe.

Now the Indians gather their forces to go against Northampton.[9] Over night one went about yelling and hooting to give notice of the design. Whereupon they fell to boiling of ground nuts, and parching of corn (as many as had it) for their provision; and in the morning away they went. During my abode in this place, Philip spake to me to make a shirt for his boy, which I

6. Job 1.21.
7. Rowlandson probably has in mind Psalm 145.4: "One generation shall praise thy works to another, and shall declare thy mighty acts."
8. I.e., among believers ("saints") as well as the unregenerate.
9. A colonial town in Western Massachusetts.

did, for which he gave me a shilling. I offered the money to my master, but he bade me keep it; and with it I bought a piece of horse flesh. Afterwards he asked me to make a cap for his boy, for which he invited me to dinner. I went, and he gave me a pancake, about as big as two fingers. It was made of parched wheat, beaten, and fried in bear's grease, but I thought I never tasted pleasanter meat[1] in my life. There was a squaw who spake to me to make a shirt for her *sannup*,[2] for which she gave me a piece of bear. Another asked me to knit a pair of stockings, for which she gave me a quart of peas. I boiled my peas and bear together, and invited my master and mistress to dinner; but the proud gossip,[3] because I served them both in one dish, would eat nothing, except one bit that he gave her upon the point of his knife. Hearing that my son was come to this place, I went to see him, and found him lying flat upon the ground. I asked him how he could sleep so? He answered me that he was not asleep, but at prayer; and lay so, that they might not observe what he was doing. I pray God he may remember these things now he is returned in safety. At this place (the sun now getting higher) what with the beams and heat of the sun, and the smoke of the wigwams, I thought I should have been blind. I could scarce discern one wigwam from another. There was here one Mary Thurston of Medfield, who seeing how it was with me, lent me a hat to wear; but as soon as I was gone, the squaw (who owned that Mary Thurston) came running after me, and got it away again. Here was the squaw that gave me one spoonful of meal. I put it in my pocket to keep it safe. Yet notwithstanding, somebody stole it, but put five Indian corns in the room of it;[4] which corns were the greatest provisions I had in my travel for one day.

The Indians returning from Northampton, brought with them some horses, and sheep, and other things which they had taken; I desired them that they would carry me to Albany upon one of those horses, and sell me for powder: for so they had sometimes discoursed. I was utterly hopeless of getting home on foot, the way that I came. I could hardly bear to think of the many weary steps I had taken, to come to this place.

The Ninth Remove[5]

But instead of going either to Albany or homeward, we must go five miles up the river, and then go over it. Here we abode a while. Here lived a sorry Indian, who spoke to me to make him a shirt. When I had done it, he would pay me nothing. But he living by the riverside, where I often went to fetch water, I would often be putting of him in mind, and calling for my pay: At last he told me if I would make another shirt, for a papoose not yet born, he would give me a knife, which he did when I had done it. I carried the knife in, and my master asked me to give it him, and I was not a little glad that I had anything that they would accept of, and be pleased with. When we were at this place, my master's maid came home; she had been gone three weeks into the Narragansett country to fetch corn, where they had stored up some in the ground. She brought home about a peck and half of corn. This was

1. Food.
2. Husband.
3. Relation, i.e., wife.

4. I.e., five kernels of corn in place of it.
5. To the Ashuelot Valley, in New Hampshire.

about the time that their great captain, Naananto, was killed in the Narragansett country. My son being now about a mile from me, I asked liberty to go and see him; they bade me go, and away I went; but quickly lost myself, traveling over hills and through swamps, and could not find the way to him. And I cannot but admire at the wonderful power and goodness of God to me, in that, though I was gone from home, and met with all sorts of Indians, and those I had no knowledge of, and there being no Christian soul near me; yet not one of them offered the least imaginable miscarriage to me. I turned homeward again, and met with my master. He showed me the way to my son. When I came to him I found him not well: and withal he had a boil on his side, which much troubled him. We bemoaned one another a while, as the Lord helped us, and then I returned again. When I was returned, I found myself as unsatisfied as I was before. I went up and down mourning and lamenting; and my spirit was ready to sink with the thoughts of my poor children. My son was ill, and I could but not think of his mournful looks, and no Christian friend was near him, to do any office of love for him, either for soul or body. And my poor girl, I knew not where she was, nor whether she was sick, or well, or alive, or dead. I repaired under these thoughts to my Bible (my great comfort in that time) and that Scripture came to my hand, "Cast thy burden upon the Lord, and He shall sustain thee" (Psalm 55.22).

But I was fain to go and look after something to satisfy my hunger, and going among the wigwams, I went into one and there found a squaw who showed herself very kind to me, and gave me a piece of bear. I put it into my pocket, and came home, but could not find an opportunity to broil it, for fear they would get it from me, and there it lay all that day and night in my stinking pocket. In the morning I went to the same squaw, who had a kettle of ground nuts boiling. I asked her to let me boil my piece of bear in her kettle, which she did, and gave me some ground nuts to eat with it: and I cannot but think how pleasant it was to me. I have sometime seen bear baked very handsomely among the English, and some like it, but the thought that it was bear made me tremble. But now that was savory to me that one would think was enough to turn the stomach of a brute creature.

One bitter cold day I could find no room to sit down before the fire. I went out, and could not tell what to do, but I went in to another wigwam, where they were also sitting round the fire, but the squaw laid a skin for me, and bid me sit down, and gave me some ground nuts, and bade me come again; and told me they would buy me, if they were able, and yet these were strangers to me that I never saw before.

The Tenth Remove[6]

That day a small part of the company removed about three-quarters of a mile, intending further the next day. When they came to the place where they intended to lodge, and had pitched their wigwams, being hungry, I went again back to the place we were before at, to get something to eat, being encouraged by the squaw's kindness, who bade me come again. When I was there, there came an Indian to look after me, who when he had found me,

6. To another location in the Ashuelot Valley.

kicked me all along. I went home and found venison roasting that night, but they would not give me one bit of it. Sometimes I met with favor, and sometimes with nothing but frowns.

The Eleventh Remove[7]

The next day in the morning they took their travel, intending a day's journey up the river. I took my load at my back, and quickly we came to wade over the river; and passed over tiresome and wearisome hills. One hill was so steep that I was fain to creep up upon my knees, and to hold by the twigs and bushes to keep myself from falling backward. My head also was so light that I usually reeled as I went; but I hope all these wearisome steps that I have taken, are but a forewarning to me of the heavenly rest: "I know, O Lord, that thy judgments are right, and that thou in faithfulness hast afflicted me" (Psalm 119.75).

The Twelfth Remove[8]

It was upon a Sabbath-day morning, that they prepared for their travel. This morning I asked my master whether he would sell me to my husband. He answered me "Nux,"[9] which did much rejoice my spirit. My mistress, before we went, was gone to the burial of a papoose, and returning, she found me sitting and reading in my Bible; she snatched it hastily out of my hand, and threw it out of doors. I ran out and catched it up, and put it into my pocket, and never let her see it afterward. Then they packed up their things to be gone, and gave me my load. I complained it was too heavy, whereupon she gave me a slap in the face, and bade me go; I lifted up my heart to God, hoping the redemption was not far off; and the rather because their insolency grew worse and worse.

But the thoughts of my going homeward (for so we bent our course) much cheered my spirit, and made my burden seem light, and almost nothing at all. But (to my amazement and great perplexity) the scale was soon turned; for when we had gone a little way, on a sudden my mistress gives out; she would go no further, but turn back again, and said I must go back again with her, and she called her *sannup,* and would have had him gone back also, but he would not, but said he would go on, and come to us again in three days. My spirit was, upon this, I confess, very impatient, and almost outrageous.[1] I thought I could as well have died as went back; I cannot declare the trouble that I was in about it; but yet back again I must go. As soon as I had the opportunity, I took my Bible to read, and that quieting Scripture came to my hand, "Be still, and know that I am God" (Psalm 46.10). Which stilled my spirit for the present. But a sore time of trial, I concluded, I had to go through, my master being gone, who seemed to me the best friend that I had of an Indian, both in cold and hunger, and quickly so it proved. Down I sat, with my heart as full as it could hold, and yet so hungry that I could not sit neither; but going out to see what I could find, and walking among

7. April 1676, near Chesterfield, New Hampshire—as far north as Rowlandson was taken.
8. Sunday, April 9.
9. Yes.
1. Outraged.

the trees, I found six acorns, and two chestnuts, which were some refreshment to me. Towards night I gathered some sticks for my own comfort, that I might not lie a-cold; but when we came to lie down they bade me to go out, and lie somewhere else, for they had company (they said) come in more than their own. I told them, I could not tell where to go, they bade me go look; I told them, if I went to another wigwam they would be angry, and send me home again. Then one of the company drew his sword, and told me he would run me through if I did not go presently. Then was I fain to stoop to this rude fellow, and to go out in the night, I knew not whither. Mine eyes have seen that fellow afterwards walking up and down Boston, under the appearance of a Friend Indian, and several others of the like cut. I went to one wigwam, and they told me they had no room. Then I went to another, and they said the same; at last an old Indian bade me to come to him, and his squaw gave me some ground nuts; she gave me also something to lay under my head, and a good fire we had; and through the good providence of God, I had a comfortable lodging that night. In the morning, another Indian bade me come at night, and he would give me six ground nuts, which I did. We were at this place and time about two miles from [the] Connecticut River. We went in the morning to gather ground nuts, to the river, and went back again that night. I went with a good load at my back (for they when they went, though but a little way, would carry all their trumpery² with them). I told them the skin was off my back, but I had no other comforting answer from them than this: that it would be no matter if my head were off too.

The Thirteenth Remove³

Instead of going toward the Bay, which was that I desired, I must go with them five or six miles down the river into a mighty thicket of brush; where we abode almost a fortnight. Here one asked me to make a shirt for her papoose, for which she gave me a mess of broth, which was thickened with meal made of the bark of a tree, and to make it the better, she had put into it about a handful of peas, and a few roasted ground nuts. I had not seen my son a pretty while, and here was an Indian of whom I made inquiry after him, and asked him when he saw him. He answered me that such a time his master roasted him, and that himself did eat a piece of him, as big as his two fingers, and that he was very good meat. But the Lord upheld my Spirit, under this discouragement; and I considered their horrible addictedness to lying, and that there is not one of them that makes the least conscience of speaking of truth. In this place, on a cold night, as I lay by the fire, I removed a stick that kept the heat from me. A squaw moved it down again, at which I looked up, and she threw a handful of ashes in mine eyes. I thought I should have been quite blinded, and have never seen more, but lying down, the water run out of my eyes, and carried the dirt with it, that by the morning I recovered my sight again. Yet upon this, and the like occasions, I hope it is not too much to say with Job, "Have pity upon me, O ye my Friends, for the Hand of the Lord has touched me."⁴ And here I cannot but remember how many times sitting in their wigwams, and musing on things past, I

2. Worthless things.
3. To Hinsdale, New Hampshire, near the

Connecticut River.
4. Job 19.21.

should suddenly leap up and run out, as if I had been at home, forgetting where I was, and what my condition was; but when I was without, and saw nothing but wilderness, and woods, and a company of barbarous heathens, my mind quickly returned to me, which made me think of that, spoken concerning Sampson, who said, "I will go out and shake myself as at other times, but he wist not that the Lord was departed from him."[5] About this time I began to think that all my hopes of restoration would come to nothing. I thought of the English army, and hoped for their coming, and being taken by them, but that failed. I hoped to be carried to Albany, as the Indians had discoursed before, but that failed also. I thought of being sold to my husband, as my master spake, but instead of that, my master himself was gone, and I left behind, so that my spirit was now quite ready to sink. I asked them to let me go out and pick up some sticks, that I might get alone, and pour out my heart unto the Lord. Then also I took my Bible to read, but I found no comfort here neither, which many times I was wont to find. So easy a thing it is with God to dry up the streams of Scripture comfort from us. Yet I can say, that in all my sorrows and afflictions, God did not leave me to have my impatience work towards Himself, as if His ways were unrighteous. But I knew that He laid upon me less than I deserved. Afterward, before this doleful time ended with me, I was turning the leaves of my Bible, and the Lord brought to me some Scriptures, which did a little revive me, as that [in] Isaiah 55.8: "For my thoughts are not your thoughts, neither are your ways my ways, saith the Lord." And also that [in] Psalm 37.5: "Commit thy way unto the Lord; trust also in him; and he shall bring it to pass." About this time they came yelping from Hadley,[6] where they had killed three Englishmen, and brought one captive with them, viz. Thomas Read. They all gathered about the poor man, asking him many questions. I desired also to go and see him; and when I came, he was crying bitterly, supposing they would quickly kill him. Whereupon I asked one of them, whether they intended to kill him; he answered me, they would not. He being a little cheered with that, I asked him about the welfare of my husband. He told me he saw him such a time in the Bay, and he was well, but very melancholy. By which I certainly understood (though I suspected it before) that whatsoever the Indians told me respecting him was vanity and lies. Some of them told me he was dead, and they had killed him; some said he was married again, and that the Governor wished him to marry; and told him he should have his choice, and that all persuaded I was dead. So like were these barbarous creatures to him who was a liar from the beginning.[7]

As I was sitting once in the wigwam here, Philip's maid came in with the child in her arms, and asked me to give her a piece of my apron, to make a flap for it. I told her I would not. Then my mistress bade me give it, but still I said no. The maid told me if I would not give her a piece, she would tear a piece off it. I told her I would tear her coat then. With that my mistress rises up, and take up a stick big enough to have killed me, and struck at me with it. But I stepped out, and she struck the stick into the mat of the wigwam. But while she was pulling of it out I ran to the maid and gave her all my apron, and so that storm went over.

5. Judges 16.20. "Wist": knew.
6. A colonial town southeast of Northampton.

7. I.e., Satan.

Hearing that my son was come to this place, I went to see him, and told him his father was well, but melancholy. He told me he was as much grieved for his father as for himself. I wondered at his speech, for I thought I had enough upon my spirit in reference to myself, to make me mindless of my husband and everyone else; they being safe among their friends. He told me also, that awhile before, his master (together with other Indians) were going to the French for powder; but by the way the Mohawks met with them, and killed four of their company, which made the rest turn back again, for it might have been worse with him, had he been sold to the French, than it proved to be in his remaining with the Indians.

I went to see an English youth in this place, one John Gilbert of Springfield.[8] I found him lying without doors, upon the ground. I asked him how he did? He told me he was very sick of a flux,[9] with eating so much blood. They had turned him out of the wigwam, and with him an Indian papoose, almost dead (whose parents had been killed), in a bitter cold day, without fire or clothes. The young man himself had nothing on but his shirt and waistcoat. This sight was enough to melt a heart of flint. There they lay quivering in the cold, the youth round like a dog, the papoose stretched out with his eyes and nose and mouth full of dirt, and yet alive, and groaning. I advised John to go and get to some fire. He told me he could not stand, but I persuaded him still, lest he should lie there and die. And with much ado I got him to a fire, and went myself home. As soon as I was got home his master's daughter came after me, to know what I had done with the Englishman. I told her I had got him to a fire in such a place. Now had I need to pray Paul's Prayer "That we may be delivered from unreasonable and wicked men" (2 Thessalonians 3.2). For her satisfaction I went along with her, and brought her to him; but before I got home again it was noised about that I was running away and getting the English youth, along with me; that as soon as I came in they began to rant and domineer, asking me where I had been, and what I had been doing? and saying they would knock him on the head. I told them I had been seeing the English youth, and that I would not run away. They told me I lied, and taking up a hatchet, they came to me, and said they would knock me down if I stirred out again, and so confined me to the wigwam. Now may I say with David, "I am in a great strait" (2 Samuel 24.14). If I keep in, I must die with hunger, and if I go out, I must be knocked in [the] head. This distressed condition held that day, and half the next. And then the Lord remembered me, whose mercies are great. Then came an Indian to me with a pair of stockings that were too big for him, and he would have me ravel them out, and knit them fit for him. I showed myself willing, and bid him ask my mistress if I might go along with him a little way; she said yes, I might, but I was not a little refreshed with that news, that I had my liberty again. Then I went along with him, and he gave me some roasted ground nuts, which did again revive my feeble stomach.

Being got out of her sight, I had time and liberty again to look into my Bible; which was my guide by day, and my pillow by night. Now that comfortable Scripture presented itself to me, "For a small moment have I forsaken thee, but with great mercies will I gather thee" (Isaiah 54.7). Thus the Lord carried me along from one time to another, and made good to me this precious

8. A colonial town southwest of Hadley. 9. Dysentery.

promise, and many others. Then my son came to see me, and I asked his master to let him stay awhile with me, that I might comb his head, and look over him, for he was almost overcome with lice. He told me, when I had done, that he was very hungry, but I had nothing to relieve him, but bid him go into the wigwams as he went along, and see if he could get anything among them. Which he did, and it seems tarried a little too long; for his master was angry with him, and beat him, and then sold him. Then he came running to tell me he had a new master, and that he had given him some ground nuts already. Then I went along with him to his new master who told me he loved him, and he should not want.[1] So his master carried him away, and I never saw him afterward, till I saw him at Piscataqua in Portsmouth.

That night they bade me go out of the wigwam again. My mistress's papoose was sick, and it died that night, and there was one benefit in it— that there was more room. I went to a wigwam, and they bade me come in, and gave me a skin to lie upon, and a mess of venison and ground nuts, which was a choice dish among them. On the morrow they buried the papoose, and afterward, both morning and evening, there came a company to mourn and howl with her; though I confess I could not much condole with them. Many sorrowful days I had in this place, often getting alone. "Like a crane, or a swallow, so did I chatter; I did mourn as a dove, mine eyes ail with looking upward. Oh, Lord, I am oppressed; undertake for me" (Isaiah 38.14). I could tell the Lord, as Hezekiah, "Remember now O Lord, I beseech thee, how I have walked before thee in truth."[2] Now had I time to examine all my ways: my conscience did not accuse me of unrighteousness toward one or other; yet I saw how in my walk with God, I had been a careless creature. As David said, "Against thee, thee only have I sinned":[3] and I might say with the poor publican, "God be merciful unto me a sinner."[4] On the Sabbath days, I could look upon the sun and think how people were going to the house of God, to have their souls refreshed; and then home, and their bodies also; but I was destitute of both; and might say as the poor prodigal, "He would fain have filled his belly with the husks that the swine did eat, and no man gave unto him" (Luke 15.16). For I must say with him, "Father, I have sinned against Heaven and in thy sight."[5] I remembered how on the night before and after the Sabbath, when my family was about me, and relations and neighbors with us, we could pray and sing, and then refresh our bodies with the good creatures of God; and then have a comfortable bed to lie down on; but instead of all this, I had only a little swill for the body and then, like a swine, must lie down on the ground. I cannot express to man the sorrow that lay upon my spirit; the Lord knows it. Yet that comfortable Scripture would often come to mind, "For a small moment have I forsaken thee, but with great mercies will I gather thee."[6]

The Fourteenth Remove[7]

Now must we pack up and be gone from this thicket, bending our course toward the Baytowns; I having nothing to eat by the way this day, but a few

1. Lack. Cf. Psalm 23.1.
2. Isaiah 38.3.
3. Psalm 51.4.
4. Luke 18.13.
5. Luke 15.21.

6. Isaiah 54.7.
7. The fourteenth to nineteenth removes (April 20 to April 28) retrace the path taken earlier. The "Baytowns" are the towns near Boston.

crumbs of cake, that an Indian gave my girl the same day we were taken. She gave it me, and I put it in my pocket; there it lay, till it was so moldy (for want of good baking) that one could not tell what it was made of; it fell all to crumbs, and grew so dry and hard, that it was like little flints; and this refreshed me many times, when I was ready to faint. It was in my thoughts when I put it into my mouth, that if ever I returned, I would tell the world what a blessing the Lord gave to such mean food. As we went along they killed a deer, with a young one in her, they gave me a piece of the fawn, and it was so young and tender, that one might eat the bones as well as the flesh, and yet I thought it very good. When night came on we sat down; it rained, but they quickly got up a bark wigwam, where I lay dry that night. I looked out in the morning, and many of them had lain in the rain all night, I saw by their reeking.[8] Thus the Lord dealt mercifully with me many times, and I fared better than many of them. In the morning they took the blood of the deer, and put it into the paunch, and so boiled it. I could eat nothing of that, though they ate it sweetly. And yet they were so nice[9] in other things, that when I had fetched water, and had put the dish I dipped the water with into the kettle of water which I brought, they would say they would knock me down; for they said, it was a sluttish trick.[1]

The Fifteenth Remove

We went on our travel. I having got one handful of ground nuts, for my support that day, they gave me my load, and I went on cheerfully (with the thoughts of going homeward), having my burden more on my back than my spirit. We came to Banquang river again that day, near which we abode a few days. Sometimes one of them would give me a pipe, another a little tobacco, another a little salt: which I would change for a little victuals. I cannot but think what a wolvish appetite persons have in a starving condition; for many times when they gave me that which was hot, I was so greedy, that I should burn my mouth, that it would trouble me hours after, and yet I should quickly do the same again. And after I was thoroughly hungry, I was never again satisfied. For though sometimes it fell out,[2] that I got enough, and did eat till I could eat no more, yet I was as unsatisfied as I was when I began. And now could I see that Scripture verified (there being many Scriptures which we do not take notice of, or understand till we are afflicted) "Thou shalt eat and not be satisfied" (Micah 6.14). Now might I see more than ever before, the miseries that sin hath brought upon us. Many times I should be ready to run against the heathen, but the Scripture would quiet me again, "Shall there be evil in a City and the Lord hath not done it?" (Amos 3.6). The Lord help me to make a right improvement of His word, and that I might learn that great lesson: "He hath showed thee (Oh Man) what is good, and what doth the Lord require of thee, but to do justly, and love mercy, and walk humbly with thy God? Hear ye the rod, and who hath appointed it" (Micah 6.8–9).

8. Steaming.
9. Fastidious.

1. Slovenly (unclean) practice.
2. I.e., it so happened.

The Sixteenth Removal

We began this remove with wading over Banquang river: the water was up to the knees, and the stream very swift, and so cold that I thought it would have cut me in sunder. I was so weak and feeble, that I reeled as I went along, and thought there I must end my days at last, after my bearing and getting through so many difficulties. The Indians stood laughing to see me stagger- ing along; but in my distress the Lord gave me experience of the truth, and goodness of that promise, "When thou passest through the waters, I will be with thee; and through the rivers, they shall not overflow thee" (Isaiah 43.2). Then I sat down to put on my stockings and shoes, with the tears running down mine eyes, and sorrowful thoughts in my heart, but I got up to go along with them. Quickly there came up to us an Indian, who informed them that I must go to Wachusett to my master, for there was a letter come from the council to the Sagamores, about redeeming the captives, and that there would be another in fourteen days, and that I must be there ready. My heart was so heavy before that I could scarce speak or go in the path; and yet now so light, that I could run. My strength seemed to come again, and recruit my feeble knees, and aching heart. Yet it pleased them to go but one mile that night, and there we stayed two days. In that time came a company of Indians to us, near thirty, all on horseback. My heart skipped within me, thinking they had been Englishmen at the first sight of them, for they were dressed in English apparel, with hats, white neckcloths, and sashes about their waists; and ribbons upon their shoulders; but when they came near, there was a vast difference between the lovely faces of Christians, and foul looks of those heathens, which much damped my spirit again.

The Seventeenth Remove

A comfortable remove it was to me, because of my hopes. They gave me a pack, and along we went cheerfully; but quickly my will proved more than my strength; having little or no refreshing, my strength failed me, and my spirits were almost quite gone. Now may I say with David, "I am poor and needy, and my heart is wounded within me. I am gone like the shadow when it declineth: I am tossed up and down like the locust; my knees are weak through fasting, and my flesh faileth of fatness" (Psalm 119.22–24). At night we came to an Indian town, and the Indians sat down by a wigwam discours- ing, but I was almost spent, and could scarce speak. I laid down my load, and went into the wigwam, and there sat an Indian boiling of horses' feet (they being wont to eat the flesh first, and when the feet were old and dried, and they had nothing else, they would cut off the feet and use them). I asked him to give me a little of his broth, or water they were boiling in; he took a dish, and gave me one spoonful of samp,[3] and bid me take as much of the broth as I would. Then I put some of the hot water to the samp, and drank it up, and my spirit came again. He gave me also a piece of the ruff or rid- ding[4] of the small guts, and I broiled it on the coals; and now may I say with Jonathan, "See, I pray you, how mine eyes have been enlightened, because

3. Porridge made of Indian corn. 4. I.e., the refuse, that which he was casting away.

I tasted a little of this honey" (1 Samuel 14.29). Now is my spirit revived again; though means be never so inconsiderable, yet if the Lord bestow His blessing upon them, they shall refresh both soul and body.

The Eighteenth Remove

We took up our packs and along we went, but a wearisome day I had of it. As we went along I saw an Englishman stripped naked, and lying dead upon the ground, but knew not who it was. Then we came to another Indian town, where we stayed all night. In this town there were four English children, captives; and one of them my own sister's. I went to see how she did, and she was well, considering her captive condition. I would have tarried that night with her, but they that owned her would not suffer it. Then I went into another wigwam, where they were boiling corn and beans, which was a lovely sight to see, but I could not get a taste thereof. Then I went to another wigwam, where there were two of the English children; the squaw was boiling horses feet; then she cut me off a little piece, and gave one of the English children a piece also. Being very hungry I had quickly eat up mine, but the child could not bite it, it was so tough and sinewy, but lay sucking, gnawing, chewing and slabbering of it in the mouth and hand. Then I took it of the child, and eat it myself, and savory it was to my taste. Then I may say as Job 6.7, "The things that my soul refused to touch are as my sorrowful meat." Thus the Lord made that pleasant refreshing, which another time would have been an abomination. Then I went home to my mistress's wigwam; and they told me I disgraced my master with begging, and if I did so any more, they would knock me in the head. I told them, they had as good knock me in [the] head as starve me to death.

The Nineteenth Remove

They said, when we went out, that we must travel to Wachusett this day. But a bitter weary day I had of it, traveling now three days together, without resting any day between. At last, after many weary steps, I saw Wachusett hills, but many miles off. Then we came to a great swamp, through which we traveled, up to the knees in mud and water, which was heavy going to one tired before. Being almost spent, I thought I should have sunk down at last, and never got out; but I may say, as in Psalm 94.18, "When my foot slipped, thy mercy, O Lord, held me up." Going along, having indeed my life, but little spirit, Philip, who was in the company, came up and took me by the hand, and said, two weeks more and you shall be mistress again. I asked him, if he spake true? He answered, "Yes, and quickly you shall come to your master again; who had been gone from us three weeks." After many weary steps we came to Wachusett, where he was: and glad I was to see him. He asked me, when I washed me? I told him not this month. Then he fetched me some water himself, and bid me wash, and gave me the glass to see how I looked; and bid his squaw give me something to eat. So she gave me a mess of beans and meat, and a little ground nut cake. I was wonderfully revived with this favor showed me: "He made them also to be pitied of all those that carried them captives" (Psalm 106.46).

My master had three squaws, living sometimes with one, and sometimes with another one, this old squaw, at whose wigwam I was, and with whom my master had been those three weeks. Another was Weetamoo[5] with whom I had lived and served all this while. A severe and proud dame she was, bestowing every day in dressing herself neat as much time as any of the gentry of the land: powdering her hair, and painting her face, going with necklaces, with jewels in her ears, and bracelets upon her hands. When she had dressed herself, her work was to make girdles of wampum[6] and beads. The third squaw was a younger one, by whom he had two papooses. By the time I was refreshed by the old squaw, with whom my master was, Weetamoo's maid came to call me home, at which I fell aweeping. Then the old squaw told me, to encourage me, that if I wanted victuals, I should come to her, and that I should lie there in her wigwam. Then I went with the maid, and quickly came again and lodged there. The squaw laid a mat under me, and a good rug over me; the first time I had any such kindness showed me. I understood that Weetamoo thought that if she should let me go and serve with the old squaw, she would be in danger to lose not only my service, but the redemption pay[7] also. And I was not a little glad to hear this; being by it raised in my hopes, that in God's due time there would be an end of this sorrowful hour. Then came an Indian, and asked me to knit him three pair of stockings, for which I had a hat, and a silk handkerchief. Then another asked me to make her a shift, for which she gave me an apron.

Then came Tom and Peter,[8] with the second letter from the council, about the captives. Though they were Indians, I got them by the hand, and burst out into tears. My heart was so full that I could not speak to them; but recovering myself, I asked them how my husband did, and all my friends and acquaintance? They said, "They are all very well but melancholy." They brought me two biscuits, and a pound of tobacco. The tobacco I quickly gave away. When it was all gone, one asked me to give him a pipe of tobacco. I told him it was all gone. Then began he to rant and threaten. I told him when my husband came I would give him some. Hang him rogue[9] (says he), I will knock out his brains, if he comes here. And then again, in the same breath they would say that if there should come an hundred without guns, they would do them no hurt. So unstable and like madmen they were. So that fearing the worst, I durst not send to my husband, though there were some thoughts of his coming to redeem and fetch me, not knowing what might follow. For there was little more trust to them than to the master they served. When the letter was come, the Sagamores met to consult about the captives, and called me to them to inquire how much my husband would give to redeem me. When I came I sat down among them, as I was wont to do, as their manner is. Then they bade me stand up, and said they were the General Court.[1] They bid me speak what I thought he would give. Now knowing that all we had was destroyed by the Indians, I was in a great strait. I thought if I should speak of but a little it would be slighted, and hinder the matter;

5. Rowlandson spells the name "Wattimore" here.
6. Beads of polished shells used by some American Indians as currency.
7. I.e., the anticipated ransom money.

8. Christian Indians.
9. I.e., I'll hang that rogue.
1. In imitation of the colonial assembly of Massachusetts.

if of a great sum, I knew not where it would be procured. Yet at a venture I said, "Twenty pounds," yet desired them to take less. But they would not hear of that, but sent that message to Boston, that for twenty pounds I should be redeemed. It was a Praying Indian that wrote their letter for them. There was another Praying Indian, who told me, that he had a brother, that would not eat horse; his conscience was so tender and scrupulous (though as large as hell, for the destruction of poor Christians). Then he said, he read that Scripture to him, "There was a famine in Samaria, and behold they besieged it, until an ass's head was sold for fourscore pieces of silver, and the fourth part of a cab of dove's dung for five pieces of silver" (2 Kings 6.25). He expounded this place to his brother, and showed him that it was lawful to eat that in a famine which is not at another time. And now, says he, he will eat horse with any Indian of them all. There was another Praying Indian, who when he had done all the mischief that he could, betrayed his own father into the English hands, thereby to purchase his own life. Another Praying Indian was at [the] Sudbury fight,[2] though, as he deserved, he was afterward hanged for it. There was another Praying Indian, so wicked and cruel, as to wear a string about his neck, strung with Christians' fingers. Another Praying Indian, when they went to [the] Sudbury fight, went with them, and his squaw also with him, with her papoose at her back. Before they went to that fight they got a company together to powwow.[3] The manner was as followeth: there was one that kneeled upon a deerskin, with the company round him in a ring who kneeled, and striking upon the ground with their hands, and with sticks, and muttering or humming with their mouths. Besides him who kneeled in the ring, there also stood one with a gun in his hand. Then he on the deerskin made a speech, and all manifested assent to it; and so they did many times together. Then they bade him with the gun go out of the ring, which he did. But when he was out, they called him in again; but he seemed to make a stand; then they called the more earnestly, till he returned again. Then they all sang. Then they gave him two guns, in either hand one. And so he on the deerskin began again; and at the end of every sentence in his speaking, they all assented, humming or muttering with their mouths, and striking upon the ground with their hands. Then they bade him with the two guns go out of the ring again; which he did, a little way. Then they called him in again, but he made a stand. So they called him with greater earnestness; but he stood reeling and wavering as if he knew not whither he should stand or fall, or which way to go. Then they called him with exceeding great vehemency, all of them, one and another. After a little while he turned in, staggering as he went, with his arms stretched out, in either hand a gun. As soon as he came in they all sang and rejoiced exceedingly a while. And then he upon the deerskin, made another speech unto which they all assented in a rejoicing manner. And so they ended their business, and forthwith went to [the] Sudbury fight. To my thinking they went without any scruple, but that they should prosper, and gain the victory. And they went out not so rejoicing, but they came home with as great a victory. For they said they had killed two captains and almost an hundred men. One Englishman they brought along with them: and he said, it was too true, for they had made sad work at

Sudbury, as indeed it proved. Yet they came home without that rejoicing and triumphing over their victory which they were wont to show at other times; but rather like dogs (as they say) which have lost their ears. Yet I could not perceive that it was for their own loss of men. They said they had not lost above five or six; and I missed none, except in one wigwam. When they went, they acted as if the devil had told them that they should gain the victory; and now they acted as if the devil had told them they should have a fall. Whether it were so or no, I cannot tell, but so it proved, for quickly they began to fall, and so held on that summer, till they came to utter ruin. They came home on a Sabbath day, and the Powwow[4] that kneeled upon the deer-skin came home (I may say, without abuse) as black as the devil. When my master came home, he came to me and bid me make a shirt for his papoose, of a holland-laced pillowbere.[5] About that time there came an Indian to me and bid me come to his wigwam at night, and he would give me some pork and ground nuts. Which I did, and as I was eating, another Indian said to me, he seems to be your good friend, but he killed two Englishmen at Sudbury, and there lie their clothes behind you: I looked behind me, and there I saw bloody clothes, with bullet-holes in them. Yet the Lord suffered not this wretch to do me any hurt. Yea, instead of that, he many times refreshed me; five or six times did he and his squaw refresh my feeble carcass. If I went to their wigwam at any time, they would always give me something, and yet they were strangers that I never saw before. Another squaw gave me a piece of fresh pork, and a little salt with it, and lent me her pan to fry it in; and I cannot but remember what a sweet, pleasant, and delightful relish that bit had to me, to this day. So little do we prize common mercies when we have them to the full.

The Twentieth Remove[6]

It was their usual manner to remove, when they had done any mischief, lest they should be found out; and so they did at this time. We went about three or four miles, and there they built a great wigwam, big enough to hold an hundred Indians, which they did in preparation to a great day of dancing. They would say now amongst themselves, that the governor would be so angry for his loss at Sudbury, that he would send no more about the captives, which made me grieve and tremble. My sister being not far from the place where we now were, and hearing that I was here, desired her master to let her come and see me, and he was willing to it, and would go with her; but she being ready before him, told him she would go before, and was come within a mile or two of the place. Then he overtook her, and began to rant as if he had been mad, and made her go back again in the rain; so that I never saw her till I saw her in Charlestown.[7] But the Lord requited many of their ill doings, for this Indian her master, was hanged afterward at Boston. The Indians now began to come from all quarters, against their merry dancing day. Among some of them came one goodwife Kettle. I told her my heart was so heavy that it was ready to break. "So is mine too," said she, but yet

4. Shaman.
5. Pillowcase.
6. April 28 to May 2, to a camp at the southern
end of Wachusett Lake, Princeton, Massachusetts.
7. Oldest neighborhood in Boston.

said, "I hope we shall hear some good news shortly." I could hear how earnestly my sister desired to see me, and I as earnestly desired to see her; and yet neither of us could get an opportunity. My daughter was also now about a mile off, and I had not seen her in nine or ten weeks, as I had not seen my sister since our first taking. I earnestly desired them to let me go and see them: yea, I entreated, begged, and persuaded them, but to let me see my daughter; and yet so hard-hearted were they, that they would not suffer it. They made use of their tyrannical power whilst they had it; but through the Lord's wonderful mercy, their time was now but short.

On a Sabbath day, the sun being about an hour high in the afternoon, came Mr. John Hoar[8] (the council permitting him, and his own foreward spirit inclining him), together with the two forementioned Indians, Tom and Peter, with their third letter from the council. When they came near, I was abroad. Though I saw them not, they presently called me in, and bade me sit down and not stir. Then they catched up their guns, and away they ran, as if an enemy had been at hand, and the guns went off apace. I manifested some great trouble, and they asked me what was the matter? I told them I thought they had killed the Englishman (for they had in the meantime informed me that an Englishman was come). They said, no. They shot over his horse and under and before his horse, and they pushed him this way and that way, at their pleasure, showing what they could do. Then they let them come to their wigwams. I begged of them to let me see the Englishman, but they would not. But there was I fain to sit their pleasure. When they had talked their fill with him, they suffered me to go to him. We asked each other of our welfare, and how my husband did, and all my friends? He told me they were all well, and would be glad to see me. Amongst other things which my husband sent me, there came a pound of tobacco, which I sold for nine shillings in money; for many of the Indians for want of tobacco, smoked hemlock, and ground ivy. It was a great mistake in any, who thought I sent for tobacco; for through the favor of God, that desire was overcome. I now asked them whether I should go home with Mr. Hoar? They answered no, one and another of them, and it being night, we lay down with that answer. In the morning Mr. Hoar invited the Sagamores to dinner; but when we went to get it ready we found that they had stolen the greatest part of the provision Mr. Hoar had brought, out of his bags, in the night. And we may see the wonderful power of God, in that one passage,[9] in that when there was such a great number of the Indians together, and so greedy of a little good food, and no English there but Mr. Hoar and myself, that there they did not knock us in the head, and take what we had, there being not only some provision, but also trading-cloth,[1] a part of the twenty pounds agreed upon. But instead of doing us any mischief, they seemed to be ashamed of the fact, and said, it were some matchit[2] Indian that did it. Oh, that we could believe that there is nothing too hard for God! God showed His power over the heathen in this, as He did over the hungry lions when Daniel was cast into the den.[3] Mr. Hoar

8. By the request of Rowlandson's husband, Hoar—a prominent lawyer and Indian missionary from Concord, Massachusetts—represented the colonial authorities at the negotiations for Rowlandson's release.

9. Incident.
1. Cloth used for barter.
2. Bad.
3. The prophet Daniel was cast into a den of lions, but they did not harm him (Daniel 6.1–29).

called them betime[4] to dinner, but they ate very little, they being so busy in dressing themselves, and getting ready for their dance, which was carried on by eight of them, four men and four squaws. My master and mistress being two. He was dressed in his holland[5] shirt, with great laces sewed at the tail of it; he had his silver buttons, his white stockings, his garters were hung round with shillings, and he had girdles of wampum upon his head and shoulders. She had a kersey[6] coat, and covered with girdles of wampum from the loins upward. Her arms from her elbows to her hands were covered with bracelets; there were handfuls of necklaces about her neck, and several sorts of jewels in her ears. She had fine red stockings, and white shoes, her hair powdered and face painted red, that was always before black. And all the dancers were after the same manner. There were two others singing and knocking on a kettle for their music. They kept hopping up and down one after another, with a kettle of water in the midst, standing warm upon some embers, to drink of when they were dry. They held on till it was almost night, throwing out wampum to the standers by. At night I asked them again, if I should go home? They all as one said no, except[7] my husband would come for me. When we were lain down, my master went out of the wigwam, and by and by sent in an Indian called James the Printer,[8] who told Mr. Hoar, that my master would let me go home tomorrow, if he would let him have one pint of liquors. Then Mr. Hoar called his own Indians, Tom and Peter, and bid them go and see whether he would promise it before them three; and if he would, he should have it; which he did, and he had it. Then Philip smelling the business called me to him, and asked me what I would give him, to tell me some good news, and speak a good word for me. I told him I could not tell what to give him. I would [give him] anything I had, and asked him what he would have? He said two coats and twenty shillings in money, and half a bushel of seed corn, and some tobacco. I thanked him for his love; but I knew the good news as well as the crafty fox. My master after he had had his drink, quickly came ranting into the wigwam again, and called for Mr. Hoar, drinking to him, and saying, he was a good man, and then again he would say, "hang him rogue." Being almost drunk, he would drink to him, and yet presently say he should be hanged. Then he called for me. I trembled to hear him, yet I was fain to go to him, and he drank to me, showing no incivility. He was the first Indian I saw drunk all the while that I was amongst them. At last his squaw ran out, and he after her, round the wigwam, with his money jingling at his knees. But she escaped him. But having an old squaw he ran to her; and so through the Lord's mercy, we were no more troubled that night. Yet I had not a comfortable night's rest; for I think I can say, I did not sleep for three nights together. The night before the letter came from the council, I could not rest, I was so full of fears and troubles, God many times leaving us most in the dark, when deliverance is nearest. Yea, at this time I could not rest night nor day. The next night I was overjoyed, Mr. Hoar being come, and that with such good tidings. The third night I was even swallowed up with the thoughts of things,

4. In good time; early.
5. Linen.
6. Coarse cloth woven from long wool and usually ribbed.

7. Unless.
8. Wowaus, who assisted the Reverend John Eliot in his printing of the Bible.

viz. that ever I should go home again; and that I must go, leaving my children behind me in the wilderness; so that sleep was now almost departed from mine eyes.

On Tuesday morning they called their General Court (as they call it) to consult and determine, whether I should go home or no. And they all as one man did seemingly consent to it, that I should go home; except Philip, who would not come among them.

But before I go any further, I would take leave to mention a few remarkable passages of providence, which I took special notice of in my afflicted time.

1. Of the fair opportunity lost in the long march, a little after the fort fight, when our English army was so numerous, and in pursuit of the enemy, and so near as to take several and destroy them, and the enemy in such distress for food that our men might track them by their rooting in the earth for ground nuts, whilst they were flying for their lives. I say, that then our army should want provision, and be forced to leave their pursuit and return homeward; and the very next week the enemy came upon our town, like bears bereft of their whelps, or so many ravenous wolves, rending us and our lambs to death. But what shall I say? God seemed to leave his People to themselves, and order all things for His own holy ends. Shall there be evil in the City and the Lord hath not done it?[9] They are not grieved for the affliction of Joseph, therefore shall they go captive, with the first that go captive.[1] It is the Lord's doing, and it should be marvelous in our eyes.

2. I cannot but remember how the Indians derided the slowness, and dullness of the English army, in its setting out. For after the desolations at Lancaster and Medfield, as I went along with them, they asked me when I thought the English army would come after them? I told them I could not tell. "It may be they will come in May," said they. Thus did they scoff at us, as if the English would be a quarter of a year getting ready.

3. Which also I have hinted before, when the English army with new supplies were sent forth to pursue after the enemy, and they understanding it, fled before them till they came to Banquaug river, where they forthwith went over safely; that that river should be impassable to the English. I can but admire to see the wonderful providence of God in preserving the heathen for further affliction to our poor country. They could go in great numbers over, but the English must stop. God had an over-ruling hand in all those things.

4. It was thought, if their corn were cut down, they would starve and die with hunger, and all their corn that could be found, was destroyed, and they driven from that little they had in store, into the woods in the midst of winter; and yet how to admiration did the Lord preserve them for His holy ends, and the destruction of many still amongst the English! strangely did the Lord provide for them; that I did not see (all the time I was among them) one man, woman, or child, die with hunger.

Though many times they would eat that, that[2] a hog or a dog would hardly touch; yet by that God strengthened them to be a scourge to His people.

9. Amos 3.6.
1. Amos 6.6–7.

2. I.e., that which.

The chief and commonest food was ground nuts. They eat also nuts and acorns, artichokes, lily roots, ground beans, and several other weeds and roots, that I know not.

They would pick up old bones, and cut them to pieces at the joints, and if they were full of worms and maggots, they would scald them over the fire to make the vermin come out, and then boil them, and drink up the liquor, and then beat the great ends of them in a mortar, and so eat them. They would eat horse's guts, and ears, and all sorts of wild birds which they could catch; also bear, venison, beaver, tortoise, frogs, squirrels, dogs, skunks, rattle-snakes; yea, the very bark of trees; besides all sorts of creatures, and provision which they plundered from the English. I can but stand in admiration to see the wonderful power of God in providing for such a vast number of our enemies in the wilderness, where there was nothing to be seen, but from hand to mouth. Many times in a morning, the generality of them would eat up all they had, and yet have some further supply against they wanted. It is said, "Oh, that my People had hearkened to me, and Israel had walked in my ways, I should soon have subdued their Enemies, and turned my hand against their Adversaries" (Psalm 81.13–14). But now our perverse and evil carriages in the sight of the Lord, have so offended Him, that instead of turning His hand against them, the Lord feeds and nourishes them up to be a scourge to the whole land.

5. Another thing that I would observe is the strange providence of God, in turning things about when the Indians was at the highest, and the English at the lowest. I was with the enemy eleven weeks and five days, and not one week passed without the fury of the enemy, and some desolation by fire and sword upon one place or other. They mourned (with their black faces) for their own losses, yet triumphed and rejoiced in their inhumane, and many times devilish cruelty to the English. They would boast much of their victories; saying that in two hours time they had destroyed such a captain and his company at such a place; and boast how many towns they had destroyed, and then scoff, and say they had done them a good turn to send them to Heaven so soon. Again, they would say this summer that they would knock all the rogues in the head, or drive them into the sea, or make them fly the country; thinking surely, Agag-like, "The bitterness of Death is past."[3] Now the heathen begins to think all is their own, and the poor Christians' hopes to fail (as to man) and now their eyes are more to God, and their hearts sigh heavenward; and to say in good earnest, "Help Lord, or we perish." When the Lord had brought His people to this, that they saw no help in anything but Himself; then He takes the quarrel into His own hand; and though they had made a pit, in their own imaginations, as deep as hell for the Christians that summer, yet the Lord hurled themselves into it. And the Lord had not so many ways before to preserve them, but now He hath as many to destroy them.

But to return again to my going home, where we may see a remarkable change of providence. At first they were all against it, except my husband would come for me, but afterwards they assented to it, and seemed much to rejoice in it; some asked me to send them some bread, others some tobacco,

3. 1 Samuel 15.32. Agag, king of Amalek, was defeated by Saul and thought himself spared, but was then slain by Samuel.

others shaking me by the hand, offering me a hood and scarf to ride in; not one moving hand or tongue against it. Thus hath the Lord answered my poor desire, and the many earnest requests of others put up unto God for me. In my travels an Indian came to me and told me, if I were willing, he and his squaw would run away, and go home along with me. I told him no: I was not willing to run away, but desired to wait God's time, that I might go home quietly, and without fear. And now God hath granted me my desire. O the wonderful power of God that I have seen, and the experience that I have had. I have been in the midst of those roaring lions, and savage bears, that feared neither God, nor man, nor the devil, by night and day, alone and in company, sleeping all sorts together, and yet not one of them ever offered me the least abuse of unchastity to me, in word or action. Though some are ready to say I speak it for my own credit; but I speak it in the presence of God, and to His Glory. God's power is as great now, and as sufficient to save, as when He preserved Daniel in the lion's den; or the three children in the fiery furnace.[4] I may well say as his Psalm 107.12, "Oh give thanks unto the Lord for he is good, for his mercy endureth for ever." Let the redeemed of the Lord say so, whom He hath redeemed from the hand of the enemy, especially that I should come away in the midst of so many hundreds of enemies quietly and peaceably, and not a dog moving his tongue. So I took my leave of them, and in coming along my heart melted into tears, more than all the while I was with them, and I was almost swallowed up with the thoughts that ever I should go home again. About the sun going down, Mr. Hoar, and myself, and the two Indians came to Lancaster, and a solemn sight it was to me. There had I lived many comfortable years amongst my relations and neighbors, and now not one Christian to be seen, nor one house left standing. We went on to a farmhouse that was yet standing, where we lay all night, and a comfortable lodging we had, though nothing but straw to lie on. The Lord preserved us in safety that night, and raised us up again in the morning, and carried us along, that before noon, we came to Concord. Now was I full of joy, and yet not without sorrow; joy to see such a lovely sight, so many Christians together, and some of them my neighbors. There I met with my brother, and my brother-in-law, who asked me, if I knew where his wife was? Poor heart! he had helped to bury her, and knew it not. She being shot down by the house was partly burnt, so that those who were at Boston at the desolation of the town, and came back afterward, and buried the dead, did not know her. Yet I was not without sorrow, to think how many were looking and longing, and my own children amongst the rest, to enjoy that deliverance that I had now received, and I did not know whether ever I should see them again. Being recruited[5] with food and raiment we went to Boston that day, where I met with my dear husband, but the thoughts of our dear children, one being dead, and the other we could not tell where, abated our comfort each to other. I was not before so much hemmed in with the merciless and cruel heathen, but now as much with pitiful, tender-hearted and compassionate Christians. In that poor, and distressed, and beggarly condition I was received in; I was kindly entertained in several houses. So much love I received from several (some of whom I knew, and others I knew not)

4. Shadrach, Meshach, and Abednego refused to worship false gods and were cast into a fiery furnace but saved from death by an angel (Daniel 3.13–30).

5. Refreshed.

that I am not capable to declare it. But the Lord knows them all by name. The Lord reward them sevenfold into their bosoms of His spirituals, for their temporals.[6] The twenty pounds, the price of my redemption, was raised by some Boston gentlemen, and Mrs. Usher, whose bounty and religious charity, I would not forget to make mention of. Then Mr. Thomas Shepard of Charlestown received us into his house, where we continued eleven weeks; and a father and mother they were to us. And many more tender-hearted friends we met with in that place. We were now in the midst of love, yet not without much and frequent heaviness of heart for our poor children, and other relations, who were still in affliction. The week following, after my coming in, the governor and council sent forth to the Indians again; and that not without success; for they brought in my sister, and goodwife Kettle. Their not knowing where our children were was a sore trial to us still, and yet we were not without secret hopes that we should see them again. That which was dead lay heavier upon my spirit, than those which were alive and amongst the heathen: thinking how it suffered with its wounds, and I was no way able to relieve it; and how it was buried by the heathen in the wilderness from among all Christians. We were hurried up and down in our thoughts, sometime we should hear a report that they were gone this way, and sometimes that; and that they were come in, in this place or that. We kept inquiring and listening to hear concerning them, but no certain news as yet. About this time the council had ordered a day of public thanksgiving. Though I thought I had still cause of mourning, and being unsettled in our minds, we thought we would ride toward the eastward, to see if we could hear anything concerning our children. And as we were riding along (God is the wise disposer of all things) between Ipswich and Rowley we met with Mr. William Hubbard, who told us that our son Joseph was come in to Major Waldron's, and another with him, which was my sister's son. I asked him how he knew it? He said the major himself told him so. So along we went till we came to Newbury; and their minister being absent, they desired my husband to preach the thanksgiving for them; but he was not willing to stay there that night, but would go over to Salisbury, to hear further, and come again in the morning, which he did, and preached there that day. At night, when he had done, one came and told him that his daughter was come in at Providence. Here was mercy on both hands. Now hath God fulfilled that precious Scripture which was such a comfort to me in my distressed condition. When my heart was ready to sink into the earth (my children being gone, I could not tell whither) and my knees trembling under me, and I was walking through the valley of the shadow of death; then the Lord brought, and now has fulfilled that reviving word unto me: "Thus saith the Lord, Refrain thy voice from weeping, and thine eyes from tears, for thy Work shall be rewarded, saith the Lord, and they shall come again from the Land of the Enemy."[7] Now we were between them, the one on the east, and the other on the west. Our son being nearest, we went to him first, to Portsmouth, where we met with him, and with the Major also, who told us he had done what he could, but could not redeem him under seven pounds, which the good people thereabouts were pleased to pay. The Lord reward the major, and all the rest, though unknown to me, for their labor of

6. Worldly goods and gifts.　　　　7. Jeremiah 31.16.

love. My sister's son was redeemed for four pounds, which the council gave order for the payment of. Having now received one of our children, we hastened toward the other. Going back through Newbury my husband preached there on the Sabbath day; for which they rewarded him many fold.

On Monday we came to Charlestown, where we heard that the governor of Rhode Island had sent over for our daughter, to take care of her, being now within his jurisdiction; which should not pass without our acknowledgments. But she being nearer Rehoboth than Rhode Island, Mr. Newman went over, and took care of her and brought her to his own house. And the goodness of God was admirable to us in our low estate, in that He raised up passionate[8] friends on every side to us, when we had nothing to recompense any for their love. The Indians were now gone that way, that it was apprehended dangerous to go to her. But the carts which carried provision to the English army, being guarded, brought her with them to Dorchester, where we received her safe. Blessed be the Lord for it, for great is His power, and He can do whatsoever seemeth Him good. Her coming in was after this manner: she was traveling one day with the Indians, with her basket at her back; the company of Indians were got before her, and gone out of sight, all except one squaw; she followed the squaw till night, and then both of them lay down, having nothing over them but the heavens and under them but the earth. Thus she traveled three days together, not knowing whither she was going; having nothing to eat or drink but water, and green hirtle-berries.[9] At last they came into Providence, where she was kindly entertained by several of that town. The Indians often said that I should never have her under twenty pounds. But now the Lord hath brought her in upon free-cost, and given her to me the second time. The Lord make us a blessing indeed, each to others. Now have I seen that Scripture also fulfilled, "If any of thine be driven out to the outmost parts of heaven, from thence will the Lord thy God gather thee, and from thence will he fetch thee. And the Lord thy God will put all these curses upon thine enemies, and on them which hate thee, which persecuted thee" (Deuteronomy 30.4–7). Thus hath the Lord brought me and mine out of that horrible pit, and hath set us in the midst of tenderhearted and compassionate Christians. It is the desire of my soul that we may walk worthy of the mercies received, and which we are receiving.

Our family being now gathered together (those of us that were living), the South Church in Boston hired an house for us. Then we removed from Mr. Shephard's, those cordial friends, and went to Boston, where we continued about three-quarters of a year. Still the Lord went along with us, and provided graciously for us. I thought it somewhat strange to set up housekeeping with bare walls; but as Solomon says, "Money answers all things"[1] and that we had through the benevolence of Christian friends, some in this town, and some in that, and others; and some from England; that in a little time we might look, and see the house furnished with love. The Lord hath been exceeding good to us in our low estate, in that when we had neither house nor home, nor other necessaries, the Lord so moved the hearts of these and those towards us, that we wanted neither food, nor raiment for ourselves or ours: "There is a Friend which sticketh closer than a Brother" (Proverbs

8. Compassionate.
9. Either blueberries or huckleberries.

1. Ecclesiastes 10.19.

18.24). And how many such friends have we found, and now living amongst? And truly such a friend have we found him to be unto us, in whose house we lived, *viz*. Mr. James Whitcomb, a friend unto us near hand, and afar off.

I can remember the time when I used to sleep quietly without workings in my thoughts, whole nights together, but now it is other ways with me. When all are fast about me, and no eye open, but His who ever waketh, my thoughts are upon things past, upon the awful dispensation of the Lord towards us, upon His wonderful power and might, in carrying of us through so many difficulties, in returning us in safety, and suffering none to hurt us. I remember in the night season, how the other day I was in the midst of thousands of enemies, and nothing but death before me. It is then hard work to persuade myself, that ever I should be satisfied with bread again. But now we are fed with the finest of the wheat, and, as I may say, with honey out of the rock.[2] Instead of the husk, we have the fatted calf.[3] The thoughts of these things in the particulars of them, and of the love and goodness of God towards us, make it true of me, what David said of himself, "I watered my Couch with my tears" (Psalm 6.6). Oh! the wonderful power of God that mine eyes have seen, affording matter enough for my thoughts to run in, that when others are sleeping mine eyes are weeping.

I have seen the extreme vanity of this world:[4] One hour I have been in health, and wealthy, wanting nothing. But the next hour in sickness and wounds, and death, having nothing but sorrow and affliction.

Before I knew what affliction meant, I was ready sometimes to wish for it. When I lived in prosperity, having the comforts of the world about me, my relations by me, my heart cheerful, and taking little care for anything, and yet seeing many, whom I preferred before myself, under many trials and afflictions, in sickness, weakness, poverty, losses, crosses,[5] and cares of the world, I should be sometimes jealous least I should have my portion in this life, and that Scripture would come to my mind, "For whom the Lord loveth he chasteneth, and scourgeth every Son whom he receiveth" (Hebrews 12.6). But now I see the Lord had His time to scourge and chasten me. The portion of some is to have their afflictions by drops, now one drop and then another; but the dregs of the cup, the wine of astonishment, like a sweeping rain that leaveth no food, did the Lord prepare to be my portion. Affliction I wanted, and affliction I had, full measure (I thought), pressed down and running over. Yet I see, when God calls a person to anything, and through never so many difficulties, yet He is fully able to carry them through and make them see, and say they have been gainers thereby. And I hope I can say in some measure, as David did, "It is good for me that I have been afflicted."[6] The Lord hath showed me the vanity of these outward things. That they are the vanity of vanities, and vexation of spirit, that they are but a shadow, a blast, a bubble, and things of no continuance. That we must rely on God Himself, and our whole dependance must be upon Him. If trouble from smaller matters begin to arise in me, I have something at hand to check myself with, and say, why am I troubled? It was but the other day that if I had

2. "He should have fed them also with the finest of the wheat: and with honey out of the rock should I have satisfied thee" (Psalm 81.16).
3. "And bring hither the fatted calf, and kill it; and let us eat, and be merry" (Luke 15.23).

4. Cf. Ecclesiastes 1.2. "Vanity": emptiness, futility.
5. Burdens.
6. Psalm 119.71.

had the world, I would have given it for my freedom, or to have been a servant to a Christian. I have learned to look beyond present and smaller troubles, and to be quieted under them. As Moses said, "Stand still and see the salvation of the Lord" (Exodus 14.13).

1682

EDWARD TAYLOR
c. 1642–1729

E dward Taylor's poetry was known only by a select circle in his own day. It was passed down in manuscript through his family for generations, until his great-grandson donated the manuscript volume to the Beinecke library, at Yale University, in 1883. Five decades later, the literary scholar Thomas H. Johnson located the manuscript there. After Johnson edited *The Poetical Works of Edward Taylor* (1939), the Puritan poet and his work became the object of sustained critical attention.

Taylor's lack of print publication in his lifetime did not mean that he thought his work unworthy. Manuscript publication remained a common practice long after the printing press had become widely available. In the seventeenth century, manuscript was a popular medium for coterie poetry, or poems shared exclusively with a small group of associates. The most eminent coterie poet may be John Donne (1572–1631), the Anglican minister whom many regard as the finest practitioner of Metaphysical poetry, an intellectual style that influenced Taylor. Donne authorized the print publication of just seven of his poems; his other 187 poems circulated exclusively in manuscript during his lifetime.

Even less of Taylor's poetry was printed in his own day—just a few fragments, notably the final two stanzas of "Upon Wedlock, and Death of Children," which Cotton Mather included at the end of a sermon that was published in London in 1689. Scholars think that Mather acquired those stanzas from a letter that Taylor wrote to his college friend Samuel Sewall, rather than from a compendium of poems. Taylor may have been less a coterie poet than a private one who wrote verses for his own satisfaction and inspiration. Yet he cared enough about future readers to copy his poems into a four-hundred-page leather-bound book, which he passed down to his descendants. Today, a number of pages from Taylor's manuscript can be viewed online at the Beinecke Library Web site.

As a youth, Taylor was schooled in English religious poetry, which he later adapted to his circumstances as the minister of a small New England village. He was probably born in Sketchly, Leicestershire County, England, and the dialect of that farming country gives some of his poems provincial charm. His father was a yeoman farmer—not a gentleman with a large estate but an independent land-holder with title to his farm. Taylor taught school for a time, perhaps after some university training. Then in 1668, rather than sign an oath of loyalty to the Church of England, he sailed to New England. He preferred self-exile in what he once called a "howling wilderness" to either compromising his religious principles as a Puritan or suffering the substantial legal consequences of refusing to do so. Once in Massachusetts, he attended Harvard College, where he prepared himself for the ministry.

In 1671 Taylor became the minister and physician in the frontier town of Westfield, Massachusetts, roughly a hundred miles west of Boston. After a delay caused partly by King Philip's War (1675–76; see the Mary Rowlandson headnote), he settled in and remained at Westfield for the rest of his life, also serving as a public servant. He married twice and had fourteen children, suffering the loss of many who died in infancy. Taylor also involved himself in the intellectual life and religious controversies of the colony. He strictly observed the "old" New England way, which called for a prospective church member to give a public account of conversion, and he fought against a movement to drop that requirement.

Taylor's grandson Ezra Stiles, who served as the president of Yale, described him as "a man of small stature, but firm; of quick Passions, yet serious and grave." Like most Harvard-trained ministers, Taylor knew Latin, Hebrew, and Greek, and his peers regarded him as a good preacher. His extensive library included theology, such as works of Augustine, and religious histories including *Foxe's Book of Martyrs* (1563); natural sciences and history, including Sir Walter Raleigh's *History of the World* (1614); and a great many works by New England authors, including a substantial number of Cotton Mather's publications and the 1678 edition of Anne Bradstreet's poems.

Taylor worked in various poetic genres, including personal lyrics, elegies on the deaths of public figures, and translations of the psalms. His verses most closely resemble those of the early Metaphysical poet George Herbert. Delighting in puns, paradoxes, and a rich profusion of metaphors and images, the Metaphysical wits explored the nature of language and its capacity to express spiritual meanings, as Taylor does in "Huswifery" and *Preparatory Meditations*. Taylor's *God's Determinations* is a long poem in the tradition of the medieval debate. "Upon Wedlock, and Death of Children" uses knotty wordplay to express emotional pain and the search for meaning and solace. Other poems, such as "Upon a Wasp Chilled with Cold," combine naturalistic detail with spiritual meaning in a more direct style. The following selections suggest Taylor's considerable range, which places him squarely in the distinguished tradition of seventeenth-century religious lyric poetry.

All of the following texts are from *Poems of Edward Taylor* (1960), edited by Donald E. Stanford.

FROM PREPARATORY MEDITATIONS[1]

Prologue

Lord, Can a Crumb of Dust the Earth outweigh,
 Outmatch all mountains, nay, the Crystal sky?
Embosom in't designs that shall Display
 And trace into the Boundless Deity?
 Yea, hand a Pen whose moisture doth guide o'er 5
 Eternal Glory with a glorious glore.[2]

1. The full title is *Preparatory Meditations before my Approach to the Lord's Supper. Chiefly upon the Doctrine preached upon the Day of Administration [of Communion]*. Taylor administered communion once a month to those members of his congregation who had made a declaration of their faith. He wrote these meditations in private; they are primarily the result of his contemplation of the biblical texts that served as the basis for the communion sermon. A total of 217 meditations survive, dating from 1682 to 1725.
2. Glory (Scottish).

If it its Pen had of an Angel's Quill,
 And sharpened on a Precious Stone ground tight,
And dipped in liquid Gold, and moved by Skill
 In Crystal leaves should golden Letters write, 10
 It would but blot and blur, yea, jag, and jar
 Unless Thou mak'st the Pen, and Scrivener.

I am this Crumb of Dust which is designed
 To make my Pen unto Thy Praise alone,
And my dull Fancy³ I would gladly grind 15
 Unto an Edge on Zion's⁴ Precious Stone.
 And Write in Liquid Gold upon Thy Name
 My Letters till Thy glory forth doth flame.

Let not th' attempts break down my Dust, I pray,
 Nor laugh Thou them to scorn but pardon give. 20
Inspire this crumb of Dust till it display
 Thy Glory through't: and then Thy dust shall live.
 Its failings then Thou'lt overlook, I trust,
 They being Slips slipped from Thy Crumb of Dust.

Thy Crumb of Dust breathes two words from its breast, 25
 That Thou wilt guide its pen to write aright
To Prove Thou art, and that Thou art the best
 And show Thy Properties to shine most bright.
 And then Thy Works will shine as flowers on Stems
 Or as in Jewelry Shops, do gems. 30

c. 1682 1939

Meditation 8 (First Series)

John 6.51. I am the Living Bread.[1]

I kenning through Astronomy Divine
 The World's bright Battlement,[2] wherein I spy
A Golden Path my Pencil cannot line,
 From that bright Throne unto my Threshold lie.
 And while my puzzled thoughts about it pour, 5
 I find the Bread of Life in't at my door.

When that this Bird of Paradise[3] put in
 This Wicker Cage (my Corpse) to tweedle praise

3. I.e., imagination.
4. In ancient Jerusalem, the hill on which King Solomon built his temple; the City of God on Earth.
1. "The Jews then murmured at him, because he said, I am the bread which came down from heaven. And they said, Is not this Jesus, the son of Joseph, whose father and mother we know? how is it then that he saith, I came down from heaven? Jesus therefore answered[,] . . . Verily, verily, I say unto you, He that believeth on me hath everlasting life. I am that bread of life" (John 6.41–48). Jesus offers a "New Covenant of Faith" in place of the "Old Covenant of Works," which Adam broke when he disobeyed God's commandment (Genesis 1–3).
2. I.e., discerning, by means of "divine astronomy," the towers of heaven. Taylor goes on to suggest an invisible golden path extends from this world to the gates of Heaven.
3. I.e., the soul, which is like a bird kept in the body's cage.

Had pecked the Fruit forbade: and so did fling
 Away its Food; and lost its golden days; 10
 It fell into Celestial Famine sore:
 And never could attain a morsel more.

Alas! alas! Poor Bird, what wilt thou do?
 The Creatures' field no food for Souls e'er gave.
And if thou knock at Angels' doors they show 15
 An Empty Barrel: they no soul bread have.
 Alas! Poor Bird, the World's White Loaf is done.
 And cannot yield thee here the smallest Crumb.

In this sad state, God's Tender Bowels[4] run
 Out streams of Grace: and He to end all strife 20
The Purest Wheat in Heaven His dear-dear son
 Grinds, and kneads up into this Bread of Life.
 Which Bread of Life from Heaven down came and stands
 Dished on Thy Table up by Angels' Hands.

Did God mold up this Bread in Heaven, and bake, 25
 Which from His Table came, and to thine goeth?
Doth He bespeak thee thus, This Soul Bread take?
 Come Eat thy fill of this thy God's White Loaf?
 It's Food too fine for Angels, yet come, take
 And Eat thy fill. It's Heaven's Sugar Cake. 30

What Grace is this knead in this Loaf? This thing
 Souls are but petty things it to admire.
Ye Angels, help: This fill would to the brim
 Heav'ns whelmed-down[5] Crystal meal Bowl, yea and higher.
 This Bread of Life dropped in thy mouth, doth Cry: 35
 Eat, Eat me, Soul, and thou shalt never die.

June 8, 1684 1939

FROM GOD'S DETERMINATIONS[1]

The Preface

Infinity, when all things it beheld
In Nothing, and of Nothing all did build,

4. Here, the interior of the body, the heart, the intestines, or the location of sympathetic emotions.
5. Turned over.
1. The subject of this "debate" poem is made clear in the full title: *God's determinations touching His Elect* [i.e., those divinely chosen for salvation]: *and the Elect's combat in their conversion, and coming up to God in Christ, together with the comfortable effects thereof.* In this group of poems, Taylor explores the progress of the human soul from the creation of the world and the fall from grace to the redemption of the Christian soul through Jesus Christ's Crucifixion: Christ's mercy triumphs over justice—the punishment that humanity deserves for disobedience—and the soul is finally carried to heaven to share in the joys of the Resurrection.

Upon what Base was fixed the Lathe wherein
He turned this Globe, and riggalled[2] it so trim?
Who blew the Bellows of His Furnace Vast? 5
Or held the Mold wherein the world was Cast?
Who laid its Corner Stone?[3] Or whose Command?
Where stand the Pillars upon which it stands?
Who Laced and Filleted[4] the earth so fine,
With Rivers like green Ribbons Smaragdine?[5] 10
Who made the Sea's its Selvage,[6] and its locks
Like a Quilt Ball[7] within a Silver Box?
Who Spread its Canopy? Or Curtains Spun?
Who in this Bowling Alley bowled the Sun?
Who made it always when it rises set 15
To go at once both down, and up to get?
Who th' Curtain rods made for this Tapestry?
Who hung the twinkling Lanthorns[8] in the Sky?
Who? who did this? or who is He? Why, know
It's Only Might Almighty this did do. 20
His hand hath made this noble work which Stands
His Glorious Handiwork not made by hands.
Who spake all things from Nothing; and with ease
Can speak all things to Nothing, if He please.
Whose Little finger at His pleasure Can 25
Out mete[9] ten thousand worlds with half a Span:
Whose Might Almighty can by half a looks
Root up the rocks and rock the hills by the roots.
Can take this mighty World up in His hand,
And shake it like a Squitchen[1] or a Wand. 30
Whose single Frown will make the Heavens shake
Like as an aspen leaf the Wind makes quake.
Oh! what a might is this Whose single frown
Doth shake the world as it would shake it down?
Which All from Nothing fet,[2] from Nothing, All: 35
Hath All on Nothing set, lets Nothing fall.
Gave All to Nothing Man indeed, whereby
Through Nothing man all might Him Glorify.
In Nothing then embossed the brightest Gem
More precious than all preciousness in them. 40
But Nothing man did throw down all by Sin:
And darkened that lightsome Gem in him.
 That now his Brightest Diamond is grown
 Darker by far than any Coalpit Stone.

c. 1685 1939

2. Grooved.
3. "Where wast thou when I laid the founda-
tions of the earth? declare, if thou hast under-
standing. Who hath laid the measures thereof, if
thou knowest? or who hath stretched the line
upon it? Whereupon are the foundations thereof
fastened? or who laid the corner stone thereof;
When the morning stars sang together, and all the
sons of God shouted for joy? Or who shut up the
sea with doors, when it brake forth, as if it had
issued out of the womb?" (Job 38.4–8).

4. Encircled, bound around.
5. Emerald green.
6. The border of woven material that prevents
unraveling.
7. A ball of wool that would unravel if it were not
kept in a box.
8. Lanterns.
9. Outmeasure.
1. Switch.
2. Made.

Upon Wedlock, and Death of Children

A Curious Knot[1] God made in Paradise,
 And drew it out enameled[2] neatly Fresh.
It was the True-Love Knot, more sweet than spice,
 And set with all the flowers of Grace's dress.
 It's Wedden's[3] Knot, that ne're can be untied: 5
 No Alexander's Sword[4] can it divide.

The slips[5] here planted, gay and glorious grow:
 Unless an Hellish breath do singe their Plumes.
Here Primrose, Cowslips, Roses, Lilies blow[6]
 With Violets and Pinks that void[7] perfumes: 10
 Whose beauteous leaves o'erlaid with Honey Dew,
 And Chanting birds Chirp out sweet Music true.

When in this Knot I planted was, my Stock[8]
 Soon knotted, and a manly flower out brake.[9]
And after it, my branch again did knot, 15
 Brought out another Flower, its sweet-breathed mate.
 One knot gave one tother[1] the tother's place.
 Whence Chuckling smiles fought in each other's face.

But Oh! a glorious hand from glory came
 Guarded with Angels, soon did crop this flower[2] 20
Which almost tore the root up of the same,
 At that unlooked for, Dolesome, darksome hour.
 In Prayer to Christ perfumed it did ascend,
 And Angels bright did it to heaven 'tend.

But pausing on't, this sweet perfumed my thought: 25
 Christ would in Glory have a Flower, Choice, Prime,
And having Choice, chose this my branch forth brought.
 Lord take't. I thank Thee, Thou tak'st ought of mine:
 It is my pledge in glory, part of me
 Is now in it, Lord, glorified with Thee. 30

But praying o're my branch, my branch did sprout,
 And bore another manly flower, and gay,[3]
And after that another, sweet brake out,
 The which the former hand soon got away.
 But Oh! the tortures, Vomit, screechings, groans, 35
 and six week's Fever would pierce hearts like stones.[4]

1. Flower bed.
2. Polished, shining.
3. I.e., wedding's.
4. Alexander the Great cut the Gordian knot devised by the king of Phyrgia when he learned that anyone who could undo it would rule Asia.
5. Cuttings.
6. Bloom.
7. Emit.
8. Stem, stalk.

9. I.e., broke out. Samuel Taylor was born on August 27, 1675, and lived to maturity.
1. To the other.
2. Elizabeth Taylor was born on December 27, 1676, and died on December 25, 1677.
3. James Taylor was born on October 12, 1678, and lived to maturity.
4. Abigail Taylor was born on August 6, 1681, and died on August 22, 1682.

Grief o'er doth flow: and nature fault would find
 Were not Thy Will, my Spell, Charm, Joy, and Gem:
That as I said, I say, take, Lord, they're Thine.
 I piecemeal pass to Glory bright in them. 40
 In joy, may I sweet flowers for glory breed,
 Whether thou get'st them green, or lets them seed.

c. 1682 1939

Upon a Wasp Chilled with Cold

The Bear that breathes the Northern blast[1]
Did numb, Torpedo-like,[2] a Wasp
Whose stiffened limbs encramped, lay bathing
In Sol's[3] warm breath and shine as saving,
Which with her hands she chafes and stands 5
Rubbing her Legs, Shanks, Thighs, and hands.
Her petty[4] toes, and fingers' ends
Nipped with this breath, she out extends
Unto the Sun, in great desire
To warm her digits at that fire. 10
Doth hold her Temples in this state
Where pulse doth beat, and head doth ache.
Doth turn, and stretch her body small,
Doth Comb her velvet Capital.[5]
As if her little brain pan were 15
A Volume of Choice precepts clear.
As if her satin jacket hot
Contained Apothecary's Shop
Of Nature's receipts,[6] that prevails
To remedy all her sad ails, 20
As if her velvet helmet high
Did turret[7] rationality.
She fans her wing up to the Wind
As if her Pettycoat were lined,
With reason's fleece, and hoists sails 25
And humming flies in thankful gales
Unto her dun Curled[8] palace Hall
Her warm thanks offering for all.

 Lord, clear my misted sight that I
 May hence view Thy Divinity, 30
 Some sparks whereof Thou up dost hasp[9]

1. The northern constellation the Big Dipper, also called Ursa Major, or the Great Bear.
2. The torpedo is a fish, like a stingray, that discharges a shock to one who touches it, causing numbness.
3. The sun personified.
4. I.e., small.
5. Head.
6. Remedies, prescriptions. "Apothecary's Shop": a drugstore or pharmacy.
7. Contain, encompass.
8. Her dark curved.
9. Enclose, fasten.

Within this little downy Wasp
In whose small Corporation[1] we
A school and a schoolmaster see,
Where we may learn, and easily find 35
A nimble Spirit bravely mind
Her work in every limb: and lace
It up neat with a vital grace,
Acting each part though ne'er so small
Here of this Fustian[2] animal, 40
Till I enravished Climb into
The Godhead on this Ladder do,
Where all my pipes inspired upraise
An Heavenly music furred[3] with praise.

1960

Huswifery[1]

Make me, O Lord, Thy Spinning Wheel complete.[2]
 Thy Holy Word my Distaff make for me.
Make mine Affections Thy Swift Flyers neat
 And make my Soul Thy holy Spool to be.
 My conversation make to be Thy Reel 5
 And reel the yarn thereon spun of Thy Wheel.

Make me Thy Loom then, knit therein this Twine:
 And make Thy Holy Spirit, Lord, wind quills:[3]
Then weave the Web Thyself. The yarn is fine.
 Thine Ordinances make my Fulling Mills.[4] 10
 Then dye the same in Heavenly Colors Choice,
 All pinked with Varnished[5] Flowers of Paradise.

Then clothe therewith mine Understanding, Will,
 Affections, Judgment, Conscience, Memory,
My Words, and Actions, that their shine may fill 15
 My ways with glory and Thee glorify.
 Then mine apparel shall display before Ye
 That I am Clothed in Holy robes for glory.[6]

1939

1. Body.
2. Coarse-clothed.
3. Trimmed or embellished, as with fur.
1. Housekeeping; here, weaving.
2. In lines 2–6, Taylor refers to the working parts of a spinning wheel. "Distaff':' holds the raw wool or flax. "Flyers": regulate the spinning. "Spool": twists the yarn. "Reel": takes up the finished thread.
3. I.e., be like a spool or bobbin.
4. Where cloth is beaten and cleansed with

fuller's earth, or soap.
5. Glossy, sparkling. "Pinked": adorned.
6. In Taylor's *Treatise Concerning the Lord's Supper*, he considers the significance of the sacrament of communion and takes as his text a passage from the New Testament: "And he saith unto him, Friend, how camest thou in hither not having a wedding garment? And he was speechless" (Matthew 22.12). Taylor argues that the wedding garment is the proper sign of the regenerate (spiritually reborn) Christian.

SAMUEL SEWALL
1652–1730

S amuel Sewall belonged to a network of New England intellectuals that included the poet-minister Edward Taylor, who had been Sewall's classmate at Harvard College, and the Boston polymath Cotton Mather. Sewall began his diary during his time at Harvard (1667–71), and he continued it until the year before his death. The diary is an ancient genre, its name derived from the Latin *diarium*, from *dies* for "day." The semiformal diary in English began to flourish after the Reformation, as self-reflection became an integral feature of everyday life for many people. Sewall's diary, first published in the nineteenth century, offers insights into both daily life in upper-class colonial Boston and events that transformed Massachusetts from a Puritan colony to a stronghold of "Yankee" ingenuity, commerce, and philanthropy. The diary also provides Sewall's perspective on some of the most sensational issues of the day, including the Salem witchcraft trials, and it reflects the first stirrings of the debate over slavery. Sewall was involved in both controversies, serving as a judge in the witchcraft proceedings and later offering a public apology for his role; and publishing *The Selling of Joseph* (1700), an early antislavery tract.

Sewall was born in England, but his parents had lived in Massachusetts before their marriage, and by the time he was nine the family had returned to the Bay Colony. After his schooling, he chose commerce and the law over the ministry. In 1676 Sewall married Hannah Hull, the only surviving child of the wealthy Boston goldsmith and merchant John Hull, and moved into Hull's Boston house, where he lived until his death. John Hull entrusted his extensive business interests to his son-in-law, and after Hull's death in 1684 Sewall became a central figure in Boston's thriving mercantile life.

In 1678, the Massachusetts General Court (that is, the Bay Colony's legislature) appointed Sewall to manage the Boston printing press. The first text he issued was John Bunyan's *Pilgrim's Progress* (1678), an influential allegory about a hero named Christian. During the nearly three years that Sewall ran the press, he published official documents, works by important Puritan thinkers, and some of his own essays.

In 1692, Sewall became one of the justices of the Superior Court of Judicature, a position he held for more than thirty-five years, the last eleven as chief justice. Earlier that same year, he was appointed to the special court inquiring into reported instances of witchcraft in Salem and other towns. The court tried dozens of cases and condemned a number of people to death. Public opinion soon turned against the court's standards of evidence. When two of his children died, Sewall feared that the deaths might be divine punishment for his involvement in the trials. He formally apologized in church for his part in the witchcraft tragedy in 1697.

When *The Selling of Joseph* appeared three years later, Sewall reported, he received "frowns and harsh words" from his fellow townspeople, including the merchant and slaveholder John Saffin, who published the pamphlet *A Brief and Candid Answer* the following year. Sewall delayed acknowledging this answer until he "saw a very severe act passing [the General Court] against Indians and Negroes" in 1705. He returned to the controversy, arranging to reprint an article from an English periodical arguing that the slave trade was "especially contrary to the great Law of Christianity." Though Sewall remained opposed to interracial marriage, his willingness to promote the antislavery cause makes him a significant figure in the emerging abolitionist movement.

From The Diary of Samuel Sewall[1]

Satterday, Jan[y] 2[d][, *1686.*] Last night had a very unusual Dream; *viz.*[2] That our Savior in the dayes of his Flesh when upon Earth, came to Boston and abode here sometime, and moreover that He Lodged in that time at Father Hull's; upon which in my Dream had two Reflections, One was how much more Boston had to say than Rome boasting of Peter's being there.[3] The other a sense of great Respect that I ought to have shewed Father Hull since Christ chose when in town, to take up His Quarters at his House. Admired the goodness and Wisdom of Christ in coming hither and spending some part of His short Life here. The Chronological absurdity never came into my mind, as I remember. Jan[y] 1, 1688, finished reading the Godly Learned ingenious Pareus on the Revelation.[4]

Sabbath, Augt. 10th[, *1690.*] Went to see Cous. [Daniel] Quinsey; read the 102. Psal. and begin 103. pray'd, and so went home. Put up a Bill[5] at his request. Just after Contribution in the Afternoon, was call'd out, Cousin being very bad, so far as I could perceive. He desired me to pray, which I did: Afterward sent for Mr. [Samuel] Willard, and He pray'd, then Cousin pull'd his hand out of the Bed, and gave it to Mr. Willard. Seem'd to pray himself; but I could hear little except Jesus Christ; breath'd quick and hard, till at last abated and He quietly expired about Seven aclock. Mother Hull and I being there. I have parted with a cordial fast Friend, such an one as I shall hardly find. The Lord fit me for my Change and help me to wait till it come. Cousin was concern'd what he should doe for Patience, but God graciously furnish'd him, and has now translated Him to that State and place wherein He has no occasion for any.

Tuesday, Augt. 12[, *1690.*] About 7. P.M. we lay the Body of Cous. Daniel Quinsey in my Father's Tomb. Mr. Serjeant, Dummer, H. Usher, Davis, Williams, Conney, Bearers. I led the Widow, then the Children, next, Mr. T. Brattle, Mis. Shepard, H. Newman, Mistress Margaret, Mr. Willard, Mother Hull, Mr. Parson, my wife and so on. *Note.* My wife was so ill could hardly get home, taking some harm in going in Pattens[6] or some wrench, so had a great flux of Blood, which amaz'd us both, at last my wife bade me call Mrs. Ellis, then Mother Hull, then the Midwife, and throw the Goodness of God was brought to Bed of a Daughter between 3. and four aclock, *Aug. 13th, 1690. mane*[7] Mrs. Elisabeth Weeden, Midwife. Had not Women nor other preparations as usually, being wholly surpris'd, my wife expecting to have gone a Moneth longer.

* * *

Augt. 17[, *1690.*] Mr. Willard keeps his Sabbath at Roxbury, and so the Baptism of my little Daughter is deferred to the next Lord's Day.

1. The text is from *The Diary of Samuel Sewall* (1973), edited by M. Halsey Thomas. To preserve the flavor of Sewall's style, the text has been only slightly modernized. The dates, however, have been changed to conform to the modern calendar.
2. Abbreviation for *videlicet*: that is to say, namely (Latin).
3. Peter, one of Jesus' original twelve disciples,

is buried in Rome.
4. The biblical Book of Revelation. "Pareus": David Pareus (1548-1622), a German theologian and biblical commentator and one of Sewall's favorite authors.
5. A legal petition.
6. Wearing high-heeled shoes.
7. Morning (Latin).

Sabbath-day, August the four and twentieth, 1690. I publish my little Daughter's name to be Judith, held her up for Mr. Willard to baptize her. She cried not at all, though a pretty deal of water was poured on her by Mr. Willard when He baptized her: Six others were baptized at the same time; Capt. Davis's Son James, and a grown person, Margaret Clifford, two of them. I named my Daughter Judith for the sake of her Grandmother and great Grandmother, who both wore that Name, and the Signification of it very good: The Lord grant that we may have great cause to praise Him on her account and help her to speak the Jews Language and to forget that of Ashdod,[8] Nehemiah 13.24. And that she may follow her Grandmother Hull, as she follows Christ, being not slothfull in Business, fervent in Spirit, serving the Lord. Her Prayers and Painstaking for all my Children are incessant, voluntary, with condescension to the meanest Services[9] night and day: that I judg'd I could in justice doe no less than endeavor her remembrance by putting her Name on one of her Grand-Daughters. I have now had my health and opportunity to offer up Nine Children to God in Baptisme. Mr. Tho. Thacher baptized the two eldest; John and Samuel; Mr. Samuel Willard baptized the Seven younger. Lord grant that I who have thus solemnly and frequently named the name of the Lord Jesus, may depart from Iniquity; and that mine may be more His than Mine, or their own.

Sept. 20[, 1690.] * * * My little Judith languishes and moans, ready to die.

Sabbath, Sept. 21[, 1690.] About 2 *mane*, I rise, read some Psalms and pray with my dear Daughter. Between 7. and 8. (Mr. Moodey preaches in the Forenoon,) I call Mr. Willard, and he prays. Told Mr. Walter of her condition * * * desiring him to give her a Lift towards heaven. Mr. Baily sat with me in the Afternoon. I acquainted Him. Between 7. and 8. in the evening the child died, and I hope sleeps in Jesus.

Sept. 22[, 1690.] In the even,[1] Mr. Moodey, Allen, Mather come from Mrs. Clark's Funeral to see us. Mr. Moodey and I went before the other came, to neighbor Hord, who lay dying; where also Mr. Allen came in. Nurse Hord told her Husband who was there, and what he had to say; whether he desir'd them to pray with him: He said with some earnestness, Hold your tongue, which was repeated three times to his wive's repeated intreaties; once he said, Let me alone, or, be quiet, (whether that made a fourth or was one of the three do not remember) and, My Spirits are gon. At last Mr. Moodey took him up pretty roundly and told him he might with the same labor have given a pertinent answer. When were ready to come away Mr. Moodey bid him put forth a little Breath to ask prayer, and said twas the last time had to speak to him; At last ask'd him, doe you desire prayer, shall I pray with you, He answer'd, Ay for the Lord's sake, and thank'd Mr. Moodey when had done. His former carriage[2] was very startling and amazing to us. About One at night he died. About 11. aclock I supposed to hear neighbor Mason at prayer with him, just as I and my wife were going to bed. Mr. Allen prayed with us when came from said Hord's.

8. I.e., be true believers and speak the language of Judah. Children of Jews who married Ashdod women were unable to speak the language of their fathers.

9. I.e., willingness to perform the least dignified kinds of childcare.

1. Evening.

2. Previous behavior.

Sept. 23[, *1690.*] Tuesday, between 5. and 6. Sir[3] Moodey carries the Body of my dear Judith to the Tomb, Solomon Rainsford receives it on the Stairs and sets it in. On the Coffin is the year 1690. made with little nails. Gov[r] Bradstreet and Lady,[4] Mrs. Moodey, Mather the Mother, Mr. Winthrop, Richards here, with many others; Ministers, Willard, Moodey, Mather.

June 2[d,] 1691. Mr. Edward Taylor puts his Son James to Mr. Steward, Shopkeeper of Ipswich, for Seven years, to serve him as an Apprentice, Term to begin the first of July next. Mr. Taylor desires me to represent himself in making the Indenture,[5] if Mr. Steward desire the accomplishment of it befor He comes down again.

Monday, Dec. 7th[, *1691.*] I ride to New-Cambridge to see Sam.[6] He could hardly speak to me, his affections were so mov'd, having not seen me for above a fortnight; his Cough is still very bad, much increas'd by his going to Cambridge on foot in the night. * * *

April 11th, 1692. Went to Salem, where, in the Meeting-house, the persons accused of Witchcraft were examined; was a very great Assembly; 'twas awfull to see how the afflicted persons were agitated. Mr. Noyes pray'd at the beginning, and Mr. Higginson concluded. [*In the margin*], Væ,[7] Væ, Væ, Witchcraft.

July 30, 1692. Mrs. Cary makes her escape out of Cambridge-Prison, who was Committed for Witchcraft.[8]

Thursday, Augt. 4[, *1692.*] At Salem, Mr. Waterhouse brings the news of the desolation at Jamaica, June 7th. 1700 persons kill'd, besides the Loss of Houses and Goods by the Earthquake.

Augt. 19th, 1692. * * * This day [*in the margin*, Dolefull Witchcraft] George Burrough, John Willard, Jn° Procter,[9] Martha Carrier and George Jacobs were executed at Salem, a very great number of Spectators being present. Mr. Cotton Mather was there, Mr. Sims, Hale, Noyes, Chiever, &c. All of them said they were innocent, Carrier and all. Mr. Mather says they all died by a Righteous Sentence. Mr. Burrough by his Speech, Prayer, protestation of his Innocence, did much move unthinking persons, which occasions their speaking hardly[1] concerning his being executed.

Augt. 25[, *1692.*] Fast at the old [*First*] Church, respecting the Witchcraft, Drought, &c.

Monday, Sept. 19, 1692. About noon, at Salem, Giles Corey was press'd to death for standing Mute;[2] much pains was used with him two days, one after another, by the Court and Capt. Gardner of Nantucket who had been of his acquaintance: but all in vain.

3. Here, meaning minister.
4. Simon Bradstreet's second wife (i.e., not the poet Anne).
5. Sewall represented the town of Westfield in the General Court of Massachusetts.
6. Sewall's thirteen-year-old son, boarding at school.
7. Woe (Latin). On May 24, 1692, Governor William Phips (1651–1695) appointed Sewall one of the seven councilors of a court of Oyer and Terminer (i.e., to hear and determine) to judge those accused of witchcraft in Salem. The court met in

Salem on June 2, and Bridget Bishop was hanged on June 10. On June 30, they met again, and five more accused were executed on July 19. Unfortunately for us, Sewall kept his entries regarding the trials at Salem to a minimum.
8. Cary was given protection in New York.
9. I.e., John Proctor.
1. Vigorously.
2. Refusing to enter a plea. Corey was eighty years old at the time. Heavy stones were placed on him until he died.

Sept. 20[, *1692.*] Now I hear from Salem that about 18 years agoe, he was suspected to have stamped and press'd a man to death, but was cleared. Twas not remembred till Anne Putnam was told of it by said Corey's Spectre the Sabbath-day night before Execution.[3]

Sept. 20, 1692. The Swan[4] brings in a rich French Prize of about 300 Tuns, laden with Claret, White Wine, Brandy, Salt, Linnen Paper, &c.

Sept. 21[, *1692.*] A petition is sent to Town in behalf of Dorcas Hoar, who now confesses: Accordingly an order is sent to the Sheriff to forbear her Execution, notwithstanding her being in the Warrant to die to morrow. This is the first condemned person who has confess'd.[5]

Nov. 6[, *1692.*] Joseph threw a knop[6] of Brass and hit his Sister Betty on the forhead so as to make it bleed and swell; upon which, and for his playing at Prayer-time, and eating when Return Thanks,[7] I whipd him pretty smartly. When I first went in (call'd by his Grandmother) he sought to shadow and hide himself from me behind the head of the Cradle: which gave me the sorrowfull remembrance of Adam's carriage.[8]

Apr. 16, 1695. My Appletree which I nourish from a kernel, has the growth of 1694[9] and is now scarce Ten inches high; removd it this Spring into the room[1] of a young Appletree that dyed.

* · * · *

Monday, April 29, 1695. The morning is very warm and Sunshiny; in the Afternoon there is Thunder and Lightening, and about 2 P.M. a very extraordinary Storm of Hail, so that the ground was made white with it, as with the blossoms when fallen; 'twas as bigg as pistoll and Musquet Bullets; It broke of the Glass of the new House about 480 Quarrels[2] of the Front; of Mr. Sergeant's about as much; Col. Shrimpton, Major General, Gov[r] Bradstreet, New Meetinghouse, Mr. Willard, &c. Mr. Cotton Mather dined with us, and was with me in the new Kitchen when this was; He had just been mentioning that more Minister Houses than others proportionably had been smitten with Lightening; enquiring what the meaning of God should be in it. Many Hail-Stones broke throw the Glass and flew to the middle of the Room, or farther: People afterward Gazed upon the House to see its Ruins. I got Mr. Mather to pray with us after this awfull Providence; He told God He had broken the brittle part of our house, and prayd that we might be ready for the time when our Clay-Tabernacles should be broken. Twas a sorrowfull thing to me to see the house so far undon again before twas finish'd. It seems at Milton on the one hand, and at Lewis's[3] on the other, there was no Hail.

Jan[y] 15[, *1697.*] * * * Copy of the Bill I put up on the Fast day;[4] giving it to Mr. Willard as he pass'd by, and standing up at the reading of it, and bowing when finished; in the Afternoon.

3. Putnam was twelve when she, along with her mother, made accusations against "witches."
4. A ship.
5. Confession of witchcraft automatically set the accused free.
6. Knob.
7. Saying grace.
8. The behavior of Adam after the fall, when he tried to hide from God (see Genesis 3).

9. It has a year's growth.
1. Place.
2. Squares.
3. The tavern in Lynn, Massachusetts, which is north of Boston. Milton is south of Boston.
4. The Massachusetts General Court made January 14, 1697, a day of fasting to atone for the events at Salem. Sewall publicly confessed his error and guilt.

Samuel Sewall, sensible of the reiterated strokes of God upon himself and family[5] and being sensible, that as to the Guilt contracted, upon the opening of the late Commission of Oyer and Terminer at Salem (to which the order for this Day relates) he is, upon many accounts, more concerned than any that he knows of, Desires to take the Blame and Shame of it, Asking pardon of Men, And especially desiring prayers that God, who has an Unlimited Authority, would pardon that Sin and all other his Sins; personal and Relative: And according to his infinite Benignity, and Soveraignty, Not Visit the Sin of him, or of any other, upon himself or any of his, nor upon the Land: But that He would powerfully defend him against all Temptations to Sin, for the future; and vouchsafe him the Efficacious, Saving Conduct of his Word and Spirit.

July 15, 1698. Mr. Edward Taylor comes to our house from Westfield. *Monday, July 18*[, *1698.*] I walk'd with Mr. Edward Taylor upon Cotton Hill, thence to Becon Hill, the Pasture, along the Stone-wall: As came back, we sat down on the great Rock, and Mr. Taylor told me his courting his first wife,[6] and Mr. Fitch his story of Mr. Dod's prayer to God to bring his Affection to close with a person pious, but hard-favored. Has God answered me in finding out one Godly and fit for me, and shall I part for fancy? When came home, my wife gave me Mr. Tappan's Letter concerning Eliza,[7] which caus'd me to reflect on Mr. Taylor's Discourse. And his Prayer was for pardon of error in our ways—which made me think whether it were not best to overlook all, and go on. This day John Ive, fishing in great Spiepond, is arrested with mortal sickness which renders him in a manner speechless and senseless; dies next day; buried at Charlestown on the Wednesday. Was a very debauched, atheistical man. I was not at his Funeral. Had Gloves sent me,[8] but the knowledge of his notoriously wicked life made me sick of going; and Mr. Mather, the president, came in just as I was ready to step out, and so I staid at home, and by that means lost a Ring:[9] but hope had no loss. Follow thou Me, was I suppose more complied with, than if had left Mr. Mather's company to go to such a Funeral.

Fourth-day, June 19, 1700. * * * Having been long and much dissatisfied with the Trade of fetching Negros from Guinea; at last I had a strong Inclination to Write something about it; but it wore off. At last reading Bayne, Ephes.[1] about servants, who mentions Blackamoors; I began to be uneasy that I had so long neglected doing any thing. When I was thus thinking, in came Bro[r] Belknap to shew me a Petition he intended to present to the Gen[L] Court for the freeing a Negro and his wife, who were unjustly held in Bondage. And there is a Motion by a Boston Committee to get a Law that all Importers of Negros shall pay 40[s2] *per* head, to discourage the bringing of

5. On May 22, 1696, Sewall buried a premature son born dead, and on December 23 his daughter Sarah died. When his son Samuel read from Matthew 12.7 ("But if ye had known what this meaneth, I will have mercy, and not sacrifice, ye would not have condemned the guiltless") it did "awfully bring to mind," Sewall noted, "the Salem tragedy."
6. Elizabeth Fitch, who died in 1689. The Mr. Fitch about to be mentioned may have been one

of her relatives.
7. Elizabeth Tappan (or Toppan) was Sewall's niece.
8. Gloves were sent as an invitation to a funeral.
9. A memorial gift.
1. Paul Baynes, *A Commentary upon the First Chapter of the Epistle of Saint Paul. Written to the Ephesians* (1618).
2. Forty shillings (£2, a considerable sum in those days).

them. And Mr. C. Mather resolves to publish a sheet to exhort Masters to labor their Conversion.[3] Which makes me hope that I was call'd of God to Write this Apology[4] for them; Let his Blessing accompany the same.

Tuesday, June 10th[, 1701.] Having last night heard that Josiah Willard had cut off his hair (a very full head of hair) and put on a Wigg, I went to him this morning. Told his Mother what I came about, and she call'd him. I enquired of him what Extremity had forced him to put off his own hair, and put on a Wigg? He answered, none at all. But said that his Hair was streight, and that it parted behinde. Seem'd to argue that men might as well shave their hair off their head, as off their face. I answered men were men before they had hair on their faces, (half of mankind have never any). God seems to have ordain'd our Hair as a Test, to see whether we can bring our minds to be content to be at his finding: or whether we would be our own Carvers, Lords, and come no more at Him. If disliked our Skin, or Nails; 'tis no Thanks to us, that for all that, we cut them not off: Pain and danger restrain us. Your Calling is to teach men self Denial. Twill be displeasing and burdensom to good men: And they that care not what men think of them care not what God thinks of them. Father, Bro[r] Simon, Mr. Pemberton, Mr. [Michael] Wigglesworth,[5] Oakes, Noyes (Oliver), Brattle of Cambridge their example. Allow me to be so far a *Censor Morum*[6] for this end of the Town. Pray'd him to read the Tenth Chapter of the Third book of Calvins Institutions.[7] I read it this morning in course, not of choice. Told him that it was condemn'd by a Meeting of Ministers at Northampton in Mr. [Solomon] Stoddards house, when the said Josiah was there. Told him of the Solemnity of the Covenant which he and I had lately entered into, which put me upon discoursing to him. He seem'd to say would leave off his Wigg when his hair was grown. I spake to his Father of it a day or two after: He thank'd me that had discoursed his Son, and told me that when his hair was grown to cover his ears, he promis'd to leave off his Wigg. If he had known of it, would have forbidden him His Mother heard him talk of it, but was afraid positively to forbid him; lest he should do it, and so be more faulty.

Sabbath, Nov[r] 30[, 1701.] * * * I spent this Sabbath at Mr. Colman's, partly out of dislike to Mr. Josiah Willard's cutting off his Hair, and wearing a Wigg: He preach'd for Mr. Pemberton in the morning; He that contemns the Law of Nature, is not fit to be a publisher of the Law of Grace.[8] * * *

Lord's Day, June 10, 1705. The Learned and pious Mr. Michael Wigglesworth dies at Malden about 9. m. Had been sick about 10. days of a Fever; 73 years and 8 moneths old. He was the Author of the Poem entituled The Day of Doom, which has been so often printed: and was very useful as a Physician.

* * *

3. Work toward their slaves' conversion to Christianity.
4. *The Selling of Joseph* was published five days later.
5. See his headnote, above.
6. Judge of morals (Latin).
7. The Protestant theologian John Calvin's *Insti-*

tutes of the Christian Religion (1536). In this chapter, "How to Use the Present Life, and the Comforts of It," Calvin recommends naturalness and moderation.
8. I.e., a minister who cuts off his hair scorns the law of nature and therefore should not be allowed to preach.

Lords day, Dec^r 17[, 1727.] I was surprised to hear Mr. Thacher of Milton, my old Friend, pray'd for as dangerously Sick. Next day. *Dec^r 18, 1727.* I am inform'd by Mr. Gerrish, that my dear friend died last night; which I doubt bodes ill to Milton and the Province, his dying at this Time, though in the 77th year of his Age. *Deus avertat Omen!*[9]

Friday, Dec^r 22[, 1727.] the day after the Fast, was inter'd.[1] Bearers Rev^d Mr. Nehemiah Walter, Mr. Joseph Baxter; Mr. John Swift, Mr. Sam^L Hunt; Mr. Joseph Sewall, Mr. Thomas Prince. I was inclin'd before, and having a pair of Gloves sent me, I determined to go to the Funeral, if the Weather prov'd favorable, which it did, and I hired Blake's Coach with four Horses; my Son, Mr. Cooper and Mr. Prince went with me. Refresh'd there with Meat and Drink; got thither about half an hour past one. It was sad to see [death] triumphed over my dear Friend! I rode in my Coach to the Burying place; not being able to get nearer by reason of the many Horses. From thence went directly up the Hill where the Smith's Shop, and so home very comfortably and easily, the ground being mollified. But when I came to my own Gate, going in, I fell down, a board slipping under my Left foot, my right Legg raised off the skin, and put me to a great deal of pain, especially when 'twas washed with Rum. It was good for me that I was thus Afflicted that my spirit might be brought into a frame more suitable to the Solemnity, which is apt to be too light; and by the loss of some of my Skin, and blood I might be awakened to prepare for my own Dissolution. Mr. Walter prayed before the Corps was carried out. I had a pair of Gloves sent me before I went, and a Ring given me there. Mr. Millar, the Church of England Minister, was there. At this Funeral I heard of the death of my good old Tenant Cap^t Nathan Niles, that very Friday morn. I have now been at the Interment of 4 of my Class-mates. First, the Rev'd Mr. William Adams at Dedham, Midweek, Augt. 19, 1685. Second, Mr. John Bowles, at Roxbury, March 31, 1691. Was one of his Bearers. Third, Capt. Samuel Phips at Charlestown. He was laid in his Son-in-Law Lemmon's Tomb. Had a good pair of Gloves, and a gold Ring. He was Clerk of the Court and Register many years. Clerk to his death, and his Son succeeded him. Was Præcentor[2] many years to the congregation. Inter'd Augt. 9, 1725. Fourth, the Rev'd Mr. Thachar at Milton. Now I can go to no more Funerals of my Classmates; nor none be at mine; for the survivers, the Rev'd Mr. Samuel Mather at Windsor, and the Rev^d Mr. Taylor at Westfield, [are] one Hundred Miles off, and are extremly enfeebled. I humbly pray that CHRIST may be graciously present with us all Three both in Life, and in Death, and then we shall safely and Comfortably walk through the shady valley that leads to Glory.

Lords-day, Dec^r 24th[, 1727.] am kept from the solemn Assembly by my bruised Shin.

October 19, 1728. Seeing this to be the same day of the week and Moneth that the Wife of my youth expired Eleven years agoe, it much affected me. I writ to my dear Son Mr. Joseph Sewall of it, desiring him to come and dine with me: or however that he would call some time to join my Condolence. He came about Noon and made an excellent Prayer in the East Chamber. *Laus Deo.*[3] I told him of the death of the Widow Wheeler yesterday morning,

9. May God turn aside all bad things (Latin).
1. I.e, interred: buried.
2. One who leads the congregation in singing.
3. Praise God (Latin).

which he had not heard of. When Sam came to read, I wrap'd up a Silver Cup with one ear,[4] weighing about 3 ounces and 12 Grains, to give his Mother, which I had promis'd her. A Minister's Wife, I told her, ought not to be without such a one. I went to looke [for] silver to make such a one, and unexpectedly met with one ready made.

Ditto, die, feria Septima.[5] I gave my dear Wife a Book of 7 Sermons, which had been my Daughter Hannah's, for whom she had labored beyond measure.

1673–1729

1878–82

The Selling of Joseph: A Memorial[1]

Forasmuch as Liberty *is in real value next unto* Life: *None ought to part with it themselves, or deprive others of it, but upon most mature Consideration.*[2]

The Numerousness of Slaves at this day in the Province, and the Uneasiness of them under their Slavery, hath put many upon thinking whether the Foundation of it be firmly and well laid; so as to sustain the Vast Weight that is built upon it. It is most certain that all Men, as they are the Sons of *Adam,* are Coheirs; and have equal Right unto Liberty, and all other outward Comforts of Life. *God hath given the Earth* [with all its Commodities] *unto the Sons of Adam, Psal* 115.16. *And hath made of One Blood, all Nations of Men, for to dwell on all the face of the Earth, and hath determined the Times before appointed, and the bounds of their habitation: That they should seek the Lord. Forasmuch then as we are the Offspring of GOD &c. Act* 17.26, 27, 29. Now although the Title given by the last ADAM, doth infinitely better Men[']s Estates, respecting GOD and themselves; and grants them a most beneficial and inviolable Lease under the Broad Seal of Heaven, who were before only Tenants at Will:[3] Yet through the Indulgence of GOD to our First Parents after the Fall, the outward Estate of all and every of their Children, remains the same, as to one another. So that Originally, and Naturally, there is no such thing as Slavery. *Joseph* was rightfully no more a Slave to his Brethren, than they were to him: and they had no more Authority to *Sell* him, than they had to *Slay* him. And if *they* had nothing to do to Sell him; the *Ishmaelites* bargaining with them, and paying down Twenty pieces of Silver could not make a Title. Neither could *Potiphar* have any better Interest in him than the *Ishmaelites* had. *Gen.* 37.20, 27, 28. For he that shall in this case plead *Alteration of Property,* seems to have forfeited a great part of his own claim to Humanity. There is no proportion between Twenty Pieces of Silver, and LIBERTY. The Commodity it self is the Claimer. If *Arabian* Gold

4. Handle.
5. Same place, the day, Sunday (Latin).
1. A public remonstrance or statement. The text is derived from the first edition (1700).
2. Translated from *De Conscientia, et eius iure, vel casibus* (1623), by the English theologian William Ames, who was the main source for Puritan ecclesiastical ideas. The last quotation in *The Selling of Joseph,* in Ames's Latin original, includes

this same passage.
3. Renters subject to immediate expulsion from rental property, as opposed to those holding a long-term lease. Here and throughout this opening passage, Sewall uses language derived from contemporary property law and practice as well as from the Bible. "Broad Seal": seal of England, affixed to land grants and patents.

be imported in any quantities, most are afraid to meddle with it, though they might have it at easy rates; lest if it should have been wrongfully taken from the Owners, it should kindle a fire to the Consumption of their whole Estate. 'tis pity there should be more Caution used in buying a Horse, or a little life-less dust; than there is in purchasing Men and Women: Whenas they are the Offspring of GOD, and their Liberty is,

. *Auro pretiosior Omni.*[4]

And seeing GOD hath said, *He that Stealeth a Man and Selleth him, or if he be found in his hand, he shall surely be put to Death.* Exod. 21.16. This Law being of Everlasting Equity, wherein Man Stealing is ranked amongst the most atrocious of Capital Crimes: What louder Cry can there be made of that Celebrated Warning,

Caveat Emptor![5]

And all things considered, it would conduce more to the Welfare of the Province, to have White Servants for a Term of Years, than to have Slaves for Life. Few can endure to hear of a Negro's being made free; and indeed they can seldom use their freedom well; yet their continual aspiring after their forbidden Liberty, renders them Unwilling Servants. And there is such a disparity in their Conditions, Colour & Hair, that they can never embody with us, and grow up into orderly Families, to the Peopling of the Land: but still remain in our Body Politick as a kind of extravasat[6] Blood. As many Negro men as there are among us, so many empty places there are in our Train Bands, and the places taken up of Men that might make Husbands for our Daughters.[7] And the Sons and Daughters of *New England* would become more like *Jacob,* and *Rachel,*[8] if this Slavery were thrust quite out of doors. Moreover it is too well known what Temptations Masters are under, to connive at the Fornication of their Slaves; lest they should be obliged to find them Wives, or pay their Fines.[9] It seems to be practically pleaded that they might be Lawless; 'tis thought much of, that the Law should have Satisfaction for their Thefts, and other Immoralities; by which means, *Holiness to the Lord,* is more rarely engraven upon this sort of Servitude. It is likewise most lamentable to think, how in taking Negros out of *Africa,* and Selling of them here, That which GOD has joyned together men do boldly rend asunder; Men from their Country, Husbands from their Wives, Parents from their Children. How horrible is the Uncleanness, Mortality, if not Murder, that the Ships are guilty of that bring great Crouds of these miserable Men, and Women. Methinks, when we are bemoaning the barbarous Usage of our Friends and Kinsfolk in *Africa:* it might not be unseasonable to enquire whether we are not culpable in forcing the *Africans* to become Slaves amongst our selves. And it may be a question whether all the Benefit received by *Negro* Slaves, will balance the Accompt[1] of Cash laid out upon them; and for the

4. More precious than all the gold (Latin).
5. Let the buyer beware! (Latin).
6. Foreign, not intrinsic.
7. "Train bands" were companies of militia. Sewall implies that black members of these militias were taking the places of white men.

8. Famous in the Bible for their courtship and abiding love.
9. I.e., extramarital sex was subject to fines in Massachusetts and other colonies.
1. Account.

Redemption of our own enslaved Friends out of *Africa*. Besides all the Persons and Estates that have perished there.

Obj. 1. *These Blackamores are of the Posterity of* Cham,[2] *and therefore are under the Curse of Slavery.* Gen. 9.25, 26, 27.

Answ. Of all Offices, one would not begg this; *viz.*[3] Uncall'd for, to be an Executioner of the Vindictive Wrath of God; the extent and duration of which is to us uncertain. If this ever was a Commission; How do we know but that it is long since out of Date? Many have found it to their Cost, that a Prophetical Denunciation of Judgment against a Person or People, would not warrant them to inflict that evil. If it would, *Hazael* might justify himself in all he did against his Master, and the *Israelites*, from 2 *Kings* 8.10, 12.

But it is possible that by cursory reading, this Text may have been mistaken. For *Canaan* is the Person Cursed three times over, without the mentioning of *Cham*. Good Expositors suppose the Curse entaild on him, and that this Prophesie was accomplished in the Extirpation of the *Canaanites*, and in the Servitude of the *Gibeonites. Vide Pareum.*[4] Whereas the Blackmores are not descended of *Canaan*, but of *Cush*. Psal. 68.31. *Princes shall come out of Egypt, Ethiopia shall soon stretch out her hands unto God.* Under which Names, all *Africa* may be comprehended; and their Promised Conversion ought to be prayed for. *Jer.* 13.23. *Can the Ethiopian change his skin?* This shows that Black Men are the Posterity of *Cush*: Who time out of mind have been distinguished by their Colour. And for want of the true, *Ovid* assigns a fabulous cause of it.

> *Sanguine tum credunt in corpora summa vocato*
> *Æthiopum populus nigrum traxisse colorem.*
> Metamorph. lib. 2.[5]

Obj. 2. *The Nigers are brought out of a Pagan Country, into places where the Gospel is Preached.*

Answ. Evil must not be done, that good may come of it. The extraordinary and comprehensive Benefit accruing to the Church of God, and to *Joseph* personally, did not rectify his brethren[']s Sale of him.

Obj. 3. *The Africans have Wars one with another: Our Ships bring lawful Captives taken in those Wars.*

Answ. For ought is known, their Wars are much such as were between *Jacob's* Sons and their Brother *Joseph.*[6] If they be between Town and Town; Provincial, or National: Every War is upon one side Unjust. An Unlawful War can't make lawful Captives. And by Receiving, we are in danger to promote, and partake in their Barbarous Cruelties. I am sure, if some Gentlemen should go down to the *Brewsters* to take the Air, and Fish: And a stronger

2. I.e., Ham, the second son of Noah and the father of Cush as well as of Canaan. In Genesis 9.25, Noah says, "Cursed be Canaan; a servant of servants shall he be unto his brethren." Apologists for slavery often insisted that Ham was the ancestor of the African peoples.

3. Abbreviation for *videlicet*: that is to say, namely (Latin).

4. See Pareus (Latin); David Pareus (1548–1622) was a German theologian and biblical commenta-

tor and one of Sewall's favorite authors.

5. From book 2 (lines 235–36) of *Metamorphoses*, by the ancient Roman poet Ovid: Then it was, as men think, that the people of Ethiopia became dark-skinned, for the blood was called to the surface of their bodies (by the heat) (Latin).

6. Joseph was sold into slavery in Egypt by his brothers. The story appears in Genesis 37. "For . . . known": i.e., for all we know.

party from *Hull*[7] should Surprise them, and Sell them for Slaves to a Ship outward bound: they would think themselves unjustly dealt with; both by Sellers and Buyers. And yet 'tis to be feared, we have no other kind of Title to our *Nigers*. *Therefore all things whatsoever ye would that men should do to you, do ye even so to them: for this is the Law and the Prophets.* Matt. 7.12.[8]

Obj. 4. Abraham *had Servants bought with his Money, and born in his House.*

Answ. Until the Circumstances of *Abraham's* purchase be recorded, no Argument can be drawn from it. In the mean time, Charity obliges us to conclude, that He knew it was lawful and good.

It is Observable that the *Israelites* were strictly forbidden the buying, or selling one another for Slaves. *Levit.* 25. 39. 46. *Jer.* 34 8. 22. And GOD gaged His Blessing in lieu of any loss they might conceipt[9] they suffered thereby. *Deut.* 15. 18. And since the partition Wall is broken down, inordinate Self love should likewise be demolished.[1] GOD expects that Christians should be of a more Ingenuous and benign frame of spirit. Christians should carry it to all the World, as the *Israelites* were to carry it one towards another. And for men obstinately to persist in holding their Neighbours and Brethren under the Rigor of perpetual Bondage, seems to be no proper way of gaining Assurance that God has given them Spiritual Freedom. Our Blessed Saviour has altered the Measures of the ancient Love-Song, and set it to a most Excellent New Tune, which all ought to be ambitious of Learning. *Matt.* 5.43, 44 *John* 13.34. These *Ethiopians*, as black as they are; seeing they are the Sons and Daughters of the First *Adam*, the Brethren and Sisters of the Last ADAM, and the Offspring of GOD; They ought to be treated with a Respect agreeable.

Servitus perfecta voluntaria, inter Christianum & Christianum, ex parte servi patientis sæpe est licita, quia est necessaria: sed ex parte domini agentis, & procurando & exercendo, vix potest esse licita: quia non convenit regulæ illi generali: Quæcunque volueritis ut faciant vobis homines, ita & vos facite eis.[2] Matt. 7. 12.

Perfecta servitus pœnæ, non potest jure locum habere, nisi ex delicto gravi quod ultimum supplicium aliquo modo meretur: quia Libertas ex naturali æstimatione proxime accedit ad vitam ipsam, & eidem a multis præferri solet.[3] Ames. Cas. Consc. Lib. 5. Cap. 23. Thes. 2, 3.

1700

7. A coastal town near Boston. The Brewsters are a group of islands at the outer entrance to Boston Harbor.
8. Since the eighteenth century, this injunction has been known as the Golden Rule.
9. Conceive.
1. Ephesians 2.12–14: "At that time ye were without Christ, being aliens from the commonwealth of Israel, and strangers to the covenants of promise, having no hope, and without God in the world: But now in Christ Jesus ye who sometimes were far off are made nigh by the blood of Christ. For he is our peace, who hath made both one, and hath broken down the middle wall of partition between us."

2. As long as it is voluntary, the total servitude of one Christian to another is often enough lawful on the part of the servant because it arises from his necessity. But on the part of the master who is the agent in procuring and managing [the servant], it is scarcely legal, for it does not conform to the general rule: Whatsoever ye would that men should do to you, do ye even so to them (Latin).
3. Total servitude, when used as a punishment, can have no place in law, unless for an offense so grave that it is deserving of the severest penalty: for liberty by common estimate is next in importance to life itself, and by many is placed even higher than life (Latin); from Ames's *De Conscientia.*

COTTON MATHER
1663–1728

Cotton Mather's writings represent the peak of New England Puritan intellectual life in its baroque phase: ornate, with a hint of decadence. The sense of a world-view a bit past its prime and straining to recover preeminence emerges from many accounts of his life and writings. Mather was the grandson of Richard Mather and John Cotton, leading first-generation ministers in the Massachusetts Bay Colony, and the son of another prominent minister, Increase Mather. These men published frequently on theology, church polity, history, and the natural sciences. Young Cotton Mather shouldered the burden of this inheritance, viewing it as a precious legacy for the colony and, indeed, all of humanity, but he did so at some personal cost. He stammered badly as a youth, and while he was able to overcome that debility well enough to become a minister, throughout his life he continued to suffer from nervous disorders that today we would probably call anxiety and depression. He had a reputation for being pushy and difficult, and he alienated people with extreme behavior, even when he acted with the best intentions.

Tutored by his father, this precocious eldest son of a distinguished family was admitted to Harvard College at the unusually young age of twelve. At Mather's graduation, in 1678, President Urian Oakes told the commencement audience that his hope was great that "in this youth, Cotton and Mather shall, in fact as well as name, join together and once more appear in life"—a reference to the young man's illustrious grandfathers. Later, the pressures associated with living up to his family heritage mounted. In 1685, his father began a long term as the president of Harvard, and for four years starting in the late 1680s he served as New England's envoy to England, where he renegotiated favorable terms for the colonial charter. These were remarkable accomplishments for any child to attempt to equal.

Mather remained for much of his adult life in his father's shadow. He studied medicine when it seemed that his stammer would prevent him from taking a pulpit, then began serving as his father's assistant pastor at Boston's Second Church after Increase became the president of Harvard. Cotton was later thwarted in his desire to follow his father into the Harvard presidency, a source of lingering bitterness to him. He finally became pastor at the Second Church after his father's death, only five years before he himself died. Frustrated professionally in certain ways, Mather devoted his considerable energy to the transatlantic republic of letters, involving himself in the major intellectual questions of his day and writing on a wide variety of topics.

Mather experienced further disappointment and tragedy in his personal life. His first two wives died, and his third wife became mentally ill. Of his fifteen children, only six survived to adulthood, and just two lived until his death. His extended family put uncomfortable demands on his financial resources. Despite these considerable responsibilities, he was passionately committed to the common good as he understood it, and he took great satisfaction in organizing societies for building churches, supporting schools for the children of slaves, and working to establish funds for indigent clergy. During Benjamin Franklin's early years in Boston, he learned a great deal from Mather about public service, and those insights became central to Franklin's life and writings.

Mather published over four hundred works. Some of his most engaging writings deal with the witchcraft trials at Salem, which exemplify central tensions between the Puritan worldview and an emerging, science-based modern order. Mather was only indirectly involved in the prosecutions. His writings on the subject, in works

such as *The Wonders of the Invisible World* (1693), contain both an apocalyptic narrative of Satan's assaults on godly New England and more neutral descriptions of the supposed supernatural manifestations and the legal proceedings designed to stamp them out. Mather embraced the natural sciences warmly enough to earn election in 1713 into London's prestigious Royal Society, an organization founded in 1660 to promote scientific investigation of the natural world. His later writings included a medical compendium, and he took a public stand in favor of inoculation during Boston's smallpox epidemic in 1721–22. These facets of Mather's intellectual life are not as contradictory as they may appear. He studied the phenomena associated with witchcraft in much the same manner as he sought to understand other physical, mental, and spiritual phenomena.

While these publications suggest a major aspect of Mather's thought, his historical writings are what have earned him a significant place in American literary history. The title page of *Magnalia Christi Americana* (1702) describes this epic work as an "ecclesiastical history of New England." In its seven volumes, however, Mather's history focuses not only on the New England churches and Harvard, where its ministers were trained, but also on representative lives of leading figures, accounts of the colony's Indian wars, and much else. His biographical sketches, modeled on the first-century Greek and Roman historian Plutarch and on Christian hagiographies (i.e., saint's lives), present some of his most compelling writing. His biographies of William Bradford, the longtime governor of the Plymouth Colony, and John Winthrop, leader of the Massachusetts Bay Colony, are among his finest literary achievements. The *Magnalia* also includes Mather's experiments in popular forms such as the captivity tale, a genre that his father had helped usher into being through his involvement with Mary Rowlandson's narrative. The younger Mather contributed to the form with his account of Hannah Dustan's experiences as a captive, "A Notable Exploit."

By the time Mather was writing his history of New England, the issues that seemed most pressing to his parishioners were political and social rather than theological. Mather defended the old order of church authority against the encroachment of an increasingly secular world, noting in a diary entry for 1700 that "there was hardly any but my father and myself to appear in defense of our invaded churches." But he also recast the Puritan perspective in ethical terms, producing what in essence were "conduct books" (represented here by selections from *Bonifacius* [1710], later reprinted as *Essays to Do Good*). These works show him seeking to replace or augment the ever-fragile political power of the clergy with moral chastisement and persuasion. Here again, Mather shared an interest with Benjamin Franklin, whose *Poor Richard's Almanack* (1732–58) offers similar lessons in a more secular idiom. In a society adjusting to new realities, Mather was a worldly Puritan.

From The Wonders of the Invisible World[1]

[A People of God in the Devil's Territories]

The New Englanders are a people of God settled in those, which were once the devil's territories; and it may easily be supposed that the devil was exceedingly disturbed, when he perceived such a people here accomplishing

1. In May 1692, Governor William Phips of Massachusetts appointed a Court of Oyer and Terminer ("hear and determine") in the cases against some nineteen people in Salem accused of witchcraft. Mather had long been interested in the subject of witchcraft, and in this work, written at the request of the judges, he describes the case against the accused. Mather, like many others, saw the evidence of witchcraft as the devil's work, a last-ditch effort to undermine the Puritan ideal. He was skeptical of much of the evidence used against the accused, especially as the trials proceeded in the summer of 1692, but like a number of prominent individuals in the community, he made no public protest. The work was first published in 1693; this text is from the reprint published by John Russell Smith in 1862.

the promise of old made unto our blessed Jesus, that He should have the utmost parts of the earth for His possession.[2] There was not a greater uproar among the Ephesians, when the Gospel was first brought among them,[3] than there was among the powers of the air (after whom those Ephesians walked) when first the silver trumpets of the Gospel here made the joyful sound. The devil thus irritated, immediately tried all sorts of methods to overturn this poor plantation: and so much of the church, as was fled into this wilderness, immediately found the serpent cast out of his mouth a flood for the carrying of it away. I believe that never were more satanical devices used for the unsettling of any people under the sun, than what have been employed for the extirpation of the vine which God has here planted, casting out the heathen, and preparing a room before it, and causing it to take deep root, and fill the land, so that it sent its boughs unto the Atlantic Sea eastward, and its branches unto the Connecticut River westward, and the hills were covered with a shadow thereof. But all those attempts of hell have hitherto been abortive, many an Ebenezer[4] has been erected unto the praise of God, by his poor people here; and having obtained help from God, we continue to this day. Wherefore the devil is now making one attempt more upon us; an attempt more difficult, more surprising, more snarled with unintelligible circumstances than any that we have hitherto encountered; an attempt so critical, that if we get well through, we shall soon enjoy halcyon days with all the vultures of hell trodden under our feet. He has wanted his incarnate legions to persecute us, as the people of God have in the other hemisphere been persecuted: he has therefore drawn forth his more spiritual ones to make an attack upon us. We have been advised by some credible Christians yet alive, that a malefactor, accused of witchcraft as well as murder, and executed in this place more than forty years ago, did then give notice of an horrible plot against the country by witchcraft, and a foundation of witchcraft then laid, which if it were not seasonably discovered, would probably blow up, and pull down all the churches in the country. And we have now with horror seen the discovery of such a witchcraft! An army of devils is horribly broke in upon the place which is the center, and after a sort, the first-born of our English settlements: and the houses of the good people there are filled with the doleful shrieks of their children and servants, tormented by invisible hands, with tortures altogether preternatural. After the mischiefs there endeavored, and since in part conquered,[5] the terrible plague of evil angels hath made its progress into some other places, where other persons have been in like manner diabolically handled. These our poor afflicted neighbors, quickly after they become infected and infested with these demons, arrive to a capacity of discerning those which they conceive the shapes of their troublers; and notwithstanding the great and just suspicion that the demons might impose the shapes of innocent persons in their spectral exhibitions upon the sufferers (which may perhaps prove no

2. After Jesus was baptized, he fasted in the desert for forty days; there, the devil tempted him and offered him the world (Luke 4).
3. Ephesus was an ancient city in Asia Minor, famous for its temples to the goddess Diana. When Saint Paul preached there, he received hostile treatment, and riots followed the sermons of missionaries who attempted to convert the

Ephesians.
4. Stone of help (Hebrew, literal trans.); a commemorative monument like the one Samuel erected to note victory over the Philistines (1 Samuel 7.12).
5. I.e., after the mischiefs were attempted there, and later partly overcome.

small part of the witch-plot in the issue), yet many of the persons thus represented, being examined, several of them have been convicted of a very damnable witchcraft: yea, more than one [and] twenty have confessed, that they have signed unto a book, which the devil showed them, and engaged in his hellish design of bewitching and ruining our land. We know not, at least I know not, how far the delusions of Satan may be interwoven into some circumstances of the confessions; but one would think all the rules of understanding human affairs are at an end, if after so many most voluntary harmonious confessions, made by intelligent persons of all ages, in sundry towns, at several times, we must not believe the main strokes wherein those confessions all agree: especially when we have a thousand preternatural things every day before our eyes, wherein the confessors do acknowledge their concernment, and give demonstration of their being so concerned. If the devils now can strike the minds of men with any poisons of so fine a composition and operation, that scores of innocent people shall unite, in confessions of a crime, which we see actually committed, it is a thing prodigious, beyond the wonders of the former ages, and it threatens no less than a sort of a dissolution upon the world. Now, by these confessions 'tis agreed that the devil has made a dreadful knot of witches in the country, and by the help of witches has dreadfully increased that knot: that these witches have driven a trade of commissioning their confederate spirits to do all sorts of mischiefs to the neighbors, whereupon there have ensued such mischievous consequences upon the bodies and estates of the neighborhood, as could not otherwise be accounted for: yea, that at prodigious witch-meetings, the wretches have proceeded so far as to concert and consult the methods of rooting out the Christian religion from this country, and setting up instead of it perhaps a more gross diabolism than ever the world saw before. And yet it will be a thing little short of miracle, if in so spread a business as this, the devil should not get in some of his juggles,[6] to confound the discovery of all the rest.

* * *

But I shall no longer detain my reader from his expected entertainment, in a brief account of the trials which have passed upon some of the malefactors lately executed at Salem, for the witchcrafts whereof they stood convicted. For my own part, I was not present at any of them; nor ever had I any personal prejudice at the persons thus brought upon the stage; much less at the surviving relations of those persons, with and for whom I would be as hearty a mourner as any man living in the world: The Lord comfort them! But having received a command so to do,[7] I can do no other than shortly relate the chief matters of fact, which occurred in the trials of some that were executed, in an abridgment collected out of the court papers on this occasion put into my hands. You are to take the truth, just as it was; and the truth will hurt no good man. There might have been more of these, if my book would not thereby have swollen too big; and if some other worthy hands did not perhaps intend something further in these collections; for which cause I have only singled out four or five, which may serve to illustrate the

6. Tricks.
7. I.e., having been requested by the judges to write about the trials.

way of dealing, wherein witchcrafts use to be concerned; and I report matters not as an advocate, but as an historian.

* * *

[The Trial of Martha Carrier]

AT THE COURT OF OYER AND TERMINER, HELD BY ADJOURNMENT AT SALEM, AUGUST 2, 1692

I. Martha Carrier was indicted for the bewitching certain persons, according to the form usual in such cases, pleading not guilty to her indictment; there were first brought in a considerable number of the bewitched persons who not only made the court sensible[8] of an horrid witchcraft committed upon them, but also deposed that it was Martha Carrier, or her shape, that grievously tormented them, by biting, pricking, pinching and choking of them. It was further deposed that while this Carrier was on her examination before the magistrates, the poor people were so tortured that every one expected their death upon the very spot, but that upon the binding of Carrier they were eased. Moreover the look of Carrier then laid the afflicted people for dead; and her touch, if her eye at the same time were off them, raised them again: which things were also now seen upon her trial. And it was testified that upon the mention of some having their necks twisted almost round, by the shape of this Carrier, she replied, "It's no matter though their necks had been twisted quite off."

II. Before the trial of this prisoner, several of her own children had frankly and fully confessed not only that they were witches themselves, but that this their mother had made them so. This confession they made with great shows of repentance, and with much demonstration of truth. They related place, time, occasion; they gave an account of journeys, meetings and mischiefs by them performed, and were very credible in what they said. Nevertheless, this evidence was not produced against the prisoner at the bar,[9] inasmuch as there was other evidence enough to proceed upon.

III. Benjamin Abbot gave his testimony that last March was a twelvemonth,[1] this Carrier was very angry with him, upon laying out some land near her husband's: her expressions in this anger were that she would stick as close to Abbot as the bark stuck to the tree; and that he should repent of it afore seven years came to an end, so as Doctor Prescot should never cure him. These words were heard by others besides Abbot himself; who also heard her say, she would hold his nose as close to the grindstone[2] as ever it was held since his name was Abbot. Presently after this, he was taken with a swelling in his foot, and then with a pain in his side, and exceedingly tormented. It bred into a sore, which was lanced by Doctor Prescot, and several gallons of corruption[3] ran out of it. For six weeks it continued very bad, and then another sore bred in the groin, which was also lanced by Doctor Prescot. Another sore then bred in his groin, which was likewise cut, and

8. Aware.
9. I.e., the defendant in court.
1. I.e., a year ago last March.
2. I.e., literally, not metaphorically, press his

face against the revolving sandstone used for grinding, smoothing, etc.
3. Pus; infected matter. "Lanced": cut open.

put him to very great misery: he was brought unto death's door, and so remained until Carrier was taken, and carried away by the constable, from which [that] very day he began to mend, and so grew better every day, and is well ever since.

Sarah Abbot also, his wife, testified that her husband was not only all this while afflicted in his body, but also that strange, extraordinary and unaccountable calamities befell his cattle; their death being such as they could guess at no natural reason for.

IV. Allin Toothaker testified that Richard, the son of Martha Carrier, having some difference with him, pulled him down by the hair of the head. When he rose again he was going to strike at Richard Carrier but fell down flat on his back to the ground, and had not power to stir hand or foot, until he told Carrier he yielded; and then he saw the shape of Martha Carrier go off his breast.

This Toothaker had received a wound in the wars; and he now testified that Martha Carrier told him he should never be cured. Just afore the apprehending of Carrier, he could thrust a knitting needle into his wound four inches deep; but presently after her being seized, he was thoroughly healed.

He further testified that when Carrier and he some times were at variance, she would clap her hands at him, and say he should get nothing by it; whereupon he several times lost his cattle, by strange deaths, whereof no natural causes could be given.

V. John Rogger also testified that upon the threatening words of this malicious Carrier, his cattle would be strangely bewitched; as was more particularly then described.

VI. Samuel Preston testified that about two years ago, having some difference with Martha Carrier, he lost a cow in a strange, preternatural, unusual manner; and about a month after this, the said Carrier, having again some difference with him, she told him he had lately lost a cow, and it should not be long before he lost another; which accordingly came to pass; for he had a thriving and well-kept cow, which without any known cause quickly fell down and died.

VII. Phebe Chandler testified that about a fortnight before the apprehension of Martha Carrier, on a Lordsday,[4] while the Psalm was singing in the Church, this Carrier then took her by the shoulder and shaking her, asked her, where she lived: she made her no answer, although as Carrier, who lived next door to her father's house, could not in reason but know who she was. Quickly after this, as she was at several times crossing the fields, she heard a voice, that she took to be Martha Carrier's, and it seemed as if it was over her head. The voice told her she should within two or three days be poisoned. Accordingly, within such a little time, one half of her right hand became greatly swollen and very painful; as also part of her face: whereof she can give no account how it came. It continued very bad for some days; and several times since she has had a great pain in her breast; and been so seized on her legs that she has hardly been able to go. She added that lately, going well to the house of God, Richard, the son of Martha Carrier, looked very earnestly upon her, and immediately her hand, which had formerly

4. Sunday.

been poisoned, as is abovesaid, began to pain her greatly, and she had a strange burning at her stomach; but was then struck deaf, so that she could not hear any of the prayer, or singing, till the two or three last words of the Psalm.

VIII. One Foster, who confessed her own share in the witchcraft for which the prisoner stood indicted, affirmed that she had seen the prisoner at some of their witch-meetings, and that it was this Carrier, who persuaded her to be a witch. She confessed that the devil carried them on a pole to a witch-meeting; but the pole broke, and she hanging about Carrier's neck, they both fell down, and she then received an hurt by the fall, whereof she was not at this very time recovered.

IX. One Lacy, who likewise confessed her share in this witchcraft, now testified, that she and the prisoner were once bodily present at a witch-meeting in Salem Village; and that she knew the prisoner to be a witch, and to have been at a diabolical sacrament, and that the prisoner was the undoing of her and her children by enticing them into the snare of the devil.

X. Another Lacy, who also confessed her share in this witchcraft, now testified, that the prisoner was at the witch-meeting, in Salem Village, where they had bread and wine administered unto them.

XI. In the time of this prisoner's trial, one Susanna Sheldon in open court had her hands unaccountably tied together with a wheel-band[5] so fast that without cutting, it could not be loosed: it was done by a specter; and the sufferer affirmed it was the prisoner's.

Memorandum. This rampant hag, Martha Carrier, was the person of whom the confessions of the witches, and of her own children among the rest, agreed that the devil had promised her she should be Queen of Hebrews.

1692 1693

5. A strap that goes around a wheel.

FROM MAGNALIA CHRISTI AMERICANA[1]

Galeacius Secundus:[2] The Life of William Bradford, Esq.,
Governor of Plymouth Colony

Omnium Somnos illius vigilantia defendit; omnium otium, illius
Labor; omnium Delicias, illius Industria; omnium vacationem,
illius occupatio.[3]

It has been a matter of some observation, that although Yorkshire be one of
the largest shires in England; yet for all the fires of martyrdom which were
kindled in the days of Queen Mary,[4] it afforded no more fuel than one poor
leaf; namely, John Leaf, an apprentice, who suffered for the doctrine of the
Reformation at the same time and stake with the famous John Bradford.[5]
But when the reign of Queen Elizabeth[6] would not admit the reformation
of worship to proceed unto those degrees, which were proposed and pur-
sued by no small number of the faithful in those days, Yorkshire was not the
least of the shires in England that afforded suffering witnesses thereunto.
The churches there gathered were quickly molested with such a raging per-
secution, that if the spirit of separation in them did carry them unto a fur-
ther extreme than it should have done, one blamable cause thereof will be
found in the extremity of that persecution. Their troubles made that cold
country too hot for them, so that they were under a necessity to seek a retreat
in the Low Countries;[7] and yet the watchful malice and fury of their adver-
saries rendered it almost impossible for them to find what they sought. For
them to leave their native soil, their lands and their friends, and go into a
strange place, where they must hear foreign language, and live meanly and
hardly, and in other employments than that of husbandry,[8] wherein they had
been educated, these must needs have been such discouragements as could
have been conquered by none, save those who sought first the kingdom of
God, and the righteousness thereof. But that which would have made these
discouragements the more unconquerable unto an ordinary faith, was the

1. A History of the Wonderful Works of Christ
in America (Latin). Mather's book is subtitled
*The ecclesiastical History of New England from
its first planting, in the year 1620, unto the year of
our Lord, 1698.* The first of the *Magnalia's* seven
books is concerned with the landing of the first
Europeans in America and the founding and his-
tory of the New England settlements. The sec-
ond presents lives of governors of New England,
including the lives of Bradford and Winthrop
(also see their headnotes, above). The third pre-
sents lives of sixty famous "Divines, by whose
ministry the churches of New England have
been planted and continued." Other books con-
tain a history of Harvard College, a record of
church ordinances passed in synods, and a record
of "illustrious" and "wonderous" events that have
been witnessed by people in New England. The
work was first published in London in 1702; this
text is from that edited by Thomas Robbins
(1853–55), with translations from the Hebrew,
Greek, and Latin by Lucius F. Robinson.
2. The Second Galeazzo (Latin). Galeazzo Car-

accioli (1517–1586) was a Neapolitan nobleman
who converted to Calvinism and moved to
Geneva, Switzerland, where John Calvin's influ-
ence was strong.
3. His vigilance defends the sleep of all; his
labor, their rest; his industry, their pleasures;
and his diligence, their leisure (Latin).
4. During the reign of Mary Tudor (1553–58),
an effort was made to restore Roman Catholi-
cism to the position of a national Church, and a
number of Protestants were executed.
5. Bradford (1510?–1555), burned at the stake
with Leaf on July 1, 1555, for their unorthodox
religious views. Their story was well known from
John Foxe's *Book of Martyrs* (1563).
6. Followed Mary Tudor to the throne (1558–
1603) and by virtue of the Act of Uniformity pre-
scribed traditional church ritual.
7. A number of English Puritans went to Hol-
land to form their own churches without being
accused of treason.
8. Farming. "Meanly": in poverty.

terrible zeal of their enemies to guard all ports, and search all ships, that none of them should be carried off. I will not relate the sad things of this kind then seen and felt by this people of God; but only exemplify those trials with one short story. Divers of these people having hired a Dutchman, then lying at Hull, to carry them over to Holland, he promised faithfully to take them in, between Grimsby and Hull;[9] but they coming to the place a day or two too soon, the appearance of such a multitude alarmed the officers of the town adjoining, who came with a great body of soldiers to seize upon them. Now it happened that one boat full of men had been carried aboard, while the women were yet in a bark that lay aground in a creek at low water. The Dutchman perceiving the storm that was thus beginning ashore, swore by the sacrament that he would stay no longer for any of them; and so taking the advantage of a fair wind then blowing, he put out to sea for Zeeland.[1] The women thus left near Grimsby-common, bereaved of their husbands, who had been hurried from them, and forsaken of their neighbors, of whom none durst in this fright stay with them, were a very rueful spectacle; some crying for fear, some shaking for cold, all dragged by troops of armed and angry men from one Justice to another, till not knowing what to do with them, they even dismissed them to shift as well as they could for themselves. But by their singular afflictions, and by their Christian behaviors, the cause for which they exposed themselves did gain considerably. In the meantime, the men at sea found reason to be glad that their families were not with them, for they were surprised with an horrible tempest, which held them for fourteen days together, in seven whereof they saw not sun, moon or star, but were driven upon the coast of Norway. The mariners often despaired of life, and once with doleful shrieks gave over all, as thinking the vessel was foundered: but the vessel rose again, and when the mariners with sunk hearts often cried out, "We sink! we sink!" the passengers, without such distraction of mind, even while the water was running into their mouths and ears, would cheerfully shout, "Yet, Lord, thou canst save! Yet, Lord, thou canst save!" And the Lord accordingly brought them at last safe unto their desired haven: and not long after helped their distressed relations thither after them, where indeed they found upon almost all accounts a new world, but a world in which they found that they must live like strangers and pilgrims.

Among these devout people was our William Bradford, who was born *Anno* 1588, in an obscure village called Austerfield, where the people were as unacquainted with the Bible, as the Jews do seem to have been with part of it in the days of Josiah;[2] a most ignorant and licentious people, and like unto their priest. Here, and in some other places, he had a comfortable inheritance left him of his honest parents, who died while he was yet a child, and cast him on the education,[3] first of his grandparents, and then of his uncles, who devoted him, like his ancestors, unto the affairs of husbandry. Soon a long sickness kept him, as he would afterwards thankfully say, from the vanities of youth, and made him the fitter for what he was afterwards to undergo. When he was about a dozen years old, the reading of the Scriptures began to

9. Ports in northeast England. "Divers": several.
1. I.e., the Netherlands.
2. King of Judah (c. 638–608 B.C.E.), who was ignorant of the book of the law of the God of

Israel and worshiped false gods (2 Kings 22f.). "*Anno*": in the year (Latin). Austerfield is in Yorkshire.
3. I.e., made his education dependent on.

cause great impressions upon him; and those impressions were much assisted and improved, when he came to enjoy Mr. Richard Clifton's[4] illuminating ministry, not far from his abode; he was then also further befriended, by being brought into the company and fellowship of such as were then called professors, though the young man that brought him into it did after become a profane and wicked apostate.[5] Nor could the wrath of his uncles, nor the scoff of his neighbors, now turned upon him, as one of the Puritans, divert him from his pious inclinations.

At last, beholding how fearfully the evangelical and apostolical church-form, whereinto the churches of the primitive times were cast by the good spirit of God, had been deformed by the apostacy of the succeeding times; and what little progress the Reformation had yet made in many parts of Christendom towards its recovery, he set himself by reading, by discourse, by prayer, to learn whether it was not his duty to withdraw from the communion of the parish-assemblies, and engage with some society of the faithful, that should keep close unto the written Word of God, as the rule of their worship. And after many distresses of mind concerning it, he took up a very deliberate and understanding resolution, of doing so; which resolution he cheerfully prosecuted, although the provoked rage of his friends tried all the ways imaginable to reclaim him from it, unto all whom his answer was:

> Were I like to endanger my life, or consume my estate by any ungodly courses, your counsels to me were very seasonable; but you know that I have been diligent and provident in my calling, and not only desirous to augment what I have, but also to enjoy it in your company; to part from which will be as great a cross as can befall me. Nevertheless, to keep a good conscience, and walk in such a way as God has prescribed in His Word; is a thing which I must prefer before you all, and above life itself. Wherefore, since 'tis for a good cause that I am like to suffer the disasters which you lay before me, you have no cause to be either angry with me, or sorry for me; yea, I am not only willing to part with every thing that is dear to me in this world for this cause, but I am also thankful that God has given me an heart so to do, and will accept me so to suffer for Him.

Some lamented him, some derided him, all dissuaded him: nevertheless, the more they did it, the more fixed he was in his purpose to seek the ordinances of the Gospel, where they should be dispensed with most of the commanded purity; and the sudden deaths of the chief relations which thus lay at him,[6] quickly after convinced him what a folly it had been to have quitted his profession, in expectation of any satisfaction from them. So to Holland he attempted a removal.

Having with a great company of Christians hired a ship to transport them for Holland, the master perfidiously betrayed them into the hands of those persecutors, who rifled and ransacked their goods, and clapped their persons into prison at Boston,[7] where they lay for a month together. But Mr. Bradford being a young man of about eighteen, was dismissed sooner than the rest, so

4. A Puritan minister (d. 1616) in the town of Scrooby, who settled in Amsterdam with the Scrooby Separatists.
5. One who denies what he formerly professed. "Professors": i.e., those who declared their Sepa-
ratist faith.
6. I.e., struck out at him and tried to make him change his beliefs.
7. In England.

that within a while he had opportunity with some others to get over to Zeeland, through perils, both by land and sea not inconsiderable; where he was not long ashore ere a viper seized on his hand—that is, an officer—who carried him unto the magistrates, unto whom an envious passenger had accused him as having fled out of England. When the magistrates understood the true cause of his coming thither, they were well satisfied with him; and so he repaired joyfully unto his brethren at Amsterdam, where the difficulties to which he afterwards stooped in learning and serving of a Frenchman at the working of silks, were abundantly compensated by the delight wherewith he sat under the shadow of our Lord, in His purely dispensed ordinances. At the end of two years, he did, being of age to do it, convert his estate in England into money; but setting up for himself, he found some of his designs by the Providence of God frowned upon, which he judged a correction bestowed by God upon him for certain decays of internal piety, whereinto he had fallen; the consumption of his estate he thought came to prevent a consumption in his virtue. But after he had resided in Holland about half a score years, he was one of those who bore a part in that hazardous and generous enterprise of removing into New England, with part of the English church at Leyden, where, at their first landing, his dearest consort[8] accidently falling overboard, was drowned in the harbor; and the rest of his days were spent in the services, and the temptations, of that American wilderness.

Here was Mr. Bradford, in the year 1621, unanimously chosen the governor of the plantation; the difficulties whereof were such, that if he had not been a person of more than ordinary piety, wisdom and courage, he must have sunk under them. He had, with a laudable industry, been laying up a treasure of experiences, and he had now occasion to use it; indeed, nothing but an experienced man could have been suitable to the necessities of the people. The potent nations of the Indians, into whose country they were come, would have cut them off, if the blessing of God upon his conduct had not quelled them; and if his prudence, justice and moderation had not overruled them, they had been ruined by their own distempers. One specimen of his demeanor is to this day particularly spoken of. A company of young fellows that were newly arrived were very unwilling to comply with the governor's order for working abroad on the public account; and therefore on Christmas Day, when he had called upon them, they excused themselves, with a pretense that it was against their conscience to work such a day.[9] The governor gave them no answer, only that he would spare them till they were better informed; but by and by he found them all at play in the street, sporting themselves with various diversions; whereupon commanding the instruments of their games to be taken from them, he effectually gave them to understand that it was against his conscience that they should play whilst others were at work, and that if they had any devotion to the day, they should show it at home in the exercises of religion, and not in the streets with pastime and frolics; and this gentle reproof put a final stop to all such disorders for the future.

For two years together after the beginning of the colony, whereof he was now governor, the poor people had a great experiment of "man's not living by bread alone";[1] for when they were left all together without one morsel of

8. Wife.
9. Puritans did not observe Christmas as a holi-
day. "Abroad": publicly.
1. Luke 4.4.

bread for many months, one after another, still the good Providence of God relieved them, and supplied them, and this for the most part out of the sea. In this low condition of affairs, there was no little exercise for the prudence and patience of the governor, who cheerfully bore his part in all; and, that industry might not flag, he quickly set himself to settle propriety among the new planters, foreseeing that while the whole country labored upon a common stock, the husbandry and business of the plantation could not flourish, as Plato[2] and others long since dreamed that it would if a community were established. Certainly, if the spirit which dwelt in the old Puritans, had not inspired these new planters, they had sunk under the burden of these difficulties; but our Bradford had a double portion of that spirit.

The plantation was quickly thrown into a storm that almost overwhelmed it, by the unhappy actions of a minister sent over from England by the adventurers[3] concerned for the plantation; but by the blessing of Heaven on the conduct of the governor, they weathered out that storm. Only the adventurers, hereupon breaking to pieces, threw up all their concernments with the infant colony; whereof they gave this as one reason, that the planters dissembled with his Majesty and their friends in their petition, wherein they declared for a church discipline, agreeing with the French and others of the reforming churches in Europe.[4] Whereas 'twas now urged, that they had admitted into their communion a person who at his admission utterly renounced the churches of England, (which person, by the way, was that very man who had made the complaints against them) and therefore, though they denied the name of Brownists,[5] yet they were the thing. In answer hereunto, the very words written by the governor were these:

> Whereas you tax us with dissembling about the French discipline, you do us wrong, for we both hold and practice the discipline of the French and other Reformed Churches (as they have published the same in the Harmony of Confessions) according to our means, in effect and substance. But whereas you would tie us up to the French discipline in every circumstance, you derogate from the liberty we have in Christ Jesus. The Apostle Paul would have none to follow him in any thing, but wherein he follows Christ; much less ought any Christian or church in the world to do it. The French may err, we may err, and other churches may err, and doubtless do in many circumstances. That honor therefore belongs only to the infallible Word of God, and pure Testament of Christ, to be propounded and followed as the only rule and pattern for direction herein to all churches and Christians. And it is too great arrogancy for any man or church to think that he or they have so sounded the Word of God unto the bottom, as precisely to set down the church's discipline without error in substance or circumstance, that no other without blame may digress or differ in any thing from the same. And it is not difficult to show that the reformed churches differ in many circumstances among themselves.

2. Greek philosopher (427?–347 B.C.E.). Much of Plato's *Republic* concerns his ideals of community and government. "Propriety": i.e., property. "Common stock": property held in common.
3. English investors.
4. In Europe, states were declared as either Protestant or Catholic. In France, the Edict of Nantes (1598) provided liberty of conscience for all without denying the authority of the Crown.
5. Robert Browne (c. 1550–1633) was a Separatist clergyman and identified with Congregationalism, a system whereby each church is independent of any national Church.

By which words it appears how far he was free from that rigid spirit of separation, which broke to pieces the Separatists themselves in the Low Countries, unto the great scandal of the reforming churches.[6] He was indeed a person of a well-tempered spirit, or else it had been scarce possible for him to have kept the affairs of Plymouth in so good a temper for thirty-seven years together; in every one of which he was chosen their governor, except the three years wherein Mr. Winslow, and the two years wherein Mr. Prince,[7] at the choice of the people, took a turn with him.

The leader of a people in a wilderness had need be a Moses;[8] and if a Moses had not led the people of Plymouth Colony, where this worthy person was the governor, the people had never with so much unanimity and importunity still called him to lead them. Among many instances thereof, let this one piece of self-denial be told for a memorial of him, wheresoever this history shall be considered: the patent of the colony was taken in his name, running in these terms: "To William Bradford, his heirs, associates, and assigns," but when the number of the freemen[9] was much increased, and many new townships erected, the General Court there desired of Mr. Bradford that he would make a surrender of the same into their hands, which he willingly and presently assented unto, and confirmed it according to their desire by his hand and seal, reserving no more for himself than was his proportion, with others, by agreement. But as he found the Providence of Heaven many ways recompensing his many acts of self-denial, so he gave this testimony to the faithfulness of the Divine Promises: that he had forsaken friends, houses and lands for the sake of the Gospel, and the Lord gave them him again. Here he prospered in his estate; and besides a worthy son which he had by a former wife, he had also two sons and a daughter by another, whom he married in this land.

He was a person for study as well as action; and hence, notwithstanding the difficulties through which he passed in his youth, he attained unto a notable skill in languages: the Dutch tongue was become almost as vernacular to him as the English; the French tongue he could also manage; the Latin and the Greek he had mastered; but the Hebrew he most of all studied, because he said he would see with his own eyes the ancient oracles of God in their native beauty. He was also well skilled in history, in antiquity, and in philosophy; and for theology he became so versed in it, that he was an irrefragable disputant against the errors, especially those of Anabaptism,[1] which with trouble he saw rising in his colony; wherefore he wrote some significant things for the confutation of those errors. But the crown of all was his holy, prayerful, watchful, and fruitful walk with God, wherein he was very exemplary.

At length he fell into an indispositon of body, which rendered him unhealthy for a whole winter; and as the spring advanced, his health yet more declined; yet he felt himself not what he counted sick, till one day, in the night after which, the God of Heaven so filled his mind with ineffable

6. By the time the movement for reform had come to an end, the movement for separating ended in dissension and mutual recrimination, with particular churches arguing which were more pure than the others. Two English Puritans even baptized themselves on the grounds that there were no churches pure enough to baptize them.
7. Thomas Prince (1600–1673). For Edward Winslow, see the "First Encounters" cluster.
8. The Hebrew lawgiver and prophet who led the Israelites out of Egypt into Canaan.
9. I.e., those who are not indentured servants and are able to work for themselves.
1. Unlike the Puritans, Anabaptists opposed the baptism of children and advocated separation of Church and state.

consolations, that he seemed little short of Paul, rapt up unto the unutterable entertainments of Paradise.[2] The next morning he told his friends that the good spirit of God had given him a pledge of his happiness in another world, and the first fruits of his eternal glory; and on the day following he died, May 9, 1657, in the 69th year of his age—lamented by all the colonies of New England as a common blessing and father to them all.

O mihi si Similis Contingat Clausula Vitae![3]
Plato's brief description of a governor, is all that I will now leave as his character, in an

<div align="center">

EPITAPH.

Νομεὺς Τροψὸς ἀγέλης ἀνθρωπίνης[4]

Men are but flocks: Bradford beheld their need,
And long did them at once both rule and feed.

</div>

<div align="right">1702</div>

Nehemias Americanus:[1] The Life of John Winthrop, Esq., Governor of the Massachusetts Colony

<div align="center">

Quicunque Venti erunt, Ars nostra certe non aberit.
—Cicero[2]

</div>

Let Greece boast of her patient Lycurgus,[3] the lawgiver, by whom diligence, temperance, fortitude, and wit were made the fashions of a therefore long-lasting and renowned commonwealth: let Rome tell of her devout Numa,[4] the lawgiver, by whom the most famous commonwealth saw peace triumphing over extinguished war and cruel plunders; and murders giving place to the more mollifying exercises of his religion. Our New England shall tell and boast of her Winthrop, a lawgiver as patient as Lycurgus, but not admitting any of his criminal disorders; as devout as Numa, but not liable to any of his heathenish madnesses; a governor in whom the excellencies of Christianity made a most improving addition unto the virtues, wherein even without those he would have made a parallel for the great men of Greece, or of Rome, which the pen of a Plutarch[5] has eternized.

A stock of heroes by right should afford nothing but what is heroical; and nothing but an extreme degeneracy would make anything less to be expected from a stock of Winthrops. Mr. Adam Winthrop, the son of a worthy

2. In 2 Corinthians 12.2–4, the Apostle Paul describes a man (himself) who experienced a moment in which he "was caught up into paradise, and heard unspeakable words, which it is not lawful for a man to utter."
3. Oh, that such an end of life might come to me (Latin).
4. Shepherd and provider of the human flock (Greek).
1. The American Nehemiah (Latin). As governor of Judea, the biblical Nehemiah rebuilt the walls of Jerusalem (Nehemiah 1.3).

2. *Epistulae ad Familiares* 12.25.5, by the Roman orator Cicero (106–43 B.C.E.): whatever winds may blow, this art of ours can never be lost (Latin).
3. Spartan reformer (ninth century B.C.E.), who reshaped the constitution of Greece and made the nation an efficient military state.
4. Numa Pompilius (715–673 B.C.E.), second legendary king of Rome.
5. Greek biographer (c. 46–120 C.E.), best known for his lives of notable Greeks and Romans.

gentleman wearing the same name, was himself a worthy, a discreet, and a learned gentleman, particularly eminent for skill in the law, nor without remark for[6] love to the gospel, under the reign of King Henry VIII, and brother to a memorable favorer of the Reformed religion in the days of Queen Mary, into whose hands the famous martyr Philpot committed his papers, which afterwards made no inconsiderable part of our martyr-books.[7] This Mr. Adam Winthrop had a son of the same name also, and of the same endowments and employments with his father; and this third Adam Winthrop was the father of that renowned John Winthrop, who was the father of New England, and the founder of a colony, which, upon many accounts, like him that founded it, may challenge the first place among the English glories of America. Our John Winthrop, thus born at the mansion-house of his ancestors, at Groton in Suffolk, on June 12, 1587,[8] enjoyed afterwards an agreeable education. But though he would rather have devoted himself unto the study of Mr. John Calvin, than of Sir Edward Cook;[9] nevertheless, the accomplishments of a lawyer were those wherewith heaven made his chief opportunities to be serviceable.

Being made, at the unusually early age of eighteen, a justice of peace, his virtues began to fall under a more general observation; and he not only so bound himself to the behavior of a Christian, as to become exemplary for a conformity to the laws of Christianity in his own conversation, but also discovered a more than ordinary measure of those qualities which adorn an officer of humane society. His justice was impartial, and used the balance to weigh not the cash, but the case of those who were before him: *prosopolatria* he reckoned as bad as *idolatria*.[1] His wisdom did exquisitely temper things according to the art of governing, which is a business of more contrivance than the seven arts of the schools; *oyer* still went before *terminer* in all his administrations.[2] His courage made him dare to do right, and fitted him to stand among the lions that have sometimes been the supporters of the throne.[3] All which virtues he rendered the more illustrious, by emblazoning them with the constant liberality and hospitality of a gentleman. This made him the terror of the wicked, and the delight of the sober, the envy of the many, but the hope of those who had any hopeful design in hand for the common good of the nation and the interests of religion.

Accordingly, when the noble design of carrying a colony of chosen people into an American wilderness was by some eminent persons undertaken, this eminent person was, by the consent of all, chosen for the Moses,[4] who must

6. I.e., notable for. Mather refers here to Winthrop's grandfather (1498–1562), father (1548–1623), and uncle William (1529–1582).
7. John Philpot (1516–1555), a Puritan martyr burned at the stake, is included in John Foxe's *Book of Martyrs* (1563). Henry VIII (1491–1547) founded the Church of England and was despised by Puritans. Mary Tudor (1516–1558), who reestablished Roman Catholicism in England in 1555, was also hated by Puritans.
8. Should read January 12, 1588.
9. I.e., he would have preferred to study for the ministry and read John Calvin's *Institutes* (1536) rather than prepare for the law by reading Lord Chief Justice Edward Coke's *Institutes of English Law* (1628–44).

1. Worship of false gods (Latin). "*Prosopolatria*": face worship (Latin, literal trans.); i.e., hero worship.
2. I.e., in the parlance of English law, hearing ("*oyer*") all the evidence came before judging ("*terminer*"). "Seven arts": a classical education consisted of the trivium (grammar, rhetoric, and logic) and the quadrivium (arithmetic, music, geometry, and astronomy).
3. Daniel was saved from the Babylonian lions by his faith (Daniel 6.23). King Solomon's throne had carved lions on both sides (1 Kings 10.19–20).
4. Moses was the Hebrew lawgiver and prophet who led the Israelites out of Egypt into Canaan.

be the leader of so great an undertaking: and indeed nothing but a Mosaic spirit could have carried him through the temptations, to which either his farewell to his own land, or his travel in a strange land, must needs expose a gentleman of his education. Wherefore, having sold a fair estate of six or seven hundred[5] a year, he transported himself with the effects of it into New England in the year 1630, where he spent it upon the service of a famous plantation, founded and formed for the seat of the most reformed Christianity: and continued there, conflicting with temptations of all sorts, as many years as the nodes of the moon take to dispatch a revolution.[6] Those persons were never concerned in a new plantation, who know not that the unavoidable difficulties of such a thing will call for all the prudence and patience of a mortal man to encounter therewithal; and they must be very insensible of the influence, which the just wrath of heaven has permitted the devils to have upon this world, if they do not think that the difficulties of a new plantation, devoted unto the evangelical worship of our Lord Jesus Christ, must be yet more than ordinary. How prudently, how patiently, and with how much resignation to our Lord Jesus Christ, our brave Winthrop waded through these difficulties, let posterity consider with admiration. And know, that as the picture of this their governor was, after his death, hung up with honor in the State House of his country, so the wisdom, courage, and holy zeal of his life, were an example well worthy to be copied by all that shall succeed him in government.

Were he now to be considered only as a Christian, we might therein propose him as greatly imitable. He was a very religious man; and as he strictly kept his heart, so he kept his house, under the laws of piety;[7] there he was every day constant in holy duties, both morning and evening, and on the Lord's days, and lectures, though he wrote not after the preacher,[8] yet such was his attention, and such his retention in hearing, that he repeated unto his family the sermons which he had heard in the congregation. But it is chiefly as a governor that he is now to be considered. Being the governor over the considerablest part of New England, he maintained the figure and honor of his place with the spirit of a true gentleman; but yet with such obliging condescension[9] to the circumstances of the colony, that when a certain troublesome and malicious calumniator, well known in those times, printed his libelous nicknames upon the chief persons here, the worst nickname he could find for the governor was John Temperwell;[1] and when the calumnies of that ill man caused the Archbishop to summon one Mr. Cleaves before the King, in hopes to get some accusation from him against the country,[2] Mr. Cleaves gave such an account of the governor's laudable carriage in all respects, and the serious devotion wherewith prayers were both publicly and privately made for his Majesty, that the King expressed himself most highly

5. I.e., English pounds.
6. Approximately the same number of years that Winthrop lived in Massachusetts: 18.6. In astronomy, a "node" is either of two diametrically opposite points at which the orbit (or revolution) of a planet intersects the ecliptic.
7. "For if a man know not how to rule his own house, how shall he take care of the church of God?" (1 Timothy 3.5).
8. I.e., although he did not take the sermon

down in shorthand. "Lectures": days on which less formal sermons were delivered.
9. Concern, care.
1. In chapter 23 of the fourth book of *New English Canaan* (1637), by Thomas Morton (see his headnote, above).
2. George Cleaves settled in Maine in 1630 and returned to England in 1636. Archbishop William Laud (1573–1645) was an enemy of the Puritans.

pleased therewithal, only sorry that so worthy a person should be no better accommodated than with the hardships of America. He was, indeed, a governor, who had most exactly studied that book which, pretending to teach politics, did only contain three leaves, and but one word in each of those leaves, which word was, MODERATION. Hence, though he were a zealous enemy to all vice, yet his practice was according to his judgment thus expressed: "In the infancy of plantations, justice should be administered with more lenity than in a settled state; because people are more apt then to transgress; partly out of ignorance of new laws and orders, partly out of oppression of business, and other straits. [LENTO GRADU][3] was the old rule; and if the strings of a new instrument be wound up unto their height, they will quickly crack." But when some leading and learned men took offense at his conduct in this matter, and upon a conference gave it in as their opinion, "That a stricter discipline was to be used in the beginning of a plantation, than after its being with more age established and confirmed," the governor being readier to see his own errors than other men's, professed his purpose to endeavor their satisfaction with less of lenity in his administrations. At that conference there were drawn up several other articles to be observed between the governor and the rest of the magistrates, which were of this import: That the magistrates, as far as might be, should aforehand ripen their consultations, to produce that unanimity in their public votes, which might make them liker to the voice of God; that if differences fell out among them in their public meetings, they should speak only to the case, without any reflection,[4] with all due modesty, and but by way of question; or desire the deferring of the cause to further time; and after sentence to imitate privately no dislike; that they should be more familiar, friendly and open unto each other, and more frequent in their visitations, and not any way expose each other's infirmities, but seek the honor of each other, and all the court; that one magistrate shall not cross the proceedings of another, without first advising with him, and that they should in all their appearances abroad, be so circumstanced as to prevent all contempt of authority; and that they should support and strengthen all under-officers. All of which articles were observed by no man more than by the governor himself.

But whilst he thus did, as our New English Nehemiah, the part of a ruler in managing the public affairs of our American Jerusalem, when there were Tobijahs and Sanballats enough to vex him,[5] and give him the experiment of Luther's observation, *Omnis qui regit est tanquam signum, in quod omnia jacula, Satan et Mundus dirigunt*;[6] he made himself still an exacter parallel unto that governor of Israel, by doing the part of a neighbor among the distressed people of the new plantation. To teach them the frugality necessary for those times, he abridged himself of a thousand comfortable things, which he had allowed himself elsewhere: his habit was not that soft raiment, which would have been disagreeable to a wilderness;[7] his table was not covered with

3. By slow degrees (Latin).
4. I.e., without imputing any ill will on the part of another.
5. Both the governor of Samaria, Sanballat, and a Persian officer, Tobijah, opposed the rebuilding of the walls of Jerusalem (Nehemiah 2.10, 4.7).

6. From the *Loci Communes*, by the Protestant reformer Martin Luther (1483–1546): a man in authority is a target at which Satan and the world launch all their darts (Latin).
7. "But what went ye out for to see? A man clothed in soft raiment? behold, they that wear soft clothing are in kings' houses" (Matthew 11.8).

the superfluities that would have invited unto sensualities: water was commonly his own drink, though he gave wine to others. But at the same time his liberality unto the needy was even beyond measure generous; and therein he was continually causing "the blessing of him that was ready to perish to come upon him, and the heart of the widow and the orphan to sing for joy,"[8] but none more than those of deceased ministers, whom he always treated with a very singular compassion; among the instances whereof we still enjoy with us the worthy and now aged son of that Reverend Higginson, whose death left his family in a wide world soon after his arrival here, publicly acknowledging the charitable Winthrop for his foster-father.[9] It was oftentimes no small trial unto his faith, to think how a table for the people should be furnished when they first came into the wilderness![1] and for very many of the people his own good works were needful, and accordingly employed for the answering of his faith. Indeed, for a while the governor was the Joseph, unto whom the whole body of the people repaired when their corn failed them,[2] and he continued relieving of them with his open-handed bounties, as long as he had any stock to do it with; and a lively faith to see the return of the "bread after many days,"[3] and not starve in the days that were to pass till that return should be seen, carried him cheerfully through those expenses.

Once it was observable that, on February 5, 1630,[4] when he was distributing the last handful of the meal in the barrel unto a poor man distressed by the "wolf at the door," at that instant they spied a ship arrived at the harbor's mouth, laden with provisions for them all. Yea, the governor sometimes made his own private purse to be the public: not by sucking into it, but by squeezing out of it; for when the public treasure had nothing in it, he did himself defray the charges of the public. And having learned that lesson of our Lord, "that it is better to give than to receive," he did, at the General Court,[5] when he was a third time chosen governor, make a speech unto this purpose: That he had received gratuities from divers[6] towns, which he accepted with much comfort and content; and he had likewise received civilities from particular persons, which he could not refuse without incivility in himself: nevertheless, he took them with a trembling heart, in regard of God's word, and the conscience of his own infirmities; and therefore he desired them that they would not hereafter take it ill if he refused such presents for the time to come. 'Twas his custom also to send some of his family upon errands unto the houses of the poor, about their mealtime, on purpose to spy whether they wanted;[7] and if it were found that they wanted, he would make that the opportunity of sending supplies unto them. And there was

8. Job 29.13.
9. Francis Higginson (1587–1630) died after only a year's residence in Salem. His "aged son" John (1616–1708) wrote an "Attestation" prefixed to the *Magnalia*.
1. "Yea, they spake against God; they said, Can God furnish a table in the wilderness?" (Psalm 78.19).
2. "And the famine was over all the face of the earth: And Joseph opened all the storehouses, and sold unto the Egyptians; and the famine waxed sore in the land of Egypt" (Genesis 41.56).
3. "Cast thy bread upon the waters: for thou shalt find it after many days" (Ecclesiastes 11.1).

4. Old Style. The present (Gregorian), calendar, designating January 1 as the first day of the year, was adopted in England in 1752. Earlier, March 25 had served as the first day of the calendar year.
5. Then the governing body of Massachusetts. "I have shewed you all things, how that so labouring ye ought to support the weak, and to remember the words of the Lord Jesus, how he said, It is more blessed to give than to receive" (Acts 20.35).
6. Several.
7. I.e., were needy.

one passage of his charity that was perhaps a little unusual: in an hard and long winter, when wood was very scarce at Boston, a man gave him a private information that a needy person in the neighborhood stole wood sometimes from his pile; whereupon the governor in a seeming anger did reply, "Does he so? I'll take a course with him;[8] go, call that man to me; I'll warrant you I'll cure him of stealing." When the man came, the governor considering that if he had stolen, it was more out of necessity than disposition, said unto him, "Friend, it is a severe winter, and I doubt you are but meanly[9] provided for wood; wherefore I would have you supply yourself at my woodpile till this cold season be over." And he then merrily asked his friends whether he had not effectually cured this man of stealing his wood.

One would have imagined that so good a man could have had no enemies, if we had not had a daily and woeful experience to convince us that goodness itself will make enemies. It is a wonderful speech of Plato (in one of his books, *De Republica*), "For the trial of true virtue, 'tis necessary that a good man μηδέν αδικῶ, δοξαν εχει την μεγιστην άδικιας: Though he do no unjust thing, should suffer the infamy of the greatest injustice."[1] The governor had by his unspotted integrity procured himself a great reputation among the people; and then the crime of popularity was laid unto his charge by such, who were willing to deliver him from the danger of having all men speak well of him.[2] Yea, there were persons eminent both for figure and for number, unto whom it was almost essential to dislike everything that came from him; and yet he always maintained an amicable correspondence with them; as believing that they acted according to their judgment and conscience, or that their eyes were held by some temptation in the worst of all their oppositions. Indeed, his right works were so many, that they exposed him unto the envy of his neighbors,[3] and of such power was that envy, that sometimes he could not stand before it; but it was by not standing that he most effectually withstood it all.[4] Great attempts were sometimes made among the freemen to get him left out from his place in the government upon little pretenses, lest by the too frequent choice of one man, the government should cease to be by choice; and with a particular aim at him, sermons were preached at the anniversary Court of Election, to dissuade the freemen from choosing one man twice together. This was the reward of his extraordinary serviceableness! But when these attempts did succeed, as they sometimes did, his profound humility appeared in that equality of mind, wherewith he applied himself cheerfully to serve the country in whatever station their votes had allotted for him. And one year when the votes came to be numbered, there were found six less for Mr. Winthrop than for another gentleman who then stood in competition: but several other persons regularly tendering their votes before the election was published, were, upon a very frivolous objection, refused by some of the magistrates that were afraid lest the election should at last fall upon Mr. Winthrop: which,

8. I.e., I'll hassle, persecute or trouble, or even thrash him.
9. Meagerly.
1. From *The Republic*, by the Greek philosopher Plato (427?–347 B.C.E.).
2. "Woe unto you, when all men shall speak well of you! for so did their fathers to the false prophets" (Luke 6.26).
3. "Again, I consider all travail, and every right work, that for this a man is envied of his neighbour. This is also vanity and vexation of spirit" (Ecclesiastes 4.4).
4. "Wrath is cruel, and anger is outrageous; but who is able to stand before envy?" (Proverbs 27.4).

though it was well perceived, yet such was the self-denial of this patriot, that he would not permit any notice to be taken of the injury. But these trials were nothing in comparison of those harsher and harder treats which he sometimes had from the forwardness of not a few in the days of their paroxysms; and from the faction of some against him, not much unlike that of the Piazzi in Florence against the family of the Medicis:[5] all of which he at last conquered by conforming to the famous Judge's motto, *Prudens qui Patiens*.[6] The oracles of God have said, "Envy is rottenness to the bones;"[7] and Gulielmus Parisiensis[8] applies it unto rulers, who are as it were the bones of the societies which they belong unto: "Envy," says he, "is often found among them, and it is rottenness unto them." Our Winthrop encountered this envy from others, but conquered it, by being free from it himself.

Were it not for the sake of introducing the exemplary skill of this wise man, at giving soft answers, one would not choose to relate those instances of wrath which he had sometimes to encounter with; but he was for his gentleness, his forbearance, and longanimity,[9] a pattern so worthy to be written *after*, that something must here be written *of* it. He seemed indeed never to speak any other language than that of Theodosius: "If any man speak evil of the governor, if it be through lightness, 'tis to be contemned;[1] if it be through madness, 'tis to be pitied; if it be through injury, 'tis to be remitted." Behold, reader, the "meekness of wisdom" notably exemplified! There was a time when he received a very sharp letter from a gentleman who was a member of the Court,[2] but he delivered back the letter unto the messengers that brought it, with such a Christian speech as this: "I am not willing to keep such a matter of provocation by me!" Afterwards the same gentleman was compelled by scarcity of provisions to send unto him that he would sell him some of his cattle; whereupon the governor prayed him to accept what he had sent for as a token of his good will; but the gentleman returned him this answer: "Sir, your overcoming of yourself hath overcome me:" and afterwards gave demonstration of it.

The French have a saying that *"Un honesté homme, est un homme mesle!"*—a good man is a mixed man; and there hardly ever was a more sensible mixture of those two things, resolution and condescension,[3] than in this good man. There was a time when the Court of Election being, for fear of tumult, held at Cambridge, May 17, 1637, the sectarian part of the country, who had the year before gotten a governor more unto their mind,[4] had a project now to have confounded the election, by demanding that the court would consider a petition then tendered before their proceeding thereunto. Mr. Winthrop saw that this was only a trick to throw all into confusion, by putting off the choice of the governor and assistants until the day should be over; and therefore he did, with a strenuous resolution, procure a disappointment unto

5. In 1478, an important member of the Medici family was assassinated by one of the Piazzis, and all Italy became involved in the war that followed. "Forwardness": brashness. "Paroxysms": paroxysms; fits of rage.
6. He is prudent who is patient (Latin), a maxim attributed to Sir Edward Coke.
7. "A sound heart is the life of the flesh: but envy the rottenness of the bones" (Proverbs 14.30).
8. William of Saint Amour (d. 1272), bishop of Paris and a satirist.

9. Patience.
1. Despised. Theodosius Flavius I (346–395 C.E.) was a Christian Roman emperor.
2. Thomas Dudley (1576–1653), who several times served as governor of the Massachusetts Bay Colony.
3. Humility.
4. Sir Henry Vane returned to England in 1637; he was sympathetic toward the views expressed by the followers of Anne Hutchinson.

that mischievous and ruinous contrivance. Nevertheless, Mr. Winthrop himself being by the voice of the freemen in this exigency chosen the governor, and all of the other party left out, that ill-affected party discovered the dirt and mire, which remained with them, after the storm was over; particularly the sergeants, whose office 'twas to attend the governor, laid down their halberds;[5] but such was the condescension of this governor, as to take no present notice of this anger and contempt, but only order some of his own servants to take the halberds; and when the country manifested their deep resentments of the affront thus offered him, he prayed them to overlook it. But it was not long before a compensation was made for these things by the doubled respects which were from all parts paid unto him. Again, there was a time when the suppression of an *Antinomian* and *Familistical* faction,[6] which extremely threatened the ruin of the country, was generally thought much owing unto this renowned man; and therefore when the friends of that faction could not wreak[7] their displeasure on him with any politic vexations, they set themselves to do it by ecclesiastical ones. Accordingly, when a sentence of banishment was passed on the ringleaders of those disturbances, who

> ——*Maria et Terras, Cœlumque profundum,*
> *Quippe ferant Rapidi, secum vertantque per Auras;*[8]

many at the church of Boston, who were then that way too much inclined, most earnestly solicited the elders of that church, whereof the governor was a member, to call him forth as an offender, for passing of that sentence. The elders were unwilling to do any such thing; but the governor understanding the ferment among the people took that occasion to make a speech in the congregation to this effect:

> BRETHREN: Understanding that some of you have desired that I should answer for an offense lately taken among you; had I been called upon so to do, I would, first, have advised[9] with the ministers of the country, whether the church had power to call in question the civil court; and I would, secondly, have advised with the rest of the court, whether I might discover their counsels unto the church. But though I know that the reverend Elders of this church, and some others, do very well apprehend that the church cannot inquire into the proceedings of the court; yet, for the satisfaction of the weaker, who do not apprehend it, I will declare my mind concerning it. If the church have any such power, they have it from the Lord Jesus Christ; but the Lord Jesus Christ hath disclaimed it, not only by practice, but also by precept, which we have in his gospel, Matt. xx. 25, 26.[1] It is true, indeed, that magistrates, as they are church-members, are accountable unto the church for their failings; but that is when they are out of their calling. When Uzziah would go

5. Weapons that are a combination spear and battle-ax.
6. Both Antinomianism and Familism (a word derived from an English religious sect called the Family of Love) hold the regenerate (i.e., "born-again") self above ecclesiastical and civil law.
7. Inflict.
8. *Aeneid* 1.59–60, by the Roman poet Virgil (70–19 B.C.E.): "Rack sea and land and sky with mingled wrath. / In the wild tumult of their stormy path."
9. Consulted.
1. "But Jesus called them unto him, and said, Ye know that the princes of the Gentiles exercise dominion over them, and they that are great exercise authority upon them. But it shall not be so among you: but whosoever will be great among you, let him be your minister."

offer incense in the temple, the officers of the church called him to an account, and withstood him; but when Asa put the prophet in prison,[2] the officers of the church did not call him to an account for that. If the magistrate shall in a private way wrong any man, the church may call him to an account for it; but if he be in pursuance of a course of justice, though the thing that he does be unjust, yet he is not accountable for it before the church. As for myself, I did nothing in the causes of any of the brethren but by the advice of the Elders of the church. Moreover, in the oath which I have taken there is this clause: "In all cases wherein you are to give your vote, you shall do as in your judgment and conscience you shall see to be just, and for the public good." And I am satisfied, it is most for the glory of God, and the public good, that there has been such a sentence passed; yea, those brethren are so divided from the rest of the country in their opinions and practices, that it cannot stand with the public peace for them to continue with us; Abraham saw that Hagar and Ishmael must be sent away.[3]

By such a speech he marvelously convinced, satisfied and mollified the uneasy brethren of the church; *Sic cunctus Pelagi cecidit Fragor*[4]———. And after a little patient waiting, the differences all so wore away, that the church, merely as a token of respect unto the governor when he had newly met with some losses in his estate, sent him a present of several hundreds of pounds.

Once more there was a time when some active spirits among the deputies of the colony, by their endeavors not only to make themselves a Court of Judicature, but also to take away the negative by which the magistrates might check their votes, had like by over-driving[5] to have run the whole government into something too democratical. And if there was a town in Spain undermined by coneys, another town in Thrace destroyed by moles, a third in Greece ranversed[6] by frogs, a fourth in Germany subverted by rats; I must on this occasion add, that there was a country in America like to be confounded by a swine. A certain stray sow being found, was claimed by two several persons with a claim so equally maintained on both sides, that after six or seven years' hunting the business from one court unto another, it was brought at last into the General Court, where the final determination was "that it was impossible to proceed unto any judgment in the case." However, in the debate of this matter, the negative of the upper-house upon the lower in that court was brought upon the stage; and agitated with so hot a zeal, that a little more, and all had been in the fire. In these agitations, the governor was informed that an offense had been taken by some eminent persons at certain passages in a discourse by him written thereabout; whereupon, with his usual condescendency, when he next came into the General Court, he made a speech of this import:

I understand that some have taken offense at something that I have lately written; which offense I desire to remove now, and begin this year

2. Asa, the third king of Judea, put the prophet Hanani in prison when he accused Asa of not relying on the Lord (2 Chronicles 16.7–10). Uzziah, king of Judea, was afflicted with leprosy when he tried to burn incense on the altar despite the protests of the priests (2 Chronicles 26.18).
3. Ishmael was the son of Abraham and Hagar, who was a servant of Abraham's wife. Abraham sent Hagar and Ishmael into the wilderness at his wife's insistence (Genesis 16.1–16, 21.9–14).
4. "To silence sunk the thunder of the wave" (*Aeneid* 1.154).
5. Pushing too hard.
6. Overturned. "Coneys": rabbits.

in a reconciled state with you all. As for the matter of my writing, I had the concurrence of my brethren; it is a point of judgment which is not at my own disposing. I have examined it over and over again by such light as God has given me, from the rules of religion, reason and custom; and I see no cause to retract anything of it: wherefore I must enjoy my liberty in that, as you do yourselves. But for the manner, this, and all that was blameworthy in it, was wholly my own; and whatsoever I might allege for my own justification therein before men, I wave it, as now setting myself before another Judgment seat. However, what I wrote was upon great provocation, and to vindicate myself and others from great aspersion; yet that was no sufficient warrant for me to allow any distemper of spirit in myself; and I doubt I have been too prodigal of my brethren's reputation; I might have maintained my cause without casting any blemish upon others, when I made that my conclusion, "And now let religion and sound reason give judgment in the case;" it looked as if I arrogated too much unto myself, and too little to others. And when I made that profession, "That I would maintain what I wrote before all the world," though such words might modestly be spoken, yet I perceive an unbeseeming pride of my own heart breathing in them. For these failings, I ask pardon of God and man.

> *Sic ait, et dicto citius Tumida Æquora placat,*
> *Collectasque fugat Nubes, Solemque reducit.*[7]

This acknowledging disposition in the governor made them all acknowledge that he was truly "a man of an excellent spirit."[8] In fine, the victories of an Alexander, an Hannibal, or a Cæsar[9] over other men were not so glorious as the victories of this great man over himself, which also at last proved victories over other men.

But the stormiest of all the trials that ever befell this gentleman was in the year 1645, when he was, in title, no more than deputy governor of the colony. If the famous Cato were forty-four times called into judgment but as often acquitted; let it not be wondered, and if[1] our famous Winthrop were one time so. There happening certain seditious and mutinous practices in the town of Hingham,[2] the deputy governor, as legally as prudently, interposed his authority for the checking of them: whereupon there followed such an enchantment[3] upon the minds of the deputies in the General Court, that upon a scandalous petition of the delinquents unto them, wherein a pretended invasion made upon the liberties of the people was complained of, the deputy governor was most irregularly called forth unto an ignominious hearing before them in a vast assembly; whereto with a sagacious humilitude he consented, although he showed them how he might have refused it. The result of that hearing was, that notwithstanding the touchy jealousy of the people about

7. "He speaks—but ere the word is said, / Each mounting billow droops its head, / And brightening clouds one moment stay / To pioneer returning day" (*Aeneid* 1.142–43).
8. "He that hath knowledge spareth his words: and a man of understanding is of an excellent spirit" (Proverbs 17.27).
9. Julius Caesar (100–44 B.C.E.), Roman general and statesman. "In fine": in conclusion. Alexander the Great (356–323 B.C.E.), king of Macedonia. Hannibal (247–183 B.C.E.), Carthaginian general.
1. "And if" is an archaic form of *if*. Cato (234–149 B.C.E.) was a Roman orator.
2. About twenty-five miles south of Boston; these challenges to authority were made against the captain of the town militia, who was appointed by the state authorities.
3. I.e., a delusion in judgment.

their liberties lay at the bottom of all this prosecution, yet Mr. Winthrop was publicly acquitted, and the offenders were severally fined and censured. But Mr. Winthrop then resuming the place of deputy governor on the bench, saw cause to speak unto the root of the matter after this manner:[4]

I shall not now speak anything about the past proceedings of this Court, or the persons therein concerned. Only I bless God that I see an issue[5] of this troublesome affair. I am well satisfied that I was publicly accused, and that I am now publicly acquitted. But though I am justified before men, yet it may be the Lord hath seen so much amiss in my administrations, as calls me to be humbled; and indeed for me to have been thus charged by men, is itself a matter of humiliation, whereof I desire to make a right use before the Lord. If Miriam's father spit in her face, she is to be ashamed.[6] But give me leave, before you go, to say something that may rectify the opinions of many people, from whence the distempers have risen that have lately prevailed upon the body of this people. The questions that have troubled the country have been about the authority of the magistracy, and the liberty of the people. It is you who have called us unto this office; but being thus called, we have our authority from God; it is the ordinance of God, and it hath the image of God stamped upon it; and the contempt of it has been vindicated by God with terrible examples of his vengeance. I entreat you to consider, that when you choose magistrates, you take them from among yourselves, "men subject unto like passions with yourselves." If you see our infirmities, reflect on your own, and you will not be so severe censurers of ours. We count him a good servant who breaks not his covenant:[7] the covenant between us and you is the oath you have taken of us, which is to this purpose, "that we shall govern you, and judge your causes, according to God's laws, and our own, according to our best skill." As for our skill, you must run the hazard of it; and if there be an error, not in the will, but only in skill, it becomes you to bear it. Nor would I have you to mistake in the point of your own liberty. There is a liberty of corrupt nature, which is affected both by men and beasts, to do what they list;[8] and this liberty is inconsistent with authority, impatient of all restraint; by this liberty, *Sumus Omnes Deteriores*,[9] 'tis the grand enemy of truth and peace, and all the ordinances of God are bent against it. But there is a civil, a moral, a federal liberty, which is the proper end and object of authority; it is a liberty for that only which is just and good; for this liberty you are to stand with the hazard of your very lives; and whatsoever crosses it is not authority, but a distemper thereof. This liberty is maintained in a way of subjection to authority; and the authority set over you will in all administrations for your good be quietly submitted unto, by all but such as have a disposition to shake off the yoke, and

4. "But ye should say, Why persecute we him, seeing the root of the matter is found in me?" (Job 19.28).
5. End, outcome.
6. Miriam, Moses' sister, was punished for challenging his choice in a wife: "And the Lord said unto Moses, If her father had but spit in her face, should she not be ashamed seven days? let her be shut out from the camp seven days, and after that let her be received in again" (Numbers 12.14).
7. Contract, formal agreement.
8. Want, like.
9. From *Heauton Timorumenos* 3.1.74, by the Roman dramatist Terence (c. 190–159 B.C.E.): "We are all the worse for it" (Latin).

lose their true liberty, by their murmuring at the honor and power of authority.

The spell that was upon the eyes of the people being thus dissolved, their distorted and enraged notions of things all vanished; and the people would not afterwards entrust the helm of the weather-beaten bark[1] in any other hands but Mr. Winthrop's until he died.

Indeed, such was the mixture of distant qualities in him, as to make a most admirable temper; and his having a certain greatness of soul, which rendered him grave, generous, courageous, resolved, well-applied, and every way a gentleman in his demeanor, did not hinder him from taking sometimes the old Roman's way to avoid confusions, namely, *Cedendo*;[2] or from discouraging some things which are agreeable enough to most that wear the name of gentlemen. Hereof I will give no instances, but only oppose two passages of his life.

In the year 1632, the governor, with his pastor, Mr. Wilson,[3] and some other gentlemen, to settle a good understanding between the two colonies, traveled as far as Plymouth, more than forty miles, through an howling wilderness, no better accommodated in those early days than the princes that in Solomon's time saw "servants on horseback," or than genus and species in the old epigram, "going on foot."[4] The difficulty of the walk was abundantly compensated by the honorable, first reception, and then dismission, which they found from the rulers of Plymouth, and by the good correspondence thus established between the new colonies, who were like the floating bottles wearing this motto: *Si Collidimur Frangimur.*[5] But there were at this time in Plymouth two ministers,[6] leavened so far with the humors of the rigid Separation, that they insisted vehemently upon the unlawfulness of calling any unregenerate man by the name of "Goodman Such-an-One,"[7] until by their indiscreet urging of this whimsy, the place began to be disquieted. The wiser people being troubled at these trifles, they took the opportunity of Governor Winthrop's being there, to have the thing publicly propounded in the congregation; who in answer thereunto, distinguished between a theological and a moral goodness; adding, that when juries were first used in England, it was usual for the crier, after the names of persons fit for that service were called over, to bid them all, "Attend, good men and true;" whence it grew to be a civil custom in the English nation, for neighbors living by one another, to call one another "Goodman Such-an-One;" and it was [a] pity now to make a stir about a civil custom, so innocently introduced. And that speech of Mr. Winthrop's put a lasting stop to the little, idle, whimsical conceits, then beginning to grow obstreperous.

Nevertheless, there was one civil custom used in (and in few but) the English nation, which this gentleman did endeavor to abolish in this country; and that was, the usage of drinking to one another. For although by

1. Ship.
2. By yielding the point (Latin).
3. John Wilson (c. 1591–1667).
4. Better on foot go, than a wicked horse to ride (adage). "Servants on horseback": a reference to Ecclesiastes 10.7 ("I have seen servants upon horses, and princes walking as servants upon the earth"). The Book of Ecclesiastes was mistakenly attributed to Solomon.

5. If we come into collision, we break (Latin).
6. Ralph Smith (1590–1661), Plymouth's first minister (1629–36), and Roger Williams, who briefly assisted him (see Williams's headnote, above), were both Separatists.
7. I.e., they reserved the title "Goodman" for those who were regenerate "saints" in full good standing with the church.

drinking to one another, no more is meant than an act of courtesy, when one going to drink, does invite another to do so too, for the same ends with himself, nevertheless the governor (not altogether unlike to Cleomenes, of whom 'tis reported by Plutarch, ἄκοντι οὐδεὶς ποτήριον προσφερε, *Nolenti poculum nunquam prœbuit*,)[8] considered the impertinency and insignificancy of this usage, as to any of those ends that are usually pretended for it; and that indeed it ordinarily served for no ends at all, but only to provoke persons unto unseasonable and perhaps unreasonable drinking, and at last produce that abominable health-drinking, which the Fathers of old[9] so severely rebuked in the pagans, and which the Papists themselves do condemn, when their casuists pronounce it, *Peccatum mortale, provocare ad Æquales Calices, et Nefas Respondere*.[1] Wherefore in his own most hospitable house he left it off; not out of any silly or stingy fancy, but merely that by his example a greater temperance, with liberty of drinking, might be recommended, and sundry inconveniences in drinking avoided; and his example accordingly began to be much followed by the sober people in this country, as it now also begins among persons of the highest rank in the English nation itself; until an order of court came to be made against that ceremony in drinking, and then, the old wont violently returned, with a *Nitimur in Vetitum*.[2]

Many were the afflictions of this righteous man![3] He lost much of his estate in a ship, and in an house, quickly after his coming to New England, besides the prodigious expense of it in the difficulties of his first coming hither. Afterwards his assiduous application unto the public affairs, (wherein *Ipse se non habuit, postquam Republica eum Gubernatorem habere cœpit*)[4] made him so much to neglect his own private interests, that an unjust[5] steward ran him £2,500 in debt before he was aware; for the payment whereof he was forced, many years before his decease, to sell the most of what he had left unto him in the country. Albeit, by the observable blessings of God upon the posterity of this liberal man, his children all of them came to fair estates, and lived in good fashion and credit. Moreover, he successively buried three wives; the first of which was the daughter and heiress of Mr. Forth, of Much Stambridge in Essex, by whom he had "wisdom with an inheritance;" and an excellent son.[6] The second was the daughter of Mr. William Clopton, of London, who died with her child, within a very little while. The third was the daughter of the truly worshipful Sir John Tyndal,[7] who made it her whole care to please, first God, and then her husband; and by whom he had four sons, which survived and honored their father. And unto all these, the addition of the distempers, ever now and then raised in the country, procured

8. Never urge the reluctant to drink (Greek, Latin). Plutarch (c. 46–120 C.E.) writes about the Spartan king Cleomenes III (r. 235–222 B.C.E.) in his *Parallel Lives*.
9. I.e., Church fathers.
1. It is a deadly sin to challenge another to a drinking match, and it is impious to accept such challenges (Latin). "Casuists": sophists; theological quibblers.
2. From *Amores* 3.4.17, by the Roman poet Ovid (43 B.C.E.–c. 17 C.E.): "A bias toward the forbidden usage" (Latin).
3. "Many are the afflictions of the righteous: but

the Lord delivereth him of them all" (Psalm 34.19).
4. He no longer belonged to himself, after the Republic had once made him her chief magistrate (Latin).
5. Injudicious.
6. Winthrop married Mary Forth (1583–1615) in 1606. They had six children but only one, John (b. 1606), survived his father. "Much Stambridge": now known as Great Stambridge.
7. Winthrop married Thomasine Clopton (1583–1616) in 1615 and Margaret Tyndal in 1618.

unto him a very singular share of trouble; yea, so hard was the measure which he found even among pious men, in the temptations of a wilderness, that when the thunder and lightning had smitten a windmill whereof he was owner, some had such things in their heads as publicly to reproach this charitablest of men as if the voice of the Almighty had rebuked, I know not what oppression, which they judged him guilty of; which things I would not have mentioned, but that the instances may fortify the expectations of my best readers for such afflictions.

He that had been for his attainments, as they said of the blessed Macarius,[8] a παιδαριογερων, (an old man, while a young one,) and that had in his young days met with many of those ill days, whereof he could say, he had "little pleasure in them;" now found old age in its infirmities advancing earlier upon him, than it came upon his much longer-lived progenitors. While he was yet seven years off of that which we call "the grand climacterical,"[9] he felt the approaches of his dissolution; and finding he could say,

> Non Habitus, non ipse Color, non Gressus Euntis,
> Non Species Eadem, quæ fuit ante, manet.[1]

He then wrote this account of himself: "Age now comes upon me, and infirmities therewithal, which makes me apprehend, that the time of my departure out of this world is not far off.[2] However, our times are all in the Lord's hand, so as we need not trouble our thoughts how long or short they may be, but how we may be found faithful when we are called for." But at last when that year came, he took a cold which turned into a fever, whereof he lay sick about a month, and in that sickness, as it hath been observed, that there was allowed unto the serpent the "bruising of the heel;"[3] and accordingly at the heel or the close of our lives the old serpent will be nibbling more than ever in our lives before; and when the devil sees that we shall shortly be, "where the wicked cease from troubling," that wicked one will trouble us more than ever; so this eminent saint now underwent sharp conflicts with the tempter, whose wrath grew great, as the time to exert it grew short; and he was buffeted with the disconsolate thoughts of black and sore desertions, wherein he could use that sad representation of his own condition:

> Nuper eram Judex; Jam Judicor; Ante Tribunal
> Subsistens paveo; Judicor ipse modo.[4]

But it was not long before those clouds were dispelled, and he enjoyed in his holy soul the great consolations of God! While he thus lay ripening for heaven, he did out of obedience unto the ordinance of our Lord send for the Elders of the church to pray with him; yea, they and the whole church fasted as well as prayed for him; and in that fast the venerable Cotton[5] preached on Psalm 35.13–14: "When they were sick, I humbled myself with fasting; I

8. A fourth-century Egyptian believed to have accomplished much while still young.
9. I.e., when he was fifty-six. "Grand climacterical"; age sixty-three.
1. From *Elegies* 1.210–11, by the sixth-century Roman poet Maximianus: "I am not what I was in form or face, / In healthful color or in vigorous pace" (Latin).
2. "For I am now ready to be offered, and the time of my departure is at hand" (2 Timothy 4.6).

3. In his anger after the Fall, God tells the devil (in the form of a serpent): "And I will put enmity between thee and the woman, and between thy seed and her seed; it shall bruise thy head, and thou shalt bruise his heel" (Genesis 3.15).
4. "I once judged others, but now trembling stand / Before a dread tribunal, to be judged" (Latin).
5. John Cotton (1584–1652), Mather's grandfather and namesake.

behaved myself as though he had been my friend or brother; I bowed down heavily, as one that mourned for his mother." From whence I find him raising that observation, "The sickness of one that is to us as a friend, a brother, a mother, is a just occasion of deep humbling our souls with fasting and prayer;" and making this application:

> Upon this occasion we are now to attend this duty for a governor, who has been to us as a friend in his counsel for all things, and help for our bodies by physic, for our estates by law, and of whom there was no fear of his becoming an enemy, like the friends of David:[6] a governor who has been unto us as a brother; not usurping authority over the church; often speaking his advice, and often contradicted, even by young men, and some of low degree; yet not replying, but offering satisfaction also when any supposed offenses have arisen; a governor who had been unto us as a mother, parent-like distributing his goods to brethren and neighbors at his first coming; and gently bearing our infirmities without taking notice of them.

Such a governor, after he had been more than ten several[7] times by the people chosen their governor, was New England now to lose; who having, like Jacob, first left his counsel and blessing with his children gathered about his bedside;[8] and, like David, "served his generation by the will of God,"[9] he "gave up the ghost," and fell asleep on March 26, 1649. Having like the dying Emperor Valentinian,[1] this above all his other victories for his triumphs, his overcoming of himself.

The words of Josephus[2] about Nehemiah, the governor of Israel, we will now use upon this governor of New England, as his

<div align="center">

EPITAPH

Ἀνὴρ 'εγενετο χρηστος την φυσιν, και δικαιος.
Και περι τους ομοεθνεις φιλοτιμοτατος
Μνημεῖον αιωνιον αυτω καταλιπων, τα τῶν
'Ιεροσολυμων τειχη.

</div>

VIR FUIT INDOLE BONUS, AC JUSTUS:
ET POPULARIUM GLORIAE AMANTISSIMUS:
QUIBUS ETERNUM RELIQUIT MONUMENTUM,
<div align="center"><i>Novanglorum</i> MOENIA.[3]</div>

<div align="right">1702</div>

6. King David's friends and counselors joined Absalom in his revolt against his father (2 Samuel). "Physic": medicine.
7. Separate.
8. The aged patriarch Jacob was the second son of Isaac and Rebekah. He called his sons about him and told them what would befall them "in the last days" of the world (Genesis 49).
9. "For David, after he had served his own generation by the will of God, fell on sleep, and was laid unto his fathers" (Acts 13.36).

1. Christian emperor of Rome (d. 375 C.E.).
2. Jewish historian (37–100? C.E.) and author of *Antiquities of the Jews*, where the following quotation appears (book II, ch. 5).
3. He was by nature a man at once benevolent and just: most zealous for the honor of his countrymen and to them he left an imperishable monument—the walls of New England (Latin). This Latin paraphrase of the Greek that precedes it substitutes *New England* for *Jerusalem*.

A Notable Exploit: *Dux Fœmina Facti*[1]

On March 15, 1697, the savages made a descent upon the skirts of Haverhill, murdering and captivating about thirty-nine persons, and burning about half a dozen houses. In this broil, one Hannah Dustan, having lain in[2] about a week, attended with her nurse, Mary Neff, a body of terrible Indians drew near unto the house where she lay, with designs to carry on their bloody devastations. Her husband hastened from his employments abroad unto the relief of his distressed family; and first bidding *seven* of his *eight* children (which were from *two* to *seventeen* years of age) to get away as fast as they could unto some garrison in the town, he went in to inform his wife of the horrible distress come upon them. Ere she could get up, the fierce Indians were got so near, that, utterly despairing to do her any service, he ran out after his children; resolving that on the horse which he had with him, he would ride away with *that*[3] which he should in this extremity find his affections to pitch most upon, and leave the rest unto the care of the Divine Providence. He overtook his children, about forty rod[4] from his door; but then such was the *agony* of his parental affections, that he found it impossible for him to distinguish any one of them from the rest; wherefore he took up a courageous resolution to live and die with them all. A party of Indians came up with him; and now, though they fired at him, and he fired at them, yet he manfully kept at the rear of his *little army* of unarmed children, while they marched off with the pace of a child of five years old; until, by the singular providence of God, he arrived safe with them all unto a place of safety about a mile or two from his house. But his house must in the mean time have more dismal *tragedies* acted at it. The nurse, trying to escape with the newborn infant, fell into the hands of the formidable savages; and those furious tawnies coming into the house, bid poor Dustan to rise immediately. Full of astonishment, she did so; and sitting down in the chimney with an heart full of most fearful *expectation*, she saw the raging dragons rifle all that they could carry away, and set the house on fire. About nineteen or twenty Indians now led these away, with about half a score other English captives; but ere they had gone many steps, they dashed out the brains of the infant against a tree; and several of the other captives, as they began to tire in the sad journey, were soon sent unto their long home;[5] the savages would presently bury their hatchets in their brains, and leave their carcasses on the ground for birds and beasts to feed upon. However, Dustan (with her nurse) notwithstanding her present condition, traveled that night about a dozen miles, and then kept up with their new masters in a long travel of an hundred and fifty miles, more or less, within a few days ensuing, without any sensible damage in their health, from the hardships of their *travel*, their *lodging*, their *diet*, and their many other difficulties.

These two poor women were now in the hands of those whose "tender mercies are cruelties;"[6] but the good God, who hath all "hearts in his own

1. The leader was a woman (Latin).
2. I.e., having been confined to bed after the birth of a child.
3. I.e., one of his children.
4. About seven hundred feet.
5. I.e., to heaven. From Ecclesiastes 12.5: "Because man goeth to his long home, and the mourners go about the streets."
6. Proverbs 12.10: "A righteous man regardeth the life of his beast: but the tender mercies of the wicked are cruel."

hands,"[7] heard the sighs of these prisoners, and gave them to find unexpected favor from the master who hath laid claim unto them. That Indian family consisted of twelve persons; two stout men, three women, and seven children; and for the shame of many an English family, that has the character of *prayerless* upon it, I must now publish what these poor women assure me. 'Tis this: in obedience to the instructions which the French have given them, they would have *prayers* in their family no less than thrice every day; in the morning, at noon, and in the evening; nor would they ordinarily let their children *eat* or *sleep*, without first saying their prayers. Indeed, these *idolaters* were, like the rest of their whiter brethren, *persecutors*, and would not endure that these poor women should retire to their English prayers, if they could hinder them. Nevertheless, the poor women had nothing but fervent prayers to make their lives comfortable or tolerable; and by being daily sent out upon business, they had opportunities, together and asunder to do like another Hannah, in "pouring out their souls before the Lord."[8] Nor did their praying friends among ourselves forbear to "pour out" supplications for them. Now, they could not observe it without some wonder, that their Indian master sometimes when he saw them dejected, would say unto them, "What need you trouble yourself? If your God will have you delivered, you shall be so!" And it seems our God would have it so to be. This Indian family was now traveling with these two captive women (and an English youth taken from Worcester, a year and a half before), unto a rendezvous of savages, which they call a *town*, some where beyond Penacook,[9] and they still told these poor women that when they came to this town, they must be stripped, and scourged, and run the *gauntlet* through the whole army of Indians. They said this was the *fashion* when the captives first came to a town; and they derided some of the faint-hearted English, which, they said, fainted and swooned away under the *torments* of this discipline. But on April 30, while they were yet, it may be, about an hundred and fifty miles from the Indian town, a little before break of day, when the whole crew was in a *dead sleep*, (reader, see if it prove not so!) one of these women took up a resolution to imitate the action of Jael upon Sisera,[1] and being where she had not her own *life* secured by any *law* unto her, she thought she was not forbidden by any *law* to take away the *life* of the *murderers* by whom her child had been butchered. She heartened the nurse and the youth to assist her in this enterprise; and all furnishing themselves with hatchets for the purpose, they struck such home blows upon the heads of their sleeping oppressors, that ere they could any of them struggle into any effectual resistance, "at the feet of these poor prisoners, they bowed, they fell, they lay down; at their feet they bowed, they fell; where they bowed, there they fell down dead."[2] Only one squaw escaped, sorely wounded, from them in the dark; and one boy, whom they reserved asleep, intending to bring him away with them, suddenly waked, and scuttled away from this desolation. But cutting off the

7. Proverbs 21.1: "The king's heart is in the hand of the Lord."
8. Hannah, sorrowful because she could not have children, "pour[ed] out [her] soul before the Lord," who thereafter allowed her to give birth to Samuel (1 Samuel 1.15).
9. A site on the Merrimack River in central New Hampshire, north of Concord.
1. Jael's brutal murder of the warrior Sisera is recounted in Judges 4–5.
2. Based on Judges 5.27, which describes Sisera's death after Jael drives a tent stake through his head while he sleeps.

scalps of the ten wretches, they came off, and received *fifty pounds* from the General Assembly of the province, as a recompense of their action; besides which, they received many "presents of congratulation" from their more private friends: but none gave them a greater taste of bounty than Colonel Nicholson the Governor of Maryland, who, hearing of their action, sent them a very generous token of his favor.[3]

1702

Bonifacius[1]

From *Essays to Do Good*

§ 1. Such *Glorious Things are Spoken* in the Oracles of our Good God, concerning them who *Devise Good*, that, A Book of Good Devices, may very reasonably demand Attention and Acceptance from them that have any Impressions of the most *Reasonable Religion* upon them. I am *Devising* Such a Book; but at the same time Offering a Sorrowful Demonstration, That if men would Set themselves to *Devise Good*, a world of *Good* might be done, more than there is, in this *Present Evil World*. It is very sure, The World has *Need Enough*. There Needs abundance to be done, That the Great GOD and His CHRIST may be more Known and Serv'd in the World; and that the *Errors* which are *Impediments* to the *Acknowledgments* wherewith men ought to Glorify their Creator and Redeemer, may be Rectified. There needs abundance to be done, That the *Evil Manners* of the World, by which men are *drowned in Perdition*, may be Reformed; and mankind rescued from the Epidemical Corruption and Slavery which has overwhelmed it. There needs abundance to be done, That the *Miseries* of the World may have *Remedies and Abatements* provided for them; and that miserable people may be Relieved and Comforted. The world has according to the Computation of Some, above Seven hundred millions of people now Living in it. What an ample Field among all these, to *Do Good* upon! In a word, *The Kingdom of God* in the World, Calls for Innumerable *Services* from us. To Do SUCH THINGS is to Do Good. Those men Devise Good, who Shape any Devices to do Things of Such a Tendency; whether the Things be of a *Spiritual* Importance, or of a *Temporal*. You see, Sirs, the General matter, appearing as Yet, but as a *Chaos*, which is to be wrought upon. *Oh! that the Good Spirit of God may now fall upon us, and carry on the Glorious work which lies before us!*

§ 2. Tis to be Supposed, my Readers will readily grant, That it is an Excellent, a Virtuous, a Laudable Thing to be full of *Devices*, to bring about Such *Noble Purposes*. For any man to Deride, or to Despise my Proposal, *That we Resolve and Study to Do as much Good in the World as we can*, would be so black a Character, that I am not willing to make a Supposal of it in any of

3. Francis Nicholson (1655–1728), at the time governor of Maryland, had served as lieutenant governor of the Dominion of New England in the previous decade. A scalp bounty in effect in Massachusetts had been rescinded before Dustan's capture, but a petition to the government signed by her husband, Thomas, secured twenty-five pounds for Hannah and the same amount to be split by Neff and the "English youth," Samuel Lennardson.

1. The text is derived from *Bonifacius : An Essay upon the Good* (1710).

those with [whom] I am Concerned. Let no man pretend unto the Name of, *A Christian*, who does not Approve the proposal of, *A Perpetual Endeavor to Do Good in the World*. What pretension can Such a man have to be, *A Follower of the Good One?* The Primitive *Christians* gladly accepted and improved the Name, when the Pagans by a mistake Styled them, *Chrestians*;[2] Because it Signified, *Useful Ones*. The *Christians* who have no Ambition to be So, Shall be condemned by the Pagans; among whom it was a Term of the Highest Honor, to be termed, *A Benefactor*; to have *Done Good*, was accounted *Honorable*. The Philosopher being asked why Every one desired so much to look upon a Fair Object! he answered, That *it was a Question of a Blind man*. If any man ask, as wanting the Sense of it, What is it worth the while to *Do Good* in the world! I must Say, *It Sounds not like the Question of a Good man*. The Αιθησις πνευματικη, as *Origen*[3] calls it, the *Spiritual Taste* of every Good Man will make him have an unspeakable *Relish* for it. Yea, Unworthy to be discoursed as a *Man*, is he, who is not for, *Doing of Good among Men*. An *Enemy* to the Proposal, *That mankind, may be the better for us*, deserves to be Reckoned, little better than, *A Common Enemy of Mankind*. How Cogently do I bespeak, a Good Reception of what is now designed! I produce not only *Religion*, but even *Humanity* itself, as full of a *Fiery Indignation against the Adversaries of the Design*. Excuse me, Sirs; I declare, that if I could have my choice, I would never *Eat* or *Drink*, or *Walk*, with such an one, as long as I Live; or, Look on him as any other than one by whom *Humanity* itself is Debased and Blemished. A very *Wicked Writer*, has yet found himself compell'd by the Force of *Reason*, to publish this Confession. *To Love the Public, to Study an Universal Good, and to Promote the Interest of the whole World, as far as is in our Power, is surely the Highest of Goodness, and makes that Temper, which we call Divine*. And, he goes on. *Is the Doing of Good for Glories Sake so Divine a thing?* (Alas, Too much *Humane*, Sir!) *Or, Is it not a Diviner to Do Good, even where it may be thought Inglorious? Even unto the Ingrateful, and unto those who are wholly Insensible of the Good they receive!*[4] A man must be far gone in *Wickedness*, who will open his Mouth, against such *Maxims* and *Actions!* A better Pen has Remark'd it; yea, the man must be much a Stranger in History, who has not made the Remark. *To Speak Truth, and to Do Good, were in the Esteem even of the Heathen World, most God-like Qualities*. God forbid, That in the Esteem of the *Christian World*, for those Qualities, there should be any Abatement!

§ 3. I Won't yet propose the *Reward* of *Well-doing*, and the glorious Things which the *Mercy* and *Truth* of God will do, for them who *Devise Good*; Because I would have to do with such, as will esteem it, a Sufficient *Reward* unto itself. I will imagine that Generous Ingenuity, in my Readers, which will dispose them to count themselves *well-Rewarded* in the Thing itself, if God will Accept them to *Do Good* in the World. It is an Invaluable *Honor*, To *Do Good*; It is an Incomparable *Pleasure*. A Man must Look upon himself as *Dignified* and *Gratified* by GOD, when an *Opportunity* to *Do Good* is put

2. By a common mistake in the early days, what the followers of Christ were called.
3. Origen Adamantius (185–254 C.E.), early Christian theologian and scholar, wrote of this "spiritual taste" in *De Principiis*, probably composed in the years 212–15.

4. From "A Letter Concerning Enthusiasm," part of *Characteristics of Men, Manners, Opinions, Times* (1711), a famous work by the worldly English philosopher Anthony Ashley Cooper, third earl of Shaftesbury (1671–1713).

into his Hands. He must Embrace it with *Rapture*, as enabling him directly to answer the Great END of his Being. He must manage it with *Rapturous Delight*, as a most Suitable Business, as a most Precious Privilege. He must *Sing in those Ways of the Lord*, wherein he cannot but find himself, while he is *Doing of Good*. As the Saint of Old Sweetly Sang, *I was glad, when they said unto me, Let us go into the House of the Lord*.[5] Thus ought we to be *Glad*, when any *Opportunity* to *Do Good*, is offered unto us. We should need no *Arguments*, to make us Entertain the Offer; but we should *Naturally* fly into the Matter, as most agreeable to the *Divine Nature* whereof we are *made Partakers*. It should *Oblige* us wonderfully! An Ingot of Gold presented unto us, not more Obliging! Think, Sirs, *Now I Enjoy what I Am for! Now I Attain what I Wish for!* Some Servants of God have been so Strongly Disposed this way, that they have cheerfully made a Tender of any *Recompense* that could be desired, (yea, rather than fail, a *Pecuniary* one,) unto any Friend that would *Think* for them, and *Supply* the *Barrenness* of their Thoughts, and *Suggest* unto them any Special and proper *Methods*, wherein they may be *Serviceable*. Certainly, To *Do Good* is a thing that brings its own *Recompense*, in the Opinion of those, who reckon a kind *Information* of a Point wherein they may *Do Good*, worthy to be by them requited with a *Recompense* to the *Informer*.[6] I will only Say; If any of you are Strangers unto such a Disposition as this, to Look upon an *Opportunity* to *Do Good*, as a thing that *Enriches* you, and to Look upon yourselves as *Enriched*, and *Favored* of God, when He does Employ you to *Do Good*: I have done with you. I would pray them, to lay the *Book* aside; It will disdain to carry on any further Conversation with 'em! It handles a Subject on which the Wretches of the House of *Caleb*,[7] will not be conversed withal. It is content with one of Dr. *Stoughton's* Introductions: *It is Enough to me, that I Speak to wise men, whose Reason shall be my Rhetoric, to Christians, whose Conscience shall be my Eloquence.*[8]

§ 4. Tho' the Assertion fly never so much like a *Chain*-Shot,[9] among us and Rake down all before it, I will again, and again Assert it; *That we might every One of us do more Good than we do.* And therefore, This is the FIRST, PROPOSAL, to be made unto us; *To be Exceedingly Humbled, that we have done so Little Good in the World.* I am not *Uncharitable*, in saying; I know not that *Assembly* of Christians upon Earth, which ought not to be a *Bochim*,[1] in this consideration. Oh! Tell me, what *Utopia*, I shall find it in! Sirs, Let us begin to bring forth some *Good Fruit*, by Lamenting our own *Great Unfruitfulness*. Verily, *Sins of Omission* must be Confessed and Bewailed; else we add unto the Number of them. The most *Useful* Men in the World, have gone out of it, crying to God, *Lord, Let my Sins of Omission be Forgiven to me!* Men that have made more than ordinary Conscience about well-Spending of their *Time*, have had their Death-bed made uneasy by this Reflection; *The Loss of Time now Sits heavy upon me.* Be sure, All *Unregenerate* Persons, are, as our

5. Psalm 122.1.
6. I.e., those who receive kindly advice about opportunities for doing good reciprocate with similar advice of their own.
7. Nabal, a man who was "churlish and evil in his doings," was of the otherwise honorable "house of Caleb" (1 Samuel 25.3).
8. John Stoughton (d. 1639), English Puritan preacher, made this point on the opening page of "The Happiness of Peace," one of his *Choice Sermons* (1640). However, as David Levin points out in his edition of *Bonifacius*, Mather edited Stoughton's prose so as to remove his original references to King James I and his courtiers, before whom the sermon was delivered.
9. Two cannon balls joined by chain, an especially destructive shot.
1. A place where the Israelites, pausing on their flight from Egypt, wept when an angel reproved them for their backsliding (Judges 2).

Bible has told us, *Unprofitable* Persons.² 'Tis not for nothing that the Comparison of *Thorns*, and *Briars*, has been used, to *Teach* us, what they are. An Unrenewed Sinner, alas, he never did *One Good Work* in all his *Life*! In all his *Life*, did I Say? You must give me that word again! He is *Dead* while he *Lives*; he is *Dead in Sins*; he has never yet begun to *Live unto God*: and, as is he, so are *all the Works of his Hands*; They are *Dead Works*. Ah! Wretched *Good-for-nothing*. Wonder, Wonder at the Patience of Heaven, which yet forbears *Cutting down*, such a *Cumberer of the Ground*. The best, and the first Advice, to be given unto such Persons, is, *Immediately to do their best, that they may get out of their woeful Unregeneracy*. Let them *Immediately* Acknowledge the *Necessity* of their Turning to God, but how *Unable* they are to do it, and how Unworthy that God should make them *Able*. *Immediately* let them lift up their *Cry* unto Sovereign *Grace*, to *Quicken* them; and let them then *Try*, whether they cannot with *Quickened* Souls, *Plead* the *Sacrifice* and *Righteousness* of a Glorious CHRIST for their Happy Reconciliation to God; Seriously Resolve upon a Life of *Obedience* to God, and *Serious Religion*; and Resign themselves up unto the *Holy Spirit*, that he may possess them, Instruct them, Strengthen them, and *for His Name Sake lead them in the paths of Holiness*. There will no *Good* be done, till this be done. The very *First-born* of all *Devices* to *Do Good*, is in being *Born again*, and in *Devising Means, that a Banished* Soul may no longer be *Expelled* from the presence of God. But you that have been brought home to God, have Sad cause, not only to deplore the *Dark Days* of your Unregeneracy, wherein you did none but the *Unfruitful Works of Darkness*; but also, that you have done *so Little*, since God has Quickened you and Enabled you, to *Do*, the Things that should be done. How Little, How Little have you Lived up, to the Strains of *Gratitude*, which might have been justly Expected, since God has brought you *into His Marvellous Light*! The best of us may mourn in our Complaint; *Lord, How Little Good have I done, to what I might have done*! Let the Sense of this cause us to *Loathe* and *Judge* ourselves before the Lord: Let it fill us with Shame, and Abase us wonderfully! How can we do any other, than with *David*, even make a Cauldron of our couch, and a Bath of our Tears, when we consider how little *Good* we have done!³ *Oh! That our Heads were Waters*, because they have been so *Dry* of all Thoughts to *Do Good*! *Oh! That our Eyes were a Fountain of Tears*, because they have been so little upon the *Look out* for Objects and Methods to *Do Good* upon! For the *Pardon* of this *Evil-doing*, Let us Fly to the Great *Sacrifice*; which is our only *Expiation*. Plead the *Blood* of that *Lamb of God*, whose Universal *Usefulness* is One of those admirable Properties, for which He has been called, *A Lamb*. The *Pardon* of our *Barrenness* at *Good Works* being thus obtained, by Faith in that *Blood which cleanses from all Sin*, that is the way for us to be rescued from a Condemnation to *Perpetual Barrenness*. The dreadful Sentence of, *Let no Fruit grow on thee forever*! will be reversed and prevented, by such a *Pardon*.⁴ Sirs, A True, Right, Evangelical Procedure to *Do Good*, must have this *Repentance* laid in the Foundation of it! We do not *Handle the Matter Wisely*, if a *Foundation* be not laid thus *Low*, and in the deepest *Self-Abasement*.

2. See Philemon 1.11.
3. Brass cauldrons were a fixture of Solomon's temple; in them, animals were cleansed for sacrifice. Mather conflates this fact with the language of Psalm 6.6: "I am weary with my groaning; all the night make I my bed to swim; I water my couch with my tears."
4. Matthew 21.19.

§ 5. How full, how full of *Devices* are we, for our own *Secular Advantage*! And how *Expert* in *Devising* many *Little Things*, to be done for ourselves! We apply our Thoughts, with a mighty Assiduity, unto the Old Question, *What shall I Eat and Drink, and wherewithal shall I be clothed?* It is with a very strong Application of our Thoughts, that we Study, what we shall do for ourselves, in our *Marriages*, in our *Voyages*, in our *Bargains*, and in many, many other concerns, wherein we are Solicitous to have our condition easy. We Solicitously *Contrive*, that we may accomplish *Good Bargains*, and that we may Steer clear of ten thousand *Inconveniencies*, to which, without some *Contrivance*, we may lie obnoxious. The *Business* of our *Personal Callings* we carry on with Numberless Thoughts, how we may *Do Well*, in what is to be done. To accomplish our Temporal *Business*, in affairs that cannot be Numbered, we *find out Witty Inventions*. But, O Rational, Immortal Heaven-born SOUL; Are thy wondrous Faculties capable of no Greater Improvements, no better Employments? Why should a *Soul* of such High Capacities, a *Soul* that may arrive to be[5] clothed in the Bright *Scarlet* of Angels, yet *Embrace a Dunghill*! O let a *Blush* coloring beyond *Scarlet*, be thy clothing for thy being found so meanly occupied! Alas, *In the Multitude of thy Thoughts within thee*, hast thou no Dispositions to Raise thy Soul, unto Some thoughts, *What may be done for* GOD, *and* CHRIST, *and for my own* SOUL, *and for the most Considerable Interests?* How many Hundreds of *Thoughts* have we, How to obtain or secure Some *Trifle* for ourselves; to *One*, How we may Serve the interests of the Glorious LORD, and of His People in the World? How can we now pretend, that we *Love Him*, or, that a carnal, and a Criminal *Self-Love*, has not the Dominion over us? I again come in, upon a *Soul* of an Heavenly Extract, and *Smite* it, as the Angel did the Sleeping Prisoner;[6] *Awake, Shake off thy Shackles, lie no longer fettered in a Base confinement unto nothing but a Meaner[7] Sort of Business.* Assume and Assert the Liberty of now and then Thinking on the *Noblest Question* in the World; *What Good may I do in the World?* There was a Time, when it was complain'd by no less a man, than *Gregory* the Great (the Bishop of *Rome*) *I am Sunk into the World*![8] It may be the complaint of a *Soul*, that minds all other things, and rarely calls to mind that *Noblest Question*. Ah! *Star, fall'n from Heav'n*, and chok'd in Dust, Rise and Soar up to something answerable to thy Original.[9] Begin a *Course of Thoughts*, which when begun, will be like a *Resurrection from the Dead*. They *which dwell in the Dust, Wake and Sing*, and a Little anticipate the *Life* which we are to Live at the *Resurrection of the Dead*, when they Livelily set themselves to Think; *How may I be a Blessing in the World?* And, *What may I do, that Righteousness, may more dwell in the World?*

* * *

1710

5. Come to be.
6. See Acts 12.6–7, where the prisoner is the apostle Peter.
7. Lesser.
8. Pope Gregory the First (c. 540–604) con-

fessed to being "sunk into the world" in the autobiographical epistle that opens his famous commentary on the Book of Job, known as *Magna Moralia* (written 578–95).
9. Origin.

JONATHAN EDWARDS
1703–1758

A pivotal figure in American literary history, the Puritan minister Jonathan Edwards created a fresh prose style that integrated contemporary theories of sensation with traditional Calvinist theology. Edwards spoke and wrote in a manner designed to give his audiences an almost visceral sense of spiritual realities. To appreciate his achievements as a religious writer, it may be helpful to consider how Edwards's focus on sensation distinguishes his prose from that of his older contemporary Cotton Mather. In many ways, Edwards and Mather were engaged in the same project, that is, updating the Calvinist tradition for their own time. Born forty years apart, both men were members of powerful New England religious dynasties, and they were also both active members of the Atlantic-world republic of letters, with an interest in the latest scientific ideas. As a writer, however, Mather frequently oriented himself toward the past, creating the baroque style that reached its apex in *Magnalia Christi Americana* (1702). Edwards focused instead on giving his audiences an immediate experience of "divine things" that could rival and even exceed the perceptions conveyed by the physical senses. The appeal of his rhetoric of sensation, as it has been called, was its capacity to make invisible things vividly present. Those things might be the theological tenets and spiritual experiences that Edwards held to be divine truths, or they might be the life stories of young girls and women (including his wife, Sarah Pierpont Edwards) that appealed to readers of the novel, a genre becoming prominent in Edwards's lifetime. Edwards is a central figure in American literary history, then, because of the way his works influenced the development of both religious and secular prose.

Born in East Windsor, Connecticut, a town not far from the major city of Hartford, Edwards was the son of the Reverend Timothy Edwards and Esther Stoddard Edwards. Edwards's mother was the daughter of the Reverend Solomon Stoddard, of Northampton, Massachusetts, one of the most influential figures in the religious life of New England. Stoddard's gifted grandson, the only male child in a family of eleven children, was groomed to be his heir. Studious and dutiful, Edwards showed remarkable gifts of observation and exposition from a young age. When he was eleven, he wrote an essay, still very readable, on the flying spider. At thirteen, he was admitted to Yale College, in New Haven; he stayed on to read theology for two years after his graduation. He was determined to perfect himself, and in one of his early notebooks he resolved "never to lose one moment of time, but to improve it in the most profitable way" he could. As a student, he always rose at four in the morning, studied thirteen hours a day, and reserved part of each day for walking. Edwards varied this routine little, even when—after two years in New York City, assisting at a Presbyterian church—he went to Northampton to assist his grandfather in his church. In 1727, he married Sarah Pierpont, a young woman from a leading New Haven clerical family. Two years later, Solomon Stoddard died, and Edwards succeeded him. In the twenty-four years that Edwards lived in Northampton, he fulfilled his duties as the pastor of a growing congregation and delivered brilliant sermons, wrote some of his most important books—concerned primarily with defining true religious experience—and raised his eleven children.

Until the mid-1740s, his relations with the town were harmonious. This period included the early years of the Great Awakening, when a spirit of revivalism transformed complacent believers all along the eastern seaboard, beginning in 1734. At

first, Edwards could do no wrong. His meetinghouse was filled with converts, and his works describing the revivals were widely published and distributed on both sides of the Atlantic. But in his attempt to restore the church to the position of authority it held in the years of his grandfather's ministry, Edwards went too far. He berated people for becoming too secularized, named backsliders from his pulpit—including members of the best families in town—and tried to return to the old order of communion, permitting the sacrament to be taken only by those who had publicly declared themselves to be saved. Throughout the Connecticut River Valley, people were tired of religious controversy, and the hysterical behavior of a few fanatics turned many against the spirit of revivalism. On June 22, 1750, by a vote of two hundred to twenty, Edwards was dismissed from his church. Although the congregation had difficulty naming a successor, they preferred to have no sermons rather than let Edwards preach.

For the next seven years, Edwards served as missionary to the Housatonic Indians in Stockbridge, Massachusetts, a town thirty-five miles west of Northampton. Founded after the 1735 Treaty of Deerfield, Stockbridge was a product of the chronic imperial warfare—between British, French, and Native forces—that disrupted western New England throughout Edwards's lifetime. At Stockbridge, Edwards wrote his monumental treatises on free will and on true virtue as "that consent, propensity, and union of heart to Being in general, that is immediately exercised in a general good will." Edwards then received, very reluctantly, a call to become president of the College of New Jersey (later renamed Princeton University) after the Reverend Aaron Burr, Sr.—Edwards's son-in-law, who had been serving as the new college's president—died of fever and overwork. However, just three months after his arrival in Princeton, Edwards died of smallpox, the result of his inoculation to prevent infection.

All of Edwards's work is of a piece and, in essence, readily graspable. He was trying to restore to his congregation and to his readers that original sense of religious commitment that he felt had been lost since the first days of the Puritan exodus to America, and he wanted to do this by transforming his congregation from mere believers who understood the logic of Christian doctrine to converted Christians who were genuinely moved by the principles of their belief. Edwards wrote that he read the work of the English philosopher John Locke (1632–1704) with more pleasure "than the greedy miser finds when gathering up handfuls of silver and gold, from some newly discovered treasure." Locke confirmed Edwards's conviction that people must do more than comprehend religious ideas; they must be *moved* by them and come to know them experientially: the difference, as he says, is like that between reading the word "fire" and actually being burned. Basic to this newly felt belief is the recognition that nothing that an individual can do warrants his or her salvation, that people are motivated entirely by self-love, and only supernatural grace alters their natural depravity. Edwards says that he experienced several steps toward real Christian commitment but that his true conversion came only when he had achieved a "full and constant sense of the absolute sovereignty of God, and a delight in that sovereignty."

The word "delight" reminds us that Edwards was trying to inculcate and describe a religious feeling that approximates a physical sensation. He held that divine grace produced a new sense in the religious convert, which he sometimes analogized to taste. He believed this new sense would enable the convert to respond to God in more vital ways. "Delight" further links him to the transatlantic community of those who recognized sentiment as the basic emotion that connects individuals to one another. In his patient and lucid prose, Edwards became a master at the art of persuading his congregants and readers that they could—and *must*—possess an intense awareness of humanity's precarious condition and experience the joys and pleasures of grace.

Personal Narrative[1]

I had a variety of concerns and exercises about my soul from my childhood; but had two more remarkable seasons of awakening[2] before I met with that change, by which I was brought to those new dispositions, and that new sense of things, that I have since had. The first time was when I was a boy, some years before I went to college, at a time of remarkable awakening in my father's congregation. I was then very much affected[3] for many months, and concerned about the things of religion, and my soul's salvation; and was abundant in duties. I used to pray five times a day in secret, and to spend much time in religious talk with other boys; and used to meet with them to pray together. I experienced I know not what kind of delight in religion. My mind was much engaged in it, and had much self-righteous pleasure; and it was my delight to abound in religious duties. I, with some of my schoolmates joined together, and built a booth in a swamp, in a very secret and retired place, for a place of prayer. And besides, I had particular secret places of my own in the woods, where I used to retire by myself; and used to be from time to time much affected. My affections seemed to be lively and easily moved, and I seemed to be in my element, when engaged in religious duties. And I am ready to think, many are deceived with such affections, and such a kind of delight, as I then had in religion, and mistake it for grace.

But in process of time, my convictions and affections wore off; and I entirely lost all those affections and delights, and left off secret prayer, at least as to any constant performance of it; and returned like a dog to his vomit, and went on in ways of sin.[4]

Indeed, I was at some times very uneasy, especially towards the latter part of the time of my being at college.[5] Till it pleased God, in my last year at college, at a time when I was in the midst of many uneasy thoughts about the state of my soul, to seize me with a pleurisy;[6] in which he brought me nigh to the grave, and shook me over the pit of hell.

But yet, it was not long after my recovery, before I fell again into my old ways of sin. But God would not suffer me to go on with any quietness; but I had great and violent inward struggles: till after many conflicts with wicked inclinations, and repeated resolutions, and bonds that I laid myself under by a kind of vows to God, I was brought wholly to break off all former wicked ways, and all ways of known outward sin; and to apply myself to seek my salvation, and practice the duties of religion: but without that kind of affection and delight, that I had formerly experienced. My concern now wrought more by inward struggles and conflicts, and self-reflections. I made seeking

1. Because of Edwards's reference to an evening in January 1739, he must have written this essay after that date. Edwards's reasons for writing it are not known, and it was not published in his lifetime. After his death, his friend Samuel Hopkins had access to his manuscripts and prepared *The Life and Character of the Late Rev. Mr. Jonathan Edwards*, which was published in 1765. In that volume, the "Personal Narrative" appeared in section IV as the chapter "An Account of His Conversion, Experiences, and Religious Exercises, Given by Himself." The text here is from *Works of Jonathan Edwards* (1998), vol. 16, edited by George Claghorn.
2. I.e., spiritual awakenings, renewals. "Exercises": agitations.
3. Emotionally aroused, as opposed to merely understanding rationally the arguments for Christian faith.
4. "As a dog returneth to his vomit, so a fool returneth to his folly" (Proverbs 26.11).
5. Edwards was an undergraduate at Yale from 1716 to 1720 and a divinity student from 1720 to 1722.
6. A respiratory disorder.

my salvation the main business of my life. But yet it seems to me, I sought after a miserable manner: which has made me sometimes since to question, whether ever it issued in that which was saving;[7] being ready to doubt, whether such miserable seeking was ever succeeded. But yet I was brought to seek salvation, in a manner that I never was before. I felt a spirit to part with all things in the world, for an interest in Christ. My concern continued and prevailed, with many exercising things and inward struggles; but yet it never seemed to be proper to express my concern that I had, by the name of terror.

From my childhood up, my mind had been wont to be full of objections against the doctrine of God's sovereignty, in choosing whom He would to eternal life and rejecting whom he pleased; leaving them eternally to perish, and be everlastingly tormented in hell. It used to appear like a horrible doctrine to me. But I remember the time very well, when I seemed to be convinced, and fully satisfied, as to this sovereignty of God, and his justice in thus eternally disposing of men, according to his sovereign pleasure. But never could give an account, how, or by what means, I was thus convinced; not in the least imagining, in the time of it, nor a long time after, that there was any extraordinary influence of God's Spirit in it: but only that now I saw further, and my reason apprehended the justice and reasonableness of it. However, my mind rested in it; and it put an end to all those cavils and objections, that had till then abode with me, all the preceeding part of my life. And there has been a wonderful alteration in my mind, with respect to the doctrine of God's sovereignty, from that day to this; so that I scarce ever have found so much as the rising of an objection against God's sovereignty, in the most absolute sense, in showing mercy on whom he will show mercy, and hardening and eternally damning whom he will.[8] God's absolute sovereignty, and justice, with respect to salvation and damnation, is what my mind seems to rest assured of, as much as of anything that I see with my eyes; at least it is so at times. But I have oftentimes since that first conviction, had quite another kind of sense of God's sovereignty, than I had then. I have often since, not only had a conviction, but a *delightful* conviction. The doctrine of God's sovereignty has very often appeared, an exceeding pleasant, bright and sweet doctrine to me: and absolute sovereignty is what I love to ascribe to God. But my first conviction was not with this.

The first that I remember that ever I found anything of that sort of inward, sweet delight in God and divine things, that I have lived much in since, was on reading those words, 1 Tim. 1.17, "Now unto the King eternal, immortal, invisible, the only wise God, be honor and glory for ever and ever, Amen." As I read the words, there came into my soul, and was as it were diffused through it, a sense of the glory of the divine being, a new sense, quite different from anything I ever experienced before. Never any words of Scripture seemed to me as these words did. I thought with myself, how excellent a Being that was; and how happy I should be, if I might enjoy that God, and be wrapt[9] up to God in heaven, and be as it were swallowed up in him. I kept saying, and as it were singing over these words of Scripture to myself; and went to prayer, to pray to God that I might enjoy him; and prayed in a

7. I.e., truly redeeming, capable of making the penitent a "saint."
8. "Therefore hath he mercy on whom he will have mercy, and whom he will he hardeneth" (Romans 9.18).
9. Lifted.

manner quite different from what I used to do, with a new sort of affection. But it never came into my thought, that there was anything spiritual, or of a saving nature in this.

From about that time, I began to have a new kind of apprehensions and ideas of Christ, and the work of redemption, and the glorious way of salvation by him. I had an inward, sweet sense of these things, that at times came into my heart; and my soul was led away in pleasant views and contemplations of them. And my mind was greatly engaged, to spend my time in reading and meditating on Christ; and the beauty and excellency of his person, and the lovely way of salvation, by free grace in him. I found no books so delightful to me, as those that treated of these subjects. Those words (Cant. 2:1) used to be abundantly with me: "I am the rose of Sharon, the lily of the valleys." The words seemed to me, sweetly to represent, the loveliness and beauty of Jesus Christ. And the whole book of Canticles[1] used to be pleasant to me; and I used to be much in reading it, about that time. And found, from time to time, an inward sweetness, that used, as it were, to carry me away in my contemplations; in what I know not how to express otherwise, than by a calm, sweet abstraction of soul from all the concerns o[f] this world; and a kind of vision, or fixed ideas and imaginations, of being alone in the mountains, or some solitary wilderness, far from all mankind, sweetly conversing with Christ, and wrapt and swallowed up in God. The sense I had of divine things, would often of a sudden as it were, kindle up a sweet burning in my heart; an ardor of my soul, that I know not how to express.

Not long after I first began to experience these things, I gave an account to my father, of some things that had passed in my mind. I was pretty much affected by the discourse we had together. And when the discourse was ended, I walked abroad alone, in a solitary place in my father's pasture, for contemplation. And as I was walking there, and looked up on the sky and clouds; there came into my mind, a sweet sense of the glorious majesty and grace of God, that I know not how to express. I seemed to see them both in a sweet conjunction: majesty and meekness joined together: it was a sweet and gentle, and holy majesty; and also a majestic meekness; an awful sweetness; a high, and great, and holy gentleness.

After this my sense of divine things gradually increased, and became more and more lively, and had more of that inward sweetness. The appearance of everything was altered: there seemed to be, as it were, a calm, sweet cast, or appearance of divine glory, in almost everything. God's excellency, his wisdom, his purity and love, seemed to appear in everything; in the sun, moon and stars; in the clouds, and blue sky; in the grass, flowers, trees; in the water, and all nature; which used greatly to fix my mind. I often used to sit and view the moon, for a long time; and so in the daytime, spent much time in viewing the clouds and sky, to behold the sweet glory of God in these things: in the meantime, singing forth with a low voice, my contemplations of the Creator and Redeemer. And scarce anything, among all the works of nature, was so sweet to me as thunder and lightning. Formerly, nothing had been so terrible to me. I used to be a person uncommonly terrified with thunder: and it used to strike me with terror, when I saw a thunderstorm rising. But now, on the contrary, it rejoiced me. I felt God at the first appearance

1. I.e., Song of Solomon.

of a thunderstorm. And used to take the opportunity at such times, to fix myself to view the clouds, and see the lightnings play, and hear the majestic and awful voice of God's thunder: which often times was exceeding entertaining, leading me to sweet contemplations of my great and glorious God. And while I viewed, used to spend my time, as it always seemed natural to me, to sing or chant forth my meditations; to speak my thoughts in soliloquies, and speak with a singing voice.

I felt then a great satisfaction as to my good estate.[2] But that did not content me. I had vehement longings of soul after God and Christ, and after more holiness; wherewith my heart seemed to be full, and ready to break: which often brought to my mind, the words of the Psalmist, Ps. 119:28, "My soul breaketh for the longing it hath." I often felt a mourning and lamenting in my heart, that I had not turned to God sooner, that I might have had more time to grow in grace. My mind was greatly fixed on divine things; I was almost perpetually in the contemplation of them. Spent most of my time in thinking of divine things, year after year. And used to spend abundance of my time, in walking alone in the woods, and solitary places, for meditation, soliloquy and prayer, and converse with God. And it was always my manner, at such times, to sing forth my contemplations. And was almost constantly in ejaculatory[3] prayer, wherever I was. Prayer seemed to be natural to me; as the breath, by which the inward burnings of my heart had vent.

The delights which I now felt in things of religion, were of an exceeding different kind, from those forementioned, that I had when I was a boy. They were totally of another kind; and what I then had no more notion or idea of, than one born blind has of pleasant and beautiful colors. They were of a more inward, pure, soul-animating and refreshing nature. Those former delights, never reached the heart; and did not arise from any sight of the divine excellency of the things of God; or any taste of the soul-satisfying, and life-giving good, there is in them.

My sense of divine things seemed gradually to increase, till I went to preach at New York; which was about a year and a half after they began. While I was there, I felt them, very sensibly,[4] in a much higher degree, than I had done before. My longings after God and holiness, were much increased. Pure and humble, holy and heavenly Christianity, appeared exceeding amiable to me. I felt in me a burning desire to be in everything a complete Christian; and conformed to the blessed image of Christ: and that I might live in all things, according to the pure, sweet and blessed rules of the gospel. I had an eager thirsting after progress in these things. My longings after it, put me upon pursuing and pressing after them. It was my continual strife day and night, and constant inquiry, how I should be more holy, and live more holily, and more becoming a child of God, and disciple of Christ. I sought an increase of grace and holiness, and that I might live an holy life, with vastly more earnestness, than ever I sought grace, before I had it. I used to be continually examining myself, and studying and contriving for likely ways and means, how I should live holily, with far greater diligence and earnestness, than ever I pursued anything in my life: but with too great a dependence on my own strength, which afterwards proved a great damage

2. Condition of being.
3. I.e., exclaimed suddenly, blurted out sponta-
neously.
4. Feelingly.

to me. My experience had not then taught me, as it has done since, my extreme feebleness and impotence, every manner of way; and the innumerable and bottomless depths of secret corruption and deceit, that there was in my heart. However, I went on with my eager pursuit after more holiness; and sweet conformity to Christ.

The Heaven I desired was a heaven of holiness; to be with God, and to spend my eternity in divine love, and holy communion with Christ. My mind was very much taken up with contemplations on heaven, and the enjoyments of those there; and living there in perfect holiness, humility and love. And it used at that time to appear a great part of the happiness of heaven, that there the saints could express their love to Christ. It appeared to me a great clog and hindrance and burden to me, that what I felt within, I could not express to God, and give vent to, as I desired. The inward ardor of my soul, seemed to be hindered and pent up, and could not freely flame out as it would. I used often to think, how in heaven, this sweet principle should freely and fully vent and express itself. Heaven appeared to me exceeding delightful as a world of love. It appeared to me, that all happiness consisted in living in pure, humble, heavenly, divine love.

I remember the thoughts I used then to have of holiness. I remember I then said sometimes to myself, I do certainly know that I love holiness, such as the gospel prescribes. It appeared to me, there was nothing in it but what was ravishingly lovely. It appeared to me, to be the highest beauty and amiableness, above all other beauties: that it was a divine beauty; far purer than anything here upon earth; and that everything else, was like mire, filth and defilement, in comparison of it.

Holiness, as I then wrote down some of my contemplations on it, appeared to me to be of a sweet, pleasant, charming, serene, calm nature. It seemed to me, it brought an inexpressible purity, brightness, peacefulness and ravishment to the soul: and that it made the soul like a field or garden of God, with all manner of pleasant flowers; that is all pleasant, delightful and undisturbed; enjoying a sweet calm, and the gently vivifying beams of the sun. The soul of a true Christian, as I then wrote my meditations, appeared like such a little white flower, as we see in the spring of the year; low and humble on the ground, opening its bosom, to receive the pleasant beams of the sun's glory; rejoicing as it were, in a calm rapture; diffusing around a sweet fragrancy; standing peacefully and lovingly, in the midst of other flowers round about; all in like manner opening their bosoms, to drink in the light of the sun.

There was no part of creature-holiness, that I then, and at other times, had so great a sense of the loveliness of, as humility, brokenness of heart and poverty of spirit: and there was nothing that I had such a spirit to long for. My heart, as it were, panted after this to lie low before GOD, and in the dust; that I might be nothing, and that God might be all; that I might become as a little child.[5]

While I was there at New York, I sometimes was much affected with reflections on my past life, considering how late it was, before I began to be truly religious; and how wickedly I had lived till then: and once so as to weep abundantly, and for a considerable time together.

5. "Verily I say unto you, Whosoever shall not receive the kingdom of God as a little child, he shall not enter therein" (Mark 10.15).

On January 12, 1722–3, I made a solemn dedication of myself to God, and wrote it down; giving up myself, and all that I had to God; to be for the future in no respect my own; to act as one that had no right to himself, in any respect. And solemnly vowed to take God for my whole portion and felicity; looking on nothing else as any part of my happiness, nor acting as if it were: and his law for the constant rule of my obedience; engaging to fight with all my might, against the world, the flesh and the devil, to the end of my life. But have reason to be infinitely humbled, when I consider, how much I have failed of answering my obligation.

I had then abundance of sweet religious conversation in the family where I lived, with Mr. John Smith, and his pious mother. My heart was knit in affection to those, in whom were appearances of true piety; and I could bear the thoughts of no other companions, but such as were holy, and the disciples of the blessed Jesus.

I had great longings for the advancement of Christ's kingdom in the world. My secret prayer used to be in great part taken up in praying for it. If I heard the least hint of anything that happened in any part of the world, that appeared to me, in some respect or other, to have a favorable aspect on the interest of Christ's kingdom, my soul eagerly catched at it; and it would much animate and refresh me. I used to be earnest to read public newsletters, mainly for that end; to see if I could not find some news favorable to the interest of religion in the world.

I very frequently used to retire into a solitary place, on the banks of Hudson's River, at some distance from the city, for contemplation on divine things, and secret converse with God; and had many sweet hours there. Sometimes Mr. Smith and I walked there together, to converse of the things of God; and our conversation used much to turn on the advancement of Christ's kingdom in the world, and the glorious things that God would accomplish for his church in the latter days.

I had then, and at other times, the greatest delight in the holy Scriptures, of any book whatsoever. Oftentimes in reading it, every word seemed to touch my heart. I felt an harmony between something in my heart, and those sweet and powerful words. I seemed often to see so much light, exhibited by every sentence, and such a refreshing ravishing food communicated, that I could not get along in reading. Used oftentimes to dwell long on one sentence, to see the wonders contained in it; and yet almost every sentence seemed to be full of wonders.

I came away from New York in the month of April 1723, and had a most bitter parting with Madam Smith and her son. My heart seemed to sink within me, at leaving the family and city, where I had enjoyed so many sweet and pleasant days. I went from New York to Weathersfield[6] by water. As I sailed away, I kept sight of the city as long as I could; and when I was out of sight of it, it would affect me much to look that way, with a kind of melancholy mixed with sweetness. However, that night after this sorrowful parting, I was greatly comforted in God at Westchester, where we went ashore to lodge: and had a pleasant time of it all the voyage to Saybrook.[7] It was sweet to me to think of meeting dear Christians in heaven, where we should never part more.

6. Wethersfield, Connecticut, is very close to Windsor.

7. Westchester and Saybrook are in New York and Connecticut, respectively.

At Saybrook we went ashore to lodge on Saturday, and there kept sabbath; where I had a sweet and refreshing season, walking alone in the fields.

After I came home to Windsor, remained much in a like frame of my mind, as I had been in at New York; but only sometimes felt my heart ready to sink, with the thoughts of my friends at New York. And my refuge and support was in contemplations on the heavenly state; as I find in my diary of May 1, 1723. It was my comfort to think of that state, where there is fulness of joy; where reigns heavenly, sweet, calm and delightful love, without alloy; where there are continually the dearest expressions of this love; where is the enjoyment of the persons loved, without ever parting; where these persons that appear so lovely in this world, will really be inexpressibly more lovely, and full of love to us. And how sweetly will the mutual lovers join together to sing the praises of God and the Lamb![8] How full will it fill us with joy, to think, that this enjoyment, these sweet exercises will never cease or come to an end; but will last to all eternity!

Continued much in the same frame in the general, that I had been in at New York, till I went to New Haven, to live there as Tutor of the College; having some special season of uncommon sweetness: particularly once at Bolton,[9] in a journey from Boston, walking out alone in the fields. After I went to New Haven, I sunk in religion; my mind being diverted from my eager and violent[1] pursuits after holiness, by some affairs that greatly perplexed and distracted my mind.

In September 1725, was taken ill at New Haven; and endeavoring to go home to Windsor, was so ill at the North Village, that I could go no further: where I lay sick for about a quarter of a year. And in this sickness, God was pleased to visit me again with the sweet influences of his spirit. My mind was greatly engaged there on divine, pleasant contemplations, and longings of soul. I observed that those who watched with me, would often be looking out for the morning, and seemed to wish for it. Which brought to my mind those words of the Psalmist, which my soul with sweetness made its own language, "My soul waiteth for the Lord more than they that watch for the morning: I say, more than they that watch for the morning."[2] And when the light of the morning came, and the beams of the sun came in at the windows, it refreshed my soul from one morning to another. It seemed to me to be some image of the sweet light of God's glory.

I remember, about that time, I used greatly to long for the conversion of some that I was concerned with. It seemed to me, I could gladly honor them, and with delight be a servant to them, and lie at their feet, if they were but truly holy.

But sometime after this, I was again greatly diverted in my mind, with some temporal concerns, that exceedingly took up my thoughts, greatly to the wounding of my soul: and went on through various exercises, that it would be tedious to relate, that gave me much more experience of my own heart, than ever I had before.

Since I came to this town, I have often had sweet complacency[3] in God in views of his glorious perfections, and the excellency of Jesus Christ. God

8. In the Book of Revelation, the symbol of Christ.
9. A town in Massachusetts, twenty-five miles from Boston.

1. I.e., intense, passionate, uncontrollable.
2. Psalm 130.6.
3. Contentment. "This town": Northampton.

has appeared to me, a glorious and lovely being, chiefly on the account of his holiness. The holiness of God has always appeared to me the most lovely of all his attributes. The doctrines of God's absolute sovereignty, and free grace, in showing mercy to whom he would show mercy; and man's absolute dependence on the operations of God's Holy Spirit, have very often appeared to me as sweet and glorious doctrines. These doctrines have been much my delight. God's sovereignty has ever appeared to me, as great part of his glory. It has often been sweet to me to go to God, and adore him as a sovereign God, and ask sovereign mercy of him.

I have loved the doctrines of the gospel: they have been to my soul like green pastures.[4] The gospel has seemed to me to be the richest treasure; the treasure that I have most desired, and longed that it might dwell richly in me. The way of salvation by Christ, has appeared in a general way, glorious and excellent, and most pleasant and beautiful. It has often seemed to me, that it would in a great measure spoil heaven, to receive it in any other way. That text has often been affecting and delightful to me, Is. 32:2, "A man shall be an hiding place from the wind, and a covert from the tempest," etc.

It has often appeared sweet to me, to be united to Christ; to have him for my head, and to be a member of his body: and also to have Christ for my teacher and prophet. I very often think with sweetness and longings and pantings of soul, of being a little child, taking hold of Christ, to be led by him through the wilderness of this world. That text, Matt. 18 at the beginning, has often been sweet to me, "Except ye be converted, and become as little children," etc. I love to think of coming to Christ, to receive salvation of him, poor in spirit, and quite empty of self; humbly exalting him alone; cut entirely off from my own root, and to grow into, and out of Christ: to have God in Christ to be all in all; and to live by faith in the Son of God, a life of humble, unfeigned confidence in him. That Scripture has often been sweet to me, Ps. 115:1, "Not unto us, O Lord, not unto us, but unto thy name give glory, for thy mercy, and for thy truth's sake." And those words of Christ, Luke 10:21, "In that hour Jesus rejoiced in spirit, and said, I thank thee, O Father, Lord of heaven and earth, that thou hast hid these things from the wise and prudent, and hast revealed them unto babes: even so Father, for so it seemed good in thy sight." That sovereignty of God that Christ rejoiced in, seemed to me to be worthy to be rejoiced in; and that rejoicing of Christ, seemed to me to show the excellency of Christ, and the spirit that he was of.

Sometimes only mentioning a single word, causes my heart to burn within me: or only seeing the name of Christ, or the name of some attribute of God. And God has appeared glorious to me, on account of the Trinity. It has made me have exalting thoughts of God, that he subsists in three persons; Father, Son, and Holy Ghost.

The sweetest joys and delights I have experienced, have not been those that have arisen from a hope of my own good estate; but in a direct view of the glorious things of the gospel. When I enjoy this sweetness, it seems to carry me above the thoughts of my own safe estate. It seems at such times

4. Edwards alludes to Psalm 23.2: "He maketh me to lie down in green pastures: he leadeth me beside the still waters."

a loss that I cannot bear, to take off my eye from the glorious, pleasant object I behold without me, to turn my eye in upon myself, and my own good estate.

My heart has been much on the advancement of Christ's kingdom in the world. The histories of the past advancement of Christ's kingdom, have been sweet to me. When I have read histories of past ages, the pleasantest thing in all my reading has been, to read of the kingdom of Christ being promoted. And when I have expected in my reading, to come to any such thing, I have lotted[5] upon it all the way as I read. And my mind has been much entertained and delighted, with the Scripture promises and prophecies, of the future glorious advancement of Christ's kingdom on earth.

I have sometimes had a sense of the excellent fullness of Christ, and his meetness and suitableness as a Savior; whereby he has appeared to me, far above all, the chief of ten thousands.[6] And his blood and atonement has appeared sweet, and his righteousness sweet; which is always accompanied with an ardency of spirit, and inward strugglings and breathings and groanings, that cannot be uttered, to be emptied of myself, and swallowed up in Christ.

Once, as I rid out into the woods for my health, *anno*[7] 1737; and having lit from my horse in a retired place, as my manner commonly has been, to walk for divine contemplation and prayer; I had a view, that for me was extraordinary, of the glory of the Son of God; as mediator between God and man; and his wonderful, great, full, pure and sweet grace and love, and meek and gentle condescension.[8] This grace, that appeared to me so calm and sweet, appeared great above the heavens. The person of Christ appeared ineffably excellent, with an excellency great enough to swallow up all thought and conception. Which continued, as near as I can judge, about an hour; which kept me, the bigger part of the time, in a flood of tears, and weeping aloud. I felt withal, an ardency of soul to be, what I know not otherwise how to express, than to be emptied and annihilated; to lie in the dust, and to be full of Christ alone; to love him with a holy and pure love; to trust in him; to live upon him; to serve and follow him, and to be totally wrapt up in the fullness of Christ; and to be perfectly sanctified and made pure, with a divine and heavenly purity. I have several other times, had views very much of the same nature, and that have had the same effects.

I have many times had a sense of the glory of the third person in the Trinity, in his office of Sanctifier; in his holy operations communicating divine light and life to the soul. God in the communications of his Holy Spirit, has appeared as an infinite fountain of divine glory and sweetness; being full and sufficient to fill and satisfy the soul: pouring forth itself in sweet communications, like the sun in its glory, sweetly and pleasantly diffusing light and life.

I have sometimes had an affecting sense of the excellency of the word of God, as a word of life; as the light of life; a sweet, excellent, life-giving word: accompanied with a thirsting after that word, that it might dwell richly in my heart.

5. Rejoiced.
6. "My beloved is white and ruddy, the chiefest among ten thousand" (Song of Solomon 5.10).
7. In the year (Latin).
8. Regard for those of lesser status.

I have often since I lived in this town, had very affecting views of my own sinfulness and vileness; very frequently so as to hold me in a kind of loud weeping, sometimes for a considerable time together: so that I have often been forced to shut myself up.[9] I have had a vastly greater sense of my wickedness, and the badness of my heart, since my conversion, than ever I had before. It has often appeared to me, that if God should mark iniquity against me, I should appear the very worst of all mankind; of all that have been since the beginning of the world of this time: and that I should have by far the lowest place in hell. When others that have come to talk with me about their soul concerns, have expressed the sense they have had of their own wickedness, by saying that it seemed to them, that they were as bad as the devil himself; I thought their expressions seemed exceeding faint and feeble, to represent my wickedness. I thought I should wonder, that they should content themselves with such expressions as these, if I had any reason to imagine, that their sin bore any proportion to mine. It seemed to me, I should wonder at myself, if I should express my wickedness in such feeble terms as they did.

My wickedness, as I am in myself, has long appeared to me perfectly ineffable, and infinitely swallowing up all thought and imagination; like an infinite deluge, or infinite mountains over my head. I know not how to express better, what my sins appear to me to be, than by heaping infinite upon infinite, and multiplying infinite by infinite. I go about very often, for this many years, with these expressions in my mind, and in my mouth, "Infinite upon infinite. Infinite upon infinite!" When I look into my heart, and take a view of my wickedness, it looks like an abyss infinitely deeper than hell. And it appears to me, that were it not for free grace, exalted and raised up to the infinite height of all the fullness and glory of the great Jehovah,[1] and the arm of his power and grace stretched forth, in all the majesty of his power, and in all the glory of his sovereignty; I should appear sunk down in my sins infinitely below hell itself, far beyond sight of everything, but the piercing eye of God's grace, that can pierce even down to such a depth, and to the bottom of such an abyss.

And yet, I ben't in the least inclined to think, that I have a greater conviction of sin than ordinary. It seems to me, my conviction of sin is exceeding small, and faint. It appears to me enough to amaze me, that I have no more sense of my sin. I know certainly, that I have very little sense of my sinfulness. That my sins appear to me so great, don't seem to me to be, because I have so much more conviction of sin than other Christians, but because I am so much worse, and have so much more wickedness to be convinced of. When I have had these turns of weeping and crying for my sins, I thought I knew in the time of it, that my repentance was nothing to my sin.

I have greatly longed of late, for a broken heart, and to lie low before God. And when I ask for humility of God, I can't bear the thoughts of being no more humble, than other Christians. It seems to me, that though their degrees of humility may be suitable for them; yet it would be a vile self-exaltation in me, not to be the lowest in humility of all mankind. Others speak of their longing to be humbled to the dust. Though that may be a proper expres-

9. I.e., retire to his study. 1. The name used for God in the Old Testament.

sion for them, I always think for myself, that I ought to be humbled down below hell. 'Tis an expression that it has long been natural for me to use in prayer to God. I ought to lie infinitely low before God.

It is affecting to me to think, how ignorant I was, when I was a young Christian, of the bottomless, infinite depths of wickedness, pride, hypocrisy and deceit left in my heart.

I have vastly a greater sense, of my universal, exceeding dependence on God's grace and strength, and mere good pleasure, of late, than I used formerly to have; and have experienced more of an abhorrence of my own righteousness. The thought of any comfort or joy, arising in me, on any consideration, or reflection on my own amiableness, or any of my performances or experiences, or any goodness of heart or life, is nauseous and detestable to me. And yet I am greatly afflicted with a proud and self-righteous spirit; much more sensibly, than I used to be formerly. I see that serpent rising and putting forth its head, continually, everywhere, all around me.

Though it seems to me, that in some respects I was a far better Christian, for two or three years after my first conversion, than I am now; and lived in a more constant delight and pleasure: yet of late years, I have had a more full and constant sense of the absolute sovereignty of God, and a delight in that sovereignty; and have had more of a sense of the glory of Christ, as a mediator, as revealed in the Gospel. On one Saturday night in particular, had a particular discovery of the excellency of the gospel of Christ, above all other doctrines; so that I could not but say to myself; "This is my chosen light, my chosen doctrine": and of Christ, "This is my chosen prophet." It appeared to me to be sweet beyond all expression, to follow Christ, and to be taught and enlightened and instructed by him; to learn of him, and live to him.

Another Saturday night, January 1738–9, had such a sense, how sweet and blessed a thing it was, to walk in the way of duty, to do that which was right and meet to be done, and agreeable to the holy mind of God; that it caused me to break forth into a kind of a loud weeping, which held me some time; so that I was forced to shut myself up, and fasten the doors. I could not but as it were cry out, "How happy are they which do that which is right in the sight of God! They are blessed indeed, they are the happy ones!" I had at the same time, a very affecting sense, how meet and suitable it was that God should govern the world, and order all things according to his own pleasure; and I rejoiced in it, that God reigned, and that his will was done.

c. 1740 1765

On Sarah Pierpont[1]

They say there is a young lady in [New Haven] who is beloved of that almighty Being, who made and rules the world, and that there are certain seasons in which this great Being, in some way or other invisible, comes to her and fills her mind with exceeding sweet delight, and that she hardly cares for any-

1. When Edwards was twenty and his future wife thirteen, he inscribed this tribute on the flyleaf of a book. It was first published in Sereno E. Dwight's *The Life of President Edwards* (1829). The text here is from *Works of Jonathan Edwards* (1998), vol. 16, edited by George Claghorn.

thing, except to meditate on him—that she expects after a while to be received up where he is, to be raised up out of the world and caught up into heaven; being assured that he loves her too well to let her remain at a distance from him always. There she is to dwell with him, and to be ravished with his love, favor and delight, forever. Therefore, if you present all the world before her, with the richest of its treasures, she disregards it and cares not for it, and is unmindful of any pain or affliction. She has a strange sweetness in her mind, and sweetness of temper, uncommon purity in her affections; is most just and praiseworthy in all her actions; and you could not persuade her to do anything thought wrong or sinful, if you would give her all the world, lest she should offend this great Being. She is of a wonderful sweetness, calmness and universal benevolence of mind; especially after those times in which this great God has manifested himself to her mind. She will sometimes go about, singing sweetly, from place to [place]; and seems to be always full of joy and pleasure; and no one knows for what. She loves to be alone, and to wander in the fields and on the mountains, and seems to have someone invisible always conversing with her.

1723 1829

Sarah Edwards's Narrative[1]

I have been particularly acquainted with many persons that have been the subjects of the high and extraordinary transports of the present day; and in the highest transports of any of the instances that I have been acquainted with, and where the affections of admiration, love and joy, so far as another could judge, have been raised to a higher pitch than in any other instances I have observed or been informed of, the following things have been united: viz[2] a very frequent dwelling, for some considerable time together, in such views of the glory of the divine perfections, and Christ's excellencies, that the soul in the meantime has been as it were perfectly overwhelmed, and swallowed up with light and love and a sweet solace, rest and joy of soul, that was altogether unspeakable; and more than once continuing for five or six hours together, without any interruption, in that clear and lively view or sense of the infinite beauty and amiableness of Christ's person, and the heavenly sweetness of his excellent and transcendent love; so that (to use the person's own expressions) the soul remained in a kind of heavenly Elysium, and did as it were swim in the rays of Christ's love, like a little mote swimming in the beams of the sun, or streams of his light that come in at a window; and the heart was swallowed up in a kind of glow of Christ's love, coming down from Christ's heart in heaven, as a constant stream of sweet light, at the same time the soul all flowing out in love to him; so that there seemed to be a constant flowing and reflowing from heart to heart. The soul dwelt on high, and was lost in God, and seemed almost to leave the body;

1. Edwards first transcribed his wife's narrative, then revised his transcription for inclusion in *Some Thoughts Concerning the Present Revival of* *Religion* (1742).
2. Abbreviation for *videlicet*: that is to say, namely (Latin).

dwelling in a pure delight that fed and satisfied the soul; enjoying pleasure without the least sting, or any interruption, a sweetness that the soul was lost in; so that (so far as the judgment and word of a person of discretion may be taken, speaking upon the most deliberate consideration) what was enjoyed in each single minute of the whole space, which was many hours, was undoubtedly worth more than all the outward comfort and pleasure of the whole life put together; and this without being in any trance, or being at all deprived of the exercise of the bodily senses: and the like heavenly delight and unspeakable joy of soul, enjoyed from time to time, for years together; though not frequently so long together, to such an height: extraordinary views of divine things, and religious affections, being frequently attended with very great effects on the body, nature often sinking under the weight of divine discoveries, the strength of the body taken away, so as to deprive of all ability to stand or speak; sometimes the hands clinched, and the flesh cold, but senses still remaining; animal nature often in a great emotion and agitation, and the soul very often, of late, so overcome with great admiration, and a kind of omnipotent joy, as to cause the person (wholly unavoidably) to leap with all the might, with joy and mighty exultation of soul; the soul at the same time being so strongly drawn towards God and Christ in heaven, that it seemed to the person as though soul and body would, as it were of themselves, of necessity mount up, leave the earth and ascend thither.

These effects on the body did not begin now in this wonderful season, that they should be owing to the influence of the example of the times, but about seven years ago; and began in a much higher degree, and greater frequency, near three years ago, when there was no such enthusiastical season, as many account this, but it was a very dead time through the land. They arose from no distemper catched from Mr. Whitefield or Mr. Tennent,[3] because they began before either of them came into the country; they began, as I said, near three years ago, in a great increase, upon an extraordinary self-dedication, and renunciation of the world, and resignation of all to God, made in a great view of God's excellency, and high exercise of love to him, and rest and joy in him; since which time they have been very frequent; and began in a yet higher degree, and greater frequency, about a year and [a] half ago, upon another new resignation of all to God, with a yet greater fervency and delight of soul; since which time the body has been very often fainting with the love of Christ; and began in a much higher degree still, the last winter, upon another resignation and acceptance of God, as the only portion and happiness of the soul, wherein the whole world, with the dearest enjoyments in it, were renounced as dirt and dung, and all that is pleasant and glorious, and all that is terrible in this world, seemed perfectly to vanish into nothing, and nothing to be left but God, in whom the soul was perfectly swallowed up, as in an infinite ocean of blessedness: since which time there have often been great agitations of body, and an unavoidable leaping for joy; and the soul as it were dwelling almost without interruption, in a kind of paradise; and very often, in high transports, disposed to speak of those great and glorious things of God and Christ, and the eternal world, that are in view, to others that are present, in a most earnest manner, and

3. George Whitefield (1714–1770) and Gilbert Tennent (1703–1764), influential revivalists.

with a loud voice, so that it is next to impossible to avoid it: these effects on the body not arising from any bodily distemper or weakness, because the greatest of all have been in a good state of health. This great rejoicing has been a rejoicing with trembling, i.e. attended with a deep and lively sense of the greatness and majesty of God, and the person's own exceeding littleness and vileness: spiritual joys in this person never were attended, either formerly or lately, with the least appearance of any laughter or lightness of countenance, or manner of speaking; but with a peculiar abhorrence of such appearances in spiritual rejoicings, especially since joys have been greatest of all. These high transports when they have been past, have had abiding effects in the increase of the sweetness, rest and humility that they have left upon the soul; and a new engagedness of heart to live to God's honor, and watch and fight against sin. And these things not in one that is in the giddy age of youth, nor in a new convert, and unexperienced Christian, but in one that was converted above twenty-seven years ago; and neither converted nor educated in that enthusiastical town of Northampton (as some may be ready to call it), but in a town and family that none that I[4] know of suspected of enthusiasm; and in a Christian that has been long, in an uncommon manner, growing in grace, and rising, by very sensible degrees, to higher love to God, and weanedness from the world, and mastery over sin and temptation, through great trials and conflicts, and long continued struggling and fighting with sin, and earnest and constant prayer and labor in religion, and engagedness of mind in the use of all means, attended with a great exactness of life: which growth has been attended, not only with a great increase of religious affections, but with a wonderful alteration of outward behavior, in many things, visible to those who are most intimately acquainted, so as lately to have become as it were a new person; and particularly in living so much more above the world, and in a greater degree of steadfastness and strength in the way of duty and self-denial, maintaining the Christian conflict against temptations, and conquering from time to time under great trials; persisting in an unmoved, untouched calm and rest; under the changes and accidents of time.

✦ The person had formerly in lower degrees of grace, been subject to unsteadiness, and many ups and downs, in the frame of mind; the mind being under great disadvantages, through a vapory habit of body,[5] and often subject to melancholy, and at times almost overborne with it, it having been so even from early youth: but strength of grace, and divine light has of a long time, wholly conquered these disadvantages, and carried the mind in a constant manner, quite above all such effects of vapors.[6] Since that resignation spoken of before, made near three years ago, everything of that nature seems to be overcome and crushed by the power of faith and trust in God, and resignation to him; the person has remained in a constant uninterrupted rest, and humble joy in God, and assurance of his favor, without one hour's melancholy or darkness, from that day to this; vapors have had great effects on the body, such as they used to have before, but the soul has been always out of their reach. And this steadfastness and constancy has remained

4. I.e., Jonathan.
5. Roughly equivalent to "hysteria."

6. Being emotionally overcome.

through great outward changes and trials; such as times of the most extreme pain, and apparent hazard of immediate death. What has been felt in late great transports is known to be nothing new in kind, but to be of the same nature with what was felt formerly, when a little child of about five or six years of age; but only in a vastly higher degree. These transporting views and rapturous affections are not attended with any enthusiastic disposition to follow impulses, or any supposed prophetical revelations; nor have they been observed to be attended with any appearance of spiritual pride, but very much of a contrary disposition, an increase of a spirit of humility and meekness, and a disposition in honor to prefer others.[7] And 'tis worthy to be remarked, that at a time remarkably distinguished from all others, wherein discoveries and holy affections were evidently at the greatest height that ever happened, the greatness and clearness of divine light being overwhelming, and the strength and sweetness of divine love altogether overpowering, which began early in the morning of the Holy Sabbath, and lasted for days together, melting all down in the deepest humility and poverty of spirit, reverence and resignation, and the sweetest meekness, and universal benevolence; I say, 'tis worthy to be observed, that there were these two things in a remarkable manner felt at that time, viz. a peculiar sensible aversion to a judging others that were professing Christians of good standing in the visible[8] church, that they were not converted, or with respect to their degrees of grace; or at all intermeddling with that matter, so much as to determine against and condemn others in the thought of the heart; it appearing hateful, as not agreeing with that lamb-like[9] humility, meekness, gentleness and charity, which the soul then, above other times, saw the beauty of, and felt a disposition to. The disposition that was then felt was, on the contrary, to prefer others to self, and to hope that they saw more of God and loved him better; though before, under smaller discoveries and feebler exercises of divine affection, there had been felt a disposition to censure and condemn others. And another thing that was felt at that time, was a very great sense of the importance of moral social duties, and how great a part of religion lay in them: there was such a new sense and conviction of this, beyond what had been before, that it seemed to be as it were a clear discovery then made to the soul. But in general, there has been a very great increase of a sense of these two things, as divine views and divine love have increased.

The things already mentioned have been attended also with the following things, viz. an extraordinary sense of the awful majesty and greatness of God, so as oftentimes to take away the bodily strength; a sense of the holiness of God, as of a flame infinitely pure and bright, so as sometimes to overwhelm soul and body; a sense of the piercing all-seeing eye of God, so as sometimes to take away the bodily strength; and an extraordinary view of the infinite terribleness of the wrath of God, which has very frequently been strongly impressed on the mind, together with a sense of the ineffable misery of sinners that are exposed to this wrath, that has been overbearing: sometimes the exceeding pollution of the person's own heart, as a sink of all manner of abomination, and a nest of vipers, and the dreadfulness of an

eternal hell of God's wrath, opened to view both together; with a clear view of a desert of that misery, without the least degree of divine pity, and that by the pollution of the best duties; yea, only by the pollution and irreverence, and want of humility that attended once speaking of the holy name of God, when done in the best manner that ever it was done; the strength of the body very often taken away with a deep mourning for sin, as committed against so holy and good a God, sometimes with an affecting sense of actual sin, sometimes especially indwelling sin, sometimes the consideration of the sin of the heart as appearing in a particular thing, as for instance, in that there was no greater forwardness and readiness to self-denial for God and Christ, that had so denied himself for us; yea, sometimes the consideration of sin that was in only speaking one word concerning the infinitely great and holy God, has been so affecting as to overcome the strength of nature: very great sense of the certain truth of the great things revealed in the Gospel; an overwhelming sense of the glory of the work of redemption, and the way of salvation by Jesus Christ; the glorious harmony of the divine attributes appearing therein, as that wherein "mercy and truth are met together, and righteousness and peace have kissed each other";[1] a sight of the fulness and glorious sufficiency of Christ, that has been so affecting as to overcome the body: a constant immovable trust in God through Christ, with a great sense of his strength and faithfulness, the sureness of his covenant,[2] and the immutability of his promises, so that the everlasting mountains and perpetual hills have appeared as mere shadows to these things: sometimes the sufficiency and faithfulness of God as the covenant God of his people, appearing in these words, "I AM THAT I AM,"[3] in so affecting a manner as to overcome the body: a sense of the glorious, unsearchable, unerring wisdom of God in his works, both of creation and providence, so as to swallow up the soul, and overcome the strength of the body: a sweet rejoicing of soul at the thoughts of God's being infinitely and unchangeably happy, and an exulting gladness of heart that God is self-sufficient, and infinitely above all dependence, and reigns over all, and does his will with absolute and uncontrollable power and sovereignty; a sense of the glory of the Holy Spirit, as the great Comforter, so as to overwhelm both soul and body; only mentioning the word, "the Comforter," has immediately taken away all strength; that word, as the person expressed it, seemed great enough to fill heaven and earth: a most vehement and passionate desire of the honor and glory of God's name; a sensible, clear and constant preference of it not only to the person's own temporal interest, but spiritual comfort in this world; and a willingness to suffer the hidings of God's face, and to live and die in darkness and horror if God's honor should require it, and to have no other reward for it but that God's name should be glorified, although so much of the sweetness of the light of God's countenance had been experienced: a great lamenting of ingratitude, and the lowness of the degree of love to God, so as to deprive of bodily strength; and very often vehement longings and faintings after more love to Christ, and greater conformity to him; especially longing after these two things, viz. to be more perfect in humility and adoration; the flesh

1. Psalm 85.10.
2. God made the Covenant of Works with Adam, who then broke it. Jesus Christ made the Covenant of Grace with fallen humanity, declaring that believers in him would be saved.
3. Exodus 3.14.

and heart seems often to cry out for a lying low before God, and adoring him with greater love and humility: the thoughts of the perfect humility with which the saints in heaven worship God, and fall down before his throne, have often overcome the body, and set it into a great agitation.

A great delight in singing praises to God and Jesus Christ, and longing that this present life may be, as it were, one continued song of praise to God; longing, as the person expressed it, to sit and sing this life away; and an overcoming pleasure in the thoughts of spending an eternity in that exercise: a living by faith to a great degree; a constant and extraordinary distrust of own strength and wisdom; a great dependence on God for his help, in order to the performance of anything to God's acceptance, and being restrained from the most horrid sins, and running upon God, even on his neck, and "on the thick bosses of his bucklers":[4] such a sense of the black ingratitude of true saints' coldness and deadness in religion, and their setting their hearts on the things of this world, as to overcome the bodily frame: a great longing that all the children of God might be lively in religion, fervent in their love, and active in the service of God; and when there have been appearances of it in others, rejoicing so in beholding the pleasing sight, that the joy of soul has been too great for the body: taking pleasure in the thoughts of watching and striving against sin, and fighting through the way to heaven, and filling up this life with hard labor, and bearing the cross for Christ, as an opportunity to give God honor; not desiring to rest from labors till arrived in heaven, but abhorring the thoughts of it, and seeming astonished that God's own children should be backward to strive and deny themselves for God: earnest longings that all God's people might be clothed with humility and meekness, like the Lamb of God, and feel nothing in their hearts but love and compassion to all mankind; and great grief when anything to the contrary seems to appear in any of the children of God, as any bitterness, or fierceness of zeal, or censoriousness, or reflecting uncharitably on others, or disputing with any appearance of heat of spirit; a deep concern for the good of others' souls; a melting compassion to those that looked on themselves as in a state of nature, and to saints under darkness, so as to cause the body to faint: an universal benevolence to mankind, with a longing as it were to embrace the whole world in the arms of pity and love; ideas of suffering from enemies the utmost conceivable rage and cruelty, with a disposition felt to fervent love and pity in such a case, so far as it could be realized in thought; fainting with pity to the world that lies in ignorance and wickedness; sometimes a disposition felt to a life given up to mourning alone in a wilderness over a lost and miserable world; compassion towards them being often to that degree, that would allow of no support or rest, but in going to God, and pouring out the soul in prayer for them; earnest desires that the work of God that is now in the land, may be carried on, and that with greater purity, and freedom from all bitter zeal, censoriousness, spiritual pride, hot disputes, etc.

A vehement and constant desire for the setting up of Christ's kingdom through the earth, as a kingdom of holiness, purity, love, peace and happiness to mankind: the soul often entertained with unspeakable delight, and bodily strength overborne at the thoughts of heaven as a world of love, where

4. Job 15.26. A buckler is a shield, and the boss is the convex side of the shield.

love shall be the saints' eternal food, and they shall dwell in the light of love, and swim in an ocean of love, and where the very air and breath will be nothing but love; love to the people of God, or God's true saints, as such that have the image of Christ, and as those that will in a very little time shine in his perfect image, that has been attended with that endearment and oneness of heart, and that sweetness and ravishment of soul, that has been altogether inexpressible; the strength very often taken away with longings that others might love God more, and serve God better, and have more of his comfortable presence, than the person that was the subject of these longings, desiring to follow the whole world to heaven, or that everyone should go before, and be higher in grace and happiness, not by this person's diminution, but by others' increase: a delight in conversing of things of religion, and in seeing Christians together, talking of the most spiritual and heavenly things in religion, in a lively and feeling manner, and very frequently overcome with the pleasure of such conversation: a great sense often expressed, of the importance of the duty of charity to the poor, and how much the generality of Christians come short in the practice of it: a great sense of the need God's ministers have of much of the Spirit of God, at this day especially; and most earnest longings and wrestlings with God for them, so as to take away the bodily strength: the greatest, fullest, longest continued, and most constant assurance of the favor of God, and of a title to future glory, that ever I saw any appearance of in any person, enjoying, especially of late (to use the person's own expression) the riches of full assurance: formerly longing to die with something of impatience, but lately, since that resignation forementioned about three years ago, an uninterrupted entire resignation to God with respect to life or death, sickness or health, ease or pain, which has remained unchanged and unshaken, when actually under extreme and violent pains, and in times of threatenings of immediate death; but though there be this patience and submission, yet the thoughts of death and the day of judgment are always exceeding sweet to the soul. This resignation is also attended with a constant resignation of the lives of dearest earthly friends; and sometimes when some of their lives have been imminently threatened, often expressing the sweetness of the liberty of having wholly left the world, and renounced all for God, and having nothing but God, in whom is an infinite fulness.

These things have been attended with a constant sweet peace and calm and serenity of soul, without any cloud to interrupt it; a continual rejoicing in all the works of God's hands, the works of nature, and God's daily works of providence, all appearing with a sweet smile upon them; a wonderful access to God by prayer, as it were[5] seeing him, and sensibly immediately conversing with him, as much oftentimes (to use the person's own expressions) as if Christ were here on earth, sitting on a visible throne, to be approached to and conversed with; frequent, plain, sensible and immediate answers of prayer; all tears wiped away; all former troubles and sorrows of life forgotten, and all sorrow and sighing fled away, excepting grief for past sins and for remaining corruption, and that Christ is loved no more, and that God is no more honored in the world, and a compassionate grief towards

5. As if.

fellow creatures; a daily sensible doing and suffering everything for God for a long time past, eating for God, and working for God, and sleeping for God, and bearing pain and trouble for God, and doing all as the service of love, and so doing it with a continual, uninterrupted cheerfulness, peace and joy. "Oh how good," said the person once, "is it to work for God in the daytime, and at night to lie down under his smiles!" High experiences and religious affections in this person have not been attended with any disposition at all to neglect the necessary business of a secular calling, to spend the time in reading and prayer, and other exercises of devotion; but worldly business has been attended with great alacrity, as part of the service of God: the person declaring that it being done thus, 'tis found to be as good as prayer. These things have been accompanied with an exceeding concern and zeal for moral duties, and that all professors[6] may with them adorn the doctrine of God their Saviour; and an uncommon care to perform relative[7] and social duties, and a noted eminence in them; a great inoffensiveness of life and conversation in the sight of others; a great meekness, gentleness and benevolence of spirit and behavior; and a great alteration in those things that formerly used to be the person's failings; seeming to be much overcome and swallowed up by the late great increase of grace, to the observation of those that are most conversant and most intimately acquainted: in times of the brightest light and highest flights of love and joy, finding no disposition to any opinion of being now perfectly free from sin (agreeable to the notion of the Wesleys and their followers,[8] and some other high pretenders to spirituality in these days); but exceedingly the contrary: at such times especially, seeing how loathsome and polluted the soul is, soul and body and every act and word appearing like rottenness and corruption in that pure and holy light of God's glory: not slighting instruction or means of grace any more for having had great discoveries; on the contrary, never more sensible[9] of the need of instruction than now. And one thing more may be added, viz. that these things have been attended with a particular dislike of placing religion much in dress,[1] and spending much zeal about those things that in themselves are matters of indifference, or an affecting to shew humility and devotion by a mean habit,[2] or a demure and melancholy countenance, or anything singular and superstitious.

Now if such things are enthusiasm, and the fruits of a distempered brain, let my brain be evermore possessed of that happy distemper! If this be distraction, I pray God that the world of mankind may be all seized with this benign, meek, beneficent, beatifical, glorious distraction!

1742

6. Those who profess faith.
7. Family.
8. John Wesley (1703-1790) and his brother, Charles (1707-1788), were English clergymen instrumental in founding Methodism.
9. Aware.
1. I.e., in superficialities.
2. I.e., through poor clothing.

A Divine and Supernatural Light[1]

IMMEDIATELY IMPARTED TO THE SOUL BY THE SPIRIT OF GOD, SHOWN TO BE BOTH A SCRIPTURAL AND RATIONAL DOCTRINE

Matthew 16.17

And Jesus answered and said unto him, Blessed art thou, Simon Barjona;[2] for flesh and blood hath not revealed it unto thee, but my Father which is in heaven.

Christ addresses these words to Peter upon occasion of his professing his faith in Him as the Son of God. Our Lord was inquiring of His disciples, whom men said that He was; not that He needed to be informed, but only to introduce and give occasion to what follows. They answer that some said He was John the Baptist, and some Elias, and others Jeremias, or one of the prophets.[3] When they had thus given an account whom others said that He was, Christ asks them, whom they said that He was? Simon Peter, whom we find always zealous and forward, was the first to answer: he readily replied to the question, Thou art Christ, the Son of the living God.

Upon this occasion, Christ says as He does to him and of him in the text: in which we may observe.

1. That Peter is pronounced blessed on this account.—Blessed art thou— "Thou art an happy man, that thou art not ignorant of this, that I am Christ, the Son of the living God. Thou art distinguishingly happy. Others are blinded, and have dark and deluded apprehensions, as you have now given an account, some thinking that I am Elias, and some that I am Jeremias, and some one thing, and some another: but none of them thinking right, all of them are misled. Happy art thou, that art so distinguished as to know the truth in this matter."

2. The evidence of this his happiness declared, viz.,[4] That God, and He only, had revealed it to him. This is an evidence of his being blessed.

First. As it shows how peculiarly favored he was of God above others; q.d., "How highly favored art thou, that others, wise and great men, the scribes, Pharisees,[5] and rulers, and the nation in general, are left in darkness, to follow their own misguided apprehensions; and that thou shouldst be singled out, as it were, by name, that My heavenly Father should thus set His love on thee, Simon Bar-jona.—This argues thee blessed, that thou shouldst thus be the object of God's distinguishing love."

Secondly. It evidences his blessedness also, as it intimates that this knowledge is above any that flesh and blood can reveal. "This is such knowledge as only my Father which is in heaven can give. It is too high and excellent to be communicated by such means as other knowledge is. Thou art blessed, that thou knowest what God alone can teach thee."

1. Edwards delivered this sermon in Northampton; it was published the following year at the request of his congregation. The text here is from *The Works of Jonathan Edwards* (1829–30), vol. 6, edited by Sereno E. Dwight.
2. Simon, son of Jona; also known as the Apostle Peter.
3. Matthew 16.14. Elias is the name used in the New Testament for the prophet Elijah.
4. Abbreviation for *videlicet*: that is to say, namely (Latin).
5. A sect hostile to Jesus and known for their arrogance and pride (Matthew 9.9–13). "Scribes": interpreters of the Jewish law. "Q.d.": abbreviation for *quasi dicat*: as if he should say (Latin).

The original of this knowledge is here declared, both negatively and positively. Positively, as God is here declared the author of it. Negatively, as it is declared, that flesh and blood had not revealed it. God is the author of all knowledge and understanding whatsoever. He is the author of all moral prudence, and of the skill that men have in their secular business. Thus it is said of all in Israel that were wise-hearted and skilled in embroidering, that God had filled them with the spirit of wisdom. Exodus 28.3.[6]

God is the author of such knowledge; yet so that flesh and blood reveals it. Mortal men are capable of imparting the knowledge of human arts and sciences, and skill in temporal affairs. God is the author of such knowledge by those means: flesh and blood is employed as the mediate or second cause of it; He conveys it by the power and influence of natural means. But this spiritual knowledge, spoken of in the text, is what God is the author of, and none else: He reveals it, and flesh and blood reveals it not. He imparts this knowledge immediately, not making use of any intermediate natural causes, as He does in other knowledge.

What had passed in the preceding discourse naturally occasioned Christ to observe this; because the disciples had been telling how others did not know Him, but were generally mistaken about him, divided and confounded in their opinions of Him: but Peter had declared his assured faith, that He was the Son of God. Now it was natural to observe how it was not flesh and blood that had revealed it to him, but God; for if this knowledge were dependent on natural causes or means, how came it to pass that they, a company of poor fishermen, illiterate men, and persons of low education, attained to the knowledge of the truth, while the Scribes and Pharisees, men of vastly higher advantages, and greater knowledge and sagacity, in other matters, remained in ignorance? This could be owing only to the gracious distinguishing influence and revelation of the Spirit of God. Hence, what I would make the subject of my present discourse from these words, is this:

Doctrine

That there is such a thing as a spiritual and divine light, immediately imparted to the soul by God, of a different nature from any that is obtained by natural means. And on this subject I would,

I. Show what this divine light is.
II. How it is given immediately by God, and not obtained by natural means.
III. Show the truth of the doctrine.
And then conclude with a brief improvement.[7]

I. I would show what this spiritual and divine light is. And in order to it would show,

First, In a few things, what it is not. And here,

1. Those convictions that natural men may have of their sin and misery, is not this spiritual and divine light. Men, in a natural condition, may have

6. This Bible passage refers to God's command to the people of Israel to make proper garments for Aaron's priesthood.

7. Literally, turning something to profit; here, the lesson to be learned.

convictions of the guilt that lies upon them, and of the anger of God, and their danger of divine vengeance. Such convictions are from the light of truth. That some sinners have a greater conviction of their guilt and misery than others is because some have more light, or more of an apprehension of truth than others. And this light and conviction may be from the Spirit of God; the Spirit convinces men of sin; but yet nature is much more concerned in it than in the communication of that spiritual and divine light that is spoken of in the doctrine; it is from the Spirit of God only as assisting natural principles, and not as infusing any new principles. Common grace differs from special in that it influences only by assisting of nature, and not by imparting grace, or bestowing anything above nature. The light that is obtained is wholly natural, or of no superior kind to what mere nature attains to, though more of that kind be obtained than would be obtained if men were left wholly to themselves; or, in other words, common grace only assists the faculties of the soul to do that more fully which they do by nature, as natural conscience or reason will by mere nature make a man sensible of guilt, and will accuse and condemn him when he has done amiss. Conscience is a principle natural to men; and the work that it doth naturally, or of itself, is to give an apprehension of right and wrong, and to suggest to the mind the relation that there is between right and wrong and a retribution. The Spirit of God, in those convictions which unregenerate men[8] sometimes have, assists conscience to do this work in a further degree than it would do if they were left to themselves. He helps it against those things that tend to stupify it, and obstruct its exercise. But in the renewing and sanctifying work of the Holy Ghost, those things are wrought in the soul that are above nature, and of which there is nothing of the like kind in the soul by nature; and they are caused to exist in the soul habitually, and according to such a stated constitution or law, that lays such a foundation for exercises in a continued course, as is called a principle of nature. Not only are remaining principles assisted to do their work more freely and fully, but those principles are restored that were utterly destroyed by the fall; and the mind thenceforward habitually exerts those acts that the dominion of sin had made it as wholly destitute of as a dead body is of vital acts.

The Spirit of God acts in a very different manner in the one case, from what He doth in the other. He may, indeed, act upon the mind of a natural man, but He acts in the mind of a saint[9] as an indwelling vital principle. He acts upon the mind of an unregenerate person as an extrinsic occasional agent; for, in acting upon them, He doth not unite himself to them: for, notwithstanding all His influences that they may possess, they are still sensual, having not the Spirit. Jude 19.[1] But He unites himself with the mind of a saint, takes him for His temple, actuates and influences him as a new supernatural principle of life and action. There is this difference, that the Spirit of God, in acting in the soul of a godly man, exerts and communicates Himself there in His own proper nature. Holiness is the proper nature

8. Those who are not yet saved.
9. Here, a living Christian who has passed from mere understanding of Christ's doctrine to heartfelt commitment; such people were often called "visible saints."
1. "These be they who separate themselves, sensual, having not the Spirit."

of the Spirit of God. The Holy Spirit operates in the minds of the godly, by uniting Himself to them, and living in them, and exerting His own nature in the exercise of their faculties. The Spirit of God may act upon a creature, and yet not in acting communicate Himself. The Spirit of God may act upon inanimate creatures, as, the Spirit moved upon the face of the waters,[2] in the beginning of the creation; so the Spirit of God may act upon the minds of men many ways, and communicate Himself no more than when He acts upon an inanimate creature. For instance, He may excite thoughts in them, may assist their natural reason and understanding, or may assist other natural principles, and this without any union with the soul, but may act, as it were, upon an external object. But as He acts in His holy influences and spiritual operations, He acts in a way of peculiar communication of Himself; so that the subject is thence denominated spiritual.

2. This spiritual and divine light does not consist in any impression made upon the imagination. It is no impression upon the mind, as though one saw anything with the bodily eyes. It is no imagination or idea of an outward light or glory, or any beauty of form or countenance, or a visible luster or brightness of any object. The imagination may be strongly impressed with such things; but this is not spiritual light. Indeed when the mind has a lively discovery of spiritual things, and is greatly affected with the power of divine light, it may, and probably very commonly doth, much affect the imagination; so that impressions of an outward beauty or brightness may accompany those spiritual discoveries. But spiritual light is not that impression upon the imagination, but an exceedingly different thing. Natural men may have lively impressions on their imaginations; and we cannot determine but that the devil, who transforms himself into an angel of light,[3] may cause imaginations of an outward beauty, or visible glory, and of sounds and speeches, and other such things; but these are things of a vastly inferior nature to spiritual light.

3. This spiritual light is not the suggesting of any new truths or propositions not contained in the word of God. This suggesting of new truths or doctrines to the mind, independent of any antecedent revelations of those propositions, either in word or writing, is inspiration; such as the prophets and apostles had, and such as some enthusiasts[4] pretend to. But this spiritual light that I am speaking of, is quite a different thing from inspiration. It reveals no new doctrine, it suggests no new proposition to the mind, it teaches no new thing of God, or Christ, or another world, not taught in the Bible, but only gives a due apprehension of those things that are taught in the word of God.

4. It is not every affecting[5] view that men have of religious things that is this spiritual and divine light. Men by mere principles of nature are capable of being affected with things that have a special relation to religion as well as other things. A person by mere nature, for instance, may be liable to be affected with the story of Jesus Christ, and the sufferings he underwent, as well as by any other tragical story. He may be the more affected with it from

2. Genesis 1.2.
3. Satan, a fallen angel, is also known as Lucifer (from the Latin for "bringing light" and originally associated with the morning star, Venus).
4. People who erroneously claim to be inspired by the spirit of God.
5. Emotionally arousing.

the interest he conceives mankind to have in it. Yea, he may be affected with it without believing it; as well as a man may be affected with what he reads in a romance, or sees acted in a stage play. He may be affected with a lively and eloquent description of many pleasant things that attend the state of the blessed in heaven, as well as his imagination be entertained by a romantic[6] description of the pleasantness of fairyland, or the like. And a common belief of the truth of such things, from education or otherwise, may help forward their affection. We read in Scripture of many that were greatly affected with things of a religious nature, who yet are there represented as wholly graceless, and many of them very ill[7] men. A person therefore may have affecting views of the things of religion, and yet be very destitute of spiritual light. Flesh and blood may be the author of this; one man may give another an affecting view of divine things with but common assistance; but God alone can give a spiritual discovery of them.—But I proceed to show.

Secondly, Positively what this spiritual and divine light is.

And it may be thus described: A true sense of the divine excellency of the things revealed in the word of God, and a conviction of the truth and reality of them thence arising. This spiritual light primarily consists in the former of these, viz., a real sense and apprehension of the divine excellency of things revealed in the word of God. A spiritual and saving conviction of the truth and reality of these things, arises from such a sight of their divine excellency and glory; so that this conviction of their truth is an effect and natural consequence of this sight of their divine glory. There is therefore in this spiritual light,

1. A true sense of the divine and superlative excellency of the things of religion; a real sense of the excellency of God and Jesus Christ, and of the work of redemption, and the ways and works of God revealed in the gospel. There is a divine and superlative glory in these things; an excellency that is of a vastly higher kind, and more sublime nature than in other things; a glory greatly distinguishing them from all that is earthly and temporal. He that is spiritually enlightened truly apprehends and sees it, or has a sense of it. He does not merely rationally believe that God is glorious, but he has a sense of the gloriousness of God in his heart. There is not only a rational belief that God is holy, and that holiness is a good thing, but there is a sense of the loveliness of God's holiness. There is not only a speculatively judging that God is gracious, but a sense how amiable God is on account of the beauty of this divine attribute.

There is a twofold knowledge of good of which God has made the mind of man capable. The first, that which is merely notional; as when a person only speculatively judges that anything is, which by the agreement of mankind, is called good or excellent, viz., that which is most to general advantage, and between which and a reward there is a suitableness,—and the like. And the other is, that which consists in the sense of the heart; as when the heart is sensible[8] of pleasure and delight in the presence of the idea of it. In the former is exercised merely the speculative faculty, or the

6. Fanciful, imaginary. 8. Aware.
7. I.e., evil.

understanding, in distinction from the will or disposition of the soul. In the latter, the will, or inclination, or heart, are mainly concerned.

Thus there is a difference between having an opinion, that God is holy and gracious, and having a sense of the loveliness and beauty of that holiness and grace. There is a difference between having a rational judgment that honey is sweet, and having a sense of its sweetness. A man may have the former, that knows not how honey tastes; but a man cannot have the latter unless he has an idea of the taste of honey in his mind. So there is a difference between believing that a person is beautiful, and having a sense of his beauty. The former may be obtained by hearsay, but the latter only by seeing the countenance. When the heart is sensible of the beauty and amiableness of a thing, it necessarily feels pleasure in the apprehension. It is implied in a person's being heartily sensible of the loveliness of a thing, that the idea of it is pleasant to his soul; which is a far different thing from having a rational opinion that it is excellent.

2. There arises from this sense of the divine excellency of things contained in the word of God, a conviction of the truth and reality of them; and that, either indirectly or directly.

First, Indirectly, and that two ways:

1. As the prejudices of the heart, against the truth of divine things, are hereby removed; so that the mind becomes susceptive of the due force of rational arguments for their truth. The mind of man is naturally full of prejudices against divine truth. It is full of enmity against the doctrines of the gospel; which is a disadvantage to those arguments that prove their truth, and causes them to lose their force upon the mind. But when a person has discovered to him the divine excellency of Christian doctrines, this destroys the enmity, removes those prejudices, sanctifies the reason, and causes it to lie open to the force of arguments for their truth.

Hence was the different effect that Christ's miracles had to convince the disciples, from what they had to convince the Scribes and Pharisees. Not that they had a stronger reason, or had their reason more improved; but their reason was sanctified, and those blinding prejudices, that the Scribes and Pharisees were under, were removed by the sense they had of the excellency of Christ, and his doctrine.

It not only removes the hindrances of reason, but positively helps reason. It makes even the speculative notions more lively. It engages the attention of the mind, with more fixedness and intenseness to that kind of objects; which causes it to have a clearer view of them, and enables it more clearly to see their mutual relations, and occasions it to take more notice of them. The ideas themselves that otherwise are dim and obscure are by this means impressed with the greater strength, and have a light cast upon them, so that the mind can better judge of them. As he that beholds objects on the face of the earth, when the light of the sun is cast upon them, is under greater advantage to discern them in their true forms and natural relations, than he that sees them in a dim twilight.

The mind, being sensible of the excellency of divine objects, dwells upon them with delight; and the powers of the soul are more awakened and enlivened to employ themselves in the contemplation of them, and exert themselves more fully and much more to the purpose. The beauty of the objects draws on the faculties, and draws forth their exercises; so that reason itself

is under far greater advantages for its proper and free exercises, and to attain its proper end, free of darkness and delusion.—But,

Secondly, A true sense of the divine excellency of the things of God's word doth more directly and immediately convince us of their truth; and that because the excellency of these things is so superlative. There is a beauty in them so divine and godlike, that it greatly and evidently distinguishes them from things merely human, or that of which men are the inventors and authors; a glory so high and great, that when clearly seen, commands assent to their divine reality. When there is an actual and lively discovery of this beauty and excellency, it will not allow of any such thought as that it is the fruit of men's invention. This is a kind of intuitive and immediate evidence. They believe the doctrines of God's word to be divine, because they see a divine, and transcendent, and most evidently distinguishing glory in them; such a glory as, if clearly seen, does not leave room to doubt of their being of God, and not of men.

Such a conviction of the truths of religion as this, arising from a sense of their divine excellency, is included in saving faith. And this original of it is that by which it is most essentially distinguished from that common assent, of which unregenerate men are capable.

II. I proceed now to the second thing proposed, viz., to show how this light is immediately given by God, and not obtained by natural means. And here,

1. It is not intended that the natural faculties are not used in it. They are the subject of this light: and in such a manner, that they are not merely passive, but active in it. God, in letting in this light into the soul, deals with man according to his nature, and makes use of his rational faculties. But yet this light is not the less immediately from God for that; the faculties are made use of as the subject, and not as the cause. As the use we make of our eyes in beholding various objects, when the sun arises, is not the cause of the light that discovers those objects to us.

2. It is not intended that outward means have no concern in this affair. It is not in this affair, as in inspiration, where new truths are suggested; for, by this light is given only a due apprehension of the same truths that are revealed in the word of God, and therefore it is not given without the word. The gospel is employed in this affair. This light is the "light of the glorious gospel of Christ" (2 Corinthians 4.3–4).[9] The gospel is as a glass, by which this light is conveyed to us (1 Corinthians 13.12): "Now we see through a glass."[1]—But,

3. When it is said that this light is given immediately by God, and not obtained by natural means, hereby is intended that it is given by God without making use of any means that operate by their own power or natural force. God makes use of means; but it is not as mediate causes to produce this effect. There are not truly any second causes of it; but it is produced by God immediately. The word of God is no proper cause of this effect, but is made use of only to convey to the mind the subject matter of this saving

9. "But if our gospel be hid, it is hid to them that are lost: In whom the god of this world hath blinded the minds of them which believe not, lest the light of the glorious gospel of Christ, who is the image of God, should shine unto them."
1. "For now we see through a glass, darkly; but then face to face."

instruction: And this indeed it doth convey to us by natural force or influence. It conveys to our minds these doctrines; it is the cause of a notion of them in our heads, but not of the sense of their divine excellency in our hearts. Indeed a person cannot have spiritual light without the word. But that does not argue, that the word properly causes that light. The mind cannot see the excellency of any doctrine, unless that doctrine be first in the mind; but seeing the excellency of the doctrine may be immediately from the Spirit of God; though the conveying of the doctrine, or proposition, itself, may be by the word. So that the notions which are the subject matter of this light are conveyed to the mind by the word of God; but that due sense of the heart, wherein this light formally consists, is immediately by the Spirit of God. As, for instance, the notion that there is a Christ, and that Christ is holy and gracious, is conveyed to the mind by the word of God: But the sense of the excellency of Christ, by reason of that holiness and grace, is nevertheless, immediately the work of the Holy Spirit.—I come now,

III. To show the truth of the doctrine; that is, to show that there is such a thing as that spiritural light that has been described, thus immediately let into the mind by God. And here I would show, briefly, that this doctrine is both scriptural and rational.

First, It is scriptural. My text is not only full to the purpose, but it is a doctrine with which the Scripture abounds. We are there abundantly taught, that the saints differ from the ungodly in this; that they have the knowledge of God, and a sight of God, and of Jesus Christ. I shall mention but few texts out of many: 1 John 3.6: "Whosoever sinneth, hath not seen him, nor known him." 3 John 11: "He that doeth good, is of God: but he that doeth evil, hath not seen God." John 14.19: "The world seeth me no more; but ye see me." John 17.3: "And this is eternal life, that they might know thee, the only true God, and Jesus Christ whom thou hast sent." This knowledge, or sight of God and Christ, cannot be a mere speculative knowledge, because it is spoken of as that wherein they differ from the ungodly. And by these scriptures, it must not only be a different knowledge in degree and circumstances, and different in its effects, but it must be entirely different in nature and kind.

And this light and knowledge is always spoken of as immediately given of God; Matthew 11.25–27: "At that time, Jesus answered and said, I thank thee, O Father, Lord of heaven and earth, because thou hast hid these things from the wise and prudent, and hast revealed them unto babes. Even so, Father, for so it seemed good in thy sight. All things are delivered unto me of my Father: and no man knoweth the Father, save the Son, and he to whomsoever the Son will reveal him." Here this effect is ascribed exclusively to the arbitrary operation and gift of God bestowing this knowledge on whom He will, and distinguishing those with it who have the least natural advantage or means for knowledge, even babes, when it is denied to the wise and prudent. And imparting this knowledge is here appropriated to the Son of God, as His sole prerogative. And again, 2 Corinthians 4.6: "For God, who commanded the light to shine out of darkness, hath shined in our hearts, to give the light of the knowledge of the glory of God, in the face of Jesus Christ." This plainly shows, that there is a discovery of the divine superlative glory and excellency of God and Christ, peculiar to the saints: and,

also, that it is as immediately from God, as light from the sun, and that it is the immediate effect of His power and will. For it is compared to God's creating the light by his powerful word in the beginning of the creation; and is said to be by the Spirit of the Lord, in the 18th verse of the preceding chapter. God is spoken of as giving the knowledge of Christ in conversion, as of what before was hidden and unseen; Galatians 1.15–16: "But when it pleased God, who separated me from my mother's womb, and called me by his grace, to reveal his son in me." The scripture also speaks plainly of such a knowledge of the word of God, as has been described as the immediate gift of God; Psalm 119.18: "Open thou mine eyes, that I may behold wondrous things out of thy law." What could the Psalmist mean, when he begged of God to open his eyes? Was he ever blind? Might he not have resort to the law, and see every word and sentence in it when he pleased? And what could he mean by those wondrous things? Were they the wonderful stories of the creation, and deluge, and Israel's passing through the Red Sea,[2] and the like? Were not his eyes open to read these strange things when he would? Doubtless, by wondrous things in God's law, he had respect to those distinguishing and wonderful excellencies, and marvelous manifestations of the divine perfections and glory contained in the commands and doctrines of the word, and those works and counsels of God that were there revealed. So the scripture speaks of a knowledge of God's dispensation, and covenant of mercy,[3] and way of grace towards His people, as peculiar to the saints, and given only by God; Psalm 25.14: "The secret of the Lord is with them that fear him; and he will show them his covenant."

And that a true and saving belief of the truth of religion is that which arises from such a discovery is, also, what the scripture teaches. As John 6.40: "And this is the will of him that sent me, that every one who seeth the Son, and believeth on him, may have everlasting life"; where it is plain that a true faith is what arises from a spiritual sight of Christ. And John 17.6–8: "I have manifested thy name unto the men which thou gavest me out of the world. Now, they have known, that all things whatsoever thou hast given me, are of thee. For I have given unto them the words which thou gavest me, and they have received them, and have known surely, that I came out from thee, and they have believed that thou didst send me"; where Christ's manifesting God's name to the disciples, or giving them the knowledge of God, was that whereby they knew that Christ's doctrine was of God, and that Christ Himself proceeded from Him, and was sent by Him. Again, John 12.44–46: "Jesus cried, and said, He that believeth on me, believeth not on me but on him that sent me. And he that seeth me, seeth him that sent me. I am come a light into the world, that whosoever believeth on me, should not abide in darkness." Their believing in Christ, and spiritually seeing Him, are parallel.

Christ condemns the Jews, that they did not know that He was the Messiah, and that His doctrine was true, from an inward distinguishing taste and relish of what was divine, in Luke 12.56–57. He having there blamed

2. The waters of the Red Sea divided for the Israelites in their exodus from Egypt (Exodus 14.21).
3. The agreement between Jesus Christ and those who believe in him that they would be saved; also known as the Covenant of Faith, as distinct from the Covenant of Works, which Adam broke.

the Jews, that, though they could discern the face of the sky and of the earth, and signs of the weather, that yet they could not discern those times—or, as it is expressed in Matthew, the signs of those times—adds, "yea, and why even of your ownselves, judge ye not what is right?" i.e., without extrinsic signs. Why have ye not that sense of true excellency, whereby ye may distinguish that which is holy and divine? Why have ye not that savor of the things of God, by which you may see the distinguishing glory, and evident divinity of me and my doctrine?

The apostle Peter mentions it as what gave him and his companions good and well-grounded assurance of the truth of the gospel, that they had seen the divine glory of Christ. 2 Peter 1.16: "For we have not followed cunningly devised fables, when we made known unto you the power and coming of our Lord Jesus Christ, but were eye-witnesses of his majesty." The apostle has respect to that visible glory of Christ which they saw in His transfiguration. That glory was so divine, having such an ineffable appearance and semblance of divine holiness, majesty, and grace, that it evidently denoted Him to be a divine person. But if a sight of Christ's outward glory might give a rational assurance of His divinity, why may not an apprehension of His spiritual glory do so too? Doubtless Christ's spiritual glory is in itself as distinguishing, and as plainly shows His divinity, as His outward glory—nay, a great deal more, for His spiritual glory is that wherein His divinity consists; and the outward glory of His transfiguration showed Him to be divine, only as it was a remarkable image or representation of that spiritual glory. Doubtless, therefore, he that has had a clear sight of the spiritual glory of Christ, may say, "I have not followed cunningly devised fables, but have been an eyewitness of His majesty, upon as good grounds as the apostle, when he had respect to the outward glory of Christ that he had seen." But this brings me to what was proposed next, viz., to show that,

Secondly, This doctrine is rational.[4]

1. It is rational to suppose, that there is really such an excellency in divine things—so transcendent and exceedingly different from what is in other things—that if it were seen, would most evidently distinguish them. We cannot rationally doubt but that things divine, which appertain to the supreme Being, are vastly different from things that are human; that there is a high, glorious, and godlike excellency in them that does most remarkably difference them from the things that are of men, insomuch that if the difference were but seen, it would have a convincing, satisfying influence upon anyone that they are divine. What reason can be offered against it unless we would argue that God is not remarkably distinguished in glory from men.

If Christ should now appear to any one as he did on the mount at His transfiguration,[5] or if He should appear to the world in His heavenly glory, as He will do at the Day of Judgment,[6] without doubt, His glory and majesty would be such as would satisfy everyone that He was a divine person, and that His religion was true; and it would be a most reasonable, and well grounded conviction too. And why may there not be that stamp of divinity

4. Capable of being grasped by the mind, understandable.
5. In Matthew 17.1–8, Christ appeared to Peter, James, and John shining "as the sun" and his garments "white as the light."
6. See Revelation 4.

or divine glory on the word of God, on the scheme and doctrine of the gospel, that may be in like manner distinguishing and as rationally convincing, provided it be but seen? It is rational to suppose, that when God speaks to the world, there should be something in His word vastly different from men's word. Supposing that God never had spoken to the world, but we had notice that He was about to reveal Himself from heaven and speak to us immediately Himself, or that He should give us a book of His own inditing;[7] after what manner should we expect that He would speak? Would it not be rational to suppose, that His speech would be exceeding different from men's speech, that there should be such an excellency and sublimity in His word, such a stamp of wisdom, holiness, majesty, and other divine perfections, that the word of men, yea of the wisest of men, should appear mean[8] and base in comparison of it? Doubtless it would be thought rational to expect this, and unreasonable to think otherwise. When a wise man speaks in the exercise of His wisdom, there is something in everything He says, that is very distinguishable from the talk of a little child. So, without doubt, and much more is the speech of God, to be distinguished from that of the wisest of men; agreeable to Jeremiah 23.28–29. God, having there been reproving the false prophets that prophesied in his name, and pretended that what they spake was His word, when indeed it was their own word, says, "The prophet that hath a dream, let him tell a dream; and he that hath my word let him speak my word faithfully: what is the chaff to the wheat? saith the Lord. Is not my word like as a fire? saith the Lord: and like a hammer that breaketh the rock in pieces?"

2. If there be such a distinguishing excellency in divine things, it is rational to suppose that there may be such a thing as seeing it. What should hinder but that it may be seen? It is no argument that there is no such distinguishing excellency, or that it cannot be seen, because some do not see it, though they may be discerning men in temporal matters. It is not rational to suppose, if there be any such excellency in divine things, that wicked men should see it. Is it rational to suppose that those whose minds are full of spiritual pollution, and under the power of filthy lusts, should have any relish or sense of divine beauty or excellency; or that their minds should be susceptive of that light that is in its own nature so pure and heavenly? It need not seem at all strange that sin should so blind the mind, seeing that men's particular natural tempers and dispositions will so much blind them in secular matters; as when men's natural temper is melancholy, jealous, fearful, proud, or the like.

3. It is rational to suppose that this knowledge should be given immediately by God, and not be obtained by natural means. Upon what account should it seem unreasonable that there should be any immediate communication between God and the creature? It is strange, that men should make any matter of difficulty of it. Why should not He that made all things still have something immediately to do with the things that He has made? Where lies the great difficulty, if we own the being of a God, and that He created all things out of nothing, of allowing some immediate influence of God on the creation still? And if it be reasonable to suppose it with respect

7. Composition. 8. Low, unethical.

to any part of the creation, it is especially so with respect to reasonable, intelligent creatures; who are next to God in the gradation of the different orders of beings, and whose business is most immediately with God; and reason teaches that man was made to serve and glorify his Creator. And if it be rational to suppose that God immediately communicates Himself to man in any affair, it is in this. It is rational to suppose that God would reserve that knowledge and wisdom, which is of such a divine and excellent nature, to be bestowed immediately by Himself, and that it should not be left in the power of second causes. Spiritual wisdom and grace is the highest and most excellent gift that ever God bestows on any creature; in this, the highest excellency and perfection of a rational creature consists. It is also immensely the most important of all divine gifts: it is that wherein man's happiness consists, and on which his everlasting welfare depends. How rational is it to suppose that God, however He has left lower gifts to second causes, and in some sort in their power, yet should reserve this most excellent, divine, and important of all divine communications in His own hands to be bestowed immediately by Himself, as a thing too great for second causes to be concerned in. It is rational to suppose that this blessing should be immediately from God, for there is no gift or benefit that is in itself so nearly related to the divine nature. Nothing which the creature receives is so much a participation of the Deity; it is a kind of emanation of God's beauty, and is related to God as the light is to the sun. It is, therefore, congruous and fit, that when it is given of God, it should be immediately from Himself, and by Himself, according to His own sovereign will.

It is rational to suppose, that it should be beyond man's power to obtain this light by the mere strength of natural reason; for it is not a thing that belongs to reason to see the beauty and loveliness of spiritual things; it is not a speculative thing, but depends on the sense of the heart. Reason, indeed, is necessary, in order to it, as it is by reason only that we are become the subjects of the means of it; which means, I have already shown to be necessary in order to it, though they have no proper causal influence in the affair.[9] It is by reason that we become possessed of a notion of those doctrines that are the subject matter of this divine light or knowledge; and reason may many ways be indirectly and remotely an advantage to it. Reason has also to do in the acts that are immediately consequent on this discovery: for, seeing the truth of religion from hence, is by reason, though it be but by one step, and the inference be immediate. So reason has to do in that accepting of and trusting in Christ that is consequent on it. But if we take reason strictly—not for the faculty of mental perception in general, but for ratiocination, or a power of inferring by arguments—the perceiving of spiritual beauty and excellency no more belongs to reason than it belongs to the sense of feeling to perceive colors, or to the power of seeing to perceive the sweetness of food. It is out of reason's province to perceive the beauty or loveliness of anything; such a perception does not belong to that faculty. Reason's work is to perceive truth and not excellency. It is not ratiocination that gives men the perception of the beauty and amiableness of a countenance, though it may be many ways indirectly an advantage to it; yet

9. I.e., it is through reason that God communicates grace via things and persons (i.e., "means").

it is no more reason that immediately perceives it than it is reason that perceives the sweetness of honey; it depends on the sense of the heart. Reason may determine that a countenance is beautiful to others, it may determine that honey is sweet to others, but it will never give me a perception of its sweetness.

I will conclude with a very brief improvement of what has been said.

First, this doctrine may lead us to reflect on the goodness of God, that has so ordered it, that a saving evidence of the truth of the Gospel is such as is attainable by persons of mean capacities and advantages, as well as those that are of the greatest parts and learning. If the evidence of the Gospel depended only on history and such reasonings as learned men only are capable of, it would be above the reach of far the greatest part of mankind. But persons with an ordinary degree of knowledge are capable, without a long and subtle train of reasoning, to see the divine excellency of the things of religion; they are capable of being taught by the Spirit of God, as well as learned men. The evidence that is this way obtained is vastly better and more satisfying than all that can be obtained by the arguings of those that are most learned and greatest masters of reason. And babes are as capable of knowing these things as the wise and prudent; and they are often hid from these when they are revealed to those. 1 Corinthians 1.26–27: "For ye see your calling, brethren, how that not many wise men, after the flesh, not many mighty, not many noble, are called. But God hath chosen the foolish things of the world."

Secondly, This doctrine may well put us upon examining ourselves, whether we have ever had this divine light let into our souls. If there be such a thing, doubtless it is of great importance whether we have thus been taught by the Spirit of God; whether the light of the glorious gospel of Christ, who is the image of God, hath shined unto us, giving us the light of the knowledge of the glory of God in the face of Jesus Christ; whether we have seen the Son, and believed on Him, or have that faith of gospel doctrines which arises from a spiritual sight of Christ.

Thirdly, All may hence be exhorted earnestly to seek this spiritual light. To influence and move to it, the following things may be considered.

1. This is the most excellent and divine wisdom that any creature is capable of. It is more excellent than any human learning; it is far more excellent than all the knowledge of the greatest philosophers or statesmen. Yea, the least glimpse of the glory of God in the face of Christ doth more exalt and ennoble the soul than all the knowledge of those that have the greatest speculative understanding in divinity without grace. This knowledge has the most noble object that can be, viz., the divine glory and excellency of God and Christ. The knowledge of these objects is that wherein consists the most excellent knowledge of the angels, yea, of God Himself.

2. This knowledge is that which is above all others sweet and joyful. Men have a great deal of pleasure in human knowledge, in studies of natural things; but this is nothing to that joy which arises from this divine light shining into the soul. This light gives a view of those things that are immensely the most exquisitely beautiful and capable of delighting the eye of the understanding. The spiritual light is the dawning of the light of glory in the heart. There is nothing so powerful as this to support persons in affliction, and to give the mind peace and brightness in this stormy and dark world.

3. This light is such as effectually influences the inclination and changes the nature of the soul. It assimilates our nature to the divine nature, and changes the soul into an image of the same glory that is beheld. 2 Corinthians 3.18: "But we all with open face, beholding as in a glass the glory of the Lord, are changed into the same image, from glory to glory, even as by the Spirit of the Lord." This knowledge will wean[1] from the world, and raise the inclination to heavenly things. It will turn the heart to God as the fountain of good, and to choose Him for the only portion. This light, and this only, will bring the soul to a saving close[2] with Christ. It conforms the heart to the gospel, mortifies its enmity and opposition against the scheme of salvation therein revealed; it causes the heart to embrace the joyful tidings, and entirely to adhere to, and acquiesce in, the revelation of Christ as our Savior; it causes the whole soul to accord and symphonize with it, admitting it with entire credit and respect, cleaving to it with full inclination and affection; and it effectually disposes the soul to give up itself entirely to Christ.

4. This light, and this only, has its fruit in an universal holiness of life. No merely notional or speculative understanding of the doctrines of religion will ever bring to this. But this light, as it reaches the bottom of the heart, and changes the nature, so it will effectually dispose to an universal obedience. It shows God as worthy to be obeyed and served. It draws forth the heart in a sincere love to God, which is the only principle of a true, gracious, and universal obedience, and it convinces of the reality of those glorious rewards that God has promised to them that obey Him.

1733 1734

Sinners in the Hands of an Angry God[1]

Deuteronomy 32.35

Their foot shall slide in due time.[2]

In this verse is threatened the vengeance of God on the wicked unbelieving Israelites, who were God's visible people, and who lived under the means of grace,[3] but who, notwithstanding all God's wonderful works towards them, remained (as in verse 28)[4] void of counsel, having no understanding in them. Under all the cultivations of heaven, they brought forth bitter and poisonous fruit, as in the two verses next preceding the text.[5] The expression I have

1. Draw us away.
2. Union.
1. Edwards delivered this sermon in Enfield, Connecticut, a town about thirty miles south of Northampton. According to Benjamin Trumbull's *A Complete History of Connecticut* (1797, 1818), Edwards read his sermon in a level voice with his sermon book in his left hand, and in spite of his calm, "there was such a breathing of distress, and weeping, that the preacher was obliged to speak to the people and desire silence, that he might be heard." The text here is from *The Works of Jonathan Edwards* (1829–30), vol. 7, edited by Sereno E. Dwight.
2. "To me belongeth vengeance, and recom-

pense; their foot shall slide in due time: for the day of their calamity is at hand, and the things that shall come upon them make haste."
3. I.e., the Ten Commandments.
4. "For they are a nation void of counsel, neither is there any understanding in them" (Deuteronomy 32.28).
5. "For their vine is of the vine of Sodom, and the fields of Gomorrah: their grapes are grapes of gall, their clusters are bitter: Their wine is the poison of dragons, and the cruel venom of asps" (Deuteronomy 32.32–33). Sodom and Gomorrah were wicked cities destroyed by a rain of fire and sulfur from heaven (Genesis 19.24).

chosen for my text, "Their foot shall slide in due time," seems to imply the following things, relating to the punishment and destruction to which these wicked Israelites were exposed.

1. That they were always exposed to destruction; as one that stands or walks in slippery places is always exposed to fall. This is implied in the manner of their destruction coming upon them, being represented by their foot sliding. The same is expressed, Psalm 73.18: "Surely thou didst set them in slippery places; thou castedst them down into destruction."

2. It implies that they were always exposed to sudden unexpected destruction. As he that walks in slippery places is every moment liable to fall, he cannot foresee one moment whether he shall stand or fall the next; and when he does fall, he falls at once without warning: which is also expressed in Psalm 73.18–19: "Surely thou didst set them in slippery places; thou castedst them down into destruction: How are they brought into desolation as in a moment!"

3. Another thing implied is, that they are liable to fall of themselves, without being thrown down by the hand of another; as he that stands or walks on slippery ground needs nothing but his own weight to throw him down.

4. That the reason why they are not fallen already, and do not fall now, is only that God's appointed time is not come. For it is said that when that due time, or appointed times comes, their foot shall slide. Then they shall be left to fall, as they are inclined by their own weight. God will not hold them up in these slippery places any longer, but will let them go; and then, at that very instant, they shall fall into destruction; as he that stands on such slippery declining ground, on the edge of a pit, he cannot stand alone, when he is let go he immediately falls and is lost.

The observation from the words that I would now insist upon is this. "There is nothing that keeps wicked men at any one moment out of hell, but the mere pleasure of God." By the mere pleasure of God, I mean His sovereign pleasure, His arbitrary will, restrained by no obligation, hindered by no manner of difficulty, any more than if nothing else but God's mere will had in the least degree, or in any respect whatsoever, any hand in the preservation of wicked men one moment. The truth of this observation may appear by the following considerations.

1. There is no want[6] of power in God to cast wicked men into hell at any moment. Men's hands cannot be strong when God rises up. The strongest have no power to resist Him, nor can any deliver[7] out of His hands. He is not only able to cast wicked men into hell, but He can most easily do it. Sometimes an earthly prince meets with a great deal of difficulty to subdue a rebel, who has found means to fortify himself, and has made himself strong by the numbers of his followers. But it is not so with God. There is no fortress that is any defense from the power of God. Though hand join in hand, and vast multitudes of God's enemies combine and associate themselves, they are easily broken in pieces. They are as great heaps of light chaff before the whirlwind; or large quantities of dry stubble before devouring flames. We find it easy to tread on and crush a worm that we see crawling on the earth; so it is easy for us to cut or singe a slender thread that any thing

6. Lack. 7. I.e., rescue others.

hangs by: thus easy is it for God, when he pleases, to cast His enemies down to hell. What are we, that we should think to stand before Him, at whose rebuke the earth trembles, and before whom the rocks are thrown down?

2. They deserve to be cast into hell; so that divine justice never stands in the way, it makes no objection against God's using His power at any moment to destroy them. Yea, on the contrary, justice calls aloud for an infinite punishment of their sins. Divine justice says of the tree that brings forth such grapes of Sodom, "Cut it down, why cumbereth it the ground?" Luke 13.7. The sword of divine justice is every moment brandished over their heads, and it is nothing but the hand of arbitrary mercy, and God's will, that holds it back.

3. They are already under a sentence of condemnation to hell. They do not only justly deserve to be cast down thither, but the sentence of the law of God, that eternal and immutable rule of righteousness that God has fixed between Him and mankind, is gone out against them, and stands against them; so that they are bound over[8] already to hell. John 3.18: "He that believeth not is condemned already." So that every unconverted man properly belongs to hell; that is his place; from thence he is, John 8.23: "Ye are from beneath." And thither he is bound; it is the place that justice, and God's word, and the sentence of his unchangeable law assign to him.

4. They are now the objects of that very same anger and wrath of God that is expressed in the torments of hell. And the reason why they do not go down to hell at each moment is not because God, in whose power they are, is not then very angry with them as He is with many miserable creatures now tormented in hell, who there feel and bear the fierceness of His wrath. Yea, God is a great deal more angry with great numbers that are now on earth: yea, doubtless, with many that are now in this congregation, who it may be are at ease, than He is with many of those who are now in the flames of hell.

So that it is not because God is unmindful of their wickedness, and does not resent it, that He does not let loose His hand and cut them off. God is not altogether such an one as themselves, though they may imagine Him to be so. The wrath of God burns against them, their damnation does not slumber; the pit is prepared, the fire is made ready, the furnace is now hot, ready to receive them; the flames do now rage and glow. The glittering sword is whet,[9] and held over them, and the pit hath opened its mouth under them.

5. The devil stands ready to fall upon them, and seize them as his own, at what moment God shall permit him. They belong to him; he has their souls in his possession, and under his dominion. The Scripture represents them as his goods, Luke 11.12.[1] The devils watch them; they are ever by them at their right hand; they stand waiting for them, like greedy hungry lions that see their prey, and expect to have it, but are for the present kept back. If God should withdraw His hand, by which they are restrained, they would in one moment fly upon their poor souls. The old serpent is gaping for them; hell opens its mouth wide to receive them; and if God should permit it, they would be hastily swallowed up and lost.

8. A legal phrase referring to the phase after an arraignment, when the accused is sent to trial. Here, it means condemned.

9. Sharpened.

1. "Or if he shall ask an egg, will he offer him a scorpion?"

6. There are in the souls of wicked men those hellish principles reigning that would presently kindle and flame out into hell fire, if it were not for God's restraints. There is laid in the very nature of carnal men a foundation for the torments of hell. There are those corrupt principles, in reigning power in them, and in full possession of them, that are seeds of hell fire. These principles are active and powerful, exceeding violent in their nature, and if it were not for the restraining hand of God upon them, they would soon break out, they would flame out after the same manner as the same corruptions, the same enmity does in the hearts of damned souls, and would beget the same torments as they do in them. The souls of the wicked are in Scripture compared to the troubled sea, Isaiah 57.20.[2] For the present, God restrains their wickedness by His mighty power, as He does the raging waves of the troubled sea, saying, "Hitherto shalt thou come, but no further;"[3] but if God should withdraw that restraining power, it would soon carry all before it. Sin is the ruin and misery of the soul; it is destructive in its nature; and if God should leave it without restraint, there would need nothing else to make the soul perfectly miserable. The corruption of the heart of man is immoderate and boundless in its fury; and while wicked men live here, it is like fire pent up by God's restraints, whereas if it were let loose, it would set on fire the course of nature; and as the heart is now a sink of sin, so if sin was not restrained, it would immediately turn the soul into a fiery oven, or a furnace of fire and brimstone.

7. It is no security to wicked men for one moment that there are no visible means of death at hand. It is no security to a natural[4] man that he is now in health and that he does not see which way he should now immediately go out of the world by any accident, and that there is no visible danger in any respect in his circumstances. The manifold and continual experience of the world in all ages, shows this is no evidence that a man is not on the very brink of eternity, and that the next step will not be into another world. The unseen, unthought-of ways and means of persons going suddenly out of the world are innumerable and inconceivable. Unconverted men walk over the pit of hell on a rotten covering, and there are innumerable places in this covering so weak that they will not bear their weight, and these places are not seen. The arrows of death fly unseen at noonday;[5] the sharpest sight cannot discern them. God has so many different unsearchable ways of taking wicked men out of the world and sending them to hell, that there is nothing to make it appear that God had need to be at the expense of a miracle, or go out of the ordinary course of His providence, to destroy any wicked man at any moment. All the means that there are of sinners going out of the world are so in God's hands, and so universally and absolutely subject to His power and determination, that it does not depend at all the less on the mere will of God whether sinners shall at any moment go to hell than if means were never made use of or at all concerned in the case.

8. Natural men's prudence and care to preserve their own lives, or the care of others to preserve them, do not secure them a moment. To this, divine

2. "But the wicked are like the troubled sea, when it cannot rest, whose waters cast up mire and dirt."
3. Job 38.11.

4. I.e., unregenerate, unsaved.
5. "Thou shalt not be afraid for the terror by night; nor for the arrow that flieth by day" (Psalm 91.5).

providence and universal experience do also bear testimony. There is this clear evidence that men's own wisdom is no security to them from death; that if it were otherwise we should see some difference between the wise and politic men of the world, and others, with regard to their liableness to early and unexpected death: but how is it in fact? Ecclesiastes 2.16: "How dieth the wise man? even as the fool."

9. All wicked men's pains and contrivance which they use to escape hell, while they continue to reject Christ, and so remain wicked men, do not secure them from hell one moment. Almost every natural man that hears of hell, flatters himself that he shall escape it; he depends upon himself for his own security; he flatters himself in what he has done, in what he is now doing, or what he intends to do. Every one lays out matters in his own mind how he shall avoid damnation, and flatters himself that he contrives well for himself, and that his schemes will not fail. They hear indeed that there are but few saved, and that the greater part of men that have died heretofore are gone to hell; but each one imagines that he lays out matters better for his own escape than others have done. He does not intend to come to that place of torment; he says within himself that he intends to take effectual care, and to order matters so for himself as not to fail.

But the foolish children of men miserably delude themselves in their own schemes, and in confidence in their own strength and wisdom; they trust to nothing but a shadow. The greater part of those who heretofore have lived under the same means of grace, and are now dead, are undoubtedly gone to hell; and it was not because they were not as wise as those who are now alive: it was not because they did not lay out matters as well for themselves to secure their own escape. If we could speak with them, and inquire of them, one by one, whether they expected when alive, and when they used to hear about hell, ever to be the subjects of that misery, we doubtless, should hear one and another reply, "No, I never intended to come here: I had laid out matters otherwise in my mind; I thought I should contrive well for myself: I thought my scheme good. I intended to take effectual care; but it came upon me unexpected; I did not look for it at that time, and in that manner; it came as a thief: Death outwitted me: God's wrath was too quick for me. Oh, my cursed foolishness! I was flattering myself, and pleasing myself with vain dreams of what I would do hereafter; and when I was saying, peace and safety, then suddenly destruction came upon me."

10. God has laid Himself under no obligation by any promise to keep any natural man out of hell one moment. God certainly has made no promises either of eternal life or of any deliverance or preservation from eternal death but what are contained in the covenant of grace,[6] the promises that are given in Christ, in whom all the promises are yea and amen. But surely they have no interest in the promises of the covenant of grace who are not the children of the covenant, who do not believe in any of the promises, and have no interest in the Mediator of the covenant.[7]

6. The original covenant God made with Adam is called the Covenant of Works; the second covenant Jesus Christ made with fallen humanity— declaring that if they believed in him they would be saved—is called the Covenant of Grace.

7. I.e., Christ, who mediated between God and humanity by taking upon himself the sins of the world and suffering for them.

So that, whatever some have imagined and pretended about promises made to natural men's earnest seeking and knocking,[8] it is plain and manifest that whatever pains a natural man takes in religion, whatever prayers he makes, till he believes in Christ, God is under no manner of obligation to keep him a moment from eternal destruction.

So that, thus it is that natural men are held in the hand of God, over the pit of hell; they have deserved the fiery pit, and are already sentenced to it; and God is dreadfully provoked. His anger is as great towards them as to those that are actually suffering the executions of the fierceness of His wrath in hell, and they have done nothing in the least to appease or abate that anger, neither is God in the least bound by any promise to hold them up one moment; the devil is waiting for them, hell is gaping for them, the flames gather and flash about them, and would fain lay hold on them, and swallow them up; the fire pent up in their own hearts is struggling to break out: and they have no interest in any Mediator, there are no means within reach that can be any security to them. In short, they have no refuge, nothing to take hold of; all that preserves them every moment is the mere arbitrary will, and uncovenanted, unobliged forbearance of an incensed God.

Application

The use of this awful[9] subject may be for awakening unconverted persons in this congregation. This that you have heard is the case of every one of you that are out of Christ. That world of misery, that lake of burning brimstone, is extended abroad under you. There is the dreadful pit of the glowing flames of the wrath of God; there is hell's wide gaping mouth open; and you have nothing to stand upon, nor any thing to take hold of; there is nothing between you and hell but the air; it is only the power and mere pleasure of God that holds you up.

You probably are not sensible[1] of this; you find you are kept out of hell, but do not see the hand of God in it; but look at other things, as the good state of your bodily constitution, your care of your own life, and the means you use for your own preservation. But indeed these things are nothing; if God should withdraw His hand, they would avail no more to keep you from falling, than the thin air to hold up a person that is suspended in it.

Your wickedness makes you as it were heavy as lead, and to tend downwards with great weight and pressure towards hell; and if God should let you go, you would immediately sink and swiftly descend and plunge into the bottomless gulf, and your healthy constitution, and your own care and prudence, and best contrivance, and all your righteousness, would have no more influence to uphold you and keep you out of hell, than a spider's web would have to stop a fallen rock. Were it not for the sovereign pleasure of God, the earth would not bear you one moment; for you are a burden to it; the creation groans with you; the creature is made subject to the bondage of your corruption, not willingly; the sun does not willingly shine upon you to give you light to serve sin and Satan; the earth does not willingly yield her increase

8. Matthew 7.7: "Ask, and it shall be given you; seek, and ye shall find; knock, and it shall be opened unto you." "Pretended": claimed.

9. Awe-inspiring.
1. Aware.

to satisfy your lusts; nor is it willingly a stage for your wickedness to be acted upon; the air does not willingly serve you for breath to maintain the flame of life in your vitals, while you spend your life in the service of God's enemies. God's creatures are good, and were made for men to serve God with, and do not willingly subserve to any other purpose, and groan when they are abused to purposes so directly contrary to their nature and end. And the world would spew you out, were it not for the sovereign hand of Him who hath subjected it in hope.[2] There are black clouds of God's wrath now hanging directly over your heads, full of the dreadful storm, and big with thunder; and were it not for the restraining hand of God, it would immediately burst forth upon you. The sovereign pleasure of God, for the present, stays His rough wind; otherwise it would come with fury, and your destruction would come like a whirlwind, and you would be like the chaff of the summer threshing floor.

The wrath of God is like great waters that are dammed for the present; they increase more and more, and rise higher and higher, till an outlet is given; and the longer the stream is stopped, the more rapid and mighty is its course when once it is let loose. It is true that judgment against your evil works has not been executed hitherto; the floods of God's vengeance have been withheld; but your guilt in the meantime is constantly increasing, and you are every day treasuring up more wrath; the waters are constantly rising, and waxing more and more mighty; and there is nothing but the mere pleasure of God that holds the waters back, that are unwilling to be stopped, and press hard to go forward. If God should only withdraw His hand from the floodgate, it would immediately fly open, and the fiery floods of the fierceness and wrath of God, would rush forth with inconceivable fury, and would come upon you with omnipotent power; and if your strength were ten thousand times greater than it is, yea, ten thousand times greater than the strength of the stoutest, sturdiest devil in hell, it would be nothing to withstand or endure it.

The bow of God's wrath is bent, and the arrow made ready on the string, and justice bends the arrow at your heart, and strains the bow, and it is nothing but the mere pleasure of God, and that of an angry God, without any promise or obligation at all, that keeps the arrow one moment from being made drunk with your blood. Thus all you that never passed under a great change of heart, by the mighty power of the Spirit of God upon your souls, all you that were never born again, and made new creatures, and raised from being dead in sin, to a state of new, and before altogether unexperienced light and life, are in the hands of an angry God. However you may have reformed your life in many things, and may have had religious affections, and may keep up a form of religion in your families and closets,[3] and in the house of God, it is nothing but His mere pleasure that keeps you from being this moment swallowed up in everlasting destruction. However unconvinced you may now be of the truth of what you hear, by and by you will be fully convinced of it. Those that are gone from being in the like circumstances with you see that it was so with them; for destruction came

2. Romans 8.20: "For the creature was made subject to vanity, not willingly, but because of Him who subjected it, in hope."

3. Studies; rooms for meditation. "Affections": feelings.

suddenly upon most of them; when they expected nothing of it and while they were saying, peace and safety: now they see that those things on which they depended for peace and safety, were nothing but thin air and empty shadows.

The God that holds you over the pit of hell, much as one holds a spider or some loathsome insect over the fire, abhors you, and is dreadfully provoked: His wrath towards you burns like fire; He looks upon you as worthy of nothing else but to be cast into the fire; He is of purer eyes than to bear to have you in His sight; you are ten thousand times more abominable in His eyes than the most hateful venomous serpent is in ours. You have offended Him infinitely more than ever a stubborn rebel did his prince; and yet it is nothing but His hand that holds you from falling into the fire every moment. It is to be ascribed to nothing else, that you did not go to hell the last night; that you was suffered to awake again in this world, after you closed your eyes to sleep. And there is no other reason to be given, why you have not dropped into hell since you arose in the morning, but that God's hand has held you up. There is no other reason to be given why you have not gone to hell, since you have sat here in the house of God, provoking His pure eyes by your sinful wicked manner of attending His solemn worship. Yea, there is nothing else that is to be given as a reason why you do not this very moment drop down into hell.

O sinner! Consider the fearful danger you are in: it is a great furnace of wrath, a wide and bottomless pit, full of the fire of wrath, that you are held over in the hand of that God, whose wrath is provoked and incensed as much against you, as against many of the damned in hell. You hang by a slender thread, with the flames of divine wrath flashing about it, and ready every moment to singe it, and burn it asunder; and you have no interest in any Mediator, and nothing to lay hold of to save yourself, nothing to keep off the flames of wrath, nothing of your own, nothing that you ever have done, nothing that you can do, to induce God to spare you one moment. And consider here more particularly.

1. Whose wrath it is: it is the wrath of the infinite God. If it were only the wrath of man, though it were of the most potent prince, it would be comparatively little to be regarded. The wrath of kings is very much dreaded, especially of absolute monarchs, who have the possessions and lives of their subjects wholly in their power, to be disposed of at their mere will. Proverbs 20.2: "The fear of a king is as the roaring of a lion: Whoso provoketh him to anger, sinneth against his own soul." The subject that very much enrages an arbitrary prince is liable to suffer the most extreme torments that human art can invent, or human power can inflict. But the greatest earthly potentates in their greatest majesty, and strength, and when clothed in their greatest terrors, are but feeble, despicable worms of the dust, in comparison of the great and almighty Creator and King of heaven and earth. It is but little that they can do, when most enraged, and when they have exerted the utmost of their fury. All the kings of the earth, before God, are as grasshoppers; they are nothing, and less than nothing: both their love and their hatred is to be despised. The wrath of the great King of kings, is as much more terrible than theirs, as His majesty is greater. Luke 12.4–5: "And I say unto you, my friends, Be not afraid of them that kill the body, and after that, have no more that they can do. But I will forewarn you whom you shall fear: fear

him, which after he hath killed, hath power to cast into hell: yea, I say unto you, Fear him."

2. It is the fierceness of His wrath that you are exposed to. We often read of the fury of God; as in Isaiah 59.18: "According to their deeds, accordingly he will repay fury to his adversaries." So Isaiah 66.15: "For behold, the Lord will come with fire, and with his chariots like a whirlwind, to render his anger with fury, and his rebuke with flames of fire." And in many other places. So, Revelation 19.15: we read of "the wine press of the fierceness and wrath of Almighty God."[4] The words are exceeding terrible. If it had only been said, "the wrath of God," the words would have implied that which is infinitely dreadful: but it is "the fierceness and wrath of God." The fury of God! the fierceness of Jehovah![5] Oh, how dreadful must that be! Who can utter or conceive what such expressions carry in them! But it is also "the fierceness and wrath of Almighty God." As though there would be a very great manifestation of His almighty power in what the fierceness of His wrath should inflict, as though omnipotence should be as it were enraged, and exerted, as men are wont to exert their strength in the fierceness of their wrath. Oh! then, what will be the consequence! What will become of the poor worms that shall suffer it! Whose hands can be strong? And whose heart can endure? To what a dreadful, inexpressible, inconceivable depth of misery must the poor creature be sunk who shall be the subject of this!

Consider this, you that are here present that yet remain in an unregenerate state. That God will execute the fierceness of His anger implies that He will inflict wrath without any pity. When God beholds the ineffable extremity of your case, and sees your torment to be so vastly disproportioned to your strength, and sees how your poor soul is crushed, and sinks down, as it were, into an infinite gloom; He will have no compassion upon you, He will not forbear the executions of His wrath, or in the least lighten His hand; there shall be no moderation or mercy, nor will God then at all stay His rough wind; He will have no regard to your welfare, nor be at all careful lest you should suffer too much in any other sense, than only that you shall not suffer beyond what strict justice requires. Nothing shall be withheld because it is so hard for you to bear. Ezekiel 8.18: "Therefore will I also deal in fury: mine eye shall not spare, neither will I have pity; and though they cry in mine ears with a loud voice, yet I will not hear them." Now God stands ready to pity you; this is a day of mercy; you may cry now with some encouragement of obtaining mercy. But when once the day of mercy is past, your most lamentable and dolorous cries and shrieks will be in vain; you will be wholly lost and thrown away of God as to any regard to your welfare. God will have no other use to put you to, but to suffer misery; you shall be continued in being to no other end; for you will be a vessel of wrath fitted to destruction; and there will be no other use of this vessel, but to be filled full of wrath. God will be so far from pitying you when you cry to Him, that it is said He will only "laugh and mock." Proverbs 1.25–26, etc.[6]

How awful are those words, Isaiah 63.3, which are the words of the great God: "I will tread them in mine anger, and will trample them in my fury,

4. "He treadeth the winepress of the fierceness and wrath of Almighty God."

5. The name used for God in the Old Testament.

6. "But ye have set at nought all my counsel, and would none of my reproof: I also will laugh at your calamity; I will mock you when your fear cometh."

and their blood shall be sprinkled upon my garments, and I will stain all my raiment." It is perhaps impossible to conceive of words that carry in them greater manifestations of these three things, viz.,[7] contempt, and hatred, and fierceness of indignation. If you cry to God to pity you, He will be so far from pitying you in your doleful case, or showing you the least regard or favor, that instead of that, He will only tread you under foot. And though He will know that you cannot bear the weight of omnipotence treading upon you, yet He will not regard that, but He will crush you under His feet without mercy; He will crush out your blood, and make it fly and it shall be sprinkled on His garments, so as to stain all His raiment. He will not only hate you, but He will have you in the utmost contempt: no place shall be thought fit for you, but under His feet to be trodden down as the mire of the streets.

3. The misery you are exposed to is that which God will inflict to that end, that He might show what that wrath of Jehovah is. God hath had it on His heart to show to angels and men both how excellent His love is, and also how terrible His wrath is. Sometimes earthly kings have a mind to show how terrible their wrath is, by the extreme punishments they would execute on those that would provoke them. Nebuchadnezzar, that mighty and haughty monarch of the Chaldean empire, was willing to show his wrath when enraged with Shadrach, Meshech, and Abednego; and accordingly gave orders that the burning fiery furnace should be heated seven times hotter than it was before; doubtless, it was raised to the utmost degree of fierceness that human art could raise it.[8] But the great God is also willing to show His wrath, and magnify His awful majesty and mighty power in the extreme sufferings of His enemies. Romans 9.22: "What if God, willing to show his wrath, and to make his power known, endure with much long-suffering the vessels of wrath fitted to destruction?" And seeing this is His design, and what He has determined, even to show how terrible the restrained wrath, the fury and fierceness of Jehovah is, He will do it to effect. There will be something accomplished and brought to pass that will be dreadful with a witness. When the great and angry God hath risen up and executed His awful vengeance on the poor sinner, and the wretch is actually suffering the infinite weight and power of His indignation, then will God call upon the whole universe to behold that awful majesty and mighty power that is to be seen in it. Isaiah 33.12–14: "And the people shall be as the burnings of lime, as thorns cut up shall they be burnt in the fire. Hear ye that are far off, what I have done; and ye that are near, acknowledge my might. The sinners in Zion are afraid; fearfulness hath surprised the hypocrites," etc.

Thus it will be with you that are in an unconverted state, if you continue in it; the infinite might, and majesty, and terribleness of the omnipotent God shall be magnified upon you, in the ineffable strength of your torments. You shall be tormented in the presence of the holy angels, and in the presence of the Lamb; and when you shall be in this state of suffering, the glorious inhabitants of heaven shall go forth and look on the awful spectacle, that they may see what the wrath and fierceness of the Almighty is; and when they have seen it, they will fall down and adore that great power and majesty.

7. Abbreviation for *videlicet*: that is to say, namely (Latin).
8. See Daniel 3.1–30.

Isaiah 66.23–24: "And it shall come to pass, that from one new moon to another, and from one sabbath to another, shall all flesh come to worship before me, saith the Lord. And they shall go forth and look upon the carcasses of the men that have transgressed against me; for their worm shall not die, neither shall their fire be quenched, and they shall be an abhorring unto all flesh."

4. It is everlasting wrath. It would be dreadful to suffer this fierceness and wrath of Almighty God one moment; but you must suffer it to all eternity. There will be no end to this exquisite horrible misery. When you look forward, you shall see a long forever, a boundless duration before you, which will swallow up your thoughts, and amaze your soul; and you will absolutely despair of ever having any deliverance, any end, any mitigation, any rest at all. You will know certainly that you must wear out long ages, millions of millions of ages, in wrestling and conflicting with this almighty merciless vengeance; and then when you have so done, when so many ages have actually been spent by you in this manner, you will know that all is but a point to what remains. So that your punishment will indeed be infinite. Oh, who can express what the state of a soul in such circumstances is! All that we can possibly say about it gives but a very feeble, faint representation of it; it is inexpressible and inconceivable: For "who knows the power of God's anger?"[9]

How dreadful is the state of those that are daily and hourly in the danger of this great wrath and infinite misery! But this is the dismal case of every soul in this congregation that has not been born again, however moral and strict, sober and religious, they may otherwise be. Oh that you would consider it, whether you be young or old! There is reason to think that there are many in this congregation now hearing this discourse that will actually be the subjects of this very misery to all eternity. We know not who they are, or in what seats they sit, or what thoughts they now have. It may be they are now at ease, and hear all these things without much disturbance, and are now flattering themselves that they are not the persons, promising themselves that they shall escape. If they knew that there was one person, and but one, in the whole congregation, that was to be the subject of this misery, what an awful thing would it be to think of! If we knew who it was, what an awful sight would it be to see such a person! How might all the rest of the congregation lift up a lamentable and bitter cry over him! But, alas! instead of one, how many is it likely will remember this discourse in hell? And it would be a wonder, if some that are now present should not be in hell in a very short time, even before this year is out. And it would be no wonder if some persons, that now sit here, in some seats of this meetinghouse, in health, quiet and secure, should be there before tomorrow morning. Those of you that finally continue in a natural condition, that shall keep out of hell longest will be there in a little time! your damnation does not slumber; it will come swiftly, and, in all probability, very suddenly upon many of you. You have reason to wonder that you are not already in hell. It is doubtless the case of some whom you have seen and known, that never deserved hell

9. "Who knoweth the power of thine anger? even according to thy fear, so is thy wrath" (Psalm 90.11).

more than you, and that heretofore appeared as likely to have been now alive as you. Their case is past all hope; they are crying in extreme misery and perfect despair; but here you are in the land of the living and in the house of God, and have an opportunity to obtain salvation. What would not those poor damned hopeless souls give for one day's opportunity such as you now enjoy!

And now you have an extraordinary opportunity, a day wherein Christ has thrown the door of mercy wide open, and stands in calling and crying with a loud voice to poor sinners; a day wherein many are flocking to Him, and pressing into the kingdom of God. Many are daily coming from the east, west, north and south; many that were very lately in the same miserable condition that you are in are now in a happy state, with their hearts filled with love to Him who has loved them, and washed them from their sins in His own blood, and rejoicing in hope of the glory of God. How awful is it to be left behind at such a day! To see so many others feasting, while you are pining and perishing! To see so many rejoicing and singing for joy of heart, while you have cause to mourn for sorrow of heart, and howl for vexation of spirit! How can you rest one moment in such a condition? Are not your souls as precious as the souls of the people at Suffield,[1] where they are flocking from day to day to Christ?

Are there not many here who have lived long in the world, and are not to this day born again? and so are aliens from the commonwealth of Israel,[2] and have done nothing ever since they have lived, but treasure up wrath against the day of wrath? Oh, sirs, your case, in an especial manner, is extremely dangerous. Your guilt and hardness of heart is extremely great. Do you not see how generally persons of your years are passed over and left, in the present remarkable and wonderful dispensation of God's mercy? You had need to consider yourselves, and awake thoroughly out of sleep. You cannot bear the fierceness and wrath of the infinite God. And you, young men, and young women, will you neglect this precious season which you now enjoy, when so many others of your age are renouncing all youthful vanities,[3] and flocking to Christ? You especially have now an extraordinary opportunity; but if you neglect it, it will soon be with you as with those persons who spent all the precious days of youth in sin, and are now come to such a dreadful pass in blindness and hardness. And you, children, who are unconverted, do not you know that you are going down to hell, to bear the dreadful wrath of that God, who is now angry with you every day and every night? Will you be content to be the children of the devil, when so many other children in the land are converted, and are become the holy and happy children of the King of kings?

And let every one that is yet out of Christ, and hanging over the pit of hell, whether they be old men and women, or middle-aged, or young people, or little children, now hearken to the loud calls of God's word and providence. This acceptable year of the Lord, a day of such great favors to some, will doubtless be a day of as remarkable vengeance to others. Men's hearts harden,

1. A town in the neighborhood [Edwards's note].
2. I.e., not among the chosen people, the saved.

3. Cf. Ecclesiastes 1.2.

and their guilt increases apace at such a day as this, if they neglect their souls; and never was there so great danger of such person being given up to hardness of heart and blindness of mind. God seems now to be hastily gathering in His elect[4] in all parts of the land; and probably the greater part of adult persons that ever shall be saved, will be brought in now in a little time, and that it will be as it was on the great outpouring of the Spirit upon the Jews in the apostles' days;[5] the election will obtain,[6] and the rest will be blinded. If this should be the case with you, you will eternally curse this day, and will curse the day that ever you was born, to see such a season of the pouring out of God's Spirit, and will wish that you had died and gone to hell before you had seen it. Now undoubtedly it is, as it was in the days of John the Baptist, the ax is in an extraordinary manner laid at the root of the trees,[7] that every tree which brings not forth good fruit, may be hewn down and cast into the fire.

Therefore, let everyone that is out of Christ, now awake and fly from the wrath to come. The wrath of Almighty God is now undoubtedly hanging over a great part of this congregation: Let everyone fly out of Sodom: "Haste and escape for your lives, look not behind you, escape to the mountain, lest you be consumed."[8]

Sunday, July 8, 1741.

1741

4. Those whom God has chosen to save.
5. In Acts 2, the Apostle Peter admonishes a crowd to repent and be converted, saying, "Save yourselves from this untoward generation. Then they that gladly received his word were baptized: and the same day there were added unto them about three thousand souls" (Acts 2.40–41).
6. I.e., during "the great outpouring of the Spirit," as in a revival, the elect will respond positively to God's call.
7. "And now also the ax is laid unto the root of the trees: therefore every tree which bringeth not forth good fruit is hewn down, and cast into the fire" (Matthew 3.10).
8. Genesis 19.17.

American Literature and the Varieties of Religious Expression

The religious revivals that Jonathan Edwards helped launch in 1734 reached a new level when the Reverend George Whitefield began touring the colonies in the late 1730s. Writing in his *Autobiography* of Whitefield's arrival in Philadelphia in 1739, Benjamin Franklin noted the popular English preacher's ability to draw "Multitudes of all Sects and Denominations." This inclusive religious impulse led to the construction of a meetinghouse "expressly for the use of any Preacher of any religious Persuasion who might desire to say something to the People of Philadelphia." Even a missionary sent "to preach Mohametanism [i.e., Islam] to us," Franklin remarked, "would find a Pulpit in his Service." The building eventually fell into disuse, and Franklin worked to repurpose it for the Academy of Philadelphia, a secondary school that evolved into the University of Pennyslvania. Yet the principle of religious inclusion embodied in the meetinghouse remained an important element in Franklin's thought, punctuating his reflections on how religion factored in his own life and in the life of the nation that was emerging even as he wrote these passages in late 1788 or early 1789.

Born in Puritan Boston and a longtime resident of Philadelphia (known as the Quaker City), Franklin was an experienced navigator of religious differences. The Quaker faith that is so prominent in Philadelphia emerged in England during the English Civil Wars (1642–51), when state control over speech, printing, and religious worship was loosened. Among the central principles distinguishing Quakers from traditional Protestants is the belief that the Bible is only one instance of the Word of God, which Quakers hold to be continuously expressed as an ongoing divine revelation in every individual, women equally with men, and made accessible through a faculty known as the Inner Light. In New England, this belief in the supremacy of immediate revelation made the Quakers deeply unpopular with Puritan leaders, who based their own challenge to religious authority on the centrality of Scripture. In the 1650s, the Massachusetts Bay Colony outlawed Quakerism, and around 1660 colonial officials executed four Quakers (including Mary Dyer, a former associate of John Winthrop's antagonist Anne Hutchinson), who came to be known as the Boston Martyrs. Despite such setbacks, the Quakers were more successful than many other radical Protestant groups at establishing a lasting institutional presence, in no small part through the efforts of the English preacher George Fox (1624–1691), who guided their transition from a loosely organized movement into the Religious Society of Friends. In 1681, Fox's associate William Penn received a royal charter to establish the colony of Pennsylvania as a haven of religious toleration.

Early Quakers practiced distinctive forms of expression related to their understanding of the Inner Light. The most pronounced of these verbal habits was their use of "plain speech," including the deliberately archaic use of "thee" and "thou" for "you." They were also known for encouraging women to preach. In the selections included here by Elizabeth Ashbridge and John Woolman, belief in the Inner Light and a commitment to plain speech are translated into language and narrative. A different aspect of Quakerism is represented in the poem here by Francis Daniel Pastorius, whose multilingual writings focus on the potential for language to foster unity within diversity. A number of prominent later American writers were influenced by Quakerism, including Charles Brockden Brown, James Fenimore Cooper, and Walt Whitman.

In Protestant writings, the Roman Catholic Church is often presented as a spiritual antagonist—characterized, for example, as the Antichrist or the Whore of Babylon. Anti-Catholic imagery in New England colonial literature tends to be closely tied to imperial rivalries with France and Spain. This political and spiritual competition was bound up with the development of rival print cultures and the production of literary works. In 1539, the first press in the Americas was established in Mexico City, a century before the press in Cambridge, Massachusetts. Spanish America developed a thriving print culture encompassing religious works, some at least partly in indigenous languages, as well as secular texts. The writings of Sor Juana Inés de la Cruz, who spent much of her life at a convent in Mexico City, demonstrate familiarity with both the secular and the religious poetic traditions of imperial Spain. Sor Juana, a contemporary of the Puritan poet Anne Bradstreet, employed distinctive themes and images tied to her religious orientation.

The Jesuit Relations are a different kind of literary enterprise altogether. Originally written in French, the Relations include reports in the form of letters sent from the missions of New France to the Paris headquarters of the Society of Jesus (i.e., the Jesuits). Filled with tales of the mission enterprise that can be surprising in their adventurousness and, at times, their violence, the printed Relations were received with great interest. The corporate authorship of these annual reports marks a distinction from the more individualist traditions of Puritan and Quaker writing. A Jesuit superior synthesized the reports from original letters and in-person accounts, as was the case with the Isaac Jogues narrative included here. Later works in the Jesuit tradition included saintly biographies—also known as hagiographies— represented by the chronicle of Kateri Tekakwitha's life.

While there are sizable bodies of Catholic and Quaker writing from pre-1820 North America, there is only a small archive of works by Jewish writers. The development of Jewish writing in the Western Hemisphere can be traced to events that took place in 1492. The year of Columbus's voyage was also the year when Ferdinand and Isabella of Spain completed the Reconquista (reconquest) of the Iberian Peninsula from the Islamic Moors. Moorish Spain had sometimes been a place of peaceful interactions between people of the major Abrahamic religions, with Christians, Jews, and Muslims living in comfortable proximity. Two months after defeating the Moors, however, the Spanish monarchs promulgated the Alhambra Decree, which declared that Spanish Jews had to make a difficult choice: either convert to Christianity or be forced to leave Spain. The extinction of Spanish Jewry was an unusually thorough instance of practices that had been prevalent throughout Europe for centuries. King Edward I of England had expelled that country's Jewish population in 1290. Oliver Cromwell orchestrated the opening of England to Jews in 1656—a shift in policy that Roger Williams supported in print and put into practice in the Providence Colony. Jewish communities in British North America grew slowly, and those who wanted to practice their religion faced numerous challenges. Rebecca Samuel was an eighteenth-century Jewish immigrant to the United States, probably from Germany. Included here are letters she wrote to her parents in 1791—the year that the First Amendment to the Constitution was adopted, establishing freedom of religion. They capture some of the complexities of Jewish life in the early United States, reflecting positively and negatively on the experience of being a religious outsider.

The two additional selections address indigenous religion in different ways. John Marrant's popular narrative of 1785 describes his life as a free black youth in Charleston, South Carolina, where a chance exposure to the eloquence of George Whitefield led to his conversion. Marrant's description of how he came to convert a Cherokee "king," while himself adopting Cherokee dress, captures the multiethnic dynamics of Protestant revivalism. In an 1805 address to the Christian missionary Jacob Cram, the Seneca chief Sagoyewatha pointedly rejects the logic of Christian conversion, asking to have indigenous beliefs respected and to be given an opportu-

nity to judge the effects of Christianity on the behavior of its white converts. Widely republished, Sagoyewatha's counternarrative of colonial settlement seems to have resonated with both Native and white audiences. The popularity of this speech shows that the desire for freedom of religion extended in many directions.

THE JESUIT RELATIONS

The Society of Jesus, or Jesuits, is a Roman Catholic religious order founded in 1534 by Ignatius of Loyola (1491–1556), a knight at the Spanish court of Ferdinand and Isabella. *The Jesuit Relations* is the name of a group of publications from the Jesuits' missionary project in New France. Published annually in Paris between 1632 and 1673, *The Jesuit Relations* narrated the major events of the year, including descriptions of indigenous life, chronicles of wars and epidemics, and accounts of stirring journeys and dramatic martyrdoms.

The first of the following two selections, relating the torture of Father Isaac Jogues (1607–1646) by Mohawks at the town of Gandaouague (Caughnawaga, New York), is drawn from the *Relation* of 1647. Father Jérôme Lalemant (1593–1673), the Provincial Superior of the Jesuits in Canada from 1645 to 1650, based his account on Jogues's spoken and written descriptions of the events represented here, which took place in 1642. After returning to France following these occurences, Jogues chose to return to North America, where he was later killed. The Church later named Jogues as the first of the "North American martyrs," a group of six Jesuit priests and two lay assistants who died while pursuing missionary activities in the 1640s.

The second selection is not from *The Jesuit Relations* proper but from *History and General Description of New France* (1744), by the Jesuit priest and writer P. F. X. Charlevoix (1682–1761). The subject of this hagiographic narrative is a young Mohawk woman, Kateri Tekakwitha (1656–1680), from what is now central New York. When she was around twenty, Tekakwitha (or Tegahkouita, as the name is rendered here) converted to Catholicism and moved to a Jesuit mission near Montreal. The narrative was translated into several languages, including English. In 2012, Tekakwitha became the first Native American to be canonized by the Roman Catholic Church.

Both selections are from *The Jesuit Relations: Natives and Missionaries in Seventeenth-Century North America* (2000), edited by Allan Greer. The bracketed insertions are Greer's.

JÉRÔME LALEMANT

From How Father Isaac Jogues Was Taken by the Iroquois, and What He Suffered on His First Entrance into Their Country

Father Isaac Jogues was born to a worthy family of the city of Orléans.[1] After he gave some evidence of his virtue in our society, he was sent to New France in the year 1636. In that very year, he went up to the Huron country, where he remained until the thirteenth of June in the year 1642, when he was sent to Quebec upon the affairs of that important and arduous mission.

From that time until his death, there occurred many remarkable things, of which one cannot without guilt deprive the public since they are honorable to God and full of consolation for souls who love to suffer for Jesus Christ. What has been said of his labors in the earlier *Relations* came, for the most part, from some Indians who had been companions in his sufferings. But what I am about to set down issued forth from his own pen and his own lips: It was necessary to use a superior's authority, along with gentle persuasion in our personal conversations, in order to discover that which the very low esteem in which he held himself kept concealed in a profound silence.

Sometime before his departure from the Hurons in order to come to Quebec, finding himself alone before the Blessed Sacrament,[2] he prostrated himself to the ground, beseeching our Lord to grant him the favor and grace of suffering for His glory. This answer was engraved in the depth of his soul, with a certainty similar to that which faith gives us: *Exaudita est oratio tua; fiet tibi sicut à me petisti. Confortare et esto robustus*, "Thy prayer is heard; what thou hast asked of me is granted thee. Be courageous and steadfast." The effects which followed have shown that these words, which were always present for him in all his sufferings, were genuinely substantial, words which issued from the lips of Him for whom saying and doing are one and the same thing.

Reverend Father Jérôme Lalemant, at that time superior of the mission among the Hurons, knowing nothing of this, sent for him and proposed to him the journey to Quebec. This would be a frightful voyage on account of the difficulty of the route, and very dangerous because of the ambushes of the Iroquois, who every year massacred a considerable number of the Indians allied to the French. Let us hear him [Father Jogues] speak upon this subject and upon the outcome of his journey.

"Authority having made me a simple proposition, and not a command, to go down to Quebec, I offered myself with all my heart. I was all the more

1. A city in north central France, south of Paris.
2. In Roman Catholicism, the bread and wine made sacred in a celebration called the Eucharist, or Holy Communion; sometimes, as here, dis-played on an altar. Catholics consider the Blessed Sacrament the actual flesh and blood of Jesus Christ.

willing, since otherwise some of our fathers who were much better than I might have been exposed to the perils and hazards that we all anticipate. And so we set out, in danger from the moment of our departure. We were obliged to disembark forty times, and forty times to carry our boats and all our baggage amid the rapids and waterfalls that one encounters on this journey of about three hundred leagues. Although the Indians who were conducting us were very skillful, we nevertheless incurred some disasters, to the great peril of our lives and with some loss of our small baggage. At last, thirty-five days after our departure from the Huron country, we arrived much fatigued at Three Rivers, and from there we descended to Quebec. We blessed God throughout for His goodness in preserving us. Our business being finished in fifteen days, we observed the Feast of Saint Ignace, and the next day, the first of August of the same year, 1642, we left Three Rivers to return to the country whence we had come.

"The first day was favorable to us, but the second caused us to fall into the hands of the Iroquois. We were forty persons, distributed in several canoes. The one that kept the vanguard discovered on the banks of the great river some tracks of men, recently imprinted on the sand and clay, and gave us warning. We put to shore. Some said that these were enemy tracks; others were sure that they were footprints of the Algonquins, our allies. In the midst of this argument, Eustache Ahatsistari, to whom all the others deferred on account of his exploits in arms and his virtue, exclaimed: 'Be they friends or enemies, it matters not. I notice by their tracks that they are not in greater number than we, so let us then advance without fear.' We had made less than half a league when the enemy, concealed among the grass and bushes, rose with a great outcry and discharged a volley of shots at our canoes. The noise of their arquebuses[3] so greatly frightened some of our Hurons that they abandoned their canoes and weapons and all their supplies to flee into the woods. This discharge had done us no great harm: No lives were lost, and only one Huron was shot through the hand. Our canoes, however, were broken in several places. We were four French, one of whom was in the rear and escaped with the Hurons, who abandoned him before approaching the enemy. Eight or ten [Hurons], both Christians and catechumens, joined us. We led them in a short prayer as they bravely faced the enemy, and though it was thirty men against twelve or fourteen, our people held on valiantly. But when they saw another band of forty Iroquois, who had been in ambush on the opposite shore of the river, coming to attack them, they lost courage, and those who were not then caught up in the fighting abandoned their comrades and took to their heels. No longer sustained by those who followed him, a Frenchman named René Goupil[4] (whose death is precious before God) was surrounded and captured, along with some of the most courageous Hurons.

"I was watching this disaster," says the father, "from a place very favorable for concealing me from the sight of the enemy, being able to hide myself in thickets and among very tall and dense reeds; but this thought could never enter my mind. 'Could I really,' I said to myself, 'abandon our French and

3. Muzzle-loaded firearms.
4. Nonclerical Jesuit missionary (1608–1642); like Jogues, one of the North American martyrs of the Roman Catholic Church.

leave those good neophytes and those poor catechumens, without giving them the succor that the church of my God has entrusted to me?' Flight seemed horrible to me. 'It must be,' I said in my heart, 'that my body suffer the fire of earth in order to deliver these poor souls from the flames of Hell. It must die a transient death, in order to procure for them an eternal life.' Having reached a decision without great opposition from my mind, I called one of the Iroquois who had remained to guard the prisoners. This man perceived me but hesitated to approach, for fear of some ambush. 'Come,' I said, 'be not afraid. Take me to the Frenchman and the Hurons whom you hold captive.' He advanced, seized me, and placed me in the number of those whom the world calls miserable. Tenderly embracing the Frenchman, I said to him: 'My dear brother, God treats us in a strange manner, but He is the master and he has done what has seemed best in his sight; he has followed his good pleasure. May His holy name be blessed forever.' This good young man at once made his confession, and I gave him absolution. I then approached the Hurons to instruct and baptize them. As more fugitives were being brought in by their pursuers every minute, I heard these too in confession, making Christians of those who had not been baptized. Finally, they brought that worthy Christian captain Eustache, who, on seeing me, exclaimed: 'Ah! My father, I swore and promised to you that I would live or die with you.' The sight of him pierced my heart. I do not remember what words I said to him.

"Another Frenchman, named Guillaume Couture, seeing that the Hurons were giving way, escaped like them into those great forests, and, as he was agile, he was soon out of the enemy's grasp. But he was seized with remorse because he had forsaken his father and his comrade. He stopped quite short, deliberating whether he should go on or retrace his steps. The fear of being regarded as treacherous made him turn around, and there he found himself facing five big Iroquois, one of whom was aiming a gun at him. The arquebus misfired, but the Frenchman did not fail to find his own mark and shot him dead on the spot. His shot spent, the four other Iroquois fell upon him like enraged lions, or rather like demons. They stripped him naked, beat him black-and-blue with clubs, and tore out his fingernails with their teeth, crushing the bleeding ends to cause him more pain. Finally, they pierced through one of his hands with a knife and led him, tied and bound in this sad plight, to the place where we were. When I recognized him, I broke away from my guards and embraced him. 'Courage, my dear brother and friend,' I urged him. 'Offer your pains and anguish to God on behalf of these men who torment you. We must not shrink back. Let us instead suffer bravely for His holy name. His glory was our only object in this journey.' The Iroquois were at first quite bewildered before these endearments, then, imagining perhaps that I was applauding this young man for killing one of their captains, they fell upon me with a mad fury. They stabbed at me and beat me and overwhelmed me with blows from their war clubs, flinging me to the ground, half-dead. When I began to catch my breath, the men who had not participated in the beating came up and used their teeth to tear out my fingernails. Then they took turns biting the ends of my two index fingers, and with the nails gone, this caused me excruciating pain, as if they were being ground and crushed between two stones until small bone splinters began to protrude. The good René Goupil was given the same treatment, though they did not at that point do any harm to the Hurons. They were angry with the French

Jesuit martyrdom. This famous tableau of Jesuit martyrdom, which was widely reproduced, combines three separate scenes. The Jesuit missionaries being tortured and killed are Isaac Jogues, Gabriel Lalemant (1610–1649), and Jean de Brébeuf (1596–1625).

because of the latter's unwillingness the year before to accept the peace conditions they had been willing to offer.

"When the hunters had returned from their chase after a human quarry and the party had reassembled, these barbarians divided up their booty among themselves, rejoicing in their prey with great shouts of joy. As I saw them engrossed in examining and distributing our spoils, I sought also for my share. I went round to all the captives, baptizing those who were not yet baptized, encouraging these poor wretches to suffer steadfastly, in the assurance that their reward would far exceed the severity of their torments. I ascertained, on this round of visits, that we were twenty-two captives, not counting three Hurons killed on the spot. An old man, aged eighty years, having just received holy baptism, said to the Iroquois who were commanding him to embark: 'It is too late for an old man like me to go visiting foreign countries. I can find death here if you refuse me life.' These words were hardly out of his mouth before they felled him.

"And so we set out, led off to a country truly foreign, where our Lord favored us with a share of His cross. During the thirteen days that we spent on that journey, I suffered bodily torments almost unendurable and, in the soul, mortal anguish: hunger, the fiercely burning sun, the threats and hatred of those leopards, and the pain of our wounds, which, in the absence of any dressing, became putrid and worm infested. All this certainly caused us much distress. But these things seemed light to me in comparison with an inward sadness

that I felt at the sight of our first and most ardent Huron Christians. I had expected them to be the pillars of that rising church, and I saw them become the victims of death. Seeing the path to salvation closed for such a long time to so many nations, people who perish every day for want of succor, made me die every hour in the depth of my soul. It is a very hard thing, a cruel thing, to see the triumph of the devils over whole nations redeemed with so much love and ransomed in the currency of a blood so adorable.

* * *

1647

P. F. X. DE CHARLEVOIX

From Catherine Tegahkouita: An Iroquois Virgin

New France has had her apostles and martyrs, and has given the church saints in all conditions, and I do not hesitate to say that they would have done honor to the primitive ages of Christianity. Several I have made known so far as the course of this history permitted me. The lives of some have been published, but God—who exalted his glory during their lifetime by the great things that he effected through them; by the luster which their sanctity has diffused over this vast continent; by the courage which he inspired in them to found with untold toil a new Christendom amid the most fearful barbarism, and to cement it with their blood—chose none of these to have all the riches of his power and mercy displayed on their tombs. Instead he conferred this honor on a young neophyte, almost unknown to the whole country during her life. For more than sixty years she has been regarded as the protectress of Canada, and it has been impossible to oppose a kind of cult publicly rendered to her.

This holy virgin, so celebrated under the name of Catherine Tegahkouita, was born in 1656 at Gandaouagué, a town in the Mohawk canton,[1] of a heathen Iroquois father and a Christian Algonquin mother. She lost her mother at the age of four and was still quite young when her father died, leaving her to the care of one of her aunts and under the control of an uncle who had the chief authority in his village. The smallpox which she had in her infancy having weakened her sight, she was long compelled as it were to remain in the corner of a cabin, her eyes being unable to stand the light, and this retirement was the first source of her happiness. What she did at first out of necessity, she continued to do by choice, thereby avoiding whatever could cause her to lose that moral purity so difficult to preserve amid idolatrous and then very dissolute youth.

1. Gandaouagué ("castle" or "fortified place" in Mohawk) is an alternative name for the historic Mohawk village of Caughnawaga, on the Mohawk River in central New York. The French ran a mission there for around a decade in the late 1600s.

As soon as she saw herself of age to act, she took on herself almost all the toil of the household, and this shielded her from two dangers fatal to most Indian girls—that is, private conversations and idleness. Her relatives, however, wished her to use the decorations common to young persons of her sex, and although she yielded from simple compliance with their wishes, and with all possible repugnance, it was a matter of much scruple to her when, favored by the light of faith, she learned how dangerous it is to seek to please men.

The first knowledge that she acquired of Christianity was imparted by some missionaries sent to the Iroquois after Monsieur de Tracy's expedition.[2] On their way they passed through the town where she lived and were received at her cabin. She was appointed to take care of them and waited on them in a manner that surprised them. She had herself, on beholding them, been moved by an impulse that excited sentiments in her heart, regarded subsequently by her as the first sparks of the heavenly fire which later inflamed her so completely. The fervor and recollection of those religious in their devotions inspired her with the desire of praying with them, and she informed them of it. They understood much more than she expressed. They instructed her in the Christian truth, as far as the short stay that they made in that town permitted them, and left her with a regret that she heartily reciprocated. Sometime after, a match [marriage] was proposed to her, but as she showed strong opposition, her relatives did not press it. However, they soon returned to the charge, and to save themselves the trouble of overcoming her resistance, they, without mentioning it to her, betrothed her to a young man who at once went to her cabin and sat down beside her. To ratify the marriage, it only required that she should remain near the husband selected for her, such being the way of these tribes, but she abruptly left the cabin and protested that she would not return till he withdrew. This conduct brought her much ill treatment, which she endured with unalterable patience. She was more sensitive to the reproach made that she lacked affection for her kindred, that she hated her nation and gave all her attachment to that to which her mother belonged. But nothing could overcome her repugnance for the state of life in which they sought to involve her.

Meanwhile Father Jacques de Lamberville[3] arrived at Gandaouagué, with orders to found a mission there. Tegahkouita then felt her former desires to become a Christian revive, but she was still for some time without mentioning it, either out of respect for her uncle, who did not relish our religion, or from pure timidity. At last an opportunity came for avowing her conviction, and she was not wanting.[4] A wound in the foot kept her in the cabin, while all the other women were busy harvesting the Indian corn. Father de Lamberville, compelled to suspend his public instructions, which no one would attend, took this time to visit the cabins and instruct those who were confined there by age or infirmity. One day he entered the cabin of Tegahkouita.

Unable to dissemble the joy that this visit caused her, she did not hesitate to open her mind to the missionary in the presence of two or three women,

2. Alexandre de Prouville de Tracy (c. 1600–1670), French military commander, served as lieutenant-general of New France in 1663–67 and led victorious campaigns against the Iroquois and the Mohawk.

3. Jesuit priest (1641–1710).

4. Not lacking (conviction; i.e., her faith was strong).

Kateri Tekakwitha. The Native American Christian woman in this painting may be Kateri Tekakwitha. The artist has not been firmly identified but may be Father Claude Chauchetière (1645–1709), a Jesuit missionary.

who were in company with her, on her design of embracing Christianity. She added that she would have great obstacles to overcome but that nothing appalled her. The energy with which she spoke, the courage she displayed, and a certain modest yet resolute air that lighted up her countenance at once told the missionary that his new proselyte would not be an ordinary Christian. Accordingly, he carefully taught her many things that he did not explain to all preparing for baptism. God doubtless infuses into hearts of which he has especially reserved possession a sort of purely spiritual sympathy, forming even in this life the sacred bond which will unite them hereafter in the abode of glory. Father de Lamberville, whom I knew well, was one of the most holy missionaries of New France. He died at Sault St. Louis,[5] spent with toil and austerity, and, if I may use the expression, in the arms of Charity. He often declared that in his first interview with Tegahkouita, he thought he could discern that God had great designs as to that virgin, yet he would not exercise any haste in conferring baptism on her. He adopted in her case all the precautions that experience had shown to be necessary to make sure [of the sincerity and commitment] of the Indians before administering the sacrament of regeneration.[6]

* * *

* * * She was baptized on Easter Sunday, 1676, and received the name of Catherine.

The grace of the sacrament, received into a heart which her uprightness and innocence had so well prepared, produced wondrous effects. Whatever impression the missionary already had of the young Iroquois maiden, he was astonished to find in her, immediately after baptism, not a neophyte needing to be confirmed in the faith, but a soul filled with the most precious gifts of Heaven who had to be guided in the most sublime spiritual ways. At the outset her virtue excited the admiration even of the people who were least inclined to imitate her. Those on whom she depended allowed her to follow every impulse of her zeal, though this freedom did not last long. The innocence of her life, the precautions which she took to avoid all that could in the least affect it, and especially her extreme reserve as to whatever could in the slightest degree offend purity, appeared to the young men of her village as a reproach toward the dissolute life they led, and many laid snares for her with the sole view of dimming a virtue which dazzled them.

On the other hand, although she had relaxed nothing in her domestic occupations and was ever found ready to give her services to all, her relatives were displeased to see her devote all her free time to prayer. In order to prevent her from suspending on Sundays and holidays the work which the church forbids on those days consecrated to the Lord, they made her pass them without food. Seeing, however, that they gained nothing by this course, they had recourse to still more violent means. They often mistreated her shamefully: When she went to the chapel, they sent young men after her to jeer and pelt her with stones, and men who

5. Then, territory in Montreal, Quebec, given to the Jesuits by the French Crown as a reserve for the protection of newly converted Mohawks.

6. Before baptizing her (regeneration meaning spiritual rebirth).

were drunk, or who pretended to be drunk, rushed upon her as though they intended to take her life. But, undismayed by these artifices and acts of violence, she continued her devotions as though she enjoyed the most perfect liberty.

One day when she was in her cabin, a young man entered abruptly, with flashing eyes, brandishing his hatchet as if intending to tomahawk her. At this sight she displayed no emotion and bowed down her head to receive the blow; but the madman, seized at this instant by a panic fear, fled as precipitately as though pursued by a war party. These first storms were succeeded by a still more dangerous persecution. Catherine's aunt was a woman of morose disposition who was displeased with all that her niece did to satisfy her, for the simple reason that she could find nothing to reprove. One day the virtuous neophyte happened to call the husband of this woman by his own name, instead of calling him Father, as usual. Her aunt imagined, or pretended to believe, that this familiar mode of speaking showed an improper connection between the uncle and niece, and she hastened on the spot to Father de Lamberville to assert that she had surprised Catherine soliciting her husband to sin. The father promised to examine the case, and when he learned on what this atrocious accusation rested, he gave the slanderer a rebuke that covered her with confusion; reactions against the priest's reproaches only resulted in further vexation for the innocent girl.

* * *

She felt well only at the foot of the altar, where, buried in profound contemplation and shedding torrents of tears, whose inexhaustible fountain was His love and the wound it had inflicted on her heart, she often so forgot the wants[7] of her body as not even to feel the cold which benumbed her whole frame. She always came from this contemplation with a renewed love of suffering, and it is difficult to conceive how ingenious her mind was in inventing means to crucify her flesh. Sometimes she walked barefoot on the ice and snow until she lost all feeling. Sometimes she covered her bed with thorns. She rolled for three days in succession on branches of thorns, which pierced deeply into her flesh, causing inexpressible pain. Another time she burned her feet, as war captives are burned, wishing thus to brand herself as a slave of Christ. But the solidity of her virtue is best seen in the unalterable gentleness, patience, joy even, that she manifested in the sufferings she experienced in her last days.

* * *

On Wednesday morning she received the sacred anointing,[8] and about three o'clock in the afternoon she expired after a gentle agony of half an hour, retaining complete consciousness and sound judgment until her last sigh. Thus lived, and thus in her twenty-fifth [sic actually her twenty-fourth] year died, Catherine Tegahkouita. The example of her most holy life had produced a very great fervor among the Iroquois of Sault St. Louis. The wonders that God soon began to work in favor of those who had recourse to

7. Needs.
8. Extreme unction, a Christian sacrament given to a critically ill person.

her intercession are still at this day, for these neophytes and indeed for all of New France, a powerful motive to serve in spirit and in truth so liberal a Master, who, without respect of persons, lavishes his most precious gifts on those who abandon themselves to Him without reserve.

* * *

Thus New France, like the capital of Old France, beheld the glory of a poor Indian girl and of a shepherdess [Ste. Genevieve][9] shining above that of so many apostolic men who were martyrs and other saints of all conditions of life, God doubtless wishing for our instruction and the consolation of the humble to glorify His saints in proportion to their smallness and obscurity on earth.

1744

9. According to legend, this young shepherdess (c. 422–512) devoted her life to God. After moving from outside Paris into the city, she practiced penitence and austerity, and her prayers protected Paris from the invading forces of Attila the Hun.

SOR JUANA INÉS DE LA CRUZ

S or Juana Inés de la Cruz (c. 1651–1695) was a prolific, celebrated, and sometimes controversial writer, who spent most of her adult life as a cloistered sister in the Convent of the Order of St. Jérôme, in Mexico City (*Sor* is Spanish for "Sister"). Born out of wedlock to a Spanish father and a Creole (i.e., Spanish American–born) mother in San Miguel Neplantla, Mexico, Juana showed an early appetite for learning and great facility with languages, including Greek, Latin, and the Aztec language, Nahuatl. She wrote her first poem when she was eight, and her other early works include several poems in Nahuatl. Determined to devote herself to her studies rather than to marry, Juana entered a convent in 1669 and remained there until her death, from the plague. Her life in the convent was very full. She entertained distinguished guests; taught music and drama; served as the convent's archivist and accountant; and had her own study and library, where she focused on music, philosophy, and the natural sciences. In the 1680s, Juana served as an unofficial court poet. Her works include verse plays, commissioned religious services, and writings for state festivals. Her verse—occasional poetry, secular love lyrics, and religious poetry—displays mastery of the Baroque style (highly ornate, richly symbolic), often coupled with rigorously logical philosophical themes.

Love Opened a Mortal Wound[1]

Love opened a mortal wound.
In agony, I worked the blade
to make it deeper. Please,
I begged, let death come quick.

1. The text is from *Sor Juana's Love Poems* (1997), translated by Joan Larkin and Jaime Manrique.

Wild, distracted, sick, 5
I counted, counted
all the ways love hurt me.
One life, I thought—a thousand deaths.

Blow after blow, my heart
couldn't survive this beating. 10
Then—how can I explain it?

I came to my senses. I said,
Why do I suffer? What lover
ever had so much pleasure?

Suspend, Singer Swan[1]

Suspend, singer swan, the sweet strain:
see how the lord that Delphi[2] sees
exchanges for you the gentle lyre for pipe
and to Admetus[3] makes a pastoral sound.

As gentle song, though strong, moved 5
stones and tamed the wrath of hell,
so it retreats, abashed, when you are heard:
your instrument blames the church itself.

For though the works of ancient builders
cannot match its columns, 10
nothing's greater than your song

when your clear voice strikes its stones,
and your sweet tones surpass it,
dwarf it, while making it grow the more.

1. The text is from poets.org. Trans. Michael Smith.
2. An ancient Greek town near Mount Parnassus; site of a famous oracle of Apollo, the god of music, poetry, truth, and prophecy, among other things.
3. In Greek mythology, the king of Pherae, in Thessaly; befriended by Apollo.

FRANCIS DANIEL PASTORIUS

Francis Daniel Pastorius (1651–c. 1720) was a man of many interests, language and literature prominent among them. Born in Bavaria, Germany, Pastorius traveled to the Philadelphia Colony in 1683, and from his friend William Penn, the colony's proprietor, he purchased 15,000 acres that became the site of the German-town settlement (now a Philadelphia neighborhood). In 1688, he was one of four authors of the Germantown Protest, the first colonial document to oppose slavery.

Pastorius was a skilled linguist and an avid reader and writer who assembled a substantial library. At his death, he left behind many works in manuscript in addi-

tion to his publications. His writings included "The Bee-hive," a monumental commonplace book in manuscript that brings together extracts from his wide reading in classical and modern texts along with his own verses. Pastorius expressed a strong interest in identifying underlying commonalities that could be used to create harmonious societies. He understood the sources of harmony to be fundamentally spiritual and mediated by language.

[In These Seven Languages][1]

In these Seven Languages I this my Book[2] do own,
Friend, if thou find it, Send the same to Germantown;
Thy Recompense shall be the half of half a Crown:[3]
But, tho' it be no more than half the half of this,
Pray! Be Content therewith, & think it not amiss. 5
Yea and if, when thou com'st, my Cash perhaps is gone,
(For Money is thus scarce, that often I have none)
A Cup of Drink may do: Or else, alas! thou must
Trust unto me a while, As I to Others Trust,
Who failing make me fail: A thing extreme unjust! 10
To which I have no lust; But must per Force, poor Dust.
 Freund, *Was du findest, wiedergieb,*
 Sonst hält man dich vor einen Dieb
 In diesem; und in jenem Leben
 Folgt anders nichts als Höllen-pein. 15
 Gott Selbst hat disz Gesetz gegeben
 Zu thun, wie man Gethan will seyn.[4]
 Quod Tibi vis fieri, hoc facias Alijs.[5]

c. after 1696 1897

1. The text is from Marion Dexter Learned, *The Life of Francis Daniel Pastorius, The Founder of Germantown* (1908).
2. I.e., his commonplace book known as "The Bee-hive."
3. A very small sum (a crown being an old British coin).
4. Friend, What thou findest, return / Otherwise you will be considered a thief / In this and in the next life / Nothing follows but the pains of hell. / God Himself has given this command / To do unto others as you would have them do onto you (German).
5. Whatever you should wish would be done to you, do this unto others (Latin).

ELIZABETH ASHBRIDGE

The life of Elizabeth Ashbridge (1713–1755) was full of tumult, adventure, and spiritual seeking. It began in England, where she was born Elizabeth Sampson to Anglican parents, and ended in Ireland, where she had gone to preach as a Quaker minister. She spent much of her adulthood in Britain's North American colonies. Her odyssey involved repeated changes in her religious affiliation, culminating in her permanent embrace of Quakerism.

One of the attractions of the Quakers was their acceptance of women's spiritual leadership. As an influential minister, Ashbridge associated with John Woolman (see the next headnote) and other leading Friends. In 1746, five years after the death of her second husband, she married Aaron Ashbridge. She composed her autobiography around 1745, and it circulated in manuscript before being published in England in 1774. The *Account* offers a remarkable view of its author's spiritual and physical journeys, including the resistance that her second husband posed to her embrace of Quakerism and to her preaching, and of the transatlantic faith communities that were an important feature of colonial life.

From Some Account of the Early Part of the Life of Elizabeth Ashbridge[1]

My life having been attended with many uncommon occurrences, I have thought proper to make some remarks on the dealings of divine goodness with me. I have often had cause, with David, to say, "It is good for me that I have been afflicted;"[2] and most earnestly I desire that they who read the following lines may take warning, and shun the evils into which I have been drawn.

I was born at Middlewich, in Cheshire,[3] in the year 1713, of honest parents, named Thomas and Mary Sampson. My father bore a good character, but he was not so strictly religious as my mother, who was a pattern of virtue to me. I was my father's only child; but my mother had a son and a daughter by a former husband. Soon after I was born, my father went to sea, and, following his profession, which was that of a surgeon, made many long voyages. He continued in his sea-faring course of life till I was twelve years old, so that the care of the early part of my education devolved upon my mother; and she discharged her duty, in endeavouring to imbue my mind with the principles of virtue. I have had reason to be thankful that I was blest with such a parent; her good advice and counsel to me have been as bread cast upon the waters.[4] She was an instructive example to all who knew her, and generally beloved; but, alas! as soon as the time came, when she might reasonably expect the benefit from her labours, and have had comfort in me, I deserted her. In my childhood I had an awful[5] regard for religion and religious people, particularly for ministers, all of whom I believed to be good men and beloved of God, which I earnestly wished to be my own case. I had also great tenderness for the poor, remembering that I had read they were beloved of the Lord. This I supposed to mean such as were poor in temporal things; whom I often visited in their cottages, and used to think that they were better off than myself; yet, if I had money, or any thing suitable for a gift, I bestowed it on them, recollecting that they who gave to such, lent unto the Lord. I made remarks on those who pretended to religion; and,

1. The text is from *Some Account of the Early Part of the Life of Elizabeth Ashbridge, Who Died, in the Truth's Service, at the House of Robert Lecky, in the County of Carlow, Ireland, the 16th of the 5th Month, 1755. Written by Herself* (1807).
2. Psalm 119.71. "David": second king of ancient Israel, traditionally considered the author of Psalms.
3. A county in northwest England.
4. Ecclesiastes 11.1: "Cast thy bread upon the waters: for thou shalt find it after many days."
5. Deeply respectful or reverential.

Quaker church. This wood engraving of a Quaker church in Philadelphia portrays a woman speaking to a congregation of both men and women. Most Christian denominations severely restricted women's speech to such mixed audiences.

when I heard people swear, I was troubled; for my mother told me that, if I used any naughty words, God would not love me.

I observed that there were several different religious societies;[6] this I often thought of, and wept with desires that I might be directed to the one which it would be best for me to join. In this frame of mind passed my younger years. I was sometimes guilty of the faults common among children, but was always sorry for what I had done amiss; and, till I was fourteen years of age, I was as innocent as most children. About this time, my sorrows (which have continued, for the greatest part of my life, ever since) began, by my giving way to a foolish passion, in setting my affections on a young man, who, without the leave of my parents, courted me till I consented to marry him; and, with sorrow of heart, I relate, that I suffered myself to be carried off in the night. We were married. My parents made all possible search for me, as soon as I was missing, but it was in vain. This precipitate act plunged me into much sorrow. I was soon smitten with remorse for thus leaving my parents, whose right it was to have disposed of me to their content, or who, at least, ought to have been consulted. But I was soon chastised for my disobedience, and convinced of my error. In five months, I was stripped of the darling of my heart, and left a young and disconsolate widow. I was now without a home. My husband had derived his livelihood only from his trade, which was that of a stocking weaver; and my father was so displeased that he would do nothing for me. My dear mother had some compassion for me, and kept

6. Faiths, or denominations.

me among the neighbours. Afterwards, by her advice, I went to a relation of hers, at Dublin. We hoped that my absence would soften my father's rigour; but he continued inflexible; he would not send for me back, and I dared not to return unless he did.

The relation I went to reside with was one of the people called Quakers. His habits were so very different to what I had been accustomed to, that the visit proved disagreeable to me. I had been brought up in the way of the Church of England, and though, as I have said, I had a religious education, yet I was allowed to sing and dance, which my cousin would not permit. The great vivacity of my natural disposition would not, in this instance, suffer me to give way to the gloomy sense of sorrow and conviction;[7] and therefore my present restraints had a wrong effect. I became more wild and airy[8] than ever; my cousin often reproved me; but I then thought his conduct was the result of singularity[9] and would not bear it, or be controlled. Having a distant relation in the West of Ireland, I went to him. I now enjoyed all the liberty I wished; for, what rendered me disagreeable to my other kinsman, was quite pleasing to this. Between these two relations I spent three years and three months.

* * *

I went from Trent-town to Philadelphia by water,[1] and from thence to my uncle's on horseback. My uncle was dead, and my aunt married again; yet, both she and her husband received me in the kindest manner. I had scarcely been three hours in the house, before my opinion of these people began to alter. I perceived a book lying upon the table, and, being fond of reading, took it up; my aunt observed me, and said, "Cousin,[2] that is a Quaker's book." She saw I was not a Quaker, and supposed I would not like it. I made her no answer, but queried with myself, what can these people write about? I have heard that they deny the scriptures, and have no other bible than George Fox's Journal,[3]—denying, also, all the holy ordinances. But, before I had read two pages, my heart burned within me, and, for fear I should be seen, I went into the garden. I sat down, and, as the piece was short, read it before I returned, though I was often obliged to stop to give vent to my tears. The fulness of my heart produced the involuntary exclamation of, "My God, must I, if ever I come to the knowledge of thy truth, be of this man's opinion, who has sought thee as I have done; and must I join this people, to whom, a few hours ago, I preferred the papists. O, thou God of my salvation, and of my life, who hath abundantly manifested thy long suffering and tender mercy, in redeeming me as from the lowest hell, I beseech thee to direct me in the right way, and keep me from error; so will I perform my covenant,[4] and think nothing too near to part with for thy name's sake. O, happy people, thus beloved of God!" After having collected myself, I washed my face, that it might not be perceived I had been weeping. In the night I got but little sleep; the enemy of mankind[5] haunted me with his insinuations, by suggesting that

7. Guilt.
8. Lacking in seriousness.
9. Peculiarity.
1. In the omitted passage, Ashbridge describes adventures, physical and spiritual, that took her to parts of Britain and the northeastern colonies. Trent-town: Trenton, New Jersey, across the Del-

aware River from Philadelphia.
2. I.e., kinswoman, relative.
3. Religious autobiography by this founder of Quakerism, published in 1694.
4. Formal agreement.
5. Satan.

I was one of those that wavered, and not steadfast in faith; and advancing several texts of scripture against me, as that, in the latter days, there should be those who would deceive the very elect;[6] that of such were the people I was among, and that I was in danger of being deluded. Warned in this manner, (from the right source as I thought,) I resolved to be aware of those deceivers, and, for some weeks, did not touch one of their books. The next day, being the first of the week, I was desirous of going to church, which was distant about four miles; but, being a stranger, and having no one to go with me, I gave up all thoughts of that, and, as most of the family were going to meeting, I went there with them. As we sat in silence,[7] I looked over the meeting, and said to myself, "How like fools these people sit; how much better would it be to stay at home, and read the Bible, or some good book, than come here and go to sleep." As for me I was very drowsy; and, while asleep, had nearly fallen down. This was the last time I ever fell asleep in a meeting. I now began to be lifted up with spiritual pride, and to think myself better than they; but this disposition of mind did not last long. It may seem strange that, after living so long with one of this society at Dublin, I should yet be so much a stranger to them. In answer, let it be considered that, while I was there, I never read any of their books, nor went to one meeting; besides, I had heard such accounts of them, as made me think that, of all societies, they were the worst. But he who knows the sincerity of the heart, looked on my weakness with pity; I was permitted to see my error, and shown that these were the people I ought to join.

*　*　*

I loved to go to meetings, but did not love to be seen going on week-days, and therefore went to them, from my school, through the woods. Notwithstanding all my care, the neighbours, (who were not friends,) soon began to revile me with the name of Quaker; adding, that they supposed I intended to be a fool, and turn preacher. Thus did I receive the same censure, which, about a year before, I had passed on one of the handmaids of the Lord in Boston. I was so weak, that I could not bear the reproach.[8] In order to change their opinion, I went into greater excess of apparel than I had freedom to do,[9] even before I became acquainted with friends. In this condition I continued till my husband came, and then began the trial of my faith.

Before he reached me, he heard I was turned Quaker; at which he stamped, and said, "I had rather have heard she was dead, well as I love her; for, if it be so, all my comfort is gone. He then came to me; it was after an absence of four months; I got up and said to him, "My dear, I am glad to see thee." At this, he flew into a great rage, exclaiming, "The devil thee, thee, thee, don't thee me."[1] I endeavoured, by every mild means, to pacify him; and, at length, got him fit to speak to my relations. As soon after this as we were alone, he said to me, "And so I see your Quaker relations have made you one;" I replied, that they had not, (which was true,) I never told them how it was

6. Those whom God has chosen to be saved.
7. Quaker meetings typically involve periods of silence until a member feels moved to speak.
8. Ashbridge felt hypocritical for having criticized a devout woman, perhaps a Quaker or a woman who had violated sanctions against female preachers.

9. Rather than wearing the attire some Quakers adopted, known as plain dress, she wore fancier clothing to disguise her Quaker leanings.
1. Ashbridge's husband objects to her use of the archaic form of the second-person pronoun, which she employs following Quaker practice.

with me. He said he would not stay amongst them; and, having found a place to his mind, hired, and came directly back to fetch me, walking, in one afternoon, thirty miles to keep me from meeting the next day, which was first day. He took me, after resting this day, to the place where he had hired, and to lodgings he had engaged at the house of a churchwarden. This man was a bitter enemy of Friends, and did all he could to irritate my husband against them.

Though I did not appear like a friend,[2] they all believed me to be one. When my husband and he used to be making their diversions and reviling, I sat in silence, though now and then an involuntary sigh broke from me; at which he would say, "There, did not I tell you your wife was a Quaker, and she will become a preacher." On such an occasion as this, my husband once came up to me, in a great rage, and shaking his hand over me, said, "You had better be hanged in that day." I was seized with horror, and again plunged into despair, which continued nearly three months. I was afraid that, by denying the Lord, the heavens would be shut against me. I walked much alone in the woods, and there, where no eye saw, or ear heard me, lamented my miserable condition. Often have I wandered, from morning till night, without food. I was brought so low that my life became a burden to me; and the devil seemed to vaunt that, though the sins of my youth were forgiven me, yet now I had committed an unpardonable sin, and hell would inevitably be my portion, and my torments would be greater than if I had hanged myself at first.

*　　*　　*

Thus, for some time, I had to go eight miles on foot to meeting, which I never thought hard.[3] My husband had a horse, but he would not suffer me to ride on it; nor, when my shoes were worn out, would he let me have a new pair; but, though he hoped, on this account, to keep me from meeting, it did not hinder me:—I have tied them-round with strings to keep them on.

Finding that all the means he had yet used could not alter my resolutions, he several times struck me with severe blows. I endeavoured to bear all with patience, believing that the time would come when he would see I was in the right. Once he came up to me, took out his penknife, and said, "If you offer to go to meeting to-morrow, with this knife I'll cripple you, for you shall not be a Quaker." I made him no answer. In the morning, I set out as usual; he did not attempt to harm me. Having despaired of recovering me himself, he fled, for help, to the priest, whom he told, that I had been a very religious woman, in the way of the Church of England, of which I was a member, and had a good certificate from Long Island;[4] that I was now bewitched, and had turned Quaker, which almost broke his heart; and, therefore, he desired that, as he[5] was one who had the care of souls, he would come and pay me a visit, and use his endeavours to reclaim me, which he hoped, by the blessing of God, would be done. The priest consented, and fixed the time for his coming, which was that day two weeks, as he said he could not come sooner. My husband came home extremely pleased, and told me of it. I replied, with

2. I.e., did not wear plain dress.
3. For many months, Ashbridge's husband continued to oppose her membership in the Society of Friends.

4. In New York.
5. I.e., the priest; the following "he" and "his" refer to the priest as well.

a smile, I trusted I should be enabled to give a reason for the hope within me; yet I believed, at the same time, that the priest would never trouble himself about me, which proved to be the case. * * *

This day, as usual, I had gone to meeting on foot. While my husband (as he afterwards told me) was lying on the bed, these words crossed his mind: "Lord, where shall I fly to shun thee," &c. upon which he arose, and, seeing it rain, got the horse and set off to fetch me, arriving just as the meeting broke up. I got on horseback as quickly as possible, lest he should hear I had been speaking; he did hear of it nevertheless, and, as soon as we were in the woods, began with saying, "Why do you mean thus to make my life unhappy? What, could you not be a Quaker, without turning fool in this manner?" I answered in tears, "My dear, look on me with pity, if thou hast any; canst thou think that I, in the bloom of my days, would bear all that thou knowest of, and much that thou knowest not of, if I did not feel it my duty." These words touched him, and, he said, "Well, I'll e'en give you up; I see it wont avail to strive; if it be of God I cannot overthrow it; and, if of yourself, it will soon fall." I saw the tears stand in his eyes, at which I was overcome with joy, and began already to reap the fruits of my obedience. But my trials were not yet over. The time appointed for the priest to visit me arrived, but no priest appeared. My husband went to fetch him, but he refused, saying he was busy, which so displeased my husband that he never went to hear him again, and, for some time, went to no place of worship.

* * *

* * * One day he said to me, "I would go to meeting, only I'm afraid I shall hear your clack, which I cannot bear." I used no persuasions. When meeting-time came, he got the horse, took me behind him, and went. For several months, if he saw me offer to rise, he went out; till, one day, I rose before he was aware and then, as he afterwards owned, he was ashamed to do it.

From this time, he left off the practice, and never hindered me from going to meeting.

ca. 1745 1774

JOHN WOOLMAN

In the catalog of American writers, John Woolman (1720–1772) stands out as a model of integrity, decency, and forthrightness. He was born on his family's farm in Burlington County, New Jersey, a few miles east of Philadelphia, and attended school in Mount Holly, New Jersey, where he later set up in business for himself. Woolman's success in business offended his Quaker belief in simplicity, and he deliberately cut back his commercial dealings. While writing a bill of sale for a slave, Woolman first became aware of the conflict between public law and private conscience that was to absorb him for the rest of his life. Although he tells us that on that first occasion he remained silent, "gave way," and wrote the bill of sale, he never made that mistake again. The next time, he informed the owner that slavery and a

religious conscience were incompatible. Woolman thereafter found his true vocation in "speaking up" fellow Quakers in their homes and at assemblies. In his "conversations" with Quakers, Woolman warned of dangers: materialist society, exploitation of workers, military conscription, paying taxes to support wars, and above all, corruptions caused by slavery.

Woolman knew Elizabeth Ashbridge and was familiar with her autobiographical narrative when he wrote his own. First published in 1774, and consistently in print ever since, Woolman's *Journal* has been admired not only for the life and temperament it reveals but also for the directness and simplicity of its style.

From The Journal of John Woolman[1]

[Early Life and Vocation]

I have often felt a motion of love to leave some hints in writing of my experience of the goodness of God, and now, in the thirty-sixth year of my age, I begin this work. I was born in Northampton, in Burlington County in West Jersey, A.D. 1720, and before I was seven years old I began to be acquainted with the operations of divine love. Through the care of my parents, I was taught to read near as soon as I was capable of it, and as I went from school one Seventh Day,[2] I remember, while my companions went to play by the way, I went forward out of sight; and sitting down, I read the twenty-second chapter of the Revelations: "He showed me a river of water, clear as crystal, proceeding out of the throne of God and the Lamb, etc."[3] And in reading it my mind was drawn to seek after that pure habitation which I then believed God had prepared for His servants. The place where I sat and the sweetness that attended my mind remains fresh in my memory.

This and the like gracious visitations[4] had that effect upon me, that when boys used ill language it troubled me, and through the continued mercies of God I was preserved from it. The pious instructions of my parents were often fresh in my mind when I happened amongst wicked children, and was of use to me. My parents, having a large family of children, used frequently on First Days after meeting[5] to put us to read in the Holy Scriptures or some religious books, one after another, the rest sitting by without much conversation, which I have since often thought was a good practice. From what I had read and heard, I believed there had been in past ages people who walked in uprightness before God in a degree exceeding any that I knew, or heard of, now living; and the apprehension of there being less steadiness and firmness amongst people in this age than in past ages often troubled me while I was a child.

I had a dream about the ninth year of my age as follows: I saw the moon rise near the west and run a regular course eastward, so swift that in about

1. The text is from *The Journal and Major Essays of John Woolman* (1971), edited by Phillips P. Mouton.

2. I.e., Saturday. Quakers substituted numbers for the days of the week both for the sake of simplicity and to discard the names of the pagan gods (e.g., Saturday was named in honor of the Roman god Saturn).

3. Revelation 22.1.

4. I.e., similar moments when he felt God's presence again.

5. Quakers refer to their assemblies as "meetings" and their church as a "meetinghouse." It is the custom for worshipers to remain silent until someone is moved to speak.

a quarter of an hour she reached our meridian, when there descended from her a small cloud on a direct line to the earth, which lighted on a pleasant green about twenty yards from the door of my father's house (in which I thought I stood) and was immediately turned into a beautiful green tree. The moon appeared to run on with equal swiftness and soon set in the east, at which time the sun arose at the place where it commonly does in the summer, and shining with full radiance in a serene air, it appeared as pleasant a morning as ever I saw.

All this time I stood still in the door in an awful[6] frame of mind, and I observed that as heat increased by the rising sun, it wrought so powerfully on the little green tree that the leaves gradually withered; and before noon it appeared dry and dead. There then appeared a being, small of size, full of strength and resolution, moving swift from the north, southward, called a sun worm.[7]

Another thing remarkable in my childhood was that once, going to a neighbor's house, I saw on the way a robin sitting on her nest; and as I came near she went off, but having young ones, flew about and with many cries expressed her concern for them. I stood and threw stones at her, till one striking her, she fell down dead. At first I was pleased with the exploit, but after a few minutes was seized with horror, as having in a sportive way killed an innocent creature while she was careful for her young. I beheld her lying dead and thought those young ones for which she was so careful must now perish for want of their dam to nourish them; and after some painful considerations on the subject, I climbed up the tree, took all the young birds and killed them, supposing that better than to leave them to pine away and die miserably, and believed in this case that Scripture proverb was fulfilled, "The tender mercies of the wicked are cruel."[8] I then went on my errand, but for some hours could think of little else but the cruelties I had committed, and was much troubled.

Thus He whose tender mercies are over all His works hath placed a principle in the human mind which incites to exercise goodness toward every living creature; and this being singly attended to, people become tenderhearted and sympathizing, but being frequently and totally rejected, the mind shuts itself up in a contrary disposition.

About the twelfth year of my age, my father being abroad, my mother reproved me for some misconduct, to which I made an undutiful reply; and the next First Day as I was with my father returning from meeting, he told me he understood I had behaved amiss to my mother and advised me to be more careful in future. I knew myself blameable, and in shame and confusion remained silent. Being thus awakened to a sense of my wickedness, I felt remorse in my mind, and getting home I retired and prayed to the Lord to forgive me, and do not remember that I ever after that spoke unhandsomely[9] to either of my parents, however foolish in other things.

Having attained the age of sixteen years, I began to love wanton[1] company, and though I was preserved from profane language or scandalous conduct, still I perceived a plant in me which produced much wild grapes. Yet

6. Full of awe.
7. I.e., sun snake, an imaginary creature.
8. Proverbs 12.10.

9. Undutifully, ungraciously.
1. Frivolous, unthinking.

my merciful Father forsook me not utterly, but at times through His grace I was brought seriously to consider my ways, and the sight of my backsliding affected me with sorrow. But for want of rightly attending to the reproofs of instruction, vanity was added to vanity,[2] and repentance to repentance; upon the whole my mind was more and more alienated from the Truth,[3] and I hastened toward destruction. While I meditate on the gulf toward which I traveled and reflect on my youthful disobedience, for these things I weep; mine eye runneth down with water.

Advancing in age the number of my acquaintance increased, and thereby my way grew more difficult. Though I had heretofore found comfort in reading the Holy Scriptures and thinking on heavenly things, I was now estranged therefrom. I knew I was going from the flock of Christ and had no resolution to return; hence serious reflections were uneasy to me and youthful vanities and diversions my greatest pleasure. Running in this road I found many like myself, and we associated in that which is reverse to true friendship.[4]

But in this swift race[5] it pleased God to visit me with sickness, so that I doubted of recovering. And then did darkness, horror, and amazement with full force seize me, even when my pain and distress of body was very great. I thought it would have been better for me never to have had a being than to see the day which I now saw. I was filled with confusion, and in great affliction both of mind and body I lay and bewailed myself. I had not confidence to lift up my cries to God, whom I had thus offended, but in a deep sense of my great folly I was humbled before Him, and at length that Word which is as a fire and a hammer broke and dissolved my rebellious heart. And then my cries were put up in contrition, and in the multitude of His mercies I found inward relief, and felt a close engagement that if He was pleased to restore my health, I might walk humbly before Him.

After my recovery this exercise[6] remained with me a considerable time; but by degrees giving way to youthful vanities, they gained strength, and getting with wanton young people I lost ground. The Lord had been very gracious and spoke peace to me in the time of my distress, and I now most ungratefully turned again to folly, on which account at times I felt sharp reproof but did not get low enough to cry for help. I was not so hardy as to commit things scandalous, but to exceed in vanity and promote mirth was my chief study. Still I retained a love and esteem for pious people, and their company brought an awe upon me.

My dear parents several times admonished me in the fear of the Lord, and their admonition entered into my heart and had a good effect for a season, but not getting deep enough to pray rightly, the tempter[7] when he came found entrance. I remember once, having spent a part of the day in wantonness, as I went to bed at night there lay in a window near my bed a Bible, which I opened, and first cast my eye on the text, "We lie down in our shame, and our confusion covers us."[8] This I knew to be my case, and meeting with so unexpected a reproof, I was somewhat affected with it and went to bed under remorse of conscience, which I soon cast off again.

2. Cf. Ecclesiastes 1.2. "Want": lack.
3. I.e., ultimate spiritual reality.
4. I.e., those ideals basic to the Religious Society of Friends.
5. Cf. Ecclesiastes 9.11.
6. Religious experience.
7. Satan.
8. Jeremiah 3.25.

Thus time passed on; my heart was replenished with mirth and wantonness, while pleasing scenes of vanity were presented to my imagination till I attained the age of eighteen years, near which time I felt the judgments of God in my soul like a consuming fire, and looking over my past life the prospect was moving. I was often sad and longed to be delivered from those vanities; then again my heart was strongly inclined to them, and there was in me a sore conflict. At times I turned to folly, and then again sorrow and confusion took hold of me. In a while I resolved totally to leave off some of my vanities, but there was a secret reserve in my heart of the more refined part of them, and I was not low enough to find true peace. Thus for some months I had great trouble, there remaining in me an unsubjected will which rendered my labors fruitless, till at length through the merciful continuance of heavenly visitations I was made to bow down in spirit before the Lord.

I remember one evening I had spent some time in reading a pious author, and walking out alone I humbly prayed to the Lord for His help, that I might be delivered from all those vanities which so ensnared me. Thus being brought low, He helped me; and as I learned to bear the cross[9] I felt refreshment to come from His presence; but not keeping in that strength which gave victory, I lost ground again, the sense of which greatly affected me; and I sought deserts[1] and lonely places and there with tears did confess my sins to God and humbly craved help of Him. And I may say with reverence He was near to me in my troubles, and in those times of humiliation opened my ear to discipline.

* * *

About the twenty-third year of my age, I had many fresh and heavenly openings in respect to the care and providence of the Almighty over his creatures in general, and over man as the most noble amongst those which are visible. And being clearly convinced in my judgment that to place my whole trust in God was best for me, I felt renewed engagements that in all things I might act on an inward principle of virtue and pursue worldly business no further than as Truth opened my way therein.

About the time called Christmas I observed many people from the country and dwellers in town who, resorting to the public houses, spent their time in drinking and vain sports, tending to corrupt one another, on which account I was much troubled. At one house in particular there was much disorder, and I believed it was a duty laid on me to go and speak to the master of that house. I considered I was young and that several elderly Friends in town had opportunity to see these things, and though I would gladly have been excused, yet I could not feel my mind clear.

The exercise was heavy, and as I was reading what the Almighty said to Ezekiel respecting his duty as a watchman,[2] the matter was set home more clearly; and then with prayer and tears I besought the Lord for His assistance, who in loving-kindness gave me a resigned heart. Then at a suitable opportunity I went to the public house, and seeing the man amongst a company, I went to him and told him I wanted to speak with him; so we went

9. I.e., live mindfully of Christ and in humility.
1. Desolate places.
2. Ezekiel was a priest and prophet to whom God said, "Son of man, I have made thee a watchman unto the house of Israel: therefore hear the word at my mouth, and give them warning from me" (Ezekiel 3.17).

aside, and there in the fear and dread of the Almighty I expressed to him what rested on my mind, which he took kindly, and afterward showed more regard to me than before. In a few years after, he died middle-aged, and I often thought that had I neglected my duty in that case it would have given me great trouble, and I was humbly thankful to my gracious Father, who had supported me herein.

My employer, having a Negro woman, sold her and directed me to write a bill of sale, the man being waiting who bought her. The thing was sudden, and though the thoughts of writing an instrument of slavery for one of my fellow creatures felt uneasy,[3] yet I remembered I was hired by the year, that it was my master who directed me to do it, and that it was an elderly man, a member of our Society, who bought her; so through weakness I gave way and wrote it, but at the executing [of] it, I was so afflicted in my mind that I said before my master and the Friend that I believed slavekeeping to be a practice inconsistent with the Christian religion. This in some degree abated my uneasiness, yet as often as I reflected seriously upon it I thought I should have been clearer if I had desired to be excused from it as a thing against my conscience, for such it was. And some time after this a young man of our Society spake to me to write an instrument of slavery, he having lately taken a Negro into his house. I told him I was not easy to write it, for though many kept slaves in our Society, as in others, I still believed the practice was not right, and desired to be excused from writing [it]. I spoke to him in good will, and he told me that keeping slaves was not altogether agreeable to his mind, but that the slave being a gift made to his wife, he had accepted of her.

1774

3. I.e., it contradicted his sense of right, so he felt ill at ease with his conscience.

JOHN MARRANT

John Marrant (1755-1791) was born in New York City into a free black family. While he was still a child, the family moved to Florida and then Georgia. When he was eleven they moved again, settling in Charleston, South Carolina. There Marrant studied music for two years and began learning a trade. He was thirteen when he heard a sermon by the evangelist George Whitefield that transformed his life and led to the adventures in his narrative. A Narrative of the Lord's Wonderful Dealings with John Marrant, a Black was immensely popular, printed at least twenty-one times between 1785 and 1835, and read on both sides of the Atlantic. An "as-told-to" text transcribed and edited by the Reverend William Aldridge, the Narrative shares features of several narrative traditions—conversion, Indian captivity, and slave—and thus encapsulates the pervasive role that themes of capture and liberation played in several of early America's most popular and influential literary genres. Some of the narrative's appeal came from its improbable story of the spiritually motivated adventures of a free black teenager.

From A Narrative of the Lord's Wonderful Dealings with John Marrant, a Black[1]

* * *

* * * I rose one morning very early, to get a little quietness and retirement, I went into the woods, and staid till eight o'clock in the morning; upon my return I found them all at breakfast;[2] I passed by them, and went up-stairs without any interruption; I went upon my knees to the Lord, and returned him thanks; then I took up a small pocket Bible and one of Dr. Watts's hymn books,[3] and passing by them went out without one word spoken by any of us. After spending some time in the fields I was persuaded to go from home altogether. Accordingly I went over the fence, about half a mile from our house, which divided the inhabited and cultivated parts of the country from the wilderness. I continued travelling in the desert all day without the least inclination of returning back.[4] * * * As I was going on, and musing upon the goodness of the Lord, an Indian hunter, who stood at some distance, saw me; he hid himself behind a tree; but as I passed along he bolted out, and put his hands on my breast, which surprised me a few moments. He then asked me where I was going? I answered I did not know; but where the Lord was pleased to guide me. Having heard me praising God before I came up to him, he enquired who I was talking to? I told him I was talking to my Lord Jesus; he seemed surprised, and asked me where he was? for he did not see him there. I told him he could not be seen with bodily eyes. After a little more talk, he insisted upon taking me home; but I refused, and added, that I would die rather than return home. He then asked me if I knew how far I was from home? I answered, I did not know; you are 55 miles and a half, says he, from home. He farther asked me how I did to live? I said I was supported by the Lord. He asked me how I slept? I answered, the Lord provided me with a bed every night; he further enquired what preserved me from being devoured by the wild beasts? I replied, the Lord Jesus Christ kept me from them. He stood astonished, and said, you say the Lord Jesus Christ do this, and do that, and do every thing for you, he must be a very fine man, where is he? I replied, he is here present. To this he made me no answer, only said, I know you, and your mother and sister, and upon a little further conversation I found he did know them, having been used in winter to sell skins[5] in our town. This alarmed me, and I wept for fear he would take me home by force; but when he saw me so affected, he said he would not take me home if I would go with him. I objected against that, for fear he would

1. The text is from the fourth edition of *A Narrative of the Lord's Wonderful Dealings with John Marrant, a Black (Now Going to Preach the Gospel in Nova Scotia) Born in New-York, in North America* (1785?).
2. Marrant was staying in Charleston with his mother and siblings, but the visit was going badly. In the preceding passage, they tormented him about his newfound faith, and he considered suicide, but he realized that "if I did destroy myself I could not come where God was."
3. The English theologian Isaac Watts (1674–1748) is known as the father of English hymnody.

4. Marrant traveled alone "in the desart" (desert, or wilderness), sleeping in trees and growing progressively weaker. At one point, he describes being reduced to eating deer grass and finding it "the best meal I ever had in my life." He writes, "I continued travelling on for nine days, feeding upon grass, and not knowing whither I was going; but the Lord Jesus Christ was very present, and that comforted me through all." His account echoes Jesus' time in the wilderness (Matthew 4.1–11, Luke 4.1–13, Mark 1.12–13).
5. I.e., having sold skins in winter.

rob me of my comfort and communion with God: But at last, being much pressed, I consented to go. Our employment for ten weeks and three days, was killing deer, and taking off their skins by day, which we afterwards hung on the trees to dry till they were sent for; the means of defence and security against our nocturnal enemies, always took up the evenings: We collected a number of large bushes, and placed them nearly in a circular form, which uniting at the extremity, afforded us both a verdant covering, and a sufficient shelter from the night dews. What moss we could gather was strewed upon the ground, and this composed our bed. A fire was kindled in the front of our temporary lodging room, and fed with fresh fuel all night, as we slept and watched by turns; and this was our defence from the dreadful animals, whose shining eyes and tremendous roar we often saw and heard during the night.

By constant conversation with the hunter, I acquired a fuller knowledge of the Indian tongue: This, together with the sweet communion I enjoyed with God, I have considered as a preparation for the great trial I was soon after to pass through.

The hunting season being now at an end, we left the woods, and directed our course towards a large Indian town, belonging to the Cherokee nation; and having reached it, I said to the hunter, they will not suffer[6] me to enter in. He replied, as I was with him, nobody would interrupt me.

There was an Indian fortification all round the town, and a guard placed at each entrance. The hunter passed one of these without molestation, but I was stopped by the guard and examined. They asked me where I came from, and what was my business there? My companion of the woods attempted to speak for me, but was not permitted; he was taken away, and I saw him no more. I was now surrounded by about 50 men, and carried to one of their chiefs to be examined by him. When I came before him, he asked me what was my business there? I told him I came there with a hunter, whom I met with in the woods. He replied, "Did I not know that whoever came there without giving a better account of themselves than I did, was to be put to death?" I said I did not know it. Observing that I answered him so readily in his own language, he asked me where I learnt it? To this I returned no answer, but burst out into a flood of tears; and calling upon my Lord Jesus. At this he stood astonished, and expressed a concern for me, and said I was young. He asked me who my Lord Jesus was? To this I gave him no answer, but continued praying and weeping. Addressing himself to the officer who stood by him, he said he was sorry; but it was the law, and it must not be broken. I was then ordered to be taken away, and put into a place of confinement. They led me from their court into a low dark place, and thrust me into it, very dreary and dismal; they made fast the door, and set a watch. The judge sent for the executioner, and gave him his warrant for my execution in the afternoon of the next day. The executioner came, and gave me notice of it, which made me very happy, as the near prospect of death made me hope for a speedy deliverance from the body: And truly this dungeon became my chapel, for the Lord Jesus did not leave me in this great trouble, but was very present, so that I continued blessing him, and singing his praises all night without ceasing: The watch hearing the noise, informed the executioner that somebody had been in the dungeon with me all night; upon

6. Allow.

which he came in to see and to examine, with a great torch lighted in his hand, who it was I had with me; but finding nobody, he turned round, and asked me who it was? I told him it was the Lord Jesus Christ; but he made no answer, turned away, went out, and locked the door. At the hour appointed for my execution I was taken out, and led to the destined spot, amidst a vast number of people. I praised the Lord all the way we went, and when we arrived at the place I understood the kind of death I was to suffer, yet, blessed be God, none of those things moved me. The executioner shewed me a basket of turpentine wood, stuck full of small pieces, like skewers; he told me I was to be stripped naked, and laid down in the basket, and these sharp pegs were to be stuck into me, and then set on fire, and when they had burnt to my body,[7] I was to be turned on the other side, and served in the same manner, and then to be taken by four men and thrown into the flame, which was to finish the execution. I burst into tears, and asked what I had done to deserve so cruel a death! To this he gave me no answer. I cried out, Lord, if it be thy will that it should be so, thy will be done: I then asked the executioner to let me go to prayer; he asked me to whom? I answered, to the Lord my God; he seemed surprized, and asked me where he was? I told him he was present; upon which he gave me leave. I desired them all to do as I did, so I fell down upon my knees, and mentioned to the Lord his delivering of the three children in the fiery furnace, and of Daniel in the lion's den,[8] and had close communion with God. I prayed in English a considerable time, and about the middle of my prayer, the Lord impressed a strong desire upon my mind to turn into their language, and pray in their tongue. I did so, and with remarkable liberty, which wonderfully affected the people. One circumstance was very singular, and strikingly displays the power and grace of God. I believe the executioner was savingly converted to God. He rose from his knees, and embraced me round the middle, and was unable to speak for about five minutes; the first words he expressed, when he had utterance, were, "No man shall hurt thee till thou hast been to the king."

I was taken away immediately, and as we passed along, and I was reflecting upon the deliverance which the Lord had wrought out for me, and hearing the praises which the executioner was singing to the Lord, I must own I was utterly at a loss to find words to praise him. I broke out in these words, what can't the Lord Jesus do! and what power is like unto his! I will thank thee for what is passed, and trust thee for what is to come. I will sing thy praise with my feeble tongue whilst life and breath shall last, and when I fail to sound thy praises here, I hope to sing them round thy throne above: And thus, with unspeakable joy, I sung two verses of Dr. Watts's hymns:

> "My God, the spring of all my joys,
> The life of my delights;
> The glory of my brightest days,
> And comfort of my nights.
> In darkest shades, if thou appear,
> My dawning is begun;
> Thou art my soul's bright morning star,
> And thou my rising sun."

7. "These pegs were to be kindled at the opposite end from the body" [Marrant's note].

8. See Daniel 6. "Three children . . . furnace": see Daniel 3.

Passing by the judge's door, he stopped us, and asked the executioner why he brought me back? The man fell upon his knees, and begged he would permit me to be carried before the king, which being granted, I went on, guarded by two hundred soldiers with bows and arrows. After many windings I entered the king's outward chamber, and after waiting some time he came to the door, and his first question was, how came I there? I answered, I came with a hunter whom I met with in the woods, and who persuaded me to come there. He then asked me how old I was? I told him not fifteen. He asked me how I was supported before I met with this man? I answered, by the Lord Jesus Christ, which seemed to confound him. He turned round, and asked me if he lived where I came from? I answered, yes, and here also. He looked about the room, and said he did not see him; but I told him I felt him. The executioner fell upon his knees, and intreated the king, and told him what he had felt of the same Lord. At this instant the king's eldest daughter came into the chamber, a person about 19 years of age, and stood at my right-hand. I had a Bible in my hand, which she took out of it, and having opened it, she kissed it; and seemed much delighted with it. When she had put it into my hand again; the king asked me what it was? and I told him, the name of my God was recorded there; and, after several questions, he bid me read it; which I did, particularly the 53d chapter of Isaiah, in the most solemn manner I was able; and also the 26th chapter of Matthew's Gospel;[9] and when I pronounced the name of Jesus, the particular effect it had upon me was observed by the king. When I had finished reading, he asked me why I read those names[1] with so much reverence? I told him, because the Being to whom those names belonged made heaven and earth, and I and he; this he denied. I then pointed to the sun, and asked him who made the sun, and moon, and stars, and preserved them in their regular order? He said there was a man in their town that did it. I laboured as much as I could to convince him to the contrary. His daughter took the book out of my hand a second time; she opened it, and kissed it again; her father bid her give it to me, which she did; but said, with much sorrow, the book would not speak to her. The executioner then fell upon his knees, and begged the king to let me go to prayer, which being granted, we all went upon our knees, and now the Lord displayed his glorious power. In the midst of the prayer some of them cried out, particularly the king's daughter, and the man who ordered me to be executed, and several others seemed under deep conviction of sin: This made the king very angry; he called me a witch, and commanded me to be thrust into the prison, and to be executed the next morning. This was enough to make me think, as old Jacob once did, "All these things are against me;"[2] for I was dragged away, and thrust into the dungeon with much indignation; but God, who never forsakes his people, was with me. Though I was weak in body, yet was I strong in the spirit: The Lord works, and who shall let it?[3] The executioner went to the king, and assured him, that if he put me to death, his daughter would never be well. They used the skill of all their doctors that afternoon and

9. Isaiah 53 begins "Who hath believed our report? And to whom is the arm of the Lord revealed?" Matthew 26 describes Jesus' actions before his Crucifixion.
1. "Or what those parts were which seemed to affect me so much, not knowing what I read, as
he did not understand the English language" [Marrant's note].
2. Genesis 42.36.
3. Who will hinder or prevent it? Cf. Isaiah 44.13.

night; but physical prescriptions were useless. In the morning the executioner came to me, and, without opening the prison door, called to me, and hearing me answer, said, "Fear not, thy God who delivered thee yesterday, will deliver thee to-day." This comforted me very much, especially to find he could trust the Lord. Soon after I was fetched out; I thought it was to be executed; but they led me away to the king's chamber with much bodily weakness, having been without food two days. When I came into the king's presence, he said to me, with much anger, if I did not make his daughter and that man well, I should be laid down and chopped into pieces before him. I was not afraid, but the Lord tried my faith sharply. The king's daughter and the other person were brought out into the outer chamber, and we went to prayer; but the heavens were locked up to my petitions. I besought the Lord again, but received no answer: I cried again, and he was intreated. He said, "Be it to thee as thou wilt;"[4] the Lord appeared most lovely and glorious; the king himself was awakened, and the others set at liberty. A great change took place among the people; the king's house became God's house; the soldiers were ordered away, and the poor condemned prisoner had perfect liberty, and was treated like a prince. Now the Lord made all my enemies to become my great friends. I remained nine weeks in the king's palace, praising God day and night: I was never out but three days all the time. I had assumed the habit of the country, and was dressed much like the king, and nothing was too good for me. The king would take off his golden ornaments, his chain and bracelets, like a child, if I objected to them, and lay them aside. Here I learnt to speak their tongue in the highest stile.[5]

1785

4. In Matthew 15.28, Jesus says this to a woman from Canaan. He has agreed to cast a devil out of her daughter.
5. Eventually, Marrant had a dramatic home-

coming at his mother's house. At the end of the *Narrative*, he is in London and preparing to depart for Nova Scotia.

REBECCA SAMUEL

Like her contemporary Abigail Adams, Rebecca Alexander Samuel (fl. 1790s) wrote letters that offer a fascinating glimpse into her cultural milieu. In Samuel's case, that milieu involved Jewish life in the early republic. Little is known about Samuel apart from her letters. She and her husband, Hyman Samuel, a silversmith and watchmaker, lived in southern cities and towns including Petersburg, Virginia; Baltimore, Maryland; and Charleston, South Carolina. They probably came originally from Germany and may have spent time in England. Writing in the German Jewish dialect of Yiddish to her parents, in Hamburg, Germany, Samuel described various challenges that her family experienced in practicing their faith and sustaining their religious identity. Samuel also emphasized her appreciation for the absence of religious coercion in the United States and the relative acceptance that they found in the southern states.

Letters to Her Parents[1]

Petersburg, January 12, 1791, Wednesday, 8th [7th?] Shebat, 5551.[2]

Dear and Worthy Parents:
I received your dear letter with much pleasure and therefrom understand that you are in good health, thank God, and that made us especially happy. The same is not lacking with us—may we live to be a hundred years. Amen.

Dear parents, you complain that you do not receive any letters from us, and my mother-in-law writes the same. I don't know what's going on. I have written more letters than I have received from you. Whenever I can and have an opportunity, I give letters to take along, and I send letters by post when I do not have any other opportunity. It is already six months since we received letters from you and from London. The last letter you sent was through Sender [Alexander], and it was the beginning of the month of Ab [July, 1790] when we received it. Now you can realize that we too have been somewhat worried. We are completely isolated here. We do not have any friends, and when we do not hear from you for any length of time, it is enough to make us sick. I hope that I will get to see some of my family. That will give me some satisfaction.

You write me that Mr. Jacob Renner's son Reuben is in Philadelphia and that he will come to us. People will not advise him to come to Virginia. When the Jews of Philadelphia or New York hear the name Virginia, they get nasty. And they are not wrong! It won't do for a Jew. In the first place it is an unhealthful district, and we are only human. God forbid, if anything should happen to us, where would we be thrown? There is no cemetery in the whole of Virginia. In Richmond, which is twenty-two miles from here, there is a Jewish community consisting of two quorums [twenty men], and the two cannot muster a quarter [quorum when needed?].

You cannot imagine what kind of Jews they have here [in Virginia]. They were all German itinerants who made a living by begging in Germany. They came to America during the war, as soldiers, and now they can't recognize themselves.

One can make a good living here, and all live at peace. Anyone can do what he wants. There is no rabbi in all of America to excommunicate anyone. This is a blessing here; Jew and Gentile are as one. There is no *galut* ["exile," rejection of Jews] here. In New York and Philadelphia there is more *galut*. The reason is that there are too many German Gentiles and Jews there. The German Gentiles cannot forsake their anti-Jewish prejudice; and the German Jews cannot forsake their disgraceful conduct; and that's what makes the *galut*.

[Rebecca Samuel]

1. The texts are from Jacob Rader Marcus, *American Jewry Documents: Eighteenth Century* (1959). Bracketed material is by Marcus.

2. The year according to the Hebrew calendar. "Shebat": variant spelling of Shabbat, the Hebrew word for Sabbath.

Touro Synagogue. Built in 1763, the Touro Synagogue, in Newport, Rhode Island, is the oldest surviving synagogue building in North America. Here, rabbis read a Torah scroll on the bima (altar).

Dear Parents:

I hope my letter will ease your mind. You can now be reassured and send me one of the family to Charleston, South Carolina.[3] This is the place to which, with God's help, we will go after Passover. The whole reason why we are leaving this place is because of [lack of] *Yehudishkeit* [Jewishness].

Dear parents, I know quite well you will not want me to bring up my children like Gentiles. Here they cannot become anything else. Jewishness is pushed aside here. There are here [in Petersburg] ten or twelve Jews, and they are not worthy of being called Jews. We have a shohet[4] here who goes to market and buys terefah [nonkosher] meat and then brings it home. On Rosh Ha-Shanah [New Year] and on Yom Kippur ["the Day of Atonement"] the people worshipped here without one sefer torah ["Scroll of the Law"], and not one of them wore the tallit [a large prayer shawl worn in the synagogue] or the *arba kanfot* [the small set of fringes worn on the body], except Hyman and my Sammy's godfather. The latter is an old man of sixty, a man from Holland. He has been in America for thirty years already; for twenty years he was in Charleston, and he has been living here for four years. He does not want to remain here any longer and will go with us to Charleston. In that place there is a blessed community of three hundred Jews.

You can believe me that I crave to see a synagogue to which I can go. The way we live now is no life at all. We do not know what the Sabbath and the holidays are. On the Sabbath all the Jewish shops are open; and they do

3. This undated letter was written before 1796, the year that Samuel moved from Petersburg to Charleston.

4. Hebrew term for the person who ritually slaughters animals according to Jewish law, producing kosher meat.

business on that day as they do throughout the whole week. But ours we do not allow to open. With us there is still some Sabbath. You must believe me that in our house we all live as Jews as much as we can.

As for the Gentiles [?], we have nothing to complain about. For the sake of a livelihood we do not have to leave here. Nor do we have to leave because of debts. I believe ever since Hyman has grown up that he has not had it so good. You cannot know what a wonderful country this is for the common man. One can live here peacefully. Hyman made a clock that goes very accurately, just like the one in the Buchenstrasse in Hamburg. Now you can imagine what honors Hyman has been getting here. In all Virginia there is no clock [like this one], and Virginia is the greatest province in the whole of America, and America is the largest section of the world. Now you know what sort of a country this is. It is not too long since Virginia was discovered. It is a young country. And it is amazing to see the business they do in this little Petersburg. At times as many as a thousand hogsheads of tobacco arrive at one time, and each hogshead contains 1,000 and sometimes 1,200 pounds of tobacco. The tobacco is shipped from here to the whole world.

When Judah [my brother?] comes here, he can become a watchmaker and a goldsmith, if he so desires. Here it is not like Germany where a watchmaker is not permitted to sell silverware. [The contrary is true in this country.] They do not know otherwise here. They expect a watchmaker to be a silversmith here. Hyman has more to do in making silverware than with watchmaking. He has a journeyman, a silversmith, a very good artisan, and he, Hyman, takes care of the watches. This work is well paid here, but in Charleston, it pays even better.

All the people who hear that we are leaving give us their blessings. They say that it is sinful that such blessed children should be brought up here in Petersburg. My children cannot learn anything here, nothing Jewish, nothing of general culture. My Schoene [my daughter], God bless her, is already three years old. I think it is time that she should learn something, and she has a good head to learn. I have taught her the bedtime prayers and grace after meals in just two lessons. I believe that no one among the Jews here can do as well as she. And my Sammy [born in 1790], God bless him, is already beginning to talk.

I could write more. However, I do not have any more paper.

I remain, your devoted daughter and servant,
Rebecca, the wife of Hayyim, the son of Samuel the Levite

I send my family, my . . . [mother-in-law?] and all my friends and good friends, my regards.

SAGOYEWATHA

The name of the Seneca leader Sagoyewatha (1758?–1830) means roughly "he keeps them awake," apparently referring to his considerable abilities as an orator. He was also known by the English name Red Jacket, after the coat that the

British awarded him for his services as a message runner during the Revolutionary War. Following the War of 1812, he negotiated with the United States government to protect Seneca lands in western New York. Among many noteworthy orations, his most famous speech was the reply he gave to the missionary Jacob Cram in 1805 outlining what has been called a "separatist" position—the notion that while the ways of white Christians may be fine for them, they are not necessarily equally fine for nonwhite indigenous peoples, who have their own religious beliefs.

Present at Red Jacket's speech was Erastus Granger, who had been appointed the postmaster and Indian agent at Buffalo Creek by President Thomas Jefferson. Granger's immediate subordinate was Joseph Parrish, who probably served as translator, as he had done on other occasions. Who-

Portrait of Sagoyewatha. Sagoyewatha dealt with American presidents from Washington (1789–97) to Jackson (1829–37), delivering major addresses to Washington, Adams, and Monroe in an effort to protect his people's lands.

ever transcribed the translation of Red Jacket's speech—perhaps Granger or Parrish—it appeared in the April 1809 issue of the *Monthly Anthology and Boston Review*, a miscellaneous magazine, and was reprinted many times throughout the nineteenth century.

Reply to the Missionary Jacob Cram[1]

FRIEND AND BROTHER: It was the will of the Great Spirit that we should meet together this day. HE orders all things, and has given us a fine day for our Council. HE has taken his garment from before the sun, and caused it to shine with brightness upon us. Our eyes are opened, that we see clearly; our ears are unstopped, that we have been able to hear distinctly the words you have spoken. For all these favors we thank the Great Spirit; and HIM *only*.

BROTHER: This council fire was kindled by you. It was at your request that we came together at this time. We have listened with attention to what you have said. You requested us to speak our minds freely. This gives us great joy; for we now consider that we stand upright before you, and can speak what we think. All have heard your voice, and all speak to you now as one man. Our minds are agreed.

1. The text is from William Leete Stone, *The Life and Times of Red-Jacket, or Sa-go-ye-wat-ha: Being the Sequel to the History of the Six Nations* (1841).

BROTHER: You say you want an answer to your talk before you leave this place. It is right you should have one, as you are a great distance from home, and we do not wish to detain you. But we will first look back a little, and tell you what our fathers have told us, and what we have heard from the white people.

BROTHER: Listen to what we say. There was a time when our forefathers owned this great island. Their seats extended from the rising to the setting sun. The Great Spirit had made it for the use of Indians. HE had created the buffalo, the deer, and other animals for food. HE had made the bear and the beaver. Their skins served us for clothing. HE had scattered them over the country, and taught us how to take them. HE had caused the earth to produce corn for bread. All this HE had done for his red children, because HE loved them. If we had some disputes about our hunting ground, they were generally settled without the shedding of much blood. But an evil day came upon us. Your forefathers crossed the great water and landed on this island. Their numbers were small. They found friends and not enemies. They told us they had fled from their own country for fear of wicked men, and had come here to enjoy their religion. They asked for a small seat. We took pity on them, granted their request; and they sat down amongst us. We gave them corn and meat; they gave us poison[2] in return.

The white people, BROTHER, had now found our country. Tidings were carried back, and more came amongst us. Yet we did not fear them. We took them to be friends. They called us brothers. We believed them and gave them a larger seat. At length their numbers had greatly increased. They wanted more land; they wanted our country. Our eyes were opened, and our minds became uneasy. Wars took place. Indians were hired to fight against Indians, and many of our people were destroyed. They also brought strong liquor amongst us. It was strong and powerful, and has slain thousands.

BROTHER: Our seats were once large and yours were small. You have now become a great people, and we have scarcely a place left to spread our blankets. You have got our country, but are not satisfied; you want to force your religion upon us.

BROTHER: Continue to listen. You say that you are sent to instruct us how to worship the Great Spirit agreeably to his mind, and, if we do not take hold of the religion which you white people teach, we shall be unhappy hereafter. You say that you are right and we are lost. How do we know this to be true? We understand that your religion is written in a book. If it was intended for us as well as you, why has not the Great Spirit given to us, and not only to us, but why did he not give to our forefathers, the knowledge of that book, with the means of understanding it rightly? We only know what you tell us about it. How shall we know when to believe, being so often deceived by the white people?

BROTHER: You say there is but one way to worship and serve the Great Spirit. If there is but one religion, why do you white people differ so much about it? Why not all agreed, as you can all read the book?

BROTHER: We do not understand these things. We are told that your religion was given to your forefathers, and has been handed down from father to son. We also have a religion, which was given to our forefathers, and has

2. Rum [Stone's note].

been handed down to us their children. We worship in that way. It teaches us to be thankful for all the favors we receive; to love each other, and to be united. We never quarrel about religion.

BROTHER: The Great Spirit has made us all, but HE has made a great difference between his white and red children. HE has given us different complexions and different customs. To you HE has given the arts. To these HE has not opened our eyes. We know these things to be true. Since HE has made so great a difference between us in other things, why may we not conclude that he has given us a different religion according to our understanding? The Great Spirit does right. HE knows what is best for his children; we are satisfied.

BROTHER: We do not wish to destroy your religion, or take it from you. We only want to enjoy our own.

* * *

BROTHER: We are told that you have been preaching to the white people in this place. These people are our neighbors. We are acquainted with them. We will wait a little while, and see what effect your preaching has upon them. If we find it does them good, makes them honest and less disposed to cheat Indians, we will then consider again of what you have said.

BROTHER: You have now heard our answer to your talk, and this is all we have to say at present. As we are going to part, we will come and take you by the hand, and hope the Great Spirit will protect you on your journey, and return you safe to your friends.

1805 1809

BENJAMIN FRANKLIN
1706–1790

To a remarkable extent, the writings of Benjamin Franklin represent the metamorphosis of New England literary culture from "Puritan" to "Yankee." They also helped inaugurate the new national sensibility that emerged after the American Revolution. These regional and national transformations can be traced in *Poor Richard's Almanac*, in his political writings, and above all in *The Autobiography*, which presents the personal history and philosophy behind Franklinian self-fashioning. *The Autobiography* begins by tracing the family's origins to the English Midlands, where they were "franklins"—nonaristocractic landowners—and dissenting Protestants in a region profoundly disrupted by the English Civil Wars (1642–51). This family history of property ownership and concern for religious and civil liberties sets the stage for the life story that unfolds in sections, which Franklin produced from the eve of the American Revolution to shortly after the ratification of the United States Constitution and the inauguration of President George Washington. Because he was writing during these tumultuous times, when he was

much occupied with public business, Franklin was able to carry his story only to his fifty-second year. Despite the narrative's incompleteness, Franklin's popular fame, the significance of his rise from obscure origins, and his lively prose style helped transform this loosely knit set of consecutive fragments into an iconic work.

Franklin's father, Josiah, was a maker of candles and soap who moved to Boston in 1682 from Ecton, Northamptonshire, England. He married Abiah Folger, whose father, Peter, was a poet, a linguist, and a missionary to the indigenous inhabitants of Nantucket Island. Benjamin was his father's youngest son in a family of seventeen children, and Josiah, who took pride in his Protestant ancestry, enrolled his son in Boston Grammar School as a preparation for the ministry. His plans were too financially ambitious, however, and Benjamin was forced to leave school and work for his father. The younger Franklin hated his father's occupation, however, and threatened to run away to sea.

A compromise was reached, and when Benjamin was twelve he was apprenticed to his brother James, a printer. This trade was a good fit for the young man, who loved books and reading and liked to write. In 1722, James unwittingly published his younger brother's first essay, when he printed an editorial left on his desk signed "Silence Dogood," the first in a series that Franklin produced over several months. The central theme of these letters is the promotion of the public interest, which Franklin had absorbed from Cotton Mather's Essays to Do Good (1710; excerpted earlier in this volume). When his brother was imprisoned in 1722 for offending Massachusetts officials, Franklin published the paper by himself.

The next year, however, Franklin broke with his brother and ran away to Philadelphia, an act of defiance that in his later telling accumulated symbolic power as a precursor to the Revolution. At seventeen, with little money in his pocket but already an expert printer, he made his way in the world, subject to numerous "errata"—as he liked to call his mistakes, using the publisher's term—but confident that he could profit from lessons learned. His most serious error was in trusting Pennsylvania governor Sir William Keith, who in 1724 sent him to London by falsely promising to sponsor a new newspaper. During his time in the British capital, Franklin worked as a typesetter and experimented with free thought, even publishing a pamphlet on the topic that he later had to explain in his Autobiography. He returned to the colonies two years later, at the very moment when print culture experienced a remarkable expansion and the printer came to play a major public role as a disseminator of information. Franklin, ever an astute businessman, turned this development to his advantage.

Franklin had an uncanny instinct for success and knew that commercialism demanded that anyone in business assume a public persona. He taught himself French, Spanish, Italian, and Latin and yet was shrewd enough to realize that people did not like to do business with merchants who put on airs. He dressed plainly and sometimes carried his own paper in a wheelbarrow through Philadelphia streets to assure prospective customers that he was hardworking and not above doing things for himself. By the time he was twenty-four, he was the sole owner of a successful printing shop as well as the editor and publisher of the Pennsylvania Gazette. He first offered his Poor Richard's Almanac for sale in 1733 and made it an American institution, preaching hard work and thrift, and filling it with maxims for achieving wealth.

Another of Franklin's popular writings was his pseudonymously published "Speech of Miss Polly Baker," which enjoyed transatlantic circulation and indicated his unusually progressive views of women for his time. Franklin had already experimented with a female persona in his Silence Dogood letters, and in 1744 he had produced an edition of Samuel Richardson's novel Pamela: or, Virtue Rewarded (1740), which portrays a young servant woman who resists the sexual overtures of her master, until he eventually marries her. Franklin, who wanted to promote the growth of the colonial population, somewhat wryly turns the tables in Polly Baker's speech to the court, where she calls for a change in the laws that punished women who bore children outside of marriage and argues that in cases of illegitimate birth, men should share equal blame with

women. These themes of the unjust and unequal punishment directed at women who violated the sexual norms of the day were emerging as central concerns in popular novels such as Richardson's *Clarissa* (1748), Susanna Rowson's *Charlotte Temple* (1791), and Hannah Webster Foster's *The Coquette* (1797; reprinted in full later in this volume). Franklin's interest in this issue was not purely intellectual or literary. In 1730, he had established a common-law marriage with Deborah Read, the daughter of his first landlady, and they went on to have two children. Around the time he married Read, Franklin fathered an illegitimate child, and Deborah accepted Franklin's son William into the household.

Before he retired from business at age forty-two, Franklin had founded a library, invented a stove, established a fire company, subscribed to an academy that would become the University of Pennsylvania, and served as secretary to the American Philosophical Society. In retirement, he intended to devote himself to public affairs and his lifelong passion for the natural sciences, especially the phenomena of sound, vapors, earthquakes, and electricity. Franklin's observations on electricity were published in London in 1751, and despite his disclaimers in *The Autobiography*, they won him the applause of British scientists. His inquiring mind was challenged most by the mechanics of

Almanac for 1739. Writing under the pseudonym Richard Saunders, Franklin became famous for the aphorisms included in his immensely popular *Poor Richard's Almanac*.

the world's seemingly ordinary phenomena, and he was convinced that his mind's rational powers could solve riddles that had puzzled humankind for centuries. Franklin believed that people were naturally innocent, that all the mysteries that charmed the religious mind could be explained in ways that would promote human well-being, and that education, properly undertaken, would transform people's lives and set them free from the tyrannies of Church and monarchy. Franklin had no illusions about the "errata" of humankind, but his editorial metaphor—unlike, say, the word "sins"— suggests that human nature can progressively change.

Franklin's later years were spent at diplomatic tables in London, Paris, and Philadelphia, where his gift for irony served him well. He was a born diplomat—detached, adaptable, witty, urbane, charming, and clever—and of the slightly more than forty years left to him after his retirement, more than half were spent abroad. In 1757 he went to England to represent the colonies, and he stayed for five years. After a brief period in Philadelphia as a legislator, Franklin returned to England as a colonial representative, and there, in 1768, he began to doubt the possibility of compromise with the British government. "Parliament can make *all* laws for the colonies or *none*,"

he said, and "I think the arguments for the latter more numerous and weighty, than those for the former." When he returned to Philadelphia in May 1775, he was chosen as a representative to the Second Continental Congress, and he served on the committee to draft the Declaration of Independence. In October 1776, he was appointed minister to France, where he successfully negotiated a treaty of allegiance and became something of a cult hero. He was a member of the American delegation to the Paris peace conference, and he signed the Treaty of Paris in 1783, officially ending the Revolutionary War.

Franklin protested his too-long stay in Europe and returned to Philadelphia in 1785, serving as a delegate to the Constitutional Convention. At that time, he acted on the antislavery beliefs that he had come to embrace, joining and eventually serving as president for the Society for Promoting the Abolition of Slavery and the Relief of Negroes Unlawfully Held in Bondage in Philadelphia. By the time he died, he had become one of the most beloved Americans. Twenty thousand people attended his funeral, and editions of his works began appearing almost immediately. He remained a cultural hero well into the nineteenth century, and his reputation helped spawn rags-to-riches tales, such as those of Horatio Alger.

By the early twentieth century, Franklin had become a figure for intellectuals to diagnose rather than emulate. In his study *The Protestant Ethic and the Spirit of Capitalism* (1905), the German sociologist Max Weber criticized Franklin as a leading theorist of the secularized asceticism that Weber found at the heart of the capitalist economic system. In *Classic Studies in American Literature* (1923), the British novelist D. H. Lawrence, influenced by the psychoanalytic theories of Sigmund Freud, charged Franklin with indifference to the darker recesses of the soul. To these readers, Franklin's capacity for detachment suggests emotional and social inauthenticity, extending to the economic oppression of others and the repression of central elements of the self. Yet Franklin the secular ascetic was just one side of a man known for both his devotion to the public good at home and his high living at the French court. When Lawrence mocks the final precept in Franklin's "Art of Virtue"—to cultivate humility, Franklin writes, one should "imitate Jesus and Socrates"—he seemingly takes Franklin at face value, missing the ironic wit that makes Franklin's works so challenging and pleasurable. As is clear in *The Autobiography*, Franklin was a deliberate prose stylist who followed such distinguished British models as Joseph Addison and Richard Steele, John Bunyan, Daniel Defoe, and Jonathan Swift. A reading of Franklin's finest prose reveals a multifaceted and agile writer alert to the best and worst in humankind—including himself.

The Way to Wealth[1]

Preface to Poor Richard Improved

Courteous Reader,

I have heard that nothing gives an author so great pleasure, as to find his works respectfully quoted by other learned authors. This pleasure I have seldom enjoyed; for though I have been, if I may say it without vanity, an eminent author of almanacs annually now a full quarter of a century, my brother

1. The text is from *The Writings of Benjamin Franklin* (1905), edited by Albert Henry Smyth. Franklin wrote this essay for the twenty-fifth anniversary issue of his *Almanac,* the first issue of which, under the fictitious editorship of "Richard Saunders," appeared in 1733. For this essay, Franklin brought together the best of his maxims in the guise of a speech by Father Abraham. It is frequently reprinted as "The Way to Wealth" but is also known by earlier titles: "Poor Richard Improved" and "Father Abraham's Speech."

authors in the same way, for what reason I know not, have ever been very sparing in their applauses, and no other author has taken the least notice of me, so that did not my writings produce me some solid pudding, the great deficiency of praise would have quite discouraged me.

I concluded at length, that the people were the best judges of my merit; for they buy my works; and besides, in my rambles, where I am not personally known, I have frequently heard one or other of my adages repeated with "as Poor Richard says" at the end on 't; this gave me some satisfaction, as it showed not only that my instructions were regarded, but discovered likewise some respect for my authority; and I own, that to encourage the practice of remembering and repeating those wise sentences, I have sometimes quoted myself with great gravity.

Judge, then, how much I must have been gratified by an incident I am going to relate to you. I stopped my horse lately where a great number of people were collected at a vendue[2] of merchant goods. The hour of sale not being come, they were conversing on the badness of the times and one of the company called to a plain clean old man, with white locks, "Pray, Father Abraham, what think you of the times? Won't these heavy taxes quite ruin the country? How shall we be ever able to pay them? What would you advise us to?" Father Abraham stood up, and replied, "If you'd have my advice, I'll give it you in short, for a *word to the wise is enough, and many words won't fill a bushel,* as Poor Richard says." They joined in desiring him to speak his mind, and gathering round him, he proceeded as follows:

"Friends," says he, "and neighbors, the taxes are indeed very heavy, and if those laid on by the government were the only ones we had to pay, we might more easily discharge them; but we have many others, and much more grievous to some of us. We are taxed twice as much by our idleness, three times as much by our pride, and four times as much by our folly; and from these taxes the commissioners cannot ease or deliver us by allowing an abatement. However, let us hearken to good advice, and something may be done for us; *God helps them that help themselves,* as Poor Richard says, in his Almanac of 1733.

"It would be thought a hard government that should tax its people one-tenth part of their time, to be employed in its service. But idleness taxes many of us much more, if we reckon all that is spent in absolute sloth, or doing of nothing, with that which is spent in idle employments, or amusements, that amount to nothing. Sloth, by bringing on diseases, absolutely shortens life. *Sloth, like rust, consumes faster than labor wears; while the used key is always bright,* as Poor Richard says. *But dost thou love life, then do not squander time, for that's the stuff life is made of,* as Poor Richard says. How much more than is necessary do we spend in sleep, forgetting that *the sleeping fox catches no poultry* and that *there will be sleeping enough in the grave,* as Poor Richard says.

"*If time be of all things the most precious, wasting time must be,* as Poor Richard says, *the greatest prodigality*; since, as he elsewhere tells us, *lost time is never found again; and what we call time enough, always proves little enough:* let us then up and be doing, and doing to the purpose; so by diligence shall

2. Auction or sale.

we do more with less perplexity. *Sloth makes all things difficult, but industry*[3] *all easy,* as Poor Richard says; *and he that riseth late must trot all day, and shall scarce overtake his business at night;* while *laziness travels so slowly, that poverty soon overtakes him,* as we read in Poor Richard, who adds, *drive thy business, let not that drive thee,* and *early to bed, and early to rise, makes a man healthy, wealthy, and wise.*

"So what signifies wishing and hoping for better times. We may make these times better, if we bestir ourselves. *Industry need not wish,* as Poor Richard says, *and he that lives upon hope will die fasting. There are no gains without pains; then help hands, for I have no lands,* or if I have, they are smartly taxed. And, as Poor Richard likewise observes, *he that hath a trade hath an estate; and he that hath a calling, hath an office of profit and honor;* but then the trade must be worked at, and the calling well followed, or neither the estate nor the office will enable us to pay our taxes. If we are industrious, we shall never starve; for, as Poor Richard says, *at the workingman's house hunger looks in, but dares not enter.* Nor will the bailiff or the constable enter, for *industry pays debts, while despair increaseth them,* says Poor Richard. What though you have found no treasure, nor has any rich relation left you a legacy, *diligence is the mother of good luck,* as Poor Richard says, and *God gives all things to industry. Then plow deep, while sluggards sleep, and you shall have corn to sell and to keep,* says Poor Dick. Work while it is called today, for you know not how much you may be hindered tomorrow, which makes Poor Richard says, *one today is worth two tomorrows,* and farther, *have you somewhat to do tomorrow, do it today.* If you were a servant, would you not be ashamed that a good master should catch you idle? Are you then your own master, *be ashamed to catch yourself idle,* as Poor Dick says. When there is so much to be done for yourself, your family, your country, and your gracious king, be up by peep of day; *let not the sun look down and say, inglorious here he lies.* Handle your tools without mittens; remember that *the cat in gloves catches no mice,* as Poor Richard says. 'Tis true there is much to be done, and perhaps you are weak-handed, but stick to it steadily; and you will see great effects, for *constant dropping*[4] *wears away stones,* and *by diligence and patience the mouse ate in two the cable;* and *little strokes fell great oaks,* as Poor Richard says in his Almanac, the year I cannot just now remember.

"Methinks I hear some of you say, 'must a man afford himself no leisure?' I will tell thee, my friend, what Poor Richard says, *employ thy time well, if thou meanest to gain leisure; and, since thou art not sure of a minute, throw not away an hour.* Leisure is time for doing something useful; this leisure the diligent man will obtain, but the lazy man never; so that, as Poor Richard says *a life of leisure and a life of laziness are two things.*[5] Do you imagine that sloth will afford you more comfort than labor? No, for as Poor Richard says, *trouble springs from idleness, and grievous toil from needless ease. Many without labor, would live by their wits only, but they break for want of stock.* Whereas industry gives comfort, and plenty, and respect: *fly*[6] *pleasures, and they'll follow you. The diligent spinner has a large shift;*[7] *and now I have a sheep and a cow, everybody bids me good morrow;* all of which is well said by Poor Richard.

3. I.e., industriousness.
4. I.e., of water.
5. I.e., two different things.

6. Flee.
7. Wardrobe.

"But with our industry, we must likewise be steady, settled, and careful, and oversee our own affairs with our own eyes, and not trust too much to others; for, as Poor Richard says

> I never saw an oft-removed tree,
> Nor yet an oft-removed family,
> That throve so well as those that settled be.

And again, *three removes*[8] *is as bad as a fire*; and again, *keep thy shop, and thy shop will keep thee*; and again, *if you would have your business done, go; if not, send.* And again,

> He that by the plow would thrive,
> Himself must either hold or drive.

And again, *the eye of a master will do more work than both his hands*; and again, *want*[9] *of care does us more damage than want of knowledge*; and again, *not to oversee workmen is to leave them your purse open.* Trusting too much to others' care is the ruin of many; for, as the Almanac says, *in the affairs of this world, men are saved, not by faith, but by the want of it*; but a man's own care is profitable; for, saith Poor Dick, *learning is to the studious*, and *riches to the careful*, as well as *power to the bold*, and *heaven to the virtuous*, and farther, *if you would have a faithful servant, and one that you like, serve yourself.* And again, he adviseth to circumspection and care, even in the smallest matters, because sometimes *a little neglect may breed great mischief*; adding, *for want of a nail the shoe was lost; for want of a shoe the horse was lost; and for want of a horse the rider was lost, being overtaken and slain by the enemy; all for want of care about a horseshoe nail.*

"So much for industry, my friends, and attention to one's own business; but to these we must add frugality, if we would make our industry more certainly successful. A man may, if he knows not how to save as he gets, keep his nose all his life to the grindstone, and die not worth a groat[1] at last. *A fat kitchen makes a lean will*, as Poor Richard says; and

> Many estates are spent in the getting,
> Since women for tea forsook spinning and knitting,
> And men for punch forsook hewing and splitting.

If you would be wealthy, says he, in another Almanac, *think of saving as well as of getting: the Indies have not made Spain rich, because her outgoes are greater than her incomes.*

"Away then with your expensive follies, and you will not then have so much cause to complain of hard times, heavy taxes, and chargeable families; for, as Poor Dick says,

> Women and wine, game[2] and deceit,
> Make the wealth small and the wants great.

And farther, *what maintains one vice would bring up two children.* You may think perhaps, that a little tea, or a little punch now and then, diet a little more costly, clothes a little finer, and a little entertainment now and then,

8. Moves.
9. Lack.

1. A silver coin worth about four pence.
2. Gambling.

can be no great matter; but remember what Poor Richard says, *many a little makes a mickle*; and farther, *Beware of little expenses; a small leak will sink a great ship*; and again, *who dainties*[3] *love shall beggars prove*; and moreover, *fools make feasts, and wise men eat them.*

"Here you are all got together at this vendue of fineries and knicknacks. You call them goods; but if you do not take care, they will prove evils to some of you. You expect they will be sold cheap, and perhaps they may for less than they cost; but if you have no occasion for them, they must be dear to you. Remember what Poor Richard says; *buy what thou hast no need of, and ere long thou shalt sell thy necessaries.* And again, *at a great penny-worth pause a while*: he means, that perhaps the cheapness is apparent only, and not real; or the bargain, by straightening[4] thee in thy business, may do thee more harm than good. For in another place he says, *many have been ruined by buying good pennyworths.* Again, Poor Richard says, *'tis foolish to lay out money in a purchase of repentance*; and yet this folly is practiced every day at vendues, for want of minding the Almanac. *Wise men*, as Poor Dick says, *learn by others' harms, fools scarcely by their own*; but *felix quem faciunt aliena pericula cautum.*[5] Many a one, for the sake of finery on the back, have gone with a hungry belly, and half-starved their families. *Silks and satins, scarlet and velvets*, as Poor Richard says, *put out the kitchen fire.*

"These are not the necessaries of life; they can scarcely be called the conveniences; and yet only because they look pretty, how many want to have them! The artificial wants of mankind thus become more numerous than the natural; and, as Poor Dick says, *for one poor person, there are an hundred indigent.* By these, and other extravagancies, the genteel are reduced to poverty, and forced to borrow of those whom they formerly despised, but who through industry and frugality have maintained their standing; in which case it appears plainly, that *a plowman on his legs is higher than a gentleman on his knees*, as Poor Richard says. Perhaps they have had a small estate left them, which they knew not the getting of; they think, " 'Tis day, and will never be night"; that a little to be spent out of so much is not worth minding; *a child and a fool*, as Poor Richard says, *imagine twenty shillings and twenty years can never be spent* but, *always taking out of the meal-tub, and never putting in, soon comes to the bottom*; as Poor Dick says, *when the well's dry, they know the worth of water.* But this they might have known before, if they had taken his advice; *if you would know the value of money, go and try to borrow some; for, he that goes a-borrowing goes a-sorrowing*; and indeed so does he that lends to such people, when he goes to get it in again. Poor Dick farther advises, and says,

> Fond[6] *pride of dress is sure a very curse;*
> *E'er*[7] *fancy you consult, consult your purse.*

And again, *pride is as loud a beggar as want, and a great deal more saucy.* When you have bought one fine thing, you must buy ten more, that your appearance may be all of a piece; but Poor Dick says, *'tis easier to suppress*

3. Delicacies, luxuries. "Mickle": lot.
4. Restricting.
5. A Latin version of the proverb just quoted.

6. Foolish.
7. Every.

the first desire, than to satisfy all that follow it. And 'tis as truly folly for the poor to ape the rich, as for the frog to swell, in order to equal the ox.

> *Great estates may venture more,*
> *But little boats should keep near shore.*

'Tis, however, a folly soon punished; for *pride that dines on vanity sups on contempt*, as Poor Richard says. And in another place, *pride breakfasted with plenty, dined with poverty, and supped with infamy*. And after all, of what use is this pride of appearance, for which so much is risked so much is suffered? It cannot promote health, or ease pain; it makes no increase of merit in the person, it creates envy, it hastens misfortune.

> *What is a butterfly? At best*
> *He's but a caterpillar dressed.*
> *The gaudy fop's his picture just,*

as Poor Richard says.

"But what madness must it be to run in debt for these superfluities! We are offered, by the terms of this vendue, *six months' credit*; and that perhaps has induced some of us to attend it, because we cannot spare the ready money, and hope now to be fine without it. But, ah, think what you do when you run in debt; you give to another power over your liberty. If you cannot pay at the time, you will be ashamed to see your creditor; you will be in fear when you speak to him; you will make poor pitiful sneaking excuses, and by degrees come to lose your veracity, and sink into base downright lying; for, as Poor Richard says, *the second vice is lying, the first is running in debt*. And again, to the same purpose, *lying rides upon debt's back*. Whereas a free-born Englishman ought not to be ashamed or afraid to see or speak to any man living. But poverty often deprives a man of all spirit and virtue: *'tis hard for an empty bag to stand upright*, as Poor Richard truly says.

"What would you think of that prince, or that government, who should issue an edict forbidding you to dress like a gentleman or a gentlewoman, on pain of imprisonment or servitude? Would you not say, that you were free, have a right to dress as you please, and that such an edict would be a breach of your privileges, and such a government tyrannical? And yet you are about to put yourself under that tyranny, when you run in debt for such dress! Your creditor has authority, at his pleasure to deprive you of your liberty, by confining you in gaol[8] for life, or to sell you for a servant, if you should not be able to pay him! When you have got your bargain, you may, perhaps, think little of payment; but *creditors*, Poor Richard tells us, *have better memories than debtors*; and in another place says, *creditors are a superstitious sect, great observers of set days and times*. The day comes round before you are aware, and the demand is made before you are prepared to satisfy it, or if you bear your debt in mind, the term which at first seemed so long will, as it lessens, appear extremely short. Time will seem to have added wings to his heels as well as shoulders. *Those have a short Lent*, saith Poor Richard, *who owe money to be paid at Easter*.[9] Then since, as he says, *The borrower is a slave to the lender, and the debtor to the creditor*, disdain the chain, preserve your

8. Jail.
9. In Christianity, Lent is the period of roughly
six weeks before Easter. Poor Richard is saying debt would make that period feel shorter.

freedom; and maintain your independency: be industrious and free; be frugal and free. At present, perhaps, you may think yourself in thriving circumstances, and that you can bear a little extravagance without injury; but,

For age and want, save while you may;
No morning sun lasts a whole day,

as Poor Richard says. Gain may be temporary and uncertain, but ever while you live, expense is constant and certain; and *'tis easier to build two chimneys than to keep one in fuel*, as Poor Richard says. So, *rather go to bed supperless than rise in debt.*

Get[1] what you can, and what you get hold;
'Tis the stone that will turn all your lead into gold,

as Poor Richard says. And when you have got the philosopher's stone,[2] sure you will no longer complain of bad times, or the difficulty of paying taxes.

"This doctrine, my friends, is reason and wisdom; but after all, do not depend too much upon your own industry, and frugality, and prudence, though excellent things, for they may all be blasted without the blessing of heaven; and therefore, ask that blessing humbly, and be not uncharitable to those that at present seem to want it, but comfort and help them. Remember, Job[3] suffered, and was afterwards prosperous.

"And now to conclude, *experience keeps a dear[4] school, but fools will learn in no other, and scarce in that*; for it is true, *we may give advice, but we cannot give conduct*, as Poor Richard says: however, remember this, *they that won't be counseled, can't be helped*, as Poor Richard says: and farther, that, *if you will not hear reason, she'll surely rap your knuckles.*"

Thus the old gentleman ended his harangue. The people heard it, and approved the doctrine, and immediately practiced the contrary, just as if it had been a common sermon; for the vendue opened, and they began to buy extravagantly, notwithstanding his cautions and their own fear of taxes. I found the good man had thoroughly studied my almanacs, and digested all I had dropped on these topics during the course of five and twenty years. The frequent mention he made of me must have tired any one else, but my vanity was wonderfully delighted with it, though I was conscious that not a tenth part of the wisdom was my own, which he ascribed to me, but rather the gleanings I had made of the sense of all ages and nations. However, I resolved to be the better for the echo of it; and though I had at first determined to buy stuff for a new coat, I went away resolved to wear my old one a little longer. Reader, if thou wilt do the same, thy profit will be as great as mine. I am, as ever, thine to serve thee,

Richard Saunders
July 7, 1757

1757

1758

1. Earn.
2. A substance much sought by alchemists, thought to transform base metals into gold.

3. The Old Testament patriarch whose faith was tested by suffering.
4. Expensive.

The Speech of Miss Polly Baker[1]

*The Speech of Miss Polly Baker, Before a Court of Judicature,
at Connecticut in New England, Where She Was Prosecuted
the Fifth Time for Having a Bastard Child; Which Influenced the
Court to Dispense with Her Punishment, and Induced One of Her
Judges to Marry Her the next Day*

May it please the Honourable Bench to indulge me a few Words: I am a poor unhappy Woman; who have no Money to Fee Lawyers to plead for me, being hard put to it to get a tolerable Living. I shall not trouble your Honours with long Speeches; for I have not the presumption to expect, that you may, by any Means, be prevailed on to deviate in your Sentence from the Law, in my Favour. All I humbly hope is, that your Honours would charitably move the Governor's Goodness on my Behalf, that my Fine may be remitted. This is the Fifth Time, Gentlemen, that I have been dragg'd before your Courts on the same Account; twice I have paid heavy Fines, and twice have been brought to public Punishment, for want of Money to pay those Fines. This may have been agreeable to the Laws; I do not dispute it: But since Laws are sometimes unreasonable in themselves, and therefore repealed; and others bear too hard on the Subject in particular Circumstances; and therefore there is left a Power somewhere to dispense with the Execution of them; I take the Liberty to say, that I think this Law, by which I am punished, is both unreasonable in itself, and particularly severe with regard to me, who have always lived an inoffensive Life in the Neighbourhood where I was born, and defy my Enemies (if I have any) to say I ever wrong'd Man, Woman, or Child. Abstracted from the Law, I cannot conceive (may it please your Honours) what the Nature of my Offence is. I have brought Five fine Children into the World, at the Risque of my Life: I have maintained them well by my own Industry, without burthening the Township, and could have done it better, if it had not been for the heavy Charges and Fines I have paid. Can it be a Crime (in the Nature of Things I mean) to add to the Number of the King's Subjects, in a new Country that really wants People? I own I should think it rather a Praise worthy, than a Punishable Action. I have debauch'd no other Woman's Husband, nor inticed any innocent Youth: These Things I never was charged with; nor has any one the least cause of Complaint against me, unless, perhaps the Minister, or the Justice, because I have had Children without being Married, by which they have miss'd a Wedding Fee. But, can even this be a Fault of mine? I appeal to your Honours. You are pleased to allow I don't want Sense; but I must be stupid to the last Degree, not to prefer the honourable State of Wedlock, to the Condition I have lived in. I always was, and still am, willing to enter into it; I doubt not my Behaving well in it, having all the Industry, Frugality, Fertility, and Skill in Oeconomy, appertaining to a good Wife's Character. I defy any Person to say I ever Refused an Offer of that Sort: On the contrary, I readily Consented to the only Proposal of Marriage that ever was made me, which was when I was a Virgin; but too easily confiding in the Person's Sincerity that made it, I

1. The text is from *Gentleman's Magazine* (London), April 1747.

unhappily lost my own Honour, by trusting to his; for he got me with Child, and then forsook me: That very Person you all know; he is now become a Magistrate of this County; and I had hopes he would have appeared this Day on the Bench, and have endeavoured to moderate the Court in my Favour; then I should have scorn'd to have mention'd it; but I must Complain of it as unjust and unequal, that my Betrayer and Undoer, the first Cause of all my Faults and Miscarriages (if they must be deemed such) should be advanced to Honour and Power, in the same Government that punishes my Misfortunes with Stripes and Infamy. I shall be told, 'tis like, that were there no Act of Assembly in the Case, the Precepts of Religion are violated by my Transgressions. If mine, then, is a religious Offence, leave it, Gentlemen, to religious Punishments. You have already excluded me from all the Comforts of your Church Communion: Is not that sufficient? You believe I have offended Heaven, and must suffer eternal Fire: Will not that be sufficient? What need is there, then, of your additional Fines and Whippings? I own, I do not think as you do; for, if I thought, what you call a Sin, was really such, I would not presumptuously commit it. But how can it be believed, that Heaven is angry at my having Children, when, to the little done by me towards it, God has been pleased to add his divine Skill and admirable Workmanship in the Formation of their Bodies, and crown'd it by furnishing them with rational and immortal Souls? Forgive me Gentlemen, if I talk a little extravagantly on these Matters; I am no Divine: But if you, great Men, (*)[2] must be making Laws, do not turn natural and useful Actions into Crimes, by your Prohibitions. Reflect a little on the horrid Consequences of this Law in particular: What Numbers of procur'd Abortions! and how many distress'd Mothers have been driven, by the Terror of Punishment and public Shame, to imbrue, contrary to Nature, their own trembling Hands in the Blood of their helpless Offspring! Nature would have induc'd them to nurse it up with a Parent's Fondness. 'Tis the Law therefore, 'tis the Law itself that is guilty of all these Barbarities and Murders. Repeal it then, Gentlemen; let it be expung'd for ever from your Books: And on the other hand, take into your wise Consideration, the great and growing Number of Batchelors in the Country, many of whom, from the mean Fear of the Expence of a Family, have never sincerely and honourably Courted a Woman in their Lives; and by their Manner of Living, leave unproduced (which I think is little better than Murder) Hundreds of their Posterity to the Thousandth Generation. Is not theirs a greater Offence against the Public Good, than mine? Compel them then, by a Law, either to Marry, or pay double the Fine of Fornication every Year. What must poor young Women do, whom Custom has forbid to solicit the Men, and who cannot force themselves upon Husbands, when the Laws take no Care to provide them any, and yet severely punish if they do their Duty without them? Yes, Gentlemen, I venture to call it a Duty; 'tis the Duty of the first and great Command of Nature, and of Nature's God, *Increase and multiply*: A Duty, from the steady Performance of which nothing has ever been able to deter me; but for it's Sake, I have hazarded the Loss of the public Esteem, and frequently incurr'd public Dis-

2. (*) Turning to some Gentlemen of the Assembly, then in Court [Franklin's note].

grace and Punishment; and therefore ought, in my humble Opinion, instead of a Whipping, to have a Statue erected to my Memory.

1747

Rules by Which a Great Empire May Be Reduced to a Small One[1]

Presented to a Late Minister,
When He Entered upon His Administration.[2]

An ancient Sage boasted, that, tho' he could not fiddle, he knew how to make a *great city* of a *little one.* The science that I, a modern simpleton, am about to communicate, is the very reverse.

I address myself to all ministers who have the management of extensive dominions, which from their very greatness are become troublesome to govern, because the multiplicity of their affairs leaves no time for *fiddling.*[3]

I. In the first place, gentlemen, you are to consider, that a great empire, like a great cake, is most easily diminished at the edges. Turn your attention, therefore, first to your *remotest* provinces; that, as you get rid of them, the next may follow in order.

II. That the possibility of this separation may always exist, take special care the provinces are never incorporated with the mother country; that they do not enjoy the same common rights, the same privileges in commerce; and that they are governed by *severer* laws, all of *your enacting,* without allowing them any share in the choice of the legislators. By carefully making and preserving such distinctions, you will (to keep to my simile of the cake) act like a wise gingerbread-baker, who, to facilitate a division, cuts his dough half through in those places where, when baked, he would have it *broken to pieces.*

III. Those remote provinces have perhaps been acquired, purchased, or conquered, at the *sole expense* of the settlers, or their ancestors, without the aid of the mother country. If this should happen to increase her *strength,* by their growing numbers, ready to join in her wars; her *commerce,* by their growing demand for her manufactures; or her *naval power,* by greater employment for her ships and seamen, they may probably suppose some merit in this, and that it entitles them to some favor; you are therefore to *forget it all, or resent it,* as if they had done you injury. If they happen to be zealous whigs,[4] friends of liberty, nurtured in revolution principles, *remember all that* to their prejudice, and resolve to punish it; for such principles, after a revolution is thoroughly established, are of *no more use;* they are even *odious* and *abominable.*

IV. However peaceably your colonies have submitted to your government, shown their affection to your interests, and patiently borne their grievances; you are to *suppose* them always inclined to revolt, and treat them accordingly.

1. The text is from *The Writings of Benjamin Franklin* (1905), edited by Albert Henry Smyth.
2. I.e., this satire purports to be a document delivered to Wills Hill (1718–1793), first Earl of Hillsborough, in 1768, when he became secretary of state to the colonies, a position he held until 1772.
3. Cheating.
4. Here, American supporters of independence from Britain.

Quarter troops among them, who by their insolence may *provoke* the rising of mobs, and by their bullets and bayonets *suppress* them. By this means, like the husband who uses his wife ill *from suspicion,* you may in time convert your *suspicions* into *realities.*

V. Remote provinces must have *Governors* and *Judges,* to represent the Royal Person, and execute everywhere the delegated parts of his office and authority. You ministers know, that much of the strength of government depends on the *opinion* of the people; and much of that opinion on the *choice of rulers* placed immediately over them. If you send them wise and good men for governors, who study the interest of the colonists, and advance their prosperity, they will think their King wise and good, and that he wishes the welfare of his subjects. If you send them learned and upright men for Judges, they will think him a lover of justice. This may attach your provinces more to his government. You are therefore to be careful whom you recommend for those offices. If you can find prodigals, who have ruined their fortunes, broken gamesters or stockjobbers,[5] these may do well as *governors;* for they will probably be rapacious, and provoke the people by their extortions. Wrangling proctors and pettifogging lawyers,[6] too, are not amiss; for they will be for ever disputing and quarrelling with their little parliaments. If withal they should be ignorant, wrong-headed, and insolent, so much the better. Attorneys' clerks and Newgate solicitors will do for *Chief Justices,* especially if they hold their places *during your pleasure;*[7] and all will contribute to impress those ideas of your government, that are proper for a people *you would wish to renounce it.*

VI. To confirm these impressions, and strike them deeper, whenever the injured come to the capital with complaints of maladministration, oppression, or injustice, punish such suitors with long delay, enormous expense, and a final judgment in favor of the oppressor. This will have an admirable effect every way. The trouble of future complaints will be prevented, and Governors and Judges will be encouraged to farther acts of oppression and injustice; and thence the people may become more disaffected, and at length desperate.

VII. When such Governors have crammed their coffers, and made themselves so odious to the people that they can no longer remain among them, with safety to their persons, *recall and reward* them with pensions. You may make them *baronets*[8] too, if that respectable order should not think fit to resent it. All will contribute to encourage new governors in the same practice, and make the supreme government, *detestable.*

VIII. If, when you are engaged in war, your colonies should vie in liberal aids of men and money against the common enemy, upon your simple requisition, and give far beyond their abilities, reflect that a penny taken from them by your power is more honorable to you, than a pound presented by their benevolence; despise therefore their voluntary grants, and resolve to harass them with novel taxes. They will probably complain to your parliaments, that they are taxed by a body in which they have no representative,

5. Broken gamblers or speculators.
6. I.e., shysters. "Proctors": civil lawyers.
7. I.e., at your pleasure. "Solicitors": lawyers. Newgate was a London prison. The phrase

"Newgate solicitors" may be akin to "ambulance chasers."
8. I.e., give them noble titles.

and that this is contrary to common right. They will petition for redress. Let the Parliaments flout their claims, reject their petitions, refuse even to suffer the reading of them, and treat the petitioners with the utmost contempt. Nothing can have a better effect in producing the alienation proposed; for though many can forgive injuries, *none ever forgave contempt.*

IX. In laying these taxes, never regard the heavy burthens those remote people already undergo, in defending their own frontiers, supporting their own provincial governments, making new roads, building bridges, churches, and other public edifices, which in old countries have been done to your lands by your ancestors, but which occasion constant calls and demands on the purses of a new people. Forget the *restraints* you lay on their trade for *your own* benefit, and the advantage a *monopoly* of this trade gives your exacting merchants. Think nothing of the wealth those merchants and your manufacturers acquire by the colony commerce; their increased ability thereby to pay taxes at home; their accumulating, in the price of their commodities, most of those taxes, and so levying them from their consuming customers; all this, and the employment and support of thousands of your poor by the colonists, you are *entirely to forget.* But remember to make your arbitrary tax more grievous to your provinces, by public declarations importing[9] that your power of taxing them has *no limits*; so that when you take from them without their consent one shilling in the pound, you have a clear right to the other nineteen. This will probably weaken every idea of *security in their property,* and convince them, that under such a government they *have nothing they can call their own*; which can scarce fail of producing the *happiest consequences!*

X. Possibly, indeed, some of them might still comfort themselves, and say, "Though we have no property, we have yet *something* left that is valuable; we have constitutional *liberty*, both of person and of conscience. This King, these Lords, and these Commons, who it seems are too remote from us to know us, and feel for us, cannot take from us our *Habeas Corpus* right, or our right of trial *by a jury of our neighbors*; they cannot deprive us of the exercise of our religion, alter our ecclesiastical constitution, and compel us to be Papists, if they please, or Mahometans."[1] To annihilate this comfort, begin by laws to perplex their commerce with infinite regulations, impossible to be remembered and observed; ordain seizures of their property for every failure; take away the trial of such property by Jury, and give it to arbitrary Judges of your own appointing, and of the lowest characters in the country, whose salaries and emoluments[2] are to arise out of the duties or condemnations, and whose appointments are *during pleasure.* Then let there be a formal declaration of both Houses, that opposition to your edicts is *treason,* and that any person suspected of treason in the provinces may, according to some obsolete law, be seized and sent to the metropolis of the empire for trial; and pass an act, that those there charged with certain other offenses, shall be sent away in chains from their friends and country to be tried in the same manner for felony. Then erect a new Court of Inquisition among them, accompanied by an armed force, with instructions to transport[3] all

9. Emphasizing.
1. I.e., Muslims. *"Habeas Corpus"*: you should have the body (Latin, literal trans.); the right to know what one is charged with. "Papists":

Roman Catholics.
2. Payments for services rendered.
3. I.e., to deport, as criminals were to the American colonies.

such suspected persons; to be ruined by the expense, if they bring over evidences to prove their innocence, or be found guilty and hanged, if they cannot afford it. And, lest the people should think you cannot possibly go any farther, pass another solemn declaratory act, "that King, Lords, Commons had, hath, and of right ought to have, full power and authority to make statutes of sufficient force and validity to bind the unrepresented provinces IN ALL CASES WHATSOEVER." This will include *spiritual* with temporal, and, taken together, must operate wonderfully to your purpose; by convincing them, that they are at present under a power something like that spoken of in the scriptures, which can not only *kill their bodies*, but *damn their souls* to all eternity, by compelling them, if it pleases, *to worship the Devil*.

XI. To make your taxes more odious, and more likely to procure resistance, send from the capital a board of officers to superintend the collection, composed of the most *indiscreet, ill-bred,* and *insolent* you can find. Let these have large salaries out of the extorted revenue, and live in open, grating luxury upon the sweat and blood of the industrious; whom they are to worry continually with groundless and expensive prosecutions before the above-mentioned arbitrary revenue Judges; *all at the cost of the party prosecuted,* tho' acquitted, because *the King is to pay no costs*. Let these men, *by your order,* be exempted from all the common taxes and burthens of the province, though they and their property are protected by its laws. If any revenue offices are *suspected* of the least tenderness for the people, discard them. If others are justly complained of, protect and reward them. If any of the under officers behave so as to provoke the people to drub them, promote those to better offices: this will encourage others to procure for themselves such profitable drubbings, by multiplying and enlarging such provocations, and *all will work towards the end you aim at*.

XII. Another way to make your tax odious, is to misapply the produce of it. If it was originally appropriated for the *defense* of the provinces, the better support of government, and the administration of justice, where it may be *necessary,* then apply none of it to that *defense,* but bestow it where it is *not necessary,* in augmented salaries or pensions to every governor, who has distinguished himself by his enmity to the people, and by calumniating them to their sovereign. This will make them pay it more unwillingly, and be more apt to quarrel with those that collect it and those that imposed it, who will quarrel again with them, and all shall contribute to your *main purpose,* of making them *weary of your government*.

XIII. If the people of any province have been accustomed to support their own Governors and Judges to satisfaction, you are to apprehend that such Governors and Judges may be thereby influenced to treat the people kindly, and to do them justice. This is another reason for applying part of that revenue in larger salaries to such Governors and Judges, given, as their commissions are, *during your pleasure* only; forbidding them to take any salaries from their provinces; that thus the people may no longer hope any kindness from their Governors, or (in Crown cases)[4] any justice from their Judges. And, as the money thus misapplied in one province is extorted from all, probably *all will resent the misapplication*.

4. Cases that were formerly appealed directly to the king.

XIV. If the parliaments of your provinces should dare to claim rights, or complain of your administration, order them to be harrassed with *repeated dissolutions*.[5] If the same men are continually returned by new elections, adjourn their meetings to some country village, where they cannot be accommodated, and there keep them *during pleasure;* for this, you know, is your PREROGATIVE; and an excellent one it is, as you may manage it to promote discontents among the people, diminish their respect, and *increase their disaffection.*

XV. Convert the brave, honest officers of your *navy* into pimping tide-waiters[6] and colony officers of the *customs.* Let those, who in time of war fought gallantly in defense of the commerce of their countrymen, in peace be taught to prey upon it. Let them learn to be corrupted by great and real smugglers; but (to show their diligence) scour with armed boats every bay, harbor, river, creek, cove, or nook throughout the coast of your colonies; stop and detain every coaster, every wood-boat, every fisherman, tumble their cargoes and even their ballast inside out and upside down; and, if a penn'orth of pins is found unentered, let the whole be seized and confiscated. Thus shall the trade of your colonists suffer more from their friends in time of peace, than it did from their enemies in war. Then let these boats' crews land upon every farm in their way, rob the orchards, steal the pigs and the poultry, and insult the inhabitants. If the injured and exasperated farmers, unable to procure other justice, should attack the aggressors, drub them, and burn their boats; you are to call this *high treason and rebellion,* order fleets and armies into their country, and threaten to carry all the offenders three thousand miles to be hanged, drawn, and quartered. *O! this will work admirably!*

XVI. If you are told of discontents in your colonies, never believe that they are general, or that you have given occasion for them; therefore do not think of applying any remedy, or of changing any offensive measure. Redress no grievance, lest they should be encouraged to demand the redress of some other grievance. Grant no request that is just and reasonable, lest they should make another that is unreasonable. Take all your informations of the state of the colonies from your Governors and officers in enmity with them. Encourage and reward these *leasing-makers;*[7] secrete their lying accusations, lest they should be confuted; but act upon them as the clearest evidence; and believe nothing you hear from the friends of the people: suppose all *their* complaints to be invented and promoted by a few factious demagogues, whom if you could catch and hang, all would be quiet. Catch and hang a few of them accordingly; and the *blood of the Martyrs* shall *work miracles* in favor of your purpose.

XVII. If you see *rival nations* rejoicing at the prospect of your disunion with your provinces, and endeavoring to promote it; if they translate, publish, and applaud all the complaints of your discontented colonists, at the same time privately stimulating you to severer measures, let not that *alarm* or offend you. Why should it, since you all mean *the same thing?*

XVIII. If any colony should at their own charge erect a fortress to secure their port against the fleets of a foreign enemy, get your Governor to betray

5. I.e., dissolutions of these provincial parliaments.
6. Customs officers who boarded a ship before it
docked.
7. I.e., liars.

that fortress into your hands. Never think of paying what it cost the country, for that would look, at least, like some regard for justice; but turn it into a citadel to awe the inhabitants and curb their commerce. If they should have lodged in such fortress the very arms they bought and used to aid you in your conquests, seize them all; it will provoke like *ingratitude* added to *robbery*. One admirable effect of these operations will be, to discourage every other colony from erecting such defenses, and so your enemies may more easily invade them; to the great disgrace of your government, and of course *the furtherance of your project*.

XIX. Send armies into their country under pretense of protecting the inhabitants; but, instead of garrisoning the forts on their frontiers with those troops, to prevent incursions, demolish those forts, and order the troops into the heart of the country, that the savages may be encouraged to attack the frontiers, and that the troops may be protected by the inhabitants. This will seem to proceed from your ill will or your ignorance, and contribute farther to produce and strengthen an opinion among them, *that you are no longer fit to govern them*.

XX. Lastly, invest the General of your army in the provinces, with great and unconstitutional powers, and free him from the control of even your own Civil Governors. Let him have troops enow[8] under his command, with all the fortresses in his possession; and who knows but (like some provincial Generals in the Roman empire, and encouraged by the universal discontent you have produced) he may take it into his head to set up for himself? If he should, and you have carefully practiced these few *excellent rules* of mine, take my word for it, all the provinces will immediately join him; and you will that day (if you have not done it sooner) get rid of the trouble of governing them, and all the *plagues* attending their *commerce* and connection from henceforth and for ever.

Q. E. D.[9]

1773

Information to Those Who Would Remove to America[1]

Many persons in Europe, having directly or by letters, expressed to the writer of this, who is well acquainted with North America, their desire of transporting and establishing themselves in that country; but who appear to have formed, through ignorance, mistaken ideas and expectations of what is to be obtained there; he thinks it may be useful, and prevent inconvenient, expensive, and fruitless removals and voyages of improper persons, if he gives

8. Enough.
9. Abbreviation for *Quod erat demonstrandum*: which was to be demonstrated (Latin); the usual conclusion to a geometry problem. In other words, "I have proved my point."
1. The text is from *The Writings of Benjamin Franklin* (1905), edited by Albert Henry Smyth.

The title is taken from an edition of this pamphlet published in London without Franklin's permission in 1784. Franklin's title was *Advice to Such As Would Remove to America,* and he used this title when he published his own edition in France in the same year. "Remove": move.

some clearer and truer notions of that part of the world, than appear to have hitherto prevailed.

He finds it is imagined by numbers, that the inhabitants of North America are rich, capable of rewarding, and disposed to reward, all sorts of ingenuity; that they are at the same time ignorant of all the sciences, and consequently, that strangers, possessing talents in the belles-lettres, fine arts, etc., must be highly esteemed, and so well paid, as to become easily rich themselves; that there are also abundance of profitable offices to be disposed of, which the natives are not qualified to fill; and that, having few persons of family among them, strangers of birth[2] must be greatly respected, and of course easily obtain the best of those offices, which will make all their fortunes; that the governments too, to encourage emigrations from Europe, not only pay the expense of personal transportation, but give lands gratis to strangers, with Negroes to work for them, utensils of husbandry, and stocks of cattle. These are all wild imaginations; and those who go to America with expectations founded upon them will surely find themselves disappointed.

The truth is, that though there are in that country few people so miserable as the poor of Europe, there are also very few that in Europe would be called rich; it is rather a general happy mediocrity[3] that prevails. There are few great proprietors of the soil, and few tenants; most people cultivate their own lands, or follow some handicraft or merchandise; very few rich enough to live idly upon their rents or incomes, or to pay the high prices given in Europe for paintings, statues, architecture, and the other works of art, that are more curious than useful. Hence the natural geniuses, that have arisen in America with such talents, have uniformly quitted that country for Europe, where they can be more suitably rewarded. It is true, that letters and mathematical knowledge are in esteem there, but they are at the same time more common than is apprehended; there being already existing nine colleges or universities, viz., four in New England, and one in each of the provinces of New York, New Jersey, Pennsylvania, Maryland, and Virginia, all furnished with learned professors; besides a number of smaller academies; these educate many of their youth in the languages, and those sciences that qualify men for the professions of divinity, law, or physic.[4] Strangers indeed are by no means excluded from exercising those professions; and the quick increase of inhabitants everywhere gives them a chance of employ, which they have in common with the natives. Of civil offices, or employments, there are few; no superfluous ones, as in Europe; and it is a rule established in some of the states, that no office should be so profitable as to make it desirable. The 36th Article of the Constitution of Pennsylvania, runs expressly in these words: "As every freeman, to preserve his independence, (if he has not a sufficient estate) ought to have some profession, calling, trade, or farm, whereby he may honestly subsist, there can be no necessity for, nor use in, establishing offices of profit; the usual effects of which are dependence, and servility, unbecoming freemen, in the possessors and expectants; faction, contention, corruption, and disorder among the people. Wherefore, whenever an office, through increase of fees or otherwise, becomes so profitable, as to occasion many to apply for it, the profits ought to be lessened by the legislature."

2. I.e., of aristocratic birth.
3. I.e., a material equality.

4. Medicine.

These ideas prevailing more or less in all the United States, it cannot be worth any man's while, who has a means of living at home, to expatriate himself, in hopes of obtaining a profitable civil office in America; and, as to military offices, they are at an end with the war,[5] the armies being disbanded. Much less is it advisable for a person to go thither, who has no other quality to recommend him but his birth. In Europe it has indeed its value; but it is a commodity that cannot be carried to a worse market than that of America, where people do not inquire concerning a stranger, *what is he?* but, *what can he do?* If he has any useful art, he is welcome; and if he exercises it, and behaves well, he will be respected by all that know him; but a mere man of quality, who, on that account, wants to live upon the public, by some office or salary, will be despised and disregarded. The husbandman is in honor there, and even the mechanic,[6] because their employments are useful. The people have a saying, that God Almighty is Himself a mechanic, the greatest in the universe; and He is respected and admired more for the variety, ingenuity, and utility of His handyworks, than for the antiquity of His family. They are pleased with the observation of a Negro, and frequently mention it, that *Boccarorra* (meaning the white men) *make de black man workee, make de horse workee, make de ox workee, make eberyting workee; only de hog. He, de hog, no workee; he eat, he drink, he walk about, he go to sleep when he please; he libb like a gentleman.* According to these opinions of the Americans, one of them would think himself more obliged to a genealogist, who could prove for him that his ancestors and relations for ten generations had been plowmen, smiths, carpenters, turners, weavers, tanners,[7] or even shoemakers, and consequently that they were useful members of society; than if he could only prove that they were gentlemen, doing nothing of value, but living idly on the labor of others, mere *fruges consumere nati*,[8] and otherwise *good for nothing*, till by their death their estates, like the carcass of the Negro's gentleman hog, come to be *cut up*.

With regard to encouragements for strangers from government, they are really only what are derived from good laws and liberty. Strangers are welcome, because there is room enough for them all, and therefore the old inhabitants are not jealous of them; the laws protect them sufficiently, so that they have no need for the patronage of great men; and every one will enjoy securely the profits of his industry. But, if he does not bring a fortune with him, he must work and be industrious to live. One or two years' residence gives him all the rights of a citizen; but the government does not at present, whatever it may have done in former times, hire people to become settlers, by paying their passages, giving land, Negroes, utensils, stock, or any other kind of emolument whatsoever. In short, America is the land of labor, and by no means what the English call *Lubberland*, and the French *Pays de Cocagne*,[9] where the streets are said to be paved with half-peck loaves,

5. I.e., the Revolutionary War.
6. Manual laborer. "Husbandman": farmer.
7. Craftspeople who convert hides into leather. "Turners": latheworkers.
8. ". . . born / Merely to eat up the corn."—Watts [Franklin's note]. The English theologian Isaac Watts (1674–1748) is known as the father of

English hymnody. Franklin is quoting from memory Watts's paraphrase of *Epistles* 1.2.27, by the ancient Roman poet Horace. The Latin literally means "born to consume the fruits (of the earth)."
9. I.e., never-never land. "*Lubberland*": a land of laziness.

the houses tiled with pancakes, and where the fowls fly about ready roasted, crying *come eat me!*

Who then are the kind of persons to whom an emigration to America may be advantageous? And what are the advantages they may reasonably expect?

Land being cheap in that country, from the vast forests still void of inhabitants, and not likely to be occupied in an age to come, insomuch that the property of an hundred acres of fertile soil full of wood may be obtained near the frontiers, in many places, for eight or ten guineas,[1] hearty young laboring men, who understand the husbandry of corn and cattle, which is nearly the same in that country as in Europe, may easily establish themselves there. A little money saved of the good wages they receive there, while they work for others, enables them to buy the land and begin their plantation,[2] in which they are assisted by the good will of their neighbors, and some credit. Multitudes of poor people from England, Ireland, Scotland, and Germany, have by this means in a few years become wealthy farmers, who, in their own countries, where all the lands are fully occupied, and the wages of labor low, could never have emerged from the poor condition wherein they were born.

From the salubrity of the air, the healthiness of the climate, the plenty of good provisions, and the encouragement to early marriages by the certainty of subsistence in cultivating the earth, the increase of inhabitants by natural generation is very rapid in America, and becomes still more so by the accession of strangers; hence there is a continual demand for more artisans of all the necessary and useful kinds, to supply those cultivators of the earth with houses, and with furniture and utensils of the grosser sorts, which cannot so well be brought from Europe. Tolerably good workmen in any of those mechanic arts are sure to find employ, and to be well paid for their work, there being no restraints preventing strangers from exercising any art they understand, nor any permission necessary. If they are poor, they begin first as servants or journeymen;[3] and if they are sober, industrious, and frugal, they soon become masters, establish themselves in business, marry, raise families, and become respectable citizens.

Also, persons of moderate fortunes and capitals, who, having a number of children to provide for, as desirous of bringing them up to industry,[4] and to secure estates for their posterity, have opportunities of doing it in America, which Europe does not afford. There they may be taught and practice profitable mechanic arts, without incurring disgrace on that account, but on the contrary acquiring respect by such abilities. There small capitals laid out in lands, which daily become more valuable by the increase of people, afford a solid prospect of ample fortunes thereafter for those children. The writer of this has known several instances of large tracts of land, bought, on what was then the frontier of Pennsylvania, for ten pounds per hundred acres, which after 20 years, when the settlements had been extended far beyond them, sold readily, without any improvement made upon them, for

1. One guinea equals a pound plus a shilling (one twentieth of a pound), so this would be about eight to eleven pounds, or roughly twenty to thirty dollars in today's currency.
2. Farm.
3. Those who have served their apprenticeship and are paid by the day.
4. To be skillful in whatever they undertake in the way of a vocation.

three pounds per acre. The acre in America is the same with the English acre, or the acre of Normandy.

Those, who desire to understand the state of government in America, would do well to read the constitutions of the several states, and the Articles of Confederation that binds the whole together for general purposes, under the direction of one assembly, called the Congress. These constitutions have been printed, by order of Congress, in America; two editions of them have also been printed in London; and a good translation of them into French has lately been published at Paris.

Several of the princes of Europe having of late years, from an opinion of advantage to arise by producing all commodities and manufactures within their own dominions, so as to diminish or render useless their importations, have endeavored to entice workmen from other countries by high salaries, privileges, etc. Many persons, pretending to be skilled in various great manufactures, imagining that America must be in want of them, and that the Congress would probably be disposed to imitate the prince above mentioned, have proposed to go over, on condition of having their passages paid, lands given, salaries appointed, exclusive privileges for terms of years, etc. Such persons, on reading the Articles of Confederation, will find, that the Congress have no power committed to them, or money out into their hands, for such purposes; and that if any such encouragement is given, it must be by the government of some separate state. This, however, has rarely been done in America; and, when it has been done, it has rarely succeeded, so as to establish a manufacture,[5] which the country was not yet so ripe for as to encourage private persons to set it up; labor being generally too dear there, and hands difficult to be kept together, every one desiring to be a master, and the cheapness of lands inclining many to leave trades for agriculture. Some indeed have met with success, and are carried on to advantage; but they are generally such as require only a few hands, or wherein great part of the work is performed by machines. Things that are bulky, and of so small value as not well to bear the expense of freight, may often be made cheaper in the country, than they can be imported; and the manufacture of such things will be profitable wherever there is a sufficient demand. The farmers in America produce indeed a good deal of wool and flax; and none is exported, it is all worked up;[6] but it is in the way of domestic manufacture, for the use of the family. The buying up quantities of wool and flax, with the design to employ spinners, weavers, etc., and form great establishments, producing quantities of linen and woollen goods for sale, has been several times attempted in different provinces; but those projects have generally failed, goods of equal value being imported cheaper. And when the governments have been solicited to support such schemes by encouragements, in money, or by imposing duties on importation of such goods, it has been generally refused, on this principle, that, if the country is ripe for the manufacture, it may be carried on by private persons to advantage; and if not, it is a folly to think of forcing Nature. Great establishments of manufacture require great numbers of poor to do the work for small wages; these poor are to be found in Europe, but will not be found in America, till the lands are all taken up

5. I.e., a large-scale industry. 6. I.e., woven into cloth.

and cultivated, and the excess of people, who cannot get land, want employment. The manufacture of silk, they say, is natural in France, as that of cloth in England, because each country produces in plenty the first material; but if England will have a manufacture of silk as well as that of cloth, and France one of cloth as well as that of silk, these unnatural operations must be supported by mutual prohibitions, or high duties on the importation of each other's goods; by which means the workmen are enabled to tax the home consumer by greater prices, while the higher wages they receive makes them neither happier nor richer, since they only drink more and work less. Therefore the governments in America do nothing to encourage such projects. The people, by this means, are not imposed on, either by the merchant or mechanic. If the merchant demands too much profit on imported shoes, they buy of the shoemaker; and if he asks too high a price, they take them of the merchant; thus the two professions are checks on each other. The shoemaker, however, has, on the whole, considerable profit upon his labor in America, beyond what he had in Europe, as he can add to his price a sum nearly equal to all the expenses of freight and commission, risk or insurance, etc., necessarily charged by the merchant. And the case is the same with the workmen in every other mechanic art. Hence it is, that artisans generally live better and more easily in America than in Europe; and such as are good economists[7] make a comfortable provision for age, and for their children. Such may, therefore, remove with advantage to America.

In the long-settled countries of Europe, all arts, trades, professions, farms, etc., are so full, that it is difficult for a poor man, who has children, to place them where they may gain, or learn to gain, a decent livelihood. The artisans, who fear creating future rivals in business, refuse to take apprentices, but upon conditions of money, maintenance, or the like, which the parents are unable to comply with. Hence the youth are dragged up in ignorance of every gainful art, and obliged to become soldiers, or servants, or thieves, for a subsistence. In America, the rapid increase of inhabitants takes away that fear of rivalship, and artisans willingly receive apprentices from the hope of profit by their labor, during the remainder of the time stipulated, after they shall be instructed. Hence it is easy for poor families to get their children instructed; for the artisans are so desirous of apprentices, that many of them will even give money to the parents, to have boys from ten to fifteen years of age bound apprentices to them till the age of twenty-one; and many poor parents have, by that means, on their arrival in the country, raised money enough to buy land sufficient to establish themselves, and to subsist the rest of their family by agriculture. These contracts for apprentices are made before a magistrate, who regulates the agreement according to reason and justice, and, having in view the formation of a future useful citizen, obliges the master to engage by a written indenture, not only that, during the time of service stipulated, the apprentice shall be duly provided with meat, drink, apparel, washing, and lodging, and, at its expiration, with a complete new suit of clothes, but also that he shall be taught to read, write, and cast accounts;[8] and that he shall be well instructed in the art or profession of his master, or some other, by which he may afterwards gain a livelihood, and be

7. I.e., prudent money managers. 8. Calculate; add up the figures in a column.

able in his turn to raise a family. A copy of this indenture is given to the apprentice or his friends, and the magistrate keeps a record of it, to which recourse may be had, in case of failure by the master in any point of performance. This desire among the masters, to have more hands employed in working for them, induces them to pay the passages of young persons, of both sexes, who, on their arrival, agree to serve them one, two, three, or four years; those, who have already learned a trade, agreeing for a shorter term, in proportion to their skill, and the consequent immediate value of their service; and those, who have none, agreeing for a longer term, in consideration of being taught an art their poverty would not permit them to acquire in their own country.

The almost general mediocrity of fortune that prevails in America obliging its people to follow some business for subsistence, those vices, that arise usually from idleness, are in a great measure prevented. Industry and constant employment are great preservatives of the morals and virtue of a nation. Hence bad examples to youth are more rare in America, which must be a comfortable consideration to parents. To this may be truly added, that serious religion, under its various denominations, is not only tolerated, but respected and practiced. Atheism is unknown there; infidelity[9] rare and secret; so that persons may live to a great age in that country, without having their piety shocked by meeting with either an atheist or an infidel. And the Divine Being seems to have manifested His approbation of the mutual forbearance and kindness with which the different sects treat each other, by the remarkable prosperity with which He has been pleased to favor the whole country.

1782 1784

Remarks Concerning the Savages of North America[1]

Savages we call them, because their manners differ from ours, which we think the perfection of civility; they think the same of theirs.

Perhaps, if we could examine the manners of different nations with impartiality, we should find no people so rude, as to be without any rules of politeness; nor any so polite, as not to have some remains of rudeness.[2]

The Indian men, when young, are hunters and warriors; when old, counselors; for all their government is by counsel of the sages; there is no force, there are no prisons, no officers to compel obedience, or inflict punishment. Hence they generally study oratory, the best speaker having the most influence. The Indian women till the ground, dress the food, nurse and bring up the children, and preserve and hand down to posterity the memory of public transactions. These employments of men and women are accounted natural and honorable. Having few artificial wants, they have abundance of leisure for improvement by conversation. Our laborious manner of life,

9. Lack of religious belief.
1. The text is from *The Writings of Benjamin Franklin* (1905), edited by Albert Henry Smyth.
2. In Franklin's time, not only unmannerly behavior but also, more broadly, unsophisticated and uncivilized behavior. "Politeness": not just mannerly behavior but also sophisticated and civilized behavior.

compared with theirs, they esteem slavish and base; and the learning, on which we value ourselves, they regard as frivolous and useless. An instance of this occurred at the Treaty of Lancaster, in Pennsylvania, *anno* 1744, between the government of Virginia and the Six Nations.[3] After the principal business was settled, the commissioners from Virginia acquainted the Indians by a speech, that there was at Williamsburg a college, with a fund for educating Indian youth; and that, if the Six Nations would send down half a dozen of their young lads to that college, the government would take care that they should be well provided for, and instructed in all the learning of the white people. It is one of the Indian rules of politeness not to answer a public proposition the same day that it is made; they think it would be treating it as a light matter, and that they show it respect by taking time to consider it, as of a matter important. They therefore deferred their answer till the day following; when their speaker began, by expressing their deep sense of the kindness of the Virginia government, in making them that offer; "for we know," says he, "that you highly esteem the kind of learning taught in those Colleges, and that the maintenance of our young men, while with you, would be very expensive to you. We are convinced, therefore, that you mean to do us good by your proposal; and we thank you heartily. But you, who are wise, must know that different nations have different conceptions of things; and you will therefore not take it amiss, if our ideas of this kind of education happen not to be the same with yours. We have had some experience of it; several of our young people were formerly brought up at the colleges of the northern provinces; they were instructed in all your sciences; but, when they came back to us, they were bad runners, ignorant of every means of living in the woods, unable to bear either cold or hunger, knew neither how to build a cabin, take a deer, or kill an enemy, spoke our language imperfectly, were therefore neither fit for hunters, warriors, nor counselors; they were totally good for nothing. We are however not the less obliged by your kind offer, though we decline accepting it; and, to show our grateful sense of it, if the gentlemen of Virginia will send us a dozen of their sons, we will take great care of their education, instruct them in all we know, and make *men* of them."

Having frequent occasions to hold public councils, they have acquired great order and decency in conducting them. The old men sit in the foremost ranks, the warriors in the next, and the women and children in the hindmost. The business of the women is to take exact notice of what passes, imprint it in their memories (for they have no writing), and communicate it to their children. They are the records of the council, and they preserve traditions of the stipulations in treaties 100 years back; which, when we compare with our writings, we always find exact. He that would speak, rises. The rest observe a profound silence. When he has finished and sits down, they leave him 5 or 6 minutes to recollect, that, if he has omitted anything he intended to say, or has anything to add, he may rise again and deliver it. To interrupt another, even in common conversation, is reckoned highly indecent. How different this from the conduct of a polite British House of Commons, where scarce a day passes without some confusion, that makes the

3. The Iroquois confederacy, consisting of the Seneca, Cayuga, Oneida, Onondaga, Mohawk, and Tuscarora tribes. *"Anno"*: in the year (Latin).

speaker hoarse in calling to *order;* and how different from the mode of conversation in many polite companies of Europe, where, if you do not deliver your sentence with great rapidity, you are cut off in the middle of it by the impatient loquacity of those you converse with, and never suffered to finish it!

The politeness of these savages in conversation is indeed carried to excess, since it does not permit them to contradict or deny the truth of what is asserted in their presence. By this means they indeed avoid disputes; but then it becomes difficult to know their minds, or what impression you make upon them. The missionaries who have attempted to convert them to Christianity all complain of this as one of the great difficulties of their mission. The Indians hear with patience the truths of the Gospel explained to them, and give their usual tokens of assent and approbation; you would think they were convinced. No such matter. It is mere civility.

A Swedish minister, having assembled the chiefs of the Susquehanah Indians, made a sermon to them, acquainting them with the principal historical facts on which our religion is founded; such as the fall of our first parents by eating an apple, the coming of Christ to repair the mischief, His miracles and suffering, etc. When he had finished, an Indian orator stood up to thank him. "What you have told us," he says, "is all very good. It is indeed bad to eat apples. It is better to make them all into cider. We are much obliged by your kindness in coming so far, to tell us these things which you have heard from your mothers. In return, I will tell you some of those we have heard from ours. In the beginning, our fathers had only the flesh of animals to subsist on; and if their hunting was unsuccessful, they were starving. Two of our young hunters, having killed a deer, made a fire in the woods to broil some part of it. When they were about to satisfy their hunger, they beheld a beautiful young woman descend from the clouds, and seat herself on that hill, which you see yonder among the blue mountains. They said to each other, it is a spirit that has smelled our broiling venison, and wishes to eat of it; let us offer some to her. They presented her with the tongue; she was pleased with the taste of it, and said, 'Your kindness shall be rewarded; come to this place after thirteen moons, and you shall find something that will be of great benefit in nourishing you and your children to the latest generations.' They did so, and, to their surprise, found plants they had never seen before; but which, from that ancient time, have been constantly cultivated among us, to our great advantage. Where her right hand had touched the ground, they found maize; where her left hand had touched it, they found kidney-beans; and where her backside had sat on it, they found tobacco." The good missionary, disgusted with this idle tale, said, "What I delivered to you were sacred truths; but what you tell me is mere fable, fiction, and falsehood." The Indian, offended, replied, "My brother, it seems your friends have not done you justice in your education; they have not well instructed you in the rules of common civility. You saw that we, who understand and practice those rules, believed all your stories; why do you refuse to believe ours?"

When any of them come into our towns, our people are apt to crowd round them, gaze upon them, and incommode them, where they desire to be private; this they esteem great rudeness, and the effect of the want of instruction in the rules of civility and good manners. "We have," say they, "as much

curiosity as you, and when you come into our towns, we wish for opportunities of looking at you, but for this purpose we hide ourselves behind bushes, where you are to pass, and never intrude ourselves into your company."

Their manner of entering one another's village has likewise its rules. It is reckoned uncivil in traveling strangers to enter a village abruptly, without giving notice of their approach. Therefore, as soon as they arrive within hearing, they stop and hollow,[4] remaining there till invited to enter. Two old men usually come out to them, and lead them in. There is in every village a vacant dwelling, called *the stranger's house*. Here they are placed, while the old men go round from hut to hut, acquainting the inhabitants, that strangers are arrived, who are probably hungry and weary; and every one sends them what he can spare of victuals, and skins to repose on. When the strangers are refreshed, pipes and tobacco are brought; and then, but not before, conversation begins, with inquiries who they are, whither bound, what news, etc.; and it usually ends with offers of service, if the strangers have occasion of guides, or any necessaries for continuing their journey; and nothing is exacted for the entertainment.[5]

The same hospitality, esteemed among them as a principal virtue, is practiced by private persons; of which Conrad Weiser, our interpreter, gave me the following instances. He had been naturalized among the Six Nations, and spoke well the Mohawk language. In going through the Indian country, to carry a message from our Governor to the Council at Onondaga, he called at the habitation of Canassatego, an old acquaintance, who embraced him, spread furs for him to sit on, placed before him some boiled beans and venison, and mixed some rum and water for his drink. When he was well refreshed, and had lit his pipe, Canassatego began to converse with him; asked how he had fared the many years since they had seen each other; whence he then came; what occasioned the journey, etc. Conrad answered all his questions; and when the discourse began to flag, the Indian, to continue it, said, "Conrad, you have lived long among the white people, and know something of their customs; I have been sometimes at Albany, and have observed, that once in seven days they shut up their shops, and assemble all in the great house; tell me what it is for? What do they do there?" "They meet there," says Conrad, "to hear and learn *good things*." "I do not doubt," says the Indian, "that they tell you so; they have told me the same; but I doubt the truth of what they say, and I will tell you my reasons. I went lately to Albany to sell my skins and buy blankets, knives, powder, rum, etc. You know I used generally to deal with Hans Hanson; but I was a little inclined this time to try some other merchant. However, I called first upon Hans, and asked him what he would give for beaver. He said he could not give any more than four shillings a pound; 'but,' says he, 'I cannot talk on business now; this is the day when we meet together to learn *good things*, and I am going to the meeting.' So I thought to myself, 'Since we cannot do any business today, I may as well go to the meeting too,' and I went with him. There stood up a man in black, and began to talk to the people very angrily. I did not understand what he said; but, perceiving that he looked much at me and at

4. Cry out; announce themselves. 5. I.e., hospitality.

Hanson, I imagined he was angry at seeing me there; so I went out, sat down near the house, struck fire, and lit my pipe, waiting till the meeting should break up. I thought too, that the man had mentioned something of beaver, and I suspected it might be the subject of their meeting. So, when they came out, I accosted my merchant. 'Well, Hans,' says I, 'I hope you have agreed to give more than four shillings a pound.' 'No,' says he, 'I cannot give so much; I cannot give more than three shillings and sixpence.' I then spoke to several other dealers, but they all sung the same song,—three and sixpence,—three and sixpence. This made it clear to me, that my suspicion was right; and, that whatever they pretended of meeting to learn *good things,* the real purpose was to consult how to cheat Indians in the price of beaver. Consider but a little, Conrad, and you must be of my opinion. If they met so often to learn *good things,* they would certainly have learned some before this time. But they are still ignorant. You know our practice. If a white man, in traveling through our country, enters one of our cabins, we all treat him as I treat you; we dry him if he is wet, we warm him if he is cold, we give him meat and drink, that he may allay his thirst and hunger; and we spread soft furs for him to rest and sleep on; we demand nothing in return. But, if I go into a white man's house at Albany, and ask for victuals and drink, they say, 'Where is your money?' and if I have none, they say, 'Get out, you Indian dog.' You see they have not yet learned those little *good things,* that we need no meetings to be instructed in, because our mothers taught them to us when we were children; and therefore it is impossible their meetings should be, as they say, for any such purpose, or have any such effect; they are only to contrive *the cheating of Indians in the price of beaver.*"[6]

1784

The Autobiography Franklin worked on the manuscript of *The Autobiography* on four different occasions over a period of nineteen years. The first part is addressed to his son William Franklin (1731–1813), governor of New Jersey when Franklin was writing this section. Franklin was visiting the country home of Bishop Jonathan Shipley at Twyford, a village about fifty miles from London. He began writing on July 30 and finished on or about August 13, 1771. Franklin did not return to the manuscript until about thirteen years later, when he was living in France and serving as minister of the newly formed United States. He wrote the last two sections in August 1788 and the winter of 1789–90, stopping because of illness. The account goes up only to 1758, so it does not cover Franklin's great triumphs as a diplomat and public servant.

In 1791, the Paris publisher Jacques Buisson issued the first part of *The Autobiography* in a French translation. William Temple Franklin, Franklin's grandson and secretary, published a London edition of 1818 that included the first three parts in English. Temple Franklin had accidentally traded his handwritten manuscript of

6. "It is remarkable that in all ages and countries hospitality has been allowed as the virtue of those whom the civilized were pleased to call barbarians. The Greeks celebrated the Scythians for it. The Saracens possessed it eminently, and it is to this day the reigning virtue of the wild Arabs. St. Paul, too, in the relation of his voyage and shipwreck on the island of Melité says "the barbarous people showed us no little kindness; for they kindled a fire, and received us every one, because of the present rain, and because of the cold" [Franklin's note; the Apostle Paul relates his visit to Melita in Acts 28].

the full text for an incomplete copy. It was not until 1868 that the American lawyer and statesman John Bigelow published all four parts of the autobiography, in a more reliable edition based on a manuscript that he bought in France.

The text reprinted here is the first one taken directly from the manuscript (other editors have merely corrected earlier printed texts). It was established by J. A. Leo Lemay and Paul Zall for their 1986 Norton Critical Edition of *The Autobiography* and is here reprinted with permission. The text has been modernized only slightly. All manuscript abbreviations and symbols have been expanded. The editors omitted short dashes, which Franklin often wrote after sentences, and punctuation marks that "have been clearly superseded by revisions or additions." Careless slips have been corrected silently but are noted in the section on emendations in their text. Lemay and Zall generously let the editors of this anthology consult their footnotes and biographical sketches. Also helpful were the edition of Leonard W. Labaree et al. (1964) and Joyce E. Chaplin's revised Norton Critical Edition (2012).

The Autobiography

[Part One]

TWYFORD, AT THE BISHOP OF ST. ASAPH'S 1771

Dear Son,

I have ever had a Pleasure in obtaining any little Anecdotes of my Ancestors. You may remember the Enquiries I made among the Remains of my Relations[1] when you were with me in England; and the Journey I took for that purpose. Now imagining it may be equally agreeable to you to know the Circumstances of *my* Life, many of which you are yet unacquainted with; and expecting a Week's uninterrupted Leisure in my present Country Retirement, I sit down to write them for you. To which I have besides some other Inducements. Having emerg'd from the Poverty and Obscurity in which I was born and bred, to a State of Affluence and some Degree of Reputation in the World, and having gone so far thro' Life with a considerable Share of Felicity, the conducting Means I made use of, which, with the Blessing of God, so well succeeded, my Posterity may like to know, as they may find some of them suitable to their own Situations, and therefore fit to be imitated. That Felicity, when I reflected on it, has induc'd me sometimes to say, that were it offer'd to my Choice, I should have no Objection to a Repetition of the same Life from its Beginning, only asking the Advantage Authors have in a second Edition to correct some Faults of the first. So would I if I might, besides correcting the Faults, change some sinister Accidents and Events of it for others more favorable, but tho' this were denied, I should still accept the Offer. However, since such a Repetition is not to be expected, the Thing most like living one's Life over again, seems to be a *Recollection* of that Life; and to make that Recollection as durable as possible, the putting it down in Writing. Hereby, too, I shall indulge the Inclination so natural in old Men, to be talking of themselves and their own past Actions, and I shall indulge it, without being troublesome to others who thro' respect to Age might think

1. I.e., the remaining representatives of his family. Franklin and his son toured England in 1758 and visited ancestral homes at Ecton and Banbury.

themselves oblig'd to give me a Hearing, since this may be read or not as any one pleases. And lastly, (I may as well confess it, since my Denial of it will be believ'd by no body) perhaps I shall a good deal gratify my own *Vanity.* Indeed I scarce ever heard or saw the introductory Words, *Without Vanity I may say,* etc. but some vain thing immediately follow'd. Most People dislike Vanity in others whatever Share they have of it themselves, but I give it fair Quarter wherever I meet with it, being persuaded that it is often productive of Good to the Possessor and to others that are within his Sphere of Action: And therefore in many Cases it would not be quite absurd if a Man were to thank God for his Vanity among the other Comforts of Life.

And now I speak of thanking God, I desire with all Humility to acknowledge, that I owe the mention'd Happiness of my past Life to his kind Providence, which led me to the Means I us'd and gave them Success. My Belief of This, induces me to *hope,* tho' I must not *presume,* that the same Goodness will still be exercis'd towards me in continuing that Happiness, or in enabling me to bear a fatal Reverso,[2] which I may experience as others have done, the Complexion of my future Fortune being known to him only: and in whose Power it is to bless to us even our Afflictions.

The Notes one of my Uncles (who had the same kind of Curiosity in collecting Family Anecdotes) once put into my Hands, furnish'd me with several Particulars, relating to our Ancestors. From those Notes I learned that the Family had liv'd in the same Village, Ecton in Northamptonshire, for 300 Years, and how much longer he knew not, (perhaps from the Time when the Name *Franklin* that before was the Name of an Order of People,[3] was assum'd by them for a Surname, when others took Surnames all over the Kingdom)[4] on a Freehold of about 30 Acres, aided by the Smith's Business which had continued in the Family till his Time, the eldest Son being always bred to that Business. A Custom which he and my Father both followed as to their eldest Sons. When I search'd the Register at Ecton, I found an Account of their Births, Marriages and Burials, from the Year 1555 only, there being no Register kept in that Parish at any time preceding. By that Register I perceiv'd that I was the youngest Son of the youngest Son for 5 Generations back. My Grandfather Thomas, who was born in 1598, lived at Ecton till he grew too old to follow Business longer, when he went to live with his Son John, a Dyer at Banbury in Oxfordshire, with whom my Father serv'd an Apprenticeship. There my Grandfather died and lies buried. We saw his Gravestone in 1758. His eldest Son Thomas liv'd in the House at Ecton, and left it with the Land to his only Child, a Daughter, who with her Husband, one Fisher of Wellingborough, sold it to Mr. Isted, now Lord of the Manor there.

My Grandfather had 4 Sons that grew up, viz., Thomas, John, Benjamin and Josiah. I will give you what Account I can of them at this distance from my Papers, and if those are not lost in my Absence, you will among them find many more Particulars. Thomas was bred a Smith under his Father, but being ingenious, and encourag'd in Learning (as all his Brothers likewise

2. I.e., a backhanded stroke; a term used in dueling with rapiers.
3. A "franklin" was a freeholder—a land owner
not of noble birth.
4. Here a note [Franklin had intended to insert a note here].

were,) by an Esquire[5] Palmer then the principal Gentleman in that Parish, he qualified himself for the Business of Scrivener,[6] became a considerable Man in the County Affairs, was a chief Mover of all public Spirited Undertakings for the County or Town of Northampton and his own Village, of which many Instances were told us at Ecton, and he was much taken Notice of and patroniz'd by the then Lord Halifax. He died in 1702, Jan. 6, old Stile,[7] just 4 Years to a Day before I was born. The Account we receiv'd of his Life and Character from some old People at Ecton, I remember struck you as something extraordinary from its Similarity to what you knew of mine. Had he died on the same Day, you said one might have suppos'd a Transmigration.[8]

John was bred a Dyer, I believe of Woollens. Benjamin was bred a Silk Dyer, serving an Apprenticeship at London. He was an ingenious Man. I remember him well, for when I was a Boy he came over to my Father in Boston, and lived in the House with us some Years. He lived to a great Age. His Grandson Samuel Franklin now lives in Boston. He left behind him two Quarto[9] Volumes, Manuscript of his own Poetry, consisting of little occasional Pieces address'd to his Friends and Relations, of which the following sent to me, is a Specimen.[1] He had form'd a Shorthand of his own, which he taught me, but never practicing it I have now forgot it. I was nam'd after this Uncle, there being a particular Affection between him and my Father. He was very pious, a great Attender of Sermons of the best Preachers, which he took down in his Shorthand and had with him many Volumes of them. He was also much of a Politician, too much perhaps for his Station. There fell lately into my Hands in London a Collection he had made of all the principal Pamphlets relating to Public Affairs from 1641 to 1717. Many of the Volumes are wanting, as appears by the Numbering, but there still remains 8 Volumes Folio, and 24 in Quarto and Octavo. A Dealer in old Books met with them, and knowing me by my sometimes buying of him, he brought them to me. It seems my Uncle must have left them here when he went to America, which was above 50 Years since. There are many of his Notes in the Margins.

This obscure Family of ours was early in the Reformation, and continu'd Protestants thro' the Reign of Queen Mary,[2] when they were sometimes in Danger of Trouble on Account of their Zeal against Popery. They had got an English Bible,[3] and to conceal and secure it, it was fastened open with Tapes under and within the Frame of a Joint Stool.[4] When my Great Great Grandfather read in it to his Family, he turn'd up the Joint Stool upon his Knees, turning over the Leaves then under the Tapes. One of the Children stood at

5. An honorific originally extended to a young man of gentle birth but extended as a courtesy to any gentleman.

6. A professional copier of documents.

7. Until 1752, England used the Julian calendar, in which the new year began on March 25. Because the Julian calendar did not have leap years, it had fallen behind the astronomical year; the English skipped eleven days when adopting the Gregorian calendar. Franklin's birthday is either January 6, 1705–06, Old Style, or January 17, 1706, New Style.

8. The passage of the soul, upon death, to another's body.

9. The terms "folio," "quarto," and "octavo" desig-

nate book sizes from large to small. A single sheet of paper folded once makes a folio, or four sides for printing; a quarto is obtained if the sheet is folded again; an octavo is the sheet folded once more.

1. Here insert it [Franklin's note, but he did not include the example].

2. Mary Tudor (1516–1558; reigned 1553–58) tried to restore Roman Catholicism as the national Church.

3. Also known as the "Geneva" version, translated by Reformed English Protestants living in Switzerland; this version, used by the Puritans, was outlawed by the Church of England.

4. A small, four-legged stool.

the Door to give Notice if he saw the Apparitor[5] coming, who was an Officer of the Spiritual Court. In that Case the Stool was turn'd down again upon its feet, when the Bible remain'd conceal'd under it as before. This Anecdote I had from my Uncle Benjamin. The Family continu'd all of the Church of England till about the End of Charles the Second's Reign,[6] when some of the Ministers that had been outed for Nonconformity, holding Conventicles[7] in Northamptonshire, Benjamin and Josiah adher'd to them, and so continu'd all their Lives. The rest of the Family remain'd with the Episcopal Church.

Josiah, my Father, married young, and carried his Wife with three Children unto New England, about 1682.[8] The Conventicles having been forbidden by Law, and frequently disturbed, induced some considerable Men of his Acquaintance to remove to that Country, and he was prevail'd with to accompany them thither, where they expected to enjoy their Mode of Religion with Freedom. By the same Wife he had 4 Children more born there, and by a second Wife ten more, in all 17, of which I remember 13 sitting at one time at his Table, who all grew up to be Men and Women, and married. I was the youngest Son and the youngest Child but two, and was born in Boston, New England.

My Mother the second Wife was Abiah Folger, a Daughter of Peter Folger, one of the first Settlers of New England, of whom honorable mention is made by Cotton Mather, in his Church History of that Country, (entitled Magnalia Christi Americana) as a *godly learned Englishman,* if I remember the Words rightly.[9] I have heard that he wrote sundry small occasional Pieces, but only one of them was printed which I saw now many Years since. It was written in 1675, in the homespun Verse of that Time and People, and address'd to those then concern'd in the Government there. It was in favor of Liberty of Conscience, and in behalf of the Baptists, Quakers, and other Sectaries,[1] that had been under Persecution; ascribing the Indian Wars and other Distresses that had befallen the Country to that Persecution, as so many Judgments of God, to punish so heinous an Offence; and exhorting a Repeal of those uncharitable Laws. The whole appear'd to me as written with a good deal of Decent Plainness and manly Freedom. The six last concluding Lines I remember, tho' I have forgotten the two first of the Stanza, but the Purport of them was that his Censures proceeded from *Goodwill,* and therefore he would be known as the Author,

> because to be a Libeler, (says he)
> I hate it with my Heart.
> From Sherburne Town[2] where now I dwell,
> My Name I do put here,
> Without Offence, your real Friend,
> It is Peter Folgier.

5. An officer of an ecclesiastical court, in this case a court established to eliminate heresy.
6. Charles II (1630–1685) reigned from 1660 to 1685.
7. Secret and illegal meetings of Nonconformists, outlawed in 1664. Nonconformists refused to adopt the rituals and acknowledge the hierarchy of the Church of England.

8. More correctly, October 1683.
9. Cotton Mather's ecclesiastical history (excerpted earlier in this volume) was published in London in 1702; the quotation is properly "an Able Godly Englishman."
1. Sectarians; believers or followers of a particular religious teaching.
2. In the Island of Nantucket [Franklin's note].

My elder Brothers were all put Apprentices to different Trades. I was put to the Grammar School at Eight Years of Age, my Father intending to devote me as the Tithe[3] of his Sons to the Service of the Church. My early Readiness in learning to read (which must have been very early, as I do not remember when I could not read) and the Opinion of all his Friends that I should certainly make a good Scholar, encourag'd him in this Purpose of his. My Uncle Benjamin too approv'd of it, and propos'd to give me all his Shorthand Volumes of Sermons, I suppose as a Stock to set up with, if I would learn his Character.[4] I continu'd however at the Grammar School not quite one Year, tho' in that time I had risen gradually from the Middle of the Class of that Year to be the Head of it, and farther was remov'd into the next Class above it, in order to go with that into the third at the End of the Year. But my Father in the meantime, from a View of the Expense of a College Education which, having so large a Family, he could not well afford, and the mean Living many so educated were afterwards able to obtain, Reasons that he gave to his Friends in my Hearing, altered his first Intention, took me from the Grammar School, and sent me to a School for Writing and Arithmetic kept by a then famous Man, Mr. George Brownell, very successful in his Profession generally, and that by mild encouraging Methods. Under him I acquired fair Writing pretty soon, but I fail'd in the Arithmetic, and made no Progress in it.

At Ten Years old, I was taken home to assist my Father in his Business, which was that of a Tallow Chandler and Soap-Boiler.[5] A Business he was not bred to, but had assumed on his Arrival in New England and on finding his Dying Trade would not maintain his Family, being in little Request. Accordingly I was employed in cutting Wick for the Candles, filling the Dipping Mold, and the Molds for cast Candles, attending the Shop, going of Errands, etc. I dislik'd the Trade and had a strong Inclination for the Sea; but my Father declar'd against it; however, living near the Water, I was much in and about it, learned early to swim well, and to manage Boats, and when in a Boat or Canoe with other Boys I was commonly allow'd to govern,[6] especially in any case of Difficulty; and upon other Occasions I was generally a Leader among the Boys, and sometimes led them into Scrapes, of which I will mention one Instance, as it shows an early projecting[7] public Spirit, tho' not then justly conducted. There was a Salt Marsh that bounded part of the Mill Pond, on the Edge of which at Highwater, we us'd to stand to fish for Minnows. By much Trampling, we had made it a mere Quagmire. My Proposal was to build a Wharf there fit for us to stand upon, and I show'd my Comrades a large Heap of Stones which were intended for a new House near the Marsh, and which would very well suit our Purpose. Accordingly in the Evening when the Workmen were gone, I assembled a Number of my Playfellows, and working with them diligently like so many Emmets,[8] sometimes two or three to a Stone, we brought them all away and built our little Wharf. The next Morning the Workmen were surpris'd at Missing the Stones; which

3. I.e., as if his son were the tenth part of his income, traditionally given to the Church.
4. Here, his system of shorthand.
5. Maker of candles and soap.
6. Steer.
7. Enterprising.
8. Ants.

were found in our Wharf; Enquiry was made after the Removers; we were discovered and complain'd of; several of us were corrected by our Fathers; and tho' I pleaded the Usefulness of the Work, mine convinc'd me that nothing was useful which was not honest.

I think you may like to know something of his Person and Character. He had an excellent Constitution of Body, was of middle Stature, but well set and very strong. He was ingenious, could draw prettily, was skill'd a little in Music and had a clear pleasing Voice, so that when he play'd Psalm Tunes on his Violin and sung withal as he some times did in an Evening after the Business of the Day was over, it was extremely agreeable to hear. He had a mechanical Genius too, and on occasion was very handy in the Use of other Tradesmen's Tools. But his great Excellence lay in a sound Understanding, and solid Judgment in prudential Matters, both in private and public Affairs. In the latter indeed he was never employed, the numerous Family he had to educate and the Straitness of his Circumstances, keeping him close to his Trade, but I remember well his being frequently visited by leading People, who consulted him for his Opinion on Affairs of the Town or of the Church he belong'd to and show'd a good deal of Respect for his Judgment and Advice. He was also much consulted by private Persons about their Affairs when any Difficulty occur'd, and frequently chosen an Arbitrator between contending Parties. At his Table he lik'd to have as often as he could, some sensible Friend or Neighbor, to converse with, and always took care to start some ingenious or useful Topic for Discourse, which might tend to improve the Minds of his Children. By this means he turn'd our Attention to what was good, just, and prudent in the Conduct of Life; and little or no Notice was ever taken of what related to the Victuals on the Table, whether it was well or ill drest, in or out of season, of good or bad flavor, preferable or inferior to this or that other thing of the kind; so that I was brought up in such a perfect Inattention to those Matters as to be quite Indifferent what kind of Food was set before me; and so unobservant of it, that to this Day, if I am ask'd I can scarce tell, a few Hours after Dinner, what I din'd upon. This has been a Convenience to me in traveling, where my Companions have been sometimes very unhappy for want of a suitable Gratification of their more delicate because better instructed Tastes and Appetites.

My Mother had likewise an excellent Constitution. She suckled all her 10 Children. I never knew either my Father or Mother to have any Sickness but that of which they died, he at 89 and she at 85 Years of age. They lie buried together at Boston, where I some Years since plac'd a Marble stone over their Grave with this Inscription:

> Josiah Franklin
> And Abiah his Wife
> Lie here interred.
> They lived lovingly together in Wedlock
> Fifty-five Years.
> Without an Estate or any gainful[9] Employment,
> By constant Labor and Industry,

9. Privileged. I.e., consistent and paid.

 With God's Blessing,
 They maintained a large Family
 Comfortably;
 And brought up thirteen Children,
 And seven Grandchildren
 Reputably.
 From this Instance, Reader,
 Be encouraged to Diligence in thy Calling,
 And distrust not Providence.
 He was a pious and prudent Man,
 She a discreet and virtuous Woman.
 Their youngest Son,
 In filial Regard to their Memory,
 Places this Stone.
 J.F. born 1655—Died 1744. Ætat[1] 89
 A.F. born 1667—died 1752——85.

By my rambling Digressions I perceive myself to be grown old. I us'd to write more methodically. But one does not dress for private Company as for a public Ball. 'Tis perhaps only Negligence.

To return. I continu'd thus employ'd in my Father's Business for two Years, that is till I was 12 Years old; and my Brother John who was bred to that Business having left my Father, married and set up for himself at Rhode Island,[2] there was all Appearance that I was destin'd to supply his Place and be a Tallow Chandler. But my Dislike to the Trade continuing, my Father was under Apprehensions that if he did not find one for me more agreeable, I should break away and get to Sea, as his Son Josiah had done to his great Vexation. He therefore sometimes took me to walk with him, and see Joiners, Bricklayers, Turners, Braziers,[3] etc. at their Work, that he might observe my Inclination, and endeavor to fix it on some Trade or other on Land. It has ever since been a Pleasure to me to see good Workmen handle their Tools; and it has been useful to me, having learned so much by it, as to be able to do little Jobs myself in my House, when a Workman could not readily be got; and to construct little Machines for my Experiments while the Intention of making the Experiment was fresh and warm in my Mind. My Father at last fix'd upon the Cutler's Trade, and my Uncle Benjamin's Son Samuel who was bred to that Business in London being about that time establish'd in Boston, I was sent to be with him some time on liking. But his Expectations of a Fee with me displeasing my Father, I was taken home again.

From a Child I was fond of Reading, and all the little Money that came into my Hands was ever laid out in Books. Pleas'd with the Pilgrim's Progress, my first Collection was of John Bunyan's Works,[4] in separate little Volumes. I afterwards sold them to enable me to buy R. Burton's[5] Historical

1. Abbreviation for *ætatis*: aged (Latin).
2. John Franklin (1690–1756), Franklin's favorite brother, later became postmaster of Boston.
3. Woodworkers, bricklayers, latheworkers, brassworkers.
4. The English preacher John Bunyan (1628–1688) published *Pilgrim's Progress* in 1678; his literary works were enormously popular and

available in cheap one-shilling editions. *Pilgrim's Progress* is an allegory in which the hero, Christian, flees the City of Destruction and makes his way to the Celestial City with the help of characters such as Mr. Worldly-Wiseman, Faithful, and Hopeful.
5. A pseudonym for Nathaniel Crouch (c. 1632–1725), a popularizer of British history.

Collections; they were small Chapmen's Books[6] and cheap, 40 or 50 in all. My Father's little Library consisted chiefly of Books in polemic Divinity, most of which I read, and have since often regretted, that at a time when I had such a Thirst for Knowledge, more proper Books had not fallen in my Way, since it was now resolv'd I should not be a Clergyman. Plutarch's Lives[7] there was, in which I read abundently, and I still think that time spent to great Advantage. There was also a Book of Defoe's called an Essay on Projects and another of Dr. Mather's call'd Essays to do Good,[8] which perhaps gave me a Turn of Thinking that had an Influence on some of the principal future Events of my Life.

This Bookish Inclination at length determin'd my Father to make me a Printer, tho' he had already one Son, (James) of that Profession. In 1717 my Brother James return'd from England with a Press and Letters[9] to set up his Business in Boston. I lik'd it much better than that of my Father, but still had a Hankering for the Sea. To prevent the apprehended Effect of such an Inclination, my Father was impatient to have me bound[1] to my Brother. I stood out some time, but at last was persuaded and signed the Indentures,[2] when I was yet but 12 Years old. I was to serve as an Apprentice till I was 21 Years of Age, only I was to be allow'd Journeyman's Wages[3] during the last Year. In a little time I made great Proficiency in the Business, and became a useful Hand to my Brother. I now had Access to better Books. An Acquaintance with the Apprentices of Booksellers enabled me sometimes to borrow a small one, which I was careful to return soon and clean. Often I sat up in my Room reading the greatest Part of the Night, when the Book was borrow'd in the Evening and to be return'd early in the Morning lest it should be miss'd or wanted. And after some time an ingenious Tradesman[4] who had a pretty[5] Collection of Books, and who frequented our Printing-House, took Notice of me, invited me to his Library, and very kindly lent me such Books as I chose to read. I now took a Fancy to Poetry, and made some little Pieces. My Brother, thinking it might turn to account encourag'd me, and put me on composing two occasional Ballads. One was called the *Light House Tragedy,* and contain'd an Account of the drowning of Capt. Worthilake with his Two Daughters; the other was a Sailor Song on the Taking of *Teach* or Blackbeard the Pirate.[6] They were wretched Stuff, in the Grubstreet Ballad Style,[7] and when they were printed he sent me about the Town to sell them. The first sold wonderfully, the Event being recent, having made a great Noise. This flatter'd my Vanity. But my Father discourag'd me, by ridiculing my Performances, and telling me Verse-makers were generally Beggars; so I escap'd being a Poet, most probably a very bad one. But as Prose Writing

6. Peddlers' books, hence inexpensive.
7. *Parallel Lives,* by the Greek biographer Plutarch (c. 46–120 C.E.), about noted Greek and Roman figures.
8. Cotton Mather's *Bonifacius: An Essay upon the Good. Essay on Projects,* by the English writer Daniel Defoe (1659?–1731), offers suggestions for economic improvement.
9. Type.
1. Apprenticed.
2. A contract binding him to work for his brother for nine years. James Franklin (1697–1735) had learned the printer's trade in England.

3. I.e., be paid for each day's work, having served his apprenticeship.
4. Mr. Matthew Adams [Franklin's note].
5. Exceptionally fine.
6. The full texts of these ballads are lost; George Worthylake, lighthouse keeper on Beacon Island, Boston Harbor, and his wife and daughter were drowned on November 3, 1718. The pirate Blackbeard, Edward Teach, was killed off the Carolina coast on November 22, 1718.
7. Grub Street in London was inhabited by poor literary hacks who churned out poems of topical interest.

has been of great Use to me in the Course of my Life, and was a principal Means of my Advancement, I shall tell you how in such a Situation I acquir'd what little Ability I have in that Way.

There was another Bookish Lad in the Town, John Collins by Name, with whom I was intimately acquainted. We sometimes disputed, and very fond we were of Argument, and very desirous of confuting one another. Which disputatious Turn, by the way, is apt to become a very bad Habit, making People often extremely disagreeable in Company, by the Contradiction that is necessary to bring it into Practice, and thence, besides souring and spoiling the Conversation, is productive of Disgusts and perhaps Enmities where you may have occasion for Friendship. I had caught it by reading my Father's Books of Dispute about Religion. Persons of good Sense, I have since observ'd, seldom fall into it, except Lawyers, University Men, and Men of all Sorts that have been bred at Edinburgh.[8] A Question was once some how or other started between Collins and me, of the Propriety of educating the Female Sex in Learning, and their Abilities for Study. He was of Opinion that it was improper; and that they were naturally unequal to it. I took the contrary Side, perhaps a little for Dispute sake. He was naturally more eloquent, had a ready Plenty of Words, and sometimes as I thought bore me down more by his Fluency than by the Strength of his Reasons. As we parted without settling the Point, and were not to see one another again for some time, I sat down to put my Arguments in Writing, which I copied fair and sent to him. He answer'd and I replied. Three or four Letters of a Side had pass'd, when my Father happen'd to find my Papers, and read them. Without entering into the Discussion, he took occasion to talk to me about the Manner of my Writing, observ'd that tho' I had the Advantage of my Antagonist in correct Spelling and pointing[9] (which I ow'd to the Printing-House) I fell far short in elegance of Expression, in Method and in Perspicuity, of which he convinc'd me by several Instances. I saw the Justice of his Remarks, and thence grew more attentive to the *Manner* in Writing, and determin'd to endeavor at Improvement.

About this time I met with an odd Volume of the Spectator.[1] I had never before seen any of them. I bought it, read it over and over, and was much delighted with it. I thought the Writing excellent, and wish'd if possible to imitate it. With that View, I took some of the Papers, and making short Hints of the Sentiment in each Sentence, laid them by a few Days, and then without looking at the Book, tried to complete the Papers again, by expressing each hinted Sentiment at length and as fully as it had been express'd before, in any suitable Words that should come to hand.

Then I compar'd my Spectator with the Original, discover'd some of my Faults and corrected them. But I found I wanted a Stock of Words or a Readiness in recollecting and using them, which I thought I should have acquir'd before that time, if I had gone on making Verses, since the continual Occasion for Words of the same Import but of different Length, to suit the Measure,[2]

8. Scottish Presbyterians were noted for their argumentative nature.
9. Punctuation. Spelling and punctuation were not standardized at this time.
1. An English periodical published daily from March 1, 1711, to December 6, 1712, and revived

in 1714. It contained essays by Joseph Addison (1672–1719) and Richard Steele (1672–1729) and addressed itself primarily to matters of literature and morality. Its aim was to "enliven morality with wit" and "temper wit with morality."
2. Meter.

or of different Sound for the Rhyme, would have laid me under a constant Necessity of searching for Variety, and also have tended to fix that Variety in my Mind, and make me Master of it. Therefore I took some of the Tales and turn'd them into Verse: And after a time, when I had pretty well forgotten the Prose, turn'd them back again. I also sometimes jumbled my Collections of Hints into Confusion, and after some Weeks, endeavor'd to reduce them into the best Order, before I began to form the full Sentences, and complete the Paper. This was to teach me Method in the Arrangement of Thoughts. By comparing my Work afterwards with the original, I discover'd many faults and amended them; but I sometimes had the Pleasure of Fancying that in certain Particulars of small Import, I had been lucky enough to improve the Method or the Language and this encourag'd me to think I might possibly in time come to be a tolerable English Writer, of which I was extremely ambitious.

My Time for these Exercises and for Reading, was at Night after Work, or before Work began in the Morning; or on Sundays, when I contrived to be in the Printing-House alone, evading as much as I could the common Attendance on public Worship, which my Father used to exact of me when I was under his Care: And which indeed I still thought a Duty; tho' I could not, as it seemed to me, afford the Time to practice it.

When about 16 Years of Age, I happen'd to meet with a Book written by one Tryon,[3] recommending a Vegetable Diet. I determined to go into it. My Brother being yet unmarried, did not keep House, but boarded himself and his Apprentices in another Family. My refusing to eat Flesh occasioned an Inconveniency, and I was frequently chid for my singularity. I made myself acquainted with Tryon's Manner of preparing some of his Dishes, such as Boiling Potatoes or Rice, making Hasty Pudding,[4] and a few others, and then propos'd to my Brother, that if he would give me Weekly half the Money he paid for my Board, I would board myself. He instantly agreed to it, and I presently found that I could save half what he paid me. This was an additional Fund for buying Books: But I had another Advantage in it. My Brother and the rest going from the Printing-House to their Meals, I remain'd there alone, and dispatching presently my light Repast, (which often was no more than a Biscuit or a Slice of Bread, a Handful of Raisins or a Tart from the Pastry Cook's, and a Glass of Water) had the rest of the Time till their Return, for Study, in which I made the greater Progress from that greater Clearness of Head and quicker Apprehension which usually attend Temperance in Eating and Drinking. And now it was that being on some Occasion made asham'd of my Ignorance in Figures, which I had twice fail'd in learning when at School, I took Cocker's Book of Arithmetic,[5] and went thro' the whole by myself with great Ease. I also read Seller's and Sturmy's Books of Navigation,[6] and became acquainted with the little Geometry they contain,

3. Thomas Tryon, whose *Way to Health, Wealth, and Happiness* appeared in 1682; a digest titled *Wisdom's Dictates* appeared in 1691.
4. I.e., cornmeal or oatmeal mush.
5. Edward Cocker's *Arithmetic,* published in 1677, was reprinted twenty times by 1700.
6. John Seller published *An Epitome of the Art of Navigation* in 1681. Samuel Sturmy published *The Mariner's Magazine: Or Sturmy's Mathematical and Practical Arts* in 1699.

but never proceeded far in that Science. And I read about this Time Locke on Human Understanding and the Art of Thinking by Messrs. du Port Royal.[7]

While I was intent on improving my Language, I met with an English Grammar (I think it was Greenwood's[8]) at the End of which there were two little Sketches of the Arts of Rhetoric and Logic, the latter finishing with a Specimen of a Dispute in the Socratic Method.[9] And soon after I procur'd Xenophon's Memorable Things of Socrates,[1] wherein there are many Instances of the same Method. I was charm'd with it, adopted it, dropped my abrupt Contradiction and positive Argumentation, and put on the humble Enquirer and Doubter. And being then, from reading Shaftesbury and Collins, became a real Doubter in many Points of our Religious Doctrine,[2] I found this Method safest for myself and very embarrassing to those against whom I used it, therefore I took a Delight in it, practic'd it continually and grew very artful and expert in drawing People even of superior Knowledge into Concessions the Consequences of which they did not foresee, entangling them in Difficulties out of which they could not extricate themselves, and so obtaining Victories that neither myself nor my Cause always deserved. I continu'd this Method some few Years, but gradually left it, retaining only the Habit of expressing myself in Terms of modest Diffidence, never using when I advance any thing that may possibly be disputed, the Words, *Certainly, undoubtedly*, or any others that give the Air of Positiveness to an Opinion; but rather say, *I conceive*, or *I apprehend* a Thing to be so or so, *It appears to me*, or *I should think it so or so for such and such Reasons*, or *I imagine* it to be so, or *it is so* if *I am not mistaken*. This Habit I believe has been of great Advantage to me, when I have had occasion to inculcate my Opinions and persuade Men into Measures that I have been from time to time engag'd in promoting. And as the chief Ends of Conversation are to *inform*, or to be *informed*, to *please* or to *persuade*, I wish well-meaning sensible Men would not lessen their Power of doing Good by a Positive assuming Manner that seldom fails to disgust, tends to create Opposition, and to defeat every one of those Purposes for which Speech was given us, to wit, giving or receiving Information, or Pleasure: For If you would *inform*, a positive dogmatical Manner in advancing your Sentiments, may provoke Contradiction and prevent a candid Attention. If you wish Information and Improvement from the Knowledge of others and yet at the same time express yourself as firmly fix'd in your present Opinions, modest sensible Men, who do not love Disputation, will probably leave you undisturb'd in the Possession of your Error; and by such a Manner you can seldom hope to recommend yourself in *pleasing* your Hearers, or to persuade those whose Concurrence you desire. Pope says, judiciously.

7. The English philosopher John Locke (1632–1704) published *An Essay Concerning Human Understanding* in 1690. The philosophers Antoine Arnauld (1612–1694) and Pierre Nicole (1625?–1695), of Port Royal, France, published the English edition of *Logic: Or the Art of Thinking* in 1687. It was originally published in Latin in 1662.
8. James Greenwood wrote *An Essay towards a Practical English Grammar* (1711).
9. I.e., in the form of a debate or dialectic, as practiced by the Greek philosopher Socrates (c.

470–399 B.C.E.).
1. Work by the Greek historian Xenophon (434?–355 B.C.E.) translated by Edward Bysshe in 1712.
2. Anthony Ashley Cooper, third Earl of Shaftesbury (1671–1713), was a religious skeptic. Anthony Collins (1676–1729) argued that the world could satisfactorily be explained in terms of itself. Perhaps Franklin read Shaftesbury's *Characteristics of Men, Manners, Opinions, Times* (1711) and Collins's *A Discourse of Free Thinking* (1713).

> Men should be taught as if you taught them not,
> And things unknown propos'd as things forgot,

farther recommending it to us,

> To speak tho' sure, with seeming Diffidence.[3]

And he might have coupled with this Line that which he has coupled with another, I think less properly,

> For want of Modesty is want of Sense.

If you ask why less properly, I must repeat the Lines;

> "Immodest Words admit of no Defence;
> For Want of Modesty is Want of Sense."[4]

Now is not Want of Sense, (where a Man is so unfortunate as to want it) some Apology for his Want of Modesty? and would not the Lines stand more justly thus?

> Immodest Words admit but this Defence,
> That Want of Modesty is Want of Sense.

This however I should submit to better Judgments.

My Brother had in 1720 or 21, begun to print a Newspaper. It was the second[5] that appear'd in America, and was called The New England Courant. The only one before it, was The Boston News Letter. I remember his being dissuaded by some of his Friends from the Undertaking, as not likely to succeed, one Newspaper being in their Judgment enough for America. At this time 1771 there are not less than five and twenty. He went on however with the Undertaking, and after having work'd in composing the Types and printing off the Sheets I was employ'd to carry the Papers thro' the Streets to the Customers. He had some ingenious Men among his Friends who amus'd themselves by writing little Pieces for this Paper, which gain'd it Credit, and made it more in Demand; and these Gentlemen often visited us. Hearing their Conversations, and their Accounts of the Approbation their Papers were receiv'd with, I was excited to try my Hand among them. But being still a Boy, and suspecting that my Brother would object to printing any Thing of mine in his Paper if he knew it to be mine, I contriv'd to disguise my Hand, and writing an anonymous Paper I put it in at Night under the Door of the Printing-House.

It was found in the Morning and communicated to his Writing Friends when they call'd in as Usual. They read it, commented on it in my Hearing, and I had the exquisite Pleasure, of finding it met with their Approbation, and that in their different Guesses at the Author none were named but Men of some Character among us for Learning and Ingenuity. I suppose now that I was rather lucky in my Judges: And that perhaps they were not really so

3. Franklin is quoting from memory lines 574–75 and 567 of An Essay on Criticism, by the English poet Alexander Pope (1688–1744). The first line should read, "Men must be taught as if you taught them not," and the third, "And speak, tho' sure, with seeming Diffidence."
4. Franklin is mistaken here: the lines are from Wentworth Dillon, fourth Earl of Roscommon (1633?–1685), from his Essay on Translated Verse, lines 113–14. The second line should read, "For want of decency is want of sense." "Want": lack.
5. Actually, the fifth; James Franklin's paper appeared on August 7, 1721.

Early American print shop. "The Printer hath metal Letters in a great
number put into Boxes (5). The Compositor (1) taketh them out one by one,
and according to the Copy (which he hath fastened before him in a Visorum
[2]) composeth words in a Composing-stick (3) till a Line be made; he putteth
these in a Galley (4) till a Page (6) be made, and those again in a Form (7),
and he locketh them up in Iron Chases (8) with Quoins (9) lest they should
drop out, and putteth them under the Press (10). Then the Press-man beateth
it over with Printer's Ink, by means of Balls (11) spreadeth upon it the Papers
put in the Frisket (12), which being put under the Spindle (14) on the Coffin
(13) and pressed down with a Bar (15) he maketh to take impression." From
Comensius's Visible World (1810), with thanks to James Green of the Library
Company of Philadelphia.

very good ones as I then esteem'd them. Encourag'd however by this, I wrote
and convey'd in the same Way to the Press several more Papers,[6] which were
equally approv'd, and I kept my Secret till my small Fund of Sense for such
Performances was pretty well exhausted, and then I discovered[7] it; when I
began to be considered a little more by my Brother's Acquaintance, and in a
manner that did not quite please him, as he thought, probably with reason,
that it tended to make me too vain. And perhaps this might be one Occa-
sion of the Differences that we began to have about this Time. Tho' a Brother,
he considered himself as my Master, and me as his Apprentice; and accord-
ingly expected the same Services from me as he would from another; while
I thought he demean'd me too much in some he requir'd of me, who from a
Brother expected more Indulgence, Our Disputes were often brought before
our Father, and I fancy I was either generally in the right, or else a better
Pleader, because the Judgment was generally in my favor. But my Brother
was passionate and had often beaten me, which I took extremely amiss; and
thinking my Apprenticeship very tedious, I was continually wishing for

6. The Silence Dogood letters (April 12–October 7. Revealed.
8, 1722), the earliest essay series in America.

some Opportunity of shortening it, which at length offered in a manner unexpected.[8]

One of the Pieces in our Newspaper, on some political Point which I have now forgotten, gave Offence to the Assembly. He was taken up, censur'd and imprison'd[9] for a Month by the Speaker's Warrant, I suppose because he would not discover his Author. I too was taken up and examin'd before the Council; but tho' I did not give them any Satisfaction, they contented themselves with admonishing me, and dismiss'd me; considering me perhaps as an Apprentice who was bound to keep his Master's Secrets. During my Brother's Confinement, which I resented a good deal, notwithstanding our private Differences, I had the Management of the Paper, and I made bold to give our Rulers some Rubs[1] in it, which my Brother took very kindly, while others began to consider me in an unfavorable Light, as a young Genius that had a Turn for Libeling and Satire.[2] My Brother's Discharge was accompanied with an Order of the House, (a very odd one) *that James Franklin should no longer print the Paper called the New England Courant.* There was a Consultation held in our Printing-House among his Friends what he should do in this Case. Some propos'd to evade the Order by changing the Name of the Paper; but my Brother seeing Inconveniences in that, it was finally concluded on as a better Way, to let it be printed for the future under the Name of *Benjamin Franklin.* And to avoid the Censure of the Assembly that might fall on him, as still printing it by his Apprentice, the Contrivance was, that my old Indenture should be return'd to me with a full Discharge on the Back of it, to be shown on Occasion; but to secure to him the Benefit of my Service I was to sign new Indentures for the Remainder of the Term, which were to be kept private. A very flimsy Scheme it was, but however it was immediately executed, and the Paper went on accordingly under my Name for several Months.[3] At length a fresh Difference arising between my Brother and me, I took upon me to assert my Freedom, presuming that he would not venture to produce the new Indentures. It was not fair in me to take this Advantage, and this I therefore reckon one of the first Errata of my Life: But the Unfairness of it weigh'd little with me, when under the Impressions of Resentment, for the Blows his Passion too often urg'd him to bestow upon me. Tho' he was otherwise not an ill-natur'd Man: Perhaps I was too saucy and provoking.

When he found I would leave him, he took care to prevent my getting Employment in any other Printing-House of the Town, by going round and speaking to every Master, who accordingly refus'd to give me Work. I then thought of going to New York as the nearest Place where there was a Printer: and I was the rather inclin'd to leave Boston, when I reflected that I had already made myself a little obnoxious to the governing Party; and from the arbitrary Proceedings of the Assembly in my Brother's Case it was likely I

8. I fancy his harsh and tyrannical Treatment of me, might be a means of impressing me with that Aversion to arbitrary Power that has stuck to me thro' my whole Life [Franklin's note].
9. On June 11, 1722, the *Courant* hinted that there was collusion between local authorities and pirates raiding off Boston Harbor. James Franklin was jailed from June 12 to July 7. "Assembly":

Massachusetts legislative body; the lower house, with representatives elected by towns of the Massachusetts General Court.
1. Insults, annoyances.
2. Satirizing.
3. The paper continued under Franklin's name until 1726, three years after he left Boston.

might if I stay'd soon bring myself into Scrapes; and farther that my indiscreet Disputations about Religion began to make me pointed at with Horror by good People, as an Infidel or Atheist; I determin'd on the Point: but my Father now siding with my Brother, I was sensible that if I attempted to go openly, Means would be used to prevent me. My Friend Collins therefore undertook to manage a little for me. He agreed with the Captain of a New York Sloop for my Passage, under the Notion of my being a young Acquaintance of his that had got a naughty Girl with Child, whose Friends would compel me to marry her, and therefore I could not appear or come away publicly. So I sold some of my Books to raise a little Money, was taken on board privately, and as we had a fair Wind, in three Days I found myself in New York near 300 Miles from home, a Boy of but 17, without the least Recommendation to or Knowledge of any Person in the Place, and with very little Money in my Pocket.

My Inclinations for the Sea, were by this time worn out, or I might now have gratified them. But having a Trade, and supposing myself a pretty good Workman, I offer'd my Service to the Printer of the Place, old Mr. William Bradford.[4] He could give me no Employment, having little to do, and Help enough already: But, says he, my Son at Philadelphia has lately lost his principal Hand, Aquila Rose, by Death. If you go thither I believe he may employ you. Philadelphia was 100 Miles farther. I set out, however, in a Boat for Amboy;[5] leaving my Chest and Things to follow me round by Sea. In crossing the Bay we met with a Squall that tore our rotten Sails to pieces, prevented our getting into the Kill, and drove us upon Long Island.[6] In our Way a drunken Dutchman, who was a Passenger too, fell overboard; when he was sinking I reach'd thro' the Water to his shock Pate[7] and drew him up so that we got him in again. His Ducking sober'd him a little, and he went to sleep, taking first out of his Pocket a Book which he desir'd I would dry for him. It prov'd to be my old favorite Author Bunyan's Pilgrim's Progress in Dutch, finely printed on good Paper with copper Cuts,[8] a Dress better than I had ever seen it wear in its own Language. I have since found that it has been translated into most of the Languages of Europe, and suppose it has been more generally read than any other Book except perhaps the Bible. Honest John was the first that I know of who mix'd Narration and Dialogue, a Method of Writing very engaging to the Reader, who in the most interesting Parts finds himself as it were brought into the Company, and present at the Discourse. Defoe in his Crusoe, his Moll Flanders, Religious Courtship, Family Instructor, and other Pieces, has imitated it with Success.[9] And Richardson has done the same in his Pamela,[1] etc.

When we drew near the Island we found it was at a Place where there could be no Landing, there being a great Surf on the stony Beach. So we dropped Anchor and swung round towards the Shore. Some People came

4. One of the first American printers (1663–1752) and father of Andrew Bradford (1686–1742), Franklin's future competitor in Philadelphia.
5. Perth Amboy, New Jersey.
6. In New York. "The Kill": the Kill van Kull, a narrow channel that separates Staten Island, New York, from New Jersey.
7. Shaggy head of hair.
8. Engravings. See n. 4, p. 473.

9. Defoe (see n. 8, p. 474) published *Robinson Crusoe* in 1719, *Moll Flanders* in 1722, *Religious Courtship* in 1772, and *The Family Instructor* in 1715–18.
1. The English writer Samuel Richardson (1689–1761) published his novel *Pamela: Or Virtue Rewarded* in 1740. Franklin reprinted it in 1744 and in doing so published the first novel in America.

down to the Water Edge and hallow'd to us, as we did to them. But the Wind was so high and the Surf so loud, that we could not hear so as to understand each other. There were Canoes on the Shore, and we made Signs and hallow'd that they should fetch us, but they either did not understand us, or thought it impracticable. So they went away, and Night coming on, we had no Remedy but to wait till the Wind should abate, and in the mean time the Boatman and I concluded to sleep if we could, and so crowded into the Scuttle[2] with the Dutchman who was still wet, and the Spray beating over the Head of our Boat, leak'd thro' to us, so that we were soon almost as wet as he. In this Manner we lay all Night with very little Rest. But the Wind abating the next Day, we made a Shift to reach Amboy before Night, having been 30 hours on the Water without Victuals, or any Drink but a Bottle of filthy Rum: The Water we sail'd on being salt.

In the Evening I found myself very feverish, and went ill to Bed. But having read somewhere that cold Water drank plentifully was good for a Fever, I follow'd the Prescription, sweat plentifully most of the Night, my Fever left me, and in the Morning crossing the Ferry, proceeded on my Journey, on foot, having 50 Miles to Burlington,[3] where I was told I should find Boats that would carry me the rest of the Way to Philadelphia.

It rain'd very hard all the Day, I was thoroughly soak'd, and by Noon a good deal tir'd, so I stopped at a poor Inn, where I stayed all Night, beginning now to wish I had never left home. I cut so miserable a Figure too, that I found by the Questions ask'd me I was suspected to be some runaway Servant, and in danger of being taken up on that Suspicion. However I proceeded the next Day, and got in the Evening to an Inn within 8 or 10 Miles of Burlington, kept by one Dr. Browne.[4]

He entered into Conversation with me while I took some Refreshment, and finding I had read a little, became very sociable and friendly. Our Acquaintance continu'd as long as he liv'd. He had been, I imagine, an itinerant Doctor, for there was no Town in England, or Country in Europe, of which he could not give a very particular Account. He had some Letters,[5] and was ingenious, but much of an Unbeliever, and wickedly undertook some Years after to travesty the Bible in doggerel Verse as Cotton had done Virgil.[6] By this means he set many of the Facts in a very ridiculous Light, and might have hurt weak minds if his Work had been publish'd: but it never was. At his House I lay that Night, and the next Morning reach'd Burlington. But had the Mortification to find that the regular Boats were gone a little before my coming, and no other expected to go till Tuesday, this being Saturday. Wherefore I return'd to an old Woman in the Town of whom I had bought Gingerbread to eat on the Water, and ask'd her Advice; she invited me to lodge at her House till a Passage by Water should offer; and being tired with my foot Traveling, I accepted the Invitation. She understanding I was a Printer, would have had me stay at that Town and follow my

2. An opening in a ship's deck, with a lid.
3. Then the capital of West Jersey, about eighteen miles north of Philadelphia.
4. Dr. John Browne (c. 1667–1737), innkeeper in Bordentown, New Jersey, and a noted religious skeptic as well as physician.
5. I.e., formal education.

6. In *Scarronides*, the English writer Charles Cotton (1630–1687) parodied the first and fourth books of the *Aeneid*, by the ancient Roman poet Virgil. Cotton's opening lines are: "I sing the Man (read it who list), / A Trojan true as ever pissed."

Business, being ignorant of the Stock necessary to begin with. She was very hospitable, gave me a Dinner of Ox Cheek with great Goodwill, accepting only of a Pot of Ale in return. And I thought myself fix'd till Tuesday should come. However walking in the Evening by the Side of the River a Boat came by, which I found was going towards Philadelphia with several People in her. They took me in, and as there was no Wind, we row'd all the Way; and about Midnight not having yet seen the City, some of the Company were confident we must have pass'd it, and would row no farther, the others knew not where we were, so we put towards the Shore, got into a Creek, landed near an old Fence with the Rails of which we made a Fire, the Night being cold, in October, and there we remain'd till Daylight. Then one of the Company knew the Place to be Cooper's Creek a little above Philadelphia, which we saw as soon as we got out of the Creek, and arriv'd there about 8 or 9 aClock, on the Sunday morning,[7] and landed at the Market Street Wharf.

I have been the more particular in this Description of my Journey, and shall be so of my first Entry into that City, that you may in your Mind compare such unlikely Beginning with the Figure I have since made there. I was in my working Dress, my best Clothes being to come round by Sea. I was dirty from my Journey; my Pockets were stuff'd out with Shirts and Stockings; I knew no Soul, nor where to look for Lodging. I was fatigu'd with Traveling, Rowing and Want of Rest. I was very hungry, and my whole Stock of Cash consisted of a Dutch Dollar and about a Shilling in Copper.[8] The latter I gave the People of the Boat for my Passage, who at first refus'd it on Account of my Rowing; but I insisted on their taking it, a Man being sometimes more generous when he has but a little Money than when he has plenty, perhaps thro' Fear of being thought to have but little. Then I walk'd up the Street, gazing about, till near the Market House I met a Boy with Bread. I had made many a Meal on Bread, and inquiring where he got it, I went immediately to the Baker's he directed me to in Second Street; and ask'd for Biscuit, intending such as we had in Boston, but they it seems were not made in Philadelphia, then I ask'd for a three-penny Loaf, and was told they had none such: so not considering or knowing the Difference of Money and the greater Cheapness nor the Names of his Bread, I bad him give me three pennyworth of any sort. He gave me accordingly three great Puffy Rolls. I was surpris'd at the Quantity, but took it, and having no Room in my Pockets, walk'd off, with a Roll under each Arm, and eating the other. Thus I went up Market Street as far as Fourth Street, passing by the Door of Mr. Read, my future Wife's Father, when she standing at the Door saw me, and thought I made as I certainly did a most awkward ridiculous Appearance. Then I turn'd and went down Chestnut Street and part of Walnut Street, eating my Roll all the Way, and coming round found myself again at Market Street Wharf, near the Boat I came in, to which I went for a Drought of the River Water, and being fill'd with one of my Rolls, gave the other two to a Woman and her Child that came down the River in the Boat with us and were waiting to go farther. Thus refresh'd I walk'd again up the Street, which by this time had many clean dress'd People in it who were all walking

7. October 6, 1723.
8. Colonial money was extraordinarily heterogeneous, as Franklin's "stock" here begins to indicate.

the same Way; I join'd them, and thereby was led into the great Meeting House of the Quakers near the Market. I sat down among them, and after looking round a while and hearing nothing said, being very drowsy thro' Labor and want of Rest the preceding Night, I fell fast asleep, and continu'd so till the Meeting broke up, when one was kind enough to rouse me. This was therefore the first House I was in or slept in, in Philadelphia.

Walking again down towards the River, and looking in the Faces of People, I met a young Quaker Man whose Countenance I lik'd, and accosting him requested he would tell me where a Stranger could get Lodging. We were then near the Sign of the Three Mariners. Here, says he, is one Place that entertains Strangers, but it is not a reputable House; if thee wilt walk with me, I'll show thee a better. He brought me to the Crooked Billet in Water Street. Here I got a Dinner. And while I was eating it, several sly Questions were ask'd me, as it seem'd to be suspected from my youth and Appearance, that I might be some Runaway. After Dinner my Sleepiness return'd: and being shown to a Bed, I lay down without undressing, and slept till Six in the Evening; was call'd to Supper; went to Bed again very early and slept soundly till the next Morning. Then I made myself as tidy as I could, and went to Andrew Bradford the Printer's. I found in the Shop the old Man his Father, whom I had seen at New York, and who traveling on horse back had got to Philadelphia before me. He introduc'd me to his Son, who receiv'd me civilly, gave me a Breakfast, but told me he did not at present want a Hand, being lately supplied with one. But there was another Printer in town lately set up, one Keimer,[9] who perhaps might employ me; if not, I should be welcome to lodge at his House, and he would give me a little Work to do now and then till fuller Business should offer.

The old Gentleman said, he would go with me to the new Printer: And when we found him, Neighbor, says Bradford, I have brought to see you a young Man of your Business, perhaps you may want such a One. He ask'd me a few Questions, put a Composing Stick[1] in my Hand to see how I work'd, and then said he would employ me soon, tho' he had just then nothing for me to do. And taking old Bradford whom he had never seen before, to be one of the Townspeople that had a Goodwill for him, enter'd into a Conversation on his present Undertaking and Prospects; while Bradford not discovering[2] that he was the other Printer's Father; on Keimer's Saying he expected soon to get the greatest Part of the Business into his own Hands, drew him on by artful Questions and starting little Doubts, to explain all his Views, what Interest he relied on, and in what manner he intended to proceed. I who stood by and heard all, saw immediately that one of them was a crafty old Sophister,[3] and the other a mere Novice. Bradford left me with Keimer, who was greatly surpris'd when I told him who the old Man was.

Keimer's Printing-House I found, consisted of an old shatter'd Press and one small worn-out Font of English,[4] which he was then using himself, composing in it an Elegy on Aquila Rose[5] before-mentioned, an ingenious young

9. Samuel Keimer (c. 1688–1742), a printer in London before moving to Philadelphia.
1. An instrument of adjustable width in which type is set before being put on a galley (an oblong, single-column tray).
2. Revealing.

3. Trickster, rationalizer.
4. An oversized type, not usable for books and newspapers.
5. Journeyman printer (c. 1695–1723) for Andrew Bradford; his son Joseph apprenticed with Franklin.

Man of excellent Character much respected in the Town, Clerk of the Assembly,[6] and a pretty Poet. Keimer made Verses, too, but very indifferently. He could not be said to write them, for his Manner was to compose them in the Types directly out of his Head; so there being no Copy, but one Pair of Cases,[7] and the Elegy likely to require all the Letter, no one could help him. I endeavor'd to put his Press (which he had not yet us'd, and of which he understood nothing) into Order fit to be work'd with; and promising to come and print off his Elegy as soon as he should have got it ready, I return'd to Bradford's who gave me a little Job to do for the present, and there I lodged and dieted.[8] A few Days after Keimer sent for me to print off the Elegy. And now he had got another Pair of Cases, and a Pamphlet to reprint, on which he set me to work.

These two Printers I found poorly qualified for their Business. Bradford had not been bred to it, and was very illiterate; and Keimer tho' something of a Scholar, was a mere Compositor, knowing nothing of Presswork. He had been one of the French Prophets[9] and could act their enthusiastic Agitations. At this time he did not profess any particular Religion, but something of all on occasion; was very ignorant of the World, and had, as I afterwards found, a good deal of the Knave in his Composition. He did not like my Lodging at Bradford's while I work'd with him. He had a House indeed, but without Furniture, so he could not lodge me: But he got me a Lodging at Mr. Read's before-mentioned, who was the Owner of his House. And my Chest and Clothes being come by this time, I made rather a more respectable Appearance in the Eyes of Miss Read, than I had done when she first happen'd to see me eating my Roll in the Street.

I began now to have some Acquaintance among the young People of the Town, that were Lovers of Reading with whom I spent my Evenings very pleasantly and gaining Money by my Industry and Frugality, I lived very agreeably, forgetting Boston as much as I could, and not desiring that any there should know where I resided except my Friend Collins who was in my Secret, and kept it when I wrote to him. At length an Incident happened that sent me back again much sooner than I had intended.

I had a Brother-in-law, Robert Homes,[1] Master of a Sloop that traded between Boston and Delaware. He being at New Castle[2] 40 Miles below Philadelphia, heard there of me, and wrote me a Letter, mentioning the Concern of my Friends in Boston at my abrupt Departure, assuring me of their Goodwill to me, and that everything would be accommodated to my Mind if I would return, to which he exhorted me very earnestly. I wrote an Answer to his Letter, thank'd him for his Advice, but stated my Reasons for quitting Boston fully, and in such a Light as to convince him I was not so wrong as he had apprehended. Sir William Keith Governor of the Province,[3] was then at New Castle, and Captain Homes happening to be in Company with him when my Letter came to hand, spoke to him of me, and show'd him the Letter.

6. One who has charge of the records, documents, and correspondence of any organized body (here, the Pennsylvania legislative council).
7. Two shallow trays that contain uppercase and lowercase type.
8. Boarded.
9. An English sect that preached doomsday and cultivated emotional fits.
1. Ship's captain (d. before 1743), husband of Franklin's sister Mary.
2. City in Delaware.
3. Keith (1680–1749), lieutenant-governor of Pennsylvania and Delaware from 1717 to 1726, fled to England in 1728 to escape creditors.

The Governor read it, and seem'd surpris'd when he was told my Age. He said I appear'd a young Man of promising Parts, and therefore should be encouraged: The Printers at Philadelphia were wretched ones, and if I would set up there, he made no doubt I should succeed; for his Part, he would procure me the public Business, and do me every other Service in his Power. This my Brother-in-Law afterwards told me in Boston. But I knew as yet nothing of it; when one Day Keimer and I being at Work together near the Window, we saw the Governor and another Gentleman (which prov'd to be Colonel French, of New Castle) finely dress'd, come directly across the Street to our House, and heard them at the Door.

Keimer ran down immediately, thinking it a Visit to him. But the Governor enquir'd for me, came up, and with a Condescension⁴ and Politeness I had been quite unus'd to, made me many Compliments, desired to be acquainted with me, blam'd me kindly for not having made myself known to him when I first came to the Place, and would have me away with him to the Tavern where he was going with Colonel French to taste as he said some excellent Madeira. I was not a little surpris'd, and Keimer star'd like a Pig poison'd. I went however with the Governor and Colonel French, to a Tavern the Corner of Third Street, and over the Madeira he propos'd my Setting up my Business, laid before me the Probabilities of Success, and both he and Colonel French assur'd me I should have their Interest and Influence in procuring the Public-Business of both Governments. On my doubting whether my Father would assist me in it, Sir William said he would give me a Letter to him, in which he would state the Advantages, and he did not doubt of prevailing with him. So it was concluded I should return to Boston in the first Vessel with the Governor's Letter recommending me to my Father.

In the meantime the Intention was to be kept secret, and I went on working with Keimer as usual, the Governor sending for me now and then to dine with him, a very great Honor I thought it, and conversing with me in the most affable, familiar, and friendly manner imaginable. About the End of April 1724, a little Vessel offer'd for Boston. I took Leave of Keimer as going to see my Friends. The Governor gave me an ample Letter, saying many flattering things of me to my Father, and strongly recommending the Project of my setting up at Philadelphia, as a Thing that must make my Fortune. We struck on a Shoal in going down the Bay and sprung a Leak, we had a blustring time at Sea, and were oblig'd to pump almost continually, at which I took my Turn. We arriv'd safe however at Boston in about a Fortnight. I had been absent Seven Months and my Friends had heard nothing of me, for my Brother Homes was not yet return'd; and had not written about me. My unexpected Appearance surpris'd the Family; all were however very glad to see me and made me Welcome, except my Brother.

I went to see him at his Printing-House: I was better dress'd than ever while in his Service, having a genteel new Suit from Head to foot, a Watch, and my Pockets lin'd with near Five Pounds Sterling in Silver. He receiv'd me not very frankly, look'd me all over, and turn'd to his Work again. The Journeymen were inquisitive where I had been, what sort of a Country it was, and how I lik'd it? I prais'd it much, and the happy Life I led in it;

4. Disregard for difference in rank or station.

expressing strongly my Intention of returning to it; and one of them asking what kind of Money we had there, I produc'd a handful of Silver and spread it before them, which was a kind of Raree-Show[5] they had not been us'd to, Paper being the Money of Boston. Then I took an Opportunity of letting them see my Watch: and lastly, (my Brother still grum and sullen) I gave them a Piece of Eight to drink[6] and took my Leave. This Visit of mine offended him extremely. For when my Mother some time after spoke to him of a Reconciliation, and of her Wishes to see us on good Terms together, and that we might live for the future as Brothers, he said, I had insulted him in such a Manner before his People that he could never forget or forgive it. In this however he was mistaken.

My Father receiv'd the Governor's Letter with some apparent Surprise; but said little of it to me for some Days; when Captain Homes returning, he show'd it to him, ask'd if he knew Keith, and what kind of a Man he was: Adding his Opinion that he must be of small Discretion, to think of setting a Boy up in Business who wanted yet 3 Years of being at Man's Estate. Homes said what he could in favor of the Project; but my Father was clear in the Impropriety of it; and at last gave a flat Denial to it. Then he wrote a civil Letter to Sir William thanking him for the Patronage he had so kindly offered me, but declining to assist me as yet in Setting up, I being in his Opinion too young to be trusted with the Management of a Business so important; and for which the Preparation must be so expensive.

My Friend and Companion Collins, who was a Clerk at the Post-Office, pleas'd with the Account I gave him of my new Country, determin'd to go thither also: And while I waited for my Father's Determination, he set out before me by Land to Rhode Island, leaving his Books which were a pretty Collection of Mathematics and Natural Philosophy,[7] to come with mine and me to New York where he propos'd to wait for me. My Father, tho' he did not approve Sir William's Proposition, was yet pleas'd that I had been able to obtain so advantageous a Character from a Person of such Note where I had resided, and that I had been so industrious and careful as to equip myself so handsomely in so short a time: therefore seeing no Prospect of an Accommodation between my Brother and me, he gave his Consent to my Returning again to Philadelphia, advis'd me to behave respectfully to the People there, endeavor to obtain the general Esteem, and avoid lampooning and libeling to which he thought I had too much Inclination; telling me, that by steady Industry and a prudent Parsimony, I might save enough by the time I was One and Twenty to set me up, and that if I came near the Matter he would help me out with the Rest. This was all I could obtain, except some small Gifts as Tokens of his and my Mother's Love, when I embark'd again for New York, now with their Approbation and their Blessing.

The Sloop putting in at Newport, Rhode Island, I visited my Brother John, who had been married and settled there some Years. He received me very affectionately, for he always lov'd me. A Friend of his, one Vernon, having some Money due to him in Pennsylvania, about 35 Pounds Currency, desired

5. A sidewalk peep show. Silver coins were rare in the colonies.
6. A Spanish dollar with which they could buy

drinks. "Grum": glum, morose.
7. I.e., natural science. "Determination": decision.

I would receive it for him, and keep it till I had his Directions what to remit it in. Accordingly he gave me an Order. This afterwards occasion'd me a good deal of Uneasiness. At Newport we took in a Number of Passengers for New York: Among which were two young Women, Companions, and a grave, sensible Matron-like Quaker-Woman with her Attendants. I had shown an obliging Readiness to do her some little Services which impress'd her I suppose with a degree of Goodwill towards me. Therefore when she saw a daily growing Familiarity between me and the two Young Women, which they appear'd to encourage, she took me aside and said, Young Man, I am concern'd for thee, as thou has no Friend with thee, and seems not to know much of the World, or of the Snares Youth is expos'd to; depend upon it those are very bad Women, I can see it in all their Actions, and if thee art not upon thy Guard, they will draw thee into some Danger: they are Strangers to thee, and I advise thee in a friendly Concern for thy Welfare, to have no Acquaintance with them. As I seem'd at first not to think so ill of them as she did, she mention'd some Things she had observ'd and heard that had escap'd my Notice; but now convinc'd me she was right. I thank'd her for her kind Advice, and promis'd to follow it. When we arriv'd at New York, they told me where they liv'd, and invited me to come and see them: but I avoided it. And it was well I did: For the next Day, the Captain miss'd a Silver Spoon and some other Things that had been taken out of his Cabin, and knowing that these were a Couple of Strumpets, he got a Warrant to search their Lodgings, found the stolen Goods, and had the Thieves punish'd. So tho' we had escap'd a sunken Rock which we scrap'd upon in the Passage, I thought this Escape of rather more Importance to me.

At New York I found my Friend Collins, who had arriv'd there some Time before me. We had been intimate from[8] Children, and had read the same Books together. But he had the Advantage of more time for Reading, and Studying and a wonderful Genius for Mathematical Learning in which he far outstripped me. While I liv'd in Boston most of my Hours of Leisure for Conversation were spent with him, and he continu'd a sober as well as an industrious Lad; was much respected for his Learning by several of the Clergy and other Gentlemen, and seem'd to promise making a good Figure in Life: but during my Absence he had acquir'd a Habit of Sotting with[9] Brandy; and I found by his own Account and what I heard from others, that he had been drunk every day since his Arrival at New York, and behav'd very oddly. He had gam'd too and lost his Money, so that I was oblig'd to discharge his Lodgings,[1] and defray his Expences to and at Philadelphia: Which prov'd extremely inconvenient to me. The then Governor of New York, Burnet,[2] Son of Bishop Burnet, hearing from the Captain that a young Man, one of his Passengers, had a great many Books, desired he would bring me to see him. I waited upon him accordingly, and should have taken Collins with me but that he was not sober. The Governor treated me with great Civility, show'd me his Library, which was a very large one, and we had a good deal of Conversation about Books and Authors. This was the second Gover-

8. I.e., since we were.
9. Getting stupefied on.
1. To pay the rent he owed.

2. William Burnet (1688–1729), governor of New York and New Jersey from 1720 to 1728 and governor of Massachusetts from 1728 to 1729.

nor who had done me the Honor to take Notice of me, which to a poor Boy like me was very pleasing.

We proceeded to Philadelphia. I received on the Way Vernon's Money, without which we could hardly have finish'd our Journey. Collins wish'd to be employ'd in some Counting House; but whether they discover'd his Dramming[3] by his Breath, or by his Behavior, tho' he had some Recommendations, he met with no Success in any Application, and continu'd Lodging and Boarding at the same House with me and at my Expense. Knowing I had that Money of Vernon's he was continually borrowing of me, still promising Repayment as soon as he should be in Business. At length he had got so much of it, that I was distress'd to think what I should do, in case of being call'd on to remit it. His Drinking continu'd, about which we sometimes quarrel'd, for when a little intoxicated he was very fractious. Once in a Boat on the Delaware with some other young Men, he refused to row in his Turn: I will be row'd home, says he. We will not row you, says I. You must, says he, or stay all Night on the Water, just as you please. The others said, Let us row; What signifies it? But my Mind being soured with his other Conduct, I continu'd to refuse. So he swore he would make me row, or throw me overboard; and coming along stepping on the Thwarts[4] towards me, when he came up and struck at me, I clapped my Hand under his Crotch, and rising, pitch'd him headforemost into the River. I knew he was a good Swimmer, and so was under little Concern about him; but before he could get round to lay hold of the Boat, we had with a few Strokes pull'd her out of his Reach. And ever when he drew near the Boat, we ask'd if he would row, striking a few Strokes to slide her away from him. He was ready to die with Vexation, and obstinately would not promise to row; however seeing him at last beginning to tire, we lifted him in; and brought him home dripping wet in the Evening. We hardly exchang'd a civil Word afterwards; and a West India Captain who had a Commission to procure a Tutor for the Sons of a Gentleman at Barbados,[5] happening to meet with him, agreed to carry him thither. He left me then, promising to remit me the first Money he should receive in order to discharge the Debt. But I never heard of him after.

The Breaking into this Money of Vernon's was one of the first great Errata of my Life. And this Affair show'd that my Father was not much out in his Judgment when he suppos'd me too Young to manage Business of Importance. But Sir William, on reading his Letter, said he was too prudent. There was great Difference in Persons, and Discretion did not always accompany Years, nor was Youth always without it. And since he will not set you up, says he, I will do it myself. Give me an Inventory of the Things necessary to be had from England, and I will send for them. You shall repay me when you are able; I am resolv'd to have a good Printer here, and I am sure you must succeed. This was spoken with such an Appearance of Cordiality, that I had not the least doubt of his meaning what he said. I had hitherto kept the Proposition of my Setting up a Secret in Philadelphia, and I still kept it. Had it been known that I depended on the Governor, probably some Friend

3. Drinking liquor.
4. The seat on which an oarsman sits.
5. Island in the British West Indies.

that knew him better would have advis'd me not to rely on him, as I afterwards heard it as his known Character to be liberal of Promises which he never meant to keep. Yet unsolicited as he was by me, how could I think his generous Offers insincere? I believ'd him one of the best Men in the World.

I presented him an Inventory of a little Printing-House, amounting by my Computation to about 100 Pounds Sterling. He lik'd it, but ask'd me if my being on the Spot in England to choose the Types and see that everything was good of the kind, might not be of some Advantage. Then, says he, when there, you may make Acquaintances and establish Correspondences in the Bookselling, and Stationery Way. I agreed that this might be advantageous. Then says he, get yourself ready to go with Annis;[6] which was the annual Ship, and the only one at that Time usually passing between London and Philadelphia. But it would be some Months before Annis sail'd, so I continu'd working with Keimer, fretting about the Money Collins had got from me, and in daily Apprehensions of being call'd upon by Vernon, which however did not happen for some Years after.

I believe I have omitted mentioning that in my first Voyage from Boston, being becalm'd off Block Island,[7] our People set about catching Cod and haul'd up a great many. Hitherto I had stuck to my Resolution of not eating animal Food; and on this Occasion, I consider'd with my Master Tryon, the taking every Fish as a kind of unprovok'd Murder, since none of them had or ever could do us any Injury that might justify the Slaughter. All this seem'd very reasonable. But I had formerly been a great Lover of Fish, and when this came hot out of the Frying Pan, it smelt admirably well. I balanc'd some time between Principle and Inclination: till I recollected, that when the Fish were opened, I saw smaller Fish taken out of their Stomachs: Then, thought I, if you eat one another, I don't see why we mayn't eat you. So I din'd upon Cod very heartily and continu'd to eat with other People, returning only now and then occasionally to a vegetable Diet. So convenient a thing it is to be a *reasonable Creature,* since it enables one to find or make a Reason for everything one has a mind to do.

Keimer and I liv'd on a pretty good familiar Footing and agreed tolerably well: for he suspected nothing of my Setting up. He retain'd a great deal of his old Enthusiasms, and lov'd an Argumentation. We therefore had many Disputations. I us'd to work him so with my Socratic Method, and had trapann'd[8] him so often by Questions apparently so distant from any Point we had in hand, and yet by degrees led to the Point, and brought him into Difficulties and Contradictions, that at last he grew ridiculously cautious, and would hardly answer me the most common Question, without asking first, *What do you intend to infer from that?* However it gave him so high an Opinion of my Abilities in the Confuting Way, that he seriously propos'd my being his Colleague in a Project he had of setting up a new Sect. He was to preach the Doctrines, and I was to confound all Opponents. When he came to explain with me upon the Doctrines, I found several Conundrums[9] which I objected to, unless I might have my Way a little too, and introduce some

6. Thomas Annis, captain of the *London Hope,* the boat on which Franklin sailed to London in 1724.

7. Off the coast of Rhode Island.
8. Trapped.
9. Puzzles, difficult questions.

of mine. Keimer wore his Beard at full Length, because somewhere in the Mosaic Law it is said, *thou shalt not mar the Corners of thy Beard.*[1] He likewise kept the seventh-day Sabbath; and these two Points were Essentials with him. I dislik'd both, but agreed to admit them upon Condition of his adopting the Doctrine of using no animal Food. I doubt, says he, my Constitution will not bear that. I assur'd him it would, and that he would be the better for it. He was usually a great Glutton, and I promis'd myself some Diversion in half-starving him. He agreed to try the Practice if I would keep him Company. I did so and we held it for three Months. We had our Victuals dress'd and brought to us regularly by a Woman in the Neighborhood, who had from me a List of 40 Dishes to be prepar'd for us at different times, in all which there was neither Fish Flesh nor Fowl, and the Whim suited me the better at this time from the Cheapness of it, not costing us about 18 Pence Sterling each, per Week. I have since kept several Lents most strictly, leaving the common Diet for that, and that for the common, abruptly, without the least Inconvenience: So that I think there is little in the Advice of making those Changes by easy Gradations. I went on pleasantly, but Poor Keimer suffer'd grievously, tir'd of the Project, long'd for the Flesh Pots of Egypt, and order'd a roast Pig.[2] He invited me and two Women Friends to dine with him, but it being brought too soon upon table, he could not resist the Temptation, and ate it all up before we came.

I had made some Courtship during this time to Miss Read. I had a great Respect and Affection for her, and had some Reason to believe she had the same for me: but as I was about to take a long Voyage, and we were both very young, only a little above 18, it was thought most prudent by her Mother to prevent our going too far at present, as a Marriage if it was to take place would be more convenient after my Return, when I should be as I expected set up in my Business. Perhaps too she thought my Expectations not so well founded as I imagined them to be.

My chief Acquaintances at this time were, Charles Osborne, Joseph Watson, and James Ralph;[3] All Lovers of Reading. The two first were Clerks to an eminent Scrivener or Conveyancer in the Town, Charles Brockden; the other was Clerk to a Merchant. Watson was a pious sensible young Man, of great integrity. The others rather more lax in their Principles of Religion, particularly Ralph, who as well as Collins had been unsettled by me, for which they both made me suffer. Osborne was sensible, candid, frank, sincere, and affectionate to his Friends; but in literary Matters too fond of Criticizing. Ralph, was ingenious, genteel in his Manners, and extremely eloquent; I think I never knew a prettier Talker. Both of them great Admirers of Poetry, and began to try their Hands in little Pieces. Many pleasant Walks we four had together, on Sundays into the Woods near Skuylkill,[4] where we read to one another and conferr'd on what we read. Ralph was

1. "Ye shall not round the corners of your heads, neither shalt thou mar the corners of thy beard" (Leviticus 19.27). Keimer probably also wore his hair long. "Mosaic Law": ancient law as revealed to the prophet Moses and set out in the first five books of the Old Testament.
2. "And the whole congregation of the children of Israel murmured against Moses and [the prophet] Aaron in the wilderness: And the children of Israel said unto them, Would to God we had died by the hand of the Lord in the land of Egypt, when we sat by the flesh pots, and when we did eat bread to the full" (Exodus 16.2–3).
3. Brockden (1683–1769) arrived in Philadelphia in 1706. "Conveyancer": one who draws up leases and deeds.
4. A river at Philadelphia.

inclin'd to pursue the Study of Poetry, not doubting but he might become eminent in it and make his Fortune by it, alledging that the best Poets must when they first began to write, make as many Faults as he did. Osborne dissuaded him, assur'd him he had no Genius for Poetry, and advis'd him to think of nothing beyond the Business he was bred to; that in the mercantile way tho' he had no Stock, he might by his Diligence and Punctuality recommend himself to Employment as a Factor,[5] and in time acquire wherewith to trade on his own Account. I approv'd the amusing oneself with Poetry now and then, so far as to improve one's Language, but no farther. On this it was propos'd that we should each of us at our next Meeting produce a Piece of our own Composing, in order to improve by our mutual Observations, Criticisms and Corrections. As Language and Expression was what we had in View, we excluded all Considerations of Invention,[6] by agreeing that the Task should be a Version of the 18th Psalm, which describes the Descent of a Deity.[7] When the Time of our Meeting drew nigh, Ralph call'd on me first, and let me know his Piece was ready. I told him I had been busy, and having little Inclination had done nothing. He then show'd me his Piece for my Opinion; and I much approv'd it, as it appear'd to me to have great Merit. Now, says he, Osborne never will allow the least Merit in any thing of mine, but makes 1000 Criticisms out of mere Envy. He is not so jealous of you. I wish therefore you would take this Piece, and produce it as yours. I will pretend not to have had time, and so produce nothing. We shall then see what he will say to it. It was agreed, and I immediately transcrib'd it that it might appear in my own hand. We met.

Watson's Performance was read: there were some Beauties in it: but many Defects. Osborne's was read: It was much better. Ralph did it Justice, remark'd some Faults, but applauded the Beauties. He himself had nothing to produce. I was backward, seem'd desirous of being excus'd, had not had sufficient Time to correct; etc., but no Excuse could be admitted, produce I must. It was read and repeated; Watson and Osborne gave up the Contest; and join'd in applauding it immoderately. Ralph only made some Criticisms and propos'd some Amendments, but I defended my Text. Osborne was against Ralph, and told him he was no better a Critic than Poet; so he dropped the Argument. As they two went home together, Osborne express'd himself still more strongly in favor of what he thought my Production, having restrain'd himself before as he said, lest I should think it Flattery. But who would have imagin'd, says he, that Franklin had been capable of such a Performance; such Painting, such Force! such Fire! He has even improv'd the Original! In his common Conversation, he seems to have no Choice of Words; he hesitates and blunders; and yet, good God, how he writes!

When we next met, Ralph discover'd the Trick we had played him, and Osborne was a little laughed at. This Transaction fix'd Ralph in his Resolution of becoming a Poet. I did all I could to dissuade him from it, but he continu'd scribbling Verses, till *Pope* cur'd him. He became however a pretty

5. Business agent.
6. I.e., of originality.

7. "He bowed the heavens also, and came down: and darkness was under his feet" (Psalm 18.9).

good Prose Writer.[8] More of him hereafter. But as I may not have occasion again to mention the other two, I shall just remark here, that Watson died in my Arms a few Years after,[9] much lamented, being the best of our Set. Osborne went to the West Indies, where he became an eminent Lawyer and made Money, but died young.[1] He and I had made a serious Agreement, that the one who happen'd first to die, should if possible make a friendly Visit to the other, and acquaint him how he found things in that separate State. But he never fulfill'd his Promise.

The Governor, seeming to like my Company, had me frequently to his House; and his Setting me up was always mention'd as a fix'd thing. I was to take with me Letters recommendatory to a Number of his Friends, besides the Letter of Credit to furnish me with the necessary Money for purchasing the Press and Types, Paper, etc. For these Letters I was appointed to call at different times, when they were to be ready, but a future time was still[2] named. Thus we went on till the ship whose Departure too had been several times postponed was on the Point of sailing. Then when I call'd to take my Leave and receive the Letters, his Secretary, Dr. Bard,[3] came out to me and said the Governor was extremely busy, in writing, but would be down at New Castle before the Ship, and there the Letters would be delivered to me.

Ralph, tho' married and having one Child, had determined to accompany me in this Voyage. It was thought he intended to establish a Correspondence, and obtain Goods to sell on Commission. But I found afterwards, that thro' some Discontent with his Wife's Relations, he purposed to leave her on their Hands, and never return again. Having taken leave of my Friends, and interchang'd some Promises with Miss Read, I left Philadelphia in the Ship, which anchor'd at New Castle. The Governor was there. But when I went to his Lodging, the Secretary came to me from him with the civilest Message in the World, that he could not then see me being engag'd in Business of the utmost Importance, but should send the Letters to me on board, wish'd me heartily a good Voyage and a speedy Return, etc. I return'd on board, a little puzzled, but still not doubting.

Mr. Andrew Hamilton, a famous Lawyer of Philadelphia, had taken Passage in the same Ship for himself and Son: and with Mr. Denham a Quaker Merchant,[4] and Messrs. Onion and Russel Masters of an Iron Work in Maryland, had engag'd the Great Cabin; so that Ralph and I were forc'd to take up with a Berth in the Steerage: And none on board knowing us, were considered as ordinary Persons. But Mr. Hamilton and his Son (it was James, since

8. Ralph (c. 1705–1762) became a well-known political journalist after trying his hand at poetry. In the second edition of the *Dunciad* (1728), a poem that attacks ignorance of all kinds, Alexander Pope (see n. 3, p. 478) responded to the slur against him in Ralph's poem *Sawney*. Pope wrote: "Silence, ye Wolves: while Ralph to Cynthia howls. / And makes Night hideous— Answer him ye Owls" (book 3, lines 159–60). In the 1742 edition, Pope included another dig at Ralph: "And see: The very Gazeteers give o'er, / Ev'n Ralph repents" (book 1, lines 215–16).
9. About 1728.
1. Osborne's dates are unknown.
2. Always.

3. Patrick Bard, or Baird, resided in Philadelphia as port physician after 1720.
4. Thomas Denham (d. 1728), merchant and benefactor, left Bristol, England, in 1715. In 1735, Andrew Hamilton (c. 1676–1741), a Scottish-born lawyer who lived in Philadelphia, successfully defended a newspaper publisher against a libel charge, establishing a precedent for freedom of the press in the colonies and earning the nickname "the Philadelphia lawyer" (now a catchphrase meaning an extremely competent lawyer). Hamilton's son James (c. 1710–1783) served as governor of Pennsylvania four times between 1748 and 1773.

Governor) return'd from New Castle to Philadelphia the Father being recall'd by a great Fee to plead for a seized Ship. And just before we sail'd Colonel French coming on board, and showing me great Respect, I was more taken Notice of, and with my Friend Ralph invited by the other Gentlemen to come into the Cabin, there being now Room. Accordingly we remov'd thither.

Understanding that Colonel French had brought on board the Governor's Dispatches, I ask'd the Captain for those Letters that were to be under my Care. He said all were put into the Bag together; and he could not then come at them; but before we landed in England, I should have an Opportunity of picking them out. So I was satisfied for the present, and we proceeded on our Voyage. We had a sociable Company in the Cabin, and lived uncommonly well, having the Addition of all Mr. Hamilton's Stores, who had laid in plentifully. In this Passage Mr. Denham contracted a Friendship for me that continued during his Life. The Voyage was otherwise not a pleasant one, as we had a great deal of bad Weather.

When we came into the Channel, the Captain kept his Word with me, and gave me an Opportunity of examining the Bag for the Governor's Letters. I found none upon which my Name was put, as under my Care; I pick'd out 6 or 7 that by the Handwriting I thought might be the promis'd Letters, especially as one of them was directed to Basket[5] the King's Printer, and another to some Stationer. We arriv'd in London the 24th of December, 1724. I waited upon the Stationer who came first in my Way, delivering the Letter as from Governor Keith. I don't know such a Person, says he: but opening the Letter, O, this is from Riddlesden,[6] I have lately found him to be a complete Rascal, and I will have nothing to do with him, nor receive any Letters from him. So putting the Letter into my Hand, he turn'd on his Heel and left me to serve some Customer. I was surprised to find these were not the Governor's Letters. And after recollecting and comparing Circumstances, I began to doubt his Sincerity. I found my Friend Denham, and opened the whole Affair to him. He let me into Keith's Character, told me there was not the least Probability that he had written any Letters for me, that no one who knew him had the smallest Dependence on him, and he laughed at the Notion of the Governor's giving me a Letter of Credit, having as he said no Credit to give. On my expressing some Concern about what I should do: He advis'd me to endeavor getting some Employment in the Way of my Business. Among the Printers here, says he, you will improve yourself; and when you return to America, you will set up to greater Advantage.

We both of us happen'd to know, as well as the Stationer, that Riddlesden the Attorney, was a very Knave. He had half ruin'd Miss Read's Father by drawing him in to be bound[7] for him. By his Letter it appear'd, there was a secret Scheme on foot to the Prejudice of Hamilton, (Suppos'd to be then coming over with us,) and that Keith was concern'd in it with Riddlesden. Denham, who was a Friend of Hamilton's, thought he ought to be acquainted with it. So when he arriv'd in England, which was soon after, partly from Resentment and Ill-Will to Keith and Riddlesden, and partly from Goodwill to him: I waited on him, and gave him the Letter. He thank'd me cordially,

5. John Baskett (d. 1742).
6. William Riddlesden (d. before 1733), well known in Maryland as a man of "infamy."

7. I.e., as a cosigner of a document and legally bound to be responsible for his debts.

the Information being of Importance to him. And from that time he became my Friend, greatly to my Advantage afterwards on many Occasions.

But what shall we think of a Governor's playing such pitiful Tricks, and imposing so grossly on a poor ignorant Boy! It was a Habit he had acquired. He wish'd to please everybody; and having little to give, he gave Expectations. He was otherwise an ingenious sensible Man, a pretty good Writer, and a good Governor for the People, tho' not for his Constituents the Proprietaries,[8] whose Instructions he sometimes disregarded. Several of our best Laws were of his Planning, and pass'd during his Administration.

Ralph and I were inseparable Companions. We took Lodgings together in Little Britain[9] at 3 shillings 6 pence per Week, as much as we could then afford. He found some Relations, but they were poor and unable to assist him. He now let me know his Intentions of remaining in London, and that he never meant to return to Philadelphia. He had brought no Money with him, the whole he could muster having been expended in paying his Passage. I had 15 Pistoles.[1] So he borrowed occasionally of me, to subsist while he was looking out for Business. He first endeavor'd to get into the Playhouse, believing himself qualified for an Actor; but Wilkes,[2] to whom he applied, advis'd him candidly not to think of that Employment, as it was impossible he should succeed in it. Then he propos'd to Roberts, a Publisher in Paternoster Row,[3] to write for him a Weekly Paper like the Spectator, on certain Conditions, which Roberts did not approve. Then he endeavor'd to get Employment as a Hackney Writer to copy for the Stationers and Lawyers about the Temple[4] but could find no Vacancy.

I immediately got into Work at Palmer's, then a famous Printing-House in Bartholomew Close;[5] and here I continu'd near a Year. I was pretty diligent; but spent with Ralph a good deal of my Earnings in going to Plays and other Places of Amusement. We had together consum'd all my Pistoles, and now just rubb'd on[6] from hand to mouth. He seem'd quite to forget his Wife and Child, and I by degrees my Engagements with Miss Read, to whom I never wrote more than one Letter, and that was to let her know I was not likely soon to return. This was another of the great Errata of my Life, which I should wish to correct if I were to live it over again. In fact, by our Expenses, I was constantly kept unable to pay my Passage.

At Palmer's I was employ'd in Composing for the second Edition of Wollaston's Religion of Nature.[7] Some of his Reasonings not appearing to me well-founded, I wrote a little metaphysical Piece, in which I made Remarks on them. It was entitled, *A Dissertation on Liberty and Necessity, Pleasure and Pain.* I inscrib'd it to my Friend Ralph. I printed a small Number. I occasion'd my being more consider'd by Mr. Palmer, as a young Man of some

8. Members of the Penn family, headed by William Penn (1644–1718), were the proprietors of Pennsylvania and its legal owners. "Constituents": those who appointed him their representative; in this case, the Penn family, which retained control of Pennsylvania until the Revolution.
9. A street in London near St. Paul's Cathedral.
1. Gold coins.
2. Robert Wilks (1665?–1732), an Irish actor, dominated London theater life from 1709 to 1730.
3. The center of the London printing business.

4. The Inner and Middle Temples were buildings in London that were centers for the legal profession. "Hackney Writer": copyist.
5. Just off Little Britain; a square known for its printers and typesetters.
6. Proceeded with difficulty.
7. The English philosopher William Wollaston's *Religion of Nature Delineated* was first printed privately in 1722. Its second edition (1724) sold so well that Franklin was here setting the type for a third edition (1725), not "the second edition."

Ingenuity, tho' he seriously expostulated with me upon the Principles of my Pamplet which to him appear'd abominable.[8] My printing this Pamphlet was another Erratum.

While I lodg'd in Little Britain I made an Acquaintance with one Wilcox a Bookseller, whose Shop was at the next Door. He had an immense Collection of second-hand Books. Circulating Libraries were not then in Use; but we agreed that on certain reasonable Terms which I have now forgotten, I might take, read and return any of his Books. This I esteem'd a great Advantage, and I made as much Use of it as I could.

My Pamphlet by some means falling into the Hands of one Lyons,[9] a Surgeon, Author of a Book entitled *The Infallibility of Human Judgment*, it occasioned an Acquaintance between us; he took great Notice of me, call'd on me often, to converse on these Subjects, carried me to the Horns a pale Ale-House in [blank] Lane, Cheapside, and introduc'd me to Dr. Mandeville, Author of the Fable of the Bees[1] who had a Club there, of which he was the Soul, being a most facetious entertaining Companion. Lyons too introduc'd me to Dr. Pemberton, at Batson's Coffee House, who promis'd to give me an Opportunity some time or other of seeing Sir Isaac Newton,[2] of which I was extremely desirous; but this never happened.

I had brought over a few Curiosities among which the principal was a Purse made of the Asbestos, which purifies by Fire. Sir Hans Sloane heard of it, came to see me, and invited me to his House in Bloomsbury Square; where he show'd me all his Curiosities,[3] and persuaded me to let him add that to the Number, for which he paid me handsomely.

In our House there lodg'd a young Woman, a Millener, who I think had a shop in the Cloisters.[4] She had been genteelly bred, was sensible and lively, and of most pleasing Conversation. Ralph read Plays to her in the Evenings, they grew intimate, she took another Lodging, and he follow'd her. They liv'd together some time, but he being still out of Business, and her Income not sufficient to maintain them with her Child, he took a Resolution of going from London, to try for a Country School, which he thought himself well qualified to undertake, as he wrote an excellent Hand, and was a Master of Arithmetic and Accounts. This however he deem'd a Business below him, and confident of future better Fortune when he should be unwilling to have it known that he once was so meanly employ'd, he chang'd his Name, and did me the Honor to assume mine. For I soon after had a Letter from him, acquainting me, that he was settled in a small Village in Berkshire, I think it was, where he taught reading and writing to 10 or a dozen Boys at 6 pence each per Week, recommending Mrs. T. to my Care, and desiring me to write to him directing for Mr. Franklin Schoolmaster at such a Place. He continu'd

8. By denying the existence of virtue and vice, Franklin opened himself to accusations of atheism.
9. William Lyons, a surgeon and author of *The Infallibility, Dignity, and Excellence of Human Judgment* (1719).
1. Bernard Mandeville (c. 1670–1733), a Dutch physician and man of letters residing in London, published *The Fable of the Bees* in 1723.
2. English mathematician and physicist (1642–1727), best known for formulating theories of gravity, light, and color. Newton was president of

the Royal Society, the British national academy of science, from 1703 to 1727. Henry Pemberton was a friend of Newton's and a member of the Society. Batson's, in Cornhill, was a favorite meeting place of physicians.
3. Sloane (1660–1753), a physician and naturalist, succeeded Newton as president of the Royal Society. His library and museum served as the basis for the present collection at the British Museum.
4. Probably near St. Bartholomew's Church, London.

to write frequently, sending me large Specimens of an Epic Poem, which he was then composing, and desiring my Remarks and Corrections. These I gave him from time to time, but endeavor'd rather to discourage his Proceeding. One of Young's Satires was then just publish'd.[5] I copied and sent him a great Part of it, which set in a strong Light the Folly of pursuing the Muses with any Hope of Advancement by them. All was in vain. Sheets of the Poem continu'd to come by every Post. In the mean time Mrs. T. having on his Account lost her Friends and Business, was often in Distresses, and us'd to send for me, and borrow what I could spare to help her out of them. I grew fond of her Company, and being at this time under no Religious Restraints, and presuming on my Importance to her, I attempted Familiarities, (another Erratum) which she repuls'd with a proper Resentment, and acquainted him with my Behavior. This made a Breach between us, and when he return'd again to London, he let me know he thought I had cancel'd all the Obligations he had been under to me. So I found I was never to expect his Repaying me what I lent to him or advanc'd for him. This was however not then of much Consequence, as he was totally unable. And in the Loss of his Friendship I found myself reliev'd from a Burden. I now began to think of getting a little Money beforehand; and expecting better Work, I left Palmer's to work at Watts's[6] near Lincoln's Inn Fields, a still greater Printing-House. Here I continu'd all the rest of my Stay in London.

At my first Admission into this Printing-House, I took to working at Press, imagining I felt a Want of the Bodily Exercise I had been us'd to in America, where Presswork is mix'd with Composing.[7] I drank only Water; the other Workmen, near 50 in Number, were great Guzzlers of Beer. On occasion I carried up and down Stairs a large Form of Types[8] in each hand, when others carried but one in both Hands. They wonder'd to see from this and several Instances that the Water-American as they call'd me was *stronger* than themselves who drunk *strong*[9] Beer. We had an Alehouse Boy who attended always in the House to supply the Workmen. My Companion at the Press drank every day a Pint before Breakfast, a Pint at Breakfast with his Bread and Cheese; a Pint between Breakfast and Dinner; a Pint at Dinner; a Pint in the Afternoon about Six o'clock, and another when he had done his Day's Work. I thought it a detestable Custom. But it was necessary, he suppos'd, to drink *strong* Beer that he might be *strong* to labor. I endeavor'd to convince him that the Bodily Strength afforded by Beer could only be in proportion to the Grain or Flour of the Barley dissolved in the Water of which it was made; that there was more Flour in a Penny-worth of Bread, and therefore if he would eat that with a Pint of Water, it would give him more Strength than a Quart of Beer. He drank on however, and had 4 or 5 Shillings to pay out of his Wages every Saturday Night for that muddling Liquor; an Expense I was free from. And thus these poor Devils keep themselves always under.[1]

Watts after some Weeks desiring to have me in the Composing-Room, I left the Pressmen. A new *Bienvenu*[2] or Sum for Drink, being 5 Shillings,

5. The English poet Edward Young (1683–1765) published the first four parts of *Love of Fame, the Universal Passion* in 1725.
6. Press belonging to John Watts (c. 1678–1763).
7. I.e., the workers do both the printing and

typesetting for it.
8. Type set and locked in metal frames.
9. With high alcohol content.
1. I.e., in poverty.
2. Welcome (French, literal trans.).

was demanded of me by the Compositors.[3] I thought it an Imposition, as I had paid below. The Master thought so too, and forbad my Paying it. I stood out two or three Weeks, was accordingly considered as an Excommunicate, and had so many little Pieces of private Mischief done me, by mixing my Sorts, transposing my Pages, breaking my Matter,[4] etc., etc. if I were ever so little out of the Room, and all ascrib'd to the Chapel[5] Ghost, which they said ever haunted those not regularly admitted, that notwithstanding the Master's Protection, I found myself oblig'd to comply and pay the Money; convinc'd of the Folly of being on ill Terms with those one is to live with continually. I was now on a fair Footing with them, and soon acquir'd considerable Influence. I propos'd some reasonable Alterations in their Chapel Laws, and carried them against all Opposition. From my Example a great Part of them, left their muddling Breakfast of Beer and Bread and Cheese, finding they could with me be supplied from a neighboring House with a large Porringer of hot Water-gruel, sprinkled with Pepper, crumb'd with Bread, and a Bit of Butter in it, for the Price of a Pint of Beer, viz., three halfpence. This was a more comfortable as well as cheaper Breakfast, and kept their Heads clearer. Those who continu'd sotting with Beer all day, were often, by not paying, out of Credit at the Alehouse, and us'd to make Interest with me to get Beer, *their Light,* as they phras'd it, *being out.* I watch'd the Pay table on Saturday Night, and collected what I stood engag'd for them, having to pay some times near Thirty Shillings a Week on their Accounts. This and my being esteem'd a pretty good Riggite,[6] that is a jocular verbal Satirist, supported my Consequence in the Society. My constant Attendance, (I never making a St. Monday),[7] recommended me to the Master; and my uncommon Quickness at Composing, occasion'd my being put upon all Work of Dispatch, which was generally better paid. So I went on now very agreeably.

My Lodging in Little Britain being too remote, I found another in Duke Street opposite to the Romish Chapel.[8] It was two pair of Stairs backwards at an Italian Warehouse. A Widow Lady kept the House; she had a Daughter and a Maid Servant, and a Journeyman who attended the Warehouse, but lodg'd abroad. After sending to enquire my Character at the House where I last lodg'd, she agreed to take me in at the same Rate, 3 Shillings 6 Pence per Week, cheaper as she said from the Protection she expected in having a Man lodge in the House. She was a Widow, an elderly Woman, had been bred a Protestant, being a Clergyman's Daughter, but was converted to the Catholic Religion by her Husband, whose Memory she much revered, had lived much among People of Distinction, and knew a 1000 Anecdotes of them as far back as the Times of Charles the second. She was lame in her Knees with the Gout, and therefore seldom stirr'd out of her Room, so sometimes wanted Company; and hers was so highly amusing to me that I was sure to spend an Evening with her whenever she desired it. Our Supper was only half an Anchovy each, on a very little Strip of Bread and Butter, and

3. Typesetters. The workers set their own customs, practices, and fines.
4. Type set up for printing. "Sorts": type, letters.
5. "A Printing House is always called a Chapel by the Workmen" [Franklin's note].

6. One who makes fun of others.
7. Taking Monday off as if it were a religious holiday.
8. The Roman Catholic Chapel of St. Anselm and St. Cecilia.

half a Pint of Ale between us. But the Entertainment was in her Conversation. My always keeping good Hours, and giving little Trouble in the Family, made her unwilling to part with me; so that when I talk'd of a Lodging I had heard of, nearer my Business, for 2 Shillings a Week, which, intent as I now was on saving Money, made some Difference; she bid me not think of it, for she would abate me two Shillings a Week for the future, so I remain'd with her at 1 Shilling 6 Pence as long as I stayed in London.

In a Garret of her House there lived a Maiden Lady of 70 in the most retired Manner, of whom my Landlady gave me this Account, that she was a Roman Catholic, had been sent abroad when young and lodg'd in a Nunnery with an Intent of becoming a Nun: but the Country not agreeing with her, she return'd to England, where there being no Nunnery, she had vow'd to lead the Life of a Nun as near as might be done in those Circumstances: Accordingly She had given all her Estate to charitable Uses, reserving only Twelve Pounds a year to live on, and out of this Sum she still gave a great deal in Charity, living herself on Watergruel only, and using no Fire but to boil it. She had lived many Years in that Garret, being permitted to remain there gratis by successive catholic Tenants of the House below, as they deem'd it a Blessing to have her there. A Priest visited her, to confess her every Day. I have ask'd her, says my Landlady, how she, as she liv'd, could possibly find so much Employment for a Confessor? O, says she, it is impossible to avoid *vain Thoughts*. I was permitted once to visit her: She was cheerful and polite, and convers'd pleasantly. The Room was clean, but had no other Furniture than a Mattress, a Table with a Crucifix and Book, a Stool, which she gave me to sit on, and a Picture over the Chimney of *St. Veronica*, displaying her Handkerchief with the miraculous Figure of Christ's bleeding Face on it,[9] which she explain'd to me with great Seriousness. She look'd pale, but was never sick, and I give it as another Instance on how small an Income Life and Health may be supported.

At Watts's Printing-House I contracted an Acquaintance with an ingenious young Man, one Wygate, who having wealthy Relations, had been better educated than most Printers, was a tolerable Latinist, spoke French, and lov'd Reading. I taught him, and a Friend of his, to swim at twice going into the River, and they soon became good Swimmers. They introduc'd me to some Gentlemen from the Country who went to Chelsea by Water to see the College and Don Saltero's Curiosities.[1] In our Return, at the Request of the Company, whose Curiosity Wygate had excited, I stripped and leaped into the River, and swam from near Chelsea to Blackfriars,[2] performing on the Way many Feats of Activity both upon and under Water, that surpris'd and pleas'd those to whom they were Novelties. I had from a Child been ever delighted with this Exercise, had studied and practic'd all Thevenot's Motions and Positions,[3] added some of my own, aiming at the graceful and easy, as well as the Useful. All these I took this Occasion of exhibiting to the

9. According to tradition, as Christ bore the Cross, St. Veronica wiped his face with a cloth that miraculously retained the image of his face.
1. I.e., the cabinets of curiosities in Don Saltero's, a coffeehouse in London's Chelsea district. "Don Saltero" was James Salter, a former servant of Sir Hans Sloane to whom Sloane had given many objects from his collection. "College": i.e., Chelsea Hospital, erected on the site of the former Chelsea College.
2. I.e., more than three miles.
3. I.e., in Melchisédech de Thevenot's *The Art of Swimming* (1699).

Company, and was much flatter'd by their Admiration. And Wygate, who was desirous of becoming a Master, grew more and more attach'd to me on that account, as well as from the Similarity of our Studies. He at length propos'd to me traveling all over Europe together, supporting ourselves every where by working at our Business. I was once inclin'd to it. But mentioning it to my good Friend Mr. Denham, with whom I often spent an Hour when I had Leisure, he dissuaded me from it; advising me to think only of returning to Pennsylvania, which he was now about to do.

I must record one Trait of this good Man's Character. He had formerly been in Business at Bristol, but fail'd in Debt to a Number of People, compounded[4] and went to America. There, by a close Application to Business as a Merchant, he acquir'd a plentiful Fortune in a few Years. Returning to England in the Ship with me, He invited his old Creditors to an Entertainment, at which he thank'd them for the easy Composition[5] they had favor'd him with, and when they expected nothing but the Treat, every Man at the first Remove[6] found under his Plate an Order on a Banker for the full Amount of the unpaid Remainder with Interest.

He now told me he was about to return to Philadelphia, and should carry over a great Quantity of Goods in order to open a Store there: He propos'd to take me over as his Clerk, to keep his Books (in which he would instruct me), copy his Letters, and attend the Store. He added, that as soon as I should be acquainted with mercantile Business he would promote me by sending me with a Cargo of Flour and Bread, etc., to the West Indies, and procure me Commissions from others; which would be profitable, and if I manag'd well, would establish me handsomely. The Thing pleas'd me, for I was grown tired of London, remember'd with Pleasure the happy Months I had spent in Pennsylvania, and wish'd again to see it. Therefore I immediately agreed, on the Terms of Fifty Pounds a Year, Pennsylvania Money; less indeed than my then Gettings as a Compositor, but affording a better Prospect.

I now took Leave of Printing, as I thought for ever, and was daily employ'd in my new Business; going about with Mr. Denham among the Tradesmen, to purchase various Articles, and see them pack'd up, doing Errands, calling upon Workmen to dispatch, etc., and when all was on board, I had a few Days' Leisure. On one of these Days I was to my Surprise sent for by a great Man I knew only by Name, a Sir William Wyndham and I waited upon him. He had heard by some means or other of my Swimming from Chelsey to Blackfriars, and of my teaching Wygate and another young Man to swim in a few Hours. He had two Sons about to set out on their Travels; he wish'd to have them first taught Swimming; and propos'd to gratify me handsomely if I would teach them. They were not yet come to Town and my Stay was uncertain, so I could not undertake it. But from this Incident I thought it likely, that if I were to remain in England and open a Swimming School, I might get a good deal of Money. And it struck me so strongly, that had the Overture been sooner made me, probably I should not so soon have returned to America. After Many Years, you and I had something of more Importance

4. Settled part payment on his debts.
5. Conditions for accepting a declaration of bankruptcy.
6. I.e., the first time the plates were cleared.

to do with one of these Sons of Sir William Wyndham,[7] become Earl of Egre-mont, which I shall mention in its Place.

Thus I spent about 18 Months in London. Most Part of the Time, I work'd hard at my Business, and spent but little upon myself except in seeing Plays, and in Books. My Friend Ralph had kept me poor. He owed me about 27 Pounds; which I was now never likely to receive; a great Sum out of my small Earnings. I lov'd him notwithstanding, for he had many amiable Qualities. Tho' I had by no means improv'd my Fortune, I had pick'd up some very ingenious Acquaintance whose Conversation was of great Advantage to me, and I had read considerably.

We sail'd from Gravesend on the 23d of July 1726. For The Incidents of the Voyage, I refer you to my Journal, where you will find them all minutely related. Perhaps the most important Part of that Journal is the *Plan*[8] to be found in it which I formed at Sea for regulating my future Conduct in Life. It is the more remarkable, as being form'd when I was so young, and yet being pretty faithfully adhered to quite thro' to old Age. We landed in Philadel-phia the 11th of October, where I found sundry Alterations. Keith was no longer Governor, being superseded by Major Gordon:[9] I met him walking the Streets as a common Citizen. He seem'd a little asham'd at seeing me, but pass'd without saying anything. I should have been as much asham'd at seeing Miss Read, had not her Friends despairing with Reason of my Return, after the Receipt of my Letter, persuaded her to marry another, one Rogers, a Potter, which was done in my Absence. With him however she was never happy, and soon parted from him, refusing to cohabit with him, or bear his Name. It being now said that he had another Wife. He was a worthless Fel-low tho' an excellent Workman which was the Temptation to her Friends. He got into Debt, and ran away in 1727 or 28, went to the West Indies, and died there. Keimer had got a better House, a Shop well supplied with Stationery, plenty of new Types, a number of Hands tho' none good, and seem'd to have a great deal of Business.

Mr. Denham took a Store in Water Street, where we open'd our Goods. I attended the Business diligently, studied Accounts, and grew in a little Time expert at selling. We lodg'd and boarded together, he counsel'd me as a Father, having a sincere Regard for me: I respected and lov'd him: and we might have gone on together very happily: But in the Beginning of February 1726/7 when I had just pass'd my 21st Year, we both were taken ill. My Dis-temper was a Pleurisy, which very nearly carried me off: I suffered a good deal, gave up the Point[1] in my own mind, and was rather disappointed when I found myself recovering; regretting in some degree that I must now some-time or other have all that disagreeable Work to do over again. I forget what his Distemper was. It held him a long time, and at length carried him off. He left me a small Legacy in a nuncupative[2] Will, as a Token of his Kind-ness for me, and he left me once more to the wide World. For the Store was taken into the Care of his Executors, and my Employment under him ended:

7. Franklin does not mention Charles Wyndham (1710–1763) again. Charles's father, Sir William (1687–1740), was an English statesman and Member of Parliament.
8. Only the outline and preamble of Franklin's *Plan* survive.
9. Patrick Gordon (1644–1736), deputy gover-nor of Pennsylvania from 1726 to 1736.
1. End; i.e., resigned himself to death.
2. Oral.

My Brother-in-law Homes, being now at Philadelphia, advis'd my Return to my Business. And Keimer tempted me with an Offer of large Wages by the Year to come and take the Management of his Printing-House that he might better attend his Stationer's Shop. I had heard a bad Character of him in London, from his Wife and her Friends, and was not fond of having any more to do with him. I tried for farther Employment as a Merchant's Clerk; but not readily meeting with any, I clos'd again with Keimer.

I found in *his* House these Hands; Hugh Meredith[3] a Welsh-Pennsylvanian, 30 Years of Age, bred to Country Work: honest, sensible, had a great deal of solid Observation, was something of a Reader, but given to drink: Stephen Potts,[4] a young Country Man of full Age, bred to the Same, of uncommon natural Parts[5] and great Wit and Humor, but a little idle. These he had agreed with at extreme low Wages, per Week, to be rais'd a Shilling every 3 Months, as they would deserve by improving in their Business, and the Expectation of these high Wages to come on hereafter was what he had drawn them in with. Meredith was to work at Press, Potts at Bookbinding, which he by Agreement, was to teach them, tho' he knew neither one nor t'other. John————a wild Irishman brought up to no Business, whose Service for 4 Years Keimer had purchas'd from the Captain of a Ship.[6] He too was to be made a Pressman. George Webb,[7] an Oxford Scholar, whose Time for 4 Years he had likewise bought, intending him for a Compositor: of whom more presently. And David Harry,[8] a Country Boy, whom he had taken Apprentice. I soon perceiv'd that the Intention of engaging me at Wages so much higher than he had been us'd to give, was to have these raw cheap Hands form'd thro' me, and as soon as I had instructed them, then, they being all articled to him, he should be able to do without me. I went on however, very cheerfully; put his Printing-House in Order, which had been in great Confusion, and brought his Hands by degrees to mind their Business and to do it better.

It was an odd Thing to find an Oxford Scholar in the Situation of a bought Servant. He was not more than 18 Years of Age, and gave me this Account of himself; that he was born in Gloucester, educated at a Grammar School there, had been distinguish'd among the Scholars for some apparent Superiority in performing his Part when they exhibited Plays; belong'd to the Witty Club there, and had written some Pieces in Prose and Verse which were printed in the Gloucester Newspapers. Thence he was sent to Oxford; there he continu'd about a Year, but not well-satisfied, wishing of all things to see London and become a Player.[9] At length receiving his Quarterly Allowance of 15 Guineas,[1] instead of discharging his Debts, he walk'd out of Town, hid his Gown in a Furz Bush, and footed it to London, where having no Friend to advise him, he fell into bad Company, soon spent his Guineas, found no means of being introduc'd among the Players,[2] grew necessitous,

3. Meredith (c. 1696–1749) was later a business partner of Franklin's.
4. Potts (d. 1758) was later a bookseller and an innkeeper.
5. I.e., handsome.
6. I.e., Keimer had paid for the Irishman's passage in exchange for his service.
7. Webb (1708–1736?) was later a member of Franklin's Junto (a small, select club for mutual improvement) and a printer.

8. A Welsh Quaker (1708–1760); later the first printer in Barbados.
9. Actor.
1. An evergreen shrub; gorse. "Gown": academic robe worn regularly by Oxford students. "15 Guineas": almost sixteen pounds.
2. An advertisement for free passage to the colonies for those who would work as indentured servants.

pawn'd his Clothes and wanted Bread. Walking the Street very hungry, and not knowing what to do with himself, a Crimp's Bill was put into his Hand, offering immediate Entertainment and Encouragement to such as would bind themselves to serve in America. He went directly, sign'd the Indentures, was put into the Ship and came over; never writing a Line to acquaint his Friends what was become of him. He was lively, witty, good-natur'd and a pleasant Companion, but idle, thoughtless and imprudent to the last Degree.

John the Irishman soon ran away. With the rest I began to live very agreeably; for they all respected me, the more as they found Keimer incapable of instructing them, and that from me they learned something daily. We never work'd on a Saturday, that being Keimer's Sabbath. So I had two Days for Reading. My Acquaintance with ingenious People in the Town increased. Keimer himself treated me with great Civility and apparent Regard; and nothing now made me uneasy but my Debt to Vernon, which I was yet unable to pay, being hitherto but a poor Economist. He however kindly made no Demand of it.

Our Printing-House often wanted Sorts, and there was no Letter Founder[3] in America. I had seen Types cast at James's[4] in London, but without much Attention to the Manner: However I now contriv'd a Mold, made use of the Letters we had as Puncheons, struck the Matrices[5] in Lead, and thus supplied in a pretty tolerable way all Deficiencies. I also engrav'd several Things on occasion. I made the Ink, I was Warehouse-man and everything, in short quite a Factotum.[6]

But however serviceable I might be, I found that my Services became every Day of less Importance, as the other Hands improv'd in the Business. And when Keimer paid my second Quarter's Wages, he let me know that he felt them too heavy, and thought I should make an Abatement. He grew by degrees less civil, put on more of the Master, frequently found Fault, was captious and seem'd ready for an Out-breaking. I went on nevertheless with a good deal of Patience, thinking that his encumber'd Circumstances were partly the Cause. At length a Trifle snapped our Connection. For a great Noise happening near the Courthouse, I put my Head out of the Window to see what was the Matter. Keimer being in the Street look'd up and saw me, call'd out to me in a loud Voice and angry Tone to mind my Business, adding some reproachful Words, that nettled me the more for their Publicity, all the Neighbors who were looking out on the same Occasion being Witnesses how I was treated. He came up immediately into the Printing-House, continu'd the Quarrel, high Words pass'd on both Sides, he gave me the Quarter's Warning we had stipulated, expressing a Wish that he had not been oblig'd to so long a Warning: I told him his Wish was unnecessary for I would leave him that Instant; and so taking my Hat walk'd out of Doors; desiring Meredith whom I saw below to take care of some Things I left, and bring them to my Lodging.

Meredith came accordingly in the Evening, when we talk'd my Affair over. He had conceiv'd a great Regard for me, and was very unwilling that I should leave the House while he remain'd in it. He dissuaded me from returning to

3. Foundry for type (sorts).
4. Thomas James's foundry.
5. Molds for casting type. "Puncheons": stamp-
ing tools.
6. Jack-of-all-trades.

my native Country[7] which I began to think of. He reminded me that Keimer was in debt for all he possess'd, that his Creditors began to be uneasy, that he kept his Shop miserably, sold often without Profit for ready Money, and often trusted without keeping Account. That he must therefore fail; which would make a Vacancy I might profit of. I objected my Want of Money. He then let me know, that his Father had a high Opinion of me, and from some Discourse that had pass'd between them, he was sure would advance Money to set us up, if I would enter into Partnership with him. My Time, says he, will be out with Keimer in the Spring. By that time we may have our Press and Types in from London: I am sensible I am no Workman. If you like it, Your Skill in the Business shall be set against the Stock I furnish; and we will share the Profits equally. The Proposal was agreeable, and I consented. His Father was in Town, and approv'd of it, the more as he saw I had great Influence with his Son, had prevail'd on him to abstain long from Dram-drinking, and he hop'd might break him of that wretched Habit entirely, when we came to be so closely connected. I gave an Inventory to the Father, who carried it to a Merchant; the Things were sent for; the Secret was to be kept till they should arrive, and in the mean time I was to get Work if I could at the other Printing-House. But I found no Vacancy there, and so remain'd idle a few Days, when Keimer, on a Prospect of being employ'd to print some Paper-money, in New Jersey, which would require Cuts and various Types that I only could supply, and apprehending Bradford might engage me and get the Job from him, sent me a very civil Message, that old Friends should not part for a few Words, the Effect of sudden Passion, and wishing me to return. Meredith persuaded me to comply, as it would give more Opportunity for his Improvement under my daily Instructions. So I return'd, and we went on more smoothly than for some time before. The New Jersey Job was obtain'd. I contriv'd a Copper-Plate Press for it, the first that had been seen in the Country. I cut several Ornaments and Checks for the Bills. We went together to Burlington,[8] where I executed the Whole to Satisfaction, and he received so large a Sum for the Work, as to be enabled thereby to keep his Head much longer above Water.

At Burlington I made an Acquaintance with many principal People of the Province. Several of them had been appointed by the Assembly a Committee to attend the Press, and take Care that no more Bills were printed than the Law directed. They were therefore by Turns constantly with us, and generally he who attended brought with him a Friend or two for Company. My Mind having been much more improv'd by Reading than Keimer's, I suppose it was for that Reason my Conversation seem'd to be more valu'd. They had me to their Houses, introduc'd me to their Friends and show'd me much Civility, while he, tho' the Master, was a little neglected. In truth he was an odd Fish, ignorant of common Life, fond of rudely opposing receiv'd Opinions, slovenly to extreme dirtiness, enthusiastic[9] in some Points of Religion, and a little Knavish withal. We continu'd there near 3 Months, and by that time I could reckon among my acquired Friends, Judge Allen, Samuel Bustill, the Secretary of the Province, Isaac Pearson, Joseph Cooper and

7. I.e., Boston.
8. City in New Jersey.

9. Highly emotional.

several of the Smiths, Members of Assembly, and Isaac Decow the Surveyor General. The latter was a shrewd sagacious old Man, who told me that he began for himself when young by wheeling Clay for the Brickmakers, learned to write after he was of Age, carried the Chain for Surveyors, who taught him Surveying, and he had now by his Industry acquir'd a good Estate; and says he, I foresee, that you will soon work this Man out of his Business and make a Fortune in it at Philadelphia. He had not then the least Intimation of my Intention to set up there or anywhere. These Friends were afterwards of great Use to me, as I occasionally was to some of them. They all continued their Regard for me as long as they lived.

Before I enter upon my public Appearance in Business, it may be well to let you know the then State of my Mind, with regard to my Principles and Morals, that you may see how far those influenc'd the future Events of my Life. My Parents had early given me religious Impressions, and brought me through my Childhood piously in the Dissenting Way.[1] But I was scarce 15 when, after doubting by turns of several Points as I found them disputed in the different Books I read, I began to doubt of Revelation itself. Some Books against Deism fell into my Hands; they were said to be the Substance of Sermons preached at Boyle's Lectures.[2] It happened that they wrought an Effect on me quite contrary to what was intended by them: For the Arguments of the Deists which were quoted to be refuted, appeared to me much Stronger than the Refutations. In short I soon became a thorough Deist. My Arguments perverted some others, particularly Collins and Ralph: but each of them having afterwards wrong'd me greatly without the least Compunction, and recollecting Keith's Conduct towards me, (who was another Freethinker) and my own towards Vernon and Miss Read which at Times gave me great Trouble, I began to suspect that this Doctrine tho' it might be true, was not very useful. My London pamphlet, which had for its Motto those Lines of Dryden

> ——Whatever is, is right
> Tho' purblind Man Sees but a Part of
> The Chain, the nearest Link,
> His Eyes not carrying to the equal Beam,
> That poizes all, above.[3]

And from the Attributes of God, his infinite Wisdom, Goodness and Power concluded that nothing could possibly be wrong in the World, and that Vice and Virtue were empty Distinctions, no such Things existing: appear'd now not so clever a Performance as I once thought it; and I doubted whether some Error had not insinuated itself unperceiv'd into my Argument, so as to infect all that follow'd, as is common in metaphysical Reasonings. I grew convinc'd that *Truth, Sincerity* and *Integrity* in Dealings between Man and Man, were of the utmost Importance to the Felicity of Life, and I form'd written

1. I.e., in the Congregational or Presbyterian way, as opposed to the Church of England way.
2. Robert Boyle (1627–1691), English physicist and chemist, endowed a series of lectures for discussing the existence of God and preaching against "infidels." Deism accepts a supreme being as the author of finite existence, but denies Chris-

tian doctrines of revelation and supernaturalism.
3. The first line is not from the English poet John Dryden (1631–1700) but from Alexander Pope's *Essay on Man* Epistle I, line 294; however, Dryden's line is close: "Whatever is, is in its Causes just." The rest of these lines are recalled accurately from Dryden's *Oedipus* (3.1.244–48).

Resolutions, (which still remain in my Journal Book) to practice them ever while I lived. Revelation had indeed no weight with me as such; but I entertain'd an Opinion, that tho' certain Actions might not be bad *because* they were forbidden by it, or good *because* it commanded them; yet probably those Actions might be forbidden *because* they were bad for us, or commanded *because* they were beneficial to us, in their own Natures, all the Circumstances of things considered. And this Persuasion, with the kind hand of Providence, or some guardian Angel, or accidental favorable Circumstances and Situations, or all together, preserved me (thro' this dangerous Time of Youth and the hazardous Situations I was sometimes in among Strangers, remote from the Eye and Advice of my Father) without any *willful* gross Immorality or Injustice that might have been expected from my Want of Religion. I say *willful*, because the Instances I have mentioned, had something of *Necessity* in them, from my Youth, Inexperience, and the Knavery of others. I had therefore a tolerable Character to begin the World with, I valued it properly, and determin'd to preserve it.

We had not been long return'd to Philadelphia, before the New Types arriv'd from London. We settled with Keimer, and left him by his Consent before he heard of it. We found a House to hire near the Market, and took it. To lessen the Rent, (which was then but 24 Pounds a Year tho' I have since known it let for 70) we took in Thomas Godfrey a Glazier,[4] and his Family, who were to pay a considerable Part of it to us, and we to board with them. We had scarce opened our Letters and put our Press in Order, before George House, an Acquaintance of mine, brought a Countryman to us; whom he had met in the Street enquiring for a Printer. All our Cash was now expended in the Variety of Particulars we had been obliged to procure, and this Countryman's Five Shillings, being our First Fruits and coming so seasonably, gave me more Pleasure than any Crown[5] I have since earn'd; and from the Gratitude I felt towards House, has made me often more ready than perhaps I should otherwise have been to assist young Beginners.

There are Croakers in every Country always boding its Ruin. Such a one then lived in Philadelphia, a Person of Note, an elderly Man, with a wise Look and very grave Manner of Speaking. His Name was Samuel Mickle. This Gentleman, a Stranger to me, stopped one Day at my Door, and ask'd me if I was the young Man who had lately opened a new Printing-House: Being answer'd in the Affirmative; He said he was sorry for me; because it was an expensive Undertaking, and the Expense would be lost, for Philadelphia was a sinking[6] Place, the People already half Bankrupts or near being so; all Appearances of the contrary such as new Buildings and the Rise of Rents, being to his certain Knowledge fallacious, for they were in fact among the Things that would soon ruin us. And he gave me such a Detail of Misfortunes now existing or that were soon to exist, that he left me half-melancholy. Had I known him before I engag'd in this Business, probably I never should have done it. This Man continu'd to live in this decaying Place, and to declaim in the same Strain, refusing for many Years to buy a House there, because all was going to Destruction, and at last I had the Pleasure

4. Godfrey (1704–1749) set glass for window-panes. He was also an optician and inventor.

5. A coin worth five shillings.

6. Economically declining.

of seeing him give five times as much for one as he might have bought it for when he first began his Croaking.

I should have mention'd before, that in the Autumn of the preceding Year, I had form'd most of my ingenious Acquaintance into a Club, for mutual Improvement, which we call'd the Junto. We met on Friday Evenings. The Rules I drew up, requir'd that every Member in his Turn should produce one or more Queries on any Point of Morals, Politics or Natural Philosophy, to be discuss'd by the Company, and once in three Months produce and read an Essay of his own Writing on any Subject he pleased. Our Debates were to be under the Direction of a President, and to be conducted in the sincere Spirit of Enquiry after Truth, without fondness for Dispute, or Desire of Victory; and to prevent Warmth, all expressions of Positiveness[7] in Opinion, or of direct Contradiction, were after some time made contraband and prohibited under small pecuniary Penalties. The first Members were, Joseph Breintnall, a Copier of Deeds for the Scriveners; a good-natur'd friendly middle-ag'd Man, a great Lover of Poetry, reading all he could meet with, and writing some that was tolerable; very ingenious in many little Nicknackeries, and of sensible Conversation.[8] Thomas Godfrey, a self-taught Mathematician, great in his Way, and afterwards Inventor of what is now call'd Hadley's Quadrant.[9] But he knew little out of his way, and was not a pleasing Companion, as like most Great Mathematicians I have met with, he expected unusual Precision in everything said, or was forever denying or distinguishing upon Trifles, to the Disturbance of all Conversation. He soon left us. Nicholas Scull,[1] a Surveyor, afterwards Surveyor-General, Who lov'd Books, and sometimes made a few Verses. William Parsons, bred a Shoemaker, but loving Reading, had acquir'd a considerable Share of Mathematics, which he first studied with a View to Astrology that he afterwards laughed at. He also became Surveyor General.[2] William Maugridge, a Joiner,[3] and a most exquisite Mechanic, and a solid sensible Man. Hugh Meredith, Stephen Potts, and George Webb, I have Characteris'd before. Robert Grace,[4] a young Gentleman of some Fortune, generous, lively and witty, a Lover of Punning and of his Friends. And William Coleman, then a Merchant's Clerk, about my Age, who had the coolest clearest Head, the best Heart, and the exactest Morals, of almost any Man I ever met with. He became afterwards a Merchant of great Note, and one of our Provincial Judges: Our Friendship continued without Interruption to his Death, upwards of 40 Years.[5] And the Club continu'd almost as long and was the best School of Philosophy, Morals and Politics that then existed in the Province; for our Queries which were read the Week preceding their Discussion, put us on reading with Attention upon the several Subjects, that we might speak more to the purpose: and here too we acquired better Habits of Conversation, everything being studied in our Rules which might prevent our disgusting each other. From hence the long Continuance of the Club, which I shall have

7. Certainty. "Warmth": anger.
8. Breintnall (d. 1746) shared Franklin's interest in science.
9. Godfrey invented this instrument for measuring altitudes in navigation and astronomy—also known as the octant—around the same time as the English inventor John Hadley (1682–1744) did.

1. Nicholas Scull II (1687–1761).
2. Parsons (1701–1757) became surveyor general in 1741 and librarian of the Library Company— the first subscription library in North America, an offshoot of the Junto.
3. A ship's carpenter (d. 1766).
4. Franklin's landlord for thirty-seven years.
5. Coleman lived from 1704 to 1769.

frequent Occasion to speak farther of hereafter; But my giving this Account of it here, is to show something of the Interest I had, everyone of these exerting themselves in recommending Business to us.

Breintnall particularly procur'd us from the Quakers, the Printing 40 Sheets of their History, the rest being to be done by Keimer: and upon this we work'd exceeding hard, for the Price was low. It was a Folio, Pro Patria Size, in Pica with Long Primer Notes.[6] I compos'd of it a Sheet a Day, and Meredith work'd it off at Press. It was often 11 at Night and sometimes later, before I had finish'd my Distribution[7] for the next day's Work: For the little Jobs sent in by our other Friends now and then put us back. But so determin'd I was to continue doing a Sheet a Day of the Folio, that one Night when having impos'd my Forms,[8] I thought my Day's Work over, one of them by accident was broken and two Pages reduc'd to Pie,[9] I immediately distributed and compos'd it over again before I went to bed. And this Industry visible to our Neighbors began to give us Character and Credit; particularly I was told, that mention being made of the new Printing Office at the Merchants' Every-night-Club, the general Opinion was that it must fail, there being already two Printers in the Place, Keimer and Bradford; but Doctor Baird (whom you and I saw many Years after at his native Place, St. Andrews in Scotland) gave a contrary Opinion; for the Industry of that Franklin, says he, is superior to anything I ever saw of the kind: I see him still at work when I go home from Club; and he is at Work again before his Neighbors are out of bed. This struck the rest, and we soon after had Offers from one of them to supply us with Stationery. But as yet we did not choose to engage in Shop Business.

I mention this Industry the more particularly and the more freely, tho' it seems to be talking in my own Praise, that those of my Posterity who shall read it, may know the Use of that Virtue, when they see its Effects in my Favor throughout this Relation.

George Webb, who had found a Friend that lent him wherewith to purchase his Time of Keimer, now came to offer himself as a Journeyman to us. We could not then employ him, but I foolishly let him know, as a Secret, that I soon intended to begin a Newspaper, and might then have Work for him. My Hopes of Success as I told him were founded on this, that the then only Newspaper,[1] printed by Bradford was a paltry thing, wretchedly manag'd, no way entertaining; and yet was profitable to him. I therefore thought a good Paper could scarcely fail of good Encouragement. I requested Webb not to mention it, but he told it to Keimer, who immediately, to be beforehand with me, published Proposals for Printing one himself, on which Webb was to be employ'd. I resented this, and to counteract them, as I could not yet begin our Paper, I wrote several Pieces of Entertainment for Bradford's Paper, under the Title of the Busy Body which Breintnall continu'd some Months.[2] By this means the Attention of the Public was fix'd on that Paper, and

6. A book, of large size, with the main text in twelve-point type and the notes in ten-point type.
7. I.e., of type, returning letters to their cases so they may be used again.
8. Locked the type into its form and readied it for printing.
9. A confused pile.
1. The *American Weekly Mercury*.
2. From February 4, 1728, to September 25, 1729.

Keimer's Proposals which we burlesqu'd and ridicul'd, were disregarded. He began his Paper however, and after carrying it on three Quarters of a Year, with at most only 90 Subscribers, he offer'd it to me for a Trifle, and I having been ready some time to go on with it, took it in hand directly, and it prov'd in a few Years extremely profitable to me.[3]

I perceive that I am apt to speak in the singular Number, though our Partnership still continu'd. The Reason may be, that in fact the whole Management of the Business lay upon me. Meredith was no Compositor, a poor Pressman, and seldom sober. My Friends lamented my Connection with him, but I was to make the best of it.

Our first Papers made a quite different Appearance from any before in the Province, a better Type and better printed: but some spirited Remarks of my Writing on the Dispute then going on between Governor Burnet[4] and the Massachusetts Assembly, struck the principal People, occasion'd the Paper and the Manager of it to be much talk'd of, and in a few Weeks brought them all to be our Subscribers. Their Example was follow'd by many, and our Number went on growing continually. This was one of the first good Effects of my having learned a little to scribble. Another was, that the leading Men, seeing a Newspaper now in the hands of one who could also handle a Pen, thought it convenient to oblige and encourage me. Bradford still printed the Votes and Laws and other Public Business. He had printed an Address of the House[5] to the Governor in a coarse blundering manner; We reprinted it elegantly and correctly, and sent one to every Member. They were sensible of the Difference, it strengthen'd the Hands of our Friends in the House, and they voted us their Printers for the Year ensuing.

Among my Friends in the House I must not forget Mr. Hamilton before-mentioned,[6] who was then returned from England and had a Seat in it. He interested himself[7] for me strongly in that Instance, as he did in many others afterwards, continuing his Patronage till his Death. Mr. Vernon about this time put me in mind of the Debt I ow'd him: but did not press me. I wrote him an ingenuous Letter of Acknowledgments, crav'd his Forbearance a little longer which he allow'd me, and as soon as I was able I paid the Principal with Interest and many Thanks. So that Erratum was in some degree corrected.

But now another Difficulty came upon me, which I had never the least Reason to expect. Mr. Meredith's Father, who was to have paid for our Printing-House according to the Expectations given me, was able to advance only one Hundred Pounds, Currency, which had been paid, and a Hundred more was due to the Merchant; who grew impatient and su'd us all. We gave Bail, but saw that if the Money could not be rais'd in time, the Suit must come to a Judgment and Execution, and our hopeful Prospects must with us be ruined, as the Press and Letters must be sold for Payment, perhaps at half-Price. In this Distress two true Friends whose Kindness I have never

3. Franklin took over Keimer's *The Universal Instructor in All Arts and Sciences: and Pennsylvania Gazette* in October 1729 and shortened the name to the *Pennsylvania Gazette*.
4. See n. 2, p. 488.
5. I.e., the Pennsylvania Assembly.

6. See n. 4, p. 493.
7. "I got his Son once £500" [Franklin's note]. Franklin was able to get the legislature to pay Governor James Hamilton his salary when they were at odds with him.

forgotten nor ever shall forget while I can remember anything, came to me separately unknown to each other, and without any Application from me, offering each of them to advance me all the Money that should be necessary to enable me to take the whole Business upon myself if that should be practicable, but they did not like my continuing the Partnership with Meredith, who as they said was often seen drunk in the Streets, and playing at low Games in Alehouses, much to our Discredit. These two Friends were *William Coleman* and *Robert Grace*.

I told them I could not propose a Separation while any Prospect remain'd of the Merediths fulfilling their Part of our Agreement. Because I thought myself under great Obligations to them for what they had done and would do if they could. But if they finally fail'd in their Performance, and our Partnership must be dissolv'd, I should then think myself at Liberty to accept the Assistance of my Friends. Thus the matter rested for some time. When I said to my Partner, perhaps your Father is dissatisfied at the Part you have undertaken in this Affair of ours, and is unwilling to advance for you and me what he would for you alone: If that is the Case, tell me, and I will resign the whole to you and go about my Business. No—says he, my Father has really been disappointed and is really unable; and I am unwilling to distress him farther. I see this is a Business I am not fit for. I was bred a Farmer, and it was a Folly in me to come to Town and put myself at 30 Years of Age an Apprentice to learn a new Trade. Many of our Welsh People are going to settle in North Carolina where Land is cheap: I am inclin'd to go with them, and follow my old Employment. You may find Friends to assist you. If you will take the Debts of the Company upon you, return to my Father the hundred Pound he has advanc'd, pay my little personal Debts, and give me Thirty Pounds and a new Saddle, I will relinquish the Partnership and leave the whole in your Hands. I agreed to this Proposal. It was drawn up in Writing, sign'd and seal'd immediately. I gave him what he demanded and he went soon after to Carolina; from whence he sent me next Year two long Letters, containing the best Account that had been given of that Country, the Climate, Soil, Husbandry, etc., for in those Matters he was very judicious. I printed them in the Papers,[8] and they gave great Satisfaction to the Public.

As soon as he was gone, I recurr'd to my two Friends; and because I would not give an unkind Preference to either, I took half what each had offered and I wanted, of one, and half of the other; paid off the Company Debts, and went on with the Business in my own Name, advertising that the Partnership was dissolved. I think this was in or about the Year 1729.[9]

About this Time there was a Cry among the People for more Paper-Money, only 15,000 Pounds being extant in the Province and that soon to be sunk.[1] The wealthy Inhabitants oppos'd any Addition, being against all Paper Currency, from an Apprehension that it would depreciate as it had done in New England to the Prejudice of all Creditors. We had discuss'd this Point in our

8. In the *Pennsylvania Gazette*, May 6 and 13, 1732.
9. More accurately, July 14, 1730.
1. Destroyed. In 1723, paper money had become so scarce that the Assembly issued new money secured by real estate mortgages; when the mortgages were paid off, the bills were "sunk." But by 1729, the value of the currency was so low that the money was recalled before the mortgages were paid.

Junto, where I was on the Side of an Addition, being persuaded that the first small Sum struck in 1723 had done much good, by increasing the Trade, Employment, and Number of Inhabitants in the Province, since I now saw all the old Houses inhabited, and many new ones building, where as I remember'd well, that when I first walk'd about the Streets of Philadelphia, eating my Roll, I saw most of the Houses in Walnut Street between Second and Front Streets with Bills[2] on their Doors, to be let; and many likewise in Chestnut Street, and other Streets; which made me then think the Inhabitants of the City were one after another deserting it. Our Debates possess'd me so fully of the Subject, that I wrote and printed an anonymous Pamphlet on it, entitled, *The Nature and Necessity of a Paper Currency.*[3] It was well receiv'd by the common People in general; but the Rich Men dislik'd it; for it increas'd and strengthen'd the Clamor for more Money; and they happening to have no Writers among them that were able to answer it, their Opposition slacken'd, and the Point was carried by a Majority in the House. My Friends there, who conceiv'd I had been of some Service, thought fit to reward me, by employing me in printing the Money,[4] a very profitable Job, and a great Help to me. This was another Advantage gain'd by my being able to write. The Utility of this Currency became by Time and Experience so evident, as never afterwards to be much disputed, so that it grew soon to 55,000 Pounds, and in 1739 to 80,000 Pounds, since which it arose during War to upwards of 350,000 Pounds—Trade, Building and Inhabitants all the while increasing. Tho' I now think there are Limits beyond which the Quantity may be hurtful.

I soon after obtain'd, thro' my Friend Hamilton, the Printing of the New Castle Paper Money,[5] another profitable Job, as I then thought it; small Things appearing great to those in small Circumstances. And these to me were really great Advantages, as they were great Encouragements. He procured me also the Printing of the Laws and Votes of that Government which continu'd in my Hands as long as I follow'd the Business.

I now open'd a little Stationer's Shop.[6] I had in it Blanks of all Sorts the correctest that ever appear'd among us, being assisted in that by my Friend Breintnall; I had also Paper, Parchment, Chapmen's Books,[7] etc. One Whitmarsh a Compositor I had known in London, an excellent Workman now came to me and work'd with me constantly and diligently,[8] and I took an Apprentice the Son of Aquila Rose. I began now gradually to pay off the Debt I was under for the Printing-House. In order to secure my Credit and Character as a Tradesman, I took care not only to be in *Reality* Industrious and frugal, but to avoid all *Appearances* of the contrary. I dressed plainly; I was seen at no Places of idle Diversion; I never went out a-fishing or shooting; a Book, indeed, sometimes debauch'd me from my Work; but that was seldom, snug, and gave no Scandal: and to show that I was not above my Business, I sometimes brought home the Paper I purchas'd at the Stores, thro' the Streets on a Wheelbarrow. Thus being esteem'd an industrious thriving

2. Signs.
3. *A Modest Inquiry into the Nature and Necessity of a Paper Currency* (April 3, 1729).
4. Franklin received the contract to print money in 1731.
5. I.e., for Delaware, which had a separate legislature but the same proprietary governor as Pennsylvania.
6. In July 1730.
7. Inexpensive paper pamphlets.
8. Thomas Whitmarsh (d. 1733) moved to South Carolina the next year.

young Man, and paying duly for what I bought, the Merchants who imported Stationery solicited my Custom, others propos'd supplying me with Books, and I went on swimmingly. In the mean time Keimer's Credit and Business declining daily, he was at last forc'd to sell his Printing-House to satisfy his Creditors. He went to Barbados, and there lived some Years, in very poor Circumstances.

His Apprentice David Harry, whom I had instructed while I work'd with him, set up in his Place at Philadelphia, having bought his Materials. I was at first apprehensive of a powerful Rival in Harry, as his Friends were very able, and had a good deal of Interest. I therefore propos'd a Partnership to him; which he, fortunately for me, rejected with Scorn. He was very proud, dress'd like a Gentleman, liv'd expensively, took much Diversion and Pleasure abroad, ran in debt, and neglected his Business, upon which all Business left him; and finding nothing to do, he follow'd Keimer to Barbados; taking the Printing-House with him. There this Apprentice employ'd his former Master as a Journeyman. They quarrel'd often. Harry went continually behind-hand, and at length was forc'd to sell his Types, and return to his Country Work in Pennsylvania. The Person that bought them employ'd Keimer to use them, but in a few years he died. There remain'd now no Competitor with me at Philadelphia, but the old one, Bradford, who was rich and easy, did a little Printing now and then by straggling Hands, but was not very anxious about the Business. However, as he kept the Post Office, it was imagined he had better Opportunities of obtaining News, his Paper was thought a better Distributer of Advertisements than mine, and therefore had many more, which was a profitable thing to him and a Disadvantage to me. For tho' I did indeed receive and send Papers by the Post, yet the public Opinion was otherwise; for what I did send was by Bribing the Riders[9] who took them privately: Bradford being unkind enough to forbid it: which occasion'd some Resentment on my Part; and I thought so meanly of him for it, that when I afterwards came into his Situation,[1] I took care never to imitate it.

I had hitherto continu'd to board with Godfrey who lived in Part of my House with his Wife and Children, and had one Side of the Shop for his Glazier's Business, tho' he work'd little, being always absorb'd in his Mathematics. Mrs. Godfrey projected a Match for me with a Relation's Daughter, took Opportunities of bringing us often together, till a serious Courtship on my Part ensu'd, the Girl being in herself very deserving. The old Folks encourag'd me by continual Invitations to Supper, and by leaving us together, till at length it was time to explain. Mrs. Godfrey manag'd our little Treaty. I let her know that I expected as much Money with their Daughter as would pay off my Remaining Debt for the Printing-House, which I believe was not then above a Hundred Pounds.[2] She brought me Word they had no such Sum to spare. I said they might mortgage their House in the Loan Office. The Answer to this after some Days was, that they did not approve the Match; that on Enquiry of Bradford they had been inform'd the Printing Business

9. I.e., the postal riders, or carriers. Franklin bribed them to have his papers delivered on the same day as Andrew Bradford's.
1. Franklin succeeded Bradford as postmaster of Philadelphia in October 1737.
2. Franklin's expectations were not unusual: marriage arrangements often hinged on agreeable financial considerations.

was not a profitable one, the Types would soon be worn out and more wanted, that S. Keimer and D. Harry had fail'd one after the other, and I should probably soon follow them; and therefore I was forbidden the House, and the Daughter shut up.

Whether this was a real Change of Sentiment, or only Artifice, on a Supposition of our being too far engag'd in Affection to retract, and therefore that we should steal a Marriage, which would leave them at Liberty to give or withhold what they pleas'd, I know not: But I suspected the latter, resented it, and went no more. Mrs. Godfrey brought me afterwards some more favorable Accounts of their Disposition, and would have drawn me on again: But I declared absolutely my Resolution to have nothing more to do with that Family. This was resented by the Godfreys, we differ'd, and they removed, leaving me the whole House, and I resolved to take no more Inmates. But this Affair having turn'd my Thoughts to Marriage, I look'd round me, and made Overtures of Acquaintance in other Places; but soon found that the Business of a Printer being generally thought a poor one, I was not to expect Money with a Wife unless with such a one, as I should not otherwise think agreeable. In the mean time, that hard-to-be-govern'd Passion of Youth, had hurried me frequently into Intrigues with low Women that fell in my Way, which were attended with some Expense and great Inconvenience, besides a continual Risk to my Health by a Distemper[3] which of all Things I dreaded, tho' by great good Luck I escaped it.

A friendly Correspondence as Neighbors and old Acquaintances, had continued between me and Mrs. Read's Family who all had a Regard for me from the time of my first Lodging in their House. I was often invited there and consulted in their Affairs, wherein I sometimes was of Service. I pitied poor Miss Read's unfortunate Situation, who was generally dejected, seldom cheerful, and avoided Company. I consider'd my Giddiness and Inconstancy when in London as in a great degree the Cause of her Unhappiness; tho' the Mother was good enough to think the Fault more her own than mine, as she had prevented our Marrying before I went thither, and persuaded the other Match in my Absence. Our mutual Affection was revived, but there were now great Objections to our Union. That Match was indeed look'd upon as invalid, a preceding Wife being said to be living in England; but this could not easily be prov'd, because of the Distance, etc. And tho' there was a Report of his Death, it was not certain. Then, tho' it should be true, he had left many Debts which his Successor might be call'd upon to pay. We ventured however, over all these Difficulties, and I took her to Wife Sept. 1, 1730.[4] None of the Inconveniencies happened that we had apprehended, she prov'd a good and faithful Helpmate, assisted me much by attending the Shop, we throve together, and have ever mutually endeavor'd to make each other happy. Thus I corrected that great Erratum as well as I could.

About this Time our Club meeting, not at a Tavern, but in a little Room of Mr. Grace's set apart for that Purpose; a Proposition was made by me, that since our Books were often referr'd to in our Disquisitions upon the Queries, it might be convenient to us to have them all together where we

3. I.e., syphilis.
4. Because there was no proof that John Rogers, Deborah Read's first husband, was dead, she and Franklin entered into a common-law marriage without civil ceremony.

met, that upon Occasion they might be consulted; and by thus clubbing our Books to a common Library, we should, while we lik'd to keep them together, have each of us the Advantage of using the Books of all the other Members, which would be nearly as beneficial as if each owned the whole. It was lik'd and agreed to, and we fill'd one End of the Room with such Books as we could best spare. The Number was not so great as we expected; and tho' they had been of great Use, yet some Inconveniencies occurring for want of due Care of them, the Collection after about a Year was separated, and each took his Books home again.

And now I set on foot my first Project of a public Nature, that for a Subscription Library. I drew up the Proposals, got them put into Form by our great Scrivener Brockden, and by the help of my Friends in the Junto, procur'd Fifty Subscribers of 40 Shillings each to begin with and 10 Shillings a Year for 50 Years, the Term our Company was to continue. We afterwards obtain'd a Charter, the Company being increas'd to 100. This was the Mother of all the North American Subscription Libraries now so numerous. It is become a great thing itself, and continually increasing. These Libraries have improv'd the general Conversation of the Americans, made the common Tradesmen and Farmers as intelligent as most Gentlemen from other Countries, and perhaps have contributed in some degree to the Stand so generally made throughout the Colonies in Defense of their Privileges.

Memo.

Thus far was written with the Intention express'd in the Beginning and therefore contains several little family Anecdotes of no Importance to others. What follows was written many Years after in compliance with the Advice contain'd in these Letters, and accordingly intended for the Public. The Affairs of the Revolution occasion'd the Interruption.

[Part Two][1]

LETTER FROM MR. ABEL JAMES,[2] WITH NOTES ON MY LIFE, (RECEIVED IN PARIS)

My dear and honored Friend.

I have often been desirous of writing to thee, but could not be reconciled to the Thought that the Letter might fall into the Hands of the British,[3] lest some Printer or busy Body should publish some Part of the Contents and give our Friends Pain and myself Censure.

Some Time since there fell into my Hands to my great Joy about 23 Sheets in thy own handwriting containing an Account of the Parentage and Life of thyself, directed to thy Son ending in the Year 1730 with which there were Notes[4] likewise in thy writing, a Copy of which I enclose in Hopes it may be a means if thou continuedst it up to a later

1. Franklin wrote the second part of his autobiography at the Hôtel de Valentenois, in Passy, a Paris suburb. He had been sent to Paris as one of the American representatives for the peace treaty that officially ended the war with Britain on September 3, 1783. Franklin remained in Paris until July 1785, when Thomas Jefferson succeeded him as a minister for trade agreements.

2. A Quaker merchant in Philadelphia (c. 1726–1790).
3. James wrote his letter in 1782, when Britain was still at war with the colonies.
4. Franklin's outline for his *Autobiography*, written in 1771; reprinted in the Yale University edition (1964).

period, that the first and latter part may be put together; and if it is not yet continued, I hope thou wilt not delay it. Life is uncertain as the Preacher tells us, and what will the World say if kind, humane and benevolent Ben Franklin should leave his Friends and the World deprived of so pleasing and profitable a Work, a Work which would be useful and entertaining not only to a few, but to millions.

The Influence Writings under that Class have on the Minds of Youth is very great, and has no where appeared so plain as in our public Friends' Journals. It almost insensibly leads the Youth into the Resolution of endeavoring to become as good and as eminent as the Journalist. Should thine for Instance when published, and I think it could not fail of it, lead the Youth to equal the Industry and Temperance of thy early Youth, what a Blessing with that Class would such a Work be. I know of no Character living nor many of them put together, who has so much in his Power as Thyself to promote a greater Spirit of Industry and early Attention to Business, Frugality and Temperance with the American Youth. Not that I think the Work would have no other Merit and Use in the World, far from it, but the first is of such vast Importance, that I know nothing that can equal it.

The foregoing letter and the minutes accompanying it being shown to a friend, I received from him the following:

LETTER FROM MR. BENJAMIN VAUGHAN[5]

MY DEAREST SIR, *Paris, January* 31, 1783.
When I had read over your sheets of minutes of the principal incidents of your life, recovered for you by your Quaker acquaintance; I told you I would send you a letter expressing my reasons why I thought it would be useful to complete and publish it as he desired. Various concerns have for some time past prevented this letter being written, and I do not know whether it was worth any expectation: happening to be at leisure however at present, I shall by writing at least interest and instruct myself; but as the terms I am inclined to use may tend to offend a person of your manners, I shall only tell you how I would address any other person, who was as good and as great as yourself, but less diffident. I would say to him, Sir, I *solicit* the history of your life from the following motives.

Your history is so remarkable, that if you do not give it, somebody else will certainly give it; and perhaps so as nearly to do as much harm, as your own management of the thing might do good.

It will moreover present a table of the internal circumstances of your country, which will very much tend to invite to it settlers of virtuous and manly minds. And considering the eagerness with which such information is sought by them, and the extent of your reputation, I do not know of a more efficacious advertisement than your Biography would give.

5. English politician, the wealthy son (1751–1835) of a West Indies merchant and Maine mother; during the Paris peace talks, unofficial emissary between the British prime minister Lord Shelburne (1737–1805; in office 1782–83) and Franklin.

All that has happened to you is also connected with the detail of the manners and situation of *a rising* people; and in this respect I do not think that the writings of Caesar and Tacitus[6] can be more interesting to a true judge of human nature and society.

But these, Sir, are small reasons in my opinion, compared with the chance which your life will give for the forming of future great men; and in conjunction with your *Art of Virtue*,[7] (which you design to publish) of improving the features of private character, and consequently of aiding all happiness both public and domestic.

The two works I allude to, Sir, will in particular give a noble rule and example of *self-education*. School and other education constantly proceed upon false principles, and show a clumsy apparatus pointed at a false mark; but your apparatus is simple, and the mark a true one; and while parents and young persons are left destitute of other just means of estimating and becoming prepared for a reasonable course in life, your discovery that the thing is in many a man's private power, will be invaluable!

Influence upon the private character late in life, is not only an influence late in life, but a weak influence. It is in *youth* that we plant our chief habits and prejudices; it is in youth that we take our party[8] as to profession, pursuits, and matrimony. In youth therefore the turn is given; in youth the education even of the next generation is given; in youth the private and public character is determined: and the term of life extending from youth to age, life ought to begin well from youth; and more especially *before* we take our party as to our principal objects.

But your Biography will not merely teach self-education, but the education of *a wise man*; and the wisest man will receive lights and improve his progress, by seeing detailed the conduct of another wise man. And why are weaker men to be deprived of such helps, when we see our race has been blundering on in the dark, almost without a guide in this particular, from the farthest trace of time. Show then, Sir, how much is to be done, *both to sons and fathers*; and invite all wise men to become like yourself; and other men to become wise.

When we see how cruel statesmen and warriors can be to the humble race, and how absurd distinguished men can be to their acquaintance, it will be instructive to observe the instances multiply of pacific acquiescing manners; and to find how compatible it is to be great and *domestic*; enviable and yet *good-humored*.

The little private incidents which you will also have to relate, will have considerable use, as we want above all things, *rules of prudence in ordinary affairs*; and it will be curious to see how you have acted in these. It will be so far a sort of key to life, and explain many things that all men ought to have once explained to them, to give them a chance of becoming wise by foresight.

6. The Roman statesman historian Gaius Julius Caesar (100–44 B.C.E.) and Publius Cornelius Tacitus (c. 56 C.E.–c. 120).
7. Vaughan is referring to Franklin's intention to write "a little work for the benefit of youth" to be

called *The Art of Virtue*. Part Two of the *Autobiography* is, in part, a response to Vaughan's reminder.
8. Make our decision.

The nearest thing to having experience of one's own, is to have other people's affairs brought before us in a shape that is interesting; this is sure to happen from your pen. Your affairs and management will have an air of simplicity or importance that will not fail to strike; and I am convinced you have conducted them with as much originality as if you had been conducting discussions in politics or philosophy; and what more worthy of experiments and system, (its importance and its errors considered) than human life!

Some men have been virtuous blindly, others have speculated fantastically, and others have been shrewd to bad purposes; but you, Sir, I am sure, will give under your hand, nothing but what is at the same moment, wise, practical, and good.

Your account of yourself (for I suppose the parallel I am drawing for Dr. Franklin, will hold not only in point of character but of private history), will show that you are ashamed of no origin; a thing the more important, as you prove how little necessary all origin is to happiness, virtue, or greatness.

As no end likewise happens without a means, so we shall find, Sir, that even you yourself framed a plan by which you became considerable; but at the same time we may see that though the event is flattering, the means are as simple as wisdom could make them; that is, depending upon nature, virtue, thought, and habit.

Another thing demonstrated will be the propriety of every man's waiting for his time for appearing upon the stage of the world. Our sensations being very much fixed to the moment, we are apt to forget that more moments are to follow the first, and consequently that man should arrange his conduct so as to suit the *whole* of a life. Your attribution appears to have been applied to your *life,* and the passing moments of it have been enlivened with content and enjoyment, instead of being tormented with foolish impatience or regrets. Such a conduct is easy for those who make virtue and themselves their standard, and who try to keep themselves in countenance by examples of other truly great men, of whom patience is so often the characteristic.

Your Quaker correspondent, Sir (for here again I will suppose the subject of my letter resembling Dr. Franklin,) praised your frugality, diligence, and temperance, which he considered as a pattern for all youth: but it is singular that he should have forgotten your modesty, and your disinterestedness, without which you never could have waited for your advancement, or found your situation in the mean time comfortable; which is a strong lesson to show the poverty of glory, and the importance of regulating our minds.

If this correspondent had known the nature of your reputation as well as I do, he would have said; your former writings and measures would secure attention to your Biography, and Art of Virtue; and your Biography and Art of Virtue, in return, would secure attention to them. This is an advantage attendant upon a various character, and which brings all that belongs to it into greater play; and it is the more useful, as perhaps more persons are at a loss for the *means* of improving their minds and characters, than they are for the time or the inclination to do it.

But there is one concluding reflection, Sir, that will show the use of your life as a mere piece of biography. This style of writing seems a little gone out of vogue, and yet it is a very useful one; and your specimen of it may be particularly serviceable, as it will make a subject of comparison with the lives of various public cut-throats and intriguers, and with absurd monastic self-tormentors, or vain literary triflers. If it encourages more writings of the same kind with your own, and induces more men to spend lives fit to be written; it will be worth all Plutarch's Lives[9] put together.

But being tired of figuring to myself a character of which every feature suits only one man in the world, without giving him the praise of it; I shall end my letter, my dear Dr. Franklin, with a personal application to your proper self.

I am earnestly desirous then, my dear Sir, that you should let the world into the traits of your genuine character, as civil broils may otherwise tend to disguise or traduce it. Considering your great age, the caution of your character, and your peculiar style of thinking, it is not likely that any one besides yourself can be sufficiently master of the facts of your life, or the intentions of your mind.

Besides all this, the immense revolution of the present period, will necessarily turn our attention towards the author of it; and when virtuous principles have been pretended in it, it will be highly important to show that such have really influenced; and, as your own character will be the principal one to receive a scrutiny, it is proper (even for its effects upon your vast and rising country, as well as upon England and upon Europe), that it should stand respectable and eternal. For the furtherance of human happiness, I have always maintained that it is necessary to prove that man is not even at present a vicious and detestable animal; and still more to prove that good management may greatly amend him; and it is for much the same reason, that I am anxious to see the opinion established, that there are fair characters existing among the individuals of the race; for the moment that all men, without exception, shall be conceived abandoned, good people will cease efforts deemed to be hopeless, and perhaps think of taking their share in the scramble of life, or at least of making it comfortable principally for themselves.

Take then, my dear Sir, this work most speedily into hand: show yourself good as you are good, temperate as you are temperate; and above all things, prove yourself as one who from your infancy have loved justice, liberty, and concord, in a way that has made it natural and consistent for you to have acted, as we have seen you act in the last seventeen years of your life. Let Englishmen be made not only to respect, but even to love you. When they think well of individuals in your native country, they will go nearer to thinking well of your country; and when your countrymen see themselves well thought of by Englishmen, they will go nearer to thinking well of England. Extend your views even further; do not stop at those who speak the English tongue, but after having settled so many points in nature and politics, think of bettering the whole race of men.

9. See 1st n. 7, p. 474.

As I have not read any part of the life in question, but know only the character that lived it, I write somewhat at hazard. I am sure however, that the life, and the treatise I allude to (on the *Art of Virtue*), will necessarily fullfil the chief of my expectations; and still more so if you take up the measure of suiting these performances to the several views above stated. Should they even prove unsuccessful in all that a sanguine admirer of yours hopes from them, you will at least have framed pieces to interest the human mind; and whoever gives a feeling of pleasure that is innocent to man, has added so much to the fair side of a life otherwise too much darkened by anxiety, and too much injured by pain.

In the hope therefore that you will listen to the prayer addressed to you in this letter, I beg to subscribe myself, my dearest Sir, etc., etc.

Signed BENJ. VAUGHAN.

CONTINUATION OF THE ACCOUNT OF MY LIFE.
BEGUN AT PASSY, 1784

It is some time since I receiv'd the above Letters, but I have been too busy till now to think of complying with the Request they contain. It might too be much better done if I were at home among my Papers, which would aid my Memory, and help to ascertain Dates. But my Return being uncertain, and having just now a little Leisure, I will endeavor to recollect and write what I can; if I live to get home, it may there be corrected and improv'd.

Not having any Copy here of what is already written, I know not whether an Account is given of the means I used to establish the Philadelphia public Library, which from a small Beginning is now become so considerable, though I remember to have come down to near the Time of that Transaction, 1730. I will therefore begin here, with an Account of it, which may be struck out if found to have been already given.

At the time I establish'd myself in Pennsylvania, there was not a good Bookseller's Shop in any of the Colonies to the Southward of Boston. In New York and Philadelphia the Printers were indeed Stationers, they sold only Paper, etc., Almanacs, Ballads, and a few common School Books. Those who lov'd Reading were oblig'd to send for their Books from England. The Members of the Junto had each a few. We had left the Alehouse where we first met, and hired a Room to hold our Club in. I propos'd that we should all of us bring our Books to that Room, where they would not only be ready to consult in our Conferences, but become a common Benefit, each of us being at Liberty to borrow such as he wish'd to read at home. This was accordingly done, and for some time contented us. Finding the Advantage of this little Collection, I propos'd to render the Benefit from Books more common by commencing a Public Subscription Library. I drew a Sketch of the Plan and Rules that would be necessary, and got a skillful Conveyancer Mr. Charles Brockden[1] to put the whole in Form of Articles of Agreement to be subscribed, by which each Subscriber engag'd to pay a certain Sum down for the first Purchase of Books and an annual Contribution for increasing them.

1. Philadelphia's leading drafter of legal documents (1683–1769). "Conveyancer": an attorney who specializes in the transfer of real estate and property.

So few were the Readers at that time in Philadelphia, and the Majority of us so poor, that I was not able with great Industry to find more than Fifty Persons, mostly young Tradesmen, willing to pay down for this purpose Forty shillings each, and Ten Shillings per Annum. On this little Fund we began. The Books were imported. The Library was open one Day in the Week for lending them to the Subscribers, on their Promissory Notes to pay Double the Value if not duly returned. The Institution soon manifested its Utility, was imitated by other Towns and in other Provinces, the Libraries were augmented by Donations, Reading became fashionable, and our People having no public Amusements to divert their Attention from Study became better acquainted with Books, and in a few Years were observ'd by Strangers to be better instructed and more intelligent than People of the same Rank generally are in other Countries.

When we were about to sign the above-mentioned Articles, which were to be binding on us, our Heirs, etc., for fifty Years, Mr. Brockden, the Scrivener, said to us, "You are young Men, but it is scarce probable that any of you will live to see the Expiration of the Term fix'd in this Instrument." A Number of us, however, are yet living: But the Instrument was after a few Years rendered null by a Charter that incorporated and gave Perpetuity to the Company.

The Objections, and Reluctances I met with in Soliciting the Subscriptions, made me soon feel the Impropriety of presenting oneself as the Proposer of any useful Project that might be suppos'd to raise one's Reputation in the smallest degree above that of one's Neighbors, when one has need of their Assistance to accomplish that Project. I therefore put myself as much as I could out of sight, and stated it as a Scheme of *a Number of Friends,* who had requested me to go about and propose it to such as they thought Lovers of Reading. In this way my Affair went on more smoothly, and I ever after practic'd it on such Occasions; and from my frequent Successes, can heartily recommend it. The present little Sacrifice of your Vanity will afterwards be amply repaid. If it remains a while uncertain to whom the Merit belongs, someone more vain than yourself will be encourag'd to claim it, and then even Envy will be dispos'd to do you Justice, by plucking those assum'd Feathers, and restoring them to their right Owner.

This Library afforded me the Means of Improvement by constant Study, for which I set apart an Hour or two each Day; and thus repair'd in some Degree the Loss of the Learned Education my Father once intended for me. Reading was the only Amusement I allow'd myself. I spent no time in Taverns, Games, or Frolics of any kind. And my Industry in my Business continu'd as indefatigable as it was necessary. I was in debt for my Printing-House, I had a young Family[2] coming on to be educated, and I had to contend with for Business two Printers who were establish'd in the Place before me. My Circumstances however grew daily easier: my original Habits of Frugality continuing. And My Father having among his Instructions to me when a Boy, frequently repeated a Proverb of Solomon, *"Seest thou a Man diligent in his Calling, he shall stand before Kings, he shall not stand before mean Men."*[3] I from thence consider'd Industry as a Means of obtaining Wealth

2. Franklin had three children: William, born c. 1731; Francis, born in 1732; and Sarah, born in 1743.
3. Proverbs 22.29.

and Distinction, which encourag'd me: tho' I did not think that I should ever literally stand before Kings, which however has since happened; for I have stood before five,[4] and even had the honor of sitting down with one, the King of Denmark, to Dinner.

We have an English Proverb that says,

> He that would thrive
> Must ask his Wife,[5]

it was lucky for me that I had one as much dispos'd to Industry and Frugality as myself. She assisted me cheerfully in my Business, folding and stitching Pamphlets, tending Shop, purchasing old Linen Rags for the Paper-makers, etc., etc. We kept no idle Servants, our Table was plain and simple, our Furniture of the cheapest. For instance my Breakfast was a long time Bread and Milk, (no Tea,) and I ate it out of a two penny earthen Porringer[6] with a Pewter Spoon. But mark how Luxury will enter Families, and make a Progress, in Spite of Principle. Being Call'd one Morning to Breakfast, I found it in a China[7] Bowl with a Spoon of Silver. They had been bought for me without my Knowledge by my Wife, and had cost her the enormous Sum of three and twenty Shillings, for which she had no other Excuse or Apology to make, but that she thought *her* Husband deserv'd a Silver Spoon and China Bowl as well as any of his Neighbors. This was the first Appearance of Plate[8] and China in our House, which afterwards in a Course of Years as our Wealth increas'd, augmented gradually to several Hundred Pounds in Value.

I had been religiously educated as a Presbyterian, and tho' some of the Dogmas of that Persuasion, such as the Eternal Decrees of God, Election, Reprobation,[9] etc., appear'd to me unintelligible, others doubtful, and I early absented myself from the Public Assemblies of the Sect, Sunday being my Studying-Day, I never was without some religious Principles; I never doubted, for instance, the Existence of the Deity, that he made the World, and govern'd it by his Providence; that the most acceptable Service of God was the doing Good to Man; that our Souls are immortal; and that all Crime will be punished and Virtue rewarded either here or hereafter; these I esteem'd the Essentials of every Religion, and being to be found in all the Religions we had in our Country I respected them all, tho' with different degrees of Respect as I found them more or less mix'd with other Articles which without any Tendency to inspire, promote or confirm Morality, serv'd principally to divide us and make us unfriendly to one another. This Respect to all, with an Opinion that the worst had some good Effects, induc'd me to avoid all Discourse that might tend to lessen the good Opinion another might have of his own Religion; and as our Province increas'd in People and new Places of worship were continually wanted, and generally erected by voluntary Contribution, my Mite[1] for such purpose, whatever might be the Sect, was never refused.

4. Louis XV and Louis XVI of France (reigned 1715–74 and 1774–92, respectively), George II and George III of England (reigned 1727–60 and 1760–1820, respectively), and Christian VI of Denmark (reigned 1730–46).
5. More commonly: "He that will thrive must ask leave of his wife."
6. Small bowl.
7. I.e., porcelain.
8. Silver.
9. Punishment. "Election": God's determining who is to be saved and who is to be damned.
1. Small contribution.

Tho' I seldom attended any Public Worship, I had still an Opinion of its Propriety, and of its Utility when rightly conducted, and I regularly paid my annual Subscription for the Support of the only Presbyterian Minister or Meeting we had in Philadelphia. He us'd to visit me sometimes as a Friend, and admonish me to attend his Administrations, and I was now and then prevail'd on to do so, once for five Sundays successively. Had he been, *in my Opinion,* a good Preacher perhaps I might have continued, notwithstanding the occasion I had for the Sunday's Leisure in my Course of Study: But his Discourses were chiefly either polemic Arguments, or Explications of the peculiar Doctrines of our Sect, and were all to me very dry, uninteresting and unedifying, since not a single moral Principle was inculcated or enforc'd, their Aim seeming to be rather to make us Presbyterians than good Citizens. At length he took for his Text that Verse of the 4th Chapter of Philippians, *Finally, Brethren, Whatsoever Things are true, honest, just, pure, lovely, or of good report, if there be any virtue, or any praise, think on these Things;*[2] and I imagin'd in a Sermon on such a Text, we could not miss of having some Morality: But he confin'd himself to five Points only as meant by the Apostle, viz., 1. Keeping holy the Sabbath Day. 2. Being diligent in Reading the Holy Scriptures. 3. Attending duly the Public Worship. 4. Partaking of the Sacrament. 5. Paying a due Respect to God's Ministers. These might be all good Things, but as they were not the kind of good Things that I expected from that Text, I despaired of ever meeting with them from any other, was disgusted, and attended his Preaching no more. I had some Years before compos'd a little Liturgy or Form of Prayer for my own private Use, viz., in 1728, entitled, *Articles of Belief and Acts of Religion.*[3] I return'd to the Use of this, and went no more to the public Assemblies. My Conduct might be blameable, but I leave it without attempting farther to excuse it, my present purpose being to relate Facts, and not to make Apologies for them.

It was about this time that I conceiv'd the bold and arduous Project of arriving at moral Perfection. I wish'd to live without committing any Fault at anytime; I would conquer all that either Natural Inclination, Custom, or Company might lead me into. As I knew, or thought I knew, what was right and wrong, I did not see why I might not *always* do the one and avoid the other. But I soon found I had undertaken a Task of more Difficulty than I had imagined: While my Care was employ'd in guarding against one Fault, I was often surpris'd by another. Habit took the Advantage of Inattention. Inclination was sometimes too strong for Reason. I concluded at length, that the mere speculative Conviction that it was our Interest to be completely virtuous, was not sufficient to prevent our Slipping, and that the contrary Habits must be broken and good Ones acquired and established, before we can have any Dependence on a steady uniform Rectitude of Conduct. For this purpose I therefore contriv'd the following Method.

In the various Enumerations of the moral Virtues I had met with in my Reading, I found the Catalog more or less numerous, as different Writers included more or fewer Ideas under the same Name. Temperance, for Example, was by some confin'd to Eating and Drinking, while by others it

2. A paraphrase of Philippians 4.8.
3. Only the first part of Franklin's two-part *Articles of Belief and Acts of Religion* survives.

was extended to mean the moderating every other Pleasure, Appetite, Inclination or Passion, bodily or mental, even to our Avarice and Ambition. I propos'd to myself, for the sake of Clearness, to use rather more Names with fewer Ideas annex'd to each, than a few Names with more Ideas; and I included after Thirteen Names of Virtues all that at that time occurr'd to me as necessary or desirable, and annex'd to each a short Precept, which fully express'd the Extent I gave to its Meaning.

These Names of Virtues with their Precepts were

1. TEMPERANCE.
Eat not to Dullness. Drink not to Elevation.

2. SILENCE.
Speak not but what may benefit others or yourself. Avoiding trifling Conversation.

3. ORDER.
Let all your Things have their Places. Let each Part of your Business have its Time.

4. RESOLUTION.
Resolve to perform what you ought. Perform without fail what you resolve.

5. FRUGALITY.
Make no Expense but to do good to others or yourself: i.e., Waste nothing.

6. INDUSTRY.
Lose no Time. Be always employ'd in something useful. Cut off all unnecessary Actions.

7. SINCERITY.
Use no hurtful Deceit. Think innocently and justly; and, if you speak; speak accordingly.

8. JUSTICE.
Wrong none, by doing Injuries or omitting the Benefits that are your Duty.

9. MODERATION.
Avoid Extremes. Forbear resenting Injuries so much as you think they deserve.

10. CLEANLINESS.
Tolerate no Uncleanness in Body, Clothes or Habitation.

11. TRANQUILITY.
Be not disturbed at Trifles, or Accidents common or unavoidable.

12. CHASTITY.
Rarely use Venery but for Health or Offspring; Never to Dullness, Weakness, or the Injury of your own or another's Peace or Reputation.

13. HUMILITY.
Imitate Jesus and Socrates.

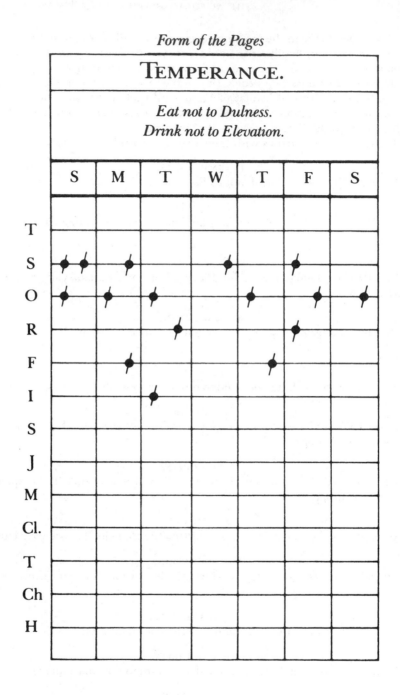

My intention being to acquire the *Habitude*[4] of all these Virtues, I judg'd it would be well not to distract my Attention by attempting the whole at once, but to fix it on one of them at a time, and when I should be Master of that, then to proceed to another, and so on till I should have gone thro' the thirteen. And as the previous Acquisition of some might facilitate the Acquisition of certain others, I arrang'd them with that View as they stand above. *Temperance* first, as it tends to procure that Coolness and Clearness of Head, which is so necessary where constant Vigilance was to be kept up, and Guard maintained, against the unremitting Attraction of ancient Habits, and the Force of perpetual Temptations. This being acquir'd and establish'd, *Silence* would be more easy, and my Desire being to gain Knowledge at the same time that I improv'd in Virtue, and considering that in Conversation it was obtain'd rather by the Use of the Ears than of the Tongue, and therefore wishing to break a Habit I was getting into of Prattling, Punning and Joking, which only made me acceptable to trifling Company, I gave *Silence* the second Place. This, and the next, *Order,* I expected would allow me more Time for attending to my Project and my studies; RESOLUTION once become habitual, would keep me firm in my Endeavors to obtain all the subsequent Virtues; *Frugality* and *Industry,* by freeing me from my remaining Debt, and producing Affluence and Independence would make more easy the Practice of *Sincerity* and *Justice,* etc., etc. Conceiving then that agreeable to the Advice of Pythagoras[5] in his Golden Verses, daily Examination would be necessary, I contriv'd the following Method for conducting that Examination.

I made a little Book in which I allotted a Page for each of the Virtues. I rul'd each Page with red Ink so as to have seven Columns, one for each Day of the Week, marking each Column with a Letter for the Day. I cross'd these Columns with thirteen red Lines, marking the Beginning of each Line with the first Letter of one of the Virtues, on which Line and in its proper Column I might mark by a little black Spot every Fault I found upon Examination, to have been committed respecting that Virtue upon that Day.

I determined to give a Week's strict Attention to each of the Virtues successively. Thus in the first Week my great Guard was to avoid every the least Offence against Temperance, leaving the other Virtues to their ordinary Chance, only marking every Evening the Faults of the Day. Thus if in the first Week I could keep my first Line marked T clear of Spots, I suppos'd the Habit of that Virtue so much strengthen'd and its opposite weaken'd, that I might venture extending my Attention to include the next, and for the following Week keep both Lines clear of Spots. Proceeding thus to the last, I could go thro' a Course complete in Thirteen Weeks, and four Courses in a Year. And like him who having a Garden to weed, does not attempt to eradicate all the bad Herbs at once, which would exceed his Reach and his Strength, but works on one of the Beds at a time, and having accomplish'd the first proceeds to a second; so I should have, (I hoped) the encouraging Pleasure of seeing on my Pages the Progress I made in Virtue, by clearing successively my Lines of their Spots, till in the End by a Number of Courses, I

4. I.e., making these virtues an integral part of his nature.
5. Greek philosopher and mathematician (c. 580–c. 500 B.C.E.). Franklin added a note here: "Insert those Lines that direct it in a Note," and

wished to include verses translated: "Let sleep not close your eyes till you have thrice examined the transactions of the day: where have I strayed, what have I done, what good have I omitted?"

should be happy in viewing a clean Book after a thirteen Weeks' daily Examination.

This my little Book had for its Motto these Lines from *Addison's Cato,*

> Here will I hold: If there is a Pow'r above us,
> (And that there is, all Nature cries aloud
> Thro' all her Works) he must delight in Virtue,
> And that which he delights in must be happy.[6]

Another from *Cicero.*

> O Vitæ Philosophia Dux! O Virtutum indagatrix, expultrixque vitiorum! Unus dies bene, et ex præceptis tuis actus, peccanti immortalitati est anteponendus.[7]

Another from the Proverbs of Solomon speaking of Wisdom or Virtue;

> Length of Days is in her right hand, and in her Left Hand Riches and Honors; Her Ways are Ways of Pleasantness, and all her Paths are Peace.

<div align="right">III, 16, 17</div>

And conceiving God to be the Fountain of Wisdom, I thought it right and necessary to solicit his Assistance for obtaining it; to this End I form'd the following little Prayer, which was prefix'd to my Tables of Examination, for daily Use.

> O Powerful Goodness! bountiful Father! merciful Guide! Increase in me that Wisdom which discovers my truest Interests; Strengthen my Resolutions to perform what that Wisdom dictates. Accept my kind Offices to thy other Children, as the only Return in my Power for thy continual Favors to me.

I us'd also sometimes a little Prayer which I took from *Thomson's* Poems, viz.,

> Father of Light and Life, thou Good supreme,
> O teach me what is good, teach me thy self!
> Save me from Folly, Vanity and Vice,
> From every low Pursuit, and fill my Soul
> With Knowledge, conscious Peace, and Virtue pure,
> Sacred, substantial, neverfading Bliss![8]

The Precept of *Order* requiring that *every Part of my Business should have its allotted Time,* one Page in my little Book contain'd the following Scheme of Employment for the Twenty-four Hours of a natural Day.

I enter'd upon the Execution of this Plan for Self-examination, and continu'd it with occasional Intermissions for some time. I was surpris'd to find myself so much fuller of Faults than I had imagined, but I had the Satisfaction of seeing them diminish. To avoid the Trouble of renewing now and then my little

6. *Cato, a Tragedy* 5.1.15–18, by the English writer Joseph Addison (1672–1719). Franklin also used these lines as an epigraph for his *Articles of Belief and Acts of Religion.*
7. From *Tusculan Disputations* 5.2.5, by the Roman philosopher and orator Marcus Tullius Cicero (106–43 B.C.E.). Several lines are omitted after *vitiorum:* Oh, philosophy, guide of life: Oh, searcher out of virtues and expeller of vices! . . . One day lived well and according to thy precepts is to be preferred to an eternity of sin (Latin).
8. *The Seasons,* "Winter," lines 218–23, by the Scottish poet James Thomson (1700–1748).

The Morning Question, What Good shall I do this Day?	5 6 7	Rise, wash, and address *Powerful Goodness;* contrive Day's Business and take the Resolution of the Day; prosecute the present Study: and breakfast.—
	8 9 10 11	Work.
	12 1	Read, or overlook my Accounts, and dine.
	2 3 4 5	Work.
	6 7 8 9	Put Things in their Places, Supper, Musick, or Diversion, or Conversation, Examination of the Day.
Evening Question, What Good have I done to day?	10 11 12 1 2 3 4	Sleep.—

Book, which by scraping out the Marks on the Paper of old Faults to make room for new Ones in a new Course, became full of Holes: I transferr'd my Tables and Precepts to the Ivory Leaves of a Memorandum Book, on which the Lines were drawn with red Ink that made a durable Stain, and on those Lines I mark'd my Faults with a black Lead Pencil, which Marks I could easily wipe out with a wet Sponge. After a while I went thro' one Course only in a Year, and afterwards only one in several Years; till at length I omitted them entirely, being employ'd in Voyages and Business abroad with a Multiplicity of Affairs, that interfered. But I always carried my little Book with me.

My Scheme of ORDER, gave me the most Trouble, and I found, that tho' it might be practicable where a Man's Business was such as to leave him the Disposition of his Time, that of a Journeyman Printer for instance, it was not possible to be exactly observ'd by a Master, who must mix with the World, and often receive People of Business at their own Hours. *Order* too, with regard to Places for Things, Papers, etc., I found extremely difficult to acquire. I had not been early accustomed to it, and having an exceeding good Memory, I was not so sensible of the Inconvenience attending Want of Method. This Article therefore cost me so much painful Attention and my Faults in it vex'd me so much, and I made so little Progress in Amendment, and had such frequent Relapses, that I was almost ready to give up the Attempt, and content myself with a faulty Character in that respect. Like the Man who in buying an Ax of a Smith my Neighbor, desired to have the whole of its Surface as bright as the Edge; the Smith consented to grind it bright for him if he would turn the Wheel. He turn'd while the Smith press'd the broad Face of the Ax hard and heavily on the Stone, which made the Turning of it very fatiguing. The Man came every now and then from the Wheel to see how the Work went on; and at length would take his Ax as it was without farther Grinding. No, says the Smith, Turn on, turn on; we shall have it bright by and by; as yet 'tis only speckled. Yes, says the Man; but—I *think I like a speckled Ax best.*—And I believe this may have been the Case with many who having for want of some such Means as I employ'd found the Difficulty of obtaining good, and breaking bad Habits, in other Points of Vice and Virtue, have given up the Struggle, and concluded that *a speckled Ax was best.* For something that pretended to be Reason was every now and then suggesting to me, that such extreme Nicety as I exacted of myself might be a kind of Foppery in Morals, which if it were known would make me ridiculous; that a perfect Character might be attended with the Inconvenience of being envied and hated; and that a benevolent Man should allow a few Faults in himself, to keep his Friends in Countenance.

In Truth I found myself incorrigible with respect to *Order;* and now I am grown old, and my Memory bad, I feel very sensibly the want of it. But on the whole, tho' I never arrived at the Perfection I had been so ambitious of obtaining, but fell far short of it, yet I was by the Endeavor made a better and a happier Man than I otherwise should have been, if I had not attempted it; As those who aim at perfect Writing by imitating the engraved Copies,[9] tho' they never reach the wish'd for Excellence of those Copies, their Hand is mended by the Endeavor, and is tolerable while it continues fair and legible.

9. I.e., the models in the printed book.

And it may be well my Posterity should be informed, that to this little Artifice, with the Blessing of God, their Ancestor ow'd the constant Felicity of his Life down to his 79th Year in which this is written. What Reverses may attend the Remainder is in the Hand of Providence: But if they arrive, the Reflection on past Happiness enjoy'd ought to help his Bearing them with more Resignation. To *Temperance* he ascribes his long-continu'd Health, and what is still left to him of a good Constitution. To *Industry* and *Frugality* the early Easiness of his Circumstances, and Acquisition of his Fortune, with all that Knowledge which enabled him to be an useful Citizen, and obtain'd for him some Degree of Reputation among the Learned. To *Sincerity* and *Justice* the Confidence of his Country, and the honorable Employs it conferr'd upon him. And to the joint Influence of the whole Mass of the Virtues, even in their imperfect State he was able to acquire them, all that Evenness of Temper, and that Cheerfulness in Conversation which makes his Company still sought for, and agreeable even to his younger Acquaintance. I hope therefore that some of my Descendants may follow the Example and reap the Benefit.

It will be remark'd[1] that, tho' my Scheme was not wholly without Religion there was in it no Mark of any of the distinguishing Tenets of any particular Sect. I had purposely avoided them; for being fully persuaded of the Utility and Excellency of my Method, and that it might be serviceable to People in all Religions, and intending some time or other to publish it, I would not have anything in it that should prejudice anyone of any Sect against it. I purposed writing a little Comment on each Virtue, in which I would have shown the Advantages of possessing it, and the Mischiefs attending its opposite Vice; and I should have called my Book the ART *of Virtue*, because it would have shown the *Means and Manner* of obtaining Virtue; which would have distinguish'd it from the mere Exhortation to be good, that does not instruct and indicate the Means; but is like the Apostle's Man of verbal Charity, who only, without showing to the Naked and the Hungry *how* or where they might get Clothes or Victuals, exhorted them to be fed and clothed. *James II*, 15, 16.[2]

But it so happened that my Intention of writing and publishing this Comment was never fulfilled. I did indeed, from time to time put down short Hints of the Sentiments, Reasonings, etc., to be made use of in it; some of which I have still by me: But the necessary close Attention to private Business in the earlier part of Life, and public Business since, have occasioned my postponing it. For it being connected in my Mind with a *great and extensive Project* that required the whole Man to execute, and which an unforeseen Succession of Employs prevented my attending to, it has hitherto remain'd unfinish'd.

In this Piece it was my Design to explain and enforce this Doctrine, that vicious Actions are not hurtful because they are forbidden, but forbidden because they are hurtful, the Nature of Man alone consider'd: That it was therefore every one's Interest to be virtuous, who wish'd to be happy even in

1. Observed.
2. "If a brother or sister be naked, and destitute of daily food, And one of you say unto them, Depart in peace, be ye warmed and filled: notwithstanding ye give them not those things which are needful to the body; what doth it profit?"

this World. And I should from this Circumstance (there being always in the World a Number of rich Merchants, Nobility, States and Princes, who have need of honest Instruments for the Management of their Affairs, and such being so rare) have endeavored to convince young Persons, that no Qualities were so likely to make a poor Man's Fortune as those of Probity and Integrity.

My List of Virtues contain'd at first but twelve: But a Quaker Friend having kindly inform'd me that I was generally thought proud; that my Pride show'd itself frequently in Conversation; that I was not content with being in the right when discussing any Point, but was overbearing and rather insolent; of which he convinc'd me by mentioning several Instances; I determined endeavoring to cure myself if I could of this Vice or Folly among the rest, and I added *Humility* to my List, giving an extensive Meaning to the Word. I cannot boast of much Success in acquiring the *Reality* of this Virtue; but I had a good deal with regard to the *Appearance* of it. I made it a Rule to forbear all direct Contradiction to the Sentiments of others, and all positive Assertion of my own. I even forbid myself, agreeable to the old Laws of our Junto, the Use of every Word or Expression in the Language that imported[3] a fix'd Opinion; such as *certainly, undoubtedly,* etc., and I adopted instead of them, I *conceive,* I *apprehend,* or I *imagine* a thing to be so or so, or it so appears to me at present. When another asserted something that I thought an Error, I denied myself the Pleasure of contradicting him abruptly, and of showing immediately some Absurdity in his Proposition; and in answering I began by observing that in certain Cases or Circumstances his Opinion would be right, but that in the present case there *appear'd* or *seem'd* to me some Difference, etc., I soon found the Advantage of this Change in my Manners. The Conversations I engag'd in went on more pleasantly. The modest way in which I propos'd my Opinions, procur'd them a readier Reception and less Contradiction; I had less Mortification when I was found to be in the wrong, and I more easily prevail'd with others to give up their Mistakes and join with me when I happen'd to be in the right. And this Mode, which I at first put on, with some violence to natural Inclination, became at length so easy and so habitual to me, that perhaps for these Fifty Years past no one has ever heard a dogmatical Expression escape me. And to this Habit (after my Character of Integrity) I think it principally owing, that I had early so much Weight with my Fellow Citizens, when I proposed new Institutions, or Alterations in the old; and so much Influence in public Councils when I became a Member. For I was but a bad Speaker, never eloquent, subject to much Hesitation in my choice of Words, hardly correct in Language, and yet I generally carried my Points.

In reality there is perhaps no one of our natural Passions so hard to subdue as *Pride.* Disguise it, struggle with it, beat it down, stifle it, mortify it as much as one pleases, it is still alive, and will every now and then peep out and show itself. You will see it perhaps often in this History. For even if I could conceive that I had completely overcome it, I should probably be proud of my Humility.

<div align="center">Thus far written at Passy, 1784.</div>

3. Suggested.

[Part Three]¹

I am now about to write at home, August 1788, but cannot have the help expected from my Papers, many of them being lost in the War. I have however found the following.

Having mentioned a *great and extensive Project* which I had conceiv'd, it seems proper that some Account should be here given of that Project and its Object. Its first Rise in my Mind appears in the following little Paper, accidentally preserv'd, viz.,

OBSERVATIONS on my Reading
History in Library, May 9, 1731.

"That the great Affairs of the World, the Wars, Revolutions, etc., are carried on and effected by Parties.

"That the View of these Parties is their present general Interest, or what they take to be such.

"That the different Views of these different Parties, occasion all Confusion.

"That while a Party is carrying on a general Design, each Man has his particular private Interest in View.

"That as soon as a Party has gain'd its general Point, each Member becomes intent upon his particular Interest, which thwarting others, breaks that Party into Divisions, and occasions more Confusion.

"That few in Public Affairs act from a mere View of the Good of their Country, whatever they may pretend; and tho' their Actings bring real Good to their Country, yet Men primarily consider'd that their own and their Country's Interest was united, and did not act from a Principle of Benevolence.

"That fewer still in public Affairs act with a View to the Good of Mankind.

"There seems to me at present to be great Occasion for raising an united Party for Virtue, by forming the Virtuous and good Men of all Nations into a regular Body, to be govern'd by suitable good and wise Rules, which good and wise Men may probably be more unanimous in their Obedience to, than common People are to common Laws.

"I at present think, that whoever attempts this aright, and is well qualified, cannot fail of pleasing God, and of meeting with Success. B. F."

Revolving this Project in my Mind, as to be undertaken hereafter when my Circumstances should afford me the necessary Leisure, I put down from time to time on Pieces of Paper such Thoughts as occur'd to me respecting it. Most of these are lost; but I find one purporting to be the Substance of an intended Creed, containing as I thought the Essentials of every known Religion, and being free of everything that might shock the Professors of any Religion. It is express'd in these Words, viz.,

"That there is one God who made all things.

"That he governs the World by his Providence.

"That he ought to be worshiped by Adoration, Prayer and Thanksgiving.

1. Franklin wrote the third part of his autobiography in Philadelphia between August 1788 and the end of May 1789.

"But that the most acceptable Service of God is doing Good to Man.

"That the Soul is immortal.

"And that God will certainly reward Virtue and punish Vice either here or hereafter."

My Ideas at that time were, that the Sect should be begun and spread at first among young and single Men only; that each Person to be initiated should not only declare his Assent to such Creed, but should have exercis'd himself with the Thirteen Weeks' Examination and Practice of the Virtues as in the before-mention'd Model; that the Existance of such a Society should be kept a Secret till it was become considerable, to prevent Solicitations for the Admission of improper Persons; but that the Members should each of them search among his Acquaintance for ingenuous well-disposed Youths, to whom with prudent Caution the Scheme should be gradually communi-cated: That the Members should engage to afford their Advice, Assistance and Support to each other in promoting one another's Interest, Business and Advancement in Life: That for Distinction we should be call'd the Society of the *Free and Easy;* Free, as being by the general Practice and Habit of the Virtues, free from the Dominion of Vice, and particularly by the Practice of Industry and Frugality, free from Debt, which exposes a Man to Confinement and a Species of Slavery to his Creditors. This is as much as I can now rec-ollect of the Project, except that I communicated it in part to two young Men, who adopted it with some Enthusiasm. But my then narrow Circum-stances, and the Necessity I was under of sticking close to my Business, occasion'd my Postponing the farther Prosecution of it at that time, and my multifarious Occupations public and private induc'd me to continue post-poning, so that it has been omitted till I have no longer Strength or Activity left sufficient for such an Enterprise: Tho' I am still of Opinion that it was a practicable Scheme, and might have been very useful, by forming a great Number of good Citizens: And I was not discourag'd by the seeming Mag-nitude of the Undertaking, as I have always thought that one Man of tolerable Abilities may work great Changes, and accomplish great Affairs among Mankind, if he first forms a good Plan, and, cutting off all Amusements or other Employments that would divert his Attention, makes the Execution of that same Plan his sole Study and Business.

In 1732 I first published my Almanac, under the Name of *Richard Saun-ders;* it was continu'd by me about 25 Years, commonly call'd *Poor Richard's* Almanac. I endeavor'd to make it both entertaining and useful, and it accord-ingly came to be in such Demand that I reap'd considerable Profit from it, vending[2] annually near ten Thousand. And observing that it was generally read, scarce any Neighborhood in the Province being without it, I consider'd it as a proper Vehicle for conveying Instruction among the common People, who bought scarce any other Books. I therefore filled all the little Spaces that occur'd between the Remarkable Days in the Calendar, with Prover-bial Sentences, chiefly such as inculcated Industry and Frugality, as the Means of procuring Wealth and thereby securing Virtue, it being more dif-ficult for a Man in Want to act always honestly, as (to use here one of those

2. Selling. *Poor Richard's Almanac* was first published on December 19, 1732. Richard Saun-ders was a London almanac maker of the seven-teenth century. Franklin may also have had in mind a London almanac published from 1661 to 1776 called *Poor Robin.*

Proverbs) *it is hard for an empty Sack to stand upright.* These Proverbs, which contained the Wisdom of many Ages and Nations, I assembled and form'd into a connected Discourse prefix'd to the Almanac of 1757, as the Harangue of a wise old Man to the People attending an Auction.[3] The bringing all these scatter'd Counsels thus into a Focus, enabled them to make greater Impression. The Piece being universally approved was copied in all the Newspapers of the Continent, reprinted in Britain on a Broadside[4] to be stuck up in Houses, two Translations were made of it in French, and great Numbers bought by the Clergy and Gentry to distribute gratis among their poor Parishioners and Tenants. In Pennsylvania, as it discouraged useless Expense in foreign Superfluities, some thought it had its share of Influence in producing that growing Plenty of Money which was observable for several Years after its Publication.

I consider'd my Newspaper also as another Means of communicating Instruction, and in that View frequently reprinted in it Extracts from the Spectator[5] and other moral Writers, and sometimes publish'd little Pieces of my own which had been first compos'd for Reading in our Junto. Of these are a Socratic Dialogue tending to prove, that, whatever might be his Parts and Abilities, a vicious Man could not properly be called a Man of Sense. And a Discourse on Self-denial, showing that Virtue was not Secure, till its Practice became a Habitude, and was free from the Opposition of contrary Inclinations. These may be found in the Papers about the beginning of 1735.[6] In the Conduct of my Newspaper I carefully excluded all Libeling and Personal Abuse, which is of late Years become so disgraceful to our Country. Whenever I was solicited to insert anything of that kind, and the Writers pleaded as they generally did, the Liberty of the Press, and that a Newspaper was like a Stage Coach in which any one who would pay had a Right to a Place, my Answer was, that I would print the Piece separately if desired, and the Author might have as many Copies as he pleased to distribute himself, but that I would not take upon me to spread his Detraction, and that having contracted with my Subscribers to furnish them with what might be either useful or entertaining, I could not fill their Papers with private Altercation in which they had no Concern without doing them manifest Injustice. Now many of our Printers make no scruple of gratifying the Malice of Individuals by false Accusations of the fairest Characters among ourselves, augmenting Animosity even to the producing of Duels, and are moreover so indiscrete as to print scurrilous Reflections on the Government of neighboring States, and even on the Conduct of our best national Allies, which may be attended with the most pernicious Consequences. These Things I mention as a Caution to young Printers, and that they may be encouraged not to pollute their Presses and disgrace their Profession by such infamous Practices, but refuse steadily; as they may see by my Example, that such a Course of Conduct will not on the whole be injurious to their Interests.

In 1733, I sent one of my Journeymen to Charleston South Carolina where a Printer was wanting. I furnish'd him with a Press and Letters, on an Agree-

3. This is the famous preface to the twenty-fifth anniversary edition, called *Father Abraham's Speech* or *The Way to Wealth* (see p. 442).
4. A sheet of paper, usually large, with printing on only one side.
5. See n. 1, p. 475.
6. I.e., in the *Pennsylvania Gazette*, February 11 and 18, 1735.

ment of Partnership, by which I was to receive One Third of the Profits of the Business, paying One Third of the Expense. He was a Man of Learning and honest, but ignorant in Matters of Account;[7] and tho' he sometimes made me Remittances, I could get no Account from him, nor any satisfactory State of our Partnership while he lived. On his Decease, the Business was continued by his Widow, who being born and bred in Holland, where as I have been inform'd the Knowledge of Accounts makes a Part of Female Education, she not only sent me as clear a State as she could find of the Transactions past, but continu'd to account with the greatest Regularity and Exactitude every Quarter afterwards; and manag'd the Business with such Success that she not only brought up reputably a Family of Children, but at the Expiration of the Term was able to purchase of me the Printing-House and establish her Son in it. I mention this affair chiefly for the Sake of recommending that Branch of Education for our young Females, as likely to be of more Use to them and their Children in Case of Widowhood than either Music or Dancing, by preserving them from Losses by Imposition of crafty Men, and enabling them to continue perhaps a profitable mercantile House with establish'd Correspondence till a Son is grown up fit to undertake and go on with it, to the lasting Advantage and enriching of the Family.

About the Year 1734, there arrived among us from Ireland, a young Presbyterian Preacher named Hemphill,[8] who delivered with a good Voice, and apparently extempore, most excellent Discourses, which drew together considerable Numbers of different Persuasions, who join'd in admiring them. Among the rest I became one of his constant Hearers, his Sermons pleasing me as they had little of the dogmatical kind, but inculcated strongly the Practice of Virtue, or what in the religious Style are called Good Works. Those however, of our Congregation, who considered themselves as orthodox Presbyterians, disapprov'd his Doctrine, and were join'd by most of the old Clergy, who arraign'd him of Heterodoxy before the Synod,[9] in order to have him silenc'd. I became his zealous Partisan, and contributed all I could to raise a Party[1] in his Favor; and we combated for him a while with some Hopes of Success. There was much Scribbling pro and con upon the Occasion; and finding that tho' an elegant Preacher he was but a poor Writer, I lent him my Pen and wrote for him two or three Pamphlets, and one Piece in the Gazette of April 1735. Those Pamphlets, as is generally the Case with controversial Writings, tho' eagerly read at the time, were soon out of Vogue, and I question whether a single Copy of them now exists.

During the Contest an unlucky Occurrence hurt his Cause exceedingly. One of our Adversaries having heard him preach a Sermon that was much admired, thought he had somewhere read that Sermon before, or at least a part of it. On Search he found that Part quoted at length in one of the British Reviews, from a Discourse of Dr. Foster's.[2] This Detection gave many of our Party Disgust, who accordingly abandoned his Cause, and occasion'd our more speedy Discomfiture in the Synod. I stuck by him, however, as I rather approv'd his giving us good Sermons compos'd by others, than bad

7. In bookkeeping.
8. Samuel Hemphill, brought to North America as assistant minister to the only regular Presbyterian minister in Philadelphia.
9. The governing body of the Presbyterian Church.

"Arraign'd him of": charged him with.
1. A group of supporters.
2. James Foster (1697–1735), well-known London Baptist preacher.

ones of his own Manufacture; tho' the latter was the Practice of our common Teachers. He afterwards acknowledg'd to me that none of those he preach'd were his own; adding that his Memory was such as enabled him to retain and repeat any Sermon after one Reading only. On our Defeat he left us, in search elsewhere of better Fortune, and I quitted the Congregation, never joining it after, tho' I continu'd many Years my Subscription for the Support of its Ministers.

I had begun in 1733 to study Languages. I soon made myself so much a Master of the French as to be able to read the Books with Ease. I then undertook the Italian. An Acquaintance who was also learning it, us'd often to tempt me to play Chess with him. Finding this took up too much of the Time I had to spare for Study, I at length refus'd to play anymore, unless on this Condition, that the Victor in every Game, should have a Right to impose a Task, either in Parts of the Grammar to be got by heart, or in Translation, etc., which Tasks the Vanquish'd was to perform upon Honor before our next Meeting. As we play'd pretty equally we thus beat one another into that Language. I afterwards with a little Pains-taking acquir'd as much of the Spanish as to read their Books also.

I have already mention'd that I had only one Year's Instruction in a Latin School, and that when very young, after which I neglected that Language entirely.—But when I had attained an Acquaintance with the French, Italian and Spanish, I was surpris'd to find, on looking over a Latin Testament,[3] that I understood so much more of that Language than I had imagined; which encouraged me to apply myself again to the Study of it, and I met with the more Success, as those preceding Languages had greatly smooth'd my Way. From these Circumstances I have thought, that there is some Inconsistency in our common Mode of Teaching Languages. We are told that it is proper to begin first with the Latin, and having acquir'd that, it will be more easy to attain those modern languages which are deriv'd from it; and yet we do not begin with the Greek in order more easily to acquire the Latin. It is true, that if you can clamber and get to the Top of a Staircase without using the Steps, you will more easily gain them in descending: but certainly if you begin with the lowest you will with more Ease ascend to the Top. And I would therefore offer it to the Consideration of those who superintend the Educating of our Youth, whether, since many of those who begin with the Latin, quit the same after spending some Years, without having made any great Proficiency, and what they have learned becomes almost useless, so that their time has been lost, it would not have been better to have begun them with the French, proceeding to the Italian, etc., for tho' after spending the same time they should quit the Study of Languages, and never arrive at the Latin, they would however have acquir'd another Tongue or two that being in modern Use might be serviceable to them in common Life.

After ten Years' Absence from Boston, and having become more easy in my Circumstances, I made a Journey thither to visit my Relations, which I could not sooner well afford. In returning I call'd at Newport, to see my Brother then settled there with his Printing-House. Our former Differences were forgotten, and our Meeting was very cordial and affectionate. He was fast declining in his Health, and requested of me that in case of his Death

3. I.e., a copy of the New Testament in Latin.

which he apprehended not far distant, I would take home his Son, then but 10 Years of Age, and bring him up to the Printing Business. This I accordingly perform'd, sending him a few Years to School before I took him into the Office. His Mother carried on the Business till he was grown up, when I assisted him with an Assortment of new Types, those of his Father being in a Manner worn out.—Thus it was that I made my Brother ample Amends for the Service I had depriv'd him of by leaving him so early.

In 1736 I lost one of my Sons, a fine Boy of 4 Years old, by the Smallpox taken in the common way. I long regretted bitterly and still regret that I had not given it to him by Inoculation.[4] This I mention for the Sake of Parents, who omit that Operation on the Supposition that they should never forgive themselves if a Child died under it; my Example showing that the Regret may be the same either way, and that therefore the safer should be chosen.

Our Club, the Junto, was found so useful, and afforded such Satisfaction to the Members, that several were desirous of introducing their Friends, which could not well be done without exceeding what we had settled as a convenient Number, viz., Twelve. We had from the Beginning made it a Rule to keep our Institution a Secret, which was pretty well observ'd. The Intention was, to avoid Applications of improper Persons for Admittance, some of whom perhaps we might find it difficult to refuse. I was one of those who were against any Addition to our Number, but instead of it made in Writing a Proposal, that every Member separately should endeavor to form a subordinate Club, with the same Rules respecting Queries,[5] etc., and without informing them of the Connection with the Junto. The Advantages propos'd were the Improvement of so many more young Citizens by the Use of our Institutions; Our better Acquaintance with the general Sentiments of the Inhabitants on any Occasion, as the Junto-Member might propose what Queries we should desire, and was to report to Junto what pass'd in his separate Club; the Promotion of our particular Interests in Business by more extensive Recommendations; and the Increase of our Influence in public Affairs and our Power of doing Good by spreading thro' the several Clubs the Sentiments of the Junto. The Project was approv'd, and every Member undertook to form his Club: but they did not all succeed. Five or six only were completed, which were call'd by different Names, as the Vine, the Union, the Band, etc. They were useful to themselves, and afforded us a good deal of Amusement, Information, and Instruction, besides answering in some considerable Degree our Views of influencing the public Opinion on particular Occasions, of which I shall give some Instances in course of time as they happened.

My first Promotion was my being chosen in 1736 Clerk of the General Assembly. The Choice was made that Year without Opposition, but the Year following when I was again propos'd (the Choice, like that of the Members being annual) a new Member made a long Speech against me in order to favor some other Candidate. I was however chosen; which was the more agreeable to me, as besides the Pay for immediate Service as Clerk, the Place gave me a better Opportunity of keeping up an Interest among the Members, which secur'd to me the Business of Printing the Votes, Laws, Paper

4. Franklin's son Francis died of smallpox because he was not inoculated against it due to an intestinal disorder.

5. I.e., questions to be discussed.

Money, and other occasional Jobs for the Public, that on the whole were very profitable. I therefore did not like the Opposition of this new Member, who was a Gentleman of Fortune, and Education, with Talents that were likely to give him in time great Influence in the House, which indeed afterwards happened. I did not however aim at gaining his Favor by paying any servile Respect to him, but after some time took this other Method. Having heard that he had in his Library a certain very scarce and curious Book, I wrote a Note to him expressing my Desire of perusing that Book, and requesting he would do me the Favor of lending it to me for a few Days. He sent it immediately; and I return'd it in about a Week, with another Note expressing strongly my Sense of the Favor. When we next met in the House he spoke to me, (which he had never done before) and with great Civility. And he ever afterwards manifested a Readiness to serve me on all Occasions, so that we became great Friends, and our Friendship continu'd to his Death. This is another Instance of the Truth of an old Maxim I had learned, which says, *He that has once done you a Kindness will be more ready to do you another, than he whom you yourself have obliged.* And it shows how much more profitable it is prudently to remove, than to resent, return and continue inimical Proceedings.

In 1737, Colonel Spotswood, late Governor of Virginia, and then Postmaster General,[6] being dissatisfied with the Conduct of his Deputy at Philadelphia, respecting some Negligence in rendering, and Inexactitude of his Accounts, took from him the Commission and offered it to me.[7] I accepted it readily, and found it of great Advantage; for tho' the Salary was small, it facilitated the Correspondence that improv'd my Newspaper, increas'd the Number demanded, as well as the Advertisements to be inserted, so that it came to afford me a very considerable Income. My old Competitor's Newspaper declin'd proportionably, and I was satisfied without retaliating his Refusal, while Postmaster, to permit my Papers being carried by the Riders. Thus He suffer'd greatly from his Neglect in due Accounting; and I mention it as a Lesson to those young Men who may be employ'd in managing Affairs for others that they should always render Accounts and make Remittances with great Clearness and Punctuality. The Character of observing Such a Conduct is the most powerful of all Recommendations to new Employments and Increase of Business.

I began now to turn my Thoughts a little to public Affairs, beginning however with small Matters. The City Watch[8] was one of the first Things that I conceiv'd to want Regulation. It was managed by the Constables of the respective Wards in Turn. The Constable warn'd a Number of Housekeepers to attend[9] him for the Night. Those who chose never to attend paid him Six Shillings a Year to be excus'd, which was suppos'd to be for hiring Substitutes; but was in Reality much more than was necessary for that purpose, and made the Constableship a Place of Profit. And the Constable for a little Drink often got such Ragamuffins about him as a Watch, that

6. Alexander Spotswood (1676–1740), English military leader, served as lieutenant governor of Virginia from 1710 to 1722 and deputy postmaster general for North America from 1730 to 1739.
7. See n. 1, p. 512. During his last nine years as postmaster Andrew Bradford did not submit accounts.
8. I.e., the night watch, or patrol.
9. Accompany. "Housekeepers": heads of households, homeowners. "Warn'd": ordered, instructed.

reputable Housekeepers did not choose to mix with. Walking the Rounds too was often neglected, and most of the Night spent in Tippling. I thereupon wrote a Paper to be read in Junto, representing these Irregularities, but insisting more particularly on the Inequality of this Six Shilling Tax of the Constables, respecting the Circumstances of those who paid it, since a poor Widow Housekeeper, all whose Property to be guarded by the Watch did not perhaps exceed the Value of Fifty Pounds, paid as much as the wealthiest Merchant who had Thousands of Pounds worth of Goods in his Stores. On the whole I proposed as a more effectual Watch, the Hiring of proper Men to serve constantly in that Business; and as a more equitable Way of supporting the Charge, the levying a Tax that should be proportion'd to Property. This Idea being approv'd by the Junto, was communicated to the other Clubs, but as arising in each of them. And tho' the Plan was not immediately carried into Execution, yet by preparing the Minds of People for the Change, it paved the Way for the Law obtain'd a few Years after,[1] when the Members of our Clubs were grown into more Influence.

About this time I wrote a Paper, (first to be read in Junto but it was afterwards publish'd)[2] on the different Accidents and Carelessnesses by which Houses were set on fire, with Cautions against them, and Means proposed of avoiding them. This was much spoken of as a useful Piece, and gave rise to a Project, which soon followed it, of forming a Company for the more ready Extinguishing of Fires, and mutual Assistance in Removing and Securing of Goods when in Danger.[3] Associates in this Scheme were presently found amounting to Thirty. Our Articles of Agreement oblig'd every Member to keep always in good Order and fit for Use, a certain Number of Leather Buckets, with strong Bags and Baskets (for packing and transporting of Goods), which were to be brought to every Fire; and we agreed to meet once a Month and spend a social Evening together, in discoursing, and communicating such Ideas as occurr'd to us upon the Subject of Fires as might be useful in our Conduct on such Occasions. The Utility of this Institution soon appear'd, and many more desiring to be admitted than we thought convenient for one Company, they were advised to form another; which was accordingly done. And this went on, one new Company being formed after another, till they became so numerous as to include most of the Inhabitants who were Men of Property; and now at the time of my Writing this, tho' upwards of Fifty Years since its Establishment, that which I first formed, called the Union Fire Company, still subsists and flourishes, tho' the first Members are all deceas'd but myself and one who is older by a Year than I am. The small Fines that have been paid by Members for Absence at the Monthly Meetings, have been applied to the Purchase of Fire Engines, Ladders, Firehooks, and other useful Implements for each Company, so that I question whether there is a City in the World better provided with the Means of putting a Stop to beginning Conflagrations; and in fact since these Institutions, the City has never lost by Fire more than one or two Houses at a time, and the Flames have often been extinguish'd before the House in which they began has been half-consumed.

1. Actually, seventeen years later.
2. In the *Pennsylvania Gazette*, February 4, 1735.

3. The Union Fire Company articles of incorporation were signed in December 1736.

In 1739 arriv'd among us from England the Rev. Mr. Whitefield,[4] who had made himself remarkable there as an itinerant Preacher. He was at first permitted to preach in some of our Churches; but the Clergy taking a Dislike to him, soon refus'd him their Pulpits and he was oblig'd to preach in the Fields. The Multitudes of all Sects and Denominations that attended his Sermons were enormous and it was matter of Speculation to me who was one of the Number, to observe the extraordinary Influence of his Oratory on his Hearers, and how much they admir'd and respected him, notwithstanding his common Abuse of them, by assuring them they were naturally *half Beasts and half Devils*. It was wonderful to see the Change soon made in the Manners of our Inhabitants; from being thoughtless or indifferent about Religion, it seem'd as if all the World were growing Religious; so that one could not walk thro' the Town in an Evening without Hearing Psalms sung in different Families of every Street. And it being found inconvenient to assemble in the open Air, subject to its Inclemencies, the Building of a House to meet in was no sooner propos'd and Persons appointed to receive Contributions, but sufficient Sums were soon receiv'd to procure the Ground and erect the Building which was 100 feet long and 70 broad, about the Size of Westminster Hall;[5] and the Work was carried on with such Spirit as to be finished in a much shorter time than could have been expected. Both House and Ground were vested in Trustees, expressly for the Use of any Preacher of any religious Persuasion who might desire to say something to the People of Philadelphia, the Design in building not being to accommodate any particular Sect, but the Inhabitants in general, so that even if the Mufti of Constantinople were to send a Missionary to preach Mahometanism to us, he would find a Pulpit at his Service.[6]

Mr. Whitefield, in leaving us, went preaching all the Way thro' the Colonies to Georgia. The Settlement of that Province had lately been begun; but instead of being made with hardy industrious Husbandmen accustomed to Labor, the only People fit for such an Enterprise, it was with Families of broken[7] Shopkeepers and other insolvent Debtors, many of indolent and idle habits, taken out of the Jails, who being set down in the Woods, unqualified for clearing Land, and unable to endure the Hardships of a new Settlement, perished in Numbers, leaving many helpless Children unprovided for. The Sight of their miserable Situation inspired the benevolent Heart of Mr. Whitefield with the Idea of building an Orphan House there, in which they might be supported and educated. Returning northward he preach'd up this charity, and made large Collections;—for his Eloquence had a wonderful Power over the Hearts and Purses of his Hearers, of which I myself was an Instance. I did not disapprove of the Design, but as Georgia was then destitute of Materials and Workmen, and it was propos'd to send them from Philadelphia at a great Expense, I thought it would have been better to have built the House here and brought the Children to it. This I advis'd, but he was resolute in his first Project, and rejected my Counsel, and I thereupon refus'd to contribute.

4. George Whitefield (1714–1770), popular Methodist preacher whose visit to the colonies escalated the spiritual revival known as the Great Awakening (1730s–40s).
5. In London.
6. The building was called New Building and was later used by the University of Pennsylvania, then called the Academy and College of Philadelphia. "Mufti": a judge who interprets Muslim religious law.
7. Bankrupt.

I happened soon after to attend one of his Sermons, in the Course of which I perceived he intended to finish with a Collection, and I silently resolved he should get nothing from me. I had in my Pocket a Handful of Copper Money, three or four silver Dollars, and five Pistoles in Gold. As he proceeded I began to soften, and concluded to give the Coppers. Another Stroke of his Oratory made me asham'd of that, and determin'd me to give the Silver; and he finish'd so admirably, that I emptied my Pocket wholly into the Collector's Dish, Gold and all. At this Sermon there was also one of our Club, who being of my Sentiments respecting the Building in Georgia, and suspecting a Collection might be intended, had by Precaution emptied his Pockets before he came from home; towards the Conclusion of the Discourse however, he felt a strong Desire to give, and apply'd to a Neighbor who stood near him to borrow some Money for the Purpose. The Application was unfortunately to perhaps the only Man in the Company who had the firmness not to be affected by the Preacher. His Answer was, *At any other time, Friend Hopkinson,*[8] *I would lend to thee freely; but not now; for thee seems to be out of thy right Senses.*

Some of Mr. Whitefield's Enemies affected to suppose that he would apply these Collections to his own private Emolument; but I, who was intimately acquainted with him, (being employ'd in printing his Sermons and Journals,[9] etc.) never had the least Suspicion of his Integrity, but am to this day decidedly of Opinion that he was in all his Conduct, a perfectly *honest Man*. And methinks my Testimony in his Favor ought to have the more Weight, as we had no religious Connection. He us'd indeed sometimes to pray for my Conversion, but never had the Satisfaction of believing that his Prayers were heard. Ours was a mere civil Friendship, sincere on both Sides, and lasted to his Death.

The following Instance will show something of the Terms on which we stood. Upon one of his Arrivals from England at Boston, he wrote to me that he should come soon to Philadelphia, but knew not where he could lodge when there, as he understood his old kind Host Mr. Benezet was remov'd to Germantown.[1] My Answer was; You know my House, if you can make shift with its scanty Accommodations you will be most heartily welcome. He replied, that if I made that kind Offer for Christ's sake, I should not miss of a Reward.—And I return'd, *Don't let me be mistaken; it was not for Christ's sake, but for your sake.* One of our common Acquaintance jocosely remark'd, that knowing it to be the Custom of the Saints,[2] when they receiv'd any favor, to shift the Burthen of the Obligation from off their own Shoulders, and place it in Heaven, I had contriv'd to fix it on Earth.

The last time I saw Mr. Whitefield was in London, when he consulted me about his Orphan House Concern, and his Purpose of appropriating it to the Establishment of a College.

He had a loud and clear Voice, and articulated his Words and Sentences so perfectly that he might be heard and understood at a great Distance, espe-

8. Thomas Hopkinson (1709–1751), a prominent Philadephia lawyer and public official.
9. In 1739–41, Franklin printed a number of Whitefield's books and journals.
1. John Stephen Benezet (1683–1751) emigrated from Europe and became one of Philadelphia's leading citizens. He arrived in Philadelphia as a Quaker but joined the Moravian Church when he moved to Germantown.
2. Living church members who are believed to be saved.

cially as his Auditors, however numerous, observ'd the most exact Silence. He preach'd one Evening from the Top of the Court House Steps, which are in the Middle of Market Street, and on the West Side of Second Street which crosses it at right angles. Both Streets were fill'd with his Hearers to a considerable Distance. Being among the hindmost in Market Street, I had the Curiosity to learn how far he could be heard, by retiring backwards down the Street towards the River, and I found his Voice distinct till I came near Front Street,[3] when some Noise in that Street, obscur'd it. Imagining then a Semicircle, of which my Distance should be the Radius, and that it were fill'd with Auditors, to each of whom I allow'd two square feet, I computed that he might well be heard by more than Thirty Thousand. This reconcil'd me to the Newspaper Accounts of his having preach'd to 25,000 People in the Fields, and to the ancient Histories of Generals haranguing whole Armies, of which I had sometimes doubted.

By hearing him often I came to distinguish easily between Sermons newly compos'd, and those which he had often preach'd in the Course of his Travels. His Delivery of the latter was so improv'd by frequent Repetitions, that every Accent, every Emphasis, every Modulation of Voice, was so perfectly well turn'd and well plac'd, that without being interested in the Subject, one could not help being pleas'd with the Discourse, a Pleasure of much the same kind with that receiv'd from an excellent Piece of Music. This is an Advantage itinerant Preachers have over those who are stationary: as the latter cannot well improve their Delivery of a Sermon by so many Rehearsals.

His Writing and Printing from time to time gave great Advantage to his Enemies. Unguarded Expressions and even erroneous Opinions delivered in Preaching might have been afterwards explain'd, or qualified by supposing others that might have accompanied them; or they might have been denied; but *litera scripta manet*.[4] Critics attack'd his Writings violently, and with so much Appearance of Reason as to diminish the Number of his Votaries,[5] and prevent their Increase: So that I am of Opinion, if he had never written anything he would have left behind him a much more numerous and important Sect. And his Reputation might in that case have been still growing, even after his Death; as there being nothing of his Writings on which to found a Censure; and give him a lower Character, his Proselytes would be left at Liberty to feign for him as great a Variety of Excellencies, as their enthusiastic Admiration might wish him to have possessed.

My Business was now continually augmenting, and my Circumstances growing daily easier, my Newspaper having become very profitable, as being for a time almost the only one in this and the neighboring Provinces. I experienc'd too the Truth of the Observation, that *after getting the first hundred Pound, it is more easy to get the second:* Money itself being of a prolific Nature: The Partnership at Carolina having succeeded, I was encourag'd to engage in others, and to promote several of my Workmen who had behaved well, by establishing them with Printing-Houses in different Colonies, on the same Terms with that in Carolina. Most of them did well, being enabled at the End of our Term, Six Years, to purchase the Types of me; and go on

3. About five hundred feet from the courthouse.
4. I.e., *vox audita perit, litera scripta manet*: the spoken word passes away, the written word

remains (Latin).
5. Those devoted to him; disciples.

working for themselves, by which means several Families were raised. Partnerships often finish in Quarrels, but I was happy in this, that mine were all carried on and ended amicably; owing I think a good deal to the Precaution of having very explicitly settled in our Articles everything to be done by or expected from each Partner, so that there was nothing to dispute, which Precaution I would therefore recommend to all who enter into Partnerships, for whatever Esteem Partners may have for and Confidence in each other at the time of the Contract, little Jealousies and Disgusts may arise, with Ideas of Inequality in the Care and Burden of the Business, etc., which are attended often with Breach of Friendship and of the Connection, perhaps with Lawsuits and other disagreeable Consequences.

I had on the whole abundant Reason to be satisfied with my being established in Pennsylvania. There were however two things that I regretted: There being no Provision for Defense, nor for a complete Education of Youth. No Militia nor any College. I therefore in 1743, drew up a Proposal[6] for establishing an Academy; and at that time thinking the Rev. Mr. Peters,[7] who was out of Employ, a fit Person to superintend such an Institution, I communicated the Project to him. But he having more profitable Views in the Service of the Proprietor,[8] which succeeded, declin'd the Undertaking. And not knowing another at that time suitable for such a Trust, I let the Scheme lie a while dormant. I succeeded better the next Year, 1744, in proposing and establishing a Philosophical Society. The Paper I wrote for that purpose[9] will be found among my Writings when collected.

With respect to Defense, Spain having been several Years at War against Britain, and being at length join'd by France, which brought us into greater Danger,[1] and the labored and long-continued Endeavors of our Governor Thomas[2] to prevail with our Quaker Assembly to pass a Militia Law, and make other Provisions for the Security of the Province having proved abortive, I determined to try what might be done by a voluntary Association of the People. To promote this I first wrote and published a Pamphlet, entitled, PLAIN TRUTH,[3] in which I stated our defenseless Situation in strong Lights, with the Necessity of Union and Discipline for our Defense, and promis'd to propose in a few Days an Association to be generally signed for that purpose. The Pamphlet had a sudden and surprising Effect. I was call'd upon for the Instrument[4] of Association: And having settled the Draft of it with a few Friends, I appointed a Meeting of the Citizens in the large Building before-mentioned.

The House was pretty full. I had prepared a Number of printed Copies, and provided Pens and Ink dispers'd all over the Room. I harangu'd them a

6. No such proposal exists, but it evidently included plans for using the New Building, built for Whitefield.
7. Richard Peters (c. 1704–1776), called "the most learned man in Pennsylvania," was an Anglican clergyman and the provincial secretary to the Penn family (see n. 8, p. 495).
8. I.e., he expected to make more money working for the proprietor than running the Academy.
9. A Proposal for Promoting Useful Knowledge among the British Plantations in America (May 14, 1743). The American Philosophical Society, cofounded by Franklin and the naturalist John Bartram, was the first learned society in North America. Its first president was Thomas Hopkin-

son, discussed above.
1. War on Spain and France had been declared by Great Britain in 1739 and 1744, respectively. Colonial shipping was, therefore, subject to attack by privateers of Spain and France. The Treaty of Aix-la-Chapelle (1748) ended this danger.
2. George Thomas (c. 1695–1774), governor of Pennsylvania 1738–47.
3. Plain Truth; or, Serious Considerations on the Present State of the City of Philadelphia, and Province of Pennsylvania, by a "tradesman of Philadelphia" (November 17, 1747).
4. Charter, probably including the bylaws.

little on the Subject, read the Paper and explain'd it, and then distributed the Copies which were eagerly signed, not the least Objection being made. When the Company separated, and the Papers were collected we found above Twelve hundred Hands; and other Copies being dispers'd in the Country the Subscribers amounted at length to upwards of Ten Thousand. These all furnish'd themselves as soon as they could with Arms; form'd themselves into Companies, and Regiments, chose their own Officers, and met every Week to be instructed in the manual Exercise, and other Parts of military Discipline. The Women, by Subscriptions among themselves, provided Silk Colors, which they presented to the Companies, painted with different Devices and Mottos which I supplied. The Officers of the Companies composing the Philadelphia Regiment, being met, chose me for their Colonel; but conceiving myself unfit, I declin'd that Station, and recommended Mr. Lawrence, a fine Person and Man of Influence, who was accordingly appointed.[5] I then propos'd a Lottery to defray the Expense of Building a Battery[6] below the Town, and furnishing it with Cannon. It filled expeditiously and the Battery was soon erected, the Merlons[7] being fram'd of Logs and fill'd with Earth. We bought some old Cannon from Boston, but these not being sufficient, we wrote to England for more, soliciting at the same Time our Proprietaries for some Assistance, tho' without much Expectation of obtaining it.

Meanwhile Colonel Lawrence, William Allen, Abraham Taylor, Esquires, and myself were sent to New York by the Associators, commission'd to borrow some Cannon of Governor Clinton. He at first refus'd us peremptorily: but at a Dinner with his Council where there was great Drinking of Madeira Wine, as the Custom at that Place then was, he soften'd by degrees, and said he would lend us Six. After a few more Bumpers[8] he advanc'd to Ten. And at length he very good-naturedly conceded Eighteen. They were fine Cannon, 18 pounders, with their Carriages, which we soon transported and mounted on our Battery, where the Associators kept a nightly Guard while the War lasted; And among the rest I regularly took my Turn of Duty there as a common Soldier.

My Activity in these Operations was agreeable to the Governor and Council; they took me into Confidence, and I was consulted by them in every Measure wherein their Concurrence was thought useful to the Association. Calling in the Aid of Religion, I propos'd to them the Proclaiming a Fast, to promote Reformation, and implore the Blessing of Heaven on our Undertaking. They embrac'd the Motion, but as it was the first Fast ever thought of in the Province, the Secretary had no Precedent from which to draw the Proclamation. My Education in New England, where a Fast is proclaim'd every Year, was here of some Advantage. I drew it in the accustomed Style, it was translated into German, printed in both Languages and divulg'd[9] thro' the Province. This gave the Clergy of the different Sects an Opportunity of Influencing their Congregations to join in the Association; and it would probably have been general among all but Quakers if the Peace had not soon interven'd.

5. Before his appointment as lieutenant colonel of the Associated Regiment of Foot for Philadelphia, Thomas Lawrence (1689–1754) had served as a city Councilman, an alderman, and three times as mayor. He later served two more times as mayor.
6. Wall or platform on which guns are placed.
7. Battlements.
8. I.e., drinking vessels filled to the brim.
9. Made known.

It was thought by some of my Friends that by my Activity in these Affairs, I should offend that Sect, and thereby lose my Interest in the Assembly where they were a great Majority. A young Gentleman who had likewise some Friends in the House, and wish'd to succeed me as their Clerk, acquainted me that it was decided to displace me at the next Election, and he therefore in goodwill advis'd me to resign, as more consistent with my Honor than being turn'd out. My Answer to him was, that I had read or heard of some Public Man, who made it a Rule never to ask for an Office, and never to refuse one when offer'd to him. I approve, says I, of his Rule, and will practice it with a small Addition; I shall never *ask*, never *refuse*, nor ever *resign* an Office.[1] If they will have my Office of Clerk to dispose of to another, they shall take it from me. I will not be giving it up, lose my Right of some time or other making Reprisals on my adversaries. I heard however no more of this. I was chosen again, unanimously as usual, at the next Election. Possibly as they dislik'd my late Intimacy with the Members of Council, who had join'd the Governors in all the Disputes about military Preparations with which the House had long been harass'd, they might have been pleas'd if I would voluntarily have left them; but they did not care to displace me on Account merely of my Zeal for the Association; and they could not well give another Reason.

Indeed I had some Cause to believe, that the Defense of the Country was not disagreeable to any of them, provided they were not requir'd to assist in it. And I found that a much greater Number of them than I could have imagined, tho' against offensive War, were clearly for the defensive. Many Pamphlets *pro and con* were publish'd on the Subject, and some by good Quakers in favor of Defense, which I believe convinc'd most of their younger People. A Transaction in our Fire Company gave me some Insight into their prevailing Sentiments. It had been propos'd that we should encourage the Scheme for building a Battery by laying out the present Stock, then about Sixty Pounds, in Tickets of the Lottery. By our Rules no Money could be dispos'd of but at the next Meeting after the Proposal. The Company consisted of Thirty Members, of which Twenty-two were Quakers, and Eight only of other Persuasions. We eight punctually attended the Meeting; but tho' we thought that some of the Quakers would join us, we were by no means sure of a Majority. Only one Quaker, Mr. James Morris,[2] appear'd to oppose the Measure: He express'd much Sorrow that it had ever been propos'd, as he said *Friends*[3] were all against it, and it would create such Discord as might break up the Company. We told him, that we saw no Reason for that; we were the Minority, and if *Friends* were against the Measure and outvoted us, we must and should, agreeable to the Usage of all Societies, submit.

When the Hour for Business arriv'd, it was mov'd to put the Vote. He allow'd we might then do it by the Rules, but as he could assure us that a Number of Members intended to be present for the purpose of opposing it, it would be but candid to allow a little time for their appearing. While we were disputing this, a Waiter came to tell me two Gentlemen below desir'd

1. Franklin here neglects to mention that he applied for the position of clerk of the assembly in 1736 and for the deputy postmaster generalship in 1751.
2. James Morris (1707–1751), prominent Phila-

delphia Quaker, assemblyman, and member of the Library Company (see n. 2, p. 507).
3. I.e., members of the Society of Friends, or Quakers. Pacifism is a basic article of their faith.

Beginnings to 1820

A Portion of the Mappa Mundi (World Map) by Juan de la Cosa, 1500

The oldest known cartographic representation of the Americas was made by Juan de la Cosa, a Spanish mariner, conquistador, and mapmaker. As pilot of the *Niña* during Columbus's second voyage (1494–95), de la Cosa learned about New World space firsthand. He also accompanied Columbus on his third voyage, and in 1499 he was the first pilot for the expedition of Alonso de Ojeda and Amerigo Vespucci. De la Cosa's map, measuring three feet by six feet, embraces the entire known world but is most notable for its attempt to portray and conceptualize the land that would come to be called the "New World" or "America." Hovering to the west (at the top) is a mystical figure of Columbus as Saint Christopher—the humble ferryman who carried Christ over the water on his back and thus supplied de la Cosa with a fitting metaphor for the looming Christianization of the Americas. The green area represents the western continents. Cuba, rendered as an island, shows up with remarkable clarity, below and to the right of the image of Columbus/Saint Christopher. The western edge of Europe is visible at the bottom.

René de Laudonnière and Chief Athore, **Jacques Le Moyne de Morgues, 1564**

When Protestant French colonists under Jean Ribault landed in Florida in the early 1560s, they erected two columns, decorated with the arms of the French king, that were intended to project their claim over the region. Jacques Le Moyne de Morgues, who as mapmaker and artist accompanied Ribault's successor, René de Laudonnière, on a second French expedition, here portrays the moment when the local Indian chief, Athore, took René de Laudonnière to Ribault's column. This engraving shows the native people "worshipping this stone as an idol," having placed before it offerings of fruit, edible roots, medicinal herbs, precious oils, and artifacts such as baskets and a bow and quiver. The artist, who escaped when the Spanish wiped out the French colony in 1565, settled in London, where he became an associate of Sir Walter Raleigh and the English artist-explorer John White.

The French Reach Port Royal, **Theodor de Bry, 1591**

Theodor de Bry, the first great illustrator of European voyages to the Americas, established the visual language through which generations of Old World inhabitants perceived the New World. In this engraving, based on a lost watercolor by Jacques Le Moyne de Morgues, de Bry shows the French fleet under Jean de Ribault reaching the coast of South Carolina at present-day St. Helena Sound, near Beaufort, in the spring of 1562. The representation of the Indian village, with its lush surroundings (pumpkins and grapes grow wild; deer, turkeys, and geese abound), offers an alluring image of America as paradise.

Indian Village of Secoton, John White, 1585

The English painter John White left an impressive visual record of places, people, and natural facts observed during several voyages to the New World in the 1580s. Collaborator at one time with the writer Thomas Harriot, White is known especially for his images of Native American life. This composite rendering of a village on the mainland of present-day North Carolina, just inside Pamlico Sound, is intended to show a wide array of Native customs and activities, from hunting and planting to everyday behavior and religious rites.

Elizabeth Clarke Freake and Baby Mary, **unknown artist, 1671–74**

Elizabeth Clarke (1642–1713), the daughter of a prosperous Boston merchant, was married in 1661 to the English-born lawyer John Freake, with whom she had eight children. Her portrait (like her husband's) was painted in 1671 by an unknown English-trained artist (now called "the Freake painter") who is believed to be responsible for several surviving portraits executed in a surprisingly rich style in the Boston area in the 1670s. When the Freakes' last child, Mary, was born in 1674, the artist or his successor added her to the portrait of Elizabeth, creating a composite of family life especially notable for the fineness of the clothes worn by the well-to-do mother.

Page from William Byrd's "Secret Diary"

For many years Byrd (1674–1744) kept an account of his daily life, both on his Virginia plantation, Westover, and on trips to London. Much of the diary was written in a code—developed by William Mason and published in 1707—designed for gentlemen to keep such writing from prying eyes. In terse but informative entries, Byrd discusses all facets of plantation life, from his religious exercises to the oversight of his many slaves. Most striking are his matter-of-fact records of his sexual encounters with slave women.

Hummingbird, from *The Natural History of Carolina, Florida and the Bahama Islands*, Mark Catesby, 1731–43

The British artist Mark Catesby produced the first large-scale natural history of the New World's flora and fauna, with which he was familiar from visits there between 1712 and 1719. In addition to birds he depicted reptiles, fish, and plant life, and in the text he discussed insects and the soil's and water's suitability for agriculture, among other topics. The engraving here is of what Catesby considered one of the New World's true wonders, the tiny ruby-throated hummingbird, near what he called a "trumpet flower." Before the development of color-printing technologies such as lithography, reproductions of this kind, including Catesby's, were hand-colored.

Benjamin Franklin Drawing Electricity from the Sky, Benjamin West, 1805

This allegorical depiction of Franklin conducting his famous experiment with a kite during a thunderstorm in the 1750s, and thereby demonstrating that lightning was electricity, suggests the almost mythic status he had achieved by the early nineteenth century, when his *Autobiography* became immensely popular. It also makes a claim for the importance of Americans to scientific inquiry in the Western world. Benjamin West (1738–1820), one of the most important American painters of this period and the first to be widely appreciated in England, made this sketch for a larger painting that he never completed. Notice the scientific apparatus to the left of Franklin. This orrery, which shows the relative positions of the planets, is being studied by childlike figures with oddly adult faces.

The Old Plantation, c. 1790–1800

This watercolor depicts slave life on an antebellum Southern plantation and is particularly important for its representation of slave quarters and of the slaves' social music. At right one man plays a gourd banjo and another keeps time with two sticks, or "bones." The man in the middle and two women do a ritual dance, probably reflecting West African cultural influences. The head wraps also reflect African influence.

Declaration of Independence, John Trumbull, c. 1817–19

This painting, measuring twelve feet by eighteen feet, depicts *the* iconic moment in American political history, the signing of the Declaration of Independence, in Philadelphia. In the center are the men who drafted the Declaration (l. to r., John Adams, Roger Sherman, Thomas Jefferson, and Benjamin Franklin), with Jefferson presenting the document to John Hancock, president of the Continental Congress. About two-thirds of the fifty-six signers are also depicted. Trumbull (1756–1843), who studied in England with the great American artist Benjamin West, is known primarily for his paintings of scenes from American history. Although completed several decades after the event it memorializes, this painting is a good example of American artists' and writers' attempts, after the War of 1812, to play a role in creating a unique and heroic American history.

Exhuming the Mastodon, **Charles Wilson Peale, 1806–08**

Peale (1741–1827) was the patriarch of a family of American artists, including his sons Rembrandt and Raphael, renowned for their portraits and still lifes. Like many eighteenth-century Americans (Thomas Jefferson included), Peale had a deep interest in natural history; he established in Philadelphia his own museum of scientific curiosities—a collection of specimens not arranged by any particular scientific method. In the early nineteenth century he organized an expedition to the Hudson Valley, in New York, to recover the recently discovered bones of a mastodon, which he and his son Rembrandt later mounted for display. This striking painting illustrates the elaborate excavation, with the apparatus in the center removing earth from the pit where the bones lie buried. Peale supervises at right. The fascination of the subject lay in its proof of America's long early history.

Elizabeth Graham's Embroidery Map

This *Plan of the City of Washington* (1800–1803) was worked in silk embroidery on linen by Elizabeth Graham, of Baltimore, Maryland, when she was about thirteen. The plan of the new capital city was originally designed by Pierre L'Enfant in 1791 and engraved by James Thackara and John Vallance in 1792. Graham decorated the map with oval cartouches showing George Washington and the figures of Justice, Hope, and Liberty, combining patriotic themes with the decorative arts.

to speak with me. I went down, and found they were two of our Quaker Members. They told me there were eight of them assembled at a Tavern just by; that they were determin'd to come and vote with us if there should be occasion, which they hop'd would not be the Case; and desir'd we would not call for their Assistance if we could do without it, as their Voting for such a Measure might embroil them with their Elders and Friends. Being thus secure of a Majority, I went up, and after a little seeming Hesitation, agreed to a Delay of another Hour. This Mr. Morris allow'd to be extremely fair. Not one of his opposing Friends appear'd, at which he express'd great Surprise; and at the Expiration of the Hour, we carried the Resolution Eight to one; And as of the 22 Quakers, Eight were ready to vote with us and, Thirteen by their Absence manifested that they were not inclin'd to oppose the Measure, I afterwards estimated the Proportion of Quakers sincerely against Defense as one to twenty-one only. For these were all regular Members of that Society, and in good Reputation among them, and had due Notice of what was propos'd at that Meeting.

The honorable and learned Mr. Logan,[4] who had always been of that Sect, was one who wrote an Address to them, declaring his Approbation of defensive War, and supporting his Opinion by many strong Arguments: He put into my Hands Sixty Pounds,[5] to be laid out in Lottery Tickets for the Battery, with Directions to apply what Prizes might be drawn wholly to that Service. He told me the following Anecdote of his old Master William Penn respecting Defense. He came over from England, when a young Man, with that Proprietary, and as his Secretary. It was War Time, and their Ship was chas'd by an armed Vessel suppos'd to be an Enemy. Their Captain prepar'd for Defense, but told William Penn and his Company of Quakers, that he did not expect their Assistance, and they might retire into the Cabin; which they did, except James Logan, who chose to stay upon Deck, and was quarter'd to a Gun. The suppos'd Enemy prov'd a Friend; so there was no Fighting. But when the Secretary went down to communicate the Intelligence, William Penn rebuk'd him severely for staying upon Deck and undertaking to assist in defending the Vessel, contrary to the Principles of *Friends*, especially as it had not been required by the Captain. This Reproof being before all the Company, piqu'd the Secretary, who answer'd, *I being thy Servant, why did thee not order me to come down: but thee was willing enough that I should stay and help to fight the Ship when thee thought there was Danger.*

My being many Years in the Assembly, the Majority of which were constantly Quakers, gave me frequent Opportunities of seeing the Embarrassment given them by their Principle against War, whenever Application was made to them by Order of the Crown to grant Aids for military Purposes. They were unwilling to offend Government on the one hand, by a direct Refusal, and their Friends the Body of Quakers on the other, by a Compliance contrary to their Principles. Hence a Variety of Evasions to avoid Complying, and Modes of disguising the Compliance when it became unavoidable. The common Mode at last was to grant Money under the Phrase of its being *for the King's Use*, and never to enquire how it was applied. But if the Demand

4. James Logan (1674–1751) moved to Philadelphia in 1699 as William Penn's secretary and oversaw Penn's business for fifty years (see n. 8, p. 495).

5. Actually two hundred and fifty.

was not directly from the Crown, that Phrase was found not so proper, and some other was to be invented. As when Powder was wanting, (I think it was for the Garrison at Louisburg,)[6] and the Government of New England solicited a Grant of some from Pennsylvania, which was much urg'd on the House by Governor Thomas, they could not grant Money to buy Powder, because that was an Ingredient of War, but they voted an Aid to New England, of Three Thousand Pounds, to be put into the hands of the Governor, and appropriated it for the Purchasing of Bread, Flour, Wheat, *or other Grain*. Some of the Council desirous of giving the House still farther Embarrassment, advis'd the Governor not to accept Provision, as not being the Thing he had demanded. But he replied, "I shall take the Money, for I understand very well their Meaning; *Other Grain*, is Gunpowder"; which he accordingly bought; and they never objected to it.

It was in Allusion to this Fact, that when in our Fire Company we feared the Success of our Proposal in favor of the Lottery, and I had said to my friend Mr. Syng,[7] one of our Members, if we fail, let us move the Purchase of a Fire Engine with the Money; the Quakers can have no Objection to that: and then if you nominate me, and I you, as a Committee for that purpose, we will buy a great Gun, which is certainly a *Fire-Engine*: I see, says he, you have improv'd by being so long in the Assembly; your equivocal Project would be just a Match for their Wheat *or other grain*.

These Embarrassments that the Quakers suffer'd from having establish'd and publish'd it as one of their Principles, that no kind of War was lawful, and which being once published, they could not afterwards, however they might change their minds, easily get rid of, reminds me of what I think a more prudent Conduct in another Sect among us; that of the Dunkers. I was acquainted with one of its Founders, Michael Welfare, soon after it appear'd.[8] He complain'd to me that they were grievously calumniated by the Zealots of other Persuasions, and charg'd with abominable Principles and Practices to which they were utter Strangers. I told him this had always been the case with new Sects; and that to put a Stop to such Abuse, I imagin'd it might be well to publish the Articles of their Belief and the Rules of their Discipline. He said that it had been propos'd among them, but not agreed to, for this Reason; "When we were first drawn together as a Society, says he, it had pleased God to enlighten our Minds so far, as to see that some Doctrines which we once esteemed Truths were Errors, and that others which we had esteemed Errors were real Truths. From time to time he has been pleased to afford us farther Light, and our Principles have been improving, and our Errors diminishing. Now we are not sure that we are arriv'd at the End of this Progression, and at the Perfection of Spiritual or Theological Knowledge; and we fear that if we should once print our Confession of Faith, we should feel ourselves as if bound and confin'd by it, and perhaps be unwilling to receive farther Improvement; and our Successors still more so, as

6. The Fortress of Louisburg was built on Cape Breton Island, Nova Scotià, to protect the St. Lawrence River approaches. It was captured in 1745 and returned to France in 1748 through the Treaty of Aix-la-Chapelle.
7. Philip Syng (1703–1789), silversmith and member of the Junto (see n. 7, p. 502).
8. In 1719, a group of German Baptists emigrated from the Netherlands to Pennsylvania. Welfare (1687–1741), also known as Wolfaert or Wohlfahrt, was a leader of a splinter group, the Seventh Day Baptist Community in Ephrata (now Lancaster), Pennsylvania. The German Baptists were called "Dunkers" because they believed in baptism by total immersion.

conceiving what we their Elders and Founders had done, to be something sacred, never to be departed from."

This Modesty in a Sect is perhaps a singular Instance in the History of Mankind, every other Sect supposing itself in Possession of all Truth, and that those who differ are so far in the Wrong: Like a Man traveling in foggy Weather: Those at some Distance before him on the Road he sees wrapped up in the Fog, as well as those behind him, and also the People in the Fields on each side; but near him all appears clear.—Tho' in truth he is as much in the Fog as any of them. To avoid this kind of Embarrassment the Quakers have of late Years been gradually declining the public Service in the Assembly and in the Magistracy.[9] Choosing rather to quit their Power than their Principle.[1]

In Order of Time I should have mentioned before, that having in 1742 invented an open Stove,[2] for the better warming of Rooms and at the same time saving Fuel, as the fresh Air admitted was warmed in Entering, I made a Present of the Model to Mr. Robert Grace, one of my early Friends, who having an Iron Furnace, found the Casting of the Plates for these Stoves a profitable Thing, as they were growing in Demand. To promote that Demand I wrote and published a Pamphlet entitled, *An Account of the New-Invented* PENNSYLVANIA FIRE PLACES: *Wherein their Construction and manner of Operation is particularly explained; their Advantages above every other Method of warming Rooms demonstrated; and all Objections that have been raised against the Use of them answered and obviated, etc.*[3] This Pamphlet had a good Effect. Governor Thomas was so pleas'd with the Construction of this Stove, as describ'd in it, that he offer'd to give me a Patent for the sole Vending of them for a Term of Years; but I declin'd it from a Principle which has ever weigh'd with me on such Occasions, viz., *That as we enjoy great Advantages from the Inventions of Others, we should be glad of an Opportunity to serve others by any Invention of ours, and this we should do freely and generously.* An Ironmonger in London, however, after assuming a good deal of my Pamphlet and working it up into his own, and making some small Changes in the Machine, which rather hurt its Operation, got a Patent for it there,[4] and made as I was told a little Fortune by it. And this is not the only Instance of Patents taken out for my Inventions by others, tho' not always with the same success: which I never contested, as having no Desire of profiting by Patents myself, and hating Disputes. The Use of these Fireplaces in very many Houses both of this and the neighboring Colonies, has been and is a great Saving of Wood to the Inhabitants.

Peace being concluded, and the Association Business therefore at an End, I turn'd my Thoughts again to the Affair of establishing an Academy. The first Step I took was to associate in the Design a Number of active Friends, of whom the Junto furnished a good Part; the next was to write and publish a Pamphlet entitled, *Proposals relating to the Education of Youth in Pennsylvania.*[5] This I distributed among the principal Inhabitants gratis; and as soon as I could suppose their Minds a little prepared by the Perusal of it, I set on

9. Courts.
1. In 1756, ten pacifist Quakers resigned from their assembly seats and three refused to run for reelection.
2. However, not the stove known today as the Franklin stove. None of Franklin's originals survives.

3. Grace paid for the publication of this pamphlet in 1744.
4. The ironmonger, or hardware merchant, was probably James Sharp, who took out such a patent in 1781. "Assuming": appropriating.
5. Published in 1749.

foot a Subscription for Opening and Supporting an Academy; it was to be paid in Quotas yearly for Five Years; by so dividing it I judg'd the Subscription might be larger, and I believe it was so, amounting to no less (if I remember right) than Five thousand Pounds.[6] In the Introduction to these Proposals, I stated their Publication not as an Act of mine, but of some *public-spirited Gentlemen*, avoiding as much as I could, according to my usual Rule, the presenting myself to the Public as the Author of any Scheme for their Benefit.

The Subscribers, to carry the Project into immediate Execution chose out of their Number Twenty-four Trustees, and appointed Mr. Francis, then Attorney General, and myself, to draw up Constitutions for the Government of the Academy, which being done and signed, an House was hired, Masters engag'd and the Schools opened I think in the same Year 1749.[7] The Scholars increasing fast, the House was soon found too small, and we were looking out for a Piece of Ground properly situated, with Intention to build, when Providence threw into our way a large House ready built, which with a few Alterations might well serve our purpose, this was the Building before-mentioned erected by the Hearers of Mr. Whitefield, and was obtain'd for us in the following Manner.

It is to be noted, that the Contributions to this Building being made by People of different Sects, Care was taken in the Nomination of Trustees, in whom the Building and Ground was to be vested, that a Predominancy should not be given to any Sect, lest in time that Predominancy might be a means of appropriating the whole to the Use of such Sect, contrary to the original Intention; it was therefore that one of each Sect was appointed, viz., one Church-of-England-man, one Presbyterian, one Baptist, one Moravian, etc. Those in case of Vacancy by Death were to fill it by Election from among the Contributors. The Moravian happen'd not to please his Colleagues, and on his Death, they resolved to have no other of that Sect. The Difficulty then was, how to avoid having two of some other Sect, by means of the new Choice. Several Persons were named and for that Reason not agreed to. At length one mention'd me, with the Observation that I was merely an honest Man, and of no Sect at all; which prevail'd with them to choose me.

The Enthusiasm which existed when the House was built, had long since abated, and its Trustees had not been able to procure fresh Contributions for paying the Ground Rent, and discharging some other Debts the Building had occasion'd, which embarrass'd them greatly. Being now a Member of both Sets of Trustees, that for the Building and that for the Academy, I had good Opportunity of negotiating with both, and brought them finally to an Agreement, by which the Trustees for the Building were to cede it to those of the Academy, the latter undertaking to discharge the Debt, to keep forever open in the Building a large Hall for occasional Preachers according to the original Intention, and maintain a Free School for the Instruction of poor Children. Writings were accordingly drawn, and on paying the Debts the Trustees of the Academy were put in Possession of the Premises, and by dividing the great and lofty Hall into Stories, and different Rooms above and below for the several Schools, and purchasing some additional Ground, the

6. Actually, two thousand pounds. 7. Actually, January 1751.

whole was soon made fit for our purpose, and the Scholars remov'd into the Building. The Care and Trouble of agreeing with the Workmen, purchasing Materials, and superintending the Work fell upon me, and I went thro' it the more cheerfully, as it did not then interfere with my private Business, having the Year before taken a very able, industrious and honest Partner, Mr. David Hall, with whose Character I was well acquainted, as he had work'd for me four Years.[8] He took off my Hands all Care of the Printing-Office, paying me punctually my Share of the Profits. This Partnership continued Eighteen Years, successfully for us both.

The Trustees of the Academy after a while were incorporated by a Charter from the Governor; their Funds were increas'd by Contributions in Britain, and Grants of Land from the Proprietaries, to which the Assembly has since made considerable Addition, and thus was established the present University of Philadelphia. I have been continued one of its Trustees from the Beginning, now near forty Years, and have had the very great Pleasure of seeing a Number of the Youth who have receiv'd their Education in it, distinguish'd by their improv'd Abilities, serviceable in public Stations, and Ornaments to their Country.

When I disengag'd myself as above-mentioned from private Business, I flatter'd myself that, by the sufficient tho' moderate Fortune I had acquir'd, I had secur'd Leisure during the rest of my Life, for Philosophical Studies[9] and Amusements; I purchas'd all Dr. Spencer's Apparatus, who had come from England to lecture here;[1] and I proceeded in my Electrical Experiments with great Alacrity; but the Public now considering me as a Man of Leisure, laid hold of me for their Purposes; every Part of our Civil Government, and almost at the same time, imposing some Duty upon me. The Governor put me into the Commission of the Peace; the Corporation of the City chose me of the Common Council, and soon after an Alderman; and the Citizens at large chose me a Burgess to represent them in Assembly.[2] This latter Station was the more agreeable to me, as I was at length tired with sitting there to hear Debates in which as Clerk I could take no part, and which were often so unentertaining, that I was induc'd to amuse myself with making magic Squares, or Circles,[3] or anything to avoid Weariness. And I conceiv'd my becoming a Member would enlarge my Power of doing Good. I would not however insinuate that my Ambition was not flatter'd by all these Promotions. It certainly was. For considering my low Beginning they were great Things to me. And they were still more pleasing, as being so many spontaneous Testimonies of the public's good Opinion, and by me entirely unsolicited.

The Office of Justice of the Peace I tried a little, by attending a few Courts, and sitting on the Bench to hear Causes. But finding that more knowledge of the Common Law than I possess'd, was necessary to act in that Station with Credit, I gradually withdrew from it, excusing myself by my being oblig'd

8. Hall (1714–1772), a Scottish printer, moved to Philadelphia in 1743 at Franklin's invitation.
9. I.e., natural science.
1. Archibald Spencer (c. 1698–1760) was a physician, natural scientist, and lecturer on electricity. Franklin heard his Boston lectures in 1743.
2. Franklin served as city councilman in 1748, justice of the peace in 1749, alderman in 1751, and

assemblyman in 1751. "Burgess": representative sent by a town to a legislative body.
3. In a magic square, numbers are arranged so that the sums of each row—horizontal, vertical, and diagonal—are equal. A magic circle is a circular configuration of numbers whose additive values equal 180 or 360 when arranged in a prescribed way.

to attend the higher Duties of a Legislator in the Assembly. My Election to this Trust was repeated every Year for Ten Years, without my ever asking any Elector for his Vote, or signifying either directly or indirectly any Desire of being chosen. On taking my Seat in the House, my Son was appointed their Clerk.

The Year following, a Treaty being to be held with the Indians at Carlisle,[4] the Governor sent a Message to the House, proposing that they should nominate some of their Members to be join'd with some Members of Council as Commissioners for that purpose. The House nam'd the Speaker (Mr. Norris) and myself; and being commission'd we went to Carlisle, and met the Indians accordingly. As those People are extremely apt to get drunk, and when so are very quarrelsome and disorderly, we strictly forbad the selling any Liquor to them; and when they complain'd of this Restriction, we told them that if they would continue sober during the Treaty, we would give them Plenty of Rum when Business was over. They promis'd this; and they kept their Promise—because they could get no Liquor—and the Treaty was conducted very orderly, and concluded to mutual Satisfaction. They then claim'd and receiv'd the Rum. This was in the Afternoon. They were near 100 Men, Women and Children, and were lodg'd in temporary Cabins built in the Form of a Square just without the Town. In the Evening, hearing a great Noise among them, the Commissioners walk'd out to see what was the Matter. We found they had made a great Bonfire in the Middle of the Square. They were all drunk, Men and Women, quarreling and fighting. Their dark-color'd Bodies, half naked, seen only by the gloomy Light of the Bonfire, running after and beating one another with Firebrands, accompanied by their horrid Yellings, form'd a Scene the most resembling our Ideas of Hell that could well be imagin'd. There was no appeasing the Tumult, and we retired to our Lodging. At Midnight a Number of them came thundering at our Door, demanding more Rum; of which we took no Notice. The next Day, sensible they had misbehav'd in giving us that Disturbance, they sent three of their old Counselors to make their Apology. The Orator acknowledg'd the Fault, but laid it upon the Rum; and then endeavor'd to excuse the Rum, by saying, "*The great Spirit who made all things made everything for some Use, and whatever Use he design'd anything for, that Use it should always be put to; Now, when he made Rum, he said,* LET THIS BE FOR INDIANS TO GET DRUNK WITH. *And it must be so.*—And indeed if it be the Design of Providence to extirpate these Savages in order to make room for Cultivators of the Earth, it seems not improbable that Rum may be the appointed Means. It has already annihilated all the Tribes who formerly inhabited the Seacoast.

In 1751 Dr. Thomas Bond, a particular Friend of mine,[5] conceiv'd the Idea of establishing a Hospital in Philadelphia for the Reception and Cure of poor sick Persons, whether Inhabitants of the Province or Strangers. A very beneficent Design, which has been ascrib'd to me, but was originally his. He was zealous and active in endeavoring to procure Subscriptions for it; but the Proposal being a Novelty in America, and at first not well understood, he met with small Success. At length he came to me, with the Compliment that

4. In Pennsylvania.

5. Bond (1712–1784) was Franklin's physician.

he found there was no such thing as carrying a public-spirited Project through, without my being concern'd in it; "for, says he, I am often ask'd by those to whom I propose Subscribing, Have you consulted Franklin upon this Business? and what does he think of it? And when I tell them that I have not, (supposing it rather out of your Line,) they do not subscribe, but say they will consider of it." I enquir'd into the Nature, and probable Utility of his Scheme, and receiving from him a very satisfactory Explanation, I not only subscrib'd to it myself, but engag'd heartily in the Design of Procuring Subscriptions from others. Previous however to the Solicitation, I endeavored to prepare the Minds of the People by writing on the Subject in the Newspapers,[6] which was my usual Custom in such Cases, but which he had omitted. The Subscriptions afterwards were more free and generous, but beginning to flag, I saw they would be insufficient without some Assistance from the Assembly, and therefore propos'd to petition for it, which was done. The Country Members did not at first relish the Project. They objected that it could only be serviceable to the City, and therefore the Citizens should alone be at the Expense of it; and they doubted whether the Citizens themselves generally approv'd of it: My Allegation on the contrary, that it met with such Approbation as to leave no doubt of our being able to raise 2000 Pounds by voluntary Donations, they considered as a most extravagant Supposition, and utterly impossible. On this I form'd my Plan; and asking Leave to bring in a Bill, for incorporating the Contributors, according to the Prayers of their Petition, and granting them a blank Sum of Money, which Leave was obtain'd chiefly on the Consideration that the House could throw the Bill out if they did not like it, I drew it so as to make the important Clause a conditional One, viz., "And be it enacted by the Authority aforesaid That when the said Contributors shall have met and chosen their Managers and Treasurer, *and shall have raised by their Contributions a Capital Stock of 2000 Pounds Value*, (the yearly Interest of which is to be applied to the Accommodating of the Sick Poor in the said Hospital, free of Charge for Diet, Attendance, Advice and Medicines) and *shall make the same appear to the Satisfaction of the Speaker of the Assembly* for the time being; that *then* it shall and may be lawful for the said Speaker, and he is hereby required to sign an Order on the Provincial Treasurer for the Payment of Two Thousand Pounds in two yearly Payments, to the Treasurer of the said Hospital, to be applied to the Founding, Building and Finishing of the same."—This Condition carried the Bill through; for the Members who had oppos'd the Grant, and now conceiv'd they might have the Credit of being charitable without the Expense, agreed to its Passage; And then in soliciting Subscriptions among the People we urg'd the conditional Promise of the Law as an additional Motive to give, since every Man's Donation would be doubled. Thus the Clause work'd both ways. The subscriptions accordingly soon exceeded the requisite Sum, and we claim'd and receiv'd the Public Gift, which enabled us to carry the Design into Execution. A convenient and handsome Building was soon erected, the Institution has by constant Experience been found useful, and flourishes to this Day. And I do not remember any of my political Maneuvers, the Success

6. *Pennsylvania Gazette*, August 8 and 15, 1751. Franklin also published *Some Account of the Pennsylvania Hospital* in 1754.

of which gave me at the time more Pleasure. Or that in after-thinking of it, I more easily excus'd myself for having made some Use of Cunning.

It was about this time that another Projector, the Revd. Gilbert Tennent,[7] came to me, with a Request that I would assist him in procuring a Subscription for erecting a new Meetinghouse. It was to be for the Use of a Congregation he had gathered among the Presbyterians who were originally Disciples of Mr. Whitefield. Unwilling to make myself disagreeable to my fellow Citizens, by too frequently soliciting their Contributions, I absolutely refus'd. He then desir'd I would furnish him with a List of the Names of Persons I knew by Experience to be generous and public-spirited. I thought it would be unbecoming in me, after their kind Compliance with my Solicitations, to mark them out to be worried by other Beggars, and therefore refus'd also to give such a List. He then desir'd I would at least give him my Advice. That I will readily do, said I; and, in the first Place, I advise you to apply to all those whom you know will give something; next to those whom you are uncertain whether they will give anything or not; and show them the List of those who have given: and lastly, do not neglect those who you are sure will give nothing; for in some of them you may be mistaken. He laugh'd, and thank'd me, and said he would take my Advice. He did so, for he ask'd of *everybody*; and he obtain'd a much larger Sum than he expected, with which he erected the capacious and very elegant Meetinghouse that stands in Arch Street.

Our City, tho' laid out with a beautiful Regularity, the Streets large, straight, and crossing each other at right Angles, had the Disgrace of suffering those Streets to remain long unpav'd, and in wet Weather the Wheels of heavy Carriages plough'd them into a Quagmire, so that it was difficult to cross them. And in dry Weather the Dust was offensive. I had liv'd near what was call'd the Jersey Market, and saw with Pain the Inhabitants wading in Mud while purchasing their Provisions. A Strip of Ground down the middle of that Market was at length pav'd with Brick, so that being once in the Market they had firm Footing, but were often over Shoes in Dirt to get there. By talking and writing on the Subject, I was at length instrumental in getting the Street pav'd with Stone between the Market and the brick'd Foot-Pavement that was on each Side next the Houses. This for some time gave an easy Access to the Market, dry-shod. But the rest of the Street not being pav'd, whenever a Carriage came out of the Mud upon this Pavement, it shook off and left its Dirt on it, and it was soon cover'd with Mire, which was not remov'd, the City as yet having no Scavengers.[8] After some Enquiry I found a poor industrious Man, who was willing to undertake keeping the Pavement clean, by sweeping it twice a week and carrying off the Dirt from before all the Neighbors' Doors, for the Sum of Sixpence per Month, to be paid by each House. I then wrote and printed a Paper, setting forth the Advantages to the Neighborhood that might be obtain'd by this small Expense; the greater Ease in keeping our Houses clean, so much Dirt not being brought in by People's Feet; the Benefit to the Shops by more Custom,[9] as Buyers could more easily get at them, and by not having in windy Weather the Dust

7. Presbyterian preacher (1703–1764) in New Brunswick, New Jersey; like George Whitefield, a leader of the Great Awakening. "Projector": someone with a proposal in mind.
8. Street cleaners.
9. Business, trade.

blown in upon their Goods, etc., etc. I sent one of these Papers to each House, and in a Day or two went round to see who would subscribe an Agreement to pay these Sixpences. It was unanimously sign'd, and for a time well executed. All the Inhabitants of the City were delighted with the Cleanlines of the Pavement that surrounded the Market; it being a Convenience to all; and this rais'd a general Desire to have all the Streets paved; and made the People more willing to submit to a Tax for that purpose.

After some time I drew a Bill for Paving the City, and brought it into the Assembly. It was just before I went to England in 1757[1] and did not pass till I was gone, and then with an Alteration in the Mode of Assessment, which I thought not for the better, but with an additional Provision for lighting as well as Paving the Streets, which was a great Improvement. It was by a private Person, the late Mr. John Clifton,[2] his giving a Sample of the Utility of Lamps by placing one at his Door, that the People were first impress'd with the Idea of enlightening[3] all the City. The Honor of this public Benefit has also been ascrib'd to me, but it belongs truly to that Gentleman. I did but follow his Example; and have only some Merit to claim respecting the Form of our Lamps as differing from the Globe Lamps we at first were supplied with from London. Those we found inconvenient in these respects; they admitted no Air below, the Smoke therefore did not readily go out above, but circulated in the Globe, lodg'd on its Inside, and soon obstructed the Light they were intended to afford; giving, besides, the daily Trouble of wiping them clean: and an accidental Stroke on one of them would demolish it, and render it totally useless. I therefore suggested the composing them of four flat Panes, with a long Funnel above to draw up the Smoke, and Crevices admitting Air below, to facilitate the Ascent of the Smoke. By this means they were kept clean, and did not grow dark in a few Hours as the London Lamps do, but continu'd bright till Morning; and an accidental Stroke would generally break but a single Pane, easily repair'd. I have sometimes wonder'd that the Londoners did not, from the Effect Holes in the Bottom of the Globe Lamps us'd at Vauxhall,[4] have in keeping them clean, learn to have such Holes in their Street Lamps. But those Holes being made for another purpose, viz., to communicate Flame more suddenly to the Wick, by a little Flax hanging down thro' them, the other Use of letting in Air seems not to have been thought of.—And therefore, after the Lamps have been lit a few Hours, the Streets of London are very poorly illuminated.

The Mention of these Improvements puts me in mind of one I propos'd when in London, to Dr. Fothergill,[5] who was among the best Men I have known, and a great Promoter of useful Projects. I had observ'd that the Streets when dry were never swept and the light Dust carried away, but it was suffer'd to accumulate till wet Weather reduc'd it to Mud, and then after lying some Days so deep on the Pavement that there was no Crossing but in Paths kept clean by poor People with Brooms, it was with great Labor rak'd together and thrown up into Carts open above, the Sides of which suffer'd some of the Slush at every jolt on the Pavement to shake out and fall,

1. Franklin went to England as an agent for the Pennsylvania Assembly to negotiate with Thomas and Richard Penn on the matter of taxing proprietary estates in common with other property.
2. Quaker apothecary (d. 1759).

3. I.e., illuminating.
4. A garden and amusement park near London.
5. John Fothergill (1712–1780), a leader of the English Quakers and Franklin's physician when he was in London.

sometimes to the Annoyance of Foot-Passengers. The Reason given for not sweeping the dusty Streets was, that the Dust would fly into the Windows of Shops and Houses. An accidental Occurrence had instructed me how much Sweeping might be done in a little Time. I found at my Door in Craven Street[6] one Morning a poor Woman sweeping my Pavement with a birch Broom. She appeared very pale and feeble as just come out of a Fit of Sickness. I ask'd who employ'd her to sweep there. She said, "Nobody; but I am very poor and in Distress, and I sweeps before Gentlefolkeses Doors, and hopes they will give me something." I bid her sweep the whole Street clean and I would give her a Shilling. This was at 9 aClock. At 12 she came for the Shilling. From the Slowness I saw at first in her Working, I could scarce believe that the Work was done so soon, and sent my Servant to examine it, who reported that the whole Street was swept perfectly clean, and all the Dust plac'd in the Gutter which was in the Middle. And the next Rain wash'd it quite away, so that the Pavement and even the Kennel[7] were perfectly clean. I then judg'd that if that feeble Woman could sweep such a Street in 3 Hours, a strong active Man might have done it in half the time. And here let me remark the Convenience of having but one Gutter in such a narrow Street, running down its Middle, instead of two, one on each Side near the Footway. For Where all the Rain that falls on a Street runs from the Sides and meets in the middle, it forms there a Current strong enough to wash away all the Mud it meets with: But when divided into two Channels, it is often too weak to cleanse either, and only makes the Mud it finds more fluid, so that the Wheels of Carriages and Feet of Horses throw and dash it up on the Foot Pavement which is thereby rendered foul and slippery, and sometimes splash it upon those who are walking. My Proposal communicated to the good Doctor, was as follows.

"For the more effectual cleaning and keeping clean the Streets of London and Westminster, it is proposed,

"That the several Watchmen be contracted with to have the Dust swept up in dry Seasons, and the Mud rak'd up at other Times, each in the several Streets and Lanes of his Round.

"That they be furnish'd with Brooms and other proper Instruments for these purposes, to be kept at their respective Stands, ready to furnish the poor People they may employ in the Service.

"That in the dry Summer Months the Dust be all swept up into Heaps at proper Distances, before the Shops and Windows of Houses are usually opened: when the Scavengers with close-covered Carts shall also carry it all away.

"That the Mud when rak'd up be not left in Heaps to be spread abroad again by the Wheels of Carriages and Trampling of Horses; but that the Scavengers be provided with Bodies of Carts, not plac'd high upon Wheels, but low upon Sliders; with Lattice Bottoms, which being cover'd with Straw, will retain the Mud thrown into them, and permit the Water to drain from it, whereby it will become much lighter, Water making the greatest Part of its Weight. These Bodies of Carts to be plac'd at convenient Distances, and the

6. In London, near Charing Cross; Franklin lived there in 1757–62 and 1764–75. 7. Gutter.

Mud brought to them in Wheelbarrows, they remaining where plac'd till the Mud is drain'd, and then Horses brought to draw them away."

I have since had Doubts of the Practicability of the latter Part of this Proposal, on Account of the Narrowness of some Streets, and the Difficulty of placing the Draining Sleds so as not to encumber too much the Passage: But I am still of Opinion that the former, requiring the dust to be swept up and carried away before the Shops are open, is very practicable in the Summer, when the Days are long. For in walking thro' the Strand and Fleet Street one Morning at 7 aClock I observ'd there was not one shop open tho' it had been Daylight and the Sun up above three Hours. The Inhabitants of London choosing voluntarily to live much by Candle Light, and sleep by Sunshine; and yet often complain, a little absurdly, of the Duty on Candles and the high Price of Tallow.

Some may think these trifling Matters not worth minding or relating. But when they consider, that tho' Dust blown into the Eyes of a single Person or into a single Shop on a windy Day, is but of small Importance, yet the great Number of the Instances in a populous City, and its frequent Repetitions give it Weight and Consequence; perhaps they will not censure very severely those who bestow some of Attention to Affairs of this seemingly low Nature. Human Felicity is produc'd not so much by great Pieces of good Fortune that seldom happen, as by little Advantages that occur every Day. Thus if you teach a poor young Man to shave himself and keep his Razor in order, you may contribute more to the Happiness of his Life than in giving him a 1000 Guineas. The Money will be soon spent, and the Regret only remaining of having foolishly consum'd it. But in the other Case he escapes the frequent Vexation of waiting for Barbers, and of their sometimes, dirty Fingers, offensive Breaths and dull Razors. He shaves when most convenient to him, and enjoys daily the Pleasure of its being done with a good Instrument.— With these Sentiments I have hazarded the few preceding Pages, hoping they may afford Hints which some time or other may be useful to a City I love, having lived many Years in it very happily, and perhaps to some of our Towns in America.

Having been for some time employed by the Postmaster General of America, as his Comptroller, in regulating the several Offices, and bringing the Officers to account, I was upon his Death in 1753 appointed jointly with Mr. William Hunter[8] to succeed him by a Commission from the Postmaster General in England. The American Office had never hitherto paid anything to that of Britain. We were to have 600 Pounds a Year between us if we could make that Sum out of the Profits of the Office. To do this, a Variety of Improvements were necessary; some of these were inevitably at first expensive; so that in the first four Years the Office became above 900 Pounds in debt to us. But it soon after began to repay us, and before I was displac'd, by a Freak of the Minister's, of which I shall speak hereafter, we had brought it to yield *three times* as much clear Revenue to the Crown as the Post-Office of Ireland. Since that imprudent Transaction, they have receiv'd from it,— Not one Farthing.[9]

8. Printer and publisher of the *Virginia Gazette* (d. 1761).

9. A former British coin worth one quarter of a penny.

The Business of the Post-Office occasion'd my taking a Journey this Year to New England, where the College of Cambridge of their own Motion, presented me with the Degree of Master of Arts. Yale College in Connecticut, had before made me a similar Compliment.[1] Thus without studying in any College I came to partake of their Honors. They were Confer'd in Consideration of my Improvements and Discoveries in the electric Branch of Natural Philosophy.

In 1754, War with France being again apprehended, a Congress of Commissioners from the different Colonies, was by an Order of the Lords of Trade, to be assembled at Albany, there to confer with the Chiefs of the Six Nations, concerning the Means of defending both their Country and ours.[2] Governor Hamilton, having receiv'd this Order, acquainted the House with it, requesting they would furnish proper Presents for the Indians to be given on this Occasion;[3] and naming the Speaker (Mr. Norris) and myself, to join Mr. Thomas Penn and Mr. Secretary Peters,[4] as Commissioners to act for Pennsylvania. The House approv'd the Nomination, and provided the Goods for the Present, tho' they did not much like treating out of the Province,[5] and we met the other Commissioners and met at Albany about the Middle of June. In our Way thither, I projected and drew up a Plan for the Union of all the Colonies, under one Government so far as might be necessary for Defense, and other important general Purposes. As we pass'd thro' New York, I had there shown my Project to Mr. James Alexander and Mr. Kennedy, two Gentlemen of great Knowledge in public Affairs,[6] and being fortified by their Approbation I ventur'd to lay it before the Congress. It then appear'd that several of the Commissioners had form'd Plans of the same kind. A previous Question was first taken whether a Union should be established, which pass'd in the Affirmative unanimously. A Committee was then appointed, One Member from each Colony, to consider the several Plans and report. Mine happen'd to be prefer'd, and with a few Amendments was accordingly reported.

By this Plan, the general Government was to be administered by a President General appointed and supported by the Crown, and a Grand Council to be chosen by the Representatives of the People of the several Colonies met in their respective Assemblies. The Debates upon it in Congress went on daily hand in hand with the Indian Business. Many Objections and Difficulties were started, but at length they were all overcome, and the Plan was unanimously agreed to, and Copies ordered to be transmitted to the Board of Trade and to the Assemblies of the several Provinces. Its Fate was singular. The Assemblies did not adopt it, as they all thought there was too much *Prerogative* in it; and in England it was judg'd to have too much of the

1. Actually, Harvard conferred the degree on July 25, 1753, and Yale on September 12.
2. At the start of the French and Indian War (1754–63), representatives from seven of the nine British colonies met with representatives from the Iroquois Confederacy (the Seneca, Cayuga, Onondaga, Oneida, Mohawk, and Tuscarora tribes) to discuss a common defense.
3. It was customary to present goods to the Indians. "Governor Hamilton": James (see n. 4, p. 493).
4. Isaac Norris (1701–1766), John (not Thomas) Penn (1729–1795), Richard Peters (1704–1776).
5. I.e., engaging in negotiations outside Pennsylvania.
6. Alexander (1691–1756) and Archibald Kennedy (1685–1763) held public offices in New York, and Kennedy wrote *The Importance of Gaining and Preserving the Friendship of the Indians* (1751).

Democratic.[7] The Board of Trade therefore did not approve of it; nor recommend it for the Approbation of his Majesty; but another Scheme was form'd (suppos'd better to answer the same Purpose) whereby the Governors of the Provinces with some Members of their respective Councils were to meet and order the raising of Troops, building of Forts, etc., etc., to draw on the Treasury of Great Britain for the Expense, which was afterwards to be refunded by an Act of Parliament laying a Tax on America. My Plan, with my Reasons in support of it, is to be found among my political Papers that are printed.[8]

Being the Winter following in Boston, I had much Conversation with Governor Shirley[9] upon both the Plans. Part of what pass'd between us on the Occasion may also be seen among those Papers. The different and contrary Reasons of dislike to my Plan, makes me suspect that it was really the true Medium; and I am still of Opinion it would have been happy for both Sides the Water if it had been adopted. The Colonies so united would have been sufficiently strong to have defended themselves; there would then have been no need of Troops from England; of course the subsequent Pretense for Taxing America, and the bloody Contest it occasioned, would have been avoided. But such Mistakes are not new; History is full of the Errors of States and Princes.

> *"Look round the habitable World, how few*
> *Know their own Good, or knowing it pursue."*[1]

Those who govern, having much Business on their hands, do not generally like to take the Trouble of considering and carrying into Execution new Projects. The best public Measures are therefore seldom *adopted from previous Wisdom*, but *forc'd by the Occasion*.

The Governor of Pennsylvania in sending it down to the Assembly, express'd his Approbation of the Plan "as appearing to him to be drawn up with great Clearness and Strength of Judgment, and therefore recommended it as well worthy their closest and most serious Attention." The House however, by the Management of a certain Member, took it up when I happen'd to be absent, which I thought not very fair, and reprobated[2] it without paying any Attention to it at all, to my no small Mortification.

In my Journey to Boston this Year I met at New York with our new Governor, Mr. Morris,[3] just arriv'd there from England, with whom I had been before intimately acquainted. He brought a Commission to supersede Mr. Hamilton, who, tir'd with the Disputes his Proprietary Instructions subjected him to, had resigned. Mr. Morris ask'd me, if I thought he must expect as uncomfortable an Administration. I said, No; you may on the contrary have a very comfortable one, if you will only take care not to enter into any Dispute with the Assembly; "My dear Friend, says he, pleasantly, how

7. "Too much *Prerogative*" means too much royal power was to be invested in the proposed governor general of all the North American colonies. "Too much of the *Democratic*" means too much power was to be given to the proposed intercolonial legislature.
8. *Political, Miscellaneous, and Philosophical Papers* (1779). Labaree points out that Franklin has oversimplified reasons for the failure of the Albany plan. The colonies feared the domination of any one colony and were wary of strong-willed

colonial assemblies and reluctant to see any one strong legislature emerge.
9. William Shirley (1694–1771), governor of Massachusetts 1741–49 and 1753–56.
1. "Satire 10," lines 1–2, by the ancient Roman writer Juvenal, translated by the seventeenth-century English writer John Dryden.
2. Totally rejected.
3. Robert Hunter Morris (c. 1700–1764), governor of Pennsylvania 1754–56.

can you advise my avoiding Disputes. You know I love Disputing; it is one of my greatest Pleasures: However, to show the Regard I have for your Counsel, I promise you I will if possible avoid them." He had some Reason for loving to dispute, being eloquent, an acute Sophister, and therefore generally successful in argumentative Conversation. He had been brought up to it from a Boy, his Father (as I have heard) accustoming his Children to dispute with one another for his Diversion while sitting at Table after Dinner. But I think the Practice was not wise, for in the Course of my Observation, these disputing, contradicting and confuting People are generally unfortunate in their Affairs. They get Victory sometimes, but they never get Good Will, which would be of more use to them. We parted, he going to Philadelphia, and I to Boston. In returning, I met at New York with the Votes of the Assembly, by which it appear'd that notwithstanding his Promise to me, he and the House were already in high Contention, and it was a continual Battle between them, as long as he retain'd the Government.

I had my Share of it; for as soon as I got back to my Seat in the Assembly, I was put on every Committee for answering his Speeches and Messages, and by the Committees always desired to make the Drafts. Our Answers as well as his Messages were often tart, and sometimes indecently abusive. And as he knew I wrote for the Assembly, one might have imagined that when we met we could hardly avoid cutting Throats. But he was so good-natur'd a Man, that no personal Difference between him and me was occasion'd by the Contest, and we often din'd together.[4] One Afternoon in the height of this public Quarrel, we met in the Street. "Franklin, says he, you must go home with me and spend the Evening. I am to have some Company that you will like;" and taking me by the Arm he led me to his House. In gay Conversation over our Wine after Supper he told us Jokingly that he much admir'd the Idea of Sancho Panza, who when it was propos'd to give him a Government, requested it might be a Government of *Blacks*, as then, if he could not agree with his People he might sell them.[5] One of his Friends who sat next me, says, "Franklin, why do you continue to side with these damn'd Quakers? had not you better sell them? the Proprietor[6] would give you a good Price." The Governor, says I, had not yet *black'd* them enough. He had indeed labor'd hard to blacken the Assembly in all his Messages, but they wip'd off his Coloring as fast as he laid it on, and plac'd it in return thick upon his own Face; so that finding he was likely to be negrified himself, he as well as Mr. Hamilton, grew tir'd of the Contest, and quitted the Government.

These public Quarrels were all at bottom owing to the Proprietaries, our hereditary Governors; who when any Expense was to be incurr'd for the Defense of their Province, with incredible Meanness instructed their Deputies to pass no Act for levying the necessary Taxes, unless their vast Estates were in the same Act expressly excused; and they had even taken Bonds of those Deputies to observe such Instructions. The Assemblies for three Years held out against this Injustice. Tho' constrain'd to bend at last. At length

4. Franklin's account of Pennsylvania politics during this period does not accurately reflect some of the real bitterness.
5. In *Don Quixote*, a novel by the Spanish writer Miguel de Cervantes (1547–1616), Sancho Panza

grieves at the prospect of ruling a kingdom of black people, then realizes he could sell his subjects.
6. At this time, Thomas Penn (1702–1775), son of William and uncle of John.

Captain Denny, who was Governor Morris's Successor, ventur'd to disobey those Instructions; how that was brought about I shall show hereafter.[7]

But I am got forward too fast with my Story; there are still some Transactions to be mentioned that happened during the Administration of Governor Morris.[8]

War being, in a manner, commenced with France the Government of Massachusetts Bay projected an Attack upon Crown Point, and sent Mr. Quincy to Pennsylvania, and Mr. Pownall, afterwards Governor Pownall, to New York to solicit Assistance.[9] As I was in the Assembly, knew its Temper, and was Mr. Quincy's Countryman, he applied to me for my Influence and Assistance. I dictated his Address to them which was well receiv'd. They voted an Aid of Ten Thousand Pounds, to be laid out in Provisions. But the Governor refusing his Assent to their Bill, (which included this with other Sums granted for the Use of the Crown) unless a Clause were inserted exempting the Proprietary Estate from bearing any Part of the Tax that would be necessary, the Assembly, tho' very desirous of making their Grant to New England effectual, were at a Loss how to accomplish it. Mr. Quincy laboured hard with the Governor to obtain his Assent, but he was obstinate. I then suggested a Method of doing the Business without the Governor, by Orders on the Trustees of the Loan-Office, which by Law the Assembly had the Right of Drawing.[1] There was indeed little or no Money at that time in the Office, and therefore I propos'd that the Orders should be payable in a Year and to bear an Interest of Five percent. With these Orders I suppos'd the Provisions might easily be purchas'd. The Assembly with very little Hesitation adopted the Proposal. The Orders were immediately printed, and I was one of the Committee directed to sign and dispose of them. The Fund for Paying them was the Interest of all the Paper Currency then extant in the Province upon Loan, together with the Revenue arising from the Excise,[2] which being known to be more than sufficient, they obtain'd instant Credit, and were not only receiv'd in Payment for the Provisions, but many money'd People who had Cash lying by them, vested it in those Orders, which they found advantageous, as they bore Interest while upon hand, and might on any Occasion be used as Money: So that they were eagerly all bought up, and in a few Weeks none of them were to be seen. Thus this important Affair was by my means completed. Mr. Quincy return'd Thanks to the Assembly in a handsome Memorial, went home highly pleas'd with the Success of his Embassy, and ever after bore for me the most cordial and affectionate Friendship.

The British Government not choosing to permit the Union of the Colonies, as propos'd at Albany, and to trust that Union with their Defense, lest they

7. The Pennsylvania Assembly had failed to get the colony's proprietors to share the expense of government. In 1759, William Denny (1709–1765), a former British Army captain who succeeded Robert Hunter Morris as governor, was pressured into signing a bill that taxed proprietary estates. However, this tax was not enforced until 1775. Franklin does not finish his account.
8. Morris was in office 1754–56; Denny, 1756–59.
9. The colonists are planning to attack Fort Saint-Frédéric, a French outpost at Lake Champlain. The French controlled the territory to the north, and three British colonies (Massachu-

setts, New Hampshire, and New York) controlled the territory to the south. Josiah Quincy (1710–1784) was a wealthy Massachusetts merchant. Thomas Pownall (1722–1805) served as governor of New Jersey (1755–56) before becoming governor of Massachusetts (1757–60).
1. The Loan Office lent paper money authorized by legislative act and secured by mortgages on real estate. Interest was received on the loans. The Assembly was empowered to direct the expenditure of these receipts.
2. A tax on articles made and used in the colonies.

should thereby grow too military, and feel their own Strength, Suspicions and Jealousies at this time being entertain'd of them, sent over General Braddock[3] with two Regiments of Regular English Troops for that purpose. He landed at Alexandria in Virginia, and thence march'd to Frederick Town in Maryland, where he halted for Carriages. Our Assembly apprehending, from some Information, that he had conceived violent Prejudices against them, as averse to the Service, wish'd me to wait upon him, not as from them, but as Postmaster General, under the guise of proposing to settle with him the Mode of conducting with most Celerity and Certainty the Dispatches between him and the Governors of the several Provinces, with whom he must necessarily have continual Correspondence, and of which they propos'd to pay the Expense. My Son accompanied me on this Journey. We found the General at Frederick Town, waiting impatiently for the Return of those he had sent thro' the back Parts of Maryland and Virginia to collect Waggons. I stayed with him several Days, Din'd with him daily, and had full Opportunity of removing all his Prejudices, by the Information of what the Assembly had before his Arrival actually done and were still willing to do to facilitate his Operations.

When I was about to depart, the Returns of Waggons to be obtain'd were brought in, by which it appear'd that they amounted only to twenty-five, and not all of those were in serviceable Condition. The General and all the Officers were surpris'd, declar'd the Expedition was then at an End, being impossible, and exclaim'd against the Ministers for ignorantly landing them in a Country destitute of the Means of conveying their Stores, Baggage, etc., not less than 150 Waggons being necessary. I happen'd to say, I thought it was pity they had not been landed rather in Pennsylvania, as in that Country almost every Farmer had his Waggon. The General eagerly laid hold of my Words, and said, "Then you, Sir, who are a Man of Interest there, can probably procure them for us; and I beg you will undertake it." I ask'd what Terms were to be offer'd the Owners of the Waggons; and I was desir'd to put on Paper the Terms that appear'd to me necessary. This I did, and they were agreed to, and a Commission and Instructions accordingly prepar'd immediately. What those Terms were will appear in the Advertisement I publish'd as soon as I arriv'd at Lancaster,[4] which being, from the great and sudden Effect it produc'd, a Piece of some Curiosity, I shall insert at length, as follows.

ADVERTISEMENT

Lancaster, April 26, 1755.

WHEREAS 150 Waggons, with 4 Horses to each Waggon, and 1500 Saddle or Pack-Horses are wanted for the Service of his Majesty's Forces now about to rendezvous at *Wills's* Creek;[5] and his Excellency General *Braddock* hath been pleased to empower me to contract for the Hire of the same; I hereby give Notice, that I shall attend for that Purpose at *Lancaster* from this Time till next *Wednesday* Evening; and at *York* from next *Thursday* Morning 'till

3. Edward Braddock (1695–1755), commander of the British forces in North America in the French and Indian War.

4. In Pennsylvania.

5. At Fort Cumberland, in Maryland.

Friday Evening; where I shall be ready to agree for Waggons and Teams, or single Horses, on the following Terms, viz.,

1st. That there shall be paid for each Waggon with 4 good Horses and a Driver, *Fifteen Shillings* per *Diem:* And for each able Horse with a Pack-Saddle or other Saddle and Furniture,[6] *Two Shillings* per *Diem.* And for each able Horse without a Saddle, *Eighteen Pence* per *Diem.*

2dly, That the Pay commence from the Time of their joining the Forces at *Wills's* Creek (which must be on or before the twentieth of *May* ensuing) and that a reasonable Allowance be made over and above for the Time necessary for their traveling to *Wills's* Creek and home again after their Discharge.

3dly, Each Waggon and Team, and every Saddle or Pack Horse is to be valued by indifferent[7] Persons, chosen between me and the Owner, and in Case of the Loss of any Waggon, Team or other Horse in the Service, the Price according to such Valuation, is to be allowed and paid.

4thly, Seven Days' Pay is to be advanced and paid in hand by me to the Owner of each Waggon and Team, or Horse, at the Time of contracting, if required; and the Remainder to be paid by General *Braddock*, or by the Paymaster of the Army, at the Time of their Discharge, or from time to time as it shall be demanded.

5thly, No Drivers of Waggons, or Persons taking care of the hired Horses, are on any Account to be called upon to do the Duty of Soldiers, or be otherwise employ'd than in conducting or taking Care of their Carriages and Horses.

6thly, All Oats, Indian Corn or other Forage,[8] that Waggons or Horses bring to the Camp more than is necessary for the Subsistence of the Horses, is to be taken for the Use of the Army, and a reasonable Price paid for it.

Note. My Son *William Franklin*, is empowered to enter into like Contracts with any Person in *Cumberland* County.

B. FRANKLIN.

To the Inhabitants of the Counties of Lancaster, York, and Cumberland.

Friends and Countrymen,

BEING occasionally at the Camp at *Frederick* a few Days since, I found the General and Officers of the Army extremely exasperated, on Account of their not being supplied with Horses and Carriages, which had been expected from this Province as most able to furnish them; but thro' the Dissensions between our Governor and Assembly, Money had not been provided nor any Steps taken for that Purpose.

It was proposed to send an armed Force immediately into these Counties, to seize as many of the best Carriages and Horses as should be wanted, and compel as many Persons into the Service as would be necessary to drive and take care of them.

I apprehended that the Progress of a Body of Soldiers thro' these Counties on such an Occasion, especially considering the Temper they are in, and their Resentment against us, would be attended with many and great Incon-

6. Tack, harnesses.
7. Objective.

8. Fodder.

veniences to the Inhabitants; and therefore more willingly undertook the Trouble of trying first what might be done by fair and equitable Means.

The People of these back Counties have lately complained to the Assembly that a sufficient Currency was wanting; you have now an Opportunity of receiving and dividing among you a very considerable Sum; for if the Service of this Expedition should continue (as it's more than probable it will) for 120 Days, the Hire of these Waggons and Horses will amount to upwards of *Thirty thousand Pounds,* which will be paid you in Silver and Gold of the King's Money.

The Service will be light and easy, for the Army will scarce march above 12 Miles per Day, and the Waggons and Baggage Horses, as they carry those Things that are absolutely necessary to the Welfare of the Army, must march with the Army and no faster, and are, for the Army's sake, always plac'd where they can be most secure, whether on a March or in Camp.

If you are really, as I believe you are, good and loyal Subjects to His Majesty, you may now do a most acceptable Service, and make it easy to yourselves; for three or four of such as cannot separately spare from the Business of their Plantations a Waggon and four Horses and a Driver, may do it together, one furnishing the Waggon, another one or two Horses, and another the Driver, and divide the Pay proportionably between you. But if you do not this Service to your King and Country voluntarily, when such good Pay and reasonable Terms are offered you, your Loyalty will be strongly suspected; the King's Business must be done; so many brave Troops, come so far for your Defense, must not stand idle, thro' your backwardness to do what may be reasonably expected from you; Waggons and Horses must be had; violent Measures will probably be used; and you will be to seek for a Recompense where you can find it, and your Case perhaps be little pitied or regarded.

I have no particular Interest in this Affair; as (except the Satisfaction of endeavouring to do Good and prevent Mischief) I shall have only my Labor for my Pains. If this Method of obtaining the Waggons and Horses is not like to succeed, I am oblig'd to send Word to the General in fourteen Days; and I suppose Sir *John St. Clair* the Hussar, with a Body of Soldiers, will immediately enter the Province, for the Purpose aforesaid, of which I shall be sorry to hear,[9] because

> I am,
>
> > *very sincerely and truly*
> > *your Friend and Well-wisher,* B. FRANKLIN

I receiv'd of the General about 800 Pounds to be disburs'd in Advance-money to the Waggon-Owners, etc.: but that Sum being insufficient, I advanc'd upwards of 200 Pounds more, and in two Weeks, the 150 Waggons with 259 carrying Horses were on their March for the Camp. The Advertisement promised Payment according to the Valuation, in case any Waggon or Horse should be lost. The Owners however, alledging they did not know

9. I.e., Franklin will be sorry because St. Clair will requisition the horses like a "hussar"—a type of cavalryman that, in eighteenth-century Europe, had a reputation for pillage and mistreatment of civilians.

General Braddock, or what Dependance might be had on his Promise, insisted on my Bond for the Performance, which I accordingly gave them.

While I was at the Camp, supping one Evening with the Officers of Colonel Dunbar's Regiment, he[1] represented to me his Concern for the Subalterns, who he said were generally not in Affluence, and could ill afford in this dear[2] Country to lay in the Stores that might be necessary in so long a March thro' a Wilderness where nothing was to be purchas'd. I commiserated their Case, and resolved to endeavor procuring them some Relief. I said nothing however to him of my Intention, but wrote the next Morning to the Committee of Assembly, who had the Disposition of some public Money, warmly recommending the Case of these Officers to their consideration, and proposing that a Present should be sent them of Necessaries and Refreshments. My Son, who had had some Experience of a Camp Life,[3] and of its Wants, drew up a List for me, which I enclos'd in my Letter. The Committee approv'd, and used such Diligence, that conducted by my Son, the Stores arrived at the Camp as soon as the Waggons. They consisted of 20 Parcels, each containing

> 6 lb. Loaf Sugar[4]
> 6 lb. good Muscovado[5] Ditto
> 1 lb. good Green Tea
> 1 lb. good Bohea[6] Ditto
> 6 lb. good ground Coffee
> 6 lb. Chocolate
> ½ Hundredweight best white Biscuit
> ½ lb. Pepper
> 1 Quart best white Wine Vinegar
> 1 Gloucester Cheese
> 1 Keg containing 20lb. good Butter
> 2 Doz. old Madeira Wine
> 2 Gallons Jamaica Spirits[7]
> 1 Bottle Flour of Mustard
> 2 well-cur'd Hams
> ½ Doz. dried Tongues
> 6 lb. Rice.
> 6 lb. Raisins.

These 20 Parcels well pack'd were plac'd on as many Horses, each Parcel with the Horse, being intended as a Present for one Officer. They were very thankfully receiv'd, and the Kindness acknowledg'd by Letters to me from the Colonels of both Regiments in the most grateful Terms. The General too was highly satisfied with my Conduct in procuring him the Waggons, etc., and readily paid my Account of Disbursements; thanking me repeatedly and requesting my farther Assistance in sending Provisions after him. I undertook this also, and was busily employ'd in it till we heard of his Defeat, advancing, for the Service, of my own Money, upwards of 1000 Pounds

1. Thomas Dunbar (d. 1767), who in 1755 replaced Braddock as commander of the North American forces.
2. Expensive. "Subalterns": officers below the rank of captain.
3. William Franklin had been an officer in a colonial army brought together to resist French

Canada.
4. In this period, sugar was either loaf-shaped or cone-shaped.
5. Brown sugar.
6. In the eighteenth century, a fine black tea.
7. Rum.

Sterling, of which I sent him an Account. It came to his Hands luckily for me a few Days before the Battle,[8] and he return'd me immediately an Order on the Paymaster for the round Sum of 1000 Pounds, leaving the Remainder to the next Account. I consider this Payment as good Luck; having never been able to obtain that Remainder; of which more hereafter.

This General was I think a brave Man, and might probably have made a Figure as a good Officer in some European War. But he had too much self-confidence, too high an Opinion of the Validity of Regular Troops,[9] and too mean a One of both Americans and Indians. George Croghan, our Indian Interpreter, join'd him on his March with 100 of those People, who might have been of great Use to his Army as Guides, Scouts, etc., if he had treated them kindly; but he slighted and neglected them, and they gradually left him.

In Conversation with him one day, he was giving me some Account of his intended Progress. "After taking Fort Duquesne,[1] says he, I am to proceed to Niagara; and having taken that, to Frontenac,[2] if the Season will allow time; and I suppose it will; for Duquesne can hardly detain me above three or four Days; and then I see nothing that can obstruct my March to Niagara."—Having before revolv'd in my Mind the long Line his Army must make in their March, by a very narrow Road to be cut for them thro' the Woods and Bushes; and also what I had read of a former Defeat of 1500 French who invaded the Iroquois Country,[3] I had conceiv'd some Doubts, and some Fears for the Event of the Campaign. But I ventur'd only to say, To be sure, Sir, if you arrive well before Duquesne, with these fine Troops so well provided with Artillery, that Place, not yet completely fortified, and as we hear with no very strong Garrison, can probably make but a short Resistance. The only Danger I apprehend of Obstruction to your March, is from Ambuscades of Indians, who by constant Practice are dextrous in laying and executing them. And the slender Line near four Miles long, which your Army must make, may expose it to be attack'd by Surprise in its Flanks, and to be cut like a Thread into several Pieces, which from their Distance cannot come up in time to support each other.

He smil'd at my Ignorance, and replied, "These Savages may indeed be a formidable Enemy to your raw American Militia; but, upon the King's regular and disciplin'd Troops, Sir, it is impossible they should make any Impression." I was conscious of an Impropriety in my Disputing with a military Man in Matters of his Profession, and said no more.—The Enemy however did not take the Advantage of his Army which I apprehended its long Line of March expos'd it to, but let it advance without Interruption till within 9 Miles of the Place,[4] and then when more in a Body, (for it had just pass'd a River, where the Front had halted till all were come over) and in a more open Part of the Woods than any it had pass'd, attack'd its advanc'd Guard; by a heavy Fire from behind Trees and Bushes; which was the first Intelligence

8. The Battle of the Monongahela (also known as the Battle of the Wilderness or Braddock's Defeat), in July 1755, nine miles south of present-day Pittsburgh. Braddock died from wounds received in the battle. George Washington directed the colonial survivors in retreat.
9. I.e., the standing army.
1. French outpost at the intersection of the Allegheny and Monongahela rivers, on the site of what is now Pittsburgh.
2. In Quebec.
3. Franklin may have in mind the campaign of the Marquis de Denonville against the Seneca tribe in 1687. The French were ambushed and forced to retreat.
4. I.e., Fort Duquesne.

the General had of an Enemy's being near him. This Guard being disordered, the General hurried the Troops up to their Assistance, which was done in great Confusion thro' Waggons, Baggage and Cattle; and presently the Fire came upon their Flank; the Officers being on Horseback were more easily distinguish'd, pick'd out as Marks, and fell very fast; and the Soldiers were crowded together in a Huddle, having or hearing no Orders, and standing to be shot at till two-thirds of them were killed, and then being seiz'd with a Panic the whole fled with Precipitation. The Waggoners took each a Horse out of his Team, and scamper'd; their Example was immediately follow'd by others, so that all the Waggons, Provisions, Artillery and Stores were left to the Enemy.

The General being wounded was brought off with Difficulty, his Secretary Mr. Shirley[5] was killed by his Side, and out of 86 Officers 63 were killed or wounded, and 714 Men killed out of 1100.[6] These 1100 had been picked Men, from the whole Army, the Rest had been left behind with Colonel Dunbar, who was to follow with the heavier Part of the Stores, Provisions and Baggage. The Fliers,[7] not being pursu'd, arriv'd at Dunbar's Camp, and the Panic they brought with them instantly seiz'd him and all his People. And tho' he had now above 1000 Men, and the Enemy who had beaten Braddock did not at most exceed 400,[8] Indians and French together; instead of Proceeding and endeavoring to recover some of the lost Honor, he order'd all the Stores, Ammunitions, etc., to be destroy'd, that he might have more Horses to assist his Flight towards the Settlements, and less Lumber[9] to remove. He was there met with Requests from the Governors of Virginia, Maryland and Pennsylvania, that he would post his Troops on the Frontiers so as to afford some Protection to the Inhabitants; but he continu'd his hasty March thro' all the Country, not thinking himself safe till he arriv'd at Philadelphia, where the Inhabitants could protect him. This whole Transaction gave us Americans the first Suspicion that our exalted Ideas of the Prowess of British Regulars had not been well founded.

In their first March too, from their Landing till they got beyond the Settlements, they had plundered and stripped the Inhabitants, totally ruining some poor Families, besides insulting, abusing and confining the People if they remonstrated. This was enough to put us out of Conceit[1] of such Defenders if we had really wanted any. How different was the Conduct of our French Friends in 1781, who during a March thro' the most inhabited Part of our Country, from Rhode Island to Virginia, near 700 Miles, occasion'd not the smallest Complaint for the Loss of a Pig, a Chicken, or even an Apple!

Captain Orme,[2] who was one of the General's Aides Camp, and being grievously wounded was brought off with him, and continu'd with him to his Death, which happen'd in a few Days, told me, that he was totally silent, all the first Day, and at Night only said, *Who'd have thought it?* that he was silent again the following Days, only saying at last, *We shall better know how to deal with them another time*; and died a few Minutes after.

5. William Shirley, Jr. (1721–1755), son of the governor of Massachusetts (see n. 9, p. 557).
6. More accurately, fourteen hundred and sixty-nine military were engaged, four hundred and fifty-six were killed, and five hundred and twenty were wounded.

7. I.e., those who ran away.
8. A more accurate estimate would be eight hundred.
9. I.e., supplies and equipment.
1. Patience.
2. Robert Orme (d. 1790).

The Secretary's Papers with all the General's Orders, Instructions and Correspondence falling into the Enemy's Hands, they selected and translated into French a Number of the Articles, which they printed to prove the hostile Intentions of the British Court before the Declaration of War. Among these I saw some Letters of the General to the Ministry speaking highly of the great Service I had rendered the Army, and recommending me to their Notice. David Hume[3] too, who was some Years after Secretary to Lord Harcourt when Minister in France, and afterwards to General Conway when Secretary of State, told me he had seen among the Papers in that Office Letters from Braddock highly recommending me. But the Expedition having been unfortunate, my Service it seems was not thought of much Value, for those Recommendations were never of any Use to me.

As to Rewards from himself, I ask'd only one, which was, that he would give Orders to his Officers not to enlist any more of our bought servants,[4] and that he would discharge such as had been already enlisted. This he readily granted, and several were accordingly return'd to their Masters on my Application. Dunbar, when the Command devolv'd on him, was not so generous. He Being at Philadelphia on his Retreat, or rather Flight, I applied to him for the Discharge of the Servants of three poor Farmers of Lancaster County that he had enlisted, reminding him of the late General's Orders on that head. He promis'd me, that if the Masters would come to him at Trenton, where he should be in a few Days on his March to New York, he would there deliver their Men to them. They accordingly were at the Expense and Trouble of going to Trenton, and there he refus'd to perform his Promise, to their great Loss and Disappointment.

As soon as the Loss of the Waggons and Horses was generally known, all the Owners came upon me for the Valuation which I had given Bond to pay. Their Demands gave me a great deal of Trouble, my acquainting them that the Money was ready in the Paymaster's Hands, but that Orders for paying it must first be obtained from General Shirley,[5] and my assuring them that I had applied to that General by Letter, but he being at a Distance an Answer could not soon be receiv'd, and they must have Patience; all this was not sufficient to satisfy, and some began to sue me. General Shirley at length reliev'd me from this terrible Situation, by appointing Commissioners to examine the Claims and ordering Payment. They amounted to near twenty Thousand Pound, which to pay would have ruined me.

Before we had the News of this Defeat, the two Doctors Bond came to me with a Subscription Paper,[6] for raising Money to defray the Expense of a grand Firework, which it was intended to exhibit at a Rejoicing on receipt of the News of our Taking Fort Duquesne. I looked grave and said, "it would, I thought, be time enough to prepare for the Rejoicing when we knew we should have occasion to rejoice."—They seem'd surpris'd that I did not immediately comply with their Proposal. "Why, the D—l," says one of them, "you surely don't suppose that the Fort will not be taken?" "I don't know that it

3. Scottish philosopher and historian (1711–1776), later secretary to Francis Seymour-Conway (1719–1749), first Marquis of Hertford.
4. I.e., indentured servants, whose masters received no compensation while they were conscripted.

5. Governor William Shirley, as commander-in-chief.
6. Document asking subscribers to contribute money. "Doctors Bond": the brothers Thomas (1713–1784) and Phineas Bond (1717–1773), Philadelphia physicians.

will not be taken; but I know that the Events of War are subject to great Uncertainty."—I gave them the Reasons of my doubting. The Subscription was dropped, and the Projectors thereby miss'd that Mortification they would have undergone if the Firework had been prepared. Dr. Bond on some other Occasions afterwards said, that he did not like Franklin's forebodings.

Governor Morris who had continually worried the Assembly with Message after Message before the Defeat of Braddock, to beat them into the making of Acts to raise Money for the Defense of the Province without Taxing among others the Proprietary Estates, and had rejected all their Bills for not having such an exempting Clause, now redoubled his Attacks, with more hope of Success, the Danger and Necessity being greater. The Assembly however continu'd firm, believing they had Justice on their side, and that it would be giving up an essential Right, if they suffered the Governor to amend their Money-Bills. In one of the last, indeed, which was for granting 50,000 Pounds, his propos'd Amendment was only of a single Word; the Bill express'd that all Estates real and personal were to be taxed, those of the Proprietaries *not* excepted. His Amendment was; For *not* read *only*. A small but very material Alteration! However, when the News of this Disaster reach'd England, our Friends there whom we had taken care to furnish with all the Assembly's Answers to the Governor's Messages, rais'd a Clamor against the Proprietaries for their Meanness and Injustice in giving their Governor such Instructions, some going so far as to say that by obstructing the Defense of their Province, they forfeited their Right to it. They were intimidated by this, and sent Orders to their Receiver General to add 5000 Pounds of their Money to whatever Sum might be given by the Assembly, for such Purpose. This being notified to the House, was accepted in Lieu of their Share of a general Tax, and a new Bill was form'd with an exempting Clause which pass'd accordingly. By this Act I was appointed one of the Commissioners for disposing of the Money, 60,000 Pounds. I had been active in modelling it, and procuring its Passage: and had at the same time drawn a Bill for establishing and disciplining a voluntary Militia, which I carried thro' the House without much Difficulty, as Care was taken in it, to leave the Quakers at their Liberty.[7]

To promote the Association necessary to form the Militia, I wrote a Dialogue,[8] stating and answering all the Objections I could think of to such a Militia, which was printed and had as I thought great Effect. While the several Companies in the City and Country were forming and learning their Exercise, the Governor prevail'd with me to take Charge of our Northwestern Frontier, which was infested by the Enemy, and provide for the Defense of the Inhabitants by raising Troops, and building a Line of Forts. I undertook this military Business, tho' I did not conceive myself well-qualified for it. He gave me a Commission with full Powers and a Parcel of blank Commissions for Officers to be given to whom I thought fit. I had but little Difficulty in raising Men, having soon 560 under my Command. My Son who had in the preceding War been an Officer in the Army rais'd

7. Franklin's bill was vetoed by the ministry on July 7, 1756. It provided exemption for conscientious objectors, made enlistment voluntary, and contained little in the way of military discipline.
8. "This Dialogue and the Militia Act are in the Gent. Magazine for February and March 1756"

[Franklin's note]. *Dialogue between X, Y, and Z* first appeared in the *Pennsylvania Gazette*, December 18, 1755, and was reprinted in *Gentleman's Magazine*, March 26, 1756. The *Militia Act* appeared in *Gentleman's Magazine* in February 1756.

against Canada, was my Aide de Camp, and of great Use to me. The Indians had burned Gnadenhut, a Village settled by the Moravians, and massacred the Inhabitants, but the Place was thought a good Situation for one of the Forts. In order to march thither, I assembled the Companies at Bethlehem, the chief Establishment of those People. I was surprised to find it in so good a Posture of Defense. The Destruction of Gnadenhut had made them apprehend Danger.[9] The principal Buildings were defended by a Stockade: They had purchased a Quantity of Arms and Ammunition from New York, and had even plac'd Quantities of small Paving Stones between the Windows of their high Stone Houses, for their Women to throw down upon the Heads of any Indians that should attempt to force into them. The armed Brethren too, kept Watch, and reliev'd[1] as methodically as in any Garrison Town. In Conversation with Bishop Spangenberg, I mention'd this my Surprise; for knowing they had obtain'd an Act of Parliament exempting them from military Duties in the Colonies, I had suppos'd they were conscientiously scrupulous of bearing Arms. He answer'd me, "That it was not one of their establish'd Principles; but that at the time of their obtaining that Act, it was thought to be a Principle with many of their People. On this Occasion, however, they to their Surprise found it adopted by but a few." It seems they were either deceiv'd in themselves, or deceiv'd the Parliament. But Common Sense aided by present Danger, will sometimes be too strong for whimsical Opinions.

It was the Beginning of January when we set out upon this Business of Building Forts. I sent one Detachment towards the Minisinks,[2] with Instructions to erect one for the Security of that upper Part of the Country; and another to the lower Part, with similar Instructions. And I concluded to go myself with the rest of my Force to Gnadenhut, where a Fort was thought more immediately necessary. The Moravians procur'd me five Waggons for our Tools, Stores, Baggage, etc. Just before we left Bethlehem, Eleven Farmers who had been driven from their Plantations by the Indians, came to me, requesting a supply of Fire Arms, that they might go back and fetch off their Cattle. I gave them each a Gun with suitable Ammunition. We had not march'd many Miles before it began to rain, and it continu'd raining all Day. There were no Habitations on the Road, to shelter us, till we arriv'd near Night, at the House of a German, where and in his Barn we were all huddled together as wet as Water could make us. It was well we were not attack'd in our March, for Our Ars were of the most ordinary Sort, and our Men could not keep their Gunlocks[3] dry. The Indians are dextrous in Contrivances for that purpose, which we had not. They met that Day the eleven poor Farmers above-mentioned and kill'd Ten of them.[4] The one who escap'd

9. The Moravians, members of the Church of the United Brethren, emigrated from Saxony in 1735 and eventually established settlements in Pennsylvania: their headquarters in Bethlehem and a smaller mission, Gnadenhütten, in present-day Lehighton. In November 1755, French-allied Natives decimated Gnadenhütten. On January 1, 1756, British troops protecting the area were killed by Natives. Franklin received his commission several days after the governor learned of this second attack.
1. I.e., relieved the guard and kept careful watch.
2. I.e., northeastern Pennsylvania. The northern Delaware Indians were called Munsees or Minisinks.
3. The firing mechanisms, which required priming powder.
4. Actually, two of the eleven escaped.

inform'd that his and his Companions' Guns would not go off, the Priming being wet with the Rain.

The next Day being fair, we continu'd our March and arriv'd at the desolated Gnadenhut.[5] There was a Saw Mill near, round which were left several Piles of Boards, with which we soon hutted ourselves; an Operation the more necessary at that inclement Season, as we had no Tents. Our first Work was to bury more effectually the Dead we found there, who had been half interr'd by the Country People. The next Morning our Fort was plann'd and mark'd out, the Circumference measuring 455 feet, which would require as many Palisades to be made of Trees one with another of a Foot Diameter each. Our Axes, of which we had 70 were immediately set to work, to cut down Trees; and our Men being dextrous in the Use of them, great Dispatch was made. Seeing the Trees fall so fast, I had the Curiosity to look at my Watch when two Men began to cut at a Pine. In 6 Minutes they had it upon the Ground; and I found it of 14 Inches Diameter. Each Pine made three Palisades of 18 Feet long, pointed at one End. While these were preparing, our other Men, dug a Trench all round of three feet deep in which the Palisades were to be planted, and our Waggons, the Body being taken off, and the fore and hind Wheels separated by taking out the Pin which united the two Parts of the Perch,[6] we had 10 Carriages with two Horses each, to bring the Palisades from the Woods to the Spot. When they were set up, our Carpenters built a Stage of Boards all round within, about 6 Feet high, for the Men to stand on when to fire thro' the Loopholes. We had one swivel Gun which we mounted on one of the Angles; and fired it as soon as fix'd, to let the Indians know, if any were within hearing, that we had such Pieces. And thus our Fort, (if such a magnificent Name may be given to so miserable a Stockade) was finished in a Week, tho' it rain'd so hard every other Day that the Men could not work.

This gave me occasion to observe, that when Men are employ'd they are best contented. For on the Days they work'd they were good-natur'd and cheerful; and with the consciousness of having done a good Day's work they spent the Evenings jollily; but on the idle Days they were mutinous and quarrelsome; finding fault with their Pork, the Bread, etc., and in continual ill-humor: which put me in mind of a Sea-Captain, whose Rule it was to keep his Men constantly at Work; and when his Mate once told him that they had done everything, and there was nothing farther to employ them about; O, says he, *make them scour the Anchor.*

This kind of Fort, however contemptible, is a sufficient Defense against Indians who have no Cannon. Finding ourselves now posted securely, and having a Place to retreat to on Occasion, we ventur'd out in Parties to scour the adjacent Country. We met with no Indians, but we found the Places on the neighboring Hills where they had lain to watch our Proceedings. There was an Art in their Contrivance of these Places that seems worth mention. It being Winter, a Fire was necessary for them. But a common Fire on the Surface of the Ground would by its Light have discover'd their Position at a Distance. They had therefore dug Holes in the Ground about three feet

5. The march from Bethlehem to Gnadenhütten took place from January 15 to 18, 1756.

6. The shaft that connects the front and rear axles.

Diameter, and somewhat deeper. We saw where they had with their Hatchets cut off the Charcoal from the Sides of burned Logs lying in the Woods. With these Coals they had made small Fires in the Bottom of the Holes, and we observ'd among the Weeds and Grass the Prints of their Bodies made by their laying all around with their Legs hanging down in the Holes to keep their Feet warm, which with them is an essential Point. This kind of Fire, so manag'd, could not discover them either by its Light, Flame, Sparks or even Smoke. It appear'd that their Number was not great, and it seems they saw we were too many to be attack'd by them with Prospect of Advantage.

We had for our Chaplain a zealous Presbyterian Minister, Mr. Beatty,[7] who complain'd to me that the Men did not generally attend his Prayers and Exhortations. When they enlisted, they were promis'd, besides Pay and Provisions, a Gill[8] of Rum a Day, which was punctually serv'd out to them, half in the Morning and the other half in the Evening, and I observ'd they were as punctual in attending to receive it. Upon which I said to Mr. Beatty, "It is perhaps below the Dignity of your Profession to act as Steward of the Rum. But if you were to deal it out, and only just after Prayers, you would have them all about you." He lik'd the Thought, undertook the Office, and with the help of a few hands to measure out the Liquor executed it to Satisfaction; and never were Prayers more generally and more punctually attended, So that I thought this Method preferable to the Punishments inflicted by some military Laws for Non-Attendance on Divine Service.

I had hardly finish'd this Business, and got my Fort well stor'd with Provisions, when I receiv'd a Letter from the Governor, acquainting me that he had called the Assembly, and wish'd my Attendance there, if the Posture of Affairs on the Frontiers was such that my remaining there was no longer necessary. My Friends too of the Assembly pressing me by their Letters to be if possible at the Meeting, and my three intended Forts being now completed,[9] and the Inhabitants contented to remain on their Farms under that Protection, I resolved to return. The more willingly as a New England Officer, Colonel Clapham,[1] experienc'd in Indian War, being on a Visit to our Establishment, consented to accept the Command. I gave him a Commission, and parading the Garrison had it read before them, and introduc'd him to them as an Officer who from his Skill in Military Affairs, was much more fit to command them than myself; and giving them a little Exhortation took my Leave. I was escorted as far as Bethlehem, where I rested a few Days, to recover from the Fatigue I had undergone. The first Night being in a good Bed, I could hardly sleep, it was so different from my hard Lodging on the Floor of our Hut at Gnaden, wrapped only in a Blanket or two.

While at Bethlehem, I enquir'd a little into the Practices of the Moravians. Some of them had accompanied me, and all were very kind to me. I found they work'd for a common Stock,[2] ate at common Tables, and slept in common Dormitories, great Numbers together. In the Dormitories I observ'd Loopholes at certain Distances all along just under the Ceiling, which I

7. Charles Clinton Beatty (c. 1715–1772).
8. Quarter of a pint.
9. Fort Allen, the stockade built under Franklin's supervision; Fort Norris, about fifteen miles northeast, and Fort Franklin, about fifteen miles southwest.
1. William Clapham (d. 1763), a well-known frontiersman.
2. I.e., shared their produce communally.

thought judiciously plac'd for Change of Air. I was at their Church, where I was entertain'd with good Music, the Organ being accompanied with Violins, Hautboys,[3] Flutes, Clarinets, etc. I understood that their Sermons were not usually preached to mix'd Congregations of Men, Women and Children, as is our common Practice; but that they assembled sometimes the married Men, at other times their Wives, then the Young Men, the young Women, and the little Children, each Division by itself. The Sermon I heard was to the latter, who came in and were plac'd in Rows on Benches, the Boys under the Conduct of a young Man their Tutor, and the Girls conducted by a young Woman. The Discourse seem'd well adapted to their Capacities, and was delivered in a pleasing familiar Manner, coaxing them as it were to be good. They behav'd very orderly, but look'd pale and unhealthy, which made me suspect they were kept too much within-doors, or not allow'd sufficient Exercise. I enquir'd concerning the Moravian Marriages, whether the Report was true that they were by Lot? I was told that Lots were us'd only in particular Cases. That generally when a young Man found himself dispos'd to marry, he inform'd the Elders of his Class, who consulted the Elder Ladies that govern'd the young Women. As these Elders of the different Sexes were well acquainted with the Tempers and Dispositions of their respective Pupils, they could best judge what Matches were suitable, and their Judgments were generally acquiesc'd in. But if for example it should happen that two or three young Women were found to be *equally* proper for the young Man, the Lot was then recurr'd to. I objected, If the Matches are not made by the mutual Choice of the Parties, some of them may chance to be very unhappy. And so they may, answer'd my Informer, if you let the Parties choose for themselves.— Which indeed I could not deny.

Being return'd to Philadelphia, I found the Association went on swimmingly, the Inhabitants that were not Quakers having pretty generally come into it, form'd themselves into Companies, and chosen their Captains, Lieutenants and Ensigns according to the new Law.[4] Dr. B.[5] visited me, and gave me an Account of the Pains he had taken to spread a general good Liking to the Law, and ascrib'd much to those Endeavors. I had had the Vanity to ascribe all to my Dialogue; However, not knowing but that he might be in the right, I let him enjoy his Opinion, which I take to be generally the best way in such Cases.—The Officers meeting chose me to be Colonel of the Regiment; which I this time accepted. I forget how many Companies we had, but We paraded about 1200 well-looking Men, with a Company of Artillery who had been furnish'd with 6 brass Field Pieces, which they had become so expert in the Use of as to fire twelve times in a Minute. The first Time I review'd my Regiment, they accompanied me to my House, and would salute me with some Rounds fired before my Door, which shook down and broke several Glasses of my Electrical Apparatus. And my new Honor prov'd not much less brittle; for all our Commissions were soon after broke by a Repeal of the Law in England.[6]

3. Oboes.
4. The militia elections were held from December 22 to 24 and caused rioting when Governor Morris refused to accept balloting at the polls as valid. "Ensigns": standard-bearers; the lowest commissioned army grade.
5. Probably Thomas Bond.
6. Franklin was commissioned on February 23, 1756. In mid-October, Philadelphians were informed that the Militia Act had been rejected.

During the short time of my Colonelship, being about to set out on a Journey to Virginia, the Officers of my Regiment took it into their heads that it would be proper for them to escort me out of town as far as the Lower Ferry. Just as I was getting on Horseback, they came to my door, between 30 and 40, mounted, and all in their Uniforms. I had not been previously acquainted with the Project, or I should have prevented it, being naturally averse to the assuming of State on any Occasion, and I was a good deal chagrin'd at their Appearance, as I could not avoid their accompanying me. What made it worse, was, that as soon as we began to move, they drew their Swords, and rode with them naked all the way. Somebody wrote an Account of this to the Proprietor, and it gave him great Offense. No such Honor had been paid him when in the Province; nor to any of his Governors; and he said it was only proper to Princes of the Blood Royal; which may be true for aught I know, who was, and still am, ignorant of the Etiquette, in such Cases. This silly Affair, however greatly increas'd his Rancor against me, which was before not a little, on account of my Conduct in the Assembly, respecting the Exemption of his Estate from Taxation, which I had always oppos'd very warmly, and not without severe Reflections on his Meanness and Injustice in contending for it. He accus'd me to the Ministry as being the great Obstacle to the King's Service, preventing by my Influence in the House the proper Forming of the Bills for raising Money; and he instanc'd this Parade with my Officers as a Proof of my having an Intention to take the Government of the Province out of his Hands by Force. He also applied to Sir Everard Fawkener, then Post Master General,[7] to deprive me of my Office. But this had no other Effect, than to procure from Sir Everard a gentle Admonition.

Notwithstanding the continual Wrangle between the Governor and the House, in which I as a Member had so large a Share, there still subsisted a civil Intercourse between that Gentleman and myself, and we never had any personal Difference. I have sometimes since thought that his little or no Resentment against me for the Answers it was known I drew up to his Messages, might be the Effect of professional Habit, and that, being bred a Lawyer, he might consider us both as merely Advocates for contending Clients in a suit, he for the Proprietaries and I for the Assembly. He would therefore sometimes call in a friendly way to advise with me on difficult Points, and sometimes, tho' not often, take my Advice. We acted in Concert to supply Braddock's Army with Provisions, and When the shocking News arriv'd of his Defeat, the Governor sent in haste for me, to consult with him on Measures for preventing the Desertion of the back Counties. I forget now the Advice I gave, but I think it was, that Dunbar should be written to and prevail'd with if possible to post his Troops on the Frontiers for their Protection, till by Reinforcements from the Colonies, he might be able to proceed on the Expedition.—And after my Return from the Frontier, he would have had me undertake the Conduct of such an Expedition with Provincial Troops, for the Reduction of Fort Duquesne, Dunbar and his Men being otherwise employ'd; and he propos'd to commission me as General. I had not so good an Opinion of my military Abilities as he profess'd to have; and I believe his Professions must have exceeded his real Sentiments:

7. Fawkener (1684–1758) was appointed postmaster general in 1745.

but probably he might think that my Popularity would facilitate the Raising of the Men, and my Influence in Assembly the Grant of Money to pay them;—and that, perhaps, without taxing the Proprietary Estate. Finding me not so forward to engage as he expected, the Project was dropped: and he soon after left the Government, being superseded by Captain Denny.

Before I proceed in relating the Part I had in public Affairs under this new Governor's Administration, it may not be amiss here to give some Account of the Rise and Progress of my Philosophical[8] Reputation.

In 1746 being at Boston, I met there with a Dr. Spencer, who was lately arrived from Scotland, and show'd me some electric Experiments.[9] They were imperfectly perform'd, as he was not very expert; but being on a Subject quite new to me, they equally surpris'd and pleas'd me. Soon after my Return to Philadelphia, our Library Company receiv'd from Mr. Peter Collinson, F.R.S. of London a Present of a Glass Tube, with some Account of the Use of it in making such Experiments.[1] I eagerly seiz'd the Opportunity of repeating what I had seen at Boston, and by much Practice acquir'd great Readiness in performing those also which we had an Account of from England, adding a Number of new Ones. I say much Practice, for my House was continually full for some time, with People who came to see these new Wonders. To divide a little this Incumbrance among my Friends, I caused a Number of similar Tubes to be blown at our Glass-House, with which they furnish'd themselves, so that we had at length several Performers. Among these the Principal was Mr. Kinnersley,[2] an ingenious Neighbor, who being out of Business, I encouraged to undertake showing the Experiments for Money, and drew up for him two Lectures, in which the Experiments were rang'd in such Order and accompanied with Explanations, in such Method, as that the foregoing should assist in Comprehending the following. He procur'd an elegant Apparatus for the purpose, in which all the little Machines that I had roughly made for myself, were nicely form'd by Instrument-makers. His Lectures were well attended and gave great Satisfaction; and after some time he went thro' the Colonies exhibiting them in every capital Town, and pick'd up some Money. In the West India Islands indeed it was with Difficulty the Experiments could be made, from the general Moisture of the Air.

Oblig'd as we were to Mr. Collinson for his Present of the Tube, etc., I thought it right he should be inform'd of our Success in using it, and wrote him several Letters containing Accounts of our Experiments. He got them read in the Royal Society, where they were not at first thought worth so much Notice as to be printed in their Transactions. One Paper which I wrote for Mr. Kinnersley, on the Sameness of Lightning with Electricity, I sent to Dr. Mitchel,[3] an Acquaintance of mine, and one of the Members also of that Society; who wrote me word that it had been read but was laughed at by the Connoisseurs:[4] The Papers however being shown to

8. Scientific.
9. See n. 1, p. 549.
1. The "Glass Tube" is a solid glass rod that, when rubbed with a cloth, produces electrical charges. Collinson (1694–1768), an English botanist and fellow of the Royal Society (the British national academy of science), is best known for his correspondence with Franklin about electricity.

2. Ebenezer Kinnersley (1711–1778), English-born scientist and scholar.
3. John Mitchell (d. 1768), English physician and mapmaker.
4. Franklin seems to have underestimated the reception of his observations by English scientists, many of whom recognized them as important.

Dr. Fothergill,[5] he thought them of too much value to be stifled, and advis'd the Printing of them. Mr. Collinson then gave them to *Cave*[6] for publication in his Gentleman's Magazine; but he chose to print them separately in a Pamphlet, and Dr. Fothergill wrote the Preface.[7] *Cave* it seems judg'd rightly for his Profit; for by the Additions that arriv'd afterwards they swell'd to a Quarto Volume, which has had five Editions, and cost him nothing for Copy-money.[8]

It was however some time before those Papers were much taken Notice of in England. A Copy of them happening to fall into the Hands of the Count de Buffon,[9] a Philosopher deservedly of great Reputation in France, and indeed all over Europe, he prevail'd with M. Dalibard[1] to translate them into French; and they were printed at Paris. The Publication offended the Abbé Nollet, Preceptor[2] in Natural Philosophy to the Royal Family, and an able Experimenter, who had form'd and publish'd a Theory of Electricity, which then had the general Vogue. He could not at first believe that such a Work came from America, and said it must have been fabricated by his Enemies at Paris, to decry his System. Afterwards having been assur'd that there really existed such a Person as Franklin of Philadelphia, which he had doubted, he wrote and published a Volume of Letters, chiefly address'd to me, defending his Theory, and denying the Verity of my Experiments and of the Positions deduc'd from them. I once purpos'd answering the Abbé, and actually began the Answer. But on Consideration that my Writings contain'd only a Description of Experiments, which any one might repeat and verify, and if not to be verified could not be defended; or of Observations, offer'd as Conjectures, and not delivered dogmatically, therefore not laying me under any Obligation to defend them; and reflecting that a Dispute between two Persons writing in different Languages might be lengthened greatly by mistranslations, and thence misconceptions of one another's Meaning, much of one of the Abbé's Letters being founded on an Error in the Translation; I concluded to let my Papers shift for themselves; believing it was better to spend what time I could spare from public Business in making new Experiments, than in Disputing about those already made. I therefore never answer'd M. Nollet; and the Event gave me no Cause to repent my Silence; for my Friend M. le Roy[3] of the Royal Academy of Sciences took up my Cause and refuted him, my Book was translated into the Italian, German and Latin Languages, and the Doctrine it contain'd was by degrees universally adopted by the Philosophers of Europe in preference to that of the Abbé, so that he liv'd to see himself the last of his Sect: except Mr. B——his Elève[4] and immediate Disciple.

What gave my Book the more sudden and general Celebrity, was the Success of one of its propos'd Experiments, made by Messrs. Dalibard and Delor,

5. John Fothergill (1712–1780), English physician and fellow of the Royal Society.
6. Edward Cave (1691–1754), English publisher of *Gentleman's Magazine* (1731–54).
7. To Franklin's *Experiments and Observations on Electricity* (1751).
8. Money paid to an author for a manuscript. "Quarto Volume": see n. 9, p. 469.
9. Georges-Louis Leclerc, Comte de Buffon (1707–1788), French naturalist.
1. Thomas-François Dalibard (1703–1799), French naturalist.

2. Instructor, tutor. Jean-Antoine Nollet (1700–1770), French scientist whose theories of electricity were corrected by Franklin's experiments.
3. Jean-Baptiste Le Roy (1720–1800), French scientist who invented the first practical generator and perfected the lightning rod.
4. Pupil (French). "Mr. B——": Mathurin-Jacques Brisson (1723–1806), French naturalist and translator of Joseph Priestley's *History and Present State of Electricity* (1767) into French. In this volume, he defended Nollet's ideas against Franklin's.

at Marly, for drawing Lightning from the Clouds.[5] This engag'd the public Attention everywhere. M. Delor, who had an Apparatus for experimental Philosophy, and lectur'd in that Branch of Science, undertook to repeat what he call'd the *Philadelphia Experiments*, and after they were performed before the King and Court, all the Curious of Paris flock'd to see them. I will not swell this Narrative with an Account of that capital Experiment, nor of the infinite Pleasure I receiv'd in the Success of a similar one I made soon after with a Kite at Philadelphia, as both are to be found in the Histories of Electricity. Dr. Wright, an English Physician[6] then at Paris, wrote to a Friend who was of the Royal Society an Account of the high Esteem my Experiments were in among the Learned abroad, and of their Wonder that my Writings had been so little noticed in England. The Society on this resum'd the Consideration of the Letters that had been read to them, and the celebrated Dr. Watson drew up a summary Account of them, and of all I had afterwards sent to England on the Subject, which he accompanied with some Praise of the Writer.[7] This Summary was then printed in their Transactions:[8] And some Members of the Society in London, particularly the very ingenious Mr. Canton, having verified the Experiment of procuring Lightning from the Clouds by a Pointed Rod,[9] and acquainting them with the Success, they soon made me more than Amends for the Slight with which they had before treated me. Without my having made any Application for that Honor, they chose me a Member, and voted that I should be excus'd the customary Payments, which would have amounted to twenty-five Guineas, and ever since have given me their Transactions gratis. They also presented me with the Gold Medal of Sir Godfrey Copley[1] for the Year 1753, the Delivery of which was accompanied by a very handsome Speech of the President Lord Macclesfield,[2] wherein I was highly honored.

Our new Governor, Captain Denny, brought over for me the beforementioned Medal from the Royal Society, which he presented to me at an Entertainment given him by the City. He accompanied it with very polite Expressions of his Esteem for me, having, as he said been long acquainted with my Character. After Dinner, when the Company as was customary at that time, were engag'd in Drinking, he took me aside into another Room, and acquainted me that he had been advis'd by his Friends in England to cultivate a Friendship with me, as one who was capable of giving him the best Advice, and of contributing most effectually to the making his Administration easy. That he therefore desired of all things to have a good Understanding with me; and he begg'd me to be assur'd of his Readiness on all Occasions to render me every Service that might be in his Power. He

5. In 1750, Franklin suggested placing a rod on a steeple to draw "electrical fluid" from thunderclouds and thus demonstrate that lightning involved electricity. Dalibard and his associate Delor (first name unknown) performed Franklin's experiment on May 10, 1752, in Marly-la-Ville, France.
6. Edward Wright (d. 1761), Scottish (not English) physician and fellow of the Royal Society. "Histories of Electricity": e.g., Priestley's.
7. William Watson (1715–1787), physician and scientist, had developed a theory of electricity similar to Franklin's. In 1756, he nominated

Franklin for membership in the Royal Society.
8. Published accounts.
9. John Canton (1718–1772), schoolmaster, was the first person in England to try Franklin's electrical experiments.
1. Copley (c. 1654–1709), English aristocrat, established this annual prize, Britain's oldest scientific honor, to be given to one who had contributed to the advancement of knowledge.
2. George Parker, second Earl of Macclesfield (c. 1697–1764), astronomer and mathematician; president of the Royal Society 1752–64.

said much to me also of the Proprietor's good Dispositions toward the Province, and of the Advantage it might be to us all, and to me in particular, if the Opposition that had been so long continu'd to his Measures, were dropped, and Harmony restor'd between him and the People, in effecting which it was thought no one could be more serviceable than myself, and I might depend on adequate Acknowledgments and Recompenses, etc., etc.

The Drinkers finding we did not return immediately to the Table, sent us a Decanter of Madeira, which the Governor made liberal Use of, and in proportion became more profuse of his Solicitations and Promises. My Answers were to this purpose, that my Circumstances, Thanks to God, were such as to make Proprietary Favors unnecessary to me; and that being a Member of the Assembly I could not possibly accept of any; that however I had no personal Enmity to the Proprietary, and that whenever the public Measures he propos'd should appear to be for the Good of the People, no one should espouse and forward them more zealously than myself, my past Opposition having been founded on this, that the Measures which had been urg'd were evidently intended to serve the Proprietary Interest with great Prejudice to that of the People. That I was much obliged to him (the Governor) for his Professions of Regard to me, and that he might rely on everything in my Power to make his Administration as easy to him as possible, hoping at the same time that he had not brought with him the same unfortunate Instructions his Predecessor had been hamper'd with.[3] On this he did not then explain himself. But when he afterwards came to do Business with the Assembly they appear'd again, the Disputes were renewed, and I was as active as ever in the Opposition, being the Penman first of the Request to have a Communication of the Instructions, and then of the Remarks upon them, which may be found in the Votes of the Time, and in the Historical Review I afterwards publish'd;[4] but between us personally no Enmity arose; we were often together, he was a Man of Letters, had seen much of the World, and was very entertaining and pleasing in Conversation. He gave me the first Information that my old Friend James Ralph was still alive, that he was esteem'd one of the best political Writers in England, had been employ'd in the Dispute between Prince Frederick and the King,[5] and had obtain'd a Pension of Three Hundred a Year; that his Reputation was indeed small as a Poet, *Pope* having damn'd his Poetry in the Dunciad, but his Prose was thought as good as any Man's.[6]

The Assembly finally, finding the Proprietaries obstinately persisted in manacling their Deputies with Instructions inconsistent not only with the Privileges of the People, but with the Service of the Crown, resolv'd to petition the King against them, and appointed me their Agent to go over to England to present and support the Petition.[7] The House had sent up a Bill to the Governor granting a Sum of Sixty Thousand Pounds for the King's

3. As proprietor of Pennsylvania, Thomas Penn gave instructions to his "governor," or deputy. The Assembly distinguished between these orders and those of the British ministry, which they were willing to obey. One issue was the appropriation of money.
4. *An Historical Review of the Constitution and Government of Pennsylvania* (1759) was written by Richard Jackson, but Franklin supplied much of

the material and paid for the book's publication.
5. Frederick Louis, Prince of Wales (1707–1751), led the opposition party to his father, King George II (1683–1760).
6. See n. 8, p. 493.
7. On September 23, 1756, the Assembly condemned private instructions to the "governor," and in 1757 Franklin was sent to London to "remove grievances we labor under."

Use, (10,000 Pounds of which was subjected to the Orders of the then General Lord Loudon,[8]) which the Governor absolutely refus'd to pass, in Compliance with his Instructions. I had agreed with Captain Morris of the Packet[9] at New York for my Passage, and my Stores were put on board, when Lord Loudon arriv'd at Philadelphia, expressly, as he told me to endeavor an Accommodation between the Governor and Assembly, that his Majesty's Service might not be obstructed by their Dissensions: Accordingly he desir'd the Governor and myself to meet him, that he might hear what was to be said on both sides.

We met and discuss'd the Business. In behalf of the Assembly I urg'd all the Arguments that may be found in the public Papers of that Time, which were of my Writing, and are printed with the Minutes of the Assembly and the Governor pleaded his Instructions, the Bond he had given to observe them, and his Ruin if he disobey'd: Yet seem'd not unwilling to hazard himself if Lord Loudon would advise it. This his Lordship did not choose to do, tho' I once thought I had nearly prevail'd with him to do it; but finally he rather chose to urge the Compliance of the Assembly; and he entreated me to use my Endeavors with them for that purpose; declaring he could spare none of the King's Troops for the Defense of our Frontiers, and that if we did not continue to provide for that Defense ourselves they must remain expos'd to the Enemy. I acquainted the House with what had pass'd, and (presenting them with a Set of Resolutions I had drawn up, declaring our Rights, and that we did not relinquish our Claim to those Rights but only suspended the Exercise of them on this Occasion thro *Force,* against which we protested) they at length agreed to drop that Bill and frame another comfortable to the Proprietary Instructions. This of course the Governor pass'd, and I was then at Liberty to proceed on my Voyage: but in the meantime the Packet had sail'd with my Sea-Stores, which was some Loss to me, and my only Recompense was his Lordship's Thanks for my Service, all the Credit of obtaining the Accommodation falling to his Share.

He set out for New York before me; and as the Time for dispatching the Packet Boats, was in his Disposition, and there were two then remaining there, one of which he said was to sail very soon, I requested to know the precise time, that I might not miss her by any Delay of mine. His Answer was, I have given out that she is to sail on Saturday next, but I may let you know *entre nous,*[1] that if you are there by Monday morning you will be in time, but do not delay longer. By some Accidental Hindrance at a Ferry, it was Monday Noon before I arrived, and I was much afraid she might have sailed as the Wind was fair, but I was soon made easy by the Information that she was still in the Harbor, and would not move till the next Day.

One would imagine that I was now on the very point of Departing for Europe. I thought so; but I was not then so well acquainted with his Lordship's Character, of which *Indecision* was one of the Strongest Features. I shall give some Instances. It was about the Beginning of April that I came to New York, and I think it was near the End of June before we sail'd.[2] There

8. John Campbell, fourth Earl of Loudon (1705–1782), served as commander-in-chief of the British forces in North America after Braddock's defeat in 1755.

9. William Morris, captain of the *Halifax* (a packet, or boat for carrying passengers and usually mail and cargo).

1. Between us, privately (French).

2. June 20, 1757.

were then two of the Packet Boats which had been long in Port, but were detain'd for the General's Letters, which were always to be ready tomorrow. Another Packet arriv'd, and she too was detain'd, and before we sail'd a fourth was expected. Ours was the first to be dispatch'd, as having been there longest. Passengers were engag'd in all, and some extremely impatient to be gone, and the Merchants uneasy about their Letters, and the Orders they had given for Insurance (it being War-time) and for Fall Goods. But their Anxiety avail'd nothing; his Lordship's Letters were not ready. And yet whoever waited on him found him always at his Desk, Pen in hand, and concluded he must needs write abundantly.

Going myself one Morning to pay my Respects, I found in his Antechamber one Innis, a Messenger of Philadelphia,[3] who had come from thence express, with a Packet from Governor Denny for the General. He deliver'd to me some Letters from my Friends there, which occasion'd my enquiring when he was to return and where he lodg'd, that I might send some Letters by him. He told me he was order'd to call tomorrow at nine for the General's Answer to the Governor, and should set off immediately. I put my Letters into his Hands the same Day. A Fortnight after I met him again in the same Place. So you are soon return'd, Innis! *Return'd*; No, I am not *gone* yet.—How so?—I have call'd here by Order every Morning these two Weeks past for his Lordship's Letter, and it is not yet ready.—Is it possible, when he is so great a Writer, for I see him constantly at his Scritoire.[4] Yes, says Innis, but he is like St. George on the Signs, *always on horseback, and never rides on.*[5] This Observation of the Messenger was it seems well founded; for when in England, I understood that Mr. Pitt[6] gave it as one Reason for Removing this General, and sending Amherst and Wolf,[7] *that the Ministers never heard from him, and could not know what he was doing.*

This daily Expectation of Sailing, and all the three Packets going down Sandy hook,[8] to join the Fleet there, the Passengers thought it best to be on board, lest by a sudden Order the Ships should sail, and they be left behind. There if I remember right we were about Six Weeks, consuming our Sea Stores, and oblig'd to procure more. At length the Fleet sail'd, the General and all his Army on board, bound to Louisburg with Intent to besiege and take that Fortress;[9] all the Packet Boats in Company, ordered to attend the General's Ship, ready to receive his Dispatches when those should be ready. We were out 5 Days before we got a Letter with Leave to part; and then our Ship quitted the Fleet and steered for England. The other two Packets he still detain'd, carried them with him to Halifax, where he stayed some time to exercise the Men in sham Attacks upon sham Forts, then alter'd his Mind as to besieging Louisburg,[1] and return'd to New York with all his Troops, together with the two Packets above-mentioned and all their Passengers. During his Absence the French and Savages had taken Fort George on the

3. James Ennis (c. 1709–1774), official courier for the government of Pennsylvania.
4. Writing desk.
5. This proverb refers to the image of St. George on horseback slaying a dragon. It was a common tavern sign.
6. William Pitt (1708–1778), prime minister of England, champion of the American cause.
7. Jeffrey Amherst (1717–1797), successor to

Lord Loudon as British commander-in-chief in North America. James Wolfe (1727–1759), commander of the British campaign to seize Quebec.
8. In eastern New Jersey.
9. The Fortress of Louisburg (see n. 6, p. 546).
1. The Earl of Loudon's attack on Fort Louisburg failed because of bad weather and superior French defenses. "Halifax": in Nova Scotia, Southwest of Cape Breton.

Frontier of that Province,[2] and the Savages had massacred many of the Garrison after Capitulation.

I saw afterwards in London, Captain Bonnell, who commanded one of those Packets.[3] He told me, that when he had been detain'd a Month, he acquainted his Lordship that his Ship was grown foul, to a degree that must necessarily hinder her fast Sailing, a Point of consequence for a Packet Boat, and requested an Allowance of Time to heave her down and clean her Bottom. He was ask'd how long time that would require. He answer'd Three Days. The General replied, If you can do it in one Day, I give leave; otherwise not; for you must certainly sail the Day after tomorrow. So he never obtain'd leave tho' detain'd afterwards from day to day during full three Months. I saw also in London one of Bonnell's Passengers, who was so enrag'd against his Lordship for deceiving and detaining him so long at New York, and then carrying him to Halifax, and back again, that he swore he would sue him for Damages. Whether he did or not I never heard; but as he represented the Injury to his Affairs it was very considerable.

On the whole I then wonder'd much, how such a Man came to be entrusted with so important a Business as the Conduct of a great Army: but having since seen more of the great World, and the means of obtaining and Motives for giving Places and Employments, my Wonder is diminished. General Shirley, on whom the Command of the Army devolved upon the Death of Braddock, would in my Opinion if continued in Place, have made a much better Campaign than that of Loudon in 1757, which was frivolous, expensive and disgraceful to our Nation beyond Conception: For tho' Shirley was not a bred Soldier, he was sensible and sagacious in himself, and attentive to good Advice from others, capable of forming judicious Plans, quick and active in carrying them into Execution. Loudon, instead of defending the Colonies with his great Army, left them totally expos'd while he paraded it idly at Halifax, by which means Fort George was lost;—besides he derang'd all our mercantile Operations, and distress'd our Trade by a long Embargo on the Exportation of Provisions, on pretense of keeping Supplies from being obtain'd by the Enemy, but in Reality for beating down their Price in Favor of the Contractors, in whose Profits it was said, perhaps from Suspicion only, he had a Share. And when at length the Embargo was taken off, by neglecting to send Notice of it to Charlestown, the Carolina Fleet was detain'd near three Months longer, whereby their Bottoms were so much damag'd by the Worm,[4] that a great Part of them founder'd in the Passage home. Shirley was I believe sincerely glad of being reliev'd from so burdensome a Charge as the Conduct of an Army must be to a Man unacquainted with military Business. I was at the Entertainment given by the City of New York, to Lord Loudon on his taking upon him the Command. Shirley, tho' thereby superseded, was present also. There was a great Company of Officers, Citizens and Strangers, and some Chairs having been borrowed in the Neighborhood, there was one among them very low which fell to the Lot of Mr. Shirley. Perceiving it as I sat by him, I said, they have given you, Sir, too low a Seat.—No Matter, says he; Mr. Franklin, I find *a low Seat* the easiest!

2. Fort William Henry, on Lake George, in present-day upper New York State.
3. John Dod Bonnell, captain of the packet *Harriott*, was wounded on Loudon's Louisburg campaign.
4. Wormlike mollusks had bored through the ships' planks.

While I was, as afore-mention'd, detain'd at New York, I receiv'd all the Accounts of the Provisions, etc., that I had furnish'd to Braddock, some of which Accounts could not sooner be obtain'd from the different Persons I had employ'd to assist in the Business. I presented them to Lord Loudon, desiring to be paid the Balance. He caus'd them to be regularly examin'd by the proper Officer, who, after comparing every Article with its Voucher, certified them to be right, and the Balance due, for which his Lordship promis'd to give me an Order on the Paymaster. This, however, was put off from time to time, and tho' I called often for it by Appointment, I did not get it. At length, just before my Departure, he told me he had on better Consideration concluded not to mix his Accounts with those of his Predecessors. And you, says he, when in England, have only to exhibit your Accounts at the Treasury, and you will be paid immediately. I mention'd, but without Effect, the great and unexpected Expense I had been put to by being detain'd so long at New York, as a Reason for my desiring to be presently paid; and On my observing that it was not right I should be put to any farther Trouble or Delay in obtaining the Money I had advanc'd, as I charg'd no Commissions for my Service. O, Sir, says he, you must not think of persuading us that you are no Gainer. We understand better those Affairs, and know that every one concern'd in supplying the Army finds means in the doing it to fill his own Pockets. I assur'd him that was not my Case, and that I had not pocketed a Farthing: but he appear'd clearly not to believe me; and indeed I have since learned that immense Fortunes are often made in such Employments.—As to my Balance, I am not paid it to this Day, of which more hereafter.

Our Captain of the Packet had boasted much before we sail'd, of the Swiftness of his Ship. Unfortunately when we came to Sea, she proved the dullest[5] of 96 Sail, to his no small Mortification. After many Conjectures respecting the Cause, when we were near another Ship almost as dull as ours, which however gain'd upon us, the Captain order'd all hands to come aft and stand as near the Ensign Staff[6] as possible. We were, Passengers included, about forty Persons. While we stood there the Ship mended her Pace, and soon left our Neighbor far behind, which prov'd clearly what our Captain suspected, that she was loaded too much by the Head. The Casks of Water it seems had been all plac'd forward. These he therefore order'd to be remov'd farther aft; on which the Ship recover'd her Character, and prov'd the best Sailor in the Fleet.

The Captain said she had once gone at the Rate of 13 Knots, which is accounted 13 Miles per hour.[7] We had on board as a Passenger Captain Kennedy[8] of the Navy, who contended that it was impossible, that no Ship ever sailed so fast, and that there must have been some Error in the Division of the Log-Line, or some Mistake in heaving[9] the Log. A Wager ensu'd between the two Captains, to be decided when there should be sufficient Wind. Kennedy thereupon examin'd rigorously the Log-line, and being satisfied with that, he determin'd to throw the Log himself. Accordingly some Days after

5. Slowest.
6. The flagpole bearing the ship's flag.
7. Thirteen nautical miles, or approximately fifteen land miles per hour.

8. Archibald Kennedy Jr. (d. 1794); Franklin had consulted with his father on the Albany plan (see n. 6, p. 556).
9. Setting up, measuring.

when the Wind blew very fair and fresh, and the Captain of the Packet (Lut-widge) said he believ'd she then went at the Rate of 13 Knots, Kennedy made the Experiment, and own'd his Wager lost.

The above Fact I give for the sake of the following Observation. It has been remark'd as an Imperfection in the Art of Shipbuilding, that it can never be known till she is tried, whether a new Ship will or will not be a good Sailor; for that the Model of a good sailing Ship has been exactly follow'd in a new One, which has prov'd on the contrary remarkably dull. I apprehend this may be partly occasion'd by the different Opinions of Seamen respecting the Modes of lading, rigging and sailing of a Ship. Each has his System. And the same Vessel laden by the Judgment and Orders of one Captain shall sail better or worse than when by the Orders of another. Besides, it scarce ever happens that a Ship is form'd, fitted for the Sea, and sail'd by the same Person. One Man builds the Hull, another rigs her, a third lades[1] and sails her. No one of these has the Advantage of knowing all the Ideas and Experience of the others, and therefore cannot draw just Conclusions from a Combination of the whole. Even in the simple Operation of Sailing when at Sea, I have often observ'd different Judgments in the Officers who commanded the successive Watches, the Wind being the same. One would have the Sails trimm'd sharper or flatter than another, so that they seem'd to have no certain Rule to govern by. Yet I think a Set of Experiments might be instituted, first to determine the most proper Form of the Hull for swift sailing; next the best Dimensions and properest Place for the Masts; then the Form and Quantity of Sail, and their Position as the Winds may be; and lastly the Disposition of her Lading. This is the Age of Experiments; and such a Set accurately made and combin'd would be of great Use. I am therefore persuaded that ere long some ingenious Philosopher will undertake it—to whom I wish Success.

We were several times chas'd on our Passage, but outsail'd everything, and in thirty Days had Soundings.[2] We had a good Observation,[3] and the Captain judg'd himself so near our Port, (Falmouth) that if we made a good Run in the Night we might be off the Mouth of that Harbor in the Morning, and by running in the Night might escape the Notice of the Enemy's Privateers,[4] who often cruis'd near the Entrance of the Channel. Accordingly all the Sail was set that we could possibly make, and the Wind being very fresh and fair, we went right before it, and made great Way. The Captain after his Observation, shap'd his Course as he thought so as to pass wide of the Scilly Isles:[5] but it seems there is sometimes a strong Indraft setting up St. George's Channel which deceives Seamen, and caus'd the Loss of Sir Cloudsley Shovel's Squadron.[6] This Indraft was probably the Cause of what happen'd to us. We had a Watchman plac'd in the Bow to whom they often call'd, *Look well out befor'e, there*; and he as often answer'd *Aye,*

1. Loads.
2. I.e., land on the bottom of the sea could be touched with a weighted line, so the ship was near shore.
3. I.e., they could determine their location by the sun's position.
4. Armed ships in private hands, commissioned by a government to seize its enemies' ships.

5. Group of islands and rocks twenty-five miles southwest of England.
6. St. George's Channel is between England and Ireland. There, in one of Britain's worst maritime disasters, four ships commanded by Cloudsley Shovell (c. 1650–1707) struck the rocks and went down on October 22, 1707.

Aye! But perhaps had his Eyes shut, and was half asleep at the time: they sometimes answering as is said mechanically: For he did not see a Light just before us, which had been hid by the Studding Sails[7] from the Man at Helm and from the rest of the Watch; but by an accidental Yaw[8] of the Ship was discover'd, and occasion'd a great Alarm, we being very near it, the light appearing to me as big as a Cart Wheel. It was Midnight, and Our Captain fast asleep. But Captain Kennedy jumping upon Deck, and seeing the Danger, ordered the Ship to wear round, all Sails standing. An Operation dangerous to the Masts, but it carried us clear, and we escap'd Shipwreck, for we were running right upon the Rocks on which the Lighthouse was erected. This Deliverance impress'd me strongly with the Utility of Lighthouses, and made me resolve to encourage the building more of them in America, if I should live to return there.

In the Morning it was found by the Soundings, etc., that we were near our Port, but a thick Fog hid the Land from our Sight. About 9 aClock the Fog began to rise, and seem'd to be lifted up from the Water like the Curtain at a Playhouse, discovering underneath the Town of Falmouth, the Vessels in its Harbor, and the Fields that surrounded it. A most pleasing Spectacle to those who had been so long without any other Prospects, than the uniform View of a vacant Ocean! And it gave us the more Pleasure, as we were now freed from the Anxieties which the State of War occasion'd.

I set out immediately with my Son for London, and we only stopped a little by the Way to view Stonehenge[9] on Salisbury Plain, and Lord Pembroke's House and Gardens, with his very curious Antiquities at Wilton.[1]

We arriv'd in London the 27th of July 1757.[2] [*Part Four*] As soon as I was settled in a Lodging Mr. Charles[3] had provided for me, I went to visit Dr. Fothergill, to whom I was strongly recommended, and whose Counsel respecting my Proceedings I was advis'd to obtain. He was against an immediate Complaint to Government, and thought the Proprietaries should first be personally applied to, who might possibly be induc'd by the Interposition and Persuasion of some private Friends to accommodate Matters amicably. I then waited on my old Friend and Correspondent Mr. Peter Collinson, who told me that John Hanbury, the great Virginia Merchant, had requested to be informed when I should arrive, that he might carry me to Lord Granville's, who was then President of the Council,[4] and wish'd to see me as soon as possible. I agreed to go with him the next Morning. Accordingly Mr. Hanbury called for me and took me in his Carriage to that Nobleman's, who receiv'd me with great Civility; and after some Questions respecting the present State of Affairs in America, and Discourse thereupon, he said to me, "You Americans have wrong Ideas of the Nature of your Constitution; you contend that the King's Instructions to his Governors are not Laws,

7. Small sails set at the sides of larger sails.
8. Movement.
9. The prehistoric British monument, about ten miles north of Salisbury.
1. Wilton House, home of the earls of Pembroke and one of the great manor houses of England.
2. Franklin arrived at Falmouth on July 17 and reached London on the evening of July 26. This sentence concludes the third part of *The Autobiography*. It was the last sentence in the manuscript printed by Franklin's son in 1818. Franklin

wrote Part Four between November 13, 1789, and his death, on April 17, 1790, at age 84.
3. Robert Charles (1706–1770), a colonist living in London and serving as colonial agent for New York and Pennsylvania.
4. In 1751–63, John Cartaret, first Earl of Granville (1690–1763), was president of the king's Privy Council, which ruled on Franklin's case against the proprietors. Collinson (see n. 1, p. 573) was a cloth merchant by trade, and Hanbury (1700–1758) was a tobacco merchant.

and think yourselves at Liberty to regard or disregard them at your own Discretion. But those Instructions are not like the Pocket Instructions given to a Minister going abroad, for regulating his Conduct in some trifling Point of Ceremony. They are first drawn up by Judges learned in the Laws; they are then considered, debated and perhaps amended in Council, after which they are signed by the King. They are then so far as relates to you, the *Law of the Land:* for THE KING IS THE LEGISLATOR OF THE COLONIES."

I told his Lordship this was new Doctrine to me. I had always understood from our Charters, that our Laws were to be made by our Assemblies, to be presented indeed to the King for his Royal Assent, but that being once given the King could not repeal or alter them. And as the Assemblies could not make permanent Laws without his Assent, so neither could he make a Law for them without theirs. He assur'd me I was totally mistaken. I did not think so however. And his Lordship's Conversation having a little alarm'd me as to what might be the Sentiments of the Court concerning us, I wrote it down as soon as I return'd to my Lodgings.—I recollected that about 20 Years before,[5] a Clause in a Bill brought into Parliament by the Ministry, had propos'd to make the King's Instructions Laws in the Colonies; but the Clause was thrown out by the Commons, for which we ador'd them as our Friends and Friends of Liberty, till by their Conduct towards us in 1765, it seem'd that they had refus'd that Point of Sovereignty to the King, only that they might reserve it for themselves.[6]

After some Days,[7] Dr. Fothergill having spoken to the Proprietaries, they agreed to a Meeting with me at Mr. J. Penn's[8] House in Spring Garden. The Conversation at first consisted of mutual Declarations of Disposition to reasonable Accommodation; but I suppose each Party had its own Ideas of what should be meant by *reasonable.* We then went into Consideration of our several Points of Complaint which I enumerated. The Proprietaries justified their Conduct as well as they could, and I the Assembly's. We now appeared very wide, and so far from each other in Our Opinions, as to discourage all Hope of Agreement. However, it was concluded that I should give them the Heads of our Complaints in Writing, and they promis'd then to consider them.—I did so soon after;[9] but they put the Paper into the Hands of their Solicitor Ferdinando John Paris,[1] who manag'd for them all their Law Business in their great Suit with the neighboring Proprietary of Maryland, Lord Baltimore,[2] who had subsisted 70 Years, and wrote for them all their Papers and Messages in their Dispute with the Assembly. He was a proud angry Man; and as I had occasionally in the Answers of the Assembly treated his Papers with some Severity, they being really weak in point of

5. Actually, in 1744. In the next sentence, Franklin leaps ahead to 1765–66.
6. After Parliament repealed the Stamp Act in 1766 it passed the Declaratory Act, which asserted the right of Parliament to legislate for the colonies without their consent. The Stamp Act of 1765 was an act of Parliament that imposed a direct tax on the colonies. In response to colonial protests, Parliament repealed this act in 1766. At the same time, it passed the Declaratory Act, which asserted Parliament's unconditional right to legislate for the colonies without their consent.
7. I.e., in July–August 1757.

8. Actually, Thomas Penn (see n. 3, p. 576), who lived in England after 1741 but remained proprietor of Pennsylvania until 1775.
9. On August 20, 1757; "Heads": i.e., chief points.
1. John Ferdinand Paris (d. 1759), attorney specializing in colonial affairs and legal adviser to the Penns.
2. Charles Calvert, the fifth Baron Baltimore (1699–1751), proprietor of Maryland. The dispute over the boundary between Pennsylvania and Maryland was settled by the survey of the Mason-Dixon Line, 1763–67.

Argument, and haughty in Expression, he had conceiv'd a mortal Enmity to me, which discovering itself whenever we met, I declin'd the Proprietary's Proposal that he and I should discuss the Heads of Complaint between our two selves, and refus'd treating with anyone but them. They then by his Advice put the Paper into the Hands of the Attorney and Solicitor General for their Opinion and Counsel upon it, where it lay unanswered a Year wanting eight Days, during which time I made frequent Demands of an Answer from the Proprietaries but without obtaining any other than that they had not yet receiv'd the Opinion of the Attorney and Solicitor General: What it was when they did receive it I never learned, for they did not communicate it to me, but sent a long Message to the Assembly drawn and signed by Paris reciting my Paper, complaining of its want of Formality as a Rudeness on my part, and giving a flimsy Justification of their Conduct, adding that they should be willing to accommodate Matters, if the Assembly would send over *some Person of Candor* to treat with them for that purpose, intimating thereby that I was not such.

The want of Formality or Rudeness, was probably my not having address'd the Paper to them with their assum'd Titles of true and absolute Proprietaries of the Province of Pennsylvania, which I omitted as not thinking it necessary in a Paper the Intention of which was only to reduce to a Certainty by writing what in Conversation I had delivered *vivâ voce*.[3] But during this Delay, the Assembly having prevail'd with Governor Denny to pass an Act taxing the Proprietary Estate in common with the Estates of the People, which was the grand Point in Dispute, they omitted answering the Message.

When the Act however came over, the Proprietaries counsel'd by Paris determin'd to oppose its receiving the Royal Assent. Accordingly they petition'd the King in Council, and a Hearing was appointed, in which two Lawyers were employ'd by them against the Act, and two by me in Support of it. They alledg'd that the Act was intended to load the Proprietary Estate in order to spare those of the People, and that if it were suffer'd to continue in force, and the Proprietaries who were in Odium with the People, left to their Mercy in proportioning the Taxes, they would inevitably be ruined. We replied that the Act had no such Intention and would have no such Effect. That the Assessors were honest and discreet Men, under an Oath to assess fairly and equitably, and that any Advantage each of them might expect in lessening his own Tax by augmenting that of the Proprietaries was too trifling to induce them to perjure themselves. This is the purport of what I remember as urg'd by both Sides, except that we insisted strongly on the mischievous Consequences that must attend a Repeal; for that the Money, 100,000 Pounds, being printed and given to the King's Use, expended in his Service, and now spread among the People, the Repeal would strike it dead in their Hands to the Ruin of many, and the total Discouragement of future Grants, and the Selfishness of the Proprietors in soliciting such a general Catastrophe, merely from a groundless Fear of their Estate being taxed too highly, was insisted on in the strongest Terms.

On this Lord Mansfield, one of the Council[4] rose, and beckoning to me, took me into the Clerk's Chamber, while the Lawyers were pleading, ask'd

3. Orally (Latin).
4. William Murray, first Earl of Mansfield (1705–1793), chief justice of the King's Bench.

me if I was really of Opinion that no Injury would be done the Proprietary Estate in the Execution of the Act. I said, Certainly. Then says he, you can have little Objection to enter into an Engagement to assure that Point. I answer'd None, at all. He then call'd in Paris, and after some Discourse his Lordship's Proposition was accepted on both Sides; a Paper to the purpose was drawn up by the Clerk of the Council, which I sign'd with Mr. Charles, who was also an Agent of the Province for their ordinary Affairs; when Lord Mansfield return'd to the Council Chamber where finally the Law was allowed to pass. Some Changes were however recommended and we also engag'd they should be made by a subsequent Law; but the Assembly did not think them necessary. For one Year's Tax having been levied by the Act before the Order of Council arrived, they appointed a Committee to examine the Proceedings of the Assessors, and On this Committee they put several particular Friends of the Proprietaries. After a full Enquiry they unanimously sign'd a Report that they found the Tax had been assess'd with perfect Equity.

The Assembly look'd on my entering into the first Part of the Engagement as an essential Service to the Province, since it secur'd the Credit of the Paper Money then spread over all the Country; and they gave me their Thanks in form when I return'd. But the Proprietaries were enrag'd at Governor Denny for having pass'd the Act, and turn'd him out, with Threats of suing him for Breach of Instructions which he had given Bond to observe. He however having done it at the Instance[5] of the General and for his Majesty's Service, and having some powerful Interest at Court, despis'd the Threats, and they were never put in Execution.

1771–90 1868

5. Urging.

SAMSON OCCOM
1723–1792

Born in a wigwam on Mohegan land near New London, Connecticut, Samson Occom (or Occum, as it is sometimes spelled) belonged to the northernmost branch of the Pequot tribe. When the religious revival known as the Great Awakening began, his mother, Sarah Occom, was among the first Mohegans to convert to evangelical, or New Light, Protestantism. In 1741, Occom himself converted to Christianity after hearing a sermon by the radical New Light preacher John Davenport. The following year, he was appointed to the Mohegan tribal council, where he served with his father, Joshua Occom. Two years later, he attended hearings in the Mason case, a land dispute between the state of Connecticut and the Mohegans where historic deeds and treaties played a large role. The case was decided in favor of Connecticut. Convinced that literacy was a crucial skill for defending native

sovereignty in their historic domains, Occom sought out the Reverend Eleazar Wheelock, a Yale graduate and New Light minister who kept a small school at Lebanon Creek, in Mohegan territory. From 1743 until 1747, Occom studied English, Hebrew, Greek, and Latin with Wheelock. After completing his studies, he taught school for a short period, then prepared for the ministry under the Reverend Benjamin Pomeroy in Hebron, Connecticut.

In 1749, Occom moved to Montauk, at the southeastern tip of Long Island, New York. There, with the support of the local Montaukett community and the Boston branch of the Company for the Propagation of the Gospel in New England, he started a school for about thirty Native and white children. He married a Montaukett former pupil, Mary Fowler, in 1751, and together they formed a traditional home in a Montauk wigwam and started a family. After eleven years with the Montauks, during which time Occom served not only as a teacher but also as a healer, judge, and counselor, he was ordained by the presbytery of Suffolk, on Long Island. In 1761, he wrote *An Account of the Montauk Indians, on Long Island*, an early example of an indigenous author writing an ethnographic account of a Native community. That same year, he undertook a mission to the Iroquois, establishing a school in Oneida, in upstate New York, and recruiting students for Moor's Indian Charity School, a small institution that Wheelock had recently opened in Lebanon to help develop a Native ministry.

Occom went to England on a speaking tour with the Reverend Nathaniel Whitaker to raise funds for the Indian Charity School in 1765. Before his departure, Occom wrote a short autobiography to clarify some details about his background for the group sponsoring his trip. Over the next two years, he delivered some three hundred sermons across England, Scotland, and Ireland, while collecting around twelve thousand pounds for the school—an enormous sum of money for the time. During his stay in London, he testified in an appeal of the Mason land case. Wheelock had promised to care for Occom's family while he was away, but when Occom returned, he found his relations sickly and in extreme poverty.

In dire financial straits, alienated from Wheelock, and feeling vulnerable as an "Indian preacher" in the Presbyterian Church, Occom wrote a ten-page autobiography by way of self-justification. Dated September 17, 1768, *A Short Narrative of My Life* was not published until 1982. It provides fascinating details of the day-to-day life of a rural minister in eighteenth-century North America. Occom describes how he tended his garden, his animals, and his congregation, and how he preached to his Native parishioners and used innovative pedagogy to teach their children to read. He speculates that some of the criticisms leveled against him arose simply because "I am a poor Indian."

When Occom learned that Wheelock intended to use the money raised on the speaking tour to expand the Indian School into a college and move it to Hanover, New Hampshire, he angrily predicted to Wheelock that his college had too much "Grandeur for the Poor Indians, they'll never have much benefit of it." He was right. The newly renamed Dartmouth College soon ceased to focus on educating Native American students, and in 1773 Occom and Wheelock broke off their long relationship.

By that time, however, Occom had established himself as a public figure. On September 2, 1772, he preached at the execution of Moses Paul, a Wampanoag man convicted of murder. His sermon was densely packed with Scriptural allusions, and it addressed several audiences at once. Noting that he was preaching "at the earnest desire and invitation of the poor condemned Criminal," Occom called upon the assembled ministers to do the work of the Lord and exhorted his Native audience to avoid "the sin of drunkenness." *A Sermon, Preached at the Execution of Moses Paul, an Indian* was first printed on October 31 and went through three further editions by the end of the year. Nineteen editions were ultimately published, an extraordinary number for any work in this period.

The Reverend M^r SAMSON OCCOM,

The first Indian Minister that ever was in Europe & who accompanied the Rev^d. Nathan^l Whitaker D.D. in an application to Great Britain for Charities to support y^e Rev^d. D^r Wheelock's Indian Academy & Missionaries among y^e Native Savages of N. America.

Publish'd according to Act of Parliament, Sept^r 20th 1768 by Henry Parker, at N^o 82 in Cornhill, LONDON.

Samson Occom. Made during Occom's speaking tour of the British Isles, this famous print shows him pointing at a Bible. A bow and arrows hang directly above.

Meanwhile, Occom preached widely, especially in New England, often to congregations of Native Christians. In 1774, he published his *Collection of Hymns and Spiritual Songs*, which included six hymns of his own composition. A prominent feature of Christian worship for centuries, hymns had become a source of friction between traditionalists and evangelical New Lights, who preferred the new hymns of the English theologians Isaac Watts and Charles Wesley to the older hymns in collections such as the *Bay Psalm Book* (excerpted earlier in this volume). Despite these tensions, hymn singing had become a central element of worship in Native Christian

communities. Occom's hymnal appealed to a wide audience, appearing in four editions, the last in 1792. It had a lasting impact on the American tradition of hymnody.

A few months after Moses Paul's execution, Occom had attended the first organizational meeting of the Brotherton group, a pantribal movement to establish a Christian Indian town in Oneida territory. The aim of the town was to provide residents with a space where they could exercise self-governance, sheltered from white influence and encroachment. Occom was closely involved with the Brotherton community for over a decade. Shortly after moving his family to Brotherton in 1789, however, Occom became frustrated by conflicts within the community over the disposition of lands to whites. In 1791, the family moved to the Native Christian town of New Stockbridge, some fifteen miles northwest of Brotherton. When Occom died there the following year, of natural causes, three hundred indigenous people attended his funeral.

From An Account of the Montauk Indians, on Long Island[1]

III. Concerning their GODS. They imagined a great number of gods. There were the gods of the four corners of the earth; the god of the east, the god of the west, the god of the north, the god of the south; and there was a god over their corn, another over their beans, another over their pumpkins, and squashes, &c. There was one god over their wigwams, another of the fire, another over the sea, another of the wind, one of the day, and another of the night; and there were four gods over the four parts of the year, &c. &c.

But they had a notion of one great and good God, that was over all the rest of the gods, which they called CAUHLUNTOOWUT, which signifies one that is possessed with supreme power. They also had a notion of a great evil god, which they called Mutcheshesunnetooh, which signifies evil power, who they say is mischievous, &c.

And to these gods they call for help under every difficulty, and to them they offered their sacrifices of various kinds, &c.

As for their images, they kept them as oracles. The powwaws[2] consult these images to know the minds of their gods; for they pretend these images tell what the people should do to the gods, either to make a dance or a feast, or give something to the old people, or sacrifice to the gods.

IV. As for the POWAWS, they say they get their art from dreams; and one has told me they get their art from the devil, but then partly by dreams or night visions, and partly by the devil's immediate appearance to them by various shapes; sometimes in the shape of one creature, sometimes in another, sometimes by a voice, &c. and their poisoning one another, and taking out poison, they say is no imaginary thing, but real. I have heard some say, that have been poisoned, it puts them into great pain, and when a powaw takes out the poison they have found immediate relief; at other times they feel no manner of pain, but feel strangely by degrees, till they are senseless, and then they will run mad. Sometimes they would run into the water; sometimes into the fire; and at other times run up to the top of high trees and tumble

1. The text is from *Collections of the Massachusetts Historical Society*, Vol. ser. 1, Vol. 10 (1809).
2. Or (as below) "powaws," and often spelled "powwows," are religious leaders, sometimes referred to as priests.

down headlong to the ground, yet receive no hurt by all these. And I don't see for my part, why it is not as true, as the English or other nation's witch-craft, but is a great mystery of darkness, &c.

V. Concerning their DEAD, BURIAL, AND MOURNING. They use[d] to wash their dead clean, and adorn them with all manner of ornaments, and paint the face of them with divers[3] colours, and make a great lamentation over their dead. When they carry the corpse to the grave, the whole company, especially of the women, make a doleful and a very mournful and loud lam-entation, all the way as they go to the grave, and at the grave; and they use[d] to bury great many things with their dead, especially the things that belonged to the dead, and what they did not bury they would give away, and they would never live in a wigwam, in which any person died, but will immediately pull it down, and they generally mourned for their dead about a year, and the time they are in mourning the women kept their faces blackt with coal mixt with grease, neither would they wear fine cloathes, nor sing, nor dance, nei-ther will the mourners mention the name by which their dead was called, nor suffer any one in the whole place to mention it till some of the relations are called by the same name; and when they put off their mourning habit, they generally made a great nightly dance. They begin it in the evening and hold it till morning.

VI. Concerning their NOTIONS OF FUTURE STATE. They believed the exis-tence of their souls after their bodies are dead. Their souls go to the west-ward a great way off, where the righteous, or those that behaved themselves well in this world, will exercise themselves in pleasurable singing and danc-ing forever, in the presence of their Sawwonnuntoh or their western god, from whom they have received their beans and corn, their pumpkins, squashes, and all such things. They suppose the wicked go to the same place or country with the righteous; but they are to be exercised in some hard ser-vile labour, or some perplexing exercise, such as fetching water in a riddle, or making a canoe with a round stone, &c.

These were common notions with all Long Island Indians.

1761 1809

A Short Narrative of My Life[1]

From My Birth till I Received the Christian Religion

I was Born a Heathen and Brought up In Heathenism, till I was between 16 & 17 years of age, at a Place Calld Mohegan, in New London, Connecticut, in New England. My Parents Livd a wandering life, for did all the Indians at Mohegan, they Chiefly Depended upon Hunting, Fishing, & Fowling for their Living and had no Connection with the English, excepting to Traffic with them in their small Trifles; and they Strictly maintained and followed their Heathenish Ways, Customs & Religion, though there was Some

3. Various.
1. The text is from *American Indian Nonfiction: An Anthology of Writings* (2007), edited by

Bernd C. Peyer. Some of the bracketed insertions are Peyer's; others have been added for this anthology.

Preaching among them. Once a Fortnight, in ye Summer Season, a Minister from New London used to come up, and the Indians to attend;[2] not that they regarded the Christian Religion, but they had Blankets given to them every Fall of the Year and for these things they would attend and there was a Sort of School kept, when I was quite young, but I believe there never was one that ever Learnt to read any thing,—and when I was about 10 Years of age there was a man who went about among the Indian Wigwams, and wherever he Could find the Indian Children, would make them read;[3] but the Children Used to take Care to keep out of his way;—and he used to Catch me Some times and make me Say over my Letters; and I believe I learnt Some of them. But this was Soon over too; and all this Time there was not one amongst us, that made a Profession of Christianity—Neither did we Cultivate our Land, nor kept any Sort of Creatures except Dogs, which we used in Hunting; and we Dwelt in Wigwams. These are a Sort of Tents, Covered with Matts, made of Flags.[4] And to this Time we were unaquainted with the English Tongue in general though there were a few, who understood a little of it.

From the Time of Our Reformation till I Left Mr. Wheelocks

When I was 16 years of age, we heard a Strange Rumor among the English, that there were Extraordinary Ministers Preaching from Place to Place and a Strange Concern among the White People.[5] This was in the Spring of the Year. But we Saw nothing of these things, till Some Time in the Summer, when Some Ministers began to visit us and Preach the Word of God; and the Common People all Came frequently and exhorted us to the things of God, which it pleased the Lord, as I humbly hope, to Bless and accompany with Divine Influence to the Conviction and Saving Conversion of a Number of us; amongst whom I was one that was Imprest with the things we had heard. These Preachers did not only come to us, but we frequently went to their meetings and Churches. After I was awakened[6] & converted, I went to all the meetings, I could come at; & Continued under Trouble of Mind about 6 months; at which time I began to Learn the English Letters; got me a Primer, and used to go to my English Neighbours frequently for Assistance in Reading, but went to no School. And when I was 17 years of age, I had, as I trust, a Discovery of the way of Salvation through Jesus Christ, and was enabl'd to put my trust in him alone for Life & Salvation. From this Time the Distress and Burden of my mind was removed, and I found Serenity and Pleasure of Soul, in Serving God. By this time I just began to Read in the New Testament without Spelling,—and I had a Stronger Desire Still to Learn to read the Word of God, and at the Same Time had an uncommon Pity and Compassion to my Poor Brethren According to the Flesh. I used to wish I was capable of Instructing my poor Kindred. I used to think, if I Could once Learn to Read I would Instruct the poor Children in Reading,—and used frequently to talk with our Indians Concerning Religion. This continued till

2. In 1729, the Harvard graduate and Congregationalist minister Eliphalet Adams occasionally preached to the Mohegans.
3. In 1733–38 the Yale graduate and Presbyterian minister Jonathan Barber occasionally taught the Mohegans.
4. I.e., woven mats, which were placed over birchbark frames.
5. I.e., the Great Awakening was underway.
6. I.e., awakened spiritually to a sense of sin.

I was in my 19th year: by this Time I Could Read a little in the Bible. At this Time my Poor Mother was going to Lebanon, and having had Some Knowledge of Mr. Wheelock and hearing he had a Number of English youth under his Tuition,[7] I had a great Inclination to go to him and be with him a week or a Fortnight, and Desired my Mother to Ask Mr. Wheelock whether he would take me a little while to Instruct me in Reading. Mother did so; and when She Came Back, She Said Mr. Wheelock wanted to See me as Soon as possible. So I went up, thinking I Should be back again in a few Days; when I got up there, he received me With kindness and Compassion and in Stead of Staying a Forthnight or 3 Weeks, I Spent 4 Years with him.—After I had been with him Some Time, he began to acquaint his Friends of my being with him, and of his Intentions of Educating me, and my Circumstances. And the good People began to give Some Assistance to Mr. Wheelock, and gave me Some old and Some New Clothes. Then he represented the Case to the Honorable Commissioners at Boston, who were Commission'd by the Honorable Society in London for Propagating the gospel among the Indians in New England and parts adjacent, and they allowed him 60 £ in old Tender, which was about 6 £ Sterling,[8] and they Continu'd it 2 or 3 years, I cant't tell exactly.—While I was at Mr. Wheelock's, I was very weakly and my Health much impaired, and at the End of 4 Years, I over Strained my Eyes to such a Degree, I Could not persue my Studies any Longer; and out of these 4 years I Lost Just about one year;—And was obliged to quit my Studies.

From the Time I left Mr. Wheelock till I Went to Europe

As soon as I left Mr. Wheelock, I endeavored to find Some Employ among the Indians; went to Nahantuck,[9] thinking they may want a School Master, but they had one; then went to Narraganset,[1] and they were Indifferent about a School, and went back to Mohegan, and heard a number of our Indians were going to Montauk, on Long Island, and I went with them, and the Indians there were very desirous to have me keep a School amongst them, and I Consented, and went back a while to Mohegan and Some time in November I went on the Island, I think it is 17 years ago last November. I agreed to keep School with them Half a Year, and left it with them to give me what they Pleased; and they took turns to Provide Food for me. I had near 30 Scholars this winter; I had an evening School too for those that could not attend the Day School—and began to Carry on their meetings, they had a Minister, one Mr. Horton, the Scotch Society's Missionary; but he Spent, I think two thirds of his Time at Sheenecock, 30 Miles from Montauk.[2] We met together 3 times for Divine Worship every Sabbath and once on every Wednesday evening. I [used] to read the Scriptures to them and used to expound upon Some particular Passages in my own Tongue. Visited the Sick and attended their Burials.—When the half year expired, they Desired me to Continue with them, which I complied with, for another half year, when

7. Instruction.
8. Probably worth about $1,400 in present-day American currency.
9. A village of the Western Niantics, in present-day East Lyme, Connecticut.

1. A village of the Narragansetts, in Charlestown, Rhode Island.
2. The Presbyterian minister Azeriah Horton, a Yale graduate, ministered primarily to the Shinnecocks on Long Island and in Rhode Island.

I had fulfilled that, they were urgent to have me Stay Longer, So I continued amongst them till I was Married, which was about 2 years after I went there. And Continued to Instruct them in the Same manner as I did before. After I was married a while, I found there was need of a Support more than I needed while I was Single,—and made my Case Known to Mr. Buell[3] and to Mr. Wheelock, and also the Needy Circumstances and the Desires of these Indians of my Continuing amongst them, and the Commissioners were so good as to grant £15 a year Sterling—And I kept on in my Service as usual, yea I had additional Service; I kept School as I did before and Carried on the Religious Meetings as often as ever, and attended the Sick and their Funerals, and did what Writings they wanted, and often Sat as a Judge to reconcile and Decide their Matters Between them, and had visitors of Indians from all Quarters; and, as our Custom is, we freely Entertain all Visitors. And was fetched often from my Tribe and from others to see into their Affairs Both Religious, Temporal,—Besides my Domestic Concerns. And it Pleased the Lord to Increase my Family fast—and Soon after I was Married, Mr. Horton left these Indians and the Shenecock & after this I was [alone] and then I had the whole care of these Indians at Montauk, and visited the Shenecock Indians often. Used to set out Saturdays towards Night and come back again Mondays. I have been obliged to Set out from Home after Sun Set, and Ride 30 Miles in the Night, to Preach to these Indians. And Some Indians at Shenecock Sent their Children to my School at Montauk, I kept one of them Some Time, and had a Young Man a half year from Mohegan, a Lad from Nahantuck who was with me almost a year; and had little or nothing for keeping them.

My Method in the School was, as Soon as the Children got together, and took their proper Seats, I Prayed with them, then began to hear them. I generally began (after some of them Could Spell and Read,) With those that were yet in their Alphabets, So around, as they were properly Seated till I got through and I obliged them to Study their Books, and to help one another. When they could not make out a hard word they Brought it to me—and I usually heard them, in the Summer Season 8 Times a Day 4 in the morning, and in [the] after Noon.—In the Winter Season 6 Times a Day, As Soon as they could Spell, they were obliged to Spell when ever they wanted to go out. I concluded with Prayer; I generally heard my Evening Scholars 3 Times Round, And as they go out the School, every one, that Can Spell, is obliged to Spell a Word, and to go out Leisurely one after another. I Catechised 3 or 4 Times a Week according to the Assembly's [Shorter] Catechism, and many Times Proposed Questions of my own, and in my own Tongue. I found Difficulty with Some Children, who were Some what Dull,[4] most of these can soon learn to Say over their Letters, they Distinguish the Sounds by the Ear, but their Eyes can't Distinguish the Letters, and the way I took to cure them was by making an Alphabet on Small bits of paper, and glued them on Small Chips of Cedar after this manner A B & C. I put these on Letters in order on a Bench then point to one Letter and bid a Child to take notice of it, and then I order the Child to fetch me the Letter from the Bench; if he Brings the Letter, it is well, if not he must go again and again till he brings

3. Samuel Buell, the Presbyterian minister and Yale graduate, who preached at Occom's ordination, in 1759.

4. Somewhat slow to learn.

[the] right Letter. When they can bring any Letters this way, then I just Jumble them together, and bid them to set them in Alphabetical order, and it is a Pleasure to them; and they soon Learn their Letters this way.—I frequently Discussed or Exhorted my Scholars, in Religious matters.—My Method in our Religious Meetings was this; Sabbath Morning we Assemble together about 10 o'C and begin with Singing; we generally Sung Dr. Watt's Psalms or Hymns.[5] I distinctly read the Psalm or Hymn first, and then gave the meaning of it to them, after that Sing, then Pray, and Sing again after Prayer. Then proceed to Read from Suitable portion of Scripture, and so Just give the plain Sense of it in Familiar Discourse and apply it to them. So continued with Prayer and Singing. In the after Noon and Evening we Proceed in the Same Manner, and so in Wednesday Evening. Some Time after Mr. Horton left these Indians, there was a remarkable revival of religion among these Indians and many were hopefully converted to the Saving knowledge of God in Jesus. It is to be observed before Mr. Horton left these Indians they had Some Prejudices infused in their minds, by Some Enthusiastical Exhorters[6] from New England, against Mr. Horton, and many of them had left him, by this means he was Discouraged, and was disposed from[7] these Indians. And being acquainted with the Enthusiasts in New England & the make and the Disposition[8] of the Indians I took a mild way to reclaim them. I opposed them not openly but let them go on in their way, and whenever I had an opportunity, I would read Such pages of the Scriptures, and I thought would confound their Notions, and I would come to them with all Authority, Saying "these Saith the Lord"; and by this means, the Lord was pleased to Bless my poor Endeavours, and they were reclaimed, and Brought to hear almost any of the ministers.—I am now to give an Account of my Circumstances and manner of Living. I Dwelt in a Wigwam, a Small Hut with Small Poles and Covered with Matts made of Flags, and I was obligd to remove[9] twice a Year, about 2 miles Distance, by reason of the Scarcity of wood, for in one Neck of Land they Planted their Corn, and in another, they had their wood, and I was obligd to have my Corn carted and my Hay also,—and I got my Ground Plow'd every year, which Cost me about 12 shillings an acre; and I kept a Cow and a Horse, for which I paid 21 shillings every year York currency, and went 18 miles to Mill for every Dust[1] of meal we used in my family. I Hired or Joined with my Neighbours to go to Mill, with a Horse or ox Cart, or on Horse Back, and Some time went myself. My Family Increasing fast, and my Visitors also. I was obligd to contrive every way to Support my Family; I took all opportunities, to get Some thing to feed my Family Daily. I Planted my own Corn, Potatoes, and Beans; I used to be out hoeing my Corn Some times before Sun Rise and after my School is Dismist,[2] and by this means I was able to raise my own Pork, for I was allowed to keep 5 Swine. Some mornings & Evenings I would be out with my Hook and Line to Catch fish, and in the Fall of Year and in the Spring, I used my gun, and fed my Family with Fowls. I Could more than pay for my Powder & Shot with Feathers. At other Times I Bound old Books for

5. The works of the great English hymnodist Isaac Watts (1674–1748).
6. Enthusiastic lay preachers.
7. Turned away from.
8. Inclination.
9. Move.
1. Particle, bit. "York": probably New York.
2. I.e., dismissed.

Easthampton People, made wooden Spoons and Ladles, Stocked Guns, & worked on Cedar to make Pails, [Piggins], and Churns & C.[3] Besides all these Difficulties I met with advers Providence, I bought a Mare, had it but a little while, and she fell into the Quick Sand and Died, After a while Bought another, I kept her about half year, and she was gone, and I never have heard of nor Seen her from that Day to this; it was Supposed Some Rogue Stole her. I got another and [it] Died with a Distemper, and last of all I Bought a Young Mare, and kept her till She had one Colt, and She broke her Leg and Died, and Presently after the [Colt] Died also. In the whole I Lost 5 Horse Kind; all these Losses helped to pull me down; and by this Time I got greatly in Debt, and acquainted my Circumstances to Some of my Friends, and they Represented my Case to the Commissioners of Boston, and Interceded with them for me, and they were pleased to vote 15 £ for my Help, and Soon after Sent a Letter to my good Friend at New London, acquainting him that they had Superseded their Vote; and my Friends were so good as to represent my Needy Circumstances Still to them, and they were so good at Last, as to Vote £ 15 and Sent it, for which I am very thankful; and the Revd Mr. Buell was so kind as to write in my behalf to the gentlemen of Boston; and he told me they were much Displeased with him, and heard also once again that they blamed me for being Extravagant; I Can't Conceive how these gentlemen would have me Live. I am ready to [forgive] their Ignorance, and I would wish they had Changed Circumstances with me but one month, that they may know, by experience what my Case really was; but I am now fully convinced, that it was not Ignorance, For I believe it can be proved to the world that these Same Gentlemen gave a young Missionary a Single man, *one Hundred Pounds* for one year, and fifty Pounds for an Interpreter, and thirty Pounds for an Introducer; so it Cost them one Hundred & Eighty Pounds in one Single Year, and they Sent too where there was no Need of a Missionary.

Now you See what difference they made between me and other missionaries; they gave me 180 Pounds for 12 years Service, which they gave for one years Services in another Mission.—In my Service (I speak like a fool,[4] but I am Constrained) I was my own Interpreter. I was both a School master and Minister to the Indians, yea I was their Ear, Eye & Hand, as Well as Mouth. I leave it with the World, as wicked as it is, to Judge, whether I ought not to have had half as much, they gave a young man Just mentioned which would have been but £ 50 a year; and if they ought to have given me that, I am not under obligations to them, I owe them nothing at all; what can be the Reason that they used me after this manner? I can't think of any thing, but this as a Poor Indian Boy Said, Who was Bound out to an English Family, and he used to Drive Plow for a young man, and he whipt and Beat him allmost every Day, and the young man found fault with him, and Complained of him to his master and the poor Boy was Called to answer for himself before his master, and he was asked, what it was he did, that he was So Complained of and beat almost every Day. He Said, he did not know, but he Supposed it was because he could not drive any better; but says he, I Drive as well as I know how; and at other Times he Beats me, because he is of a

3. I.e., et cetera. "Piggins": small, wooden pails.
4. Cf. 2 Corinithians 11.23.

mind to beat me; but says he believes he Beats me for the most of the Time "because I am an Indian".

So I am *ready* to Say, they have used me thus, because I Can't Influence the Indians so well as other missionaries; but I can assure them I have endeavoured to teach them as well as I know how;—but I *must Say*, "I believe it is because I am a poor Indian". I Can't help that God has made me So; I did not make my self so.

September 17, 1768 1982

From A Sermon at the Execution of Moses Paul, an Indian[1]

The ADDRESS

By the melancholy providence of God, and at the earnest desire and invitation of the poor condemned criminal,[2] I am here before this great concourse of people at this time, to give the last discourse to the poor miserable object who is to be executed this day before your eyes, for the due reward of his folly, and madness, and enormous wickedness. It is an unwelcome task to me to speak upon such an occasion; but since it is the desire of the poor man himself, in conscience I cannot deny him; I must endeavour to do the great work the dying man requests. I conclude that this great concourse of people have come together to see the execution of justice upon this poor Indian; and I suppose the biggest part of you look upon yourselves Christians, and as such I hope you will demean[3] yourselves; and that you will have suitable commiseration towards this poor object. Though you cannot in justice pray for his life to be continued in this world, you can pray earnestly for the salvation of his poor soul. Let this be therefore, the fervent exercise of our souls; for this is the last day we have to pray for him.—As for you that do not regard religion, it cannot be expected, that you will put up one petition for this miserable creature: yet I would intreat you seriously to consider the frailty of corrupt nature, and behave yourselves as becomes rational creatures.

And in a word, let us all be suitably affected with the melancholy occasion of the day, knowing that we are all dying creatures, and accountable unto God. Though this poor condemned criminal will in a few minutes know more than all of us, either in unutterable joy, or inconceivable woe; yet we shall certainly know as much as he, in a few days.

The sacred words that I have chosen to speak from upon this undesirable occasion, are found written in Romans vi. 23.

1. The text is from Samson Occom, *A Sermon at the Execution of Moses Paul, an Indian; Who had been guilty of Murder, Preached at New Haven in America* (1788).
2. Moses Paul, a Wampanoag man, was convicted of the murder of a white man, Moses Cook, and sentenced to death. Paul unsuccess- fully appealed his conviction, charging the all-white jury with racial bias. Paul then wrote to Occom asking him to preach at his execution, which took place in 1772 at the Brick Meeting House in New Haven, Connecticut.
3. Behave.

FOR THE WAGES OF SIN IS DEATH, BUT THE GIFT OF GOD
IS ETERNAL LIFE THROUGH JESUS CHRIST OUR LORD.

Death is called the King of Terrors, and it ought to be the subject of every man and woman's thoughts daily; because it is that unto which they are liable every moment of their lives: and therefore, it cannot be unseasonable to think, speak and hear of it at any time, and especially on this mournful occasion; for we must all come to it, how soon we cannot tell; whether we are prepared or not prepared, ready or not ready, whether death is welcome or not welcome, we must feel the force of it: whether we concern ourselves with death or not, it will concern itself with us. Seeing that this is the case with every one of us, what manner of persons ought we to be in all holy conversation and godliness; how ought men to exert themselves in preparation for death continually; for they know not what a day or an hour may bring forth, with respect to them. But, alas! according to the appearance of mankind in general, death is the least thought of. They go on from day to day, as if they were to live here for ever, as if this was the only life. They contrive, rack their inventions, disturb their rest, and even hazard their lives in all manner of dangers, both by sea and land; yea they leave no stone unturned that they may live in the world, and at the same time have little or no contrivance to die well: God and their souls are neglected, and heaven and eternal happiness are disregarded; Christ and his religion are despised—yet most of these very men intend to be happy when they come to die, not considering that there must be great preparation in order to die well. Yea there is none so fit to live as those that are fit to die; those that are not fit to die are not fit to live. Life and death are nearly connected: we generally own that it is a great and solemn thing to die. But I say again, how little do mankind realize these things? They are busy about the things of this world as if there was no death before them. Dr. Watts pictures them out to the life in his psalms:

> See the vain race of mortals move
> Like shadows o'er the plain,
> They rage and strive, desire and love,
> But all their noise is vain.

> Some walk in honor's gaudy show,
> Some dig for golden ore,
> They toil for heirs they know not who,
> And strait are seen no more.[4]

Eternal life is shamefully disregarded by men in general, and eternal death is chosen rather than life.[5] This is the general complaint of the bible from the beginning to the end. As long as Christ is neglected, life is refused, and as long as sin is cherished, death is chosen; and this seems to be the woful case of mankind of all nations, according to their appearance in these days; for it is too plain to be denied, that vice and immortality, and floods of iniquity are abounding every where amongst all nations, and all orders and ranks of men, and in every sect of people. Yea there is a great agreement and harmony among all nations, and from the highest to the lowest to practise sin and iniquity; and the pure religion of Jesus Christ is turned out of doors, and is dying without; or, in other words, the Lord Jesus Christ is turned out of doors by men in general, and even by his professed people. "He came to his own, and his own

4. Psalm 39, "Teach Me the Measure of My Days," verses 3 and 4, by the English hymnodist Isaac Watts (1674–1748).
5. Cf. Deuteronomy 30.19.

received him not."[6] But the devil is admitted, he has free access to the houses and hearts of the children of men: Thus life is refused and death is chosen.

But in further speaking upon our text, by divine assistance, I shall consider those two general propositions:

 I. That sin is the cause of all the miseries that befall the children of men, both as to their bodies and souls, for time and eternity.

 II. That eternal life and happiness is the free gift of God, through Jesus Christ our Lord.

In speaking to the first proposition, I shall first consider the nature of sin; and secondly, shall consider the consequences of sin, or the wages of sin, which is death.

First then, we are to describe the nature of sin.

Sin is the transgression of the law:—This is the scripture definition of sin. Now the law of God being holy, just and good; sin must be altogether unholy, unjust and evil. If I was to define sin, I should call it a contrariety to God; and as such it must be the vilest thing in the world; it is full of all evil; it is the evil of evils; the only evil, in which dwells no good thing; and is most destructive to God's creation, where ever it takes effect. It was sin that transformed the very angels of heaven into devils; and it was sin that caused hell to be made. If it had not been for sin, there never would have been such a thing as hell or devil, death or misery.

And if sin is such a thing as we have just described; it must be worse than the devils and hell itself.—Sin is full of deadly poison; it is full of malignity and hatred against God, against all his divine perfections and attributes, against his wisdom, against his power, against his holiness and goodness, against his mercy and justice, against his written law and gospel; yea, against his very being and existence. Were it in the power of sin, it would even dethrone God, and set itself on the throne.

* * *

2. I shall endeavour to shew the sad consequences or effects of sin upon the children of men.

Sin has poisoned them, and made them distracted or fools. The Psalmist says, The fool hath said in his heart, there is no God.[7] And Solomon, through his Proverbs, calls ungodly sinners fools;[8] and their sin he calls their folly and foolishness. The Apostle James says, "But the tongue can no man tame, it is an unruly evil, full of deadly poison." It is the heart that is in the first place full of this "deadly poison." The tongue is only an interpreter of the heart. Sin has vitiated the whole man, both soul and body; all the powers are corrupted; it has turned the minds of men against all good, towards all evil. So poisoned are they, according to the Prophet Isaiah v. 20. "Wo unto them that call evil good, and good evil; that put darkness for light, and light for darkness; that put bitter for sweet, and sweet for bitter." And Christ Jesus saith in John iii. 19, 20. "And this is the condemnation, that light is come into the world, and men loved darkness rather than light, because their deeds

6. John 1.11.

7. Psalm 14.1. "The Psalmist": David, the second king of ancient Israel, traditionally considered the author of the Book of Psalms.

8. James 3.8. Cf., e.g., Proverbs 14.9, 15.2, 26.4. "Solomon": a son of David who became a king of Israel, traditionally considered the author of the Book of Proverbs.

were evil. For every one that doth evil hateth the light, neither cometh to the light, lest his deeds should be reproved." Sin has stupified mankind, they are now ignorant of God their maker; neither do they enquire after him. And they are ignorant of themselves, they know not what is good for them, neither do they understand their danger; and they have no fear of God before their eyes.

* * *

The next thing I shall consider, is the actual death of the body, or separation between soul and body. At the cessation of natural life, there is an end of all the enjoyments of this life: there is no more joy nor sorrow; no more hope nor fear, as to the body; no more contrivance and carrying on any business; no more merchandizing and trading; no more farming; no more buying and selling; no more building of any kind, no more contrivance at all to live in the world; no more flatteries nor frowns from the world; no more honor nor reproach; no more praise; no more good report, nor evil report; no more learning of any trades, arts or sciences in the world; no more sinful pleasures, they are all at an end; recreations, visiting, tavern haunting, music and dancing, chambering[9] and carousing, playing at dice and cards, or any game whatsoever; cursing and swearing, and profaning the holy name of God, drunkenness, fighting, debauchery, lying and cheating, in this world, must cease for ever. Not only so, sinners must bid an eternal farewell to all the world; bid farewell to all their beloved sins and pleasures: and the places and possessions that knew them once, shall know them no more for ever. And further, they must bid adieu to all sacred and divine things. They are obliged to leave the Bible, and all the ordinances thereof; and to bid farewell to preachers, and all sermons and all Christian people, and Christian conversation; they must bid a long farewell to sabbaths and seasons, and opportunities of worship; yea, an eternal farewell to God the Father, Son and Holy Ghost, and adieu to heaven and all happiness, to saints and all the inhabitants of the upper world. At your leisure please to read the destruction of Babylon; Rev. the 18th, most of that description will apply to the case of dying sinners.

Mean while, the poor departed soul must take up its lodging in sorrow, woe and misery, in the lake that burns with fire and brimstone, where the worm dieth not, and the fire is not quenched; where a multitude of frightful deformed devils dwell, and the damned ghosts of Adam's race; where darkness, horror and despair reigns, where hope never comes, and where poor guilty naked souls will be tormented with exquisite torments, even the wrath of the Almighty poured out upon their damned souls; the smoke of their torments ascending up for ever and ever; and hellish groans, howlings, cries and shrieks all round them, and merciless devils upbraiding them for their folly and madness, and tormenting them incessantly.—And there they must endure the most unsatiable, fruitless desire, and the most overwhelming shame and confusion, and the most horrible fear, and the most doleful sorrow, and the most racking despair. When they cast their flaming eyes to heaven, with Dives in torments,[1] they behold an angry and frowning God,

9. Illicit sexual intercourse.
1. The parable of Dives the rich man and Lazarus appears in Luke 16.19–31.

whose eyes are as a flaming fire, and they are struck with ten thousand darts of pain; and the sight of the happiness of the saints above, adds to their pains and aggravates their misery. And when they reflect upon their past folly and madness, in neglecting the great salvation in their day, it will pierce them with ten thousand inconceivable torments; it will as it were enkindle their hell afresh; and it will cause them to curse themselves bitterly, and curse the day in which they were born, and curse their parents that were the instruments of their being in the world; yea they will curse, bitterly curse; and with that very God that gave them their being, to be in the same condition with them in hell torments. This is what is called the second death, and it is the last death, and an eternal death to a guilty soul.

And O eternity, eternity, eternity! Who can measure it? Who can count the years thereof? Arithmetic must fail, the thoughts of men and angels are drowned in it; how shall we describe eternity? To what shall we compare it? Were it possible to employ a fly to carry off this globe by the small particles thereof, and to carry them to such a distance that it should return once in ten thousand years for another particle, and so continue until it has carried off all this globe, and framed them together in some unknown space, until it has made just such a world as this is; after all, eternity would remain the fame unexhausted duration. This must be the unavoidable portion of all impenitent sinners, let them be who they will, great or small, honorable or ignoble, rich or poor, bond or free. Negroes, Indians, English, or of what nations forever, all that die in their sins, must go to hell together, for the wages of sin is death.

The next thing that I was to consider is this:

II. That eternal life and happiness is the free gift of God, through Jesus Christ our Lord.

Under this proposition I shall endeavour to shew, what this life and happiness is.

The life that is mentioned in our text, begins with a *spiritual* life: it is the life of the soul, a restoration of soul from sin to holiness, from darkness to light, a translation from the kingdom and dominion of Satan, to the kingdom of God's grace. In other words, it is being restored to the image of God, and delivered from the image of Satan. And this life consists in union of the soul to God, and communion with God; a real participation of the divine nature, or in the apostle's words, it is Christ formed within us; "I live," says he, "yet not I, but Christ liveth in me."[2] And the apostle John saith, "God is love, and he that dwelleth in love, dwelleth in God, and God in him."[3] * * * This life is called eternal life, because God has planted a living principle in the soul; and whereas he was dead before, now he is made alive unto God; there is an active principle within him towards God, he now moves towards God in his religious devotions and exercises; is daily, comfortably and sweetly walking with God, in all his ordinances and commands; his delight is in the ways of God; he breathes towards God, a living breath, in praises, prayers, adorations and thanksgivings; his prayers are now heard in the heavens, and his praises delight the ears of the Almighty,

2. Galatians 2.20. "The apostle": Jesus' apostle Paul. 3. 1 John 4.16.

and his thanksgivings are accepted. So alive is he now to God, that it is his meat and drink, yea more than his meat and drink, to do the will of his heavenly Father. It is his delight, his happiness and pleasure to serve God. He does not drag himself to his duties now, but he does them out of choice, and with alacrity of soul. Yea, so alive is he to God, that he gives up himself and all that he has entirely to God, to be for him and none other; his whole aim is to glorify God in all things, whether by life or death, all the same to him.

We have a bright example of this in St Paul. After he was converted, he was all alive to God; he regarded not himself, but was willing to spend, and be spent in the service of his God;[4] he was hated, reviled, despised, laughed at, and called by all manner of evil names; was scourged, stoned and imprisoned;— and all could not stop his activity towards God. He would boldly and courageously go on in preaching the gospel of the Lord Jesus Christ, to poor, lost, and undone sinners; he would do the work God set him about, in spite of all opposition he met with, either from men or devils, earth or hell; come death, or come life, none of these things moved him, because he was alive unto God. Though he suffered hunger and thirst, cold and heat, poverty and nakedness by day and by night, by sea and land, and was in danger all ways; yet he would serve God amidst all these dangers. Read his amazing account in 2 Cor. xi. 23. and on.

Another instance of marvellous love towards God, we have in Daniel. When there was a proclamation, sent by the king, to all his subjects, forbidding them to call upon their gods, for thirty days; which was done by envious men, that they might find occasion against Daniel, the servant of the Most High God; yet he having the life of God in his soul, regarded not the king's decree, but made his petitions to his God, as often as he used to do, though death was threatened to the disobedient. But he feared not the hell they had prepared; the den resembled hell, and the lions the devils. Thus Daniel and Paul went through fire and water, as the common saying is, because they had *eternal* life in their souls in an eminent manner; and they regarded not *this* life, for the cause and glory of God. And thus it has been in all ages with true Christians. Many of the fore-fathers of the English, in this country, had this life, and are gone the same way that the holy prophets and apostles went. Many of them went through all manner of sufferings for God; and a great number of them are gone home to heaven, in chariots of fire. I have seen the place in London, called Smithfield, where numbers were burnt to death for the religion of Jesus Christ.[5] And there is the same life in true Christians now in these days; and if there should persecutions arise in our day, I verily believe, true Christians would suffer with the same spirit and temper of mind, as those did, who suffered in days past.

We proceed to shew, that this life which we have described, is the free gift of God, through Jesus Christ our Lord.

Sinners have forfeited all mercy into the hand of divine justice, and have merited hell and damnation to themselves; for the wages of sin is everlasting death, but heaven and happiness is a free gift; it comes by favour; and

4. 2 Corinthians 12.15.
5. At this location, Protestants were executed during the reigns of Henry VIII (1509–47),

Edward VI (1547–53), Mary I (1553–58), Elizabeth I (1558–1603), and James I (1603–1625).

all merit is excluded: and especially if we consider that we are fallen sinful creatures, and there is nothing in us that can recommend us to the favour of God. * * * And it is said, that this life is given in and through the Lord Jesus Christ. It could not be given in any other way, but in and through the death and sufferings of Christ; Christ himself is a gift, and he is the Christian's life. "For God so loved the world, that he gave his only begotten Son, that whosoever believeth in him should not perish, but have everlasting life."[6] The word says further, "For by grace ye are saved, through faith, and that not of yourselves, it is the gift of God."[7] This is given through Jesus Christ our Lord; Christ obtained it with his own blood, by the influence of his spirit he prepares us for it; and by his divine grace preserves us for it. In a word, he is all in all in our eternal salvation; all this is the free gift of God.

I have now gone through what I proposed from my text. And I shall now make some application of the whole.

First to the criminal in particular; and then to the auditory in general.[8]

My poor unhappy brother MOSES;

As it was your own desire that I should preach to you this last discourse, so I shall speak plainly to you.—You are the bone of my bone, and flesh of my flesh. You are an Indian, a despised creature; but you have despised yourself; yea, you have despised God more; you have trodden under foot his authority; you have despised his commands and precepts: and now, as God says, "be sure your sins will find you out;[9] so now, poor Moses, your sins have found you out, and they have overtaken you this day; the day of your death is now come; the King of Terrors is at hand; you have but a very few moments to breathe in this world.—The just laws of man, and the holy law of Jehovah, call aloud for the destruction of your mortal life; God says, "Whoso sheddeth man's blood, by man shall his blood be shed."[1] This is the ancient decree of heaven, and it is to be executed by man; nor have you the least gleam of hope of escape, for the unalterable sentence is past; the terrible day of execution is come, the unwelcome guard is about you; and the fatal instruments of death are now made ready; your coffin and your grave, your last lodging, are open ready to receive you.

Alas! poor Moses, now you know, by sad, by woful experience, the living truth of our text, that the wages of sin is death. You have been already dead; yea twice dead: by nature spiritually dead, and since the awful sentence of death has been past upon you, you have been dead to all the pleasures of this life: or all the pleasures, lawful or unlawful, have been dead to you: And death which is the wages of sin, is standing even on this side of your grave ready to put a final period to your mortal life; and just beyond the grave, eternal death awaits your poor soul, and the devils are ready to drag your miserable soul down to their bottomless den, where everlasting woe and horror reigns; the place is filled with doleful shrieks, howls and groans of the damned. Oh! to what a miserable, forlorn, and wretched condition, have your extravagant folly and wickedness brought you, i.e. if you die in your sins. And O! what manner of repentance ought you to manifest! How ought your

6. John 3.16.
7. Ephesians 2.8.
8. The assembled listeners, including numerous

clergymen.
9. Numbers 32.23.
1. Genesis 9.6.

heart to bleed for what you have done! How ought you to prostrate your soul before a bleeding God! And under self-condemnation, cry out, Ah Lord, ah Lord, what have I done!—Whatever partiality, injustice and error there may be among the judges of the earth, remember that you have deserved a thousand deaths, and a thousand hells, by reason of your sins, at the hands of a holy God. Should God come out against you in strict justice, alas! what could you say for yourself? for you have been brought up under the bright sunshine, and plain, and loud sound of the gospel; and you have had a good education; you can read and write well; and God has given you a good natural understanding: and therefore your sins are so much more aggravated. You have not sinned in such an ignorant manner as others have done; but you have sinned with both your eyes open as it were, under the light, even the glorious light of the gospel of the Lord Jesus Christ.—You have sinned against the light of your own conscience, against your knowledge and understanding; you have sinned against the pure and holy laws of God, and the just laws of men; you have sinned against heaven and earth; you have sinned against all the mercies and goodness of God; you have sinned against the whole Bible, against the Old and New-Testament; you have sinned against the blood of Christ, which is the blood of the everlasting covenant.[2] O poor Moses, see what you have done! and now repent, repent, I say again repent; see how the blood you shed cries against you, and the avenger of blood is at your heels. O fly, fly to the Blood of the Lamb of God, for the pardon of all your aggravated sins.

But let us now turn to a more pleasant theme.—Though you have been a great sinner, a heaven daring sinner; yet hark! O hear the joyful sound from heaven, even from the King of kings, and Lord of lords; that the gift of God is eternal life, through Jesus Christ our Lord. It is a free gift, and bestowed on the greatest sinners, and upon their true repentance towards God and faith in the Lord Jesus Christ, they shall be welcome to the life, which we have spoken of; it is granted upon free terms. He that hath no money may come; he that hath no righteousness, no goodness, may come; the call is to poor undone sinners; the call is not to the righteous, but sinners, inviting them to repentance. Hear the voice of the Son of the most high God, "Come unto me, all ye that labour and are heavy laden, and I will give you rest."[3] This is a call, a gracious call to you, poor Moses, under your present burdens and distresses. * * * O poor Moses, believe on the Lord Jesus Christ with all your heart, and thou shalt be saved eternally. Come just as you are, with all your sins and abominations, with all your blood-guiltiness, with all your condemnation, and lay hold of the hope set before you this day. This is the last day of salvation with your soul; you will be beyond the bounds of mercy in a few minutes more. O, what a joyful day will it be if you now openly believe in, and receive the Lord Jesus Christ; it would be the beginning of heavenly days with your poor soul; instead of a melancholy day, it would be a wedding day to your soul; it would cause the very angels in heaven to rejoice, and the saints on earth to be glad; it would cause the angels to

2. In Calvinist theology, God established the Covenant of Works with Adam, who then broke it. Jesus Christ established the Covenant of Grace with those who believe in him and will thus be saved.

3. Matthew 11.28.

come down from the realms above, and wait hovering about your gallows, ready to convey your soul to the heavenly mansions, there to take the possession of eternal glory and happiness, and join the heavenly choirs in singing the song of Moses and the Lamb; there to sit down forever with Abraham, Isaac and Jacob[4] in the kingdom of God's glory; and your shame and guilt shall be forever banished from the place, and all sorrow and fear forever fly away, and tears be wiped from your face; and there shall you forever admire the astonishing and amazing and infinite mercy of God in Christ Jesus, in pardoning such a monstrous sinner as you have been; there you will claim the highest note of praise, for the riches of free grace in Christ Jesus. But if you will not accept of a Saviour proposed to your acceptance in this last day of your life, you must this very day bid farewell to God the Father, Son and Holy Ghost, to heaven and all the saints and angels that are there; and you must bid all the saints in this lower world an eternal farewell, and even the whole world. And so I must leave you in the hands of God; and must turn to the whole auditory.

Sirs, We may plainly see, from what we have heard, and from the miserable object before us, into what a doleful condition sin has brought mankind, even into a state of death and misery. We are by nature as certainly under sentence of death from God, as this miserable man is, by the the just determination of man; and we are all dying creatures, this is the dreadful fruit of sin. O! let us then fly from all appearance of sin; let us fight against it with all our might; let us repent and turn to God, and believe on the Lord Jesus Christ, that we may live forever; let us all prepare for death, for we know not how soon, nor how suddenly we may be called out of the world.

Permit me *reverend gentlemen and fathers* in Israel, to speak a few words to you, though I am well sensible that I need to be taught the first principles of the oracles of God, by the least of you. But since the providence of God has so ordered it, that I must speak here on this occasion, I beg that you would not be offended nor be angry with me.

God has raised *you* up, from among your brethren, and has qualified, and authorised you to do his great work; and *you* are the servants of the Most High God, and ministers of the Lord Jesus, the Son of the living God: *you* are Christ's ambassadors; *you* are called Shepherds, watchmen, overseers, or bishops, and *you* are rulers of the temples of God, or of the assemblies of God's people; *you* are God's angels, and as such you have nothing to do but to wait upon God, and to do the work the Lord Jesus Christ your blessed Lord and Master has set you about, not fearing the face of any man, nor seeking to please men, but your Master. * * * But what need I speak any more? Let us *all* attend, and hear the great Apostle of the Gentiles speaking unto us in Eph[esians] vi from the 10th verse and onward. "Finally, my brethren, be strong in the Lord, and in the power of his might; put on the whole armour of God, that ye may be able to stand against the wiles of the devil. For we wrestle not against flesh and blood, but against principalities, against powers, against the rulers of the darkness of this world, against spiritual wickedness in high places. Wherefore take unto you the whole armour of God, that ye may be able to stand in the evil day, and having done all to

4. The patriarchs of the Hebrew Bible.

stand. Stand therefore, having your loins girt about with truth, and having on the breast-plate of righteousness; and your feet shod with the preparation of the gospel of peace: above all, taking the shield of faith, wherewith ye shall be able to quench all the fiery darts of the wicked; and take the helmet of salvation, and the sword of the spirit, which is the word of God; praying always with all prayer and supplication in the spirit, and watching thereunto with all perseverance, and supplication for all saints."

I shall now address myself to the *Indians*, my brethren and kindred according to the flesh.

MY POOR KINDRED,

You see the woful consequences of sin, by seeing this our poor miserable country-man now before us, who is to die this day for his sins and great wickedness. And it was the sin of drunkenness that has brought this destruction and untimely death upon him. There is a dreadful woe denounced from the Almighty against drunkards; and it is this sin, this abominable, this beastly and accursed sin of drunkenness, that has stript us of every desirable comfort in this life; by this we are poor, miserable and wretched; by this sin we have no name nor credit in the world among polite nations; for this sin we are despised in the world, and it is all right and just, for we despise ourselves more; and if we do not regard ourselves, who will regard us? And it is for our sins, and especially for that accursed, that most hateful sin of drunkenness that we suffer every day. For the love of strong drink we spend all that we have, and every thing we can get. By this sin we cannot have comfortable houses, nor any thing comfortable in our houses; neither food nor raiment, nor decent utensils. We are obliged to put up any sort of shelter just to screen us from the severity of the weather; and we go about with very mean,[5] ragged and dirty clothes, almost naked. And we are half starved, for most of the time obliged to pick up any thing to eat.—And our poor children are suffering every day for want[6] of the necessaries of life; they are very often crying for want of food, and we have nothing to give them; and in the cold weather they are shivering and crying, being pinched with the cold——All this is for the love of strong drink. And this is not all the misery and evil we bring on ourselves in this world; but when we are intoxicated with strong drink, we drown our rational powers, by which we are distinguished from the brutal creation; we unman ourselves, and bring ourselves not only level with the beasts of the field, but seven degrees beneath them; yea we bring ourselves level with the devils; I do not know but we make ourselves worse than the devils, for I never heard of drunken devils.

My poor kindred, do consider what a dreadful abominable sin drunkenness is. God made us men, and we choose to be beasts and devils; God made us rational creatures, and we chuse to be fools. Do consider further, and behold a drunkard, and see how he looks, when he has drowned his reason; how deformed and shameful does he appear? He disfigures every part of him, both soul and body, which was made after the image of God. He appears with awful deformity, and his whole visage is disfigured; if he attempts to speak he cannot bring out his words distinct, so as to be understood; if

5. Poor, shabby. 6. Lack.

he walks he reels and staggers to and fro, and tumbles down. And see how he behaves, he is now laughing, and then he is crying; he is singing, and the next minute he is mourning; and is all love to every one, and anon he is raging, and for fighting, and killing all before him, even the nearest and the dearest relations and friends: Yea nothing is too bad for a drunken man to do. He will do that which he would not do for the world, in his right mind.

Further, when a person is drunk, he is just good for nothing in the world; he is of no service to himself, to his family, to his neighbours, or his country; and how much more unfit is he to serve God: yet he is just as fit for the service of the devil.

Again, a man in drukenness is in all manner of dangers, he may be killed by his fellow-men, by wild beasts, and tame beasts; he may fall into the fire, into the water, or into a ditch; or he may fall down as he walks along, and break his bones or his neck; he may cut himself with edge tools.—Further, if he has any money or any thing valuable, he may lose it all, or may be robbed, or he may make a foolish bargain, and be cheated out of all he has.

I believe you know the truth of what I have just now said, many of you, by sad experience; yet you will go on still in your drunkenness. Though you have been cheated over and over again, and you have lost your substance by drunkenness, yet you will venture to go on in this most destructive sin. O fools when will ye be wise?—We all know the truth of what I have been saying, by what we have seen and heard of drunken deaths. How many have been drowned in our rivers, and how many have been frozen to death in the winter seasons! yet drunkards go on without fear and consideration: alas, alas! What will become of all such drunkards? Without doubt they must all go to hell, except they truly repent and turn to God. Drunkenness is so common amongst us, that even our young men and young women are not ashamed to get drunk. Our young men will get drunk as soon as they will eat when they are hungry—It is generally esteemed amongst men, more abominable for a woman to be drunk, than a man; and yet there is nothing more common amongst us than female drunkards. Women ought to be more modest than men; the holy scriptures recommend modesty to women in particular:—but drunken women have no modesty at all. It is more intolerable for a woman to get drunk, if, we consider further, that she is in great danger of falling into the hands of the sons of Belial,[7] or wicked men, and being shamefully treated by them.

And here I cannot but observe, we find in sacred writ, a woe denounced against men, who put their bottles to their neighbours' mouth to make them drunk, that they may see their nakedness;[8] and no doubt there are such devilish men now in our day, as there were in the days of old.

And to conclude, consider my poor kindred, you that are drunkards, into what a miserable condition you have brought yourselves. There is a dreadful woe thundering against you every day, and the Lord says, that drunkards shall not inherit the kingdom of God.

7. A name in the Hebrew Bible that later became identified with the devil.
8. See Genesis 9.22, where Ham sees the naked- ness of his father, Noah. In some accounts, this led to the curse of Ham, which was said to explain the enslavement of Africans.

And now let me exhort you all to break off from your drunkenness, by a gospel repentance, and believe on the Lord Jesus and you shall be saved. Take warning by this doleful sight before us, and by all the dreadful judgments that have befallen poor drunkards. O let us all reform our lives, and live as becomes dying creatures, in time to come. Let us be persuaded that we are accountable creatures to God, and we must be called to an account in a few days. You that have been careless all your days, now awake to righteousness, and be concerned for your poor and never dying souls. Fight against all sins, and especially the sin that easily besets you, and behave in time to come as becomes rational creatures; and above all things, receive and believe on the Lord Jesus Christ, and you shall have eternal life; and when you come to die, your souls will be received into heaven, there to be with the Lord Jesus in eternal happiness, and with all the saints in glory; which God of his infinite mercy grant, through Jesus Christ our Lord. Amen.

September 2, 1772 1788

HYMNS[1]

The Sufferings of Christ, or Throughout the Saviour's Life We Trace

Throughout the Saviour's Life we trace,
Nothing but Shame and deep Disgrace,
No period else is seen;
Till he a spotless Victim fell,
Tasting in Soul a painful Hell, 5
Caus'd by the Creature's Sin.
On the cold Ground methinks I see
My Jesus kneel, and pray for me;
For this I him adore;
Siez'd with a chilly sweat throughout, 10
Blood-drops did force their Passage out
Through ev'ry open'd Pore.
A pricking Thorn his Temples bore;
His Back with Lashes all was tore,
Till one the Bones might see; 15
Mocking, they push'd him here and there,
Marking his Way with Blood and Tear,
Press'd by the heavy Tree.[2]
Thus up the Hill he painful came,
Round him they mock, and make their Game, 20

1. The texts are from Samson Occom, *A Choice Collection of Hymns and Spiritual Songs* (1774), as reprinted in *The Collected Writings of Samson Occom, Mohegan* (2006), edited by Joanna Brooks.
2. I.e., the cross that Jesus carried to the site of his Crucifixion.

At length his Cross they rear;
And can you see the mighty God,
Cry out beneath sin's heavy Load,
Without one thankful Tear?
Thus vailed in Humanity, 25
He dies in Anguish on the Tree;
What Tongue his Grief can tell?
The shudd'ring Rocks their Heads recline,
The mourning Sun refuse to shine,
When the Creator fell.[3] 30
Shout, Brethren, shout in songs divine,
He drank the Gall to give us Wine,[4]
To quench our parching Thirst;
Seraphs advance your Voices higher;
Bride of the Lamb,[5] unite the Choir, 35
And Laud thy precious Christ.

A Morning Hymn, or Now the Shades of Night Are Gone

Now the shades of night are gone,
Now the morning light is come:
Lord, we would be thine to-day,
Drive the shades of sin away.
Make our souls as noon-day clear, 5
Banish every doubt and fear;
In thy vineyard, Lord, to-day
We would labor, we would pray.
Keep our haughty passions bound,
Rising up and sitting down, 10
Going out and coming in,[6]
Keep us safe from every sin.
When our work of life is past,
O receive us then at last;
Labor then will all be o'er, 15
Night of sin will be no more.

3. During the three-hour period called the Crucifixion darkness, the sun disappeared as Jesus died on the cross.
4. According to the New Testament accounts of the Crucifixion, Jesus was offered unappetizing beverages while on the cross. E.g., in Matthew 27.34, he is offered a cup of gall (bile) mixed with vinegar (also translated as wine). However, John 2.1–11 describes the first miracle attributed to Jesus, earlier in his life: turning water into wine. Here, he performs a similar miracle.
5. Bride of Christ. The phrase is variously interpreted.
6. Cf. Psalm 121.8.

A Son's Farewell, or I Hear the Gospel's Joyful Sound

I hear the gospel's joyful sound,
 An organ I shall be,
For to sound forth redeeming love,
 And sinner's misery.
Honor'd parents fare you well, 5
 My Jesus doth me call,
I leave you here with God until
 I meet you once for all.
My due affections I'll forsake,
 My parents and their house, 10
And to the wilderness betake,
 To pay the Lord my vows.
Then I'll forsake my chiefest mates,
 That nature could afford,
And wear the shield into the field, 15
 To wait upon the Lord.
Then thro' the wilderness I'll run,
 Preaching the gospel free;
O be not anxious for your son,
 The Lord will comfort me. 20
And if thro' preaching I shall gain
 True subjects to my Lord,
'Twill more than recompence my pain,
 To see them love the Lord.
My soul doth wish mount Zion[7] well, 25
 Whate'er becomes of me;
There my best friends and kindred dwell,
 And there I long to be.

7. Mount Zion is a hill in Jerusalem; by extension, it means Israel, the chosen people: here, the elect, or the faithful.

Ethnographic and Naturalist Writings

B roadly defined, the genre of literary ethnography is the written description of peoples, cultures, and societies. In this sense, literary ethnography involves a wide variety of styles and can be adapted to many different purposes. Descriptions of nature—naturalist writings, or natural histories as they are sometimes called—have a similarly multivalent character. Virtually all of the earliest "American" literature offers instances of ethnographic and naturalist writing, as the sustained European encounter with the Americas that began in 1492 provided writers with a treasure trove of new material. Descriptions of the land, its peoples, and its natural resources are central to narratives of contact and exploration, and they dominate promotional writings designed to encourage investment and colonization. Often enthusiastic in tone, such works typically describe marvels that can at first be puzzling, perhaps even a bit threatening, but are ultimately enticing.

A second register in these narratives, one that became more pronounced over time, involved a religiously inflected language of wonders and portents, sometimes associated with demonic influence. Drawing on folk beliefs as well as Christian traditions, works such as Cotton Mather's *Wonders of the Invisible World* (excerpted earlier in this volume) recorded observations in a quasi-scientific language influenced by the rise of empiricism—that is, the theory that all knowledge derives from sense experience—but they applied that language to events, or objects, that were not empirically observable in any direct way. Popular works in this vein appeared in early newspapers, almanacs, and broadsides, where occurrences such as earthquakes or the birth of misshapen fetuses ("monsters") were sometimes presented as curiosities but at other times interpreted as evidence of divine displeasure.

The eighteenth-century writings included in this cluster are distinguished from these earlier works by a deepening empiricism and a complexly self reflective tone that is often manifested through humor. The empiricism and the humor align these works with English novels such as Daniel Defoe's *Robinson Crusoe* (1719) and Henry Fielding's *Joseph Andrews* (1742). Novelistic elements are especially prominent in the first three selections here, by Sarah Kemble Knight, William Byrd, and Alexander Hamilton. Their travel narratives, paying substantial attention to the communities and landscapes they encountered on their journeys, offer rich instances of authors seeking new ways to understand cultures and natural environments.

The final two selections have different emphases. William Bartram's charming "Anecdotes of a Crow" invites reflection on enduring questions about human and animal behavior. An instance of the popular naturalist essay, "Anecdotes of a Crow" shows the same interest in environment and social context that animates works such as J. Hector St. John de Crèvecoeur's *Letters from an American Farmer* (1782), excerpted after this cluster. In "History of the Muh-he-con-nuk Indians," the Mahican writer Hendrick Aupaumut provides an insider's view of tribal traditions. Along with works included elsewhere in this volume by David Cusick ("The Iroquois Creation Story") and Samson Occom ("An Account of the Montauk Indians, on Long Island"), Aupaumut's history signals the growing role of Native authors in representing indigenous communities.

SARAH KEMBLE KNIGHT

The Bostonian Sarah Kemble Knight (1666–1727) was a woman of many talents. She kept a boardinghouse and taught school (thus she was sometimes called Madam Knight) and supposedly numbered Benjamin Franklin and members of the Mather family among her pupils. She also taught penmanship, made copies of court records, and wrote letters for people having business with the courts. She educated herself about the law and had a reputation for skillfully settling estates. Such engagement in public affairs was not unusual; in the early eighteenth century, many women played significant economic roles.

While her husband was abroad in 1704, Knight settled her cousin Caleb Trowbridge's estate on behalf of his widow. To do so, she traveled to New Haven, Connecticut, on Monday, October 2, 1704. From there, she went to New York, and she returned home to Boston in March 1705. The journey was hazardous, not undertaken lightly in those years, and unusual for a woman traveling alone.

Like numerous classics of early American literature, *The Private Journal of a Journey from Boston to New York in the Year 1704* that Knight kept was not published until the nineteenth century, when it was transcribed from shorthand and edited by Theodore Dwight. It provides a striking contrast to the soul-searching journals of Knight's Puritan contemporaries, having more of a Yankee flavor. Her literary allusions and passages of poetry remind us that early Americans absorbed transatlantic literary models to express the most common and intimate details of their lives. A keen ethnographic observer of provincial America, Knight was a sharply humorous commentator on its sometimes crude or ridiculous features. Her journal depicts everyday life in the northeastern colonies at the turn of the eighteenth century, while revealing that its author shared some of her society's most troubling prejudices.

From The Private Journal of a Journey from Boston to New York in the Year 1704[1]

Saturday, October the Seventh

We set out early in the morning and being something unacquainted with the way, having asked it of some we met, they told us we must ride a mile or two and turn down a lane on the right hand, and by their direction we rode on but not yet coming to the turning, we met a young fellow and asked him how far it was to the lane which turned down towards Guilford.[2] He said we must ride a little further and turn down by the corner of Uncle Sam's lot. My guide vented his spleen at the lubber,[3] and we soon after came into the road, and keeping still on, without anything further remarkable, about two o'clock afternoon we arrived at New Haven, where I was received with all possible respects and civility. Here I discharged Mr. Wheeler with a reward

1. The text is from *The Journal of Madame Knight* (1920), edited by George P. Winship.

2. Town in Connecticut.
3. Clumsy fellow.

to his satisfaction, and took some time to rest after so long and toilsome a journey, and informed myself of the manners and customs of the place and at the same time employed myself in the affair I went there upon.

They are governed by the same laws as we in Boston (or little differing) throughout this whole colony of Connecticut, and much the same way of church government, and many of them good, sociable people, and I hope religious too. But a little too much independent in their principles, and, as I have been told, were formerly in their zeal very rigid in their administrations towards such as their laws made offenders, even to a harmless kiss or innocent merriment among young people, whipping being a frequent and counted an easy punishment, about which as other crimes, the judges were absolute in their sentences. They told me a pleasant story about a pair of justices in those parts, which I may not omit the relation of.

A negro slave belonging to a man in the town stole a hogshead[4] from his master and gave or sold it to an Indian, native of the place. The Indian sold it in the neighborhood, and so the theft was found out. Thereupon the heathen[5] was seized and carried to the justice's house to be examined. But his Worship (it seems) was gone into the field, with a brother in office to gather in his pompions.[6] Whither the malefactor is hurried, and complaint made and satisfaction in the name of justice demanded. Their Worships can't proceed in form without a bench: whereupon they order one to be immediately erected, which, for want of fitter materials, they made with pompions—which being finished, down sets their Worships, and the malefactor called and by the senior Justice interrogated after the following manner: You, Indian, why did you steal from this man? You shouldn't do so—it's a grandy wicked thing to steal. "Hol't, hol't," cries Justice junior. "Brother, you speak negro to him. I'll ask him." "You, sirrah, why did you steal this man's hogshead?" "Hogshead?" (replies the Indian), "Me no stomany."[7] "No?" says his Worship, and pulling off his hat, patted his own head with his hand, says, "Tatapa[8]you, Tatapa—you; all one this. Hogshead all one this." "Hah!" says Netop, "Now me stomany that." Whereupon the company fell into a great fit of laughter, even to roaring. Silence is commanded, but to no effect: for they continued perfectly shouting. "Nay," says his Worship in an angry tone, "If it be so, *take me off the bench.*"

Their diversions in this part of the country are on lecture days and training days[9] mostly: on the former there is riding from town to town.

And on training days the youth divert themselves by shooting at the target, as they call it (but it very much resembles a pillory[1]), where he that hits nearest the white has some yards of red ribbon presented him which being tied to his hatband, the two ends streaming down his back, he is led away in triumph with great applause as the winners of the Olympiack games. They generally marry very young: the males oftener, as I am told, under twenty than above. They generally make public weddings and have a way something

4. A large barrel or cask.
5. I.e., the Indian.
6. Pumpkins.
7. I.e., understand.
8. Equal to, the same as. The joke plays on the justice's head being the same as the head of a hog (a hog's head).

9. Days set aside for military exercises. "Lecture days": days when a less formal sermon was offered than the one prepared for Sundays.
1. A wooden frame on a post, with holes for the head and arms, used as public punishment for offenders.

singular (as they say) in some of them, *viz.* just before joining hands the bridegroom quits the place, who is soon followed by the bridesmen and, as it were, dragged back to duty—being the reverse to the former practice among us, to steel[2] man's pride.

There are great plenty of oysters all along by the seaside as far as I rode in the colony and those very good. And they generally lived very well and comfortably in their families. But too indulgent (especially the farmers) to their slaves, suffering too great familiarity from them, permitting them to sit at table and eat with them (as they say, to save time), and into the dish goes the black hoof as freely as the white hand. They told me that there was a farmer lived near the town where I lodged who had some difference with his slave concerning something the master had promised him and did not punctually perform, which caused some hard words between them. But at length they put the matter to arbitration and bound themselves to stand to the award of such as they named—which done, the arbitrators having heard the allegations of both parties, order the master to pay 40[3] to black face and acknowledge his fault. And so the matter ended, the poor master very honestly standing to[4] the award.

There are everywhere in the towns as I passed a number of Indians the natives of the country, and are the most savage[5] of all the savages of that kind that I had ever seen: little or no care taken (as I heard upon inquiry) to make them otherwise. They have in some places lands of their own, and governed by laws of their own making;—they marry many wives and at pleasure put them away, and on the least dislike or fickle humor, on either side. Saying *"stand away"* to one another is a sufficient divorce. And, indeed, those uncomely *"stand aways"* are too much in vogue among the English in this (indulgent colony) as their records plentifully prove, and that on very trivial matters, of which some have been told me, but are not proper to be related by a female pen, though some of that foolish sex have had too large a share in the story.

If the natives commit any crime on their own precincts among themselves the English takes no cognezens[6] of. But if on the English ground they are punishable by our laws. They mourn for their dead by blacking their faces and cutting their hair after an awkerd and frightful manner, but can't bear you should mention the names of their dead relations to them. They trade most for rum, for which they would hazard their very lives, and the English fit[7] them generally as well by seasoning it plentifully with water.

They give the title of merchant to every trader who rate their goods according to the time and spetia[8] they pay in: *viz.* pay, money, pay as money, and trusting. *Pay* is grain, pork, beef, &c. at the prices set by the General Court that year; *money* is pieces of eight, rials, or Boston or Bay shillings[9] (as they call them,) or good hard money, as sometimes silver coin is termed by them; also wampum, *viz.* Indian beads which serves for change. *Pay as money* is provisions, as aforesaid, one third cheaper than as the Assembly or General Court sets it, and *trust* as they and the merchant agree for time.

2. Fortify against.
3. Shillings, or two English pounds.
4. I.e., paying.
5. Unchristian.
6. Cognizance; recognition.
7. Fix; cheat.

8. Specie; actual coin or money. "Rate": calculate the price of.
9. Coin minted in the Massachusetts Bay Colony. "Pieces of eight": Spanish silver coins. "Rials": former English gold coins worth ten shillings.

Now, when the buyer comes to ask for a commodity, sometimes before the merchant answers that he has it, he says, *"Is your pay ready?"* Perhaps the chap replies "Yes." "What do you pay in?" says the merchant. The buyer having answered, then the price is set; as suppose he wants a sixpenny knife, in pay it is 12d[1]—in pay as money eight pence, and hard money its own price, *viz. 6d.* It seems a very intricate way of trade and what *Lex Mercatoria*[2] had not thought of.

Being at a merchant's house, in comes a tall country fellow, with his alfogeos[3] full of tobacco; for they seldom lose their cud, but keep chewing and spitting as long as their eyes are open. He advanced to the middle of the room, makes an awkward nod, and spitting a large deal of aromatic tincture, he gave a scrape with his shovel-like shoe, leaving a small shovel full of dirt on the floor, made a full stop, hugging his own pretty body with his hands under his arms, stood staring round him like a cat let out of a basket. At last, like the creature Balaam rode on,[4] he opened his mouth and said: "Have you any ribinen for hatbands to sell, I pray?" The questions and answers about the pay being passed, the ribin is brought and opened. Bumpkin simpers, cries "It's confounded gay[5] I vow"; and beckning to the door, in comes Joan Tawdry,[6] dropping about 50 curtsies, and stands by him. He shows her the ribin. *"Law, you,"* says she, *"it's right gent,* do you take it, *tis dreadful[7] pretty."* Then she inquires *"Have you any hood silk[8] I pray?"* which being brought and bought, "Have you any *thread silk to sew it with?"* says she, which being accommodated with they departed. They generally stand after they come in a great while speechless, and sometimes don't say a word till they are asked what they want, which I impute to the awe they stand in of the merchants, who they are constantly almost indebted to, and must take what they bring without liberty to choose for themselves. But they serve them as well,[9] making the merchants stay long enough for their pay.

We may observe here the great necessity and benefit both of education and conversation; for these people have as large a portion of mother wit,[1] and sometimes a larger, than those who have been brought up in cities, but for want of improvements render themselves almost ridiculous, as above. I should be glad if they would leave such follies and am sure all that love clean houses (at least) would be glad on't too.[2]

They are generally very plain in their dress, throughout all the colony, as I saw, and follow one another in their modes, that you may know where they belong, especially the women, meet them where you will.

Their chief red-letter day is St. Election,[3] which is annually observed according to charter, to choose their government, a blessing they can never be thankful enough for, as they will find if ever it be their hard fortune to lose it. The present governor in Connecticut is the Honorable John Winthrop,

1. Twelve pence; "d" is from *denarius*, an ancient Roman coin.
2. The law of merchants (Latin).
3. Cheeks like saddlebags (from the Spanish *alforjas*: pouches).
4. I.e., talking, like the ass ridden by the Old Testament prophet Balaam (Numbers 22).
5. Vibrant; brilliant in color.
6. Slang for lower-class woman.
7. Extremely. "Gent": genteel, stylish. "Law": Lord.

8. Silk cloth suitable for a hood.
9. I.e., treat them equally badly.
1. Of native intelligence.
2. Knight criticizes country people for desiring luxuries and for chewing tobacco, which they spit in the house of the merchant where they go to purchase ribbons and such.
3. I.e., Election Day, which Knight mockingly suggests they treat as a sacred holiday.

A View of Fort George with the City of New York from the S.W. An engraving of New York from the southwest, showing the skyline (primarily church steeples) as it might have appeared to Sarah Kemble Knight in the early eighteenth century.

Esq.[4] A gentleman of an ancient and honorable family whose father was governor here sometime before, and his grandfather had been governor of the Massachusetts.[5] This gentleman is a very courteous and affable person, much given to hospitality, and has by his good services gained the affection of the people as much as any who had been before him in that post.

From *December the Sixth*

* * *

The city of New York is a pleasant, well-compacted place, situated on a commodious river which is a fine harbor for shipping. The buildings brick generally, very stately and high, though not altogether like ours in Boston. The bricks in some of the houses are of divers colors and laid in checkers,[6] being glazed look very agreeable. The inside of them are neat to admiration, the wooden work, for only the walls are plastered, and the sumers and gist[7] are planed and kept very white scowered as so is all the partitions if made of boards. The fireplaces have no jambs (as ours have) but the backs run flush with the walls, and the hearth is of tiles and is as far out into the room at the ends as before the fire, which is generally five foot in the lower rooms, and the piece over where the mantle tree should be is made as ours with joiners' work,[8] and as I suppose is fastened to iron rods inside. The house

4. Fitz-John Winthrop (1638–1707), governor of Connecticut 1698–1707.
5. John Winthrop (1606–1676), father of Fitz-John, governor of Connecticut 1659–76. John Winthrop (1588–1649), grandfather of Fitz-John, founding governor of Massachusetts Bay.

6. I.e., alternating. "Divers": various.
7. The main beams and joists.
8. Joiners were craftsmen who constructed things by joining pieces of wood together. Their work was more finished than a carpenter's. "Mantle tree": a wood beam over the opening of a fireplace.

where the vendue[9] was, had chimney corners like ours, and they and the hearths were laid with the finest tile that I ever see, and the staircases laid all with white tile which is ever clean, and so are the walls of the kitchen which had a brick floor. They were making great preparations to receive their governor, Lord Cornbury from the Jerseys,[1] and for that end raised the militia to guard him on shore to the fort.

They are generally of the Church of England and have a New England gentleman for their minister, and a very fine church set out with all customary requisites. There are also a Dutch and divers conventicles as they call them, viz. Baptist, Quakers, etc. They are not strict in keeping the Sabbath as in Boston and other places where I had been, but seem to deal with great exactness as far as I see or deal with. They are sociable to one another and courteous and civil to strangers and fare well in their houses. The English go very fashionable in their dress. But the Dutch, especially the middling sort, differ from our women, in their habit go loose,[2] wear French muchets which are like a cap and a headband in one, leaving their ears bare, which are set out with jewels of a large size and many in number. And their fingers hooped with rings, some with large stones in them of many colors as were their pendants in their ears, which you should see very old women wear as well as young.

They have vendues very frequently and make their earnings very well by them, for they treat with good liquor liberally, and the customers drink as liberally and generally pay for't as well, by paying for that which they bid up briskly for, after the sack[3] has gone plentifully about, though sometimes good penny worths' are got there. Their diversions in the winter is riding sleighs about three or four miles out of town, where they have houses of entertainment at a place called the Bowery,[4] and some go to friends' houses who handsomely treat them. Mr. Burroughs carried his spouse and daughter and myself out to one Madame Dowes, a gentlewoman that lived at a farm house, who gave us a handsome entertainment of five or six dishes and choice beer and metheglin,[5] cider, etc. all which she said was the produce of her farm. I believe we met 50 or 60 sleighs that day—they fly with great swiftness and some are so furious that they'll turn out of the path for none except a loaden cart. Nor do they spare for any diversion the place affords, and sociable to a degree, their tables being as free to their neighbors as to themselves.

Having here transacted the affair I went upon and some other that fell in the way, after about a fortnight's stay there I left New York with no little regret[.] * * *

9. Auction.
1. Edward Hyde (1661–1723), Viscount Cornbury, governor of New York and New Jersey 1701–08.
2. Are more casual in appearance. "Middling": middle class.

3. Wine; specifically, white wine imported from Spain or the Canaries.
4. Now a street in lower Manhattan.
5. A spiced variety of fermented beverage. The cider offered was probably also alcoholic.

WILLIAM BYRD

William Byrd (1674–1744) was the son of a wealthy Virginia planter, merchant, and Indian trader. His mother, Mary Horsmanden, came from a family of Royalist refugees who fled the English Civil Wars (1642–51). Byrd was educated in England and spent the formative years of his life in London, where he learned the skills to manage his father's estate.

After spending more than half of his life in England, Byrd returned to Virginia in 1726 to stay. In a letter of that year to his friend Charles Boyle, Earl of Orrery, Byrd described the satisfactions he derived from the role of the Virginia planter:

> Besides the advantage of pure air, we abound in all kinds of provisions without expense (I mean we who have plantations). I have a large family of my own, and my doors are open to everybody, yet I have no bills to pay, and half-a-crown will rest undisturbed in my pockets for many moons altogether. Like one of the patriarchs [in the Old Testament], I have my flock and herds, my bondmen and bondwomen, and every sort of trade amongst my own servants, so that I live in a kind of independence on everyone but Providence. . . . Thus, my Lord, we are very happy in our Canaans [our "promised lands"] if we could but forget the onions and fleshpots of Egypt [where the Israelites had been enslaved yet enjoyed luxuries].

Byrd's "new Canaan" is a self-sufficient, earthly garden, combining the best of civilized and rural life—all, of course, based on slave labor. He recorded details of plantation life in his secret diary.

In 1728, Byrd accepted a commission to survey the much-disputed boundary line between Virginia and North Carolina. The diary that he kept on his trip served as the sourcebook for his *History of the Dividing Line*. He planned to have the *History of the Dividing Line* published in London, and although that project failed and the book did not appear in print until 1841, Byrd's manuscript was circulated among his London friends, and later naturalists such as Thomas Jefferson knew of it. In its wealth of natural detail and Indian lore, as well as its frequently contemptuous portrayals of provincials, the *History* helped satisfy the London metropolis's curiosity about America.

From The Secret Diary of William Byrd of Westover
1710–1712[1]

[December] 31. [1710] I rose at 5 o'clock and read a chapter in Hebrew and four leaves in Lucian.[2] I said my prayers and ate boiled milk for breakfast. My daughter was very sick all night and vomited a great deal but was a little better this morning. All my sick people were better, thank God, and I had another girl come down sick from the quarters.[3] I danced my dance.[4] Then I read a sermon in Dr. Tillotson[5] and after that walked in the garden till

1. The text is from *The Secret Diary of William Byrd of Westover 1709–1712*, edited by Louis B. Wright and Marion Tinling (1941).
2. I.e., four pages of Lucian, a Greek satirist of the second century C.E.

3. I.e., slave quarters.
4. I.e., performed my calisthenics.
5. Dr. John Tillotson (1620–1694), archbishop of Canterbury, one of Byrd's favorite writers.

dinner. I ate roast venison. In the afternoon I looked over my sick people and then took a walk about the plantation. The weather was very warm still. My wife walked with me and when she came back she was very much indisposed and went to bed. In the evening I read another sermon in Dr. Tillotson. About 8 o'clock the wind came to northwest and it began to be cold. I said my prayers and had good health, good thoughts, and good humor, thank God Almighty.

Some night this month I dreamed that I saw a flaming sword in the sky and called some company to see it but before they could come it was disappeared, and about a week after my wife and I were walking and we discovered in the clouds a shining cloud exactly in the shape of a dart and seemed to be over my plantation but it soon disappeared likewise. Both these appearances seemed to foretell some misfortune to me which afterwards came to pass in the death of several of my negroes after a very unusual manner. My wife about two months since dreamed she saw an angel in the shape of a big woman who told her the time was altered and the seasons were changed and that several calamities would follow that confusion. God avert His judgment from this poor country.

[January] 2. [1711] I rose at 5 o'clock and read a chapter in Hebrew and nothing in Greek because of the company that was here. I said my prayers and ate boiled milk for breakfast. I had six sick negroes come down from the quarters. About 9 o'clock my company went away. My wife was a little better and so was my child, thank God, but C-l-y was extremely ill and so was A-g-y.[6] I tended them as much as I could but God is pleased to afflict me with His judgment for my sins. His holy will be done. I ate some wild turkey. The wind was northeast and it was cold. In the afternoon I read a little English but could not be easy because poor C-l-y was so very ill. I took a melancholy walk. In the evening about 6 o'clock C-l-y died and all the people was grieved at it. I read a little English and gave the necessary orders about the sick people who were 12 in number. I said my prayers and had good health, good thoughts, and good humor, thank God Almighty.

[January] 6. [1711] I rose at 5 o'clock and read two chapters in Hebrew and six leaves in Lucian. I said my prayers and ate boiled milk for breakfast. Poor old S-r-y died this night to make up the number of the dead. God save the rest. A-g-y seemed to be a little better and so did the rest of the sick, God be praised, except Jenny and she seemed to be worse. The weather threatened rain all day. I removed several things out of the Doctor's closet[7] into mine and was very little with my cousin. I was out of humor with my wife. I ate boiled pork for dinner. In the afternoon Mrs. Dunn[8] went away in the rain. I spent most of my time in looking after my sick. In the evening it rained extremely, and all night. My cousin and I took a walk about the plantation. I said my prayers and had good health, good thoughts, and good humor, thank God Almighty.

[January] 7. [1711] I rose at 5 o'clock and read two chapters in Hebrew and some Greek in Lucian. I said my prayers and ate boiled milk for breakfast. My sick people were some worse and some well enough to go home to the quarters. Jenny and A-g-y were much as they were. The weather held up so

6. Both were servants.
7. Small private room.

8. A frequent visitor, the wife of the minister of Hungar's Parish, Northampton County, Virginia.

that I and my cousin [Guy] went to church, but my wife was afflicted with the headache and stayed at home. People condoled the sickness of my family. Mr. Anderson gave us a sermon. After church I carried him home with me to dinner and to see my sick people. I ate fish for dinner. Mr. Anderson advised me to give my people cordials since other physic failed, which I did. In the afternoon I did nothing but mind them. In the evening my cousin and we talked till 8 o'clock. I said a short prayer and had good health, good thoughts, and good humor, thank God Almighty.

[January] 22. [1711] I rose at 3 o'clock and read a chapter in Hebrew and some Greek in Lucian. I said my prayers and ate boiled milk for breakfast. I danced my dance. I ordered the sloop to be unloaded. Redskin Peter pretended to be sick and I put a [branding-iron] on the place he complained of and put the [bit] upon him.[9] The boy called the Doc was sent from Falling Creek with a swollen thigh. My sick people were better, thank God Almighty. I received a courteous letter from the Governor by Tom, who brought no news. I ate boiled pork for dinner. Mr. Mumford came down after dinner and told me all was well at Appomattox. When he had got some victuals we took a walk to see the people load the sloop and afterwards about the plantation. In the evening G-r-l came and let me know things were well at Falling Creek. He brought me a letter from Tom Turpin[1] in which he agreed to stay with me for £25 a year. I ate some roast beef for supper. I neglected to say my prayers, but had good health, good thoughts, and good humor, thank God.

[January] 23. [1711] I rose at 5 o'clock and read a chapter in Hebrew and some Greek in Lucian. I said my prayers and ate boiled milk for breakfast. I danced my dance. My sick people were better, thank God, and Redskin Peter was particularly well and worked as well as anybody. * * *

1710–12 1941

From The History of the Dividing Line[1]

We encamp't about two Miles beyond the River, where we made good Chear[2] upon a very fat Buck, that luckily fell in our way. The Indian[3] likewise shot a Wild Turkey, but confest he wou'd not bring it us, lest we shou'd continue to provoke the Guardian of the Forrest, by cooking the Beasts of the Field, and the Birds of the Air together in one Vessel.

This Instance of Indian Superstition I confess is countenanc'd in some measure by the Levitical Law, which forbad the mixing things of a Different Nature together in the same field, or in the same Garment, and why then not in the same Kettle?[4]

9. A device something like a horse's bit and fastened in the mouth.
1. An overseer.
1. The text is from *The Dividing Line Histories of William Byrd II of Westover* (2013), edited by Kevin Joel Berland.
2. Ate well. "The River": the Dan River, which weaves back and forth across the boundary between Virginia and North Carolina that Byrd's company was in the process of marking with poles. Byrd is credited with the first recorded mention of this name.
3. Ned Bearskin, the surveyors' Saponi Indian guide.
4. In the biblical Books of Leviticus and Deuteronomy, dietary laws prohibit various kinds of mixing, such as meat and milk, though not two kinds of meat in one pot.

But after all, if the Jumbleing of two Sorts of Flesh together be a Sin, how intolerable an Offence must it be to make a Spanish Oleo, that is a Hotch-potch of every kind of thing that is eatable, and the good People of England wou'd have a great deal to answer for, for beating up so many different Ingredients into a Pudding.

We were so cruelly intangled with Bushes, and Grape-Vines all day, that we could advance the Line no farther than 5 Miles and 28 Poles.[5]

The Vines grew very thick in these Woods, twineing lovingly round the Trees almost every where, especially to the Saplins.[6] This makes it evident how natural both the Soil, and Climate of this Country are to Vines, tho' I believe most to our own Vines.

The Grapes, we commonly met with were black, tho' there be two or three kinds of White Grapes that grow wild. The black are very sweet, but small, because the Strength of the Vine spends itself in Wood, tho' without Question a proper Culture wou'd make the same Grapes both larger and sweeter. But with all these Disadvantages I have drunk tolerable good Wine prest from them, tho' made without Skill. There is then good Reason to believe, it might admit of great Improvement if rightly managed.

Our Indian kill'd a Bear of two years old, that was feasting on these Grapes. He was very fat as they generally are, in that Season of the year. In the fall the Flesh of this Animal has a high Relish,[7] different from that of other Creatures, tho' inclining nearest to that of Pork, or rather Wild Boar.

A true Woodsman prefers this sort of meat to that of the fattest Venison, not only for the Haut-gout[8] but also because the Fat of it is well tasted, and never rises in the Stomach. Another proof of the goodness of this meat is, that it is less apt to corrupt, than any other we are acquainted with.

As agreeable as such rich Diet was to the men, yet we who were not accustom'd to it, tasted it at first with some sort of Squemishness, that Animal being of the Dog-kind[9] tho' a little use soon reconcil'd us to this American Venison. And that its being of the Dog kind might give us less disgust, we had the Example of that Ancient and polite People the Chinese, who reckon Dog's Flesh too good for any under the Quality of Mandarin.[1]

This Beast is in truth a very clean Feeder, living while the Season lasts upon [Acorns], Chesnuts, and Chinkapens,[2] Wild-Hony, and wild Grapes. They are naturally not carnivorous, unless Hunger constrain them to it, after the Mast[3] is all gone, and the Product of the Woods quite exhausted.

They are not provident enough to lay up any Hoard, like the Squirrels, nor can they after all live very long upon licking their Paws, as Sir John Mandevil and some Travellers tell us,[4] but are forc't in the Winter Months to quit the Mountains, and visit the Inhabitants.

5. A pole is a surveyor's tool and unit of measurement equal to sixteen and a half feet.
6. Saplings: young trees.
7. An appetizing flavor.
8. A strong flavor with a slight element of decay in it (from French *haut goût*: high taste). "Venison": in Byrd's day, game, not specifically deer meat.
9. Some early systems for classifying animals grouped bears with dogs.
1. I.e., they consider dog meat a delicacy fit for only the highest level of society.

2. A close relative of the chestnut. "A very clean Feeder": i.e., a creature that eats clean foods.
3. The fruit of forest trees, particularly as food for wild animals.
4. The pseudonymous travel writer Sir John Mandeville (fl. c. 1356) does not mention bears in *The Voyages and Travels of Sir John Mandeville*, but the claim that bears hoard food appears in the works of the Roman naturalists Pliny the Elder (23–79 C.E.) and Aelian (c. 170–c. 235 C.E.).

Their Errand is then to surprise a poor Hog at a Pinch to keep them from starving. And to shew they are not Flesh Eaters by Trade, they devour their Prey very awkwardly.

They don't kill it right out, and feast upon its Blood and Entrails, like other Ravenous Beasts, but having after a fair pursuit seiz'd it with their Paws, they begin first upon the Rump, and so devour one Collop[5] after another til they come to the Vitals, the poor Animal crying all the while for several Minutes together. However in so doing Bruin[6] acts a little imprudently, because the dismal outcry of the Hog alarms the Neighbourhood, and 'tis odds but he pays the forfeit with his Life, before he can secure his Retreat.

But Bears soon grow weary of this unnatural Diet, and about January, when there is nothing to be got in the Woods, they retire into some cave or hollow Tree, where they sleep away two or three Months very comfortably. But then they quit their Holes in March when the Fish begin to run up the Rivers, on which they are forc't to keep Lent[7] till some Fruit or Berry comes in Season.

But Bears are fondest of Chesnuts, which grow plentifully towards the Mountains upon very large Trees, where the Soil happens to be rich. We were curious to know how it happen'd that many of the outward Branches of those Trees came to be broke off in that solitary Place, and were inform'd, that the Bears are so discreet, as not to trust their unwieldy Bodies on the smaller Limbs of the Tree, that would not bear their Weight. But after venturing as far as is safe, which they can juge to an Inch, they bite off the End of the Branch, which falling down, they are content to finish their Repast on the Ground. In the same Cautious Manner they secure the Acorns, that grow on the weaker Limbs of the Oak. And it must be allow'd, that in these Instances a Bear carries Instinct a great way, and acts more reasonably than many of his Betters, who indiscreetly venture upon frail Projects[8] that won't bear them.

* * *

In the Evening we examin'd our Friend Bearskin, concerning the Religion of his Country, and he explained it to us, without any of that Reserve, to which his Nation is Subject.

He told us he believ'd there was one Supreme God, who had several Subaltern Deities under Him. And that this Master-God made the World a long time ago. That he told the Sun, the Moon, and Stars, their Business in the Beginning, which they with good looking after have faithfully perform'd ever since.

That the same Power, that made all things at first, has taken Care to keep them in the same Method and Motion ever since.

He believed that God had form'd many Worlds before he form'd this, but that those Worlds either grew old and ruinous, or were destroyed for the Dishonesty of the Inhabitants.

That God is very just and very good, ever well pleas'd with those men who possess those God-like Qualities. That he takes good People into his safe Protection, makes them very rich, fills their Bellies plentifully, preserves them from Sickness, and from being surprizd, or overcome by their Enemies.

But all such as tell Lies, and cheat those they have Dealings with, he never fails to punish with Sickness, Poverty, and Hunger, and after all that, suf-

5. Piece of flesh.
6. A name for a bear.
7. I.e., fast as during the Christian observation of

Lent, a period of roughly six weeks before Easter.
8. Projections; i.e., branches.

fers them to be knock't on the Head and scalp't by those that fight against them.

He believ'd that after Death both good and bad People are conducted by a strong Guard into a great Road in which departed Souls travel together for some time, Til at a certain Distance this Road forks into two Paths, the one extremely Levil,[9] and the other Stony and Mountainous.

Here the good are parted from the Bad, by a flash of Lightening, the first being hurry'd away to the Right, the other to the Left. The Right Hand Road leads to a charming warm Country, where the Spring is everlasting, and every Month is May, and as the year is always in its Youth, so are the People, and particularly the Women are bright as Stars, and never scold.

That in this happy Climate there are Deer, Turkeys, Elks, and Buffalos innumerable, perpetually fat and gentle, while the Trees are loaded with delicious Fruit quite throughout the four seasons.

That the Soil brings forth Corn spontaneously, without the Curse of Labour, and so very wholesome, that None who have the happiness to eat of it, are ever sick, grow old, or dy.

Near the Entrance into this Blessed Land sits a venerable old Man on a Mat richly woven, who examins strictly all that are brought before Him, and if they have behav'd well, the Guards are order'd to open the Chrystal Gate, and let them enter into the Land of Delights.

The left hand Path is very rugged and uneaven, leading to a dead and barren Country, where it is always Winter. The Ground is the whole year round cover'd with Snow, and nothing is to be seen upon the Trees, but Icicles.

All the People are hungry, yet have not a Morsel of anything to eat, except a bitter kind of Potatoe, that gives them the Dry-Gripes[1] and fills their whole Body, with loathsome Ulcers, that stink and are insupportably painfull.

Here all the Women are old and ugly, having claws like a Panther, with which they fly upon the Men, that slight their Passion. For it seems these haggard old Furies are intolerably fond[2] and expect a vast deal of Cherishing. They talk much and exceedingly shrill, giving exquisite Pain to the Drum of the Ear, which in that Place of the Torment is so tender that every sharp Note wounds it to the Quick.

At the end of this Path sits a dreadful Old Woman on a monstrous Toad-Stool, whose head is cover'd with Rattle Snakes instead of Tresses, with glaring white Eyes, that strike a Terror unspeakable into all that behold her.

This Hag pronounces Sentence of Woe upon all the miserable Wretches that hold up their hands at her Tribunal. After this they are deliver'd over to huge Turkey-Buzzards, like Harpys, that fly away with them, to the Place above mentioned.

Here after they have been tormented a certain number of Years, according to their several Degrees of Guilt, they are again driven back into this World, to try if they will mend their Manners, and merit a place the next time in the Regions of Bliss.

This was the Substance of Bearskins Religion, and was as much to the purpose as could be expected from a meer State of Nature, without one glimps of Revelation or Philosophy.[3]

9. Level.
1. Stomach cramps.
2. Infatuated, foolish, silly.

3. Byrd distinguishes between Bearskin's natural perspective and the philosophy of the ancients or the religion of the moderns.

It contain'd however the three Great Articles of Natural Religion, The Belief of a God. The Moral Distinction betwixt Good and Evil, and the Expectation of Rewards and Punishments in another World.

Indeed the Indian Notion of a Future Happiness is a little Gross and Sensual, like Mahomet's Paradise.[4] But how can it be otherwise in a People, that are contented with Nature, as they find Her, and have no other Lights but what they receive from purblind Tradition.[5]

There having been great Signs of Rain yesterday Evening, we had taken our Precautions in securing the Bread, and Trenching in our Tent.

* * *

As I sat in the Tent I overheard a learn'd Conversation between one of our Men and the Indian. He ask't the Englishman what it was that made that rumbling Noise when it Thunder'd?

The Man told him merrily, that the God of the English was firing his great Guns upon the God of the Indians, which made all that roaring in the Clouds, and that the Lightening was only the Flash of those Guns.

The Indian carrying on the Humour, reply'd very gravely, He believ'd that might be the Case indeed, and that the Rain which follow'd upon the Thunder must be occasion'd by the Indian God's being so scar'd he cou'd not hold his Water.

1728 1841

4. The idea of paradise in Islam (founded by the prophet Muhammad) is popularly identified with the presence of seventy-two virgins. "Gross": materialistic.
5. Traditional beliefs based on poor perception, lack of intellect, or both.

ALEXANDER HAMILTON

Alexander Hamilton (1712–1756) was a product of the Scottish Enlightenment, a period distinguished by a rich literary and intellectual culture that helped lay the foundations of the modern human sciences, such as sociology and economics. Not to be confused with the first secretary of the U.S. treasury, this Alexander Hamilton belonged to minor Scottish gentry. The twelfth child of a professor of divinity at the University of Edinburgh, Hamilton entered the university at age thirteen. After earning a Master of Arts degree, he studied medicine, completing his training in 1737. Hamilton believed in both the value of local identity and advancement within the British Empire, and in 1739 he followed an elder brother to Maryland in search of greater opportunity than he could find in Edinburgh. He settled in Maryland's capital, Annapolis, where he found the disorder and lack of culture disheartening and the conditions unhealthy, as he experienced directly when he contracted malaria.

Hamilton's rocky start in the colony took a turn for the better in 1743, when he was elected to Annapolis's governing body, the Common Council. The next year, he spent four months traveling around the northeast, accompanied by his slave Dromo. In the *Itinerarium*, an account of the journey based on his diary, Hamilton takes

notice of the natural and human landscapes on this more than sixteen-hundred-mile-long tour. Some of his best writing involves character portraits, which are novelistic in their detail—perhaps unsurprisingly, since early in the trip he read *Joseph Andrews*, the first novel by the English writer Henry Fielding (1707–1754) and, in fact, one of the first English-language novels. He also provided detailed descriptions, in an ethnographic mode, of several of colonial America's urban centers: New York City, Boston, and Newport, Rhode Island. Hamilton gave the manuscript of the *Itinerarium* to an Italian friend, who probably took it to Italy. Following a lengthy disappearance, the manuscript was first published in 1906.

From Hamilton's Itinerarium[1]

[May 31, 1744] Leaving Joppa[2] I fell in company with one Captain Waters and with Mr. D——gs, a virtuoso in botany. He affected some knowledge in Natural Philosophy,[3] but his learning that way was but superficial.

* * *

He showed me a print or figure of the Gensing,[4] which he told me was to be found in the rich bottoms near Susquehanna.[5] The plant is of one stem or stalk, and jointed. From each joint issues four small branches, at the extremity of each of these is a cinquefoil, or five leaves, somewhat oblong, notched and veined. Upon the top of the stem it bears a bunch of red berries, but I could not learn if it had any apparent flower, the colour of that flower, or at what season of the year it blossomed or bore fruit. I intended, however, to look for it upon the branches of Susquehanna, not that I imagined it of any singular virtue, for I think it has really no more than what may be in the common liquorice root, mixed with an aromatick, or spicy drug, but I had a curiosity to see a thing which has been so famous.

After parting with this company, I put up at one Tradaway's, about ten miles from Joppa. The road here is pretty hilly, stony, and full of a small gravel. I observed some stone, which I thought looked like limestone.

Just as I dismounted at Tradaway's, I found a drunken Club dismissing.[6] Most of them had got upon their horses, and were seated in an oblique situation, deviating much from a perpendicular to the horizontal plane, a posture quite necessary for keeping the center of gravity within its proper base, for the support of the superstructure; hence we deduce the true physical reason why our heads overloaded with liquor become too ponderous for our heels. Their discourse was as oblique as their position: the only thing intelligible in it was oaths and Goddamnes; the rest was an inarticulate sound like Rabelais' frozen words a-thawing[7] interlaced with hickupings and belch-

1. The text is from *Hamilton's Itinerarium Being a Narrative of a Journey from Annapolis, Maryland through Delaware, Pennsylvania, New York, New Jersey, Connecticut, Rhode Island, Massachusetts and New Hampshire from May to September, 1744* (1907), edited by Albert Bushnell Hart, LL.D.
2. Or Joppa Town, seat of Baltimore County 1712–68.
3. I.e., in science.
4. Ginseng (the more common spelling), a popu-

lar medicinal plant.
5. I.e., in the nutrient-rich soil below water near the Susquehanna River.
6. Leaving, or breaking up a meeting.
7. In *The Life of Gargantua and Pantagruel*, a series of novels by the French monk François Rabelais (c. 1494–1553), the noise of a winter battle melts and is heard by the crew of a ship that passes the site of the conflict the following spring.

ings. I was uneasy till they were gone, and my landlord, seeing me stare, made that trite apology,—That indeed he did not care to have such disorderly fellows come about his house; he was always noted far and near for keeping a quiet house and entertaining only gentlemen or such like; but these were country people, his neighbours, and it was not prudent to disoblige them upon slight occasions. "Alas, sir!" added he, "we that entertain travellers must strive to oblige everybody, for it is our daily bread." While he spoke thus our Bacchanalians[8] finding no more rum in play, rid off helter-skelter, as if the devil had possessed them, every man sitting his horse in a seesaw manner like a bunch of rags tied upon the saddle. I found nothing particular or worth notice in my landlord's character or conversation, only as to his bodily make. He was a fat pursy man, and had large bubbies[9] like a woman. I supped upon fried chickens and bacon, and after supper the conversation turned upon politicks, news, and the dreaded French war;[1] but it was so very lumpish and heavy that it disposed me mightily to sleep. This learned company consisted of the landlord, his overseer and miller, and another greasy-thumbed fellow, who, as I understood, professed physick[2] and particularly surgery in the drawing of teeth.

He practised upon the housemaid, a dirty piece of lumber, who made such screaming and squawling as made me imagine there was murder going forwards in the house. However, the artist got the tooth out at last, with a great clumsy pair of blacksmith's forceps; and indeed it seemed to require such an instrument, for when he showed it to us it resembled a horsenail[3] more than a tooth.

The miller I found professed musick, and would have tuned his crowd to us,[4] but unfortunately the two middle strings betwixt the bass and treble were broke. This man told us that he could play by the book.[5]

After having had my fill of this elegant company, I went to bed at ten o'clock.

Friday, June 1st.—The sun rose in a clear horizon, and the air in these highlands was for two hours in the morning very cool and refreshing. I breakfasted upon some dirty chocolate, but the best that the house could afford, and took horse about half an hour after six in the morning. For the first thirteen miles the road seemed gravelly and hilly, and the land but indifferent.

* * *

When I came near Susquehanna Ferry,[6] I looked narrowly in the bottoms for the gensing, but could not discover it. The lower ferry of Susquehanna, which I crossed, is above a mile broad.[7] It is kept by a little old man, whom I found at vittles with his wife and family upon a homely dish of fish, without any kind of sauce. They desired me to eat, but I told them I had no stomach.[8]

8. Drunken revelers; from the devotees of Bacchus, the Roman god of wine and intoxication.
9. Breasts. "Pursy": short of breath, asthmatic; fat.
1. King George's War (1744–48), between England and France; sometimes called the third French and Indian War.
2. Claimed to practice medicine—in this case, dentistry.

3. A nail used to secure a horseshoe to the horse's hoof.
4. Entertained us with a tune on his crowd, a stringed instrument played with a bow.
5. By reading music, generally considered more advanced than playing by rote or by ear.
6. A crossable passage of the Susquehanna.
7. Over a mile wide.
8. Appetite.

They had no cloth upon the table, and their mess was in a dirty, deep, wooden dish, which they evacuated[9] with their hands, cramming down skins, scales, and all. They used neither knife, fork, spoon, plate, or napkin, because, I suppose, they had none to use. I looked upon this as a picture of that primitive simplicity practised by our forefathers, long before the mechanic arts[1] had supplied them with instruments for the luxury and elegance of life. I drank some of their cider, which was very good, and crossed the ferry in company with a certain Scots-Irishman, by name Thomas Quiet. The land about Susquehanna is pretty high and woody, and the channel of the river rocky.

Mr. Quiet rid a little scrub bay mare, which he said was sick and ailing, and could not carry him, and therefore he lighted every half mile and ran a couple of miles at a footman's pace, to "spell the poor beast" (as he termed it). He informed me he lived at Monocosy,[2] and had been out three weeks in quest of his creatures (horses), four of which had strayed from his plantation. I condoled his loss, and asked him what his mare's distemper was, resolving to prescribe for her, but all that I could get out of him was that the poor silly beast had choaked herself in eating her oats; so I told him that if she was choaked she was past my art to recover. This fellow I observed had a particular down-hanging look, which made me suspect he was one of our New-light bigots.[3]

I guessed right, for he introduced a discourse concerning Whitefield, and enlarged pretty much and with some warmth upon the doctrines of that apostle, speaking much in his praise. I took upon me, in a ludicrous manner, to impugn some of his doctrines, which by degrees put Mr. Quiet in a passion. He told me flatly that I was damned without redemption. I replied that I thought his name and behaviour were very incongruous, and desired him to change it with all speed, for it was very improper that such an angry turbulent mortal as he should be called by the name of Thomas Quiet.

1744 1906

9. Emptied. "Mess": meal.
1. The construction of tools.
2. Near Frederick, Maryland, northwest of Baltimore.
3. Evangelical Protestants, which in Hamilton's

day prominently included followers of the British Anglican revivalist George Whitefield (1714–1770), mentioned below, who toured the colonies on several occasions.

WILLIAM BARTRAM

The son of the internationally famous botanist John Bartram, William Bartram (1739–1823) became an important naturalist in his own right. During his early years in Philadelphia, William accompanied his father on expeditions in the eastern American colonies to collect plants and served as an illustrator for his father's writings. He participated in the far-flung intellectual networks that included the local luminary Benjamin Franklin and the Swedish naturalist Carl von Linné, more familiarly known as Linnaeus, who developed the organism-naming system still used by biologists. For three years, Bartram attended the Philadelphia Academy (later the University of Pennsylvania). He then moved to the Cape Fear region of North Carolina to live with his uncle.

After France ceded Florida to England in 1765, Bartram traveled extensively in the southeastern United States, at first with his father and later on his own. In 1777, John Bartram died, leaving his botanical garden to William's brother, and William returned to Philadelphia to assist with its management. Among the Bartrams' most prominent customers were the United States presidents George Washington and Thomas Jefferson and the writer J. Hector St. John de Crèvecoeur.

William Bartram's most famous literary work derived from his journeys in the southeast. He published *Travels through North and South Carolina, East and West Florida, the Cherokee Country, the Extensive Territories of the Muscolgulges, or Creek Confederacy, and the Country of the Chactaws* in 1791. This account influenced numerous writers, including the eighteenth-century British Romantic poets Samuel Taylor Coleridge and William Wordsworth. In later years, Bartram continued to be active in naturalist circles and published several essays, including the following selection.

Anecdotes of an American Crow[1]

It is a difficult task to give a history of our Crow. And I hesitate not to aver, that it would require the pen of a very able biographer to do justice to his talents.

Before I enter on this subject minutely, it may be necessary to remark, that we do not here speak of the crow, collectively, as giving an account of the whole race[2] (since I am convinced, that these birds differ as widely as men do from each other, in point of talents and acquirements), but of a particular bird of that species, which I reared from the nest.

He was, for a long time, comparatively a helpless, dependent creature, having a very small degree of activity or vivacity, every sense seeming to be asleep, or in embryo, until he had nearly attained his finished dimensions, and figure, and the use of all his members. Then, we were surprised, and daily amused with the progressive developement of his senses, expanding and maturating as the wings of the youthful phalæna,[3] when disengaged from its nympha-shell.

These senses, however, seemed, as in man, to be only the organs or instruments of his intellectual powers, and of their effects, as directed towards the accomplishment of various designs, and the gratification of the passions.

This was a bird of a happy temper, and good disposition. He was tractable and benevolent, docile and humble, whilst his genius demonstrated extraordinary acuteness, and lively sensations. All these good qualities were greatly in his favour, for they procured him friends and patrons, even among *men*, whose society and regard contributed to illustrate the powers of his understanding. But what appeared most extraordinary, he seemed to have the wit to select and treasure up in his mind, and the sagacity to practise, that kind of knowledge which procured him the most advantage and profit.

He had great talents, and a strong propensity to imitation. When I was engaged in weeding in the garden, he would often fly to me, and, after very attentively observing me in pulling up the small weeds and grass, he would fall to work, and with his strong beak, pluck up the grass; and the more so, when I complimented him with encouraging expressions. He enjoyed great

1. The text is from *The Philadelphia Medical and Physical Journal*, Part 1, Vol. 1 (1804).
2. In the biological sense of a distinct popula-
tion within a species.
3. Linnaeus's now obsolete term for most moths.

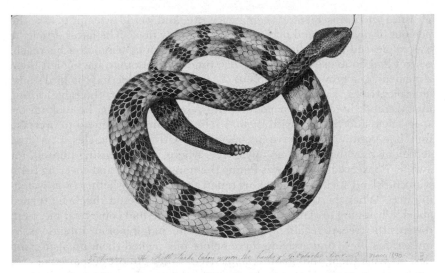

Timber rattler. William Bartram was a talented nature painter as well as being a naturalist writer. He encountered this timber rattler in the backwoods of colonial New Jersey.

Snapping turtle. Bartram produced this painting, which he titled "The great Mud Tortoise from Pennsylvania—called the snap[p]ing Turtle," around 1760.

pleasure and amusement in seeing me write, and would attempt to take the pen out of my hand, and my spectacles from my nose. The latter article he was so pleased with, that I found it necessary to put them out of his reach, when I had done using them. But, one time, in particular, having left them a moment, the crow being then out of my sight, recollecting the bird's mischievous tricks, I returned quickly, and found him upon the table, rifling my inkstand, books, and paper. When he saw me coming, he took up my spectacles, and flew off with them. I found it vain[4] to pretend to overtake him; but standing to observe his operations with my spectacles, I saw him settle down at the root of an apple-tree, where, after amusing himself, for awhile, I observed, that he was hiding them in the grass, and covering them with chips and sticks, often looking round about, to see whether I was watching him. When he thought he had sufficiently secreted them, he turned about, advancing towards me, at my call. When he had come near me, I ran towards the tree, to regain my property. But he, judging of my intentions, by my actions, flew, and arriving there before me, picked them up again, and flew off with them, into another apple-tree. I now almost despaired of ever getting them again. However, I returned back to a house, a little distance off, and there secreting myself, I had a full view of him, and waited to see the event. After some time had elapsed, during which I heard a great noise and talk from him, of which I understood not a word, he left the tree, with my spectacles dangling in his mouth, and alighted, with them, on the ground. After some time, and a great deal of caution and contrivance in choosing and rejecting different places, he hid them again, as he thought very effectually, in the grass, carrying and placing over them chips, dry leaves, &c., and often pushing them down with his bill. After he had finished this work, he flew up into a tree, hard by, and there continued a long time, talking to himself, and making much noise; bragging, as I supposed, of his achievements. At last, he returned to the house, where not finding me, he betook himself to other amusements. Having noted the place, where he had hid my spectacles, I hastened thither, and after some time recovered them.

This bird had an excellent memory. He soon learned the name which we had given him, which was Tom; and would commonly come when he was called, unless engaged in some favourite amusement, or soon after correction: for when he had run to great lengths in mischief, I was under the necessity of whipping him; which I did with a little switch. He would, in general, bear correction with wonderful patience and humility, supplicating with piteous and penitent cries and actions. But sometimes, when chastisement became intolerable, he would suddenly start off, and take refuge in the next tree. Here he would console himself with chattering, and adjusting his feathers, if he was not lucky enough to carry off with him some of my property, such as a pen-knife, or a piece of paper; in this case, he would boast and brag very loudly. At other times, he would soon return, and with every token of penitence and submission, approach me for forgiveness and reconciliation. On these occasions, he would sometimes return, and settle on the ground, near my feet, and diffidently advance, with soft-soothing expressions, and a sort of circumlocution; and sit silently by me, for a considerable time. At other times, he would confidently come and settle

4. Useless.

upon my shoulder, and there solicit my favour and pardon, with soothing expressions, and caressing gesticulations; not omitting to tickle me about the neck, ears, &c.

Tom appeared to be influenced by a lively sense of domination (an attribute prevalent in the animal creation): but, nevertheless, his ambition, in this respect, seemed to be moderated by a degree of reason, or reflection. He was, certainly, by no means tyrannical, or cruel. It must be confessed, however, that he aimed to be master of every animal around him, in order to secure his independence and his self-preservation, and for the acquisition and defence of his natural rights. Yet, in general, he was peaceable and social with all the animals about him.

He was the most troublesome and teazing to a large dog, whom he could never conquer. This old dog, from natural fidelity, and a particular attachment, commonly lay down near me, when I was at rest, reading or writing under the shade of a pear-tree, in the garden, near the house. Tom (I believe from a passion of jealousy) would approach me, with his usual caresses, and flattery, and after securing my notice and regard, he would address the dog in some degree of complaisance, and by words and actions; and, if he could obtain access to him, would tickle him with his bill, jump upon him, and compose himself, for a little while. It was evident, however, that this seeming sociability was mere artifice to gain an opportunity to practise some mischievous trick; for no sooner did he observe the old dog to be dozing, than he would be sure to pinch his lips, and pluck his beard. At length, however, these bold and hazardous achievements had nearly cost him his life: for, one time, the dog being highly provoked, he made so sudden and fierce a snap, that the crow narrowly escaped with his head. After this, Tom was wary, and used every caution and deliberation in his approaches, examining the dog's eyes and movements, to be sure that he was really asleep, and at last would not venture nearer than his tail, and then by slow, silent, and wary steps, in a sideways, or oblique manner, spreading his legs, and reaching forward. In this position, he would pluck the long hairs of the dog's tail. But he would always take care to place his feet in such a manner as to be ready to start off, when the dog was roused and snapped at him.

1804

HENDRICK AUPAUMUT

Hendrick Aupaumut (1757–1830) produced one of the first ethnographies of a Native community written by an indigenous author: his "History of the Muh-he-con-nuk [Mahican] Indians" (1791). The path that led him to this project suggests many of the complexities facing Native American intellectuals in the eighteenth century.

Born in the Native Christian town of Stockbridge, Massachusetts, Aupaumut entered a community that had recently been ministered to by the Puritan divine Jonathan Edwards. Edwards served at Stockbridge from 1751 until late 1757, long enough to have baptized Aupaumut. Schooled by a Protestant minister, possibly

Edwards's son Timothy, Aupaumut learned to speak, read, and write in English. In 1775 he wrote to Timothy Edwards, asking to borrow copies of some of his father's works, including the treatise on the freedom of the will that Edwards had written at Stockbridge.

When the Revolutionary War broke out, Aupaumut joined the Continental Army, forming a company along with other Stockbridge Indians. He earned a reputation as a good soldier, was commissioned as a captain, and saw extensive service, winning a commendation from George Washington, then the commanding general of the Continental Army. In the mid-1780s, Aupaumut led the Stockbridge community as it relocated to New Stockbridge, in central New York, where Samson Occom briefly joined him.

During the early 1790s, Aupaumut served as an emissary from President George Washington's administration to a pan-Indian alliance in the Great Lakes region of the Northwest Territory. His diplomatic initiatives continued for nearly two decades and were directed at finding peaceful resolutions to conflicts between the United States and Native communities. In the 1800s, he opposed Tecumseh's efforts to create a pantribal alliance to wage frontier warfare.

Even as Aupaumut pursued negotiated settlements between the United States and Indian groups on the western frontier, he began searching for land where the residents of New Stockbridge could relocate again, in order to be relieved of the pressures of white encroachment on their New York lands. In 1829, he joined the last group of Stockbridges to remove to the Fox River in Wisconsin, which is where he died.

In addition to numerous speeches and letters published during his lifetime, Aupaumut's writings include a narrative reporting on his diplomatic initiative to the Iroquois and Northwest tribes. The following selection is from the tribal history that he wrote in 1791, probably in connection with his proposal to serve as a negotiator for the Washington administration.

From History of the Muh-he-con-nuk Indians[1]

"Our ancestors, before they ever enjoyed Gospel revelation acknowledged one Supreme Being who dwells above, whom they styled Waun-theet Monnit-toow, or the Great, Good Spirit, the author of all things in heaven and on earth and governs all events; and he is good to all his creatures. They also believed that there is an evil one, called Mton-toow or Wicked Spirit that loves altogether to do mischief; that he excites person or persons to tell a lie—angry, fight, hate, steal, to commit murder, and to be envious, malicious, and evil-talking; also excites nations to war with one another, to violated their friendship which the Great, Good Spirit given them to maintain for their mutual good, and their children after them.

"In order to please the Great, Good Spirit which they acknowledged to be their dependence, and on the other hand to withstand the evil one—therefore, the following custom was observed, which handed down to them by their forefathers, and considered as communicated to them by Good Spirit.

"The Head of each family—man or woman—would began with all tenderness as soon as daylight, to waken up their children and teach them, as follows:—

1. The text is from Electa F. Jones, *Stockbridge, Past and Present; or, Records of an Old Mission Station* (1854).

"'My Children—you must remember that it is by the goodness of the Great, Good Spirit we are preserved through the night. My Children, you must listen to my words. If you wish to see many good days and evenings you must love to all men, and be kind to all people.

"'If you see any that are in distress, you must try to help them. Remember that you will also be in distress some time or other. If you see any one hungry you must give him something to eat; though you should have but little cake, give him half of it, for you also liable to hunger. If you see one naked, you must cover him with your own raiment.[2] For you must consider that some future time you will also stand in need of such help; but if you will not assist, or have compassion for the poor, you will displease the Good Spirit; you will be called Uh-wu-theet, or hard-hearted and nobody will pity on you the time of your distress, but will mock at you.

* * *

"'My Children—at all times you must obey your Sachem and Chiefs,[3] in all good counsels they give; never to speak evil against them, for they have taken much pains in promoting your happiness. And if you do not observe this, you will be looked upon worse than the beasts are.'

"Thus they inculcate instruction to their children day after day until they are grown up; and after they are grown, yet they would teach them occasionally. And when young people have children they also teach theirs in like manner.—This custom is handed down from generation to another; at the same time it may be observed that there were some that did not take no pains to instruct their children, but would set bad examples before them, as well as there are such among civilized nations. But such men were roving about, and could not be contented to stay at one place.

"Our ancestors' Government was a Democratical. They had Wi-gow-wauw, or Chief Sachem, successively, as well as other nations had, chosen by the nation, whom they looked upon as conductor and promoter of their general welfare, and rendered him obedience as long as he behaved himself agreeably to the office of a Sachem.[4] And this office was hereditary by the lineage of a female's offspring, but not on man's line, but on woman's part. That is— when Wi-gow-wauw is fallen by death, one of his Nephews, (if he has any) will be appointed to succeed his Uncle as a Sachem, and not any of his sons.[5]

The Sachem always have Woh-weet-quan-pe-chee, or Counselors, and one Mo-quau-pauw, or Hero, and one Mkhooh-que-thoth, or Owl, and one Un-nuh-kau-kun, or Messenger, or Runner; and the rest of the men are called young men. (But the Six Nations[6] call young men Warriors.) The Sachem is looked upon as a great tree under whose shade the whole nation is sit. His business is to contemplate the welfare of his people day and night—how to promote their peace and happiness. He also ever take pains to maintain and brighten the belt of friendship with all their allies. When he find any busi-

2. Cf. Matthew 25.34–40. Aupaumut may have purposefully highlighted similarities between Christian and Mahican beliefs.
3. Supreme leader and subordinates.
4. I.e., the Chief Sachem serves as long as he pleases the people.
5. I.e., the position was passed down through the female line, to the sons of the Chief Sachems' sisters.
6. The Iroquois Confederacy, consisting of the Mohawk, Oneida, Onondaga, Cayuga, Seneca, and Tuscarora tribes. Aupaumut compares the organizational structure of Mahican political society to that of the Iroquois, at a time when they were living in proximity to one another in central New York.

ness of public nature, he is to call his counselors together to consult with them; and then they will determine what is good for the Nation. The Sachem must be a peaceable man—has nothing to do with wars—but he is at times go from house to house to exhort his people to live in unity and peace.

"The Sachem has no stated salary for his services; for it was a disgrace or reproach any man to ask reward for any of his public services; but whatever he does for his nation must be done out of friendship and good will. But it was the custom to help their Sachem voluntarily in building a long We-ko-wohm, or wigwam, all complete; and the hunters, when they returned from hunting each man give him a skin. The women also at times, some give him Mkith-non, or Muk-sens, some belts for the body, others garters, and some other ornaments—as wampum[7] to be for his own use. They are also to bring victuals to Sachem's to enable him to feed strangers;—for whenever strangers arrived at their fire-place[8] they are directed to go to Sachem's house. There they stay until their business is completed.

"The Sachem is allowed to keep Mno-ti, or peaceable bag, or bag of peace, containing about one bushel, some less.—This bag is made of Weeth-kuhn-pauk, or bitter sort of hemp; grows on intervals, about three or four feet long; and sometimes made of Wau-pon-nep-pauk, or white hemp, which grows by the side of rivers, or edge of marshes,—amazing strong and lasting—of which they make strings, and die part of the strings of different colors; then worked and made into bag of different marks. In this bag they keep various Squau-tho-won, or belts of wampum; also strings; which belts and strings they used to establish peace and friendship with different nations, and to use them on many occasions, and passed as coin. In this bag they keep all belts and strings which they received of their allies of different nations. This bag is, as it were, unmoveable; but it is always remain at Sachem's house, as hereditary with the office of a Sachem; and he is to keep the Pipe of Peace, made of red hard stone—a long stem to it. Besides this bag, they keep other smaller bags which they called Ne-mau-won-neh Mno-ti, or Scrip, which contains nourishment on journey, which they carry with them when they go out to hold treaties with other fire-places.[9] In such scrips they occasionally put belts and strings for transacting business abroad. When they find the wampum will be fall short, besides what is kept in the bag, the Sachem and his counselors would sent their runner to gather, or collect wampum from their women, which business they called mauw-peen, or sitting into one place.

"The office of Counselors was not gotten by hereditary, but it was elective; therefore, the wise men were only entitled the office of Counselors. They are called Chiefs. Their business is to consult with their Sachems in promoting peace and happiness for their people. They will also at all times exhort young people to every good work.

"The title of Mo-quau-pauw, or Hero, is gotten only by merit; by remarkable conduct in the wars, by great courage and prudence. The business of Heroes in time of peace is to sit with their Sachem and Counselors in all their councils, and to confirm their agreements, but never to contradict them; for which they are beloved by their Sachem and Counselors, and by all their people. But when any warfare is sounded in their ears, then they will all meet

7. Currency, consisting of shells beaded on string. Wampum belts were also used to symbolize diplomatic agreements, similar to treaties.

8. I.e., a central spot, similar to a town center.
9. Here, meeting places for intertribal diplomacy.

together to hold a general Council: and when they find themselves under necessity of joining to such war, then the Sachem and Counselors will put the business in the hands of Heroes, exhorting them to be courageous and prudent, to take good care of their young men. But when the offers of peace is proposed, then the Hero will put the business in the hands of the Sachem and Counselors, who will cut or break the string of the bow, and bury the Puhwi, and by certain ceremony or emblem wipe off all tears and blood, and cleanse their beds, scattered all dark clouds, that they may enjoy pleasant days again.

"The office of Owl is come by merit also; who must have strong memory, and must be good speaker, and have strong voice. He is to sit by the side of his Sachem; his business is to proclaim the orders of his Sachem to the people with loud voice. And he is also to get up every morning as soon as daylight. In the first place he is to make noise like an Owl, then shouted to wake the people, and then ordered them to their respective lawful duties for the day.

"And the business of the Runner is to carry messages, or carry tidings; and he is always ready to run. He is to give notice to the people to attend. And when they go out another town to hold council, he is to run to inform the Chiefs that live in that town that his Chiefs will arrive—such a time. And when they hold treaty with any nation he is to light his Sachem's Pipe. And he must be man of veracity: for if he tell a falsehood, his feathers will be pulled off.

"Our Nation was divided into three clans or tribes, as Bear Tribe. Wolf Tribe, and Turtle Tribe. Our ancestors had particular opinion for each tribe to which they belonged. The Bear Tribe formerly considered as the head of the other tribes, and claims the title of hereditary office of Sachem. Yet they ever united as one family.

"And at the death of Sachem they considered as though their light is put out, and sitting under dark clouds, and in the situation of mourning, until another is appointed to succeed in the office; which must be done by the consent and approbation of the whole nation. Yet no other person has right to succeed but one of the nephews of the deceased Sachem, either the eldest, or the likeliest.

"One of the wisest of their Counselors is employed on such occasions. In the first place, when all things are ready, He will address the whole Nation as follows,—

"'My friends—grand-fathers, Uncles, Brothers, Cousins, attend. You also, my women—grand-mothers, Mothers, and Sisters, listen. You, the Children—you must also hear me attentively. It is the will of the Great, Wise, Good Spirit—our great tree has been fallen to the ground, and great darkness has been spread over our fire-place these many days, whereby we become as fatherless children. According to the custom of our good ancestors, and by the help of the Great Good Spirit. I now remove all dark clouds which hangs over our fire-place. [Strings of Wampum delivered.]

"'Again listen: I now raise your heads which has been hang downwards, and wipe off all your tears from your face, so that you may see clear, and open your ears that you may hear, and set your hearts right again, that you may understand distinctly.'" [Strings of Wampum again delivered.]

This ceremony has passed so entirely out of use that the Tribe are unable to give the remainder; indeed they have not retained even thus much of this

interesting document. They, however, have retained their wampum. The *meaning* of a belt is remembered by the Indian Tribes in this manner. The whole body frequently assemble, and being seated, each piece is passed from hand to hand, every person repeating the words as he takes it. Then again the color conveys some idea. A blood-colored hatchet readily gives an impression of something warlike, while white speaks of peace.[1]

1791

1. Aupaumut describes a peace-building process resembling the Iroquois Condolence Ritual, a diplomatic ritual used by the Iroquois and other Native groups.

J. HECTOR ST. JOHN DE CRÈVECOEUR
1735–1813

J. Hector St. John de Crèvecoeur is a writer with a divided reputation, as well as a mysterious and fascinating past. Like Benjamin Franklin, another master of irony and disguise, Crèvecoeur rewards the reader's close attention but only rarely provides firm conclusions about the author's views and intentions. In "What Is an American?"—the most famous essay in his internationally acclaimed *Letters from an American Farmer* (1782)—Crèvecoeur offers an idealistic portrait of the soon-to-be United States, one that resonated with later depictions of the nation as a melting pot and a land of opportunity. Farmer James, Crèvecoeur's persona in the *Letters*, is at his happiest and most hopeful here, and these qualities have sometimes been taken as his creator's entire understanding of "the American, this new man." The full text of the *Letters* tells a different story. It includes a shocking depiction of a slave suffering a brutal punishment; and it ends with Farmer James having moved his family to a frontier Indian village out of despair over the fratricidal violence unleashed by the Revolution. The complexity of Crèvecoeur's stance toward Revolutionary-era American society is greatly magnified by the uncertainties surrounding the author's ultimate commitments. The uncertainties associated with the work itself are amplified by the differences between the English and French editions.

Born Michel-Guillaume Jean de Crèvecoeur in Caen, Normandy, the son of a minor nobleman, he was educated by Jesuits. However, he came to reject Catholicism as oppressive, and perhaps for this reason he broke with his father as a teenager, sailed to England, and lived there with distant relatives. In 1755 he traveled to French Canada. He enlisted in the Canadian militia, served the government as a surveyor and cartographer, and was wounded in the defense of Quebec during one of the major battles of the French and Indian War (1754–63). After his military career ended in 1759, he traveled to New York, where he was naturalized as a British colonial subject in 1765 and changed his name to Hector St. John. Sometimes he went by James Hector St. John, a moniker suggesting that he identified with his persona Farmer James. He later expanded his surname to St. John de Crèvecoeur and added an initial. For the next ten years, Crèvecoeur traveled extensively in the colonies as a surveyor and a trader with American Indians. In 1769, he married a wealthy Protestant woman, Mehetabel Tippet; bought land in Orange County, New

York; and settled into life on his farm there, Pine Hill. The couple gave their three children names that evoked Crèvecoeur's French background; a daughter was named América-Francés. In his first year at Pine Hill, Crèvecoeur began to write a series of essays about America based on his travels and experience as a farmer.

The advent of the American Revolution prompted Crèvecoeur's wish to reestablish ownership of family lands in France. Although he seems to have held Loyalist sympathies and was suspected of being a British spy, he was arrested and imprisoned as an American spy in 1779, when he tried to sail from the British-held port of New York. (Some have suspected him of being a double agent.) His delayed departure was probably related to France's recognition of the United States and entrance into the war against Britain in 1778. Crèvecoeur reached London in 1780, and the following year he sold his manuscript to a publishing house there, leading to the 1782 edition of *Letters*. There is evidence to suggest that the British edition was partially rewritten by an unknown editor to draw out its republican themes. In France, Crèvecoeur reconciled with his father, then moved to Paris. There, he was celebrated by the French intellectuals known as the philosophes, who encouraged him to publish a French translation of the *Letters*. The text that appeared in 1784 was recast more favorably toward France.

In 1783, Crèvecoeur returned to the now victorious United States. He then learned that his farm had been burned in an Indian attack, his wife was dead, and his children were housed with strangers. After regaining custody of his children and moving to New York City, Crèvecoeur was made French consul to New York, Connecticut, and New Jersey. A great success as a diplomat, he was named an honorary citizen of several American cities; the town of St. Johnsbury, Vermont, was named in his honor; and he became an adopted member of the Oneida Nation. He returned to Paris in 1790, at the height of the French Revolution. Three years later, he retired to Normandy. His three-volume sequel to *Letters* (1801) was not well received. He died at his daughter's home outside Paris.

In the conceit that structures Crèvecoeur's work, Farmer James writes his letters in response to queries from an English visitor, who wishes to better understand America. The personal letter was a central genre in eighteenth-century literary culture, featured in epistolary novels as well as popular travelers' and naturalists' accounts, both factual and fictional. Works ranging from the French political philosopher Baron de Montesquieu's *Persian Letters* (1721) to the English poet Lady Mary Wortley Montagu's *Turkish Embassy Letters* (1763) to the English novelist Laurence Sterne's *A Sentimental Journey through France and Italy* (1768) embody aspects of the form as Crèvecoeur employed it. The American farmer was already a well-established figure in the political and social debates of the day, notably employed by the statesman John Dickinson in his *Letters from a Farmer in Pennsylvania* (1767–68).

Crèvecoeur's *Letters* engage the revolutionary-era debates over human nature and political organization vividly but unspecifically. He inserted himself into the same transatlantic debates over Americanness and its effects on humankind that Thomas Jefferson pursued in *Notes on the State of Virginia* (1785; excerpted below); but in contrast to Jefferson, with whom he later corresponded, Crèvecoeur's philosophical themes are woven through his work rather than presented discursively. This allusiveness distinguishes Crèvecoeur's *Letters* from the political writings of the day and lends the collection its lasting fascination.

From Letters from an American Farmer[1]

From *Letter III. What Is an American?*

I wish I could be acquainted with the feelings and thoughts which must agitate the heart and present themselves to the mind of an enlightened Englishman, when he first lands on this continent. He must greatly rejoice that he lived at a time to see this fair country discovered and settled; he must necessarily feel a share of national pride, when he views the chain of settlements which embellishes these extended shores. When he says to himself, this is the work of my countrymen, who, when convulsed by factions,[2] afflicted by a variety of miseries and wants, restless and impatient, took refuge here. They brought along with them their national genius,[3] to which they principally owe what liberty they enjoy, and what substance they possess. Here he sees the industry of his native country displayed in a new manner, and traces in their works the embryos of all the arts, sciences, and ingenuity which flourish in Europe. Here he beholds fair cities, substantial villages, extensive fields, an immense country filled with decent houses, good roads, orchards, meadows, and bridges, where an hundred years ago all was wild, woody, and uncultivated! What a train of pleasing ideas this fair spectacle must suggest; it is a prospect which must inspire a good citizen with the most heartfelt pleasure. The difficulty consists in the manner of viewing so extensive a scene. He is arrived on a new continent; a modern society offers itself to his contemplation, different from what he had hitherto seen. It is not composed, as in Europe, of great lords who possess everything, and of a herd of people who have nothing. Here are no aristocratical families, no courts, no kings, no bishops, no ecclesiastical dominion, no invisible power giving to a few a very visible one; no great manufacturers employing thousands, no great refinements of luxury. The rich and the poor are not so far removed from each other as they are in Europe. Some few towns excepted, we are all tillers of the earth, from Nova Scotia to West Florida. We are a people of cultivators, scattered over an immense territory, communicating with each other by means of good roads and navigable rivers, united by the silken bands of mild government, all respecting the laws, without dreading their power, because they are equitable. We are all animated with the spirit of an industry which is unfettered and unrestrained, because each person works for himself. If he travels through our rural districts he views not the hostile castle, and the haughty mansion, contrasted with the clay-built hut and miserable cabin, where cattle and men help to keep each other warm, and dwell in meanness,[4] smoke, and indigence. A pleasing uniformity of decent competence appears throughout our habitations. The meanest of our log-houses is a dry and comfortable habitation. Lawyer or merchant are the fairest[5] titles our towns afford; that of a farmer is the only appellation of the rural inhabitants of our country. It must take some time ere he can reconcile himself to our dictionary, which is but short in words of dignity, and

1. The text is from *Letters from an American Farmer*, edited by Albert Boni and Charles Boni (1925).
2. Disputes.
3. Spirit; distinctive character.
4. Poorness, shabbiness.
5. Most important.

names of honor. There, on a Sunday, he sees a congregation of respectable farmers and their wives, all clad in neat homespun, well mounted, or riding in their own humble wagons. There is not among them an esquire, saving the unlettered magistrate. There he sees a parson as simple as his flock, a farmer who does not riot[6] on the labor of others. We have no princes, for whom we toil, starve, and bleed; we are the most perfect society now existing in the world. Here man is free as he ought to be; nor is this pleasing equality so transitory as many others are. Many ages will not see the shores of our great lakes replenished with inland nations, nor the unknown bounds of North America entirely peopled. Who can tell how far it extends? Who can tell the millions of men whom it will feed and contain? for no European foot has as yet traveled half the extent of this mighty continent!

The next wish of this traveler will be to know whence came all these people? They are a mixture of English, Scotch, Irish, French, Dutch, Germans and Swedes. From this promiscuous breed, that race now called Americans have arisen. The eastern provinces[7] must indeed be excepted, as being the unmixed descendants of Englishmen. I have heard many wish that they had been more intermixed also: for my part, I am no wisher, and think it much better as it has happened. They exhibit a most conspicuous figure in this great and variegated picture; they too enter for a great share in the pleasing perspective displayed in these thirteen provinces. I know it is fashionable to reflect on[8] them, but respect them for what they have done; for the accuracy and wisdom with which they have settled their territory; for the decency of their manners; for their early love of letters; their ancient college,[9] the first in this hemisphere; for their industry,[1] which to me who am but a farmer is the criterion of everything. There never was a people, situated as they are, who with so ungrateful a soil have done more in so short a time. Do you think that the monarchical ingredients which are more prevalent in other governments have purged them from all foul stains? Their histories assert the contrary.

In this great American asylum,[2] the poor of Europe have by some means met together, and in consequence of various causes; to what purpose should they ask one another what countrymen they are? Alas, two thirds of them had no country. Can a wretch who wanders about, who works and starves, whose life is a continual scene of sore affliction or pinching penury, can that man call England or any other kingdom his country? A country that had no bread for him, whose fields procured him no harvest, who met with nothing but the frowns of the rich, the severity of the laws, with jails and punishments; who owned not a single foot of the extensive surface of this planet? No! Urged by a variety of motives, here they came. Everything has tended to regenerate them; new laws, a new mode of living, a new social system; here they are become men: in Europe they were as so many useless plants, wanting vegetative mold and refreshing showers; they withered, and were mowed down by want, hunger, and war; but now by the power of transplantation, like all other plants they have taken root and flourished! Formerly they were not numbered in any civil lists[3] of their country, except in those

6. I.e., indulge himself.
7. New England.
8. To censure or blame.
9. Harvard College, founded in 1636.
1. Industriousness.

2. Place of refuge (e.g., as from religious persecution).
3. Recognized employees of the civil government: ambassadors, judges, secretaries, etc.

of the poor; here they rank as citizens. By what invisible power has this surprising metamorphosis been performed? By that of the laws and that of their industry. The laws, the indulgent laws, protect them as they arrive, stamping on them the symbol of adoption; they receive ample rewards for their labors; these accumulated rewards procure them lands; those lands confer on them the title of freemen, and to that title every benefit is affixed which men can possibly require. This is the great operation daily performed by our laws. From whence proceed these laws? From our government. Whence the government? It is derived from the original genius and strong desire of the people ratified and confirmed by the crown. This is the great chain which links us all, this is the picture which every province exhibits, Nova Scotia excepted. There the crown has done all; either there were no people who had genius, or it was not much attended to: the consequence is that the province is very thinly inhabited indeed; the power of the crown in conjunction with the mosquitoes has prevented men from settling there. Yet some parts of it flourished once, and it contained a mild, harmless set of people. But for the fault of a few leaders, the whole were banished.[4] The greatest political error the crown ever committed in America was to cut off men from a country which wanted nothing but men!

What attachment can a poor European emigrant have for a country where he had nothing? The knowledge of the language, the love of a few kindred as poor as himself, were the only cords that tied him: his country is now that which gives him land, bread, protection, and consequence: *Ubi panis ibi patria*[5] is the motto of all emigrants. What then is the American, this new man? He is either a European, or the descendant of a European, hence that strange mixture of blood, which you will find in no other country. I could point out to you a family whose grandfather was an Englishman, whose wife was Dutch, whose son married a French woman, and whose present four sons have now four wives of different nations. *He* is an American, who, leaving behind him all his ancient prejudices and manners, receives new ones from the new mode of life he has embraced, the new government he obeys, and the new rank he holds. He becomes an American by being received in the broad lap of our great *Alma Mater.*[6] Here individuals of all nations are melted into a new race of men, whose labors and posterity will one day cause great changes in the world. Americans are the western pilgrims, who are carrying along with them that great mass of arts, sciences, vigor, and industry which began long since in the east; they will finish the great circle. The Americans were once scattered all over Europe; here they are incorporated into one of the finest systems of population which has ever appeared, and which will hereafter become distinct by the power of the different climates they inhabit. The American ought therefore to love this country much better than that wherein either he or his forefathers were born. Here the rewards of his industry follow with equal steps the progress of his labor; his labor is founded on the basis of nature, *self-interest*; can it want a stronger allurement? Wives and children, who before in vain demanded of him a morsel of bread, now, fat and frolicsome, gladly help their father to clear those

4. In 1755, as part of the French and Indian War, the French Acadians—settlers who had lived in Nova Scotia for about one hundred and twenty-five years—were banished by the British, who had taken the province in 1710.
5. Where there is bread, there is one's fatherland (Latin).
6. Dear mother (Latin, literal trans.).

fields whence exuberant crops are to arise to feed and to clothe them all; without any part being claimed, either by a despotic prince, a rich abbot, or a mighty lord. Here religion demands but little of him; a small voluntary salary to the minister, and gratitude to God; can he refuse these? The American is a new man, who acts upon new principles; he must therefore entertain new ideas, and form new opinions. From involuntary idleness, servile dependence, penury, and useless labor, he has passed to toils of a very different nature, rewarded by ample subsistence.—This is an American.

British America is divided into many provinces, forming a large association, scattered along a coast 1,500 miles extent and about 200 wide. This society I would fain examine, at least such as it appears in the middle provinces; if it does not afford that variety of tinges and gradations which may be observed in Europe, we have colors peculiar to ourselves. For instance, it is natural to conceive that those who live near the sea must be very different from those who live in the woods; the intermediate space will afford a separate and distinct class.

Men are like plants; the goodness and flavor of the fruit proceeds from the peculiar soil and exposition in which they grow. We are nothing but what we derive from the air we breathe, the climate we inhabit, the government we obey, the system of religion we profess, and the nature of our employment. Here you will find but few crimes; these have acquired as yet no root among us. I wish I was able to trace all my ideas; if my ignorance prevents me from describing them properly, I hope I shall be able to delineate a few of the outlines, which are all I propose.

Those who live near the sea feed more on fish than on flesh, and often encounter that boisterous element.[7] This renders them more bold and enterprising; this leads them to neglect the confined occupations of the land. They see and converse with a variety of people, their intercourse[8] with mankind becomes extensive. The sea inspires them with a love of traffic,[9] a desire of transporting produce from one place to another; and leads them to a variety of resources which supply the place of labor. Those who inhabit the middle settlements, by far the most numerous, must be very different; the simple cultivation of the earth purifies them, but the indulgences of the government, the soft remonstrances of religion, the rank of independent freeholders,[1] must necessarily inspire them with sentiments, very little known in Europe among people of the same class. What do I say? Europe has no such class of men; the early knowledge they acquire, the early bargains they make, give them a great degree of sagacity. As freemen they will be litigious; pride and obstinancy are often the cause of lawsuits; the nature of our laws and governments may be another. As citizens it is easy to imagine that they will carefully read the newspapers, enter into every political disquisition, freely blame or censure governors and others. As farmers they will be careful and anxious to get as much as they can, because what they get is their own. As northern men they will love the cheerful cup. As Christians, religion curbs them not in their opinions; the general indulgence leaves everyone to think for themselves in spiritual matters; the laws inspect our actions, our thoughts are left to God. Industry, good living, selfishness,

7. I.e., the sea.
8. Social experience.

9. Trade.
1. Nonaristocratic landowners.

litigiousness, country politics, the pride of freemen, religious indifference are their characteristics. If you recede still farther from the sea, you will come into more modern settlements; they exhibit the same strong lineaments, in a ruder appearance. Religion seems to have still less influence, and their manners are less improved.

Now we arrive near the great woods, near the last inhabited districts;[2] there men seem to be placed still farther beyond the reach of government, which in some measure leaves them to themselves. How can it pervade every corner; as they were driven there by misfortunes, necessity of beginnings, desire of acquiring large tracts of land, idleness, frequent want of economy,[3] ancient debts; the reunion of such people does not afford a very pleasing spectacle. When discord, want of unity and friendship; when either drunkenness or idleness prevail in such remote districts; contention, inactivity, and wretchedness must ensue. There are not the same remedies to these evils as in a long-established community. The few magistrates they have are in general little better than the rest; they are often in a perfect state of war; that of man against man, sometimes decided by blows, sometimes by means of the law; that of man against every wild inhabitant of these venerable woods, of which they are come to dispossess them. There men appear to be no better than carnivorous animals of a superior rank, living on the flesh of wild animals when they can catch them, and when they are not able, they subsist on grain. He who would wish to see America in its proper light, and have a true idea of its feeble beginnings and barbarous rudiments, must visit our extended line of frontiers where the last settlers dwell, and where he may see the first labors of settlement, the mode of clearing the earth, in all their different appearances; where men are wholly left dependent on their native tempers and on the spur of uncertain industry, which often fails when not sanctified by the efficacy of a few moral rules. There, remote from the power of example and check of shame, many families exhibit the most hideous parts of our society. They are a kind of forlorn hope, preceding by ten or twelve years the most respectable army of veterans which come after them. In that space, prosperity will polish some, vice and the law will drive off the rest, who uniting again with others like themselves will recede still farther; making room for more industrious people, who will finish their improvements, convert the loghouse into a convenient habitation, and rejoicing that the first heavy labors are finished, will change in a few years that hitherto barbarous country into a fine fertile, well-regulated district. Such is our progress, such is the march of the Europeans toward the interior parts of this continent. In all societies these are offcasts; this impure part serves as our precursors or pioneers; my father himself was one of that class,[4] but he came upon honest principles, and was therefore one of the few who held fast; by good conduct and temperance, he transmitted to me his fair inheritance, when not above one in fourteen of his contemporaries had the same good fortune.

Forty years ago his smiling country was thus inhabited; it is now purged, a general decency of manners prevails throughout, and such has been the fate of our best countries.

2. I.e., the frontier; the land west of the original colonies and east of the Mississippi.
3. I.e., they were improvident and spent beyond their means. "Want": lack.
4. Crèvecoeur's father, unlike Farmer John's, never went to America.

Exclusive of those general characteristics, each province has its own, founded on the government, climate, mode of husbandry, customs, and peculiarity of circumstances. Europeans submit insensibly to these great powers, and become, in the course of a few generations, not only Americans in general, but either Pennsylvanians, Virginians, or provincials under some other name. Whoever traverses the continent must easily observe those strong differences, which will grow more evident in time. The inhabitants of Canada, Massachusetts, the middle provinces, the southern ones will be as different as their climates; their only points of unity will be those of religion and language.

As I have endeavored to show you how Europeans become Americans, it may not be disagreeable to show you likewise how the various Christian sects introduced wear out, and how religious indifference becomes prevalent. When any considerable number of a particular sect happen to dwell contiguous to each other, they immediately erect a temple, and there worship the Divinity agreeably to their own peculiar ideas. Nobody disturbs them. If any new sect springs up in Europe it may happen that many of its professors[5] will come and settle in America. As they bring their zeal with them, they are at liberty to make proselytes if they can, and to build a meeting and to follow the dictates of their consciences; for neither the government nor any other power interferes. If they are peaceable subjects, and are industrious, what is it to their neighbors how and in what manner they think fit to address their prayers to the Supreme Being? But if the sectaries are not settled close together, if they are mixed with other denominations, their zeal will cool for want of fuel, and will be extinguished in a little time. Then the Americans become as to religion what they are as to country, allied to all. In them the name of Englishman, Frenchman, and European is lost, and in like manner, the strict modes of Christianity as practiced in Europe are lost also. This effect will extend itself still farther hereafter, and though this may appear to you as a strange idea, yet it is a very true one. I shall be able perhaps hereafter to explain myself better; in the meanwhile, let the following example serve as my first justification.

Let us suppose you and I to be traveling; we observe that in this house, to the right, lives a Catholic, who prays to God as he has been taught, and believes in transubstantiation;[6] he works and raises wheat, he has a large family of children, all hale and robust; his belief, his prayers offend nobody. About one mile farther on the same road, his next neighbor may be a good honest plodding German Lutheran, who addresses himself to the same God, the God of all, agreeably to the modes he has been educated in, and believes in consubstantiation;[7] by so doing he scandalizes nobody; he also works in his fields, embellishes the earth, clears swamps, etc. What has the world to do with his Lutheran principles? He persecutes nobody, and nobody persecutes him, he visits his neighbors, and his neighbors visit him. Next to him lives a seceder,[8] the most enthusiastic of all sectaries; his zeal is hot and fiery, but separated as he is from others of the same complexion, he has no congregation

5. Believers.
6. The Roman Catholic doctrine that the substance of the bread and wine used in the sacrament of communion is changed at the consecration to the substance of the body and blood of Christ.
7. As distinguished from transubstantiation; the doctrine that Christ's body is not present in or under the elements of bread and wine, but the bread and wine are signs of Christ's presence through faith.
8. One who dissents or withdraws from an established church.

of his own to resort to, where he might cabal and mingle religious pride with worldly obstinacy. He likewise raises good crops, his house is handsomely painted, his orchard is one of the fairest in the neighborhood. How does it concern the welfare of the country, or of the province at large, what this man's religious sentiments are, or really whether he has any at all? He is a good farmer, he is a sober, peaceable, good citizen: William Penn[9] himself would not wish for more. This is the visible character, the invisible one is only guessed at, and is nobody's business. Next again lives a Low Dutchman, who implicitly believes the rules laid down by the synod of Dort.[1] He conceives no other idea of a clergyman than that of a hired man; if he does his work well he will pay him the stipulated sum; if not he will dismiss him, and do without his sermons, and let his church be shut up for years. But notwithstanding this coarse idea, you will find his house and farm to be the neatest in all the country; and you will judge by his wagon and fat horses that he thinks more of the affairs of this world than of those of the next. He is sober and laborious, therefore he is all he ought to be as to the affairs of this life; as for those of the next, he must trust to the great Creator. Each of these people instruct their children as well as they can, but these instructions are feeble compared to those which are given to the youth of the poorest class in Europe. Their children will therefore grow up less zealous and more indifferent in matters of religion than their parents. The foolish vanity, or rather the fury of making proselytes, is unknown here; they have no time, the seasons call for all their attention, and thus in a few years, this mixed neighborhood will exhibit a strange religious medley, that will be neither pure Catholicism nor pure Calvinism. A very perceptible indifference, even in the first generation, will become apparent; and it may happen that the daughter of the Catholic will marry the son of the seceder, and settle by themselves at a distance from their parents. What religious education will they give their children? A very imperfect one. If there happens to be in the neighborhood any place of worship, we will suppose a Quaker's meeting; rather than not show their fine clothes, they will go to it, and some of them may perhaps attach themselves to that society. Others will remain in a perfect state of indifference; the children of these zealous parents will not be able to tell what their religious principles are, and their grandchildren still less. The neighborhood of a place of worship generally leads them to it, and the action of going thither is the strongest evidence they can give of their attachment to any sect. The Quakers are the only people who retain a fondness for their own mode of worship; for be they ever so far separated from each other, they hold a sort of communion with the society, and seldom depart from its rules, at least in this country. Thus all sects are mixed as well as all nations; thus religious indifference is imperceptibly disseminated from one end of the continent to the other; which is at present one of the strongest characteristics of the Americans. Where this will reach no one can tell, perhaps it may leave a vacuum fit to receive other systems. Persecution, religious pride, the love of contradiction are the food of what the world commonly calls religion. These motives have ceased here; zeal in Europe is confined; here it

9. English Quaker and founder of Pennsylvania (1644–1718).
1. An ecclesiastical assembly held in Dordrecht, or Dordt, Holland, in 1618 to settle disputes between Protestant Reformed churches. "Low Dutchman": someone from Holland, not Belgium.

evaporates in the great distance it has to travel; there it is a grain of powder inclosed,[2] here it burns away in the open air, and consumes without effect.

But to return to our back settlers. I must tell you that there is something in the proximity of the woods which is very singular. It is with men as it is with the plants and animals that grow and live in the forests; they are entirely different from those that live in the plains. I will candidly tell you all my thoughts but you are not to expect that I shall advance any reasons. By living in or near the woods, their actions are regulated by the wildness of the neighborhood. The deer often come to eat their grain, the wolves to destroy their sheep, the bears to kill their hogs, the foxes to catch their poultry. This surrounding hostility immediately puts the gun into their hands; they watch these animals, they kill some; and thus by defending their property, they soon become professed hunters; this is the progress; once hunters, farewell to the plow. The chase renders them ferocious, gloomy, and unsociable; a hunter wants no neighbor, he rather hates them, because he dreads the competition. In a little time their success in the woods makes them neglect their tillage. They trust to the natural fecundity of the earth, and therefore do little; carelessness in fencing often exposes what little they sow to destruction; they are not at home to watch; in order therefore to make up the deficiency, they go oftener to the woods. That new mode of life brings along with it a new set of manners, which I cannot easily describe. These new manners, being grafted on the old stock, produce a strange sort of lawless profligacy, the impressions of which are indelible. The manners of the Indian natives are respectable, compared with this European medley. Their wives and children live in sloth and inactivity; and having no proper pursuits, you may judge what education the latter receive. Their tender minds have nothing else to contemplate but the example of their parents; like them they grow up a mongrel breed, half civilized, half savage, except nature stamps on them some constitutional propensities. That rich, that voluptuous sentiment is gone that struck them so forcibly; the possession of their freeholds[3] no longer conveys to their minds the same pleasure and pride. To all these reasons you must add their lonely situation, and you cannot imagine what an effect on manners the great distances they live from each other has! Consider one of the last settlements in its first view: of what is it composed? Europeans who have not that sufficient share of knowledge they ought to have, in order to prosper; people who have suddenly passed from oppression, dread of government, and fear of laws into the unlimited freedom of the woods. This sudden change must have a very great effect on most men, and on that class particularly. Eating of wild meat, whatever you may think, tends to alter their temper: though all the proof I can adduce is that I have seen it: and having no place of worship to resort to, what little society this might afford is denied them. The Sunday meetings, exclusive of religious benefits, were the only social bonds that might have inspired them with some degree of emulation in neatness. Is it then surprising to see men thus situated, immersed in great and heavy labors, degenerate a little? It is rather a wonder the effect is not more diffusive. The Moravians[4] and the Quakers are the only instances in

2. I.e., like gunpowder in a gun.
3. Parcels of land held outright for specified periods of time.
4. The Moravian Church, or Unity of Brethren, originated in Bohemia and Moravia in the fifteenth century. In the following two centuries, persecution forced groups of Moravians to emigrate to other lands.

exception to what I have advanced. The first never settle singly, it is a colony of the society which emigrates; they carry with them their forms, worship, rules, and decency:[5] the others never begin so hard, they are always able to buy improvements,[6] in which there is a great advantage, for by that time the country is recovered from its first barbarity. Thus our bad people are those who are half cultivators and half hunters; and the worst of them are those who have degenerated altogether into the hunting state. As old plowmen and new men of the woods, as Europeans and new-made Indians, they contract the vices of both; they adopt the moroseness and ferocity of a native, without his mildness, or even his industry at home. If manners are not refined, at least they are rendered simple and inoffensive by tilling the earth; all our wants[7] are supplied by it, our time is divided between labor and rest, and leaves none of the commission of great misdeeds. As hunters it is divided between the toil of the chase, the idleness of repose, or the indulgence of inebriation. Hunting is but a licentious idle life, and if it does not always pervert good dispositions; yet, when it is united with bad luck, it leads to want:[8] want stimulates that propensity to rapacity and injustice, too natural to needy men, which is the fatal gradation. After this explanation of the effects which follow by living in the woods, shall we yet vainly flatter ourselves with the hope of converting the Indians? We should rather begin with converting our back-settlers; and now if I dare mention the name of religion, its sweet accents would be lost in the immensity of these woods. Men thus placed are not fit either to receive or remember its mild instructions; they want[9] temples and ministers, but as soon as men cease to remain at home, and begin to lead an erratic life, let them be either tawny or white, they cease to be its disciples.

* * *

Europe contains hardly any other distinctions but lords and tenants; this fair country alone is settled by freeholders, the possessors of the soil they cultivate, members of the government they obey, and the framers of their own laws, by means of their representatives. This is a thought which you have taught me to cherish; our difference from Europe, far from diminishing, rather adds to our usefulness and consequence as men and subjects. Had our forefathers remained there, they would only have crowded it, and perhaps prolonged those convulsions which had shook it so long. Every industrious European who transports himself here may be compared to a sprout growing at the foot of a great tree; it enjoys and draws but a little portion of sap; wrench it from the parent roots, transplant it, and it will become a tree bearing fruit also. Colonists are therefore entitled to the consideration due to the most useful subjects; a hundred families barely existing in some parts of Scotland will here in six years cause an annual exportation of 10,000 bushels of wheat; 100 bushels being but a common quantity for an industrious family to sell, if they cultivated good land. It is here then that the idle may be employed, the useless become useful, and the poor become rich; but by riches I do not mean gold and silver, we have but little of those metals; I

5. The Moravians were family communities who gave up private property and were noted for their industry and thrift.
6. I.e., Quaker settlers had more money than the Moravians.
7. Needs.
8. Neediness, poverty.
9. Lack.

mean a better sort of wealth, cleared lands, cattle, good houses, good clothes, and an increase of people to enjoy them.

There is no wonder that this country has so many charms, and presents to Europeans so many temptations to remain in it. A traveler in Europe becomes a stranger as soon as he quits his own kingdom; but it is otherwise here. We know, properly speaking, no strangers; this is every person's country; the variety of our soils, situations, climates, governments, and produce hath something which must please everybody. No sooner does a European arrive, no matter of what condition, than his eyes are opened upon the fair prospect; he hears his language spoken, he retraces many of his own country manners, he perpetually hears the names of families and towns with which he is acquainted; he sees happiness and prosperity in all places disseminated; he meets with hospitality, kindness, and plenty everywhere; he beholds hardly any poor; he seldom hears of punishments and executions; and he wonders at the elegance of our towns, those miracles of industry and freedom. He cannot admire enough our rural districts, our convenient roads, good taverns, and our many accommodations; he involuntarily loves a country where everything is so lovely.

* * *

After a foreigner from any part of Europe is arrived, and become a citizen, let him devoutly listen to the voice of our great parent, which says to him, "Welcome to my shores, distressed European; bless the hour in which thou didst see my verdant fields, my fair navigable rivers, and my green mountains!—If thou wilt work, I have bread for thee; if thou wilt be honest, sober, and industrious, I have greater rewards to confer on thee—ease and independence. I will give thee fields to feed and clothe thee; a comfortable fireside to sit by, and tell thy children by what means thou hast prospered; and a decent bed to repose on. I shall endow thee beside with the immunities of a freeman. If thou wilt carefully educate thy children, teach them gratitude to God, and reverence to that government, the philanthropic government, which has collected here so many men and made them happy. I will also provide for thy progeny; and to every good man this ought to be the most holy, the most powerful, the most earnest wish he can possibly form, as well as the most consolatory prospect when he dies. Go thou and work and till; thou shalt prosper, provided thou be just, grateful, and industrious."

From *Letter IX. Description of Charles-Town; Thoughts on Slavery; on Physical Evil; A Melancholy Scene*

Charles-Town is, in the north, what Lima is in the south;[1] both are capitals of the richest provinces of their respective hemispheres: you may therefore conjecture, that both cities must exhibit the appearances necessarily resulting from riches. Peru abounding in gold, Lima is filled with inhabitants who enjoy all those gradations of pleasure, refinement, and luxury, which proceed from wealth. Carolina produces commodities, more valuable perhaps than gold, because they are gained by greater industry; it exhibits also on our northern stage, a display of riches and luxury, inferior indeed to the

1. Charles-Town (now Charleston), South Carolia; Lima, Peru.

former, but far superior to what are to be seen in our northern towns. Its situation is admirable, being built at the confluence of two large rivers, which receive in their course a great number of inferior streams; all navigable in the spring, for flat-boats. Here the produce of this extensive territory concenters; here therefore is the seat of the most valuable exportation; their wharfs, their docks, their magazines,[2] are extremely convenient to facilitate this great commercial business. The inhabitants are the gayest[3] in America; it is called the center of our beau monde, and it [is] always filled with the richest planters of the province, who resort hither in a quest of health and pleasure. Here are always to be seen a great number of valetudinarians from the West Indies, seeking for the renovation of health, exhausted by the debilitating nature of their sun, air, and modes of living. Many of these West Indians have I seen, at thirty, loaded with the infirmities of old age; for nothing is more common in those countries of wealth, than for persons to lose the abilities of enjoying the comforts of life, at a time when we northern men just begin to taste the fruits of our labor and prudence. The round of pleasure, and the expenses of those citizens' tables, are much superior to what you would imagine: indeed the growth of this town and province has been astonishingly rapid. It is [a] pity that the narrowness of the neck[4] on which it stands prevents it from increasing; and which is the reason why houses are so dear.[5] The heat of the climate, which is sometimes very great in the interior parts of the country, is always temperate in Charles-Town; though sometimes when they have no sea breezes the sun is too powerful. The climate renders excesses of all kinds very dangerous, particularly those of the table; and yet, insensible or fearless of danger, they live on, and enjoy a short and a merry life: the rays of their sun seem to urge them irresistably to dissipation and pleasure: on the contrary, the women, from being abstemious, reach to a longer period of life, and seldom die without having had several husbands. An European at his first arrival must be greatly surprised when he sees the elegance of their houses, their sumptuous furniture, as well as the magnificence of their tables. Can he imagine himself in a country, the establishment of which is so recent?

The three principal classes of inhabitants are, lawyers, planters, and merchants; this is the province which has afforded to the first the richest spoils, for nothing can exceed their wealth, their power, and their influence. They have reached the *ne plus ultra* of worldly felicity; no plantation is secured, no title is good, no will is valid, but what they dictate, regulate, and approve. The whole mass of provincial property is become tributary to this society; which, far above priests and bishops, disdain to be satisfied with the poor Mosaical portion of the tenth.[6] I appeal to the many inhabitants, who, while contending perhaps for their right to a few hundred acres, have lost by the mazes of the law their whole patrimony. These men are more properly law givers than interpreters of the law; and have united here, as well as in most other provinces, the skill and dexterity of the scribe with the power and ambition of the prince: who can tell where this may lead in a future day? The

2. Warehouses.
3. Liveliest, most vibrant.
4. I.e., of the land, extending into the harbor.
5. Expensive.
6. The practice of tithing (offering a tenth of one's worldly goods to God) was begun by the biblical patriarch Abraham (Genesis 14.20). It is "Mosaical" because the first five Books of the Old Testament (starting with Genesis) are traditionally ascribed to Moses.

nature of our laws, and the spirit of freedom, which often tends to make us litigious, must necessarily throw the greatest part of the property of the colonies into the hands of these gentlemen. In another century, the law will possess in the north, what now the church possesses in Peru and Mexico.

While all is joy, festivity, and happiness in Charles-Town, would you imagine that scenes of misery overspread in the country? Their ears by habit are become deaf, their hearts are hardened; they neither see, hear, nor feel for the woes of their poor slaves, from whose painful labors all their wealth proceeds. Here the horrors of slavery, the hardship of incessant toils, are unseen; and no one thinks with compassion of those showers of sweat and of tears which from the bodies of Africans, daily drop, and moisten the ground they till. The cracks of the whip urging these miserable beings to excessive labor, are far too distant from the gay capital to be heard. The chosen race eat, drink, and live happy, while the unfortunate one grubs up the ground, raises indigo, or husks the rice; exposed to a sun full as scorching as their native one; without the support of good food, without the cordials of any cheering liquor. This great contrast has often afforded me subjects of the most afflicting meditation. On the one side, behold a people enjoying all that life affords most bewitching and pleasurable, without labor, without fatigue, hardly subjected to the trouble of wishing. With gold, dug from Peruvian mountains, they order vessels to the coasts of Guinea; by virtue of that gold, wars, murders, and devastations are committed in some harmless, peaceable African neighborhood, where dwelt innocent people, who even knew not but that all men were black. The daughter torn from her weeping mother, the child from the wretched parents, the wife from the loving husband; whose families swept away and brought through storms and tempests to this rich metropolis! There, arranged like horses at a fair, they are branded like cattle, and then driven to toil, to starve, and to languish for a few years on the different plantations of these citizens. And for whom must they work? For persons they know not, and who have no other power over them than that of violence; no other right than what this accursed metal has given them! Strange order of things! Oh, Nature, where are thou?—Are not these blacks thy children as well as we? On the other side, nothing is to be seen but the most diffusive misery and wretchedness, unrelieved even in thought or wish! Day after day they drudge on without any prospect of ever reaping for themselves; they are obliged to devote their lives, their limbs, their will, and every vital exertion to swell the wealth of masters; who look not upon them with half the kindness and affection with which they consider their dogs and horses. Kindness and affection are not the portion of those who till the earth, who carry the burdens, who convert the logs into useful boards. This reward, simple and natural as one would conceive it, would border on humanity; and planters must have none of it!

* * *

A clergyman settled a few years ago at George-Town,[7] and feeling as I do now, warmly recommended to the planters, from the pulpit, a relaxation of severity; he introduced the benignity of Christianity, and pathetically made use of the admirable precepts of that system to melt the hearts of his

7. Then a colony in South Carolina.

congregation into a greater degree of compassion toward their slaves than had been hitherto customary; "Sir (said one of his hearers) we pay you a genteel salary to read to us the prayers of the liturgy, and to explain to us such parts of the Gospel as the rule of the church directs; but we do not want you to teach us what we are to do with our blacks." The clergyman found it prudent to withhold any farther admonition. Whence this astonishing right, or rather this barbarous custom, for most certainly we have no kind of right beyond that of force? We are told, it is true, that slavery cannot be so repugnant to human nature as we at first imagine, because it has been practiced in all ages, and in all nations: the Lacedemonians[8] themselves, those great assertors of liberty, conquered the Helotes with the design of making them their slaves; the Romans, whom we consider as our masters in civil and military policy, lived in the exercise of the most horrid oppression; they conquered to plunder and to enslave. What a hideous aspect the face of the earth must then have exhibited! Provinces, towns, districts, often depopulated; their inhabitants driven to Rome, the greatest market in the world, and there sold by thousands! The Roman dominions were tilled by the hands of unfortunate people, who had once been, like their victors free, rich, and possessed of every benefit society can confer; until they became subject to the cruel right of war, and to lawless force. Is there then no superintending power who conducts the moral operations of the world, as well as the physical? The same sublime hand which guides the planets round the sun with so much exactness, which preserves the arrangement of the whole with such exalted wisdom and paternal care, and prevents the vast system from falling into confusion; doth it abandon mankind to all the errors, the follies, and the miseries, which their most frantic rage, and their most dangerous vices and passions can produce?

* * *

Everywhere one part of the human species are taught the art of shedding the blood of the other; of setting fire to their dwellings; of leveling the works of their industry: half of the existence of nations regularly employed in destroying other nations. What little political felicity is to be met with here and there, has cost oceans of blood to purchase; as if good was never to be the portion of unhappy man. Republics, kingdoms, monarchies, founded either on fraud or successful violence, increase by pursuing the steps of the same policy, until they are destroyed in their turn, either by the influence of their own crimes, or by more successful but equally criminal enemies.

If from this general review of human nature, we descend to the examination of what is called civilized society; there the combination of every natural and artificial want, makes us pay very dear for what little share of political felicity we enjoy. It is a strange heterogeneous assemblage of vices and virtues, and of a variety of other principles, forever at war, forever jarring, forever producing some dangerous, some distressing extreme. Where do you conceive then that nature intended we should be happy? Would you prefer

8. Lacedemonia was a country in the Peloponnese region of the ancient world. The inhabitants of its capital, Sparta—who were known as Spartans or Lacedemonians—enslaved the inhabitants of the town of Helos, who were known as Helotes.

the state of men in the woods, to that of men in a more improved situation? Evil preponderates in both; in the first they often eat each other for want of food, and in the other they often starve each other for want of room. For my part, I think the vices and miseries to be found in the latter, exceed those of the former; in which real evil is more scarce, more supportable, and less enormous. Yet we wish to see the earth peopled; to accomplish the happiness of kingdoms, which is said to consist in numbers. Gracious God! to what end is the introduction of so many beings into a mode of existence in which they must grope amidst as many errors, commit as many crimes, and meet with as many diseases, wants, and sufferings!

The following scene will I hope account for these melancholy reflections, and apologize for the gloomy thoughts with which I have filled this letter: my mind is, and always has been, oppressed since I became a witness to it. I was not long since invited to dine with a planter who lived three miles from——, where he then resided. In order to avoid the heat of the sun, I resolved to go on foot, sheltered in a small path, leading through a pleasant wood. I was leisurely traveling along, attentively examining some peculiar plants which I had collected, when all at once I felt the air strongly agitated; though the day was perfectly calm and sultry. I immediately cast my eyes toward the cleared ground, from which I was but at a small distance, in order to see whether it was not occasioned by a sudden shower; when at that instant a sound resembling a deep rough voice, uttered, as I thought, a few inarticulate monosyllables. Alarmed and surprised, I precipitately looked all round, when I perceived at about six rods distance something resembling a cage, suspended to the limbs of a tree; all the branches of which appeared covered with large birds of prey, fluttering about, and anxiously endeavoring to perch on the cage. Actuated by an involuntary motion of my hands, more than by any design of my mind, I fired at them; they all flew to a short distance, with a most hideous noise: when, horrid to think and painful to repeat, I perceived a Negro, suspended in the cage, and left there to expire! I shudder when I recollect that the birds had already picked out his eyes, his cheek bones were bare; his arms had been attacked in several places, and his body seemed covered with a multitude of wounds. From the edges of the hollow sockets and from the lacerations with which he was disfigured, the blood slowly dropped, and tinged the ground beneath. No sooner were the birds flown, than swarms of insects covered the whole body of this unfortunate wretch, eager to feed on his mangled flesh and to drink his blood. I found myself suddenly arrested by the power of affright and terror; my nerves were convulsed; I trembled, I stood motionless, involuntarily contemplating the fate of this Negro, in all its dismal latitude. The living specter, though deprived of his eyes, could still distinctly hear, and in his uncouth dialect begged me to give him some water to allay his thirst. Humanity herself would have recoiled back with horror; she would have balanced whether to lessen such reliefless distress, or mercifully with one blow to end this dreadful scene of agonizing torture! Had I had a ball in my gun, I certainly should have dispatched him; but finding myself unable to perform so kind an office, I sought, though trembling, to relieve him as well as I could. A shell ready fixed to a pole, which had been used by some Negroes, presented itself to me; filled it with water, and with trembling hands I guided it to the quivering lips of the wretched sufferer. Urged by the irresistible power of thirst,

he endeavored to meet it, as he instinctively guessed its approach by the noise it made in passing through the bars of the cage. "Tankè, you whitè man, tankè you, putè somè poison and givè me." "How long have you been hanging there?" I asked him. "Two days, and me no die; the birds, the birds; aaah me!" Oppressed with the reflections which this shocking spectacle afforded me, I mustered strength enough to walk away, and soon reached the house at which I intended to dine. There I heard that the reason for this slave being thus punished was on account of his having killed the overseer of the plantation. They told me that the laws of self-preservation rendered such executions necessary; and supported the doctrine of slavery with the arguments generally made use of to justify the practice; with the repetition of which I shall not trouble you at present.

ADIEU.

From *Letter X. On Snakes; and on the Humming Bird*

* * *

As I was one day sitting solitary and pensive in my primitive arbor, my attention was engaged by a strange sort of rustling noise at some paces distant. I looked all around without distinguishing anything, until I climbed one of my great hemp stalks; when to my astonishment, I beheld two snakes of considerable length, the one pursuing the other with great celerity through a hemp stubble field. The aggressor was of the black kind, six feet long; the fugitive was a water snake, nearly of equal dimensions. They soon met, and in the fury of their first encounter, they appeared in an instant firmly twisted together; and whilst their united tails beat the ground, they mutually tried with open jaws to lacerate each other. What a fell[9] aspect did they present! their heads were compressed to a very small size, their eyes flashed fire; and after this conflict had lasted about five minutes, the second found means to disengage itself from the first, and hurried toward the ditch. Its antagonist instantly assumed a new posture, and half creeping and half erect, with a majestic mien, overtook and attacked the other again, which placed itself in the same attitude, and prepared to resist. The scene was uncommon and beautiful; for thus opposed they fought with their jaws, biting each other with the utmost rage; but notwithstanding this appearance of mutual courage and fury, the water snake still seemed desirous of retreating toward the ditch, its natural element. This was no sooner perceived by the keen-eyed black one, than twisting its tail twice round a stalk of hemp, and seizing its adversary by the throat, not by means of its jaws, but by twisting its own neck twice round that of the water snake, pulled it back from the ditch. To prevent a defeat the latter took hold likewise of a stalk on the bank, and by the acquisition of that point of resistance became a match for its fierce antagonist. Strange was this to behold; two great snakes strongly adhering to the ground mutually fastened together by means of the writhings which lashed them to each other, and stretched at their full length, they pulled but pulled in vain, and in the moments of greatest exertions that part of their bodies which was entwined, seemed extremely small, while the rest

9. Evil.

appeared inflated, and now and then convulsed with strong undulations, rapidly following each other. Their eyes seemed on fire, and ready to start out of their heads; at one time the conflict seemed decided; the water-snake bent itself into two great folds, and by that operation rendered the other more than commonly outstretched; the next minute the new struggles of the black one gained an unexpected superiority, it acquired two great folds likewise, which necessarily extended the body of its adversary in proportion as it had contracted its own. These efforts were alternate; victory seemed doubtful, inclining sometimes to the one side and sometimes to the other; until at last the stalk to which the black snake fastened, suddenly gave way, and in consequence of this accident they both plunged into the ditch. The water did not extinguish their vindictive rage; for by their agitations I could trace, though not distinguish their mutual attacks. They soon reappeared on the surface twisted together, as in their first onset; but the black snake seemed to retain its wonted superiority, for its head was exactly fixed above that of the other, which it incessantly pressed down under the water, until it was stifled, and sunk. The victor no sooner perceived its enemy incapable of farther resistance, than abandoning it to the current, it returned on shore and disappeared.

From *Letter XII. Distresses of a Frontier Man*

I wish for a change of place; the hour is come at last, that I must fly from my house and abandon my farm! But what course shall I steer, enclosed as I am? The climate best adapted to my present situation and humor[1] would be the polar regions, where six months day and six months night divide the dull year: nay, a simple Aurora Borealis would suffice me, and greatly refresh my eyes, fatigued now by so many disagreeable objects. The severity of those climates, that great gloom, where melancholy dwells, would be perfectly analogous to the turn of my mind. Oh, could I remove my plantation to the shores of the Oby,[2] willingly would I dwell in the hut of a Samoyede, with cheerfulness would I go and bury myself in the cavern of a Laplander. Could I but carry my family along with me, I would winter at Pello, or Tobolsky, in order to enjoy the peace and innocence of that country. But let me arrive under the pole, or reach the antipodes,[3] I never can leave behind me the remembrance of the dreadful scenes to which I have been a witness; therefore never can I be happy! Happy, why would I mention that sweet, that enchanting word? Once happiness was our portion; now it is gone from us, and I am afraid not to be enjoyed again by the present generation! Whichever way I look, nothing but the most frightful precipices present themselves to my view, in which hundreds of my friends and acquaintances have already perished: of all animals that live on the surface of this planet, what is man when no longer connected with society; or when he finds himself surrounded by a convulsed and a half-dissolved one? He cannot live in solitude, he must belong to some community bound by some ties, however imperfect. Men

1. Temperament.
2. A river in Siberia, the approximate region referred to in this sentence and the next one. Samoyedes are a Siberian people. Laplanders can be the Sami people or others living in Lapland, a far-northern region near Siberia. Pello is a town in Lapland. Tobolsky, or Tobolsk, is a town in Siberia.
3. I.e., even if I travel far south—below the south pole on to Australia and New Zealand.

mutually support and add to the boldness and confidence of each other; the weakness of each is strengthened by the force of the whole. I had never before these calamitous times formed any such ideas; I lived on, labored and prospered, without having ever studied on what the security of my life and the foundation of my prosperity were established: I perceived them just as they left me. Never was a situation so singularly terrible as mine, in every possible respect, as a member of an extensive society, as a citizen of an inferior division of the same society, as a husband, as a father, as a man who exquisitely feels for the miseries of others as well as for his own! But alas! so much is everything now subverted among us, that the very word misery, with which we were hardly acquainted before, no longer conveys the same ideas; or rather tired with feeling for the miseries of others, everyone feels now for himself alone. When I consider myself as connected in all these characters, as bound by so many cords, all uniting in my heart, I am seized with a fever of the mind, I am transported beyond that degree of calmness which is necessary to delineate our thoughts. I feel as if my reason wanted to leave me, as if it would burst its poor weak tenement: again I try to compose myself, I grow cool, and preconceiving the dreadful loss, I endeavor to retain the useful guest.

<p style="text-align:center">* * *</p>

Must I then bid farewell to Britain, to that renowned country? Must I renounce a name so ancient and so venerable? Alas, she herself, that once indulgent parent, forces me to take up arms against her. She herself first inspired the most unhappy citizens of our remote districts with the thoughts of shedding the blood of those whom they used to call by the name of friends and brethren. That great nation which now convulses the world; which hardly knows the extent of her Indian kingdoms; which looks toward the universal monarchy of trade, of industry, of riches, of power: why must she strew our poor frontiers with the carcasses of her friends, with the wrecks of our insignificant villages, in which there is no gold? When, oppressed by painful recollection, I revolve all these scattered ideas in my mind; when I contemplate my situation, and the thousand streams of evil with which I am surrounded; when I descend into the particular tendency even of the remedy I have proposed, I am convulsed—convulsed sometimes to that degree, as to be tempted to exclaim—Why has the master of the world permitted so much indiscriminate evil throughout every part of this poor planet, at all times, and among all kinds of people? It ought surely to be the punishment of the wicked only. I bring that cup to my lips, of which I must soon taste, and shudder at its bitterness. What then is life, I ask myself, is it a gracious gift? No, it is too bitter; a gift means something valuable conferred, but life appears to be a mere accident, and of the worst kind: we are born to be victims of diseases and passions, of mischances and death: better not to be than to be miserable.—Thus impiously I roam, I fly from one erratic thought to another, and my mind, irritated by these acrimonious reflections, is ready sometimes to lead me to dangerous extremes of violence. When I recollect that I am a father, and a husband, the return of these endearing ideas strikes deep into my heart. Alas! they once made it to glow with pleasure and with every ravishing exultation; but now they fill it with sorrow. At other times, my wife industriously rouses me out of these dreadful meditations, and

soothes me by all the reasoning she is mistress of; but her endeavors only serve to make me more miserable, by reflecting that she must share with me all these calamities, the bare apprehensions of which I am afraid will subvert her reason. Nor can I with patience think that a beloved wife, my faithful helpmate, throughout all my rural schemes, the principal hand which has assisted me in rearing the prosperous fabric of ease and independence I lately possessed, as well as my children, those tenants of my heart, should daily and nightly be exposed to such a cruel fate. Self-preservation is above all political precepts and rules, and even superior to the dearest opinions of our minds; a reasonable accommodation of ourselves to the various exigencies of the times in which we live is the most irresistible precept. To this great evil I must seek some sort of remedy adapted to remove or to palliate it; situated as I am, what steps should I take that will neither injure nor insult any of the parties, and at the same time save my family from that certain destruction which awaits it if I remain here much longer. Could I insure them bread, safety, and subsistence, not the bread of idleness, but that earned by proper labor as heretofore; could this be accomplished by the sacrifice of my life, I would willingly give it up. I attest before heaven that it is only for these I would wish to live and to toil: for these whom I have brought into this miserable existence. I resemble, methinks, one of the stones of a ruined arch, still retaining that pristine form that anciently fitted the place I occupied, but the center is tumbled down; I can be nothing until I am replaced, either in the former circle or in some stronger one. I see one on a smaller scale, and at a considerable distance, but it is within my power to reach it: and since I have ceased to consider myself as a member of the ancient state now convulsed, I willingly descend into an inferior one. I will revert into a state approaching nearer to that of nature, unencumbered either with voluminous laws or contradictory codes, often galling the very necks of those whom they protect; and at the same time sufficiently remote from the brutality of unconnected savage nature. Do you, my friend, perceive the path I have found out? it is that which leads to the tenants of the great——village of——, where, far removed from the accursed neighborhood of Europeans, its inhabitants live with more ease, decency, and peace than you imagine: where, though governed by no laws, yet find, in uncontaminated simple manners all that laws can afford. Their system is sufficiently complete to answer all the primary wants of man and to constitute him a social being, such as he ought to be in the great forest of nature. There it is that I have resolved at any rate to transport myself and family: an eccentric thought, you may say, thus to cut asunder all former connections, and to form new ones with a people whom nature has stamped with such different characteristics! But as the happiness of my family is the only object of my wishes, I care very little where we be, or where we go, provided that we are safe and all united together.

* * *

You may therefore, by means of anticipation, behold me under the Wigwam;[4] I am so well acquainted with the principal manners of these people, that I

4. I.e., living as an American Indian. A wigwam is a hut or lodge, usually built of poles and covered with skins, mats, or bark.

entertain not the least apprehension from them. I rely more securely on their strong hospitality than on the witnessed compacts of many Europeans. As soon as possible after my arrival, I design to build myself a wigwam, after the same manner and size with the rest, in order to avoid being thought singular, or giving occasion for any railleries; though these people are seldom guilty of such European follies. I shall erect it hard by[5] the lands which they propose to allot me, and will endeavor that my wife, my children, and myself may be adopted soon after our arrival. Thus becoming truly inhabitants of their village, we shall immediately occupy that rank within the pale[6] of their society which will afford us all the amends we can possibly expect for the loss we have met with by the convulsions of our own. According to their customs we shall likewise receive names from them, by which we shall always be known. My youngest children shall learn to swim and to shoot with the bow, that they may acquire such talents as will necessarily raise them into some degree of esteem among the Indian lads of their own age; the rest of us must hunt with the hunters. I have been for several years an expert marksman; but I dread lest the imperceptible charm of Indian education may seize my younger children and give them such a propensity to that mode of life as may preclude their returning to the manners and customs of their parents. I have but one remedy to prevent this great evil; and that is, to employ them in the labor of the fields as much as I can; I am even resolved to make their daily subsistence depend altogether on it. As long as we keep ourselves busy in tilling the earth, there is no fear of any of us becoming wild; it is the chase and the food it procures that have this strange effect. Excuse a simile—those hogs which range in the woods, and to whom grain is given once a week, preserve their former degree of tameness; but if, on the contrary, they are reduced to live on ground nuts, and on what they can get, they soon become wild and fierce. For my part, I can plow, sow, and hunt, as occasion may require; but my wife, deprived of wool and flax, will have no room for industry,[7] what is she then to do? like the other squaws, she must cook for us the nasaump, the ninchické,[8] and such other preparations of corn as are customary among these people. She must learn to bake squashes and pumpkins under the ashes; to slice and smoke the meat of our own killing, in order to preserve it; she must cheerfully adopt the manners and customs of her neighbors, in their dress, deportment, conduct, and internal economy, in all respects. Surely if we can have fortitude enough to quit all we have, to remove so far, and to associate with people so different from us, these necessary compliances are but part of the scheme. The change of garments, when those they carry with them are worn out, will not be the least of my wife's and daughter's concerns: though I am in hopes that self-love will invent some sort of reparation. Perhaps you would not believe that there are in the woods looking-glasses, and paint of every color; and that the inhabitants take as much pains to adorn their faces and their bodies, to fix their bracelets of silver, and plait their hair, as our forefathers the Picts[9] used to do in the time of the Romans. Not that I would wish to see either my wife or daughter adopt those savage customs; we can live in great peace and harmony with them without descending to every article; the interrup-

5. Built it right near.
6. Bounds.
7. Household work.

8. Like nasaump, a kind of cornmeal mush.
9. Ancient people of northern Britain.

tion of trade hath, I hope, suspended this mode of dress. My wife understands inoculation perfectly well, she inoculated all our children one after another, and has successfully performed the operation on several scores of people, who, scattered here and there through our woods, were too far removed from all medical assistance. If we can persuade but one family to submit to it, and it succeeds, we shall then be as happy as our situation will admit of; it will raise her into some degree of consideration, for whoever is useful in any society will always be respected. If we are so fortunate as to carry one family through a disorder, which is the plague[1] among these people, I trust to the force of example, we shall then become truly necessary, valued, and beloved; we indeed owe every kind office to a society of men who so readily offer to admit us into their social partnership, and to extend to my family the shelter of their village, the strength of their adoption, and even the dignity of their names. God grant us a prosperous beginning, we may then hope to be of more service to them than even missionaries who have been sent to preach to them a Gospel they cannot understand.

As to religion, our mode of worship will not suffer much by this removal from a cultivated country, into the bosom of the woods; for it cannot be much simpler than that which we have followed here these many years: and I will with as much care as I can, redouble my attention, and twice a week, retrace to them the great outlines of their duty to God and to man. I will read and expound to them some part of the decalogue,[2] which is the method I have pursued ever since I married.

<p style="text-align:center">*　*　*</p>

Thus then in the village of——, in the bosom of that peace it has enjoyed ever since I have known it, connected with mild hospitable people, strangers to our political disputes, and having none among themselves; on the shores of a fine river, surrounded with woods, abounding with game; our little society united in perfect harmony with the new adoptive one, in which we shall be incorporated, shall rest I hope from all fatigues, from all apprehensions, from our present terrors, and from our long watchings. Not a word of politics shall cloud our simple conversation; tired either with the chase or the labor of the field, we shall sleep on our mats without any distressing want, having learnt to retrench every superfluous one: we shall have but two prayers to make to the Supreme Being, that He may shed His fertilizing dew on our little crops, and that He will be pleased to restore peace to our unhappy country. These shall be the only subject of our nightly prayers, and of our daily ejaculations:[3] and if the labor, the industry, the frugality, the union of men can be an agreeable offering to Him, we shall not fail to receive His paternal blessings. There I shall contemplate Nature in her most wild and ample extent; I shall carefully study a species of society, of which I have at present but very imperfect ideas; I will endeavor to occupy with propriety that place which will enable me to enjoy the few and sufficient benefits it confers. The solitary and unconnected mode of life I have lived in my youth must fit me for this trial, I am not the first who has attempted it; Europeans did not, it is true, carry to the wilderness numerous families; they went there

1. Smallpox.
2. The Ten Commandments.
3. Prayers.

as merely speculators; I, as a man seeking a refuge from the desolation of war. They went there to study the manner of the aborigines; I to conform to them, whatever they are; some went as visitors, as travelers; I as a sojourner, as a fellow hunter and laborer, go determined industriously to work up among them such a system of happiness as may be adequate to my future situation, and may be a sufficient compensation for all my fatigues and for the misfortunes I have borne: I have always found it at home, I may hope likewise to find it under the humble roof of my wigwam.

O Supreme Being! if among the immense variety of planets, inhabited by Thy creative power, Thy paternal and omnipotent care deigns to extend to all the individuals they contain; if it be not beneath Thy infinite dignity to cast Thy eye on us wretched mortals; if my future felicity is not contrary to the necessary effects of those secret causes which Thou hast appointed, receive the supplications of a man, to whom in Thy kindness Thou hast given a wife and an offspring: View us all with benignity, sanctify this strong conflict of regrets, wishes, and other natural passions; guide our steps through these unknown paths, and bless our future mode of life. If it is good and well meant, it must proceed from Thee; Thou knowest, O Lord, our enterprise contains neither fraud, nor malice, nor revenge. Bestow on me that energy of conduct now become so necessary, that it may be in my power to carry the young family Thou hast given me through this great trial with safety and in Thy peace. Inspire me with such intentions and such rules of conduct as may be most acceptable to Thee. Preserve, O God, preserve the companion of my bosom, the best gift Thou hast given me: endue her with courage and strength sufficient to accomplish this perilous journey. Bless the children of our love, those portions of our hearts; I implore Thy divine assistance, speak to their tender minds, and inspire them with the love of that virtue which alone can serve as the basis of their conduct in this world, and of their happiness with Thee. Restore peace and concord to our poor afflicted country, assuage the fierce storm which has so long ravaged it. Permit, I beseech Thee, O Father of Nature, that our ancient virtues, and our industry, may not be totally lost: and that as a reward for the great toils we have made on this new land, we may be restored to our ancient tranquillity, and enabled to fill it with successive generations, that will constantly thank Thee for the ample subsistence Thou hast given them.

The unreserved manner in which I have written must give you a convincing proof of that friendship and esteem, of which I am sure you never yet doubted. As members of the same society, as mutually bound by the ties of affection and old acquaintance, you certainly cannot avoid feeling for my distresses; you cannot avoid mourning with me over that load of physical and moral evil with which we are all oppressed. My own share of it I often overlook when I minutely contemplate all that hath befallen our native country.

c. 1769–80 1782

ANNIS BOUDINOT STOCKTON
1736–1801

Annis Boudinot Stockton spent her life surrounded by influential people, a fact that was closely related to her poetic pursuits. Shortly after her birth, in Darby, Pennsylvania, her parents moved to Philadelphia, where they lived next to Benjamin Franklin's post office; in 1751, they enrolled her brothers John and Elias in the Academy and College of Philadelphia, a secondary school cofounded by Franklin. After the family moved to Princeton, New Jersey, some two years later, they lived for a time in a house rented from the Reverend Aaron Burr, then serving as the president of Princeton University, and his wife, Esther Edwards Burr, the daughter of Jonathan Edwards. (The Burrs' son, Aaron, Jr., who was born in 1756, became the vice president of the United States in 1801 and, three years later, famously killed the statesman Alexander Hamilton in a duel.) Annis and Esther became quite close. Around 1757, Annis married Richard Stockton, a prominent lawyer and a favorite of Loyalist New Jersey governor William Franklin (Benjamin's illegitimate son, to whom the first part of *The Autobiography* is addressed). Stockton eventually joined the patriot cause, and as a New Jersey delegate to the Second Continental Congress, he signed the Declaration of Independence in 1776. That same year, Annis and Richard's daughter Julia married Benjamin Rush, a leading physician, intellectual, and public servant, who also signed the Declaration. Annis's brother Elias was a delegate to the Second Continental Congress and served for a year as its president. Long after his sister's death, Elias became the first president of the American Bible Society and the benefactor of Buck Watie, the Cherokee tribal leader and editor of the *Cherokee Phoenix*, who took Elias Boudinot's name as a gesture of respect. In short, Annis Boudinot Stockton was at the center of a network of socially prominent and politically influential men. The women who were associated with those men often exerted influence in ways that were less direct but could be at least equally significant.

In her roles as Richard's wife and Elias's sister, Stockton served in a semipublic capacity as the hostess at Morven, the Stocktons' elegant estate in Princeton, where she counted George and Martha Custis Washington among her guests. With its lavish gardens—a source of enjoyment and inspiration for Annis—the property required a considerable labor force, and enslaved people provided at least part of that labor. Richard had been raised a Quaker, but the Stocktons owned slaves at a time when the Society of Friends was becoming increasingly firm in its opposition to the practice. Annis (whose background was French Huguenot, i.e., Protestant) appears to have continued to own slaves after Richard's death, perhaps because she wished to remain at her beloved Morven rather than move in with her daughter.

Residing within a network of social privilege and political power, Annis Stockton assumed the authority of her station in various ways, one of which was by writing and publishing poetry. Several of her topical poems that address leading events and figures of the day were printed in newspapers, and she sent some of her strongly nationalist poems in celebration of George Washington to the object of her praise. While her associations with influential male figures are important for understanding Stockton's work, so too are her networks of friends, mainly though not exclusively women. Women such as Esther Burr provided Stockton with an intellectual atmosphere and an audience for her poetry that shaped the poems themselves.

Stockton's milieu and her writings defy certain common ideas about poetry. In William Wordsworth's preface to the second edition of *Lyrical Ballads* (1800), the

Annis Boudinot Stockton. This undated painting of Stockton is by an unidentified American artist.

groundbreaking Romantic work that he coauthored with Samuel Taylor Coleridge, Wordsworth defined poetry as "the spontaneous overflow of powerful feelings" that "takes its origin from emotion recollected in tranquility." This definition seems to suggest that solitude is essential to poetic composition, but the writing and reading of poetry were and often continued to be intensely social activities. In Boudinot's day, poems might be composed at regular social gatherings in private homes, called "salons." Works written there or composed elsewhere were often read aloud to the assembled guests, and later circulated in manuscript. Some participants in these literary networks kept "commonplace books," that is, manuscript books where they recorded their own and one another's poems. At other times, writers circulated manuscript collections of their own work, as did Stockton's close friend Elizabeth Graeme Fergusson, a writer and intellectual described by one admirer as "the most learned woman in America." The network involving Stockton and Fergusson also included

Hannah Griffitts, Deborah Logan, Milcah Martha Moore, and Susanna Wright. Moore kept a commonplace book that contains the only known copies of many works by these women. Stockton collected the main body of her poetry in a large manuscript volume that she labeled "Only for the Eye of a Friend." Held in the archives of the New Jersey Historical Society, the volume first appeared in print in 1995.

The poetry that was the coin of such literary networks was typically modeled on the work of British neoclassical poets, notably John Dryden and Alexander Pope. In Protestant America, John Milton was another important influence. Stockton produced works in all the major poetic genres, including odes, elegies, sonnets, and hymns. Her subjects ranged from the battle of the sexes, to pastoral celebrations of rural life, to the major events of the Revolution and early republic. She also wrote elegies, including annual tributes to Richard after his death. The scope of her work is remarkable, and at its best so is its wit, technical mastery, sensibility, and intelligence.

The following texts are from *Only for the Eye of a Friend: The Poems of Annis Boudinot Stockton* (1995), edited by Carla Mulford. The bracketed insertions are Mulford's.

A Hymn Written in the Year 1753

1

Jesus thy Servant is resign'd
To thy unerring will;
Oh; may my heart be more inclin'd
Thy precepts to fulfill.

2

Do with me what thou thinkest best, 5
Conform my soul to thee,
Stamp thy dear image on my breast
And ne'er depart from me

3

For in thy blissful smiles I live—
More sweet than life's thy love, 10
And in thy favour is Contain'd
The heaven I hope above.

4

Thou art my soul's honour and wealth
Her bliss and friendship too,
The source of all her peace and health 15
And every joy in view.

5

Then lead me thro the giddy path
Of youth's deceitful road,
Nor leave me to the tempter's wrath
My Saviour and my God 20

6

And at the last and gloomy hour
When death my flesh invades,
Oh! let thy staff thy crook thy power
Support me through the shades.

7

Then with thy presence gild the gloom 25
Of that tremendous vale
O! guide the wandering exile home
Nor let my foes prevail.

8

But let thy spirit whisper peace,
And shew my sins forgiven; 30
Make ev'ry doubt and sorrow cease,
And antedate my heaven[1]

1753 1995

An Elegiack Ode on the 28th Day of February [1782]. The Anniversary of Mr. [Stockton's] Death

Mr. COLLINS,

The following elegant little ode, written by a lady on the anniversary of her husband's death, tho' it deserves a more lasting remembrance than a Gazette can give it, yet, in the mean-time, may serve to entertain your ingenious readers. Sent to me as a friend, I have to beg her excuse for thus exposing her grief to the eyes of the publick, while I wish to shew it, her wit.

A.B.[1]

I've heard the tempest howl along the plain,
And screaming winds pour forth a dreadful blast;
While fleaks[2] of snow and sheets of driving rain
Presented nature as a dreary waste.

1. That is, make heaven present to her during her life.
1. This poem was submitted by "A.B." (possibly Aaron Burr, Jr.,) to the *New Jersey Gazette*, where it was first published.
2. Flakes.

Howl now ye tempests, blow ye winds around— 5
Your gloomy sounds are music to my ear;
Such as I never yet in zephyrs[3] found,
Tho' fan'd by purple wings of vernal air.

The gloomy sound, according with my wo,
Spreads a soft melancholy o'er my mind, 10
That sooths my pangs, and gives the tender flow
Of lenient drops, to sorrow ever kind.

Ah! what avails my sorrows' sad complaint,
While in the grave my Lucius[4] breathless lies?
The turf enshrines the dust; the skies the saint; 15
But left behind the hapless mourner dies.

Each day I find the anguish more severe;
In *crouds*, in *solitude*, at *home, abroad*—
Bereav'd of all my inmost soul held dear,
I find her sinking fast beneath the load. 20

No change of circumstance, no varying scene,
Can draw the deep, envenom'd, barbed dart:
Tho' care maternal, prompts the look serene;[5]
The anxious sigh, still wrings the mother's heart.

Oh! on this day, may each revolving year, 25
Be mark'd by nature's sympathetic groan!
Nor sighing gales, deny the pitying tear,
While at his tomb, I make my silent moan!

The weeping winds, report my tender grief—
And see! a group celestial hastening down, 30
To share my wo, and bring my pain relief,
By holding up a bright immortal crown!

Religion first, with Heaven's resplendent beam,
Presents a glass to meet my tearful eye—
Behold! behind this life's impervious screen, 35
My fav'rite son, and wipe your sorrows dry.

Then friendship, science, liberty, and truth,
Write on his tomb, in characters sublime,
Approve the efforts, of his age and youth,
To hand their influence down to future time. 40

The graces too, by eloquence led on,
With cypress garlands strew his hallowed grave:[6]
For they had fondly mark'd him as their own—
But vain their power, and influence to save!

In times when civil discord holds her court; 45
And vice triumphant, keeps his ancient post:
When most is needed, such a firm support,
They mourn with me, their friend and patron lost.

EMELIA.

February 28, 1782 April 24, 1782

3. Breezes.
4. A pseudonym for Richard, as Emelia, at the
end of the poem, is a pseudonym for Annis.
5. I.e., the widow "looks serene" for her children's
sake.

6. Since classical times, cypress has been
associated with death. "Graces": Greek god-
desses of qualities such as charm, beauty, and
creativity.

On a Little Boy Going to Play on a Place
from Whence He Had Just Fallen[1]

So the wreckd mariner who tos'd on shore
Hears the wind whistle and the billows roar
Hous'd in some humble cot he vows in vain
Never to trust the faithless deep again
But warm'd and cloath'd to the first port repairs 5
And in a can of flip[2] forgets his fears.
The Seamens Register[3] he hastes to seek
And sets his name to sail within a week

c. 1783 1995

Addressed to General Washington, in the Year 1777,
after the Battles of Trenton and Princeton[1]

The muse affrighted at the clash of arms,
And all the dire calamities of war,
From Morven's[2] peaceful shades has long retir'd,
And left her faithful votary to mourn,
In sighs, not numbers, o'er her native land. 5
Dear native land, whom George's hostile slaves[3]
Have drench'd with blood, and spread destruction round,
But thou, thy country's better genius come,
Heroic Washington, and aid my song!
While I the wonders of thy deeds relate, 10
Thy martial ardor, and thy temp'rate zeal—
Describe the fortitude, the saint like patience,
With which thou hast sustain'd the greatest load,
That ever guardian of his country bore.
What muse can sing the hardships thou endur'd; 15
Unarm'd, uncloth'd, undisciplin'd thy men;[4]
In winter's cold unhospitable reign;
And press'd by numerous hosts of veteran troops,
All well appointed for the hardy fight:
When quite deserted by the tatter'd bands 20
Which form'd thy camp (all but a chosen few,
Of spirits like thy own) was forced to fly

1. Elizabeth Graeme Fergusson wrote out this poem in her copybook with a note explaining that it referred to Stockton's grandson John Rush, the eldest son of Julia Stockton Rush and Benjamin Rush, who was six at the time the poem was composed.
2. A type of alcoholic beverage.
3. Where sailors registered with an official before going to sea.

1. Elias Boudinot may have sent Washington a written copy of this poem in 1779. The poem was first published in *Columbian Magazine* 1.
2. Stockton's home in Princeton, New Jersey.
3. King George III's British Army; possibly also a reference to Hessians, i.e., German mercenary soldiers.
4. Richard Stockton had inspected Washington's troops in the late fall of 1776.

From Hudson's side[5] before the victor foe.
Ah! who can paint the horrors of that morn,
When fame, with brazen trumpet, sounded loud, 25
That Washington retreats! Caesaria's maids,[6]
Old men and matrons, children at the breast,
With hair dishevell'd, and with streaming eyes,
Implore the God of battles to protect
Thee, their best hope, and now their only care. 30
—Oh, greatly favour'd by the God of hosts!
He gave to thee to turn the battle's fate,[7]
And shew his power to potentates below:
While lines of Hessian captive slaves[8] announce
Thy triumph, and their haughty lords disgrace. 35
—Not good Æneas who his father bore,
And all his houshold gods from ruin'd Troy,
Was more the founder of the Latian realm,[9]
Than thou the basis of this mighty fabric,
Now rising to my view, of arms, of arts; 40
The seat of glory in the western world.
—For thee awaits the patriots shining crown;
The laurel blooms in blest elysian groves,[1]
That twin'd by angel hands shall grace thy brow.
A vacant seat among the ancient heroes, 45
Of purple, amarynth and fragrant myrtle,[2]
Awaits for thee—high rais'd above the rest,
By Cato, Sydney, and the sacred shades[3]
Of bright illustrious line, from Greece and Rome,
Gallic,[4] American or British shores, 50
And long to hail thee welcome to the bower.[5]
—Late may they lead thee to the blest abode,
And may'st thou meet the plaudit of thy God,
While future ages shall enroll thy name
In sacred annals of immortal fame. 55

 EMELIA.

1777 January 1787

5. Washington had been defeated twice in the Hudson River region: on Long Island in August 1776 and in White Plains in October. The British continued to advance across the Hudson, pushing Washington's troops through New Jersey. To escape the British, the Stocktons left Princeton in November.

6. The women of New Jersey. Stockton alludes to the name given to the region (*Nova Caesaria*) in a 1664 land grant from King Charles II to his brother James, the Duke of York and future King James II.

7. I.e., in Washington's famous crossing of the Delaware River before his successful attack on Trenton on December 26, 1776.

8. Captured German mercenary soldiers, presented in a manner that evokes the ancient Roman treatment of captives.

9. The Roman Empire. In his epic the *Aeneid*, the Roman poet Virgil (70–19 B.C.E.) relates Aeneas's rescue of his father and others after the destruction of their city, Troy, and Aeneas's subsequent founding of Rome's parent town.

1. In Elysium, the ancient Greek Isles of the Blessed, where heroes and patriots went after death. "Laurel": an evergreen plant traditionally used to crown heroes and other famous people.

2. Classical symbols of majesty.

3. Spirits. Marcus Porcius Cato (95–46 B.C.E) was the Roman defender of republican liberty and opponent of Julius Caesar. Sir Philip Sidney (1554–86)—English poet, statesman, and soldier—was a major exponent of classical republicanism in the time of Queen Elizabeth I.

4. French.

5. Arbor, attractive dwelling or retreat.

[L]ines on Hearing of the Death of Doctor Franklin[1]

Why do I see the power of Genius droop
As if on earth they'd lost their only prop?
Why do I hear the philanthrophist sigh,
And meet each neighbour with a tearful eye;
They shake their heads and pensive beat their breast 5
And say alas the friend of man's at rest.—
Franklin no more—his vast unbounded mind
Set free to rove with knowledge unconfin'd
From globe to globe their magnitudes to scan
Observe their distance motion and their plan 10
View systems new in beauteous order rise
And fixed stars that flame in other Skies[2]
Thro boundless depths of ether[3] to survey
The electric fluid find it self a way
In forked lightnings wild excentric play[4] 15
Ah what a scene for philosophic lore—
But think of this and ye will weep no more—
How rapid is the soul's immortal growth—
How great its progress in the search of truth—
Compar'd to this all former efforts faint— 20
And the deep sage perfected in the saint.—[5]

1995

1. Franklin died in 1790.
2. Franklin's scientific work included astronomy.
3. Here, the clear sky.
4. Franklin experimented to determine if light-
ning involved electricity.
5. All of Franklin's achievements pale in com-
parison to the "immortal growth" he has experi-
enced in death.

JOHN ADAMS
1735–1826

ABIGAIL ADAMS
1744–1818

The correspondence between Abigail Adams and John Adams provides a com-
pelling glimpse into the ways that personal lives and political aspirations inter-
sected in the months leading up to the American Declaration of independence. The
couple exchanged exceptionally vivid letters from the time of their courtship until
John's retirement. Passionate and articulate, they exchanged details of their daily
activities and wrote about their hopes and fears in ways that bring the meaning of
the Revolution alive.

Abigail Smith and John Adams were married on October 25, 1764, and they
remained the closest of partners until Abigail's death, more than fifty years later.
She was the daughter of a wealthy Congregational minister from Weymouth, on
the South Shore of Massachusetts, and he—a man who was to become the second

president of the United States—was the son of a farmer from nearby Braintree (now a part of Quincy, Massachusetts). Abigail had no formal schooling because, as she often explained, she was frequently ill as a child. Although this was true, she observed in later years that girls and boys in her youth were not treated equally and that "daughters" were "wholly neglected in point of Literature." She grew up in her grandmother's house, where "instruction and amusement" were blended together. With a remarkable native intelligence, easy access to her father's library, and a good ear for assimilating conversation heard in the parsonage, she developed both a grasp of the Greek and Roman classics, which were constant references for the Revolutionary generation, and an appreciation for modern literature.

John Adams graduated from Harvard College in 1755. He taught school for a short time in Worcester, Massachusetts, but the roles of teacher and preacher were too closely joined for his taste, and he was made uncomfortable by any association with "frigid" Calvinism. He studied law instead and was admitted to the Boston bar in 1758. The following year, he met Abigail. Although he preferred a country law practice to one in the city and treasured his Braintree farm, he found it impossible to support a growing family—the Adamses eventually had five children—with only a country clientele, so in 1768 they moved to Boston. John Adams's opposition to the British Parliament's Stamp Act of 1765 and his defense of Massachusetts radicals such as John Hancock identified him as one who would support the cause of independence, and in June 1774 he was elected as a Massachusetts delegate to the First Congress of the Colonies, later known as the First Continental Congress. He left Braintree for Philadelphia on August 10, and for the next twenty-six years, ten of them spent abroad, he was a famous and sometimes controversial figure in American public life. He was elected vice president under George Washington for two terms (1788 and 1792) and president in 1796. After losing the presidential election of 1800 to Thomas Jefferson, he retired to Braintree, eager to lead the rural life he had spoken about so wistfully while holding public office. During John's public career, Abigail oversaw the daily life of the farm, astutely managing money, property, animals, and people.

From the time that John Adams left Massachusetts in 1774 until he returned from Paris in 1783, the couple exchanged more than three hundred letters. Their grandson published a selection in the nineteenth century, and new editions continue to appear. Their correspondence was exceptional but not unusual. The artfully composed personal letter, often intended for public or semipublic circulation, already had a long history when the English novelist Samuel Richardson helped make it an essential middle class genre with his influential writing guide, *Letters Written to and for Particular Friends, on the Most Important Occasions* (1741). Richardson, who also wrote the popular epistolary novels *Pamela; or Virtue Rewarded* (1740) and *Clarissa: or, the History of a Young Lady* (1748), made the letter form accessible to more kinds of writers, especially women.

An admirer of Richardson's fiction, Abigail crafted her epistolary style with care. When she remonstrated with John, writing "That your Sex are Naturally Tyrannical is a Truth so thoroughly established as to admit of no dispute," and pointedly instructed him to "Remember the Ladies" in the new "Code of Laws" then being contemplated or they would "foment a rebellion," she used a language born in part from Richardson's works. John, too, was influenced by Richardson, in one famous passage alluding to *Clarissa*: more skeptical of extending political and legal rights than his wife, John Adams complained to a different correspondent, "Democracy is Lovelace, and the people are Clarissa. The artful villain will pursue the innocent lovely girl to her ruin and her death." Notwithstanding this difference in perspective, the letters between Abigail and John provide an extraordinary record of a long and happy marriage as well as a vivid portrait of a nation seeking its identity.

Abigail Adams and John Adams. Benjamin Blyth executed these pastel portraits of the Adamses in 1766. Perhaps the most famous married couple in the new republic, the Adamses carried on an extensive and revealing correspondence about political as well as domestic matters.

From The Letters[1]

Abigail Adams to John Adams

[CLASSICAL PARALLELS]

Braintree August 19 1774

The great distance between us, makes the time appear very long to me. It seems already a month since you left me.[2] The great anxiety I feel for my Country, for you and for our family renders the day tedious, and the night unpleasant. The Rocks and quick Sands appear upon every Side. What course you can or will take is all wrapt in the Bosom of futurity. Uncertainty and expectation leave the mind great Scope. Did ever any Kingdom or State regain their Liberty, when once it was invaded [,] without Blood shed? I cannot think of it without horror.

Yet we are told that all the Misfortunes of Sparta were occasiond by their too great Sollicitude for present tranquility, and by an excessive love of peace they neglected the means of making it sure and lasting.[3] They ought to have reflected says Polibius that as there is nothing more desirable, or advantages[4] than peace, when founded in justice and honour, so there is nothing more

1. The texts are from *Adams Family Correspondence* (1963), two vols., edited by L. H. Butterfield. The original spellings are unchanged. The bracketed insertions are Butterfield's. Words in angle brackets identify the writer's earlier choice of a word.
2. John had left Braintree on August 10.
3. In 338 B.C.E., Philip II, king of Macedon

(382–336 B.C.E.), invaded Greece. The citizens of the Greek city of Sparta protected only their own territory and not the other Greek city-states. As a result Greece fell and subsequently was transformed from a democracy into a monarchy.
4. Advantageous. "Polibius": Polybius (c. 205–125 B.C.E.), Greek historian and author of a history of Rome.

shameful and at the same time more pernicious when attained by bad measures, and purchased at the price of liberty.

I have received a most charming Letter from our Friend Mrs. W[arre]n.[5] She desires me to tell you that her best wishes attend you thro your journey both as a Friend and patriot—hopes you will have no uncommon difficulties to surmount or Hostile Movements to impeade you—but if the Locrians should interrupt you, she hop[e]s you will beware that no future Annals may say you chose an ambitious Philip for your Leader, who subverted the noble order of the American Amphyctions, and built up a Monarchy on the Ruins of the happy institution.[6]

I have taken a very great fondness for reading Rollin's ancient History since you left me.[7] I am determined to go thro with it if possible in these my days of solitude. I find great pleasure and entertainment from it, and I have perswaided Johnny[8] to read me a page or two every day, and hope he will from his desire to oblige me entertain a fondness for it.—We have had a charming rain which lasted 12 hours and has greatly revived the dying fruits of the earth.

I want much to hear from you. I long impatiently to have you upon the Stage of action. The first of September or the month of September, perhaps may be of as much importance to Great Britan as the Ides of March were to Ceaser.[9] I wish you every Publick as well, as private blessing, and that wisdom which is profitable both for instruction and edification to conduct you in this difficult day.—The little flock remember Pappa, and kindly wish to see him. So does your most affectionate

Abigail Adams

1774 1848

John Adams to Abigail Adams

[PRAYERS AT THE CONGRESS]

Phyladelphia Septr. 16. 1774

Having a Leisure Moment, while the Congress is assembling, I gladly embrace it to write you a Line.

When the Congress first met, Mr. Cushing[1] made a Motion, that it should be opened with Prayer. It was opposed by Mr. Jay of N. York and Mr. Rutledge of South Carolina,[2] because we were so divided in religious Sentiments, some Episcopalians, some Quakers, some Anabaptists, some Presbyterians, and some Congregationalists, so that We could not join in the same Act of Worship.—Mr. S. Adams[3] arose and said he was no Bigot, and could hear a Prayer from a Gentleman of Piety and Virtue, who was at the same Time a Friend to his Country. He was a Stranger in Phyladelphia, but had heard

5. Mercy Otis Warren (1728–1814), Massachusetts writer, well known as a correspondent and friend of the leading political figures of her day; wife of the statesman James Warren (1726–1808).
6. Philip of Macedon had invaded Greece under the pretext that part of a Greek tribe known as the Locrians, in the town of Amphissa, were resisting the authority of the Amphictionic League, a neighboring council of states.
7. John owned the fifth edition (1768) of *Ancient History*, by Charles Rollion (1661–1741), rector of

the University of Paris.
8. Their seven-year-old son.
9. Julius Caesar died on the Ides of March in 44 B.C.E.
1. Thomas Cushing (1725–1788), a Massachusetts delegate to the Continental Congress.
2. John Rutledge (1739–1800), later governor of South Carolina. John Jay (1745–1829), New York jurist.
3. Samuel Adams (1722–1803), a Massachusetts patriot.

that Mr. Duchè (Dushay they pronounce it) deserved that Character, and therefore he moved that Mr. Duchè, an episcopal Clergyman,[4] might be desired, to read Prayers to the Congress, tomorrow Morning. The Motion was seconded and passed in the Affirmative. Mr. Randolph our President, waited on[5] Mr. Duchè, and received for Answer that if his Health would permit, he certainly would. Accordingly next Morning he appeared with his Clerk and in his Pontificallibus, and read several Prayers, in the established Form;[6] and then read the Collect for the seventh day of September, which was the Thirty fifth Psalm.[7]—You must remember this was the next Morning after we heard the horrible Rumour, of the Cannonade[8] of Boston.—I never saw a greater Effect upon an Audience. It seemed as if Heaven had ordained that Psalm to be read on that Morning.

After this Mr. Duchè, unexpected to every Body struck out into an extemporary Prayer, which filled the Bosom of every Man present. I must confess I never heard a better Prayer or one, so well pronounced. Episcopalian as he is, Dr. Cooper[9] himself never prayed with such fervour, such Ardor, such Earnestness and Pathos, and in Language so elegant and sublime—for America, for the Congress, for The Province of Massachusetts Bay, and especially the Town of Boston. It has had an excellent Effect upon every Body here.

I must beg you to read that Psalm. If there was any Faith in the sortes Virgilianæ, or sortes Homericæ, or especially the Sortes biblicæ, it would be thought providential.[1]

It will amuse your Friends to read this Letter and the 35th. Psalm to them. Read it to your Father and Mr. Wibirt.—I wonder what our Braintree Churchmen would think of this?—Mr. Duchè is one of the most ingenious[2] Men, and best Characters, and greatest orators in the Episcopal order, upon this Continent—Yet a Zealous Friend of Liberty and his Country.[3]

I long to see my dear Family. God bless, preserve and prosper it. Adieu.

John Adams

1774 1875

John Adams to Abigail Adams

[DR. FRANKLIN]

July 23 1775

My Dear

You have more than once in your Letters mentioned Dr. Franklin,[4] and in one intimated a Desire that I should write you something concerning him.

4. Jacob Duché (1737–1798), assistant rector of Christ Church and St. Peter's in Philadelphia.
5. Made a formal call on. Peyton Randolph (1721?–1775), a public official from Virginia, was president of the Continental Congress.
6. I.e., in the form set down by the Church of England. "Pontificallibus": priestly attire.
7. "Plead my cause, O Lord, with them that strive with me: fight against them that fight against me" (Psalm 35.1). "Collect": the prayer assigned to be read before the Epistle, or liturgical lesson.
8. Bombardment.
9. Samuel Cooper (1725–1783), minister of the Brattle Street Church, Boston.
1. The Bible and the works of the Roman poet

Virgil (70–19 B.C.E.) and the Greek epic poet Homer were thought to have magical properties: a passage opened to at random (in Latin the sortes, or "chance oracles") had relevance to one's life and future. I.e., the choice of Psalm 35 is prophetic.
2. Showing discernment.
3. Duché later supported the Crown and fled to England.
4. Benjamin Franklin (1706–1790; see his headnote, above) returned to Philadelphia from England in May 1775. The Pennsylvania Assembly then elected him to the Second Continental Congress (May 1775–March 1781).

Dr. Franklin has been very constant in his Attendance on Congress from the Beginning. His Conduct has been composed and grave and in the Opinion of many Gentlemen very reserved. He has not assumed any Thing, nor affected to take the lead; but has seemed to choose that the Congress should pursue their own Principles and sentiments and adopt their own Plans: Yet he has not been backward: has been very usefull, on many occasions, and discovered[5] a Disposition entirely American. He does not hesitate at our boldest Measures, but rather seems to think us, too irresolute, and backward. He thinks us at present in an odd State, neither in Peace nor War, neither dependent nor independent. But he thinks that We shall soon assume a Character more decisive.

He thinks, that We have the Power of preserving ourselves, and that even if We should be driven to the disagreable Necessity of assuming a total Independency, and set up a separate state, We could maintain it. The People of England, have thought that the Opposition in America, was wholly owing to Dr. Franklin: and I suppose their scribblers will attribute the Temper, and Proceedings of this Congress to him: but there cannot be a greater Mistake. He has had but little share farther than to co operate and assist. He is however a great and good Man. I wish his Colleagues from this City were All like him, particularly one, whose Abilities and Virtues, formerly trumpeted so much in America, have been found wanting.[6]

There is a young Gentleman from Pensylvania whose Name is Wilson, whose Fortitude, Rectitude, and Abilities too, greatly outshine his Masters.[7] Mr. Biddle, the Speaker, has been taken off, by Sickness.[8] Mr. Mifflin is gone to the Camp, Mr. Morton is ill too, so that this Province has suffered by the Timidity of two overgrown Fortunes.[9] The Dread of Confiscation, or Caprice, I know not what has influenced them too much: Yet they were for taking Arms and pretended to be very valiant.—This Letter must be secret my dear—at least communicated with great Discretion. Yours,

John Adams

1775 1875

John Adams to Abigail Adams

[PREJUDICE IN FAVOR OF NEW ENGLAND]

Octr. 29. 1775

There is, in the human Breast, a social Affection, which extends to our whole Species. Faintly indeed; but in some degree. The Nation, Kingdom, or Community to which We belong is embraced by it more vigorously. It is stronger still towards the Province to which we belong, and in which We had our Birth. It is stronger and stronger, as We descend to the County, Town, Parish, Neighbourhood, and Family, which We call our own.—And

5. Revealed.
6. John Dickinson (1732–1808), elected to the Continental Congress by the Pennsylvania Assembly, wrote two petitions—one in 1774, the other at the start of July 1775—that attempted but failed to reconcile with Great Britain.
7. James Wilson (1742–1798), a lawyer, was elected to the Second Continental Congress by

the Pennsylvania Assembly along with Thomas Willing (1732–1821), a banker, and Franklin.
8. Edward Biddle (1738–1779), a lawyer, was often ill.
9. I.e., Dickinson and Willing. Thomas Mifflin (1744–1800), a merchant, had left for the army ("Camp"). John Morton (1724?–1777), a jurist, was often ill.

here We find it often so powerfull as to become partial, to blind our Eyes, to darken our Understandings and pervert our Wills.

It is to this Infirmity, in my own Heart, that I must perhaps attribute that local Attachment, that partial Fondness, that overweening Prejudice in favour of New England, which I feel very often and which I fear sometimes, leads me to expose myself to just Ridicule.

New England has in many Respects the Advantage of every other Colony in America, and indeed of every other Part of the World, that I know any Thing of.

1. The People are purer English Blood, less mixed with Scotch, Irish, Dutch, French, Danish, Sweedish &c. than any other; and descended from Englishmen too who left Europe, in purer Times than the present and less tainted with Corruption than those they left behind them.

2. The Institutions in New England for the Support of Religion, Morals and Decency, exceed any other, obliging every Parish to have a Minister, and every Person to go to Meeting &c.[1]

3. The public Institutions in New England for the Education of Youth, supporting Colledges at the public Expence and obliging Towns to maintain Grammar schools, is not equalled and never was in any Part of the World.

4. The Division of our Territory, that is our Counties into Townships, empowering Towns to assemble, choose officers, make Laws, mend roads, and twenty other Things, gives every Man an opportunity of shewing and improving that Education which he received at Colledge or at school, and makes Knowledge and Dexterity at public Business common.

5. Our Laws for the Distribution of Intestate Estates[2] occasions a frequent Division of landed Property and prevents Monopolies, of Land.

But in opposition to these We have laboured under many Disadvantages. The exorbitant Prerogatives of our Governors &c. which would have overborn our Liberties, if it had not been opposed by the five preceding Particulars.

1775 1875

Abigail Adams to John Adams

[THE BUILDING UP A GREAT EMPIRE]

November 27 1775

Tis a fortnight to Night since I wrote you a line during which, I have been confined with the Jaundice, Rhumatism and a most voilent cold; I yesterday took a puke which has releived me, and I feel much better to day. Many, very many people who have had the dysentery, are now afflicted both with the Jaundice and Rhumatisim, some it has left in Hecticks, some in dropsies.[3]

The great and incessant rains we have had this fall, (the like cannot be recollected) may have occasiond some of the present disorders. The Jaundice is very prevelant in the Camp. We have lately had a week of very cold weather, as cold as January, and a flight of snow, which I hope will purify the air of some of the noxious vapours. It has spoild many hundreds of

1. I.e., to attend a Congregational church unless specifically exempted.
2. The distribution of property when no will exists.
3. Some have fevers, and some have unnatural retention of water in any part of the body.

Bushels of Apples, which were designd for cider, and which the great rains had prevented people from making up. Suppose we have lost 5 Barrels by it.

Col. Warren[4] returnd last week to Plymouth, so that I shall not hear any thing from you till he goes back again which will not be till the last of <next> this month.

He Damp'd my Spirits greatly by telling me that the Court had prolonged your Stay an other month.[5] I was pleasing myself with the thoughts that you would soon be upon your return. Tis in vain to repine. I hope the publick will reap what I sacrifice.

I wish I knew what mighty things were fabricating.[6] If a form of Goverment is to be established here what one will be assumed? Will it be left to our assemblies to chuse one? and will not many men have many minds? and shall we not run into Dissentions among ourselves?

I am more and more convinced that Man is a dangerous creature, and that power whether vested in many or a few is ever grasping, and like the grave cries give, give. The great fish swallow up the small, and he who is most strenuous for the Rights of the people, when vested with power, is as eager after the perogatives of Government. You tell me of degrees of perfection to which Humane Nature is capable of arriving, and I believe it, but at the same time lament that our admiration should arise from the scarcity of the instances.

The Building up a Great Empire, which was only hinted at by my correspondent may now I suppose be realized even by the unbelievers. Yet will not ten thousand Difficulties arise in the formation of it? The Reigns of Government have been so long slakned, that I fear the people will not quietly submit to those restraints which are necessary for the peace, and security, of the community; if we seperate from Brittain, what Code of Laws will be established. How shall we be governd so as to retain our Liberties? Can any government be free which is not adminstred by general stated Laws? Who shall frame these Laws? Who will give them force and energy? Tis true your Resolution[s] as a Body have heithertoo had the force of Laws. But will they continue to have?

When I consider these things and the prejudices of people in favour of Ancient customs and Regulations, I feel anxious for the fate of our Monarchy or Democracy or what ever is to take place. I soon get lost in a Labyrinth of perplexities, but whatever occurs, may justice and righteousness be the Stability of our times, and order arise out of confusion. Great difficulties may be surmounted, by patience and perserverance.

I believe I have tired you with politicks. As to news we have not any at all. I shudder at the approach of winter when I think I am to remain desolate. Suppose your weather is warm yet. Mr. Mason and Thaxter[7] live with me, and render some part of my time less disconsolate. Mr. Mason is a youth who will please you, he has Spirit, taste and Sense. His application to his Studies is constant and I am much mistaken if he does not make a very good figure in his profession.

4. James Warren (see n. 5, p. 667).
5. On November 11, the Massachusetts House of Representatives extended the commissions of the delegates to the Continental Congress.

6. Being made.
7. John Thaxter, Jr. (1775–1791), Abigail's cousin and a law clerk. Jonathan Mason (1756–1831), at the time a law clerk.

I have with me now, the only Daughter of your Brother; I feel a tenderer affection for her as she has lost a kind parent.[8] Though too young to be sensible of her own loss, I can pitty her. She appears to be a child of a very good Disposition—only wants to be a little used to company.

Our Little ones send Duty to pappa and want much to see him. Tom says he[9] wont come home till the Battle is over—some strange notion he has got into his head. He has got a political cread to say to him when he returns.

I must bid you good night. Tis late for one who am much of an invalide. I was dissapointed last week in receiving a packet by the post, and upon unsealing it found only four news papers. I think you are more cautious than you need be. All Letters I believe have come safe to hand. I have Sixteen from you, and wish I had as many more. Adieu. Yours.

1775 1848

Abigail Adams to John Adams

[REMEMBER THE LADIES]

Braintree March 31 1776

I wish you would ever write me a Letter half as long as I write you; and tell me if you may where your Fleet are gone? What sort of Defence Virginia can make against our common Enemy? Whether it is so situated as to make an able Defence?[1] Are not the Gentery Lords and the common people vassals, are they not like the uncivilized Natives Brittain represents us to be? I hope their Riffel Men who have shewen themselves very savage and even Blood thirsty; are not a specimen of the Generality of the people.

I am willing to allow the Colony great merit for having produced a Washington but they have been shamefully duped by a Dunmore.[2]

I have sometimes been ready to think that the passion for Liberty cannot be Eaquelly Strong in the Breasts of those who have been accustomed to deprive their fellow Creatures of theirs. Of this I am certain that it is not founded upon that generous and christian principal of doing to others as we would that others should do unto us.

Do not you want to see Boston; I am fearfull of the small pox, or I should have been in before this time. I got Mr. Crane[3] to go to our House and see what state it was in. I find it has been occupied by one of the Doctors of a Regiment, very dirty, but no other damage has been done to it. The few things which were left in it are all gone. Cranch has the key which he never deliverd up. I have wrote to him for it and am determined to get it cleand as soon as possible and shut it up. I look upon it a new acquisition of property,

8. Susanna Adams (1766–1826) was the daughter of Elihu and Thankful Adams. Elihu, John's younger brother, died of dysentery while serving in the Continental Army.
9. Like "him" in the next sentence, pappa (i.e., John).
1. On March 17, 1776, the British evacuated Boston, having been defeated by General George Washington and his forces. Abigail anticipates that the front will move to Virginia (rather than

New York, as proved to be the case).
2. In 1775, John Murray, Lord Dunmore (1730-1809), a Scottish nobleman who served as Virginia's final royal governor, proclaimed martial law in that colony to thwart the rebel cause. George Washington was born in Westmoreland County, Virginia.
3. Probably Richard Cranch (1726-1811), Massachusetts legislator and husband of Abigail's sister Mary (1741-1811).

a property which one month ago I did not value at a single Shilling, and could with pleasure have seen it in flames.

The Town in General is left in a better state than we expected, more oweing to a percipitate flight than any Regard to the inhabitants, tho some individuals discoverd a sense of honour and justice and have left the rent of the Houses in which they were, for the owners and the furniture unhurt, or if damaged sufficent to make it good.

Others have committed abominable Ravages. The Mansion House of your President is safe and the furniture unhurt whilst both the House and Furniture of the Solisiter General[4] have fallen a prey to their own merciless party. Surely the very Fiends feel a Reverential awe for Virtue and patriotism, whilst they Detest the paricide[5] and traitor.

I feel very differently at the approach of spring to what I did a month ago. We knew not then whether we could plant or sow with safety, whether when we had toild we could reap the fruits of our own industery,[6] whether we could rest in our own Cottages, or whether we should not be driven from the sea coasts to seek shelter in the wilderness, but now we feel as if we might sit under our own vine and eat the good of the land.

I feel a gaieti de Coar[7] to which before I was a stranger. I think the Sun looks brighter, the Birds sing more melodiously, and Nature puts on a more chearfull countanance. We feel a temporary peace, and the poor fugitives are returning to their deserted habitations.

Tho we felicitate ourselves, we sympathize with those who are trembling least the Lot of Boston should be theirs.[8] But they cannot be in similar circumstances unless pusilanimity[9] and cowardise should take possession of them. They have time and warning given them to see the Evil and shun it—I long to hear that you have declared an independancy—and by the way in the new Code of Laws which I suppose it will be necessary for you to make I desire you would Remember the Ladies, and be more generous and favourable to them than your ancestors. Do not put such unlimited power into the hands of the Husbands. Remember all Men would be tyrants if they could. If perticuliar care and attention is not paid to the Laidies we are determined to foment a Rebelion, and will not hold ourselves bound by any Laws in which we have no voice, or Representation.

That your Sex are Naturally Tyrannical is a Truth so thoroughly established as to admit of no dispute, but such of you as wish to be happy willingly give up the harsh title of Master for the more tender and endearing one of Friend. Why then, not put it out of the power of the vicious and the Lawless to use us with cruelty and indignity with impunity. Men of Sense in all Ages abhor those customs which treat us only as the vassals of your Sex. Regard us then as Beings placed by providence under your protection and in immitation of the Supreem Being make use of that power only for our happiness.

1776

4. Samuel Quincy (1735-1793). "Your president": John Hancock (1737-1793), president of the Second Continental Congress.
5. I.e., patricide: killer of one's own father.
6. I.e., industry: labor.

7. I.e., *gaieté de Coeur*: gaiety of heart (French).
8. Boston was under siege from April 19, 1775, through March 17, 1776. "Least": i.e., lest.
9. I.e., pusillanimity: timidity.

John Adams to Abigail Adams
[THESE COLONIES ARE FREE AND INDEPENDENT STATES]

Philadelphia July 3. 1776

Your Favour of June 17. dated at Plymouth, was handed me, by Yesterdays Post. I was much pleased to find that you had taken a Journey to Plymouth, to see your Friends in the long Absence of one whom you may wish to see. The Excursion will be an Amusement, and will serve your Health. How happy would it have made me to have taken this Journey with you?

I was informed, a day or two before the Receipt of your Letter, that you was gone to Plymouth, by Mrs. Polly Palmer,[1] who was obliging enough in your Absence, to inform me, of the Particulars of the Expedition to the lower Harbour against the Men of War.[2] Her Narration is executed, with a Precision and Perspicuity, which would have become the Pen of an accomplished Historian.

I am very glad you had so good an opportunity of seeing one of our little American Men of War. Many Ideas, new to you, must have presented themselves in such a Scene; and you will in future, better understand the Relations of Sea Engagements.

I rejoice extreamly at Dr. Bulfinches Petition to open an Hospital.[3] But I hope, the Business will be done upon a larger Scale. I hope, that one Hospital will be licensed in every County, if not in every Town. I am happy to find you resolved, to be with the Children, in the first Class.[4] Mr. Whitney and Mrs. Katy Quincy,[5] are cleverly through Innoculation, in this City.

I have one favour to ask, and that is, that in your future Letters, you would acknowledge the Receipt of all those you may receive from me, and mention their Dates. By this Means I shall know if any of mine miscarry.

The Information you give me of our Friends refusing his Appointment, has given me much Pain, Grief and Anxiety.[6] I believe I shall be obliged to follow his Example. I have not Fortune enough to support my Family, and what is of more Importance, to support the Dignity of that exalted Station. It is too high and lifted up, for me; who delight in nothing so much as Retreat, Solitude, Silence, and Obscurity. In private Life, no one has a Right to censure me for following my own Inclinations, in Retirement, Simplicity, and Frugality: in public Life, every Man has a Right to remark as he pleases, at least he thinks so.

Yesterday the greatest Question was decided, which ever was debated in America, and a greater perhaps, never was or will be decided among Men. A Resolution was passed without one dissenting Colony "that these united Colonies, are, and of right ought to be free and independent States, and as such, they have, and of Right ought to have full Power to make War, conclude Peace, establish Commerce, and to do all the other Acts and Things,

1. Miss Mary Palmer ("Mrs." here stands for "Mistress"; 1746–1791), a niece of Richard and Mary Cranch.
2. I.e., to see the Continental Navy's warships (men-o'-war).
3. Thomas Bulfinch (1728–1802), an M.D., inoculated Abigail Adams, her children, and her friends and family members against smallpox.
4. I.e., the first group to be inoculated.
5. Katherine Quincy (1733–1804), a relative of Abigail's. Peter Whitney (1744–1816), minister and patriot.
6. In an earlier letter, Abigail had informed John that James Warren had declined an appointment as associate justice of the Massachusetts Superior Court.

which other States may rightfully do." You will see in a few days a Declaration setting forth the Causes, which have impell'd Us to this mighty Revolution, and the Reasons which will justify it, in the Sight of God and Man.[7] A Plan of Confederation will be taken up in a few days.

When I look back to the Year 1761, and recollect the Argument concerning Writs of Assistance, in the Superiour Court, which I have hitherto considered as the Commencement of the Controversy, between Great Britain and America,[8] and run through the whole Period from that Time to this, and recollect the series of political Events, the Chain of Causes and Effects, I am surprized at the Suddenness, as well as Greatness of this Revolution. Britain has been fill'd with Folly, and America with Wisdom, at least this is my Judgment.—Time must determine. It is the Will of Heaven, that the two Countries should be sundered forever. It may be the Will of Heaven that America shall suffer Calamities still more wasting and Distresses yet more dreadfull. If this is to be the Case, it will have this good Effect, at least: it will inspire Us with many Virtues, which We have not, and correct many Errors, Follies, and Vices, which threaten to disturb, dishonour, and destroy Us.—The Furnace of Affliction produces Refinement, in States as well as Individuals. And the new Governments we are assuming, in every Part, will require a Purification from our Vices, and an Augmentation of our Virtues or they will be no Blessings. The People will have unbounded Power. And the People are extreamly addicted to Corruption and Venality, as well as the Great.—I am not without Apprehensions from this Quarter. But I must submit all my Hopes and Fears, to an overruling Providence, in which, unfashionable as the Faith may be, I firmly believe.

1776 1792

John Adams to Abigail Adams

[REFLECTIONS ON THE DECLARATION OF INDEPENDENCE]

Philadelphia July 3d. 1776

Had a Declaration of Independency been made seven Months ago, it would have been attended with many great and glorious Effects.[9] . . . We might before this Hour, have formed Alliances with foreign States.—We should have mastered Quebec and been in Possession of Canada[1]. . . . You will perhaps wonder, how such a Declaration would have influenced our Affairs, in Canada, but if I could write with Freedom I could easily convince you, that it would, and explain to you the manner how.—Many Gentlemen in high Stations and of great Influence have been duped, by the ministerial Bubble

7. Butterfield notes that this letter "and the next one of the same date were written *between* the act of independence itself and the adoption of the statement designed to 'justify it in the sight of God and man.'" On June 7, Richard Henry Lee (1732–1794), from Virginia, moved "that these United Colonies are, and of right ought to be, Free and Independent States." Lee's motion was carried on July 2 after vigorous debate. A committee was appointed to prepare a formal declaration, and this document, written largely by Thomas Jefferson, was adopted July 4, 1776.

8. Writs of assistance were general search warrants and, as such, a threat to civil liberty.
9. Here and below, the ellipses are in the manuscript.
1. The Continental Army invaded Canada in June 1775. Their aim was to win control of Quebec and recruit French Canadians to their side. They were defeated in an assault on Quebec City in December of that year. The army suffered badly from smallpox, which contributed to the defeat.

of Commissioners to treat.[2] . . . And in real, sincere Expectation of this Event, which they so fondly wished, they have been slow and languid, in promoting Measures for the Reduction[3] of that Province. Others there are in the Colonies who really wished that our Enterprise in Canada would be defeated, that the Colonies might be brought into Danger and Distress between two Fires, and be thus induced to submit. Others really wished to defeat the Expedition to Canada, lest the Conquest of it, should elevate the Minds of the People too much to hearken to those Terms of Reconciliation which they believed would be offered Us. These jarring Views, Wishes and Designs, occasioned an opposition to many salutary Measures, which were proposed for the Support of that Expedition, and caused Obstructions, Embarrassments and studied Delays, which have finally, lost Us the Province.

All these Causes however in Conjunction would not have disappointed Us, if it had not been for a Misfortune, which could not be foreseen, and perhaps could not have been prevented, I mean the Prevalence of the small Pox among our Troops. . . . This fatal Pestilence compleated our Destruction.—It is a Frown of Providence upon Us, which We ought to lay to heart.

But on the other Hand, the Delay of this Declaration to this Time, has many great Advantages attending it.—The Hopes of Reconciliation, which were fondly entertained by Multitudes of honest and well meaning tho weak and mistaken People, have been gradually and at last totally extinguished.— Time has been given for the whole People, maturely to consider the great Question of Independence and to ripen their Judgments, dissipate their Fears, and allure their Hopes, by discussing it in News Papers and Pamphletts, by debating it, in Assemblies, Conventions, Committees of Safety and Inspection, in Town and County Meetings, as well as in private Conversations, so that the whole People in every Colony of the 13, have now adopted it, as their own Act.—This will cement the Union, and avoid those Heats and perhaps Convulsions which might have been occasioned, by such a Declaration Six Months ago.

But the Day is past. The Second Day of July 1776, will be the most memorable Epocha, in the History of America.—I am apt to believe that it will be celebrated, by succeeding Generations, as the great anniversary Festival. It ought to be commemorated, as the Day of Deliverance by solemn Acts of Devotion to God Almighty. It ought to be solemnized with Pomp and Parade, with Shews, Games, Sports, Guns, Bells, Bonfires and Illuminations from one End of this Continent to the other from this Time forward forever more.

You will think me transported with Enthusiasm but I am not.—I am well aware of the Toil and Blood and Treasure, that it will cost Us to maintain this Declaration, and support and defend these States.—Yet through all the Gloom I can see the Rays of ravishing Light and Glory. I can see that the End is more than worth all the Means. And that Posterity will tryumph in that Days Transaction, even altho We should rue it, which I trust in God We shall not.

1776 1792

2. Negotiate. 3. Conquest.

Abigail Adams to John Adams

[THE DECLARATION. SMALLPOX. THE GREY HORSE]

* * *

Sunday july 14 [1776]

By yesterdays post I received two Letters dated 3 and 4 of July and tho your Letters never fail to give me pleasure, be the subject what it will, yet it was greatly heightned by the prospect of the future happiness and glory of our Country; nor am I a little Gratified when I reflect that a person so nearly connected with me has had the Honour of being a principal actor, in laying a foundation for its future Greatness. May the foundation of our new constitution, be justice, Truth and Righteousness. Like the wise Mans house may it be founded upon those Rocks and then neither storms or temptests will overthrow it.[4]

I cannot but feel sorry that some of the most Manly Sentiments in the Declaration are Expunged from the printed coppy. Perhaps wise reasons induced it.[5]

Poor Canady I lament Canady but we ought to be in some measure sufferers for the past folly of our conduct. The fatal effects of the small pox there, has led almost every person to consent to Hospitals in every Town. In many Towns, already arround Boston the Selectmen have granted Liberty for innoculation. I hope the necessity is now fully seen.

I had many dissagreable Sensations at the Thoughts of comeing myself, but to see my children thro it I thought my duty, and all those feelings vanished as soon as I was innoculated and I trust a kind providence will carry me safely thro. Our Friends from Plymouth came into Town yesterday. We have enough upon our hands in the morning. The Little folks are very sick then and puke every morning but after that they are comfortable. I shall write you now very often. Pray inform me constantly of every important transaction. Every expression of tenderness is a cordial to my Heart. Unimportant as they are to the rest of the world, to me they are *every Thing*.

We have had during all the month of June a most severe Drougth which cut of all our promising hopes of english Grain and the first crop of Grass, but since july came in we have had a plenty of rain and now every thing looks well. There is one Misfortune in our family which I have never mentioned in hopes it would have been in my power to have remedied it, but all hopes of that kind are at an end. It is the loss of your Grey Horse. About 2 months ago, I had occasion to send Jonathan of an errant to my unkle Quincys[6] (the other Horse being a plowing). Upon his return a little below the church she trod upon a rolling stone and lamed herself to that degree that it was with great difficulty that she could be got home. I immediately sent for Tirrel[7] and every thing was done for her by Baths, ointments, polticeing, Bleeding &c. that could be done. Still she continued extreem lame tho not so bad as

4. Matthew 7.24–25 describes "a wise man, which built his house upon a rock: And the rain descended, and the winds blew, and beat upon that house; and it fell not: for it was founded upon a rock."

5. On these revisions, see Thomas Jefferson's account, later in this volume.
6. Norton Quincy (1716–1801), public servant. "Jonathan": Abigail's servant or farm boy.
7. A veterinarian in Braintree.

at first. I then got her carried to Domet[8] but he pronounces her incurable, as a callous is grown upon her footlock joint. You can hardly tell, not even by your own feelings how much I lament her. She was not with foal, as you immagined, but I hope she is now as care has been taken in that Respect.

I suppose you have heard of a fleet which came up pretty near the Light[9] and kept us all with our mouths open ready to catch them, but after staying near a week and makeing what observations they could set sail and went of to our great mortification who were [prepared?][1] for them in every respect. If our Ship of 32 Guns which [was] Built at Portsmouth[2] and waiting only for Guns and an other of [. . .] at Plimouth in the same state, had been in readiness we should in all probability been Masters of them. Where the blame lies in that respect I know not, tis laid upon Congress, and Congress is also blamed for not appointing us a General.—But Rome was not Built in a day.

I hope the Multiplicity of cares and avocations which invellope you will not be too powerfull for you. I have many anxietyes upon that account. Nabby[3] and Johnny send duty and desire Mamma to say that an inflamation in their Eyes which has been as much of a distemper as the small pox, has prevented their writing, but they hope soon to be able to acquaint Pappa of their happy recovery from the Distemper.—Mr. C[ranch] and wife, Sister B[etsy][4] and all our Friend[s] desire to be rememberd to you and foremost in that Number stands your

Portia[5]

PS A little India herb[6] would have been mighty agreable now.

1776 1875

John Adams to Abigail Adams

[DO MY FRIENDS THINK I HAVE FORGOTTEN MY WIFE AND CHILDREN?]

Philadelphia July 20, 1776

This has been a dull day to me: I waited the Arrival of the Post with much Solicitude and Impatience, but his Arrival made me more solicitous still.—"To be left at the Post Office" in your Hand Writing, on the back of a few Lines from the Dr.[7] were all that I could learn of you, and my little Folks. If you was too busy to write, I hoped that some kind Hand would have been found to let me know something about you.

Do my Friends think that I have been a Politician so long as to have lost all feeling? Do they suppose I have forgotten my Wife and Children? Or are they so panic struck with the Loss of Canada, as to be afraid to correspond with me? Or have they forgotten that you have an Husband and your Children a Father? What have I done, or omitted to do, that I should be thus forgotten

8. Another veterinarian.
9. Lighthouse.
1. The manuscript is torn here and below.
2. In New Hampshire.
3. Their daughter Abigail's nickname.
4. Abigail's sister Elizabeth (1742–1816).
5. Abigail's pseudoym refers to Portia Catonis (c. 70–43 B.C.E.), wife of the Roman politician Marcus Junius Brutus (85–42 B.C.E.). Brutus is the most famous assassin of the Roman statesman and general Julius Caesar (100–44 B.C.E.).
6. Tea, an import of the British East India company.
7. Dr. Cotton Tufts (1732–1815), Abigail's uncle by marriage.

and neglected in the most tender and affecting scæne of my Life! Dont mistake me, I dont blame you. Your Time and Thoughts must have been wholly taken up, with your own and your Families situation and Necessities.— But twenty other Persons might have informed me.

I suspect, that you intended to have run slyly, through the small Pox with the family, without letting me know it, and then have sent me an Account that you were all well. This might be a kind Intention, and if the design had succeeded, would have made me very joyous. But the secret is out, and I am left to conjecture. But as the Faculty[8] have this distemper so much under Command I will flatter myself with the Hope and Expectation of soon hearing of your Recovery.

1776 1875

Abigail Adams to John Adams

[SMALLPOX. THE PROCLAMATION FOR INDEPENDENCE READ ALOUD]

July 21 1776 Boston

I have no doubt but that my dearest Friend is anxious to know how his Portia does, and his little flock of children under the opperation of a disease once so formidable.

I have the pleasure to tell him that they are all comfortable tho some of them complaining. Nabby has been very ill, but the Eruption begins to make its appearance upon her, and upon Johnny. Tommy is so well that the Dr. innoculated him again to day fearing it had not taken. Charlly has no complaints yet, tho his arm has been very soar.

I have been out to meeting[9] this forenoon, but have so many dissagreable Sensations this afternoon that I thought it prudent to tarry at home. The Dr. says they are very good feelings. Mr. Cranch has passed thro the preparation and the Eruption is comeing out cleverly upon him without any Sickness at all. Mrs. Cranch is cleverly and so are all her children. Those who are broke out are pretty full for the new method as tis call'd, the Suttonian[1] they profess to practice upon. I hope to give you a good account when I write next, but our Eyes are very weak and the Dr. is not fond of either writing or reading for his patients. But I must transgress a little.

I received a Letter from you by wedensday Post 7 of July and tho I think it a choise one in the Litterary Way, containing many usefull hints and judicious observations which will greatly assist me in the future instruction of our Little ones, yet it Lacked some essential engredians to make it compleat. Not one word respecting yourself, your Health or your present Situation. My anxiety for your welfare will never leave me but with my parting Breath, tis of more importance to me than all this World contains besides. The cruel Seperation to which I am necessatated cuts of half the enjoyments of life, the other half are comprised in the hope I have that what I do and what I suffer may be serviceable to you, to our Little ones and our Country;

8. The medical profession.
9. Church service.
1. Named after Daniel Sutton (1735–1819), of Essex, Massachusetts. His method required only a small puncture instead of the customary gash to infect the subject.

I must beseach you therefore for the future never to omit what is so essential to my happiness.

Last Thursday after hearing a very Good Sermon I went with the Multitude into Kings Street[2] to hear the proclamation for independance read and proclamed. Some Field peices with the Train were brought there, the troops appeard under Arms and all the inhabitants assembled there (the small pox prevented many thousand from the Country).[3] When Col. Crafts read from the Belcona[4] of the State House the Proclamation, great attention was given to every word. As soon as he ended, the cry from the Belcona, was God Save our American States and then 3 cheers which rended the air, the Bells rang, the privateers[5] fired, the forts and Batteries, the cannon were discharged, the platoons followed and every face appeard joyfull. Mr. Bowdoin then gave a Sentiment,[6] Stability and perpetuity to American independance. After dinner the kings arms were taken down from the State House and every vestage of him from every place in which it appeard and burnt in King Street. Thus ends royall Authority in this State, and all the people shall say Amen.

I have been a little surprized that we collect no better accounts with regard to the horrid conspiricy at New York, and that so little mention has been made of it here. It made a talk for a few days but now seems all hushed in Silence. The Tories say that it was not a conspiricy but an association, and pretend that there was no plot to assasinate the General.[7] Even their hardned Hearts <Blush> feel——the discovery. We have in G[e]orge a match for a Borgia and a Catiline,[8] a Wretch Callous to every Humane feeling. Our worthy preacher told us that he believed one of our Great Sins for which a righteous God has come out in judgment against us, was our Biggoted attachment to so wicked a Man. May our repentance be sincere.

<div align="right">Monday morg. july 22</div>

I omitted many things yesterday in order to be better informed. I have got Mr. Cranch to inquire and write you, concerning a French Schooner from Martineco which came in yesterday and a prize from Ireland. My own infirmities prevents my writing. A most Excruciating pain in my head and every Limb and joint I hope portends a speedy Eruption and prevents my saying more than that I am forever Yours.

The children are not yet broke out. Tis the Eleventh Day with us.

1776 1875

2. Now Boston's State Street; site, in 1770, of the Boston Massacre, in which British Army soldiers killed and injured civilians, enraging colonists. "Thursday": July 18, 1776.
3. Countryside. "Some . . . train": i.e., field guns with their vehicles.
4. Balcony. Thomas Crafts (1740–1799), colonel in the Continental Army.
5. Privately owned armed vessels with a government commission.

6. A personal reflection. James Bowdoin (1726–1790), Massachusetts merchant and statesman; author of an influential report on the Boston Massacre.
7. George Washington.
8. Abigail compares King George III of England (1738–1820) to the Italian statesman and cardinal Cesare Borgia (1475–1507), famous for his cruelty, and to Catiline (108?–62 B.C.E.), Roman politician and conspirator against the state.

THOMAS PAINE
1737–1809

The author of two of the most popular books in eighteenth-century America, and the most persuasive rhetorician of the cause for independence, Thomas Paine was born in England and did not move to the colonies until he was thirty-seven years old and the rebellion was looming. Paine's early years prepared him to support the Revolution. The discrepancy between his high intelligence and the limitations imposed on him in England's hierarchical society made him long for a new social order. The son of a Quaker father and an Anglican mother, he once said that a sermon he heard at age eight convinced him of the cruelty inherent in Christianity and made him a rebel forever.

By the time he arrived in Philadelphia with letters of introduction from Benjamin Franklin, recommending him as an "ingenious, worthy young man," Paine had already led a remarkably full life. He attended grammar school until he was thirteen and was then apprenticed in his father's corset shop; at nineteen, he ran away from home to go to sea. From 1757 to 1774, he was, by turns, a corset maker, a tobacconist and grocer, a schoolteacher, and an exciseman (i.e., a government employee who taxed goods). Hoping to force Parliament to raise the salary of the excisemen, he engaged in some of the first efforts at labor organizing. His efforts failed, however, and he lost his job when he admitted that he had stamped goods as inspected when in fact they had not been examined. His first wife died less than a year after their marriage, and he was separated from his second wife after three years. Scandals about his private life and questions about his integrity provided his critics with ammunition for the rest of his life. Franklin was right, however, in recognizing Paine's genius; like Franklin, Paine was self-taught and curious about everything from the philosophy of law to natural science.

In Philadelphia, Paine transformed himself into a journalist. He quickly made his way in that city, first as a spokesman against slavery and then as the anonymous author of *Common Sense* (1776), the first pamphlet published in the colonies to urge immediate independence from Britain. Paine was obviously the right man in the right place at the right time. Relations with England were at their lowest ebb: Boston was under siege, and the Second Continental Congress had convened in Philadelphia. *Common Sense* sold phenomenally well and was quickly reprinted in cities along the eastern seaboard and in France, Germany, and England. Meanwhile, Paine enlisted in the Revolutionary Army and served as an aide-de-camp in battles in New York, New Jersey, and Pennsylvania. He followed the triumph of *Common Sense* with the first of sixteen pamphlets titled *The Crisis* (1776-83). The first *Crisis* paper ("These are the times that try men's souls") reportedly was read to General George Washington's troops at Trenton, New Jersey, and did much to shore up the spirits of the ultimately victorious Revolutionary soldiers.

After the war, Paine received a number of political appointments as rewards for his services as a writer for the American cause, but too indiscreet and hot-tempered for public employment, he misused his privileges and lost the most lucrative offices. In 1787, he returned to England, where he wrote his second-most successful work, *Rights of Man* (1791–92), an impassioned plea against hereditary monarchy. Paine was charged with treason and fled to France, where he was made a citizen and lionized as a spokesman for revolution. The horrors of the French Revolution, however, brought home to Paine that the overthrow of monarchy did not necessarily usher in

enlightenment and order. When he protested the execution of Louis XVI, he was accused of sympathy with the Crown and imprisoned. He was saved from trial by the American ambassador, the future president James Monroe, who offered him renewed American citizenship and safe passage back to New York.

Paine spent the last years of his life in New York City and in New Rochelle, New York. During these years of unhappiness and impoverishment, his reputation suffered enormously as a result of his public rejection of organized religion in *The Age of Reason* (1794). Paine's attempt to define his beliefs was viewed as an attack on Christianity and, by extension, on conventional society. He was ridiculed and despised. Even George Washington, who had supported Paine's early writing, thought English criticism of him was "not a bad thing." Paine was buried on his farm at New Rochelle after his request for a Quaker gravesite was refused. Ten years later, an admirer exhumed his bones with the intention of having him reburied in England, but this plan came to nothing, and Paine's remains have never been found.

Paine's role in shaping American literature took numerous forms. He began his writing career in Philadelphia as the contributing editor of a magazine—then a new publication format—where he learned to address a wide audience, a skill that he turned to advantage in his polemical pamphlets. He made important contributions to the development of copyright and to the professionalization of authorship. But it was as a stylist of "plainness" that Paine made his greatest gift to American literature. Reflecting on his prose style, he said he needed no "ceremonious expressions." He wrote: "It is my design to make those who can scarcely read understand," to put arguments in a language "as plain as the alphabet," and to shape everything "to fit the powers of thinking and the turn of language to the subject, so as to bring out a clear conclusion that shall hit the point in question and nothing else."

Like Franklin, Thomas Jefferson admired Paine's use of the new populist rhetorical style then emerging to challenge the classical rhetoric associated with political elites. Having cut a controversial path through the age of democratic revolution, Paine inspired later radicals, such as the journalist and poet Walt Whitman (in Volume B of this anthology), who eulogized his hero in 1877: "That he labor'd well and wisely for the States in the trying period of their parturition, and in the seeds of their character, there seems to me no question. I dare not say how much of what our Union is owning and enjoying to day—its independence—its ardent belief in, and substantial practice of, radical human rights—and the severance of its government from all ecclesiastical and superstitious dominion—I dare not say how much of all this is owing to Thomas Paine, but I am inclined to think a good portion of it decidedly is."

From Common Sense[1]

Introduction

Perhaps the sentiments contained in the following pages are not yet sufficiently fashionable to procure them general favor; a long habit of not think-

1. The full title is *Common Sense: Addressed to the Inhabitants of America, on the Following Interesting Subjects: viz.* [i.e., namely]: *I. Of the Origin and Design of Government in General; with Concise Remarks on the English Constitution. II. Of Monarchy and Hereditary Succes-* sion. *III. Thoughts on the Present State of American Affairs. IV. Of the Present Ability of America; with some Miscellaneous Reflections.* The text is from *The Writings of Thomas Paine* (1894–96), vol. 1, edited by M. D. Conway.

ing a thing wrong gives it a superficial appearance of being right, and raises at first a formidable outcry in defence of custom. But the tumult soon subsides. Time makes more converts than reason.

As a long and violent abuse of power is generally the means of calling the right of it in question (and in matters too which might never have been thought of, had not the sufferers been aggravated into the inquiry), and as the King of England[2] hath undertaken in his own right, to support the Parliament in what he calls theirs, and as the good people of this country are grievously oppressed by the combination, they have an undoubted privilege to inquire into the pretensions of both, and equally to reject the usurpation of either.

In the following sheets, the author hath studiously avoided everything which is personal among ourselves. Compliments as well as censure to individuals make no part thereof. The wise and the worthy need not the triumph of a pamphlet; and those whose sentiments are injudicious or unfriendly will cease of themselves, unless too much pains is bestowed upon their conversions.

The cause of America is in a great measure the cause of all mankind. Many circumstances have, and will, arise which are not local, but universal, and through which the principles of all lovers of mankind are affected, and in the event of which their affections are interested. The laying a country desolate with fire and sword, declaring war against the natural rights of all mankind, and extirpating the defenders thereof from the face of the earth, is the concern of every man to whom nature hath given the power of feeling; of which class, regardless of party censure, is

THE AUTHOR

From III. Thoughts on the Present State of American Affairs

In the following pages I offer nothing more than simple facts, plain arguments, and common sense: and have no other preliminaries to settle with the reader, than that he will divest himself of prejudice and prepossession, and suffer his reason and his feelings to determine for themselves: that he will put on, or rather that he will not put off, the true character of a man, and generously enlarge his views beyond the present day.

Volumes have been written on the subject of the struggle between England and America. Men of all ranks have embarked in the controversy, from different motives, and with various designs; but all have been ineffectual, and the period of debate is closed. Arms as the last resource decide the contest; the appeal was the choice of the King, and the continent has accepted the challenge.

It hath been reported of the late Mr. Pelham[3] (who though an able minister was not without his faults) that on his being attacked in the House of Commons on the score that his measures were only of a temporary kind, replied, "they will last my time." Should a thought so fatal and unmanly possess the colonies in the present contest, the name of ancestors will be remembered by future generations with detestation.

2. George III (1738–1820; reigned 1760–1820). 3. Henry Pelham (1696–1754; prime minister of Britain 1743–54).

The sun never shined on a cause of greater worth. 'Tis not the affair of a city, a county, a province, or a kingdom; but of a continent—of at least one eighth part of the habitable globe. 'Tis not the concern of a day, a year, or an age; posterity are virtually involved in the contest, and will be more or less affected even to the end of time, by the proceedings now. Now is the seed time of continental union, faith and honor. The least fracture now will be like a name engraved with the point of a pin on the tender rind of a young oak; the wound would enlarge with the tree, and posterity read it in full grown characters.

By referring the matter from argument to arms, a new era for politics is struck—a new method of thinking hath arisen. All plans, proposals, etc., prior to the nineteenth of April, i.e., to the commencement of hostilities,[4] are like the almanacs of the last year; which though proper then, are super-seded and useless now. Whatever was advanced by the advocates on either side of the question then, terminated in one and the same point, viz., a union with Great Britain; the only difference between the parties was the method of effecting it; the one proposing force, the other friendship; but it hath so far happened that the first hath failed, and the second hath withdrawn her influence.

As much hath been said of the advantages of reconciliation, which, like an agreeable dream, hath passed away and left us as we were, it is but right that we should examine the contrary side of the argument, and inquire into some of the many material injuries which these colonies sustain, and always will sustain, by being connected with and dependent on Great Britain. To examine that connection and dependence, on the principles of nature and common sense, to see what we have to trust to, if separated, and what we are to expect, if dependent.

I have heard it asserted by some, that as America has flourished under her former connection with Great Britain, the same connection is neces-sary towards her future happiness, and will always have the same effect. Nothing can be more fallacious than this kind of argument. We may as well assert that because a child has thrived upon milk, that it is never to have meat, or that the first twenty years of our lives is to become a precedent for the next twenty. But even this is admitting more than is true; for I answer roundly, that America would have flourished as much, and probably much more, had no European power taken any notice of her. The commerce by which she hath enriched herself are the necessaries of life, and will always have a market while eating is the custom of Europe.

But she has protected us, say some. That she hath engrossed[5] us is true, and defended the continent at our expense as well as her own, is admitted; and she would have defended Turkey from the same motive, viz., for the sake of trade and dominion.

Alas! we have been long led away by ancient prejudices and made large sacrifices to superstition. We have boasted the protection of Great Britain without considering that her motive was interest not attachment; and that she did not protect us from our enemies on our account; but from her enemies

4. On April 19, 1775, in the first armed conflict of the American Revolution, the Minutemen of Lexington, Massachusetts, defended their ammu-

nition stores against the British.
5. Dominated.

on her own account, from those who had no quarrel with us on any other account, and who will always be our enemies on the same account. Let Britain waive her pretensions to the continent, or the continent throw off the dependence, and we should be at peace with France and Spain, were they at war with Britain. The miseries of Hanover's last war[6] ought to warn us against connections.

It hath lately been asserted in Parliament, that the colonies have no relation to each other but through the parent country, i.e., that Pennsylvania and the Jerseys,[7] and so on for the rest, are sister colonies by the way of England; this is certainly a very roundabout way of proving relationship, but it is the nearest and only true way of proving enmity (or enemyship, if I may so call it). France and Spain never were, nor perhaps ever will be, our enemies as Americans, but as our being the subjects of Great Britain.

But Britain is the parent country, say some. Then the more shame upon her conduct. Even brutes do not devour their young, nor savages make war upon their families; wherefore, the assertion, if true, turns to her reproach; but it happens not to be true, or only partly so, and the phrase parent or mother country hath been jesuitically[8] adopted by the King and his parasites, with a low papistical design of gaining an unfair bias on the credulous weakness of our minds. Europe, and not England, is the parent country of America. This new world hath been the asylum for the persecuted lovers of civil and religious liberty from every part of Europe. Hither have they fled, not from the tender embraces of the mother, but from the cruelty of the monster; and it is so far true of England, that the same tyranny which drove the first emigrants from home, pursues their descendants still.

In this extensive quarter of the globe, we forget the narrow limits of three hundred and sixty miles (the extent of England) and carry our friendship on a larger scale; we claim brotherhood with every European Christian, and triumph in the generosity of the sentiment.

It is pleasant to observe by what regular gradations we surmount the force of local prejudices, as we enlarge our acquaintance with the world. A man born in any town in England divided into parishes, will naturally associate most with his fellow parishioners (because their interests in many cases will be common) and distinguish him by the name of neighbor; if he meet him but a few miles from home, he drops the narrow idea of a street, and salutes him by the name of townsman; if he travel out of the county and meet him in any other, he forgets the minor divisions of street and town, and calls him countryman, i.e., countyman: but if in their foreign excursions they should associate in France, or any other part of Europe, their local remembrance would be enlarged into that of Englishmen. And by a just parity of reasoning, all Europeans meeting in America, or any other quarter of the globe, are countrymen; for England, Holland, Germany, or Sweden, when compared with the whole, stand in the same places on the larger scale, which

6. King George III was a descendant of the German House of Hanover. Paine is referring to the Seven Years' War (1756–63), which originally involved Prussia and Austria and grew to include all the major European powers. The war was settled in Britain's favor, but the North American component, the French and Indian War (1754–63), resulted in heavy colonial losses.
7. The province of New Jersey was divided into East and West Jersey.
8. I.e., cunningly (from the historical intrigues of the Jesuits, a Roman Catholic order of priests and brothers).

the divisions of street, town, and county do on the smaller ones; distinctions too limited for continental minds. Not one third of the inhabitants, even of this province,[9] are of English descent. Wherefore, I reprobate the phrase of parent or mother country applied to England only, as being false, selfish, narrow and ungenerous.

But, admitting that we were all of English descent, what does it amount to? Nothing. Britain, being now an open enemy, extinguishes every other name and title: and to say that reconciliation is our duty is truly farcical. The first King of England of the present line (William the Conqueror)[1] was a Frenchman, and half the peers of England are descendants from the same country; wherefore, by the same method of reasoning, England ought to be governed by France.

Much hath been said of the united strength of Britain and the colonies, that in conjunction they might bid defiance to the world: but this is mere presumption; the fate of war is uncertain, neither do the expressions mean anything; for this continent would never suffer itself to be drained of inhabitants to support the British arms in either Asia, Africa, or Europe.

Besides, what have we to do with setting the world at defiance? Our plan is commerce, and that, well attended to, will secure us the peace and friendship of all Europe; because it is the interest of all Europe to have America a free port. Her trade will always be a protection, and her barrenness of gold and silver secure her from invaders.

I challenge the warmest advocate for reconciliation to show a single advantage that this continent can reap by being connected with Great Britain. I repeat the challenge; not a single advantage is derived. Our corn[2] will fetch its price in any market in Europe, and our imported goods must be paid for buy them where we will.

But the injuries and disadvantages which we sustain by that connection, are without number; and our duty to mankind at large, as well as to ourselves, instruct us to renounce the alliance: because, any submission to, or dependence on, Great Britain tends directly to involve this continent in European wars and quarrels, and set us at variance with nations who would otherwise seek our friendship, and against whom we have neither anger nor complaint. As Europe is our market for trade, we ought to form no partial connection with any part of it. It is the true interest of America to steer clear of European contentions, which she never can do, while, by her dependence on Britain, she is made the makeweight in the scale of British politics.

Europe is too thickly planted with kingdoms to be long at peace, and whenever a war breaks out between England and any foreign power, the trade of America goes to ruin, because of her connection with Britain. The next war may not turn out like the last, and should it not, the advocates for reconciliation now will be wishing for separation then, because neutrality in that case would be a safer convoy than a man of war.[3] Everything that is right or reasonable pleads for separation. The blood of the slain, the weeping voice of nature cries, " 'Tis time to part." Even the distance at which the Almighty

9. I.e., Pennsylvania.
1. William I (c. 1028–1087; reigned 1066–87) conquered England when he was duke of the French region of Normandy, his homeland.

2. I.e., wheat, not what Americans now call corn.
3. A naval warship. "Like the last": the Seven Years' War ended in Britain's favor.

hath placed England and America is a strong and natural proof that the authority of the one over the other was never the design of Heaven. The time likewise at which the continent was discovered adds weight to the argument, and the manner in which it was peopled increases the force of it. The Reformation was preceded by the discovery of America: as if the Almighty graciously meant to open a sanctuary to the persecuted in future years, when home should afford neither friendship nor safety.

The authority of Great Britain over this continent is a form of government which sooner or later must have an end: and a serious mind can draw no true pleasure by looking forward, under the painful and positive conviction that what he calls "the present constitution" is merely temporary. As parents, we can have no joy, knowing that this government is not sufficiently lasting to insure anything which we may bequeath to posterity: and by a plain method of argument, as we are running the next generation into debt, we ought to do the work of it, otherwise we use them meanly and pitifully. In order to discover the line of our duty rightly, we should take our children in our hand, and fix our station a few years farther into life; that eminence will present a prospect which a few present fears and prejudices conceal from our sight.

Though I would carefully avoid giving unnecessary offense, yet I am inclined to believe that all those who espouse the doctrine of reconciliation may be included within the following descriptions.

Interested men who are not to be trusted, weak men who cannot see, prejudiced men who will not see, and a certain set of moderate men who think better of the European world than it deserves; and this last class, by an ill-judged deliberation, will be the cause of more calamities to this continent than all the other three.

It is the good fortune of many to live distant from the scene of present sorrow; the evil is not sufficiently brought to their doors to make them feel the precariousness with which all American property is possessed. But let our imaginations transport us a few moments to Boston;[4] that seat of wretchedness will teach us wisdom, and instruct us forever to renounce a power in whom we can have no trust. The inhabitants of that unfortunate city, who but a few months ago were in ease and affluence, have now no other alternative than to stay and starve, or turn out to beg. Endangered by the fire of their friends if they continue within the city,[5] and plundered by the soldiery if they leave it, in their present situation they are prisoners without the hope of redemption, and in a general attack for their relief they would be exposed to the fury of both armies.

Men of passive tempers look somewhat lightly over the offenses of Great Britain, and, still hoping for the best, are apt to call out, "Come, come, we shall be friends again for all this." But examine the passions and feelings of mankind: bring the doctrine of reconciliation to the touchstone of nature, and then tell me whether you can hereafter love, honor, and faithfully serve the power that hath carried fire and sword into your land? If you cannot do all these, then are you only deceiving yourselves, and by your delay bringing

4. Boston was under British military occupation and was blockaded for six months.

5. I.e., liable to be caught in "friendly fire" from colonial rebels.

ruin upon posterity. Your future connection with Britain, whom you can neither love nor honor, will be forced and unnatural, and, being formed only on the plan of present convenience, will in a little time fall into a relapse more wretched than the first. But if you say, you can still pass the violations over, then I ask, hath your house been burnt? Hath your property been destroyed before your face? Are your wife and children destitute of a bed to lie on, or bread to live on? Have you lost a parent or a child by their hands, and yourself the ruined and wretched survivor? If you have not, then are you not a judge of those who have. But if you have, and can still shake hands with the murderers, then are you unworthy the name of husband, father, friend, or lover, and whatever may be your rank or title in life, you have the heart of a coward, and the spirit of a sycophant.

This is not inflaming or exaggerating matters, but trying them by those feelings and affections which nature justifies, and without which we should be incapable of discharging the social duties of life, or enjoying the felicities of it. I mean not to exhibit horror for the purpose of provoking revenge, but to awaken us from fatal and unmanly slumbers, that we may pursue determinately some fixed object. 'Tis not in the power of Britain or of Europe to conquer America, if she doth not conquer herself by delay and timidity. The present winter is worth an age if rightly employed, but if lost or neglected the whole continent will partake of the misfortune; and there is no punishment which that man doth not deserve, be he who, or what, or where he will, that may be the means of sacrificing a season so precious and useful.

'Tis repugnant to reason, to the universal order of things, to all examples from former ages, to suppose that this continent can long remain subject to any external power. The most sanguine in Britain doth not think so. The utmost stretch of human wisdom cannot, at this time, compass a plan, short of separation, which can promise the continent even a year's security. Reconciliation is now a fallacious dream. Nature hath deserted the connection, and art cannot supply her place. For, as Milton wisely expresses, "never can true reconcilement grow where wounds of deadly hate have pierced so deep."[6]

* * *

A government of our own is our natural right: and when a man seriously reflects on the precariousness of human affairs, he will become convinced that it is infinitely wiser and safer to form a constitution of our own in a cool deliberate manner, while we have it in our power, than to trust such an interesting event to time and chance. If we omit it now, some Massanello[7] may hereafter arise, who, laying hold of popular disquietudes, may collect together the desperate and the discontented, and by assuming to themselves the powers of government, finally sweep away the liberties of the continent like a deluge. Should the government of America return again into the hands of Britain, the tottering situation of things will be a temptation for some desperate adventurer to try his fortune; and in such a case, what relief can

6. *Paradise Lost* 4.98–99, by the English poet John Milton (1608–1674).
7. Thomas Anello, otherwise Massanello [i.e., Tommaso Aniello (1622–1647), known as Masaniello], a fisherman of Naples, who after spiriting up his countrymen in the public market place, against the oppression of the Spaniards, to whom the place was then subject, prompted them to revolt, and in the space of a day became King [Paine's note].

Britain give? Ere she could hear the news, the fatal business might be done; and ourselves suffering like the wretched Britons under the oppression of the conqueror. Ye that oppose independence now, ye know not what ye do: ye are opening a door to eternal tyranny by keeping vacant the seat of government. There are thousands and tens of thousands, who would think it glorious to expel from the continent that barbarous and hellish power, which hath stirred up the Indians and the Negroes to destroy us; the cruelty hath a double guilt: it is dealing brutally by us, and treacherously by them.

To talk of friendship with those in whom our reason forbids us to have faith, and our affections wounded through a thousand pores instruct us to detest, is madness and folly. Every day wears out the little remains of kindred between us and them; and can there be any reason to hope, that as the relationship expires, the affection will increase, or that we shall agree better when we have ten times more and greater concerns to quarrel over than ever?

Ye that tell us of harmony and reconciliation, can ye restore to us the time that is past? Can ye give to prostitution its former innocence? Neither can ye reconcile Britain and America. The last cord now is broken, the people of England are presenting addresses against us. There are injuries which nature cannot forgive; she would cease to be nature if she did. As well can the lover forgive the ravisher of his mistress, as the continent forgive the murders of Britain. The Almighty hath implanted in us these unextinguishable feelings for good and wise purposes. They are the guardians of His image in our hearts. They distinguish us from the herd of common animals. The social compact would dissolve, and justice be extirpated from the earth, or have only a casual existence were we callous to the touches of affection. The robber and the murderer would often escape unpunished, did not the injuries which our tempers sustain provoke us into justice.

O! ye that love mankind! Ye that dare oppose not only the tyranny but the tyrant, stand forth! Every spot of the old world is overrun with oppression. Freedom hath been hunted round the globe. Asia and Africa have long expelled her. Europe regards her like a stranger, and England hath given her warning to depart. O! receive the fugitive, and prepare in time an asylum[8] for mankind.

1776

The Crisis, No. 1[9]

These are the times that try men's souls. The summer soldier and the sunshine patriot will, in this crisis, shrink from the service of their country; but he that stands it now, deserves the love and thanks of man and woman. Tyranny, like hell, is not easily conquered; yet we have this consolation with us,

8. Refuge.
9. Paine sometimes referred to this essay, the first of the sixteen Crisis pamphlets, as The American Crisis. In one week in 1776, he published three editions: one undated, one dated December 19, and the one reprinted here, dated December 23. The text is from The Writings of Thomas Paine (1894–96), vol. 1, edited by M. D. Conway.

that the harder the conflict, the more glorious the triumph. What we obtain too cheap, we esteem too lightly: it is dearness[1] only that gives everything its value. Heaven knows how to put a proper price upon its goods; and it would be strange indeed if so celestial an article as freedom should not be highly rated. Britain, with an army to enforce her tyranny, has declared that she has a right (not only to tax) but "to bind us in all cases whatsoever,"[2] and if being bound in that manner is not slavery, then is there not such a thing as slavery upon earth. Even the expression is impious; for so unlimited a power can belong only to God.

Whether the independence of the continent was declared too soon, or delayed too long, I will not now enter into as an argument; my own simple opinion is, that had it been eight months earlier, it would have been much better. We did not make a proper use of last winter, neither could we, while we were in a dependent state. However, the fault, if it were one, was all our own;[3] we have none to blame but ourselves. But no great deal is lost yet. All that Howe has been doing for this month past is rather a ravage than a conquest, which the spirit of the Jerseys,[4] a year ago, would have quickly repulsed, and which time and a little resolution will soon recover.

I have as little superstition in me as any man living, but my secret opinion has ever been, and still is, that God Almighty will not give up a people to military destruction, or leave them unsupportedly to perish, who have so earnestly and so repeatedly sought to avoid the calamities of war, by every decent method which wisdom could invent. Neither have I so much of the infidel in me as to suppose that He has relinquished the government of the world, and given us up to the care of devils; and as I do not, I cannot see on what grounds the King of Britain can look up to heaven for help against us: a common murderer, a highwayman, or a housebreaker has as good a pretense as he.

'Tis surprising to see how rapidly a panic will sometimes run through a country. All nations and ages have been subject to them: Britain has trembled like an ague[5] at the report of a French fleet of flat-bottomed boats; and in the fourteenth century the whole English army, after ravaging the kingdom of France, was driven back like men petrified with fear; and this brave exploit was performed by a few broken forces collected and headed by a woman, Joan of Arc.[6] Would that heaven might inspire some Jersey maid to spirit up her countrymen, and save her fair fellow sufferers from ravage and ravishment! Yet panics, in some cases, have their uses; they produce as much good as hurt. Their duration is always short; the mind soon grows through

1. Costliness.
2. Cf. the Second Continental Congress's "Declaration Setting Forth the Causes and Necessity of [the Massachusetts Assembly's] Taking Up Arms" (July 6, 1775): "By one statute [Parliament's Declaratory Act of 1766] it is declared that Parliament can 'of right make laws to bind us in all cases whatsoever.' What is to defend us against so enormous, so unlimited a power?"
3. "The present winter is worth an age, if rightly employed; but, if lost or neglected, the whole continent will partake of the evil; and there is no punishment that man does not deserve, be he who, or what, or where he will, that may be the means of sacrificing a season so precious and useful" [Paine's note, taken from *Common Sense*]. Paine wanted an immediate declaration of independence, uniting the colonies and enlisting the aid of France and Spain.
4. The province of New Jersey was divided into East and West Jersey. Lord William Howe (1729–1814), commander of the British Army in America (1775–78).
5. I.e., like one who is chilled.
6. Joan of Arc (1412–1431) led the French to victory over the English in 1429 (not "the fourteenth century").

them, and acquires a firmer habit than before. But their peculiar advantage is that they are the touchstones of sincerity and hypocrisy, and bring things and men to light, which might otherwise have lain forever undiscovered. In fact, they have the same effect on secret traitors, which an imaginary apparition would have upon a private murderer. They sift out the hidden thoughts of man, and hold them up in public to the world. Many a disguised tory[7] has lately shown his head, that shall penitentially solemnize with curses the day on which Howe arrived upon the Delaware.[8]

As I was with the troops at Fort Lee, and marched with them to the edge of Pennsylvania, I am well acquainted with many circumstances, which those who live at a distance know but little or nothing of. Our situation there was exceedingly cramped, the place being a narrow neck of land between the North River[9] and the Hackensack. Our force was inconsiderable, being not one fourth so great as Howe could bring against us. We had no army at hand to have relieved the garrison, had we shut ourselves up and stood on our defense. Our ammunition, light artillery, and the best part of our stores had been removed on the apprehension that Howe would endeavor to penetrate the Jerseys, in which case Fort Lee could be of no use to us; for it must occur to every thinking man, whether in the army or not, that these kind of field forts are only for temporary purposes, and last in use no longer than the enemy directs his force against the particular object, which such forts are raised to defend. Such was our situation and condition at Fort Lee on the morning of the 20th of November, when an officer arrived with information that the enemy with 200 boats had landed about seven miles above: Major General Green,[1] who commanded the garrison, immediately ordered them under arms, and sent express to General Washington at the town of Hackensack, distant, by the way of the ferry, six miles. Our first object was to secure the bridge over the Hackensack, which laid up the river between the enemy and us, about six miles from us, and three from them. General Washington arrived in about three quarters of an hour, and marched at the head of the troops towards the bridge, which place I expected we should have a brush for; however, they did not choose to dispute it with us, and the greatest part of our troops went over the bridge, the rest over the ferry, except some which passed at a mill on a small creek, between the bridge and the ferry, and made their way through some marshy grounds up to the town of Hackensack, and there passed the river. We brought off as much baggage as the wagons could contain, the rest was lost. The simple object was to bring off the garrison, and march them on till they could be strengthened by the Jersey or Pennsylvania militia, so as to be enabled to make a stand. We staid four days at Newark, collected our outposts with some of the Jersey militia, and marched out twice to meet the enemy, on being informed that they were advancing, though our numbers were greatly inferior to theirs. Howe, in my little opinion, committed a great error in generalship in not throwing a body of forces off from Staten Island through Amboy, by which means he might have seized all our stores at Brunswick, and intercepted our march into

7. Supporter of the king.
8. The Delaware River, which played a major part in the 1776 battles—in New York, New Jersey, and Pennsylvania—that Paine details below.

9. The Hudson River.
1. Major General Nathanael Greene (1742–1786). Paine was his aide-de-camp.

Pennsylvania; but if we believe the power of hell to be limited, we must likewise believe that their agents are under some providential control.[2]

I shall not now attempt to give all the particulars of our retreat to the Delaware; suffice it for the present to say, that both officers and men, though greatly harassed and fatigued, frequently without rest, covering, or provision, the inevitable consequences of a long retreat, bore it with a manly and martial spirit. All their wishes centered in one, which was that the country would turn out and help them to drive the enemy back. Voltaire has remarked that King William never appeared to full advantage but in difficulties and in action;[3] the same remark may be made on General Washington, for the character fits him. There is a natural firmness in some minds which cannot be unlocked by trifles, but which, when unlocked, discovers a cabinet[4] of fortitude; and I reckon it among those kind of public blessings, which we do not immediately see, that God hath blessed him with uninterrupted health, and given him a mind that can even flourish upon care.

I shall conclude this paper with some miscellaneous remarks on the state of our affairs; and shall begin with asking the following question: Why is it that the enemy have left the New England provinces, and made these middle ones the seat of war? The answer is easy: New England is not infested with tories, and we are. I have been tender in raising the cry against these men, and used numberless arguments to show them their danger, but it will not do to sacrifice a world either to their folly or their baseness. The period is now arrived, in which either they or we must change our sentiments, or one or both must fall. And what is a tory? Good God! what is he? I should not be afraid to go with a hundred whigs[5] against a thousand tories, were they to attempt to get into arms. Every tory is a coward; for servile, slavish, self-interested fear is the foundation of toryism; and a man under such influence, though he may be cruel, never can be brave.

But, before the line of irrecoverable separation be drawn between us, let us reason the matter together: Your conduct is an invitation to the enemy, yet not one in a thousand of you has heart enough to join him. Howe is as much deceived by you as the American cause is injured by you. He expects you will all take up arms, and flock to his standard, with muskets on your shoulders. Your opinions are of no use to him, unless you support him personally, for 'tis soldiers, and not tories, that he wants.

I once felt all that kind of anger, which a man ought to feel, against the mean principles that are held by the tories: a noted one, who kept a tavern at Amboy,[6] was standing at his door, with as pretty a child in his hand, about eight or nine years old, as I ever saw, and after speaking his mind as freely as he thought was prudent, finished with this unfatherly expression, "Well! give me peace in my day." Not a man lives on the continent but fully believes that a separation must some time or other finally take place, and a generous parent should have said, "If there must be trouble, let it be in my day, that my child may have peace"; and this single reflection, well applied, is suffi-

2. The American losses were larger than Paine implies. General Howe took three thousand prisoners and a large store of military supplies when he captured Fort Lee.
3. The French writer François-Marie Arouet (1694–1778), known as Voltaire, made this remark about King William III of England (1650–1702) in his *History of Louis the Fourteenth*.
4. Storehouse.
5. Supporters of the Revolution.
6. Paine was stationed at Perth Amboy, New Jersey, while in the Continental Army.

cient to awaken every man to duty. Not a place upon earth might be so happy as America. Her situation is remote from all the wrangling world, and she has nothing to do but to trade with them. A man can distinguish himself between temper and principle, and I am as confident, as I am that God governs the world, that America will never be happy till she gets clear of foreign dominion. Wars, without ceasing, will break out till that period arrives, and the continent must in the end be conqueror; for though the flame of liberty may sometimes cease to shine, the coal can never expire.

America did not, nor does not, want[7] force; but she wanted a proper application of that force. Wisdom is not the purchase of a day, and it is no wonder that we should err at the first setting off. From an excess of tenderness, we were unwilling to raise an army, and trusted our cause to the temporary defense of a well-meaning militia. A summer's experience has now taught us better; yet with those troops, while they were collected, we were able to set bounds to the progress of the enemy, and thank God! they are again assembling. I always considered militia as the best troops in the world for a sudden exertion, but they will not do for a long campaign. Howe, it is probable, will make an attempt on this city;[8] should he fail on this side of the Delaware, he is ruined: if he succeeds, our cause is not ruined. He stakes all on his side against a part on ours; admitting[9] he succeeds, the consequence will be that armies from both ends of the continent will march to assist their suffering friends in the middle states; for he cannot go everywhere, it is impossible. I consider Howe as the greatest enemy the tories have; he is bringing a war into their country, which, had it not been for him and partly for themselves, they had been clear of. Should he now be expelled, I wish with all the devotion of a Christian, that the names of whig and tory may never more be mentioned; but should the tories give him encouragement to come, or assistance if he come, I as sincerely wish that our next year's arms may expel them from the continent, and the congress appropriate their possessions to the relief of those who have suffered in well-doing. A single successful battle next year will settle the whole. America could carry on a two years' war by the confiscation of the property of disaffected persons, and be made happy by their expulsion. Say not that this is revenge; call it rather the soft resentment of a suffering people, who, having no object in view but the good of all, have staked their own all upon a seemingly doubtful event. Yet it is folly to argue against determined hardness; eloquence may strike the ear, and the language of sorrow draw forth the tear of compassion, but nothing can reach the heart that is steeled with prejudice.

Quitting this class of men, I turn with the warm ardor of a friend to those who have nobly stood, and are yet determined to stand the matter out: I call not upon a few, but upon all: not on this state or that state, but on every state: up and help us; lay your shoulders to the wheel; better have too much force than too little, when so great an object is at stake. Let it be told to the future world that in the depth of winter, when nothing but hope and virtue could survive, that the city and the country, alarmed at one common danger, came forth to meet and to repulse it. Say not that thousands are gone,

7. Lack.
8. I.e., Philadelphia.
9. If.

turn out your tens of thousands;[1] throw not the burden of the day upon Providence, but "show your faith by your works"[2] that God may bless you. It matters not where you live, or what rank of life you hold, the evil or the blessing will reach you all. The far and the near, the home counties and the back,[3] the rich and poor will suffer or rejoice alike. The heart that feels not now is dead: the blood of his children will curse his cowardice who shrinks back at a time when a little might have saved the whole, and made them happy. I love the man that can smile in trouble, that can gather strength from distress, and grow brave by reflection. 'Tis the business of little minds to shrink; but he whose heart is firm, and whose conscience approves his conduct, will pursue his principles unto death. My own line of reasoning is to myself as straight and clear as a ray of light. Not all the treasures of the world, so far as I believe, could have induced me to support an offensive war, for I think it murder; but if a thief breaks into my house, burns and destroys my property, and kills or threatens to kill me, or those that are in it, and to "bind me in all cases whatsoever" to his absolute will, am I to suffer it? What signifies it to me, whether he who does it is a king or a common man; my countryman or not my countryman; whether it be done by an individual villain, or an army of them? If we reason to the root of things we shall find no difference; neither can any just cause be assigned why we should punish in the one case and pardon in the other. Let them call me rebel, and welcome, I feel no concern from it; but I should suffer the misery of devils were I to make a whore of my soul by swearing allegiance to one whose character is that of a sottish, stupid, stubborn, worthless, brutish man. I conceive likewise a horrid idea in receiving mercy from a being, who at the last day shall be shrieking to the rocks and mountains to cover him, and fleeing with terror from the orphan, the widow, and the slain of America.

There are cases which cannot be overdone by language, and this is one. There are persons, too, who see not the full extent of the evil which threatens them; they solace themselves with hopes that the enemy, if he succeed, will be merciful. It is the madness of folly to expect mercy from those who have refused to do justice; and even mercy, where conquest is the object, is only a trick of war; the cunning of the fox is as murderous as the violence of the wolf, and we ought to guard equally against both. Howe's first object is, partly by threats and partly by promises, to terrify or seduce the people to deliver up their arms and receive mercy. The ministry recommended the same plan to Gage, and this is what the tories call making their peace, "a peace which passeth all understanding"[4] indeed! A peace which would be the immediate forerunner of a worse ruin than any we have yet thought of. Ye men of Pennsylvania, do reason upon these things! Were the back counties to give up their arms, they would fall an easy prey to the Indians, who are all armed: this perhaps is what some tories would not be sorry for. Were the home counties to deliver up their arms, they would be exposed to the resentment of the back counties, who would then have it in their power to

1. "Saul hath slain his thousands, and David his ten thousands" (1 Samuel 18.7).
2. "Shew me thy faith without thy works, and I will shew thee my faith by my works" (James 2.18).
3. I.e., the backwoods.

4. "And the peace of God, which passeth all understanding, shall keep your hearts and minds through Christ Jesus" (Philippians 4.7). General Thomas Gage (1721–1787) commanded the British armies in America from 1763 to 1775, before Howe.

chastise their defection at pleasure. And were any one state to give up its arms, that state must be garrisoned by all Howe's army of Britons and Hessians[5] to preserve it from the anger of the rest. Mutual fear is the principal link in the chain of mutual love, and woe be to that state that breaks the compact. Howe is mercifully inviting you to barbarous destruction, and men must be either rogues or fools that will not see it. I dwell not upon the vapors of imagination: I bring reason to your ears, and, in language as plain as A, B, C, hold up truth to your eyes.

I thank God that I fear not. I see no real cause for fear. I know our situation well, and can see the way out of it. While our army was collected, Howe dared not risk a battle; and it is no credit to him that he decamped from the White Plains,[6] and waited a mean opportunity to ravage the defenseless Jerseys; but it is great credit to us, that, with a handful of men, we sustained an orderly retreat for near an hundred miles, brought off our ammunition, all our field pieces, the greatest part of our stores, and had four rivers to pass. None can say that our retreat was precipitate, for we were near three weeks in performing it, that the country[7] might have time to come in. Twice we marched back to meet the enemy, and remained out till dark. The sign of fear was not seen in our camp, and had not some of the cowardly and disaffected inhabitants spread false alarms through the country, the Jerseys had never been ravaged. Once more we are again collected and collecting; our new army at both ends of the continent is recruiting fast, and we shall be able to open the next campaign with sixty thousand men, well armed and clothed. This is our situation, and who will may know it. By perseverance and fortitude we have the prospect of a glorious issue; by cowardice and submission, the sad choice of a variety of evils—a ravaged country—a depopulated city—habitations without safety, and slavery without hope—our homes turned into barracks and bawdyhouses for Hessians, and a future race to provide for, whose fathers we shall doubt of. Look on this picture and weep over it! and if there yet remains one thoughtless wretch who believes it not, let him suffer it unlamented.

Common Sense

1776

From The Age of Reason[1]

Chapter I. The Author's Profession of Faith

It has been my intention, for several years past, to publish my thoughts upon religion; I am well aware of the difficulties that attend the subject, and from that consideration had reserved it to a more advanced period of life. I intended it to be the last offering I should make to my fellow citizens of all nations, and that at a time when the purity of the motive that induced me to it could not admit of a question, even by those who might disapprove the work.

5. German mercenaries.
6. In New York, where, on October 28, 1776, General Howe successfully overcame Washington's troops but failed to take full advantage of

his victory.
7. I.e., the local volunteers.
1. The text is from *The Writings of Thomas Paine* (1894–96), vol. 4, edited by M. D. Conway.

The circumstance that has now taken place in France, of the total abolition of the whole national order of priesthood, and of everything appertaining to compulsive systems of religion, and compulsive articles of faith,[2] has not only precipitated my intention, but rendered a work of this kind exceedingly necessary lest, in the general wreck of superstition, of false systems of government, and false theology, we lose sight of morality, of humanity, and of the theology that is true.

As several of my colleagues and others of my fellow citizens of France have given me the example of making their voluntary and individual profession of faith, I also will make mine; and I do this with all that sincerity and frankness with which the mind of man communicates with itself.

I believe in one God, and no more; and I hope for happiness beyond this life.

I believe in the equality of man, and I believe that religious duties consist in doing justice, loving mercy, and endeavoring to make our fellow creatures happy.

But, lest it should be supposed that I believe many other things in addition to these, I shall, in the progress of this work, declare the things I do not believe, and my reasons for not believing them.

I do not believe in the creed professed by the Jewish church, by the Roman church, by the Greek church, by the Turkish church, by the Protestant church, nor by any church that I know of. My own mind is my own church.

All national institutions of churches, whether Jewish, Christian, or Turkish, appear to me no other than human inventions set up to terrify and enslave mankind, and monopolize power and profit.

I do not mean by this declaration to condemn those who believe otherwise; they have the same right to their belief as I have to mine. But it is necessary to the happiness of man that he be mentally faithful to himself. Infidelity does not consist in believing, or in disbelieving; it consists in professing to believe what he does not believe.

It is impossible to calculate the moral mischief, if I may so express it, that mental lying has produced in society. When a man has so far corrupted and prostituted the chastity of his mind as to subscribe his professional belief to things he does not believe, he has prepared himself for the commission of every other crime. He takes up the trade of a priest for the sake of gain, and, in order to qualify himself for that trade, he begins with a perjury. Can we conceive anything more destructive to morality than this?

Soon after I had published the pamphlet *Common Sense,* in America, I saw the exceeding probability that a revolution in the system of government would be followed by a revolution in the system of religion. The adulterous connection of church and state, wherever it had taken place, whether Jewish, Christian, or Turkish, had so effectually prohibited, by pains and penalties, every discussion upon established creeds and upon first principles of religion, that until the system of government should be changed, those subjects could not be brought fairly and openly before the world; but that whenever this should be done, a revolution in the system of religion would follow.

2. By 1792, leaders of the French Revolution had discredited the Roman Catholic Church in France and closed the churches.

Human inventions and priestcraft would be detected; and man would return to the pure, unmixed, and unadulterated belief of one God, and no more.

Chapter II. Of Missions and Revelations

Every national church or religion has established itself by pretending some special mission from God, communicated to certain individuals. The Jews have their Moses; the Christians their Jesus Christ, their apostles and saints; and the Turks their Mahomet;[3] as if the way to God was not open to every man alike.

Each of those churches shows certain books, which they call revelation, or the Word of God. The Jews say that their Word of God was given by God to Moses face to face; the Christians say that their Word of God came by divine inspiration; and the Turks say that their Word of God (the Koran) was brought by an angel from heaven. Each of those churches accuses the other of unbelief; and, for my own part, I disbelieve them all.

As it is necessary to affix right ideas to words, I will, before I proceed further into the subject, offer some observations on the word revelation. Revelation when applied to religion, means something communicated immediately from God to man.

No one will deny or dispute the power of the Almighty to make such a communication if He pleases. But admitting, for the sake of a case, that something has been revealed to a certain person, and not revealed to any other person, it is revelation to that person only. When he tells it to a second person, a second to a third, a third to a fourth, and so on, it ceases to be a revelation to all those persons. It is revelation to the first person only, and hearsay to every other, and, consequently, they are not obliged to believe it.

It is a contradiction in terms and ideas to call anything a revelation that comes to us at secondhand, either verbally or in writing. Revelation is necessarily limited to the first communication. After this, it is only an account of something which that person says was a revelation made to him; and though he may find himself obliged to believe it, it cannot be incumbent on me to believe it in the same manner, for it was not a revelation made to me, and I have only his word for it that it was made to him.

When Moses told the children of Israel that he received the two tables of the commandments from the hand of God, they were not obliged to believe him, because they had no other authority for it than his telling them so; and I have no other authority for it than some historian telling me so, the commandments carrying no internal evidence of divinity with them. They contain some good moral precepts such as any man qualified to be a lawgiver or a legislator could produce himself, without having recourse to supernatural intervention.[4]

When I am told that the Koran was written in Heaven, and brought to Mahomet by an angel, the account comes to near the same kind of hearsay

3. The prophet Muhammad (c. 570–632), founder of Islam. "Moses": Old Testament prophet, traditionally considered the author of the first five Books of the Bible.
4. It is, however, necessary to except the decla- ration which says that God *visits the sins of the fathers upon the children* [see, e.g., Exodus 34. 6–7]. This is contrary to every principle of moral justice [Paine's note].

evidence and secondhand authority as the former. I did not see the angel myself, and therefore I have a right not to believe it.

When also I am told that a woman, called the Virgin Mary, said, or gave out, that she was with child without any cohabitation with a man, and that her betrothed husband, Joseph, said that an angel told him so, I have a right to believe them or not: such a circumstance required a much stronger evidence than their bare word for it: but we have not even this; for neither Joseph nor Mary wrote any such matter themselves. It is only reported by others that they said so. It is hearsay upon hearsay, and I do not choose to rest my belief upon such evidence.

It is, however, not difficult to account for the credit that was given to the story of Jesus Christ being the Son of God. He was born when the heathen mythology had still some fashion and repute in the world, and that mythology had prepared the people for the belief of such a story. Almost all the extraordinary men that lived under the heathen mythology were reputed to be the sons of some of their gods. It was not a new thing at that time to believe a man to have been celestially begotten; the intercourse of gods with women was then a matter of familiar opinion. Their Jupiter,[5] according to their accounts, had cohabited with hundreds; the story therefore had nothing in it either new, wonderful, or obscene; it was conformable to the opinions that then prevailed among the people called Gentiles, or mythologists, and it was those people only that believed it. The Jews, who had kept strictly to the belief of one god, and no more, and who had always rejected the heathen mythology, never credited the story.

It is curious to observe how the theory of what is called the Christian Church, sprung out of the tail of the heathen mythology. A direct incorporation took place in the first instance, by making the reputed founder to be celestially begotten. The trinity of gods that then followed was no other than a reduction of the former plurality, which was about twenty or thirty thousand. The statue of Mary succeeded the statue of Diana of Ephesus.[6] The deification of heroes changed into the canonization of saints. The mythologists had gods for everything; the Christian mythologists had saints for everything. The church became as crowded with the one, as the Pantheon[7] had been with the other; and Rome was the place of both. The Christian theory is little else than the idolatry of the ancient mythologists, accommodated to the purposes of power and revenue; and it yet remains to reason and philosophy to abolish the amphibious[8] fraud.

Chapter XI. Of the Theology of the Christians, and the True Theology

As to the Christian system of faith, it appears to me as a species of atheism; a sort of religious denial of God. It professes to believe in a man rather than in God. It is a compound made up chiefly of man-ism with but little deism, and is as near to atheism as twilight is to darkness. It introduces between man and his Maker an opaque body, which it calls a redeemer, as the moon introduces her opaque self between the earth and the sun, and it produces

5. Roman god of the heavens, king of the gods.
6. In the ancient city of Ephesus, in Asia Minor, a temple honored the Greek fertility goddess Artemis. The Romans identified Artemis with Diana, their virgin goddess of women and childbirth.
7. A temple in Rome dedicated to all the gods.
8. Combining two characteristics.

by this means a religious or an irreligious eclipse of light. It has put the whole orbit of reason into shade.

The effect of this obscurity has been that of turning everything upside down, and representing it in reverse; and among the revolutions it has thus magically produced, it has made a revolution in theology.

That which is now called natural philosophy, embracing the whole circle of science, of which astronomy occupies the chief place, is the study of the works of God, and of the power and wisdom of God in His works, and is the true theology.

As to the theology that is now studied in its place, it is the study of human opinions and of human fancies concerning God. It is not the study of God Himself in the works that He has made, but in the works or writings that man has made; and it is not among the least of the mischiefs that the Christian system has done to the world, that it has abandoned the original and beautiful system of theology, like a beautiful innocent, to distress and reproach, to make room for the hag of superstition.

The Book of Job and the 19th Psalm, which even the church admits to be more ancient than the chronological order in which they stand in the book called the Bible, are theological orations conformable to the original system of theology.[9] The internal evidence of those orations proves to [be] a demonstration that the study and contemplation of the works of creation, and of the power and wisdom of God revealed and manifested in those works, made [up] a great part of the religious devotion of the times in which they were written; and it was this devotional study and contemplation that led to the discovery of the principles upon which what are now called sciences are established; and it is to the discovery of these principles that almost all the arts that contribute to the convenience of human life owe their existence. Every principal art has some science for its parent, though the person who mechanically performs the work does not always, and but very seldom, perceive the connection.

It is a fraud of the Christian system to call the sciences human inventions; it is only the application of them that is human. Every science has for its basis a system of principles as fixed and unalterable as those by which the universe is regulated and governed. Man cannot make principles; he can only discover them.

For example: every person who looks at an almanac sees an account when an eclipse will take place, and he sees also that it never fails to take place according to the account there given. This shows that man is acquainted with the laws by which the heavenly bodies move. But it would be something worse than ignorance, were any church on earth to say that those laws are an human invention.

It would also be ignorance, or something worse, to say that the scientific principles, by the aid of which man is enabled to calculate and foreknow when an eclipse will take place, are an human invention. Man cannot invent

9. In the Old Testament, Job comes before the Book of Psalms, but the author of Job alludes to some lines of Psalms, which must have come earlier. Paine thinks that both Job and Psalm 19 ("The heavens declare the glory of God; and the firmament sheweth his handiwork") conform "to the original system of theology," because they convey immediate responses to the world that God made.

anything that is eternal and immutable; and the scientific principles he employs for this purpose must, and are, of necessity, as eternal and immutable as the laws by which the heavenly bodies move, or they could not be used as they are to ascertain the time when, and the manner how, an eclipse will take place.

The scientific principles that man employs to obtain the foreknowledge of an eclipse, or of anything else relating to the motion of the heavenly bodies, are contained chiefly in that part of science that is called trigonometry, or the properties of a triangle, which, when applied to the study of the heavenly bodies, is called astronomy; when applied to direct the course of a ship on the ocean, it is called navigation; when applied to the construction of figures drawn by a rule and compass, it is called geometry; when applied to the construction of plans of edifices, it is called architecture; when applied to the measurement of any portion of the surface of the earth, it is called land surveying. In fine, it is the soul of science. It is an eternal truth: it contains the mathematical demonstration of which man speaks, and the extent of its uses are unknown.

It may be said, that man can make or draw a triangle, and therefore a triangle is an human invention.

But the triangle, when drawn, is no other than the image of the principle: it is a delineation to the eye, and from thence to the mind, of a principle that would otherwise be imperceptible. The triangle does not make the principle any more than a candle taken into a room that was dark makes the chairs and tables that before were invisible. All the properties of a triangle exist independently of the figure, and existed before any triangle was drawn or thought of by man. Man had no more to do in the formation of those properties or principles than he had to do in making the laws by which the heavenly bodies move; and therefore the one must have the same divine origin as the other.

In the same manner as, it may be said, that man can make a triangle, so also, may it be said, he can make the mechanical instrument called a lever. But the principle by which the lever acts is a thing distinct from the instrument, and would exist if the instrument did not; it attaches itself to the instrument after it is made; the instrument, therefore, can act no otherwise than it does act; neither can all the efforts of human invention make it act otherwise. That which, in all such cases, man calls the effect, is no other than the principle itself rendered perceptible to the senses.

Since, then, man cannot make principles, from whence did he gain a knowledge of them, so as to be able to apply them, not only to things on earth, but to ascertain the motion of bodies so immensely distant from him as all the heavenly bodies are? From whence, I ask, could he gain that knowledge, but from the study of the true theology?

It is the structure of the universe that has taught this knowledge to man. That structure is an ever-existing exhibition of every principle upon which every part of mathematical science is founded. The offspring of this science is mechanics; for mechanics is no other than the principles of science applied practically. The man who proportions the several parts of a mill uses the same scientific principles as if he had the power of constructing an universe, but as he cannot give to matter that invisible agency by which all the component parts of the immense machine of the universe have influence upon

each other, and act in motional unison together, without any apparent contact, and to which man has given the name of attraction, gravitation, and repulsion, he supplies the place of that agency by the humble imitation of teeth and cogs. All the parts of man's microcosm must visibly touch. But could he gain a knowledge of that agency, so as to be able to apply it in practice, we might then say that another canonical book of the word of God[1] had been discovered.

If man could alter the properties of the lever, so also could he alter the properties of the triangle: for a lever (taking that sort of lever which is called a steelyard, for the sake of explanation) forms, when in motion, a triangle. The line it descends from (one point of that line being in the fulcrum), the line it descends to, and the chord of the arc, which the end of the lever describes in the air, are the three sides of a triangle. The other arm of the lever describes also a triangle; and the corresponding sides of those two triangles, calculated scientifically, or measured geometrically—and also the sines, tangents, and secants generated from the angles, and geometrically measured—have the same proportions to each other as the different weights have that will balance each other on the lever, leaving the weight of the lever out of the case.

It may also be said that man can make a wheel and axis; that he can put wheels of different magnitudes together, and produce a mill. Still the case comes back to the same point, which is, that he did not make the principle that gives the wheels those powers. This principle is as unalterable as in the former cases, or rather it is the same principle under a different appearance to the eye.

The power that two wheels of different magnitudes have upon each other is in the same proportion as if the semidiameter of the two wheels were joined together and made into that kind of lever I have described, suspended at the part where the semidiameters join; for the two wheels, scientifically considered, are no other than the two circles generated by the motion of the compound lever.

It is from the study of the true theology that all our knowledge of science is derived; and it is from that knowledge that all the arts have originated.

The Almighty lecturer, by displaying the principles of science in the structure of the universe, has invited man to study and to imitation. It is as if He had said to the inhabitants of this globe that we call ours, "I have made an earth for man to dwell upon, and I have rendered the starry heavens visible, to teach him science and the arts. He can now provide for his own comfort, and learn from my munificence to all, to be kind to each other."

Of what use is it, unless it be to teach man something, that his eye is endowed with the power of beholding, to an incomprehensible distance, an immensity of worlds revolving in the ocean of space? Or of what use is it that this immensity of worlds is visible to man? What has man to do with the Pleiades, with Orion, with Sirius, with the star he calls the North Star, with the moving orbs he has named Saturn, Jupiter, Mars, Venus, and Mercury, if no uses are to follow from their being visible? A less power of vision would have been sufficient for man, if the immensity he now possesses were

1. I.e., a book that would form a part of Scripture.

given only to waste itself, as it were, on an immense desert of space glittering with shows.

It is only by contemplating what he calls the starry heavens, as the book and school of science, that he discovers any use in their being visible to him, or any advantage resulting from his immensity of vision. But when he contemplates the subject in this light, he sees an additional motive for saying, that nothing was made in vain; for in vain would be this power of vision if it taught man nothing.

1793 1794

THOMAS JEFFERSON
1743–1826

In June 1776, the Second Continental Congress met in Philadelphia to consider whether to declare their alliance of colonies independent of Great Britain. The delegates turned to a thirty-two-year-old representative from Virginia, Thomas Jefferson, to be the principal drafter of a statement that the full congress would then debate, amend, and vote to either accept or reject. Jefferson was an awkward speaker but a talented prose stylist, and his reputation as a writer had preceded him to Philadelphia. While serving in the Virginia House of Burgesses in 1774, he had written an influential and daring pamphlet, A Summary View of the Rights of British America, which denied all parliamentary authority over America and argued that ties to the British monarchy were voluntary and not irrevocable. On June 11, 1776, after some maneuvering by John Adams, Jefferson was chosen to head the committee charged with drafting a declaration of independence. The other members of the committee who helped Jefferson refine his draft were Adams, Benjamin Franklin, Roger Sherman, and Robert Livingston. On June 28, the draft declaration was presented to Congress, where it underwent some further modifications before it could pass unanimously, as it did on July 4. These alterations were a source of regret to Jefferson. In his Autobiography (1829), he included the original draft and indicated changes made by the Congress.

One of the omitted passages speaks to a central tension of Jefferson's legacy. Admired as a prophet of equality and liberty, he is also widely recognized as an owner of some two hundred slaves, including several men and women who were most likely his children with the enslaved woman Sally Hemings. This paradox in Jefferson's personal life resonates with a larger circumstance memorably captured by the English writer Samuel Johnson in his 1775 pamphlet "Taxation No Tyranny." "Why is it," Johnson asked, "we hear the loudest yelps for liberty among the drivers of negroes?" In his draft declaration, Jefferson seeks to turn the tables by blaming George III, "the christian king of Great Britain," for refusing to allow the colonists to limit the slave trade and inciting enslaved people "to rise in arms among us, . . . thus paying off former crimes committed against the LIBERTIES of one people, with crimes which he urges them to commit against the lives of another." In this formulation, Jefferson proposes an equivalence between the colonists, who are said to be resisting "slavery" to Great Britain, and those subjected to race-based chattel

slavery. At the same time, he invokes the specter of racial warfare—of whites against the "merciless Indian savages" as well as black slaves—to unite the colonists against the Crown.

Jefferson wrote his *Autobiography* in 1821, and he may have been prompted to restore this passage of the draft declaration by a national crisis regarding whether to admit Missouri to the Union as a slave state and Maine as a free state. On March 3, 1820, the Missouri Compromise legislated a balance between free and slave states. Writing of the slave system in April 1820, he observed that "we have the wolf by the ear, and we can neither hold him, nor safely let him go. Justice is in one scale, and self-preservation in the other." As the restored text of the Declaration shows, Jefferson's fear of race war had long been a powerful—and powerfully distorting—factor in his thought. In the 1780s, it led him in *Notes on the State of Virginia* to support the colonization movement that sought to remove people of African descent from the United States.

Jefferson's complex stance is related to his roots in the Virginia planter society that had developed over the eighteenth century. He was born at the Shadwell plantation, in what is now Albemarle County, Virginia. His mother, Jane Randolph, came from one of the state's most prominent families. His father, Peter Jefferson, was a county official and surveyor. When Thomas was fourteen, his father died, and he inherited twenty-seven hundred acres of land and slaves to work it. Over the years he added to this expanse of property, which reached a peak of almost ten thousand acres.

In 1760 Jefferson entered the College of William and Mary, in Williamsburg, the capital of Virginia. There Jefferson met three men who strongly influenced his life: Governor Francis Fauquier, a fellow of the Royal Society, a famous scientific organization based in England; George Wythe, one of the best teachers of law in the colonies; and Dr. William Small, an emigrant from Scotland who introduced Jefferson to the Scottish Enlightenment, including the work of Francis Hutcheson, author of *An Inquiry into the Original of Our Ideas of Beauty and Virtue* (1725), and Henry Home, Lord Kames, author of *Essays on the Principles of Morality and Natural Religion* (1751), whose ideas shaped his aesthetic and political thought. Jefferson remained in Williamsburg to study law after graduation and was admitted to the bar in 1765.

Three years later he began clearing the mountaintop at his plantation, named Monticello, Italian for "little mountain." There, he eventually built the neoclassical mansion of his own design, completing the project in 1808. The year after he started his building project, he was elected to the Virginia House of Burgesses and began a prominent career in the legislature. After serving in the Continental Congress during the catalytic summer of 1776, he left to take up a seat in the Virginia House of Delegates that September. He was elected governor in 1779 and reelected the following year. Jefferson's term of office came to an ignominious end after the British captured Richmond in 1781. Jefferson and the legislature moved to Charlottesville, and he and the legislators barely escaped imprisonment when the pursuing British Army descended on them at Monticello. Jefferson's ensuing resignation and the lack of preparations for the defense of the city were held against him, and it was some time before he regained the confidence of Virginians.

From 1781 to late 1783, Jefferson withdrew from public life and remained for stretches of time at Monticello, completing his only book, *Notes on the State of Virginia*, a work of natural and social history that also presents Jefferson's thinking on a range of volatile issues, including slavery and race, religious liberty, and the economic basis of the future United States. He was elected to the Continental Congress in 1783, and in early 1784 he was among the Congressional delegates who signed the Treaty of Paris, ending the Revolutionary War. He was elected Minister to France in May 1784 and sailed from Boston on July 5 of that year. He returned to Monticello in 1789, and the following year George Washington appointed him to be the first secretary of state under the newly adopted Constitution. After three years, Jefferson retired once again

and temporarily withdrew to Monticello. He ran for president in 1796, losing to John Adams and taking the office of vice president instead, as was then the practice. However, he won the watershed election of 1800, becoming the nation's third president and the first to be inaugurated in Washington, D.C. He named Benjamin Latrobe surveyor of public buildings and worked with Latrobe in planning a great city to be the new nation's capital.

When Jefferson returned to Monticello in 1809, his public life was over. In his later years, he kept up a copious correspondence. His exchanges with John Adams offer a study in contrasting personalities as well as fascinating insights into revolutionary history. On the Fourth of July, 1826—the fiftieth anniversary of the Declaration of Independence—Jefferson died a few hours before Adams, his longtime collaborator, rival, and correspondent. At the time of his death, he was deeply in debt, and his family was forced to sell Monticello. Despite the discomfort with the slave system that he frequently expressed, Jefferson ultimately freed a total of just seven of the people he held in bondage, all members of the extended Hemings family.

President of the United States, first secretary of state, minister to France, governor of Virginia, and congressman, Thomas Jefferson once said that he wished to be remembered for only three things: drafting the Declaration of Independence, writing and supporting the Virginia Statute for Religious Freedom (1786), and founding the University of Virginia (1819). Jefferson might well have included a number of other accomplishments in this list: a remarkable architect, he designed not just Monticello but also the Virginia state capitol and the original buildings for the University of Virginia; he had a library of some ten thousand volumes, which served as the basis for the Library of Congress, and a collection of paintings and sculpture that made him the greatest patron of the arts in the early United States; and he was known the world over for his spirit of scientific inquiry and as the creator of several remarkable inventions.

The three acts for which he wished to be remembered testify to Jefferson's lifelong passion to liberate the human mind from tyranny, whether imposed by the state, the Church, or human ignorance. The fact that he was unable to liberate his own mind from the tyranny of racialist thought remains part of his ambiguous legacy. The Declaration of Independence has directly influenced independence movements around the world, from Haiti to India and from Venezuela to Rhodesia. It offers an important argument for viewing "Life, Liberty and the pursuit of Happiness" as "unalienable Rights" best achieved through the exercise of popular government.

From The Autobiography of Thomas Jefferson[1]

From The Declaration of Independence

* * *

It appearing in the course of these debates, that the colonies of New York, New Jersey, Pennsylvania, Delaware, Maryland, and South Carolina were not yet matured for falling from the parent stem, but that they were fast

1. On June 7, 1776, Richard Henry Lee of Virginia proposed to the Second Continental Congress, meeting in Philadelphia, that "these united Colonies are, and of a right ought to be, free and independent states." Lee's resolution was passed on July 2, and the Declaration was adopted on July 4 with the changes noted by Jefferson in this text, taken from his *Autobiography*. On August 2, a copy on parchment was signed by all the delegates but three, who signed later. The text is from *The Writings of Thomas Jefferson* (1903), edited by A. A. Lipscomb and A. E. Bergh.

advancing to that state, it was thought most prudent to wait a while for them, and to postpone the final decision to July 1st; but, that this might occasion as little delay as possible, a committee was appointed to prepare a Declaration of Independence. The committee were John Adams, Dr. Franklin, Roger Sherman, Robert R. Livingston, and myself. Committees were also appointed, at the same time, to prepare a plan of confederation for the colonies, and to state the terms proper to be proposed for foreign alliance. The committee for drawing the Declaration of Independence, desired me to do it. It was accordingly done, and being approved by them, I reported it to the House on Friday, the 28th of June, when it was read, and ordered to lie on the table.[2] On Monday, the 1st of July, the House resolved itself into a committee of the whole, and resumed the consideration of the original motion made by the delegates of Virginia, which, being again debated through the day, was carried in the affirmative by the votes of New Hampshire, Connecticut, Massachusetts, Rhode Island, New Jersey, Maryland, Virginia, North Carolina and Georgia. South Carolina and Pennsylvania voted against it. Delaware had but two members present, and they were divided. The delegates from New York declared they were for it themselves, and were assured their constituents were for it; but that their instructions having been drawn near a twelve-month before, when reconciliation was still the general object, they were enjoined by them to do nothing which should impede that object. They, therefore, thought themselves not justifiable in voting on either side, and asked leave to withdraw from the question: which was given them. The committee rose and reported their resolution to the House. Mr. Edward Rutledge, of South Carolina, then requested the determination might be put off to the next day, as he believed his colleagues, though they disapproved of the resolution, would then join in it for the sake of unanimity. The ultimate question, whether the House would agree to the resolution of the committee, was accordingly postponed to the next day, when it was again moved, and South Carolina concurred in voting for it. In the meantime, a third member had come post[3] from the Delaware counties, and turned the vote of that colony in favor of the resolution. Members of a different sentiment attending that morning from Pennsylvania also, her vote was changed, so that the whole twelve colonies who were authorized to vote at all, gave their voices for it; and, within a few days, the convention of New York approved of it, and thus supplied the void occasioned by the withdrawing of her delegates from the vote.

Congress proceeded the same day to consider the Declaration of Independence, which had been reported and lain on the table the Friday preceding, and on Monday referred to a committee of the whole. The pusillanimous idea that we had friends in England worth keeping terms with, still haunted the minds of many. For this reason, those passages which conveyed censures on the people of England were struck out, lest they should give them offense. The clause too, reprobating the enslaving the inhabitants of Africa, was struck out in complaisance to South Carolina and Georgia, who had never attempted to restrain the importation of slaves, and who, on the contrary,

2. A parliamentary procedure calling for the consideration of the proposal (British usage). 3. Posthaste: speedily.

still wished to continue it. Our northern brethren also, I believe, felt a little tender under those censures; for though their people had very few slaves themselves, yet they had been pretty considerable carriers of them to others. The debates, having taken up the greater parts of the 2d, 3d, and 4th days of July, were, on the evening of the last, closed; the Declaration was reported by the committee, agreed to by the House, and signed by every member present, except Mr. Dickinson.[4] As the sentiments of men are known not only by what they receive, but what they reject also, I will state the form of the Declaration as originally reported. The parts struck out by Congress shall be distinguished by a black line drawn under them, and those inserted by them shall be placed in the margin, or in a concurrent column.

A DECLARATION BY THE REPRESENTATIVES OF THE UNITED STATES OF AMERICA, IN GENERAL CONGRESS ASSEMBLED.

When, in the course of human events, it becomes necessary for one people to dissolve the political bands which have connected them with another, and to assume among the powers of the earth the separate and equal station to which the laws of nature and of nature's God entitle them, a decent respect to the opinions of mankind requires that they should declare the causes which impel them to the separation.

We hold these truths to be self evident: that all men are created equal; that they are endowed by their Creator with certain inherent and inalienable rights; that among these are life, liberty, and the pursuit of happiness;[5] that to secure these rights, governments are instituted among men, deriving their just powers from the consent of the governed; that whenever any form of government becomes destructive of these ends, it is the right of the people to alter or to abolish it, and to institute new government, laying its foundation on such principles, and organizing its powers in such form, as to them shall seem most likely to effect their safety and happiness. Prudence, indeed, will dictate that governments long established should not be changed for light and transient causes; and accordingly all experience hath shown that mankind are more disposed to suffer while evils are sufferable, than to right themselves by abolishing the forms to which they are accustomed. But when a long train of abuses and usurpations, begun at a distinguished[6] period and pursuing invariably the same object, evinces a design to reduce them under absolute despotism, it is their right, it is their duty to throw off such government, and to provide new guards for their future security. Such has been the patient sufferance of these colonies; and such is now the necessity which constrains them to

4. John Dickinson of Pennsylvania, who opposed it.
5. Jefferson's phrase "life, liberty, and the pursuit of happiness" echoes "life, liberty, and property," from the English philosopher John Locke (1632–1704). However, Jefferson may have been more influenced by the Scottish Enlightenment philosophers, particularly Hutcheson.
6. I.e., discernible.

expunge their former systems of government. The history of the present king of Great Britain[7] is a history of unremitting injuries and usurpations, among which appears no solitary fact to contradict the uniform tenor of the rest, but all have in direct object the establishment of an absolute tyranny over these states. To prove this, let facts be submitted to a candid world for the truth of which we pledge a faith yet unsullied by falsehood.

alter

repeated

all having

He has refused his assent to laws the most wholesome and necessary for the public good.

He has forbidden his governors to pass laws of immediate and pressing importance, unless suspended in their operation till his assent should be obtained; and, when so suspended, he has utterly neglected to attend to them.

He has refused to pass other laws for the accommodation of large districts of people, unless those people would relinquish the right of representation in the legislature, a right inestimable to them, and formidable to tyrants only.

He has called together legislative bodies at places unusual, uncomfortable, and distant from the depository of their public records, for the sole purpose of fatiguing them into compliance with his measures.

He has dissolved representative houses repeatedly and continually for opposing with manly firmness his invasions on the rights of the people.

He has refused for a long time after such dissolutions to cause others to be elected, whereby the legislative powers, incapable of annihilation, have returned to the people at large for their exercise, the state remaining, in the meantime, exposed to all the dangers of invasion from without and convulsions within.

He has endeavored to prevent the population of these states; for that purpose obstructing the laws for naturalization of foreigners, refusing to pass others to encourage their migrations hither, and raising the conditions of new appropriations of lands.

He has suffered the administration of justice totally to cease in some of these states refusing his assent to laws for establishing judiciary powers.

obstructed

by

He has made our judges dependent on his will alone for the tenure of their offices, and the amount and payment of their salaries.

He has erected a multitude of new offices, by a self-assumed power and sent hither swarms of new officers to harass our people and eat out their substance.[8]

He has kept among us in times of peace standing armies and ships of war without the consent of our legislatures.

7. King George III (1738–1820; reigned 1760–1820).

8. I.e., consume the local people's food and other staple goods.

He has affected to render the military independent of, and superior to, the civil power.

He has combined with others[9] to subject us to a jurisdiction foreign to our constitutions and unacknowledged by our laws, giving his assent to their acts of pretended legislation for quartering large bodies of armed troops among us; for protecting them by a mock trial from punishment for any murders which they should commit on the inhabitants of these states; for cutting off our trade with all parts of the world; for imposing taxes on us without our consent; for depriving us [] *[margin: in many cases]* of the benefits of trial by jury; for transporting us beyond seas to be tried for pretended offenses; for abolishing the free system of English laws in a neighboring province, establishing therein an arbitrary government, and enlarging its boundaries, so as to render it at once an example and fit instrument for introducing the same absolute rule into these <u>states;</u>[1] *[margin: colonies;]* for taking away our charters, abolishing our most valuable laws, and altering fundamentally the forms of our governments; for suspending our own legislatures, and declaring themselves invested with power to legislate for us in all cases whatsoever.

He has abdicated government here <u>withdrawing his governors, and declaring us out of his allegiance and protection.</u> *[margin: by declaring us out of his protection, and waging war against us.]*

He has plundered our seas, ravaged our coasts, burnt our towns, and destroyed the lives of our people.

He is at this time transporting large armies of foreign mercenaries[2] to complete the works of death, desolation and tyranny already begun with circumstances of cruelty and perfidy [] unworthy the head of a civilized nation. *[margin: scarcely paralleled in the most barbarous ages, and totally]*

He has constrained our fellow citizens taken captive on the high seas, to bear arms against their country, to become the executioners of their friends and brethren, or to fall themselves by their hands.

He has [] endeavored to bring on the inhabitants of our frontiers, the merciless Indian savages, whose known rule of warfare is an undistinguished destruction of all ages, sexes and conditions <u>of existence.</u> *[margin: excited domestic insurrection among us, and has]*

<u>He has incited treasonable insurrections of our fellow citizens, with the allurements of forfeiture and confiscation of our property.</u>

<u>He has waged cruel war against human nature itself, violating its most sacred rights of life and liberty in the persons of a distant people who never offended him, captivating and carrying them into slavery in another hemisphere, or to incur miserable death in their transportation thither. This piratical</u>

9. I.e., the British Parliament.
1. The Quebec Act of 1774 recognized the Roman Catholic religion in Quebec and extended the borders of the province to the Ohio River; it restored French civil law and thus angered the New England colonies. It was often referred to as one of the "intolerable acts."
2. German soldiers hired by the king for colonial service.

warfare, the opprobrium of infidel powers, is the warfare of the christian king of Great Britain. Determined to keep open a market where men should be bought and sold, he has prostituted his negative[3] for suppressing every legislative attempt to prohibit or to restrain this execrable commerce. And that this assemblage of horrors might want no fact of distinguished die,[4] he is now exciting those very people to rise in arms among us, and to purchase that liberty of which he has deprived them, by murdering the people on whom he also obtruded them: thus paying off former crimes committed against the LIBERTIES of one people, with crimes which he urges them to commit against the lives of another.

In every stage of these oppressions we have petitioned for redress in the most humble terms: our repeated petitions have been answered only by repeated injuries.

A prince[5] whose character is thus marked by every act which may define a tyrant is unfit to be the ruler of a [] people who mean to be free. Future ages will scarcely believe that the hardiness of one man adventured,[6] within the short compass of twelve years only, to lay a foundation so broad and so undisguised for tyranny over a people fostered and fixed in principles of freedom. *[free]*

Nor have we been wanting in attentions[7] to our British brethren. We have warned them from time to time of attempts by their legislature to extend a jurisdiction over these our states. We have reminded them of the circumstances of our emigration and settlement here, no one of which could warrant so strange a pretension: that these were effected at the expense of our own blood and treasure, unassisted by the wealth or the strength of Great Britain: that in constituting indeed our several forms of government, we had adopted one common king, thereby laying a foundation for perpetual league and amity with them: but that submission to their parliament was no part of our constitution, nor ever in idea, if history may be credited: and, we [] appealed to their native justice and magnanimity as well as to the ties of our common kindred to disavow these usurpations which were likely *to* interrupt our connection and correspondence. They too have been deaf to the voice of justice and of consanguinity, and when occasions have been given them, by the regular course of their laws, of removing from their councils the disturbers of our harmony, they have, by their free election, reestablished them in power. At this very time too, they are permitting their chief magistrate to send over not only soldiers of our common blood, but Scotch and foreign mercenaries to invade and destroy us. These facts have given the *[an unwarrantable / us]* *[have / and we have / conjured / them by / would inevitably]*

3. I.e., vetoed legislation to end the slave trade.
4. Might lack nothing.
5. King George III.

6. Engaged.
7. Lacking attention.

last stab to agonizing affection, and manly spirit bids us to renounce forever these unfeeling brethren. We must endeavor to forget our former love for them, and hold them as we hold the rest of mankind, enemies in war, in peace friends. We might have been a free and a great people together; but a communication of grandeur and of freedom, it seems, is below their dignity. Be it so, since they will have it. The road to happiness and to glory is open to us, too. We will tread it apart from them, and acquiesce in the necessity which denounces[8] our eternal separation []!

and hold them as we hold the rest of mankind, enemies in war, in peace friends.

We therefore the representatives of the United States of America in General Congress assembled, do in the name, and by the authority of the good people of these states reject and renounce all allegiance and subjection to the kings of Great Britain and all others who may hereafter claim by, through or under them; we utterly dissolve all political connection which may heretofore have subsisted between us and the people or parliament of Great Britain: and finally we do assert and declare these colonies to be free and independent states, and that as free and independent states, they have full power to levy war, conclude peace, contract alliances, establish commerce, and to do all other acts and things which independent states may of right do.

And for the support of this declaration, we mutually pledge to each other our lives, our fortunes, and our sacred honor.

We, therefore, the representatives of the United States of America in General Congress assembled, appealing to the supreme judge of the world for the rectitude of our intentions, do in the name, and by the authority of the good people of these colonies, solemnly publish and declare, that these united colonies are, and of right ought to be free and independent states; that they are absolved from all allegiance to the British crown, and that all political connection between them and the state of Great Britain is, and ought to be, totally dissolved; and that as free and independent states, they have full power to levy war, conclude peace, contract alliances, establish commerce, and to do all other acts and things which independent states may of right do.

And for the support of this declaration, with a firm reliance on the protection of divine providence, we mutually pledge to each other our lives, our fortunes, and our sacred honor.

The Declaration thus signed on the 4th, on paper, was engrossed[9] on parchment, and signed again on the 2d of August.

1821 1829

8. Proclaims. 9. Written in a legal hand.

From Notes on the State of Virginia[1]

From *Query V. Cascades*

* * *

[NATURAL BRIDGE][2]

The *Natural bridge,* the most sublime of Nature's works, though not comprehended under the present head, must not be pretermitted.[3] It is on the ascent of a hill, which seems to have been cloven through its length by some great convulsion. The fissure, just at the bridge, is by some admeasurements, 270 feet deep, by others only 205. It is about 45 feet wide at the bottom, and 90 feet at the top; this of course determines the length of the bridge, and its height from the water. Its breadth in the middle, is about 60 feet, but more at the ends, and the thickness of the mass at the summit of the arch, about 40 feet. A part of this thickness is constituted by a coat of earth, which gives growth to many large trees. The residue, with the hill on both sides, is one solid rock of lime-stone. The arch approaches the Semi-elliptical form; but the larger axis of the ellipsis, which would be the cord[4] of the arch, is many times longer than the transverse. Though the sides of this bridge are provided in some parts with a parapet of fixed rocks, yet few men have resolution to walk to them and look over into the abyss. You involuntarily fall on your hands and feet, creep to the parapet and peep over it. Looking down from this height about a minute, gave me a violent head ach. If the view from the top be painful and intolerable, that from below is delightful in an equal extreme. It is impossible for the emotions arising from the sublime, to be felt beyond what they are here: so beautiful an arch, so elevated, so light, and springing as it were up to heaven, the rapture of the spectator is really indescribable! The fissure continuing narrow, deep, and streight for a considerable distance above and below the bridge, opens a short but very pleasing view of the North mountain on one side, and Blue ridge on the other, at the distance each of them of about five miles. This bridge is in the country of Rock bridge, to which it has given name, and affords a public and commodious passage over a valley, which cannot be crossed elsewhere for a considerable distance. The stream passing under it is called Cedar creek. It is a water of James river, and sufficient in the driest seasons to turn a grist-mill, though its fountain is not more than two miles above.

1. In 1781, the year Jefferson resigned as governor of Virginia, he received a request from the Marquis de Barbé-Marbois (1745–1837), secretary of the French legation at Philadelphia, to answer twenty-three questions concerning the geographical boundaries, the ecology, and the social history of Virginia. Jefferson took the occasion to make some observations on slavery, manufacturing, and government. He wanted especially to counter the notion, prevalent among European naturalists (especially Georges Louis Leclerc, Comte de Buffon [1707–1788]), that North American species, human and nonhuman, had degenerated and were inferior to Old World types. Jefferson's replies were published privately in 1784–85. The threat of an unauthorized French translation prompted Jefferson to publish an authorized edition of this heterogeneous work in London in 1787.

2. Jefferson owned the land near Lexington, Virginia, on which the Natural Bridge stands.

3. I.e., though it is not a cascade, it must not be omitted.

4. Chord (a term in geometry).

From *Query XIV. Laws*

* * *

[SLAVERY]

To emancipate all slaves born after passing the act.[5] The bill reported by the revisors does not itself contain this proposition; but an amendment containing it was prepared, to be offered to the legislature whenever the bill should be taken up, and further directing, that they should continue with their parents to a certain age, then be brought up, at the public expence, to tillage, arts or sciences, according to their geniusses,[6] till the females should be eighteen, and the males twenty-one years of age, when they should be colonized to such place as the circumstances of the time should render most proper, sending them out with arms, implements of household and of the handicraft arts, seeds, pairs of the useful domestic animals, &c. to declare them a free and independent people, and extend to them our alliance and protection, till they shall have acquired strength; and to send vessels at the same time to other parts of the world for an equal number of white inhabitants; to induce whom to migrate hither, proper encouragements were to be proposed. It will probably be asked, Why not retain and incorporate the blacks into the state, and thus save the expence of supplying, by importation of white settlers, the vacancies they will leave? Deep rooted prejudices entertained by the whites; ten thousand recollections, by the blacks, of the injuries they have sustained; new provocations; the real distinctions which nature has made; and many other circumstances, will divide us into parties, and produce convulsions which will probably never end but in the extermination of the one or the other race.—To these objections, which are political, may be added others, which are physical and moral. The first difference which strikes us is that of colour. Whether the black of the negro resides in the reticular membrane between the skin and scarf-skin, or in the scarf-skin itself; whether it proceeds from the colour of the blood, the colour of the bile, or from that of some other secretion, the difference is fixed in nature, and is as real as if its seat and cause were better known to us. And is this difference of no importance? Is it not the foundation of a greater or less share of beauty in the two races? Are not the fine mixtures of red and white, the expressions of every passion by greater or less suffusions of colour in the one, preferable to that eternal monotony, which reigns in the countenances, that immoveable veil of black which covers all the emotions of the other race? Add to these, flowing hair, a more elegant symmetry of form, their own judgment in favour of the whites, declared by their preference of them, as uniformly as is the preference of the Oranootan for the black women over those of his own species. The circumstance of superior beauty, is thought worthy attention in the propagation of our horses, dogs, and other domestic animals; why not in that of man? Besides those of colour, figure, and hair, there are other physical distinctions proving a difference of race. They have less hair on the face and body. They secrete less by the kidnies, and more by the glands of the skin, which gives them a very strong and disagreeable odour. This

5. This sentence fragment represents a proposed revision to the Virginia state constitution ("the act").

6. Abilities, capacities.

greater degree of transpiration renders them more tolerant of heat, and less so of cold, than the whites. Perhaps too a difference of structure in the pulmonary apparatus, which a late ingenious experimentalist[7] has discovered to be the principal regulator of animal heat, may have disabled them from extricating, in the act of inspiration, so much of that fluid from the outer air, or obliged them in expiration, to part with more of it. They seem to require less sleep. A black, after hard labour through the day, will be induced by the slightest amusements to sit up till midnight, or later, though knowing he must be out with the first dawn of the morning. They are at least as brave, and more adventuresome. But this may perhaps proceed from a want of forethought, which prevents their seeing a danger till it be present. When present, they do not go through it with more coolness or steadiness than the whites. They are more ardent after their female: but love seems with them to be more an eager desire, than a tender delicate mixture of sentiment and sensation. Their griefs are transient. Those numberless afflictions, which render it doubtful whether heaven has given life to us in mercy or in wrath, are less felt, and sooner forgotten with them. In general, their existence appears to participate more of sensation than reflection. To this must be ascribed their disposition to sleep when abstracted from their diversions, and unemployed in labour. An animal whose body is at rest, and who does not reflect, must be disposed to sleep of course. Comparing them by their faculties of memory, reason, and imagination, it appears to me, that in memory they are equal to the whites; in reason much inferior, as I think one could scarcely be found capable of tracing and comprehending the investigations of Euclid;[8] and that in imagination they are dull, tasteless, and anomalous. It would be unfair to follow them to Africa for this investigation. We will consider them here, on the same stage with the whites, and where the facts are not apocryphal on which a judgment is to be formed. It will be right to make great allowances for the difference of condition, of education, of conversation, of the sphere in which they move. Many millions of them have been brought to, and born in America. Most of them indeed have been confined to tillage, to their own homes, and their own society: yet many have been so situated, that they might have availed themselves of the conversation of their masters; many have been brought up to the handicraft arts, and from that circumstance have always been associated with the whites. Some have been liberally educated, and all have lived in countries where the arts and sciences are cultivated to a considerable degree, and have had before their eyes samples of the best works from abroad. The Indians, with no advantages of this kind, will often carve figures on their pipes not destitute of design and merit. They will crayon out an animal, a plant, or a country, so as to prove the existence of a germ in their minds which only wants cultivation. They astonish you with strokes of the most sublime oratory; such as prove their reason and sentiment strong, their imagination glowing and elevated. But never yet could I find that a black had uttered a thought above the level of plain narration; never see even an elementary trait of painting or sculpture. In music they are more generally gifted than the whites with

7. Crawford [Jefferson's note]. British scientist Adair Crawford (1748–1795).

8. Greek mathematician (fl. c. 300 B.C.E.).

accurate ears for tune and time, and they have been found capable of imagining a small catch. Whether they will be equal to the composition of a more extensive run of melody, or of complicated harmony, is yet to be proved. Misery is often the parent of the most affecting touches in poetry.—Among the blacks is misery enough, God knows, but no poetry. Love is the peculiar œstrum[9] of the poet. Their love is ardent, but it kindles the senses only, not the imagination. Religion indeed has produced a Phyllis Whately,[1] but it could not produce a poet. The compositions published under her name are below the dignity of criticism. The heroes of the Dunciad are to her, as Hercules to the author of that poem.[2] Ignatius Sancho[3] has approached nearer to merit in composition; yet his letters do more honour to the heart than the head. They breathe the purest effusions of friendship and general philanthropy, and shew how great a degree of the latter may be compounded with strong religious zeal. He is often happy in the turn of his compliments, and his stile is easy and familiar, except when he affects a Shandean[4] fabrication of words. But his imagination is wild and extravagant, escapes incessantly from every restraint of reason and taste, and, in the course of its vagaries, leaves a tract of thought as incoherent and eccentric, as is the course of a meteor through the sky. His subjects should often have led him to a process of sober reasoning: yet we find him always substituting sentiment for demonstration. Upon the whole, though we admit him to the first place among those of his own colour who have presented themselves to the public judgment, yet when we compare him with the writers of the race among whom he lived, and particularly with the epistolary class, in which he has taken his own stand, we are compelled to enroll him at the bottom of the column. This criticism supposes the letters published under his name to be genuine, and to have received amendment from no other hand; points which would not be of easy investigation. The improvement of the blacks in body and mind, in the first instance of their mixture with the whites, has been observed by every one, and proves that their inferiority is not the effect merely of their condition of life. We know that among the Romans, about the Augustan age especially,[5] the condition of their slaves was much more deplorable than that of the blacks on the continent of America. The two sexes were confined in separate apartments, because to raise a child cost the master more than to buy one. Cato, for a very restricted indulgence to his slaves in this particular, took from them a certain price. But in this country the slaves multiply as fast as the free inhabitants. Their situation and manners place the commerce between the two sexes almost without restraint.—The same Cato, on a principle of œconomy, always sold his sick

9. Estrus: period of (sexual) receptivity and fertility; heat.
1. Phillis Wheatley (c. 1753–1784), the first published African American female poet, whose poems appear later in this volume.
2. In his mock-heroic Dunciad, the English poet Alexander Pope (1688–1744) satirizes hack writers. Jefferson is saying that just as the severely unhealthy and deformed Pope was not the mythological hero Hercules, so Wheatley was less talented than Pope's targets.

3. Black Briton, composer, actor, and writer (c. 1729–1780), known for his posthumously published letters, an early account of African slavery by a former slave.
4. As in the highly inventive novel Tristram Shandy, by the Anglo-Irish writer Laurence Sterne (1713–1768).
5. I.e., during the period when Augustus (63 B.C.E.–14 C.E.) was Rome's first emperor (27 B.C.E.–14 C.E.).

and superannuated slaves. He gives it as a standing precept to a master visiting his farm, to sell his old oxen, old wagons, old tools, old and diseased servants, and every thing else become useless. "Vendat boves vetulos, plaustrum vetus, ferramenta vetera, servum senem, servum morbosum, & si quid aliud supersit vendat." Cato de re rusticâ. c. 2.[6] The American slaves cannot enumerate this among the injuries and insults they receive. It was the common practice to expose in the island of Æsculapius, in the Tyber,[7] diseased slaves, whose cure was like to become tedious. The Emperor Claudius,[8] by an edict, gave freedom to such of them as should recover, and first declared, that if any person chose to kill rather than to expose them, it should be deemed homicide. The exposing them is a crime of which no instance has existed with us; and were it to be followed by death, it would be punished capitally. We are told of a certain Vedius Pollio,[9] who, in the presence of Augustus, would have given a slave as food to his fish, for having broken a glass. With the Romans, the regular method of taking the evidence of their slaves was under torture. Here it has been thought better never to resort to their evidence. When a master was murdered, all his slaves, in the same house, or within hearing, were condemned to death. Here punishment falls on the guilty only, and as precise proof is required against him as against a freeman. Yet notwithstanding these and other discouraging circumstances among the Romans, their slaves were often their rarest artists. They excelled too in science, insomuch as to be usually employed as tutors to their master's children. Epictetus, Terence, and Phædrus,[1] were slaves. But they were of the race of whites. It is not their condition then, but nature, which has produced the distinction.—Whether further observation will or will not verify the conjecture, that nature has been less bountiful to them in the endowments of the head, I believe that in those of the heart she will be found to have done them justice. That disposition to theft with which they have been branded, must be ascribed to their situation, and not to any depravity of the moral sense. The man, in whose favour no laws of property exist, probably feels himself less bound to respect those made in favour of others. When arguing for ourselves, we lay it down as a fundamental, that laws, to be just, must give a reciprocation of right: that, without this, they are mere arbitrary rules of conduct, founded in force, and not in conscience: and it is a problem which I give to the master to solve, whether the religious precepts against the violation of property were not framed for him as well as his slave? And whether the slave may not as justifiably take a little from one, who has taken all from him, as he may slay one who would slay him? That a change in the relations in which a man is placed should change his ideas of moral right and wrong, is neither new, nor peculiar to the colour of the blacks. Homer tells us it was so 2600 years ago.

6. I.e., from chapter 2 of *De Re Rusticâ*, also known as *De Agri Cultura* (Latin for *Of Agriculture* or *Of Farming*), by the Roman statesman Cato the Elder (234–149 B.C.E.). The Latin quotation is preceded by its English translation.
7. Present-day Tiber Island, in the Tiber River, which runs through Rome. "Expose": abandon to die.

8. Tiberius Claudius Drusus Nero (10 B.C.E.–54 C.E., reigned 41–54).
9. Publius Vedius Pollio (d. 15 B.C.E.), Roman equestrian and friend of Augustus.
1. Respectively, Greek philosopher in Rome (c. 55–135 C.E.), Roman dramatist (186 or 185–?159 B.C.E.), and Roman Fabulist (c. 15 B.C.E–c. 50 C.E.).

'Ημισυ, γαζ τ' ἀρετῆς ἀποαίνυῖαι εὐρύθπα Ζεὺς.
'Ανερος, ευτ' ἂν μιν κατὰ δȢλιον ἦμαζ ἕλησιν.
Od. 17. 323.[2]

Jove fix'd it certain, that whatever day
Makes man a slave, takes half his worth away.

But the slaves of which Homer speaks were whites. Notwithstanding these considerations which must weaken their respect for the laws of property, we find among them numerous instances of the most rigid integrity, and as many as among their better instructed masters, of benevolence, gratitude, and unshaken fidelity.—The opinion, that they are inferior in the faculties of reason and imagination, must be hazarded with great diffidence. To justify a general conclusion, requires many observations, even where the subject may be submitted to the Anatomical knife, to Optical glasses, to analysis by fire, or by solvents. How much more then where it is a faculty, not a substance, we are examining; where it eludes the research of all the senses; where the conditions of its existence are various and variously combined; where the effects of those which are present or absent bid defiance to calculation; let me add too, as a circumstance of great tenderness, where our conclusion would degrade a whole race of men from the rank in the scale of beings which their Creator may perhaps have given them. To our reproach it must be said, that though for a century and a half we have had under our eyes the races of black and of red men, they have never yet been viewed by us as subjects of natural history. I advance it therefore as a suspicion only, that the blacks, whether originally a distinct race, or made distinct by time and circumstances, are inferior to the whites in the endowments both of body and mind. It is not against experience to suppose, that different species of the same genus, or varieties of the same species, may possess different qualifications. Will not a lover of natural history then, one who views the gradations in all the races of animals with the eye of philosophy, excuse an effort to keep those in the department of man as distinct as nature has formed them? This unfortunate difference of colour, and perhaps of faculty, is a powerful obstacle to the emancipation of these people. Many of their advocates, while they wish to vindicate the liberty of human nature, are anxious also to preserve its dignity and beauty. Some of these, embarrassed by the question "What further is to be done with them?" join themselves in opposition with those who are actuated by sordid avarice only. Among the Romans emancipation required but one effort. The slave, when made free, might mix with, without staining the blood of his master. But with us a second is necessary, unknown to history. When freed, he is to be removed beyond the reach of mixture.

2. I.e., book 17, line 323 of the *Odyssey*, by the ancient Greek epic poet Homer. The Greek quotation is followed by Alexander Pope's translation (1726).

Query XVII

[RELIGION]

The first settlers in this country[3] were emigrants from England, of the English church, just at a point of time when it was flushed with complete victory over the religious of all other persuasions. Possessed, as they became, of the powers of making, administering, and executing the laws, they showed equal intolerance in this country with their Presbyterian brethren, who had emigrated to the northern government. The poor Quakers were flying from persecution in England. They cast their eyes on these new countries as asylums[4] of civil and religious freedom; but they found them free only for the reigning sect. Several acts of the Virginia assembly of 1659, 1662, and 1693, had made it penal in parents to refuse to have their children baptized; had prohibited the unlawful assembling of Quakers; had made it penal for any master of a vessel to bring a Quaker into the state; had ordered those already here, and such as should come thereafter, to be imprisoned till they should abjure[5] the country; provided a milder punishment for their first and second return, but death for their third; had inhibited all persons from suffering their meetings in or near their houses, entertaining them individually, or disposing[6] of books which supported their tenets. If no capital execution took place here, as did in New-England, it was not owing to the moderation of the church, or spirit of the legislature, as may be inferred from the law itself; but to historical circumstances which have not been handed down to us. The Anglicans retained full possession of the country about a century. Other opinions began then to creep in, and the great care of the government to support their own church, having begotten an equal degree of indolence in its clergy, two-thirds of the people had become dissenters at the commencement of the present revolution. The laws indeed were still oppressive on them, but the spirit of the one party had subsided into moderation, and of the other had risen to a degree of determination which commanded respect.

The present state of our laws on the subject of religion is this. The convention of May 1776, in their declaration of rights, declared it to be a truth, and a natural right, that the exercise of religion should be free;[7] but when they proceeded to form on that declaration the ordinance of government, instead of taking up every principle declared in the bill of rights, and guarding it by legislative sanction, they passed over that which asserted our religious rights, leaving them as they found them.[8] The same convention, however, when they met as a member of the general assembly in October 1776, repealed all *acts of parliament* which had rendered criminal the maintaining any opinions in matters of religion, the forbearing to repair to church, and the exercising any mode of worship; and suspended the laws giving salaries to the clergy, which suspension was made perpetual in October 1779.

3. This land; i.e., Virginia, as opposed to the "northern government," or colonies, referred to below.
4. Refuges.
5. I.e., swear to leave.
6. Distributing. "Inhibited": prohibited. "Suffering their meetings": hosting their religious services.

7. Jefferson is referring to Article XVI of Virginia's Declaration of Rights (adopted June 12, 1776, by the fifth Virginia Convention).
8. I.e., the Constitution of Virginia (adopted June 29, 1776, by the Fifth Virginia Convention) incorporates the entire Declaration of Rights.

Statutory oppressions in religion being thus wiped away, we remain at present under those only imposed by the common law, or by our own acts of assembly. At the common law, *heresy* was a capital offense, punishable by burning. Its definition was left to the ecclesiastical judges, before whom the conviction was, till the statute of the 1 El. c. 1.[9] circumscribed it, by declaring, that nothing should be deemed heresy, but what had been so determined by authority of the canonical scriptures, or by one of the four first general councils, or by some other council having for the grounds of their declaration the express and plain words of the scriptures. Heresy, thus circumscribed, being an offense at the common law, our act of assembly of October 1777, c. 17. gives cognizance of it to the general court, by declaring, that the jurisdiction of that court shall be general in all matters at the common law. The execution is by the writ *De hæretico comburendo.*[1] By our own act of assembly of 1705, c. 30, if a person brought up in the Christian religion denies the being of a God, or the Trinity, or asserts there are more Gods than one, or denies the Christian religion to be true, or the scriptures to be of divine authority, he is punishable on the first offense by incapacity to hold any office or employment ecclesiastical, civil, or military; on the second by disability to sue, to take any gift or legacy, to be guardian, executor, or administrator, and by three years' imprisonment, without bail. A father's right to the custody of his own children being founded in law on his right of guardianship, this being taken away, they may of course be severed from him, and put, by the authority of a court, into more orthodox hands. This is a summary view of that religious slavery, under which a people have been willing to remain, who have lavished their lives and fortunes for the establishment of their civil freedom. The error seems not sufficiently eradicated, that the operations of the mind, as well as the acts of the body, are subject to the coercion of the laws[2] But our rulers can have authority over such natural rights only as we have submitted to them. The rights of conscience we never submitted, we could not submit. We are answerable for them to our God. The legitimate powers of government extend to such acts only as are injurious to others. But it does me no injury for my neighbour to say there are twenty gods, or no god. It neither picks my pocket nor breaks my leg. If it be said, his testimony in a court of justice cannot be relied on, reject it then, and be the stigma on him. Constraint may make him worse by making him a hypocrite, but it will never make him a truer man. It may fix him obstinately in his errors, but will not cure them. Reason and free enquiry are the only effectual agents against error. Give a loose to them,[3] they will support the true religion, by bringing every false one to their tribunal, to the test of their investigation. They are the natural enemies of error, and of error only. Had not the Roman government permitted free inquiry, Christianity could never have been introduced. Had not free inquiry been indulged, at the æra of the reformation, the corruptions of Christianity could not have been

9. That is, chapter 1 of the first year (1558–59) of the reign of Elizabeth.
1. On the burning of a heretic (Latin).
2. Furneaux passim [Jefferson's note]. Philip Furneaux (1726–1783), English minister and author of *Letters to the Honorable Mr. Justice Blackstone, Concerning His Exposition of the* *Act of Toleration, and Some Positions Relative to Religious Liberty, in His Celebrated Commentaries on the Laws of England* (1770). "Passim," Latin for "here and there," means Jefferson is citing various parts of Furneaux's work.
3. I.e., leave them unrestrained.

purged away. If it be restrained now, the present corruptions will be protected, and new ones encouraged. Was the government to prescribe to us our medicine and diet, our bodies would be in such keeping as our souls are now. Thus in France the emetic was once forbidden as a medicine, and the potato as an article of food. Government is just as infallible too when it fixes systems in physics. Galileo[4] was sent to the Inquisition for affirming that the earth was a sphere: the government had declared it to be as flat as a trencher, and Galileo was obliged to abjure his error. This error however at length prevailed, the earth became a globe, and Descartes[5] declared it was whirled round its axis by a vortex. The government in which he lived was wise enough to see that this was no question of civil jurisdiction, or we should all have been involved by authority in vortices. In fact, the vortices have been exploded, and the Newtonian[6] principle of gravitation is now more firmly established, on the basis of reason, than it would be were the government to step in, and to make it an article of necessary faith. Reason and experiment have been indulged, and error has fled before them. It is error alone which needs the support of government. Truth can stand by itself. Subject opinion to coercion: whom will you make your inquisitors? Fallible men; men governed by bad passions, by private as well as public reasons. And why subject it to coercion? To produce uniformity. But is uniformity of opinion desirable? No more than of face and stature. Introduce the bed of Procrustes[7] then, and as there is danger that the large men may beat the small, make us all of a size, by lopping the former and stretching the latter. Difference of opinion is advantageous in religion. The several sects perform the office of a Censor morum[8] over each other. Is uniformity attainable? Millions of innocent men, women, and children, since the introduction of Christianity, have been burnt, tortured, fined, imprisoned; yet we have not advanced one inch towards uniformity. What has been the effect of coercion? To make one half the world fools, and the other half hypocrites. To support roguery and error all over the earth. Let us reflect that it is inhabited by a thousand millions of people. That these profess probably a thousand different systems of religion. That ours is but one of that thousand. That if there be but one right, and ours that one, we should wish to see the 999 wandering sects gathered into the fold of truth. But against such a majority we cannot effect this by force. Reason and persuasion are the only practicable instruments. To make way for these, free inquiry must be indulged; and how can we wish others to indulge it while we refuse it ourselves. But every state, says an inquisitor, has established some religion. No two, say I, have established the same. Is this a proof of the infallibility of establishments? Our sister states of Pennsylvania and New York, however, have long subsisted without any establishment at all. The experiment was new and doubtful when they made it. It has answered beyond conception. They flourish infinitely. Religion is well supported; of various kinds, indeed, but all good enough; all sufficient to preserve peace and order: or if a sect arises, whose tenets would subvert morals, good sense has fair play, and reasons and laughs it out of doors, without

4. Galileo Galilei (1564–1642), Italian astronomer and physicist.
5. René Descartes (1596–1650), French scientist and philosopher.
6. Formulated by the English mathematician and physicist Sir Isaac Newton (1642–1727).
7. In classical mythology, a highwayman who either streched or cut off the legs of his captors to fit their bodies into his iron bed.
8. Critic of morals or customs (Latin).

suffering the state to be troubled with it. They do not hang more malefactors than we do. They are not more disturbed with religious dissensions. On the contrary, their harmony is unparalleled, and can be ascribed to nothing but their unbounded tolerance, because there is no other circumstance in which they differ from every nation on earth. They have made the happy discovery, that the way to silence religious disputes, is to take no notice of them. Let us too give this experiment fair play, and get rid, while we may, of those tyrannical laws. It is true, we are as yet secured against them by the spirit of the times. I doubt whether the people of this country would suffer an execution for heresy, or a three years' imprisonment for not comprehending the mysteries of the Trinity. But is the spirit of the people an infallible, a permanent reliance? Is it government? Is this the kind of protection we receive in return for the rights we give up? Besides, the spirit of the times may alter, will alter. Our rulers will become corrupt, our people careless. A single zealot may commence persecutor, and better men be his victims. It can never be too often repeated, that the time for fixing every essential right on a legal basis is while our rulers are honest, and ourselves united. From the conclusion of this war we shall be going down hill. It will not then be necessary to resort every moment to the people for support. They will be forgotten, therefore, and their rights disregarded. They will forget themselves, but in the sole faculty of making money, and will never think of uniting to effect a due respect for their rights. The shackles, therefore, which shall not be knocked off at the conclusion of this war, will remain on us long, will be made heavier and heavier, till our rights shall revive or expire in a convulsion.

Query XIX

[MANUFACTURES]

We never had an interior trade of any importance. Our exterior commerce has suffered very much from the beginning of the present contest. During this time we have manufactured within our families the most necessary articles of clothing. Those of cotton will bear some comparison with the same kinds of manufacture in Europe; but those of wool, flax and hemp are very coarse, unsightly, and unpleasant: and such is our attachment to agriculture, and such our preference for foreign manufactures, that be it wise or unwise, our people will certainly return as soon as they can, to the raising raw materials, and exchanging them for finer manufactures than they are able to execute themselves.

The political œconomists of Europe have established it as a principle that every state should endeavour to manufacture for itself: and this principle, like many others, we transfer to America, without calculating the difference of circumstance which should often produce a difference of result. In Europe the lands are either cultivated, or locked up against the cultivator. Manufacture must therefore be resorted to of necessity not of choice, to support the surplus of their people. But we have an immensity of land courting the industry of the husbandman.[9] Is it best then that all our citizens should be

9. Farmer.

employed in its improvement, or that one half should be called off from that to exercise manufactures and handicraft arts for the other? Those who labour in the earth are the chosen people of God, if ever he had a chosen people, whose breasts he has made his peculiar deposit for substantial and genuine virtue. It is the focus in which he keeps alive that sacred fire, which otherwise might escape from the face of the earth. Corruption of morals in the mass of cultivators is a phænomenon of which no age nor nation has furnished an example. It is the mark set on those, who not looking up to heaven, to their own soil and industry, as does the husbandman, for their subsistence, depend for it on the casualties and caprice of customers. Dependance begets subservience and venality, suffocates the germ of virtue, and prepares fit tools for the designs of ambition. This, the natural progress and consequence of the arts, has sometimes perhaps been retarded by accidental circumstances: but, generally speaking, the proportion which the aggregate of the other classes of citizens bears in any state to that of its husbandmen, is the proportion of its unsound to its healthy parts, and is a good-enough barometer whereby to measure its degree of corruption. While we have land to labour then, let us never wish to see our citizens occupied at a workbench, or twirling a distaff.[1] Carpenters, masons, smiths, are wanting in husbandry: but, for the general operations of manufacture, let our workshops remain in Europe. It is better to carry provisions and materials to workmen there, than bring them to the provisions and materials, and with them their manners and principles. The loss by the transportation of commodities across the Atlantic will be made up in happiness and permanence of government. The mobs of great cities add just so much to the support of pure government, as sores do to the strength of the human body. It is the manners and spirit of a people which preserve a republic in vigour. A degeneracy in these is a canker which soon eats to the heart of its laws and constitution.

1780–81 1787

1. A short stick on which wool or flax is wound.

THE FEDERALIST

When Richard Henry Lee, a Virginia delegate to the Continental Congress, proposed his resolution for independence from Britain on June 7, 1776, he also suggested that a "plan of confederation be prepared and transmitted to the respective colonies for their consideration and approbation." On July 12, 1776, the Articles of Confederation were presented to Congress. They were debated for a year and then ratified and adopted as the bylaws of the nation on March 1, 1781. The central question before the Constitutional Convention, meeting in Philadelphia six years

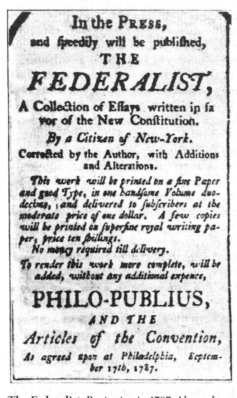

In the PRESS,

and speedily will be published,

THE
FEDERALIST,

A Collection of Essays written in favor of the New Constitution.

By a Citizen of New-York.

Corrected by the Author, with Additions and Alterations.

This work will be printed on a fine Paper and good Type, in one handsome Volume duodecimo, and delivered to subscribers at the moderate price of one dollar. A few copies will be printed on superfine royal writing paper, price ten shillings.

No money required till delivery.

To render this work more complete, will be added, without any additional expence,

PHILO-PUBLIUS,

AND THE

Articles of the Convention,

As agreed upon at Philadelphia, September 17th, 1787.

The Federalist. Beginning in 1787, Alexander Hamilton, James Madison, and John Jay wrote eighty-five essays in support of the new Constitution that eventually were published in book form as *The Federalist*.

later, was whether to salvage these articles through complicated amendments or to design a new national government. The Convention delegates decided on the latter and, in September 1787, received copies of the proposed Constitution, which they were to submit to their state legislatures for ratification. Advocates of the new Constitution, dubbed Federalists, and their Anti-Federalist opponents quickly rose to the occasion, and a great debate followed. Many feared what they saw as the loss of states' rights and the power of a large, impersonal federal government to dominate the lives of individual citizens, and they cited the absence of a bill of rights as a particular concern; others thought that the Constitution favored urban over rural populations; still others bemoaned the proposed end of the slave trade.

The debate took ten months, nowhere more seriously than in the state of New York, where adoption was not inevitable. The discussion there produced significant documents, the most enduring of which were the eighty-five essays that appeared in New York newspapers from October 1787 to April 1788 and were later collected in two volumes called *The Federalist*. These essays were written by Alexander Hamilton (1757–1804), a brilliant and quick-tempered man, born in the West Indies, who was an aide to General George Washington and, later, secretary of the Treasury; John Jay (1745–1829), who would be first chief justice of the United States Supreme Court and governor of the state of New York; and a Virginian, James Madison (1751–1836), a lawyer of distinction who would be fourth president of the United States. They used the pseudonym Publius (Latin for "public"), but the authorship was generally known.

As originally conceived, *The Federalist* had only one purpose: to persuade reluctant New Yorkers to adopt the proposed new Constitution. It did not set out to define the nature of government, yet it has proven to be far more lasting than most political treatises. Although authored individually, the essays comprising *The Federalist* share certain themes and rhetorical strategies, and they collectively respond to the writings of the ancient Greek philosopher Aristotle, the English thinkers Thomas Hobbes and John Locke, as well as David Hume and other Scottish Enlightenment philosophers. The text prominently registers the tension between the states and the union, which is sometimes referred to as "the empire," alluding to expectations that the nation would expand westward.

The underlying moral emphasis of *The Federalist* also marks the epochal shift in public authority away from the clergy to the legal profession. All three authors had

studied law, and Hamilton and Jay had practiced it. Aspects of the legal culture then emerging to prominence in the early republic—including the authors' training in deliberative (or persuasive) and forensic (or judicial) rhetoric—are clearly visible in the text. Its essential argument is that individuals have a natural right to "liberty, dignity, and happiness" and that to ensure these rights government must "secure the public good, and private rights, against the dangers of a majority," at the same time preserving the "spirit and form of a popular government." This difficult balancing of interests that *The Federalist* argues for goes to the very heart of American democracy.

From The Federalist[1]

No. 1

[ALEXANDER HAMILTON]

To the People of the State of New York. October 27, 1787

After an unequivocal experience of the inefficacy of the subsisting[2] federal government, you are called upon to deliberate on a new Constitution for the United States of America. The subject speaks its own importance; comprehending in its consequences nothing less than the existence of the Union, the safety and welfare of the parts of which it is composed, the fate of an empire, in many respects, the most interesting in the world. It has been frequently remarked that it seems to have been reserved to the people of this country, by their conduct and example, to decide the important question whether societies of men are really capable or not of establishing good government from reflection and choice, or whether they are forever destined to depend, for their political constitutions, on accident and force. If there be any truth in the remark, the crisis at which we are arrived may with propriety be regarded as the era in which that decision is to be made; and a wrong election of the part we shall act, may, in this view, deserve to be considered as the general misfortune of mankind.

This idea will add the inducements of philanthropy to those of patriotism to heighten the solicitude, which all considerate and good men must feel for the event. Happy will it be if our choice should be directed by a judicious estimate of our true interests, unperplexed and unbiased by considerations not connected with the public good. But this is a thing more ardently to be wished than seriously to be expected. The plan offered to our deliberations affects too many particular interests, innovates[3] upon too many local institutions, not to involve in its discussion a variety of objects foreign to its merits, and of views, passions and prejudices little favorable to the discovery of truth.

Among the most formidable of the obstacles which the new Constitution will have to encounter may readily be distinguished the obvious interest of a certain class of men in every state to resist all changes which may hazard a diminution of the power, emolument and consequence of the offices they

1. The text is from *The Federalist* (1961), edited by Jacob E. Cooke.

2. Existing, present.
3. Makes changes to.

hold under the state establishments—and the perverted ambition of another class of men, who will either hope to aggrandize themselves by the confusions of their country, or will flatter themselves with fairer prospects of elevation from the subdivision of the empire into several partial confederacies, than from its union under one government.

It is not, however, my design to dwell upon observations of this nature. I am well aware that it would be disingenuous to resolve indiscriminately the opposition of any set of men (merely because their situations might subject them to suspicion) into interested or ambitious views: candor will oblige us to admit, that even such men may be actuated by upright intentions; and it cannot be doubted that much of the opposition which has made its appearance, or may hereafter make its appearance, will spring from sources, blameless at least, if not respectable, the honest errors of minds led astray by preconceived jealousies and fears. So numerous indeed and so powerful are the causes, which serve to give a false bias to the judgment, that we upon many occasions see wise and good men on the wrong as well as on the right side of questions of the first magnitude to society. This circumstance, if duly attended to, would furnish a lesson of moderation to those, who are ever so much persuaded of their being in the right in any controversy. And a further reason for caution, in this respect, might be drawn from the reflection that we are not always sure that those who advocate the truth are influenced by purer principles than their antagonists. Ambition, avarice, personal animosity, party opposition, and many other motives, not more laudable than these, are apt to operate as well upon those who support as upon those who oppose the right side of a question. Were there not even these inducements to moderation, nothing could be more ill judged than that intolerant spirit, which has, at all times, characterized political parties. For, in politics as in religion, it is equally absurd to aim at making proselytes by fire and sword. Heresies in either can rarely be cured by persecution.

And yet however just these sentiments will be allowed to be, we have already sufficient indications that it will happen in this as in all former cases of great national discussion. A torrent of angry and malignant passions will be let loose. To judge from the conduct of the opposite parties, we shall be led to conclude that they will mutually hope to evince the justness of their opinions, and to increase the number of their converts by the loudness of their declamations, and by the bitterness of their invectives. An enlightened zeal for the energy and efficiency of government will be stigmatized, as the offspring of a temper fond of despotic power and hostile to the principles of liberty. An overscrupulous jealousy of danger to the rights of the people, which is more commonly the fault of the head than of the heart, will be represented as mere pretense and artifice; the bait for popularity at the expense of public good. It will be forgotten, on the one hand, that jealousy is the usual concomitant of violent love, and that the noble enthusiasm of liberty is too apt to be infected with a spirit of narrow and illiberal distrust. On the other hand, it will be equally forgotten that the vigor of government is essential to the security of liberty; that in the contemplation of a sound and well-informed judgment, their interest can never be separated; and that a dangerous ambition more often lurks behind the specious mask of

zeal for the rights of the people than under the forbidding appearance of zeal for the firmness and efficiency of government. History will teach us that the former has been found a much more certain road to the introduction of despotism than the latter, and that of those men who have overturned the liberties of republics the greatest number have begun their career by paying an obsequious court to the people, commencing demagogues and ending tyrants.

In the course of the preceding observations I have had an eye, my fellow citizens, to putting you upon your guard against all attempts, from whatever quarter, to influence your decision in a matter of the utmost moment to your welfare by any impressions other than those which may result from the evidence of truth. You will, no doubt, at the same time, have collected from the general scope of them that they proceed from a source not unfriendly to the new Constitution. Yes, my countrymen, I own to you, that, after having given it an attentive consideration, I am clearly of opinion it is your interest to adopt it. I am convinced that this is the safest course for your liberty, your dignity, and your happiness. I effect not reserves, which I do not feel. I will not amuse you with an appearance of deliberation, when I have decided. I frankly acknowledge to you my convictions, and I will freely lay before you the reasons on which they are founded. The consciousness of good intentions disdains ambiguity. I shall not however multiply professions on this head. My motives must remain in the depository of my own breast: my arguments will be open to all, and may be judged of by all. They shall at least be offered in a spirit which will not disgrace the cause of truth.

I propose in a series of papers to discuss the following interesting particulars—the utility of the Union to your political prosperity—the insufficiency of the present confederation to preserve that Union—the necessity of a government at least equally energetic with the one proposed to the attainment of this object—the conformity of the proposed constitution to the true principles of republican government—its analogy to your own state constitution—and lastly, the additional security which its adoption will afford to the preservation of that species of government, to liberty and to property.

In the progress of this discussion I shall endeavor to give a satisfactory answer to all the objections which shall have made their appearance that may seem to have any claim to your attention.

It may perhaps be thought superfluous to offer arguments to prove the utility of the Union, a point, no doubt, deeply engraved on the hearts of the great body of the people in every state, and one, which it may be imagined, has no adversaries. But the fact is that we already hear it whispered in the private circles of those who oppose the new constitution that the thirteen states are of too great extent for any general system, and that we must of necessity resort to separate confederacies of distinct portions of the whole.[4] This doctrine will, in all probability, be gradually propagated, till it has votaries enough to countenance an open avowal of it. For nothing can be more evident, to those who are able to take an enlarged view of the subject, than

4. The same idea, tracing the arguments to their consequences, is held out in several of the late publications against the new Constitution [Publius's note].

the alternative of an adoption of the new Constitution, or a dismemberment of the Union. It will therefore be of use to begin by examining the advantages of that Union, the certain evils and the probable dangers to which every state will be exposed from its dissolution. This shall accordingly constitute the subject of my next address.

Publius

No. 10

[JAMES MADISON]

To the People of the State of New York. November 22, 1787
Among the numerous advantages promised by a well-constructed Union, none deserves to be more accurately developed than its tendency to break and control the violence of faction. The friend of popular governments never finds himself so much alarmed for their character and fate as when he contemplates their propensity to this dangerous vice. He will not fail therefore to set a due value on any plan which, without violating the principles to which he is attached, provides a proper cure for it. The instability, injustice and confusion introduced into the public councils have in truth been the mortal diseases under which popular governments have everywhere perished; as they continue to be the favorite and fruitful topics from which the adversaries to liberty derive their most specious declamations. The valuable improvements made by the American constitutions on the popular models, both ancient and modern, cannot certainly be too much admired; but it would be an unwarrantable partiality to contend that they have as effectually obviated the danger on this side as was wished and expected. Complaints are everywhere heard from our most considerate and virtuous citizens, equally the friends of public and private faith and of public and personal liberty; that our governments are too unstable; that the public good is disregarded in the conflicts of rival parties; and that measures are too often decided not according to the rules of justice and the rights of the minor party, but by the superior force of an interested and overbearing majority. However anxiously we may wish that these complaints had no foundation, the evidence of known facts will not permit us to deny that they are in some degree true. It will be found indeed, on a candid review of our situation, that some of the distresses under which we labor have been erroneously charged on the operation of our governments; but it will be found, at the same time, that other causes will not alone account for many of our heaviest misfortunes; and particularly, for that prevailing and increasing distrust of public engagements, and alarm for private rights, which are echoed from one end of the continent to the other. These must be chiefly, if not wholly, effects of the unsteadiness and injustice with which a factious spirit has tainted our public administrations.

By a faction I understand a number of citizens, whether amounting to a majority or minority of the whole, who are united and actuated by some common impulse of passion or of interest, adverse to the rights of other citizens, or to the permanent and aggregate interests of the community.

There are two methods of curing the mischiefs of faction: the one, by removing its causes; the other, by controlling its effects.

There are again two methods of removing the causes of faction: the one by destroying the liberty which is essential to its existence; the other, by giving to every citizen the same opinions, the same passions, and the same interests.

It could never be more truly said than of the first remedy, that it is worse than the disease. Liberty is to faction, what air is to fire, an aliment[5] without which it instantly expires. But it could not be a less folly to abolish liberty, which is essential to political life, because it nourishes faction, than it would be to wish the annihilation of air, which is essential to animal life, because it imparts to fire its destructive agency.

The second expedient is as impracticable as the first would be unwise. As long as the reason of man continues fallible, and he is at liberty to exercise it, different opinions will be formed. As long as the connection subsists between his reason and his self-love, his opinions and his passions will have a reciprocal influence on each other; and the former will be objects to which the latter will attach themselves. The diversity in the faculties of men from which the rights of property originate is not less an insuperable obstacle to a uniformity of interests. The protection of these faculties is the first object of government. From the protection of different and unequal faculties of acquiring property, the possession of different degrees and kinds of property immediately results: and from the influence of these on the sentiments and views of the respective proprietors ensues a division of the society into different interests and parties.

The latent causes of faction are thus sown in the nature of man; and we see them everywhere brought into different degrees of activity, according to the different circumstances of civil society. A zeal for different opinions concerning religion, concerning government and many other points, as well of speculation as of practice; an attachment to different leaders ambitiously contending for pre-eminence and power; or to persons of other descriptions whose fortunes have been interesting to the human passions have in turn divided mankind into parties, inflamed them with mutual animosity, and rendered them much more disposed to vex and oppress each other than to cooperate for their common good. So strong is this propensity of mankind to fall into mutual animosities that where no substantial occasion presents itself, the most frivolous and fanciful distinctions have been sufficient to kindle their unfriendly passions and excite their most violent conflicts. But the most common and durable source of factions has been the various and unequal distribution of property. Those who hold and those who are without property have ever formed distinct interests in society. Those who are creditors and those who are debtors fall under a like discrimination. A landed interest, a manufacturing interest, a mercantile interest, a monied interest, with many lesser interests, grow up of necessity in civilized nations, and divide them into different classes, actuated by different sentiments and views. The regulation of these various and interfering interests forms the principal task of modern legislation, and involves the spirit of party and faction in the necessary and ordinary operations of government.

5. Nutriment; sustenance.

No man is allowed to be a judge in his own cause, because his interest would certainly bias his judgment and, not improbably, corrupt his integrity. With equal, nay with greater, reason a body of men are unfit to be both judges and parties at the same time; yet what are many of the most important acts of legislation but so many judicial determinations, not indeed concerning the rights of single persons, but concerning the rights of large bodies of citizens; and what are the different classes of legislators but advocates and parties to the causes which they determine? Is a law proposed concerning private debts? It is a question to which the creditors are parties on one side and the debtors on the other. Justice ought to hold the balance between them. Yet the parties are and must be themselves the judges; and the most numerous party, or, in other words, the most powerful faction, must be expected to prevail. Shall domestic manufactures be encouraged, and in what degree, by restrictions on foreign manufactures? are questions which would be differently decided by the landed and the manufacturing classes; and probably by neither, with a sole regard to justice and the public good. The apportionment of taxes on the various descriptions of property is an act which seems to require the most exact impartiality; yet, there is perhaps no legislative act in which greater opportunity and temptation are given to a predominant party to trample on the rules of justice. Every shilling with which they overburden the inferior number is a shilling saved to their own pockets.

It is in vain to say that enlightened statesmen will be able to adjust these clashing interests and render them all subservient to the public good. Enlightened statesmen will not always be at the helm; nor, in many cases, can such an adjustment be made at all, without taking into view indirect and remote considerations, which will rarely prevail over the immediate interest which one party may find in disregarding the rights of another, or the good of the whole.

The inference to which we are brought is that the *causes* of faction cannot be removed, and that relief is only to be sought in the means of controlling its *effects*.

If a faction consists of less than a majority, relief is supplied by the republican principle, which enables the majority to defeat its sinister views by regular vote. It may clog the administration, it may convulse the society, but it will be unable to execute and mask its violence under the forms of the Constitution. When a majority is included in a faction, the form of popular government on the other hand enables it to sacrifice to its ruling passion or interest both the public good and the rights of other citizens. To secure the public good and private rights against the danger of such a faction, and at the same time to preserve the spirit and the form of popular government, is then the great object to which our inquiries are directed. Let me add that it is the great desideratum[6] by which alone this form of government can be rescued from the opprobrium under which it has so long labored and be recommended to the esteem and adoption of mankind.

By what means is this object attainable? Evidently by one of two only. Either the existence of the same passion or interest in a majority at the same

6. Thing which is desired; that which is felt to be missing and needed (Latin).

time must be prevented; or the majority, having such co-existent passion or interest, must be rendered, by their number and local situation, unable to concert and carry into effect schemes of oppression. If the impulse and the opportunity be suffered to coincide, we well know that neither moral nor religious motives can be relied on as an adequate control. They are not found to be such on the injustice and violence of individuals, and lose their efficacy in proportion to the number combined together; that is, in proportion as their efficacy becomes needful.

From this view of the subject, it may be concluded, that a pure democracy, by which I mean a society consisting of a small number of citizens who assemble and administer the government in person, can admit of no cure for the mischiefs of faction. A common passion or interest will, in almost every case, be felt by a majority of the whole; a communication and concert[7] results from the form of government itself; and there is nothing to check the inducements to sacrifice the weaker party, or an obnoxious individual. Hence it is that such democracies have ever been spectacles of turbulence and contention; have ever been found incompatible with personal security, or the rights of property; and have in general been as short in their lives, as they have been violent in their deaths. Theoretic[8] politicians, who have patronized this species of government, have erroneously supposed that by reducing mankind to a perfect equality in their political rights, they would, at the same time, be perfectly equalized and assimilated in their possessions, their opinions, and their passions.

A republic, by which I mean a government in which the scheme of representation takes place, opens a different prospect, and promises the cure for which we are seeking. Let us examine the points in which it varies from pure democracy, and we shall comprehend both the nature of the cure, and the efficacy which it must derive from the Union.

The two great points of difference between a democracy and a republic are, first, the delegation of the government, in the latter, to a small number of citizens elected by the rest: secondly, the greater number of citizens, and greater sphere of country, over which the latter may be extended.

The effect of the first difference is, on the one hand, to refine and enlarge the public views by passing them through the medium of a chosen body of citizens, whose wisdom may best discern the true interest of their country, and whose patriotism and love of justice will be least likely to sacrifice it to temporary or partial considerations. Under such a regulation, it may well happen that the public voice pronounced by the representatives of the people will be more consonant to the public good than if pronounced by the people themselves convened for the purpose. On the other hand, the effect may be inverted. Men of factious tempers, of local prejudices, or of sinister designs may, by intrigue, by corruption or by other means, first obtain the suffrages,[9] and then betray the interests of the people. The question resulting is whether small or extensive republics are most favorable to the election of proper guardians of the public weal: and it is clearly decided in favor of the latter by two obvious considerations.

7. Agreement, union.
8. Theoretical.

9. Votes.

In the first place it is to be remarked that however small the republic may be, the representatives must be raised to a certain number in order to guard against the cabals[1] of a few; and that however large it may be, they must be limited to a certain number in order to guard against the confusion of a multitude. Hence the number of representatives in the two cases, not being in proportion to that of the constituents, and being proportionally greatest in the small republic, it follows, that if the proportion of fit characters be not less in the large than in the small republic, the former will present a greater option, and consequently a greater probability of a fit choice.

In the next place, as each representative will be chosen by a greater number of citizens in the large than in the small republic, it will be more difficult for unworthy candidates to practice with success the vicious arts, by which elections are too often carried; and the suffrages of the people being more free will be more likely to center on men who possess the most attractive merit, and the most diffusive and established characters.

It must be confessed that in this, as in most other cases, there is a mean, on both sides of which inconveniencies will be found to lie. By enlarging too much the number of electors, you render the representative too little acquainted with all their local circumstances and lesser interests; as by reducing it too much, you render him unduly attached to these, and too little fit to comprehend and pursue great and national objects. The federal Constitution forms a happy combination in this respect; the great and aggregate interests being referred to the national, the local, and, particular, to the state legislatures.

The other point of difference is the greater number of citizens and extent of territory which may be brought within the compass of republican, than of democratic government; and it is this circumstance principally which renders factious combinations less to be dreaded in the former than in the latter. The smaller the society, the fewer probably will be the distinct parties and interests composing it; the fewer the distinct parties and interests, the more frequently will a majority be found of the same party; and the smaller the number of individuals composing a majority, and smaller the compass within which they are placed, the more easily will they concert and execute their plans of oppression. Extend the sphere, and you take in a greater variety of parties and interests; you make it less probable that a majority of the whole will have a common motive to invade the rights of other citizens; or if such a common motive exists, it will be more difficult for all who feel it to discover their own strength, and to act in unison with each other. Besides other impediments, it may be remarked, that where there is a consciousness of unjust or dishonorable purposes, communication is always checked by distrust, in proportion to the number whose concurrence is necessary.

Hence it clearly appears that the same advantage which a republic has over a democracy, in controlling the effects of faction, is enjoyed by a large over a small republic—is enjoyed by the Union over the states composing it. Does this advantage consist in the substitution of representatives, whose enlightened views and virtuous sentiments render them superior to local prejudices, and to schemes of injustice? It will not be denied, that the repre-

1. Plots.

sentation of the Union will be most likely to possess these requisite endowments. Does it consist in the greater security afforded by a greater variety of parties, against the event of any one party being able to outnumber and oppress the rest? In an equal degree does the increased variety of parties, comprised within the Union, increase this security? Does it, in fine,[2] consist in the greater obstacles opposed to the concert and accomplishment of the secret wishes of an unjust and interested majority? Here, again, the extent of the Union gives it the most palpable advantage.

The influence of factious leaders may kindle a flame within their particular states, but will be unable to spread a general conflagration through the other states: a religious sect may degenerate into a political faction in a part of the confederacy,[3] but the variety of sects dispersed over the entire face of it must secure the national councils against any danger from that source: a rage for paper money, for an abolition of debts, for an equal division of property, or for any other improper or wicked project, will be less apt to pervade the whole body of the Union than a particular member of it; in the same proportion as such a malady is more likely to taint a particular county or district than an entire state.

In the extent and proper structure of the Union, therefore, we behold a republican remedy for the diseases most incident to republican government. And according to the degree of pleasure and pride we feel in being republicans, ought to be our zeal in cherishing the spirit, and supporting the character of Federalists.

<div align="right">Publius</div>

1787 1788

OLAUDAH EQUIANO
1745?–1797

I n 1789, *The Interesting Narrative of the Life of Olaudah Equiano, or Gustavus Vassa, the African* was published by Equiano in London, and it found an enthusiastic American audience when it was reprinted in New York two years later. Over the next five years *The Interesting Narrative* went through eight more editions, and it was reprinted on several occasions in the United States during the pre–Civil War period. This publication history suggests both the book's centrality to the antislavery cause and the powerful appeal of Equiano's narrative voice. No black person before the abolitionist Frederick Douglass (1817–1895) spoke so movingly to American readers about the inhumanity of slavery, and no work before Douglass's *Narrative* had such an impact on the antislavery movement. Incorporating the vocabulary and ideals of the Enlightenment—particularly the belief that sentiment linked all human beings and

2. In short; to sum up. 3. Alliance, union.

thus provided a basis for universal claims to human rights—Equiano made a powerful case for the countless disenfranchised and exploited workers whose labor fueled the new mercantilism. In American literature, replete with self-made figures who voyage from innocence to experience, Equiano's story stands in a class by itself, both for the challenges he faced and for the transformations he experienced. He defined himself as neither African American (his first owner in the New World was a Virginian) nor Anglo African (after he settled in London); instead, he came to exemplify the Atlantic Rim, presenting himself as someone who at various times called Africa, the Americas, and Europe his home.

Equiano wrote that he was born around 1745 in what is now Nigeria, in an otherwise unknown Ibo village called Essaka. He was sold to British slavers in 1756 and transported first to Barbadoes, in the West Indies, and then to a plantation in Virginia. Recent scholarship has questioned these claims, suggesting that Equiano may have been born in the Carolinas. If this proves to be the case, it means that he made the decision to assume an African heritage for his life story, which then can be understood as an example of a witness narrative, that is, the testimony of someone from a marginalized group who speaks in the first person for the entire group's history. To make his life appear more representative, Equiano may have merged his experiences with those of the voiceless Africans who endured the horrors of the Middle Passage.

While the facts of his early life are uncertain, his account of his later years is corroborated by existing documents. He was with his second owner, Lieutenant Michael Henry Pascal, throughout the Seven Years' War (1756–63), in which England and France led opposing coalitions of nations. He was present at the siege of Fort Louisburg, on Cape Breton Island, Nova Scotia. Eventually, Equiano was sold to a Quaker merchant from Philadelphia, Robert King, who conducted much of his business in the West Indies. King often traded in "live cargo," or slaves, and Equiano saw much that made him grateful for his Quaker master's treatment of him, though he was also sensitive to the freedom being denied him. He saw the ugliest side of American life in both the North and the South. Even in Philadelphia, a city built on the premise of brotherly love, Equiano observed that the freed black was treated with profound contempt, "plundered" and "universally insulted," with no possibility of redress. King, however, did make it possible for Equiano to purchase his freedom in 1766. Having gained his liberty by paying forty pounds—money earned by carrying on his own business while managing King's—he never set foot on American soil again.

It was Equiano's intention to settle in London for the rest of his life. He made his living there as a free servant, a musician (he played the French horn), and a barber. Eventually Equiano's skill as a seaman, and his remarkable curiosity, made him yearn for new adventures. Before he died he had traveled as far as Turkey; attended the opera in Rome; participated in an expedition to search for a Northwest Passage through the arctic to the Pacific Ocean; and seen Jamaica, Honduras, and Nicaragua.

In 1783 Equiano brought to the British public's attention the case of the infamous ship *Zong*, whose owners had thrown one hundred and thirty-two shackled slaves overboard and later made insurance claims against their loss. He lectured widely on the abolition of slavery and urged a project to resettle poor blacks in Sierra Leone, Africa. He was given an official post in this undertaking, but lost it after he made accusations of corruption against British government officials. Although he spoke about his desire to return to Africa, it always lay beyond his reach. In a letter to his hosts in Birmingham, England, after he had lectured there, he wrote evocatively about an imagined scene:

These acts of kindness and hospitality have filled me with a longing desire to see these worthy friends on my own estate in Africa, where the richest produce of it should be devoted to their entertainment. There they should partake of the luxuriant pineapples, and the well-flavored virgin palm-wine, and to heighten the bliss I would burn a certain tree, that would afford us light as clear and brilliant as the virtue of my guests.

In 1792 Equiano married Susanna Cullen, and their marriage was considered of sufficient public interest to be reported in the London *Gentleman's Magazine.* Five years later, he died of uncertain causes, and one of his daughters died shortly after.

From The Interesting Narrative of the Life of Olaudah Equiano, or Gustavas Vassa, the African, Written by Himself[1]

From *Chapter I*

I believe it is difficult for those who publish their own memoirs to escape the imputation of vanity; nor is this the only disadvantage under which they labor: it is also their misfortune, that what is uncommon is rarely, if ever, believed, and what is obvious we are apt to turn from with disgust, and to charge the writer with impertinence. People generally think those memoirs only worthy to be read or remembered which abound in great or striking events; those, in short, which in a high degree excite either admiration or pity: all others they consign to contempt and oblivion. It is therefore, I confess, not a little hazardous in a private and obscure individual, and a stranger too, thus to solicit the indulgent attention of the public; especially when I own[2] I offer here the history of neither a saint, a hero, nor a tyrant. I believe there are few events in my life, which have not happened to many: it is true the incidents of it are numerous; and, did I consider myself an European, I might say my sufferings were great: but when I compare my lot with that of most of my countrymen, I regard myself as a *particular favorite of Heaven,* and acknowledge the mercies of Providence in every occurrence of my life. If, then, the following narrative does not appear sufficiently interesting to engage general attention, let my motive be some excuse for its publication. I am not so foolishly vain as to expect from it either immortality or literary reputation. If it affords any satisfaction to my numerous friends, at whose request it has been written, or in the smallest degree promotes the interests of humanity, the ends for which it was undertaken will be fully attained, and every wish of my heart gratified. Let it therefore be remembered, that, in wishing to avoid censure, I do not aspire to praise.

That part of Africa, known by the name of Guinea, to which the trade for slaves is carried on, extends along the coast above 3400 miles, from Senegal to Angola, and includes a variety of kingdoms. Of these the most considerable is the kingdom of Benin, both as to extent and wealth, the richness

1. The text is from the first edition, published in two volumes in 1789. The original paragraphing has been altered to facilitate reading.
2. Acknowledge.

and cultivation of the soil, the power of its king, and the number and warlike disposition of the inhabitants. It is situated nearly under the line,[3] and extends along the coast about 170 miles, but runs back into the interior part of Africa to a distance hitherto, I believe, unexplored by any traveler; and seems only terminated at length by the empire of Abyssinnia, near 1500 miles from its beginning. This kingdom is divided into many provinces or districts: in one of the most remote and fertile of which, I was born, in the year 1745, situated in a charming fruitful vale, named Essaka. The distance of this province from the capital of Benin and the sea coast must be very considerable: for I had never heard of white men or Europeans, nor of the sea; and our subjection to the king of Benin was little more than nominal; for every transaction of the government, as far as my slender observation extended, was conducted by the chief or elders of the place. The manners and government of a people who have little commerce with other countries, are generally very simple; and the history of what passes in one family or village, may serve as a specimen of the whole nation. My father was one of those elders or chiefs I have spoken of, and was styled Embrenche; a term, as I remember, importing the highest distinction, and signifying in our language a *mark* of grandeur. This mark is conferred on the person entitled to it, by cutting the skin across at the top of the forehead, and drawing it down to the eyebrows: and while it is in this situation applying a warm hand, and rubbing it until it shrinks up into a thick *weal* across the lower part of the forehead. Most of the judges and senators were thus marked; my father had long borne it: I had seen it conferred on one of my brothers, and I also was *destined* to receive it by my parents. Those Embrenche or chief men, decided disputes and punished crimes; for which purpose they always assembled together. The proceedings were generally short: and in most cases the law of retaliation prevailed.* * *

We are almost a nation of dancers, musicians and poets. Thus every great event, such as a triumphant return from battle, or other cause of public rejoicing, is celebrated in public dances, which are accompanied with songs and music suited to the occasion. The assembly is separated into four divisions, which dance either apart or in succession, and each with a character peculiar to itself. The first division contains the married men, who in their dances frequently exhibit feats of arms, and the representation of a battle. To these succeed the married women, who dance in the second division. The young men occupy the third: and the maidens the fourth. Each represents some interesting scene of real life, such as a great achievement, domestic employment, a pathetic[4] story, or some rural sport; and as the subject is generally founded on some recent event, it is therefore ever new. This gives our dances a spirit and variety which I have scarcely seen elsewhere.[5]

* * *

3. I.e., the equator.
4. Emotionally moving.
5. When I was in Smyrna I have frequently

seen the Greeks dance after this manner [Equiano's note].

Chapter II

I hope the reader will not think I have trespassed on his patience in introducing myself to him, with some account of the manners and customs of my country. They had been implanted in me with great care, and made an impression on my mind, which time could not erase, and which all the adversity and variety of fortune I have since experienced, served only to rivet and record; for, whether the love of one's country be real or imaginary, or a lesson of reason, or an instinct of nature, I still look back with pleasure on the first scenes of my life, though that pleasure has been for the most part mingled with sorrow.

I have already acquainted the reader with the time and place of my birth. My father, besides many slaves, had a numerous family, of which seven lived to grow up, including myself and a sister, who was the only daughter. As I was the youngest of the sons, I became, of course, the greatest favorite with my mother, and was always with her; and she used to take particular pains to form my mind. I was trained up from my earliest years in the art of war: my daily exercise was shooting and throwing javelins; and my mother adorned me with emblems, after the manner of our greatest warriors. In this way I grew up till I was turned the age of eleven, when an end was put to my happiness in the following manner:—generally when the grown people in the neighborhood were gone far in the fields to labor, the children assembled together in some of the neighboring premises to play; and commonly some of us used to get up a tree to look out for any assailant, or kidnapper, that might come upon us—for they sometimes took those opportunities of our parents' absence, to attack and carry off as many as they could seize. One day as I was watching at the top of a tree in our yard, I saw one of those people come into the yard of our next neighbor but one to kidnap, there being many stout[6] young people in it. Immediately on this I gave the alarm of the rogue, and he was surrounded by the stoutest of them, who entangled him with cords, so that he could not escape till some of the grown people came and secured him. But, alas! ere long it was my fate to be thus attacked, and to be carried off, when none of the grown people were nigh. One day, when all our people were gone out to their works as usual, and only I and my dear sister were left to mind the house, two men and a woman got over our walls, and in a moment seized us both, and, without giving us time to cry out, or make resistance, they stopped our mouths, and ran off with us into the nearest wood. Here they tied our hands, and continued to carry us as far as they could, till night came on, when we reached a small house, where the robbers halted for refreshment, and spent the night. We were then unbound, but were unable to take any food; and, being quite overpowered by fatigue and grief, our only relief was some sleep, which allayed our misfortune for a short time. The next morning we left the house, and continued traveling all the day. For a long time we had kept the woods, but at last we came into a road which I believed I knew. I had now some hopes of being delivered; for we had advanced but a little way before I discovered some people at a distance, on which I began to cry out for their assistance; but my cries had no other effect than to make

6. Strong.

them tie me faster and stop my mouth, and then they put me into a large sack. They also stopped my sister's mouth, and tied her hands; and in this manner we proceeded till we were out of sight of these people. When we went to rest the following night, they offered us some victuals, but we refused it; and the only comfort we had was in being in one another's arms all that night, and bathing each other with our tears. But alas! we were soon deprived of even the small comfort of weeping together. The next day proved a day of greater sorrow than I had yet experienced; for my sister and I were then separated, while we lay clasped in each other's arms. It was in vain that we besought them not to part us; she was torn from me, and immediately carried away, while I was left in a state of distraction not to be described. I cried and grieved continually; and for several days did not eat any thing but what they forced into my mouth. At length, after many days traveling, during which I had often changed masters, I got into the hands of a chieftain, in a very pleasant country. This man had two wives and some children, and they all used[7] me extremely well, and did all they could to comfort me; particularly the first wife, who was something like my mother. Although I was a great many days' journey from my father's house, yet these people spoke exactly the same language with us. This first master of mine, as I may call him, was a smith,[8] and my principal employment was working his bellows, which were the same kind as I had seen in my vicinity. They were in some respects not unlike the stoves here in gentlemen's kitchens, and were covered over with leather; and in the middle of that leather a stick was fixed, and a person stood up, and worked it in the same manner as is done to pump water out of a cask with a hand pump. I believe it was gold he worked, for it was of a lovely bright yellow color, and was worn by the women on their wrists and ankles. I was there I suppose about a month, and they at last used to trust me some little distance from the house. This liberty I used in embracing every opportunity to inquire the way to my own home; and I also sometimes, for the same purpose, went with the maidens, in the cool of the evenings, to bring pitchers of water from the springs for the use of the house. I had also remarked where the sun rose in the morning, and set in the evening, as I had traveled along; and I had observed that my father's house was towards the rising of the sun. I therefore determined to seize the first opportunity of making my escape, and to shape my course for that quarter; for I was quite oppressed and weighed down by grief after my mother and friends; and my love of liberty, ever great, was strengthened by the mortifying circumstance of not daring to eat with the free-born children, although I was mostly their companion. While I was projecting my escape one day, an unlucky event happened, which quite disconcerted my plan, and put an end to my hopes. I used to be sometimes employed in assisting an elderly slave to cook and take care of the poultry; and one morning, while I was feeding some chickens, I happened to toss a small pebble at one of them, which hit it on the middle, and directly killed it. The old slave, having soon after missed the chicken, inquired after it; and on my relating the accident (for I told her the truth, for my mother would never suffer me to tell a lie), she flew into a violent passion, and threatened that I should suffer for it; and, my master being out, she immediately went and told her mistress what I had done. This alarmed me very much, and I

7. Treated.

8. A metalworker; here, a goldsmith.

expected an instant flogging, which to me was uncommonly dreadful, for I had seldom been beaten at home. I therefore resolved to fly; and accordingly I ran into a thicket that was hard by, and hid myself in the bushes. Soon afterwards my mistress and the slave returned, and, not seeing me, they searched all the house, but not finding me, and I not making answer when they called to me, they thought I had run away, and the whole neighborhood was raised in the pursuit of me. In that part of the country, as in ours, the houses and villages were skirted with woods, or shrubberies, and the bushes were so thick that a man could readily conceal himself in them, so as to elude the strictest search. The neighbors continued the whole day looking for me, and several times many of them came within a few yards of the place where I lay hid. I expected every moment, when I heard a rustling among the trees, to be found out, and punished by my master; but they never discovered me, though they were often so near that I even heard their conjectures as they were looking about for me; and I now learned from them that any attempts to return home would be hopeless. Most of them supposed I had fled towards home; but the distance was so great, and the way so intricate, that they thought I could never reach it, and that I should be lost in the woods. When I heard this I was seized with a violent panic, and abandoned myself to despair. Night, too, began to approach, and aggravated all my fears. I had before entertained hopes of getting home, and had determined when it should be dark to make the attempt; but I was now convinced it was fruitless, and began to consider that, if possibly I could escape all other animals, I could not those of the human kind; and that, not knowing the way, I must perish in the woods. Thus was I like the hunted deer—

—"Every leaf and every whisp'ring breath,
Convey'd a foe, and every foe a death."[9]

I heard frequent rustlings among the leaves, and being pretty sure they were snakes, I expected every instant to be stung by them. This increased my anguish, and the horror of my situation became now quite insupportable. I at length quitted the thicket, very faint and hungry, for I had not eaten or drank any thing all the day, and crept to my master's kitchen, from whence I set out at first, which was an open shed, and laid myself down in the ashes with an anxious wish for death, to relieve me from all my pains. I was scarcely awake in the morning, when the old woman slave, who was the first up, came to light the fire, and saw me in the fire place. She was very much surprised to see me, and could scarcely believe her own eyes. She now promised to intercede for me, and went for her master, who soon after came, and, having slightly reprimanded me, ordered me to be taken care of, and not ill treated.

Soon after this, my master's only daughter, and child by his first wife, sickened and died, which affected him so much that for some time he was almost frantic, and really would have killed himself, had he not been watched and prevented. However, in short time afterwards he recovered, and I was again sold. I was now carried to the left of the sun's rising, through many

9. Near quotation of lines 287–88 of "Cooper's Hill," a poem by the Anglo-Irish writer and statesman Sir John Denham (1615–1669).

dreary wastes and dismal woods, amidst the hideous roarings of wild beasts. The people I was sold to used to carry me very often, when I was tired, either on their shoulders or on their backs. I saw many convenient well built sheds along the road, at proper distances, to accommodate the merchants and travelers, who lay in those buildings along with their wives, who often accompany them; and they always go well armed.

From the time I left my own nation, I always found somebody that understood me till I came to the sea coast. The languages of different nations did not totally differ, nor were they so copious as those of the Europeans, particularly the English. They were therefore, easily learned; and, while I was journeying thus through Africa, I acquired two or three different tongues. In this manner I had been traveling for a considerable time, when, one evening, to my great surprise, whom should I see brought to the house where I was but my dear sister! As soon as she saw me, she gave a loud shriek, and ran into my arms—I was quite overpowered: neither of us could speak; but, for a considerable time, clung to each other in mutual embraces, unable to do any thing but weep. Our meeting affected all who saw us; and, indeed, I must acknowledge, in honor of those sable[1] destroyers of human rights, that I never met with any ill treatment, or saw any offered to their slaves, except tying them, when necessary, to keep them from running away. When these people knew we were brother and sister, they indulged us to be together; and the man, to whom I supposed we belonged, lay with us, he in the middle, while she and I held one another by the hands across his breast all night; and thus for a while we forgot our misfortunes, in the joy of being together; but even this small comfort was soon to have an end; for scarcely had the fatal morning appeared when she was again torn from me forever! I was now more miserable, if possible, than before. The small relief which her presence gave me from pain was gone, and the wretchedness of my situation was redoubled by my anxiety after her fate, and my apprehensions lest her sufferings should be greater than mine, when I could not be with her to alleviate them. Yes, thou dear partner of all my childish sports! thou sharer of my joys and sorrows! happy should I have ever esteemed myself to encounter every misery for you and to procure your freedom by the sacrifice of my own.—Though you were early forced from my arms, your image has been always riveted in my heart, from which neither time nor fortune have been able to remove it; so that, while the thoughts of your sufferings have damped my prosperity, they have mingled with adversity and increased its bitterness. To that Heaven which protects the weak from the strong, I commit the care of your innocence and virtues, if they have not already received their full reward, and if your youth and delicacy have not long since fallen victims to the violence of the African trader, the pestilential stench of a Guinea ship, the seasoning in the European colonies, or the lash and lust of a brutal and unrelenting overseer.

I did not long remain after my sister. I was again sold, and carried through a number of places, till after traveling a considerable time, I came to a town called Tinmah, in the most beautiful country I had yet seen in Africa. It was extremely rich, and there were many rivulets which flowed through it,

1. Black.

and supplied a large pond in the center of the town, where the people washed. Here I first saw and tasted cocoa nuts, which I thought superior to any nuts I had ever tasted before; and the trees which were loaded, were also interspersed among the houses, which had commodious shades adjoining, and were in the same manner as ours, the insides being neatly plastered and whitewashed. Here I also saw and tasted for the first time, sugar cane. Their money consisted of little white shells, the size of the finger nail. I was sold here for one hundred and seventy-two of them, by a merchant who lived and brought me there. I had been about two or three days at his house, when a wealthy widow, a neighbor of his, came there one evening, and brought with her an only son, a young gentleman about my own age and size. Here they saw me; and, having taken a fancy to me, I was bought of the merchant, and went home with them. Her house and premises were situated close to one of those rivulets I have mentioned, and were the finest I ever saw in Africa: they were very extensive, and she had a number of slaves to attend her. The next day I was washed and perfumed, and when mealtime came, I was led into the presence of my mistress, and ate and drank before her with her son. This filled me with astonishment; and I could scarce help expressing my surprise that the young gentleman should suffer[2] me, who was bound, to eat with him who was free; and not only so, but that he would not at any time either eat or drink till I had taken first, because I was the eldest, which was agreeable to our custom. Indeed, every thing here, and all their treatment of me, made me forget that I was a slave. The language of these people resembled ours so nearly, that we understood each other perfectly. They had also the very same customs as we. There were likewise slaves daily to attend us, while my young master and I, with other boys, sported with our darts and bows and arrows, as I had been used to do at home. In this resemblance to my former happy state, I passed about two months; and I now began to think I was to be adopted into the family, and was beginning to be reconciled to my situation, and to forget by degrees my misfortunes, when all at once the delusion vanished; for, without the least previous knowledge, one morning early, while my dear master and companion was still asleep, I was awakened out of my reverie to fresh sorrow, and hurried away even amongst the uncircumcised.

Thus, at the very moment I dreamed of the greatest happiness, I found myself most miserable; and it seemed as if fortune wished to give me this taste of joy only to render the reverse more poignant.—The change I now experienced, was as painful as it was sudden and unexpected. It was a change indeed, from a state of bliss to a scene which is inexpressible by me, as it discovered[3] to me an element I had never before beheld, and till then had no idea of, and wherein such instances of hardship and cruelty continually occurred, as I can never reflect on but with horror.

All the nations and people I had hitherto passed through, resembled our own in their manners, customs, and language: but I came at length to a country, the inhabitants of which differed from us in all those particulars. I was very much struck with this difference, especially when I came among a people who did not circumcise, and ate without washing their hands.

2. Allow. 3. Revealed.

They cooked also in iron pots, and had European cutlasses and cross bows, which were unknown to us, and fought with their fists among themselves. Their women were not so modest as ours, for they ate, and drank, and slept with their men. But above all, I was amazed to see no sacrifices or offerings among them. In some of those places the people ornamented themselves with scars, and likewise filed their teeth very sharp. They wanted sometimes to ornament me in the same manner, but I would not suffer them; hoping that I might some time be among a people who did not thus disfigure themselves, as I thought they did. At last I came to the banks of a large river which was covered with canoes, in which the people appeared to live with their household utensils, and provisions of all kinds. I was beyond measure astonished at this, as I had never before seen any water larger than a pond or a rivulet: and my surprise was mingled with no small fear when I was put into one of these canoes, and we began to paddle and move along the river. We continued going on thus till night, and when we came to land, and made fires on the banks, each family by themselves; some dragged their canoes on shore, others stayed and cooked in theirs, and laid in them all night. Those on the land had mats, of which they made tents, some in the shape of little houses; in these we slept; and after the morning meal, we embarked again and proceeded as before. I was often very much astonished to see some of the women, as well as the men, jump into the water, dive to the bottom, come up again, and swim about.—Thus I continued to travel, sometimes by land, sometimes by water, through different countries and various nations, till, at the end of six or seven months after I had been kidnapped, I arrived at the sea coast. It would be tedious and uninteresting to relate all the incidents which befell me during this journey, and which I have not yet forgotten; of the various hands I passed through, and the manners and customs of all the different people among whom I lived—I shall therefore only observe, that in all the places where I was, the soil was exceedingly rich; the pumpkins, eadas,[4] plaintains, yams, etc., etc., were in great abundance, and of incredible size. There were also vast quantities of different gums, though not used for any purpose, and every where a great deal of tobacco. The cotton even grew quite wild, and there was plenty of red-wood. I saw no mechanics[5] whatever in all the way, except such as I have mentioned. The chief employment in all these countries was agriculture, and both the males and females, as with us, were brought up to it, and trained in the arts of war.

The first object which saluted my eyes when I arrived on the coast, was the sea, and a slave ship, which was then riding at anchor, and waiting for its cargo. These filled me with astonishment, which was soon converted into terror, when I was carried on board. I was immediately handled, and tossed up to see if I were sound, by some of the crew; and I was now persuaded that I had gotten into a world of bad spirits, and that they were going to kill me. Their complexions, too, differing so much from ours, their long hair, and the language they spoke (which was very different from any I had ever heard), united to confirm me in this belief. Indeed, such were the horrors of my views and fears at the moment, that, if ten thousand worlds had been my own, I would have freely parted with them all to have exchanged

4. Or eddoes, edible roots found in the tropics. 5. Artisans, manual workers.

my condition with that of the meanest[6] slave in my own country. When I looked round the ship too, and saw a large furnace[7] of copper boiling, and a multitude of black people of every description chained together, every one of their countenances expressing dejection and sorrow, I no longer doubted of my fate; and, quite overpowered with horror and anguish, I fell motionless on the deck and fainted. When I recovered a little, I found some black people about me, who I believed were some of those who had brought me on board, and had been receiving their pay; they talked to me in order to cheer me, but all in vain. I asked them if we were not to be eaten by those white men with horrible looks, red faces, and long hair. They told me I was not: and one of the crew brought me a small portion of spirituous liquor in a wine glass, but, being afraid of him, I would not take it out of his hand. One of the blacks, therefore, took it from him and gave it to me, and I took a little down my palate, which, instead of reviving me, as they thought it would, threw me into the greatest consternation at the strange feeling it produced, having never tasted any such liquor before. Soon after this, the blacks who brought me on board went off, and left me abandoned to despair.

I now saw myself deprived of all chance of returning to my native country, or even the least glimpse of hope of gaining the shore, which I now considered as friendly; and I even wished for my former slavery in preference to my present situation, which was filled with horrors of every kind, still heightened by my ignorance of what I was to undergo. I was not long suffered to indulge my grief; I was soon put down under the decks, and there I received such a salutation in my nostrils as I had never experienced in my life: so that, with the loathsomeness of the stench, and crying together, I became so sick and low that I was not able to eat, nor had I the least desire to taste any thing. I now wished for the last friend, death, to relieve me; but soon, to my grief, two of the white men offered me eatables; and, on my refusing to eat, one of them held me fast by the hands, and laid me across, I think the windlass, and tied my feet, while the other flogged me severely. I had never experienced any thing of this kind before, and although not being used to the water, I naturally feared that element the first time I saw it, yet, nevertheless, could I have got over the nettings, I would have jumped over the side, but I could not; and besides, the crew used to watch us very closely who were not chained down to the decks, lest we should leap into the water; and I have seen some of these poor African prisoners most severely cut, for attempting to do so, and hourly whipped for not eating. This indeed was often the case with myself. In a little time after, amongst the poor chained men, I found some of my own nation, which in a small degree gave ease to my mind. I inquired of these what was to be done with us? They gave me to understand we were to be carried to these white people's country to work for them. I then was a little revived, and thought, if it were no worse than working, my situation was not so desperate; but still I feared I should be put to death, the white people looked and acted, as I thought, in so savage a manner; for I had never seen among any people such instances of brutal cruelty; and this not only shown towards us blacks, but also to some of the whites themselves. One white man in particular I saw, when we were permitted to be

6. Most poorly treated. 7. Smelting furnace.

on deck, flogged so unmercifully with a large rope near the foremast, that he died in consequence of it; and they tossed him over the side as they would have done a brute. This made me fear these people the more; and I expected nothing less than to be treated in the same manner. I could not help expressing my fears and apprehensions to some of my countrymen; I asked them if these people had no country, but lived in this hollow place (the ship)? They told me they did not, but came from a distant one. "Then," said I, "how comes it in all our country we never heard of them?" They told me because they lived so very far off. I then asked where were their women? had they any like themselves? I was told they had. "And why," said I, "do we not see them?" They answered, because they were left behind. I asked how the vessel could go? they told me they could not tell; but that there was cloth put upon the masts by the help of the ropes I saw, and then the vessel went on; and the white men had some spell or magic they put in the water when they liked, in order to stop the vessel. I was exceedingly amazed at this account, and really thought they were spirits. I therefore wished much to be from amongst[8] them, for I expected they would sacrifice me; but my wishes were vain—for we were so quartered that it was impossible for any of us to make our escape.

While we stayed on the coast I was mostly on deck; and one day, to my great astonishment, I saw one of these vessels coming in with the sails up. As soon as the whites saw it, they gave a great shout, at which we were amazed; and the more so, as the vessel appeared larger by approaching nearer. At last, she came to an anchor in my sight, and when the anchor was let go, I and my countrymen who saw it, were lost in astonishment to observe the vessel stop—and were now convinced it was done by magic. Soon after this the other ship got her boats out, and they came on board of us, and the people of both ships seemed very glad to see each other.—Several of the strangers also shook hands with us black people, and made motions with their hands, signifying I suppose, we were to go to their country, but we did not understand them.

At last, when the ship we were in had got in all her cargo, they made ready with many fearful noises, and we were all put under deck, so that we could not see how they managed the vessel. But this disappointment was the least of my sorrow. The stench of the hold while we were on the coast was so intolerably loathsome, that it was dangerous to remain there for any time, and some of us had been permitted to stay on the deck for the fresh air; but now that the whole ship's cargo were confined together, it became absolutely pestilential. The closeness of the place, and the heat of the climate, added to the number in the ship, which was so crowded that each had scarcely room to turn himself, almost suffocated us. This produced copious perspirations, so that the air soon became unfit for respiration, from a variety of loathsome smells, and brought on a sickness among the slaves, of which many died—thus falling victims to the improvident avarice, as I may call it, of their purchasers. This wretched situation was again aggravated by the galling of the chains, now become insupportable, and the filth of the necessary tubs,[9] into which the children often fell, and were almost suffocated. The shrieks of the women, and the groans of the dying, rendered the whole a scene of horror almost inconceivable. Happily perhaps, for myself, I was soon reduced so low here that it was thought necessary to keep me

8. I.e., away from. 9. I.e., for excretion.

almost always on deck; and from my extreme youth I was not put in fetters. In this situation I expected every hour to share the fate of my companions, some of whom were almost daily brought upon deck at the point of death, which I began to hope would soon put an end to my miseries. Often did I think many of the inhabitants of the deep much more happy than myself. I envied them the freedom they enjoyed, and as often wished I could change my condition for theirs. Every circumstance I met with, served only to render my state more painful, and heightened my apprehensions, and my opinion of the cruelty of the whites.

One day they had taken a number of fishes; and when they had killed and satisfied themselves with as many as they thought fit, to our astonishment who were on deck, rather than give any of them to us to eat, as we expected, they tossed the remaining fish into the sea again, although we begged and prayed for some as well as we could, but in vain; and some of my countrymen, being pressed by hunger, took an opportunity, when they thought no one saw them, of trying to get a little privately; but they were discovered, and the attempt procured them some very severe floggings. One day, when we had a smooth sea and moderate wind, two of my wearied countrymen who were chained together (I was near them at the time), preferring death to such a life of misery, somehow made through the nettings and jumped into the sea: immediately, another quite dejected fellow, who, on account of his illness, was suffered to be out of irons, also followed their example; and I believe many more would very soon have done the same, if they had not been prevented by the ship's crew, who were instantly alarmed. Those of us that were the most active, were in a moment put down under the deck, and there was such a noise and confusion amongst the people of the ship as I never heard before, to stop her, and get the boat out to go after the slaves. However, two of the wretches were drowned, but they got the other, and afterwards flogged him unmercifully, for thus attempting to prefer death to slavery. In this manner we continued to undergo more hardships than I can now relate, hardships which are inseparable from this accursed trade. Many a time we were near suffocation from the want of fresh air, which we were often without for whole days together. This, and the stench of the necessary tubs, carried off many.

During our passage, I first saw flying fishes, which surprised me very much; they used frequently to fly across the ship, and many of them fell on the deck. I also now first saw the use of the quadrant; I had often with astonishment seen the mariners make observations with it, and I could not think what it meant. They at last took notice of my surprise; and one of them, willing to increase it, as well as to gratify my curiosity, made me one day look through it. The clouds appeared to me to be land, which disappeared as they passed along. This heightened my wonder; and I was now more persuaded than ever, that I was in another world, and that every thing about me was magic. At last, we came in sight of the island of Barbadoes, at which the whites on board gave a great shout, and made many signs of joy to us. We did not know what to think of this; but as the vessel drew nearer, we plainly saw the harbor, and other ships of different kinds and sizes, and we soon anchored amongst them, off Bridgetown. Many merchants and planters now came on board, though it was in the evening. They put us in separate parcels,[1] and

1. Groups.

examined us attentively. They also made us jump, and pointed to the land, signifying we were to go there. We thought by this, we should be eaten by these ugly men, as they appeared to us; and, when soon after we were all put down under the deck again, there was much dread and trembling among us, and nothing but bitter cries to be heard all the night from these apprehensions, insomuch, that at last the white people got some old slaves from the land to pacify us. They told us we were not to be eaten, but to work, and were soon to go on land, where we should see many of our country people. This report eased us much. And sure enough, soon after we were landed, there came to us Africans of all languages.

We were conducted immediately to the merchant's yard, where we were all pent up together, like so many sheep in a fold, without regard to sex or age. As every object was new to me, every thing I saw filled me with surprise. What struck me first, was, that the houses were built with bricks and stories,[2] and in every other respect different from those I had seen in Africa; but I was still more astonished on seeing people on horseback. I did not know what this could mean; and, indeed, I thought these people were full of nothing but magical arts. While I was in this astonishment, one of my fellow prisoners spoke to a countryman of his, about the horses, who said they were the same kind they had in their country. I understood them, though they were from a distant part of Africa; and I thought it odd I had not seen any horses there; but afterwards, when I came to converse with different Africans, I found they had many horses amongst them, and much larger than those I then saw.

We were not many days in the merchant's custody, before we were sold after their usual manner, which is this:—On a signal given (as the beat of a drum), the buyers rush at once into the yard where the slaves are confined, and make choice of that parcel they like best. The noise and clamor with which this is attended, and the eagerness visible in the countenances of the buyers, serve not a little to increase the apprehension of terrified Africans, who may well be supposed to consider them as the ministers of that destruction to which they think themselves devoted. In this manner, without scruple, are relations and friends separated, most of them never to see each other again. I remember, in the vessel in which I was brought over, in the men's apartment, there were several brothers, who, in the sale, were sold in different lots; and it was very moving on this occasion, to see and hear their cries at parting. O, ye nominal Christians![3] might not an African ask you— Learned you this from your God, who says unto you, Do unto all men as you would men should do unto you? Is it not enough that we are torn from our country and friends, to toil for your luxury and lust of gain? Must every tender feeling be likewise sacrificed to your avarice? Are the dearest friends and relations, now rendered more dear by their separation from their kindred, still to be parted from each other, and thus prevented from cheering the gloom of slavery, with the small comfort of being together, and mingling their sufferings and sorrows? Why are parents to lose their children, brothers their sisters, or husbands their wives? Surely, this is a new refinement in cruelty, which, while it has no advantage to atone for it, thus aggravates distress, and adds fresh horrors even to the wretchedness of slavery.

2. I.e., the buildings were two-storied. 3. Christians in name only.

From *Chapter III*

I now totally lost the small remains of comfort I had enjoyed in conversing with my countrymen; the women too, who used to wash and take care of me were all gone different ways, and I never saw one of them afterwards.

I stayed in this island for a few days; I believe it could not be above a fortnight; when I, and some few more slaves, that were not salable amongst the rest, from very much fretting, were shipped off in a sloop for North America. On the passage we were better treated than when we were coming from Africa, and we had plenty of rice and fat pork. We were landed up a river a good way from the sea, about Virginia county, where we saw few or none of our native Africans, and not one soul who could talk to me. I was a few weeks weeding grass, and gathering stones in a plantation; and at last all my companions were distributed different ways, and only myself was left. I was now exceedingly miserable, and thought myself worse off than any of the rest of my companions; for they could talk to each other, but I had no person to speak to that I could understand. In this state, I was constantly grieving and pining,[4] and wishing for death rather than any thing else. While I was in this plantation, the gentleman, to whom I suppose the estate belonged, being unwell, I was one day sent for to his dwelling house to fan him; when I came into the room where he was I was very much affrighted at some things I saw, and the more so as I had seen a black woman slave as I came through the house, who was cooking the dinner, and the poor creature was cruelly loaded with various kinds of iron machines; she had one particularly on her head, which locked her mouth so fast that she could scarcely speak; and could not eat nor drink. I was much astonished and shocked at this contrivance, which I afterwards learned was called the iron muzzle. Soon after I had a fan put in my hand, to fan the gentleman while he slept; and so I did indeed with great fear. While he was fast asleep I indulged myself a great deal in looking about the room, which to me appeared very fine and curious. The first object that engaged my attention was a watch which hung on the chimney, and was going. I was quite surprised at the noise it made, and was afraid it would tell the gentleman any thing I might do amiss; and when I immediately after observed a picture hanging in the room, which appeared constantly to look at me, I was still more affrighted, having never seen such things as these before. At one time I thought it was something relative to magic; and not seeing it move, I thought it might be some way the whites had to keep their great men when they died, and offer them libations as we used to do our friendly spirits. In this state of anxiety I remained till my master awoke, when I was dismissed out of the room, to my no small satisfaction and relief; for I thought that these people were all made up of wonders. In this place I was called Jacob; but on board the African Snow, I was called Michael. I had been some time in this miserable forlorn, and much dejected state, without having any one to talk to, which made my life a burden, when the kind and unknown hand of the Creator (who in very deed leads the blind in a way they know not) now began to appear, to my comfort; for one day the captain of a merchant ship, called the Industrious Bee, came on some business to my master's house. This gentleman, whose name was Michael Henry Pascal, was

4. Suffering.

a lieutenant in the royal navy, but now commanded this trading ship, which was somewhere in the confines of the county many miles off. While he was at my master's house, it happened that he saw me, and liked me so well that he made a purchase of me. I think I have often heard him say he gave thirty or forty pounds sterling for me; but I do not remember which. However, he meant me for a present to some of his friends in England: and as I was sent accordingly from the house of my then master (one Mr. Campbell), to the place where the ship lay; I was conducted on horseback by an elderly black man (a mode of traveling which appeared very odd to me). When I arrived I was carried on board a fine large ship, loaded with tobacco, etc., and just ready to sail for England. I now thought my condition much mended; I had sails to lie on, and plenty of good victuals to eat; and everybody on board used me very kindly, quite contrary to what I had seen of any white people before; I therefore began to think that they were not all of the same disposition. A few days after I was on board we sailed for England. I was still at a loss to conjecture my destiny. By this time, however, I could smatter a little imperfect English; and I wanted to know as well as I could where we were going. Some of the people of the ship used to tell me they were going to carry me back to my own country, and this made me very happy. I was quite rejoiced at the idea of going back; and thought if I could get home what wonders I should have to tell. But I was reserved for another fate, and was soon undeceived when we came within sight of the English coast. While I was on board this ship, my captain and master named me *Gustavus Vassa*. I at that time began to understand him a little, and refused to be called so, and told him as well as I could that I would be called Jacob; but he said I should not, and still called me Gustavus: and when I refused to answer to my new name, which I at first did, it gained me many a cuff; so at length I submitted, and by which I have been known ever since. The ship had a very long passage; and on that account we had very short allowance of provisions. Towards the last, we had only one pound and a half of bread per week, and about the same quantity of meat, and one quart of water a day. We spoke with only one vessel the whole time we were at sea, and but once we caught a few fishes. In our extremities the captain and people told me in jest they would kill and eat me; but I thought them in earnest, and was depressed beyond measure, expecting every moment to be my last. While I was in this situation, one evening they caught, with a good deal of trouble, a large shark, and got it on board. This gladdened my poor heart exceedingly, as I thought it would serve the people to eat instead of their eating me; but very soon, to my astonishment, they cut off a small part of the tail, and tossed the rest over the side. This renewed my consternation; and I did not know what to think of these white people, though I very much feared they would kill and eat me. There was on board the ship a young lad who had never been at sea before, about four or five years older than myself: his name was Richard Baker. He was a native of America, had received an excellent education, and was of a most amiable temper. Soon after I went on board, he showed me a great deal of partiality and attention, and in return I grew extremely fond of him. We at length became inseparable; and, for the space of two years, he was of very great use to me, and was my constant companion and instructor. Although this dear youth had many slaves of his own, yet he and I have gone through many sufferings together on shipboard; and we have many

nights lain in each other's bosoms when we were in great distress. Thus such a friendship was cemented between us as we cherished till his death, which, to my very great sorrow, happened in the year 1759, when he was up the Archipelago, and on board his Majesty's ship the Preston: an event which I have never ceased to regret, as I lost at once a kind interpreter, an agreeable companion, and a faithful friend; who, at the age of fifteen, discovered a mind superior to prejudice; and who was not ashamed to notice, to associate with, and to be the friend and instructor of one who was ignorant, a stranger, of a different complexion, and a slave!

* * *

From *Chapter IV*

It was now between two and three years since I first came to England, a great part of which I had spent at sea; so that I became inured[5] to that service, and began to consider myself as happily situated, for my master treated me always extremely well; and my attachment and gratitude to him were very great. From the various scenes I had beheld on shipboard, I soon grew a stranger to terror of every kind, and was, in that respect at least, almost an Englishman. I have often reflected with surprise that I never felt half the alarm at any of the numerous dangers I have been in, that I was filled with at the first sight of the Europeans, and at every act of theirs, even the most trifling, when I first came among them, and for some time afterwards. That fear, however, which was the effect of my ignorance, wore away as I began to know them. I could now speak English tolerably well, and I perfectly understood every thing that was said. I not only felt myself quite easy with these new countrymen, but relished their society and manners. I no longer looked upon them as spirits, but as men superior to us; and therefore I had the stronger desire to resemble them, to imbibe their spirit, and imitate their manners. I therefore embraced every occasion of improvement, and every new thing that I observed I treasured up in my memory. I had long wished to be able to read and write; and for this purpose I took every opportunity to gain instruction, but had made as yet very little progress. However, when I went to London with my master, I had soon an opportunity of improving myself, which I gladly embraced. Shortly after my arrival, he sent me to wait upon the Miss Guerins, who had treated me with much kindness when I was there before;[6] and they sent me to school.

While I was attending these ladies, their servants told me I could not go to Heaven unless I was baptized. This made me very uneasy, for I had now some faint idea of a future state. Accordingly I communicated my anxiety to the eldest Miss Guerin, with whom I was become a favorite, and pressed her to have me baptized; when to my great joy, she told me I should. She had formerly asked my master to let me be baptized, but he had refused. However she now insisted on it; and he being under some obligation to her brother, complied with her request. So I was baptized in St. Margaret's church, Westminster, in February, 1759, by my present name. The clergyman at the same time, gave me a book, called a Guide to the Indians, written by the Bishop

5. Accustomed.
6. Elizabeth Martha Guerin and Mary Guerin were Pascal's cousins. Toward the end of

Chapter III, Equiano calls them "very amiable ladies, who took much notice and great care of me."

of Sodor and Man.[7] On this occasion, Miss Guerin did me the honor to stand as god-mother, and afterwards gave me a treat. I used to attend these ladies about the town, in which service I was extremely happy; as I had thus many opportunities of seeing London, which I desired of all things. I was sometimes, however, with my master at his rendezvous house,[8] which was at the foot of Westminster bridge. Here I used to enjoy myself in playing about the bridge stairs, and often in the waterman's wherries,[9] with other boys. On one of these occasions there was another boy with me in a wherry, and we went out into the current of the river; while we were there, two more stout boys came to us in another wherry, and abusing us for taking the boat, desired me to get into the other wherry boat. Accordingly, I went to get out of the wherry I was in, but just as I had got one of my feet into the other boat, the boys shoved it off, so that I fell into the Thames; and, not being able to swim, I should unavoidably have been drowned, but for the assistance of some watermen who providentially came to my relief.

The Namur being again got ready for sea, my master, with his gang,[1] was ordered on board; and, to my no small grief, I was obliged to leave my schoolmaster, whom I liked very much, and always attended while I stayed in London, to repair[2] on board with my master. Nor did I leave my kind patronesses, the Miss Guerins, without uneasiness and regret. They often used to teach me to read, and took great pains to instruct me in the principles of religion and the knowledge of God. I therefore parted from those amiable ladies with reluctance, after receiving from them many friendly cautions how to conduct myself, and some valuable presents.

When I came to Spithead,[3] I found we were destined for the Mediterranean, with a large fleet, which was now ready to put to sea. We only waited for the arrival of the Admiral, who soon came on board. And about the beginning of the spring of 1759, having weighed anchor, and got under way, sailed for the Mediterranean; and in eleven days, from the Land's End, we got to Gibralter. While we were here I used to be often on shore, and got various fruits in great plenty, and very cheap.

I had frequently told several people, in my excursions on shore, the story of my being kidnapped with my sister, and of our being separated, as I have related before; and I had as often expressed my anxiety for her fate, and my sorrow at having never met her again. One day, when I was on shore, and mentioning these circumstances to some persons, one of them told me he knew where my sister was, and if I would accompany him, he would bring me to her. Improbable as this story was, I believed it immediately, and agreed to go with him, while my heart leaped for joy; and, indeed, he conducted me to a black young woman, who was so like my sister, that at first sight, I really thought it was her; but I was quickly undeceived. And, on talking to her, I found her to be of another nation.

While we lay here, the Preston came in from the Levant.[4] As soon as she arrived, my master told me I should now see my old companion, Dick, who was gone in her when she sailed for Turkey. I was much rejoiced at this news,

7. Present-day Hebrides and the Isle of Man.
8. Private residence.
9. Small rowboats.
1. I.e., crew.
2. Go; return. "Attended": visited.

3. On the southern coast of England; a common rendezvous for the British fleet.
4. The eastern shore of the Mediterranean. "Lay": i.e., remained, harbored.

and expected every minute to embrace him; and when the captain came on board of our ship, which he did immediately after, I ran to inquire after my friend; but, with inexpressible sorrow, I learned from the boat's crew that the dear youth was dead! and that they had brought his chest, and all his other things, to my master. These he afterwards gave to me, and I regarded them as a memorial of my friend, whom I loved, and grieved for, as a brother.

* * *

After our ship was fitted out again for service, in September she went to Guernsey,[5] where I was very glad to see my old hostess, who was now a widow, and my former little charming companion, her daughter. I spent some time here very happily with them, till October, when we had orders to repair to Portsmouth. We parted from each other with a great deal of affection; and I promised to return soon, and see them again, not knowing what all powerful fate had determined for me. Our ship having arrived at Portsmouth, we went into the harbor, and remained there till the latter end of November, when we heard great talk about a peace,[6] and, to our very great joy, in the beginning of December we had orders to go up to London with our ship, to be paid off. We received this news with loud huzzas, and every other demonstration of gladness; and nothing but mirth was to be seen throughout every part of the ship. I, too, was not without my share of the general joy on this occasion. I thought now of nothing but being freed, and working for myself, and thereby getting money to enable me to get a good education; for I always had a great desire to be able at least to read and write; and while I was on ship-board, I had endeavored to improve myself in both. While I was in the Etna, particularly, the captain's clerk taught me to write, and gave me a smattering of arithmetic, as far as the Rule of Three.[7] There was also one Daniel Queen, about forty years of age, a man very well educated, who messed[8] with me on board this ship, and he likewise dressed and attended the captain. Fortunately this man soon became very much attached to me, and took very great pains to instruct me in many things. He taught me to shave and dress hair a little, and also to read in the Bible, explaining many passages to me, which I did not comprehend. I was wonderfully surprised to see the laws and rules of my own country written almost exactly here; a circumstance which I believe tended to impress our manners and customs more deeply on my memory. I used to tell him of this resemblance, and many a time we have sat up the whole night together at this employment. In short, he was like a father to me, and some even used to call me after his name; they also styled me the black Christian. Indeed, I almost loved him with the affection of a son. Many things I have denied myself that he might have them; and when I used to play at marbles, or any other game, and won a few half-pence, or got any little money, which I sometimes did, for shaving any one, I used to buy him a little sugar or tobacco, as far as my stock of money would go. He used to say, that he and I never should part; and that when our ship was paid off, as I was as free as himself, or any other man on board, he would instruct me in his business, by which I might gain a good livelihood. This gave me

5. One of the Channel Islands, in the English Channel.
6. I.e., to the Seven Years' War.
7. A method of finding a fourth (unknown) number from three given numbers. Etna was the name of the ship.
8. Took meals.

new life and spirits; and my heart burned within me, while I thought the time long till I obtained my freedom. For though my master had not promised it to me, yet, besides the assurances I had received, that he had no right to detain me, he always treated me with the greatest kindness, and reposed in me an unbounded confidence; he even paid attention to my morals, and would never suffer me to deceive him, or tell lies, of which he used to tell me the consequences; and that if I did so, God would not love me. So that, from all this tenderness, I had never once supposed, in all my dreams of freedom, that he would think of detaining me any longer than I wished.

In pursuance of our orders, we sailed from Portsmouth for the Thames, and arrived at Deptford the 10th of December, where we cast anchor just as it was high water. The ship was up about half an hour, when my master ordered the barge to be manned; and all in an instant, without having before given me the least reason to suspect any thing of the matter, he forced me into the barge, saying, I was going to leave him, but he would take care I should not. I was so struck with the unexpectedness of this proceeding, that for some time I did not make a reply, only I made an offer to go for my books and chest of clothes, but he swore I should not move out of his sight, and if I did, he would cut my throat, at the same time taking his hanger.[9] I began, however, to collect myself, and plucking up courage, I told him I was free, and he could not by law serve me so. But this only enraged him the more: and he continued to swear, and said he would soon let me know whether he would or not, and at that instant sprung himself into the barge from the ship, to the astonishment and sorrow of all on board. The tide, rather unluckily for me, had just turned downward, so that we quickly fell down the river along with it, till we came among some outward-bound West Indiamen; for he was resolved to put me on board the first vessel he could get to receive me. The boat's crew, who pulled against their will, became quite faint, different times, and would have gone ashore, but he would not let them. Some of them strove then to cheer me, and told me he could not sell me, and that they would stand by me, which revived me a little, and I still entertained hopes; for, as they pulled along, he asked some vessels to receive me, but they would not. But, just as we had got a little below Gravesend, we came along side of a ship which was going away the next tide for the West Indies. Her name was the Charming Sally. Captain James Doran, and my master went on board, and agreed with him for me; and in a little time I was sent for into the cabin. When I came there, Captain Doran asked me if I knew him. I answered that I did not. "Then," said he, "you are now my slave." I told him my master could not sell me to him, nor to any one else. "Why," said he, "did not your master buy you?" I confessed he did. "But I have served him," said I, "many years, and he has taken all my wages and prize money, for I had only got one sixpence during the war; besides this I have been baptized, and by the laws of the land no man has a right to sell me." And I added that I had heard a lawyer and others at different times tell my master so. They both then said that those people who told me so were not my friends; but I replied, "It was very extraordinary that other people did not know the law as well as they." Upon this, Captain Doran said I talked too much English; and if I did not behave myself well, and be quiet, he had a method on board

9. Small sword.

to make me. I was too well convinced of his power over me to doubt what he said; and my former sufferings in the slave ship presenting themselves to my mind, the recollection of them made me shudder. However, before I retired I told them that, as I could not get any right among men here, I hoped I should hereafter in Heaven; and I immediately left the cabin, filled with resentment and sorrow. The only coat I had with me my master took away with him, and said, "If your prize money had been £ 10,000, I had a right to it all, and would have taken it." I had about nine guineas, which, during my long seafaring life, I had scraped together from trifling perquisites and little ventures; and I hid it at that instant, lest my master should take that from me likewise, still hoping that by some means or other I should make my escape to the shore; and indeed some of my old shipmates told me not to despair, for they would get me back again; and that, as soon as they could get their pay, they would immediately come to Portsmouth to me, where the ship was going. But, alas! all my hopes were baffled, and the hour of my deliverance was as yet far off. My master, having soon concluded his bargain with the captain, came out of the cabin, and he and his people got into the boat and put off. I followed them with aching eyes as long as I could, and when they were out of sight I threw myself on the deck, with a heart ready to burst with sorrow and anguish.

From *Chapter V*

* * *

About the middle of May, when the ship was got ready to sail for England, I all the time believing that fate's blackest clouds were gathering over my head, and expecting their bursting would mix me with the dead, Captain Doran sent for me ashore one morning, and I was told by the messenger that my fate was then determined. With trembling steps and fluttering heart, I came to the captain, and found with him one Mr. Robert King, a Quaker, and the first merchant in the place. The captain then told me my former master had sent me there to be sold; but that he had desired him to get me the best master he could, as he told him I was a very deserving boy, which Captain Doran said he found to be true; and if he were to stay in the West Indies, he would be glad to keep me himself; but he could not venture to take me to London, for he was very sure that when I came there I would leave him. I at that instant burst out a crying, and begged much of him to take me to England with him, but all to no purpose. He told me he had got me the very best master in the whole island, with whom I should be as happy as if I were in England, and for that reason he chose to let him have me, though he could sell me to his own brother-in-law for a great deal more money than what he got from this gentleman. Mr. King, my new master, then made a reply, and said the reason he had bought me was on account of my good character; and as he had not the least doubt of my good behavior, I should be very well off with him. He also told me he did not live in the West Indies, but at Philadelphia, where he was going soon; and, as I understood something of the rules of arithmetic, when we got there he would put me to school, and fit me for a clerk. This conversation relieved my mind a little, and I left those gentlemen considerably more at ease in myself than when I came to them; and

I was very thankful to Captain Doran, and even to my old master, for the character[1] they had given me. A character which I afterwards found of infinite service to me. I went on board again, and took leave of all my shipmates, and the next day the ship sailed. When she weighed anchor, I went to the waterside and looked at her with a very wishful and aching heart, and followed her with my eyes until she was totally out of sight. I was so bowed down with grief, that I could not hold up my head for many months; and if my new master had not been kind to me, I believe I should have died under it at last. And, indeed, I soon found that he fully deserved the good character which Captain Doran gave me of him; for he possessed a most amiable disposition and temper, and was very charitable and humane. If any of his slaves behaved amiss he did not beat or use them ill, but parted with them. This made them afraid of disobliging him; and as he treated his slaves better than any other man on the island, so he was better and more faithfully served by them in return. By this kind treatment I did at last endeavor to compose myself; and with fortitude, though moneyless, determined to face whatever fate had decreed for me. Mr. King soon asked me what I could do; and at the same time said he did not mean to treat me as a common slave. I told him I knew something of seamanship, and could shave and dress hair pretty well; and I could refine wines, which I had learned on shipboard, where I had often done it; and that I could write, and understood arithmetic tolerably well, as far as the Rule of Three. He then asked me if I knew any thing of gauging;[2] and, on my answering that I did not, he said one of his clerks should teach me to gauge.

Mr. King dealt in all manner of merchandize, and kept from one to six clerks. He loaded many vessels in a year; particularly to Philadelphia, where he was born; and was connected with a great mercantile house in that city. He had, besides, many vessels and droggers,[3] of different sizes, which used to go about the island; and others, to collect rum, sugar, and other goods. I understood pulling and managing those boats very well. And this hard work, which was the first that he set me to, in the sugar seasons used to be my constant employment. I have rowed the boat, and slaved at the oars, from one hour to sixteen in the twenty-four; during which I had fifteen pence sterling per day to live on, though sometimes only ten pence. However, this was considerably more than was allowed to other slaves that used to work often with me, and belonged to other gentlemen on the island. Those poor souls had never more than nine-pence per day, and seldom more than six-pence, from their masters or owners, though they earned them three or four pistareens.[4] For it is a common practice in the West Indies for men to purchase slaves, though they have not plantations themselves, in order to let them out to planters and merchants at so much a piece by the day, and they give what allowance they choose out of this product of their daily work to their slaves, for subsistence; this allowance is often very scanty. My master often gave the owners of the slaves two and a half of these pieces per day, and found the poor fellows in victuals himself,[5] because

1. Favorable estimate, good reputation.
2. Determining how fully loaded a ship is by measuring its depth in the water.
3. Slow West Indian vessels that sail along the coast.

4. These pistareens are of a value of a shilling [Equiano's note].
5. I.e., King was generous to the owners in terms of payment and to the slaves in terms of food.

he thought their owners did not feed them well enough according to the work they did.

* * *

Once, for a few days, I was let out to fit[6] a vessel, and I had no victuals allowed me by either party; at last I told my master of this treatment, and he took me away from it. In many of the estates, on the different islands where I used to be sent for rum or sugar, they would not deliver it to me, or any other negro; he was therefore obliged to send a white man along with me to those places; and then he used to pay him from six to ten pistareens a day. From being thus employed, during the time I served Mr. King, in going about the different estates on the island,[7] I had all the opportunity I could wish for, to see the dreadful usage of the poor men; usage that reconciled me to my situation, and made me bless God for the hands into which I had fallen.

I had the good fortune to please my master in every department in which he employed me; and there was scarcely any part of his business, or household affairs, in which I was not occasionally engaged. I often supplied the place[8] of a clerk, in receiving and delivering cargoes to the ships, in tending stores, and delivering goods. And besides this, I used to shave and dress my master when convenient, and take care of his horse; and when it was necessary, which was very often, I worked likewise on board of different vessels of his. By these means I became very useful to my master, and saved him, as he used to acknowledge, above a hundred pounds a year. Nor did he scruple to say I was of more advantage to him than any of his clerks; though their usual wages in the West Indies are from sixty to a hundred pounds current a year.

I have sometimes heard it asserted that a Negro cannot earn his master the first cost; but nothing can be further from the truth. I suppose nine tenths of the mechanics throughout the West Indies are Negro slaves; and I well know the coopers among them earn two dollars a day, the carpenters the same, and often times more; as also the masons, smiths, and fisherman, etc. And I have known many slaves whose masters would not take a thousand pounds current for them. But surely this assertion refutes itself; for, if it be true, why do the planters and merchants pay such a price for slaves? And, above all, why do those who make this assertion exclaim the most loudly against the abolition of the slave trade? So much are men blinded, and to such inconsistent arguments are they driven by mistaken interest! I grant, indeed, that slaves are sometimes, by half-feeding, half-clothing, over-working and stripes,[9] reduced so low, that they are turned out as unfit for service, and left to perish in the woods, or expire on the dunghill.

My master was several times offered, by different gentlemen, one hundred guineas for me, but he always told them he would not sell me, to my great joy. And I used to double my diligence and care, for fear of getting into the hands of those men who did not allow a valuable slave the common support of life. Many of them even used to find fault with my master for feeding his slaves so well as he did; although I often went hungry, and an Englishman might think my fare very indifferent;[1] but he used to tell

6. Hired out to help equip.
7. Equiano remained in the West Indies from 1763 to 1766.
8. Held the position.
9. Lashes.
1. Poor, unsatisfactory.

them he always would do it, because the slaves thereby looked better and did more work.

While I was thus employed by my master, I was often a witness to cruelties of every kind, which were exercised on my unhappy fellow slaves. I used frequently to have different cargoes of new Negroes in my care for sale; and it was almost a constant practice with our clerks, and other whites, to commit violent depredations on the chastity of the female slaves; and these I was, though with reluctance, obliged to submit to at all times, being unable to help them. When we have had some of these slaves on board my master's vessels, to carry them to other islands, or to America, I have known our mates to commit these acts most shamefully, to the disgrace, not of Christians only, but of men. I have even known them to gratify their brutal passion with females not ten years old; and these abominations, some of them practiced to such scandalous excess, that one of our captains discharged the mate and others on that account. And yet in Montserrat[2] I have seen a Negro man staked to the ground, and cut most shockingly, and then his ears cut off bit by bit, because he had been connected with a white woman, who was a common prostitute. As if it were no crime in the whites to rob an innocent African girl of her virtue; but most heinous in a black man only to gratify a passion of nature, where the temptation was offered by one of a different color, though the most abandoned woman of her species.

Another Negro man was half hanged, and then burnt, for attempting to poison a cruel overseer. Thus, by repeated cruelties, are the wretched first urged to despair, and then murdered, because they still retain so much of human nature about them as to wish to put an end to their misery, and retaliate on their tyrants! These overseers are indeed for the most part persons of the worst character of any denomination of men in the West Indies. Unfortunately, many humane gentlemen, but not residing on their estates, are obliged to leave the management of them in the hands of these human butchers, who cut and mangle the slaves in a shocking manner on the most trifling occasions, and altogether treat them in every respect like brutes. They pay no regard to the situation of pregnant women, nor the least attention to the lodging of the field Negroes. Their huts, which ought to be well covered, and the place dry where they take their little repose, are often open sheds, built in damp places; so that when the poor creatures return tired from the toils of the field, they contract many disorders, from being exposed to the damp air in this uncomfortable state, while they are heated, and their pores are open. This neglect certainly conspires with many others to cause a decrease in the births as well as in the lives of the grown Negroes. I can quote many instances of gentlemen who reside on their estates in the West Indies, and then the scene is quite changed; the Negroes are treated with lenity and proper care, by which their lives are prolonged, and their masters profited. To the honor of humanity, I knew several gentlemen who managed their estates in this manner, and they found that benevolence was their true interest. And, among many I could mention in several of the islands, I knew one in Montserrat whose slaves looked remarkably well, and never needed any fresh supplies of Negroes; and there are many other estates, especially in Barbadoes, which, from such judicious treatment, need no fresh

2. An island in the West Indies, seven miles from Antigua.

stock of Negroes at any time. I have the honor of knowing a most worthy and humane gentleman, who is a native of Barbadoes, and his estates there.[3] This gentleman has written a treatise on the usage of his own slaves. He allows them two hours of refreshment at midday, and many other indulgencies and comforts, particularly in their lodging; and, besides this, he raises more provisions on his estate than they can destroy; so that by these attentions he saves the lives of his Negroes, and keeps them healthy, and as happy as the condition of slavery can admit. I myself, as shall appear in the sequel,[4] managed an estate, where, by those attentions, the Negroes were uncommonly cheerful and healthy, and did more work by half than by the common mode of treatment they usually do. For want,[5] therefore, of such care and attention to the poor Negroes, and otherwise oppressed as they are, it is no wonder that the decrease should require 20,000 new Negroes annually, to fill up the vacant places of the dead.

* * *

From *Chapter VI*

In the preceding chapter I have set before the reader a few of those many instances of oppression, extortion, and cruelty, which I have been a witness to in the West Indies; but were I to enumerate them all, the catalog would be tedious and disgusting. The punishments of the slaves on every trifling occasion are so frequent, and so well known, together with the different instruments with which they are tortured, that it cannot any longer afford novelty to recite them; and they are too shocking to yield delight either to the writer or the reader. I shall therefore hereafter only mention such as incidentally befell myself in the course of my adventures.

* * *

Some time in the year 1763, kind Providence seemed to appear rather more favorable to me. One of my master's vessels, a Bermudas sloop, about sixty tons burthen, was commanded by one captain Thomas Farmer, an Englishman, a very alert and active man, who gained my master a great deal of money by his good management in carrying passengers from one island to another; but very often his sailors used to get drunk and run away from the vessel, which hindered him in his business very much. This man had taken a liking to me, and many times begged of my master to let me go a trip with him as a sailor; but he would tell him he could not spare me, though the vessel sometimes could not go for want of hands, for sailors were generally very scarce in the island. However, at last, from necessity or force, my master was prevailed on, though very reluctantly, to let me go with this captain; but he gave him great charge to take care that I did not run away, for if I did he would make him pay for me. This being the case, the captain had for some time a sharp eye upon me whenever the vessel anchored; and as soon as she returned I was sent for on shore again. Thus was I slaving, as it were, for life, sometimes at one thing, and sometimes at another. So that the captain and I were nearly the most useful men in my master's employment. I also became so

3. Two of Equiano's notes identifying these men are omitted.
4. I.e., later.
5. Lack.

useful to the captain on ship-board, that many times, when he used to ask for me to go with him, though it should be but for twenty-four hours, to some of the islands near us, my master would answer he could not spare me, at which the captain would swear, and would not go the trip, and tell my master I was better to him on board than any three white men he had; for they used to behave ill in many respects, particularly in getting drunk; and then they frequently got the boat stove,[6] so as to hinder the vessel from coming back as soon as she might have done. This my master knew very well; and at last, by the captain's constant entreaties, after I had been several times with him, one day to my great joy, told me the captain would not let him rest, and asked whether I would go aboard as a sailor, or stay on shore and mind the stores, for he could not bear any longer to be plagued in this manner. I was very happy at this proposal, for I immediately thought I might in time stand some chance by being on board to get a little money, or possibly make my escape if I should be used ill. I also expected to get better food, and in greater abundance; for I had oftentimes felt much hunger, though my master treated his slaves, as I have observed, uncommonly well. I therefore, without hesitation, answered him, that I would go and be a sailor if he pleased. Accordingly I was ordered on board directly. Nevertheless, between the vessel and the shore, when she was in port, I had little or no rest, as my master always wished to have me along with him. Indeed he was a very pleasant gentleman, and but for my expectations on ship-board, I should not have thought of leaving him. But the captain liked me also very much, and I was entirely his right hand man. I did all I could to deserve his favor, and in return I received better treatment from him than any other, I believe, ever met with in the West Indies, in my situation.

After I had been sailing for some time with this captain, at length I endeavored to try my luck, and commence merchant. I had but a very small capital to begin with; for one single half bit,[7] which is equal to three pence in England, made up my whole stock. However, I trusted to the Lord to be with me; and at one of our trips to St. Eustatia,[8] a Dutch island, I bought a glass tumbler with my half bit, and when I came to Montserrat, I sold it for a bit, or six pence. Luckily we made several successive trips to St. Eustatia (which was a general mart for the West Indies, about twenty leagues from Montserrat), and in our next, finding my tumbler so profitable, with this one bit I bought two tumblers more; and when I came back, I sold them for two bits, equal to a shilling sterling. When we went again, I bought with these two bits four more of these glasses, which I sold for four bits on our return to Montserrat. And in our next voyage to St. Eustatia, I bought two glasses with one bit, and with the other three I bought a jug of Geneva,[9] nearly about three pints in measure. When we came to Montserrat, I sold the gin for eight bits, and the tumblers for two, so that my capital now amounted in all to a dollar, well husbanded[1] and acquired in the space of a month or six weeks, when I blessed the Lord that I was so rich. As we sailed to different islands, I laid this money out in various things occasionally, and it used to turn out to very good account, especially when we went to Guadaloupe, Grenada, and

6. Put a hole in the boat.
7. In the West Indies, a small silver coin worth a fraction of the Spanish dollar (Spanish dollars were common units of currency throughout the British colonies).

8. I.e., St. Eustatius, one of the Leeward Islands, in the West Indies.
9. A type of gin.
1. Managed.

the rest of the French islands. Thus was I going all about the islands upwards of four years, and ever trading as I went, during which I experienced many instances of ill usage, and have seen many injuries done to other Negroes in our dealings with whites. And, amidst our recreations, when we have been dancing and merry-making, they, without cause, have molested and insulted us. Indeed, I was more than once obliged to look up to God on high, as I had advised the poor fisherman some time before. And I had not been long trading for myself in the manner I have related above, when I experienced the like trial in company with him as follows:—This man, being used to the water, was upon an emergency put on board of us by his master, to work as another hand, on a voyage to Santa Cruz; and at our sailing he had brought his little all for a venture, which consisted of six bits' worth of limes and oranges in a bag; I had also my whole stock, which was about twelve bits' worth of the same kind of goods, separate in two bags, for we had heard these fruits sold well in that island. When we came there, in some little convenient time, he and I went ashore to sell them; but we had scarcely landed, when we were met by two white men, who presently took our three bags from us. We could not at first guess what they meant to do, and for some time we thought they were jesting with us; but they too soon let us know otherwise, for they took our ventures immediately to a house hard by, and adjoining the fort, while we followed all the way begging of them to give us our fruits, but in vain. They not only refused to return them, but swore at us, and threatened if we did not immediately depart they would flog us well. We told them these three bags were all we were worth in the world, and that we brought them with us to sell when we came from Montserrat, and showed them the vessel. But this was rather against us, as they now saw we were strangers, as well as slaves. They still therefore swore, and desired us to be gone, and even took sticks to beat us; while we, seeing they meant what they said, went off in the greatest confusion and despair. Thus, in the very minute of gaining more by three times than I ever did by any venture in my life before, was I deprived of every farthing I was worth. An unsupportable misfortune! but how to help ourselves we knew not. In our consternation we went to the commanding officer of the fort, and told him how we had been served by his people, but we obtained not the least redress. He answered our complaints only by a volley of imprecations against us, and immediately took a horse-whip, in order to chastise us, so that we were obliged to turn out much faster than we came in. I now, in the agony of distress and indignation, wished that the ire of God in his forked lightning might transfix these cruel oppressors among the dead. Still, however, we persevered; went back again to the house, and begged and besought them again and again for our fruits, till at last some other people that were in the house asked if we would be contented if they kept one bag and gave us the other two. We, seeing no remedy whatever, consented to this; and they, observing one bag to have both kinds of fruit in it, which belonged to my companion, kept that; and the other two, which were mine, they gave us back. As soon as I got them, I ran as fast as I could, and got the first Negro man I could to help me off. My companion, however, stayed a little longer to plead; he told them the bag they had was his, and likewise all that he was worth in the world; but this was of no avail, and he was obliged to return without it. The poor old man wringing his hands, cried bitterly for his loss; and, indeed, he then did look up to God on high, which so moved me in pity

for him, that I gave him nearly one-third of my fruits. We then proceeded to the markets to sell them; and Providence was more favorable to us than we could have expected, for we sold our fruits uncommonly well; I got for mine about thirty-seven bits. Such a surprising reverse of fortune in so short a space of time seemed like a dream, and proved no small encouragement for me to trust the Lord in any situation. My captain afterwards frequently used to take my part, and get me my right, when I have been plundered or used ill by these tender Christian depredators; among whom I have shuddered to observe the unceasing blasphemous execrations which are wantonly thrown out by persons of all ages and conditions, not only without occasion, but even as if they were indulgencies and pleasure.

* * *

The reader cannot but judge of the irksomeness of this situation to a mind like mine, in being daily exposed to new hardships and impositions, after having seen many better days, and been, as it were, in a state of freedom and plenty; added to which, every part of the world I had hitherto been in, seemed to me a paradise in comparison to the West Indies. My mind was therefore hourly replete with inventions and thoughts of being freed, and, if possible, by honest and honorable means; for I always remembered the old adage, and I trust it has ever been my ruling principle, that "honesty is the best policy;" and likewise that other golden precept—"To do unto all men as I would they should do unto me." However, as I was from early years a predestinarian, I thought whatever fate had determined must ever come to pass; and, therefore, if ever it were my lot to be freed, nothing could prevent me, although I should at present see no means or hope to obtain my freedom; on the other hand, if it were my fate not to be freed, I never should be so, and all my endeavors for that purpose would be fruitless. In the midst of these thoughts, I therefore looked up with prayers anxiously to God for my liberty; and at the same time used every honest means, and did all that was possible on my part to obtain it. In process of time, I became master of a few pounds, and in a fair way of making more, which my friendly captain knew very well; this occasioned him sometimes to take liberties with me; but whenever he treated me waspishly, I used plainly to tell him my mind, and that I would die before I would be imposed upon as other Negroes were, and that to my life had lost its relish when liberty was gone. This I said, although I foresaw my then well-being or future hopes of freedom (humanly speaking) depended on this man. However, as he could not bear the thoughts of my not sailing with him, he always became mild on my threats. I therefore continued with him; and, from my great attention to his orders and his business, I gained him credit, and through his kindness to me, I at last procured my liberty. While I thus went on, filled with the thoughts of freedom, and resisting oppression as well as I was able, my life hung daily in suspense, particularly in the surfs I have formerly mentioned, as I could not swim. These are extremely violent throughout the West Indies, and I was ever exposed to their howling rage and devouring fury in all the islands. I have seen them strike and toss a boat right up on end, and maim several on board. Once in the Grenada islands, when I and about eight others were pulling a large boat with two puncheons[2]

2. Large casks.

of water in it, a surf struck us, and drove the boat, and all in it, about half a stone's throw, among some trees, and above the high water mark. We were obliged to get all the assistance we could from the nearest estate to mend the boat, and launch it into the water again. At Montserrat, one night, in pressing hard to get off the shore on board, the punt was overset with us four times, the first time I was very near being drowned; however, the jacket I had on kept me up above water a little space of time, when I called on a man near me, who was a good swimmer, and told him I could not swim; he then made haste to me, and, just as I was sinking, he caught hold of me, and brought me to sounding, and then he went and brought the punt[3] also. As soon as we had turned the water out of her, lest we should be used ill for being absent, we attempted again three times more, and as often the horrid surfs served us as at first; but at last, the fifth time we attempted, we gained our point, at the imminent hazard of our lives. One day also, at Old Road, in Montserrat, our captain, and three men besides myself, were going in a large canoe in quest of rum and sugar, when a single surf tossed the canoe an amazing distance from the water, and some of us, near a stone's throw from each other. Most of us were very much bruised; so that I and many more often said, and really thought, that there was not such another place under the heavens as this. I longed, therefore, much to leave it, and daily wished to see my master's promise performed, of going to Philadelphia.

While we lay in this place, a very cruel thing happened on board our sloop, which filled me with horror; though I found afterwards such practices were frequent. There was a very clever and decent free young mulatto man, who sailed a long time with us; he had a free woman for his wife, by whom he had a child, and she was then living on shore, and all very happy. Our captain and mate, and other people on board, and several elsewhere, even the natives of Bermudas, all knew this young man from a child that he was always free, and no one had ever claimed him as their property. However, as might too often overcomes right in these parts, it happened that a Bermudas captain, whose vessel lay there for a few days in the road, came on board of us, and seeing the mulatto man, whose name was Joseph Clipson, he told him he was not free, and that he had orders from his master to bring him to Bermudas. The poor man could not believe the captain to be in earnest, but he was very soon undeceived, his men laying violent hands on him; and although he showed a certificate of his being born free in St. Kitts, and most people on board knew that he served his time to[4] boat building, and always passed for a free man, yet he was forcibly taken out of our vessel. He then asked to be carried ashore before the Secretary or Magistrates, and these infernal invaders of human rights promised him he should; but instead of that, they carried him on board of the other vessel. And the next day, without giving the poor man any hearing on shore, or suffering him even to see his wife or child, he was carried away, and probably doomed never more in this world to see them again. Nor was this the only instance of this kind of barbarity I was a witness to. I have since often seen in Jamaica and other islands, free men, whom I have known in America, thus villainously trepanned[5] and held in bondage. I have heard of two similar

3. Narrow, flat-bottomed boat. "Sounding": i.e., where one could stand.
4. Was apprenticed at.
5. Trapped.

practices even in Philadelphia. And were it not for the benevolence of the Quakers in that city, many of the sable race, who now breathe the air of liberty, would, I believe, be groaning indeed under some planter's chains. These things opened my mind to a new scene of horror, to which I had been before a stranger. Hitherto I had thought slavery only dreadful, but the state of a free negro appeared to me now equally so at least, and in some respects even worse, for they live in constant alarm for their liberty; which is but nominal, for they are universally insulted and plundered, without the possibility of redress; for such is the equity of the West Indian laws, that no free Negro's evidence will be admitted in their courts of justice. In this situation, is it surprising that slaves, when mildly treated, should prefer even the misery of slavery to such a mockery of freedom? I was now completely disgusted with the West Indies, and thought I never should be entirely free until I had left them.

* * *

About the latter end of the year 1764, my master bought a larger sloop, called the Prudence, about seventy or eighty tons, of which my captain had the command. I went with him in this vessel, and we took a load of new slaves for Georgia and Charlestown.[6] My master now left me entirely to the captain, though he still wished me to be with him; but I, who always much wished to lose sight of the West Indies, was not a little rejoiced at the thoughts of seeing any other country. Therefore, relying on the goodness of my captain, I got ready all the little venture I could; and, when the vessel was ready, we sailed, to my great joy. When we got to our destined places, Georgia and Charlestown, I expected I should have an opportunity of selling my little property to advantage. But here, particularly in Charlestown, I met with buyers, white men, who imposed on me as in other places. Notwithstanding, I was resolved to have fortitude, thinking no lot or trial too hard when kind Heaven is the rewarder.

We soon got loaded again, and returned to Montserrat; and there, amongst the rest of the islands, I sold my goods well; and in this manner I continued trading during the year 1764—meeting with various scenes of imposition, as usual. After this, my master fitted out his vessel for Philadelphia, in the year 1765; and during the time we were loading her, and getting ready for the voyage, I worked with redoubled alacrity, from the hope of getting money enough by these voyages to buy my freedom, in time, if it should please God; and also to see the town of Philadelphia, which I had heard a great deal about for some years past. Besides which, I had always longed to prove my master's promise the first day I came to him. In the midst of these elevated ideas, and while I was about getting my little stock of merchandize in readiness, one Sunday my master sent for me to his house. When I came there, I found him and the captain together; and, on my going in, I was struck with astonishment at his telling me he heard that I meant to run away from him when I got to Philadelphia. "And therefore," said he, "I must tell you again, you cost me a great deal of money, no less than forty pounds sterling; and it will not do to lose so much. You are a valuable fellow," continued he, "and I can get any day for you one hundred guineas, from

6. Charleston, South Carolina.

many gentlemen in this island." And then he told me of Captain Doran's brother-in-law, a severe master, who ever wanted to buy me to make me his overseer. My captain also said he could get much more than a hundred guineas for me in Carolina. This I knew to be a fact; for the gentleman that wanted to buy me came off several times on board of us, and spoke to me to live with him, and said he would use me well. When I asked him what work he would put me to, he said, as I was a sailor, he would make me a captain of one of his rice vessels. But I refused; and fearing at the same time, by a sudden turn I saw in the captain's temper, he might mean to sell me, I told the gentleman I would not live with him on any condition, and that I certainly would run away with his vessel: but he said he did not fear that, as he would catch me again, and then he told me how cruelly he would serve me if I should do so. My captain, however, gave him to understand that I knew something of navigation, so he thought better of it; and, to my great joy, he went away. I now told my master, I did not say I would run away in Philadelphia; neither did I mean it, as he did not use me ill, nor yet the captain; for if they did, I certainly would have made some attempts before now; but as I thought that if it were God's will I ever should be freed, it would be so, and, on the contrary, if it was not His will, it would not happen. So I hoped if ever I were freed, whilst I was used well, it should be by honest means; but as I could not help myself, he must do as he pleased; I could only hope and trust to the God of Heaven; and at that instant my mind was big with inventions, and full of schemes to escape. I then appealed to the captain, whether he ever saw any sign of my making the least attempt to run away, and asked him if I did not always come on board according to the time for which he gave me liberty; and, more particularly, when all our men left us at Guadeloupe, and went on board of the French fleet, and advised me to go with them, whether I might not, and that he could not have got me again. To my no small surprise, and very great joy, the captain confirmed every syllable that I had said, and even more; for he said he had tried different times to see if I would make any attempt of this kind, both at St. Eustatia and in America, and he never found that I made the smallest; but, on the contrary, I always came on board according to his orders; and he did really believe, if I ever meant to run away, that, as I could never have had a better opportunity, I would have done it the night the mate and all the people left our vessel at Guadeloupe. The captain then informed my master, who had been thus imposed on by our mate (though I did not know who was my enemy), the reason the mate had for imposing this lie upon him; which was, because I had acquainted the captain of the provisions the mate had given away or taken out of the vessel. This speech of the captain was like life to the dead to me, and instantly my soul glorified God; and still more so, on hearing my master immediately say that I was a sensible fellow, and he never did intend to use me as a common slave; and that but for the entreaties of the captain, and his character of me, he would not have let me go from the shores about as I had done. That also, in so doing, he thought by carrying one little thing or other to different places to sell, I might make money. That he also intended to encourage me in this, by crediting me with half a puncheon of rum and half a hogshead[7] of sugar at a time; so that, from being careful, I might have money enough, in some time, to purchase my

7. Large barrel.

freedom; and, when that was the case, I might depend upon it he would let me have it for forty pounds sterling money, which was only the same price he gave for me. This sound gladdened my poor heart beyond measure; though indeed it was no more than the very idea I had formed in my mind of my master long before, and I immediately made him this reply: "Sir, I always had that very thought of you, indeed I had, and that made me so diligent in serving you." He then gave me a large piece of silver coin, such as I never had seen or had before, and told me to get ready for the voyage, and he would credit me with a tierce[8] of sugar, and another of rum; he also said that he had two amiable sisters in Philadelphia, from whom I might get some necessary things. Upon this my noble captain desired me to go aboard; and, knowing the African metal,[9] he charged me not to say any thing of this matter to any body; and he promised that the lying mate should not go with him any more. This was a change indeed: in the same hour to feel the most exquisite pain, and in the turn of a moment the fullest joy. It caused in me such sensations as I was only able to express in my looks; my heart was so overpowered with gratitude, that I could have kissed both of their feet. When I left the room, I immediately went, or rather flew, to the vessel; which being loaded, my master, as good as his word, trusted me with a tierce of rum, and another of sugar, when we sailed, and arrived safe at the elegant town of Philadelphia. I sold my goods here pretty well; and in this charming place I found every thing plentiful and cheap.

While I was in this place, a very extraordinary occurrence befell me. I had been told one evening of a wise woman, a Mrs. Davis, who revealed secrets, foretold events, etc., etc. I put little faith in this story at first, as I could not conceive that any mortal could foresee the future disposals of Providence, nor did I believe in any other revelation than that of the Holy Scriptures; however, I was greatly astonished at seeing this woman in a dream that night, though a person I never before beheld in my life. This made such an impression on me, that I could not get the idea the next day out of my mind, and I then became as anxious to see her as I was before indifferent. Accordingly in the evening, after we left off working, I inquired where she lived, and being directed to her, to my inexpressible surprise, beheld the very woman in the very same dress she appeared to me to wear in the vision. She immediately told me I had dreamed of her the preceding night; related to me many things that had happened with a correctness that astonished me, and finally told me I should not be long a slave. This was the more agreeable news; as I believed it the more readily from her having so faithfully related the past incidents of my life. She said I should be twice in very great danger of my life within eighteen months, which, if I escaped, I should afterwards go on well. So, giving me her blessing, we parted. After staying here sometime till our vessel was loaded, and I had bought in my little traffic, we sailed from this agreeable spot for Montserrat, once more to encounter the raging surfs.

* * *

We soon came to Georgia, where we were to complete our landing, and here worse fate than ever attended me; for one Sunday night, as I was with

8. A third of a barrel. 9. I.e., character.

some negroes in their master's yard, in the town of Savannah, it happened that their master, one Doctor Perkins, who was a very severe and cruel man, came in drunk; and not liking to see any strange negroes in his yard, he and a ruffian of a white man, he had in his service, beset me in an instant, and both of them struck me with the first weapons they could get hold of. I cried out as long as I could for help and mercy; but, though I gave a good account of myself, and he knew my captain, who lodged hard[1] by him, it was to no purpose. They beat and mangled me in a shameful manner, leaving me near dead. I lost so much blood from the wounds I received, that I lay quite motionless, and was so benumbed that I could not feel any thing for many hours. Early in the morning, they took me away to the jail. As I did not return to the ship all night, my captain, not knowing where I was, and being uneasy that I did not then make my appearance, made inquiry after me; and having found where I was, immediately came to me. As soon as the good man saw me so cut and mangled, he could not forbear weeping; he soon got me out of jail to his lodgings, and immediately sent for the best doctors in the place, who at first declared it as their opinion that I could not recover. My captain on this went to all the lawyers in the town for their advice, but they told him they could do nothing for me as I was a negro. He then went to Doctor Perkins, the hero who had vanquished me, and menaced him, swearing he would be revenged on him, and challenged him to fight.—But cowardice is ever the companion of cruelty—and the Doctor refused. However, by the skillfullness of one Dr. Brady of that place, I began at last to amend; but, although I was so sore and bad with the wounds I had all over me, that I could not rest in any posture, yet I was in more pain on account of the captain's uneasiness about me, than I otherwise should have been. The worthy man nursed and watched me all the hours of the night; and I was, through his attention and that of the doctor, able to get out of bed in about sixteen or eighteen days. All this time I was very much wanted on board, as I used frequently to go up and down the river for rafts, and other parts of our cargo, and stow them, when the mate was sick or absent. In about four weeks, I was able to go on duty, and in a fortnight after, having got in all our lading, our vessel set sail for Montserrat; and in less than three weeks we arrived there safe towards the end of the year. This ended my adventures in 1764, for I did not leave Montserrat again till the beginning of the following year.

From *Chapter VII*

Every day now brought me nearer my freedom, and I was impatient till we proceeded again to sea, that I might have an opportunity of getting a sum large enough to purchase it. I was not long ungratified; for, in the beginning of the year 1766, my master bought another sloop, named the Nancy, the largest I had ever seen. She was partly laden, and was to proceed to Philadelphia; our captain had his choice of three, and I was well pleased he chose this, which was the largest; for, from his having a large vessel, I had more room, and could carry a larger quantity of goods with me. Accordingly, when we had delivered our old vessel, the Prudence, and completed the lading of the Nancy, having made near three hundred per cent. by four

1. I.e., close.

barrels of pork I brought from Charlestown, I laid in as large a cargo as I could, trusting to God's providence to prosper my undertaking. With these views I sailed for Philadelphia. On our passage, when we drew near the land, I was for the first time surprised at the sight of some whales, having never seen any such large sea monsters before; and as we sailed by the land, one morning, I saw a puppy whale close by the vessel; it was about the length of a wherry boat, and it followed us all the day till we got within the Capes.[2] We arrived safe, and in good time at Philadelphia, and I sold my goods there chiefly to the Quakers. They always appeared to be a very honest, discreet sort of people, and never attempted to impose on[3] me; I therefore liked them, and ever after chose to deal with them in preference to any others.

One Sunday morning, while I was here, as I was going to church, I chanced to pass a meetinghouse. The doors being open, and the house full of people, it excited my curiosity to go in. When I entered the house, to my great surprise, I saw a very tall woman standing in the midst of them, speaking in an audible voice something which I could not understand. Having never seen any thing of this kind before, I stood and stared about me for some time, wondering at this odd scene. As soon as it was over, I took an opportunity to make inquiry about the place and people, when I was informed they were called Quakers. I particularly asked what that woman I saw in the midst of them had said, but none of them were pleased to satisfy me; so I quitted them, and soon after, as I was returning, I came to a church crowded with people; the churchyard was full likewise, and a number of people were even mounted on ladders looking in at the windows. I thought this a strange sight, as I had never seen churches, either in England or the West Indies, crowded in this manner before. I therefore made bold to ask some people the meaning of all this, and they told me the Rev. Mr. George Whitefield was preaching. I had often heard of this gentleman, and had wished to see and hear him; but I never before had an opportunity. I now therefore resolved to gratify myself with the sight, and pressed in amidst the multitude. When I got into the church, I saw this pious man exhorting the people with the greatest fervor and earnestness, and sweating as much as I ever did while in slavery on Montserrat beach. I was very much struck and impressed with this; I thought it strange I had never seen divines exert themselves in this manner before, and was no longer at a loss to account for the thin congregations they preached to.

When we had discharged our cargo here, and were loaded again, we left this fruitful land once more, and set sail for Montserrat. My traffic had hitherto succeeded so well with me, that I thought, by selling my goods when we arrived at Montserrat, I should have enough to purchase my freedom. But as soon as our vessel arrived there, my master came on board, and gave orders for us to go to St. Eustatia, and discharge our cargo there, and from thence proceed for Georgia. I was much disappointed at this; but thinking, as usual, it was of no use to encounter with the decrees of fate, I submitted without repining, and we went to St. Eustatia. After we had discharged our cargo there, we took in a live cargo (as we call a cargo of slaves). Here I sold my goods tolerably well; but, not being able to lay out all my money in this small island to as much advantage as in many other places,

2. Possibly Cape May, in southern New Jersey. 3. Cheat.

I laid out only part, and the remainder I brought away with me net.[4] We sailed from hence for Georgia, and I was glad when we got there, though I had not much reason to like the place from my last adventure in Savannah; but I longed to get back to Montserrat and procure my freedom, which I expected to be able to purchase when I returned. As soon as we arrived here, I waited on my careful doctor, Mr. Brady, to whom I made the most grateful acknowledgments in my power, for his former kindness and attention during my illness.

* * *

When we had unladen the vessel, and I had sold my venture, finding myself master of about forty-seven pounds—I consulted my true friend, the captain, how I should proceed in offering my master the money for my freedom. He told me to come on a certain morning, when he and my master would be at breakfast together. Accordingly, on that morning I went, and met the captain there, as he had appointed. When I went in I made my obeisance to my master, and with my money in my hand, and many fears in my heart, I prayed him to be as good as his offer to me, when he was pleased to promise me my freedom as soon as I could purchase it. This speech seemed to confound him, he began to recoil, and my heart that instant sunk within me. "What," said he, "give you your freedom? Why, where did you get the money? Have you got forty pounds sterling?" "Yes, sir," I answered. "How did you get it?" replied he. I told him, very honestly. The captain then said he knew I got the money honestly, and with much industry, and that I was particularly careful. On which my master replied, I got money much faster than he did; and said he would not have made me the promise he did if he had thought I should have got the money so soon. "Come, come," said my worthy captain, clapping my master on the back, "Come, Robert (which was his name), I think you must let him have his freedom;—you have laid your money out very well; you have received a very good interest for it all this time, and here is now the principal at last. I know Gustavus has earned you more than a hundred a year, and he will save you money, as he will not leave you.—Come, Robert, take the money." My master then said he would not be worse than his promise; and, taking the money, told me to go to the Secretary at the Register Office, and get my manumission drawn up. These words of my master were like a voice from Heaven to me. In an instant all my trepidation was turned into unutterable bliss; and I most reverently bowed myself with gratitude, unable to express my feelings, but by the overflowing of my eyes, and a heart replete with thanks to God, while my true and worthy friend, the captain, congratulated us both with a peculiar degree of heartfelt pleasure. As soon as the first transports of my joy were over, and that I had expressed my thanks to these my worthy friends, in the best manner I was able, I rose with a heart full of affection and reverence, and left the room, in order to obey my master's joyful mandate of going to the Register Office. As I was leaving the house I called to mind the words of the Psalmist,[5] in the 126th Psalm, and like him, "I glorified God in my heart, in whom I trusted." These words had

4. In total, without further deductions.
5. David, the second king of ancient Israel, tra-

ditionally considered the author of the biblical Book of Psalms.

been impressed on my mind from the very day I was forced from Deptford to the present hour, and I now saw them, as I thought, fulfilled and verified. My imagination was all rapture as I flew to the Register Office; and, in this respect, like the apostle Peter[6] (whose deliverance from prison was so sudden and extraordinary, that he thought he was in a vision), I could scarcely believe I was awake. Heavens! who could do justice to my feelings at this moment! Not conquering heroes themselves, in the midst of a triumph—Not the tender mother who has just regained her long lost infant, and presses it to her heart—Not the weary hungry, mariner, at the sight of the desired friendly port—Not the lover, when he once more embraces his beloved mistress, after she has been ravished from his arms! All within my breast was tumult, wildness, and delirium! My feet scarcely touched the ground, for they were winged with joy; and, like Elijah, as he rose to Heaven,[7] they "were with lightning sped as I went on." Every one I met I told of my happiness, and blazed about the virtue of my amiable master and captain.

When I got to the office and acquainted the Register with my errand, he congratulated me on the occasion, and told me he would draw up my manumission for half price, which was a guinea.[8] I thanked him for his kindness; and, having received it, and paid him, I hastened to my master to get him to sign it, that I might be fully released. Accordingly he signed the manumission that day; so that, before night, I, who had been a slave in the morning, trembling at the will of another, was become my own master, and completely free. I thought this was the happiest day I had ever experienced; and my joy was still heightened by the blessings and prayers of many of the sable race, particularly the aged, to whom my heart had ever been attached with reverence.

* * *

As the form of my manumission has something peculiar in it, and expresses the absolute power and dominion one man claims over his fellow, I shall beg leave to present it before my readers at full length:

Montserrat.—To all men unto whom these presents[9] shall come: I, Robert King, of the parish of St. Anthony, in the said island, merchant, send greeting. Know ye, that I, the aforesaid Robert King, for and in consideration of the sum of seventy pounds current money of the said island,[1] to me in hand paid, and to the intent that a negro man slave, named Gustavus Vassa, shall and may become free, having manumitted, emancipated, enfranchised, and set free, and by these presents do manumit, emancipate, enfranchise, and set free, the aforesaid negro man slave, named Gustavus Vassa, for ever; hereby giving, granting, and releasing unto him, the said Gustavus Vassa, all right, title, dominion, sovereignty, and property, which, as lord and master over the aforesaid Gustavus Vassa, I had, or now have, or by any means whatsoever I may or can hereafter possibly have over him, the aforesaid negro, for ever. In witness whereof, I, the above said Robert King, have unto

6. "Acts xii.9" [Equiano's note]. "And he went out and followed him; and wist not that it was true which was done by the angel; but thought he saw a vision."
7. God takes Elijah into heaven in 2 Kings 2.11.
8. A unit of British currency, equal to twenty-one shillings.
9. The present words; this document.
1. Because the exchange rate favored the West Indians in this period, the forty pounds sterling that Equiano paid equaled seventy pounds in "local" currency.

these presents set my hand and seal, this tenth day of July, in the year of our Lord one thousand seven hundred and sixty-six.

ROBERT KING.

Signed, sealed, and delivered in the presence of Terry Legay, Montserrat.

Registered the within manumission at full length, this eleventh day of July, 1766, in liber² D.

TERRY LEGAY, REGISTER.

* * *

From *Chapter IX*

* * *

The same day I went into the city in quest of a master.³ I was extremely fortunate in my inquiry; for I soon heard of a gentleman who had a ship going to Italy and Turkey, and he wanted a man who could dress hair well. I was overjoyed at this, and went immediately on board of his ship, as I had been directed, which I found to be fitted up with great taste, and I already foreboded no small pleasure in sailing in her. Not finding the gentleman on board, I was directed to his lodgings, where I met with him the next day, and gave him a specimen of my dressing. He liked it so well that he hired me immediately, so that I was perfectly happy; for the ship, master, and voyage, were entirely to my mind. The ship was called the Delawar, and my master's name was John Jolly, a neat smart good humoured man, just such an one as I wished to serve. We sailed from England in July following, and our voyage was extremely pleasant. We went to Villa Franca, Nice, and Leghorn;⁴ and in all these places I was charmed with the richness and beauty of the countries, and struck with the elegant buildings with which they abound. We had always in them plenty of extraordinary good wines and rich fruits, which I was very fond of; and I had frequent occasions of gratifying both my taste and curiosity; for my captain always lodged on shore in those places, which afforded me opportunities to see the country around. I also learned navigation of⁵ the mate, which I was very fond of. When we left Italy we had delightful sailing among the Archipelago islands, and from thence to Smyrna in Turkey. This is a very ancient city; the houses are built of stone, and most of them have graves adjoining to them; so that they sometimes present the appearance of church-yards. Provisions are very plentiful in this city, and good wine less than a penny a pint. The grapes, pomegranates, and many other fruits, were also the richest and largest I ever tasted. The natives are well looking and strong made, and treated me always with great civility. In general I believe they are fond of black people; and several of them gave me pressing invitations to stay amongst them, although they keep the franks, or

2. Book (Latin).
3. After his emancipation, Equiano traded throughout the West Indies and in Georgia before moving to London, where he worked as a hairdresser. Low wages drove him to return to work as a sailor. He had many adventures, including the travels described here.
4. The Italian port city of Livorno. "Villa Franca": Vila Franca de Campo, port town in the Azores. "Nice": port city in France.
5. From.

Christians,[6] separate, and do not suffer them to dwell immediately amongst them. I was astonished in not seeing women in any of their shops, and very rarely any in the streets; and whenever I did they were covered with a veil from head to foot, so that I could not see their faces, except when any of them out of curiosity uncovered them to look at me, which they sometimes did. I was surprised to see how the Greeks are, in some measure, kept under by the Turks, as the negroes are in the West Indies by the white people.[7] The less refined Greeks, as I have already hinted, dance here in the same manner as we do in my nation. On the whole, during our stay here, which was about five months, I liked the place and the Turks extremely well. I could not help observing one very remarkable circumstance there: the tails of the sheep are flat, and so very large, that I have known the tail even of a lamb to weight from eleven to thirteen pounds. The fat of them is very white and rich, and is excellent in puddings, for which it is much used. Our ship being at length richly loaded with silk, and other articles, we sailed for England.

In May 1769, soon after our return from Turkey, our ship made a delightful voyage to Oporto in Portugal, where we arrived at the time of the carnival.[8] On our arrival, there were sent on board to us thirty-six articles to observe, with very heavy penalties if we should break any of them; and none of us even dared to go on board any other vessel or on shore till the Inquisition had sent on board and searched for every thing illegal, especially bibles.[9] Such as were produced, and certain other things, were sent on shore till the ships were going away; and any person in whose custody a bible was found concealed was to be imprisoned and flogged, and sent into slavery for ten years. I saw here many very magnificent sights, particularly the garden of Eden, where many of the clergy and laity went in procession in their several orders with the host, and sung Te Deum.[1] I had a great curiosity to go into some of their churches, but could not gain admittance without using the necessary sprinkling of holy water at my entrance. From curiosity, and a wish to be holy, I therefore complied with this ceremony, but its virtues were lost on me, for I found myself nothing the better for it. This place abounds with plenty of all kinds of provisions. The town is well built and pretty, and commands a fine prospect. Our ship having taken in a load of wine, and other commodities, we sailed for London, and arrived in July following. Our next voyage was to the Mediterranean. The ship was again got ready, and we sailed in September for Genoa. This is one of the finest cities I ever saw; some of the edifices were of beautiful marble, and made a most noble appearance; and many had very curious fountains before them. The churches were rich and magnificent, and curiously adorned both in the inside and out. But all this grandeur was in my eyes disgraced by the galley slaves,[2] whose condi-

6. The term "franks" derives from the Franks, ancient German tribes who converted to Christianity and extended into parts of the Eastern Roman Empire.
7. The Ottoman Turks controlled Greece from the mid-fifteenth century until 1832, when Greece was recognized as an independent state following a revolution that began in 1821.
8. Festivities before the beginning of Lent; i.e., springtime.
9. Ownership of a Bible indicated Protestantism and therefore was proscribed by the Inquisi-tion, officially the Holy Office, an ecclesiastical tribunal established by the Roman Catholic Church in the thirteenth century to identify and prosecute heretics. The Portuguese Inquisition, established in 1536, was disbanded in 1821.
1. An early Christian hymn of praise, sung in Latin. "Host": communion wafer.
2. Often prisoners of war, galley slaves were rowers in galleys: low, flat ships used in war and trade.

tion both there and in other parts of Italy is truly piteous and wretched. After we had stayed there some weeks, during which we bought many different things which we wanted, and got them very cheap, we sailed to Naples, a charming city, and remarkably clean. The bay is the most beautiful I ever saw; the moles for shiping[3] are excellent. I thought it extraordinary to see grand operas acted here on Sunday nights, and even attended by their majesties. I too, like these great ones, went to those sights, and vainly served God in the day while I thus served mammon effectually at night. While we remained here there happened an eruption of mount Vesuvius,[4] of which I had a perfect view. It was extremely awful; and we were so near that the ashes from it used to be thick on our deck. After we had transacted our business at Naples we sailed with a fair wind once more for Smyrna, where we arrived in December. A raskier[5] or officer took a liking to me here, and wanted me to stay, and offered me two wives; however I refused the temptation. The merchants here travel in caravans or large companies. I have seen many caravans from India, with some hundreds of camels, laden with different goods. The people of these caravans are quite brown. Among other articles, they brought with them a great quantity of locusts, which are a kind of pulse,[6] sweet and pleasant to the palate, and in shape resembling French beans, but longer. Each kind of goods is sold in a street by itself, and I always found the Turks very honest in their dealings. They let no Christians into their mosques or churches, for which I was very sorry; as I was always fond of going to see the different modes of worship of the people where ever I went. The plague broke out while we were in Smyrna, and we stopped taking goods into the ship till it was over. She was then richly laden, and we sailed in about March 1770 for England. One day in our passage we met with an accident which was near burning the ship. A black cook, in melting some fat, overset the pan into the fire under the deck, which immediately began to blaze, and the flame went up very high under the foretop. With the fright the poor cook became almost white, and altogether speechless. Happily however we got the fire out without doing much mischief. After various delays in this passage, which was tedious, we arrived in Standgate creek[7] in July; and, at the latter end of the year, some new event occurred, so that my noble captain, the ship, and I all separated.

<p style="text-align:center">*　*　*</p>

<p style="text-align:right">1789</p>

3. Long piers or artificial breakwaters, here in the Mediterranean.
4. The only active volcano on Europe's mainland, located on Italy's western coast overlooking Naples. Vesuvius is best known as the volcano that erupted in 79 c.e., burying the Roman town of Pompeii. The ruins of Pompeii were discovered in 1748.
5. An Ottoman title for an army commander.
6. Edible seed of a plant in the legume family. "Locusts": locust beans.
7. Stangate Creek, on the river Medway, in southeast England.

JUDITH SARGENT MURRAY
1751–1820

Judith Sargent Murray addressed her most important subject—the independent
female mind—in her first published essay, "Desultory Thoughts upon the Utility
of Encouraging a Degree of Self-Complacency, Especially in Female Bosoms" (1784).
Writing under the pen name "Constantia," she advised young women that though a
"pleasing form is undoubtedly advantageous," a developed mind is far more mean-
ingful. An intellectual woman in a culture that regarded women as men's mental
inferiors, a professional writer in an era when almost no one—male or female—
made a living by writing, Murray went on to demonstrate the validity of her own
precepts.

Judith Sargent was born and spent much of her life in Gloucester, Massachusetts,
a coastal town about forty miles north of Boston. Her parents, Judith Saunders and
Winthrop Sargent, came from seafaring families. Along with her younger brother
Winslow, Judith was tutored by the local clergyman in college preparatory subjects
including Latin, Greek, and mathematics. Another distinctive feature of her
upbringing was her parents' liberal theology, which questioned the strict Calvinist
doctrine of election, that is, the belief that God had destined each soul to either
salvation or damnation. They embraced instead the teachings of the English Univer-
salist James Relly, who proclaimed that salvation was available to anyone who
accepted Jesus Christ. Relly was sure that a rational God would never condemn
believers to hell. The Sargents and John Stevens, whom Judith married in 1769,
were thus ready to welcome Relly's greatest disciple, John Murray, who had left
England to preach in the eastern colonies, reaching Gloucester in 1774. In 1788,
about a year after the death of John Stevens in the West Indies, Judith Sargent
married John Murray. Meanwhile the first Universalist church in America had
been dedicated in Gloucester in 1780. The denomination went on to be a leader in
the effort to ordain women as ministers. As this suggests, Judith Sargent Murray's
advocacy of cultivating independent, intellectually alert women was highly com-
patible with her religious beliefs.

Murray's career as a writer began in earnest soon after she married Murray. In
an increasingly secular world, essays and novels with moral subtexts fashioned
readers into secular "congregations," and periodicals such as Boston's *Massachusetts
Magazine* and *The Gentleman's and Lady's Town and Country Magazine: or, Reposi-
tory of Instruction and Entertainment*, where "The Utility of Encouraging a Degree
of Self-Complacency, Especially in Female Bosoms" first appeared, would supplant
or supplement many pulpits in the years to come. Eighteenth-century readers liked
a moral without the theology. But while Murray found an audience early on, it was
not easy for her to make a living by the pen. In the volatile world of print culture,
magazines changed hands frequently and many of them disappeared, while pub-
lishers assumed that contributors would be so eager to see their names in print that
no payment was necessary.

Murray's most important publication and her greatest financial success was a
three-volume compilation of her work, published in 1798 as *The Gleaner*, which she
dedicated to Abigail and John Adams. She seems to have published nothing new
from 1796 to 1802, when she offered some poems in a Boston publication that
hoped to take up where the defunct *Massachusetts Magazine* left off. Her major

"Keep within Compass," c. **1795.** This engraving encourages women to remain outside the public sphere occupied by men. Judith Sargent Murray was among the thinkers of the time who challenged this view.

efforts during these years went to the care of her ailing and improvident husband and to editing his *Letters and Sketches of Sermons* (1812–13) and his posthumously published autobiography (1816). With her work on Murray's behalf completed, she left New England and made a final home with her daughter in Natchez, Mississippi, where she died in 1820.

At the beginning of her writing career, in 1779, Murray drafted "On the Equality of the Sexes," which offers a defense of women's intellectual abilities. The essay did not appear in print until 1790, the same year as the English writer Catherine Macaulay's similarly themed *Letters on Education.* Two years later the English writer Mary Wollstonecraft published *Vindication of the Rights of Woman,* a landmark political treatise and statement of women's rights. As these parallels suggest, Murray was at the forefront of the movement in the revolutionary Atlantic world to extend the promise of equality in the Declaration of Independence to women as well as men.

On the Equality of the Sexes[1]

Part I

That minds are not alike, full well I know,
This truth each day's experience will show.
To heights surprising some great spirits soar,
With inborn strength mysterious depths explore;
Their eager gaze surveys the path of light, 5
Confessed it stood to Newton's piercing sight.[2]
 Deep science, like a bashful maid retires,
And but[3] the *ardent* breast her worth inspires;
By perseverance the coy fair is won,
And Genius, led by Study, wears the crown. 10
 But some there are who wish not to improve,
Who never can the path of knowledge love,
Whose souls almost with the dull body one,
With anxious care each mental pleasure shun.
Weak is the leveled, enervated mind, 15
And but while here to vegetate designed.
The torpid spirit mingling with its clod
Can scarcely boast its origin from God.
Stupidly dull—they move progressing on—
They eat, and drink, and all their work is done, 20
While others, emulous of sweet applause,
Industrious seek for each event a cause,
Tracing the hidden springs whence knowledge flows,
Which nature all in beauteous order shows.
 Yet cannot I their sentiments imbibe 25
Who this distinction to the sex ascribe,
As if a woman's form must needs enroll
A weak, a servile, an inferior soul;
And that the guise of man must still proclaim
Greatness of mind, and him, to be the same. 30
Yet as the hours revolve fair proofs arise
Which the bright wreath of growing fame supplies,
And in past times some men have *sunk* so *low*,
That female records nothing *less* can show.
But imbecility[4] is still confined, 35
And by the lordly sex to us consigned.
They rob us of the power t'improve,
And then declare we only trifles love.
Yet haste the era when the world shall know
That such distinctions only dwell below. 40
The soul unfettered to no sex confined,
Was for the abodes of cloudless day designed.

1. The text is from *The Massachusetts Magazine, or, Monthly Museum of Knowledge and Rational Entertainment,* published in March and April 1790. Both the poem and the essay are by Murray.
2. Sir Isaac Newton (1642–1727), English scien-
tist and philosopher, broke up white light into the colors of the spectrum by means of a prism and likewise recombined the colors.
3. And only.
4. Stupidity.

> Meantime we emulate their manly fires,
> Though erudition all their thoughts inspires,
> Yet nature with *equality* imparts, 45
> And *noble passions,* swell e'en *female hearts.*

Is it upon mature consideration we adopt the idea that nature is thus partial in her distributions? Is it indeed a fact that she hath yielded to one half of the human species so unquestionable a mental superiority? I know that to both sexes elevated understandings, and the reverse, are common. But, suffer me to ask, in what the minds of females are so notoriously deficient, or unequal? May not the intellectual powers be ranged under these four heads—imagination, reason, memory and judgment? The province of imagination hath long since been surrendered up to us, and we have been crowned undoubted sovereigns of the regions of fancy. Invention is perhaps the most arduous effort of the mind; this branch of imagination hath been particularly ceded to us, and we have been time out of mind invested with that creative faculty. Observe the variety of fashions (here I bar the contemptuous smile) which distinguish and adorn the female world; how continually are they changing, insomuch that they almost render the wise man's assertion problematical, and we are ready to say, *there is something new under the sun.*[5] Now what a playfulness, what an exuberance of fancy, what strength of inventive imagination, doth this continual variation discover?[6] Again, it hath been observed that if the turpitude of the conduct of our sex hath been ever so enormous, so extremely ready are we, that the very first thought presents us with an apology so plausible as to produce our actions even in an amiable light. Another instance of our creative powers is our talent for slander. How ingenious are we at inventive scandal? What a formidable story can we in a moment fabricate merely from the force of a prolific imagination? How many reputations in the fertile brain of a female have been utterly despoiled? How industrious are we at improving[7] a hint? Suspicion[8] how easily do we convert into conviction, and conviction, embellished by the power of eloquence, stalks abroad to the surprise and confusion of unsuspecting innocence. Perhaps it will be asked if I furnish these facts as instances of excellency in our sex. Certainly not; but as proofs of a creative faculty, of a lively imagination. Assuredly great activity of mind is thereby discovered, and was this activity properly directed what beneficial effects would follow. Is the needle and kitchen sufficient to employ the operations of a soul thus organized? I should conceive not. Nay, it is a truth that those very departments leave the intelligent principle vacant, and at liberty for speculation. Are we deficient in reason? We can only reason from what we know, and if an opportunity of acquiring knowledge hath been denied us, the inferiority of our sex cannot fairly be deduced from thence. Memory, I believe, will be allowed us in common, since every one's experience must testify that a loquacious old woman is as frequently met with as a communicative old man; their subjects are alike drawn from the fund of other times, and the transactions of their youth, or of maturer life, entertain, or perhaps fatigue you, in the evening of their lives. "But our judgment is not so strong—we do not distinguish so well."—Yet it

5. "There is no new thing under the sun" (Ecclesiastes 1.8).
6. Reveal.

7. Making use of.
8. Imagine.

may be questioned, from what doth this superiority in this determining faculty of the soul, proceed? May we not trace its source in the difference of education, and continued advantages? Will it be said that the judgment of a male of two years old is more sage than that of a female's of the same age? I believe the reverse is generally observed to be true. But from that period what partiality! How is the one exalted and the other depressed by the contrary modes of education which are adopted! The one is taught to aspire and the other is early confined and limited. As their years increase the sister must be wholly domesticated, while the brother is led by the hand through all the flowery paths of science. Grant that their minds are by nature equal, yet who shall wonder at the *apparent* superiority, if indeed custom becomes *second nature*; nay if it taketh place of nature, and that it doth the experience of each day will evince. At length arrived at womanhood, the uncultivated fair one feels a void which the employments allotted her are by no means capable of filling. What can she do? To books she may not apply; or if she doth, *to those only of the novel kind*,[9] lest she merit the appellation of a *learned lady*; and what ideas have been affixed to this term, the observation of many can testify. Fashion, scandal, and sometimes what is still more reprehensible are then called in to her relief; and who can say to what lengths the liberties she takes may proceed. Meantime she herself is most unhappy; she feels the want of a cultivated mind. Is she single, she in vain seeks to fill up time from sexual[1] employments or amusements. Is she united to a person whose soul nature made equal to her own, education hath set him so far above her that in those entertainments which are productive of such rational felicity she is not qualified to accompany him. She experiences a mortifying consciousness of inferiority which embitters every enjoyment. Doth the person to whom her adverse fate hath consigned her possess a mind incapable of improvement, she is equally wretched in being so closely connected with an individual whom she cannot but despise. Now was she permitted the same instructors as her brother (with an eye however to their particular departments) for the employment of a rational mind an ample field would be opened. In astronomy she might catch a glimpse of the immensity of the Deity and thence she would form amazing conceptions of the August and supreme Intelligence. In geography she would admire Jehovah in the midst of His benevolence; thus adapting this globe to the various wants and amusements of its inhabitants. In natural philosophy she would adore the infinite majesty of heaven, clothed in condescension[2] and as she traversed the reptile world, she would hail the goodness of a creating God. A mind thus filled would have little room for the trifles with which our sex are, with too much justice, accused of amusing themselves, and they would thus be rendered fit companions for those who should one day wear them as their crown. Fashions, in their variety, would then give place to conjectures, which might perhaps conduce to the improvement of the literary world; and there would be no leisure for slander or detraction. Reputation would not then be blasted, but serious speculations would occupy the lively imaginations of the sex. Unnecessary visits would be precluded, and that custom would only be indulged by way of relaxation, or to answer the demands of consanguinity and friendship. Females would

9. I.e., fiction.
1. Defined by gender roles.

2. A gracious disregard of its superiority. "Natural philosophy": i.e., natural science.

become discreet, their judgments would be invigorated, and their partners for life being circumspectly chosen, an unhappy Hymen[3] would then be as rare as is now the reverse.

Will it be urged that those acquirements would supersede our domestic duties? I answer that every requisite in female economy[4] is easily attained; and, with truth, I can add that when once attained they require no further *mental attention*. Nay, while we are pursuing the needle, or the superintendency of the family, I repeat, that our minds are at full liberty for reflection; that imagination may exert itself in full vigor; and that if a just foundation is early laid, our ideas will then be worthy of rational beings. If we were industrious we might easily find time to arrange them upon paper, or should avocations press too hard for such an indulgence, the hours allotted for conversation would at least become more refined and rational. Should it still be vociferated, "Your domestic employments are sufficient"—I would calmly ask, is it reasonable that a candidate for immortality, for the joys of heaven, an intelligent being, who is to spend an eternity in contemplating the works of Deity, should at present be so degraded as to be allowed no other ideas than those which are suggested by the mechanism of a pudding, or the sewing the seams of a garment? Pity that all such censurers of female improvement do not go one step further and deny their[5] future existence; to be consistent they surely ought.

Yes, ye lordly, ye haughty sex, our souls are by nature *equal* to yours; the same breath of God animates, enlivens, and invigorates us; and that we are not fallen lower than yourselves, let those witness who have greatly towered above the various discouragements by which they have been so heavily oppressed. And though I am unacquainted with the list of celebrated characters on either side, yet from the observations I have made in the contracted circle in which I have moved, I dare confidently believe that from the commencement of time to the present day there hath been as many females, as males, who, by the *mere force of natural powers*, have merited the crown of applause; who, *thus unassisted*, have seized the wreath of fame. I know there are [those] who assert that as the animal powers of the one sex are superior of course their mental faculties also must be stronger; thus attributing strength of mind to the transient organization of this earth born tenement.[6] But if this reasoning is just, man must be content to yield the palm[7] [to] many of the brute creation, since by not a few of his brethren of the field he is far surpassed in bodily strength. Moreover, was this argument admitted, it would prove too much, for ocular demonstration evinceth that there are many robust masculine ladies, and effeminate gentlemen. Yet I fancy that Mr. Pope, though clogged with an enervated body, and distinguished by a diminutive stature,[8] could nevertheless lay claim to greatness of soul, and perhaps there are many other instances which might be adduced to combat so unphilosophical an opinion. Do we not often see that when the clay built tabernacle[9] is well nigh dissolved, when it is just ready to mingle with the parent soil, the immortal inhabitant aspires to and even attaineth heights the most sublime and which were before wholly unexplored? Besides, were

3. Marriage. In classical mythology, Hymen is the god of marriage.
4. Housekeeping.
5. Women's.
6. I.e., of the human body.

7. The palm branch, a classical symbol of victory.
8. The English poet Alexander Pope (1688–1744) suffered an early illness that left his body deformed.
9. I.e., the body, which houses the soul.

we to grant that animal strength proved anything, taking into consideration the accustomed impartiality of nature, we should be induced to imagine that she had invested the female mind with superior strength as an equivalent for the bodily powers of man. But waving this however palpable advantage, for *equality only*, we wish to contend.

Part II

I am aware that there are many passages in the sacred oracles which seem to give the advantage to the other sex, but I consider all these as wholly metaphorical. Thus David was a man after God's own heart, yet see him enervated by his licentious passions! Behold him following Uriah to the death[1] and show me wherein could consist the immaculate Being's complacency. Listen to the curses which Job bestoweth upon the day of his nativity,[2] and tell me where is his perfection, where his patience—*literally* it existed not. David and Job were types of Him who was to come;[3] and the superiority of man, as exhibited in scripture, being also emblematical, all arguments deduced from thence of course fall to the ground. The exquisite delicacy of the female mind proclaimeth the exactness of its texture, while its nice[4] sense of honor announceth its innate, its native grandeur. And indeed, in one respect, the preeminence seems to be tacitly allowed us, for after an education which limits and confines, and employments and recreations which naturally tend to enervate the body and debilitate the mind, after we have from early youth been adorned with ribbons and other gewgaws,[5] dressed out like the ancient victims previous to a sacrifice, being taught by the care of our parents in collecting the most showy materials that the ornamenting [of] our exterior ought to be the principal object of our attention; after, I say, fifteen years thus spent, we are introduced into the world amid the united adulation of every beholder. Praise is sweet to the soul; we are immediately intoxicated by large draughts of flattery, which being plentifully administered, is to the pride of our hearts the most acceptable incense. It is expected that with the other sex we should commence immediate war, and that we should triumph over the machinations of the most artful. We must be constantly upon our guard; prudence and discretion must be our characteristics, and we must rise superior to, and obtain a complete victory over, those who have been long adding to the native strength of their minds by an unremitted study of men and books, and who have, moreover, conceived from the loose characters which they have seen portrayed in the extensive variety of their reading a most contemptible opinion of the sex. Thus unequal, we are, notwithstanding, forced to the combat, and the infamy which is consequent upon the smallest deviation in our conduct proclaims the high idea which was formed of our native strength; and thus, indirectly at least, is the preference acknowledged to be our due. And if we are allowed an equality of acquirement, let serious studies equally employ our minds and we

1. When King David lusted after Bathsheba, he contrived to send her husband, Uriah, into battle to be killed so that David might marry her. See 2 Samuel 11.3–27.
2. Although Job's faith survives many testings, he curses the day he was born (Job 3).
3. Medieval exegetes argued that Old Testament persons and events took on their full meaning in the New Testament. Job and David are thus, in their sufferings, types (i.e., prefigurations) of Jesus.
4. Refined. "Exactness": high finish or quality.
5. Trinkets.

will bid our souls arise to equal strength. We will meet upon even ground the despot man; we will rush with alacrity to the combat, and, crowned by success, we shall then answer the exalted expectations which are formed. Though sensibility, soft compassion, and gentle commiseration are inmates in the female bosom, yet against every deep laid art, altogether fearless of the event, we will set them in array; for assuredly the wreath of victory will encircle the spotless brow. If we meet an equal, a sensible friend, we will reward him with the hand of amity, and through life we will be assiduous to promote his happiness; but from every deep laid scheme for our ruin, retiring into ourselves, amid the flowery paths of science, we will indulge in all the refined and sentimental pleasures of contemplation. And should it still be urged that the studies thus insisted upon would interfere with our more peculiar department,[6] I must further reply that *early hours* and close application will do wonders; and to her who is from the first dawn of reason taught to fill up time rationally, both the requisites will be easy. I grant that niggard[7] fortune is too generally unfriendly to the mind; and that much of that valuable treasure, time, is necessarily expended upon the wants of the body; but it should be remembered that in embarrassed circumstances our companions have as little leisure for literary improvement as is afforded to us; for most certainly their provident care is at least as requisite as our exertions. Nay, we have even more leisure for sedentary pleasures, as our avocations are more retired, much less laborious, and, as hath been observed, by no means require that avidity of attention which is proper to the employments of the other sex. In high life, or, in other words, where the parties are in possession of affluence, the objection respecting time is wholly obviated, and, of course, falls to the ground. And it may also be repeated that many of those hours which are at present swallowed up in fashion and scandal might be redeemed were we habituated to useful reflections. But in one respect, O ye arbiters of our fate! we confess that the superiority is indubitably yours; you are by nature formed for our protectors; we pretend not to vie with you in bodily strength; upon this point we will never contend for victory. Shield us then, we beseech you, from external evils, and in return *we* will transact *your* domestic affairs. Yes, *your*, for are you not equally interested in those matters with ourselves? Is not the elegancy of neatness as agreeable to your sight as to ours; is not the well favored viand equally delightful to your taste; and doth not your sense of hearing suffer as much from the discordant sounds prevalent in an ill regulated family produced by the voices of children and many *et ceteras?*[8]

<div align="right">CONSTANTIA.</div>

By way of supplement to the foregoing pages, I subjoin the following extract from a letter, wrote to a friend in the December of 1780.

And now assist me, O thou genius of my sex, while I undertake the arduous task of endeavoring to combat that vulgar, that almost universal error, which hath, it seems, enlisted even Mr. P—under its banners. The superiority of your sex hath, I grant, been time out of mind esteemed a truth incontrovertible; in consequence of which persuasion every plan of education hath

6. I.e., with duties belonging more particularly to women.

7. Stingy.

8. Unspecified other things (Latin).

been calculated to establish this favorite tenet. Not long since, weak and presuming as I was, I amused myself with selecting some arguments from nature, reason, and experience, against this so generally received idea. I confess that to sacred testimonies[9] I had not recourse. I held them to be merely metaphorical and thus regarding them, I could not persuade myself that there was any propriety in bringing them to decide in this *very important debate*. However, as you, sir, confine yourself entirely to the sacred oracles, I mean to bend the whole of my artillery against those supposed proofs which you have from thence provided, and from which you have formed an entrenchment *apparently* so invulnerable. And first, to begin with our great progenitors;[1] but here, suffer me to premise, that it is for mental strength I mean to contend, for with respect to animal powers, I yield them undisputed to that sex, which enjoys them in common with the lion, the tiger, and many other beasts of prey; therefore your observations respecting the *rib under the arm*,[2] *at a distance from the head*, etc., etc., in no sort militate against my view. Well, but the woman was first in the transgression. Strange how blind *self love* renders you men. Were you not wholly absorbed in a partial admiration of your own abilities, you would long since have acknowledged the force of what I am now going to urge. It is true some ignoramuses have absurdly enough informed us that the beauteous fair of paradise was seduced from her obedience by a malignant demon *in the guise of a baleful serpent*; but we, who are better informed, know that the fallen spirit presented himself to her view *a shining angel still*; for thus, saith the critics in the Hebrew tongue, ought the word to be rendered.[3] Let us examine her motive— Hark! the seraph declares that she shall attain a perfection of knowledge; for is there aught which is not comprehended under one or other of the terms *good* and *evil*. It doth not appear that she was governed by any one sensual appetite, but merely by a desire of adorning her mind. A laudable ambition fired her soul and a thirst for knowledge impelled the predilection so fatal in its consequences. Adam could not plead the same deception; assuredly he was not deceived; nor ought we to admire his superior strength, or wonder at his sagacity, when we so often confess that example is much more influential than precept. His gentle partner stood before him, a melancholy instance of the direful effects of disobedience; he saw her not possessed of that wisdom which she had fondly hoped to obtain, but he beheld the once blooming female disrobed of that innocence which had heretofore rendered her so lovely. To him, then, deception became impossible, as he had proof positive of the fallacy of the argument which the deceiver had suggested. What then could be his inducement to burst the barriers, and to fly directly in the face of that command, which *immediately* from the mouth of Deity *he* had received, since, I say, he could not plead that fascinating stimulus, the accumulation of knowledge, as indisputable conviction was so visibly portrayed before him. What mighty cause impelled him to sacrifice myriads of beings yet unborn, and by one impious act, which *he saw* would be productive of such fatal effects, entail undistinguished ruin upon a race of beings which

9. I.e., to the Bible.
1. Ancestors; here, Adam and Eve.
2. "And the rib, which the Lord God had taken from man, made he a woman, and brought her unto the man" (Genesis 2.22).

3. The earliest connection of Satan and light is in Isaiah 14.12: "How are thou fallen from heaven, O Lucifer, son of the morning!" *Lucifer* in Latin means "light bearer."

he was yet to produce. Blush, ye vaunters of fortitude, ye boasters of resolution, ye haughty lords of the creation; blush when ye remember that he was influenced by no other motive than a bare pusillanimous attachment to a woman! by sentiments so exquisitely soft that all his sons have from that period, when they have designed to degrade them, described as highly feminine. Thus it should seem that all the arts of the grand deceiver (since means adequate to the purpose are, I conceive, invariably pursued) were requisite to mislead our general mother, while the father of mankind forfeited his own, and relinquished the happiness of posterity, merely in compliance with the blandishments of a female. The subsequent subjection the apostle Paul explains as a figure; after enlarging upon the subject, he adds, "*This is a great mystery; but I speak concerning Christ and the church.*"[4] Now we know with what consummate wisdom the unerring father of eternity hath formed his plans; all the types which he hath displayed he hath permitted *materially* to fail, in the very virtue for which *they* were famed. The reason for this is obvious; we might otherwise mistake his economy and render that honor to the creature which is due only to the creator. I know that Adam was a figure of Him who was to come.[5] The Grace contained in this figure is the reason of my rejoicing, and while I am very far from prostrating before the shadow, I yield joyfully in all things the preeminence to the Second Federal Head.[6] Confiding faith is prefigured by Abraham, yet he exhibits a contrast to affiance when he says of his fair companion, she is my sister.[7] Gentleness was the characteristic of Moses,[8] yet he hesitated not to reply to Jehovah Himself. With unsaintlike tongue he murmured at the waters of strife, and with rash hands he break the Tables which were inscribed by the finger of divinity.[9] David, dignified with the title of the man after God's own heart, and yet how stained was his life. Solomon was celebrated for wisdom, but folly is wrote in legible characters upon his almost every action.[1] Lastly, let us turn our eyes to man in the aggregate. He is manifested as the figure of strength, but that we may not regard him as any thing more than a figure, his soul is formed in no sort superior, but every way equal to the mind of her who is the emblem of weakness and whom he hails the gentle companion of his better days.

1790, 1995

4. Ephesians 5.32.
5. Adam prefigures Jesus.
6. Jesus is the "Second Federal Head" because he made a Covenant of Faith with humanity after Adam broke God's Covenant of Works. *Federal* comes from the Latin word meaning "compact" or "treaty."
7. When Abraham, the first patriarch and progenitor of the Hebrews, is about to enter Egypt with his wife, he fears the Egyptians will kill him to take her, so he asks her: "Say, I pray thee, thou art my sister: that it may be well with me for thy sake; and my soul shall live because of thee" (Genesis 12.13). "Affiance": plighted faith; marriage.
8. The lawgiver who led the Israelites out of Egypt: "Now the man Moses was very meek, above all the men which were upon the face of the earth" (Numbers 12.3).
9. God inscribed the Ten Commandments on stone tablets ("Tables"), and Moses broke the first of those tablets (Exodus 32.19).
1. Solomon, third king of ancient Israel, was famously rich and wise, but worshiped false gods and failed to keep God's commandments (1 Kings 11.1–10).

PHILIP FRENEAU
1752–1832

I t has been said that Philip Freneau failed at almost everything he did. An accomplished journalist and political pamphleteer as well as a poet, Freneau did not fail at everything, but he was not able to support himself as a writer. His lack of success in this regard was partly a consequence of the immature print market in the United States. A generation later, Washington Irving and James Fenimore Cooper became the first American writers to support themselves with their pens.

Apart from the issue of the developing print market, there is the matter of Freneau's style. His most sympathetic readers believe that his genuine lyric gifts were always in conflict with his political pamphleteering. Another possibility emerges from the poems themselves, which reveal a writer poised between two eighteenth-century traditions: the neoclassical Augustan poetry exemplified by Alexander Pope, and the not-yet-fledged Romantic poetry inaugurated by Samuel Taylor Coleridge and William Wordsworth in their joint collection *Lyrical Ballads* (1798). Often characterized as a literary response to the age of democratic revolution, the Romantic poetics of Coleridge and Wordsworth called for the poet to be "a man speaking to men" in a natural sounding idiom and to employ freer verse forms than the heroic couplet (i.e., rhymed pairs of iambic pentameter lines) that was the mainstay of neoclassical poetry. Freneau, like his contemporary Phillis Wheatley (see her headnote, below), moved in the direction of Romantic themes and forms without accomplishing the transformation in poetics that his British contemporaries achieved.

Raised in Manhattan, Freneau had all the advantages of wealth and social position, which included an early introduction to the arts. Well-known writers and painters frequented the Freneau household. Educated in childhood by tutors, he entered the sophomore class at the College of New Jersey (now Princeton University) when he was just fifteen. At Princeton he became close friends with his roommate, James Madison, who would one day become the fourth president of the United States, and a classmate, Hugh Henry Brackenridge, who would become a judge and successful novelist. In their senior year Freneau and Brackenridge composed an ode, "On the Rising Glory of America," which Brackenridge read at commencement. It offers an early instance of Freneau's recurrent vision of a glorious future in which America fulfills the collective hope of humankind:

> Paradise anew
> Shall flourish, by no second Adam lost,
> No dangerous tree with deadly fruit shall grow,
> No tempting serpent to allure the soul
> From native innocence. . . . The lion and the lamb
> In mutual friendship linked, shall browse the shrub,
> And timorous deer with softened tigers stray
> O'er mead, or lofty hill, or grassy plain.

For a short time Freneau taught school, even as he hoped to make a career as a writer. When he was offered a position as secretary on a plantation in the West Indies in 1776, he sailed to St. Croix and remained there almost three years. On

that island—where "Sweet orange groves in lonely valleys rise," as he put it—Freneau wrote some of his most sensuous lyrics. As he remarks in "To Sir Toby," however, he could not talk only of "blossoms" and an "endless spring" in a land that abounded in poverty and misery, where the plantation owners grew wealthy on slave labor. In 1778 he returned home and enlisted as a seaman on a blockade runner; two years later he was captured at sea and imprisoned on the British ship *Scorpion*, anchored in New York harbor. He was treated cruelly, an experience he describes in "The British Prison Ship" (1781), his most popular poem with his contemporaries.

After Freneau regained his health, he moved to Philadelphia, where he worked in the post office and won his reputation as a journalist, satirist, and poet. As editor of the *Freeman's Journal*, Freneau wrote impassioned verse in support of the American Revolution, turned all his rhetorical gifts against loyalists to the British monarchy, and became identified as "the poet of the American Revolution." In 1791 Thomas Jefferson, then serving as secretary of state, hired Freneau as a translator in his department. At that point Philadelphia was the nation's capital, so Freneau remained in that city, devoting much of his time to editing the *National Gazette*, a newspaper associated with Jefferson's political party. That party, the Democratic-Republicans, favored a democratic republic rather than the strong federal government favored by the opposing Federalist party. Freneau had a sharp eye for anyone not sympathetic to the democratic cause. He strongly supported the French Revolution and had a special grudge against Alexander Hamilton, secretary of the Treasury, chief spokesman for the Federalists, who viewed the French Revolution skeptically. President George Washington, officially nonpartisan, found it ironic that "that rascal Freneau" should be employed by his administration when he attacked it outspokenly.

The *National Gazette* ceased publication in 1793, and after Jefferson resigned his office, Freneau left Philadelphia for good, alternating between ship's captain (a job that he had held on and off since 1778) and newspaper editor in New York and New Jersey. He spent his last years on his New Jersey farm, unable to make it self-supporting and with no hope of further employment. Year after year he sold off the land he had inherited from his father. Although he received a pension as a veteran of the American Revolution, he died impoverished and unknown, lost in a blizzard.

Freneau was a prolific writer of prose and poetry, addressing many topics including revolution and slavery, the fate of Native Americans, the sea, and nature. His best poems have a compelling lyricism. They reveal his interest in the beautiful, transient things of nature, and the conflict in his art between the sensuous and the didactic.

The following texts are from *The Poems of Freneau* (1929), edited by H. H. Clark, except as indicated.

The Wild Honey Suckle

Fair flower, that dost so comely grow,
Hid in this silent, dull retreat,
Untouched thy honeyed blossoms blow,[1]
Unseen thy little branches greet:
 No roving foot shall crush thee here, 5
 No busy hand provoke a tear.

1. Bloom.

By Nature's self in white arrayed,
She bade thee shun the vulgar² eye,
And planted here the guardian shade,
And sent soft waters murmuring by; 10
 Thus quietly thy summer goes,
 Thy days declining to repose.

Smit with those charms, that must decay,
I grieve to see your future doom;
They died—nor were those flowers more gay, 15
The flowers that did in Eden bloom;
 Unpitying frosts, and Autumn's power
 Shall leave no vestige of this flower.

From morning suns and evening dews
At first thy little being came: 20
If nothing once, you nothing lose,
For when you die you are the same;
 The space between, is but an hour,
 The frail duration of a flower.

 1786

The Indian Burying Ground

In spite of all the learned have said,
I still my old opinion keep;
The *posture*, that *we* give the dead,
Points out the soul's eternal sleep.

Not so the ancients of these lands— 5
The Indian, when from life released,
Again is seated¹ with his friends,
And shares again the joyous feast.

His imaged birds, and painted bowl,
And venison, for a journey dressed, 10
Bespeak the nature of the soul,
Activity, that knows no rest.

His bow, for action ready bent,
And arrows, with a head of stone,
Can only mean that life is spent, 15
And not the old ideas gone.

Thou, stranger, that shalt come this way,
No fraud upon the dead commit—

Observe the swelling turf, and say
They do not *lie*, but here they *sit*. 20

Here still a lofty rock remains,
On which the curious eye may trace
(Now wasted, half, by wearing rains)
The fancies of a ruder race.

Here still an agéd elm aspires, 25
Beneath whose far-projecting shade
(And which the shepherd still admires)
The children of the forest played!

There oft a restless Indian queen
(Pale Sheba,[2] with her braided hair) 30
And many a barbarous form is seen
To chide the man that lingers there.

By midnight moons, o'er moistening dews,
In habit for the chase arrayed,
The hunter still the deer pursues, 35
The hunter and the deer, a shade![3]

And long shall timorous fancy see
The painted chief, and pointed spear,
And Reason's self shall bow the knee
To shadows and delusions here. 40

1788

To Sir Toby[1]

*A Sugar Planter in the Interior Parts of Jamaica,
Near the City of San Jago de la Vega (Spanish Town), 1784*

> *"The motions of his spirit are black as night,
> And his affections dark as Erebus."*
> —Shakespeare[2]

If there exists a hell—the case is clear—
Sir Toby's slaves enjoy that portion here:
Here are no blazing brimstone lakes—'tis true;
But kindled rum too often burns as blue;
In which some fiend, whom nature must detest, 5

2. The queen who visited King Solomon to test his renowned wisdom (1 Kings 10.1–13).
3. Has double meaning as shadow and spirit.
1. The text is from *The Poems of Philip Freneau* (1902), edited by F. L. Pattee.

2. *The Merchant of Venice* 5.1. 86–87. Freneau has substituted "black" for "dull." "Erebus": in Greek mythology, a place of darkness in the underworld, through which the dead must pass before entering Hades.

Steeps Toby's brand, and marks poor Cudjoe's[3] breast.
 Here whips on whips excite perpetual fears,
And mingled howlings vibrate on my ears:
Here Nature's plagues abound, to fret and tease,
Snakes, scorpions, despots, lizards, centipedes— 10
No art, no care escapes the busy lash;
All have their dues—and all are paid in cash—
The eternal driver keeps a steady eye
On a black herd, who would his vengeance fly,
But chained, imprisoned, on a burning soil, 15
For the mean avarice of a tyrant toil![4]
The lengthy cart-whip guards this monster's reign—
And cracks, like pistols, from the fields of cane.
 Ye powers! who formed these wretched tribes, relate,
What had they done, to merit such a fate! 20
Why were they brought from Eboe's[5] sultry waste,
To see that plenty which they must not taste—
Food, which they cannot buy, and dare not steal;
Yams and potatoes—many a scanty meal!—
 One, with a gibbet[6] wakes his negro's fears, 25
One to the windmill nails him by the ears;
One keeps his slave in darkened dens, unfed,
One puts the wretch in pickle ere he's dead:
This, from a tree suspends him by the thumbs,
That, from his table grudges even the crumbs! 30
 O'er yond' rough hills a tribe of females go,
Each with her gourd,[7] her infant, and her hoe;
Scorched by a sun that has no mercy here,
Driven by a devil, whom men call overseer—
In chains, twelve wretches to their labors haste; 35
Twice twelve I saw, with iron collars graced!—
 Are such the fruits that spring from vast domains?
Is wealth, thus got, Sir Toby, worth your pains!—
Who would your wealth on terms, like these, possess,
Where all we see is pregnant with distress— 40
Angola's[8] natives scourged by ruffian hands,
And toil's hard product shipped to foreign lands.
 Talk not of blossoms, and your endless spring;
What joy, what smile, can scenes of misery bring?—
Though Nature, here, has every blessing spread, 45
Poor is the laborer—and how meanly fed!—
 Here Stygian[9] paintings light and shade renew,
Pictures of hell, that Virgil's[1] pencil drew:

3. "This passage has a reference to the West Indian custom (sanctioned by law) of branding a newly imported slave on the breast, with a red hot iron, as evidence of the purchaser's property" [Freneau's note]. Cudge or Cudjoe was a common name for a slave.
4. Lines 13–16 were added in 1809.
5. A small Negro kingdom near the river Senegal [Freneau's note].
6. Gallows.
7. Water cup.

8. West African Portuguese colony.
9. Hellish; taken from the river Styx, over which, in Greek mythology, souls of the dead must cross.
1. "See *Aeneid*, Book 6th.—and Fenelon's Telemachus, Book 18" [Freneau's note]. Aeneas descends to the underworld in the sixth book of the epic of the Roman poet Virgil (70–19 B.C.E.). The French theologian François de Salignac de la Mothe-Fénelon (1651–1715) wrote *Télémaque* (1699), a didactic romance concerning the son of Ulysses as he searches for his father.

Here, surly Charons[2] make their annual trip,
And ghosts arrive in every Guinea ship,[3] 50
To find what beasts these western isles afford,
Plutonian[4] scourges, and despotic lords:—
 Here, they, of stuff determined to be free,
Must climb the rude cliffs of the Liguanee;[5]
Beyond the clouds, in sculking haste repair, 55
And hardly safe from brother traitors[6] there.—

1784 1791, 1809

On Mr. Paine's Rights of Man[1]

Thus briefly sketched the sacred rights of man,
How inconsistent with the royal plan!
Which for itself exclusive honor craves,
Where some are masters born, and millions slaves.
With what contempt must every eye look down 5
On that base, childish bauble called a *crown*,
The gilded bait, that lures the crowd, to come,
Bow down their necks, and meet a slavish doom;
The source of half the miseries men endure,
The quack[2] that kills them, while it seems to cure, 10
 Roused by the reason of his manly page,
Once more shall Paine a listening world engage:
From Reason's source, a bold reform he brings,
In raising up *mankind*, he pulls down *kings*,
Who, source of discord, patrons of all wrong, 15
On blood and murder have been fed too long:
Hid from the world, and tutored to be base,
The curse, the scourge, the ruin of our race,
Theirs was the task, a dull designing few,
To shackle beings that they scarcely knew, 20
Who made this globe the residence of slaves,
And built their thrones on systems formed by knaves
—Advance, bright years, to work their final fall,
And haste the period that shall crush them all.
 Who, that has read and scanned the historic page 25
But glows, at every line, with kindling rage,
To see by them the rights of men aspersed,
Freedom restrained, and Nature's law reversed,

2. In Greek mythology, Charon ferries the souls of the dead over the river Styx to Hades.
3. Every slave ship from West Africa.
4. Hellish; in Roman mythology, Pluto was the god of the underworld.
5. The mountains northward of the kingdom [Freneau's note].
6. Alluding to the *Independent* negroes in the blue mountains, who, for a stipulated reward, deliver up every fugitive that falls into their hands, to the English Government [Freneau's note].

1. The original title was "To a Republican with Mr. Paine's Rights of Man." Thomas Paine (see his headnote, above) read the British statesman Edmund Burke's "Reflections on the French Revolution" (1790), a defense of monarchy and an attack on revolution, when he was living in England. In *The Rights of Man* (1791–92), Paine argued for the overthrow of monarchy and the right of the people to govern themselves.
2. One pretending to be a physician.

Men, ranked with beasts, by monarchs willed away,
And bound young fools, or madmen to obey: 30
Now driven to wars, and now oppressed at home,
Compelled in crowds o'er distant seas to roam,
From India's climes the plundered prize to bring
To glad the strumpet, or to glut the king.
　　Columbia,[3] hail! immortal be thy reign: 35
Without a king, we till the smiling plain;
Without a king, we trace the unbounded sea,
And traffic round the globe, through each degree;
Each foreign clime our honored flag reveres,
Which asks no monarch, to support the stars: 40
Without a *king*, the laws maintain their sway,
While honor bids each generous heart obey.
Be ours the task the ambitious to restrain,
And this great lesson teach—that kings are vain;
That warring realms to certain ruin haste, 45
That kings subsist by war, and wars are waste:
So shall our nation, formed on Virtue's plan,
Remain the guardian of the Rights of Man,
A vast republic, famed through every clime,
Without a king, to see the end of time. 50

　　　　　　　　　　　　　　　　　　　　　　　　　　　　　1795

On the Religion of Nature

The power, that gives with liberal hand
　　The blessings man enjoys, while here,
And scatters through a smiling land
　　Abundant products of the year;
　　　　That power of nature, ever blessed, 5
　　　　Bestowed religion with the rest.

Born with ourselves, her early sway
　　Inclines the tender mind to take
The path of right, fair virtue's way
　　Its own felicity to make. 10
　　　　This universally extends
　　　　And leads to no mysterious ends.

Religion, such as nature taught,
　　With all divine perfection suits;
Had all mankind this system sought 15
　　Sophists would cease their vain[1] disputes,
　　　　And from this source would nations know
　　　　All that can make their heaven below.

3. The personification of America (from Christopher Columbus).

1. Pointless. "Sophists": teachers of philosophy.

This deals not curses on mankind,
 Or dooms them to perpetual grief, 20
If from its aid no joys they find,
 It damns them not for unbelief;
 Upon a more exalted plan
 Creatress nature dealt with man—

Joy to the day, when all agree 25
 On such grand systems to proceed,
From fraud, design, and error free,
 And which to truth and goodness lead:
 Then persecution will retreat
 And man's religion be complete. 30

1815

PHILLIS WHEATLEY
c. 1753–1784

Phillis Wheatley was either nineteen or twenty years old in September 1773, when her *Poems on Various Subjects, Religious and Moral* was published in London. At the time of the volume's publication, she was the object of considerable public attention because, in addition to being a child prodigy, Wheatley was an enslaved person. Her books included a testimonial from eighteen prominent citizens—including the governor of Massachusetts and the merchant and statesman John Hancock—who bore witness that "under the Disadvantage of serving as a Slave in a Family in this Town," Wheatley "had been examined and thought qualified to write them." While the circumstances and nature of the examination remain unclear, the need for such a testimonial indicates the obstacles that Wheatley faced in pursuing her literary art.

Born in Africa (probably in present-day Senegal or Gambia), she was captured by slavers and brought to Boston in 1761. A wealthy tailor, John Wheatley, purchased her as a companion for his wife, Susanna, and she was named after the vessel that carried her to America. Wheatley was fortunate in her surroundings, for Susanna Wheatley was sympathetic toward this frail and remarkably intelligent child. At a time when even few white women were given an education, Wheatley was taught to read and write, and before long she began to read Latin writers. She came to know the Bible well, and three English poets—John Milton, Alexander Pope, and Thomas Gray—strongly influenced her verse. The Wheatleys moved in a circle of enlightened Boston Christians, and Phillis was introduced to a community that was coming to view the keeping of slaves as incompatible with Christian life.

Wheatley became internationally famous after the publication of her poetic eulogy celebrating George Whitefield, the great English evangelist who made several visits

Phillis Wheatley. This engraving—by Scipio Moorhead (see "To S. M.," on p. 795)—was the frontispiece to Wheatley's book.

to America, frequently toured New England, and died in Newburyport, Massachusetts, in 1770. In June 1773 she traveled to London in the company of the Wheatleys' son Nathaniel, partly for reasons of health and partly to seek support for her first book of poems. Benjamin Franklin and the lord mayor of London were among those who paid their respects. To her admirers, her literary gifts, intelligence, and piety exemplified the triumph of the human spirit over circumstance.

Just before her book could be published, Wheatley was called back to Boston by the news that Susanna Wheatley was dying. Early in the fall of 1773 she was granted manumission. Susanna Wheatley died in 1774. In the year that John Wheatley died, 1778, Wheatley married John Peters, a freedman, about whom almost nothing is known other than that the Wheatleys did not like him, that he petitioned for a license to sell liquor in 1784, and that he may have been in debtor's prison when Phillis Wheatley died, having endured poverty and the loss of two children in her last years. On her deathbed her third child lay ill beside her and succumbed shortly after Wheatley herself. They were buried together in an unmarked grave. Five years earlier, Wheatley had run advertisements for her second volume of poetry, to include thirteen letters and thirty-three poems. Her hoped-for subscribers did not respond, however, so she never published that volume. Most of the poems and letters are lost.

Wheatley's poetry was rediscovered in the 1830s by the New England abolitionists, but she has never been better understood than at the present. Her recent critics have not only corrected a number of biographical errors but, more important, have provided a context in which her work can be more fully interpreted. This reconsideration shows Wheatley to be a bold and canny spokesperson for her faith and her politics. She early joined the cause of American independence and supported the abolition of slavery, anticipating her friend the Reverend Samuel Hopkins's complaint that when African Americans first heard the "sons of liberty" cry out for freedom they were shocked by the indifference to their own "abject slavery and utter wretchedness." In a public letter to the Presbyterian minister and Mohegan leader Samson Occom, Wheatley stressed that the exercise of slavery cannot be reconciled with a "principle" that God has implanted in every human breast, "Love of Freedom"; and in her poem addressed to the conservative Earl of Dartmouth, she wrote that there could be no justice anywhere if people in authority were deaf to the cries of human sorrow. She promoted the cause of American independence in her poem celebrating George Washington as well, perhaps with the idea that he might encourage greater support for the rights of African Americans.

In her prosody Wheatley employed the dominant neoclassical verse form of the heroic couplet, while the themes of her poetry—including spiritual and political liberty, the sublime wonders of nature, and the qualities of vision and imagination—are more in keeping with the emerging Romantic tradition. A number of scholars have suggested that Wheatley's poetry includes allusions to her African childhood,

some overt, others more subtle. Her work is enriched by the tension between traditional form and transformational ideas.

The following texts are from *The Poems of Phillis Wheatley* (1966, rev. 1989), edited by Julian D. Mason. Wheatley's spelling and punctuation have been retained.

On Being Brought from Africa to America

'Twas mercy brought me from my pagan land,
Taught my benighted soul to understand
That there's a God, that there's a Savior too:
Once I redemption neither sought nor knew.
Some view our sable[1] race with scornful eye, 5
"Their color is a diabolic dye."
Remember, Christians, Negroes, black as Cain,[2]
May be refined, and join the angelic train.

1773

To the Right Honourable William, Earl of Dartmouth,[1] His Majesty's Principal Secretary of State for North America, &c.

Hail, happy day, when, smiling like the morn,
Fair Freedom rose New England to adorn:
The northern clime beneath her genial ray,
Dartmouth, congratulates thy blissful sway:
Elate with hope her race no longer mourns, 5
Each soul expands, each grateful bosom burns,
While in thine hand with pleasure we behold
The silken reins, and Freedom's charms unfold.
Long lost to realms beneath the northern skies
She shines supreme, while hated faction dies: 10
Soon as appeared the Goddess[2] long desired,
Sick at the view, she[3] languished and expired;
Thus from the splendors of the morning light
The owl in sadness seeks the caves of night.

No more, America, in mournful strain 15
Of wrongs, and grievance unredressed complain,
No longer shalt thou dread the iron chain,
Which wanton Tyranny with lawless hand
Had made, and with it meant t' enslave the land.

1. Black.
2. Cain slew his brother Abel and was "marked" by God for doing so. This mark has sometimes been taken to be the origin of dark-skinned peoples (Genesis 4.1–15).
1. William Legge, second Earl of Dartmouth

(1731–1801), was appointed secretary in charge of the American colonies in August 1772. He was sympathetic to the Methodist movement in England but not to the American Revolution.
2. Freedom.
3. Faction.

Should you, my lord, while you peruse my song, 20
Wonder from whence my love of Freedom sprung,
Whence flow these wishes for the common good,
By feeling hearts alone best understood,
I, young in life, by seeming cruel fate
Was snatch'd from Afric's fancied happy seat: 25
What pangs excruciating must molest,
What sorrows labor in my parent's breast?
Steeled was that soul and by no misery moved
That from a father seized his babe beloved:
Such, such my case. And can I then but pray 30
Others may never feel tyrannic sway?

For favors past, great Sir, our thanks are due,
And thee we ask thy favors to renew,
Since in thy power,[4] as in thy will before,
To sooth the griefs, which thou did'st once deplore. 35
May heavenly grace the sacred sanction give
To all thy works, and thou forever live
Not only on the wings of fleeting Fame,
Though praise immortal crowns the patriot's name,
But to conduct to heavens refulgent fane,[5] 40
May fiery coursers sweep th' ethereal plain,[6]
And bear thee upwards to that blest abode,
Where, like the prophet,[7] thou shalt find thy God.

1773

To the University of Cambridge,[1] in New England

While an intrinsic ardor prompts to write,
The muses promise to assist my pen;
'Twas not long since I left my native shore
The land of errors, and Egyptian gloom:[2]
Father of mercy, 'twas Thy gracious hand 5
Brought me in safety from those dark abodes.

Students, to you 'tis given to scan the heights
Above, to traverse the ethereal space,
And mark the systems of revolving worlds.
Still more, ye sons of science[3] ye receive 10
The blissful news by messengers from Heaven,
How Jesus' blood for your redemption flows.

4. I.e., since it is in thy power.
5. Heaven's shining temple.
6. The heavens. "Coursers": spirited horses.
7. In 2 Kings 11, a chariot of fire with fiery horses appears, and the prophet Elijah is taken up to heaven by a whirlwind.
1. Harvard.

2. "And Moses stretched forth his hand toward heaven; and there was a thick darkness in all the land of Egypt three days" (Exodus 10.22). "Errors": i.e., theological errors, because Africa was unconverted.
3. I.e., knowledge.

See Him with hands out-stretched upon the cross;
Immense compassion in his bosom glows;
He hears revilers, nor resents their scorn:⁣ ⁣ ⁣ ⁣ ⁣ ⁣ ⁣ ⁣ ⁣ ⁣ ⁣ ⁣ ⁣ ⁣ 15
What matchless mercy in the Son of God!
When the whole human race by sin had fallen,
He deigned to die that they might rise again,
And share with Him in the sublimest skies,
Life without death, and glory without end.⁣ ⁣ ⁣ ⁣ ⁣ ⁣ ⁣ ⁣ ⁣ ⁣ 20

⁣ ⁣ ⁣ Improve[4] your privileges while they stay,
Ye pupils, and each hour redeem, that bears
Or good or bad report of you to Heaven.
Let sin, that baneful evil to the soul,
By you be shunned, nor once remit your guard;⁣ ⁣ ⁣ ⁣ ⁣ ⁣ 25
Suppress the deadly serpent in its egg.
Ye blooming plants of human race divine,
An Ethiop[5] tells you 'tis your greatest foe;
Its transient sweetness turns to endless pain,
And in immense perdition sinks the soul.⁣ ⁣ ⁣ ⁣ ⁣ ⁣ ⁣ ⁣ ⁣ 30

1767⁣ 1773

On the Death of the Rev. Mr. George Whitefield, 1770[1]

Hail, happy saint, on thine immortal throne,
Possessed of glory, life, and bliss unknown;
We hear no more the music of thy tongue,
Thy wonted auditories[2] cease to throng.
Thy sermons in unequalled accents flow'd,⁣ ⁣ ⁣ ⁣ ⁣ ⁣ ⁣ ⁣ ⁣ ⁣ ⁣ 5
And every bosom with devotion glowed;
Thou didst in strains of eloquence refined
Inflame the heart, and captivate the mind.
Unhappy we the setting sun deplore,
So glorious once, but ah! it shines no more.⁣ ⁣ ⁣ ⁣ ⁣ ⁣ ⁣ ⁣ 10

⁣ ⁣ ⁣ Behold the prophet in his towering flight!
He leaves the earth for heav'n's unmeasured height,
And worlds unknown receive him from our sight.
There Whitefield wings with rapid course his way,
And sails to Zion[3] through vast seas of day.⁣ ⁣ ⁣ ⁣ ⁣ ⁣ ⁣ 15
Thy prayers, great saint, and thine incessant cries
Have pierced the bosom of thy native skies.
Thou moon hast seen, and all the stars of light,
How he has wrestled with his God by night.
He prayed that grace in every heart might dwell,⁣ ⁣ ⁣ ⁣ 20
He longed to see America excel;

4. Take advantage of.
5. Ethiopian. In Wheatley's time, "Ethiopian" was a conventional name for the black peoples of Africa.

1. Whitefield, born in 1714, was the best-known revivalist in the eighteenth century.
2. I.e., thy customary listeners.
3. Here, the heavenly city of God.

He charged[4] its youth that every grace divine
Should with full luster in their conduct shine;
That Savior, which his soul did first receive,
The greatest gift that even a God can give, 25
He freely offered to the numerous throng,
That on his lips with listening pleasure hung.

"Take Him, ye wretched, for your only good,
Take Him ye starving sinners, for your food;
Ye thirsty, come to this life-giving stream, 30
Ye preachers, take Him for your joyful theme;
Take Him my dear Americans, he said,
Be your complaints on His kind bosom laid:
Take Him, ye Africans, He longs for you,
Impartial Savior is His title due: 35
Washed in the fountain of redeeming blood,
You shall be sons, and kings, and priests to God."

Great *Countess*,[5] we Americans revere
Thy name, and mingle in thy grief sincere;
New England deeply feels, the orphans mourn, 40
Their more than father will no more return.

But, though arrested by the hand of death,
Whitefield no more exerts his laboring breath,
Yet let us view him in the eternal skies,
Let every heart to this bright vision rise; 45
While the tomb safe retains its sacred trust,
Till life divine re-animates his dust.

1770 1770, 1773

Thoughts on the Works of Providence

Arise, my soul, on wings enraptured, rise
To praise the monarch of the earth and skies,
Whose goodness and beneficence appear
As round its center moves the rolling year,
Or when the morning glows with rosy charms, 5
Or the sun slumbers in the ocean's arms:
Of light divine be a rich portion lent
To guide my soul, and favor my intent.
Celestial muse, my arduous flight sustain
And raise my mind to a seraphic[1] strain! 10

4. Exhorted.
5. Selina Shirley Hastings (c. 1707–1791), Countess of Huntingdon, head of a small society of evangelical churches, was a strong supporter of George Whitefield. Wheatley visited her in England in 1773.
1. Angelic.

Adored for ever be the God unseen,
Which round the sun revolves this vast machine,
Though to His eye its mass a point appears:
Adored the God that whirls surrounding spheres,
Which first ordained that mighty Sol² should reign 15
The peerless monarch of the ethereal train:
Of miles twice forty millions is His height,
And yet His radiance dazzles mortal sight
So far beneath—from Him the extended earth
Vigor derives, and every flowery birth: 20
Vast through her orb she moves with easy grace
Around her Phoebus³ in unbounded space;
True to her course the impetuous storm derides,
Triumphant o'er the winds, and surging tides.

Almighty, in these wond'rous works of Thine, 25
What Power, what Wisdom, and what Goodness shine!
And are Thy wonders, Lord, by men explored,
And yet creating glory unadored!

Creation smiles in various beauty gay,
While day to night, and night succeeds to day: 30
That Wisdom, which attends Jehovah's ways,
Shines most conspicuous in the solar rays:
Without them, destitute of heat and light,
This world would be the reign of endless night:
In their excess how would our race complain, 35
Abhorring life! how hate its lengthened chain!
From air adust⁴ what numerous ills would rise?
What dire contagion taint the burning skies?
What pestilential vapors, fraught with death,
Would rise, and overspread the lands beneath? 40

Hail, smiling morn, that from the orient main⁵
Ascending dost adorn the heav'nly plain!
So rich, so various are thy beauteous dyes,
That spread through all the circuit of the skies,
That, full of thee, my soul in rapture soars, 45
And thy great God, the cause of all adores.⁶

O'er beings infinite His love extends,
His Wisdom rules them, and His Pow'r defends.
When tasks diurnal⁷ tire the human frame,
The spirits faint, and dim the vital flame, 50
Then too that ever active bounty shines,
Which not infinity of space confines.
The sable⁸ veil, that Night in silence draws,

2. The sun.
3. Apollo, the Greek sun god.
4. Dried up.
5. From the eastern ocean.

6. I.e., God created everything (including the "smiling morn").
7. Daily.
8. Black.

Conceals effects, but shows the Almighty Cause,
Night seals in sleep the wide creation fair,[9] 55
And all is peaceful but the brow of care.
Again, gay Phoebus, as the day before,
Wakes every eye, but what shall wake no more;
Again the face of nature is renewed,
Which still appears harmonious, fair, and good. 60
May grateful strains salute the smiling morn,
Before its beams the eastern hills adorn!

 Shall day to day, and night to night conspire
To show the goodness of the Almighty Sire?
This mental voice shall man regardless hear, 65
And never, never raise the filial prayer?
Today, O hearken, nor your folly mourn
For time mispent, that never will return.

 But see the sons of vegetation rise,
And spread their leafy banners to the skies. 70
All-wise Almighty providence we trace
In trees, and plants, and all the flowery race;
As clear as in the nobler frame of man,
All lovely copies of the Maker's plan.
The power the same that forms a ray of light, 75
That called creation from eternal night.
"Let there be light," He said. From his profound[1]
Old Chaos heard, and trembled at the sound:
Swift as the word, inspired by power divine,
Behold the light around its Maker shine, 80
The first fair product of the omnific[2] God,
And now through all his works diffused abroad.

 As reason's powers by day our God disclose,
So we may trace Him in the night's repose:
Say what is sleep? and dreams how passing strange! 85
When action ceases, and ideas range
Licentious and unbounded o'er the plains,
Where Fancy's[3] queen in giddy triumph reigns.
Hear in soft strains the dreaming lover sigh
To a kind fair,[4] or rave in jealousy; 90
On pleasure now, and now on vengeance bent,
The lab'ring passions struggle for a vent.
What power, O man! thy reason then restores,
So long suspended in nocturnal hours?
What secret hand returns the mental train, 95
And gives improv'd thine active powers again?
From thee, O man, what gratitude should rise!
And, when from balmy sleep thou op'st thine eyes,

9. Beautiful.
1. Depths. "And God said, Let there be light: and
there was light" (Genesis 1.3).

2. Omnificent: unlimited in creative power.
3. The imagination in its image-making aspect.
4. Woman.

Let thy first thoughts be praises to the skies.
How merciful our God who thus imparts 100
O'erflowing tides of joy to human hearts,
When wants and woes might be our righteous lot,
Our God forgetting, by our God forgot!

Among the mental powers a question rose,
"What most the image of the Eternal shows?" 105
When thus to Reason (so let Fancy rove)
Her great companion spoke, immortal Love.

"Say, mighty power, how long shall strife prevail,
And with its murmurs load the whispering gale?
Refer the cause to Recollection's shrine, 110
Who loud proclaims my origin divine,
The cause whence heaven and earth began to be,
And is not man immortalized by me?
Reason let this most causeless strife subside."
Thus Love pronounced, and Reason thus replied. 115

 "Thy birth, celestial queen! 'tis mine to own,
In thee resplendent is the Godhead shown;
Thy words persuade, my soul enraptured feels
Resistless beauty which thy smile reveals."
Ardent she spoke, and, kindling at her charms, 120
She clasped the blooming goddess in her arms.

 Infinite Love where'er we turn our eyes
Appears: this every creature's wants supplies;
This most is heard in Nature's constant voice,
This makes the morn, and this the eve rejoice; 125
This bids the fostering rains and dews descend
To nourish all, to serve one gen'ral end,
The good of man: yet man ungrateful pays
But little homage, and but little praise.
To him, whose works arrayed with mercy shine, 130
What songs should rise, how constant, how divine!

1773

To S. M.,[1] a Young African Painter, on Seeing His Works

To show the laboring bosom's deep intent,
And thought in living characters to paint,
When first thy pencil did those beauties give,
And breathing figures learnt from thee to live,
How did those prospects give my soul delight, 5
A new creation rushing on my sight?
Still, wondrous youth! each noble path pursue,

1. Scipio Moorhead, a servant to the Reverend John Moorhead of Boston.

On deathless glories fix thine ardent view:
Still may the painter's and the poet's fire
To aid thy pencil, and thy verse conspire! 10
And may the charms of each seraphic[2] theme
Conduct thy footsteps to immortal fame!
High to the blissful wonders of the skies
Elate thy soul, and raise thy wishful eyes.
Thrice happy, when exalted to survey 15
That splendid city, crown'd with endless day,
Whose twice six gates[3] on radiant hinges ring:
Celestial Salem[4] blooms in endless spring.

 Calm and serene thy moments glide along,
And may the muse inspire each future song! 20
Still, with the sweets of contemplation blest,
May peace with balmy wings your soul invest!
But when these shades of time are chased away,
And darkness ends in everlasting day,
On what seraphic pinions shall we move, 25
And view the landscapes in the realms above?
There shall thy tongue in heavenly murmurs flow,
And there my muse with heavenly transport glow:
No more to tell of Damon's[5] tender sighs,
Or rising radiance of Aurora's[6] eyes, 30
For nobler themes demand a nobler strain,
And purer language on the ethereal plain.
Cease, gentle muse! the solemn gloom of night
Now seals the fair creation from my sight.

1773

To His Excellency General Washington[1]

Sir. I have taken the freedom to address your Excellency in the enclosed poem, and entreat your acceptance, though I am not insensible of its inaccuracies. Your being appointed by the Grand Continental Congress to be Generalissimo of the armies of North America, together with the fame of your virtues, excite sensations not easy to suppress. Your generosity, therefore, I presume, will pardon the attempt. Wishing your Excellency all possible success in the great cause you are so generously engaged in. I am,

Your Excellency's most obedient humble servant,
Phillis Wheatley

2. Angelic.
3. Heaven, like Jerusalem in antiquity, is thought to have had twelve gates (as many gates as tribes of Israel).
4. Heavenly Jerusalem.
5. In classical mythology, Damon pledged his life for his friend Pythias.

6. The Roman goddess of the dawn.
1. This poem was first published in the *Pennsylvania Magazine* when Thomas Paine (see his headnote, earlier in this volume) was editor. After reading it, Washington invited Wheatley to meet him in Cambridge, Massachusetts, in February 1776.

Providence, Oct. 26, 1775.[2]
His Excellency Gen. Washington.

 Celestial choir! enthroned in realms of light,
 Columbia's[3] scenes of glorious toils I write.
 While freedom's cause her anxious breast alarms,
 She flashes dreadful in refulgent arms.
 See mother earth her offspring's fate bemoan, 5
 And nations gaze at scenes before unknown!
 See the bright beams of heaven's revolving light
 Involved in sorrows and the veil of night!
 The goddess comes, she moves divinely fair,
 Olive and laurel[4] binds her golden hair: 10
 Wherever shines this native of the skies,
 Unnumbered charms and recent graces rise.
 Muse! bow propitious while my pen relates
 How pour her armies through a thousand gates,
 As when Eolus[5] heaven's fair face deforms, 15
 Enwrapped in tempest and a night of storms;
 Astonished ocean feels the wild uproar,
 The refluent surges beat the sounding shore;
 Or thick as leaves in Autumn's golden reign,
 Such, and so many, moves the warrior's train. 20
 In bright array they seek the work of war,
 Where high unfurled the ensign[6] waves in air.
 Shall I to Washington their praise recite?
 Enough thou know'st them in the fields of fight.
 Thee, first in place and honors—we demand 25
 The grace and glory of thy martial band.
 Famed for thy valor, for thy virtues more,
 Hear every tongue thy guardian aid implore!
 One century scarce performed its destined round,
 When Gallic powers Columbia's fury found;[7] 30
 And so may you, whoever dares disgrace
 The land of freedom's heaven-defended race!
 Fixed are the eyes of nations on the scales,
 For in their hopes Columbia's arm prevails.
 Anon Britannia droops the pensive head, 35
 While round increase the rising hills of dead.
 Ah! cruel blindness to Columbia's state!
 Lament thy thirst of boundless power too late.
 Proceed, great chief, with virtue on thy side,
 Thy every action let the goddess guide. 40
 A crown, a mansion, and a throne that shine,
 With gold unfading, WASHINGTON! be thine.

1775–76 1776, 1834

2. When the British occupied Boston in summer 1775, Wheatley and her former master's family moved to Providence, Rhode Island, for safety.
3. This reference to America as "the land Columbus found" is believed to be the first in print.

4. Classical emblems of victory.
5. Mythological ruler of the winds.
6. Flag or banner.
7. The French and Indian War (1754–63), between France and England, ended the French colonial empire in North America.

Letters

To John Thornton,[1] London

[THE BIBLE MY CHIEF STUDY]

[Boston, April 21, 1772]

Hon'd, Sir

I rec'd your instructive fav[r2] of Feb. 29, for which, return you ten thousand thanks, I did not flatter myself with the tho'ts of your honouring me with an Answer to my letter, I thank you for recommending the Bible to be my chief Study, I find and Acknowledge it the best of Books, it contains an endless treasure of wisdom, and knowledge. O that my eyes were more open'd to see the real worth, and true excellence of the word of truth, my flinty heart Soften'd with the grateful dews of divine grace and the Stubborn will, and affections, bent on God alone their proper object, and the vitiated palate may be corrected to relish heav'nly things. It has pleas'd God to lay me on a bed of Sickness, and I knew not but my deathbed, but he has been graciously pleas'd to restore me in a great measure. I beg your prayers, that I may be made thankful for his paternal corrections, and that I may make a proper use of them to the glory of his grace. I am Still very weak & the Physicians, seem to think there is danger of a consumpsion.[3] And O that when my flesh and my heart fail me God would be my strength and portion for ever, that I might put my whole trust and Confidence in him, who has promis'd never to forsake those who Seek him with the whole heart. You could not, I am sure have express greater tenderness and affection for me, than by being a welwisher to my Soul, the friends of Souls bear Some resemblance to the father of Spirits and are made partakers of his divine Nature. I am affraid I have entruded on your patient, but if I had not tho't it ungrateful to omit writing in answer to your favour Should not have troubl'd you, but I can't expect you to answer this,

I am Sir with greatest respect,
your very hum. sert.[4]
Phillis Wheatley

1989

To Rev. Samson Occom,[1] New London, Connecticut

[THE NATURAL RIGHTS OF NEGROES]

[February 11, 1774]

Rev'd and honor'd Sir,

I have this Day received your obliging kind Epistle, and am greatly satisfied with your Reasons respecting the Negroes, and think highly reasonable what you offer in Vindication of their natural Rights: Those that invade them

1. A London merchant (1720–1790) who was a devout Anglican and lived outside London at Clapham, where a small group of Christians were committed to helping the poor and abolishing slavery. He was a friend of John and Susanna Wheatley and sent them money to be used for work among the American Indians.
2. Favor, i.e., letter.

3. Disease of the lungs.
4. I.e., humble servant.
1. See his headnote, earlier in this volume. Wheatley first corresponded with Occom in 1765. He later suggested to Wheatley that she go to Africa as a missionary, but she rejected the idea. This extract was published in several New England newspapers.

cannot be insensible that the divine Light is chasing away the thick Darkness[2] which broods over the Land of Africa; and the Chaos which has reign'd so long, is converting into beautiful Order, and [r]eveals more and more clearly, the glorious Dispensation of civil and religious Liberty, which are so inseparably united, that there is little or no Enjoyment of one without the other: Otherwise, perhaps, the Israelites had been less solicitous for their Freedom from Egyptian slavery; I do not say they would have been contented without it, by no means, for in every human Breast, God has implanted a Principle, which we call Love of Freedom; it is impatient of Oppression, and pants for Deliverance; and by the Leave of our modern Egyptians I will assert, that the same Principle lives in us. God grant Deliverance in his own Way and Time, and get him honour upon all those whose Avarice impels them to countenance and help forward the Calamities of their fellow Creatures. This I desire not for their Hurt, but to convince them of the strange Absurdity of their Conduct whose Words and Actions are so diametrically opposite. How well the Cry for Liberty, and the reverse Disposition for the exercise of oppressive Power over others agree,—I humbly think it does not require the Penetration of a philosopher to determine.

1774, 1989

2. "And Moses stretched forth his hand toward heaven; and there was a thick darkness in all the land of Egypt three days" (Exodus 10.22).

ROYALL TYLER
1757–1826

B ritish North America did not produce the rich theatrical culture that thrived elsewhere in the Atlantic world. Few places had a dense enough population of English speakers to support a theater, and both Puritans and Quakers disapproved in principle of "the devil's drawing-room," as the Yankee yokel Jonathan terms it in Royall Tyler's play *The Contrast*. Nevertheless, British acting companies occasionally toured the major cities, amateur theatricals were staged in southern colonies, and college students performed dramatic readings. These activities diminished during the Revolution, when the Continental Congress banned the theater, but even then George Washington allowed a production of the English writer Joseph Addison's *Cato* (1712)—a historical tragedy that juxtaposes individual liberty and government tyranny—to be staged at Valley Forge, the Continental Army's military camp in winter 1777–78. After the Revolution, the project of nurturing a national drama would become part of the search for a cultural identity. Bans against theater were lifted, older acting companies returned, and others were formed to occupy the new playhouses, which mainly offered British plays, or translations of German and French dramas. Tyler was one of the few new playwrights to emerge. Tyler's first play, *The Contrast*, became an immediate hit when it opened at the Johns Street Theater in New York in April 1787, just weeks before the Constitutional Convention

convened. The play was staged in other cities including Philadelphia, where the Convention met, and it appeared in a printed version there in 1790.

Born William Clark Tyler into a wealthy Boston family, the author was an accomplished young man with a flair for letters, who earned degrees simultaneously at Harvard College and Yale College in 1776, then enlisted in the Continental Army and fought under the future statesman John Hancock. He was admitted to the bar in 1780 and began practicing law in New England. In early adulthood Tyler acquired a reputation as a profligate and a rake. For several years he courted Abigail "Nabby" Adams, John and Abigail's daughter, who ultimately broke off the relationship and, in 1786, married another man. Tyler was crushed. He eventually married, but rumors of extramarital relationships and children born out of wedlock shadowed him.

Tyler was a member of the militia that put down Shays's Rebellion (1786–87), an agrarian movement to resist debt collection, centered in western Massachusetts and led by the Continental Army captain Daniel Shays. Shays's Rebellion and similar movements elsewhere helped catalyze the writing of the United States Constitution. Tyler, who was in New York in 1787 to solicit aid in suppressing the rebellion, mentions it twice in *The Contrast*. By 1790 he had moved to Vermont and established himself as a lawyer, and in his later years, he was both chief justice of the Supreme Court of Vermont and professor of law at the University of Vermont.

Although Tyler was an amateur who wrote *The Contrast* in a mere three weeks, the play reads like a polished professional creation. In part this level of finish can be attributed to its basis in the Irish playwright Richard Brinsley Sheridan's famous comedy *The School for Scandal* (1777), which Tyler saw in New York the month before he wrote *The Contrast*. From Sheridan's play Tyler took the essential story line, which contrasts mean, shallow, but fashionable elites with a world of honest and wholesome sentiment: the latter, of course, triumphs. Tyler repays his debt to Sheridan handsomely in the scene where Jonathan thinks he has witnessed real life in a private home but has actually been watching *The School for Scandal*.

Tyler deliberately Americanized Sheridan's plot to create *The Contrast*, and the play offers a window into what one version of American identity might come to mean. His fashionable New Yorkers ape British modes—most especially the deceitful villain, a young man who runs his life according to the dictates of the English statesman Lord Chesterfield, who in his posthumously published *Letters* (1774) offered advice about social maneuvering that struck many readers as deeply cynical. By contrast the hero, Captain Manly, is a model of thoughtful rectitude; a veteran of the Revolution, he embodies the idea—later represented by George Washington—that these officer veterans were America's best hope. Manly's servant Jonathan is one of the first examples of an enduring dramatic type: the comic Yankee. Jonathan is the butt of fun because of his ignorance of city ways, but he is also a shrewd voice of common sense. Manly and Jonathan embody an American virtue capable of resisting the temptations of British luxury represented by other characters.

Tyler continued to write for the rest of his life, in a variety of genres: other plays, satirical essays, verses, and *The Algerine Captive* (1797), a picaresque novel about slavery in the Atlantic world, and one of the first works by an American to be published in both the U.S. and England. Whereas *The Algerine Captive* obliquely tackles the presence of slavery in a nation ostensibly devoted to freedom, *The Contrast* stands out for its good humor and brash, sunny nationalism. It shows an American self-image forming even as the nation's political institutions were being refashioned.

The Contrast[1]

Prologue

[*Written by a* YOUNG GENTLEMAN *of New York,
and Spoken by* MR. WIGNELL]

Exult each patriot heart!—this night is shewn
A piece, which we may fairly call our own;
Where the proud titles of "My Lord! Your Grace!"
To humble Mr. and plain Sir give place.
Our Author pictures not from foreign climes
The fashions, or the follies of the times;
But has confin'd the subject of his work
To the gay scenes—the circles of New York.
On native themes his Muse displays her pow'rs;
If ours the faults, the virtues too are ours.
Why should our thoughts to distant countries roam,
When each refinement may be found at home?
Who travels now to ape the rich or great,
To deck an equipage[2] and roll in state;
To court the graces,[3] or to dance with ease,
Or by hypocrisy to strive to please?
Our free-born ancestors such arts despis'd;
Genuine sincerity alone they priz'd;
Their minds, with honest emulation fir'd.
To solid good—not ornament—aspir'd;
Or, if ambition rous'd a bolder flame,
Stern virtue throve, where indolence was shame.

But modern youths, with imitative sense,
Deem taste in dress the proof of excellence;
And spurn the meanness of your homespun arts,
Since homespun habits would obscure their parts;
Whilst all, which aims at splendor and parade,
Must come from Europe, and be ready made.
Strange! we should thus our native worth disclaim,
And check the progress of our rising fame.
Yet one, whilst imitation bears the sway,
Aspires to nobler heights, and points the way,
Be rous'd, my friends! his bold example view;
Let your own Bards be proud to copy you!
Should rigid critics reprobate our play,
At least the patriotic heart will say,
"Glorious our fall, since in a noble cause.
"The bold attempt alone demands applause."

1. The text is from the first edition (1790), published in Philadelphia by the actor and theater manager Thomas Wignell (1753–1803). Born in England, Wignell moved to New York in the 1780s and originated the role of Jonathan in *The Contrast*. He became a prominent comic actor and George Washington's favorite comedian, and he later ran one of the new country's most successful theaters, the Chestnut Street Theater, in Philadelphia.
2. Coach.
3. Greek goddesses who personified charm and beauty.

Still may the wisdom of the Comic Muse
Exalt your merits, or your faults accuse.
But think not, 'tis her aim to be severe;—
We all are mortals, and as mortals err.
If candor pleases, we are truly blest;
Vice trembles, when compell'd to stand confess'd.
Let not light Censure on your faults offend,
Which aims not to expose them, but amend.
Thus does our Author to your candor trust;
Conscious, the free are generous, as just.

Act First

SCENE I

An apartment AT CHARLOTTE's.

[CHARLOTTE *and* LETITIA *discovered.*]

LETITIA And so, Charlotte, you really think the pocket-hoop[4] unbecoming.

CHARLOTTE No, I don't say so: It may be very becoming to saunter round the house of a rainy day; to visit my grand-mamma, or go to Quakers' meeting: but to swim in a minuet, with the eyes of fifty well-dressed beaux upon me, to trip it in the Mall, or walk on the battery,[5] give me the luxurious, jaunty, flowing, bell-hoop. It would have delighted you to have seen me the last evening, my charming girl! I was dangling o'er the battery with Billy Dimple; a knot of young fellows were upon the platform; as I passed them I faultered with one of the most bewitching false steps you ever saw, and then recovered myself with such a pretty confusion, flirting my hoop to discover a jet black shoe and brilliant buckle. Gad! how my little heart thrilled to hear the confused reptures of—"Demme,[6] Jack, what a delicate foot!" "Ha! General, what a well-turn'd—"

LETITIA Fie! fie! Charlotte [*stopping her mouth*], I protest you are quite a libertine.

CHARLOTTE Why, my dear little prude, are we not all such libertines? Do you think, when I sat tortured two hours under the hands of my friseur, and an hour more at my toilet,[7] that I had any thoughts of my aunt Susan, or my cousin Betsey? though they are both allowed to be critical judges of dress.

LETITIA Why, who should we dress to please, but those who are judges of its merits?

CHARLOTTE Why a creature who does not know *Buffon* from *Souflee*[8]— Man!—my Letitia—Man! for whom we dress, walk, dance, talk, lisp, languish, and smile. Does not the grave Spectator[9] assure us, that even

4. A type of hoopskirt; hoopskirts became fashionable about 1700. The "pocket hoop," confined to the hips, was smaller than the bell hoop (mentioned below).
5. Area at the southern tip of Manhattan (named for the seventeenth-century military fortification there). "Well-dressed beaux": i.e., dandies. "The Mall": fashionable promenade north of the Battery.
6. Affected version of "Damn me."
7. Dressing table, vanity. "Friseur": hairdresser.
8. I.e., soufflé, a puffy dish made with eggs and sauce. "Buffon": a pun on Georges-Louis Leclerc, Comte de Buffon (1707–1788), French naturalist, and "bouffant," puffed out, as in a hairdo.
9. *The Spectator* (1711–12), a popular periodical that consisted of essays on morals, manners, and literature.

our much bepraised diffidence, modesty, and blushes, are all directed to make ourselves good wives and mothers as fast as we can. Why, I'll undertake with one flirt of this hoop to bring more beaux to my feet in one week, than the grave Maria, and her sentimental circle, can do, by sighing sentiment till their hairs are grey.

LETITIA Well, I won't argue with you; you always out talk me; let us change the subject. I hear that Mr. Dimple and Maria are soon to be married.

CHARLOTTE You hear true. I was consulted in the choice of the wedding clothes. She is to be married in a delicate white satin, and has a monstrous pretty brocaded lutestring[1] for the second day. It would have done you good to have seen with what an affected indifference the dear sentimentalist turned over a thousand pretty things, just as if her heart did not palpitate with her approaching happiness, and at last made her choice, and arranged her dress with such apathy, as if she did not know that plain white satin, and a simple blond lace, would shew her clear skin, and dark hair, to the greatest advantage.

LETITIA But they say her indifference to dress, and even to the gentleman himself, is not entirely affected.

CHARLOTTE How?

LETITIA It is whispered, that if Maria gives her hand to Mr. Dimple, it will be without her heart.

CHARLOTTE Though the giving the heart is one of the last of all laughable considerations in the marriage of a girl of spirit, yet I should like to hear what antiquated notions the dear little piece of old fashioned prudery has got in her head.

LETITIA Why you know that old Mr. John-Richard-Robert-Jacob-Isaac-Abraham-Cornelius Van Dumpling, Billy Dimple's father (for he has thought fit to soften his name, as well as manners, during his English tour) was the most intimate friend of Maria's father. The old folks, about a year before Mr. Van Dumpling's death, proposed this match: the young folks were accordingly introduced, and told they must love one another. Billy was then a good natured, decent, dressing young fellow, with a little dash of the coxcomb,[2] such as our young fellows of fortune usually have. At this time, I really believe she thought she loved him; and had they then been married, I doubt not, they might have jogged on, to the end of the chapter, a good kind of a sing-song lack-a-daysaical life, as other honest married folks do.

CHARLOTTE Why did they not then marry?

LETITIA Upon the death of his father, Billy went to England to see the world, and rub off a little of the patroon rust.[3] During his absence, Maria like a good girl, to keep herself constant to her *nown*[4] true-love, avoided company, and betook herself, for her amusement, to her books, and her dear Billy's letters. But, alas! how many ways has the mischievous demon of inconstancy of stealing into a woman's heart! Her love was destroyed by the very means she took to support it.

1. A glossy silk.
2. I.e., a bit conceited.
3. I.e., get a bit of old-fashioned country style or manners.
4. I.e., own (probably from a popular song).

CHARLOTTE How?—Oh! I have it—some likely young beau found the way to her study.

LETITIA Be patient, Charlotte—your head so runs upon beaux.—Why she read Sir Charles Grandison, Clarissa Harlow, Shenstone, and the Sentimental Journey,[5] and between whiles, as I said, Billy's letters. But as her taste improved, her love declined. The contrast was so striking betwixt the good sense of her books, and the flimsiness of her love-letters, that she discovered she had unthinkingly engaged her hand without her heart; and then the whole transaction managed by the old folks, now appeared so unsentimental, and looked so like bargaining for a bale of goods, that she found she ought to have rejected, according to every rule of romance, even the man of her choice, if imposed upon her in that manner—Clary Harlow would have scorned such a match.

CHARLOTTE Well, how was it on Mr. Dimple's return? Did he meet a more favorable reception than his letters?

LETITIA Much the same. She spoke of him with respect abroad, and with contempt in her closet.[6] She watched his conduct and conversation, and found that he had by traveling acquired the wickedness of Lovelace[7] without his wit, and the politeness of Sir Charles Grandison without his generosity. The ruddy youth who washed his face at the cistern every morning, and swore and looked eternal love and constancy, was now metamorphosed into a flippant, palid, polite beau, who devotes the morning to his toilet, reads a few pages of Chesterfield's letters,[8] and then minces out, to put the infamous principles in practice upon every woman he meets.

CHARLOTTE But, if she is so apt at conjuring up these sentimental bugbears, why does she not discard him at once?

LETITIA Why, she thinks her word too sacred to be trifled with. Besides, her father, who has a great respect for the memory of his deceased friend, is ever telling her how he shall renew his years in their union, and repeating the dying injunctions of old Van Dumpling.

CHARLOTTE A mighty pretty story! And so you would make me believe, that the sensible Maria would give up Dumpling manor, and the all-accomplished Dimple as a husband, for the absurd, ridiculous reason, forsooth, because she despises and abhors him. Just as if a lady could not be privileged to spend a man's fortune, ride in his carriage, be called after his name, and call him her *nown dear lovee* when she wants money, without loving and respecting the great he-creature. Oh! my dear girl, you are a monstrous prude.

LETITIA I don't say what I would do; I only intimate how I suppose she wishes to act.

CHARLOTTE No, no, no! A fig for sentiment. If she breaks, or wishes to break, with Mr. Dimple, depend upon it, she has some other man in her

5. References to sentimental English literature of the period, when reading novels was considered a woman's occupation. *Sir Charles Grandison* and *Clarissa* (i.e., Harlowe) are novels by Samuel Richardson (1689–1761). *A Sentimental Journey through France and Italy* is a novel by Laurence Sterne (1713–1768). William Shenstone (1714–1763) was a popular poet.
6. Private apartment or room.

7. The handsome, dashing villain in *Clarissa*.
8. Letters written to his illegitimate son by the English statesman Philip Stanhope, fourth Earl of Chesterfield (1694–1773), on deportment and manners in polite society, published in 1774. They were described by the English writer Samuel Johnson (1709–1784) as teaching "the morals of a whore and the manners of a dancing master."

eye. A woman rarely discards one lover, until she is sure of another.—
Letitia little thinks what a clue I have to Dimple's conduct. The generous
man submits to render himself disgusting to Maria, in order that she
may leave him at liberty to address me. I must change the subject [*Aside,
and rings a bell.*]

 [*Enter* SERVANT.]

Frank, order the horses to.—Talking of marriage—did you hear that Sally
Bloomsbury is going to be married next week to Mr. Indigo, the rich Caro-
linian?

LETITIA Sally Bloomsbury married!—Why, she is not yet in her teens.

CHARLOTTE I do not know how that is, but, you may depend upon it, 'tis
a done affair. I have it from the best authority. There is my aunt Wyer-
ley's Hannah (you know Hannah—though a black, she is a wench that
was never caught in a lie in her life); now Hannah has a brother who
courts Sarah, Mrs. Catgut the milliner's girl, and she told Hannah's
brother, and Hannah, who, as I said before, is a girl of undoubted verac-
ity, told it directly to me, that Mrs. Catgut was making a new cap for Miss
Bloomsbury, which, as it was very dressy, it is very probable is designed
for a wedding cap: now, as she is to be married, who can it be to, but to
Mr. Indigo? Why, there is no other gentleman that visits at her papa's.

LETITIA Say not a word more, Charlotte. Your intelligence[9] is so direct
and well grounded, it is almost a pity that it is not a piece of scandal.

CHARLOTTE Oh! I am the pink of prudence. Though I cannot charge
myself with ever having discredited a tea-party by my silence, yet I take
care never to report any thing of my acquaintance, especially if it is to
their credit,—*discredit*, I mean—until I have searched to the bottom of
it. It is true, there is infinite pleasure in this charitable pursuit. Oh! how
delicious to go and condole with the friends of some backsliding sister,
or to retire with some old dowager or maiden aunt of the family, who love
scandal so well, that they cannot forbear gratifying their appetite at the
expence of the reputation of their nearest relations! And then to return
full fraught with a rich collection of circumstances, to retail to the next
circle of our acquaintance under the strongest injunctions of secrecy,—
ha, ha, ha!—interlarding the melancholy tale with so many doleful
shakes of the head, and more doleful, "Ah! who would have thought it! so
amiable, so prudent a young lady, as we all thought her, what a mon-
strous pity! well, I have nothing to charge myself with; I acted the part of
a friend, I warned her of the principles of that rake,[1] I told her what
would be the consequence; I told her so, I told her so."—Ha, ha, ha!

LETITIA Ha, ha, ha! Well, but Charlotte, you don't tell me what you think
of Miss Bloomsbury's match.

CHARLOTTE Think! why I think it is probable she cried for a plaything, and
they have given her a husband. Well, well, well, the puling chit[2] shall not
be deprived of her plaything: 'tis only exchanging London dolls for Amer-
ican babies—Apropos, of babies, have you heard what Mrs. Affable's
high-flying notions of delicacy have come to?

LETITIA Who, she that was Miss Lovely?

9. I.e., news.
1. Dissolute person.

2. The whimpering child.

CHARLOTTE The same; she married Bob Affable of Schenectady. Don't you remember?

 [*Enter* SERVANT.]

SERVANT Madam, the carriage is ready.

LETITIA Shall we go to the stores first, or visiting?

CHARLOTTE I should think it rather too early to visit; especially Mrs. Prim: you know she is so particular.

LETITIA Well, but what of Mrs. Affable?

CHARLOTTE Oh, I'll tell you as we go; come, come, let us hasten. I hear Mrs. Catgut has some of the prettiest caps arrived, you ever saw. I shall die if I have not the first sight of them. [*Exeunt.*]

<div align="center">SCENE 2</div>

A room in VAN ROUGH's *house.*

[MARIA *sitting disconsolate at a Table, with Books, etc.*]

<div align="center">SONG[3]</div>

<div align="center">I</div>

The sun sets in night, and the stars shun the day;
But glory remains when their lights fade away!
Begin, ye tormentors! your threats are in vain,
For the son of Alknomook[4] shall never complain.

<div align="center">II</div>

Remember the arrows he shot from his bow;
Remember your chiefs by his hatchet laid low:
Why so slow?—do you wait till I shrink from the pain?
No—the son of Alknomook will never complain.

<div align="center">III</div>

Remember the wood where in ambush we lay;
And the scalps which we bore from your nation away:
Now the flame rises fast, you exult in my pain;
But the son of Alknomook can never complain.

<div align="center">IV</div>

I go to the land where my father is gone;
His ghost shall rejoice in the fame of his son:
Death comes like a friend, he relieves me from pain;
And thy son, Oh Alknomook! has scorn'd to complain.

There is something in this song which ever calls forth my affections. The manly virtue of courage, that fortitude which steels the heart against the keenest misfortunes, which interweaves the laurel of glory amidst the instru-

3. This anonymous composition, widely reprinted with variations and various titles in the early 1780s, became popular in the early republic after Tyler's use of it here.
4. An Indian name.

ments of torture and death, displays something so noble, so exalted, that in despite of the prejudices of education, I cannot but admire it, even in a savage. The prepossession which our sex is supposed to entertain for the character of a soldier, is, I know, a standing piece of raillery among the wits. A cockade, a lapel'd coat, and a feather,[5] they will tell you, are irresistible by a female heart. Let it be so.—Who is it that considers the helpless situation of our sex, that does not see we each moment stand in need of a protector, and that a brave one too. Formed of the more delicate materials of nature, endowed only with the softer passions, incapable, from our ignorance of the world, to guard against the wiles of mankind, our security for happiness often depends upon their generosity and courage:—Alas! how little of the former do we find. How inconsistent! that man should be leagued to destroy that honor, upon which, solely rests his respect and esteem. Ten thousand temptations allure us, ten thousand passions betray us; yet the smallest deviation from the path of rectitude is followed by the contempt and insult of man, and the more remorseless pity of woman: years of penitence and tears cannot wash away the stain, nor a life of virture obliterate its remembrance. Reputation is the life of woman; yet courage to protect it, is masculine and disgusting; and the only safe asylum a woman of delicacy can find, is in the arms of a man of honor. How naturally then, should we love the brave, and the generous; how gratefully should we bless the arm raised for our protection, when nerv'd by virtue, and directed by honor! Heaven grant that the man with whom I may be connected—may be connected!—Whither has my imagination transported me—whither does it now lead me?—Am I not indissolubly engaged by every obligation of honor, which my own consent, and my father's approbation can give, to a man who can never share my affections, and whom a few days hence, it will be criminal for me to disapprove—to disapprove! would to heaven that were all—to despise. For, can the most frivolous manners, actuated by the most depraved heart, meet, or merit, anything but contempt from every woman of delicacy and sentiment?

 [VAN ROUGH, *without.*] Mary!

MARIA Ha, my father's voice—Sir!

 [*Enter* VAN ROUGH.]

VAN ROUGH What, Mary, always singing doleful ditties, and moping over these plaguy[6] books.

MARIA I hope, Sir, that it is not criminal to improve my mind with books; or to divert my melancholy with singing at my leisure hours.

VAN ROUGH Why, I don't know that, child; I don't know that. They us'd to say when I was a young man, that if a woman knew how to make a pudding, and to keep herself out of fire and water, she knew enough for a wife. Now, what good have these books done you? have they not made you melancholy? as you call it. Pray, what right has a girl of your age to be in the dumps? haven't you every thing your heart can wish; ain't you going to be married to a young man of great fortune; ain't you going to have the quit-rent[7] of twenty miles square?

MARIA One hundredth part of the land, and a lease for life of the heart of a man I could love, would satisfy me.

5. I.e., items of military dress; the "feather" adorns a hat, much as a "cockade" is a badge worn on a hat.

6. Annoying.

7. Small, fixed rent.

VAN ROUGH Pho, pho, pho! child; nonsense, downright nonsense, child. This comes of your reading your story-books; your Charles Grandisons, your Sentimental Journals, and your Robinson Crusoes, and such other trumpery.[8] No, no, no! child, it is money makes the mare go; keep your eye upon the main chance,[9] Mary.

MARIA Marriage, Sir, is, indeed, a very serious affair.

VAN ROUGH You are right, child; you are right. I am sure I found it so to my cost.

MARIA I mean, Sir, that as marriage is a portion for life, and so intimately involves our happiness, we cannot be too considerate in the choice of our companion.

VAN ROUGH Right, child; very right. A young woman should be very sober when she is making her choice, but when she has once made it, as you have done, I don't see why she should not be as merry as a grig, I am sure she has reason enough to be so—Solomon says, that "there is a time to laugh, and a time to weep";[1] now a time for a young woman to laugh is when she has made sure of a good rich husband. Now a time to cry, according to you, Mary, is when she is making choice of him: but, I should think, that a young woman's time to cry was, when she despaired of *getting* one.—Why, there was your mother now; to be sure when I popp'd the question to her, she did look a little silly; but when she had once looked down on her apron-strings, as all modest young women us'd to do, and drawled out ye-s, she was as brisk and as merry as a bee.

MARIA My honored mother, Sir, had no motive to melancholy; she married the man of her choice.

VAN ROUGH The man of her choice! And pray, Mary, ain't you going to marry the man of your choice—what trumpery notion is this?—It is these vile books [*throwing them away*]. I'd have you to know, Mary, if you won't make young Van Dumpling the man of *your* choice, you shall marry him as the man of *my* choice.

MARIA You terrify me, Sir. Indeed, Sir, I am all submission. My will is yours.

VAN ROUGH Why, that is the way your mother us'd to talk. "My will is yours, my dear Mr. Van Rough, my will is yours": but she took special care to have her own way though for all that.

MARIA Do not reflect upon my mother's memory, Sir—

VAN ROUGH Why not, Mary, why not? She kept me from speaking my mind all *her* life, and do you think she shall henpeck me now she is *dead* too? Come, come; don't go to sniveling: be a good girl, and mind the main chance. I'll see you well settled in the world.

MARIA I do not doubt your love, Sir; and it is my duty to obey you.—I will endeavor to make my duty and inclination go hand in hand.

VAN ROUGH Well, well, Mary; do you be a good girl, mind the main chance, and never mind inclination.—Why, do you know that I have been down in the cellar this very morning to examine a pipe of Madeira[2]

8. Worthless nonsense. *Robinson Crusoe* (1719) is a novel by the English writer Daniel Defoe (c. 1660–1731).
9. I.e., the biggest advantage.
1. "A time to weep, and a time to laugh" (Eccle-

siastes 3.4); Ecclesiastes is thought to have been written by Solomon. "Grig": lighthearted young person.
2. A big cask of wine.

which I purchased the week you were born, and mean to tap on your wedding day.—That pipe cost me fifty pounds sterling. It was well worth sixty pounds; but I over-reached Ben Bulkhead, the supercargo.[3] I'll tell you the whole story. You must know that—

[*Enter* SERVANT.]

SERVANT Sir, Mr. Transfer, the broker, is below. [*Exit.*]

VAN ROUGH Well, Mary, I must go.—Remember, and be a good girl, and mind the main chance. [*Exit.*]

MARIA [*alone*] How deplorable is my situation! How distressing for a daughter to find her heart militating with her filial duty! I know my father loves me tenderly, why then do I reluctantly obey him? Heaven knows! with what reluctance I should oppose the will of a parent, or set an example of filial disobedience; at a parent's command I could wed awkwardness and deformity. Were the heart of my husband good, I would so magnify his good qualities with the eye of conjugal affection, that the defects of his person and manners should be lost in the emanation of his virtues. At a father's command, I could embrace poverty. Were the poor man my husband, I would learn resignation to my lot; I would enliven our frugal meal with good humor, and chase away misfortune from our cottage with a smile. At a father's command, I could almost submit, to what every female heart knows to be the most mortifying, to marry a weak man, and blush at my husband's folly in every company I visited.—But to marry a depraved wretch, whose only virtue is a polished exterior; who is actuated by the unmanly ambition of conquering the defenceless; whose heart, insensible to the emotions of patriotism, dilates at the plaudits of every unthinking girl: whose laurels are the sighs and tears of the miserable victims of his specious behavior.—Can he, who has no regard for the peace and happiness of other families, ever have a due regard for the peace and happiness of his own? Would to heaven that my father were not so hasty in his temper! Surely, if I were to state my reasons for declining this match, he would not compel me to marry a man—whom, though my lips may solemnly promise to honor, I find my heart must ever despise. [*Exit.*]

Act Second

SCENE I

CHARLOTTE's *apartment.*

[*Enter* CHARLOTTE *and* LETITIA.]

CHARLOTTE [*at entering*] Betty, take those things out of the carriage and carry them to my chamber; see that you don't tumble[4] them.—My dear, I protest, I think it was the homeliest of the whole. I declare I was almost tempted to return and change it.

LETITIA Why would you take it?

CHARLOTTE Didn't Mrs. Catgut say it was the most fashionable?

3. On a merchant ship, the officer concerned with the voyage's commercial aspects.

4. Rumple, disorder.

LETITIA But, my dear, it will never sit becomingly on you.

CHARLOTTE I know that; but did not you hear Mrs. Catgut say it was fashionable?

LETITIA Did you see that sweet airy cap with the white sprig?

CHARLOTTE Yes, and I longed to take it; but, my dear, what could I do?—Did not Mrs. Catgut say it was the most fashionable; and if I had not taken it, was not that awkward gawky, Sally Slender, ready to purchase it immediately?

LETITIA Did you observe how she tumbled over the things at the next shop, and then went off without purchasing any thing, nor even thanking the poor man for his trouble?—But of all the awkward creatures, did you see Miss Blouze, endeavoring to thrust her unmerciful arm into those small kid gloves?

CHARLOTTE Ha, ha, ha, ha!

LETITIA Then did you take notice, with what an affected warmth of friendship she and Miss Wasp met? when all their acquaintances know how much pleasure they take in abusing each other in every company?

CHARLOTTE Lud!⁵ Letitia, is that so extraordinary? Why, my dear, I hope you are not going to turn sentimentalist.—Scandal, you know, is but amusing ourselves with the faults, foibles, follies, and reputations of our friends;—indeed, I don't know why we should have friends, if we are not at liberty to make use of them. But no person is so ignorant of the world as to suppose, because I amuse myself with a lady's faults, that I am obliged to quarrel with her person, every time we meet; believe me, my dear, we should have very few acquaintances at that rate.

[SERVANT *enters and delivers a letter to* CHARLOTTE, *and exits.*]

CHARLOTTE You'll excuse me, my dear. [*Opens and reads to herself.*]

LETITIA Oh, quite excusable.

CHARLOTTE As I hope to be married, my brother Henry is in the city.

LETITIA What, your brother, Colonel Manly?

CHARLOTTE Yes, my dear; the only brother I have in the world.

LETITIA Was he never in this city?

CHARLOTTE Never nearer than Harlem Heights,⁶ where he lay with his regiment.

LETITIA What sort of a being is this brother of yours? If he is as chatty, as pretty, as sprightly as you, half the belles in the city will be pulling caps for⁷ him.

CHARLOTTE My brother is the very counterpart and reverse of me: I am gay, he is grave; I am airy, he is solid; I am ever selecting the most pleasing objects for my laughter, he has a tear for every pitiful one. And thus, whilst he is plucking the briars and thorns from the path of the unfortunate, I am strewing on my own path with roses.

LETITIA My sweet friend, not quite so poetical, and little more particular.

CHARLOTTE Hands off, Letitia. I feel the rage of simile⁸ upon me; I can't talk to you in any other way. My brother has a heart replete with the noblest sentiments, but then, it is like—it is like—Oh! you provoking girl, you have deranged all my ideas—it is like—Oh! I have it—his heart

5. I.e., Lord!
6. The site of a Revolutionary War battle at the northern end of Manhattan Island.

7. I.e., setting their caps for; setting their sights on.
8. I.e., the desire to make poetic comparisons.

is like an old maiden lady's band-box;[9] it contains many costly things, arranged with the most scrupulous nicety, yet the misfortune is, that they are too delicate, costly, and antiquated, for common use.

LETITIA By what I can pick out of your flowery description, your brother is no beau.

CHARLOTTE No, indeed; he makes no pretension to the character. He'd ride, or rather fly, an hundred miles to relieve a distressed object, or to do a gallant act in the service of his country: but, should you drop your fan or bouquet in his presence, it is ten to one that some beau at the farther end of the room would have the honor of presenting it to you, before he had observed that it fell. I'll tell you one of his antiquated, anti-gallant notions.—He said once in my presence, in a room full of company—would you believe it—in a large circle of ladies, that the best evidence a gentleman could give a young lady of his respect and affection, was, to endeavor in a friendly manner to rectify her foibles. I protest I was crimson to the eyes, upon reflecting that I was known as his sister.

LETITIA Insupportable creature! tell a lady of her faults! If he is so grave, I fear I have no chance of captivating him.

CHARLOTTE His conversation is like a rich old fashioned brocade,[1] it will stand alone; every sentence is a sentiment. Now you may judge what a time I had with him in my twelve months' visit to my father. He read me such lectures, out of pure brotherly affection, against the extremes of fashion, dress, flirting, and coquetry, and all the other dear things which he knows I doat upon, that, I protest, his conversation made me as melancholy as if I had been at church; and heaven knows, though I never prayed to go there but on one occasion, yet I would have exchanged his conversation for a psalm and a sermon. Church is rather melancholy, to be sure; but then I can ogle the beaux, and be regaled with "here endeth the first lesson"; but his brotherly *here*, you would think had no end. You captivate him! Why, my dear, he would as soon fall in love with a box of Italian flowers. There is Maria now, if she were not engaged, she might do something.—Oh, how I should like to see that pair of pensorosos[2] together, looking as grave as two sailors' wives of a stormy night, with a flow of sentiment meandering through their conversation like purling streams in modern poetry.

LETITIA Oh! my dear fanciful—

CHARLOTTE Hush! I hear some person coming through the entry.

[*Enter* SERVANT.]

SERVANT Madam, there's a gentleman below who calls himself Colonel Manly; do you chuse to be at home?

CHARLOTTE Shew him in. [*Exit* SERVANT.] Now for a sober face.

[*Enter* COLONEL MANLY.]

MANLY My dear Charlotte, I am happy that I once more enfold you within the arms of fraternal affection. I know you are going to ask (amiable impatience!) how our parents do,—the venerable pair transmit you their blessing by me—they totter on the verge of a well-spent life, and wish only to see their children settled in the world, to depart in peace.

9. Cylindrical box for clothes; its lid was held on by a band of ribbon.
1. A rich, stiff fabric.

2. Melancholy, thoughtful people (from "Il Penseroso," a poem about such a person by the English poet John Milton [1608–1674]).

CHARLOTTE I am very happy to hear that they are well. [*Coolly.*] Brother, will you give me leave to introduce you to our uncle's ward, one of my most intimate friends.

MANLY [*saluting* LETITIA] I ought to regard your friends as my own.

CHARLOTTE Come, Letitia, do give us a little dash of your vivacity; my brother is so sentimental, and so grave, that I protest he'll give us the vapors.[3]

MANLY Though sentiment and gravity, I know, are banished the polite world, yet, I hoped, they might find some countenance in the meeting of such near connections as brother and sister.

CHARLOTTE Positively, brother, if you go one step further in this strain, you will set me crying, and that, you know, would spoil my eyes; and then I should never get the husband which our good papa and mamma have so kindly wished me—never be established in the world.

MANLY Forgive me, my sister—I am no enemy to mirth; I love your sprightliness; and I hope it will one day enliven the hours of some worthy man; but when I mention the respectable authors of my existence,— the cherishers and protectors of my helpless infancy, whose hearts glow with such fondness and attachment, that they would willingly lay down their lives for my welfare, you will excuse me, if I am so unfashionable as to speak of them with some degree of respect and reverence.

CHARLOTTE Well, well, brother; if you won't be gay, we'll not differ; I will be as grave as you wish. [*Affects gravity.*] And so, brother, you have come to the city to exchange some of your commutation notes[4] for a little pleasure.

MANLY Indeed, you are mistaken; my errand is not of amusement, but business; and as I neither drink nor game, my expences will be so trivial, I shall have no occasion to sell my notes.

CHARLOTTE Then you won't have occasion to do a very good thing. Why, there was the Vermont General—he came down some time since, sold all his musty notes at one stroke, and then laid the cash out in trinkets for his dear Fanny. I want a dozen pretty things myself; have you got the notes with you?

MANLY I shall be ever willing to contribute as far as it is in my power, to adorn, or in any way to please my sister; yet, I hope, I shall never be obliged for this, to sell my notes. I may be romantic, but I preserve them as a sacred deposit. Their full amount is justly due to me, but as embarrassments, the natural consequences of a long war, disable my country from supporting its credit, I shall wait with patience until it is rich enough to discharge them. If that is not in my day, they shall be transmitted as an honorable certificate to posterity, that I have humbly imitated our illustrious Washington, in having exposed my health and life in the service of my country, without reaping any other reward than the glory of conquering in so arduous a contest.

CHARLOTTE Well said heroics. Why, my dear Henry, you have such a lofty way of saying things, that I protest I almost tremble at the thought of introducing you to the polite circles in the city. The belles would think

3. I.e., depress us.
4. Notes given to Continental Army officers after the Revolution, promising payment of a pension when the notes came due; they could be cashed in earlier for less than the face amount.

you were a player[5] run mad, with your head filled with old scraps of tragedy: and, as to the beaux, they might admire, because they would not understand you.—But, however, I must, I believe, venture to introduce you to two or three ladies of my acquaintance.

LETITIA And that will make him acquainted with thirty or forty beaux.

CHARLOTTE Oh! brother, you don't know what a fund of happiness you have in store.

MANLY I fear, sister, I have not refinement sufficient to enjoy it.

CHARLOTTE Oh! you cannot fail being pleased.

LETITIA Our ladies are so delicate and dressy.

CHARLOTTE And our beaux so dressy and delicate.

LETITIA Our ladies chat and flirt so agreeably.

CHARLOTTE And our beaux simper and bow so gracefully.

LETITIA With their hair so trim and neat.

CHARLOTTE And their faces so soft and sleek.

LETITIA Their buckles so tonish[6] and bright.

CHARLOTTE And their hands so slender and white.

LETITIA I vow, Charlotte, we are quite poetical.

CHARLOTTE And then, brother, the faces of the beaux are of such a lily white hue! None of that horrid robustness of constitution, that vulgar corn-fed glow of health, which can only serve to alarm an unmarried lady with apprehensions, and prove a melancholy memento to a married one, that she can never hope for the happiness of being a widow. I will say this to the credit of our city beaux, that such is the delicacy of their complexion, dress, and address, that, even had I no reliance upon the honor of the dear Adonises,[7] I would trust myself in any possible situation with them, without the least apprehensions of rudeness.

MANLY Sister Charlotte!

CHARLOTTE Now, now, now brother [interrupting him], now don't go to spoil my mirth with a dash of your gravity; I am so glad to see you, I am in tip-top spirits. Oh! that you could be with us at a little snug party. There is Billy Simper, Jack Chassé, and Colonel Van Titter, Miss Promonade, and the two Miss Tambours, sometimes make a party, with some other ladies, in a side-box at the play.[8] Everything is conducted with such decorum,—first we bow round to the company in general, then to each one in particular, then we have so many inquiries after each other's health, and we are so happy to meet with each other, and it is so many ages since we last had that pleasure, and, if a married lady is in company, we have such a sweet dissertation upon her son Bobby's chin-cough, then the curtain rises, then our sensibility[9] is all awake, and then by the mere force of apprehension, we torture some harmless expression into a double meaning, which the poor author never dreamt of, and then we have recourse to our fans, and then we blush, and then the gentlemen jog one another, peep under the fan, and make the prettiest remarks; and then we giggle and they simper, and they giggle and we simper, and then the curtain drops, and then for nuts and oranges, and then we

5. Actor.
6. Smart, fashionable (from the French ton).
7. I.e., handsome youths; from the beautiful young man beloved by Venus, the Roman goddess of love and beauty. "Address": bearing.
8. I.e., in box seats, near the stage.
9. Responsiveness. "Chin-cough": whooping cough.

bow, and it's pray Ma'am take it, and pray Sir keep it, and oh! not for the world, Sir: and then the curtain rises again, and then we blush, and giggle, and simper, and bow, all over again. Oh! the sentimental charms of a side-box conversation! [*All laugh.*]

MANLY Well, sister, I join heartily with you in the laugh; for, in my opinion, it is as justifiable to laugh at folly, as it is reprehensible to ridicule misfortune.

CHARLOTTE Well, but brother, positively, I can't introduce you in these clothes: why, your coat looks as if it were calculated for the vulgar purpose of keeping yourself comfortable.

MANLY This coat was my regimental coat in the late war. The public tumults of our state[1] have induced me to buckle on the sword in support of that government which I once fought to establish. I can only say, sister, that there was a time when this coat was respectable, and some people even thought that those men who had endured so many winter campaigns in the service of their country, without bread, clothing, or pay, at least deserved that the poverty of their appearance should not be ridiculed.

CHARLOTTE We agree in opinion entirely, brother, though it would not have done for me to have said it: it is the coat makes the man respectable. In the time of the war, when we were almost frightened to death, why, your coat was respectable, that is, fashionable; now another kind of coat is fashionable, that is, respectable. And pray direct the taylor to make yours the height of the fashion.

MANLY Though it is of little consequence to me of what shape my coat is, yet, as to the height of the fashion, there you will please to excuse me, sister. You know my sentiments on that subject. I have often lamented the advantage which the French have over us in the particular. In Paris, the fashions have their dawnings, their routine and declensions,[2] and depend as much upon the caprice of the day as in other countries; but there every lady assumes a right to deviate from the general *ton*, as far as will be of advantage to her own appearance. In America, the cry is, what is the fashion? and we follow it, indiscriminately, because it is so.

CHARLOTTE Therefore it is, that when large hoops are in fashion, we often see many a plump girl lost in the immensity of a hoop petticoat, whose want of height and *em-bon-point*[3] would never have been remarked in any other dress. When the high head-dress is the mode, how then do we see a lofty cushion, with a profusion of gauze, feathers, and ribband, supported by a face no bigger than an apple; whilst a broad full-faced lady, who really would have appeared tolerably handsome in a large headdress, looks with her smart *chapeau*[4] as masculine as a soldier.

MANLY But remember, my dear sister, and I wish all my fair countrywomen would recollect, that the only excuse a young lady can have for going extravagantly into a fashion, is, because it makes her look extravagantly handsome.—Ladies, I must wish you a good morning.

CHARLOTTE But, brother, you are going to make home with us.

1. The young nation's problems, especially the financial ones, were not solved by the Revolution. Manly may be referring to Shays's Rebellion (1787).
2. I.e., their pattern and fall.
3. Stoutness (here, hyphenated to emphasize its derivation from the French for "in good condition," i.e., robust). "Want": lack.
4. Hat (French).

MANLY Indeed, I cannot. I have seen my uncle, and explained that matter.

CHARLOTTE Come and dine with us, then. We have a family dinner about half past four o'clock.

MANLY I am engaged to dine with the Spanish ambassador. I was introduced to him by an old brother officer; and instead of freezing me with a cold card of compliment[5] to dine with him ten days hence, he, with the true old Castilian frankness, in a friendly manner, asked me to dine with him to-day—an honor I could not refuse. Sister, adieu—Madam, your most obedient—[*Exit.*]

CHARLOTTE I will wait upon you to the door, brother; I have something particular to say to you. [*Exit.*]

LETITIA [*alone*] What a pair!—She the pink of flirtation, he the essence of everything that is *outré*[6] and gloomy.—I think I have completely deceived Charlotte by my manner of speaking of Mr. Dimple; she's too much the friend of Maria to be confided in. He is certainly rendering himself disagreeable to Maria, in order to break with her and proffer his hand to me. This is what the delicate fellow hinted in our last conversation. [*Exit.*]

SCENE 2

The Mall.

[*Enter* JESSAMY.]

JESSAMY Positively this Mall is a very pretty place. I hope the city won't ruin it by repairs. To be sure, it won't do to speak of in the same day with Ranelagh or Vauxhall;[7] however, it's a fine place for a young fellow to display his person to advantage. Indeed, nothing is lost here; the girls have taste, and I am very happy to find they have adopted the elegant London fashion of looking back, after a genteel fellow like me has passed them. Ah! who comes here! This, by his awkwardness, must be the Yankee colonel's servant. I'll accost him.

[*Enter* JONATHAN.]

Votre très—humble *serviteur*, Monsieur.[8] I understand Colonel Manly, the Yankee officer, has the honor of your services.

JONATHAN Sir!—

JESSAMY I say, Sir, I understand that Colonel Manly has the honor of having you for a servant.

JONATHAN Servant! Sir, do you take me for a neger,—I am Colonel Manly's waiter.[9]

JESSAMY A true Yankee distinction egad, without a difference. Why, Sir, do you not perform all the offices of a servant? Do you not even blacken his boots?

JONATHAN Yes; I do grease them a bit sometimes; but I am a true blue son of liberty, for all that. Father said I should come as Colonel Manly's waiter to see the world, and all that; but no man shall master me: my father has as good a farm as the colonel.

5. An invitation card.
6. Bizarre (French).
7. London pleasure gardens.

8. Your very humble servant, sir (French).
9. Valet, manservant.

JESSAMY Well, Sir, we will not quarrel about terms upon the eve of an acquaintance, from which I promise myself so much satisfaction,— therefore *sans cérémonie*[1]—

JONATHAN What?—

JESSAMY I say, I am extremely happy to see Colonel Manly's waiter.

JONATHAN Well, and I vow, too, I am pretty considerably glad to see you— but what the dogs need of all this outlandish lingo? Who may you be, Sir, if I may be so bold?

JESSAMY I have the honor to be Mr. Dimple's servant, or, if you please, waiter. We lodge under the same roof, and should be glad of the honor of your acquaintance.

JONATHAN You a waiter! By the living jingo, you look so topping, I took you for one of the agents to Congress.[2]

JESSAMY The brute has discernment notwithstanding his appearance.— Give me leave to say I wonder then at your familiarity.

JONATHAN Why, as to the matter of that, Mr.—pray, what's your name?

JESSAMY Jessamy, at your service.

JONATHAN Why, I swear we don't make any great matter of distinction in our state, between quality and other folks.

JESSAMY This is, indeed, a leveling principle. I hope, Mr. Jonathan, you have not taken part with the insurgents.

JONATHAN Why, since General Shays has sneaked off, and given us the bag to hold, I don't care to give my opinion; but you'll promise not to tell—put your ear this way—you won't tell?—I vow, I did think the sturgeons[3] were right.

JESSAMY I thought, Mr. Jonathan, you Massachusetts men always argued with a gun in your hand.—Why didn't you join them?

JONATHAN Why, the colonel is one of those folks called the Shin—shin— dang it all, I can't speak them *lignum vitæ* words—you know who I mean—there is a company of them—they wear a China goose at their buttonhole—a kind of gilt thing.[4]—Now the colonel told father and brother,—you must know there are, let me see—there is Elnathan, Silas, and Barnabas, Tabitha,—no, no, she's a she—tarnation, now I have it— there's Elnathan, Silas, Barnabas, Jonathan, that's I—seven of us, six went into the wars, and I staid at home to take care of mother. Colonel said that it was burning shame for the true blue Bunker-hill sons of liberty, who had fought Governor Hutchinson, Lord North,[5] and the Devil, to have any hand in kicking up a cursed dust against a government, which we had every mother's son of us a hand in making.

JESSAMY Bravo!—Well, have you been abroad in the city since your arrival? What have you seen that is curious and entertaining?

JONATHAN Oh! I have seen a power of fine sights. I went to see two marble-stone men and a leaden horse, that stands out in doors in all

1. Without ceremony (French).
2. I.e., an ambassador.
3. Jonathan's awkward mispronunciation of Jessamy's "insurgents," above; being from Massachusetts, he is on Shays's side.
4. The badge of the Society of the Cincinnati, a Revolutionary officers' fraternal group, was a gold eagle. *"Lignum vitae"*: staff of life (Latin,

literal trans.); here, the tough wood of a tropical tree recently introduced into New England.
5. Frederick North, second Earl of Guilford (1732–1792; prime minister of England 1770– 82). Bunker Hill, in the Charlestown section of Boston, site of an early engagement in the Revolution. Thomas Hutchinson (1711–1780; British governor of Massachusetts 1771–74).

weathers; and when I came where they was, one had got no head, and t'other wer'nt there. They said as how the leaden man was a damn'd tory,[6] and that he took wit in his anger and rode off in the time of the troubles.

JESSAMY But this was not the end of your excursion.

JONATHAN Oh, no; I went to a place they call Holy Ground.[7] Now I counted this was a place where folks go to meeting,[8] so I put my hymn-book in my pocket, and walked softly and grave as a minister; and when I came there, the dogs a bit of a meeting-house could I see. At last I spied a young gentlewoman standing by one of the seats, which they have here at the doors—I took her to be the deacon's daughter, and she looked so kind, and so obliging, that I thought I would go and ask her the way to lecture, and would you think it—she called me dear, and sweeting, and honey, just as if we were married; by the living jingo, I had a month's mind to buss[9] her.

JESSAMY Well, but how did it end?

JONATHAN Why, as I was standing talking with her, a parcel of sailor men and boys got round me, the snarl headed curs fell a-kicking and cursing of me at such a tarnal[1] rate, that, I vow, I was glad to take to my heels and split home, right off, tail on end like a stream of chalk.

JESSAMY Why, my dear friend, you are not acquainted with the city; that girl you saw was a—[Whispers.]

JONATHAN Mercy on my soul! was that young woman a harlot!—Well, if this is New York Holy Ground, what must the Holy-day Ground be!

JESSAMY Well, you should not judge of the city too rashly. We have a number of elegant fine girls here, that make a man's leisure hours pass very agreeably. I would esteem it an honor to announce[2] you to some of them.— Gad! that announce is a select word; I wonder where I picked it up.

JONATHAN I don't want to know them.

JESSAMY Come, come, my dear friend, I see that I must assume the honor of being the director of your amusements. Nature has given up passions, and youth and opportunity stimulate to gratify them. It is no shame, my dear Blueskin,[3] for a man to amuse himself with a little gallantry.

JONATHAN Girl huntry! I don't altogether understand. I never played at that game. I know how to play hunt the squirrel, but I can't play anything with the girls; I am as good as married.

JESSAMY Vulgar, horrid brute! Married, and above a hundred miles from his wife, and think that an objection to his making love to every woman he meets! He never can have read, no, he never can have been in a room with a volume of the divine Chesterfield.—So you are married?

JONATHAN No, I don't say so; I said I was as good as married, a kind of promise.

JESSAMY As good as married!—

JONATHAN Why, yes; there's Tabitha Wymen, the deacon's daughter, at home, she and I have been courting a great while, and folks say as how we are to be married; and so I broke a piece of money with her when we

6. British loyalist.
7. New York's whorehouse district, apparently so called because Trinity Church owned much of the land.
8. Church service.

9. Kiss.
1. Mild oath (from "eternal"). "Parcel": pack.
2. Present.
3. I.e., Yankee (from the blue of the Revolutionary Army uniform); also, possibly, mulatto.

parted,[4] and she promised not to spark it with Solomon Dyer while I am gone. You wouldn't have me false to my true love, would you?

JESSAMY May be you have another reason for constancy; possibly the young lady has a fortune? Ha! Mr. Jonathan, the solid charms; the chains of love are never so binding as when the links are made of gold.

JONATHAN Why, as to fortune, I must needs say her father is pretty dumb rich; he went representative for our town last year. He will give her—let me see—four times seven is—seven times four—nought and carry one;— he will give her twenty acres of land—somewhat rocky though—a Bible, and a cow.

JESSAMY Twenty acres of rock, a Bible, and a cow! Why, my dear Mr. Jonathan, we have servant maids, or, as you would more elegantly express it, wait'resses, in this city, who collect more in one year from their mistress' cast[5] clothes.

JONATHAN You don't say so!—

JESSAMY Yes, and I'll introduce you to one of them. There is a little lump of flesh and delicacy that lives at next door, wait'ress to Miss Maria; we often see her on the stoop.

JONATHAN But are you sure she would be courted by me?

JESSAMY Never doubt it; remember a faint heart never—blisters of my tongue—I was going to be guilty of a vile proverb;[6] flat against the authority of Chesterfield.—I say there can be no doubt, that the brilliancy of your merit will secure you a favorable reception.

JONATHAN Well, but what must I say to her?

JESSAMY Say to her! why, my dear friend, though I admire your profound knowledge on every other subject, yet, you will pardon my saying, that your want of opportunity has made the female heart escape the poignancy of your penetration. Say to her!—Why, when a man goes a-courting, and hopes for success, he must begin with doing, and not saying.

JONATHAN Well, what must I do?

JESSAMY Why, when you are introduced you must make five or six elegant bows.

JONATHAN Six elegant bows! I understand that; six, you say? Well—

JESSAMY Then you must press and kiss her hand; then press and kiss, and so on to her lips and cheeks; then talk as much as you can about hearts, darts, flames, nectar and ambrosia—the more incoherent the better.

JONATHAN Well, but suppose she should be angry with I?

JESSAMY Why, if she should pretend—please to observe, Mr. Jonathan— if she should pretend to be offended, you must—But I'll tell you how my master acted in such a case: He was seated by a young lady of eighteen upon a sofa, plucking with a wanton hand the blooming sweets of youth and beauty. When the lady thought it necessary to check his ardor, she called up a frown upon her lovely face, so irresistably alluring, that it would have warmed the frozen bosom of age: remember, said she, putting her delicate arm upon his, remember your character and my honor. My master instantly dropped upon his knees, with eyes swimming with love, cheeks glowing with desire, and in the gentlest modulation of voice,

4. A country custom: a parting couple broke a coin, and each person kept one piece.

5. I.e., cast-off.

6. I.e., a faint heart never won a fair lady.

he said—My dear Caroline, in a few months our hands will be indissolu-
bly united at the altar; our hearts I feel are already so—the favors you
now grant as evidence of your affection, are favors indeed; yet when the
ceremony is once past, what will now be received with rapture, will then
be attributed to duty.

JONATHAN Well, and what was the consequence?

JESSAMY The consequence!—Ah! forgive me, my dear friend, but you New
England gentlemen have such a laudable curiosity of seeing the bottom of
every thing;—why, to the honest, I confess I saw the blooming cherub of
a consequence smiling in its angelic mother's arms, about ten months
afterwards.

JONATHAN Well, if I follow all your plans, make them six bows, and all
that; shall I have such little cherubim consequences?

JESSAMY Undoubtedly.—What are you musing upon?

JONATHAN You say you'll certainly make me acquainted?—Why, I was
thinking then how I should contrive to pass this broken piece of silver—
won't it buy a sugar-dram?[7]

JESSAMY What is that, the love-token from the deacon's daughter?—You
come on bravely. But I must hasten to my master. Adieu, my dear friend.

JONATHAN Stay, Mr. Jessamy—must I buss her when I am introduced
to her?

JESSAMY I told you, you must kiss her.

JONATHAN Well, but must I buss her?

JESSAMY Why, kiss and buss, and buss and kiss, is all one.

JONATHAN Oh! my dear friend, though you have a profound knowledge of
all, a pugnancy[8] of tribulation, you don't know everything. [*Exit.*]

JESSAMY [*alone*] Well, certainly I improve; my master could not have insin-
uated himself with more address into the heart of a man he despised.—
Now will this blundering dog sicken Jenny with his nauseous pawings,
until she flies into my arms for very ease. How sweet will the contrast be,
between the blundering Jonathan, and the courtly and accomplished
Jessamy.

Act Third

SCENE I

DIMPLE's *room.*

[DIMPLE *discovered at a Toilet,*[9] *reading.*]

DIMPLE "Women have in general but one object, which is their beauty."
Very true, my lord; positively very true. "Nature has hardly formed a woman
ugly enough to be insensible to flattery upon her person." Extremely just,
my lord; every day's delightful experience confirms this. "If her face is so
shocking, that she must, in some degree, be conscious of it, her figure
and air, she thinks, make ample amends for it." The sallow Miss Wan is a
proof of this.—Upon my telling the distasteful wretch, the other day, that

7. I.e., a small amount of sugar.
8. Another awkward mispronunciation: of Jes-
samy's "poignancy," above.

9. I.e., revealed sitting at a dressing table. He is
reading Chesterfield's *Letters.*

her countenance spoke the pensive language of sentiment, and that Lady Wortley Montague declared, that if the ladies were arrayed in the garb of innocence, the face would be the last part which would be admired as Monsieur Milton expresses it, she grin'd horribly a ghastly smile.[1] "If her figure is deformed, she thinks her face counterbalances it."

[*Enter* JESSAMY *with letters.*]

DIMPLE Where got you these, Jessamy?

JESSAMY Sir, the English packet[2] is arrived.

[DIMPLE *opens and reads a letter enclosing notes.*]

"SIR,

"I have drawn bills on you in favor of Messrs. Van Cash and Co. as per margin. I have taken up your note to Col. Piquet, and discharged your debts to my Lord Lurcher and Sir Harry Rook. I herewith enclose you copies of the bills, which I have no doubt will be immediately honored. On failure, I shall empower some lawyer in your country to recover the amounts.

"I am, Sir,

"Your most humble servant,

"JOHN HAZARD."

Now, did not my lord expressly say, that it was unbecoming a well-bred man to be in a passion, I confess I should be ruffled. [*Reads.*] "There is no accident so unfortunate, which a wise man may not turn to his advantage; nor any accident so fortunate, which a fool will not turn to his disadvantage." True, my lord: but how advantage can be derived from this, I can't see. Chesterfield himself, who made, however, the worst practice of the most excellent precepts, was never in so embarrassing a situation. I love the person of Charlotte, and it is necessary I should command the fortune of Letitia. As to Maria!—I doubt not by my *sang-froid*[3] behavior I shall compel her to decline the match; but the blame must not fall upon me. A prudent man, as my lord says, should take all the credit of a good action to himself, and throw the discredit of a bad one upon others. I must break with Maria, marry Letitia, and as for Charlotte—why, Charlotte must be a companion to my wife.—Here, Jessamy!

[*Enter* JESSAMY.]

[DIMPLE *folds and seals two letters.*]

DIMPLE Here, Jessamy, take this letter to my love. [*Gives one.*]

JESSAMY To which of your honor's loves?—Oh! [*reading*] to Miss Letitia, your honor's rich love.

DIMPLE And this [*delivers another*] to Miss Charlotte Manly. See that you deliver them privately.

JESSAMY Yes, your honor. [*Going.*]

DIMPLE Jessamy, who are these strange lodgers that came to the house last night?

JESSAMY Why, the master is a Yankee colonel; I have not seen much of him; but the man is the most unpolished animal your honor ever disgraced your eyes by looking upon. I have had one of the most *outré* conversations with him!—He really has a most prodigious effect upon my risibility.

1. "Death / Grinned horrible a ghastly smile," *Paradise Lost* 2.845–46, by John Milton. Lady Mary Wortley Montagu (1689–1762), English poet and letter writer.
2. Passenger boat carrying mail and cargo.
3. Cool, unperturbable (French).

DIMPLE I ought, according to every rule of Chesterfield, to wait on him[4] and insinuate myself into his good graces.—Jessamy, wait on the colonel with my compliments, and if he is disengaged, I will do myself the honor of paying him my respects.—Some ignorant unpolished boor—
 [JESSAMY *goes off and returns.*]

JESSAMY Sir, the colonel is gone out, and Jonathan, his servant, says that he is gone to stretch his legs upon the Mall—Stretch his legs! what an indelicacy of diction!

DIMPLE Very well. Reach me my hat and sword. I'll accost him there, in my way to Letitia's, as by accident; pretend to be struck with his person and address, and endeavor to steal into his confidence. Jessamy, I have no business for you at present. [*Exit.*]

JESSAMY [*taking up the book*] My master and I obtain our knowledge from the same source;—though, gad! I think myself much the prettier fellow of the two. [*Surveying himself in the glass.*] That was a brilliant thought, to insinuate that I folded my master's letters for him; the folding is so neat, that it does honor to the operator. I once intended to have insinuated that I wrote his letters too; but that was before I saw them; it won't do now! no honor there, positively.—"Nothing looks more vulgar [*reading affectedly*], ordinary, and illiberal, than ugly, uneven, and ragged nails; the ends of which should be kept even and clean, not tipped with black, and cut in small segments of circles"—Segments of circles! surely my lord did not consider that he wrote for the beaux. Segments of circles! what a crabbed term! Now I dare answer, that my master, with all his learning, does not know that this means, according to the present mode, to let the nails grow long, and then cut them off even at top. [*Laughing without.*] Ha! that's Jenny's titter. I protest I despair of ever teaching that girl to laugh; she has something so execrably natural in her laugh, that I declare it absolutely discomposes my nerves. How came she into our house!—[*Calls.*] Jenny!
 [*Enter* JENNY.]

JESSAMY Prythee, Jenny, don't spoil your fine face with laughing.

JENNY Why, mustn't I laugh, Mr. Jessamy?

JESSAMY You may smile; but, as my lord says, nothing can authorize a laugh.[5]

JENNY Well, but I can't help laughing—Have you seen him, Mr. Jessamy? Ha, ha, ha!

JESSAMY Seen whom?—

JENNY Why, Jonathan, the New England colonel's servant. Do you know he was at the play last night, and the stupid creature don't know where he has been. He would not go to a play for the world; he thinks it was a show, as he calls it.

JESSAMY As ignorant and unpolished as he is, do you know, Miss Jenny, that I propose to introduce him to the honor of your acquaintance.

JENNY Introduce him to me! for what?

JESSAMY Why, my lovely girl, that you may take him under your protection, as Madam Ramboulliet did young Stanhope; that you may, by your

4. Pay him a formal call.
5. "To my mind, there is nothing so illiberal and so ill-bred, as audible laughter"—Chesterfield's *Letters.*

plastic[6] hand, mould this uncouth cub into a gentleman. He is to make love to you.

JENNY Make love to me!—

JESSAMY Yes, Mistress Jenny, make love to you; and, I doubt not, when he shall become domesticated in your kitchen, that this boor, under your auspices, will soon become *un aimable petit Jonathan*.[7]

JENNY I must say, Mr. Jessamy, if he copies after me, he will be vastly monstrously polite.

JESSAMY Stay here one moment, and I will call him.—Jonathan!—Mr. Jonathan!—[*Calls.*]

JONATHAN [*within*] Holla! there—[*Enters.*] You promise to stand by me— six bows you say. [*Bows.*]

JESSAMY Mrs. Jenny, I have the honor of presenting Mr. Jonathan, Colonel Manly's waiter, to you. I am extremely happy that I have it in my power to make two worthy people acquainted with each other's merit.

JENNY So Mr. Jonathan, I hear you were at the play last night.

JONATHAN At the play! why, did you think I went to the devil's drawing- room!

JENNY The devil's drawing-room!

JONATHAN Yes; why ain't cards and dice the devil's device; and the play-house the shop where the devil hangs out the vanities of the world, upon the tenterhooks of temptation. I believe you have not heard how they were acting the old boy one night, and the wicked one came among them sure enough; and went right off in a storm, and carried one quar- ter of the play-house with him. Oh! no, no, no! you won't catch me at a play-house, I warrant you.

JENNY Well, Mr. Jonathan, though I don't scruple your veracity, I have some reasons for believing you were there; pray, where were you about six o'clock?

JONATHAN Why, I went to see one Mr. Morrison, the *hocus pocus* man; they said as how he could eat a café knife.[8]

JENNY Well, and how did you find the place?

JONATHAN As I was going about here and there, to and again, to find it, I saw a great croud of folks going into a long entry, that had lanterns over the door; so I asked a man, whether that was not the place where they played *hocus pocus*? He was a very civil kind man, though he did speak like the Hessians,[9] he lifted up his eyes and said—"they play *hocus pocus* tricks enough there, Got knows, mine friend."

JENNY Well—

JONATHAN So I went right in, and they shewed me away clean up to the garret, just like a meeting-house gallery. And so I saw a power of top- ping folks, all sitting round in little cabins,[1] just like father's corncribs;— and then there was such a squeaking with the fiddles, and such a tarnal blaze with the lights, my head was near turned. At last the people that

6. Creative.
7. A well-behaved little Jonathan (French).
8. I.e., a restaurant knife: Morrison was evi- dently not only a conjurer ("*hocus-pocus* man") but also a sword swallower.

9. Germans, especially ones from Hesse, hired by the British as mercenary troops for the Revolu- tionary War.
1. I.e., in boxes in the theater.

sat near me set up such a hissing—hiss—like so many mad cats; and then they went thump, thump, thump, just like our Peleg threshing wheat, and stampt away, just like the nation;[2] and called out for one Mr. Langolee,—I suppose he helps act the tricks.

JENNY Well, and what did you do all this time?

JONATHAN Gor, I—I liked the fun, and so I thumpt away, and hiss'd as lustily as the best of 'em. One sailor-looking man that sat by me, seeing me stamp, and knowing I was a cute fellow, because I could make a roaring noise, clapt me on the shoulder and said, you are a d—d hearty cock, smite my timbers! I told him so I was, but I thought he need not swear so, and make use of such naughty words.

JESSAMY The savage!—Well, and did you see the man with his tricks?

JONATHAN Why, I vow, as I was looking out for him, they lifted up a great green cloth, and let us look right into the next neighbor's house. Have you a good many houses in New York made so in that 'ere way?

JENNY Not many: but did you see the family?

JONATHAN Yes, swamp it; I see'd the family.

JENNY Well, and how did you like them?

JONATHAN Why, I vow they were pretty much like other families;—there was a poor, good natured, curse of a husband, and a sad rantipole[3] of a wife.

JENNY But did you see no other folks?

JONATHAN Yes. There was one youngster, they called him Mr. Joseph; he talked as sober and as pious as a minister; but like some ministers that I know, he was a fly tike[4] in his heart for all that: He was going to ask a young woman to spark it with him, and—the Lord have mercy on my soul!—she was another man's wife!

JESSAMY The Wabash![5]

JENNY And did you see any more folks?

JONATHAN Why they came on as thick as mustard. For my part, I thought the house was haunted. There was a soldier fellow, who talked about his row de dow dow, and courted a young woman:[6] but of all the cute folk I saw, I liked one little fellow—

JENNY Aye! who was he?

JONATHAN Why, he had red hair, and a little round plump face like mine, only not altogether so handsome. His name was Darby:—that was his baptizing name, his other name I forgot. Oh! it was, Wig—Wag—Wagall, Darby Wagall;—pray, do you know him?—I should like to take a fling[7] with him, or a drap of cyder with a pepper-pod in it, to make it warm and comfortable.

JENNY I can't say I have that pleasure.

2. I.e., tarnation (interjection).

3. Unruly person.

4. I.e., an artful kid. The "rantipole" wife and the "pious" Joseph had by this time clued in contemporary audiences to the fact that the play Jonathan has taken for real life is Richard Brinsley Sheridan's *The School for Scandal* (1777), which had been performed in New York the previous month—a production that Tyler saw.

5. Perhaps "the scoundrel!"

6. As there is no "soldier fellow" in *The School for Scandal*, Jonathan is probably now talking about *The Poor Soldier* (1783), a comic opera played on the same bill as Sheridan's play. "Row de dow dow": noisy disturbance.

7. Other texts read "sling"—an alcoholic drink. "Wagall": i.e., Thomas Wignell, one of whose famous parts was Darby in *The Poor Soldier*.

JONATHAN I wish you did, he is a cute fellow. But there was one thing I didn't like in that Mr. Darby; and that was, he was afraid of some of them 'ere shooting irons, such as your troopers wear on training days. Now, I'm a true born Yankee American son of liberty, and I never was afraid of a gun yet in all my life.

JENNY Well, Mr. Jonathan, you were certainly at the play-house.

JONATHAN I at the play-house!—Why didn't I see the play then?

JENNY Why, the people you saw were players.

JONATHAN Mercy on my soul! did I see the wicked players?—Mayhap that 'ere Darby that I liked so, was the old serpent himself, and had his cloven foot in his pocket. Why, I vow, now I come to think on 't, the candles seemed to burn blue, and I am sure where I sat it smelt tarnally of brimstone.

JESSAMY Well, Mr. Jonathan, from your account, which I confess is very accurate, you must have been at the play-house.

JONATHAN Why, I vow I began to smell a rat. When I came away, I went to the man for my money again: you want your money, says he; yes, says I; for what, says he; why, says I, no man shall jocky me out of my money; I paid my money to see sights, and the dogs a bit of a sight have I seen, unless you call listening to people's private business a sight. Why says he, it is the School for Scandalization.—The School for Scandalization—Oh, ho! no wonder you New York folks are so cute at it, when you go to school to learn it: and so I jogged off.[8]

JESSAMY My dear Jenny, my master's business drags me from you; would to heaven I knew no other servitude than to your charms.

JONATHAN Well, but don't go; you won't leave me so.—

JESSAMY Excuse me.—Remember the cash. [*Aside to him, and—Exit.*]

JENNY Mr. Jonathan, won't you please to sit down. Mr. Jessamy tells me you wanted to have some conversation with me.
 [*Having brought forward two chairs, they sit.*]

JONATHAN Ma'am!—

JENNY Sir!—

JONATHAN Ma'am!—

JENNY Pray, how do you like the city, Sir?

JONATHAN Ma'am!—

JENNY I say, Sir, how do you like New York?

JONATHAN Ma'am!—

JENNY The stupid creature! but I must pass some little time with him, if it is only to endeavor to learn, whether it was his master that made such an abrupt entrance into our house, and my young mistress's heart, this morning. [*Aside.*] As you don't seem to like to talk, Mr. Jonathan—do you sing?

JONATHAN Gor, I—I am glad she asked that, for I forgot what Mr. Jessamy bid me say, and I dare as well be hanged as act what he bid me do, I'm so ashamed. [*Aside.*] Yes, Ma'am, I can sing—I can sing Mear, Old Hundred, and Bangor.[9]

8. Trotted off.
9. Popular names for hymn tunes. "Mear" is probably "Meae Animac Amator" ("Jesus, Lover of My Soul"). "Old Hundred" is "All People That on Earth Do Dwell." "Bangor" is "Eternal God, We Look to Thee."

JENNY Oh, I don't mean psalm tunes. Have you no little song to please the ladies; such as Roslin Castle, or the Maid of the Mill?[1]

JONATHAN Why, all my tunes go to meeting tunes, save one, and I count you won't altogether like that 'ere.

JENNY What is it called?

JONATHAN I am sure you have heard folks talk about it, it is called Yankee Doodle.

JENNY Oh! it is the tune I am fond of; and, if I know anything of my mistress, she would be glad to dance to it. Pray, sing?

JONATHAN [sings]

> Father and I went to camp,—
> Along with Captain Goodwin;
> And there we saw the men and boys,
> As thick as hasty pudding.[2]
> Yankee Doodle do, etc.
>
> And there we saw a swamping[3] gun,
> Big as log of maple,
> On a little deuced[4] cart,
> A load for father's cattle.[5]
> Yankee Doodle do, etc.
>
> And every time they fired it off,
> It took a horn of powder,
> It made a noise—like father's gun,
> Only a nation louder.
> Yankee Doodle do, etc.
>
> There was a man in our town,
> His name was—

No, no, that won't do. Now, if I was with Tabitha Wymen and Jemima Cawley, down at father Chase's, I shouldn't mind singing this all out before them you would be affronted if I was to sing that, though that's a lucky thought; if you should be affronted, I have something dang'd cute, which Jessamy told me to say to you.

JENNY Is that all! I assure you I like it of all things.

JONATHAN No, no; I can sing more, some other time, when you and I are better acquainted, I'll sing the whole of it—no, no—that's a fib—I can't sing but a hundred and ninety verses; our Tabitha at home can sing it all.— [Sings]

> Marblehead's a rocky place,
> And Cape-Cod is sandy;
> Charleston is burnt down,
> Boston is the dandy.
> Yankee Doodle do, etc.

1. Popular songs of the time.
2. Breakfast dish made from Indian corn and water.

3. Big, overwhelming.
4. I.e., damned.
5. I.e., oxen.

I vow, my own town song has put me into such topping spirits, that I believe I'll begin to do a little, as Jessamy says we must when we go a courting— [*Runs and kisses her.*] Burning rivers! cooling flames! red hot roses! pignuts! hasty-pudding and ambrosia!

JENNY What means this freedom! you insulting wretch. [*Strikes him.*]

JONATHAN Are you affronted?

JENNY Affronted! with what looks shall I express my anger?

JONATHAN Looks! why, as to the matter of looks, you look as cross as a witch.

JENNY Have you no feeling for the delicacy of my sex?

JONATHAN Feeling! Gor, I—I feel the delicacy of your sex pretty smartly [*rubbing his cheek*], though, I vow, I thought when you city ladies courted and married, and all that, you put feeling out of the question. But I want to know whether you are really affronted, or only pretend to be so? 'Cause, if you are certainly right down affronted, I am at the end of my tether;—Jessamy didn't tell me what to say to you.

JENNY Pretend to be affronted!

JONATHAN Aye, aye, if you only pretend, you shall hear how I'll go to work to make cherubim consequences. [*Runs up to her.*]

JENNY Begone, you brute!

JONATHAN That looks like mad; but I won't lose my speech. My dearest Jenny—your name is Jenny, I think? My dearest Jenny, though I have the highest esteem for the sweet favors you have just now granted me— Gor, that's a fib though, but Jessamy says it is not wicked to tell lies to the women. [*Aside.*] I say, though I have the highest esteem for the favors you have just now granted me, yet, you will consider, that as soon as the dissolvable knot is tied, they will no longer be favors, but only matters of duty, and matters of course.

JENNY Marry you! you audacious monster! get out of my sight, or rather let me fly from you. [*Exit hastily.*]

JONATHAN Gor! she's gone off in a swinging passion, before I had time to think of consequences. If this is the way with your city ladies, give me the twenty acres of rocks, the Bible, the cow, and Tabitha, and a little peaceable bundling.[6]

SCENE 2

The Mall.

[*Enter* MANLY.]

MANLY It must be so, Montague! and it is not at all the tribe of Mandevilles[7] shall convince me, that a nation, to become great, must first become dissipated. Luxury is surely the bane of a nation: Luxury! which enervates both soul and body, by opening a thousand new sources of enjoyment, opens, also, a thousand new sources of contention and want: Luxury! which renders a people weak at home, and accessible to bribery, corruption, and force from abroad. When the Grecian states knew no

6. An old courtship custom, in which a couple occupied the same bed without undressing.
7. The English statesman Edward Montagu (1713–1776), son of Lady Mary Wortley Montagu, and the Anglo-Dutch philosopher Bernard Mandeville (1670–1733) wrote books on, respectively, the decline of civilizations and the folly of humankind.

other tools than the axe and the saw, the Grecians were a great, a free, and a happy people. The kings of Greece devoted their lives to the service of their country, and her senators knew no other superiority over their fellow-citizens than a glorious preeminence in danger and virtue. They exhibited to the world a noble spectacle,—a number of independent states united by a similarity of language, sentiment, manners, common interest, and common consent, in one grand mutual league of protection.—And, thus united, long might they have continued the cherishers of arts and sciences, the protectors of the oppressed, the scourge of tyrants, and the safe asylum of liberty: But when foreign gold, and still more pernicious, foreign luxury, had crept among them, they sapped the vitals of their virtue. The virtues of their ancestors were only found in their writings. Envy and suspicion, the vices of little minds, possessed them. The various states engendered jealousies of each other; and, more unfortunately, growing jealous of their great federal council, the Amphictyons,[8] they forgot that their common safety had existed, and would exist, in giving them an honorable extensive prerogative. The common good was lost in the pursuit of private interest; and that people, who, by uniting, might have stood against the world in arms, by dividing, crumbled into ruin;—their name is now only known in the page of the historian, and what they once were, is all we have left to admire. Oh! that America! Oh! that my country, would in this her day, learn the things which belong to her peace!

[*Enter* DIMPLE.]

DIMPLE You are Colonel Manly, I presume?

MANLY At your service, Sir.

DIMPLE My name is Dimple, Sir. I have the honor to be a lodger in the same house with you, and hearing you were in the Mall, came hither to take the liberty of joining you.

MANLY You are very obliging, Sir.

DIMPLE As I understand you are a stranger here, Sir, I have taken the liberty to introduce myself to your acquaintance, as possibly I may have it in my power to point out some things in this city worthy your notice.

MANLY An attention to strangers is worthy a liberal mind, and must ever be gratefully received. But to a soldier, who has no fixed abode, such attentions are particularly pleasing.

DIMPLE Sir, there is no character so respectable as that of a soldier. And, indeed, when we reflect how much we owe to those brave men who have suffered so much in the service of their country, and secured to us those inestimable blessings that we now enjoy, our liberty and independence, they demand every attention which gratitude can pay. For my own part, I never meet an officer, but I embrace him as my friend, nor a private in distress, but I insensibly extend my charity to him.—I have hit the Bumpkin[9] off very tolerably. [*Aside.*]

MANLY Give me your hand, Sir! I do not proffer this hand to everybody; but you steal into my heart. I hope I am as insensible to flattery as most men; but I declare (it may be my weak side), that I never hear the name of soldier mentioned with respect, but I experience a thrill of pleasure, which I never feel on any other occasion.

8. Religious associations of Greek states. 9. Rustic.

DIMPLE Will you give me leave, my dear colonel, to confer an obligation on myself, by shewing you some civilities during your stay here, and giving a similar opportunity to some of my friends?

MANLY Sir, I thank you; but I believe my stay in this city will be very short.

DIMPLE I can introduce you to some men of excellent sense, in whose company you will esteem yourself happy; and, by way of amusement, to some fine girls, who will listen to your soft things with pleasure.

MANLY Sir, I should be proud of the honor of being acquainted with those gentlemen;—but, as for the ladies, I don't understand you.

DIMPLE Why, Sir, I need not tell you, that when a young gentleman is alone with a young lady, he must say some soft things to her fair cheek—indeed the lady will expect it. To be sure, there is not much pleasure, when a man of the world and a finished coquette meet, who perfectly know each other; but how delicious is it to excite the emotions of joy, hope, expectation, and delight, in the bosom of a lovely girl, who believes every tittle of what you say to be serious.

MANLY Serious, Sir! In my opinion, the man, who, under pretensions of marriage, can plant thorns in the bosom of an innocent, unsuspecting girl, is more detestable than a common robber, in the same proportion, as private violence is more despicable than open force, and money of less value than happiness.

DIMPLE How he awes me by the superiority of his sentiments. [*Aside.*] As you say, Sir, a gentleman should be cautious how he mentions marriage.

MANLY Cautious, Sir! No person more approves of an intercourse between the sexes than I do. Female conversation softens our manners, whilst our discourse, from the superiority of our literary advantages, improves their minds. But, in our young country, where there is no such thing as gallantry, when a gentleman speaks of love to a lady, whether he mentions marriage, or not, she ought to conclude, either that he meant to insult her, or, that his intentions are the most serious and honorable. How mean, how cruel, is it, by a thousand tender assiduities, to win the affections of an amiable girl, and though you leave her virtue unspotted, to betray her into the appearance of so many tender partialities, that every man of delicacy would suppress his inclination towards her, by supposing her heart engaged! Can any man, for the trivial gratification of his leisure hours, affect the happiness of a whole life! His not having spoken of marriage, may add to his perfidy, but can be no excuse for his conduct.

DIMPLE Sir, I admire your sentiments;—they are mine. The light observations that fell from me, were only a principle of the tongue; they came not from the heart—my practice has ever disapproved these principles.

MANLY I believe you, Sir. I should with reluctance suppose that those pernicious sentiments could find admittance into the heart of a gentleman.

DIMPLE I am now, Sir, going to visit a family, where, if you please, I will have the honor of introducing you. Mr. Manly's ward, Miss Letitia, is a young lady of immense fortune; and his niece, Miss Charlotte Manly is a young lady of great sprightliness and beauty.

MANLY That gentleman, Sir, is my uncle, and Miss Manly is my sister.

DIMPLE The devil she is! [*Aside.*] Miss Manly your sister, Sir? I rejoice to hear it, and feel a double pleasure in being known to you.—Plague on him! I wish he was at Boston again with all my soul. [*Aside.*]

MANLY Come, Sir, will you go?

DIMPLE I will follow you in a moment, Sir. [*Exit* MANLY.]

Plague on it! this is unlucky. A fighting brother is a cursed appendage to a fine girl. Egad! I just stopped in time; had he not discovered himself, in two minutes more I should have told him how well I was with his sister.—Indeed, I cannot see the satisfaction of an intrigue, if one can't have the pleasure of communicating it to our friends. [*Exit.*]

Act Fourth

SCENE I

CHARLOTTE's *apartment.*

[CHARLOTTE *leading in* Maria.]

CHARLOTTE This is so kind, my sweet friend, to come to see me at this moment. I declare, if I were going to be married in a few days, as you are, I should scarce have found time to visit my friends.

MARIA Do you think then that there is an impropriety in it?—How should you dispose of your time?

CHARLOTTE Why, I should be shut up in my chamber; and my head would so run upon—upon—upon the solemn ceremony that I was to pass through—I declare it would take me above two hours merely to learn that little monosyllable—*Yes.* Ah! my dear, your sentimental imagination does not conceive what that little tiny word implies.

MARIA Spare me your raillery, my sweet friend; I should love your agreeable vivacity at any other time.

CHARLOTTE Why this is the very time to amuse you. You grieve me to see you look so unhappy.

MARIA Have I not reason to look so?

CHARLOTTE What new grief distresses you?

MARIA Oh! how sweet it is, when the heart is borne down with misfortune, to recline and repose on the bosom of friendship! Heaven knows, that, although it is improper for a young lady to praise a gentleman, yet I have ever concealed Mr. Dimple's foibles, and spoke of him as of one whose reputation I expected would be linked with mine: but his late conduct towards me, has turned my coolness into contempt. He behaves as if he meant to insult and disgust me; whilst my father, in the last conversation on the subject of our marriage, spoke of it as a matter which laid near his heart, and in which he would not bear contradiction.

CHARLOTTE This works well: oh! the generous Dimple. I'll endeavor to excite her to discharge him. [*Aside.*] But, my dear friend, your happiness depends on yourself:—Why don't you discard him? Though the match has been of long standing, I would not be forced to make myself miserable: no parent in the world should oblige me to marry the man I did not like.

MARIA Oh! my dear, you never lived with your parents, and do not know what influence a father's frowns have upon a daughter's heart. Besides, what have I to allege against Mr. Dimple, to justify myself to the world? He carries himself so smoothly, that every one would impute the blame to me, and call me capricious.

CHARLOTTE And call her capricious! Did ever such an objection start into the heart of woman? For my part, I wish I had fifty lovers to discard, for no other reason, than because I did not fancy them. My dear Maria, you will forgive me; I know your candor and confidence in me; but I have at times, I confess, been led to suppose, that some other gentleman was the cause of your aversion to Mr. Dimple.

MARIA No, my sweet friend, you may be assured, that though I have seen many gentlemen I could prefer to Mr. Dimple, yet I never saw one that I thought I could give my hand to, until this morning.

CHARLOTTE This morning!

MARIA Yes;—one of the strangest accidents in the world. The odious Dimple, after disgusting me with his conversation, had just left me, when a gentleman, who, it seems, boards in the same house with him, saw him coming out of our door, and the houses looking very much alike, he came into our house instead of his lodgings; nor did he discover his mistake until he got into the parlor, where I was: he then bowed so gracefully; made such a genteel apology, and looked so manly and noble!—

CHARLOTTE I see some folks, though it is so great an impropriety, can praise a gentleman, when he happens to be the man of their fancy. [*Aside.*]

MARIA I don't know how it was,—I hope he did not think me indelicate— but I asked him, I believe, to sit down, or pointed to a chair. He sat down and instead of having recourse to observations upon the weather, or hackneyed criticisms upon the theater, he entered readily into a conversation worthy a man of sense to speak, and a lady of delicacy and sentiment to hear. He was not strictly handsome, but he spoke the language of sentiment, and his eyes looked tenderness and honor.

CHARLOTTE Oh! [*eagerly*] you sentimental grave girls, when your hearts are once touched, beat us rattles a bar's length. And so, you are quite in love with this he-angel?

MARIA In love with him! How can you rattle so, Charlotte? am I not going to be miserable? [*Sighs.*] In love with a gentleman I never saw but one hour in my life, and don't know his name!—No: I only wished that the man I shall marry, may look, and talk, and act, just like him. Besides, my dear, he is a married man.

CHARLOTTE Why, that was good natured.—He told you so, I suppose, in mere charity, to prevent your falling in love with him?

MARIA He didn't tell me so [*peevishly*]; he looked as if he was married.

CHARLOTTE How, my dear, did he look sheepish?

MARIA I am sure he has a susceptible heart, and the ladies of his acquaintance must be very stupid not to—

CHARLOTTE Hush! I hear some person coming.
 [*Enter* LETITIA.]

LETITIA My dear Maria, I am happy to see you. Lud! what a pity it is that you purchased your wedding clothes.

MARIA I think so. [*Sighing.*]

LETITIA Why, my dear, there is the sweetest parcel of silks come over you ever saw. Nancy Brilliant has a full suit come; she sent over her measure, and it fits her to a hair; it is immensely dressy, and made for a court-hoop. I thought they said the large hoops were going out of fashion.

CHARLOTTE Did you see the hat?—Is it a fact, that the deep laces round the border is still the fashion?

DIMPLE [*Within*] Upon my honor, Sir!

MARIA Ha! Dimple's voice! My dear, I must take leave of you. There are some things necessary to be done at our house.—Can't I go through the other room?

[*Enter* DIMPLE *and* MANLY.]

DIMPLE Ladies, your most obedient.

CHARLOTTE Miss Van Rough, shall I present my brother Henry to you? Colonel Manly, Maria,—Miss Van Rough, brother.

MARIA Her brother! [*Turns and sees* MANLY.] Oh! my heart! The very gentleman I have been praising.

MANLY The same amiable girl I saw this morning!

CHARLOTTE Why, you look as if you were acquainted.

MANLY I unintentionally intruded into this lady's presence this morning, for which she was so good as to promise me her forgiveness.

CHARLOTTE Oh! ho! is that the case! Have these two penserosos been together? Were they Henry's eyes that looked so tenderly? [*Aside.*] And so you promised to pardon him? and could you be so good natured?—have you really forgiven him? I beg you would do it for my sake. [*Whispering loud to* MARIA.] But, my dear, as you are in such haste, it would be cruel to detain you: I can show you the way through the other room.

MARIA Spare me, sprightly friend.

MANLY The lady does not, I hope, intend to deprive us of the pleasure of her company so soon.

CHARLOTTE She has only a mantua-maker[1] who waits for her at home. But, as I am to give my opinion of the dress, I think she cannot go yet. We were talking of the fashions when you came in; but I suppose the subject must be changed to something of more importance now.—Mr. Dimple, will you favor us with an account of the public entertainments?

DIMPLE Why, really, Miss Manly, you could not have asked me a question more *mal-apropos*.[2] For my part, I must confess, that to a man who has traveled, there is nothing that is worthy the name of amusement to be found in this city.

CHARLOTTE Except visiting the ladies.

DIMPLE Pardon me, Madam; that is the avocation of a man of taste. But, for amusement, I positively know of nothing that can be called so, unless you dignify with that title the hopping once a fortnight to the sound of two or three squeaking fiddles, and the clattering of the old tavern windows, or sitting to see the miserable mummers, whom you call actors, murder comedy, and make a farce of tragedy.

MANLY Do you never attend the theater, Sir?

DIMPLE I was tortured there once.

CHARLOTTE Pray, Mr. Dimple, was it a tragedy or a comedy?

DIMPLE Faith, Madam, I cannot tell; for I sat with my back to the stage all the time, admiring a much better actress than any there;—a lady who played the fine woman to perfection;—though, by the laugh of the horrid creatures around me, I suppose it was comedy. Yet, on second thoughts,

1. I.e., dressmaker. 2. Inappropriate (French).

it might be some hero in a tragedy, dying so comically as to set the whole house in an uproar.—Colonel, I presume you have been in Europe?

MANLY Indeed, Sir, I was never ten leagues from the continent.

DIMPLE Believe me, Colonel, you have an immense pleasure to come; and when you shall have seen the brilliant exhibitions of Europe, you will learn to despise the amusements of this country as much as I do.

MANLY Therefore I do not wish to see them; for I can never esteem that knowledge valuable, which tends to give me a distaste for my native country.

DIMPLE Well, Colonel, though you have not traveled, you have read.

MANLY I have, a little; and by it have discovered that there is a laudable partiality, which ignorant, untraveled men entertain for everything that belongs to their native country. I call it laudable;—it injures no one; adds to their own happiness; and, when extended, becomes the noble principle of patriotism. Traveled gentlemen rise superior, in their own opinion, to this: but, if the contempt which they contract for their country is the most valuable acquisition of their travels, I am far from thinking that their time and money are well spent.

MARIA What noble sentiments!

CHARLOTTE Let my brother set out from where he will in the fields of conversation, he is sure to end his tour in the temple of gravity.

MANLY Forgive me, my sister. I love my country; it has its foibles undoubtedly;—some foreigners will with pleasure remark them—but such remarks fall very ungracefully from the lips of her citizens.

DIMPLE You are perfectly in the right, Colonel—America has her faults.

MANLY Yes, Sir; and we, her children, should blush for them in private, and endeavor, as individuals, to reform them. But, if our country has its errors in common with other countries, I am proud to say America, I mean the United States, have displayed virtues and achievements which modern nations may admire, but of which they have seldom set us the example.

CHARLOTTE But, brother, we must introduce you to some of our gay folks, and let you see the city, such as it is. Mr. Dimple is known to almost every family in town;—he will doubtless take a pleasure in introducing you.

DIMPLE I shall esteem every service I can render your brother an honor.

MANLY I fear the business I am upon will take up all my time, and my family will be anxious to hear from me.

MARIA His family! But what is it to me that he is married! [*Aside.*] Pray, how did you leave your lady, Sir?

CHARLOTTE My brother is not married [*observing her anxiety*]; it is only an odd way he has of expressing himself.—Pray, brother, is this business which you make your continual excuse, a secret?

MANLY No sister, I came hither to solicit the honorable Congress that a number of my brave old soldiers may be put upon the pension-list, who were, at first, not judged to be so materially wounded as to need the public assistance.—My sister says true: [*To* MARIA.] I call my late soldiers my family.—Those who were not in the field in the late glorious contest, and those who were, have their respective merits; but, I confess, my old brother-soldiers are dearer to me than the former description. Friendships

made in adversity are lasting; our countrymen may forget us; but that is no reason why we should forget one another. But I must leave you; my time of engagement approaches.

CHARLOTTE Well, but brother, if you will go, will you please to conduct my fair friend home? You live in the same street;—I was to have gone with her myself—[*Aside.*] A lucky thought.

MARIA I am obliged to your sister, Sir, and was just intending to go. [*Going.*]

MANLY I shall attend her with pleasure.
 [*Exit with* MARIA, *followed by* DIMPLE *and* CHARLOTTE.]

MARIA Now, pray don't betray me to your brother.

CHARLOTTE [*just as she sees him make a motion to take his leave*]. One word with you, brother, if you please. [*Follows them out.*]
 [*Manent* DIMPLE *and* LETITIA.][3]

DIMPLE You received the billet[4] I sent you, I presume?

LETITIA Hush!—Yes.

DIMPLE When shall I pay my respects to you?

LETITIA At eight I shall be unengaged.
 [*Reenter* CHARLOTTE.]

DIMPLE Did my lovely angel receive my billet? [*To* CHARLOTTE.]

CHARLOTTE Yes.

DIMPLE What hour shall I expect with impatience?

CHARLOTTE At eight I shall be at home, unengaged.

DIMPLE Unfortunate! I have a horrid engagement of business at that hour.—Can't you finish your visit earlier, and let six be the happy hour?

CHARLOTTE You know your influence over me. [*Exeunt severally.*]

SCENE 2

VAN ROUGH's *house*.

[VAN ROUGH, *alone*.]

VAN ROUGH It cannot possibly be true! The son of my old friend can't have acted so unadvisedly. Seventeen thousand pounds! in bills!—Mr. Transfer must have been mistaken. He always appeared so prudent, and talked so well upon money-matters, and even assured me that he intended to change his dress for a suit of clothes which would not cost so much, and look more substantial, as soon as he married. No, no, no! it can't be; it cannot be.—But, however, I must look out sharp. I did not care what his principles or his actions were, so long as he minded the main chance. Seventeen thousand pounds!—If he had lost it in trade, why the best men may have ill-luck; but to game it away, as Transfer says—why, at this rate, his whole estate may go in one night, and, what is ten times worse, mine into the bargain. No, no; Mary is right. Leave women to look out in these matters; for all they look as if they didn't know a journal from a ledger, when their interest is concerned, they know what's what; they mind the main chance as well as the best of us.—I wonder Mary did not tell me she knew of his spending his money so foolishly. Seventeen thousand pounds! Why, if my daughter was standing up to be married,

3. I.e., Dimple and Letitia remain (Latin). 4. Letter, note.

I would forbid the banns, if I found it was to a man who did not mind the main chance.—Hush! I hear somebody coming. 'Tis Mary's voice: a man with her too! I shouldn't be surprized if this should be the other string to her bow.—Aye, aye, let them alone; women understand the main chance.—Though, i' faith, I'll listen a little. [*Retires into a closet.*]
[MANLY *leading in* MARIA.]

MANLY I hope you will excuse my speaking upon so important a subject, so abruptly; but the moment I entered your room, you struck me as the lady whom I had long loved in imagination, and never hoped to see.

MARIA Indeed, Sir, I have been led to hear more upon this subject than I ought.

MANLY Do you then disapprove my suit, Madam, or the abruptness of my introducing it? If the latter, my peculiar situation, being obliged to leave the city in a few days, will, I hope, be my excuse; if the former, I will retire: for I am sure I would not give a moment's inquietude to her, whom I could devote my life to please. I am not so indelicate as to seek your immediate approbation; permit me only to be near you, and by a thousand tender assiduities to endeavor to excite a grateful return.

MARIA I have a father, whom I would die to make happy—he will disapprove—

MANLY Do you think me so ungenerous as to seek a place in your esteem without his consent? You must—you ever ought to consider that man as unworthy of you, who seeks an interest in your heart, contrary to a father's approbation. A young lady should reflect, that the loss of a lover may be supplied, but nothing can compensate for the loss of a parent's affection. Yet, why do you suppose your father would disapprove? In our country, the affections are not sacrificed to riches, or family aggrandizement:— should you approve, my family is decent, and my rank honorable.

MARIA You distress me, Sir.

MANLY Then I will sincerely beg your excuse for obtruding so disagreeable a subject and retire. [*Going.*]

MARIA Stay, Sir! Your generosity and good opinion of me deserve a return; but why must I declare what, for these few hours, I have scarce suffered myself to think?—I am—

MANLY What?—

MARIA Engaged, Sir;—and, in a few days, to be married to the gentleman you saw at your sister's.

MANLY Engaged to be married! And have I been basely invading the rights of another? Why have you permitted this—Is this the return for the partiality I declared for you?

MARIA You distress me, Sir. What would you have me to say? You are too generous to wish the truth: ought I to say that I dared not suffer myself to think of my engagement, and that I am going to give my hand without my heart?—Would you have me confess a partiality for you? If so, your triumph is complete; and can be only more so, when days of misery, with the man I cannot love, will make me think of him whom I could prefer.

MANLY [*after a pause*] We are both unhappy; but it is your duty to obey your parent,—mine to obey my honor. Let us, therefore, both follow the path of rectitude; and of this we may be assured, that if we are not

happy, we shall, at least deserve to be so. Adieu! I dare not trust myself longer with you. [*Exeunt severally.*[5]]

Act Fifth

SCENE I

DIMPLE's *lodgings.*

[JESSAMY *meeting* JONATHAN.]

JESSAMY Well, Mr. Jonathan, what success with the fair?[6]

JONATHAN Why, such a tarnal cross tike[7] you never saw!—You would have counted she had lived upon crabapples and vinegar for a fortnight. But what the rattle makes you look so tarnation glum?

JESSAMY I was thinking, Mr. Jonathan, what could be the reason of her carrying herself so coolly to you.

JONATHAN Coolly, do you call it? Why, I vow, she was fire-hot angry: may be it was because I buss'd her.

JESSAMY No, no, Mr. Jonathan; there must be some other cause: I never yet knew a lady angry at being kissed.

JONATHAN Well, if it is not the young woman's bashfulness, I vow I can't conceive why she shou'd n't like me.

JESSAMY May be it is because you have not the Graces, Mr. Jonathan.

JONATHAN Grace! Why, does the young woman expect I must be converted before I court her?[8]

JESSAMY I mean graces of person; for instance, my lord tells us that we must cut off our nails even at top, in small segments of circles;—though you won't understand that—In the next place, you must regulate your laugh.

JONATHAN Maple-log sieze it! don't I laugh natural?

JESSAMY That's the very fault, Mr. Jonathan. Besides, you absolutely mis place it. I was told by a friend of mine that you laughed outright at the play the other night, when you ought only to have tittered.

JONATHAN Gor! I—what does one go to see fun for if they can't laugh?

JESSAMY You may laugh;—but you must laugh by rule.

JONATHAN Swamp it—laugh by rule! Well, I should like that tarnally.

JESSAMY Why you know, Mr. Jonathan, that to dance, a lady to play with her fan, or a gentleman with his cane, and all other natural motions, are regulated by art. My master has composed an immensely pretty gamut,[9] by which any lady, or gentleman, with a few years' close application, may learn to laugh as gracefully as if they were born and bred to it.

JONATHAN Mercy on my soul! A gamut for laughing—just like fa, la, sol?

JESSAMY Yes. It comprises every possible display of jocularity, from an *affetuoso* smile to a *piano* titter, or full chorus *fortissimo*[1] ha, ha, ha! My master employs his leisure-hours in marking out the plays, like a cathedral chanting-book, that the ignorant may know where to laugh; and that pit, box, and gallery may keep time together, and not have a snigger in one

5. Separately.
6. I.e., the fair sex.
7. Churlish person.
8. Jonathan takes "grace" in its religious sense.

9. Full range (of musical notes).
1. Very loud. *"Affetuoso"*: passionate. *"Piano"*: soft. These are all musical terms.

part of the house, a broad grin in the other, and a d—d grum[2] look in the third. How delightful to see the audience all smile together, then look on their books, then twist their mouths into an agreeable simper, then altogether shake the house with a general ha, ha, ha! loud as a full chorus of Handel's, at an Abbey-commemoration.[3]

JONATHAN Ha, ha, ha! that's dang'd cute, I swear.

JESSAMY The gentlemen, you see, will laugh the tenor; the ladies will play the counter-tenor; the beaux will squeak the treble; and our jolly friends in the gallery a thorough bass,[4] ho, ho, ho!

JONATHAN Well, can't you let me see that gamut?

JESSAMY Oh! yes, Mr. Jonathan; here it is. [*Takes out a book.*] Oh! no, this is only a titter with its variations. Ah, here it is. [*Takes out another.*] Now you must know, Mr. Jonathan, this is a piece written by Ben Jonson,[5] which I have set to my master's gamut. The places where you must smile, look grave, or laugh outright, are marked below the line. Now look over me.—"There was a certain man"—now you must smile.

JONATHAN Well, read it again; I warrant I'll mind my eye.

JESSAMY "There was a certain man, who had a sad scolding wife,"—now you must laugh.

JONATHAN Tarnation! That's no laughing matter, though.

JESSAMY "And she lay sick a-dying";—now you must titter.

JONATHAN What, snigger when the good woman's a-dying! Gor, I—

JESSAMY Yes; the notes say you must—"And she asked her husband leave to make a will,"—now you must begin to look grave;—"and her husband said"—

JONATHAN Ay, what did her husband say?—Something dang'd cute, I reckon.

JESSAMY "And her husband said, you have had your will all your life time, and would you have it after you are dead too?"

JONATHAN Ho, ho, ho! There the old man was even with her; he was up to the notch—ha, ha, ha!

JESSAMY But, Mr. Jonathan, you must not laugh so. Why, you ought to have tittered *piano*, and you have laughed *fortissimo*. Look here; you see these marks, A. B. C. and so on; these are the references to the other part of the book. Let us turn to it, and you will see the directions how to manage the muscles. This [*turns over*] was note D you blundered at.—"You must purse the mouth into a smile, then titter, discovering the lower part of the three front upper teeth."

JONATHAN How! read it again.

JESSAMY "There was a certain man"—very well!—"who had a sad scolding wife,"—why don't you laugh?

JONATHAN Now, that scolding wife sticks in my gizzard so pluckily, that I can't laugh for the blood and nowns[6] of me. Let me look grave here, and I'll laugh your belly full where the old creature's a-dying.—

2. Surly, grim. "Chanting-book": i.e., hymnal. "Pit": playhouse area nearest the stage. "Gallery": balcony.
3. I.e., in an oratorio by the German-born British composer George Frederic Handel (1685–1759), performed at Westminster Abbey, in London.
4. In Baroque music, the bass part.
5. English dramatist (1572–1637).
6. From the oath "God's blood and wounds." "Pluckily": perhaps pun to go with "gizzard," for "pluck" means not only courage but also the heart, liver, and lungs of a slaughtered animal.

JESSAMY "And she asked her husband"—[*Bell rings.*] My master's bell! he's returned, I fear—Here, Mr. Jonathan, take this gamut; and, I make no doubt but with a few years' close application, you may be able to smile gracefully. [*Exeunt severally.*]

SCENE 2

CHARLOTTE's *apartment.*

[*Enter* MANLY]

MANLY What, no one at home? How unfortunate to meet the only lady my heart was ever moved by, to find her engaged to another, and confessing her partiality for me! Yet engaged to a man, who, by her intimation, and his libertine conversation with me, I fear, does not merit her. Aye! there's the sting; for, were I assured that Maria was happy, my heart is not so selfish, but that it would dilate in knowing it, even though it were with another.—But to know she is unhappy!—I must drive these thoughts from me. Charlotte has some books; and this is what I believe she calls her little library. [*Enters a closet.*]

[*Enter* DIMPLE *leading* LETITIA.]

LETITIA And will you pretend to say, now, Mr. Dimple, that you propose to break with Maria? Are not the banns published?[7] Are not the clothes purchased? Are not the friends invited? In short, is it not a done affair?

DIMPLE Believe me, my dear Letitia, I would not marry her.

LETITIA Why have you not broke with her before this, as you all along deluded me by saying you would?

DIMPLE Because I was in hopes she would ere this have broke with me.

LETITIA You could not expect it.

DIMPLE Nay, but be calm a moment; 'twas from my regard to you that I did not discard her.

LETITIA Regard to me!

DIMPLE Yes; I have done everything in my power to break with her, but the foolish girl is so fond of me, that nothing can accomplish it. Besides, how can I offer her my hand, when my heart is indissolubly engaged to you?—

LETITIA There may be reason in this; but why so attentive to Miss Manly?

DIMPLE Attentive to Miss Manly! For heaven's sake, if you have no better opinion of my constancy, pay not so ill a compliment to my taste.

LETITIA Did I not see you whisper her to-day?

DIMPLE Possibly I might—but something of so very trifling a nature, that I have already forgot what it was.

LETITIA I believe, she has not forgot it.

DIMPLE My dear creature, how can you for a moment suppose I should have any serious thoughts of that trifling, gay, flighty coquette, that disagreeable—

[*Enter* CHARLOTTE.]

DIMPLE My dear Miss Manly, I rejoice to see you; there is a charm in your conversation that always marks your entrance into company as fortunate.

LETITIA Where have you been, my dear?

7. I.e., the marriage been publicly announced.

CHARLOTTE Why, I have been about to twenty shops, turning over pretty things, and so have left twenty visits unpaid. I wish you would step into the carriage and whisk round, make my apology, and leave my cards where our friends are not at home; that you know will serve as a visit. Come, do go.

LETITIA So anxious to get me out! but I'll watch you. [*Aside.*] Oh! yes, I'll go; I want a little exercise.—Positively [DIMPLE *offering to accompany her*], Mr. Dimple, you shall not go, why, half my visits are cake and caudle[8] visits; it won't do, you know, for you to go.—

[*Exit, but returns to the door in the back scene and listens.*]

DIMPLE This attachment of your brother to Maria is fortunate.

CHARLOTTE How did you come to the knowledge of it?

DIMPLE I read it in their eyes.

CHARLOTTE And I had it from her mouth. It would have amused you to have seen her! She that thought it so great an impropriety to praise a gentleman, that she could not bring out one word in your favor, found a redundancy to praise him.

DIMPLE I have done everything in my power to assist his passion there: your delicacy, my dearest girl, would be shocked at half the instances of neglect and misbehavior.

CHARLOTTE I don't know how I should bear neglect; but Mr. Dimple must misbehave himself indeed, to forfeit my good opinion.

DIMPLE Your good opinion, my angel, is the pride and pleasure of my heart; and if the most respectful tenderness for you and an utter indifference for all your sex besides, can make me worthy of your esteem, I shall richly merit it.

CHARLOTTE All my sex besides, Mr. Dimple—you forgot your *tête-à-tête*[9] with Letitia.

DIMPLE How can you, my lovely angel, cast a thought on that insipid, wry-mouthed, ugly creature!

CHARLOTTE But her fortune may have charms?

DIMPLE Not to a heart like mine. The man who has been blessed with the good opinion of my Charlotte, must despise the allurements of fortune.

CHARLOTTE I am satisfied.

DIMPLE Let us think no more on the odious subject, but devote the present hour to happiness.

CHARLOTTE Can I be happy, when I see the man I prefer going to be married to another?

DIMPLE Have I not already satisfied my charming angel that I can never think of marrying the puling Maria. But, even if it were so, could that be any bar to our happiness; for, as the poet sings—

Love, free as air, at sight of human ties,
Spreads his light wings, and in a moment flies.[1]

Come then, my charming angel! why delay our bliss! The present moment is ours; the next is in the hand of fate. [*Kissing her.*]

8. Warm ale or wine, mixed with bread, sugar, eggs, and spices.
9. Private conversation of two people (French).

1. Lines 75–76 of "Eloisa to Abelard," by the English poet Alexander Pope (1688–1744).

CHARLOTTE Begone, Sir! By your delusions you had almost lulled my honour asleep.

DIMPLE Let me lull the demon to sleep again with kisses. [*He struggles with her; she screams.*]

> [*Enter* MANLY.]

MANLY Turn, villain! and defend yourself.—

> [*Draws.* VAN ROUGH *enters and beats down their swords.*]

VAN ROUGH Is the devil in you? are you going to murder one another? [*Holding* DIMPLE.]

DIMPLE Hold him, hold him,—I can command my passion.

> [*Enter* JONATHAN.]

JONATHAN What are the rattle ails you? Is the old one[2] in you? Let the colonel alone, can't you? I feel chock full of fight,—do you want to kill the colonel?—

MANLY Be still, Jonathan; the gentleman does not want to hurt me.

JONATHAN Gor! I—I wish he did; I'd shew him Yankee boys play, pretty quick—Don't you see you have frightened the young woman into the *hystrikes*?[3]

VAN ROUGH Pray, some of you explain this; what has been the occasion of all this racket?

MANLY That gentleman can explain it to you; it will be a very diverting story for an intended father-in-law to hear.

VAN ROUGH How was this matter, Mr. Van Dumpling?

DIMPLE Sir, upon my honor—all I know is, that I was talking to this young lady, and this gentleman broke in on us, in a very extraordinary manner.

VAN ROUGH Why, all this is nothing to the purpose: can you explain it, Miss? [*To* CHARLOTTE.]

> [*Enter* LETITIA *through the back scene.*[4]]

LETITIA I can explain it to that gentleman's confusion. Though long betrothed to your daughter [*to* VAN ROUGH], yet allured by my fortune, it seems (with shame do I speak it), he has privately paid his addresses to me. I was drawn in to listen to him by his assuring me that the match was made by his father without his consent, and that he proposed to break with Maria, whether he married me or not. But whatever were his intentions respecting your daughter, Sir, even to me he was false; for he has repeated the same story, with some cruel reflections upon my person, to Miss Manly.

JONATHAN What a tarnal curse!

LETITIA Nor is this all, Miss Manly. When he was with me this very morning, he made the same ungenerous reflections upon the weakness of your mind as he has so recently done upon the defects of my person.

JONATHAN What a tarnal curse and damn too!

DIMPLE Ha! since I have lost Letitia, I believe I had as good make it up with Maria—Mr. Van Rough, at present I cannot enter into particulars; but, I believe I can explain everything to your satisfaction in private.

VAN ROUGH There is another matter, Mr. Van Dumpling, which I would have you explain:—pray, Sir, have Messrs. Van Cash and Co. presented you those bills for acceptance?

2. I.e., the devil.
3. Awkward pronunciation of "hysterics."

4. I.e., from the rear of the acting area.

DIMPLE The deuce! Has he heard of those bills! Nay, then, all's up with Maria, too; but an affair of this sort can never prejudice me among the ladies; they will rather long to know what the dear creature possesses to make him so agreeable. [*Aside.*] Sir, you'll hear from me. [*To* MANLY.]

MANLY And you from me, Sir.—

DIMPLE Sir, you wear a sword.—

MANLY Yes, Sir:—This sword was presented to me by that brave Gallic hero, the Marquis De La Fayette.[5] I have drawn it in the service of my country, and in private life, on the only occasion where a man is justified in drawing his sword, in defence of a lady's honor. I have fought too many battles in the service of my country to dread the imputation of cowardice.—Death from a man of honor would be a glory you do not merit; you shall live to bear the insult of man, and the contempt of that sex, whose general smiles afforded you all your happiness.

DIMPLE You won't meet me, Sir?—Then I'll post you[6] a coward.

MANLY I'll venture that, Sir.—The reputation of my life does not depend upon the breath of a Mr. Dimple. I would have you to know, however, Sir, that I have a cane to chastise the insolence of a scoundrel, and a sword and the good laws of my country, to protect me from the attempts of an assassin.—

DIMPLE Mighty well! Very fine, indeed!—ladies and gentlemen, I take my leave, and you will please to observe, in the case of my deportment, the contrast between a gentleman, who has read Chesterfield and received the polish of Europe, and an unpolished, untraveled American. [*Exit.*]
 [*Enter* MARIA.]

MARIA Is he indeed gone?—

LETITIA I hope never to return.

VAN ROUGH I am glad I heard of those bills; though it's plaguy unlucky; I hoped to see Mary married before I died.

MANLY Will you permit a gentleman, Sir, to offer himself as a suitor to your daughter? Though a stranger to you, he is not altogether so to her, or unknown in this city. You may find a son-in-law of more fortune, but you can never meet with one who is richer in love for her, or respect for you.

VAN ROUGH Why, Mary, you have not let this gentleman make love to[7] you without my leave?

MANLY I did not say, Sir—

MARIA Say, Sir!—I—the gentleman, to be sure, met me accidentally.

VAN ROUGH Ha, ha, ha! Mark me, Mary; young folks think old folks to be fools; but old folks know young folks to be fools.—Why, I knew all about this affair:—This was only a cunning way I had to bring it about—Hark ye! I was in the closet when you and he were at our house. [*Turns to the company.*] I heard that little baggage say she loved her old father, and would die to make him happy! Oh! how I loved the little baggage!—And you talked very prudently, young man. I have inquired into your character, and find you to be a man of punctuality and mind the main chance. And so, as you love Mary, and Mary loves you, you shall have my consent

5. French statesman and general (1757–1834) who fought with the Continental Army in 1780 and 1781.

6. I.e., denounce you as.

7. I.e., court.

immediately to be married. I'll settle my fortune on you, and go and live with you the remainder of my life.

MANLY Sir, I hope—

VAN ROUGH Come, come, no fine speeches; mind the main chance, young man, and you and I shall always agree.

LETITIA I sincerely wish you joy [*advancing to* MARIA]; and hope your pardon for my conduct.

MARIA I thank you for your congratulations, and hope we shall at once forget the wretch who has given us so much disquiet, and the trouble that he has occasioned.

CHARLOTTE And I, my dear Maria,—how shall I look up to you for forgiveness? I, who, in the practice of the meanest arts, have violated the most sacred rights of friendship? I can never forgive myself, or hope charity from the world, but I confess I have much to hope from such a brother! and I am happy that I may soon say, such a sister.—

MARIA My dear, you distress me; you have all my love.

MANLY And mine.

CHARLOTTE If repentance can entitle me to forgiveness, I have already much merit; for I despise the littleness of my past conduct. I now find, that the heart of any worthy man cannot be gained by invidious attacks upon the rights and characters of others;—by countenancing the addresses of a thousand;—or that the finest assemblage of features, the greatest taste in dress, the genteelest address, or the most brilliant wit, cannot eventually secure a coquette from contempt and ridicule.

MANLY And I have learned that probity, virtue, honor, though they should not have received the polish of Europe, will secure to an honest American the good graces of his fair countrywoman, and, I hope, the applause of THE PUBLIC.

[*Curtain.*]

1787 1790

HANNAH WEBSTER FOSTER
1758–1840

The development of the American novel lagged behind that of its English counterpart by half a century, with colonists reading works imported from Britain and the Continent. The Revolution inspired nationalistic literary energies, and after 1789—which saw the publication of William Hill Brown's *The Power of Sympathy*, usually considered the first homegrown American novel—several important novelists emerged, including Hill Brown (1765–1793), Hugh Henry Brackenridge (1748–1816), and Susanna Rowson (c. 1762–1824). Most of the pioneering American novels derived from English literary traditions: either the Gothic fiction initiated by

Horace Walpole's *The Castle of Otranto* (1764) or the seduction tale typified by Samuel Richardson's *Clarissa, or, The History of a Young Lady* (1747–48). In the United States, these and other European models lent themselves to new uses as writers sought to examine the implications of the political and social transformations that the Revolution set in motion. These transformations were particularly evident in the fiction of early American women writers such as Hannah Webster Foster.

Foster was born in the seacoast town of Salisbury, Massachusetts. Her father, Grant Webster, was a wealthy merchant whose wife, Hannah Wainwright, died four years after their daughter's birth. Well-educated, probably at one of the female academies that proliferated during this period, Hannah Webster had moved to Boston by her early teens, and there she began writing essays for newspapers and periodicals. In 1785 she married John Foster, a Congregational clergyman who had graduated from Dartmouth College. They settled in Brighton, Massachusetts, south of Boston, where Foster ministered until 1827 and where the couple raised their six children. After John's death in 1829, Hannah moved to Montreal, Canada, to live with her daughters, Harriet Vaughan Cheney and Eliza Lanesford Cushing, both writers themselves.

Foster wrote two novels, *The Coquette; or, The History of Eliza Wharton; A Novel; Founded on Fact. By a Lady of Massachusetts* (1797) and *The Boarding School; or, Lessons of a Preceptress to Her Pupils* (1798). The latter, her lesser-known work, treats female education in a young ladies' academy and consists of the teacher's advice to her students, as well as letters from students to each other where they comment on the effectiveness of her lessons. This work, though interesting for what it suggests about Foster's educational background and for its advocacy of women's education at a time when even elite women had few opportunities for formal schooling, lacks the narrative drive and psychological complexity of her more famous and much reprinted work, *The Coquette*.

Many of Foster's contemporaries distrusted "fiction"—late-eighteenth-century Americans preferred straightforward didactic works based on "true" experiences—and, as her subtitle indicates, Foster responded to this preference for "fact," drawing *The Coquette* at least partly from a sensational event that had preoccupied New Englanders a decade earlier. The basic circumstances of that incident are that Elizabeth Whitman, a well-regarded young woman from Hartford, Connecticut, rejected a number of suitors who did not meet her expectations. She then became enamored of and was seduced by a man who abandoned her when he learned she was pregnant. Whitman traveled alone to a public inn, then lived there until she delivered a stillborn child. Her own death, from complications of the childbirth, followed quickly and made her the subject of countless warnings about the dangers of unchecked passions. Fruitless speculation about the seducer's identity occupied the curious for years, and suspicion fell on a number of prominent citizens, including a grandson of the famed revivalist minister Jonathan Edwards.

The strength of Foster's approach to this episode resides in her attempt to understand how the character she calls Eliza Wharton could have gotten into such a desperate situation. Wharton is not immoral, but she values her independence and fears its loss if she marries. She is attracted to Peter Sanford, a pretentious rake who becomes infatuated with her and, recognizing her weakness in the face of flattery, sets out to add her name to the list of those he has seduced. He lures her with flowery words, apparent wealth, and a relish for living luxuriously, which arouse the suspicions of Wharton's friends but appeal to her own love of pleasure. Wharton's other suitor, the Reverend Boyer, shares many qualities and expectations with her father and her fiancé, both recently deceased. By contrast, Sanford seems fresh and exciting.

Written as an epistolary novel, with Wharton baring her soul to her confidantes and Sanford bragging rudely to a friend, *The Coquette* cuts two ways. It shows how

women of the new nation were prevented from attaining psychological as well as social and intellectual equality in a patriarchal society, even as it counsels middle-class women to give up dreams better suited to an aristocratic way of life. Intelligent, lively, and forthright, Wharton yearns for more than a one-sided contract— marriage—that circumscribes women's ambitions. Her pitiful end is not just a warning against the seducer's wiles but an indictment of cultural norms that, at best, prescribed a subordinate role for women and, at worst, punished women when they did not meet social expectations.

The Coquette; or, The History of Eliza Wharton. A Novel. Founded on Fact. By a Lady of Massachusetts.[1]

Letter I

TO MISS LUCY FREEMAN

NEW-HAVEN

An unusual sensation possesses my breast; a sensation, which I once thought could never pervade it on any occasion whatever. It is *pleasure*; pleasure, my dear Lucy, on leaving my paternal roof! Could you have believed that the darling child of an indulgent and dearly beloved mother would feel a gleam of joy at leaving her? But so it is. The melancholy, the gloom, the condolence, which surrounded me for a month after the death of Mr. Haly, had depressed my spirits, and palled every enjoyment of life. Mr. Haly was a man of worth; a man of real and substantial merit. He is therefore deeply, and justly regretted by *his* friends; he was chosen to be a future guardian, and companion for me, and was, therefore, beloved by *mine*. As their choice; as a good man, and a faithful friend, I esteemed him. But no one acquainted with the disparity of our tempers and dispositions, our views and designs, can suppose my heart much engaged in the alliance. Both nature and education had instilled into my mind an implicit obedience to the will and desires of my parents. To them, of course, I sacrificed my fancy in this affair; determined that my reason should concur with theirs; and on that to risk my future happiness. I was the more encouraged, as I saw, from our first acquaintance, his declining health; and expected, that the event would prove as it has. Think not, however, that I rejoice in his death. No; far be it from me; for though I believe that I never felt the passion of love for Mr. Haly; yet a habit of conversing with him, of hearing daily the most virtuous, tender, and affectionate sentiments from his lips, inspired emotions of the sincerest friendship and esteem.

He is gone. His fate is unalterably, and I trust, happily fixed. He lived the life, and died the death of the righteous. O that my last end may be like his! This event will, I hope, make a suitable and abiding impression upon my mind; teach me the fading nature of all sublunary enjoyments, and the little dependence which is to be placed on earthly felicity. Whose situation was more agreeable; whose prospects more flattering, than Mr. Haly's? Social,

1. The text is from the first edition (1797).

domestic, and connubial joys were fondly anticipated, and friends, and fortune seemed ready to crown every wish! Yet animated by still brighter hopes, he cheerfully bid them all adieu. In conversation with me, but a few days before his exit; "There is" said he, "but one link in the chain of life, undissevered; that, my dear Eliza, is my attachment to you. But God is wise and good in all his ways; and in this, as in all other respects, I would cheerfully say, His will be done."

You, my friend, were witness to the concluding scene; and therefore, I need not describe it.

I shall only add, on the subject, that if I have wisdom and prudence to follow his advice and example; if his prayers for my temporal and eternal welfare be heard and answered, I shall be happy indeed.

The disposition of mind, which I now feel, I wish to cultivate. Calm, placid, and serene; thoughtful of my duty, and benevolent to all around me, I wish for no other connection than that of friendship.

This letter is all egotism. I have even neglected to mention the respectable and happy friends with whom I reside; but will do it in my next. Write soon, and often; and believe me sincerely yours,

ELIZA WHARTON.

Letter II

TO THE SAME

NEW-HAVEN

Time, which effaces every occasional impression, I find gradually dispelling the pleasing pensiveness, which the melancholy event, the subject of my last, had diffused over my mind. Naturally cheerful, volatile, and unreflecting, the opposite disposition, I have found to contain sources of enjoyment, which I was before unconscious of possessing.

My friends, here, are the picture of conjugal felicity. The situation is delightful. The visiting parties perfectly agreeable. Everything tends to facilitate the return of my accustomed vivacity. I have written to my mother, and received an answer. She praises my fortitude, and admires the philosophy which I have exerted, under what she calls, my heavy bereavement. Poor woman! She little thinks that my heart was untouched; and when that is unaffected, other sentiments and passions make but a transient impression. I have been, for a month or two, excluded from the gay world; and, indeed, fancied myself soaring above it. It is now that I begin to descend, and find my natural propensity for mixing in the busy scenes and active pleasures of life returning. I have received your letter; your moral lecture rather; and be assured, my dear, your monitorial lessons and advice shall be attended to. I believe I shall never again resume those airs, which you term *coquettish*, but which I think deserve a softer appellation; as they proceed from an innocent heart, and are the effusions of a youthful, and cheerful mind. We are all invited to spend the day, tomorrow, at Col. Farington's, who has an elegant seat in this neighborhood. Both he and his Lady are strangers to me; but the friends, by whom I am introduced, will procure me a welcome reception. Adieu.

ELIZA WHARTON.

Letter III

TO THE SAME

NEW-HAVEN

Is it time for me to talk again of conquests? or must I only enjoy them in silence? I must write to you the impulses of my mind; or I must not write at all. You are not so morose, as to wish me to become a nun, would our country and religion allow it. I ventured yesterday to throw aside the habiliments of mourning, and to array myself in those more adapted to my taste. We arrived at Col. Farington's about one o'clock. The Col. handed me out of the carriage, and introduced me to a large company assembled in the hall. My name was pronounced with an *emphasis*; and I was received with the most flattering tokens of respect. When we were summoned to dinner, a young gentleman in a clerical dress offered me his hand, and led me to a table furnished with an elegant and sumptuous repast, with more gallantry and address than commonly fall to the share of students. He sat opposite me at table; and whenever I raised my eye, it caught his. The ease and politeness of his manners, with his particular attention to me, raised my curiosity, and induced me to ask Mrs. Laiton who he was? She told me that his name was Boyer; that he was descended from a worthy family; had passed with honor and applause through the university where he was educated; had since studied divinity with success; and now had a call to settle as a minister in one of the first parishes in a neighbouring state.

The gates of a spacious garden were thrown open, at this instant; and I accepted with avidity an invitation to walk in it. Mirth and hilarity prevailed, and the moments fled on downy wings; while we traced the beauties of art and nature, so liberally displayed, and so happily blended in this delightful retreat. An enthusiastic admirer of scenes like these, I had rambled some way from the company, when I was followed by Mrs. Laiton to offer her condolence on the supposed loss, which I had sustained, in the death of Mr. Haly. My heart rose against the woman, so ignorant of human nature, as to think such conversation acceptable at such a time. I made her little reply, and waved[2] the subject, though I could not immediately dispel the gloom which it excited.

The absurdity of a custom, authorizing people at a first interview to revive the idea of griefs, which time has lulled; perhaps obliterated, is intolerable. To have our enjoyments arrested by the empty compliments of unthinking persons, for no other reason, than a compliance with fashion is to be treated in a manner, which the laws of humanity forbid.

We were soon joined by the gentlemen, who each selected his partner, and the walk was prolonged.

Mr. Boyer offered me his arm, which I gladly accepted; happy to be relieved from the impertinence of my female companion. We returned to tea, after which the ladies sung and played by turns on the Piano Forte; while some of the gentlemen accompanied with the flute, the clarinet, and the violin, forming in the whole a very decent concert. An elegant supper, and half an hour's conversation after it, closed the evening; when we returned home,

2. Dismissed.

delighted with our entertainment and pleased with ourselves and each other. My imagination is so impressed with the festive scenes of the day, that Morpheus[3] waves his ebon-wand in vain. The evening is fine beyond the power of description! All nature is serene and harmonious; in perfect unison with my present disposition of mind. I have been taking a retrospect of my past life; and a few juvenile follies excepted, which I trust the recording angel has blotted out with the tear of charity, find an approving conscience, and a heart at ease. Fortune, indeed, has not been very liberal of her gifts to me; but I presume on a large stock in the bank of friendship, which, united with health and innocence, give me some pleasing anticipations of future felicity.

Whatever my fate may be, I shall always continue your

ELIZA WHARTON.

Letter IV

TO MR. SELBY

NEW-HAVEN

You ask me, my friend, whether I am in pursuit of truth, or a lady? I answer, both. I hope and trust they are united; and really expect to find truth and the virtues and graces besides in a fair form. If you mean by the first part of your question, whether I am searching into the sublimer doctrines of religion? To these I would by no means be inattentive; but to be honest my studies of that kind have been very much interrupted of late. The respectable circle of acquaintances with which I am honored here, has rendered my visits very frequent and numerous. In one of these I was introduced to Miss Eliza Wharton; a young lady whose elegant person, accomplished mind, and polished manners have been much celebrated. Her fame has often reached me; but, as the queen of Sheba said to Solomon, the half was not told me.[4] You will think, that I talk in the style of a lover. I confess it, nor am I ashamed to rank myself among the professed admirers of this lovely fair one. I am in no danger, however, of becoming an enthusiastic devotee. No, I mean to act upon just and rational principles. Expecting soon to settle in an eligible situation, if such a companion as I am persuaded she will make me, may fall to my lot, I shall deem myself as happy as this state of imperfection will admit. She is now resident at Gen. Richman's. The general and his lady are her particular friends. They are warm in her praises. They tell me, however, that she is naturally of a gay disposition. No matter for that; it is an agreeable quality, where there is discretion sufficient for its regulation. A cheerful friend, much more a cheerful wife is peculiarly necessary to a person of a studious and sedentary life. They dispel the gloom of retirement, and exhilarate the spirits depressed by intense application. She was formerly addressed by the late Mr. Haly of Boston. He was not, it seems, the man of her choice; but her parents were extremely partial to him, and wished the connection to take place. She, like a dutiful child, sacrificed her own inclination to their

3. In Greek mythology, the god of sleep and dreams.
4. See 1 Kings 10. The Queen of Sheba had heard of Solomon's wisdom, and when she met him, she asked him many questions, all of which he answered. Hence she was impressed and spoke these words to indicate that she had not been told how wise he really was.

pleasure, so far as to acquiesce in his visits. This she more easily accomplished, as his health, which declined from their first acquaintance, led her to suppose, as the event has proved, that he would not live to enter into any lasting engagements. Her father, who died some months before him, invited him to reside at his house, for the benefit of a change of air, agreeably to the advice of his physicians. She attended him during his last illness, with all the care and assiduity of a nurse; and with all the sympathizing tenderness of a sister.

I have had several opportunities of conversing with her. She discovers[5] an elevated mind, a ready apprehension, and an accurate knowledge of the various subjects which have been brought into view. I have not yet introduced the favorite subject of my heart. Indeed she seems studiously to avoid noticing any expression which leads towards it. But she must hear it soon. I am sure of the favor and interest of the friends with whom she resides. They have promised to speak previously in my behalf. I am to call as if accidentally this afternoon, just as they are to ride abroad. They are to refer me to Miss Wharton for entertainment, till their return. What a delightful opportunity for my purpose! I am counting the hours, nay, the very moments. Adieu. You shall soon hear again from your most obedient,

J. BOYER.

Letter V

TO MISS LUCY FREEMAN

NEW-HAVEN

These bewitching charms of mine have a tendency to keep my mind in a state of perturbation. I am so pestered with these admirers; not that I am so very handsome neither; but I don't know how it is, I am certainly very much the taste of the other sex. Followed, flattered, and caressed, I have cards and compliments in profusion. But I must try to be serious; for I have, alas! one serious lover. As I promised you to be particular in my writing, I suppose I must proceed methodically. Yesterday we had a party to dine. Mr. Boyer was of the number. His attention was immediately engrossed; and I soon perceived that every word, every action, and every look was studied to gain my approbation. As he sat next me at dinner, his assiduity and politeness were pleasing; and as we walked together afterwards, his conversation was improving. Mine was sentimental and sedate; perfectly adapted to the taste of my gallant. Nothing, however, was said particularly expressive of his apparent wishes. I studiously avoided every kind of discourse which might lead to this topic. I wish not for a declaration from anyone, especially from one whom I could not repulse and do not intend to encourage at present. His conversation, so similar to what I had often heard from a similar character, brought a deceased friend to mind, and rendered me somewhat pensive. I retired directly after supper. Mr. Boyer had just taken leave.

Mrs. Richman came into my chamber as she was passing to her own. Excuse my intrusion, Eliza, said she; I thought I would just step in and ask you if you have passed a pleasant day?

5. Reveals.

Perfectly so, madam; and I have now retired to protract the enjoyment by recollection. What, my dear, is your opinion of our favorite Mr. Boyer? Declaring him your favorite, madam, is sufficient to render me partial to him. But to be frank, independent of that, I think him an agreeable man. Your heart, I presume, is now free? Yes, and I hope it will long remain so. Your friends, my dear, solicitous for your welfare, wish to see you suitably and agreeably connected. I hope my friends will never again interpose in my concerns of that nature. You, madam, who have ever known my heart, are sensible, that had the Almighty spared life, in a certain instance, I must have sacrificed my own happiness, or incurred their censure. I am young, gay, volatile. A melancholy event has lately extricated me from those shackles, which parental authority had imposed on my mind. Let me then enjoy that freedom which I so highly prize. Let me have opportunity, unbiassed by opinion, to gratify my natural disposition in a participation of those pleasures which youth and innocence afford. Of such pleasures, no one, my dear, would wish to deprive you. But beware, Eliza!—Though strowed[6] with flowers, when contemplated by your lively imagination, it is, after all, a slippery, thorny path. The round of fashionable dissipation is dangerous. A phantom is often pursued, which leaves its deluded votary the real form of wretchedness. She spoke with an emphasis, and taking up her candle, wished me a good night. I had not power to return the compliment. Something seemingly prophetic in her looks and expressions cast a momentary gloom upon my mind! But I despise those contracted ideas which confine virtue to a cell. I have no notion of becoming a recluse. Mrs. Richman has ever been a beloved friend of mine; yet I always thought her rather prudish. Adieu,

<div align="right">ELIZA WHARTON.</div>

<div align="center">

Letter VI

TO THE SAME

</div>

<div align="right">*NEW-HAVEN*</div>

I had scarcely seated myself at the breakfast table this morning, when a servant entered with a card of invitation from Major Sanford, requesting the happiness of my hand this evening, at a ball, given by Mr. Atkins, about three miles from this. I showed the billet to Mrs. Richman, saying, I have not much acquaintance with this gentleman, madam; but I suppose his character sufficiently respectable to warrant an affirmative answer. He is a gay man, my dear, to say no more, and such are the companions we wish, when we join a party avowedly formed for pleasure. I then stepped into my apartment, wrote an answer, and dispatched the servant. When I returned to the parlour, something disapprobating appeared in the countenances of both my friends. I endeavored without seeming to observe, to dissipate it by chit chat; but they were better pleased with each other than with me; and soon rising, walked into the garden, and left me to amuse myself alone. My eyes followed them through the window. Happy pair, said I. Should it ever

6. Strewn.

be my fate to wear the hymenial chain,[7] may I be thus united! The purest and most ardent affection, the greatest consonance of taste and disposition, and the most congenial virtue and wishes distinguish this lovely couple. Health and wealth with every attendant blessing preside over their favored dwelling, and shed their benign influence without alloy. The consciousness of exciting their displeasure gave me pain; but I consoled myself with the idea that it was ill founded.

They should consider, said I, that they have no satisfaction to look for beyond each other.

There every enjoyment is centered; but I am a poor solitary being, who needs some amusement beyond what I can supply myself. The mind, after being confined at home for a while, sends the imagination abroad in quest of new treasures, and the body may as well accompany it, for ought I can see.

General Richman and lady have ever appeared solicitous to promote my happiness since I have resided with them. They have urged my acceptance of invitations to join parties, though they have not been much themselves, of late; as Mrs. Richman's present circumstances render her fond of retirement. What reason can be assigned for their apparent reluctance to this evening's entertainment is to me incomprehensible; but I shall apply the chemical powers of friendship, and extract the secret from Mrs. Richman tomorrow if not before. Adieu. I am now summoned to dinner, and after that shall be engaged in preparation till the wished for hour of hilarity and mirth engrosses every faculty of your

ELIZA WHARTON.

Letter VII

TO MR. SELBY

NEW-HAVEN

Divines need not declaim, nor philosophers expatiate on the disappointments of human life! Are they not legibly written on every page of our existence? Are they not predominantly prevalent over every period of our lives?

When I closed my last letter to you, my heart exulted in the pleasing anticipation of promised bliss; my wishes danced on the light breezes of hope, and my imagination dared to arrest the attention, and even claim a return of affection from the lovely Eliza Wharton! But imagination only, it has proved; and that dashed with the bitter ranklings of jealousy and suspicion.

But to resume my narrative. I reached the mansion of my friend about four. I was disagreeably struck with the appearance of a carriage at the door, as it raised an idea of company which might frustrate my plan; but still more disagreeable were my sensations, when, on entering the parlour, I found Major Sanford evidently in a waiting posture. I was very politely received; and when Eliza entered the room with a brilliance of appearance and gaiety of manner, which I had never before connected with her character, I rose, as did Major Sanford who offered his hand, and led her to a chair. I forgot to sit down again, but stood transfixed by the pangs of disappointment. Miss Whar-

7. I.e., to enter the marital bond. In Greek mythology, Hymen is the god of marriage.

ton appeared somewhat confused; but soon resuming her vivacity, desired me to be seated; inquired after my health, and made some commonplace remarks on the weather. Then apologizing for leaving me, gave her hand again to Major Sanford, who had previously risen, and reminded her that the time and their engagements made it necessary to leave the good company; which, indeed, they both appeared very willing to do. General Richman and lady took every method in their power to remove my chagrin, and atone for the absence of my fair one, but ill did they succeed. They told me that Miss Wharton had not the most distant idea of my visiting there, this afternoon; much less of the design of my visit; that for some months together, she had been lately confined by the sickness of Mr. Haly, whom she attended during the whole of his last illness; which confinement had eventually increased her desire of indulging her natural disposition for gaiety. She had, however, they said, an excellent heart and reflecting mind, a great share of sensibility, and a temper peculiarly formed for the enjoyments of social life. But this gentleman, madam, who is her gallant this evening—is his character unexceptionable? Will a lady of delicacy associate with an immoral, not to say profligate man? The rank and fortune of Major Sanford, said Mrs. Richman, procure him respect.

His specious manners render him acceptable in public company; but I must own that he is not the person with whom I wish my cousin to be connected, even for a moment. She never consulted me so little on any subject as on that of his card this morning. Before I had time to object, she dismissed the servant; and I forbore to destroy her expected happiness, by acquainting her with my disapprobation of her partner. Her omission was not design; it was juvenile indiscretion. We must, my dear sir, continued she, look with a candid eye on such eccentricities. Faults, not foibles, require the severity of censure. Far, madam, be it from me to censure any conduct, which as yet I have observed in Miss Wharton; she has too great an interest in my heart to admit of that.

We now went into more general conversation. Tea was served; and I soon after took leave. General Richman, however, insisted on my dining with him on Thursday, which I promised. And here I am again over head and ears in the hypo.[8] A disease, you will say, peculiar to students. I believe it peculiar to lovers; and with that class I must now rank myself, though I did not know, until this evening, that I was so much engaged as I find I really am. I knew, indeed, that I was extremely pleased with this amiable girl; that I was interested in her favor; that I was happier in her company than anywhere else, with innumerable other circumstances, which would have told me the truth, had I examined them. But be that as it may; I hope, and trust that I am, and ever shall be a reasonable creature; and not suffer my judgment to be misled by the operations of a blind passion.

I shall now lay aside this subject, endeavor to divest even my imagination of the charmer, and return until Thursday, to the contemplation of those truths and duties, which have a happy tendency to calm the jarring elements which compose our mortal frame. Adieu.

<div style="text-align:right">J. BOYER.</div>

8. In a depressed state ("hypo" being Greek for "down").

Letter VIII

TO MR. CHARLES DEIGHTON

NEW-HAVEN

We had an elegant ball, last night, Charles; and what is still more to the taste of your old friend, I had an elegant partner; one exactly calculated to please my fancy; gay, volatile, apparently thoughtless of everything but present enjoyment. It was Miss Eliza Wharton, a young lady, whose agreeable person, polished manners, and refined talents have rendered her the toast of the country around for these two years; though for half that time she has had a clerical lover imposed on her by her friends; for I am told it was not agreeable to her inclination. By this same clerical lover of hers, she was for several months confined as a nurse. But his death has happily relieved her, and she now returns to the world with redoubled luster. At present she is a visitor to Mrs. Richman, who is a relation. I first saw her on a party of pleasure at Mr. Frazier's where we walked, talked, sung, and danced together. I thought her cousin watched her with a jealous eye; for she is, you must know, a prude and immaculate, more so than you or I must be the man who claims admission to her society. But I fancy this young lady is a coquette; and if so, I shall avenge my sex, by retaliating the mischiefs she meditates against us. Not that I have any ill designs; but only to play off her own artillery, by using a little unmeaning[9] gallantry. And let her beware of the consequences. A young clergyman came in at Gen. Richman's yesterday, while I was waiting for Eliza, who was much more cordially received by the general and his lady, than was your humble servant: but I lay that up.

When she entered the room, an air of mutual embarrassment was evident. The lady recovered her assurance much more easily than the gentleman. I am just going to ride, and shall make it in my way to call and inquire after the health of my dulcinea.[1] Therefore, adieu for the present.

PETER SANFORD.

Letter IX

TO MISS LUCY FREEMAN

NEW-HAVEN

I am not so happy today in the recollection of last evening's entertainment, as I was in the enjoyment.

The explanation which I promised you from Mrs. Richman yesterday, I could not obtain. When I went down to dinner, some friends of General Richman's had accidentally dropped in, which precluded all particular conversation. I retired soon to dress, and saw Mrs. Richman no more, till I was informed that Major Sanford waited for me. But I was surprised on going into the parlour to find Mr. Boyer there. I blushed and stammered; but I know not why; for certain I am, that I neither love nor fear the good man yet, whatever I may do some future day. I would not be understood

9. Insincere.
1. In the novel *Don Quixote* (1605), by the Spanish writer Miguel de Cervantes (1547–1616), the title character calls the woman he loves Dulcinea.

that I do not respect and esteem him; for I do both. But these are calm passions, which soothe rather than agitate the mind. It was not the consciousness of any impropriety of conduct, for I was far from feeling any. The entertainment for which I was prepared was such as virtue would not disapprove, and my gallant was a man of fortune, fashion, and for ought I knew, of unblemished character.

But Mr. Boyer was much more disconcerted than myself. Indeed he did not recover his philosophy while I stayed. I believe, by some hints I have received since, that he had some particular views, in which he was disappointed.

Our ball had every charm which could render a ball delightful. My partner was all ease, politeness, and attention; and your friend was as much flattered and caressed as variety itself could wish. We returned to General Richman's about two. Major Sanford asked leave to call and inquire after my health, this morning, and I am now expecting him. I rose to breakfast. The late hour of retiring to rest had not depressed, but rather exhilarated my spirits. My friends were waiting for me in the parlor. They received me sociably, inquired after my health, my last evening's entertainment, the company, &c. When, after a little pause, Mrs. Richman said, and how do you like Major Sanford, Eliza? Very well indeed, madam: I think him a finished gentleman. Will you, who are a connoisieur, allow him that title? No, my dear: in my opinion, he falls far below it; since he is deficient in one of the great essentials of the character, and that is, *virtue*. I am surprised, said I: but how has he incurred so severe a censure? By being a professed libertine; by having but too successfully practised the arts of seduction; by triumphing in the destruction of innocence and the peace of families!

O, why was I not informed of this before? But, perhaps these are old affairs; the effects of juvenile folly; crimes of which he may have repented, and which charity ought to obliterate. No, my dear, they are recent facts; facts which he dares not deny; facts for which he ought to be banished from all virtuous society. I should have intimated this to you before, but your precipitate acceptance of his invitation deprived me of an opportunity, until it was too late to prevent your going with him; and we thought it best to protract your enjoyment as long as possible, not doubting but your virtues and delicacy would, in future, guard you against the like deception.

Must I then become an avowed prude at once and refuse him admission, if he call, in compliance with the customary forms? By no means. I am sensible, that even the false maxims[2] of the world must be complied with in a degree. But a man of Major Sanford's art can easily distinguish between a forbidding and an encouraging reception. The former may, in this case, be given without any breach of the rules of politeness. Astonished and mortified, I knew not what further to say. I had been so pleased with the man, that I wished to plead in his favor; but virtue and prudence forbade. I therefore rose and retired. He is this moment, I am told, below stairs.[3] So that I must bid you adieu, until the next post.

<div align="right">ELIZA WHARTON</div>

2. Rules of conduct. 3. I.e., downstairs.

Letter X

TO THE SAME

NEW-HAVEN

Upon closing my last, I walked down, and found Major Sanford alone. He met me at the door of the parlor; and taking my hand with an air of affectionate tenderness, led me to a seat, and took one beside me. I believe the gloom of suspicion had not entirely forsaken my brow. He appeared, however, not to notice it; but after the compliments of the day had passed, entered into an easy and agreeable conversation on the pleasures of society: a conversation perfectly adapted to my taste, and calculated to dissipate my chagrin, and pass the time imperceptibly. He inquired the place of my native abode; and having informed him, he said he had thoughts of purchasing the seat of Capt. Pribble, in that neighborhood, for his residence; and could he be assured of my society and friendship, his resolution would be fixed. I answered his compliment only by a slight bow. He took leave, and I retired to dress for the day, being engaged to accompany my cousin to dine at Mr. Laurence's, a gentleman of fortune and fashion, in this vicinity. Mr. Laurence has but one daughter, heiress to a large estate, with an agreeable form, but a countenance, which to me, indicates not much soul. I was surprised in the afternoon to see Major Sanford alight at the gate. He entered with the familiarity of an old acquaintance; and, after accosting each of the company, told me, with a low bow, that he did not expect the happiness of seeing me again so soon. I received his compliment with a conscious awkwardness. Mrs. Richman's morning lecture still rung in my head; and her watchful eye now traced every turn of mine, and every action of the major's. Indeed, his assiduity was painful to me; yet I found it impossible to disengage myself a moment from him, till the close of the day brought our carriage to the door; when he handed me in, and pressing my hand to his lips, retired.

What shall I say about this extraordinary man? Shall I own to you, my friend, that he is pleasing to me? His person, his manners, his situation, all combine to charm my fancy; and to my lively imagination, strew the path of life with flowers. What a pity, my dear Lucy, that the graces and virtues are not oftner united! They must, however, meet in the man of my choice; and till I find such a one, I shall continue to subscribe my name

ELIZA WHARTON.

Letter XI

TO MR. CHARLES DEIGHTON

NEW-HAVEN

Well, Charles, I have been maneuvring today, a little revengefully. That, you will say, is out of character. So baleful a passion does not easily find admission among those softer ones, which you well know I cherish. However, I am a mere Proteus,[4] and can assume any shape that will best answer my purpose.

4. In Greek mythology, a sea god who could change his shape at will.

I called this forenoon, as I told you I intended, at Gen. Richman's. I waited some time in the parlor alone, before Eliza appeared; and when she did appear, the distant reserve of her manners and the pensiveness of her countenance convinced me that she had been vexed, and I doubted not but Peter Sanford was the occasion. Her wise cousin, I could have sworn, had been giving her a detail of the vices of her gallant; and warning her against the danger of associating with him in future. Notwithstanding, I took no notice of any alteration in her behavior; but entered with the utmost facetiousness into a conversation which I thought most to her taste. By degrees, she assumed her usual vivacity; cheerfulness and good humor again animated her countenance. I tarried as long as decency would admit. She having intimated that they were to dine at my friend Lawrence's, I caught at this information; and determined to follow them, and tease the jealous Mrs. Richman, by playing off all the gallantry I was master of in her presence.

I went, and succeeded to the utmost of my wishes, as I read in the vexation, visible in the one; and the ease and attention displayed by the other. I believe too, that I have charmed the eye at least, of the amiable Eliza. Indeed, Charles, she is a fine girl. I think it would hurt my conscience to wound her mind or reputation. Were I disposed to marry, I am persuaded she would make an excellent wife; but that you know is no part of my plan, so long as I can keep out of the noose. Whenever I do submit to be shackled, it must be from a necessity of mending my fortune. This girl would be far from doing that. However, I am pleased with her acquaintance, and mean not to abuse her credulity and good nature, if I can help it.

PETER SANFORD.

Letter XII

TO MISS LUCY FREEMAN

NEW-HAVEN

The heart of your friend is again besieged. Whether it will surrender to the assailants or not, I am unable at present to determine. Sometimes I think of becoming a predestinarian, and submitting implicitly to fate, without any exercise of free will; but, as mine seems to be a wayward one, I would counteract the operations of it, if possible.

Mrs. Richman told me this morning, that she hoped I should be as agreeably entertained this afternoon, as I had been the preceding; that she expected Mr. Boyer to dine, and take tea; and doubted not but he would be as attentive and sincere to me, if not as gay and polite as the gentleman who obtruded his civilities yesterday. I replied that I had no reason to doubt the sincerity of the one, or the other, having never put them to the test, nor did I imagine I ever should. Your friends, Eliza, said she, would be very happy to see you united to a man of Mr. Boyer's worth; and so agreeably settled, as he has a prospect of being. I hope, said I, that my friends are not so weary of my company, as to wish to dispose of me. I am too happy in my present connections to quit them for new ones. Marriage is the tomb of friendship. It appears to me a very selfish state. Why do people, in general, as soon as they are married, center all their cares, their concerns, and pleasures in

their own families? Former acquaintances are neglected or forgotten. The tenderest ties between friends are weakened or dissolved; and benevolence itself moves in a very limited sphere. It is the glory of the marriage state, she rejoined, to refine, by circumscribing our enjoyments. Here we can repose in safety.

> "The friendships of the world are oft
> Confed'racies in vice, or leagues in pleasure:
> Our's has the purest virtue for its basis;
> And such a friendship ends not but with life."[5]

True, we cannot always pay that attention to former associates, which we may wish; but the little community which we superintend is quite as important an object; and certainly renders us more beneficial to the public. True benevolence, though it may change its objects, is not limited by time or place. Its effects are the same, and aided by a second self, are rendered more diffusive and salutary.

Some pleasantry passed, and we retired to dress. When summoned to dinner, I found Mr. Boyer below. If what is sometimes said be true, that love is diffident, reserved, and unassuming, this man must be tinctured with it. These symptoms were visible in his deportment when I entered the room. However, he soon recovered himself, and the conversation took a general turn. The festive board was crowned with sociability, and we found in reality, "The feast of reason, and the flow of soul."[6] After we rose from table, a walk in the garden was proposed, an amusement we are all peculiarly fond of. Mr. Boyer offered me his arm. When at a sufficient distance from our company, he begged leave to congratulate himself on having an opportunity which he had ardently desired for some time, of declaring to me his attachment; and of soliciting an interest in my favor; or, if he might be allowed the term, affection. I replied, that, sir, is indeed laying claim to an important interest. I believe you must substitute some more indifferent epithet for the present. Well then, said he, if it must be so, let it be esteem or friendship. Indeed, sir, said I, you are entitled to them both. Merit has always a share in that bank; and I know of none, who has a larger claim on that score, than Mr. Boyer. I suppose my manner was hardly serious enough for what he considered a weighty cause. He was a little disconcerted; but soon regaining his presence of mind, entreated me, with an air of earnestness, to encourage his suit, to admit his addresses, and, if possible, to reward his love. I told him, that this was rather a sudden affair to me; and that I could not answer him without consideration. Well then, said he, take what time you think proper, only relieve my suspense, as soon as may be. Shall I visit you again tomorrow? O, not so soon, said I. Next Monday, I believe will be early enough. I will endeavor to be at home. He thanked me even for that favor, recommended himself once more to my kindness; and we walked towards the company, returned with them to the house, and he soon took leave. I immediately retired to write this letter, which I shall close, without a single observation on the subject, until I know your opinion.

ELIZA WHARTON

5. Lines from the tragedy *Cato* (1712), by the English writer Joseph Addison (1672–1719).
6. Line 130 of "The First Satire of the Second Book of Horace" (1733), by the English poet Alexander Pope (1688–1744).

Letter XIII

HARTFORD

And so you wish to have my opinion before you know the result of your own. This is playing a little too much with my patience. But, however, I will gratify you this once, in hopes that my epistle may have a good effect. You will ask, perhaps, whether I would influence your judgment? I answer, no; provided you will exercise it yourself: but I am a little apprehensive that your fancy will mislead you. Methinks I can gather from your letters, a predilection for this Major Sanford. But he is a rake, my dear friend; and can a lady of your delicacy and refinement think of forming a connection with a man of that character? I hope not. Nay, I am confident you do not. You mean only to exhibit a few more girlish airs, before you turn matron. But I am persuaded, if you wish to lead down the dance of life with regularity, you will not find a more excellent partner than Mr. Boyer. Whatever you can reasonably expect in a lover, husband, or friend, you may perceive to be united in this worthy man. His taste is undebauched, his manners not vitiated, his morals uncorrupted. His situation in life is, perhaps, as elevated as you have a right to claim. Forgive my plainness, Eliza. It is the task of friendship, sometimes to tell disagreeable truths. I know your ambition is to make a distinguished figure in the first class of polished society, to shine in the gay circle of fashionable amusements, and to bear off the palm amidst the votaries of pleasure. But these are fading honors, unsatisfactory enjoyments; incapable of gratifying those immortal principles of reason and religion, which have been implanted in your mind by nature; assiduously cultivated by the best of parents, and exerted, I trust, by yourself. Let me advise you then, in conducting this affair; an affair, big, perhaps, with your future fate, to lay aside those coquettish airs which you sometimes put on; and remember that you are not dealing with a fop, who will take advantage of every concession; but with a man of sense and honor, who will properly estimate your condescension and frankness. Act then with that modest freedom, that dignified unreserve which bespeaks conscious rectitude and sincerity of heart.

I shall be extremely anxious to hear the process and progress of this business. Relieve my impatience, as soon as possible, and believe me yours, with undissembled affection.

LUCY FREEMAN.

Letter XIV

NEW-HAVEN

I have received, and read again and again, your friendly epistle. My reason and judgment entirely coincide with your opinion; but my fancy claims some share in the decision: and I cannot yet tell which will preponderate. This was the day fixed for deciding Mr. Boyer's cause. My friends here gave me a long dissertation on his merits. Your letter, likewise, had its weight, and I was candidly summing up the *pros* and *cons* in the garden, whither I

had walked (Gen. Richman and lady having rode out) when I was informed that he was waiting in the parlor. I went immediately in (a good symptom, you will say) and received him very graciously. After the first compliments were over, he seemed eager to improve the opportunity to enter directly on the subject of his present visit. It is needless for me to recite to you, who have long been acquainted with the whole process of courtship, the declarations, propositions, protestations, entreaties, looks, words and actions of a lover. They are, I believe, much the same, in the whole sex, allowing for their different dispositions, educations, and characters. But you are impatient I know for the conclusion. You have hastily perused the preceding lines, and are straining your eye forward to my part of the farce; for such it may prove after all. Well then, not to play too long with the curiosity, which I know to be excited, and actuated by real friendship, I will relieve it. I think you would have been pleased to have seen my gravity, on this important occasion. With all the candor and frankness which I was capable of assuming, I thus answered his long harangue, to which I had listened, without interrupting him. Self-knowledge, sir, that most important of all sciences, I have yet to learn. Such have been my situations in life, and the natural volatility of my temper, that I have looked but little into my own heart, in regard to its future wishes and views. From a scene of constraint and confinement, ill suited to my years and inclination, I have just launched into society. My heart beats high in expectation of its fancied joys. My sanguine imagination paints, in alluring colors, the charms of youth and freedom, regulated by virtue and innocence. Of these, I wish to partake. While I own myself under obligations for the esteem which you are pleased to profess for me, and in return, acknowledge, that neither your person nor manners are disagreeable to me, I recoil at the thought of immediately forming a connection, which must confine me to the duties of domestic life, and make me dependent for happiness, perhaps too, for subsistence, upon a class of people, who will claim the right of scrutinizing every part of my conduct; and by censuring those foibles, which I am conscious of not having prudence to avoid, may render me completely miserable. While, therefore, I receive your visits, and cultivate towards you sentiments of friendship and esteem, I would not have you consider me as consigned to your society, or obligated to a future connection. Our short acquaintance renders it impossible for me to decide what the operations of my mind may hereafter be. You must either quit the subject, or leave me to the exercise of my free will, which perhaps may coincide with your present wishes. Madam, said he, far is the wish from me to restrain your person or mind. In your breast I will repose my cause. It shall be my study to merit a return of affection; and I doubt not, but generosity and honor will influence your conduct towards me. I expect soon to settle among a generous and enlightened people, where I flatter myself I shall be exempt from those difficulties, and embarrassments, to which too many of my brethren are subject. The local situation is agreeable, the society refined and polished; and if, in addition, I may obtain that felicity which you are formed to bestow, in a family connection, I shall be happy indeed.

He spoke with emphasis. The tear of sensibility sparkled in his eye. I involuntarily gave him my hand, which he pressed with ardor to his lips. Then rising, he walked to the window to conceal his emotion. I rang the bell and ordered tea; during and after which, we shared that social converse, which

is the true zest of life, and which, I am persuaded, none but virtuous minds can participate. General Richman and lady returned with the shades of the evening. The penetrating eye of my cousin traced in *our* countenances the progress of the cause, and the smile of approbation animated *hers*. Mr. Boyer asked the favor of my company to ride tomorrow morning, which was granted. He tarried to supper, and took his leave. I retired immediately to my chamber, to which I was followed by Mrs. Richman. I related to her the conversation, and the encouragement which I had given to Mr. Boyer. She was pleased but insisted that I should own myself somewhat engaged to him. This, I told her I should never do to any man, before the indissoluble knot was tied. That, said I, will be time enough to resign my freedom. She replied that I had wrong ideas of freedom and matrimony; but she hoped that Mr. Boyer would happily rectify them.

I have now, my dear friend, given you an account of my present situation, and leave you to judge for yourself concerning it. Write me your opinion, and believe me ever yours.

<div align="right">Eliza Wharton.</div>

<div align="center">*Letter XV*</div>

<div align="center">TO MISS ELIZA WHARTON</div>

<div align="right">Hartford</div>

I congratulate you, my dear Eliza, on the stability of your conduct towards Mr. Boyer. Pursue the system which you have adopted, and I dare say, that happiness will crown your future days. You are indeed very tenacious of your freedom, as you call it; but that is a play about words. A man of Mr. Boyer's honor and good sense will never abridge any privileges which virtue can claim.

When do you return to embellish our society, here? I am impatient to see you, and likewise this amiable man. I am much interested in his favor. By the way, I am told that Major Sanford has been to look at the seat of Captain Pribble, which is upon sale. It is reported that he will probably purchase it. Many of our gentry are pleased with the prospect of such a neighbor. As an accomplished gentleman, say they, he will be an agreeable addition to our social parties; and as a man of property and public spirit, he will be an advantage to the town; but, from what I have heard of him, I am far from supposing him a desirable acquisition in either of these respects. A man of a vicious character cannot be a good member of society. In order to that, his principles and practice must be uncorrupted: in his morals, at least, he must be a man of probity and honor. Of these qualifications, if I mistake not, this gallant of yours cannot boast. But I shall not set up for a censor. I hope neither you nor I shall have much connection with him. My swain interests himself very much in your affairs. You will possibly think him impertinent; but I give his curiosity a softer name. Should I own to you that I place great confidence in his integrity and honor, you would, perhaps, laugh at my weakness; but, my dear, I have pride enough to keep me above coquetry, or prudery; and discretion enough, I hope, to secure me from the errors of both. With him I have determined to walk the future round of life. What folly then would it be to affect reserve and distance, relative to an affair in which I have so much interest?

Not that I am going to betray your secrets. These I have no right to divulge; but I must be the judge what may and what may not be communicated. I am very much pressed for an early day of consummation; but I shall not listen to a request of that kind, till your return. Such is my regard for you, that a union of love would be imperfect, if friendship attended not the rites. Adieu.

<div align="right">LUCY FREEMAN.</div>

Letter XVI

TO MISS LUCY FREEMAN

<div align="right">NEW-HAVEN</div>

We go on charmingly here; almost as soft and smooth as your ladyship. It seems to me that love must stagnate, if it have not a light breeze of discord once in a while to keep it in motion. We have not tried any yet, however. We had a lovely tour this forenoon, were out three long hours, and returned to dinner in perfect harmony.

Mr. Boyer informed me that he should set out tomorrow morning, for his future residence, and soon put on the sacred bands.[7] He solicited an epistolary correspondence, at the same time, as an alleviation of the care which that weighty charge would bring on his mind. I consented; telling him, that he must not expect anything more than general subjects from me.

We were somewhat interrupted in our confidential intercourse, in the afternoon, by the arrival of Major Sanford. I cannot say that I was not agreeably relieved. So sweet a repast, for several hours together, was rather sickening to my taste. My enamorato[8] looked a little mortified at the cheerful reception which I gave the intruder, and joined not so placidly in the social conversation, as I could have wished.

When Mr. Boyer, after the Major took leave, pressed me to give him some assurance of my constancy, I only reminded him of the terms of our engagement. Seeing me decided, he was silent on the subject, and soon bid me an affectionate adieu; not expecting, as he told me, the pleasure of a personal interview again, for two or three months.

Thus far we have proceeded in this sober business. A good beginning, you will say. Perhaps it is. I do not, however, feel myself greatly interested in the progress of the negotiation. Time may consolidate my affections, and enable me to fix them on some particular object. At present the most lively emotions of my heart are those of friendship; that friendship which I hope you will soon participate with your faithful.

<div align="right">ELIZA WHARTON</div>

Letter XVII

TO MR. SELBY

<div align="right">NEW-HAVEN</div>

I have succeeded in my addresses to the lovely Eliza Wharton; as far at least as I had any reason to expect from our short acquaintance. I find the graces

7. To assume the ministerial robes; to be ordained. 8. Inamorato: lover.

of her person and mind rise in my esteem; and have already enjoyed, in her society, some of the happiest hours of my life. She is kind, affable, and condescending;[9] yet I must own that I have not been able to infuse into her bosom the ardor which I feel in my own. I know that the native modesty of the sex would restrain the discovery; but there is an animation of countenance, which betrays the sensations of the heart, that I find wanting in hers on this occasion.

I have just taken leave of my fair, and propose returning tomorrow morning; to take upon me the solemn charge, which lies with such weight upon my mind, that I need every support, both human and divine. Eliza has promised to correspond with me. From this I anticipate a source of pleasure, which alone can atone for her absence. I am, &c.

<div align="right">J. Boyer.</div>

Letter XVIII

TO MR. CHARLES DEIGHTON

<div align="right">*New-Haven*</div>

Do you know, Charles, that I have commenced lover? I was always a general one; but now I am somewhat particular. I shall be the more interested, as I am likely to meet with difficulties; and it is the glory of a rake, as well as a christian to combat obstacles. This same Eliza, of whom I have told you, has really made more impression on my heart, than I was aware of; or than the sex, take them as they rise, are wont to do. But she is besieged by a priest (a likely[1] lad though.) I know not how it is, but they are commonly successful with the girls, even the gayest of them. This one, too, has the interest of all her friends, as I am told. I called yesterday, at General Richman's, and found this pair together, apparently too happy in each other's society for my wishes. I must own, that I felt a glow of jealousy, which I never experienced before; and vowed revenge for the pain it gave me, though but momentary. Yet Eliza's reception of me was visibly cordial; nay, I fancied my company as pleasing to her as that which she had before. I tarried not long, but left him to the enjoyment of that pleasure which I flatter myself will be short-lived. O, I have another plan in my head; a plan of necessity, which, you know, is the mother of invention. It is this: I am very much courted and caressed by the family of Mr. Lawrence, a man of large property in this neighborhood. He has only one child; a daughter, with whom I imagine the old folks intend to shackle me in the bonds of matrimony. The girl looks very well. She has no soul though, that I can discover. She is heiress, nevertheless, to a great fortune; and that is all the soul I wish for in a wife. In truth, Charles, I know of no other way to mend my circumstances. But lisp not a word of my embarrassments for your life. Show and equipage are my hobby-horse; and if any female wish to share them with me, and will furnish me with the means of supporting them, I have no objection. Could I conform to the sober rules of wedded life, and renounce those dear enjoyments of dissipation, in which I have so long indulged, I know not the lady in the world with whom I would sooner form a connection of this sort than with Eliza Wharton. But it will

9. Humble. 1. Promising.

never do. If my fortune or hers were better, I would risk a union; but as they are, no idea of the kind can be admitted. I shall endeavor, notwithstanding, to enjoy her company as long as possible. Though I cannot possess her wholly myself, I will not tamely see her the property of another.

I am now going to call at General Richman's, in hopes of an opportunity to profess my devotion to her. I know I am not a welcome visitor to the family; but I am independent of their censure or esteem, and mean to act accordingly.

<div align="right">PETER SANFORD.</div>

<div align="center">

Letter XIX

TO MISS LUCY FREEMAN

</div>

<div align="right">NEW-HAVEN</div>

I find the ideas of sobriety, and domestic solitude, I have been cultivating for three days past, somewhat deranged by the interruption of a visitor, with whom, I know, you will not be pleased. It is no other than Major Sanford. I was walking alone in the garden yesterday, when he suddenly appeared to my view. How happy am I, said he, seizing my hand, in this opportunity of finding you alone; an opportunity, Miss Wharton, which I must improve in expatiating on a theme, that fills my heart, and solely animates my frame.

I was startled at his impetuosity, and displeased with his freedom. With-drawing my hand, I told him, that my retirement was sacred. He bowed sub-missively; begged pardon for his intrusion, alledged, that he found nobody but the servants in the house; that they informed him, I was alone in the garden, which intelligence was too pleasing for him to consult any forms of ceremony for the regulation of his conduct. He then went on rhapsodically to declare his passion, his suspicions, that I was forming a connection with Mr. Boyer, which would effectually destroy all his hopes of future happiness. He painted the restraint, the confinement, the embarrassments to which a woman, connected with a man of Mr. Boyer's profession, must be subjected; however agreeable his person might be. He asked if my generous mind could submit to cares and perplexities like these; whether I could not find greater sources of enjoyment in a more elevated sphere of life, or share pleasures better suited to my genius and disposition, even in a single state? I listened to him involuntarily. My heart did not approve his sentiments, but my ear was charmed with his rhetoric, and my fancy captivated by his address.

He invited my confidence, by the most ardent professions of friendship, and labored to remove my suspicions by vows of sincerity. I was induced by his importunity, gradually to disclose the state of affairs between Mr. Boyer and myself. He listened eagerly; wished not, he said, to influence me unduly; but if I were not otherwise engaged, might he presume to solicit a place in my friendship and esteem; be admitted to enjoy my society, to visit me as an acquaintance, and to attend my excursions and amusements, as a brother, if no more? I replied, that I was a pensioner of friendship, at present; that my friends were extremely refined in their notions of propriety, and that I had no right to receive visitants independent of them. I understand you, madam, said he. You intimate that my company is not agreeable to them: but I know not why. Surely my rank in life is as elevated; and my knowledge of, and

acceptance in the world, are as extensive as General Richman's. I hope, said I, since we are engaged in the conversation, that you will excuse my frankness, if I tell you, that the understanding and virtue of this worthy couple induce them, without any regard to rank, to bestow their esteem wherever it is merited. I cannot say that you are not a sharer. Your own heart can best determine, whether upon their principles, you are, or not! He appeared mortified and chagrined; and we had walked some distance without exchanging a word, or a look. At last, he rejoined, I plead guilty to the charge, madam, which they have undoubtedly brought against me, of imprudence and folly in many particulars; yet of malignancy and vice I am innocent. Brought up in affluence; innured from my infancy to the gratification of every passion; the indulgence of every wish, it is not strange, that a life of dissipation and gaiety should prove alluring to a youthful mind, which had no care but to procure what it deemed enjoyment. In this pursuit I have perhaps deviated from the rigid rules of discretion, and the harsher laws of morality.

But let the veil of charity be drawn over my faults; let the eye of candor impartially examine my present behavior; let the kind and lenient hand of friendship assist in directing my future steps; and, perhaps, I may not prove unworthy of associating with the respectable inhabitants of this happy mansion; for such I am sure it must be, while honored with Miss Wharton's presence. But, circumstanced as you and I are, at present, I will not sue for your attention, as a lover; but rest contented, if possible, with that share of kindness, and regard, which your benevolence may afford me as a friend. I bowed in approbation of his resolution. He pressed my hand with ardor to his lips; and at that instant General Richman entered the garden. He approached us cheerfully, offered Major Sanford his hand with apparent cordiality, and told us pleasantly, that he hoped he should not be considered as an intruder. By no means, sir, said Major Sanford. It is I who have incurred that imputation. I called this afternoon to pay you my respects; when being informed that you and your lady were abroad, and that Miss Wharton was in the garden, I took the liberty to invade her retirement. She has graciously forgiven my crime, and I was just affixing the seal to my pardon as you entered.

We then returned into the house. Mrs. Richman received us politely. During tea, the conversation turned on literary subjects, in which I cannot say that the Major bore a very distinguished part. After he was gone, Mrs. Richman said, I hope you have been agreeably entertained, Miss Wharton? I did not choose my company, madam, said I. Nor, said she, did you refuse it, I presume. Would you not have me respect the rights of hospitality towards your guests, when you are absent, madam? If you had acted from that motive, I own my obligations to you, my dear; but even that consideration can hardly reconcile me to the sacrifice of time, which you have made to the amusement of a seducer. I hope, madam, you do not think me an object of seduction! I do not think you seducible; nor was Richardson's Clarissa, till she made herself the victim, by her own indiscretion. Pardon me, Eliza, this is a second Lovelace.[2] I am alarmed by his artful intrusions. His insinuating attention to you are characteristic of the man. Come, I presume you are not interested to keep his secrets, if you know them. Will you give me a little

2. In Richardson's *Clarissa*, the title character is an innocent virgin whom Lovelace, the rake, wishes to seduce.

sketch of his conversation? Most willingly, said I; and, accordingly, related the whole. When I had concluded, she shook her head, and replied, beware, my friend, of his arts. Your own heart is too sincere to suspect treachery and dissimulation in another; but suffer not your ear to be charmed by the siren voice of flattery; nor your eye to be caught by the phantom of gaiety and pleasure. Remember your engagements to Mr. Boyer. Let sincerity and virtue be your guides, and they will lead you to happiness and peace. She waited not for an answer, but immediately rising, begged leave to retire, alleging that she was fatigued. Gen. Richman accompanied her, and I hastened to my apartment, where I have written thus far, and shall send it on for your comments. I begin to think of returning soon to your circle. One inducement is, that I may be free from the intrusions of this man. Adieu.

ELIZA WHARTON.

Letter XX

TO MRS. M. WHARTON

NEW-HAVEN

From the conversation of the polite, the sedate, the engaging and the gay; from corresponding with the learned, the sentimental and the refined, my heart and my pen turn with ardor and alacrity to a tender and affectionate parent, the faithful guardian and guide of my youth; the unchanging friend of my riper years. The different dispositions of various associates sometimes perplex the mind, which seeks direction; but in the disinterested affection of the maternal breast, we fear no dissonance of passion, no jarring interests, no disunion of love. In this seat of felicity is every enjoyment which fancy can form, or friendship, with affluence, bestow; but still my mind frequently returns to the happy shades of my nativity. I wish there to impart my pleasures and share the counsels of my best, my long tried and experienced friend. At this time, my dear mamma, I am peculiarly solicitous for your advice. I am again importuned to listen to the voice of love; again called upon to accept the addresses of a gentleman of merit and respectability. You will know the character of the man, when I tell you, it is Mr. Boyer. But his situation in life! I dare not enter it. My disposition is not calculated for that sphere. There are duties arising from the station, which I fear I should not be able to fulfil; cares and restraints to which I could not submit. *This* man is not disagreeable to me; but if I must enter the connubial state, are there not *others*, who may be equally pleasing in their persons, and whose profession may be more conformable to my taste? You, madam, have passed through this scene of trial, with honor and applause. But alas! Can your volatile daughter ever acquire your wisdom; ever possess your resolution, dignity and prudence?

I hope soon to converse with you personally upon the subject, and to profit by your precepts and example. I anticipate the hour of my return to your bosom, with impatience. My daily thoughts and nightly dreams restore me to the society of my beloved mamma; and, till I enjoy it in reality, I subscribe myself your dutiful daughter,

ELIZA WHARTON.

Letter XXI

TO MISS ELIZA WHARTON

HARTFORD

How welcome to me, my dear Eliza, are the tidings of your return? My widowed heart has mourned your absence, and languished for the company of its now, dearest connection. When stripped of one dependence, the mind naturally collects and rests itself in another. Your father's death deprived me, for a while, of every enjoyment. But a reviving sense of the duties which I owed to a rising family roused me from the lethargy of grief. In my cares I found an alleviation of my sorrows. The expanding virtues of my children soothed and exhilarated my drooping spirits; and my attention to their education, and interest, was amply rewarded by their proficiency and duty. In them, every hope, every pleasure now centers. They are the axis on which revolves the temporal felicity of their mother. Judge then, my dear, how anxiously I must watch, how solicitously I must regard every circumstance which relates to their welfare and prosperity! Exquisitely alive to these sensations, your letter awakens my hopes and my fears. As you are young and charming, a thousand dangers lurk unseen around you. I wish you to find a friend and protector, worthy of being rewarded by your love and your society. Such a one, I think, Mr. Boyer will prove. I am, therefore, sorry, since there can be no other, that his profession should be an objection in your mind. You say, that I have experienced the scenes of trial connected with that station. I have, indeed; and I will tell you the result of this experience. It is, that I have found it replete with happiness. No class of society has domestic enjoyment more at command than clergymen. Their circumstances are generally a decent competency. They are removed alike from the perplexing cares of want, and from the distracting parade of wealth. They are respected by all ranks, and partakers of the best company. With regard to its being a dependent situation, what one is not so? Are we not all links in the great chain of society, some more, some less important; but each upheld by others, throughout the confederated whole? In whatever situation we are placed, our greater or less degree of happiness must be derived from ourselves. Happiness is in a great measure the result of our own dispositions and actions. Let us conduct uprightly and justly; with propriety and steadiness; nor servilely cringing for favor, nor arrogantly claiming more attention and respect than our due; let us bear with fortitude the providential and unavoidable evils of life, and we shall spend our days with respectability and contentment, at least.

I will not expatiate on the topic of your letter, till we have a personal interview, for which I am, indeed, impatient. Return, my daughter, as soon as politeness will allow, to your expecting friends; more especially, to the fond embraces of your affectionate mother,

M. WHARTON.

Letter XXII

TO MISS ELIZA WHARTON

HAMPSHIRE

Can time, can distance, can absence allay or extinguish the sentiments of refined affection, the ardor of true love? No, my dear Eliza. If I may judge by my own heart, I shall say they cannot. Amidst the parade which has attended me, the interesting scenes in which I have been engaged, and the weighty cares, which have occupied my attention, your idea has been the solace of my retired moments; the soother of every anxious thought. I recall, with pleasure, the conversation which we have shared. I dwell with rapture on the marks of favor which I have received from you. My first wish is the continuance and increase of these favors; my highest ambition, to deserve them. I look forward and anticipate with impatience, the future enjoyment of your society; and hope we shall one day experience the reality of those beautiful lines of Thomson:

> —An elegant sufficiency,
> Content, retirement, rural quiet, friendship;
> Books, ease and alternate labor, useful life;
> Progressive virtue, and approving heaven;
> These are the matchless joys of virtuous love.[3]

Mr. Selby, my particular friend, will have the honor of delivering this letter. He will be able to give you any information, relative to our public transactions, which you may wish. May I solicit the favor of a line, through him, in return? It will relieve, in some measure, the tediousness of this separation. I intend to pay my respects to you personally, in about a fortnight; till when, I subscribe myself your sincere and affectionate friend,

J. BOYER.

Letter XXIII

TO THE REV. J. BOYER

NEW-HAVEN

I have executed your commission, and been amply rewarded for my trouble, by the pleasure I enjoyed in the society of the agreeable family to which I was introduced; especially of the amiable and accomplished lady, who is the object of your particular regard. I think she fully justifies your partiality to her. She appears to possess both the virtues and the graces. Her form is fine, and her countenance interests us at once in her favor. There is a mixture of dignity and ease, which commands respect and conciliates affection. After these encomiums, will you permit me to say, there is an air of gaiety in her appearance and deportment, which favors a little of coquetry. I am persuaded, however, that she has too much good sense to practise its arts. She received your letter very graciously, asked leave to retire a few

3. Lines from the "Spring" section of *The Seasons* (1730), by the Scottish poet James Thomson (1700–1748).

moments; and returned with a smile of complacency on her brow, which I construe favorably to you.

There was a Mr. Laurence, with his lady and daughter, and a certain Major Sanford, at the house. The latter, I believe, in the modern sense of the phrase, *is much of a gentleman*, that is, a man of show and fashion.

Miss Wharton asked me, when I should leave town, and when I should return, or have an opportunity of conveyance to Hampshire? I told her I should write by the next post, and if she had any commands, would be happy to execute them. She would send a line to her friend, she said, if I would take the trouble to inclose it in my letter. I readily consented and told her that I would call and receive her favor tomorrow morning. This chitchat was a little aside, but I could not but observe, that the foresaid Major Sanford had dropped his part in the conversation of the rest of the company, and was attending to us, though he endeavored to conceal his attention, by looking carelessly over a play, which lay on the window by him. Yet he evidently watched every word and action of Miss Wharton, as if he were really interested in her movements.

It is said she has many admirers, and I conceive it very possible that this may be one of them; though, truly, I do not think that she would esteem such a conquest any great honor. I now joined in the general topic of conversation, which was politics. Mrs. Richman and Miss Wharton judiciously, yet modestly bore a part; while the other ladies amused themselves with Major Sanford, who was making his sage remarks on the play, which he still kept in his hand. General Richman at length observed, that we had formed into parties. Major Sanford, upon this, laid aside his book. Miss Laurence simpered and looked as if she was well pleased with being in a party with so fine a man; while her mother replied, that she never meddled with politics; she thought they did not belong to ladies. Miss Wharton and I, said Mrs. Richman, must beg leave to differ from you, madam. We think ourselves interested in the welfare and prosperity of our country; and, consequently, claim the right of inquiring into those affairs, which may conduce to or interfere with the commonweal. We shall not be called to the senate or the field to assert its privileges, and defend its rights, but we shall feel for the honor and safety of our friends and connections, who are thus employed. If the community flourish and enjoy health and freedom, shall we not share in the happy effects? If it be oppressed and disturbed, shall we not endure our proportion of the evil? Why then should the love of our country be a masculine passion only? Why should government, which involves the peace and order of the society, of which we are a part, be wholly excluded from our observation? Mrs. Laurence made some slight reply and waved the subject. The gentlemen applauded Mrs. Richman's sentiments as truly Roman; and what was more, they said, truly republican.

I rose to take leave, observing to Miss Wharton, that I should call tomorrow as agreed. Upon this, Gen. Richman politely requested the favor of my company at dinner. I accepted his invitation, and bid them good night. I shall do the same to you for the present; as I intend, tomorrow to scribble the cover, which is to inclose your Eliza's letter.

T. SELBY.

Letter XXIV

TO THE REV. J. BOYER

NEW-HAVEN

I resume my pen, having just returned from Gen. Richman's; not with an expectation, however, of your reading this, till you have perused and reperused the enclosed. I can bear such neglect, in this case, as I have been alike interested myself.

I went to Gen. Richman's at twelve o'clock. About a mile from thence, upon turning a corner, I observed a gentleman and lady on horseback, some way before me, riding a very moderate pace, and seemingly in close conversation. I kept at the same distance from them, till I saw them stop at the General's gate. I then put on, and coming up with them, just as they alighted, and was surprised to find them no other than Major Sanford and Miss Wharton. They were both a little disconcerted at my salutation; I know not why. Miss Wharton invited him in; but he declined, being engaged to dine. Gen. Richman received us at the door. As I handed Miss Wharton in, he observed jocosely, that she had changed company. Yes sir, she replied, more than once, since I went out, as you doubtless observed. I was not aware, said Mrs. Richman, that Major Sanford was to be of your party to day. It was quite accidental, madam, said Miss Wharton. Miss Laurence and I had agreed last evening, to take a little airing, this forenoon. A young gentleman, a relation of hers, who is making them a visit, was to attend us. We had not rode more than two miles, when we were overtaken by Major Sanford, who very politely asked leave to join our party. Miss Laurence very readily consented; and we had a very sociable ride. The fineness of the day induced me to protract the enjoyment of it abroad; but Miss Laurence declined riding so far as I proposed, as she had engaged company to dine. We therefore parted till evening, when we are to meet again. What, another engagement! said Mrs. Richman. Only to the assembly, madam. May I inquire after your gallant, my dear? But I have no right, perhaps, to be inquisitive, said Mrs. Richman. Miss Wharton made no reply; and the conversation took a general turn. Miss Wharton sustained her part with great propriety. Indeed, she discovers a fund of useful knowledge and extensive reading, which render her peculiarly entertaining; while the brilliancy of her wit, the fluency of her language, the vivacity and ease of her manners, are inexpressibly engaging. I am going myself to the assembly this evening, though I did not mention it to General Richman; I therefore took my leave soon after dinner.

I have heard so much in praise of Miss Wharton's penmanship, in addition to her other endowments, that I am almost tempted to break the seal of her letter to you; but I forbear. Wishing you much happiness in the perusal of it, and more in the possession of its writer, I subscribe myself, yours, &c.

T. SELBY.

Letter XXV

TO THE REV. J. BOYER

NEW-HAVEN

SIR,

Your favor of the 4th inst. came to hand yesterday. I received it with pleasure, and embrace this early opportunity of contributing my part to a correspondence, tending to promote a friendly and social intercourse. An epistolary communication between the sexes has been with some a subject of satire and censure; but unjustly, in my opinion. With persons of refinement and information, it may be a source of entertainment and utility. The knowledge and masculine virtues of your sex may be softened and rendered more diffusive by the inquisitiveness, vivacity, and docility of ours; drawn forth and exercised by each other.

In regard to the *particular* subject of your's I shall be silent. Ideas of that kind are better conveyed, on my part, by words, than by the pen.

I congratulate you on your agreeable settlement, and hope it will be productive of real and lasting happiness. I am convinced that felicity is not confined to any particular station or condition in life; yet methinks some are better calculated to afford it to me, than others.

Your extract from a favorite poet is charmingly descriptive; but is it not difficult to ascertain what we can pronounce "an elegant sufficiency?" Perhaps you will answer as some others have done. We can attain it by circumscribing our wishes within the compass of our abilities. I am not very avaricious; yet I must own that I should like to enjoy it without so much trouble as that would cost me.

Excuse my seeming levity. You have flattered my cheerfulness by commending it; and must, therefore, indulge me in the exercise of it. I cannot conveniently be at the pains of restraining its sallies, when I write in confidence.

Is a sprightly disposition, in your view, indicative of a giddy mind, or an innocent heart? Of the latter, I presume; for I know you are not a misanthrope.

We expect the pleasure of Mr. Selby's company to dinner. You are, certainly, under obligations to his friendship for the liberal encomiums he bestowed on you and your prospects yesterday. Mrs. Richman rallied me after he was gone, on my listening ear. The General and she unite in requesting me to present their respects. Wishing you health and happiness, I subscribe myself your friend,

ELIZA WHARTON.

Letter XXVI

TO MISS LUCY FREEMAN

NEW-HAVEN

I am perplexed and embarrassed, my friend, by the assiduous attentions of this Major Sanford. I shall write circumstantially and frankly to you, that I may have the benefit of your advice. He came here, last Monday, in company with Mr. Laurence, his wife, and daughter, to make us a visit. While

they were present, a Mr. Selby, a particular friend of Mr. Boyer, came in and delivered me a letter from him. I was really happy in the reception of this proof of his affection. His friend gave a very flattering account of his situation and prospects.

The watchful eye of Major Sanford traced every word and action, respecting Mr. Boyer, with an attention, which seemed to border on anxiety. That, however, did not restrain, but rather accelerate my vivacity and inquisitiveness on the subject; for I wished to know whether it would produce any real effect upon him, or not.

After Mr. Selby's departure, he appeared pensive, and thoughtful, the remainder of the evening; and evidently sought an opportunity of speaking to me aside; which I studiously avoided. Miss Laurence and I formed an engagement to take an airing in the morning on horseback; attended by a relation of hers, who is now with them. They called for me about ten, when we immediately set out upon our preconcerted excursion. We had not proceeded far, before we were met by Major Sanford. He was extremely polite, and finding our destination was not particular, begged leave to join our party. This was granted, and we had an agreeable tour for several miles; the time being passed in easy and unstudied remarks upon obvious occurrences. Maj. Sanford could not, however, conceal his particular attention to me, which rather nettled Miss Laurence. She grew somewhat serious and declined riding so far as we had intended; alledging that she expected company to dine.

Major Sanford understanding that she was going to the assembly in the evening with Mr. Gordon, solicited me to accept a ticket and form a party with them. The entertainment was alluring, and I consented. When we had parted with Miss Laurence, Major Sanford insisted on my riding a little farther; saying, he must converse with me on a particular subject; and if I refused him this opportunity, that he must visit me, at my residence, let it offend whom it would. I yielded to his importunity; and we rode on. He then told me that his mind was in a state of suspense and agitation, which was very painful to bear; and which I only could relieve; that my cheerful reception of Mr. Boyer's letter, yesterday, and deportment respecting him, had awakened in his breast all the pangs of jealousy, which the most ardent love could feel; that my treatment of Mr. Boyer's friend convinced him that I was more interested in his affairs than I was willing to own; that he foresaw himself to be condemned to an eternal separation; and the total loss of my favor and society, as soon as time and circumstances would allow.

His zeal, his pathos, alarmed me. I begged him to be calm. To you, said I, as a friend, I have intrusted my situation in relation to Mr. Boyer. You know that I am under no special obligation to him; and I do not intend to form any immediate connection. Mr. Boyer must have different ideas, madam; and he has reason for them, if I may judge by appearances. When do you expect another visit from him? In about a fortnight. And is my fate to be then decided; and so decided, as I fear it will be, through the influence of your friends, if not by your own inclination? My friends, sir, will not control; they will only advise to what they think most for my interest; and I hope, that my conduct will not be unworthy of their approbation. Pardon me, my dear Eliza, said he, if I am impertinent; it is my regard for you which impels me to the presumption. Do you intend to give your hand to Mr. Boyer? I do not intend to give my hand to any man at present. I have but lately entered society; and wish,

for a while, to enjoy my freedom, in the participation of pleasures suited to my age and sex. These, said he, you are aware, I suppose, when you form a connection with that man, you must renounce and content yourself with a confinement to the tedious round of domestic duties, the pedantic conversation of scholars, and the invidious criticisms of a whole town. I have been accustomed, said I, and am therefore attached to men of letters; and as to the praise or censure of the populace, I hope always to enjoy that approbation of conscience, which will render me superior to both. But you forget your promise, not to talk in this style; and have deviated far from the character of a friend and brother, with which you consented to rest satisfied. Yes, but I find myself unequal to the task. I am not stoic enough, tamely to make so great a sacrifice. I must plead for an interest in your favor, till you banish me from your presence, and tell me plainly that you hate me. We had by this time reached the gate; and as we dismounted, were unexpectedly accosted by Mr. Selby, who had come agreeably to his promise, to dine with us, and receive my letter to Mr. Boyer.

Major Sanford took his leave as General Richman appeared at the door. The General and his lady rallied me on my change of company; but very prudently concealed their sentiments of Major Sanford, while Mr. Selby was present. Nothing material occurred before and during dinner; soon after which, Mr. Selby went away. I retired to dress for the assembly; and had nearly completed the labor of the toilet, when Mrs. Richman entered. My friendship for you, my dear Eliza, said she, interests me so much in your affairs, that I cannot repress my curiosity to know who has the honor of your hand, this evening. If it be any honor, said I, it will be conferred on Major Sanford. I think it far too great to be thus bestowed, returned she. It is perfectly astonishing to me, that the virtuous part of my sex will countenance, caress, and encourage those men, whose profession it is to blast their reputation, destroy their peace, and triumph in their infamy! Is this, madam, the avowed design of Major Sanford? I know not what he avows; but his practice too plainly bespeaks his principles and views. Does he now practice the arts you mention; or do you refer to past follies? I cannot answer for his present conduct; his past has established his character. You, madam, are an advocate for charity; that, perhaps, if exercised in this instance might lead you to think it possible for him to reform; to become a valuable member of society; and, when connected with a lady of virtue and refinement, to be capable of making a good husband. I cannot conceive that such a lady would be willing to risk her all upon the slender prospect of his reformation. I hope the one with whom I am conversing has no inclination to so hazardous an experiment. Why, not much. Not much! If you have any, why do you continue to encourage Mr. Boyer's addresses? I am not sufficiently acquainted with either yet, to determine which to take. At present, I shall not confine myself in any way. In regard to these men, my fancy and my judgment are in scales. Sometimes one preponderates, sometimes the other. Which will finally outweigh, time alone can reveal. O my cousin, beware of the delusions of fancy! Reason must be our guide, if we would expect durable happiness. At this instant a servant opened the door, and told me that Major Sanford waited in the parlor. Being ready, I wished Mrs. Richman a good evening, and went down. Neither General Richman nor his lady appeared.

He therefore handed me immediately into his phaeton, and we were soon in the assembly room.

I was surprised, on my entrance, to find Mr. Selby there, as he did not mention, at dinner, his intention of going. He attached himself to our party; and, in the intervals of dancing, took every opportunity of conversing with me. These, however, were not many; for Major Sanford assiduously precluded the possibility of my being much engaged by anyone else. We passed the evening very agreeably; but the Major's importunity was rather troublesome, as we returned home. He insisted upon my declaring whether Mr. Boyer really possessed my affections; and whether I intended to confer myself on him or not. If, said he, you answer me in the affirmative, I must despair; but if you have not absolutely decided against me, I will still hope, that my persevering assiduity, my faithful love, may at last be rewarded. I told him that I was under no obligation to give him any account of my disposition towards another; and that he must remember the terms of our present association, to which he had subscribed. I therefore begged him to wave the subject now, if not forever. He asked my pardon, if he had been impertinent; but desired leave to renew his request, that I would receive his visits, his friendly visits. I replied, that I could not grant this; and that he must blame himself, not me, if he was an unwelcome guest at General Richman's. He lamented the prejudices which my friends had imbibed against him; but flattered himself that I was more liberal than to be influenced by them, without any positive proof of demerit; as it was impossible that his conduct towards me should ever deviate from the strictest rules of honor and love.

What shall I say now, my friend? This man, to an agreeable person has superadded, graceful manners, an amiable temper, and a fortune sufficient to ensure the enjoyments of all the pleasing varieties of social life. Perhaps a gay disposition and a lax education may have betrayed him into some scenes of dissipation. But is it not an adage generally received, that *"a reformed rake makes the best husband?"*[4] My fancy leads me for happiness to the festive haunts of fashionable life. I am at present, and know not but I ever shall be, too volatile for a confinement to domestic avocations and sedentary pleasures. I dare not, therefore, place myself in a situation where these must be indispensable. Mr. Boyer's person and character are agreeable. I really esteem the man. My reason and judgment, as I have observed before, declare for a connection with him, as a state of tranquillity and rational happiness. But the idea of relinquishing those delightful amusements and flattering attentions, which wealth and equipage bestow, is painful. Why were not the virtues of the one, and the graces and affluence of the other combined? I should then have been happy indeed! But, as the case now stands, I am loath to give up either; being doubtful which will conduce most to my felicity.

Pray write me impartially; let me know your real sentiments, for I rely greatly upon your opinion. I am, &c.

ELIZA WHARTON.

4. An eighteenth-century adage.

Letter XXVII

TO THE REV. MR. BOYER

NEW-HAVEN

I am quite a convert to Pope's assertion, that "Every woman is, at heart, a rake."[5] How else can we account for the pleasure which they evidently receive from the society, the flattery, the caresses of men of that character? Even the most virtuous of them seem naturally prone to gaiety, to pleasure, and, I had almost said, to dissipation! How else shall we account for the existence of this disposition, in your favorite fair? It cannot be the result of her education. Such a one as she has received is calculated to give her a very different turn of mind. You must forgive me, my friend, for I am a little vexed and alarmed on your account. I went last evening to the assembly, as I told you in my last that I intended. I was purposely without a partner, that I might have the liberty to exercise my gallantry, as circumstances should invite. Indeed, I must own, that my particular design was, to observe Miss Wharton's movements, being rather inclined to jealousy in your behalf. She was handed into the assembly room by Major Sanford. The brilliance of their appearance, the levity of their manners, and the contrast of their characters I found to be a general subject of speculation. I endeavored to associate with Miss Wharton, but found it impossible to detach her a moment from the coxcomb who attended her. If she has any idea of a connection with you, why does she continue to associate with another, especially with one of so opposite a description? I am seriously afraid, that there is more intimacy between them, than there ought to be, considering the encouragement she has given you.

I hope you will not be offended by my freedom in this matter. It originates in a concern for your honor and future happiness. I am anxious, lest you should be made the dupe of a coquette, and your peace of mind fall a sacrifice to an artful debauchee. Yet I must believe, that Miss Wharton has, in reality, all that virtue and good sense of which she enjoys the reputation; but her present conduct is mysterious.

I have said enough (more than I ought, perhaps) to awaken your attention to circumstances, which *may* lead to important events. If they appear of little, or no consequence to you, you will at least ascribe the mention of them to motives of sincere regard, in your friend and humble servant,

T. SELBY.

Letter XXVIII

TO MR. CHARLES DEIGHTON

NEW-HAVEN

I go on finely with my amour. I have every encouragement that I could wish. Indeed my fair one does not verbally declare in my favor; but then, according to the vulgar proverb, *that actions speak louder than words*, I have no reason to complain; since she evidently approves my gallantry, is pleased with

5. From line 216 of "Epistle II. To a Lady. Of the Characters of Women" (1735), by Alexander Pope.

my company, and listens to my flattery. Her sagacious[6] friends have undoubt-
edly given her a detail of my vices. If, therefore, my past conduct has been
repugnant to her notions of propriety, why does she not act consistently and
refuse at once to associate with a man whose character she cannot esteem?
But no; that, Charles, is no part of the female plan: our entrapping a few of
their sex, only discovers the gaiety of our dispositions, the insinuating
graces of our manners, and the irresistible charms of our persons and
address. These qualifications are very alluring to the sprightly fancy of the
fair. They think to enjoy the pleasures which result from this source; while
their vanity and ignorance prompt each one to imagine herself superior to
delusion; and to anticipate the honor of reclaiming the libertine, and
reforming the rake! I don't know, however, but this girl will really have that
merit with me; for I am so much attached to her, that I begin to suspect I
should sooner become a convert to sobriety than lose her. I cannot find that
I have made much impression on her heart as yet. Want of success in this
point mortifies me extremely, as it is the first time I ever failed. Besides,
I am apprehensive that she is prepossessed in favor of the other swain, the
clerical lover, whom I have mentioned to you before. The chord, therefore,
upon which I play the most, is the dissimilarity of their dispositions and
pleasures. I endeavor to detach her from him, and disaffect her towards
him; knowing, that if I can separate them entirely, I shall be more likely to
succeed in my plan. Not that I have any thoughts of marrying her myself;
that will not do at present. But I love her too well to see her connected with
another for life. I must own myself a little revengeful too in this affair. I wish
to punish her friends, as she calls them, for their malice towards me; for
their cold and negligent treatment of me whenever I go to the house. I know
that to frustrate their designs of a connection between Mr. Boyer and Eliza
would be a grievous disappointment. I have not yet determined to seduce
her, though, with all her pretensions to virtue, I do not think it impossible.
And if I should, she can blame none but herself, since she knows my char-
acter, and has no reason to wonder if I act consistently with it. If she will
play with a lion, let her beware of his paw, I say. At present, I wish inno-
cently to enjoy her society; it is a luxury which I never tasted before. She is
the very soul of pleasure. The gayest circle is irradiated by her presence,
and the highest entertainment receives its greatest charm from her smiles.
Besides, I have purchased the seat of Capt. Pribble, about a mile from her
mother's; and can I think of suffering her to leave the neighborhood, just as
I enter it? I shall exert every nerve to prevent that, and hope to meet with
the usual success of

PETER SANFORD.

Letter XXIX

TO MISS ELIZA WHARTON

HARTFORD

You desire me to write to you, my friend; but if you had not, I should by no
means have refrained. I tremble at the precipice on which you stand; and

6. Wise.

must echo, and re-echo the seasonable admonition of the excellent Mrs. Richman, "Beware of the delusions of fancy!" You are strangely infatuated by them! Let not the magic arts of that worthless Sanford lead you, like an *ignis fatuus*[7] from the path of rectitude and virtue!

I do not find, in all your conversations with him, that one word about marriage drops from his lips. This is mysterious? No, it is characteristic of the man. Suppose, however, that his views are honorable; yet what can you expect, what can you promise yourself from such a connection? "A reformed rake," you say, "makes the best husband;" a trite, but a very erroneous maxim, as the fatal experience of thousands of our sex can testify. In the first place, I believe that rakes very seldom *do* reform, while their fortunes and constitutions enable them to pursue their licentious pleasures. But even allowing this to happen, can a woman of refinement and delicacy enjoy the society of a man, whose mind has been corrupted, whose taste has been vitiated, and who has contracted a depravity both of sentiment and manners, which no degree of repentance can wholly efface? Besides, of true love they are absolutely incapable. Their passions have been too much hackneyed to admit so pure a flame. You cannot anticipate sincere and lasting respect from them. They have been so long accustomed to the company of those of our sex, who observe no esteem; that the greatest dignity and purity of character can never excite it in their breasts. They are naturally prone to jealousy. Habituated to an intercourse with the baser part of the sex, they level the whole, and seldom believe any to be incorruptible. They are always hard-hearted and cruel. How else could they triumph in the miseries which they frequently occasion? Their specious manners may render them agreeable companions abroad; but at home the evil propensities of their minds will invariably predominate. They are steeled against the tender affections, which render domestic life delightful; strangers to the kind, the endearing sympathies of husband, father, and friend! The thousand nameless attentions which soften the rugged path of life are neglected, and deemed unworthy of notice by persons who have been innured to scenes of dissipation and debauchery! And is a man of this description to be the partner, the companion, the bosom friend of my Eliza? Forbid it heaven! Let not the noble qualities, so lavishly bestowed upon her, be thus unworthily sacrificed!

You seem to be particularly charmed with the fortune of Major Sanford; with the gaiety of his appearance; with the splendor of his equipage; with the politeness of his manners; with what you call the graces of his person! These, alas! are superficial, ensnaring endowments. As to fortune, prudence, economy, and regularity are necessary to preserve it, when possessed. Of these Major Sanford is certainly destitute; unless common fame (which more frequently tells truth than some are willing to allow) does him great injustice. As to external parade, it will not satisfy the rational mind, when it aspires to those substantial pleasures for which yours is formed. And as to the graces of person and manners, they are but a wretched substitute for those virtues which adorn and dignify human life. Can you, who have always been used to serenity and order in a family, to rational, refined and improving conversation, relinquish them, and launch into the whirlpool of frivolity,

7. Phosphorescent light found in swampy areas at night, probably from decomposing matter. In popular usage, an illusion.

where the correct taste and the delicate sensibility which you possess must constantly be wounded by the frothy and illiberal sallies of licentious wit?

This, my dear, is but a faint picture of the situation to which you seem inclined! Reverse the scene, and you will perceive the alternative, which is submitted to your option, in a virtuous connection with Mr. Boyer. Remember that you are acting for life; and that your happiness in this world, perhaps in the next, depends on your present choice!

I called, last evening, to see your mamma. She is fondly anticipating your return; and rejoicing in the prospect of your agreeable and speedy settlement. I could not find it in my heart to distress her by intimating that you had other views. I wish her benevolent bosom never more to feel the pangs of disappointed hope.

I am busily engaged in preparing for my nuptials. The solemn words "as long as ye both shall live," render me thoughtful and serious. I hope for your enlivening presence soon; which will prove a seasonable cordial to the spirits of your

<div align="right">LUCY FREEMAN.</div>

Letter XXX

TO MISS LUCY FREEMAN

<div align="right">NEW-HAVEN</div>

I believe your spirits need a cordial indeed, my dear Lucy; after drawing so dreadful a portrait of my swain. But I call him mine no longer. I renounce him entirely. My friends shall be gratified. And if their predictions are verified, I shall be happy in a union with the man of their choice. General Richman and lady have labored abundantly to prove that my ruin was inevitable if I did not immediately break all intercourse with Major Sanford. I promised a compliance with their wishes; and have accomplished the task, though a hard one I found it. Last Thursday he was here, and desired leave to spend an hour with me. I readily consented, assuring my friends it should be the last hour, which I would ever spend in his company.

He told me that he was obliged to leave town for a few days; and, as I should probably see Mr. Boyer, before his return, he could not depart in peace without once more endeavoring to interest me in his favor; to obtain some token of esteem, some glimpse of hope, that I would not utterly reject him, to support him in his absence. I thanked him for the polite attention he had paid me, since our acquaintance; told him that I should ever retain a grateful sense of his partiality to me; that he would ever share my best wishes; but that all connection of the kind, to which he alluded, must from that time, forever cease.

He exerted all his eloquence to obtain a retraction of that sentence, and ran, with the greatest volubility, through all the protestations, prayers, entreaties, professions and assurances which love could feel or art contrive. I had resolution, however, to resist them, and to command my own emotions on the occasion, better than my natural sensibility gave me reason to expect.

Finding every effort vain, he rose precipitately, and bade me adieu. I urged his tarrying to tea; but he declined, saying, that he must retire to his chamber, being, in his present state of mind, unfit for any society, as he was

banished from mine. I offered him my hand, which he pressed with ardor to his lips, and bowing in silence, left the room.

Thus terminated this affair; an affair, which, perhaps, was only the effect of mere gallantry on his part, and of unmeaning pleasantry on mine; and which, I am sorry to say, has given my friends so much anxiety and concern. I am under obligations to them for their kind solicitude, however causeless it may have been.

As an agreeable companion, as a polite and finished gallant, Major Sanford is all that the most lively fancy could wish. And as you have always affirmed that I was a little inclined to coquetry, can you wonder at my exercising it upon so happy a subject? Besides, when I thought more seriously, his liberal fortune was extremely alluring to me, who, you know, have been hitherto confined to the rigid rules of prudence and economy, not to say, necessity in my finances.

Miss Laurence called on me yesterday, as she was taking the air, and asked me whether Major Sanford took leave of me when he left town? He was here last week, said I, but I did not know that he was gone away. O yes, she replied, he is gone to take possession of his seat, which he has lately purchased of Captain Pribble. I am told it is superb; and it ought to be, if it have the honor of his residence. Then you have a great opinion of Major Sanford, said I. Certainly; and has not everybody else? said she. I am sure he is a very fine gentleman. Mrs. Richman smiled rather contemptuously, and I changed the subject.

I believe that the innocent heart of this simple girl is a little taken in.

I have just received a letter from Mr. Boyer, in the usual style. He expects the superlative happiness of kissing my hand next week. O dear! I believe I must begin to fix my phiz.[8] Let me run to the glass and try if I can make up one that will look *madamish*. Yes, I succeed very well.

I congratulate you on your new neighbor; but I advise friend George to have the guardian knot tied immediately, lest you should be ensnared by this bewitching 'squire.

I have been trying to seduce General Richman to accompany me to the assembly, this evening, but cannot prevail. Were Mrs. Richman able to go with us, he would be very happy to wait on us together; but to tell the truth, he had rather enjoy her company at home, than any which is to be found abroad. I rallied him on his old-fashioned taste; but my heart approved and applauded his attachment. I despise the married man or woman, who harbors an inclination to partake of separate pleasures.

I am told, that a servant man inquires for me below; the messenger of some enamoured swain, I suppose. I will step down and learn what message he brings———

Nothing extraordinary; it is only a card of compliments from a Mr. Emmons, a respectable merchant of this city, requesting the honor to wait on me to the assembly this evening. A welcome request, which I made no hesitation to grant. If I must resign these favorite amusements, let me enjoy as large a share as possible, till the time arrive. Adieu. I must repair to the toilet and adorn for a new conquest, the person of

ELIZA WHARTON.

8. Countenance (from "physiognomy").

Letter XXXI

TO MISS ELIZA WHARTON

HARTFORD

I am very happy to find you are in so good spirits, Eliza, after parting with your favorite swain. For I perceive that he is really the favorite of your fancy, though your heart cannot esteem him; and, independent of that, no sensations can be durable.

I can tell you some news of this strange man. He has arrived, and taken possession of his seat. Having given general invitations he has been called upon and welcomed by most of the neighboring gentry. Yesterday he made an elegant entertainment. Friend George (as you call him) and I were of the number, who had cards. Twenty-one couple went, I am told. We did not go. I consider my time too valuable to be spent in cultivating acquaintance with a person from whom neither pleasure nor improvement are to be expected. His profuseness may bribe the unthinking multitude to show him respect; but he must know, that though

> Places and honors have been bought for gold,
> Esteem and love were never to be told.[9]

I look upon the vicious habits and abandoned character of Major Sanford, to have more pernicious effects on society, than the perpetrations of the robber and the assassin. These, when detected, are rigidly punished by the laws of the land. If their lives be spared, they are shunned by society, and treated with every mark of disapprobation and contempt. But to the disgrace of humanity and virtue, the assassin of honor, the wretch, who breaks the peace of families, who robs virgin innocence of its charms, who triumphs over the ill-placed confidence of the inexperienced, unsuspecting, and too credulous fair, is received, and caressed, not only by his own sex, to which he is a reproach, but even by ours, who have every conceivable reason to despise and avoid him. Influenced by these principles, I am neither ashamed nor afraid openly to avow my sentiments of this man, and my reasons for treating him with the most pointed neglect.

I write warmly on the subject; for it is a subject in which I think the honor and happiness of my sex concerned. I wish they would more generally espouse their own cause. It would conduce to the public weal, and to their personal respectability. I rejoice, heartily, that you have had resolution to resist his allurements, to detect and repel his artifices. Resolution, in such a case, is absolutely necessary; for,

> In spite of all the virtue we can boast,
> The woman that deliberates is lost.[1]

As I was riding out, yesterday, I met your mamma. She wondered that I was not one of the party at our new neighbor's. The reason, madam, said I, is that I do not like the character of the man. I know nothing of him, said she; he is quite a stranger to me, only as he called at my house, last week, to

9. Cf. *An Essay on Man* (1733–34) 4.185–88, by Alexander Pope.

1. From Addison's *Cato* 4.1.29–31, where they are spoken by the virtuous central female character.

pay me his respects, as he said, for the sake of my late husband, whose memory he revered; and because I was the mother of Miss Eliza Wharton, with whom he had the honor of some little acquaintance. His manners are engaging, and I am sorry to hear that his morals are corrupt.

This, my dear, is a very extraordinary visit. I fear that he has not yet laid aside his arts. Be still on your guard, is the advice of your sincere and faithful friend,

LUCY FREEMAN

Letter XXXII

TO MR. CHARLES DEIGHTON

HARTFORD

I am really banished and rejected; desired never more to think of the girl I love, with a view of indulging that love, or of rendering it acceptable to its object! You will perhaps, dispute the propriety of the term, and tell me it is not love, it is only gallantry, and a desire to exercise it with her, as a favorite nymph. I neither know, nor care by what appellation you distinguish it, but it truly gives me pain. I have not felt one sensation of genuine pleasure since I heard my sentence; yet I acquiesced in it, and submissively took my leave; though I doubt not but I shall retaliate the indignity one time or other.

I have taken possession of my new purchase, an elegant and delightful residence. It is rendered more so by being in the vicinity of my charmer's native abode. This circumstance will conduce much to my enjoyment, if I can succeed in my plan of separating her from Mr. Boyer. I know that my situation and mode of life are far more pleasing to her than his, and shall therefore trust to my appearance and address for a reestablishment in her favor. I intend, if possible, to ingratiate myself with her particular friends. For this purpose, I called last week at her mother's, to pay my respects to her (so I told the good woman) as an object of my particular regard; and as the parent of a young lady, whom I had the honor to know and admire. She received me very civilly, thanked me for my attention, and invited me to call whenever I had opportunity; which was the very thing I wanted. I intend likewise, to court popularity. I don't know but I must accept, by and by, some lucrative office in the civil department. Yet I cannot bear the idea of confinement to business. It appears to me quite inconsistent with the character of a gentleman; I am sure it is, with that of a man of pleasure. But something I must do; for I tell you, in confidence, that I was obliged to mortgage this place, because I had not wherewithal to pay for it. But I shall manage matters very well, I have no doubt, and keep up the appearance of affluence, till I find some lady in a strait for a husband, whose fortune will enable me to extricate myself from these embarrassments. Do come and see me, Charles; for, notwithstanding all my gaiety and parade, I have some turns of the hypo, some qualms of conscience, you will call them; but I meddle not with such obsolete words. And so good-bye to you, says

PETER SANFORD.

Letter XXXIII

TO MISS LUCY FREEMAN

NEW-HAVEN

MY DEAR FRIEND,

I believe I must begin to assume airs of gravity; and they will not be quite so foreign to my feelings now, as at some other times. You shall know the reason. I have been associated for three days, with sentiment and sobriety, in the person of Mr. Boyer. I don't know but this man will seduce me into matrimony. He is very eloquent upon the subject; and his manners are so solemn, that I am strongly tempted, yet I dare not to laugh. Really, Lucy, there is something extremely engaging and soothing too, in virtuous and refined conversation. It is a source of enjoyment which cannot be realised by the dissolute and unreflecting. But then, this particular theme of his, is not a favorite one to me; I mean, as connected with its consequences, care and confinement. However, I have compounded the matter with him, and conditioned that he shall expatiate on the subject, and call it by what name he pleases, *platonic* or *conjugal*, provided he will let me take my own time for the consummation. I have consented that he shall escort me, next week, to see my mamma and my Lucy. O, how the idea of returning to that revered mansion, to those beloved friends, exhilarates my spirits!

General Richman's politeness to me has induced him to invite a large party of those gentlemen and ladies who have been particularly attentive to me, during my residence here, to dine and take tea, tomorrow. After that, I expect to be engaged in making farewell visits, till I leave the place. I shall, therefore, forego the pleasure of telling you any occurrences, subsequent to this date, until you see and converse with your sincere friend,

ELIZA WHARTON.

Letter XXXIV

TO MRS. RICHMAN

HARTFORD

DEAR MADAM,

The day after I left your hospitable dwelling brought me safe to that of my honored mamma; to the seat of maternal and filial affection; of social ease and domestic peace; of every species of happiness which can result from religion and virtue; from refinement in morals and manners.

I found my brother and his wife, with Lucy Freeman and Mr. Sumner, waiting to receive and bid me welcome. I flew with ecstasy to the bosom of my mamma, who received me with her accustomed affection, testified by the expressive tears of tenderness which stole silently down her widowed cheek. She was unable to speak. I was equally so. We therefore indulged, a moment, the pleasing emotions of sympathizing sensibility. When disengaged from her fond embrace, I was saluted by the others in turn; and having recovered myself, I presented Mr. Boyer to each of the company, and each of the company to him. He was cordially received by all, but more especially by my mamma.

The next day I was called upon and welcomed by several of my neighboring acquaintance; among whom I was not a little surprised to see Major Sanford. He came in company with Mr. Stoddard and Lady, whom he overtook, as he told me, nearby; and, as they informed him that the design of their visit was to welcome me home, he readily accepted their invitation to partake of the pleasure which everyone must receive on my return. I bowed slightly at his compliment, taking no visible notice of any peculiarity of expression either in his words or looks.

His politeness to Mr. Boyer appeared to be the result of habit. Mr. Boyer's to him to be forced by respect to the company to which he had gained admission. I dare say, that each felt a conscious superiority; the one on the score of merit; the other on that of fortune. Which ought to outweigh, the judicious mind will easily decide. The scale, as I once observed to you, will turn as fancy or reason preponderates. I believe the esteem which I now have for Mr. Boyer will keep me steady; except, perhaps, some little eccentricities, now and then, just by way of variety. I am going tomorrow morning to spend a few days with Lucy Freeman; to assist in the preparation for and the solemnization of her nuptials. Mr. Boyer, in the meantime, will tarry among his friends in town. My mamma is excessively partial to him; though I am not yet jealous that she means to rival me. I am not certain, however, but it might be happy for him if she should. For I suspect, notwithstanding the disparity of her age, that she is better calculated to make him a good wife than I am or ever shall be.

But to be sober. Please, madam, to make my compliments acceptable to those of your neighbors, whose politeness and attention to me, while at your house, have laid me under particular obligations of gratitude and respect. My best regards attend General Richman. Pray tell him, that though I never expect to be so good a wife as he is blessed with; yet I intend, after a while (when I have sowed all my wild oats) to make a tolerable one.

I am anxious to hear of a wished-for event, and of your safety. All who know you feel interested in your health and happiness; but none more warmly than your obliged and affectionate

ELIZA WHARTON.

Letter XXXV

TO MISS ELIZA WHARTON

NEW-HAVEN

I write a line, at Mrs. Richman's request, just to inform you, Eliza, that yesterday, that lovely and beloved woman presented me with a daughter. This event awakens new sensations in my mind; and calls into exercise a kind of affection which had before lain dormant. I feel already the tenderness of a parent; while imagination fondly traces the mother's likeness in the infant form. Mrs. Richman expects to receive your congratulations in a letter by the next post. She bids me tell you, moreover, that she hopes soon to receive an invitation, and be able to attend to the consummation you talk of. Give Mrs. Richman's and my particular regards to your excellent mother and to the worthy Mr. Boyer. With sentiments of esteem and friendship, I am, &c.

S. RICHMAN.

Letter XXXVI

TO MRS. RICHMAN

HARTFORD

From the scenes of festive mirth, from the conviviality of rejoicing friends and from the dissipating amusements of the gay world, I retire with alacrity, to hail my beloved friend on the important charge which she has received; on the accession to her family, and, may I not say, on the addition to her care; since that care will be more than counterbalanced by the pleasure it confers. Hail happy babe! Ushered into the world by the best of mothers; entitled by birthright to virtue and honor; defended by parental love, from the weakness of infancy and childhood, by guardian wisdom from the perils of youth, and by affluent independence from the griping hand of poverty, in more advanced life! May these animating prospects be realized by your little daughter; and may you long enjoy the rich reward of seeing her all that you wish!

Yesterday, my dear friend, Lucy Freeman gave her hand to the amiable and accomplished Mr. George Sumner. A large circle of congratulating friends were present. Her dress was such as wealth and elegance required. Her deportment was everything that modesty and propriety could suggest. They are, indeed, a charming couple. The consonance of their dispositions, the similarity of their tastes, and the equality of their ages are a sure pledge of happiness. Every eye beamed with pleasure on the occasion, and every tongue echoed the wishes of benevolence. Mine only was silent. Though not less interested in the felicity of my friend than the rest, yet the idea of a separation perhaps, of an alienation of affection, by means of her entire devotion to another, cast an involuntary gloom over my mind. Mr. Boyer took my hand, after the ceremony was past. Permit me, Miss Wharton, said he, to lead you to your lovely friend; her happiness must be heightened by your participation of it. Oh no; said I, I am too selfish for that. She has conferred upon another that affection which I wished to engross. My love was too fervent to admit a rival. Retaliate then, said he, this fancied wrong, by doing likewise. I observed that this was not a proper time to discuss that subject; and, resuming my seat, endeavored to put on the appearance of my accustomed vivacity. I need not relate the remaining particulars of the evening's entertainment. Mr. Boyer returned with my mamma, and I remained at Mrs. Freeman's.

We are to have a ball here, this evening. Mr. Boyer has been with us, and tried to monopolize my company; but in vain. I am too much engaged by the exhilarating scenes around, for attending to a subject which affords no variety. I shall not close this till tomorrow.

———I am rather fatigued with the amusements of last night, which were protracted to a late hour. Mr. Boyer was present; and I was pleased to see him not averse to the entertainment, though his profession prevented his taking an active part. As all the neighboring gentry were invited, Mr. Freeman would, by no means, omit Major Sanford, which his daughter earnestly solicited. It happened (unfortunately, shall I say?) that I drew him for a partner. Yet I must own, that I felt very little reluctance to my lot. He is an excellent dancer, and well calculated for a companion in the hours of mirth and gaiety. I regretted Mr. Boyer's being present, however; because

my enjoyment seemed to give him pain. I hope he is not inclined to the passion of jealousy. If he is, I fear it will be somewhat exercised.

Lucy Freeman, now Mrs. Sumner, removes, next week, to Boston. I have agreed to accompany her, and spend a month or two in her family. This will give variety to the journey of life. Be so kind as to direct your next letter to me there.

Kiss the dear little babe for me. Give love, compliments, &c. as respectively due; and believe me, with every sentiment of respect, your affectionate

ELIZA WHARTON.

Letter XXXVII

TO MR. CHARLES DEIGHTON

HARTFORD

DEAR CHARLES,

My hopes begin to revive. I am again permitted to associate with my Eliza; invited to the same entertainment! She does not refuse to join with me in the mazy dance, and partake the scenes of festive mirth. Nay, more; she allows me to press her hand to my lips; and listens to the sighing accents of love. Love her, I certainly do. Would to heaven I could marry her! Would to heaven I had preserved my fortune; or she had one to supply its place! I am distracted at the idea of losing her forever. I am sometimes tempted to solicit her hand in serious earnest; but if I should, poverty and want must be the consequence. Her disappointment in the expectation of affluence and splendor, which I believe her ruling passion, would afford a perpetual source of discontent and mutual wretchedness.

She is going to Boston with her friend, Mrs. Sumner. I must follow her. I must break the connection, which is rapidly forming, between her and Mr. Boyer; and enjoy her society a while longer, if no more.

I have had a little intimation from New-Haven, that Miss Laurence is partial to me, and might easily be obtained, with a handsome property into the bargain. I am neither pleased with, nor averse to the girl. But she has money, and that may supply the place of love, by enabling me to pursue independent pleasures. This she must expect, if she marries a man of my cast. She doubtless knows my character; and if she is so vain of her charms or influence, as to think of reforming or confining me, she must bear the consequences.

However, I can keep my head up, at present, without recourse to the noose of matrimony; and shall, therefore, defer any particular attention to her, till necessity requires it.

I am, &c.

PETER SANFORD.

Letter XXXVIII

TO MRS. M. WHARTON

BOSTON

You commanded me, my dear mamma, to write you. That command, I cheerfully obey, in testimony of my ready submission and respect. No other

avocation could arrest my time, which is now completely occupied in scenes of amusement.

Mrs. Sumner is agreeably settled and situated. She appears to be possessed of every blessing which can render life desirable. Almost every day, since our arrival, has been engrossed by visitants. Our evenings, we have devoted to company abroad; and that more generally than we should otherwise have done, as my stay is limited to so short a period. The museum, the theatres, the circus and the assemblies have been frequented.

Mrs. Sumner has made me several presents, notwithstanding which, the articles requisite to a fashionable appearance, have involved me in considerable expense. I fear that you will think me extravagant when you are told how much.

Mr. Boyer tarried in town about a week, having business. He appeared a little concerned at my taste for dissipation, as he once termed it. He even took the liberty to converse seriously on the subject.

I was displeased with his freedom; and reminded him that I had the disposal of my own time, as yet; and that while I escaped the censure of my own heart, I hoped that no one else would presume to arraign it. He apologized and gave up his argument.

I was much surprised, the first time I went to the play, to see Major Sanford in the very next box. He immediately joined our party; and wherever I have been since, I have been almost sure to meet him.

Mr. Boyer has taken his departure; and I do not expect to see him again, till I return home.

O mamma! I am embarrassed about this man. His worth I acknowledge; nay, I esteem him very highly. But can there be happiness with such a disparity of dispositions?

I shall soon return to the bosom of domestic tranquillity, to the arms of maternal tenderness, where I can deliberate and advise at leisure, about this important matter. Till when,

I am, &c.

ELIZA WHARTON.

Letter XXXIX

TO MR. T. SELBY

HAMPSHIRE

DEAR SIR,

I believe that I owe you an apology for my long silence. But my time has been much engrossed of late; and my mind much more so. When it will be otherwise, I cannot foresee. I fear, my friend, that there is some foundation for your suspicions respecting my beloved Eliza. What pity it is, that so fair a form, so accomplished a mind, should be tarnished, in the smallest degree, by the follies of coquetry! If this be the fact, which I am loth to believe, all my regard for her shall never make me the dupe of it.

When I arrived at her residence, at New-Haven, where, I told you in my last, I was soon to go, she gave me a most cordial reception. Her whole behavior to me was correspondent with those sentiments of esteem and affection which she modestly avowed. She permitted me to accompany her

to Hartford, to restore her to her mother, and to declare my wish to receive her again from her hand. Thus far, all was harmony and happiness. As all my wishes were consistent with virtue and honor, she readily indulged them. She took apparent pleasure in my company, encouraged my hopes of a future union, and listened to the tender accents of love.

But the scenes of gaiety, which invited her attention, reversed her conduct. The delightful hours of mutual confidence, of sentimental converse, and of the interchange of refined affection were no more! Instead of these, parties were formed, unpleasing to my taste; and every opportunity was embraced to join in diversions, in which she knew I could not consistently take a share. I, however, acquiesced in her pleasure, though I sometimes thought myself neglected, and even hinted it to her mother. The old lady apologized for her daughter, by alleging that she had been absent for a long time; that her acquaintances were rejoiced at her return, and welcomed her by striving to promote her amusement.

One of her most intimate friends was married during my stay; and she appeared deeply interested in the event. She spent several days in assisting her, previous to the celebration. I resided, in the meantime, at her mamma's, visiting her at her friend's, where Major Sanford, among others, was received as a guest. Mrs. Sumner acquainted me that she had prevailed on Miss Wharton to go and spend a few weeks with her at Boston, whither she was removing; and urged my accompanying them. I endeavored to excuse myself, as I had been absent from my people a considerable time, and my return was now expected. But their importunity was so great, and Eliza's declaration that it would be very agreeable to her, so tempting, that I consented. Here I took lodgings and spent about a week, taking every opportunity to converse with Eliza, striving to discover her real disposition towards me. I mentioned the inconvenience of visiting her so often as I wished, and suggested my desire to enter, as soon as might be, into a family relation. I painted in the most alluring colors the pleasures resulting from domestic tranquillity, mutual confidence, and conjugal affection; and insisted on her declaring frankly whether she designed to share this happiness with me, and when it should commence. She owned that she intended to give me her hand; but when she should be ready, she could not yet determine. She pretended a promise from me to wait her time; to consent that she should share the pleasures of the fashionable world, as long as she chose, &c.

I then attempted to convince her of her mistaken ideas of pleasure; that the scenes of dissipation, of which she was so passionately fond, afforded no true enjoyment; that the adulation of the coxcomb could not give durability to her charms, or secure the approbation of the wise and good; nor could the fashionable amusements of brilliant assemblies, and crowded theatres furnish the mind with

> "That which nothing earthly gives, or can destroy,
> The soul's calm sunshine, and the heart felt joy."[2]

These friendly suggestions, I found were considered as the theme of a priest; and my desire to detach her from such empty pursuits, as the selfishness of a lover. She was even offended at my freedom; and warmly affirmed,

2. From Alexander Pope's *An Essay on Man* 4.167–79.

that no one had a right to arraign her conduct. I mentioned Major Sanford who was then in town, and who (though she went to places of public resort with Mr. and Mrs. Sumner) always met and gallanted her home. She rallied me upon my jealousy, as she termed it; wished that I would attend her myself, and then she should need no other gallant. I answered that I had rather resign that honor to another; but wished, for her sake, that he might be a gentleman whose character would not disgrace the company with which he associated. She appeared mortified and chagrined in the extreme. However, she studiously suppressed her emotions; and even soothed me with the blandishments of female softness. We parted amicably. She promised to return soon, and prepare for a compliance with my wishes. I cannot refuse to believe her! I cannot cease to love her! My heart is in her possession. She has a perfect command of my passions. Persuasion dwells on her tongue. With all the boasted fortitude and resolution of our sex, we are but mere machines. Let love once pervade our breasts; and its object may mould us into any form that pleases her fancy, or even caprice!

I have just received a letter from Eliza, informing me of her return to Hartford. Tomorrow I shall set out on a visit to the dear girl; for, my friend, notwithstanding all her foibles, she is very dear to me. Before you hear from me again, I expect that the happy day will be fixed; the day which shall unite, in the most sacred bands, this lovely maid and your faithful friend,

<div align="right">J. Boyer.</div>

<div align="center">

Letter XL

TO MR. T. SELBY

</div>

<div align="right">HAMPSHIRE</div>

I have returned; and the day, indeed, is fixed; but Oh! how different from my fond expectations! It is not the day of union, but the day of final separation; the day which divides me from my charmer; the day which breaks asunder the bands of love; the day on which my reason assumes its empire, and triumphs over the arts of a finished coquette! Congratulate me, my friend, that I have thus overcome my feelings, and repelled the infatuating wiles of a deceitful girl. I would not be understood to impeach Miss Wharton's virtue; I mean her chastity. Virtue in the common acceptation of the term, as applied to the sex, is confined to that particular, you know. But in my view, this is of little importance, where all other virtues are wanting!

When I arrived at Mrs. Wharton's, and inquired for Eliza, I was told that she had rode out; but was soon expected home. An hour after, a phaeton[3] stopped at the door, from which my fair one alighted and was handed into the house by Major Sanford, who immediately took leave. I met her and offered my hand, which she received with apparent tenderness.

When the family had retired after supper, and left us to talk on our particular affairs, I found the same indecision, the same loathness to bring our courtship to a period, as formerly. Her previous excuses were renewed, and her wishes to have a union still longer delayed were zealously urged. She could not bear the idea of confinement to the cares of a married life at

3. Carriage.

present; and begged me to defer all solicitation on that subject to some future day. I found my temper rise, and told her plainly, that I was not thus to be trifled with; that if her regard for me was sincere; if she really intended to form a connection with me, she could not thus protract the time, try my patience, and prefer every other pleasure to the rational interchange of affection, to the calm delights of domestic life. But in vain did I argue against her false notions of happiness; in vain did I represent the dangerous system of conduct, which she now pursued, and urge her to accept, before it was too late, the hand and heart which were devoted to her service. That, she said, she purposed, ere long to do; and hoped amply to reward my faithful love; but she could not fix the time this evening. She must consider a little further; and likewise consult her mother. Is it not Major Sanford whom you wish to consult, madam? Said I. She blushed, and gave me no answer. Tell me, Eliza, I continued, tell me frankly, if he has not supplanted me in your affections; if he be not the cause of my being thus evasively, thus cruelly treated? Major Sanford, sir, replied she, has done you no harm. He is a particular friend of mine; a polite gentleman, and an agreeable neighbor; and therefore I treat him with civility; but he is not so much interested in my concerns, as to alter my disposition towards any other person. Why, said I, do you talk of friendship with a man of his character? Between his society and mine there is a great contrast. Such opposite pursuits and inclinations cannot be equally pleasing to the same taste. It is therefore necessary, that you renounce the one, to enjoy the other. I will give you time to decide which. I am going to a friend's house to spend the night; and will call on you tomorrow, if agreeable, and converse with you further upon the matter. She bowed assent, and I retired.

The next afternoon I went as agreed; and found her mamma and her alone in the parlor. She was very pensive and appeared to have been in tears. The sight affected me. The idea of having treated her harshly, the evening before, disarmed me of my resolution to insist on her decision that day. I invited her to ride with me and visit a friend, to which she readily consented. We spent our time agreeably. I forebore to press her on the subject of our future union; but strove rather to soothe her mind, and inspire her with sentiments of tenderness towards me. I conducted her home, and returned early in the evening to my friend's, who met me at the door; and jocosely told me, that he expected I should now rob them of their agreeable neighbor. But, added he, we have been apprehensive that you would be rivalled, if you delayed your visit much longer. I did not suspect a rival, said I. Who can the happy man be? I can say nothing from personal observation, said he; but fame, of late, has talked loudly of Major Sanford and Miss Wharton. Be not alarmed, continued he, seeing me look grave. I presume no harm is intended. The Major is a man of gallantry, and Miss Wharton is a gay lady; but I dare say that your connection will be happy, *if it be formed*. I noticed a particular emphasis on the word *if*; and as we were alone, I followed him with questions, till the whole affair was developed. I informed him of my embarrassment; and he gave me to understand that Eliza's conduct had, for some time past, been a subject of speculation in the town; that formerly, her character was highly esteemed; but that her intimacy with a man of Sanford's known libertinism; more especially as she was supposed to be engaged to another, had rendered her very censurable; that they were often together; that wherever

she went, he was sure to follow, as if by appointment; that they walked, talked, sung and danced together in all companies; that some supposed he would marry her; others, that he only meditated adding her name to the black catalogue of deluded wretches, whom he had already ruined!

I rose, and walked the room in great agitation. He apologized for his freedom; was sorry if he had wounded my feelings; but friendship alone had induced him frankly to declare the truth, that I might guard against duplicity and deceit.

I thanked him for his kind intentions; and assured him that I should not quit the town till I had terminated this affair, in one way or another.

I retired to bed, but sleep was a stranger to my eyes. With the dawn I rose; and after breakfast walked to Mrs. Wharton's, who informed me, that Eliza was in her chamber, writing to a friend, but would be down in a few minutes. I entered into conversation with the old lady on the subject of her daughter's conduct, hinted my suspicions of the cause, and declared my resolution of knowing my destiny immediately. She endeavored to extenuate and excuse her as much as possible; but frankly owned that her behavior was mysterious; that no pains had been wanting, on her part, to alter and rectify it; that she had remonstrated, expostulated, advised and entreated, as often as occasion required. She hoped that my resolution would have a good effect, as she knew that her daughter esteemed me very highly.

In this manner we conversed till the clock struck twelve; and Eliza, not appearing, I desired her mamma to send up word that I waited to see her. The maid returned with an answer that she was indisposed, and had lain down. Mrs. Wharton observed, that she had not slept for several nights, and complained of the headache in the morning. The girl added, that she would wait on Mr. Boyer in the evening. Upon this information I rose and abruptly took my leave. I went to dine with a friend, to whom I had engaged myself the day before; but my mind was too much agitated to enjoy either the company or the dinner. I excused myself from tarrying to tea, and returned to Mrs. Wharton's. On inquiry, I was told that Eliza had gone to walk in the garden; but desired that no person might intrude on her retirement. The singularity of the request awakened my curiosity, and determined me to follow her. I sought her in vain, in different parts of the garden, till, going towards an arbor, almost concealed from sight, by surrounding shrubbery, I discovered her, sitting in close conversation with Major Sanford! My blood chilled in my veins, and I stood petrified with astonishment, at the disclosure of such baseness and deceit. They both rose in visible confusion. I dared not trust myself to accost them. My passions were raised, and I feared that I might say or do something unbecoming my character. I therefore gave them a look of indignation and contempt, and retreated to the house. I traversed the parlor hastily, overwhelmed with chagrin and resentment! Mrs. Wharton inquired the cause. I attempted to tell her, but my tongue refused utterance! While in this situation, Eliza entered the room. She was not less discomposed than myself. She sat down at the window and wept. Her mamma wept likewise. At length she recovered herself, in a degree, and desired me to sit down. I answered no; and continued walking. Will you, said she, permit me to vindicate my conduct and explain my motives? Your conduct, said I, cannot be vindicated; your motives need no explanation; they are too apparent! How, Miss Wharton, have I merited this treatment

from you? But I can bear it no longer. Your indifference to me proceeds from an attachment to another; and forgive me, if I add, to one, who is the disgrace of his own sex, and the destroyer of yours. I have been too long the dupe of your dissimulation and coquetry. Too long has my peace of mind been sacrificed to the arts of a woman, whose conduct has proved her unworthy of my regard; insensible to love, gratitude and honor!

To you, madam, said I, turning to her mother, I acknowledge my obligations for your friendship, politeness and attention. I once hoped for the privilege of rocking for you the cradle of declining age. I am deprived of that privilege; but I pray that you may never want a child, whose love and duty shall prove a source of consolation and comfort!

Farewell! If we never meet again in this life, I hope and trust we shall in a better; where the parent's eye shall cease to weep for the disobedience of a child; and the lover's heart to bleed for the infidelity of his mistress!

I turned to Eliza, and attempted to speak; but her extreme emotion softened me, and I could not command my voice. I took her hand, and bowing, in token of an adieu, went precipitately out of the house. The residence of my friend, with whom I lodged, was at no great distance, and thither I repaired. As I met him in the entry, I rushed by him, and betook myself to my chamber.

The fever of resentment and the tumult of passion began now to give place to the softer emotions of the soul. I found myself perfectly unmanned. I gave free scope to the sensibility of my heart; and the effeminate relief of tears materially lightened the load which oppressed me.

After this arduous struggle I went to bed; and slept more calmly than for several nights before. The next morning I wrote a farewell letter to Eliza (a copy of which I shall enclose to you) and ordering my horse to be brought, left town immediately.

My resentment of her behavior has much assisted me in erasing her image from my breast. In this exertion I have succeeded beyond my most sanguine expectations. The more I reflect on her temper and disposition, the more my gratitude is enlivened towards the wise Disposer of all events for enabling me to break asunder the snares of the deluder. I am convinced that the gaiety and extravagance of her taste, the frivolous levity of her manners disqualify her for the station in which I wished to have placed her. These considerations, together with that resignation to an overruling providence which the religion I profess, and teach, required me to cultivate, induce me cheerfully to adopt the following lines of an ingenious poet:

Since all the downward tracts of time,
 God's watchful eye surveys,
Oh, who so wise to choose our lot,
 Or regulate our ways?

Since none can doubt his equal love,
 Unmeasurably kind,
To his unerring gracious will,
 Be every wish resign'd.

Good, when he gives, supremely good,
 Not less when he denies;

E'en crosses from his sovereign hand,
Are blessings in disguise.

I am, &c.[4]

J. BOYER.

TO MISS ELIZA WHARTON

Enclosed in the foregoing

HARTFORD

MADAM,

Fearing, that my resolution may not be proof against the eloquence of those charms, which have so long commanded me, I take this method of bidding you a final adieu. I write not as a lover. That connection between us is forever dissolved; but I address you as a friend; a friend to your happiness, to your reputation, to your temporal and eternal welfare. I will not rehearse the innumerable instances of your imprudence and misconduct, which have fallen under my observation. Your own heart must be your monitor! Suffice it for me to warn you against the dangerous tendency of so dissipated a life; and to tell you that I have traced (I believe aright) the cause of your dissimulation and indifference to me. They are an aversion to the sober, rational frugal mode of living, to which my profession leads; a fondness for the parade, the gaiety, not to say, the licentiousness of a station calculated to gratify such a disposition; and a prepossession for Major Sanford, infused into your giddy mind by the frippery, flattery and artifice of that worthless and abandoned man. Hence you preferred a connection with him, if it could be accomplished; but a doubt, whether it could, together with the advice of your friends, who have kindly espoused my cause, have restrained you from the avowal of your real sentiments, and led you to continue your civilities to me. What the result of your coquetry would have been, had I waited for it, I cannot say, nor have I now any desire or interest to know. I tear from my breast the idea which I have long cherished of future union and happiness with you in the conjugal state. I bid a last farewell to these fond hopes, and leave you forever!

For your own sake, however, let me conjure you to review your conduct and before you have advanced beyond the possibility of returning to rectitude and honor, to restrain your steps from the dangerous path in which you now tread!

Fly Major Sanford. That man is a deceiver. Trust not his professions. They are certainly insincere; or he would not affect concealment; he would not induce you to a clandestine intercourse! Many have been the victims of his treachery! O Eliza! Add not to the number! Banish him from your society, if you wish to preserve your virtue unsullied, your character unsuspicious! It already begins to depreciate. Snatch it from the envenomed tongue of slander, before it receives an incurable wound!

Many faults have been visible to me; over which my affection once drew a veil. That veil is now removed. And, acting the part of a disinterested

4. Derived from the prose meditation "Reflections on a Flower Garden," by the English writer James Hervey (1714–1758).

friend, I shall mention some few of them with freedom. There is a levity in your manners, which is inconsistent with the solidity and decorum becoming a lady who has arrived to years of discretion. There is also an unwarrantable extravagance betrayed in your dress. Prudence and economy are such necessary, at least, such decent virtues, that they claim the attention of every female, whatever be her station or her property. To these virtues you are apparently inattentive. Too large a portion of your time is devoted to the adorning of your person.

Think not that I write thus plainly from resentment. No. It is from benevolence. I mention your foibles, not to reproach you with them, but that you may consider their nature and effects, and renounce them.

I wish you to regard this letter as the legacy of a friend; and to improve it accordingly. I shall leave town before you receive it. O, how different are my sensations at going, from what they were when I came! But I forbear description.

Think not, Eliza, that I leave you with indifference! The conflict is great; the trial is more than I can calmly support! Yet the consciousness of duty affords consolation. A duty I conceive it to be, which I owe to myself; and to the people of my charge, who are interested in my future connection.

I wish not for an answer; my resolution is unalterably fixed. But should you hereafter be convinced of the justice of my conduct; and become a convert to my advice, I shall be happy to hear it.

That you may have wisdom to keep you from falling, and conduct you safely through this state of trial to the regions of immortal bliss, is the fervent prayer of your sincere friend, and humble servant,

J. BOYER.

Letter XLI

TO MRS. LUCY SUMNER

HARTFORD

The retirement of my native home is not so gloomy, since my return from Boston, as I expected, from the contrast between them.

Indeed, the customs and amusements of this place are materially altered, since the residence of Major Sanford among us. The dull, old-fashioned sobriety which formerly prevailed, is nearly banished; and cheerfulness, vivacity, and enjoyment are substituted in its stead. Pleasure is now diffused through all ranks of the people, especially the rich; and surely it ought to be cultivated, since the wisest of men informs us, that "a merry heart doth good like a medicine."[5] As human life has many diseases, which require medicines, are we not right in selecting the most agreeable and palatable? Major Sanford's example has had great influence upon our society in general; and though some of our old dons think him rather licentious; yet, for ought I can see, he is as strict an observer of decorum, as the best of them. True, he seldom goes to church; but what of that? The Deity is not confined to temples made with hands. He may worship him as devoutly elsewhere, if he chooses; and who has a right to say he does not?

5. Proverbs 17.22.

His return from Boston was but a day or two after mine. He paid me an early visit; and, indeed, has been very attentive ever since. My mamma is somewhat precise in her notions of propriety; and of course, blames me for associating so freely with him. She says, that my engagements to Mr. Boyer ought to render me more sedate and more indifferent to the gallantry of mere *pleasure-hunters*, to use her phrase. But I think otherwise. If I am to become a recluse, let me, at least, enjoy those amusements, which are suited to my taste, a short time first. Why should I refuse the polite attentions of this gentleman? They smoothe the rugged path of life, and wonderfully accelerate the lagging wheels of time.

Indeed, Lucy, he has an admirable talent for contributing to vary and increase amusement. We have few hours unimproved. Some new plan of pleasure and sociability is constantly courting our adoption. He lives in all the magnificence of a prince; and why should I, who can doubtless share that magnificence if I please, forego the advantages and indulgences it offers, merely to gratify those friends who pretend to be better judges of my happiness than I am myself.

I have not yet told my mamma that he entertains me with the lover's theme; or, at least, that I listen to it. Yet I must own to you, from whom I have never concealed an action or idea, that his situation in life charms my imagination; that the apparent fervor and sincerity of his passion affect my heart. Yet there is something extremely problematical in his conduct. He is very urgent with me to dissolve my connection with Mr. Boyer, and engage not to marry him without his consent or knowledge, to say no more. He warmly applauds my wish, still longer to enjoy the freedom and independence of a single state; and professedly adopts it for his own. While he would disconnect me from another, he mysteriously conceals his own intentions and views. In conversation with him yesterday, I plainly told him that his conduct was unaccountable; that if his professions and designs were honorable he could not neglect to mention them to my mamma; that I should no longer consent to carry on a clandestine intercourse with him; that I hourly expected Mr. Boyer, whom I esteemed, and who was the favorite of my friends; and that unless he acted openly in this affair before his arrival, I should give my hand to him.

He appeared thunderstruck at this declaration. All his words and actions were indicative of the most violent emotions of mind. He entreated me to recall the sentence; for I knew not, he said, his motives for secrecy; yet he solemnly swore that they were honorable. I replied in the words of the poet,

> Trust not a man, they are by nature cruel,
> False, deceitful, treacherous, and inconstant.
> When a man talks of love, with caution hear him;
> But if he swear, he'll certainly deceive you.[6]

He begged that he might know by what means he had provoked my suspicions; by what means he had forfeited my confidence? His importunity vanquished my fortitude; and before we parted, I again promised to make him acquainted, from time to time, with the progress of my connection with Mr. Boyer.

6. From *The Orphan* (1680) 2.286–89, by the English dramatist Thomas Otway (1652–1685).

Now, my dear friend, I want your advice more than ever. I am inadvertently embarrassed by this man; and how to extricate myself, I know not. I am sensible that the power is in my hands; but the disposition (shall I confess it) is wanting!

> I know the right, and I approve it too;
> I know the wrong and yet the wrong pursue![7]

I have just received a card from Major Sanford, inviting me to ride this afternoon. At first I thought of returning a negative answer; but recollecting that Mr. Boyer must soon be here, I concluded it best to embrace this opportunity, of talking further with him. I must now prepare to go; but shall not close this letter, for I intend writing in continuation, as events occur, till this important business is decided.

Tuesday evening. The little tour which I mentioned to you this afternoon, was not productive of a final determination. The same plea was repeated over, and over again, without closing the cause. On my return I found Mr. Boyer waiting to receive me. My heart beat an involuntary welcome. I received him very cordially, though with a kind of pleasure mixed with apprehension. I must own that his conversation and manners are much better calculated to bear the scrutinizing eye of a refined understanding and taste, than Major Sanford's. But whether the fancy ought not to be consulted about our settlement for life is with me a question.

When we parted last, I had promised Mr. Boyer to inform him positively, at this visit, when my hand should be given. He therefore came, as he told me in the course of our conversation, with the resolution of claiming the fulfilment of this promise.

I begged absolution; told him, that I could not possibly satisfy his claim; and sought still to evade and put off the important decision. He grew warm; and affirmed that I treated him ungenerously, and made needless delays. He even accused me of indifference towards him; and of partiality to another. Major Sanford he believed, was the man who robbed him of the affection which he had supposed his due. He warned me against any intercourse with him, and insisted that I must renounce the society of the one or the other immediately. He would leave me, he said, this evening and call tomorrow to know the result of my determination. It was late before he bade me good night; since which I have written these particulars. It is now time to lay aside my pen, and deliberate what course to take.

Wednesday Evening. Last night I closed not my eyes. I rose this morning with the sun, and went into the garden till breakfast. My mamma doubtless saw the disorder of my mind, but kindly avoided any inquiry about it. She was affectionately attentive to me, but said nothing of my particular concerns. I mentioned not my embarrassment to her. She had declared herself in favor of Mr. Boyer; therefore I had no expectation, that she would advise impartially. I retired to my chamber, and remained in a kind of reverie, for more than an hour; when I was roused by the rattling of a carriage at the door. I hastened to the window, and saw Major Sanford just driving away. The idea of his having been to converse with my mamma gave me new sensations. A thousand perplexities occurred to my mind relative to the part

7. Derived from *Metamorphoses* 7.17, by the Roman poet Ovid (43 B.C.E.–17 C.E.).

most proper for me to act in this critical situation. All these might have been avoided, had I gone down and inquired into the matter; but this I delayed till dinner. My mamma then informed me, that Major Sanford had been with her, and inquired for me; but that she thought it unnecessary to call me, as she presumed I had no particular business with him. I knew the motives by which she was actuated, and was vexed at her evasions. I told her plainly, that she would never carry her point in this way; that I thought myself capable of conducting my own affairs and wished her not to interfere, except by her advice, which I should always listen to, and comply with when I could possibly make it consistent with my inclination and interest. She wept at my undutiful anger (of which I have severely repented since) and affectionately replied, that my happiness was the object of her wishes and prayers; conformably to which she felt constrained, freely to speak her mind, though it incurred my displeasure. She then went through again with all the comparative circumstances and merits of the two candidates for my favor, which have perpetually rung in my ears for months. I shed tears at the idea of my embarrassment; and in this condition Mr. Boyer found us. He appeared to be affected by my visible disorder; and without inquiring the cause, endeavored to dissipate it. This was kindly done. He conversed upon indifferent subjects; and invited me to ride, and take tea with your mamma, to which I readily consented. We found her at home; and passed the time agreeably, excepting the alloy of your absence. Mr. Boyer touched lightly on the subject of our last evening's debate; but expatiated largely on the pleasing power of love; and hoped that we should one day both realize and exemplify it in perfection. When we returned, he observed that it was late, and took his leave; telling me that he should call tomorrow; and begged that I would then relieve his suspense. As I was retiring to bed, the maid gave me a hint that Major Sanford's servant had been here and left a letter. I turned instantly back to my mamma, and telling her my information, demanded the letter. She hesitated, but I insisted on having it; and seeing me resolute, she reluctantly gave it into my hand. It contained the following words:

"Am I forsaken? Am I abandoned? Oh my adorable Eliza, have you sacrificed me to my rival? Have you condemned me to perpetual banishment, without a hearing?

I came this day, to plead my cause at your feet; but was cruelly denied the privilege of seeing you! My mind is all anarchy and confusion! My soul is harrowed up with jealousy! I will be revenged on those who separate us, if that distracting event take place! But it is from your lips only that I can hear my sentence! You must witness its effects! To what lengths my despair may carry me, I know not! You are the arbitress of my fate!

Let me conjure you to meet me in your garden tomorrow at any hour you shall appoint. My servant will call for an answer in the morning. Deny me not an interview; but have pity on your faithful Sanford."

I wrote for answer, that I would meet him tomorrow, at five o'clock in the afternoon.

I have now before me another night for consideration; and shall pass it in that employment. I purpose not to see Mr. Boyer, till I have conversed with Major Sanford.

Thursday Morning. The morning dawns and ushers in the day; a day, perhaps big with the fate of your friend! What that fate may be is wrapped in the womb of futurity; that futurity which a kind Providence has wisely concealed from the penetration of mortals!

After mature consideration; after revolving and re-revolving every circumstance on both sides of the question, I have nearly determined, in compliance with the advice of my friends, and the dictates of my own judgment, to give Mr. Boyer the preference, and with him to tread the future round of life.

As to the despair of Major Sanford, it does not much alarm me. Such violent passions are seldom so deeply rooted, as to produce lasting effects. I must, however, keep my word, and meet him according to promise.

Mr. Boyer is below. My mamma has just sent me word that he wished to see me. My reply was that I had lain down, which was a fact.

One o'Clock. My mamma, alarmed by my indisposition, has visited my apartment. I soon convinced her that it was but trifling, owing principally to the want of sleep; and that an airing in the garden, which I intended towards night, would restore me.

Ten o'clock, at night.—The day is past! And such a day it has been, as I hope never more to see!

At the hour appointed, I went tolerably composed and resolute into the garden. I had taken several turns, and retired into the little arbor, where you and I have spent so many happy hours, before Major Sanford entered. When he appeared, a consciousness of the impropriety of this clandestine intercourse suffused my cheek, and gave a coldness to my manners. He immediately penetrated the cause, and observed that my very countenance told him he was no longer a welcome guest to me. I asked him if he ought so to be; since his motives for seeking admission were unworthy of being communicated to my friends? That he said was not the case, but that prudence in the present instance required a temporary concealment.

He then undertook to exculpate himself from blame, assuring me that as soon as I should discountenance the expectations of Mr. Boyer, and discontinue the reception of his address, his intentions should be made known. He was enlarging upon this topic, when we heard a footstep approaching us; and looking up saw Mr. Boyer within a few paces of the arbor.—Confusion seized us both! We rose involuntarily from our seats, but were mute as statues! He spoke not a word, but casting a look of indignant accusation at me, a glance which penetrated my very soul, turned on his heel, and walked hastily back to the house.

I stood a few moments, considering what course to take, though shame and regret had almost taken from me the power of thought.

Major Sanford took my hand. I withdrew it from him. I *must* leave you, said I. Where will you go? said he. I will go and try to retrieve my character. It has suffered greatly by this fatal interview.

He threw himself at my feet and exclaimed, leave me not. Eliza, I conjure you not to leave me. Let me go now, I rejoined, or I bid you farewell for ever. I flew precipitately by him, and went into the parlor, where I found Mr. Boyer and my mamma, the one traversing the room in the greatest agitation; the other in flood of tears! Their appearance affected me; and I wept like an infant! When I had a little recovered myself, I

begged him to sit down; he answered no. I then told him, that however unjustifiable my conduct might appear, perhaps I might explain it to his satisfaction, if he would hear me; that my motives were innocent, though they doubtless wore the aspect of criminality, in his view. He sternly replied, that no palliation could avail; that my motives were sufficiently notorious! He accused me of treating him ill, of rendering him the dupe of coquetting artifice, of having an intrigue with Major Sanford, and declared his determination to leave me forever, as unworthy of his regard, and incapable of love, gratitude, or honor!—There was too much reason in support of his accusations for me to gainsay them, had his impetuosity suffered me to attempt it.

But in truth I had no inclination to self defence. My natural vivacity had forsaken me; and I listened without interrupting him to the fluency of reproachful language, which his resentment inspired. He took a very solemn and affectionate leave of my mamma; thanking her for her politeness, and wishing her much future felicity. He attempted to address me, I suppose somewhat in the same way, but his sensibility overcame him; and he only took my hand, and bowing in silence, departed.

The want of rest for two long nights together, the exercise of mind, and conflict of passions, which now tortured my breast, were too much for me to support!

When I saw that he was gone; that he had actually forsaken me, I fainted. My mamma, with the assistance of the maid, soon restored me.

When I opened my eyes, and beheld this amiable and tender parent, watching and attending me with the most anxious concern; without one reproachful word, without one accusing look, my reflections upon the part I had acted, in defeating her benevolent wishes, were exquisitely afflictive! But we mutually forbore to mention the occasion of my illness; and I complied with her advice to take some refreshment, and retire to my chamber. I am so much fatigued by the exertions of the day, that rest is absolutely necessary; and I lay aside my pen to seek it.

Friday Morning. When I shall again receive the balmy influence of sleep, I know not. It has absolutely forsaken me at present. I have had a most restless night. Every awakening idea presented itself to my imagination; whether I had sustained a real loss in Mr. Boyer's departure; reflections on my own misconduct, with the censure of my friends, and the ill-natured remarks of my enemies, excited the most painful anxiety in my mind!

I am going down, but how shall I see my mamma? To her will I confess my faults, in her maternal breast repose my cares, and by her friendly advice regulate my conduct. Had I done this before, I might have escaped this trouble, and saved both her and myself many distressing emotions!

Friday Evening. I have had a long conversation with my mamma, which has greatly relieved my mind. She has soothed me with the most endearing tenderness.

Mr. Atkins, with whom Mr. Boyer lodged while in town, called here this afternoon. I did not see him, but he told my mamma that Mr. Boyer had returned home, and left a letter for me, which he had promised to convey with his own hand. By this letter I am convinced that the dye is absolutely cast, with respect to him, and that no attempts on my part to bring about a reconciliation would be either prudent or successful. He has penetrated the

cause of my proceedings; and such is his resentment, that I am inclined not much to regret his avoiding another interview.

My excuses would be deemed utterly insufficient, and truth would not befriend and justify me.

As I know you are impatient to hear from me, I will now dispatch this long letter without any other addition, than that I am your sincere friend.

ELIZA WHARTON.

Letter XLII

TO MR. CHARLES DEIGHTON

HARTFORD

Well, Charles, the show is over, as we yankees say; and the girl is my own. That is, if I will have her. I shall take my own time for that, however. I have carried my point, and am amply revenged on the whole posse of those dear friends of her's. She was entangled by a promise (not to marry this priest without my knowledge,) which her conscience would not let her break. Thank God, I have no conscience. If I had, I believe it would make wretched work with me! I suppose she intended to have one, or the other of us; but preferred me. I have escaped the noose, this time, and I'll be fairly hanged, if I ever get so near it again. For indeed Charles, I was seriously alarmed. I watched all their motions; and the appearances of harmony between them awakened all my activity and zeal. So great was my infatuation, that I verily believe I should have asked her in marriage, and risked the consequences, rather than to have lost her!

I went to the house, while Mr. Boyer was in town, but her mamma refused to call her, or to acquaint her that I was there. I then wrote a despairing letter, and obtained a conference with her in the garden. This was a fortunate event for me. True, Eliza was very haughty, and resolutely insisted on immediate declaration or rejection. And I cannot say what would have been the result, if Mr. Boyer had not surprized us together. He gave us a pretty harsh look and retired without speaking a word.

I endeavored to detain Eliza, but in vain. She left me on my knees, which are always ready to bend on such occasions.

This finished the matter, it seems. I rose, and went into a near neighbor's to observe what happened; and in about half an hour saw Mr. Boyer come out, and go to his lodgings.

This, said I to myself, is a good omen. I went home, and was informed next day, that he had mounted his horse and departed.

I heard nothing more of her till yesterday, when I determined to know how she stood affected towards me. I therefore paid her a visit, her mamma being luckily abroad.

She received me very placidly, and told me, on inquiry, that Mr. Boyer's resentment at her meeting me in the garden was so great, that he had bid her a final adieu. I congratulated myself on having no rival; hoped that her favor would now be unbiassed, and that in due time I should reap the reward of my fidelity. She begged me not to mention the subject; said she had been perplexed by our competition, and wished not to hear anything further about

it at present. I bowed in obedience to her commands and changed the discourse.

I informed her, that I was about making a tour to the southward; that I should be absent several months, and trusted that on my return her embarrassments would be over.

I left her with regret. After all, Charles, she is the *summum bonum*[8] of my life. I must have her in some way or other. Nobody else shall, I am resolved.

I am making preparations for my journey; which between you and me, is occasioned by the prospect of making a speculation, by which I hope to mend my affairs. The voyage will at least lessen my expenses, and screen me from the importunity of creditors till I can look about me.

<div style="text-align: right">PETER SANFORD.</div>

Letter XLIII

TO MISS ELIZA WHARTON

<div style="text-align: right">NEW-HAVEN</div>

MY DEAR ELIZA,

Through the medium of my friends at Hartford I have been informed of the progress of your affairs, as they have transpired. The detail which my sister gave me of your separation from Mr. Boyer was painful; as I had long contemplated a happy union between you. But still more disagreeable sensations possessed my breast, when told that you had suffered your lively spirits to be depressed, and resigned yourself to solitude and dejection!

Why, my dear friend, should you allow this event thus to affect you? Heaven, I doubt not, has happiness still in store for you—perhaps greater than you could have enjoyed in that connection. If the conviction of any misconduct on your part gives you pain, dissipate it by the reflection, that unerring rectitude is not the lot of mortals, that few are to be found who have not deviated in a greater or less degree from the maxims of prudence. Our greatest mistakes may teach lessons which will be useful through life.

But I will not moralize. Come and see us; and we will talk over the matter once, and then dismiss it forever. Do prevail on your mamma to part with you a month or two, at least. I wish you to witness how well I manage my nursery business. You will be charmed with little Harriot. I am already enough of the mother to think her a miniature of beauty and perfection.

How natural, and how easy the transition from one stage of life to another! Not long since I was a gay, volatile girl; seeking satisfaction in fashionable circles and amusements; but now I am thoroughly domesticated. All my happiness is centered within the limits of my own walls; and I grudge every moment that calls me from the pleasing scenes of domestic life. Not that I am so selfish as to exclude my friends from my affection or society. I feel interested in their concerns, and enjoy their company. I must own, however, that conjugal and parental love are the main springs of my life. The conduct of some mothers in depriving their helpless offspring of the care and kindness which none but a mother can feel, is to me unaccountable. There are many nameless attentions which nothing short of maternal tenderness and

8. Greatest good (Latin).

solicitude can pay; and for which the endearing smiles and progressive improvements of the lovely babe are an ample reward.

How delightful to trace from day to day the expansion of reason and the dawnings of intelligence! Oh, how I anticipate the time, when these faculties shall be displayed by the organs of speech; when the lisping accent shall heighten our present pleasure, and the young idea be capable of direction "how to shoot"! General Richman is not less interested by these enjoyments than myself. All the father beams in his eye! All the husband reigns in his heart, and pervades his every action!

Miss Lawrence is soon to be married to Mr. Laiton. I believe he is a mere fortune-hunter. Indeed she has little to recommend her to any other. Nature has not been very bountiful, either to her body or mind. Her parents have been shamefully deficient in her education; but have secured to her what they think the chief good; not considering that happiness is by no means the invariable attendant of wealth.

I hope this incoherent scroll will amuse, while it induces you speedily to favor us with another visit.

My best wishes attend your honored mamma; while I subscribe myself, &c.

A. RICHMAN.

Letter XLIV

TO MRS. LUCY SUMNER

HARTFORD

I am extremely depressed, my dear Lucy! The agitating scenes, through which I have lately passed, have broken my spirits, and rendered me unfit for society.

Major Sanford has visited me, and taken his leave. He is gone to the southward on a tour of two or three months. I declined any further conversation with him, on the subject of love. At present, I wish not to hear it mentioned by anyone.

I have received a very friendly and consolatory letter from Mrs. Richman. She invites me to spend a few months with her; which with my mamma's consent I shall do. I hope the change of situation and company will dissipate the gloom which hangs over my mind.

It is a common observation, that we know not the value of a blessing but by deprivation.

This is strictly verified in my case. I was insensible of my regard for Mr. Boyer, till this fatal separation took place. His merit and worth now appear in the brightest colors. I am convinced of that excellence which I once slighted; and the shade of departed happiness haunts me perpetually! I am sometimes tempted to write him, and confess my faults; to tell him the situation of my mind, and to offer him my hand. But he has precluded all hopes of success, by the severity of his letter to me. At any rate, I shall do nothing of the kind, till my return from New-Haven.

I am the more willing to leave home, as my affairs are made a town talk. My mamma persuades me to disregard it. But how can I rise superior to "The world's dread laugh, which scarce the firm philosopher can scorn?"

Pray remember me to Mr. Sumner. You are happy, my friend, in the love and esteem of a worthy man; but more happy still, in deserving them. Adieu.

ELIZA WHARTON.

Letter XLV

TO THE SAME

HARTFORD

I have returned to the once smiling feat of maternal affection; but I find not repose and happiness, even there!

In the society of my amiable friends at New-Haven, I enjoyed everything that friendship could bestow; but rest to a disturbed mind was not in their power.

I was on various parties of pleasure, and passed through different scenes of amusement; but with me they have lost their charms. I relished them not as formerly.

Mrs. Richman advises me to write to Mr. Boyer, and I have concluded to act accordingly. If it answer no other purpose, it will be a relief to my mind. If he ever felt for me the tenderness and regard which he professed, me-thinks they cannot be entirely obliterated. If they still remain, perhaps I may rekindle the gentle flame, and we may both be happy. I may at least recall his esteem, and that will be a satisfaction to my conscious mind.

I wonder what has become of Major Sanford! Has he too forsaken me? Is it possible for him wilfully to neglect me? I will not entertain so injurious a suspicion.

Yet, if it were the case, it would not affect me like Mr. Boyer's disaffection; for I frankly own, that my fancy, and a taste for gaity of life, induced me to cherish the idea of a connection with Major Sanford; while Mr. Boyer's real merit has imprinted those sentiments of esteem and love in my heart, which time can never efface.

Instead of two or three, more than twelve months have elapsed, and I have not received a line from Major Sanford in all that time, which I fully expected, though he made no mention of writing; nor have I heard a sylla-ble about him, except a report circulated by his servants, that he is on the point of marrying, which I do not believe. No, it is impossible! I am per-suaded that his passion for me was sincere, however deceitful he may have been with others. But I will not bestow an anxious thought upon him. My design relative to Mr. Boyer, demands my whole attention.

My hopes and fears alternately prevail, and my resolution is extremely fluc-tuating. How it finally terminates you shall hear in my next. Pray write to me soon. I stand in need of the consoling power of friendship. Nothing can beguile my pensive hours, and exhilarate my drooping spirits, like your letters.

Let me know how you are to be entertained this winter at the theatre. That, you know, is a favorite amusement of mine. You see I can step out of myself a little. Afford an assisting hand, and perhaps I may again be fit for society.

ELIZA WHARTON.

Letter XLVI

TO THE REV. J. BOYER

HARTFORD

SIR,

It is partly in compliance with your desire, in your last letter to me, in which you told me, "that when I am convinced of the justice of your conduct, and become a convert to your advice, you shall be happy to hear it;" and partly from a wish to inform you, that such is in truth my present state of mind, that I now write to you.

I cannot but hope that this letter coming from the hand which you once sought, will not be unacceptable.

Pope very justly observes, "that every year is a critic on the last."[9] The truth of this observation is fully exemplified in my years! How severely this condemns the follies of the preceding, my own heart alone can testify!

I shall not offer any palliation or apology for my misconduct. You told me it admitted none. I frankly confess it; and if the most humble acknowledgement of my offences, with an assurance that they have cost me the deepest repentance, can in any degree atone for them, I now make that atonement. Casting off the veil of dissimulation, I shall write with frankness; believing you possessed of more honor than to make any ungenerous use of the confidence reposed in you.

To say that I ever esteemed you, may, perhaps, appear paradoxical, when compared with certain circumstances which occurred during our acquaintance; but to assert that I loved you may be deemed still more so. Yet these are real facts, facts of which I was then sensible, and by which I am now more than ever affected.

I think you formerly remarked, that absence served but to heighten real love. This I find by experience. Need I blush to declare these sentiments, when occasion like this, calls for the avowal? I will go even further, and offer you that heart which once you prized; that hand which you once solicited. The sentiments of affection, which you then cultivated, though suppressed, I flatter myself are not wholly obliterated. Suffer me then to rekindle the latent flame; to revive that friendship and tenderness, which I have so foolishly neglected. The endeavor of my future life shall be to reward your benevolence, and perhaps we may yet be happy together.

But let not this offer of myself constrain you. Let not pity influence your conduct. I would have you return, if that pleasing event take place, a voluntary act. Receive or consent not to confer happiness.

I thought it a duty which I owed to you, and to myself, to make this expiation; this sacrifice of female reserve, for the wrongs I have done you. As such I wish you to accept it; and if your affections are entirely alienated, or otherwise engaged; if you cannot again command the respect and love which I would recall, do not despise me for the concessions I have made. Think as favorably of my past faults, and of my present disposition, as charity will allow. Continue, if possible, to be my friend, though you cease to be my lover.

9. Cf. Alexander Pope's *Essay on Criticism* (1711), line 573: "And make each day a critic on the last."

Should this letter find you in the full possession of happiness, let not the idea of your once loved Eliza, thus intruding itself again upon your thoughts, interrupt your enjoyments. May some distinguished female, as deserving, as fair, partake with you of that bliss which I have forfeited.

Whatever may be my destiny, my best wishes shall ever attend you, and a pleasing remembrance of your honorable attentions preside, till death, in the breast of,

<div style="text-align: right">ELIZA WHARTON.</div>

Letter XLVII

TO MISS ELIZA WHARTON

<div style="text-align: right">HAMPSHIRE</div>

MADAM,

As I was sitting last evening in my study, a letter was handed me by a servant; upon which I no sooner cast my eye, than I recognized, with surprise, the hand and seal of my once loved, but to me long lost Eliza! I opened it hastily, and with still greater surprise, read the contents!

You write with frankness. I shall answer in the same manner.

On reviewing our former intercourse, be assured, that I have not an accusing thought in my heart. The regard which I felt for you was tender and animated, but it was not of that passionate kind which ends in death or despair. It was governed by reason, and had a nobler object in view, than mere sensual gratification. It was excited by the appearance of excellent qualities. Your conduct, at length, convinced me it was misplaced; that you possessed not, in reality, those charms which I had fondly ascribed to you. They were inconsistent, I conceived, with that artifice and dissimulation, of which you strove to render me the dupe. But thank heaven, the snare was broken. My eyes were opened to discover your folly; and my heart, engaged, as it was, exerted resolution and strength to burst asunder the chain by which you held me enslaved, and to assert the rights of an injured man.

The parting scene, you remember. I reluctantly bade you adieu. I tore myself from you, determined to eradicate your idea from my breast! Long and severe was the struggle. I at last vanquished, as I thought, every tender passion of my soul, (for they all centered in you) and resigned myself to my God and my duty; devoting those affections to friendship, which had been disappointed in love. But they are again called into exercise. The virtuous, the amiable, the accomplished Maria Selby possesses my entire confidence and esteem; and I trust I am not deceived, when I think her highly deserving of both. With her I expect soon to be united in the most sacred and endearing of human relations; with her to pass my future days in serenity and peace.

Your letter, therefore, came too late; were there no other obstacle to the renewal of our connection. I hope at the close of life, when we take a retrospect of the past, that neither of us shall have reason to regret our separation.

Permit me to add, that for your own sake, and for the sake of your ever valued friends, I sincerely rejoice that your mind has regained its native strength and beauty; that you have emerged from the shade of fanciful vanity. For although to adopt your own phrase, I cease to style myself your lover,

among the number of your friends, I am happy to be reckoned. As such, let me conjure you, by all that is dear and desirable, both in this life, and another, to adhere, with undeviating exactness, to the path of rectitude and innocence; and to improve the noble talents, which heaven has liberally bestowed upon you, in rendering yourself amiable, and useful to your friends. Thus will you secure your own, while you promote the happiness of all around you.

I shall ever cherish sentiments of kindness towards you, and with gratitude remember your condescension, in the testimony of regard, which you have given me in your last letter.

I hope soon to hear that your heart and hand are bestowed on some worthy man, who deserves the happiness you are formed to communicate. Whatever we may have called errors, will, on my part, be forever buried in oblivion; and for your own peace of mind, I entreat you to forget that any idea of a connection between us ever existed.

I shall always rejoice at the news of your welfare, and my ardent prayers will daily arise for your temporal and eternal felicity.

I am, &c.

J. BOYER.

Letter XLVIII

TO MRS. LUCY SUMNER

HARTFORD

Health, placid serenity, and every domestic pleasure are the lot of my friend; while I, who once possessed the means of each, and the capacity of tasting them, have been tossed upon the waves of folly, till I am shipwrecked on the shoals of despair!

Oh my friend, I am undone! I am slighted, rejected by the man who once sought my hand, by the man who still retains my heart! And what adds an insupportable poignancy to the reflection, is self-condemnation! From this inward torture, where shall I flee? Where shall I seek that happiness which I have madly trifled away?

The enclosed letters[1] will show you whence this tumult of soul arises. But I blame not Mr. Boyer. He has acted nobly. I approve his conduct, though it operates my ruin!

He is worthy of his intended bride, and she is what I am not, worthy of him. Peace and joy be their portion, both here and hereafter! But what are now my prospects? What are to be the future enjoyments of my life?

Oh that I had not written to Mr. Boyer! By confessing my faults, and by avowing my partiality to him, I have given him the power of triumphing in my distress; of returning to my tortured heart all the pangs of slighted love! And what have I now to console me? My bloom is decreasing; my health is sensibly impaired. Those talents, with the possession of which I have been flattered, will be of little avail when unsupported by respectability of character!

My mamma, who knows too well the distraction of my mind, endeavors to soothe and compose me, on christian principles; but they have not their desired effect. I dare not converse freely with her on the subject of my present

1. See the two preceding letters [Foster's note].

uneasiness, lest I should distress her. I am therefore, obliged to conceal my disquietude, and appear as cheerful as possible in her company, though my heart is ready to burst with grief!

Oh that you were near me, as formerly, to share and alleviate my cares! To have some friend in whom I could repose confidence, and with whom I could freely converse, and advise, on this occasion, would be an unspeakable comfort!

Such a one, next to yourself, I think Julia Granby to be. With your leave and consent I should esteem it a special favor if she would come and spend a few months with me. My mamma joins in this request. I would write to her on the subject, but cannot compose myself at present. Will you prefer my petition for me?

If I have not forfeited your friendship, my dear Mrs. Sumner, write to me, and pour its healing balm into the wounded mind of your

ELIZA WHARTON.

Letter XLIX

TO MISS ELIZA WHARTON

BOSTON

Your truly romantic letter came safe to hand. Indeed, my dear, it would make a very pretty figure in a novel. A bleeding heart, slighted love, and all the *et ceteras* of romance enter into the composition!

Excuse this raillery; and I will now write more seriously. You refer yourself to my friendship for consolation. It shall be exerted for the purpose. But I must act the part of a skilful surgeon, and probe the wound, which I undertake to heal.

Where, O Eliza Wharton! Where is that fund of sense and sentiment which once animated your engaging form? Where that strength of mind, that independence of soul, that alacrity and sprightliness of deportment, which formerly raised you superior to every adverse occurrence? Why have you resigned these valuable endowments, and suffered yourself to become the sport of contending passions?

You have now emerged from that mist of fanciful folly, which, in a measure obscured the brilliance of your youthful days.

True, you figured among the first-rate coquettes; while your friends, who knew your accomplishments, lamented the misapplication of them; but now they rejoice at the returning empire of reason.

True, you have erred; misled by the gaiety of your disposition, and that volatility, and inconsideration, which were incident to your years; but you have seen and nobly confessed your errors. Why do you talk of slighted love? True, Mr. Boyer, supposing you disregarded him, transferred his affections to another object; but have you not your admirers still, among men of real merit? Are you not esteemed and caressed by numbers, who know you capable of shining in a distinguished sphere of life? Turn then, my friend, from the gloomy prospect, which your disturbed imagination has brought into view. Let reason and religion erect their throne in your breast; obey their dictates and be happy. Past experience will point out the quicksands which you are to avoid in your future course.

Date then, from this, a new era of life; and may every moment be attended with felicity. Follow Mr. Boyer's advice, and forget all former connections.

Julia accepts your invitation. Nothing short of your request could induce me to part with her. She is a good girl; and her society will amuse and instruct you.

<div style="text-align:center">I am, &c.</div>

<div style="text-align:right">LUCY SUMNER.</div>

<div style="text-align:center">Letter L</div>

<div style="text-align:center">TO MRS. LUCY SUMNER</div>

<div style="text-align:right">HARTFORD</div>

My Julia Granby has arrived. She is all that I once was; easy, sprightly, debonair. Already has she done much towards relieving my mind. She endeavors to divert and lead my thoughts into a different channel from that to which they are now prone. Yesterday, we had each an invitation to a ball. She labored hard to prevail on me to go; but I obstinately refused. I cannot yet mix with gay and cheerful circles. I therefore alleged that I was indisposed, and persuaded her to go without me.

The events of my life have always been unaccountably wayward. In many instances I have been ready to suppose that some evil genius presided over my actions, which has directed them contrary to the sober dictates of my own judgment.

I am sometimes tempted to adopt the sentiment expressed in the following lines of the poet,

> To you, great gods, I make my last appeal;
> O, clear my conscience, or my crimes reveal!
> If wand'ring through the paths of life I've run;
> And backward trod the steps, I fought to shun,
> Impute my errors to your own decree;
> My feet were guilty, but my heart was free.[2]

I suppose you will tell me, that the fate I accuse, through the poet, is only the result of my own imprudence. Well, be it what it may; either the impulse of my own passions, or some higher efficiency; sure I am, that I pay dear for its operation.

I have heard it remarked, that experience is the preceptor of fools; but that the wise need not its instruction. I believe I must be content to rank accordingly, and endeavor to reap advantage from its tuition.

Julia urges me to revisit the scenes of amusements and pleasure; in which she tells me, she is actuated by selfish motives. She wishes it for her own sake. She likes neither to be secluded from them, nor to go alone. I am sometimes half inclined to seek, in festive mirth, a refuge from thought and reflection. I would escape, if possible, from the idea of Mr. Boyer. This I have never been able to accomplish, since he dropped a tear upon my hand, and left me.

2. Derived from *Oedipus, a Tragedy* (1679) 3.1.588–93, by the English poet and dramatist John Dryden (1631–1700); here, Oedipus learns that he has married his mother, Jocasta.

I marked the spot with my eye; and twenty times in a day, do I view it, and fondly imagine it still there! How could I give him pain! I hope his happy Maria never will! I hope she will reward that merit, which I have slighted! But I forbear. This theme carries away my pen, if I but touch upon it. And no wonder; for it is the sole exercise of my thoughts! Yet I will endeavor to divert them. Send me some new books; not such, however, as will require much attention. Let them be plays or novels, or anything else, that will amuse and extort a smile.

Julia and I have been rambling in the garden. She insisted upon my going with her into the arbor, where I was surprised with Major Sanford. What a crowd of painful ideas rushed upon my imagination! I believe she repented her rashness. But no more of this. I must lay aside my pen; for I can write nothing else!

ELIZA WHARTON.

Letter LI

TO MRS. LUCY SUMNER

HARTFORD

DEAR MADAM,
You commanded me to write you respecting Miss Wharton; and I obey. But I cannot describe to you the surprising change, which she has undergone. Her vivacity has entirely forsaken her; and she has actually become, what she once dreaded above all things, a recluse! She flies from company, as eagerly as she formerly sought it! Her mamma is exceedingly distressed by the settled melancholy which appears in her darling child; but neither of us think it best to mention the subject to her. We endeavor to find means to amuse her; and we flatter ourselves that the prospect of success rather increases. It would add greatly to my happiness, to contribute, in any degree, to restore her to herself, to her friends, and to society.

We are all invited to dine abroad tomorrow; and to oblige me, she has consented to go.

Pray madam, write to her often. Your letters may do much for her. She is still feelingly alive to the power of friendship; and none can exercise it upon her to greater acceptance or with more advantage than yourself.

Major Sanford's house is undergoing a complete repair. The report is, that he is soon to be married. Miss Wharton has heard, but does not believe it. I hope, for her sake, it will prove true. For, at any rate, he is about returning; and from her mamma's account of his past conduct towards Eliza, were he to return unconnected, he would probably renew his attentions; and though they might end in marriage, her happiness would not be secured. She has too nice a sense of love and honor, to compound with his licentious principles. A man, who has been dissolute before marriage, will very seldom be faithful afterwards.

I went into Eliza's chamber the other day, and found her with a miniature picture in her hand. You pretend to be a physiognomist, Julia, said she. What can you trace in that countenance? I guessed whose it was; and looking wistfully at it, replied, I believe the original is an artful, designing man.

He looks to me like a Chesterfieldian.[3] Pray who is he? Major Sanford, said she; and I am afraid you have hit his character exactly. Sure I am, that the appearance of those traits in it has made my heart ache! She wept, as she spoke it.

Poor girl! I wish he may never give you greater cause to weep! She is strongly blind to the vices and imperfections of this man. Though naturally penetrating, he has somehow or other cast a deceptious mist over her imagination, with respect to himself. She professes neither to love, nor esteem him; and owns that his ungenerous artifice misled her in her treatment of Mr. Boyer. Yet she has forgiven him, and thinks him a pleasing companion!

How prone to error is the human mind! How much lighter than the breath of zephyrs the operations of fancy! Strange then, it should ever preponderate over the weightier powers of the understanding!

But I will not moralize. My business here is to dissipate, not to collect ideas; and I must regulate myself accordingly.

I am endeavoring to prepare Eliza, by degrees, to accompany me to Boston, the ensuing winter; but think it doubtful whether I shall succeed. I shall, however, return myself; till when, I am, &c.

JULIA GRANBY.

Letter LII

TO MISS ELIZA WHARTON

BOSTON

MY DEAR ELIZA,

I received yours of the 24th. ult.[4] and thank you for it; though it did not afford me those lively sensations of pleasure, which I usually feel at the perusal of your letters. It inspired me both with concern and chagrin. With concern, lest your dejection of mind should affect your health; and with chagrin at your apparent indulgence of melancholy. Indeed, my friend, your own happiness and honor require you to dissipate the cloud which hangs over your imagination.

Rise then above it; and prove yourself superior to the adverse occurrences which have befallen you. It is by surmounting difficulties, not by sinking under them, that we discover our fortitude. True courage consists not in flying from the storms of life; but in braving and steering through them with prudence. Avoid solitude. It is the bane of a disordered mind; though of great utility to a healthy one. Your once favorite amusements court your attention. Refuse not their solicitations. I have contributed my mite, by sending you a few books; such as you requested. They are of the lighter kind of reading; yet perfectly chaste; and if I mistake not, well adapted to your taste.

You wish to hear from our theatre. I believe it will be well supplied with performers this winter. Come and see whether they can afford you any entertainment. Last evening I attended a tragedy; but never will I attend

3. Reference to the advice book *Letters to His Son*, by Philip Stanhope, fourth Earl of Chesterfield (1694–1773), which counsels duplicitous behavior to make one's way with women and in the world.
4. Ultimo, i.e., of the previous month (Latin).

another. I have not yet been able to erase the gloom which it impressed upon my mind. It was Romeo and Juliet. Distressing enough to sensibility this! Are there not real woes (if not in our own families, at least among our own friends and neighbors) sufficient to exercise our sympathy and pity, without introducing fictitious ones into our very diversions? How can that be a diversion, which racks the soul with grief, even though that grief be imaginary. The introduction of a funeral solemnity, upon the stage, is shocking indeed!

Death is too serious a matter to be sported with! An opening grave cannot be a source of amusement to any considerate mind! The closing scene of life can be no pastime, when realized! It must therefore awaken painful sensations; in the representation!

The circus is a place of fashionable resort of late, but not agreeable to me. I think it inconsistent with the delicacy of a lady, even to witness the indecorums, which are practised there; especially, when the performers of equestrian feats are of our own sex. To see a woman depart so far from the female character, as to assume the masculine habit and attitudes; and appear entirely indifferent, even to the externals of modesty, is truly disgusting, and ought not to be countenanced by our attendance, much less by our approbation. But setting aside this circumstance, I cannot conceive it to be a pleasure to sit a whole evening, trembling with apprehension, lest the poor wight of a horseman, or juggler, or whatever he is to be called, should break his neck in contributing to our entertainment.

With Mr. Bowen's museum,[5] I think you were much pleased. He has made a number of judicious additions to it, since you were here. It is a source of rational and refined amusement. Here the eye is gratified, the imagination charmed, and the understanding improved. It will bear frequent reviews without palling on the taste. It always affords something new; and for one, I am never a weary spectator.

Our other public and private places of resort are much as you left them.

I am happy in my present situation; but when the summer returns, I intend to visit my native home. Again, my Eliza, will we ramble together in those retired shades which friendship has rendered so delightful to us. Adieu, my friend, till then. Be cheerful, and you will yet be happy.

LUCY SUMNER.

Letter LIII

TO MRS. LUCY SUMNER

HARTFORD

Gracious Heaven! What have I heard? Major Sanford is married! Yes, the ungrateful, the deceitful wretch, is married! He has forsworn, he has perjured, and given himself to another! That, you will say, is nothing strange. It is characteristic of the man. It may be so; but I could not be convinced of his perfidy, till now!

5. In 1791, Daniel Bowen established Boston's first museum, filled with paintings, war statues, and preserved animals, among other curiosities.

Perhaps it is all for the best. Perhaps, had he remained unconnected, he might still have deceived me; but now I defy his arts!

They tell me he has married a woman of fortune. I suppose he thinks, as I once did, that wealth can ensure happiness. I wish he may enjoy it.

This event would not affect me at all, were it not for the depression of spirits which I feel, in consequence of a previous disappointment; since which, everything of the kind agitates and overcomes me. I will not see him. If I do, I shall betray my weakness, and flatter his vanity; as he will doubtless think he has the power of mortifying me by his connection with another.

Before this news discomposed me, I had attained to a good degree of cheerfulness. Your kind letter, seconded by Julia's exertions, had assisted me in regulating my sensibility. I have been frequently into company, and find my relish for it gradually returning.

I intend to accept the pleasure to which you invite me, of spending a little time with you, this winter. Julia and I will come together. Varying the scene may contribute effectually to dissipate the gloom of my imagination. I would fly to almost any resort, rather than my own mind. What a dreadful thing it is to be afraid of one's own reflections, which ought to be a constant source of enjoyment! But I will not moralize. I am sufficiently melancholy, without any additional cause to increase it!

<div align="right">ELIZA WHARTON</div>

<div align="center">

Letter LIV

TO MR. CHARLES DEIGHTON

</div>

<div align="right">HARTFORD</div>

DEAR DEIGHTON,

Who do you think is writing to you? Why, it is your old friend, metamorphosed into *a married man!* You stare, and can hardly credit the assertion. I cannot realize it myself; yet, I assure you, Charles, it is absolutely true! Necessity, dire necessity, forced me into this dernier resort. I told you, some time ago, it would come to this.

I stood aloof, as long as possible; but in vain did I attempt to shun the noose. I must either fly to this resource; or give up all my show, equipage, and pleasure, and degenerate into a downright plodding money-catcher, for a subsistance. I chose the first; and who would not? Yet I feel some remorse at taking the girl to wife, from no better motives. She is really too good for such an imposition. But she must blame herself, if she suffers hereafter; for she was visibly captivated by my external appearance; and wanted but very little solicitation to confer herself and fortune on so charming a fellow. Her parents opposed her inclination, for a while, because I was a stranger, and rather too gay for their taste. But she had not been used to contradiction, and could not bear it; and therefore they ventured not to cross her. So I bore off the prize; and prize she really is. Five thousand pounds in possession, and more in reversion, if I do not forfeit it. This will compensate for some of my past mistakes, and set matters right for the present. I think it doing much better than to have taken the little Laurence girl, I told you of, with half the sum. Besides, my Nancy is handsomer, and a more agreeable person. But that is of little consequence to me, you know. "Beauty soon grows

familiar to the lover."[6] Were I a lover, it would be of no great avail. A lover I am; yet not of my wife. The dart which I received from Miss Wharton sticks fast in my heart; and I assure you, I could hardly persuade myself even to appear unfaithful to her. O, Eliza, accuse me not of infidelity; for your image is my constant companion! A thousand times have I cursed the unpropitious stars, which withheld from her a fortune. That would have enabled me to marry her; and with her, even wedlock would have been supportable.

I am told that she is still single. Her sober lover never returned. Had he loved as I did, and do, he could not have been so precipitate. But these stoic souls are good for nothing, that I know of, but

> Fix'd like a plant, to one peculiar spot,
> To draw nutrition, propagate, and rot.[7]

I want to see Eliza, and I must see her; yet I dread an interview. I shall frankly confess my motives for marrying; and the reasons of my conduct, before I went away. I shall own that my circumstances would not allow me to possess her; and yet that I could not resign her to another.

When I make up the matter with her, I shall solicit her friendship for my wife. By this means I may enjoy her society, at least, which will alleviate the confinement of a married state. To my spouse I must be as civil as possible. I really wish she had less merit, that I might have a plausible excuse for neglecting her.

Tomorrow I shall go to Mrs. Wharton's. I am very much taken up with complimental visits, at present. What deference is always paid to equipage! They may talk of this virtue, their learning, and what not; but without either of them, I shall bear off the palm of respect from those, who have them, unadorned with gold, and its shining appendages.

Everything hereabouts recalls Eliza to my mind. I impatiently anticipate the hour, which will convey me to her presence.

PETER SANFORD.

Letter LV

TO MRS. LUCY SUMNER

Hartford

A new scene has opened upon us today, my dear Mrs. Sumner; a visit from Major Sanford. My mamma, Miss Granby, and myself were sitting together in the chamber. Miss Granby was entertaining us by reading aloud in Millot's elements of history,[8] when a servant rapped at the door, and handed in the following billet.

"Will Miss Wharton condescend to converse a few moments with her once favored Sanford? He is but too sensible that he has forfeited all claim to the privilege. He therefore presumes not to request it on the score of merit, or of former acquaintance; but solicits it from her benevolence and pity."

6. From Joseph Addison's *Cato* 1.1.143–46.
7. From Alexander Pope's *An Essay on Man*, Epistle 2, lines 59–66.
8. *The Elements of General History*, a widely known work by the French historian Claude-François-Xavier Millot (1726–1785).

I read and showed it to my mamma and Julia. What, said I, shall I do? I wish not to see him. His artifice has destroyed my peace of mind; and his presence may open the wounds which time is closing. Act, said my mamma, agreeably to the dictates of your own judgment. I see no harm in conversing with him, said Julia. Perhaps it may remove some disagreeable thoughts, which now oppress and give you pain. And as he is no longer a candidate for your affections, added she, with a smile, it will be less hazardous than formerly. He will not have the insolence to speak; nor you the folly to hear, the language of love.

He was accordingly invited in. When I rose to go down, I hesitated, and even trembled. I fear, said I, to myself, it will be too much for me; yet why should it? Conscious innocence will support me. This he has not. When I entered the room he stepped forward to meet me. Confusion and shame were visibly depicted in his countenance. He approached me hastily; and without uttering a word, took my hand. I withdrew it. O! Miss Wharton, said he, despise me not. I am convinced that I deserve your displeasure and disdain; but my own heart has avenged your cause. To your own heart, then, said I, I will leave you! But why do you again seek an interview with one whom you have endeavored to mislead; with one whom you have treated with unmerited neglect? Justice to myself required my appearing before you; that by confessing my faults, and obtaining your forgiveness, I might soften the reproaches of my own mind. Will you be seated, sir? said I. Will you, rejoined he, condescend to sit with me, Eliza? I will, sir, answered I. The rights of hospitality I shall not infringe. In my own house, therefore, I shall treat you with civility. Indeed, said he, you are very severe; but I have provoked all the coldness and reserve which you can inflict!

I am a married man, Eliza. So I understand, said I; and I hope you will never treat your wife with that dissimulation and falsehood, which you have exercised towards me. Would to heaven, exclaimed he, that you were my wife! I should not then fail in my love or duty as a husband! Yet she is an amiable girl; and, had I a heart to give her, I might still be happy! But that, alas! I can never recall. Why, then, said I, did you marry her? You were doubtless master of your own actions. No, said he, I was not. The embarrassed state of my affairs precluded the possibility of acting as I wished. Loving you most ardently, I was anxious to prevent your union with another, till I could so far improve my circumstances, as to secure you from poverty and want in a connection with me. My regard was too sincere to permit me to deceive you, by a marriage which might have proved unhappy for us both. My pride forbad my telling you the motives of my delay; and I left you to see if I could place myself in a situation worthy of your acceptance. This I could not effect; and therefore have run the risk of my future happiness, by marrying a lady of affluence. This secures to me the externals of enjoyment; but my heart, I fear, will never participate it. Yet it affords me some degree of satisfaction that I have not involved you in distress. The only alleviation of which my banishment from you is capable, is your forgiveness. In compassion then, refuse it not! It cannot injure you! To me it will be worth millions! He wept! Yes, Lucy, this libertine; this man of pleasure and gallantry wept! I really pitied him from my heart. I forgive you, said I, and wish you happy; yet, on this condition only, that you never again pollute my ears with the recital of your infamous passion. Yes, infamous, I call it, for what softer appellation

can be given to such professions from a married man? Harbor not an idea of me, in future, inconsistent with the love and fidelity which you owe your wife; much less, presume to mention it, if you wish not to be detested by me; and forever banished from my presence. He expressed gratitude for his absolution even upon these terms; and hoped his future conduct would entitle him to my friendship and esteem. That, I replied, time only can determine.

One favor more he begged leave to solicit; which was, that I would be a neighbor to his wife. She was a stranger, he said, and would deem my society a particular privilege. This, I told him, I could not grant, at present, whatever I might do hereafter. He did not urge it any further but inquired after my mamma, and expressed a wish to see her. I rung the bell, and ordered her and Miss Granby to be called. When they came, he was very polite to them both; and, after usual compliments, told my mamma that he was happy in having obtained my forgiveness, to which he was anxious to have her seal affixed. My daughter, said she, is the injured party; and if she be satisfied, I shall not complain. He thanked her for her condescension; informed her that he was married, and requested her to visit his wife. We then conversed upon different subjects for a short time, and he took his leave: a sigh escaped him as he departed; and a gloom was visible in his countenance, which I never observed before.

I must acknowledge that this interview has given me satisfaction. I have often told you that if I married Major Sanford, it would be from a predilecton for his situation in life. How wretched must have been my lot, had I discovered, too late, that he was by no means possessed of the independence, which I fondly anticipated. I knew not my own heart, when I contemplated a connection with him. Little did I think that my regard for Mr. Boyer was so deeply rooted, as I now find it. I foolishly imagined that I could turn my affections into what channel I pleased. What then must have been my feelings, when I found myself deprived both of inward peace and outward enjoyment! I begin now to emerge from the darkness, in which I have been long benighted! I hope the tragic comedy, in which I have acted so conspicuous a part, will come to a happy end.

Julia and I talk, now and then, of a journey to Boston. As yet I have not resolution to act with much decision upon the subject. But, wherever I am, and whatever may be my fate, I shall always be your's in truth,

<div align="right">Eliza Wharton.</div>

Letter LVI

TO MRS. LUCY SUMNER

<div align="right">Hartford</div>

I begin to hope we shall come to rights here, by and by. Major Sanford has returned; has made us a visit; and a treaty of peace, and amity (but not of commerce,) is ratified.

Eliza appears to be rapidly returning to her former cheerfulness, if not gaity. I hope she will not diverge too far from her present sedateness and solidity; yet I am not without apprehensions of danger on that score. One extreme commonly succeeds another. She tells me, that she assiduously cultivates her natural vivacity; that she finds her taste for company and amusements

increasing; that she dreads being alone, because past scenes arise to view which vex and discompose her.

These are indications of a mind not perfectly right. I flatter myself, however, that the time is not far distant, when her passions will vibrate with regularity.

I need not repeat to you anything relative to Major Sanford's conciliatory visit. Eliza has given you a particular, and I believe, a faithful detail. I was called down to see this wonderful man; and disliked him exceedingly. I am astonished that Eliza's penetrating eye, has not long since read his vices in his very countenance. I am told by a friend, who has visited them, that he has an agreeable wife; and I wish she may find him a husband of the same description; but I very much doubt the accomplishment of my wish. For I have no charity for these reformed rakes.

We were walking abroad the other afternoon, and met Major Sanford and lady. Eliza did not see them till they were very near us. She started, turned pale, and then colored like crimson. I cannot but think, a little envy rankled in her heart. Major Sanford very politely accosted us; and congratulated Mrs. Sanford on this opportunity of introducing her to a particular friend; presenting Eliza. She received her with an easy dignity, and bid her welcome to this part of the country. Mrs. Sanford answered her modestly; hoped for the pleasure of a further acquaintance; and urged us, as we were not far from their house, to return with them to tea. We declined; and, wishing each other a good evening, parted. Major Sanford's eyes were riveted on Eliza, the whole time we were together; and he seemed loath to remove them, when we separated. I suspect there is some truth in his tale of love. I shall therefore discourage Eliza from associating with him under any pretext whatever. She appeared more pensive and thoughtful than common, as we returned home; and said little the rest of the evening; but next morning was as chatty as ever.

She is warm in the praises of Mrs. Sanford, thinks her an accomplished woman, and wonders that the major could suggest an idea of marrying her for her money. She intends, she says, to visit her soon; and wishes me to accompany her. This, for her own sake, I shall defer, as long as possible.

I am, &c.

JULIA GRANBY.

Letter LVII

TO MRS. LUCY SUMNER

HARTFORD

By Julia's advice, we have neglected the repeated invitations of Major Sanford, to visit and commence neighborhood with them, till yesterday; when we received a polite billet, requesting the honor of our company to dine. My mamma declined going; but said she had no objection to our compliance with the message, if we thought proper. Julia and I accordingly went. We found a large company assembled in a spacious hall, splendidly furnished and decorated. They were all very polite and attentive to me; but none more so than Major Sanford and his lady, who jointly strove to dissipate the pensiveness of my mind, which I found it impossible to conceal. When we were

summoned to dinner, the major being near me, offered his hand, and leading me into the dining room, seated me at a table furnished with all the variety which could please the eye, or regale the taste of the most luxurious epicure. The conversation turned on various subjects, literary, political, and miscellaneous. In the evening we had a ball. Major Sanford gave the hand of his wife to a Mr. Grey, alledging that he was a stranger, and therefore, entitled to particular attention; and then solicited mine for himself. I was on the point of refusing him, but recollecting that it might have the appearance of continued resentment, contrary to my declaration of forgiving what was past, I complied. He was all kindness and assiduity; the more so, I imagine, with a view to make amends for his former ingratitude and neglect. Tenderness is now peculiarly soothing to my wounded heart. He took an opportunity of conversing with his wife and me together; hoped she would be honored with my friendship and acquaintance; and begged, for her sake, that I would not be a stranger at his house. His Nancy, he said, was far removed from her maternal friends; but I could supply their place, if I would generously undertake the task. She joined in expressing the same sentiments and wishes. Alas! Sir, said I, Eliza Wharton is not now what she once was! I labor under a depression of spirits, which must render my company rather painful than pleasing to my friends. The idea of what I had been, contrasted with what I then was, touched my sensibility; and I could not restrain the too officious tear from stealing down my cheek. He took me by the hand, and said, you distress me, Miss Wharton, indeed, you distress me! Happiness must, and shall attend you! Cursed be the wretch who could wound a heart like yours!

Julia Granby now joined us. An inquisitive concern was visible in her countenance.

I related this conversation to her, after we returned home; but she approved it not.

She thought Major Sanford too particularly attentive to me, considering what had previously happened. She said it would be noticed by others, and the world would make unfavorable remarks upon any appearance of intimacy between us. I care not for that, said I. It is an ill-natured, misjudging world; and I am not obliged to sacrifice my friends to its opinion. Were Major Sanford a single man I should avoid his society; but since he is married; since his wife is young, beautiful and lovely, he can have no temptation to injure me. I therefore see no evil, which can arise from the cultivation of friendship with *her*, at least. I relish company so little, that I may surely be indulged in selecting that which is most agreeable to my taste, to prevent my becoming quite a misanthrope.

I thank you, my dear Mrs. Sumner, for your kind letter. It was a seasonable cordial to my mind; and I will endeavor to profit by your advice.

Your remarks on the public entertainments are amusing, and as far as I am a judge, perfectly just.

I think it a pity they have not female managers for the theatre. I believe it would be under much better regulations, than at present.

With cordial respects to Mr. Sumner, I subscribe myself, yours in sincerity,

ELIZA WHARTON.

Letter LVIII

TO MR. CHARLES DEIGHTON

HARTFORD

Rejoice with me, my friend, that I have made my peace with the mistress of my heart. No devotee could have been more sincere in his penitence, than I was in mine. Indeed, Charles, I never knew I had so much sensibility before! Why, I was as much a woman as the very weakest of the sex!

But I dealt very plainly and sincerely with her, to be sure; and this atones for all past offences, and procures absolution for many others yet to be committed.

The dear girl was not inexorable; she was as placable and condescending as I could expect, considering the nature of the crime, which was apparently slighting her person and charms, by marrying another. This you know is one of the nicest points with the ladies. Attack their honor, that is their chastity, and they construe it to be the effect of excessive love, which hurries you a little beyond the bounds of prudence. But touch their vanity, by preferring another, and they will seldom pardon you. You will say I am very severe upon the sex. And have I not reason to be so, since I have found so many frail ones among them. This, however, is departing from my subject.

Eliza is extremely altered! Her pale dejected countenance, with the sedateness of her manners, so different from the lively glow of health, cheerfulness and activity which formerly animated her appearance and deportment, struck me very disagreeably.

With all my gallantry and fluency in love matters, I was unable to acquit myself tolerably; or to address her with any degree of ease and confidence. She was very calm; and spoke with great indifference about my marriage, &c. which mortified me exceedingly. Yet I cannot consent to believe that her present depression of spirits arises solely from Mr. Boyer's infidelity. I flatter myself that I am of sufficient consequence to her to have contributed in a degree.

When I inquired after her health, she told me she had been indisposed; but was now much better. This indisposition, I am informed, was purely mental; and I am happy to observe her recovering from it. I frequently visit her, sometimes with and sometimes without my wife; of whom, through my mediation, she has become a favorite. I have married, and according to the general opinion, reformed. Yet I suspect my reformation, like most others of the kind will prove instable as "the baseless fabric of a vision;" unless I banish myself entirely from her society. But that I can never do; for she is still lovely in my eyes, and I cannot control my passions. When absent from her, I am lost to everything but her idea. My wife begins to rally me on my fondness for Miss Wharton. She asked me the other day if she had a fortune? No, said I, if she had I should have married her. This wounded her sensibility. I repented of my sincerity, and made my peace for that time. Yet, I find myself growing extremely irritable, and she must take heed how she provokes me; for I do not love her; and I think the name of wife becomes more and more distasteful to me every day.

In my mind Eliza has no competitor. But I must keep up appearances, though I endeavor to regain her love. I imagine that the enjoyment of her

society, as a neighbor and friend may content me for the present, and render my condition supportable.

Farewell, Charles. I hope you will never be embarrassed with a wife, nor lack some favorite nymph to supply the place of one.

<div align="right">PETER SANFORD.</div>

Letter LIX

TO MRS. LUCY SUMNER

<div align="right">HARTFORD</div>

DEAR LUCY,

I intended, this week, to have journeyed to Boston with Julia Granby; but my resolution fails me. I find it painful even to think of mixing again with the gay multitude. I believe the melancholy reflections, by which I am oppressed, will be more effectually, if not more easily surmounted, by tarrying where they are rendered familiar, than by going from them awhile, and then returning.

Julia will therefore go without me. I envy her no enjoyment there, except your company.

The substitution of friendship in the place of love for Major Sanford, I find productive of agreeable sensations. With him, he assures me, it is a far more calm and rational pleasure. *He* treats me with the affection and tenderness of a brother; and his *wife*, who exceeds him in professions of regard, with all the consoling softness and attention of a sister. Indeed, their politeness has greatly contributed to revive the cheerfulness of my natural disposition.

I believe the major's former partiality to me, as a lover, is entirely obliterated; and for my part, I feel as little restraint in his company, and his lady's, as in that of any other in the neighborhood.

I very much regret the departure of Julia; and hope you will permit her to return to me again, as soon as possible. She is a valuable friend. Her mind is well cultivated; and she has treasured up a fund of knowledge and information, which renders her company both agreeable and useful in every situation of life. We lately spent the afternoon and evening at Mr. Smith's. They had a considerable number of visitants; and among the rest, Major Sanford. His wife was expected, but did not come, being indisposed.

I believe, my friend, you must excuse me if my letters are shorter than formerly. Writing is not so agreeable to me as it used to be. I love my friends as well as ever; but I think they must be weary of the gloom and dullness which pervades my present correspondence. When my pen shall have regained its original fluency and alertness, I will resume and prolong the pleasing task.

I am, my dear Lucy, your's most affectionately,

<div align="right">ELIZA WHARTON.</div>

Letter LX

HARTFORD

DEAR MADAM,

Agreeably to your desire, every art has been tried, every allurement held out, every argument used, and every plan adopted which Mrs. Wharton and I could devise to induce Eliza to accompany me to Boston; but all in vain. Sometimes she has been almost persuaded to a compliance with our united request; but soon has resolutely determined against it. I have observed her sentiments to be suddenly changed after being in company with Major Sanford. This alarms us exceedingly. Indeed the major seems to have insinuated himself into her good opinion more than ever. She is flattered into the belief that his attention to her is purely the result of friendship and benevolence.

I have not so favorable an opinion of the man, as to suppose him capable of either. He has become very familiar here. He calls in almost every day. Sometimes he but just inquires after our health; and sometimes makes long visits. The latter is his invariable practice, when he finds Eliza alone. Mrs. Wharton always avoids seeing him if she can. She dreads, she says, his approaching the house.

I entered the parlor the other day, somewhat suddenly, and found him sitting very near Eliza, in a low conversation. They both rose in apparent confusion, and he soon retired.

When he was gone; I suspect, said I, that the major was whispering a tale of love, Eliza? Do you imagine, said she, that I would listen to such a theme from a married man? I hope not, said I; but his conduct towards you indicates a revival of his former sentiments, at least. I was not aware of that, said she. As yet I have observed nothing in his behavior to me inconsistent with the purest friendship.

We drank tea not long since at Mr. Smith's. Late in the afternoon, Major Sanford made his appearance to apologize, as he said, for Mrs. Sanford, who was indisposed, and could not enjoy the pleasure of the visit she had contemplated. He was very gay the whole evening; and when the company separated, he was the first to present his arm to Eliza, who accepted it without hesitation. A Mr. Newhall attended me, and we endeavored to keep them company; but they evidently chose to walk by themselves. Mr. Newhall observed, that if Major Sanford were not married, he should suspect he still intended a union with Miss Wharton. I replied, that their former intercourse having terminated in friendship, rendered them more familiar with each other, than with the generality of their acquaintance.

When we reached the house, Mr. Newhall chose not to go in, and took his leave. I waited at the door for Eliza and Major Sanford. At some little distance I saw him press her hand to his lips. It vexed me exceedingly; and no sooner had they come up, than I sullenly bade him good night, and walked directly in. Eliza soon followed me. I sat down by the fire in a thoughtful posture. She did the same. In this situation we both remained for some time, without speaking a word. At length she said, you seem not to have enjoyed your walk, Miss Granby; did you not like your gallant? Yes, said I, very

well; but I am mortified that you were not better provided for. I make no complaint, rejoined she; I was very well entertained. That is what displeases me, said I; I mean your visible fondness for the society of such a man. Were you averse to it, as you ought to be, there would be no danger. But he has an alluring tongue and a treacherous heart. How can you be pleased and entertained by his conversation? To me it appears totally repugnant to that refinement and delicacy for which you have always been esteemed.

His assiduity and obtrusion ought to alarm you. You well know what his character has been. Marriage has not changed his disposition. It is only a cloak which conceals it. Trust him not then, my dear Eliza! If you do, depend upon it, you will find his professions of friendship to be mere hypocrisy and deceit! I fear that he is acting over again the same unworthy arts, which formerly misled you. Beware of his wiles! Your friends are anxious for you. They tremble at your professed regard and apparent intimacy with that unprincipled man. My friends, said she, are very jealous of me, lately. I know not how I have forfeited their confidence, or incurred their suspicion. By encouraging that attention, I warmly replied, and receiving those caresses from a married man, which are due from him to none but his wife! He is a villain, if he deceived her into marriage by insincere professions of love. If he had then an affection for her, and has already discarded it, he is equally guilty! Can *you* expect sincerity from the man, who withholds it from an amiable and deserving wife? No, Eliza; it is not love, which induces him to entertain you with the subject! It is a baser passion; and if you disdain not his artifice; if you listen to his flattery, you will, I fear, fall a victim to his evil machinations! If he conducted like a man of honor, he would merit your esteem; but his behavior is quite the reverse! Yet vile as he is, he would not dare to lisp his insolent hopes of your regard, if you punished his presumption with the indignation it deserves; if you spurned from your presence the ungrateful wretch, who would requite your condescension by triumphing in your ruin!

She now burst into tears, and begged me to drop the subject. Her mind, she said, was racked by her own reflections. She could bear but little. Kindness deceived and censure distressed her!

I assured her of my good intentions; that as I saw her danger, I thought it a duty of the friendship and affection I bore her, solemnly to warn her against it before we parted. We talked over the matter more calmly, till she professed herself resolved in future to avoid his company, and reject his insinuations.

The next day, as I walked out, I met Major Sanford. He accosted me very civilly. I barely bid him good morning, and passed on.

I made it in my way to call at his house, and bid Mrs. Sanford adieu; not expecting another opportunity equally favorable. When I entered the parlor, she was playing a melancholy air on the harpsicord. She rose, and gave me a polite and graceful reception. I told her, as I was soon to leave town, I called to take my leave of her; a compliment, which her attention to me required. Are you going to leave us then, Miss Granby? said she. I shall regret your departure exceedingly. I have so few friends in this part of the country, that it will give me sensible pain to part with one I so highly value.

I told her in the course of conversation, that I expected the pleasure of seeing her yesterday at Mr. Smith's; and was very sorry for the indisposition,

which prevented her favoring us with her company. Indeed, said she, I did not know I was expected there! Were you there pray? Yes, said I; and Major Sanford excused your not coming, on the account I have mentioned. Well, said she, this is the first word I ever heard about it; he told me that business led him abroad! Did he gallant any lady? O, said I, he was with us all together. We had no particular gallants.

Seeing her curiosity excited, I heartily repented saying anything of the matter, and waved the subject. Little did I suspect him to have been guilty of so base an artifice! It was evidently contrived to facilitate an interview with Eliza.

When I returned I related this affair to Mrs. Wharton and her daughter. The old lady and I expatiated largely on the vileness of this conduct; and endeavored to expose it to Eliza's view in its true colors. She pretended not to justify it. Yet she looked as if she wished it in her power.

I am now preparing for my journey to Boston; which I must however defer another week, for the sake of a more agreeable passage in the stage. I regret leaving Eliza! I tremble at her danger! She has not the resolution to resist temptation, which she once possessed. Her mind is surprisingly weakened! She appears sensible of this; yet adds to it by yielding to her own imbecility. You will receive a letter from her with this; though I had much difficulty to persuade her to write. She has unfortunately become very averse to this, her once favorite amusement.

As I shall soon have the pleasure of conversing with you personally, I conclude without any other addition to this scroll, than the name of your obliged

JULIA GRANBY.

Letter LXI

TO MISS ELIZA WHARTON

BOSTON

MY DEAR FRIEND,
I have received your letters, and must own to you that the perusal of them gave me pain. Pardon my suspicions, Eliza: they are excited by real friendship. Julia, you say, approves not Major Sanford's particular attention to you. Neither do I. If you recollect, and examine his conversation in his conciliatory visit, you will find it replete with sentiments, for the avowal of which, he ought to be banished from all virtuous society.

Does he not insidiously declare that you are the only object of his affections; that his union with another was formed from interested views; and though that other is acknowledged to be amiable and excellent, still he has not a heart to bestow and expects not happiness with her? Does this discover even the appearance of amendment? Has he not, by false pretensions, misled a virtuous woman, and induced her to form a connection with him? She was a stranger to his manner of life; and doubtless allured, as you have been, by flattery, deceit, and external appearance, to trust his honor; little thinking him wholly devoid of that sacred tie! What is the reward of her confidence? Insensibility to her charms, neglect of her person, and professed attachment to another!

Is he the man, my dear Eliza, whose friendship you wish to cultivate? Can that heavenly passion reside in a breast, which is the seat of treachery, duplicity, and ingratitude? You are too sensible of its purity and worth, to suppose it possible. The confessions of his own mouth condemn him. They convince me that he is still the abandoned libertine; and that marriage is but the cloak of his intrigues. His officious attentions to you are alarming to your friends. You own your mind weakened, and peculiarly susceptible of tender impressions. Beware how you receive them from him. Listen not a moment to his flattering professions. It is an insult upon your understanding for him to offer them. It is derogatory to virtue for you to hear them.

Slight not the opinion of the world. We are dependent beings; and while the smallest traces of virtuous sensibility remain, we must feel the force of that dependence, in a greater or less degree. No female whose mind is uncorrupted can be indifferent to reputation. It is an inestimable jewel, the loss of which can never be repaired. While retained, it affords conscious peace to our own minds, and ensures the esteem and respect of all around us.

Blessed with the company of so disinterested and faithful a friend as Julia Granby, some deference is certainly due to her opinion and advice. To an enlarged understanding, a cultivated taste, and an extensive knowledge of the world, she unites the most liberal sentiments, with a benevolence, and candor of disposition, which render her equally deserving of your confidence and affection.

I cannot relinquish my claim to a visit from you this winter. Marriage has not alienated or weakened my regard for my friends. Come, then, to your faithful Lucy. Have you sorrows? I will sooth and alleviate them. Have you cares? I will dispel them. Have you pleasures? I will heighten them. Come then, let me fold you to my expecting heart. My happiness will be partly suspended till your society render it complete. Adieu.

LUCY SUMNER.

Letter LXII

TO MISS JULIA GRANBY

HARTFORD

DEAR JULIA,

I hope Mrs. Sumner and you will excuse my writing but one letter, in answer to the number I have received from you both. Writing is an employment, which suits me not at present. It was pleasing to me formerly, and therefore, by recalling the idea of circumstances and events which frequently occupied my pen in happier days, it now gives me pain. Yet I have just written a long consolatory letter to Mrs. Richman. She has buried her babe; her little Harriot, of whom she was dotingly fond.

It was a custom with some of the ancients, we are told, to weep at the birth of their children.

Often should we be impelled to a compliance with this custom, could we foresee the future incidents of their lives. I think, at least, that the uncertainty of their conduct and condition in more advanced age, may reconcile us to their removal to a happier state, before they are capable of tasting the bitterness of woe.

> Happy the babe, who, priviledg'd by fate,
> To shorter labors, and a lighter weight,
> Receiv'd but yesterday the gift of breath;
> Order'd to morrow, to return to death.[9]

Our domestic affairs are much as when you left us. Nothing remarkable has occurred in the neighborhood, worth communicating. The company and amusements of the town are as usual, I suppose. I frequent neither of them. Having incurred so much censure by the indulgence of a gay disposition, I am now trying what a recluse and solitary mode of life will produce. You will call me splenetic. I own it. I am pleased with nobody; still less with myself. I look around for happiness, and find it not. The world is to me a desert! If I indulge myself in temporary enjoyment, the consciousness or apprehension of doing amiss, destroys my peace of mind. And, when I have recourse to books, if I read those of serious description, they remind me of an awful futurity, for which I am unprepared; if history, it discloses facts in which I have no interest; if novels, they exhibit scenes of pleasure which I have no prospect of realizing!

My mamma is solicitously attentive to my happiness; and though she fails of promoting it; yet I endeavor to save her the pangs of disappointment, by appearing what she wishes.

I anticipate, and yet I dread your return; a paradox this, which time alone can solve.

Continue writing to me, and entreat Mrs. Sumner, in my name, to do likewise. Your benevolence must be your reward.

<div align="right">ELIZA WHARTON.</div>

Letter LXIII

TO MISS ELIZA WHARTON

<div align="right">BOSTON</div>

A paradox, indeed, is the greater part of your letter to us, my dear Eliza. We had fondly flattered ourselves that the melancholy of your mind was exterminated. I hope no new cause has revived it. Little did I intend, when I left you, to have been absent so long; but Mrs. Sumner's disappointment, in her plan of spending the summer at Hartford, induced me, in compliance with her request, to prolong my residence here.

But for your sake, she now consents to my leaving her, in hopes I may be so happy as to contribute to your amusement.

I am both pleased and instructed by the conduct of this amiable woman. As I always endeavored to imitate her discreet and modest behavior in a single state; so likewise shall I take her for a pattern, should I ever enter a married life. She is most happily united. Mr. Sumner, to all the graces and accomplishments of the gentleman, adds the still more important and essential properties of virtue, integrity and honor. I was once present when a person was recommended to her for a husband. She objected that he was a rake. True, said the other, he has been, but he has reformed. That will never do for

9. Derived from *Solomon on the Vanity of the World* 2.225–26, by the English poet Matthew Prior (1664–1721), as redacted by James Hervey in his *Meditations and Contemplations* (1745–47).

me, rejoined she; I wish my future companion to need no reformation: a sentiment worthy the attention of our whole sex; the general adoption of which, I am persuaded, would have a happy influence upon the manners of the other.

I hope neither you, nor I, Eliza, shall ever be tried by a man of debauched principles. Such characters I conceive to be totally unfit for the society of women who have any claim to virtue and delicacy.

I intend to be with you, in about a month. If agreeable to you, we will visit, and spend a few weeks with the afflicted Mrs. Richman. I sincerely sympathize with her, under her bereavement. I know her fondness for you will render your company very consoling to her; and I flatter myself that I should not be an unwelcome guest.

Make my respects to your mamma; and believe me ever yours,

JULIA GRANBY.

Letter LXIV

TO MRS. LUCY SUMNER

HARTFORD

DEAR MADAM,
I have arrived in safety, to the mansion of our once happy and social friends. But I cannot describe to you, how changed, how greatly changed this amiable family appears since I left it. Mrs. Wharton met me at the door; and tenderly embracing, bade me a cordial welcome. You are come, Julia, said she, I hope, to revive and comfort us. We have been very solitary during your absence. I am happy madam, said I, to return; and my endeavors to restore cheerfulness and content shall not be wanting. But, where is Eliza? By this time we had reached the back parlor, whither Mrs. Wharton led me; and the door being open, I saw Eliza, reclined on a settee, in a very thoughtful posture. When I advanced to meet her, she never moved; but sat "like patience on a monument, smiling at grief!"[1]

I stopped involuntarily, and involuntarily raising my eyes to heaven, exclaimed, is that Eliza Wharton! She burst into tears; and attempted to rise, but sunk again into her seat. Seeing her thus affected, I sat down by her; and throwing my arm about her neck, why these tears? said I. Why this distress, my dear friend? Let not the return of your Julia give you pain! She comes to sooth you with the consolations of friendship! It is not pain, said she, clasping me to her breast; it is pleasure, too exquisite for my weak nerves to bear! See you not, Julia, how I am altered? Should you have known me for the sprightly girl, who was always welcome at the haunts of hilarity and mirth? Indeed, said I, you appear indisposed, but I will be your physician. Company and change of air will, I doubt not, restore you. Will these cure disorders of the mind, Julia? They will have a powerful tendency to remove them, if rightly applied; and I profess considerable skill in that art. Come, continued I, we will try these medicines in the morning. Let us rise early, and step into the chaise; and after riding a few miles, call and breakfast with Mrs. Freeman. I have some commissions from her daughter. We shall be agreeably entertained there, you know.

1. Cf. Shakespeare's *Twelfth Night* 2.4.111–12.

Being summoned to supper, I took her by the hand, and we walked into another room, where we found her brother, and his wife, with her mamma waiting for us. We were all very chatty; even Eliza resumed, in a degree, her former sociability. A settled gloom, notwithstanding, brooded on her countenance; and a deep sigh often escaped her, in spite of her evident endeavors to suppress it. She went to bed before us; when her mamma informed me that her health had been declining for some months, that she never complained, but studiously concealed every symptom of indisposition. Whether it were any real disorder of body, or whether it arose from her depression of spirits, she could not tell; but supposed they operated together, and mutually heightened each other.

I inquired after Major Sanford; whether he and Eliza had associated together during my absence? Sometimes, she said, they seemed on good terms; and he frequently called to see her; at others, they had very little, if any correspondence at all. She told me that Eliza never went abroad, and was very loath to see company at home; that her chief amusement consisted in solitary walks; that the dreadful idea of her meeting Major Sanford in these walks had now and then intruded upon her imagination; that she had not the least evidence of the fact, however; and indeed, was afraid to make any inquiries into the matter, lest her own suspicions should be discovered; that the major's character was worse than ever; that he was much abroad, and frequently entertained large parties of worthless bacchanalians at his house; that common report said he treated his wife with indifference, neglect, and ill nature; with many other circumstances, which it is not material to relate.

Adieu, my dear friend, for the present. When occasion requires, you shall hear again from your affectionate

JULIA GRANBY.

Letter LXV

TO MR. CHARLES DEIGHTON

HARTFORD

Good news, Charles, good news! I have arrived to the utmost bounds of my wishes; the full possession of my adorable Eliza! I have heard a quotation from a certain book; but what book it was I have forgotten, if I ever knew. No matter for that; the quotation is, that "stolen waters are sweet, and bread eaten in secret is pleasant."[2] If it has reference to the pleasures, which I have enjoyed with Eliza, I like it hugely, as Tristram Shandy's father said of Yorick's sermon;[3] and I think it fully verified.

I had a long and tedious siege. Every method which love could suggest, or art invent, was adopted. I was sometimes ready to despair, under an idea that her resolution was unconquerable, her virtue impregnable. Indeed, I should have given over the pursuit long ago, but for the hopes of success I entertained from her parleying with me, and in reliance upon her own strength, endeavoring to combat and counteract my designs. Whenever this

2. Proverbs 9.17.
3. In the very popular novel *Tristram Shandy*, by the British novelist Laurence Sterne (1713–
1768), a clergyman is named Yorick (an allusion to Shakespeare's *Hamlet*).

has been the case, Charles, I have never yet been defeated in my plan. If a lady will consent to enter the lists against the antagonist of her honor, she may be sure of losing the prize. Besides, were her delicacy genuine, she would banish the man at once, who presumed to doubt, which he certainly does, who attempts to vanquish it!

But, far be it from me to criticize the pretensions of the sex. If I gain the rich reward of my dissimulation and gallantry, that you know is all I want.

To return then to the point. An unlucky, but not a miraculous accident[4] has taken place, which must soon expose our amour. What can be done? At the first discovery, absolute distraction seized the soul of Eliza, which has since terminated in a fixed melancholy. Her health too is much impaired. She thinks herself rapidly declining; and I tremble when I see her emaciated form!

My wife has been reduced very low, of late. She brought me a boy a few weeks past, a dead one though.

These circumstances give me neither pain nor pleasure. I am too much engrossed by my divinity, to take an interest in anything else. True, I have lately suffered myself to be somewhat engaged here and there, by a few jovial lads, who assist me in dispelling the anxious thoughts, which my perplexed situation excites. I must, however, seek some means to relieve Eliza's distress. My finances are low; but the last fraction shall be expended in her service, if she need it.

Julia Granby is expected at Mrs. Wharton's every hour. I fear that her inquisitorial eye will soon detect our intrigue, and obstruct its continuation. Now there's a girl, Charles, I should never attempt to seduce; yet she is a most alluring object, I assure you. But the dignity of her manners forbid all assaults upon her virtue. Why, the very expression of her eye, blasts in the bud every thought derogatory to her honor; and tells you plainly, that the first insinuation of the kind would be punished with eternal banishment and displeasure! Of her there is no danger! But I can write no more, except that I am, &c.

<div align="right">PETER SANFORD.</div>

Letter LXVI

TO MRS. LUCY SUMNER

<div align="right">HARTFORD</div>

Oh, my friend! I have a tale to unfold; a tale which will rend every nerve of sympathizing pity, which will rack the breast of sensibility, and unspeakably distress your benevolent heart! Eliza—Oh the ruined, lost Eliza!

I want words to express the emotions of indignation and grief which oppress me! But I will endeavor to compose myself; and relate the circumstances as they came to my knowledge.

After my last letter, Eliza remained much in the same gloomy situation as I found her. She refused to go, agreeably to her promise, to visit your mamma; and under one pretext or another, has constantly declined accompanying me anywhere else, since my arrival.

4. Eliza is pregnant with Sanford's child.

Till last Thursday night she slept in the same bed with me; when she excused herself, by saying she was restless, and should disturb my repose. I yielded to her humor of taking a different apartment, little suspecting the real cause! She frequently walked out; and though I sometimes followed, I very seldom found her. Two or three times, when I happened to be awake, I heard her go downstairs; and on inquiry in the morning, she told me that she was very thirsty, and went down for water. I observed a degree of hesitancy in her answers, for which I could not account. But last night, the dreadful mystery was developed! A little before day, I heard the front door opened with great caution. I sprang from my bed, and running to the window, saw by the light of the moon, a man going from the house. Soon after I perceived a footstep upon the stairs, which carefully approached and entered Eliza's chamber.

Judge of my astonishment, my surprise, my feelings, upon this occasion! I doubted not but Major Sanford was the person I had seen; and the discovery of Eliza's guilt, in this infamous intrigue, almost deprived me of thought and recollection! My blood thrilled with horror at this sacrifice of virtue! After a while I recovered myself, and put on my clothes. But what to do, I knew not; whether to go directly to her chamber, and let her know that she was detected; or to wait another opportunity.

I resolved on the first. The day had now dawned. I tapped at her door; and she bid me come in. She was sitting in an easy chair by the side of her bed. As I entered she withdrew her handkerchief from her face; and looking earnestly at me, said, what procures me the favor of a visit, at this early hour, Miss Granby? I was disturbed, said I, and wished not to return to my bed. But what breaks your rest; and calls you up so unseasonably, Eliza? Remorse, and despair, answered she, weeping. After what I have witnessed, this morning, rejoined I, I cannot wonder at it! Was it not Major Sanford whom I saw go from the house some time ago? She was silent, but tears slowed abundantly. It is too late, continued I, to deny or evade. Answer my question sincerely; for, believe me, Eliza, it is not malice, but concern for you, which prompts it. I will answer you, Julia, said she. You have discovered a secret which harrows up my very soul! A secret, which I wished you to know, but could not exert resolution to reveal! Yes! It was Major Sanford; the man who has robbed me of my peace; who has triumphed in my destruction; and who will cause my sun to set at noon!

I shudder, said I, at your confession! Wretched, deluded girl! Is this a return for your parent's love, and assiduous care; for your friends' solicitude and premonitory advice? You are ruined, you say! You have sacrificed your virtue to an abandoned, despicable profligate! And you live to acknowledge and bear your infamy! I do, said she; but not long shall I support this burden! See you not, Julia, my decaying frame, my faded cheek, and tottering limbs? Soon shall I be insensible to censure and reproach! Soon shall I be sequestered in that mansion, "where the wicked cease from troubling, and where the weary are at rest!"[5] Rest! said I, can you expect to find rest either in this world, or another, with such a weight of guilt on your head? She exclaimed, with great emotion, add not to the upbraidings of a wounded spirit! Have pity upon me. Oh! my friend, have pity upon me!

5. Job 3.17.

Could you know what I suffer, you would think me sufficiently punished! I wish you no other punishment, said I, than what may effect your repentance and reformation. But your mother, Eliza! She cannot long be ignorant of your fall; and I tremble to think of her distress! It will break her widowed heart! How has she loved; how has she doted upon you! Dreadful is the requital which you have made! My mother, rejoined she—Oh, name her not! The very sound is distraction to me! Oh! my Julia, if your heart be not shut against mercy and compassion towards me, aid me through this trying scene! Let my situation call forth your pity, and induce you, undeserving as I am, to exert it in my behalf!

During this time, I had walked the chamber. My spirits had been raised above their natural key and were exhausted. I sat down, but thought I should have fainted, till a copious flood of tears gave me relief. Eliza was extremely affected. The appearance of calamity which she exhibited would have softened the most obdurate anger. Indeed, I feared some immediate and fatal effect. I therefore seated myself beside her; and assuming an air of kindness, compose yourself, Eliza, said I; I repeat what I told you before, it is the purest friendship, which thus interests me in your concerns. This, under the direction of charity, induces me again to offer you my hand. Yet you have erred against knowledge and reason; against warning and counsel. You have forfeited the favor of your friends; and reluctant will be their forgiveness. I plead guilty, said she, to all your charges. From the general voice I expect no clemency. If I can make my peace with my mother, it is all I seek or wish on this side the grave.

In your benevolence I confide for this. In you, I hope to find an intercessor. By the remembrance of our former affection and happiness, I conjure you, refuse me not. At present, I entreat you to conceal from her this distressing tale. A short reprieve is all I ask. Why, said I, should you defer it? When the painful task is over, you may find relief in her lenient kindness. After she knows my condition, I cannot see her, resumed she, till I am assured of her forgiveness. I have not strength to support the appearance of her anger and grief. I will write to her what I cannot speak. You must bear the melancholy message, and plead for me, that her displeasure may not follow me to the grave; whither I am rapidly hastening. Be assured, replied I, that I will keep your secret as long as prudence requires. But I must leave you now: your mamma will wonder at our being thus closeted together. When opportunity presents, we will converse further on the subject. In the meantime, keep yourself as composed as possible, if you would avoid suspicion. She raised her clasped hands, and with a piteous look, threw her handkerchief over her face, and reclined in her chair, without speaking a word. I returned to my chamber, and endeavored to dissipate every idea which might tend to disorder my countenance, and break the silence I wished to observe, relative to what had happened.

When I went down, Mrs. Wharton desired me to step up and inform Eliza that breakfast was ready. She told me she could not yet compose herself sufficiently to see her mamma; and begged me to excuse her absence as I thought proper. I accordingly returned for answer to Mrs. Wharton, that Eliza had rested but indifferently, and being somewhat indisposed, would not come down, but wished me to bring her a bowl of chocolate, when we had breakfasted. I was obliged studiously to suppress even my thoughts

concerning her, lest the emotions they excited might be observed. Mrs. Wharton conversed much of her daughter, and expressed great concern about her health and state of mind. Her return to this state of dejection, after having recovered her spirits and cheerfulness in a great degree, was owing, she feared, to some cause unknown to her; and she entreated me to extract the secret, if possible. I assured her of my best endeavors, and doubted not, I told her, but I should be able in a few days to effect what she wished.

Eliza came down and walked in the garden before dinner; at which she commanded herself much better than I expected. She said that a little ride might, she imagined, be of service to her; and asked me if I would accompany her a few miles in the afternoon. Her mamma was much pleased with the proposition; and the chaise was accordingly ordered.

I observed to Eliza, as we rode, that with her natural and acquired abilities, with her advantages of education, with her opportunities of knowing the world, and of tracing the virtues and vices of mankind to their origin, I was surprised at her becoming the prey of an insidious libertine, with whose character she was well acquainted, and whose principles she was fully apprised would prompt him to deceive and betray her. Your surprise is very natural, said she. The same will doubtless be felt and expressed by everyone to whom my sad story is related. But the cause may be found in that unrestrained levity of disposition, that fondness for dissipation and coquetry which alienated the affections of Mr. Boyer from me. This event fatally depressed and enfeebled my mind. I embraced with avidity the consoling power of friendship, ensnaringly offered by my seducer; vainly inferring from his marriage with a virtuous woman, that he had seen the error of his ways, and forsaken his licentious practices, as he affirmed, and I, fool that I was, believed it!

It is needless for me to rehearse the perfidious arts, by which he insinuated himself into my affections, and gained my confidence. Suffice it to say, he effected his purpose! But not long did I continue in the delusive dream of sensual gratification. I soon awoke to a most poignant sense of his baseness, and of my own crime and misery. I would have fled from him; I would have renounced him forever; and by a life of sincere humility and repentance, endeavored to make my peace with heaven, and to obliterate, by the rectitude of my future conduct, the guilt I had incurred; but I found it too late! My circumstances called for attention; and I had no one to participate my cares, to witness my distress, and to alleviate my sorrows, but him. I could not therefore prevail on myself, wholly to renounce his society. At times I have admitted his visits; always meeting him in the garden or grove adjoining; till of late, the weather and my ill health induced me to comply with his solicitations, and receive him into the parlor.

Not long, however, shall I be subject to these embarrassments. Grief has undermined my constitution. My health has fallen a sacrifice to a disordered mind. But I regret not its departure! I have not a single wish to live. Nothing which the world affords can restore my former serenity and happiness!

The little innocent I bear will quickly disclose its mother's shame! God Almighty grant it may not live as a monument of my guilt and a partaker of the infamy and sorrow, which is all I have to bequeath it! Should it be continued in life, it will never know the tenderness of a parent; and, perhaps, want and disgrace may be its wretched portion! The greatest consolation

I can have will be to carry it with me to a state of eternal rest; which, vile as I am, I hope to obtain, through the infinite mercy of heaven, as revealed in the gospel of Christ.

I must see Major Sanford again. It is necessary to converse further with him, in order to carry my plan of operation into execution. What is this plan of operation, Eliza? said I. I am on the rack of anxiety for your safety. Be patient, continued she, and you shall soon be informed. Tomorrow I shall write my dreadful story to my mother. She will be acquainted with my future intentions; and you shall know, at the same time, the destination of your lost friend. I hope, said I, that you have formed no resolution against your own life. God forbid, rejoined she. My breath is in his hands, let him do what seemeth good in his sight! Keep my secret one day longer, and I will never more impose so painful a silence upon you.

By this time we had reached home. She drank tea with composure and soon retired to rest. Mrs. Wharton eagerly inquired whether I had found out the cause of Eliza's melancholy. I have urged her, said I, on the subject; but she alleges that she has particular reasons for present concealment. She has, notwithstanding, promised to let me know, the day after tomorrow. Oh, said she, I shall not rest till the period arrives. Dear, good woman, said I to myself, I fear you will never rest afterwards!

This is our present situation. Think what a scene rises to the view of your Julia! She must share the distresses of others, though her own feelings, on this unhappy occasion, are too keen to admit a moment's serenity! My greatest relief is in writing to you; which I shall do again by the next post. In the meantime, I must beg leave to subscribe myself, sincerely yours,

JULIA GRANBY.

Letter LXVII

TO THE SAME

HARTFORD

All is now lost; lost, indeed! She is gone! Yes, my dear friend, our beloved Eliza, is gone! Nevermore shall we behold this once amiable companion, this once innocent and happy girl. She has forsaken, and, as she says, bid an everlasting adieu to her home, her afflicted parent and her friends! But I will take up my melancholy story where I left it in my last.

She went, as she told me she expected, into the garden, and met her detestable paramour. In about an hour she returned, and went directly to her chamber. At one o'clock I went up, and found her writing and weeping. I begged her to compose herself, and go down to dinner. No; she said, she could not eat; and was not fit to appear before anybody. I remonstrated against her immoderate grief; represented the injury she must sustain by the indulgence of it, and conjured her to suppress the violence of its emotions.

She entreated me to excuse her to her mamma; said she was writing to her, and found it a task too painful to be performed with any degree of composure; that she was almost ready to sink under the weight of her affliction; but hoped and prayed for support, both in this, and another trying scene, which awaited her. In compliance with her desire, I now left her; and told her mamma that she was very busy in writing; wished not to be interrupted at

present; but would take some refreshment, an hour or two hence. I visited her again, about four o'clock; when she appeared more calm and tranquil.

It is finished, said she, as I entered her apartment, it is finished. What said I, is finished? No matter, replied she; you will know all tomorrow, Julia. She complained of excessive fatigue, and expressed an inclination to lie down; in which I assisted her, and then retired. Sometime after her mamma went up, and found her still on the bed. She rose, however, and accompanied her downstairs. I met her at the door of the parlor, and taking her by the hand, inquired how she did? Oh, Julia, miserably indeed, said she. How severely does my mother's kindness reproach me! How insupportably it increases my self-condemnation! She wept; she wrung her hands, and walked the room in the greatest agony! Mrs. Wharton was exceedingly distressed by her appearance. Tell me, Eliza, said she, tell me the cause of your trouble! Oh, kill me not by your mysterious concealment! My dear child, let me, by sharing, alleviate your affliction! Ask me not, madam, said she; O my mother, I conjure you not to insist on my divulging tonight, the fatal secret which engrosses and distracts my mind! Tomorrow I will hide nothing from you. I will press you no further, rejoined her mamma. Choose your own time, my dear; but remember, I must participate your grief, though I know not the cause.

Supper was brought in; and we endeavored to prevail on Eliza to eat, but in vain. She sat down, in compliance with our united importunities; but neither of us tasted food. It was removed untouched. For a while, Mrs. Wharton and I gazed in silent anguish upon the spectacle of woe before us! At length, Eliza rose to retire. Julia, said she, will you call at my chamber, as you pass to your own? I assented. She then approached her mamma, fell upon her knees before her, and clasping her hand, said, in broken accents, Oh madam! can you forgive a wretch who has forfeited your love, your kindness, and your compassion? Surely, Eliza, said she, you are not that being! No, it is impossible! But however great your transgression, be assured of my forgiveness, my compassion, and my continued love! Saying this, she threw her arms about her daughter's neck and affectionately kissed her. Eliza struggled from her embrace, and looking at her with wild despair, exclaimed, this is too much! Oh, this unmerited goodness is more than I can bear! She then rushed precipitately out of the room, and left us overwhelmed in sympathy and astonishment!

When Mrs. Wharton had recovered herself a little, she observed, that Eliza's brain was evidently disordered. Nothing else, continued she, could impel her to act in this extraordinary manner. At first she was resolved to follow her; but I dissuaded her from it, alleging, that as she had desired me to come into her chamber, I thought it better for me to go alone. She acquiesced; but said she should not think of going to bed; but would, however, retire to her chamber, and seek consolation there. I bade her good night; and went up to Eliza, who took me by the hand and led me to the toilet, upon which she laid the two enclosed letters, the one to her mamma, and the other to me. These, said she, contain what I had not resolution to express. Promise me, Julia, that they shall not be opened till tomorrow morning. I will, said I. I have thought and wept, continued she, till I have almost exhausted my strength, and my reason. I would now obtain a little respite, that I may prepare my mind for the account I am one day to give at a higher tribunal than

that of earthly friends. For this purpose, what I have written, and what I shall yet say to you, must close the account between you and me. I have certainly no balance against you, said I. In my breast, you are fully acquitted. Your penitential tears have obliterated your guilt and blotted your errors with your Julia. Henceforth, be they all forgotten. Live, and be happy. Talk not, said she, of life. It would be a vain hope, though I cherished it myself.

> That I must die, it is my only comfort;
> Death is the privilege of human nature;
> And life without it were not worth our taking.
> Thither the poor, the prisoner and the mourner
> Fly for relief, and lay their burdens down![6]

You have forgiven me, Julia; my mother has assured me of her forgiveness, and what have I more to wish? My heart is much lightened by these kind assurances; they will be a great support to me in the dreadful hour which awaits me! What mean you, Eliza? said I. I fear some desperate purpose labors in your mind. Oh, no, she replied; you may be assured your fear is groundless. I know not what I say; my brain is on fire; I am all confusion! Leave me, Julia; when I have had a little rest, I shall be composed. These letters have almost distracted me; but they are written, and I am comparatively easy. I will not leave you, Eliza, said I, unless you will go directly to bed, and endeavor to rest. I will, said she, and the sooner the better. I tenderly embraced her, and retired, though not to bed. About an hour after, I returned to her chamber, and opening the door very softly, found her apparently asleep. I acquainted Mrs. Wharton with her situation, which was a great consolation to us both; and encouraged us to go to bed. Having suffered much in my mind, and being much fatigued, I soon fell asleep; but the rattling of a carriage, which appeared to stop at a little distance from the house, awoke me. I listened a moment, and heard the door turn slowly on its hinges. I sprang from my bed, and reached the window just in time to see a female handed into a chaise by a man who hastily followed her, and drove furiously away! I at once concluded they could be no other than Eliza and Major Sanford. Under this impression I made no delay, but ran immediately to her chamber. A candle was burning on the table; but Eliza was not there! I thought it best to acquaint her mamma with the melancholy discovery; and stepping to her apartment for the purpose, found her rising. She had heard me walk, and was anxious to know the cause. What is the matter, Julia, said she; what is the matter? Dear madam, said I, arm yourself with fortitude! What new occurrence demands it? rejoined she. Eliza has left us! Left us! What mean you? She is just gone! I saw her handed into a chaise, which instantly disappeared!

At this intelligence she gave a shriek, and fell back on her bed! I alarmed the family, and by their assistance soon recovered her. She desired me to inform her of every particular relative to her elopement, which I did; and then delivered her the letter which Eliza had left for her. I suspect, said she, as she took it; I have long suspected, what I dared not believe! The anguish of my mind has been known only to myself, and my God! I could not answer her, and therefore withdrew. When I had read Eliza's letter to me, and wept

6. From the tragedy *The Fair Penitent* (1703) 5.1.132–37, by the English writer Nicholas Rowe (1674–1718).

over the sad fall; and, as I fear, the total loss of this once amiable and accomplished girl, I returned to Mrs. Wharton. She was sitting in her easy chair; and still held the fatal letter in her hand. When I entered, she fixed her streaming eyes upon me, and exclaimed, O Julia, this is more than the bitterness of death! True, madam, said I, your affliction must be great; yet that all-gracious Being, who controls every event, is able, and I trust, disposed to support you! To Him, replied she, I desire humbly to resign myself; but I think I could have borne almost any other calamity with greater resignation and composure than this. With how much comparative ease could I have followed her to the grave, at any period since her birth! Oh, my child, my child! Dear, very dear hast thou been to my fond heart! Little did I think it possible for you to prepare so dreadful a cup of sorrow for your widowed mother! But where, continued she, where can the poor fugitive have fled? Where can she find that protection and tenderness, which, notwithstanding her great apostacy, I should never have withheld? From whom can she receive those kind attentions, which her situation demands.

The agitation of her mind had exhausted her strength; and I prevailed on her to refresh, and endeavor to compose herself to rest; assuring her of my utmost exertions to find out Eliza's retreat, and restore her to a mother's arms.

I am obliged to suppress my own emotions; and to bend all my thoughts towards the alleviation of Mrs. Wharton's anxiety and grief.

Major Sanford is from home, as I expected; and I am determined, if he return, to see him myself, and extort from him the place of Eliza's concealment. Her flight, in her present state of health, is inexpressibly distressing to her mother; and, unless we find her soon, I dread the effects!

I shall not close this, till I have seen or heard from the vile miscreant who has involved a worthy family in wretchedness!

Friday Morning—Two days have elapsed without affording us much relief. Last evening, I was told that Major Sanford was at home. I immediately wrote him a billet, entreating and conjuring him to let me know where the hapless Eliza had fled. He returned me the following answer.

"Miss Granby need be under no apprehensions, respecting the situation of our beloved Eliza. She is well provided for, conveniently accommodated, and has everything to make her happy, which love or affluence can give.

Major Sanford has solemnly sworn not to discover her retreat. She wishes to avoid the accusations of her friends, till she is better able to bear them.

Her mother may rest assured of immediate information, should any danger threaten her amiable daughter; and also of having seasonable notice of her safety."

Although little dependence can be placed upon this man; yet these assurances have, in a great degree, calmed our minds. We are, however, contriving means to explore the refuge of the wanderer; and hope, by tracing his steps, to accomplish our purpose. This we have engaged a friend to do.

I know, my dear Mrs. Sumner, the kind interest you will take in this disastrous affair. I tremble to think what the event may be! To relieve your suspense, however, I shall write you every circumstance, as it occurs. But at present, I shall only enclose Eliza's letters to her mamma, and me, and, subscribe myself your sincere and obliged friend,

JULIA GRANBY.

Letter LXVIII

TO MRS. M. WHARTON

Tuesday

MY HONORED AND DEAR MAMMA,

In what words, in what language shall I address you? What shall I say on a subject which deprives me of the power of expression? Would to God I had been totally deprived of that power before so fatal a subject required its exertion! Repentance comes too late, when it cannot prevent the evil lamented. For your kindness, your more than maternal affection towards me, from my infancy to the present moment, a long life of filial duty and unerring rectitude could hardly compensate. How greatly deficient in gratitude must I appear then, while I confess, that precept and example, counsel and advice, instruction and admonition, have been all lost upon me!

Your kind endeavors to promote my happiness have been repaid by the inexcusable folly of sacrificing it. The various emotions of shame and remorse, penitence and regret, which torture and distract my guilty breast, exceed description. Yes, madam, your Eliza has fallen; fallen, indeed! She has become the victim of her own indiscretion, and of the intrigue and artifice of a designing libertine, who is the husband of another! She is polluted, and no more worthy of her parentage! She flies from you, not to conceal her guilt, that she humbly and penitently owns; but to avoid what she has never experienced, and feels herself unable to support, a mother's frown; to escape the heart-rending sight of a parent's grief, occasioned by the crimes of her guilty child!

I have become a reproach and disgrace to my friends. The consciousness of having forfeited their favor, and incurred their disapprobation and resentment, induces me to conceal from them the place of my retirement; but, lest your benevolence should render you anxious for my comfort in my present situation, I take the liberty to assure you that I am amply provided for.

I have no claim even upon your pity; but from my long experience of your tenderness, I presume to hope it will be extended to me. Oh, my mother, if you knew what the state of my mind is, and has been, for months past, you would surely compassionate my case! Could tears efface the stain which I have brought upon my family, it would long since have been washed away! But, alas, tears are vain; and vain is my bitter repentance! It cannot obliterate my crime, nor restore me to innocence and peace! In this life I have no ideas of happiness. These I have wholly resigned! The only hope which affords me any solace is that of your forgiveness. If the deepest contrition can make an atonement; if the severest pains, both of body and mind, can restore me to your charity, you will not be inexorable! Oh, let my sufferings be deemed a sufficient punishment; and add not the insupportable weight of a parent's wrath! At present, I cannot see you. The effect of my crime is too obvious to be longer concealed, to elude the invidious eye of curiosity. This night, therefore, I leave your hospitable mansion! This night I become a wretched wanderer from thy paternal roof! Oh, that the grave were this night to be my lodging! Then should I lie down and be at rest! Trusting in the mercy of God, through the mediation of his son; I think I could meet my heavenly father with more composure and confidence, than my earthly parent!

Let not the faults and misfortunes of your daughter oppress your mind. Rather let the conviction of having faithfully discharged your duty to your lost child support and console you in this trying scene.

Since I wrote the above, you have kindly granted me your forgiveness, though you knew not how great, how aggravated was my offence! You forgive me, you say: Oh, the harmonious, the transporting sound! It has revived my drooping spirits; and will enable me to encounter, with resolution, the trials before me!

Farewell, my dear mamma! pity and pray for your ruined child; and be assured, that affection and gratitude will be the last sentiments which expire in the breast of your repenting daughter,

ELIZA WHARTON.

Letter LXIX

TO MISS JULIA GRANBY

TUESDAY

MY DEAR FRIEND,

By that endearing title you permit me still to address you, and such you have always proved yourself, by a participation of my distresses, as well as by the consoling voice of pity and forgiveness. What destiny Providence designs for me, I know not; but I have my forebodings that this is the last time I shall ever accost you! Nor does this apprehension arise merely from a disturbed imagination. I have reason to think myself in a confirmed consumption, which commonly proves fatal to persons in my situation. I have carefully concealed every complaint of the kind from my mamma, for fear of distressing her; yet I have never been insensible of their probable issue, and have bidden a sincere welcome to them, as the harbingers of my speedy release from a life of guilt and woe!

I am going from you, Julia. This night separates us, perhaps, forever! I have not resolution to encounter the tears of my friends; and therefore seek shelter among strangers; where none knows, or is interested in my melancholy story. The place of my seclusion I studiously conceal; yet I shall take measures that you may be apprized of my fate.

Should it please God to spare and restore me to health, I shall return, and endeavor, by a life of penitence and rectitude, to expiate my past offences. But should I be called from this scene of action; and leave behind me a helpless babe, the innocent sufferer of its mother's shame, Oh, Julia, let your friendship for me extend to the little stranger! Intercede with my mother to take it under her protection; and transfer to it all her affection for me; to train it up in the ways of piety and virtue, that it may compensate her for the afflictions which I have occasioned!

One thing more I have to request. Plead for me with my two best friends, Mrs. Richman and Mrs. Sumner. I ask you not to palliate my faults; that cannot be done; but to obtain, if possible, their forgiveness. I cannot write all my full mind suggests on this subject. You know the purport; and can better express it for me.

And now, my dear Julia, recommending myself again to your benevolence, to your charity and (may I add?) to your affection; and entreating that the

fatal consequences of my folly, now fallen upon my devoted head, may suffice for my punishment; let me conjure you to bury my crimes in the grave with me, and to preserve the remembrance of my former virtues, which engaged your love and confidence; more especially of that ardent esteem for you, which will glow till the last expiring breath of your despairing

ELIZA WHARTON.

Letter LXX

TO MR. CHARLES DEIGHTON

HARTFORD

I have, at last, accomplished the removal of my darling girl from a place where she thought every eye accused and every heart condemned her.

She has become quite romantic in her notions. She would not permit me to accompany her, lest it should be reported that we had eloped together. I provided amply for her future exigencies, and conveyed her by night to the distance of ten or twelve miles, where we met the stage, in which I had previously secured her a seat. The agony of her grief at being thus obliged to leave her mother's house baffles all description.

It very sensibly affected me, I know. I was almost a penitent. I am sure I acted like one, whether I were sincere or not. She chose to go where she was totally unknown. She would leave the stage, she said, before it reached Boston, and take passage in a more private carriage to Salem, or its vicinity, where she would fix her abode; chalking the initials of my name over the door as a signal to me of her residence.

She is exceedingly depressed; and says she neither expects nor wishes to survive her lying in. Insanity, for aught I know, must be my lot, if she should die. But I will not harbor the idea. I hope, one time or other, to have the power to make her amends, even by marriage. My wife may be provoked, I imagine, to sue for a divorce. If she should, she would find no difficulty in obtaining it; and then I would take Eliza in her stead. Though I confess that the idea of being thus connected with a woman whom I have been able to dishonor would be rather hard to surmount. It would hurt even my delicacy, little as you may think me to possess, to have a wife whom I know to be seducible. And, on this account, I cannot be positive that even Eliza would retain my love.

My Nancy and I have lived a pretty uncomfortable life, of late. She has been very suspicious of my amour with Eliza; and now and then expressed her jealous sentiments a little more warmly than my patience would bear. But the news of Eliza's circumstances and retirement, being publicly talked of, have reached her ears, and rendered her quite outrageous. She tells me she will no longer brook my indifference and infidelity; intends soon to return to her father's house, and extricate herself from me entirely. My general reply to all this, is, that she knew my character before we married, and could reasonably expect nothing less than what has happened. I shall not oppose her leaving me, as it may conduce to the execution of the plan I have hinted above.

Tomorrow I shall set out to visit my disconsolate fair one. From my very soul I pity her; and wish I could have preserved her virtue consistently with the indulgence of my passion. To her I lay not the principal blame, as in like

cases, I do to the sex in general. My finesse was too well planned for detection, and my snares too deeply laid for anyone to escape who had the least warmth in her constitution, or affection in her heart. I shall, therefore, be the less whimsical about a future connection, and the more solicitous to make her reparation, should it ever be in my power.

Her friends are all in arms about her. I dare say I have the imprecations of the whole fraternity. They may thank themselves in part; for I always swore revenge for their dislike and coldness towards me. Had they been politic, they would have conducted more like the aborigines of the country, who are said to worship the devil out of fear.

I am afraid I shall be obliged to remove my quarters; for Eliza was so great a favorite in town, that I am looked upon with an evil eye. I pled with her before we parted last to forgive my seducing her; alleged my ardent love, and my inability to possess her in any other way. How, said she, can that be love which destroys its object? But granting what you say, you have frustrated your own purpose. You have deprived yourself of my society, which might have been innocently enjoyed. You have cut me off from life in the midst of my days. You have rendered me the reproach of my friends, the disgrace of my family, and a dishonor to virtue and my sex! But I forgive you, added she. Yes, Sanford, I forgive you; and sincerely pray for your repentance and reformation. I hope to be the last wretched female sacrificed by you to the arts of falsehood and seduction!

May my unhappy story serve as a beacon to warn the American fair of the dangerous tendency and destructive consequences of associating with men of your character, of destroying their time, and risking their reputation by the practice of coquetry and its attendant follies! But for these, I might have been honorably connected; and capable, at this moment, of diffusing and receiving happiness! But for your arts, I might have remained a blessing to society, as well as the delight and comfort of my friends!

Your being a married man unspeakably aggravates both your guilt and mine. This circumstance annexes indelible shame to our crime! You have rent asunder the tenderest ties of nature! You have broken the bonds of conjugal love, which ought ever to be kept sacred and inviolate! You have filled with grief and discontent the heart of your amiable wife, whom gratitude, if no other principle, should have induced you to cherish with tenderness; and I, wretch that I am, have been your accomplice!

But I cease to reproach you. You have acted but too consistently with the character which I was sufficiently apprised you sustained. The blame then may be retorted on myself, for disregarding the counsels, warnings and admonitions of my best friends. You have prided yourself in the character of a libertine. Glory no longer in your shame! You have accomplished your designs; your dreadful designs against me! Let this suffice. Add not to the number of those deluded creatures who will one day rise up in judgment against you and condemn you.

By this time we had nearly reached the inn, and were soon to part, I seized her hand and exclaimed, you must not leave me, Eliza, with that awful anathema on your lips! Oh, say that you will forget my past faults. That, said she, I shall soon do; for in the grave there is no remembrance! This to my mind, was a harsher sentence than the other; and almost threw me into despair. Never was I so wrought upon before! I knew not what to say or

do! She saw my distress, and kindly softened her manner. If I am severe, said she, it is because I wish to impress your mind with such a sense of your offences against your Maker, your friends and society in general, as may effect your repentance and amendment. I wish not to be your accuser, but your reformer. On several accounts, I view my own crime in a more aggravated light than yours; but my conscience is awakened to a conviction of my guilt. Yours, I fear is not. Let me conjure you to return home, and endeavor by your future kindness and fidelity to your wife, to make her all the amends in your power. By a life of virtue and religion, you may yet become a valuable member of society, and secure happiness both here and hereafter.

I begged leave to visit her retirement next week, not in continuation of our amour, but as a friend, solicitous to know her situation and welfare. Unable to speak, she only bowed assent. The stage being now ready, I whispered some tender things in her ear, and kissing her cheek, which was all she would permit, suffered her to depart.

My body remains behind; but my soul, if I have any, went with her!

This was a horrid lecture, Charles! She brought every charge against me which a fruitful and gloomy imagination could suggest! But I hope, when she recovers, she will resume her former cheerfulness, and become as kind and agreeable as ever. My anxiety for her safety is very great. I trust, however, it will soon be removed; and peace and pleasure be restored to your humble servant.

<div style="text-align: right">PETER SANFORD.</div>

Letter LXXI

TO MRS. LUCY SUMNER

<div style="text-align: right">HARTFORD</div>

The drama is now closed! A tragical one indeed it has proved!

How sincerely, my dear Mrs. Sumner, must the friends of our departed Eliza sympathize with each other; and with her afflicted, bereaved parent!

You have doubtless seen the account, in the public papers, which gave us the melancholy intelligence. But I will give you a detail of circumstances.

A few days after my last was written, we heard that Major Sanford's property was attached, and he a prisoner in his own house. He was the last man, to whom we wished to apply for information respecting the forlorn wanderer; yet we had no other resource. And after waiting a fortnight in the most cruel suspense, we wrote a billet, entreating him, if possible, to give some intelligence concerning her. He replied, that he was unhappily deprived of all means of knowing himself; but hoped soon to relieve his own and our anxiety about her.

In this situation we continued, till a neighbor (purposely, we since concluded) sent us a Boston paper. Mrs. Wharton took it, and unconscious of its contents, observed that the perusal might divert her, a few moments. She read for some time; when it suddenly dropped upon the floor. She clasped her hands together, and raising her streaming eyes to heaven, exclaimed, It is the Lord; let him do what he will! Be still, O my soul, and know that he is God!

What, madam, said I, can be the matter? She answered not; but with inexpressible anguish depicted in her countenance, pointed to the paper. I

took it up, and soon found the fatal paragraph. I shall not attempt to paint our heartfelt grief and lamentation upon this occasion; for we had no doubt of Eliza's being the person described, as a stranger, who died at Danvers, last July. Her delivery of a child; her dejected state of mind; the marks upon her linen; indeed, every circumstance in the advertisement convinced us beyond dispute, that it could be no other. Mrs. Wharton retired immediately to her chamber, where she continued overwhelmed with sorrow that night and the following day. Such, in fact, has been her habitual frame ever since; though the endeavors of her friends, who have sought to console her, have rendered her somewhat more conversable. My testimony of Eliza's penitence, before her departure, is a source of comfort to this disconsolate parent. She fondly cherished the idea, that having expiated her offence by sincere repentance and amendment, her deluded child finally made a happy exchange of worlds. But the desperate resolution, which she formed and executed of becoming a fugitive; of deserting her mother's house and protection, and of wandering and dying among strangers, is a most distressing reflection to her friends; especially to her mother, in whose breast so many painful ideas arise, that she finds it extremely difficult to compose herself to that resignation, which she evidently strives to exemplify.

Eliza's brother has been to visit her last retreat; and to learn the particulars of her melancholy exit. He relates, that she was well accommodated, and had every attention and assistance, which her situation required. The people where she resided appear to have a lively sense of her merit and misfortunes. They testify her modest deportment, her fortitude under the sufferings to which she was called, and the serenity and composure, with which she bid a last adieu to the world. Mr. Wharton has brought back several scraps of her writing, containing miscellaneous reflections on her situation, the death of her babe, and the absence of her friends. Some of these were written before, some after her confinement. These valuable testimonies of the affecting sense and calm expectation she entertained of her approaching dissolution, are calculated to sooth and comfort the minds of mourning connections. They greatly alleviate the regret occasioned by her absence, at this awful period.

Her elopement can be equalled only by the infatuation which caused her ruin.

> But let no one reproach her memory.
> Her life has paid the forfeit of her folly.
> Let that suffice.[7]

I am told that Major Sanford is quite frantic. Sure I am that he has reason to be. If the mischiefs he has brought upon others return upon his own head, dreadful indeed must be his portion! His wife has left him, and returned to her parents. His estate, which has been long mortgaged, is taken from him; and poverty and disgrace await him! Heaven seldom leaves injured innocence unavenged! Wretch, that he is, he ought for ever to be banished from human society! I shall continue with Mrs. Wharton, till the lenient hand of time has assuaged her sorrows; and then make my promised visit to you. I will bring Eliza's posthumous papers with me, when I come to Boston, as I have not time to copy them now.

7. Source unidentified.

I foresee, my dear Mrs. Sumner, that this disastrous affair will suspend your enjoyments, as it has mine. But what are our feelings, compared with the pangs which rend a parent's heart? This parent, I here behold, inhumanly stripped of the best solace of her declining years, by the ensnaring machinations of a profligate debauchee! Not only the life, but what was still dearer, the reputation and virtue of the unfortunate Eliza, have fallen victims at the shrine of *libertinism!* Detested be the epithet! Let it henceforth bear its true signature, and candor itself shall call it *lust* and *brutality!*

Execrable is the man, however arrayed in magnificence, crowned with wealth, or decorated with the external graces and accomplishments of fashionable life, who shall presume to display them, at the expense of virtue and innocence! Sacred names! Attended with real blessings; blessings too useful and important to be trifled away! My resentment at the base arts, which must have been employed to complete the seduction of Eliza, I cannot suppress. I wish them to be exposed, and stamped with universal ignominy! Nor do I doubt but you will join with me in execrating the measures by which *we* have been robbed of so valuable a friend; and *society*, of so ornamental a member.

I am, &c.

JULIA GRANBY.

Letter LXXII

TO MR. CHARLES DEIGHTON

HARTFORD

Confusion, horror and despair are the portion of your wretched, unhappy friend! Oh, Deighton, I am undone! Misery irremediable is my future lot! She is gone; yes, she is gone forever! The darling of my soul, the center of all my wishes and enjoyments is no more! Cruel fate has snatched her from me, and she is irretrievably lost! I rave, and then reflect: I reflect, and then rave! I have not patience to bear this calamity, nor power to remedy it! Where shall I fly from the upbraidings of my mind, which accuses me as the murderer of my Eliza? I would fly to death, and seek a refuge in the grave; but the forebodings of a retribution to come, I cannot away with! Oh, that I had seen her; that I had once more asked her forgiveness! But even that privilege, that consolation was denied me! The day on which I meant to visit her, most of my property was attached, and to secure the rest, I was obliged to shut my doors, and become a prisoner in my own house! High living, and old debts, incurred by extravagance, had reduced the fortune of my wife to very little, and I could not satisfy the clamorous demands of my creditors.

I would have given millions, had I possessed them, to have been at liberty to see, and to have had power to preserve Eliza from death! But in vain was my anxiety; it could not relieve; it could not liberate me! When I first heard the dreadful tidings of her exit, I believe I acted like a madman! Indeed, I am little else now!

I have compounded with my creditors, and resigned the whole of my property.

Thus, that splendor and equipage, to secure which, I have sacrificed a virtuous woman, is taken from me; that poverty, the dread of which prevented my forming an honorable connection with an amiable and accomplished

girl, the only one I ever loved, has fallen, with redoubled vengeance, upon my guilty head; and I must become a vagabond in the earth!

I shall fly my country as soon as possible; I shall go from every object which reminds me of my departed Eliza! But never, never shall I eradicate from my bosom the idea of her excellence; or the painful remembrance of the injuries I have done her! Her shade will perpetually haunt me! The image of her, as she appeared when mounting the carriage which conveyed her forever from my sight, she waved her hand in token of a last adieu, will always be present to my imagination! The solemn counsel she gave me before we parted, never more to meet, will not cease to resound in my ears!

While my being is prolonged, I must feel the disgraceful and torturing effects of my guilt in seducing her! How madly have I deprived her of happiness, of reputation, of life! Her friends, could they know the pangs of contrition, and the horror of conscience which attend me, would be amply revenged!

It is said, she quitted the world with composure and peace. Well she might! She had not that insupportable weight of iniquity, which sinks me to despair! She found consolation in that religion, which I have ridiculed as priestcraft and hypocrisy! But whether it be true, or false, would to heaven I could now enjoy the comforts, which its votaries evidently feel!

My wife has left me. As we lived together without love, we parted without regret.

Now, Charles, I am to bid you a long, perhaps, a last farewell. Where I shall roam in future, I neither know nor care; I shall go where the name of Sanford is unknown; and his person and sorrows unnoticed.

In this happy clime I have nothing to induce my stay. I have not money to support me with my profligate companions; nor have I any relish, at present, for their society. By the virtuous part of the community, I am shunned as the pest and bane of social enjoyment. In short I am debarred from every kind of happiness. If I look back, I recoil with horror from the black catalogue of vices, which have stained my past life, and reduced me to indigence and contempt. If I look forward, I shudder at the prospects which my foreboding mind presents to view, both in this and a coming world! This is a deplorable, yet just picture of myself! How totally the reverse of what I once appeared!

Let it warn you, my friend, to shun the dangerous paths which I have trodden, that you may never be involved in the hopeless ignominy and wretchedness of

<div style="text-align: right">PETER SANFORD.</div>

<div style="text-align: center">

Letter LXXIII

TO MISS JULIA GRANBY

</div>

<div style="text-align: right">BOSTON</div>

A melancholy tale have you unfolded, my dear Julia; and tragic indeed is the concluding scene!

Is she then gone! gone in this most distressing manner! Have I lost my once loved friend; lost her in a way which I could never have conceived to be possible.

Our days of childhood were spent together in the same pursuits, in the same amusements. Our riper years increased our mutual affection, and

maturer judgment most firmly cemented our friendship. Can I then calmly resign her to so severe a fate! Can I bear the idea of her being lost to honor, to fame, and to life! No; she shall still live in the heart of her faithful Lucy, whose experience of her numerous virtues and engaging qualities has imprinted her image too deeply on the memory to be obliterated. However she may have erred, her sincere repentance is sufficient to restore her to charity.

Your letter gave me the first information of this awful event. I had taken a short excursion into the country, where I had not seen the papers; or if I had, paid little or no attention to them. By your directions I found the distressing narrative of her exit. The poignancy of my grief, and the unavailing lamentations which the intelligence excited, need no delineation. To scenes of this nature, you have been habituated in the mansion of sorrow, where you reside.

How sincerely I sympathize with the bereaved parent of the dear, deceased Eliza, I can feel, but have not power to express. Let it be her consolation that her child is at rest. The resolution which carried this deluded wanderer thus far from her friends, and supported her through her various trials, is astonishing! Happy would it have been, had she exerted an equal degree of fortitude in repelling the first attacks upon her virtue! But she is no more; and heaven forbid that I should accuse or reproach her!

Yet, in what language shall I express my abhorrence of the monster whose detestable arts have blasted one of the fairest flowers in creation? I leave him to God, and his own conscience! Already is he exposed in his true colors! Vengeance already begins to overtake him! His sordid mind must now suffer the deprivation of those sensual gratifications, beyond which he is incapable of enjoyment!

Upon your reflecting and steady mind, my dear Julia, I need not inculcate the lessons which may be drawn from this woe-fraught tale; but for the sake of my sex in general, I wish it engraved upon every heart, that virtue alone, independent of the trappings of wealth, the parade of equipage, and the adulation of gallantry, can secure lasting felicity. From the melancholy story of Eliza Wharton, let the American fair learn to reject with disdain every insinuation derogatory to their true dignity and honor. Let them despise and forever banish the man who can glory in the seduction of innocence and the ruin of reputation. To associate, is to approve; to approve, is to be betrayed!

I am, &c.

LUCY SUMNER.

Letter LXXIV

TO MRS. M. WHARTON

BOSTON

DEAR MADAM,

We have paid the last tribute of respect to your beloved daughter. The day after my arrival, Mrs. Sumner proposed that we should visit the sad spot which contains the remains of our once amiable friend. The grave of Eliza Wharton, said she, shall not be unbedewed by the tears of friendship.

Yesterday we went accordingly, and were much pleased with the apparent sincerity of the people, in their assurances that everything in their power

had been done to render her situation comfortable. The minutest circumstances were faithfully related; and from the state of her mind, in her last hours, I think much comfort may be derived to her afflicted friends.

We spent a mournful hour in the place where she is interred, and then returned to the inn, while Mrs. Sumner gave orders for a decent stone to be erected over her grave, with the following inscription:

"THIS HUMBLE STONE,
IN MEMORY *OF*

ELIZA WHARTON,

IS INSCRIBED BY HER WEEPING FRIENDS,
TO WHOM SHE ENDEARED HERSELF BY UNCOMMON
TENDERNESS AND AFFECTION.
ENDOWED WITH SUPERIOR ACQUIREMENTS,
SHE WAS STILL MORE DISTINGUISHED BY
HUMILITY AND BENEVOLENCE.
LET CANDOR THROW A VEIL OVER HER FRAILTIES,
FOR GREAT WAS HER CHARITY TO OTHERS.
SHE SUSTAINED THE LAST
PAINFUL SCENE, FAR FROM EVERY FRIEND;
AND EXHIBITED AN EXAMPLE
OF CALM RESIGNATION.
HER DEPARTURE WAS ON THE 25th DAY OF
JULY, A. D. ———,
IN THE 37th YEAR OF HER AGE,
AND THE TEARS OF STRANGERS WATERED HER
G R A V E."

I hope, madam, that you will derive satisfaction from these exertions of friendship, and that, united to the many other sources of consolation with which you are furnished, they may alleviate your grief; and while they leave

the pleasing remembrance of her virtues, add the supporting persuasion, that
your Eliza is happy.

<div align="center">I am, &c.</div>

<div align="right">JULIA GRANBY.</div>

<div align="right">FINIS.</div>

<div align="center">1797</div>

CHARLES BROCKDEN BROWN
1771–1810

C harles Brockden Brown had extraordinary insight into fiction's capacity to
gauge emotional depths. Influenced by the gothic tradition in fiction—as
exemplified by the work of English writers such as the political philosophers and
novelists William Godwin and Mary Wollstonecraft—Brown used the emergent
genre of the novel to test, celebrate, and sometimes reject the radical implications
of revolutionary ideology. For Brown, the sentimental plots made popular by the
English novelist Samuel Richardson and adapted by American novelists including
Susanna Rowson and Hannah Webster Foster became a starting point for very differ-
ent explorations. His fiction overturned readers' Enlightenment faith in the ratio-
nality of human behavior and indicated that the emotional and obsessive, as much
as the logical, were basic elements of character. Brown thus began to explore a rich
vein in American fiction that Edgar Allan Poe, Herman Melville, and Nathaniel
Hawthorne mined in the nineteenth century with great success.

Brown was born into a Quaker family in Philadelphia, then the cultural and
political center of the thirteen colonies and subsequently the first capital of the
United States. (Benjamin Franklin mentions Brown's great-uncle in his *Autobiogra-
phy*, and Brown was a member of the Belles Lettres Club, which sometimes met at
Franklin's house.) During the American Revolution, Brown's father remained
steadfast in the pacifist principles of the Quakers, refusing to bear arms or take a
patriot oath, and he suffered the pillaging of his business and eight months of
imprisonment in Virginia as a consequence. These events profoundly shaped
Brown's attitudes toward revolution, which came to be reflected in his fiction. He
prepared for a career in law, completing his schooling in 1787, the year that the
Constitutional Convention met in Philadelphia. As the time approached for him to
launch a legal career, however, he gravitated instead to the world of belles lettres.
He might well have succeeded in Philadelphia, which by the 1790s had become a
large, culturally sophisticated city where a writer could aspire to the newly possible
profession of authorship.

Brown opted instead for New York City, where he met and befriended contempo-
raries who shared his intellectual ambitions. They included the Hartford wit and
future president of Yale University, Timothy Dwight; the lexicographer Noah Web-
ster; and Elihu Hubbard Smith, who in 1793 published the first anthology of Amer-
ican poetry. Encouraged by the Friendly Club, an association of young writers,

physicians, and attorneys that met weekly for intellectual conversation, Brown read widely in English literature and published six novels in the gothic mode. *Wieland; or The Transformation: An American Tale* (1798), Brown's best-known work, is a tale of psychological and spiritual revolution, based on a true story about a man who believes God has instructed him to kill his family. In *Ormond* (1799) the main character, a freethinker recently returned from the Continent, tests the virtue of Constantia, who is an epitome of republican womanhood. *Edgar Huntly* (1799) capitalized on the public's continuing interest in tales of Indian captivity and the wilderness generally, even as Brown teased readers with a rational explanation—sleepwalking—for the strange behavior of one of his central characters. Brown turned to his home city for the setting of *Arthur Mervyn* (1799–1800), whose melodramatic plot has as its background Philadelphia's yellow fever outbreak of 1793. Brown concluded his career as a novelist with the lesser-read sentimental novels *Clara Howard* and *Jane Talbot* (both 1801).

In 1827 Brown's novels were reissued in a uniform edition, making him the first American novelist to have this (posthumous) honor. In his lifetime, however, Brown abandoned the novel because he could not make a living by writing fiction. To augment his income he involved himself in other publishing ventures. Over the course of a decade, for example, he founded and edited *The Monthly Magazine and American Review* (1799–1800), *The Literary Magazine and American Register* (1803–07), and the *American Register, or General Repository of History, Politics, and Science* (1807–10), all of which provided outlets for his varied talents and ambitions. He contributed many essays to these and other journals, his most important effort being *Alcuin*, a lengthy dialogue on women's rights that shows Wollstonecraft's influence. *Alcuin* appeared first in the *Philadelphia Weekly Magazine* and was published as a book in 1798. His pamphlet *An Address to the Government of the United States on the Cession of Louisiana to the French* (1803) helped sway public opinion toward the purchase of the Louisiana Territory, and his translation of C. F. Volney's *A View of the Soil and Climate of the United States of America* (1804), with his own commentary, introduced this important French philosopher to many Americans. His work on *A Complete System of Geography* was interrupted by his death, from tuberculosis.

Although he is sometimes called America's first professional author, Brown did not enjoy the kind of success achieved a few years later by Washington Irving and James Fenimore Cooper, primarily because the technological infrastructure for the rapid production and widespread distribution of printed materials was not yet fully developed in the United States. Brown's significance thus resides in his ability to identify those topics—like the limits of rationality and the role of the senses in epistemology—that were of growing interest to an American and international readership and in his willingness to explore the implications of republican ideology on a range of psychological, philosophical, and social topics, including gender relations.

In his novella *Memoirs of Carwin the Biloquist*, Brown provides the early history of Frank Carwin, the mysterious character in his novel *Wieland; or The Transformation* who has an uncanny ability to project his voice while imitating the voices of others. (Biloquism as Brown uses the term is similar to what today is known as ventriloquism.) In *Wieland*, Carwin uses these powers in ways that fatally disrupt the Wieland family and their Enlightenment community. Brown began *Memoirs* while he was at work on *Wieland*, and he serialized the shorter work between November 1803 and March 1805 in his *Literary Magazine*. In certain ways *Memoirs* is directly tied to *Wieland*, especially in the novella's middle section, where Carwin obliquely addresses the young woman Clara, *Wieland*'s narrator, revealing that his memoirs explain and apologize for actions that may have contributed to the deaths of her relatives. But the interest of *Memoirs* goes well beyond this plot device, distilling major concerns that appear throughout Brown's fiction.

In the opening pages of *Memoirs*, Carwin describes his adolescent years, when intellectual curiosity and a love of reading, coupled with distaste for physical labor, bring him into conflict with his father, a domineering and socially conservative farmer. Language of all sorts is of particular interest to Carwin. He learns through experiment to throw his voice and to imitate the way others speak; he also teaches his dog, suggestively named "Damon" (similar to the classical "daemon," or godlike power) to understand his gestures and create the illusion of speech.

Shortly after Carwin moves in with an aunt in Philadelphia, he meets an Irishman named Ludloe, who guesses at his secret capability, or "art," as he calls it. Although Carwin resists full disclosure of his talent, Ludloe takes him to Dublin and begins grooming him to join a mysterious conspiratorial organization. Carwin's training involves an extended stay in Spain, where he studies the Roman Catholic Church and learns about the Jesuits. After returning to Ireland, he is brought deeper into Ludloe's world when he is given access to his secret library. The novella concludes in the midst of things with a test of wills that involves Carwin's sense of self. Among the compelling themes that *Memoirs* explores in a transatlantic context are the interplay of power and perversity and the role of mystery in narrative. Through Carwin's biloquism, Brown examines the attractions and dangers of art in a democracy, while the figure of Ludloe speaks to a concern that is a pervasive theme in the literature of the early republic: the appeal and risks of social utopianism.

Memoirs of Carwin the Biloquist[1]

I was the second son of a farmer, whose place of residence was a western district of Pennsylvania. My eldest brother seemed fitted by nature for the employment to which he was destined. His wishes never led him astray from the hay-stack and the furrow. His ideas never ranged beyond the sphere of his vision, or suggested the possibility that to-morrow could differ from to-day. He could read and write, because he had no alternative between learning the lesson prescribed to him, and punishment. He was diligent, as long as fear urged him forward, but his exertions ceased with the cessation of this motive. The limits of his acquirements consisted in signing his name, and spelling out a chapter in the bible.

My character was the reverse of his. My thirst of knowledge was augmented in proportion as it was supplied with gratification. The more I heard or read, the more restless and unconquerable my curiosity became. My senses were perpetually alive to novelty, my fancy teemed with visions of the future, and my attention fastened upon every thing mysterious or unknown.

My father intended that my knowledge should keep pace with that of my brother, but conceived that all beyond the mere capacity to write and read was useless or pernicious. He took as much pains to keep me within these limits, as to make the acquisitions of my brother come up to them, but his efforts were not equally successful in both cases. The most vigilant and jealous scrutiny was exerted in vain: reproaches and blows, painful privations and ignominious penances had no power to slacken my zeal and abate my perseverance. He might enjoin upon me the most laborious tasks, set the envy of my brother to watch me during the performance, make the most diligent search after my books, and destroy them without mercy, when they were

1. The text is from *The Literary Magazine and American Register* (1803–05).

found; but he could not outroot my darling propensity. I exerted all my powers to elude his watchfulness. Censures and stripes[2] were sufficiently unpleasing to make me strive to avoid them. To affect[3] this desirable end, I was incessantly employed in the invention of stratagems and the execution of expedients.

My passion was surely not deserving of blame, and I have frequently lamented the hardships to which it subjected me; yet, perhaps, the claims which were made upon my ingenuity and fortitude were not without beneficial effects upon my character.

This contention lasted from the sixth to the fourteenth year of my age. My father's opposition to my schemes was incited by a sincere though unenlightened desire for my happiness. That all his efforts were secretly eluded or obstinately repelled, was a source of the bitterest regret. He has often lamented, with tears, what he called my incorrigible depravity, and encouraged himself to perseverance by the notion of the ruin that would inevitably overtake me if I were allowed to persist in my present career. Perhaps the sufferings which arose to him from the disappointment, were equal to those which he inflicted on me.

In my fourteenth year, events happened which ascertained[4] my future destiny. One evening I had been sent to bring cows from a meadow, some miles distant from my father's mansion. My time was limited, and I was menaced with severe chastisement if, according to my custom, I should stay beyond the period assigned.

For some time these menaces rung in my ears, and I went on my way with speed. I arrived at the meadow, but the cattle had broken the fence and escaped. It was my duty to carry home the earliest tidings of this accident, but the first suggestion was to examine the cause and manner of this escape. The field was bounded by cedar railing. Five of these rails were laid horizontally from post to post. The upper one had been broken in the middle, but the rest had merely been drawn out of the holes on one side, and rested with their ends on the ground. The means which had been used for this end, the reason why one only was broken, and that one the uppermost, how a pair of horns could be so managed as to effect that which the hands of man would have found difficult, supplied a theme of meditation.

Some accident recalled me from this reverie, and reminded me how much time had thus been consumed. I was terrified at the consequences of my delay, and sought with eagerness how they might be obviated.[5] I asked myself if there were not a way back shorter than that by which I had come. The beaten road was rendered circuitous by a precipice that projected into a neighbouring stream, and closed up a passage by which the length of the way would have been diminished one half: at the foot of the cliff the water was of considerable depth, and agitated by an eddy. I could not estimate the danger which I should incur by plunging into it, but I was resolved to make the attempt. I have reason to think, that this experiment, if it had been tried, would have proved fatal, and my father, while he lamented my untimely fate, would have been wholly unconscious that his own unreasonable demands had occasioned it.

I turned my steps towards the spot. To reach the edge of the stream was by no means an easy undertaking, so many abrupt points and gloomy hollows

2. Reprimands and blows.
3. Bring about.
4. Made certain.
5. Removed.

were interposed. I had frequently skirted and penetrated this tract, but had never been so completely entangled in the maze as now: hence I had remained unacquainted with a narrow pass, which, at the distance of an hundred yards from the river, would conduct me, though not without danger and toil, to the opposite side of the ridge.

This glen was now discovered, and this discovery induced me to change my plan. If a passage could be here effected, it would be shorter and safer than that which led through the stream, and its practicability was to be known only by experiment. The path was narrow, steep, and overshadowed by rocks. The sun was nearly set, and the shadow of the cliff above, obscured the passage almost as much as midnight would have done: I was accustomed to despise danger when it presented itself in a sensible[6] form, but, by a defect common in every one's education, goblins and spectres were to me the objects of the most violent apprehensions. These were unavoidably connected with solitude and darkness, and were present to my fears when I entered this gloomy recess.

These terrors are always lessened by calling the attention away to some indifferent[7] object. I now made use of this expedient, and began to amuse myself by hallowing as loud as organs of unusual compass and vigour would enable me. I uttered the words which chanced to occur to me, and repeated in the shrill tones of a Mohock[8] savage . . . "Cow! cow! come home! home!" . . . These notes were of course reverberated from the rocks which on either side towered aloft, but the echo was confused and indistinct.

I continued, for some time, thus to beguile the way, till I reached a space more than commonly abrupt, and which required all my attention. My rude ditty was suspended till I had surmounted this impediment. In a few minutes I was at leisure to renew it. After finishing the strain, I paused. In a few seconds a voice as I then imagined, uttered the same cry from the point of a rock some hundred feet behind me; the same words, with equal distinctness and deliberation, and in the same tone, appeared to be spoken. I was startled by this incident, and cast a fearful glance behind, to discover by whom it was uttered. The spot where I stood was buried in dusk, but the eminences were still invested with a luminous and vivid twilight. The speaker, however, was concealed from my view.

I had scarcely begun to wonder at this occurrence, when a new occasion for wonder, was afforded me. A few seconds, in like manner, elapsed, when my ditty[9] was again rehearsed, with a no less perfect imitation, in a different quarter. . . . To this quarter I eagerly turned my eyes, but no one was visible. . . . The station, indeed, which this new speaker seemed to occupy, was inaccessible to man or beast.

If I were surprized at this second repetition of my words, judge how much my surprise must have been augmented, when the same calls were a third time repeated, and coming still in a new direction. Five times was this ditty successively resounded, at intervals nearly equal, always from a new quarter, and with little abatement of its original distinctness and force.

A little reflection was sufficient to shew that this was no more than an echo of an extraordinary kind. My terrors were quickly supplanted by delight. The motives to dispatch were forgotten, and I amused myself for an hour,

6. Perceptible.
7. Neutral.
8. A member of the Mohawk tribe (one of the original Five Nations of the Iroquois Confederacy, in western New York).
9. A short, simple song.

with talking to these cliffs: I placed myself in new positions, and exhausted my lungs and my invention in new clamours.

The pleasures of this new discovery were an ample compensation for the ill treatment which I expected on my return. By some caprice in my father I escaped merely with a few reproaches. I seized the first opportunity of again visiting this recess, and repeating my amusement; time, and incessant repetition, could scarcely lessen its charms or exhaust the variety produced by new tones and new positions.

The hours in which I was most free from interruption and restraint were those of moonlight. My brother and I occupied a small room above the kitchen, disconnected, in some degree, with the rest of the house. It was the rural custom to retire early to bed and to anticipate the rising of the sun. When the moonlight was strong enough to permit me to read, it was my custom to escape from bed, and hie[1] with my book to some neighbouring eminence, where I would remain stretched on the mossy rock, till the sinking or beclouded moon, forbade me to continue my employment. I was indebted for books to a friendly person in the neighbourhood, whose compliance with my solicitations was prompted partly by benevolence and partly by enmity to my father, whom he could not more egregiously offend than by gratifying my perverse and pernicious curiosity.

In leaving my chamber I was obliged to use the utmost caution to avoid rousing my brother, whose temper disposed him to thwart me in the least of my gratifications. My purpose was surely laudable, and yet on leaving the house and returning to it, I was obliged to use the vigilance and circumspection of a thief.

One night I left my bed with this view. I posted first to my vocal glen, and thence scrambling up a neighbouring steep, which overlooked a wide extent of this romantic country, gave myself up to contemplation and the perusal of Milton's Comus.[2]

My reflections were naturally suggested by the singularity of this echo. To hear my own voice speak at a distance would have been formerly regarded as prodigious. To hear too, that voice, not uttered by another, by whom it might easily be mimicked, but by myself! I cannot now recollect the transition which led me to the notion of sounds, similar to these, but produced by other means than reverberation. Could I not so dispose my organs as to make my voice appear at a distance?

From speculation I proceeded to experiment. The idea of a distant voice, like my own, was intimately present to my fancy. I exerted myself with a most ardent desire, and with something like a persuasion that I should succeed. I started with surprise, for it seemed as if success had crowned my attempts. I repeated the effort, but failed. A certain position of the organs took place on the first attempt, altogether new, unexampled and as it were, by accident, for I could not attain it on the second experiment.

You[3] will not wonder that I exerted myself with indefatigable zeal to regain what had once, though for so short a space, been in my power. Your

1. Go quickly.
2. Formally titled *A Mask Presented at Ludlow Castle, 1634* (1637), this work by the English poet John Milton (1608–1674) takes its colloquial name from a central character modeled after the god of revelry.
3. The second-person address here is one of several indicators that *Memoirs* was conceived as an epistolary work.

own ears have witnessed the success of these efforts. By perpetual exertion I gained it a second time, and now was a diligent observer of the circumstances attending it. Gradually I subjected these finer and more subtle motions to the command of my will. What was at first difficult, by exercise and habit, was rendered easy. I learned to accommodate my voice to all the varieties of distance and direction.

It cannot be denied that this faculty is wonderful and rare, but when we consider the possible modifications of muscular motion, how few of these are usually exerted, how imperfectly they are subjected to the will, and yet that the will is capable of being rendered unlimited and absolute, will not our wonder cease?

We have seen men who could hide their tongues so perfectly that even an Anatomist, after the most accurate inspection that a living subject could admit, has affirmed the organ to be wanting, but this was effected by the exertion of muscles unknown and incredible to the greater part of mankind.

The concurrence of teeth, palate and tongue, in the formation of speech should seem to be indispensable, and yet men have spoken distinctly though wanting a tongue, and to whom, therefore, teeth and palate were superfluous. The tribe of motions requisite to this end, are wholly latent and unknown, to those who possess that organ.

I mean not to be more explicit. I have no reason to suppose a peculiar conformation or activity in my own organs, or that the power which I possess may not, with suitable directions and by steady efforts, be obtained by others, but I will do nothing to facilitate the acquisition. It is by far, too liable to perversion for a good man to desire to possess it, or to teach it to another.

There remained but one thing to render this instrument as powerful in my hands as it was capable of being. From my childhood, I was remarkably skilful at imitation. There were few voices whether of men or birds or beasts which I could not imitate with success. To add my ancient, to my newly acquired skill, to talk from a distance, and at the same time, in the accents of another, was the object of my endeavours, and this object, after a certain number of trials, I finally obtained.

In my present situation every thing that denoted intellectual exertion was a crime, and exposed me to invectives if not to stripes. This circumstance induced me to be silent to all others, on the subject of my discovery. But, added to this, was a confused belief, that it might be made, in some way instrumental to my relief from the hardships and restraints of my present condition. For some time I was not aware of the mode in which it might be rendered subservient to this end.

My father's sister was an ancient lady resident in Philadelphia, the relict of a merchant, whose decease left her the enjoyment of a frugal competence.[4] She was without children, and had often expressed her desire that her nephew Frank, whom she always considered as a sprightly and promising lad, should be put under her care. She offered to be at the expense of my education, and to bequeath to me at her death her slender patrimony.

This arrangement was obstinately rejected by my father, because it was merely fostering and giving scope to propensities, which he considered as hurtful, and because his avarice desired that this inheritance should fall to no

4. Small inheritance, enough to live on modestly. "Relict": widow.

one but himself. To me, it was a scheme of ravishing felicity, and to be debarred from it was a source of anguish known to few. I had too much experience of my father's pertinaciousness ever to hope for a change in his views; yet the bliss of living with my aunt, in a new and busy scene, and in the unbounded indulgence of my literary passion, continually occupied my thoughts: for a long time these thoughts were productive only of despondency and tears.

Time only enhanced the desirableness of this scheme; my new faculty would naturally connect itself with these wishes, and the question could not fail to occur whether it might not aid me in the execution of my favourite plan.

A thousand superstitious tales were current in the family. Apparitions had been seen, and voices had been heard on a multitude of occasions. My father was a confident believer in supernatural tokens. The voice of his wife, who had been many years dead, had been twice heard at midnight whispering at his pillow. I frequently asked myself whether a scheme favourable to my views might not be built upon these foundations. Suppose (thought I) my mother should be made to enjoin upon him compliance with my wishes?

This idea bred in me a temporary consternation. To imitate the voice of the dead, to counterfeit a commission from heaven, bore the aspect of presumption and impiety. It seemed an offence which could not fail to draw after it the vengeance of the deity. My wishes for a time yielded to my fears, but this scheme in proportion as I meditated on it, became more plausible; no other occurred to me so easy and so efficacious. I endeavoured to persuade myself that the end proposed, was, in the highest degree praiseworthy, and that the excellence of my purpose would justify the means employed to attain it.

My resolutions were, for a time, attended with fluctuations and misgivings. These gradually disappeared, and my purpose became firm; I was next to devise the means of effecting my views, this did not demand any tedious deliberation. It was easy to gain access to my father's chamber without notice or detection, cautious footsteps and the suppression of breath would place me, unsuspected and unthought of, by his bed side. The words I should use, and the mode of utterance were not easily settled, but having at length selected these, I made myself by much previous repetition, perfectly familiar with the use of them.

I selected a blustering and inclement night, in which the darkness was augmented by a veil of the blackest clouds. The building we inhabited was slight in its structure, and full of crevices through which the gale found easy way, and whistled in a thousand cadencies. On this night the elemental music was remarkably sonorous, and was mingled not unfrequently with *thunder heard remote*.[5]

I could not divest myself of secret dread. My heart faultered with a consciousness of wrong. Heaven seemed to be present and to disapprove my work; I listened to the thunder and the wind, as to the stern voice of this disapprobation. Big drops stood on my forehead, and my tremors almost incapacitated me from proceeding.

These impediments however I surmounted; I crept up stairs at midnight, and entered my father's chamber. The darkness was intense and I sought with outstretched hands for his bed. The darkness, added to the trepidation

5. Cf. Milton's *Paradise Lost* 2.477.

of my thoughts, disabled me from making a right estimate of distances: I was conscious of this, and when I advanced within the room, paused.

I endeavoured to compare the progress I had made with my knowledge of the room, and governed by the result of this comparison, proceeded cautiously and with hands still outstretched in search of the foot of the bed. At this moment lightning flashed into the room: the brightness of the gleam was dazzling, yet it afforded me an exact knowledge of my situation. I had mistaken my way, and discovered that my knees nearly touched the bedstead, and that my hands at the next step, would have touched my father's cheek. His closed eyes and every line in his countenance, were painted, as it were, for an instant on my sight.

The flash was accompanied with a burst of thunder, whose vehemence was stunning. I always entertained a dread of thunder, and now recoiled, overborne with terror. Never had I witnessed so luminous a gleam and so tremendous a shock, yet my father's slumber appeared not to be disturbed by it.

I stood irresolute and trembling; to prosecute my purpose in this state of mind was impossible. I resolved for the present to relinquish it, and turned with a view of exploring my way out of the chamber. Just then a light seen through the window, caught my eye. It was at first weak but speedily increased; no second thought was necessary to inform me that the barn, situated at a small distance from the house, and newly stored with hay, was in flames, in consequence of being struck by the lightning.

My terror at this spectacle made me careless of all consequences relative to myself. I rushed to the bed and throwing myself on my father, awakened him by loud cries. The family were speedily roused, and were compelled to remain impotent spectators of the devastation. Fortunately the wind blew in a contrary direction, so that our habitation was not injured.

The impression that was made upon me by the incidents of that night is indelible. The wind gradually rose into an hurricane; the largest branches were torn from the trees, and whirled aloft into the air; others were uprooted and laid prostrate on the ground. The barn was a spacious edifice, consisting wholly of wood, and filled with a plenteous harvest. Thus supplied with fuel, and fanned by the wind, the fire raged with incredible fury; meanwhile clouds rolled above, whose blackness was rendered more conspicuous by reflection from the flames; the vast volumes of smoke were dissipated in a moment by the storm, while glowing fragments and cinders were borne to an immense height, and tossed everywhere in wild confusion. Ever and anon the sable[6] canopy that hung around us was streaked with lightning, and the peals, by which it was accompanied, were deafening, and with scarcely any intermission.

It was, doubtless, absurd to imagine any connexion between this portentous scene and the purpose that I had meditated, yet a belief of this connexion, though wavering and obscure, lurked in my mind; something more than a coincidence merely casual, appeared to have subsisted between my situation, at my father's bed side, and the flash that darted through the window, and diverted me from my design. It palsied my courage, and strengthened my conviction, that my scheme was criminal.

After some time had elapsed, and tranquility was, in some degree, restored in the family, my father reverted to the circumstances in which I had been

6. Black.

discovered on the first alarm of this event. The truth was impossible to be told. I felt the utmost reluctance to be guilty of a falsehood, but by falsehood only could I elude detection. That my guilt was the offspring of a fatal necessity, that the injustice of others gave it birth and made it unavoidable, afforded me slight consolation. Nothing can be more injurious than a lie, but its evil tendency chiefly respects our future conduct. Its direct consequences may be transient and few, but it facilitates a repetition, strengthens temptation, and grows into habit. I pretended some necessity had drawn me from my bed, and that discovering the condition of the barn, I hastened to inform my father.

Some time after this, my father summoned me to his presence. I had been previously guilty of disobedience to his commands, in a matter about which he was usually very scrupulous. My brother had been privy to my offence, and had threatened to be my accuser. On this occasion I expected nothing but arraignment and punishment. Weary of oppression, and hopeless of any change in my father's temper and views, I had formed the resolution of eloping from his house, and of trusting, young as I was, to the caprice of fortune. I was hesitating whether to abscond[7] without the knowledge of the family, or to make my resolutions known to them, and while I avowed my resolution, to adhere to it in spite of opposition and remonstrances, when I received this summons.

I was employed at this time in the field; night was approaching, and I had made no preparation for departure; all the preparation in my power to make, was indeed small; a few clothes made into a bundle, was the sum of my possessions. Time would have little influence in improving my prospects, and I resolved to execute my scheme immediately.

I left my work intending to seek my chamber, and taking what was my own, to disappear forever. I turned a stile that led out of the field into a bye path,[8] when my father appeared before me, advancing in an opposite direction; to avoid him was impossible, and I summoned my fortitude to a conflict with his passion.

As soon as we met, instead of anger and upbraiding, he told me, that he had been reflecting on my aunt's proposal, to take me under her protection, and had concluded that the plan was proper; if I still retained my wishes on that head, he would readily comply with them, and that, if I chose, I might set off for the city next morning, as a neighbour's wagon was preparing to go.

I shall not dwell on the rapture with which this proposal was listened to: it was with difficulty that I persuaded myself that he was in earnest in making it, nor could divine the reasons, for so sudden and unexpected a change in his maxims. . . . These I afterwards discovered. Some one had instilled into him fears, that my aunt, exasperated at his opposition to her request, respecting the unfortunate Frank, would bequeath her property to strangers; to obviate this evil, which his avarice prompted him to regard as much greater than any mischief, that would accrue to me, from the change of my abode, he embraced her proposal.

I entered with exultation and triumph on this new scene; my hopes were by no means disappointed. Detested labour was exchanged for luxurious idleness. I was master of my time, and the chooser of my occupations. My

7. Leave secretly and in a hurry.
8. Private or little-used footway. "Stile": steps that allow people but not animals to climb over a fence or wall.

kinswoman, on discovering that I entertained no relish for the drudgery of colleges, and was contented with the means of intellectual gratification, which I could obtain under her roof, allowed me to pursue my own choice.

Three tranquil years passed away, during which, each day added to my happiness, by adding to my knowledge. My biloquial faculty was not neglected. I improved it by assiduous exercise; I deeply reflected on the use to which it might be applied. I was not destitute of pure intentions; I delighted not in evil; I was incapable of knowingly contributing to another's misery, but the sole or principal end of my endeavours was not the happiness of others.

I was actuated by ambition. I was delighted to possess superior power; I was prone to manifest that superiority, and was satisfied if this were done, without much solicitude concerning consequences. I sported frequently with the apprehensions of my associates and threw out a bait for their wonder, and supplied them with occasions for the structure of theories. It may not be amiss to enumerate one or two adventures in which I was engaged.

I had taken much pains to improve the sagacity of a favourite Spaniel. It was my purpose, indeed, to ascertain to what degree of improvement the principles of reasoning and imitation could be carried in a dog. There is no doubt that the animal affixes distinct ideas to sounds. What are the possible limits of his vocabulary no one can tell. In conversing with my dog I did not use English words, but selected simple monosyllables. Habit likewise enabled him to comprehend my gestures. If I crossed my hands on my breast he understood the signal and laid down behind me. If I joined my hands and lifted them to my breast, he returned home. If I grasped one arm above the elbow he ran before me. If I lifted my hand to my forehead he trotted composedly behind. By one motion I could make him bark; by another I could reduce him to silence. He would howl in twenty different strains of mournfulness, at my bidding. He would fetch and carry with undeviating faithfulness.

His actions being thus chiefly regulated by gestures, that to a stranger would appear indifferent or casual, it was easy to produce a belief that the animal's knowledge was much greater than in truth, it was.

One day, in a mixed company, the discourse turned upon the unrivaled abilities of *Damon*.[9] Damon had, indeed, acquired in all the circles which I frequented, an extraordinary reputation. Numerous instances of his sagacity were quoted and some of them exhibited on the spot. Much surprise was excited by the readiness with which he appeared to comprehend sentences of considerable abstraction and complexity, though he in reality attended to nothing but the movements of hand or fingers with which I accompanied my words. I enhanced the astonishment of some and excited the ridicule of others, by observing that my dog not only understood English when spoken by others, but actually spoke the language himself, with no small degree of precision.

This assertion could not be admitted without proof; proof, therefore, was readily produced. At a known signal, Damon began a low interrupted noise, in which the astonished hearers clearly distinguished English words. A dialogue began between the animal and his master, which was maintained,

9. In Greek mythology, Damon and Pythias are men who represent an idealized friendship. The dog's name also evokes the Latin term *daemon*, which refers to a godlike power, often a benevolent nature spirit or a guardian spirit.

on the part of the former, with great vivacity and spirit. In this dialogue the dog asserted the dignity of his species and capacity of intellectual improvement. The company separated, lost in wonder, but perfectly convinced by the evidence that had been produced.

On a subsequent occasion a select company was assembled at a garden, at a small distance from the city. Discourse glided through a variety of topics, till it lighted at length on the subject of invisible beings. From the speculations of philosophers we proceeded to the creations of the poet. Some maintained the justness of Shakespeare's delineations of aerial beings, while others denied it. By no violent transition, Ariel[1] and his songs were introduced, and a lady, celebrated for her musical skill, was solicited to accompany her pedal harp with the song of "Five fathom deep thy father lies"[2] . . . She was known to have set, for her favourite instrument, all the songs of Shakespeare.

My youth made me little more than an auditor on this occasion. I sat apart from the rest of the company, and carefully noted every thing. The track which the conversation had taken, suggested a scheme which was not thoroughly digested when the lady began her enchanting strain.

She ended and the audience were mute with rapture. The pause continued, when a strain was wafted to our ears from another quarter. The spot where we sat was embowered by a vine. The verdant arch was lofty and the area beneath was spacious.

The sound proceeded from above. At first it was faint and scarcely audible; presently it reached a louder key, and every eye was cast up in expectation of beholding a face among the pendant clusters. The strain was easily recognized, for it was no other than that which Ariel is made to sing when finally absolved from the service of the wizard.

> In the Cowslip's bell I lie,
> On the Bat's back I do fly . . .
> After summer merrily, &c.[3]

Their hearts palpitated as they listened: they gazed at each other for a solution of the mystery. At length the strain died away at a distance, and an interval of silence was succeded by an earnest discussion of the cause of this prodigy. One supposition only could be adopted, which was, that the strain was uttered by human organs. That the songster was stationed on the roof of the arbour, and having finished his melody had risen into the viewless fields of air.

I had been invited to spend a week at this house: this period was nearly expired when I received information that my aunt was suddenly taken sick, and that her life was in imminent danger. I immediately set out on my return to the city, but before my arrival she was dead.

This lady was entitled to my gratitude and esteem; I had received the most essential benefits at her hand. I was not destitute of sensibility, and was deeply affected by this event: I will own, however, that my grief was lessened by reflecting on the consequences of her death, with regard to my own condition. I had been ever taught to consider myself as her heir, and her death, therefore, would free me from certain restraints.

1. In Shakespeare's *The Tempest*, a spirit bound to serve Prospero, a magician.

2. *The Tempest* 1.2.395, slightly misquoted.
3. *The Tempest* 5.1.89, 91–92.

My aunt had a female servant, who had lived with her for twenty years: she was married, but her husband, who as an artisan, lived apart from her: I had no reason to suspect the woman's sincerity and disinterestedness; but my aunt was no sooner consigned to the grave than a will was produced, in which Dorothy was named her sole and universal heir.

It was in vain to urge my expectations and my claims. . . . The instrument was legibly and legally drawn up. . . . Dorothy was exasperated by my opposition and surmises, and vigorously enforced her title. In a week after the decease of my kinswoman, I was obliged to seek a new dwelling. As all my property consisted in my cloths and my papers, this was easily done.

My condition was now calamitous and forlorn. Confiding[4] in the acquisition of my aunt's patrimony, I had made no other provision for the future; I hated manual labour, or any task of which the object was gain. To be guided in my choice of occupations by any motive but the pleasure which the occupation was qualified to produce, was intolerable to my proud, indolent, and restive temper.

This resource was now cut off; the means of immediate subsistence were denied me: If I had determined to acquire the knowledge of some lucrative art, the acquisition would demand time, and, meanwhile, I was absolutely destitute of support. My father's house was, indeed, open to me, but I preferred to stifle myself with the filth of the kennel, rather than to return to it.

Some plan it was immediately necessary to adopt. The exigence of my affairs, and this reverse of fortune, continually occupied my thoughts; I estranged myself from society and from books, and devoted myself to lonely walks and mournful meditation.

One morning as I ranged along the bank of Schuylkill,[5] I encountered a person, by name Ludloe, of whom I had some previous knowledge. He was from Ireland; was a man of some rank and apparently rich: I had met with him before, but in mixed companies, where little direct intercourse had taken place between us. Our last meeting was in the arbour where Ariel was so unexpectedly introduced.

Our acquaintance merely justified a transient salutation; but he did not content himself with noticing me as I passed, but joined me in my walk and entered into conversation. It was easy to advert to the occasion on which we had last met, and to the mysterious incident which then occurred. I was solicitous to dive into his thoughts upon this head and put some questions which tended to the point that I wished.

I was somewhat startled when he expressed his belief, that the performer of this mystic strain was one of the company then present, who exerted, for this end, a faculty not commonly possessed. Who this person was he did not venture to guess, and could not discover, by the tokens which he suffered to appear, that his suspicions glanced at me.[6] He expatiated with great profoundness and fertility of ideas, on the uses to which a faculty like this might be employed. No more powerful engine, he said, could be conceived, by which the ignorant and credulous might be moulded to our purposes; managed by a man of ordinary talents, it would open for him the straightest and surest avenues to wealth and power.

4. Trusting.
5. River in Pennsylvania.

6. I.e., he did not speculate on the person's identity, nor did he indicate that he suspected me.

His remarks excited in my mind a new strain of thoughts. I had not hitherto considered the subject in this light, though vague ideas of the importance of this art could not fail to be occasionally suggested: I ventured to inquire into his ideas of the mode, in which an art like this could be employed, so as to effect the purposes he mentioned.

He dealt chiefly in general representations. Men, he said, believed in the existence and energy of invisible powers, and in the duty of discovering and conforming to their will. This will was supposed to be sometimes made known to them through the medium of their senses. A voice coming from a quarter where no attendant form could be seen would, in most cases, be ascribed to supernal[7] agency, and a command imposed on them, in this manner, would be obeyed with religious scrupulousness. Thus men might be imperiously directed in the disposal of their industry, their property, and even of their lives. Men, actuated by a mistaken sense of duty, might, under this influence, be led to the commission of the most flagitious,[8] as well as the most heroic acts: If it were his desire to accumulate wealth, or institute a new sect, he should need no other instrument.

I listened to this kind of discourse with great avidity, and regretted when he thought proper to introduce new topics. He ended by requesting me to visit him, which I eagerly consented to do. When left alone, my imagination was filled with the images suggested by this conversation. The hopelessness of better fortune, which I had lately harboured, now gave place to cheering confidence. Those motives of rectitude which should deter me from this species of imposture, had never been vivid or stable, and were still more weakened by the artifices of which I had already been guilty. The utility or harmlessness of the end, justified, in my eyes, the means.

No event had been more unexpected, by me, than the bequest of my aunt to her servant. The will, under which the latter claimed, was dated prior to my coming to the city. I was not surprised, therefore, that it had once been made, but merely that it had never been cancelled or superseded by a later instrument. My wishes inclined me to suspect the existence of a later will, but I had conceived that, to ascertain its existence, was beyond my power.

Now, however, a different opinion began to be entertained. This woman like those of her sex and class was unlettered and superstitious. Her faith in spells and apparitions, was of the most lively kind. Could not her conscience be awakened by a voice from the grave! Lonely and at midnight, my aunt might be introduced, upbraiding her for her injustice, and commanding her to atone for it by acknowledging the claim of the rightful proprietor.

True it was, that no subsequent will might exist, but this was the fruit of mistake, or of negligence. She probably intended to cancel the old one, but this act might, by her own weakness, or by the artifices of her servant, be delayed till death had put it out of her power. In either case a mandate from the dead could scarcely fail of being obeyed.

I considered this woman as the usurper of my property. Her husband as well as herself, were laborious[9] and covetous; their good fortune had made no change in their mode of living, but they were as frugal and as eager to

7. Heavenly, celestial.
8. Criminal, villainous.
9. Industrious.

accumulate as ever. In their hands, money was inert and sterile, or it served to foster their vices.[1] To take it from them would, therefore, be a benefit both to them and to myself; not even an imaginary injury would be inflicted. Restitution, if legally compelled to it, would be reluctant and painful, but if enjoined by Heaven would be voluntary, and the performance of a seeming duty would carry with it, its own reward.

These reasonings, aided by inclination, were sufficient to determine me. I have no doubt but their fallacy would have been detected in the sequel,[2] and my scheme have been productive of nothing but confusion and remorse. From these consequences, however, my fate interposed, as in the former instance, to save me.

Having formed my resolution, many preliminaries to its execution were necessary to be settled. These demanded deliberation and delay; meanwhile I recollected my promise to Ludloe, and paid him a visit. I met a frank and affectionate reception. It would not be easy to paint the delight which I experienced in this man's society. I was at first oppressed with the sense of my own inferiority in age, knowledge and rank. Hence arose numberless reserves and incapacitating diffidences; but these were speedily dissipated by the fascinations of this man's address. His superiority was only rendered, by time, more conspicuous, but this superiority, by appearing never to be present to his own mind, ceased to be uneasy to me. My questions required to be frequently answered, and my mistakes to be rectified; but my keenest scrutiny, could detect in his manner, neither arrogance nor contempt. He seemed to talk merely from the overflow of his ideas, or a benevolent desire of imparting information.

My visits gradually became more frequent. Meanwhile my wants increased, and the necessity of some change in my condition became daily more urgent. This incited my reflections on the scheme which I had formed. The time and place suitable to my design, were not selected without much anxious inquiry and frequent waverings of purpose. These being at length fixed, the interval to elapse, before the carrying of my design into effect, was not without perturbation and suspense. These could not be concealed from my new friend and at length prompted him to inquire into the cause.

It was not possible to communicate the whole truth; but the warmth of his manner inspired me with some degree of ingenuousness.[3] I did not hide from him my former hopes and my present destitute condition. He listened to my tale with no expressions of sympathy, and when I had finished, abruptly inquired whether I had any objection to a voyage to Europe? I answered in the negative. He then said that he was preparing to depart in a fortnight and advised me to make up my mind to accompany him.

This unexpected proposal gave me pleasure and surprise, but the want of money occurred to me as an insuperable objection. On this being mentioned, Oho! said he, carelessly, that objection is easily removed, I will bear all expenses of your passage myself.

1. Carwin offers several, not entirely compatible, reasons why Dorothy and her husband should not have inherited his aunt's fortune. His assertion about inert and sterile money refers to beliefs about the social value of allowing money to circulate, for instance by lending it out.
2. I.e., in what follows.
3. Frankness, trustfulness.

The extraordinary beneficence of this act as well as the air of uncautiousness attending it, made me doubt the sincerity of his offer, and when new declarations removed this doubt, I could not forbear expressing at once my sense of his generosity and of my own unworthiness.

He replied that generosity had been expunged from his catalogue as having no meaning or a vicious one. It was the scope of his exertions to be just. This was the sum of human duty, and he that fell short, ran beside, or outstripped justice was a criminal. What he gave me was my due or not my due. If it were my due, I might reasonably demand it from him and it was wicked to withhold it. Merit on one side or gratitude on the other, were contradictory and unintelligible.

If I were fully convinced that this benefit was not my due and yet received it, he should hold me in contempt. The rectitude of my principles and conduct would be the measure of his approbation, and no benefit should he ever bestow which the receiver was not entitled to claim, and which it would not be criminal in him to refuse.

These principles were not new from the mouth of Ludloe, but they had, hitherto, been regarded as the fruits of a venturous speculation in my mind. I had never traced them into their practical consequences, and if his conduct on this occasion had not squared with his maxims, I should not have imputed to him inconsistency. I did not ponder on these reasonings at this time: objects of immediate importance engrossed my thoughts.

One obstacle to this measure was removed. When my voyage was performed how should I subsist in my new abode? I concealed not my perplexity and he commented on it in his usual manner. How did I mean to subsist, he asked, in my own country? The means of living would be, at least, as much within my reach there as here. As to the pressure of immediate and absolute want, he believed I should be exposed to little hazard. With talents such as mine, I must be hunted by a destiny peculiarly malignant, if I could not provide myself with necessaries wherever my lot were cast.

He would make allowances, however, for my diffidence and self-distrust, and would obviate my fears by expressing his own intentions with regard to me. I must be apprised, however, of his true meaning. He laboured to shun all hurtful and vicious things, and therefore carefully abstained from making or confiding *in promises*. It was just to assist me in this voyage, and it would probably be equally just to continue to me similar assistance when it was finished. That indeed was a subject, in a great degree, within my own cognizance. His aid would be proportioned to my wants and to my merits, and I had only to take care that my claims were just, for them to be admitted.

This scheme could not but appear to me eligible. I thirsted after an acquaintance with new scenes; my present situation could not be changed for a worse; I trusted to the constancy of Ludloe's friendship; to this at least it was better to trust than to the success of my imposture on Dorothy, which was adopted merely as a desperate expedient: finally I determined to embark with him.

In the course of this voyage my mind was busily employed. There were no other passengers beside ourselves, so that my own condition and the character of Ludloe, continually presented themselves to my reflections. It will be supposed that I was not a vague or indifferent observer.

There were no vicissitudes in the deportment or lapses in the discourse of my friend. His feelings appeared to preserve an unchangeable tenor, and

his thoughts and words always to flow with the same rapidity. His slumber was profound and his wakeful hours serene. He was regular and temperate in all his exercises and gratifications. Hence were derived his clear perceptions and exuberant health.

This treatment of me, like all his other mental and corporal operations, was modelled by one inflexible standard. Certain scruples and delicacies were incident to my situation. Of the existence of these he seemed to be unconscious, and yet nothing escaped him inconsistent with a state of absolute equality.

I was naturally inquisitive as to his fortune and the collateral circumstances of his condition. My notions of politeness hindered me from making direct inquiries. By indirect means I could gather nothing but that his state was opulent and independent, and that he had two sisters whose situation resembled his own.

Though, in conversation, he appeared to be governed by the utmost candour; no light was let in upon the former transactions of his life. The purpose of his visit to America I could merely guess to be the gratification of curiosity.

My future pursuits must be supposed chiefly to occupy my attention. On this head I was destitute of all stedfast views. Without profession or habits of industry or sources of permanent revenue, the world appeared to me an ocean on which my bark was set afloat, without compass or sail. The world into which I was about to enter, was untried and unknown, and though I could consent to profit by the guidance I was unwilling to rely on the support of others.

This topic being nearest my heart, I frequently introduced into conversation with my friend; but on this subject he always allowed himself to be led by me, while on all others, he was zealous to point the way. To every scheme that I proposed he was sure to cause objections. All the liberal professions[4] were censured as perverting the understanding, by giving scope to the sordid motive of gain, or embuing the mind with erroneous principles. Skill was slowly obtained, and success, though integrity and independence must be given for it, dubious and instable. The mechanical trades were equally obnoxious; they were vicious by contributing to the spurious gratifications of the rich and multiplying the objects of luxury; they were destruction to the intellect and vigour of the artizan; they enervated his frame and brutalized his mind.

When I pointed out to him the necessity of some species of labour, he tacitly admitted that necessity, but refused to direct me in the choice of a pursuit, which though not free from defect should yet have the fewest inconveniences. He dwelt on the fewness of our actual wants, the temptations which attend the possession of wealth, the benefits of seclusion and privacy, and the duty of unfettering our minds from the prejudices which govern the world.

His discourse tended merely to unsettle my views and increase my perplexity. This effect was so uniform that I at length desisted from all allusions to this theme and endeavoured to divert my own reflections from it. When our voyage should be finished, and I should actually tread this new

4. Professions requiring special training in the arts and sciences; they include law, architecture, and medicine. The mechanical trades, mentioned below, require knowledge of tools and machinery.

stage, I believed that I should be better qualified to judge of the measures to be taken by me.

At length we reached Belfast. From thence we immediately repaired to Dublin. I was admitted as a member of his family. When I expressed my uncertainty as to the place to which it would be proper for me to repair, he gave me a blunt but cordial invitation to his house. My circumstances allowed me no option and I readily complied. My attention was for a time engrossed by a diversified succession of new objects. Their novelty however disappearing, left me at liberty to turn my eyes upon myself and my companion, and here my reflections were supplied with abundant food.

His house was spacious and commodious, and furnished with profusion and elegance. A suite of apartments was assigned to me, in which I was permitted to reign uncontrolled and access was permitted to a well furnished library. My food was furnished in my own room, prepared in the manner which I had previously directed. Occasionally Ludloe would request my company to breakfast, when an hour was usually consumed in earnest or sprightly conversation. At all other times he was invisible, and his apartments, being wholly separate from mine, I had no opportunity of discovering in what way his hours were employed.

He defended this mode of living as being most compatible with liberty. He delighted to expatiate on the evils of cohabitation.[5] Men, subjected to the same regimen, compelled to eat and sleep and associate at certain hours, were strangers to all rational independence and liberty. Society would never be exempt from servitude and misery, till those artificial ties which held human beings together under the same roof were dissolved. He endeavoured to regulate his own conduct in pursuance of these principles, and to secure to himself as much freedom as the present regulations of society would permit. The same independence which he claimed for himself he likewise extended to me. The distribution of my own time, the selection of my own occupations and companions should belong to myself.

But these privileges, though while listening to his arguments I could not deny them to be valuable, I would have willingly dispensed with. The solitude in which I lived became daily more painful. I ate and drank, enjoyed clothing and shelter, without the exercise of forethought or industry; I walked and sat, went out and returned for as long and at what seasons I thought proper, yet my condition was a fertile source of discontent.

I felt myself removed to a comfortless and chilling distance from Ludloe. I wanted to share in his occupations and views. With all his ingenuousness of aspect and overflow of thoughts, when he allowed me his company, I felt myself painfully bewildered with regard to his genuine condition and sentiments.

He had it in his power to introduce me to society, and without an introduction, it was scarcely possible to gain access to any social circle or domestic fireside. Add to this, my own obscure prospects and dubious situation. Some regular intellectual pursuit would render my state less irksome, but I had hitherto adopted no scheme of this kind.

Time tended, in no degree, to alleviate my dissatisfaction. It increased till the determination became at length formed of opening my thoughts to

5. Living with others in a shared arrangement.

Ludloe. At the next breakfast interview which took place, I introduced the subject, and expatiated without reserve, on the state of my feelings. I concluded with intreating him to point out some path in which my talents might be rendered useful to himself or to mankind.

After a pause of some minutes, he said, What would you do? You forget the immaturity of your age. If you are qualified to act a part in the theatre of life, step forth; but you are not qualified. You want knowledge, and with this you ought previously to endow yourself. . . . Means, for this end, are within your reach. Why should you waste your time in idleness, and torment yourself with unprofitable wishes? Books are at hand . . . books from which most sciences and languages can be learned. Read, analyze, digest; collect facts, and investigate theories: ascertain the dictates of reason, and supply yourself with the inclination and the power to adhere to them. You will not, legally speaking, be a man in less than three years. Let this period be devoted to the acquisition of wisdom. Either stay here, or retire to an house I have on the banks of Killarney,[6] where you will find all the conveniences of study.

I could not but reflect with wonder at this man's treatment of me. I could plead none of the rights of relationship; yet I enjoyed the privileges of a son. He had not imparted to me any scheme, by pursuit of which I might finally compensate him for the expense to which my maintainance and education would subject him. He gave me reason to hope for the continuance of his bounty. He talked and acted as if my fortune were totally disjoined from his; yet was I indebted to him for the morsel which sustained my life. Now it was proposed to withdraw myself to studious leisure, and romantic solitude. All my wants, personal and intellectual, were to be supplied gratuitously and copiously. No means were prescribed by which I might make compensation for all these benefits. In conferring them he seemed to be actuated by no view to his own ultimate advantage. He took no measures to secure my future services.

I suffered these thoughts to escape me, on this occasion, and observed that to make my application successful, or useful, it was necessary to pursue some end. I must look forward to some post which I might hereafter occupy beneficially to myself or others; and for which all the efforts of my mind should be bent to qualify myself.

These hints gave him visible pleasure; and now, for the first time, he deigned to advise me on this head. His scheme, however, was not suddenly produced. The way to it was circuitous and long. It was his business to make every new step appear to be suggested by my own reflections. His own ideas were the seeming result of the moment, and sprung out of the last idea that was uttered. Being hastily taken up, they were, of course, liable to objection. These objections, sometimes occurring to me and sometimes to him, were admitted or contested with the utmost candour. One scheme went through numerous modifications before it was proved to be ineligible, or before it yielded place to a better. It was easy to perceive, that books alone were insufficient to impart knowledge: that man must be examined with our own eyes to make us acquainted with their nature: that ideas collected from observation and reading, must correct and illustrate each other:

6. I.e., in the region of the Lakes of Killarney, in southwestern Ireland.

that the value of all principles, and their truth, lie in their practical effects. Hence, gradually arose the usefulness of travelling, of inspecting the habits and manners of a nation, and investigating, on the spot, the causes of their happiness and misery. Finally, it was determined that Spain was more suitable than any other, to the views of a judicious traveller.

My language, habits, and religion were mentioned as obstacles to close and extensive views; but these difficulties successively and slowly vanished. Converse with books, and natives of Spain, a steadfast purpose and unwearied diligence would efface all differences between me and a Castilian with respect to speech.[7] Personal habits were changeable, by the same means. The bars to unbounded intercourse, rising from the religion of Spain being irreconcilably opposite to mine, cost us no little trouble to surmount, and here the skill of Ludloe was eminently displayed.

I had been accustomed to regard as unquestionable, the fallacy of the Romish faith.[8] This persuasion was habitual and the child of prejudice, and was easily shaken by the artifices of this logician. I was first led to bestow a kind of assent on the doctrines of the Roman church; but my convictions were easily subdued by a new species of argumentation, and, in a short time, I reverted to my ancient disbelief, so that, if an exterior conformity to the rights of Spain were requisite to the attainment of my purpose, that conformity must be dissembled.

My moral principles had hitherto been vague and unsettled. My circumstances had led me to the frequent practice of insincerity; but my transgressions as they were slight and transient, did not much excite my previous reflections, or subsequent remorse. My deviations, however, though rendered easy by habit, were by no means sanctioned by my principles. Now an imposture, more profound and deliberate, was projected; and I could not hope to perform well my part, unless steadfastly and thoroughly persuaded of its rectitude.

My friend was the eulogist[9] of sincerity. He delighted to trace its influence on the happiness of mankind; and proved that nothing but the universal practice of this virtue was necessary to the perfection of human society. His doctrine was splendid and beautiful. To detect its imperfections was no easy task; to lay the foundations of virtue in utility, and to limit, by that scale, the operation of general principles; to see that the value of sincerity, like that of every other mode of action, consisted in its tendency to good, and that, therefore the obligation to speak truth was not paramount or intrinsical: that my duty is modelled on a knowledge and foresight of the conduct of others; and that, since men in their actual state, are infirm and deceitful, a just estimate of consequences may sometimes make dissimulation my duty were truths that did not speedily occur. The discovery, when made, appeared to be a joint work. I saw nothing in Ludloe but proofs of candour, and a judgment incapable of bias.

The means which this man employed to fit me for his purpose, perhaps owed their success to my youth and ignorance. I may have given you exaggerated ideas of his dexterity and address. Of that I am unable to judge. Certain it is, that no time or reflection has abated my astonishment at the

7. On the Iberian peninsula, Castilian Spanish is the dominant form of the language. "A Castilian": a resident of Castile, a region in north-central Spain.
8. I.e., Roman Catholicism.
9. One who speaks in praise.

profoundness of his schemes, and the perseverence with which they were pursued by him. To detail their progress would expose me to the risk of being tedious, yet none but minute details would sufficiently display his patience and subtlety.

It will suffice to relate, that after a sufficient period of preparation and arrangements being made for maintaining a copious intercourse with Ludloe, I embarked for Barcelona.[1] A restless curiosity and vigorous application have distinguished my character in every scene. Here was spacious field for the exercise of all my energies. I sought out a preceptor[2] in my new religion. I entered into the hearts of priests and confessors, the *hidalgo* and the peasant, the monk and the prelate, the austere and voluptuous devotee were scrutinized in all their forms.[3]

Man was the chief subject of my study, and the social sphere that in which I principally moved; but I was not inattentive to inanimate nature, nor unmindful of the past. If the scope of virtue were to maintain the body in health, and to furnish its highest enjoyments to every sense, to increase the number, and accuracy, and order of our intellectual stores, no virtue was ever more unblemished than mine. If to act upon our conceptions of right, and to acquit ourselves of all prejudice and selfishness in the formation of our principles, entitle us to the testimony of a good conscience, I might justly claim it.

I shall not pretend to ascertain my rank in the moral scale. Your notions of duty differ widely from mine. If a system of deceit, pursued merely from the love of truth; if voluptuousness, never gratified at the expense of health, may incur censure, I am censurable. This, indeed, was not the limit of my deviations. Deception was often unnecessarily practised, and my biloquial faculty did not lie unemployed. What has happened to yourselves may enable you, in some degree, to judge of the scenes in which my mystical[4] exploits engaged me. In none of them, indeed, were the effects equally disastrous, and they were, for the most part, the result of well digested projects.

To recount these would be an endless task. They were designed as mere specimens of power, to illustrate the influence of superstition: to give sceptics the consolation of certainty: to annihilate the scruples of a tender female, or facilitate my access to the bosoms of courtiers and monks.

The first achievement of this kind took place in the convent of the Escurial.[5] For some time the hospitality of this brotherhood allowed me a cell in that magnificent and gloomy fabric. I was drawn hither chiefly by the treasures of Arabian literature, which are preserved here in the keeping of a learned Maronite, from Lebanon.[6] Standing one evening on the steps of the great altar this devout friar expatiated on the miraculous evidences of his religion; and, in a moment of enthusiasm, appealed to San Lorenzo[7] whose martyrdom was displayed before us. No sooner was the appeal made than

1. Coastal city in northeastern Spain.
2. Teacher, tutor.
3. Carwin refers to types of Spanish Catholics, including the *hidalgo*, or gentleman; the prelate, a bishop or other high-ranking Church dignitary; and the female worshiper, or devotee, who might be self-denying ("austere") or sensuous ("voluptuous").
4. Relating to spiritual mysteries or to religious mysticism.

5. Built in the late sixteenth century by Philip II, the Royal Site of San Lorenzo de El Escorial is a historic residence of the king of Spain that encompasses a monastery, museum, and school.
6. The Maronite Church is an eastern rite Catholic Church that uses Aramaic (the language spoken by the historical Jesus) in parts of its worship service.
7. Saint Lawrence, a third-century Christian martyr.

the saint, obsequious to the summons, whispered his responses from the shrine, and commanded the heretic to tremble and believe. This event was reported to the convent. With whatever reluctance, I could not refuse my testimony to its truth, and its influence on my faith was clearly shewn in my subsequent conduct.

A lady of rank, in Seville, who had been guilty of many unauthorized indulgences,[8] was, at last, awakened to remorse, by a voice from Heaven, which she imagined had commanded her to expiate her sins by an abstinence from all food for thirty days. Her friends found it impossible to outroot this persuasion, or to overcome her resolution even by force. I chanced to be one in a numerous company where she was present. This fatal illusion was mentioned, and an opportunity afforded to the lady of defending her scheme. At a pause in the discourse, a voice was heard from the ceiling, which confirmed the truth of her tale; but, at the same time revoked the command, and, in consideration of her faith, pronounced her absolution. Satisfied with this proof, the auditors dismissed their unbelief, and the lady consented to eat.

In the course of a copious correspondence with Ludloe, the observations I had collected were given. A sentiment, which I can hardly describe, induced me to be silent on all adventures connected with my bivocal projects. On other topics, I wrote fully, and without restraint. I painted, in vivid hues, the scenes with which I was daily conversant, and pursued, fearlessly, every speculation on religion and government that occurred. This spirit was encouraged by Ludloe, who failed not to comment on my narrative, and multiply deductions from my principles.

He taught me to ascribe the evils that infest society to the errors of opinion. The absurd and unequal distribution of power and property gave birth to poverty and riches, and these were the sources of luxury and crimes. These positions were readily admitted; but the remedy for these ills, the means of rectifying these errors were not easily discovered. We have been inclined to impute them to inherent defects in the moral constitution of men: that oppression and tyranny grow up by a sort of natural necessity, and that they will perish only when the human species is extinct. Ludloe laboured to prove that this was, by no means, the case: that man is the creature of circumstances: that he is capable of endless improvement: that his progress has been stopped by the artificial impediment of government: that by the removal of this, the fondest dreams of imagination will be realized.

From detailing and accounting for the evils which exist under our present institutions, he usually proceeded to delineate some scheme of Utopian felicity, where the empire of reason should supplant that of force: where justice should be universally understood and practised; where the interest of the whole and of the individual should be seen by all to be the same; where the public good should be the scope of all activity; where the tasks of all should be the same, and the means of subsistence equally distributed.

No one could contemplate his pictures without rapture. By their comprehensiveness and amplitude they filled the imagination. I was unwilling to believe that in no region of the world, or at no period could these ideas be

8. In Roman Catholicism, an indulgence is a way to reduce punishment for sins; it can be granted for, e.g., saying a specific prayer or visiting a certain shrine. Unauthorized indulgences are issued without the Pope's grant of authority. "Seville": city and province in south-central Spain.

realized. It was plain that the nations of Europe were tending to greater depravity, and would be the prey of perpetual vicissitude. All individual attempts at their reformation would be fruitless. He therefore who desired the diffusion of right principles, to make a just system be adopted by a whole community, must pursue some extraordinary method.

In this state of mind I recollected my native country, where a few colonists from Britain had sown the germ of populous and mighty empires.[9] Attended, as they were, into their new abode, by all their prejudices, yet such had been the influence of new circumstances, of consulting for their own happiness, of adopting simple forms of government, and excluding nobles and kings from their system, that they enjoyed a degree of happiness far superior to their parent state.

To conquer the prejudices and change the habits of millions, are impossible. The human mind, exposed to social influences, inflexibly adheres to the direction that is given to it; but for the same reason why men, who begin in error will continue, those who commence in truth, may be expected to persist. Habit and example will operate with equal force in both instances.

Let a few, sufficiently enlightened and disinterested, take up their abode in some unvisited region. Let their social scheme be founded in equity, and how small soever their original number may be, their growth into a nation is inevitable. Among other effects of national justice, was to be ranked the swift increase of numbers. Exempt from servile obligations and perverse habits, endowed with property, wisdom, and health, hundreds will expand, with inconceivable rapidity into thousands and thousands, into millions; and a new race, tutored in truth, may, in a few centuries, overflow the habitable world.

Such were the visions of youth! I could not banish them from my mind. I knew them to be crude; but believed that deliberation would bestow upon them solidity and shape. Meanwhile I imparted them to Ludloe.

In answer to the reveries and speculations which I sent to him respecting this subject, Ludloe informed me, that they had led his mind into a new sphere of meditation. He had long and deeply considered in what way he might essentially promote my happiness. He had entertained a faint hope that I would one day be qualified for a station like that to which he himself had been advanced. This post required an elevation and stability, of views which human beings seldom reach, and which could be attained by me only by a long series of heroic labours. Hitherto every new stage in my intellectual progress had added vigour to his hopes, and he cherished a stronger belief than formerly that my career would terminate auspiciously. This, however, was necessarily distant. Many preliminaries must first be settled; many arduous accomplishments be first obtained; and my virtue be subjected to severe trials. At present it was not in his power to be more explicit; but if my reflections suggested no better plan, he advised me to settle my affairs in Spain, and return to him immediately. My knowledge of this country would be of the highest use, on the supposition of my ultimately arriving at the honours to which he had alluded; and some of these preparatory measures could be taken only with his assistance, and in his company.

This intimation was eagerly obeyed, and, in a short time, I arrived at Dublin. Meanwhile my mind had copious occupation in commenting on my

9. The colonies of British North America.

friend's letter. This scheme, whatever it was, seemed to be suggested by my mention of a plan of colonization, and my preference of that mode of producing extensive and permanent effects on the condition of mankind. It was easy therefore to conjecture that this mode had been pursued under some mysterious modifications and conditions.

It had always excited my wonder that so obvious an expedient had been overlooked. The globe which we inhabit was very imperfectly known. The regions and nations unexplored, it was reasonable to believe, surpassed in extent, and perhaps in populousness, those with which we were familiar. The order of Jesuits[1] had furnished an example of all the errors and excellencies of such a scheme. Their plan was founded on erroneous notions of religion and policy, and they had absurdly chosen a scene[2] within reach of the injustice and ambition of an European tyrant.

It was wise and easy to profit by their example. Resting on the two props of fidelity and zeal, an association might exist for ages in the heart of Europe, whose influence might be felt, and might be boundless, in some region of the southern hemisphere; and by whom a moral and political structure might be raised, the growth of pure wisdom, and totally unlike those fragments of Roman and Gothic barbarism, which cover the face of what are called the civilized nations.[3] The belief now rose in my mind that some such scheme had actually been prosecuted, and that Ludloe was a coadjutor.[4] On this supposition, the caution with which he approached to his point, the arduous probation which a candidate for a part on this stage must undergo, and the rigours of that test by which his fortitude and virtue must be tried, were easily explained. I was too deeply imbued with veneration for the effects of such schemes, and too sanguine in my confidence in the rectitude of Ludloe, to refuse my concurrence in any scheme by which my qualifications might at length be raised to a due point.

Our interview was frank and affectionate. I found him situated just as formerly. His aspect, manners, and deportment were the same. I entered once more on my former mode of life, but our intercourse became more frequent. We constantly breakfasted together, and our conversation was usually prolonged through half the morning.

For a time our topics were general. I thought proper to leave to him the introduction of more interesting themes: this, however, he betrayed no inclination to do. His reserve excited some surprise, and I began to suspect that whatever design he had formed with regard to me, had been laid aside. To ascertain this question, I ventured, at length, to recall his attention to the subject of his last letter, and to enquire whether subsequent reflection had made any change in his views.

He said that his views were too momentous to be hastily taken up, or hastily dismissed; the station, my attainment of which depended wholly on myself, was high above vulgar heads, and was to be gained by years of solicitude and labour. This, at least, was true with regard to minds ordinarily

1. Or the Society of Jesus, a male religious congregation of the Catholic Church.
2. Paraguay [Brown's note]. Beginning in the seventeenth century, Jesuit missionaries tried to establish model communities of Paraguayan natives. The effort generated tensions with colonial officials, leading to the Jesuits' being expelled from Spanish America in 1767.
3. Possible reference to the Bavarian Illuminati, a secret society founded in 1776 that was devoted to spreading rationalist thought and eradicating religious influence on the state.
4. Helper, assistant.

constituted; I, perhaps, deserved to be regarded as an exception, and might be able to accomplish in a few months that for which others were obliged to toil during half their lives.

Man, continued he, is the slave of habit. Convince him to-day that his duty leads straight forward: he shall advance, but at every step his belief shall fade; habit will resume its empire, and to-morrow he shall turn back, or betake himself to oblique paths.

We know not our strength till it be tried. Virtue, till confirmed by habit, is a dream. You are a man imbued by errors, and vincible[5] by slight temptations. Deep enquiries must bestow light on your opinions, and the habit of encountering and vanquishing temptation must inspire you with fortitude. Till this be done, you are unqualified for that post, in which you will be invested with divine attributes, and prescribe the condition of a large portion of mankind.

Confide not in the firmness of your principles, or the stedfastness of your integrity. Be always vigilant and fearful. Never think you have enough of knowledge, and let not your caution slumber for a moment, for you know not when danger is near.

I acknowledged the justice of his admonitions, and professed myself willing to undergo any ordeal which reason should prescribe. What, I asked, were the conditions, on the fulfilment of which depended my advancement to the station he alluded to? Was it necessary to conceal from me the nature and obligations of this rank?

These enquiries sunk him more profoundly into meditation than I had ever before witnessed. After a pause, in which some perplexity was visible, he answered:

I scarcely know what to say. As to promises, I claim them not from you. We are now arrived at a point, in which it is necessary to look around with caution, and that consequences should be fully known. A number of persons are leagued together for an end of some moment. To make yourself one of these is submitted to your choice. Among the conditions of their alliance are mutual fidelity and secrecy.

Their existence depends upon this: their existence is known only to themselves. This secrecy must be obtained by all the means which are possible. When I have said thus much, I have informed you, in some degree, of their existence, but you are still ignorant of the purpose contemplated by this association, and of all the members, except myself. So far no dangerous disclosure is yet made: but this degree of concealment is not sufficient. Thus much is made known to you, because it is unavoidable. The individuals which compose this fraternity are not immortal, and the vacancies occasioned by death must be supplied from among the living. The candidate must be instructed and prepared, and they are always at liberty to recede. Their reason must approve the obligations and duties of their station, or they are unfit for it. If they recede, one duty is still incumbent upon them: they must observe an inviolable silence. To this they are not held by any promise. They must weigh consequences, and freely decide; but they must not fail to number among these consequences their own death.

Their death will not be prompted by vengeance. The executioner will say, he that has once revealed the tale is likely to reveal it a second time; and, to

5. Capable of being overcome.

prevent this, the betrayer must die. Nor is this the only consequence: to prevent the further revelation, he, to whom the secret was imparted, must likewise perish. He must not console himself with the belief that his tresspass will be unknown. The knowledge cannot, by human means, be withheld from this fraternity. Rare, indeed, will it be that his purpose to disclose is not discovered before it can be effected, and the disclosure prevented by his death.

Be well aware of your condition. What I now, or may hereafter mention, mention not again. Admit not even a doubt as to the propriety of hiding it from all the world. There are eyes who will discern this doubt amidst the closest folds of your heart, and your life will instantly be sacrificed.

At present be the subject dismissed. Reflect deeply on the duty which you have already incurred. Think upon your strength of mind, and be careful not to lay yourself under impracticable obligations. It will always be in your power to recede. Even after you are solemnly enrolled a member, you may consult the dictates of your own understanding, and relinquish your post; but while you live, the obligation to be silent will perpetually attend you.

We seek not the misery or death of any one, but we are swayed by an immutable calculation. Death is to be abhorred, but the life of the betrayer is productive of more evil than his death: his death, therefore, we choose, and our means are instantaneous and unerring.

I love you. The first impulse of my love is to dissuade you from seeking to know more. Your mind will be full of ideas; your hands will be perpetually busy to a purpose into which no human creature, beyond the verge of your brotherhood, must pry. Believe me, who have made the experiment, that compared with this task, the task of inviolable secrecy, all others are easy. To be dumb will not suffice; never to know any remission in your zeal or your watchfulness will not suffice. If the sagacity of others detect your occupations, however strenuously you may labour for concealment, your doom is ratified, as well as that of the wretch whose evil destiny led him to pursue you.

Yet if your fidelity fail not, great will be your recompence. For all your toils and self-devotion, ample will be the retribution.[6] Hitherto you have been wrapt in darkness and storm; then will you be exalted to a pure and unruffled element. It is only for a time that temptation will environ you, and your path will be toilsome. In a few years you will be permitted to withdraw to a land of sages, and the remainder of your life will glide away in the enjoyments of beneficence and wisdom.

Think deeply on what I have said. Investigate your own motives and opinions, and prepare to submit them to the test of numerous hazards and experiments.

Here my friend passed to a new topic. I was desirous of reverting to this subject, and obtaining further information concerning it, but he assiduously repelled all my attempts, and insisted on my bestowing deep and impartial attention on what had already been disclosed. I was not slow to comply with his directions. My mind refused to admit any other theme of contemplation than this.

As yet I had no glimpse of the nature of this fraternity. I was permitted to form conjectures, and previous incidents bestowed but one form upon my thoughts. In reviewing the sentiments and deportment of Ludloe, my belief

6. Reward.

continually acquired new strength. I even recollected hints and ambiguous allusions in his discourse, which were easily solved, on the supposition of the existence of a new model of society, in some unsuspected corner of the world.

I did not fully perceive the necessity of secrecy; but this necessity perhaps would be rendered apparent, when I should come to know the connection that subsisted between Europe and this imaginary colony. But what was to be done? I was willing to abide by these conditions. My understanding might not approve of all the ends proposed by this fraternity, and I had liberty to withdraw from it, or to refuse to ally myself with them. That the obligation of secrecy should still remain, was unquestionably reasonable.

It appeared to be the plan of Ludloe rather to damp than to stimulate my zeal. He discouraged all attempts to renew the subject in conversation. He dwelt upon the arduousness of the office to which I aspired, the temptations to violate my duty with which I should be continually beset, the inevitable death with which the slightest breach of my engagements would be followed, and the long apprenticeship which it would be necessary for me to serve, before I should be fitted to enter into this conclave.

Sometimes my courage was depressed by these representations My zeal, however, was sure to revive; and at length Ludloe declared himself willing to assist me in the accomplishment of my wishes. For this end, it was necessary, he said, that I should be informed of a second obligation, which every candidate must assume. Before any one could be deemed qualified, he must be thoroughly known to his associates. For this end, he must determine to disclose every fact in his history, and every secret of his heart. I must begin with making these confessions, with regard to my past life, to Ludloe, and must continue to communicate, at stated seasons, every new thought, and every new occurrence, to him. This confidence was to be absolutely limitless: no exceptions were to be admitted, and no reserves to be practised; and the same penalty attended the infraction of this rule as of the former. Means would be employed, by which the slightest deviation, in either case, would be detected, and the deathful consequence would follow with instant and inevitable expedition. If secrecy were difficult to practise, sincerity, in that degree in which it was here demanded, was a task infinitely more arduous, and a period of new deliberation was necessary before I should decide. I was at liberty to pause: nay, the longer was the period of deliberation which I took, the better; but, when I had once entered this path, it was not in my power to recede. After having solemnly avowed my resolution to be thus sincere in my confession, any particle of reserve or duplicity would cost me my life.

This indeed was a subject to be deeply thought upon. Hitherto I had been guilty of concealment with regard to my friend. I had entered into no formal compact, but had been conscious [of] a kind of tacit obligation to hide no important transaction of my life from him. This consciousness was the source of continual anxiety. I had exerted, on numerous occasions, my bivocal faculty,[7] but, in my intercourse with Ludloe, had suffered not the slightest intimation to escape me with regard to it. This reserve was not easily explained. It was, in a great degree, the product of habit; but I likewise considered that the efficacy of this instrument depended upon its existence being unknown.

7. A variant term for ventriloquism.

To confide the secret to one, was to put an end to my privilege: how widely the knowledge would thenceforth be diffused, I had no power to foresee.

Each day multiplied the impediments to confidence. Shame hindered me from acknowledging my past reserves. Ludloe, from the nature of our intercourse, would certainly account my reserve, in this respect, unjustifiable, and to excite his indignation or contempt was an unpleasing undertaking. Now, if I should resolve to persist in my new path, this reserve must be dismissed: I must make him master of a secret which was precious to me beyond all others; by acquainting him with past concealments, I must risk incurring his suspicion and his anger. These reflections were productive of considerable embarrassment.

There was, indeed, an avenue by which to escape these difficulties, if it did not, at the same time, plunge me into greater. My confessions might, in other respects, be unbounded, but my reserves, in this particular, might be continued. Yet should I not expose myself to formidable perils? Would my secret be for ever unsuspected and undiscovered?

When I considered the nature of this faculty, the impossibility of going farther than suspicion, since the agent could be known only by his own confession, and even this confession would not be believed by the greater part of mankind, I was tempted to conceal it.

In most cases, if I had asserted the possession of this power, I should be treated as a liar; it would be considered as an absurd and audacious expedient to free myself from the suspicion of having entered into compact with a dæmon, or of being myself an emissary of the grand foe.[8] Here, however, there was no reason to dread a similar imputation, since Ludloe had denied the preternatural pretensions of these airy sounds.

My conduct on this occasion was nowise influenced by the belief of any inherent sanctity in truth. Ludloe had taught me to model myself in this respect entirely with a view to immediate consequences. If my genuine interest, on the whole, was promoted by veracity, it was proper to adhere to it; but, if the result of my investigation were opposite, truth was to be sacrificed without scruple.

Meanwhile, in a point of so much moment, I was not hasty to determine. My delay seemed to be, by no means, unacceptable to Ludloe, who applauded my discretion, and warned me to be circumspect. My attention was chiefly absorbed by considerations connected with this subject, and little regard was paid to any foreign occupation or amusement.

One evening, after a day spent in my closet,[9] I sought recreation by walking forth. My mind was chiefly occupied by the review of incidents which happened in Spain. I turned my face towards the fields, and recovered not from my reverie, till I had proceeded some miles on the road to Meath.[1] The night had considerably advanced, and the darkness was rendered intense, by the setting of the moon. Being somewhat weary, as well as undetermined in what manner next to proceed, I seated myself on a grassy bank beside the road. The spot which I had chosen was aloof from passengers, and shrouded in the deepest obscurity.

Some time elapsed, when my attention was excited by the slow approach of an equipage.[2] I presently discovered a coach and six horses, but unattended,

8. I.e., Satan.
9. Apartment or small room.

1. County in Ireland, northwest of Dublin.
2. A carriage.

except by coachman and postillion,[3] and with no light to guide them on their way. Scarcely had they passed the spot where I rested, when some one leaped from beneath the hedge, and seized the head of the fore-horses. Another called upon the coachman to stop, and threatened him with instant death if he disobeyed. A third drew open the coach-door, and ordered those within to deliver their purses. A shriek of terror showed me that a lady was within, who eagerly consented to preserve her life by the loss of her money.

To walk unarmed in the neighbourhood of Dublin, especially at night, has always been accounted dangerous. I had about me the usual instruments of defence. I was desirous of rescuing this person from the danger which surrounded her, but was somewhat at a loss how to effect my purpose. My single strength was insufficient to contend with three ruffians. After a moment's debate, an expedient was suggested, which I hastened to execute.

Time had not been allowed for the ruffian who stood beside the carriage to receive the plunder, when several voices, loud, clamorous, and eager, were heard in the quarter whence the traveller had come. By trampling with quickness, it was easy to imitate the sound of many feet. The robbers were alarmed, and one called upon another to attend. The sounds increased, and, at the next moment, they betook themselves to flight, but not till a pistol was discharged. Whether it was aimed at the lady in the carriage, or at the coachman, I was not permitted to discover, for the report affrighted the horses, and they set off at full speed.

I could not hope to overtake them: I knew not whither the robbers had fled, and whether, by proceeding, I might not fall into their hands. These considerations induced me to resume my feet, and retire from the scene as expeditiously as possible. I regained my own habitation without injury.

I have said that I occupied separate apartments from those of Ludloe. To these there were means of access without disturbing the family. I hasted[4] to my chamber, but was considerably surprized to find, on entering my apartment, Ludloe seated at a table, with a lamp before him.

My momentary confusion was greater than his. On discovering who it was, he assumed his accustomed looks, and explained appearances, by saying, that he wished to converse with me on a subject of importance, and had therefore sought me at this secret hour, in my own chamber. Contrary to his expectation, I was absent. Conceiving it possible that I might shortly return, he had waited till now. He took no further notice of my absence, nor manifested any desire to know the cause of it, but proceeded to mention the subject which had brought him hither. These were his words.

You have nothing which the laws permit you to call your own. Justice entitles you to the supply of your physical wants, from those who are able to supply them; but there are few who will acknowledge your claim, or spare an atom of their superfluity to appease your cravings. That which they will not spontaneously give, it is not right to wrest from them by violence. What then is to be done?

Property is necessary to your own subsistence. It is useful, by enabling you to supply the wants of others. To give food, and clothing, and shelter, is

3. Rider of the leading left-hand horse.
4. I.e., hastened.

to give life, to annihilate temptation, to unshackle virtue, and propagate felicity. How shall property be gained?

You may set your understanding or your hands at work. You may weave stockings, or write poems, and exchange them for money; but these are tardy[5] and meager schemes. The means are disproportioned to the end, and I will not suffer you to pursue them. My justice will supply your wants.

But dependence on the justice of others is a precarious condition. To be the object is a less ennobling state than to be the bestower of benefit. Doubtless you desire to be vested with competence and riches, and to hold them by virtue of the law, and not at the will of a benefactor. . . . He paused as if waiting for my assent to his positions. I readily expressed my concurrence, and my desire to pursue any means compatible with honesty. He resumed.

There are various means, besides labour, violence, or fraud. It is right to select the easiest within your reach. It happens that the easiest is at hand. A revenue of some thousands a year, a stately mansion in the city, and another in Kildare,[6] old and faithful domestics, and magnificent furniture, are good things. Will you have them?

A gift like that, replied I, will be attended by momentous conditions. I cannot decide upon its value, until I know these conditions.

The sole condition is your consent to receive them. Not even the airy obligation of gratitude will be created by acceptance. On the contrary, by accepting them, you will confer the highest benefit upon another.

I do not comprehend you. Something surely must be given in return.

Nothing. It may seem strange that, in accepting the absolute control of so much property, you subject yourself to no conditions; that no claims of gratitude or service will accrue; but the wonder is greater still. The law equitably enough fetters the gift with no restraints, with respect to you that receive it; but not so with regard to the unhappy being who bestows it. That being must part, not only with property but liberty. In accepting the property, you must consent to enjoy the services of the present possessor. They cannot be disjoined.

Of the true nature and extent of the gift, you should be fully apprized. Be aware, therefore, that, together with this property, you will receive absolute power over the liberty and person of the being who now possesses it. That being must become your domestic slave; be governed, in every particular, by your caprice.

Happily for you, though fully invested with this power, the degree and mode in which it will be exercised will depend upon yourself. You may either totally forbear the exercise, or employ it only for the benefit of your slave. However injurious, therefore, this authority may be to the subject of it, it will, in some sense, only enhance the value of the gift to you.

The attachment and obedience of this being will be chiefly evident in one thing. Its duty will consist in conforming, in every instance, to your will. All the powers of this being are to be devoted to your happiness; but there is one relation between you, which enables you to confer, while exacting, pleasure. This relation is *sexual*. Your slave is a woman; and the bond, which transfers her property and person to you, is . . . *marriage*.

5. Slow, sluggish.
6. Town and county southwest of Dublin.

My knowledge of Ludloe, his principles, and reasonings, ought to have precluded that surprise which I experienced at the conclusion of his discourse. I knew that he regarded the present institution of marriage as a contract of servitude, and the terms of it unequal and unjust. When my surprise had subsided, my thoughts turned upon the nature of his scheme. After a pause of reflection, I answered:

Both law and custom have connected obligations with marriage, which, though heaviest on the female, are not light upon the male. Their weight and extent are not immutable and uniform; they are modified by various incidents, and especially by the mental and personal qualities of the lady.

I am not sure that I should willingly accept the property and person of a woman decrepit with age, and enslaved by perverse habits and evil passions: whereas youth, beauty, and tenderness would be worth accepting, even for their own sake, and disconnected with fortune.

As to altar vows, I believe they will not make me swerve from equity. I shall exact neither service nor affection from my spouse. The value of these, and, indeed, not only the value, but the very existence, of the latter depends upon its spontaneity. A promise to love tends rather to loosen than strengthen the tie.

As to myself, the age of illusion is past. I shall not wed, till I find one whose moral and physical constitution will make personal fidelity easy. I shall judge without mistiness or passion, and habit will come in aid of an enlightened and deliberate choice.

I shall not be fastidious in my choice. I do not expect, and scarcely desire, much intellectual similitude between me and my wife. Our opinions and pursuits cannot be in common. While women are formed by their education, and their education continues in its present state, tender hearts and misguided understandings are all that we can hope to meet with.

What are the character, age, and person of the woman to whom you allude? and what prospect of success would attend my exertions to obtain her favour?

I have told you she is rich.[7] She is a widow, and owes her riches to the liberality of her husband, who was a trader of great opulence, and who died while on a mercantile adventure to Spain. He was not unknown to you. Your letters from Spain often spoke of him. In short, she is the widow of Benington, whom you met at Barcelona. She is still in the prime of life; is not without many feminine attractions; has an ardent and credulent[8] temper: and is particularly given to devotion. This temper it would be easy to regulate according to your pleasure and your interest, and I now submit to you the expediency of an alliance with her.

I am a kinsman, and regarded by her with uncommon deference; and my commendations, therefore, will be of great service to you, and shall be given.

I will deal ingenuously[9] with you. It is proper you should be fully acquainted with the grounds of this proposal. The benefits of rank, and property, and independence, which I have already mentioned as likely to accrue to you from this marriage, are solid and valuable benefits; but these are not the sole advantages, and to benefit you, in these respects, is not my whole view.

7. The speaker is Ludloe.
8. Credulous.

9. Candidly, sincerely.

No. My treatment of you henceforth will be regulated by one principle. I regard you only as one undergoing a probation or apprenticeship; as subjected to trials of your sincerity and fortitude. The marriage I now propose to you is desirable, because it will make you independent of me. Your poverty might create an unsuitable bias in favour of proposals, one of whose effects would be to set you beyond fortune's reach. That bias will cease, when you cease to be poor and dependent.

Love is the strongest of all human delusions. That fortitude, which is not subdued by the tenderness and blandishments of woman, may be trusted; but no fortitude, which has not undergone that test, will be trusted by us.

This woman is a charming enthusiast. She will never marry but him whom she passionately loves. Her power over the heart that loves her will scarcely have limits. The means of prying into your transactions, of suspecting and sifting your thoughts, which her constant society with you, while sleeping and waking, her zeal and watchfulness for your welfare, and her curiosity, adroitness, and penetration will afford her, are evident. Your danger, therefore, will be imminent. Your fortitude will be obliged to have recourse, not to flight, but to vigilance. Your eye must never close.

Alas! what human magnanimity can stand this test! How can I persuade myself that you will not fail? I waver between hope and fear. Many, it is true, have fallen, and dragged with them the author of their ruin, but some have soared above even these perils and temptations, with their fiery energies unimpaired, and great has been, as great ought to be, their recompence.

But you are doubtless aware of your danger. I need not repeat the consequences of betraying your trust, the rigour of those who will judge your fault, the unerring and unbounded scrutiny to which your actions, the most secret and indifferent, will be subjected.

Your conduct, however, will be voluntary. At your own option be it, to see or not to see this woman. Circumspection, deliberation, forethought, are your sacred duties and highest interest.

Ludloe's remarks on the seductive and bewitching powers of women, on the difficulty of keeping a secret which they wish to know, and to gain which they employ the soft artillery of tears and prayers, and blandishments and menaces, are familiar to all men, but they had little weight with me, because they were unsupported by my own experience. I had never had any intellectual or sentimental connection with the sex. My meditations and pursuits had all led a different way, and a bias had gradually been given to my feelings, very unfavourable to the refinements of love. I acknowledge, with shame and regret, that I was accustomed to regard the physical and sensual consequences of the sexual relation as realities, and every thing intellectual, disinterested, and heroic, which enthusiasts connect with it as idle dreams. Besides, said I, I am yet a stranger to the secret, on the preservation of which so much stress is laid, and it will be optional with me to receive it or not. If, in the progress of my acquaintance with Mrs. Benington, I should perceive any extraordinary danger in the gift, cannot I refuse, or at least delay to comply with any new conditions from Ludloe? Will not his candour and his affection for me rather commend than disapprove my diffidence? In fine, I resolved to see this lady.

She was, it seems, the widow of Benington, whom I knew in Spain. This man was an English merchant settled at Barcelona, to whom I had been

commended by Ludloe's letters, and through whom my pecuniary supplies were furnished. Much intercourse and some degree of intimacy had taken place between us, and I had gained a pretty accurate knowledge of his character. I had been informed, through different channels, that his wife was much his superior in rank, that she possessed great wealth in her own right, and that some disagreement of temper or views occasioned their separation. She had married him for love, and still doted on him: the occasions for separation having arisen, it seems, not on her side but on his. As his habits of reflection were nowise friendly to religion, and as hers, according to Ludloe, were of the opposite kind, it is possible that some jarring had arisen between them from this source. Indeed, from some casual and broken hints of Benington, especially in the latter part of his life, I had long since gathered this conjecture. Something, thought I, may be derived from my acquaintance with her husband favourable to my views.

I anxiously waited for an opportunity of acquainting Ludloe with my resolution. On the day of our last conversation, he had made a short excursion from town, intending to return the same evening, but had continued absent for several days. As soon as he came back, I hastened to acquaint him with my wishes.

Have you well considered this matter, said he. Be assured it is of no trivial import. The moment at which you enter the presence of this woman will decide your future destiny. Even putting out of view the subject of our late conversations, the light in which you shall appear to her will greatly influence your happiness, since, though you cannot fail to love her, it is quite uncertain what return she may think proper to make. Much, doubtless, will depend on your own perseverance and address, but you will have many, perhaps insuperable obstacles to encounter on several accounts, and especially in her attachment to the memory of her late husband. As to her devout temper, this is nearly allied to a warm imagination in some other respects, and will operate much more in favour of an ardent and artful lover, than against him.

I still expressed my willingness to try my fortune with her.

Well, said he, I anticipated your consent to my proposal, and the visit I have just made was to her. I thought it best to pave the way, by informing her that I had met with one for whom she had desired me to look out. You must know that her father was one of these singular men who set a value upon things exactly in proportion to the difficulty of obtaining or comprehending them. His passion was for antiques, and his favourite pursuit during a long life was monuments in brass, marble, and parchment, of the remotest antiquity. He was wholly indifferent to the character or conduct of our present sovereign and his ministers, but was extremely solicitous about the name and exploits of a king of Ireland that lived two or three centuries before the flood. He felt no curiosity to know who was the father of his wife's child, but would travel a thousand miles, and consume months, in investigating which son of Noah it was that first landed on the coast of Munster.[1] He would give a hundred guineas[2] from the mint for a piece of

1. Province of southwestern Ireland. According to some legends, the biblical patriarch Noah's son Japhet or Japeth is the father of the Gaels in Ireland. In other legends, the father of this Irish people is Bith, a son of Noah who does not appear in the Bible.
2. British gold coins, in use from 1663 to 1817.

old decayed copper no bigger than his nail, provided it had awkward charac-
ters upon it, too much defaced to be read. The whole stock of a great book-
seller was, in his eyes, a cheap exchange for a shred of parchment, containing
half a homily written by St. Patrick.[3] He would have gratefully given all
his patrimonial domains to one who should inform him what pendragon or
druid it was who set up the first stone on Salisbury plain.[4]

This spirit, as you may readily suppose, being seconded by great wealth
and long life, contributed to form a very large collection of venerable lum-
ber[5] which, though beyond all price to the collector himself, is of no value
to his heiress but so far as it is marketable. She designs to bring the whole
to auction, but for this purpose a catalogue and description are necessary.
Her father trusted to a faithful memory, and to vague and scarcely legible
memorandums, and has left a very arduous task to any one who shall be
named to the office. It occurred to me, that the best means of promoting
your views was to recommend you to this office.

You are not entirely without the antiquarian frenzy yourself. The employ-
ment, therefore, will be somewhat agreeable to you for its own sake. It will
entitle you to become an inmate of the same house, and thus establish an
incessant intercourse between you, and the nature of the business is such,
that you may perform it in what time, and with what degree of diligence
and accuracy you please.

I ventured to insinuate that, to a woman of rank and family, the charac-
ter of a hireling[6] was by no means a favourable recommendation.

He answered, that he proposed, by the account he should give of me, to
obviate[7] every scruple of that nature. Though my father was no better than a
farmer, it is not absolutely certain but that my remoter ancestors had princely
blood in their veins: but as long as proofs of my low extraction did not imper-
tinently intrude themselves, my silence, or, at most, equivocal surmises, sea-
sonably made use of, might secure me from all inconveniences on the score
of birth. He should represent me, and I was such, as his friend, favourite,
and equal, and my passion for antiquities should be my principal induce-
ment to undertake this office, though my poverty would make no objection
to a reasonable pecuniary recompense.

Having expressed my acquiescence in his measures, he thus proceeded:
My visit was made to my kinswoman, for the purpose, as I just now told you, of
paving your way into her family; but, on my arrival at her house, I found noth-
ing but disorder and alarm. Mrs. Benington, it seems, on returning from a
longer ride than customary, last Thursday evening, was attacked by robbers.
Her attendants related an imperfect tale of somebody advancing at the critical
moment to her rescue. It seems, however, they did more harm than good;
for the horses took to flight and overturned the carriage, in consequence of
which Mrs. Benington was severely bruised. She has kept her bed ever since,
and a fever was likely to ensue, which has only left her out of danger to-day.

As the adventure before related, in which I had so much concern,
occurred at the time mentioned by Ludloe, and as all other circumstances

3. Fifth-century bishop known as the primary
patron saint of Ireland.
4. Plateau in central England; the location of
Stonehenge and other prehistoric monuments.
"Pendragon": the title given to several traditional
kings of the Britons, including King Arthur.

"Druid": member of an educated, priestly class
among the Iron Age Celts.
5. Old and useless things.
6. A person paid to undertake menial work.
7. Remove.

were alike, I could not doubt that the person whom the exertion of my mysterious powers had relieved was Mrs. Benington: but what an ill-omened interference was mine! The robbers would probably have been satisfied with the few guineas[8] in her purse, and, on receiving these, would have left her to prosecute her journey in peace and security, but, by absurdly offering a succor,[9] which could only operate upon the fears of her assailants, I endangered her life, first by the desperate discharge of a pistol, and next by the fright of the horses. . . . My anxiety, which would have been less if I had not been, in some degree, myself the author of the evil, was nearly removed by Ludloe's proceeding to assure me that all danger was at an end, and that he left the lady in the road to perfect health. He had seized the earliest opportunity of acquainting her with the purpose of his visit, and had brought back with him her cheerful acceptance of my services. The next week was appointed for my introduction.

With such an object in view, I had little leisure to attend to any indifferent object. My thoughts were continually bent upon the expected introduction, and my impatience and curiosity drew strength, not merely from the character of Mrs. Benington, but from the nature of my new employment. Ludloe had truly observed, that I was infected with somewhat of this antiquarian mania myself, and I now remembered that Benington had frequently alluded to this collection in possession of his wife. My curiosity had then been more than once excited by his representations, and I had formed a vague resolution of making myself acquainted with this lady and her learned treasure, should I ever return to Ireland. . . . Other incidents had driven this matter from my mind.

Meanwhile, affairs between Ludloe and myself remained stationary. Our conferences, which were regular and daily, related to general topics, and though his instructions were adapted to promote my improvement in the most useful branches of knowledge, they never afforded a glimpse towards that quarter where my curiosity was most active.

The next week now arrived, but Ludloe informed me that the state of Mrs. Benington's health required a short excursion into the country, and that he himself proposed to bear her company. The journey was to last about a fortnight, after which I might prepare myself for an introduction to her.

This was a very unexpected and disagreeable trial to my patience. The interval of solitude that now succeeded would have passed rapidly and pleasantly enough, if an event of so much moment were not in suspense. Books, of which I was passionately fond, would have afforded me delightful and incessant occupation, and Ludloe, by way of reconciling me to unavoidable delays, had given me access to a little closet, in which his rarer and more valuable books were kept.

All my amusements, both by inclination and necessity, were centered in myself and at home. Ludloe appeared to have no visitants, and though frequently abroad, or at least secluded from me, had never proposed my introduction to any of his friends, except Mrs. Benington. My obligations to him were already too great to allow me to lay claim to new favors and indulgences, nor, indeed, was my disposition such as to make society needful to my happiness. My character had been, in some degree, modeled by the

8. British gold coins, in use from 1663 to 1817.
9. Aid, help.

faculty which I possessed. This deriving all its supposed value from impenetrable secrecy, and Ludloe's admonitions tending powerfully to impress me with the necessity of wariness and circumspection in my general intercourse with mankind, I had gradually fallen into sedate, reserved, mysterious, and unsociable habits. My heart wanted not a friend.

In this temper of mind, I set myself to examine the novelties which Ludloe's private book-cases contained. 'Twill be strange, thought I, if his favorite volumes do not show some marks of my friend's character. To know a man's favorite or most constant studies cannot fail of letting in some little light upon his secret thoughts, and though he would not have given me the reading of these books, if he had thought them capable of unveiling more of his concerns than he wished, yet possibly my ingenuity may go one step farther than he dreams of. You shall judge whether I was right in my conjectures.

The books which composed this little library were chiefly the voyages and travels of the missionaries of the sixteenth and seventeenth centuries. Added to these were some works upon political economy and legislation. Those writers who have amused themselves with reducing their ideas to practice, and drawing imaginary pictures of nations or republics, whose manners or government came up to their standard of excellence, were, all of whom I had ever heard, and some I had never heard of before, to be found in this collection. A translation of Aristotle's republic, the political romances of sir Thomas Moore, Harrington, and Hume,[1] appeared to have been much read, and Ludloe had not been sparing of his marginal comments. In these writers he appeared to find nothing but error and absurdity; and his notes were introduced for no other end than to point out groundless principles and false conclusions. . . . The style of these remarks was already familiar to me. I saw nothing new in them, or different from the strain of those speculations with which Ludloe was accustomed to indulge himself in conversation with me.

After having turned over the leaves of the printed volumes, I at length lighted on a small book of maps, from which, of course, I could reasonably expect no information, on that point about which I was most curious. It was an atlas, in which the maps had been drawn by the pen. None of them contained any thing remarkable, so far as I, who was indeed a smatterer in geography, was able to perceive, till I came to the end, when I noticed a map, whose prototype I was wholly unacquainted with. It was drawn on a pretty large scale, representing two islands, which bore some faint resemblance, in their relative proportions, at least, to Great Britain and Ireland. In shape they were widely different, but as to size there was no scale by which to measure them. From the great number of subdivisions, and from signs, which apparently represented towns and cities, I was allowed to infer, that the country was at least as extensive as the British isles. This map was apparently unfinished, for it had no names inscribed upon it.

I have just said, my geographical knowledge was imperfect. Though I had not enough to draw the outlines of any country by memory, I had still sufficient to recognize what I had before seen, and to discover that none of the

1. David Hume (1711–1776), Scottish philosopher, author of the essay "The Idea of a Perfect Commonwealth"; Plato (not Aristotle), ancient Greek philosopher, author of the dialogue *Republic*; Sir Thomas More (1478–1535), English states-man, author of the combination of fictional and political philosophy *Utopia*; James Harrington (1611–1677), English statesman, author of the work of political philosophy *The Commonwealth of Oceana*.

larger islands in our globe resembled the one before me. Having such and so strong motives to curiosity, you may easily imagine my sensations on surveying this map. Suspecting, as I did, that many of Ludloe's intimations alluded to a country well known to him, though unknown to others, I was, of course, inclined to suppose that this country was now before me.

In search of some clue to this mystery, I carefully inspected the other maps in this collection. In a map of the eastern hemisphere I soon observed the outlines of islands, which, though on a scale greatly diminished, were plainly similar to that of the land above described.

It is well known that the people of Europe are strangers to very nearly one half of the surface of the globe.[2] From the south pole up to the equator, it is only the small space occupied by southern Africa and by South America with which we are acquainted. There is a vast extent, sufficient to receive a continent as large as North America, which our ignorance has filled only with water. In Ludloe's maps nothing was still to be seen, in these regions, but water, except in that spot where the transverse parallels of the southern tropic and the 150th degree east longitude intersect each other.[3] On this spot were Ludloe's islands placed, though without any name or inscription whatever.

I needed not to be told that this spot had never been explored by any European voyager, who had published his adventures. What authority had Ludloe for fixing a habitable land in this spot? and why did he give us nothing but the courses of shores and rivers, and the site of towns and villages, without a name?

As soon as Ludloe had set out upon his proposed journey of a fortnight, I unlocked his closet, and continued rummaging among these books and maps till night. By that time I had turned over every book and almost every leaf[4] in this small collection, and did not open the closet again till near the end of that period. Meanwhile I had many reflections upon this remarkable circumstance. Could Ludloe have intended that I should see this atlas? It was the only book that could be styled a manuscript on these shelves, and it was placed beneath several others, in a situation far from being obvious and forward to the eye or the hand. Was it an oversight in him to leave it in my way, or could he have intended to lead my curiosity and knowledge a little farther onward by this accidental disclosure? In either case how was I to regulate my future deportment toward him? Was I to speak and act as if this atlas had escaped my attention or not? I had already, after my first examination of it, placed the volume exactly where I found it. On every supposition I thought this was the safest way, and unlocked the closet a second time, to see that all was precisely in the original order. . . . How was I dismayed and confounded on inspecting the shelves to perceive that the atlas was gone. This was a theft, which, from the closet being under lock and key, and the key always in my own pocket, and which, from the very nature of the thing stolen, could not be imputed to any of the domestics. After a few moments a suspicion occurred, which was soon changed into certainty by applying to the housekeeper, who told me that Ludloe had returned,

2. "The reader must be reminded that the incidents of this narrative are supposed to have taken place before the voyages of Bougainville and Cook"—EDITOR [Brown's note]. The French admiral Louis-Antoine, Comte de Bougainville (1729–1811) and the English captain James Cook (1728–1779) undertook separate explorations in the Pacific Ocean in the late 1760s.
3. I.e., at what we know as the approximate location of Australia.
4. Page.

apparently in much haste, the evening of the day on which he had set out upon his journey, and just after I had left the house, that he had gone into the room where this closet of books was, and, after a few minutes' stay, came out again and went away. She told me also, that he had made general enquiries after me, to which she had answered, that she had not seen me during the day, and supposed that I had spent the whole of it abroad. From this account it was plain, that Ludloe had returned for no other purpose but to remove this book out of my reach. But if he had a double key to this door, what should hinder his having access, by the same means, to every other locked up place in the house?

This suggestion made me start with terror. Of so obvious a means for possessing a knowledge of every thing under his roof, I had never been till this moment aware. Such is the infatuation which lays our most secret thoughts open to the world's scrutiny. We are frequently in most danger when we deem ourselves most safe, and our fortress is taken sometimes through a point, whose weakness nothing, it should seem, but the blindest stupidity could overlook.

My terrors, indeed, quickly subsided when I came to recollect that there was nothing in any closet or cabinet of mine which could possibly throw light upon subjects which I desired to keep in the dark. The more carefully I inspected my own drawers, and the more I reflected on the character of Ludloe, as I had known it, the less reason did there appear in my suspicions; but I drew a lesson of caution from this circumstance, which contributed to my future safety.

From this incident I could not but infer Ludloe's unwillingness to let me so far into his geographical secret, as well as the certainty of that suspicion, which had very early been suggested to my thoughts, that Ludloe's plans of civilization had been carried into practice in some unvisited corner of the world. It was strange, however, that he should betray himself by such an inadvertency. One who talked so confidently of his own powers, to unveil any secret of mine, and, at the same time, to conceal his own transactions, had surely committed an unpardonable error in leaving this important document in my way. My reverence, indeed, for Ludloe was such, that I sometimes entertained the notion that this seeming oversight was, in truth, a regular contrivance to supply me with a knowledge, of which, when I came maturely to reflect, it was impossible for me to make any ill use. There is no use in relating what would not be believed; and should I publish to the world the existence of islands in the space allotted by Ludloe's maps to these *incognitæ*,[5] what would the world answer? That whether the space described was sea or land was of no importance. That the moral and political condition of its inhabitants was the only topic worthy of rational curiosity. Since I had gained no information upon this point; since I had nothing to disclose but vain and fantastic surmises; I might as well be ignorant of every thing. Thus, from secretly condemning Ludloe's imprudence, I gradually passed to admiration of his policy. This discovery had no other effect than to stimulate my curiosity; to keep up my zeal to prosecute the journey I had commenced under his auspices.

I had hitherto formed a resolution to stop where I was in Ludloe's confidence: to wait till the success should be ascertained of my projects with

5. Unknown territories (Latin).

respect to Mrs. Benington, before I made any new advance in the perilous and mysterious road into which he had led my steps. But, before this tedious fortnight had elapsed, I was grown extremely impatient for an interview, and had nearly resolved to undertake whatever obligation he should lay upon me.

This obligation was indeed a heavy one, since it included the confession of my vocal powers. In itself the confession was little. To possess this faculty was neither laudable nor culpable, nor had it been exercised in a way which I should be very much ashamed to acknowledge. It had led me into many insincerities and artifices, which, though not justifiable by any creed, was entitled to some excuse, on the score of youthful ardour and temerity. The true difficulty in the way of these confessions was the not having made them already. Ludloe had long been entitled to this confidence, and, though the existence of this power was venial or wholly innocent, the obstinate concealment of it was a different matter, and would certainly expose me to suspicion and rebuke. But what was the alternative? To conceal it. To incur those dreadful punishments awarded against treason in this particular. Ludloe's menaces still rung in my ears, and appalled my heart. How should I be able to shun them? By concealing from every one what I concealed from him? How was my concealment of such a faculty to be suspected or proved? Unless I betrayed myself, who could betray me?

In this state of mind, I resolved to confess myself to Ludloe in the way that he required, reserving only the secret of this faculty. Awful, indeed, said I, is the crisis of my fate. If Ludloe's declarations are true, a horrid catastrophe awaits me: but as fast as my resolutions were shaken, they were confirmed anew by the recollection—Who can betray me but myself? If I deny, who is there can prove? Suspicion can never light upon the truth. If it does, it can never be converted into certainty. Even my own lips cannot confirm it, since who will believe my testimony?

By such illusions was I fortified in my desperate resolution. Ludloe returned at the time appointed. He informed me that Mrs. Benington expected me next morning. She was ready to depart for her country residence, where she proposed to spend the ensuing summer, and would carry me along with her. In consequence of this arrangement, he said, many months would elapse before he should see me again. You will indeed, continued he, be pretty much shut up from all society. Your books and your new friend will be your chief, if not only companions. Her life is not a social one, because she has formed extravagant notions of the importance of lonely worship and devout solitude. Much of her time will be spent in meditation upon pious books in her closet.[6] Some of it in long solitary rides in her coach, for the sake of exercise. Little will remain for eating and sleeping, so that unless you can prevail upon her to violate her ordinary rules for your sake, you will be left pretty much to yourself. You will have the more time to reflect upon what has hitherto been the theme of our conversations. You can come to town when you want to see me. I shall generally be found in these apartments.

In the present state of my mind, though impatient to see Mrs. Benington, I was still more impatient to remove the veil between Ludloe and myself. After some pause, I ventured to enquire if there was any impediment to

6. Private room.

my advancement in the road he had already pointed out to my curiosity and ambition.

He replied, with great solemnity, that I was already acquainted with the next step to be taken in this road. If I was prepared to make him my confessor, as to the past, the present, and the future, *without exception or condition*, but what arose from defect of memory, he was willing to receive my confession.

I declared myself ready to do so.

I need not, he returned, remind you of the consequences of concealment or deceit. I have already dwelt upon these consequences. As to the past, you have already told me, perhaps, all that is of any moment to know. It is in relation to the future that caution will be chiefly necessary. Hitherto your actions have been nearly indifferent to the ends of your future existence. Confessions of the past are required, because they are an earnest[7] of the future character and conduct. Have you then—but this is too abrupt. Take an hour to reflect and deliberate. Go by yourself; take yourself to severe task, and make up your mind with a full, entire, and unfailing resolution; for the moment in which you assume this new obligation will make you a new being. Perdition or felicity will hang upon that moment.

This conversation was late in the evening. After I had consented to postpone this subject, we parted, he telling me that he would leave his chamber door open, and as soon as my mind was made up I might come to him.

I retired accordingly to my apartment, and spent the prescribed hour in anxious and irresolute reflections. They were no other than had hitherto occurred, but they occurred with more force than ever. Some fatal obstinacy, however, got possession of me, and I persisted in the resolution of concealing *one thing*. We become fondly attached to objects and pursuits, frequently for no conceivable reason but the pain and trouble they cost us. In proportion to the danger in which they involve us do we cherish them. Our darling potion is the poison that scorches our vitals.

After some time, I went to Ludloe's apartment. I found him solemn, and yet benign, at my entrance. After intimating my compliance with the terms prescribed, which I did, in spite of all my labor for composure, with accents half faltering, he proceeded to put various questions to me, relative to my early history.

I knew there was no other mode of accomplishing the end in view, but by putting all that was related in the form of answers to questions; and when meditating on the character of Ludloe, I experienced excessive uneasiness as to the consummate art and penetration which his questions would manifest. Conscious of a purpose to conceal, my fancy invested my friend with the robe of a judicial inquisitor, all whose questions should aim at extracting the truth, and entrapping the liar.

In this respect, however, I was wholly disappointed. All his inquiries were general and obvious.—They betokened curiosity, but not suspicion; yet there were moments when I saw, or fancied I saw, some dissatisfaction betrayed in his features; and when I arrived at that period of my story which terminated with my departure, as his companion, for Europe, his pauses were, I thought, a little longer and more museful than I liked. At this period,

7. A pledge.

our first conference ended. After a talk, which had commenced at a late hour, and had continued many hours, it was time to sleep, and it was agreed that next morning the conference should be renewed.

On retiring to my pillow, and reviewing all the circumstances of this interview, my mind was filled with apprehension and disquiet. I seemed to recollect a thousand things, which showed that Ludloe was not fully satisfied with my part in this interview. A strange and nameless mixture of wrath and of pity appeared, on recollection, in the glances which, from time to time, he cast upon me. Some emotion played upon his features, in which, as my fears conceived, there was a tincture of resentment and ferocity. In vain I called my usual sophistries to my aid. In vain I pondered on the inscrutable nature of my peculiar faculty. In vain I endeavoured to persuade myself, that, by telling the truth, instead of entitling myself to Ludloe's approbation, I should only excite his anger, by what he could not but deem an attempt to impose upon his belief an incredible tale of impossible events. I had never heard or read of any instance of this faculty. I supposed the case to be absolutely singular, and I should be no more entitled to credit in proclaiming it, than if I should maintain that a certain billet[8] of wood possessed the faculty of articulate speech. It was now, however, too late to retract. I had been guilty of a solemn and deliberate concealment. I was now in the path in which there was no turning back, and I must go forward.

The return of day's encouraging beams in some degree quieted my nocturnal terrors, and I went, at the appointed hour, to Ludloe's presence. I found him with a much more cheerful aspect than I expected, and began to chide myself, in secret, for the folly of my late[9] apprehensions.

After a little pause, he reminded me, that he was only one among many, engaged in a great and arduous design. As each of us, continued he, is mortal, each of us must, in time, yield his post to another.—Each of us is ambitious to provide himself a successor, to have his place filled by one selected and instructed by himself. All our personal feelings and affections are by no means intended to be swallowed up by a passion for the general interest; when they can be kept alive and be brought into play, in subordination and subservience to the *great end*, they are cherished as useful, and revered as laudable; and whatever austerity and rigor you may impute to my character, there are few more susceptible of personal regards than I am.

You cannot know, till *you* are what *I* am, what deep, what all-absorbing interest I have in the success of my tutorship on this occasion. Most joyfully would I embrace a thousand deaths, rather than that you should prove a recreant.[1] The consequences of any failure in your integrity will, it is true, be fatal to yourself: but there are some minds, of a generous texture, who are more impatient under ills they have inflicted upon others, than of those they have brought upon themselves; who had rather perish, themselves, in infamy, than bring infamy or death upon a benefactor.

Perhaps of such noble materials is your mind composed. If I had not thought so, you would never have been an object of my regard, and therefore, in the motives that shall impel you to fidelity, sincerity, and perseverance, some regard to my happiness and welfare will, no doubt, have place.

8. Thick piece (of wood).
9. Recent.

1. Coward; one unfaithful to a belief, apostate.

And yet I exact nothing from you on this score. If your own safety be insufficient to control you, you are not fit for us. There is, indeed, abundant need of all possible inducements to make you faithful. The task of concealing nothing from me must be easy. That of concealing every thing from others must be the only arduous one. The *first* you can hardly fail of performing, when the exigence requires it, for what motive can you possibly have to practice evasion or disguise with me? You have surely committed no crime; you have neither robbed, nor murdered, nor betrayed. If you have, there is no room for the fear of punishment or the terror of disgrace to step in, and make you hide your guilt from me. You cannot dread any further disclosure, because I can have no interest in your ruin or your shame: and what evil could ensue the confession of the foulest murder, even before a bench of magistrates, more dreadful than that which will inevitably follow the practice of the least concealment to me, or the least undue disclosure to others?

You cannot easily conceive the emphatical solemnity with which this was spoken. Had he fixed piercing eyes on me while he spoke; had I perceived him watching my looks, and laboring to penetrate my secret thoughts, I should doubtless have been ruined: but he fixed his eyes upon the floor, and no gesture or look indicated the smallest suspicion of my conduct. After some pause, he continued, in a more pathetic tone, while his whole frame seemed to partake of his mental agitation.

I am greatly at a loss by what means to impress you with a full conviction of the truth of what I have just said. Endless are the sophistries by which we seduce ourselves into perilous and doubtful paths. What we do not see, we disbelieve, or we heed not. The sword may descend upon our infatuated head from above, but we who are, meanwhile, busily inspecting the ground at our feet, or gazing at the scene around us, are not aware or apprehensive of its irresistible coming. In this case, it must not be seen before it is felt, or before the time comes when the danger of incurring it is over. I cannot withdraw the veil, and disclose to your view the exterminating angel. All must be vacant and blank, and the danger that stands armed with death at your elbow must continue to be totally invisible, till that moment when its vengeance is provoked or unprovokable. I will do my part to encourage you in good, or intimidate you from evil. I am anxious to set before you all the motives which are fitted to influence your conduct; but how shall I work on your convictions?

Here another pause ensued, which I had not courage enough to interrupt. He presently resumed.

Perhaps you recollect a visit which you paid, on Christmas day, in the year——, to the cathedral church at Toledo.[2] Do you remember?

A moment's reflection recalled to my mind all the incidents of that day. I had good reason to remember them. I felt no small trepidation when Ludloe referred me to that day, for, at the moment, I was doubtful whether there had not been some bivocal agency exerted on that occasion. Luckily, however, it was almost the only similar occasion in which it had been wholly silent.

I answered in the affirmative. I remember them perfectly.

And yet, said Ludloe, with a smile that seemed intended to disarm this declaration of some of its terrors, I suspect your recollection is not as exact

2. City in central Spain, whose cathedral is one of the great examples of Gothic architecture.

as mine, nor, indeed, your knowledge as extensive. You met there, for the first time, a female, whose nominal uncle, but real father, a dean of that ancient church, resided in a blue stone house, the third from the west angle of the square of St. Jago.

All this was exactly true.

This female, continued he, fell in love with you. Her passion made her deaf to all the dictates of modesty and duty, and she gave you sufficient intimations, in subsequent interviews at the same place, of this passion; which, she being fair and enticing, you were not slow in comprehending and returning. As not only the safety of your intercourse, but even of both your lives, depended on being shielded even from suspicion, the utmost wariness and caution was observed in all your proceedings. Tell me whether you succeeded in your efforts to this end.

I replied, that, at the time, I had no doubt but I had.

And yet, said he, drawing something from his pocket, and putting it into my hand, there is the slip of paper, with the preconcerted[3] emblem inscribed upon it, which the infatuated girl dropped in your sight, one evening, in the left aisle of that church. That paper you imagined you afterwards burnt in your chamber lamp. In pursuance of this token, you deferred your intended visit, and next day the lady was accidentally drowned, in passing a river. Here ended your connection with her, and with her was buried, as you thought, all memory of this transaction.

I leave you to draw your own inference from this disclosure. Meditate upon it when alone. Recall all the incidents of that drama, and labour to conceive the means by which my sagacity has been able to reach events that took place so far off, and under so deep a covering. If you cannot penetrate these means, learn to reverence my assertions, that I cannot be deceived; and let sincerity be henceforth the rule of your conduct towards me, not merely because it is right, but because concealment is impossible.

We will stop here. There is no haste required of us. Yesterday's discourse will suffice for to-day, and for many days to come. Let what has already taken place be the subject of profound and mature reflection. Review, once more, the incidents of your early life, previous to your introduction to me, and, at our next conference, prepare to supply all those deficiences occasioned by negligence, forgetfulness, or design on our first. There must be some. There must be many. The whole truth can only be disclosed after numerous and repeated conversations. These must take place at considerable intervals, and when *all* is told, then shall you be ready to encounter the final ordeal, and load yourself with heavy and terrific sanctions.

I shall be the proper judge of the completeness of your confession.— Knowing previously, and by unerring means, your whole history, I shall be able to detect all that is deficient, as well as all that is redundant. Your confessions have hitherto adhered to the truth, but deficient they are, and they must be, for who, at a single trial can detail the secrets of his life? whose recollection can fully serve him at an instant's notice? who can free himself, by a single effort, from the dominion of fear and shame? We expect no miracles of fortitude and purity from our disciples. It is our discipline, our

3. Predetermined.

wariness, our laborious preparation that creates the excellence we have among us. We find it not ready made.

I counsel you to join Mrs. Benington without delay. You may see me when and as often as you please. When it is proper to renew the present topic, it shall be renewed. Till then we will be silent.—Here Ludloe left me alone, but not to indifference or vacuity. Indeed I was overwhelmed with the reflections that arose from this conversation. So, said I, I am still saved, if I have wisdom enough to use the opportunity, from the consequences of past concealments. By a distinction which I had wholly overlooked, but which could not be missed by the sagacity and equity of Ludloe, I have praise for telling the truth, and an excuse for withholding some of the truth. It was, indeed, a praise to which I was entitled, for I have made no *additions* to the tale of my early adventures. I had no motive to exaggerate or dress out in false colours. What I sought to conceal, I was careful to exclude entirely, that a lame or defective narrative might awaken no suspicions.

The allusion to incidents at Toledo confounded and bewildered all my thoughts. I still held the paper he had given me. So far as memory could be trusted, it was the same which, an hour after I had received it, I burnt, as I conceived, with my own hands. How Ludloe came into possession of this paper; how he was apprised of incidents, to which only the female mentioned and myself were privy; which she had too good reason to hide from all the world, and which I had taken infinite pains to bury in oblivion, I vainly endeavoured to conjecture.

To be continued.

Native American Eloquence:
Negotiation and Resistance

The eloquence of Native American orators impressed Europeans from the early years of contact. Exploration narratives often included descriptions of Native speakers and sometimes offered versions of what they were purported to have said, as in two selections in the "Native American Oral Traditions" cluster: the description of the Drake company's encounter with Coast Miwok leaders and John Smith's report on his negotiations with Powhatan. By the eighteenth century, as interest in political oratory and classical republicanism grew, white readers came to recognize the eloquent Indian as a literary type, and Indian speeches figured prominently in schoolbooks such as the popular elocution manuals designed to teach young American citizens to engage in public affairs. Meanwhile, oratory remained a central form of verbal art in indigenous communities, and it was an important element in formal exchanges with white Americans. The words of Native orators appeared in official state documents, treaty proceedings, and ethnographic and historical works, and orations attributed to Native speakers appeared in novels, poems, and plays. The literary fashion for Native eloquence was grounded in real practices and closely tied to matters of political exigency. The vogue reached a peak in the 1820s, when debates over Indian Removal gave added urgency to the Native resistance expressed in a number of widely circulated speeches.

The selections included here exemplify some seventy years of written or printed representations of Native eloquence. A speech by the Iroquois leader Canassatego, which achieved strikingly wide circulation on both sides of the Atlantic, shows him to be a consummate diplomat as he argues for indigenous sovereignty. Two decades later Pontiac, citing a charismatic prophet of the Delawares, attempts to persuade Huron and Pottawatomi leaders to join his Ottawa people in armed resistance to the British, in much the same way that the Shawnee leader Tecumseh later seeks to forge an Indian alliance against the expansionist Americans. The Mingo warrior Logan explains the reasons for his violent resistance to the colonists whom his people had earlier welcomed. Finally, a group of Cherokee women diplomats marshal the rhetoric of political motherhood to call for peaceful and friendly relations.

Before the nineteenth century, published texts of Native American oratory were almost all produced by hands other than those of the orators themselves—the works of Samson Occom and Hendrick Aupaumut, both included in this volume, are important exceptions—and they vary in authenticity and accuracy. Some widely reprinted speeches are now known to be largely or entirely invented, while others approximate the speaker's actual words. Somewhere between these extremes are speeches that might be called "bicultural composites," probably based on what an Indian person said but rendered in an English text that owes much to translators, transcribers, editors, and publishers. No known fabrications have been included here, and the provenance of each speech is indicated as specifically as possible.

CANASSATEGO

anassatego (b. c. 1680; sometimes Canasatego) was an Onondaga Indian. The Onondagas—whose traditional homeland is in central New York, near present-day Syracuse—were one of the original Five (later Six) Nations of the Iroquois (or Haudenosaunee) League. Canassatego had no apparent connection to the heredi-tary sachems, or leaders, of the Onondagas, but around 1740, in the years leading to the final struggle between France and England for control of North America, he rose to prominence as a negotiator of several important treaties between the Iroquois and the English colonies. He probably achieved this status through his skills as an orator and a political tactician. His influence depended partly on his close relation-ship with Conrad Weiser (1696–1760), a German-born translator and Indian agent who cultivated a reputation as an honest broker between Pennsylvania authorities and the Iroquois leadership. Canassatego first appears in the written record for 1742, when he played a significant role in the negotiations with the Pennsylvania govern-ment over compensation for land. He played a larger role in the Lancaster Treaty proceedings of 1744, the source for the selection included here, and in meetings at Albany (1745) and Philadelphia (1749). He died in 1750, possibly a victim of poison. His successor was an ally of France and a professed Roman Catholic, indicating that schisms existed within Canassatego's Onondaga community.

The printed version of the Lancaster Treaty of 1744 circulated widely in the colo-nies and in England. Benjamin Franklin, the Pennsylvania colony's official printer, laid out the text of the treaty proceedings to resemble a printed play and sent copies to his business partners in London, New York, and Annapolis. A second edition appeared in Williamsburg, Virginia. Whatever literary appeal the proceedings had was closely tied to the significance of its content, which highlighted the central place of the Iroquois in the imperial contest between England and France. Canassatego used his position of relative power on this occasion to demand compensation for land that the Iroquois claimed after defeating the Susquehanna Indians. The colonial governments were reluctant to fulfill these claims, arguing that they had previously purchased the land from the Susquehannas. In the following speech, which was probably translated by Weiser, Canassatego asserts the priority of indigenous claims to sovereignty over those of the English.

Speech at Lancaster[1]

* * *

Brother, the Governor of Maryland,
When you mentioned the Affair of the Land Yesterday, you went back to old Times, and told us, you had been in Possession of the Province of *Maryland* above One Hundred Years; but what is One Hundred Years in Comparison of the Length of Time since our Claim began since we came out of this Ground? For we must tell you, that long before One Hundred Years our Ancestors came out of this very Ground, and their Children have remained here ever

1. The text is from *A Treaty, Held at the Town of Lancaster, in Pennsylvania: by the Honourable the Lieutenant-governor of the Province, and the Honourable the Commissioners for the Provinces* of Virginia and Maryland, with the Indians of the Six Nations, in June, 1744 (printed and sold by Benjamin Franklin, 1744).

since. You came out of the Ground in a Country that lies beyond the Seas, there you may have a just Claim, but here you must allow us to be your elder Brethren, and the Lands to belong to us long before you knew any thing of them. It is true, that above One Hundred Years ago the *Dutch* came here in a Ship, and brought with them several Goods; such as Awls, Knives, Hatchets, Guns, and many other Particulars, which they gave us; and when they had taught us how to use their Things, and we saw what sort of People they were, we were so well pleased with them, that we tied their Ship to the Bushes on the Shore;[2] and afterwards, liking them still better the longer they staid with us, and thinking the Bushes too tender, we removed the Rope, and tied it to the Trees; and as the Trees were liable to be blown down by high Winds, or to decay of themselves, we, from the Affection we bore them, again removed the Rope, and tied it to a strong and big Rock [*here the Interpreter said, They mean the* Oneido *Country*] and not content with this, for its further Security we removed the Rope to the big Mountain [*here the Interpreter says they mean the* Onandago *Country*] and there we tied it very fast, and rowll'd[3] Wampum about it; and, to make it still more secure, we stood upon the Wampum, and sat down upon it, to defend it, and to prevent any Hurt coming to it, and did our best Endeavours that it might remain uninjured for ever. During all this Time the New-comers, the *Dutch*, acknowledged our Right to the Lands, and sollicited us, from Time to Time, to grant them Parts of our Country, and to enter into League and Covenant with us, and to become one People with us.

After this the *English* came into the Country, and, as we were told, became one People with the *Dutch*.[4] About two Years after the Arrival of the *English*, an *English* Governor came to *Albany*, and finding what great Friendship subsisted between us and the *Dutch*, he approved it mightily, and desired to make as strong a League, and to be upon as good Terms with us as the *Dutch* were, with whom he was united, and to become one People with us: And by his further Care in looking into what had passed between us, he found that the Rope which tied the Ship to the great Mountain was only fastened with Wampum, which was liable to break and rot, and to perish in a Course of Years; he therefore told us, he would give us a Silver Chain, which would be much stronger, and would last for ever. This we accepted, and fastened the Ship with it, and it has lasted ever since. Indeed we have had some small Differences with the *English*, and, during these Misunderstandings, some of their young Men would, by way of Reproach, be every now and then telling us, that we should have perished if they had not come into the Country and furnished us with Strowds[5] and Hatchets, and Guns, and other Things necessary for the Support of Life; but we always gave them to understand that they were mistaken, that we lived before they came amongst us, and as well, or better, if we may believe what our Forefathers have told us. We had then Room enough, and Plenty of Deer, which was easily caught; and tho' we had not Knives, Hatchets, or Guns, such as we have now, yet we had Knives of Stone, and Hatchets of Stone, and Bows and Arrows, and those served our Uses as well then as the *English* ones do

2. The following passage uses metaphors that suggest Iroquois control over their alliance with the Dutch. In this passage, the addition of wampum enhances the strength and importance of the ties between the Iroquois and the Dutch.

3. Rolled.
4. The British seized New Amsterdam from the Dutch in 1664, renaming it New York.
5. Blankets made of stroud, a coarse woolen fabric.

now. We are now straitened, and sometimes in want of Deer, and liable to many other Inconveniences since the *English* came among us, and particularly from that Pen-and-Ink Work that is going on at the Table (*pointing to the Secretary*) and we will give you an Instance of this. Our Brother *Onas*,[6] a great while ago, came to *Albany* to buy the *Sasquahannah* Lands of us, but our Brother, the Governor of *New-York*, who, as we suppose, had not a good understanding with our Brother *Onas*, advised us not to sell him any Land, for he would make an ill Use of it; and, pretending to be our good Friend, he advised us, in order to prevent *Onas*'s, or any other person's imposing upon us, and that we might always have our Land when we should want it, to put it into his Hands; and told us, he would keep it for our life, and never open his Hands, but keep them close shut, and not part with any of it, but at our Request. Accordingly we trusted him, and put our Land into his Hands, and charged him to keep it safe for our Use; but, some Time after, he went to *England*, and carried our Land with him, and there sold it to our Brother *Onas* for a large Sum of Money; and when, at the Instance of our Brother *Onas*, we were minded to sell him some Lands, he told us, we had sold the *Sasquahannah* Lands already to the Governor of *New-York*, and that he had bought them from him in *England*; tho', when he came to understand how the Governor of *New-York* had deceived us, he very generously paid us for our Lands over again.

Tho' we mention this Instance of an Imposition put upon us by the Governor of *New-York*, yet we must do the *English* the Justice to say, we have had their hearty Assistances in our Wars with the *French*, who were no sooner arrived amongst us than they began to render us uneasy, and to provoke us to War, and we have had several Wars with them; during all which we constantly received Assistance from the *English*, and, by their Means, we have always been able to keep up our Heads against their Attacks.

We now come nearer home. We have had your Deeds interpreted to us, and we acknowledge them to be good and valid, and that the *Conestogoe* or *Sasquahannah Indians* had a Right to sell those Lands to you, for they were then theirs; but since that Time we have conquered them, and their Country now belongs to us, and the Lands we demanded Satisfaction for are no Part of the Lands comprized in those Deeds; they are the *Cohongorontas* Lands; those, we are sure, you have not possessed One Hundred Years, no, nor above Ten Years, and we made our Demands so soon as we knew your People were settled in those Parts. These have never been sold, but remain still to be disposed of; and we are well pleased to hear you are provided with Goods, and do assure you of our Willingness to treat with you for those unpurchased Lands; in Confirmation whereof, we present you with this Belt of Wampum.

Which was received with the usual Ceremonies.

6. Originally a name given to William Penn (1644–1718), the founder of Pennsylvania, "Brother Onas" was later used to refer to any governor of Pennsylvania. "Onas" means feather, and, by extension, a quill pen.

PONTIAC

Pontiac (1720?–1769) was an Ottawa Indian, born in the area between Lake Erie and Lake Huron, near present-day Detroit. "Ottawa" derives from the Algonquian word for commerce or trade, and in the eighteenth century the Ottawas had strong trading and diplomatic alliances with the French. But in 1760 the British defeated the French at Fort Detroit, and in 1762, Sir Jeffrey Amherst (1717–1797), commander-in-chief of British forces in North America, turned command of Detroit over to Henry Gladwin (1730–1791), a man who shared Amherst's contempt for Indians. Gladwin continued his predecessor's policies of refusing to supply food, arms, and, critically, gunpowder to the Indians as the French had done. He also discarded the French policy of treating Indians as allies in favor of treating them as subjects of the British Crown.

Pontiac is said to have given the speech printed here to an assembly of Ottawa, Huron, and Pottawatomi leaders on April 27, 1763. He relates the vision of Neolin, the Delaware prophet, who around 1760 began to preach the necessity of abandoning European customs and returning to traditional Native practices. Neolin's nativist message spread widely, catalyzing resistance to the expanding British presence that followed their defeat of the French. Pontiac does not seem to have encountered the Delaware prophet, but he knew Neolin's message, which led him to organize what non-Indians called a "conspiracy" against the British. He allegedly gave this speech to persuade other tribes to join the Ottawas in his resistance movement.

All reprintings of Pontiac's speech derive from Francis Parkman's *The Conspiracy of Pontiac* (1851). Parkman, a leading romantic historian, gives as his source for the speech the *"Pontiac, MS."* taken from the *"M'Dougal, MSS."* This information seems to point to Lieutenant John McDougall, who was intimately involved with the history of this period—indeed, he was taken prisoner by the Indians and managed to escape. But no manuscript by him has been found. Did McDougall hear Pontiac speak? If so, who translated and transcribed Pontiac's words? The historical record is silent. Pontiac's speech can be understood as a bicultural composite, on the assumption—a guess—that there is a strong likelihood that he spoke words to this effect based on his knowledge of the Delaware prophet.

Speech at Detroit

* * *

"A Delaware Indian," said Pontiac, "conceived an eager desire to learn wisdom from the Master of Life; but, being ignorant where to find him, he had recourse to fasting, dreaming, and magical incantations. By these means it was revealed to him, that, by moving forward in a straight, undeviating course, he would reach the abode of the Great Spirit. He told his purpose to no one; and having provided the equipments of a hunter,—gun, powderhorn, ammunition, and a kettle for preparing his food,—he set out on his errand. For some time he journeyed on in high hope and confidence. On the evening of the eighth day, he stopped by the side of a brook at the edge of a meadow, where he began to make ready his evening meal, when, looking up, he saw three large openings in the woods before him, and three well-beaten paths which entered them. He was much surprised; but his wonder increased, when, after it had grown dark, the three paths were more clearly

visible than ever. Remembering the important object of his journey, he could neither rest nor sleep; and, leaving his fire, he crossed the meadow, and entered the largest of the three openings. He had advanced but a short distance into the forest, when a bright flame sprang out of the ground before him, and arrested his steps. In great amazement, he turned back, and entered the second path, where the same wonderful phenomenon again encountered him; and now, in terror and bewilderment, yet still resolved to persevere, he took the last of the three paths. On this he journeyed a whole day without interruption, when at length, emerging from the forest, he saw before him a vast mountain, of dazzling whiteness. So precipitous was the ascent, that the Indian thought it hopeless to go farther, and looked around him in despair: at that moment, he saw, seated at some distance above, the figure of a beautiful woman arrayed in white who arose as he looked upon her, and thus accosted him: 'How can you hope, encumbered as you are, to succeed in your design? Go down to the foot of the mountain, throw away your gun, your ammunition, your provisions, and your clothing; wash yourself in the stream which flows there, and you will then be prepared to stand before the Master of Life.' The Indian obeyed, and again began to ascend among the rocks, while the woman, seeing him still discouraged, laughed at his faintness of heart, and told him that, if he wished for success, he must climb by the aid of one hand and one foot only. After great toil and suffering, he at length found himself at the summit. The woman had disappeared, and he was left alone. A rich and beautiful plain lay before him, and at a little distance he saw three great villages, far superior to the squalid wigwams of the Delawares. As he approached the largest, and stood hesitating whether he should enter, a man gorgeously attired stepped forth, and, taking him by the hand, welcomed him to the celestial abode. He then conducted him into the presence of the Great Spirit, where the Indian stood confounded at the unspeakable splendor which surrounded him. The Great Spirit bade him be seated, and thus addressed him:—

"'I am the Maker of heaven and earth, the trees, lakes, rivers, and all things else. I am the Maker of mankind; and because I love you, you must do my will. The land on which you live I have made for you, and not for others. Why do you suffer the white men to dwell among you? My children, you have forgotten the customs and traditions of your forefathers. Why do you not clothe yourselves in skins, as they did, and use the bows and arrows, and the stone-pointed lances, which they used? You have bought guns, knives, kettles, and blankets, from the white men, until you can no longer do without them; and, what is worse, you have drunk the poison fire-water, which turns you into fools. Fling all these things away; live as your wise forefathers lived before you. And as for these English,—these dogs dressed in red,[1] who have come to rob you of your hunting-grounds, and drive away the game,—you must lift the hatchet against them. Wipe them from the face of the earth, and then you will win my favor back again, and once more be happy and prosperous. The children of your great father, the King of France,[2] are not like the English. Never forget that they are your brethren. They are very dear to me, for they love the red men, and understand the true mode of worshiping me.'"

1. British soldiers wore red jackets. 2. Louis XV (1710–1774).

The Great Spirit next gave his hearer various precepts of morality and religion, such as the prohibition to marry more than one wife; and a warning against the practice of magic, which is worshipping the devil. A prayer, embodying the substance of all that he had heard, was then presented to the Delaware. It was cut in hieroglyphics upon a wooden stick, after the custom of his people; and he was directed to send copies of it to all the Indian villages.

* * *

LOGAN

Although he was a person of considerable renown, the exact origins and identity of the man known as Chief Logan (1725?–1780) are not entirely clear. He was a Mingo—the term widely used for Iroquoian Natives living outside their nations' homelands—of either Oneida or Cayuga background. His Indian name was probably Tachnedorus, but he was known in English as John Logan. In 1774 agents of Virginia governor Lord Dunmore provoked a brief "war" with the aim of appropriating Native lands. A particularly brutal event of this war was the Yellow Creek massacre, on the upper Ohio River. Daniel Greathouse led a party that killed and scalped nine Indians, among them Logan's pregnant sister, who was mutilated along with her unborn child. At the end of the war, Logan was asked to attend a treaty meeting with Dunmore. He refused, but apparently sent a message through John Gibson that eventually was transformed into a speech in English. Gibson, although married to Logan's sister, had fought against the Indians in this war (and lost his wife and unborn child; his daughter survived). He would have understood whichever Iroquoian language Logan spoke.

Thomas Jefferson said he heard Logan's speech directly from Gibson and that he wrote it down in his memo book. The speech first appeared in print in the *Pennsylvania Journal* on January 20, 1775, based on a copy sent by James Madison. (How Madison got the speech is unknown.) Jefferson's text is almost identical to the Madison version. The mystery surrounding the text deepens in light of the discrepancies between the historical facts as they have been uncovered and various statements attributed to Logan. Logan is said to have asserted that Michael Cresap perpetrated the massacre, not Daniel Greathouse. And while Logan claims to have no surviving kin, he was later killed by a nephew.

Jefferson included Logan's speech in "Query VI. Productions Mineral, Vegetable, and Animal" of *Notes on the State of Virginia* (1787). In that volume Jefferson argued that the American Indians were not inherently inferior to Europeans and offered a strong defense of their "genius," pointing especially to their capacity for noble oratory. To illustrate this claim, but also to confirm the notion that Indians were a "vanishing race," he quoted Chief Logan's speech. When skeptics asserted that the speech was a fraud, Jefferson printed twenty-three pages of affidavits testifying to its authenticity in the 1801 edition of *Notes*. Nonetheless, it remains unclear just how much of this speech represents words that Logan actually spoke. Known as "Logan's Lament," the speech became famous, appearing, for example, in the fourth and fifth editions of the *McGuffey Readers*, textbooks widely used in nineteenth-century classrooms. It is the most famous instance of Indian oratory as a popular nineteenth-century American literary genre.

From Chief Logan's Speech[1]

Notes on the State of Virginia, Query VI

* * *

I may challenge the whole orations of Demosthenes and Cicero,[2] and of any more eminent orator, if Europe has furnished more eminent, to produce a single passage, superior to the speech of Logan, a Mingo chief, to Lord Dunmore,[3] when governor of this state. And, as a testimony of their talents in this line, I beg leave to introduce it, first stating the incidents necessary for understanding it. In the spring of the year 1774, a robbery was committed by some Indians on certain land-adventurers on the river Ohio. The whites in that quarter, according to their custom, undertook to punish this outrage in a summary way. Captain Michael Cresap, and a certain Daniel Great-house,[4] leading on these parties, surprised, at different times, traveling and hunting parties of the Indians, having their women and children with them, and murdered many. Among these were unfortunately the family of Logan, a chief celebrated in peace and war, and long distinguished as the friend of the whites. This unworthy return provoked his vengeance. He accordingly signalized himself in the war which ensued. In the autumn of the same year a decisive battle was fought at the mouth of the Great Kanhaway, between the collected forces of the Shawanese, Mingoes, and Delawares, and a detachment of the Virginia militia. The Indians were defeated, and sued for peace. Logan however disdained to be seen among the suppliants. But, lest the sincerity of a treaty should be distrusted, from which so distinguished a chief absented himself, he sent by a messenger[5] the following speech to be delivered to Lord Dunmore.

"I appeal to any white man to say, if ever he entered Logan's cabin hungry, and he gave him not meat; if ever he came cold and naked, and he clothed him not. During the course of the last long and bloody war, Logan remained idle in his cabin, an advocate for peace. Such was my love for the whites, that my countrymen pointed as they passed, and said, 'Logan is the friend of white men.' I had even thought to have lived with you, but for the injuries of one man. Col. Cresap, the last spring, in cold blood, and unprovoked, murdered all the relations of Logan, not sparing even my women and children. There runs not a drop of my blood in the veins of any living creature. This called on me for revenge. I have sought it: I have killed many: I have fully glutted my vengeance. For my country, I rejoice at the beams of peace. But do not harbor a thought that mine is the joy of fear. Logan never felt fear. He will not turn on his heel to save his life. Who is there to mourn for Logan?—Not one."

1. The text is from Thomas Jefferson, *Notes on the State of Virginia* (1787), edited by William Peden (1954).
2. The two most renowned classical orators. Demosthenes (c. 385–322 B.C.E.) was an Athenian. Marcus Tullius Cicero (106–43 B.C.E.) was a Roman.
3. John Murray, Earl of Dunmore (1732–1809), was the colonial governor of Virginia from 1771 to 1775.
4. Maryland-born settler in Virginia (c. 1752–1775). Cresap (1724–1775), Maryland-born soldier and settler.
5. John Gibson (1740–1882), Pennsylvania-born soldier and settler.

CHEROKEE WOMEN

In traditional matriarchal Cherokee society, women held authority within their families, supervised land usage, occupied political offices such as Beloved Woman (or Ghighua), and participated in diplomacy. Motherhood was an organizing concept used to ground women's claims to power. The diplomatic rhetoric of Cherokee women often focused on the physical and emotional bonds between mothers and children as a compelling reason to sustain peaceful relations with rival powers. In this address of September 8, 1787, to Benjamin Franklin, then serving as the governor of Pennsylvania and as a delegate to the Constitutional Convention, several representatives of the Cherokee Women's Council ask Congress to pay attention to their desire for peace.

To Governor Benjamin Franklin[1]

Brother,

I am in hopes my Brothers & the Beloved men near the water side will heare from me. This day I filled the pipes that they smoaked in piece,[2] and I am in hopes the smoake has Reached up to the skies above. I here send you a piece of the same Tobacco, and am in hopes you & your Beloved men will smoake it in Friendship—and I am glad in my heart that I am the mother of men that will smoak it in piece.

Brother,

I am in hopes if you Rightly consider it that woman is the mother of All— and that woman Does not pull Children out of Trees or Stumps nor out of old Logs, but out of their Bodies, so that they ought to mind what a woman says, and look upon her as a mother—and I have Taken the privelage to Speak to you as my own Children, & the same as if you had sucked my Breast—and I am in hopes you have a beloved woman amongst you who will help to put her Children Right if they do wrong, as I shall do the same—the great men have all promised to Keep the path clear & straight, as my Children shall Keep the path clear & white so that the Messengers shall go & come in safety Between us—the old people is never done Talking to their Children—which makes me say so much as I do. The Talk you sent to me was to talk to my Children, which I have done this day, and they all liked my Talk well, which I am in hopes you will heare from me Every now & then that I keep my Children in piece—tho' I am a woman giving you this Talk, I am in hopes that you and all the Beloved men in Congress will pay particular Attention to it, as I am Delivering it to you from the Bottom of my heart, that they will Lay this on the white stool in Congress, wishing them all well & success in all their undertakings—I hold fast the good Talk I Received from you my Brother, & thanks you kindly for your good Talks, & your presents, & the kind usage you gave to my son.

From KATTEUHA, The Beloved woman of Chota.[3]

[Indorsed by Kaattahee, Scolecutta, and Kaattahee, Cherokee Indian Women.]

1. The text is from *Transatlantic Feminisms in the Age of Revolutions* (2012), edited by Lisa L. Moore, Joanna Brooks, and Caroline Wigginton.
2. I.e., peace (as in "keep my Children in piece," below).
3. Cherokee town in Tennessee. Katteuha's identity is unknown.

TECUMSEH

In 1846 the historian Henry Trumbull called Tecumseh (1775?–1813) "the most extraordinary Indian that has appeared in history." In 1961 the historian Alvin Josephy echoed Trumbull in denominating Tecumseh "the Greatest Indian." These high estimates are noteworthy in part because Tecumseh was unwaveringly hostile to the white Americans who relentlessly encroached on the lands of his people, the Shawnees, in areas of the Old Northwest Territory, present-day Ohio and Indiana. In the Treaty of Fort Wayne in 1809, the Shawnees—despite the opposition of Tecumseh and his charismatic brother, Tenkswatawa, known as the Prophet—ceded huge tracts of land to the United States. In response Tecumseh attempted to organize a multitribal resistance to the Americans. A turning point came in 1811, when William Henry Harrison (1773–1841), then governor of the Indiana Territory, decisively defeated the Prophet's forces at Tippecanoe (near present-day Lafayette). (In 1840, Harrison would be elected president of the United States, with James Tyler as his vice president, running on the slogan "Tippecanoe and Tyler too!") Tecumseh was not present at the battle. The defeat left the Prophet's followers disillusioned, and Tecumseh had no further success in bringing the tribes together in resistance. He fought on the side of the British in the War of 1812 and was killed at the Battle of the Thames, in southern Ontario.

The brief speech printed here derives from the captivity narrative of John Dunn Hunter, published in 1823. Hunter, born about 1802, was taken captive by Osage Indians when he was no more than two or three years old and lived among them until about 1816. He claimed to have heard Tecumseh speak to the Osages in 1811 or 1812. Although Tecumseh's visit to the Osages has not been substantiated, it is quite possible that he spoke to them and that the young and impressionable John Dunn Hunter was there. This bicultural composite was crafted by Hunter, who wrote that he was deeply moved by the words of "this untutored native of the forest . . . as no audience . . . either in ancient or modern times ever before witnessed."

Speech to the Osages[1]

When the Osages and distinguished strangers had assembled, Tecumseh arose; and after a pause of some minutes, in which he surveyed his audience in a very dignified, though respectfully complaisant and sympathizing manner, he commenced as follows:

Brothers—We all belong to one family; we are all children of the Great Spirit; we walk in the same path; slake our thirst at the same spring; and now affairs of the greatest concern lead us to smoke the pipe around the same council fire!

Brothers—We are friends; we must assist each other to bear our burdens. The blood of many of our fathers and brothers has run like water on the ground, to satisfy the avarice of the white men. We, ourselves, are threatened with a great evil; nothing will pacify them but the destruction of all the red men.

1. The text is from John Dunn Hunter, *Memoirs of a Captivity among the Indians of North America* (1823), edited by Richard Drinnon (1973).

Brothers—When the white men first set foot on our grounds, they were hungry; they had no place on which to spread their blankets, or to kindle their fires. They were feeble; they could do nothing for themselves. Our fathers commiserated their distress, and shared freely with them whatever the Great Spirit had given his red children. They gave them food when hungry, medicine when sick, spread skins for them to sleep on, and gave them grounds, that they might hunt and raise corn. Brothers, the white people are like poisonous serpents: when chilled, they are feeble and harmless; but invigorate them with warmth, and they sting their benefactors to death.

The white people came among us feeble; and now we have made them strong, they wish to kill us, or drive us back, as they would wolves and panthers.

Brothers—The white men are not friends to the Indians: at first, they only asked for land sufficient for a wigwam; now, nothing will satisfy them but the whole of our hunting grounds, from the rising to the setting sun.

Brothers—The white men want more than our hunting grounds; they wish to kill our warriors; they would even kill our old men, women, and little ones.

Brothers—Many winters ago, there was no land; the sun did not rise and set: all was darkness. The Great Spirit made all things. He gave the white people a home beyond the great waters. He supplied these grounds with game, and gave them to his red children; and he gave them strength and courage to defend them.

Brothers—My people wish for peace; the red men all wish for peace: but where the white people are, there is no peace for them, except it be on the bosom of our mother.[2]

Brothers—The white men despise and cheat the Indians; they abuse and insult them; they do not think the red men sufficiently good to live.

The red men have borne many and great injuries; they ought to suffer them no longer. My people will not; they are determined on vengeance; they have taken up the tomahawk; they will make it fat with blood; they will drink the blood of the white people.

Brothers—My people are brave and numerous; but the white people are too strong for them alone. I wish you to take up the tomahawk with them. If we all unite, we will cause the rivers to stain the great waters with their blood.

Brothers—If you do not unite with us, they will first destroy us, and then you will fall an easy prey to them. They have destroyed many nations of red men because they were not united, because they were not friends to each other.

Brothers—The white people send runners[3] amongst us; they wish to make us enemies, that they may sweep over and desolate our hunting grounds, like devastating winds, or rushing waters.

Brothers—Our Great Father, over the great waters, is angry with the white people, our enemies. He will send his brave warriors against them; he will send us rifles, and whatever else we want—he is our friend, and we are his children.

Brothers—Who are the white people that we should fear them? They cannot run fast, and are good marks to shoot at: they are only men; our

2. The earth. 3. Messengers.

fathers have killed many of them: we are not squaws, and we will stain the earth red with their blood.

Brothers—The Great Spirit is angry with our enemies; he speaks in thunder, and the earth swallows up villages, and drinks up the Mississippi. The great waters will cover their lowlands; their corn cannot grow; and the Great Spirit will sweep those who escape to the hills from the earth with his terrible breath.

Brothers—We must be united; we must smoke the same pipe; we must fight each other's battles; and more than all, we must love the Great Spirit: he is for us; he will destroy our enemies, and make all his red children happy.

WASHINGTON IRVING
1783–1859

Washington Irving had an unusually long and varied career, publishing his first satirical essays in 1802, when he was nineteen, and his last book, a five-volume life of George Washington, just a few months before he died at age seventy-six. Celebrated by Americans for his contributions to a burgeoning national literature, Irving also became the first American writer of the nineteenth century to achieve an international literary reputation. He created two of the most popular and enduring figures in American culture, Rip Van Winkle and Sleepy Hollow's Ichabod Crane, who figure in paintings, comic books, plays, films, and other media. Although he was regarded as a genial and comic writer, Irving regularly addressed darker and more complex themes of historical transformation and personal dislocation. His innovative travel sketches blurred the line between the personal essay and fiction, and he is considered one of the "inventors" of the modern short story. During a time in which there were no international copyright agreements, he managed to secure simultaneous British and American copyrights for his work. His canny understanding of the literary marketplace helped him to become the first American who was able to support himself solely through his writing.

Irving was born in New York City on April 3, 1783, the last of eleven children of a Scottish-born father and English-born mother. He read widely in English literature at home, modeling his early prose on *The Spectator*, a daily paper published in 1711–12 by Joseph Addison and Richard Steele. Among the many other writers he delighted in were Shakespeare, Oliver Goldsmith, and Laurence Sterne. His brothers enjoyed writing poems and essays as companionable recreation, and, inspired by their example, he wrote a series of satirical essays on the theater and New York society under the pseudonym "Jonathan Oldstyle." Nine of these essays were published in his brother Peter's newspaper, the *Morning Chronicle*, during 1802–03.

When Irving showed signs of tuberculosis in 1804, his brothers sent him abroad for a two-year tour of Europe. On his return in 1806, he studied law with Josiah Hoffman, a former New York State attorney general, and he was admitted to the bar soon afterward. More important for his literary career, he and his brother William (along with William's brother-in-law, James Kirke Paulding) started a satirical magazine, *Salmagundi* (the name of a spicy hash), which ran from 1807 to 1808 with poems, sketches, and essays on a range of topics. In 1808 Irving began work on *A*

History of New-York from the Beginning of the World to the End of the Dutch Dynasty, at first conceiving it as a parody of Samuel Lathem Mitchell's *The Picture of New-York* (1807), then taking on a variety of satiric targets, including President Thomas Jefferson (see his headnote, earlier in this volume), whom he portrayed as an early Dutch governor of New Amsterdam, William the Testy. Narrated by the comical invented character Diedrich Knickerbocker, who dabbles in historical research, *A History of New-York* (1809) brought Irving his first literary celebrity once his authorship of the pseudonymously published work was recognized. That same year Hoffman's daughter Matilda, to whom Irving was engaged, died suddenly from consumption. Most biographers attribute Irving's lifelong bachelorhood to his grief over Matilda's death. But her death freed him from the commitment he had made to her father to devote himself to the law, which he hated; and in the figure of his most famous alter ego, the genial bachelor Geoffrey Crayon, and even in his most famous fictional creation, Rip Van Winkle, there are hints that the single life suited Irving just fine.

In May 1815 Irving moved to Europe, and he remained there for seventeen years. At first he worked in Liverpool, England, with his brother Peter, an importer of English hardware, but in 1818, shortly after their mother died in New York, Peter went bankrupt. Grief-stricken, and yet grateful to be freed from the responsibilities of working for the family firm, Irving once again took up writing. He met the Scottish poet and novelist Sir Walter Scott, an admirer of the Knickerbocker *History*, who directed him to the wealth of unused literary material in German folktales. There, Irving found sources for tales such as "Rip Van Winkle" and "The Legend of Sleepy Hollow." Some passages of "Rip Van Winkle," for instance, closely paraphrase J. C. C. N. Otmar's "Peter Klaus" (1800), which also depicts a protagonist sleeping for twenty years. Irving began sending sections of *The Sketch Book* to the United States for publication in what would turn out to be seven installments published from 1819 to 1820. When the two-volume complete *Sketch Book* was printed in England in 1820, it made Irving even more famous and brought him the friendship of many of the leading British writers of the time. As Irving knew, part of his success derived from British reviewers' pleasure that a book by an American, as the Scottish literary critic Frances Jeffrey wrote in the *Edinburgh Review,* "should be written throughout with the greatest care and accuracy, and worked up to great purity and beauty of diction, on the model of the most elegant and polished of our native writers." Addison lay behind Irving's depiction of English country life, and Oliver Goldsmith influenced his sketch of Westminster Abbey. But among *The Sketch Book*'s graceful tributes to English scenes and characters were the two immensely popular tales set in rural New York, "Rip Van Winkle" and "The Legend of Sleepy Hollow," as well as "Traits of Indian Character" and "Philip of Pokanoket," a tribute to the Wampanoag leader who led the alliance against the English in 1675.

Irving's next two books, *Bracebridge Hall* (1822) and *Tales of a Traveller* (1824), were less successful, and in 1824 he accepted an invitation from the American minister to Spain to work with original manuscripts in Madrid to produce an account of Columbus's voyages. In 1828 he published *The Life and Voyages of Christopher Columbus*, which became the basis for standard schoolroom accounts of Columbus during the nineteenth and early twentieth centuries. Out of Irving's Spanish years came also *The Conquest of Granada* (1829), *Voyages and Discoveries of the Companions of Columbus* (1831), and *The Alhambra* (1832), which soon became known as "the Spanish *Sketch Book*."

In 1829 Irving was appointed secretary to the American legation in London. When he finally returned to the United States in 1832, critics wondered openly about whether this much admired "native" writer had become Europeanized. Setting out to reclaim his Americanness, Irving proclaimed his love for his country and headed west, taking a horseback journey into what is now Oklahoma. His trav-

els and research resulted in three major works on the American West: *A Tour of the Prairies* (1835); *Astoria* (1836), an account of John Jacob Astor's fur-trading colony in Oregon; and *The Adventures of Captain Bonneville, U.S.A.* (1837), a narrative of explorations in the Rockies and the Far West.

In the late 1830s Irving bought and began refurbishing a house near Tarrytown, along the Hudson River, north of New York City. But before settling down, in 1842 he accepted an appointment as minister to Spain and returned to Europe, spending four years in Madrid. After his return to the United States in 1846, he arranged with G.P. Putnam to publish a collected edition of his writings; he also prepared a biography of Oliver Goldsmith (1849). Irving's main work after 1850 was his long-contemplated life of George Washington, which he regarded as his greatest literary accomplishment. He collapsed just after finishing the last of its five volumes, and he died a few months later, on November 28, 1859.

Cooper, Hawthorne, and many other American writers were inspired by the success of *The Sketch Book*. Although Melville, in his essay on Hawthorne's *Mosses from an Old Manse*, declared his preference for creative geniuses over adept imitators such as Irving, he could not escape Irving's influence, which emerges both in his short stories and in a late poem, "Rip Van Winkle's Lilacs." From the beginning, many readers identified with Rip as a counterhero, an anti–Benjamin Franklin who made a success of failure. Subsequent generations have also responded profoundly to Irving's pervasive theme of mutability, especially his portrayal of the bewildering rapidity of change in American life.

From A History of New-York from the Beginning of the World to the End of the Dutch Dynasty, by Diedrich Knickerbocker[1]

New Amsterdam. An etching from around 1640 shows the colony when it was under Dutch government.

Book II

Treating of the first settlement of the province of Nieuw Nederlants.

CHAP. I

How Master Hendrick Hudson,[2] *voyaging in search of a north-west passage discovered the famous bay of New York, and likewise the great river Mohegan—*

1. The text is from Diedrich Knickerbocker [Washington Irving], *A History of New-York, from the Beginning of the World to the End of the Dutch Dynasty*, Vol. 1 (1809).

2. I.e., Sir Henry Hudson (d. 1611), English sea explorer who navigated in the New York area as an employee of the Dutch East India Company, a trading company in Amsterdam, Holland.

and how he was magnificently rewarded by the munificence of their High Mightinesses.

In the ever memorable year of our Lord 1609, on the five and twentieth day of March (O. S.)—a fine Saturday morning, when jocund Phœbus,[3] having his face newly washed, by gentle dews and spring time showers, looked from the glorious windows of the east, with a more than usually shining countenance—"that worthy and irrecoverable discoverer, Master Henry Hudson" set sail from Holland in a stout vessel,[4] called the Half Moon, being employed by the Dutch East India Company, to seek a north-west passage to China.

Of this celebrated voyage we have a narration still extant, written with true log-book brevity, by master Robert Juet of Lime house,[5] mate of the vessel; who was appointed historian of the voyage, partly on account of his uncommon literary talents, but chiefly, as I am credibly informed, because he was a countryman and schoolfellow of the great Hudson, with whom he had often played truant and sailed chip boats, when he was a little boy. I am enabled however to supply the deficiencies of master Juet's journal, by certain documents furnished me by very respectable Dutch families, as likewise by sundry family traditions, handed down from my great great Grandfather, who accompanied the expedition in the capacity of cabin boy.

From all that I can learn, few incidents worthy of remark happened in the voyage; and it mortifies me exceedingly that I have to admit so noted an expedition into my work, without making any more of it.—Oh! that I had the advantages of that most authentic writer of yore, Apollonius Rhodius,[6] who in his account of the famous Argonautic expedition, has the whole mythology at his disposal, and elevates Jason and his compeers into heroes and demi-gods; though all the world knows them to have been a mere gang of sheep stealers, on a marauding expedition—or that I had the privileges of Dan Homer and Dan Virgil to enliven my narration, with giants and Lystrigo-nians;[7] to entertain our honest mariners with an occasional concert of syrens and mermaids, and now and then with the rare shew of honest old Nep-tune[8] and his fleet of frolicksome cruisers. But alas! the good old times have long gone by, when your waggish deities would descend upon the ter-raqueous globe, in their own proper persons, and play their pranks, upon its wondering inhabitants. Neptune has proclaimed an embargo in his domin-ions, and the sturdy tritons, like disbanded sailors, are out of employ, unless old Charon[9] has charitably taken them into his service, to sound their

3. The Greek sun god. "O. S." (Old Style): refers to the Julian calendar, which was used in Britain until 1752, when the Gregorian calendar was adopted. In the Julian system, the year began on March 25.

4. "Ogilvie calls it a frigate" [Irving's note]; elsewhere, Irving references Ogilvie's *History of America*—probably *America: Being an Accurate Description of the New World* (1671), by Arnoldus Montanus (1625?–1683) and John Ogilby (1600–1676). A frigate is a light, fast vessel for rowing or sailing.

5. A district in east London. Juet, whose narrative is excerpted in this volume, helped lead a mutiny that resulted in Hudson's being set adrift

in a boat, never to be seen again.

6. Author (third century B.C.E.) of *The Argonautica*, an epic poem about the quest for the Golden Fleece.

7. In Greek mythology, a tribe of giant canni-bals. "Dan Homer and Dan Virgil": authors, respectively, of the ancient Greek epics *Iliad* and *Odyssey* and of *Aeneid*, the epic of Rome's found-ing. "Dan" is an archaic equivalent of "Sir."

8. The Roman god of the sea. "Syrens": i.e., Sirens; creatures in Greek mythology famed for their seductive songs.

9. In Greek mythology, the ferryman to the underworld. "Tritons": Greek gods, sons of Po-seidon (the Greek version of Neptune).

conchs, and ply as his ferry-men. Certain it is, no mention has been made of them by any of our modern navigators, who are not behind their ancient predecessors in tampering with the marvelous—nor has any notice been taken of them, in that most minute and authentic chronicle of the seas, the New York Gazette[1] edited by Solomon Lang. Even Castor and Pollux,[2] those flaming meteors that blaze at the masthead of tempest tost vessels, are rarely beheld in these degenerate days—and it is but now and then, that our worthy sea captains fall in with that portentous phantom of the seas, that terror to all experienced mariners, that shadowy spectrum of the night— the flying Dutchman![3]

Suffice it then to say, the voyage was prosperous and tranquil—the crew being a patient people, much given to slumber and vacuity, and but little troubled with the disease of thinking—a malady of the mind, which is the sure breeder of discontent. Hudson had laid in abundance of gin and sour crout,[4] and every man was allowed to sleep quietly at his post, unless the wind blew. True it is, some slight dissatisfaction was shewn on two or three occasions, at certain unreasonable conduct of Commodore Hudson. Thus for instance, he forbore to shorten sail[5] when the wind was light, and the weather serene, which was considered among the most experienced Dutch seamen, as certain *weather breeders*, or prognostics, that the weather would change for the worse. He acted, moreover, in direct contradiction to that ancient and sage rule of the Dutch navigators, who always took in sail at night—put the helm a-port,[6] and turned in—by which precaution they had a good night's rest—were sure of knowing where they were the next morning, and stood but little chance of running down a continent in the dark. He likewise prohibited the seamen from wearing more than five jackets, and six pair of breeches, under pretence of rendering them more alert;[7] and no man was permitted to go aloft, and hand in sails,[8] with a pipe in his mouth, as is the invariable Dutch custom, at the present day—All these grievances, though they might ruffle for a moment, the constitutional tranquility of the honest Dutch tars,[9] made but transient impression; they eat hugely, drank profusely, and slept immeasurably, and being under the especial guidance of providence, the ship was safely conducted to the coast of America; where, after sundry unimportant touching and standings off and on, she at length, on the fourth day of September entered that majestic bay, which at this day expands its ample bosom, before the city of New York, and which had never before been visited by any European.

True it is—and I am not ignorant of the fact, that in a certain apocryphal book of voyages, complied by one Hacluyt, is to be found a letter written to Francis the First, by one Giovanne, or John Verazzani,[1] on which

1. Manhattan's first newspaper, which began publishing in 1725.
2. Twins who feature in Greek and Roman mythology.
3. Fabled ghost ship that sails endlessly, unable to come into port.
4. I.e., sauerkraut.
5. Take in part of the sail.
6. Position the tiller (i.e., the helm) to the left (port) side of the ship.
7. Hudson prevented his men from wearing extra clothing for warmth; he wanted them to be chilly so they would stay awake.

8. Climb into the rigging to take down sails.
9. Sailors (from "tarpaulins," an archaic term for "sailors").
1. I.e., Giovanni da Verrazzano (c. 1485–c. 1528), Italian explorer employed by Francis I (1494–1547), king of France 1515–47, to chart the eastern coast of North America from the Carolinas to New Foundland. He entered New York harbor in 1524. "Hacluyt": i.e., Richard Hakluyt (c. 1552–1616), English geographer and proponent of English settlement in the Americas, who published important collections of writings about European exploration in the hemisphere.

some writers are inclined to found a belief that this delightful bay had been visited nearly a century previous to the voyage of the enterprising Hudson. Now this (albeit it has met with the countenance of certain very judicious and learned men) I hold in utter disbelief, and that for various good and substantial reasons—*First*, Because on strict examination it will be found, that the description given by this Verazzani, applies about as well to the bay of New York, as it does to my night cap—*Secondly*, Because that this John Verazzani, for whom I already begin to feel a most bitter enmity, is a native of Florence; and every body knows the crafty wiles of these lose Florentines, by which they filched away the laurels, from the arms of the immortal Colon, (vulgarly called Columbus) and bestowed them on their officious townsman, Amerigo Vespucci[2]—and I make no doubt they are equally ready to rob the illustrious Hudson, of the credit of discovering this beauteous island, adorned by the city of New York, and placing it beside their usurped discovery of South America. And *thirdly*, I award my decision in favour of the pretensions of Hendrick Hudson, inasmuch as his expedition sailed from Holland, being truly and absolutely a Dutch enterprize—and though all the proofs in the world were introduced on the other side, I would set them at naught as undeserving my attention. If these three reasons are not sufficient to satisfy every burgher[3] of this ancient city—all I can say is, they are degenerate descendants from their venerable Dutch ancestors, and totally unworthy the trouble of convincing. Thus, therefore, the title of Hendrick Hudson, to his renowned discovery is fully vindicated.

It has been traditionary in our family, that when the great navigator was first blessed with a view of this enchanting island, he was observed, for the first and only time in his life, to exhibit strong symptoms of astonishment and admiration. He is said to have turned to master Juet, and uttered these remarkable words, while he pointed towards this paradise of the new world—"see! there!"—and thereupon, as was always his way when he was uncommonly pleased, he did puff out such clouds of dense tobacco smoke, that in one minute the vessel was out of sight of land, and master Juet was fain to wait, until the winds dispersed this impenetrable fog.

It was indeed—as my great great grandfather used to say—though in truth I never heard him, for he died, as might be expected, before I was born.—"It was indeed a spot, on which the eye might have reveled forever, in ever new and never ending beauties." The island of Manna-hata, spread wide before them, like some sweet vision of fancy, or some fair creation of industrious magic. Its hills of smiling green swelled gently one above another, crowned with lofty trees of luxuriant growth; some pointing their tapering foliage towards the clouds, which were gloriously transparent; and others, loaded with a verdant burthen of clambering vines, bowing their branches to the earth, that was covered with flowers. On the gentle declivities of the hills were scattered in gay profusion, the dog wood, the sumach, and the wild briar, whose scarlet berries and white blossoms glowed brightly among the deep green of the surrounding foliage; and here and there, a curling column of smoke rising from the little glens that opened along the shore,

2. Florentine explorer (1454–1512) after whom America was named in 1507. "Laurels": honors; from the ancient practice of bestowing crowns of laurels as honors. "Colon": i.e., Cristóbal Colón, the Spanish rendering of the name of Christopher Columbus (1451–1506).
3. Citizen.

seemed to promise the weary voyagers, a welcome at the hands of their fellow creatures. As they stood gazing with entranced attention on the scene before them, a red man crowned with feathers, issued from one of these glens, and after contemplating in silent wonder, the gallant ship, as she sat like a stately swan swimming on a silver lake, sounded the war-whoop, and bounded into the woods, like a wild deer, to the utter astonishment of the phlegmatic Dutchmen, who had never heard such a noise, or witnessed such a caper in their whole lives.

Of the transactions of our adventurers with the savages, and how the latter smoked copper pipes, and eat dried currants; how they brought great store of tobacco and oysters; how they shot one of the ship's crew, and how he was buried, I shall say nothing, being that I consider them unimportant to my history. After tarrying a few days in the bay, in order to smoke their pipes and refresh themselves after their sea-faring, our voyagers weighed anchor, and adventurously ascended a mighty river which emptied into the bay. This river it is said was known among the savages by the name of the *Shatemuck*; though we are assured in an excellent little history published in 1674, by John Josselyn, Gent. that it was called the *Mohegan*,[4] and master Richard Bloome,[5] who wrote some time afterwards, asserts the same—so that I very much incline in favour of the opinion of these two honest gentlemen. Be this as it may, the river is at present denominated the Hudson; and up this stream the shrewd Hendrick had very little doubt he should discover the much looked for passage to China!

The journal goes on to make mention of divers[6] interviews between the crew and the natives, in the voyage up the river, but as they would be impertinent to my history, I shall pass them over in silence, except the following dry joke, played off by the old commodore and his school-fellow Robert Juet; which does such vast credit to their experimental philosophy, that I cannot refrain from inserting it. "Our master and his mate determined to try some of the chiefe men of the countrey, whether they had any treacherie in them. So they tooke them downe into the cabin and gave them so much wine and acqua vitæ[7] that they were all merrie; and one of them had his wife with him, which sate so modestly, as any of our countrey women would do in a strange place. In the end, one of them was drunke, which had been aboarde of our ship all the time that we had beene there, and that was strange to them, for they could not tell how to take it."[8]

Having satisfied himself by this profound experiment, that the natives were an honest, social race of jolly roysters,[9] who had no objection to a drinking bout, and were very merry in their cups, the old commodore chuckled hugely to himself, and thrusting a double quid of tobacco in his cheek, directed master Juet to have it carefully recorded, for the satisfaction of all

4. "This river is likewise laid down in Ogilvy's map as Manhattan—Noordt—Montaigne and Mauritius river" [Irving's note]. The reference is to various names given to the Hudson River. John Josselyn (1608–1675), English traveler, author of *Account of Two Voyages to New-England Made during the Years 1638, 1663* (1674).
5. I.e., Richard Blome (1635–1705), London publisher of cartographic and illustrated books, including a world atlas.
6. Various.
7. I.e., aqua vitae: strong liquor, such as brandy.
8. "Juet's Journ. Purch. Pil." [Irving's note]. The passage from Juet's journal appears in this volume's selection. The other work referenced is *Purchas His Pilgrimage,* a compendium of travel writings by the English cleric Samuel Purchas (c. 1575–1626).
9. I.e., roisters: riotous people.

the natural philosophers of the university of Leyden[1]—which done, he proceeded on his voyage, with great self-complacency. After sailing, however, above an hundred miles up the river, he found the watery world around him, began to grow more shallow and confined, the current more rapid and perfectly fresh—phenomena not uncommon in the ascent of rivers, but which puzzled the honest Dutchmen prodigiously. A consultation of our modern Argonauts was therefore called, and having deliberated full six hours, they were brought to a determination, by the ship's running aground—whereupon they unanimously concluded, that there was but little chance of getting to China in this direction. A boat, however, was dispatched to explore higher up the river, which on its return, confirmed the opinion— upon this the ship was warped off and put about, with great difficulty, being like most of her sex,[2] exceedingly hard to govern; and the adventurous Hudson, according to the account of my great great grandfather, returned down the river—with a prodigious flea in his ear!

Being satisfied that there was little likelihood of getting to China, unless like the blind man, he returned from whence he sat out and took a fresh start; he forthwith re-crossed the sea to Holland, where he was received with great welcome by the honourable East India Company, who were very much rejoiced to see him come back safe—with their ship; and at a large and respectable meeting of the first merchants and burgomasters[3] of Amsterdam, it was unanimously determined, that as a munificent reward for the eminent services he had performed, and the important discovery he had made, the great river Mohegan should be called after his name!—and it continues to be called Hudson river unto this very day.

1809

Rip Van Winkle[1]

The following Tale was found among the papers of the late Diedrich Knickerbocker, an old gentleman of New-York, who was very curious in the Dutch history of the province, and the manners of the descendants from its primitive settlers. His historical researches, however, did not lay so much among books, as among men; for the former are lamentably scanty on his favourite topics; whereas he found the old burghers, and still more, their wives, rich in that legendary lore, so invaluable to true history. Whenever, therefore, he happened upon a genuine Dutch family, snugly shut up in its low-roofed farm house, under a spreading sycamore, he looked upon it as a little clasped volume of black-letter,[2] and studied it with the zeal of a bookworm.

The result of all these researches was a history of the province, during the reign of the Dutch governors, which he published some years since.

1. City in the Netherlands (where the Pilgrims settled in 1609, before eventually leaving for New England).
2. Ships traditionally are characterized as female.
3. Chief magistrates; more generally, leading citizens.

1. The text is from the first installment of *The Sketch Book* (May 1819).
2. Typeface in early printed books, resembling medieval script; such books, because of their value, were often equipped with clasps so they could be shut tightly and even locked.

There have been various opinions as to the literary character of his work, and, to tell the truth, it is not a whit better than it should be. Its chief merit is its scrupulous accuracy, which, indeed, was a little questioned, on its first appearance, but has since been completely established; and it is now admitted into all historical collections, as a book of unquestionable authority.[3]

The old gentleman died shortly after the publication of his work, and now, that he is dead and gone, it cannot do much harm to his memory, to say, that his time might have been much better employed in weightier labours. He, however, was apt to ride his hobby his own way; and though it did now and then kick up the dust a little in the eyes of his neighbours, and grieve the spirit of some friends, for whom he felt the truest deference and affection; yet his errors and follies are remembered "more in sorrow than in anger,"[4] and it begins to be suspected, that he never intended to injure or offend. But however his memory may be appreciated by critics, it is still held dear among many folk, whose good opinion is well worth having; particularly certain biscuit bakers, who have gone so far as to imprint his likeness on their new year cakes, and have thus given him a chance for immortality, almost equal to being stamped on a Waterloo medal, or a Queen Anne's farthing.[5]

Rip Van Winkle
A Posthumous Writing of Diedrich Knickerbocker

> By Woden, God of Saxons,
> From whence comes Wensday, that is Wodensday,
> Truth is a thing that ever I will keep
> Unto thylke day in which I creep into
> My sepulchre—
> —CARTWRIGHT[6]

Whoever has made a voyage up the Hudson, must remember the Kaatskill mountains.[7] They are a dismembered branch of the great Appalachian family, and are seen away to the west of the river, swelling up to a noble height, and lording it over the surrounding country. Every change of season, every change of weather, indeed, every hour of the day, produces some change in the magical hues and shapes of these mountains, and they are regarded by all the good wives, far and near, as perfect barometers. When the weather is fair and settled, they are clothed in blue and purple, and print their bold outlines on the clear evening sky; but some times, when the rest of the landscape is cloudless, they will gather a hood of gray vapours about their summits, which, in the last rays of the setting sun, will glow and light up like a crown of glory.

3. Irving comically alludes to the deliberate inaccuracies of his/Knickerbocker's *History of New-York* (see above).
4. Shakespeare's *Hamlet* 1.2.231. To this quotation Irving appended the following footnote: "Vide [see] the excellent discourse of G. C. Verplanck, Esq. before the New-York Historical Society." If Irving's friend Gulian C. Verplanck ever made such an address about a fictional character, it would have been in fun.
5. Waterloo medals were minted liberally after the defeat there of Napoléon Bonaparte (1769–1821), emperor of France, in 1815. Farthings (tiny coins) from the reign of Anne (1665–1714), queen of Great Britain 1702–14, were commonly but wrongly considered rare.
6. From the play *The Ordinary* 3.1.1050–54, by the English writer William Cartwright (1611–1643). "Woden": Old English for "Odin," the chief Norse god.
7. Catskill Mountains, a range in southeastern New York.

At the foot of these fairy mountains, the voyager may have descried the light smoke curling up from a village, whose shingle roofs gleam among the trees, just where the blue tints of the upland melt away into the fresh green of the nearer landscape. It is a little village of great antiquity, having been founded by some of the Dutch colonists, in the early times of the province, just about the beginning of the government of the good Peter Stuyvesant,[8] (may he rest in peace!) and there were some of the houses of the original settlers standing within a few years, with lattice windows, gable fronts surmounted with weathercocks, and built of small yellow bricks brought from Holland.

In that same village, and in one of these very houses, (which, to tell the precise truth, was sadly time worn and weather beaten,) there lived many years since, while the country was yet a province of Great Britain, a simple good natured fellow, of the name of Rip Van Winkle. He was a descendant of the Van Winkles who figured so gallantly in the chivalrous days of Peter Stuyvesant, and accompanied him to the siege of Fort Christina. He inherited, however, but little of the martial character of his ancestors. I have observed that he was a simple good natured man; he was moreover a kind neighbour, and an obedient, henpecked husband. Indeed, to the latter circumstance might be owing that meekness of spirit which gained him such universal popularity; for those men are most apt to be obsequious and conciliating abroad, who are under the discipline of shrews at home. Their tempers, doubtless, are rendered pliant and malleable in the fiery furnace of domestic tribulation, and a curtain lecture[9] is worth all the sermons in the world for teaching the virtues of patience and long suffering. A termagant[1] wife may, therefore, in some respects, be considered a tolerable blessing; and if so, Rip Van Winkle was thrice blessed.

Certain it is, that he was a great favourite among all the good wives of the village, who, as usual with the amiable sex, took his part in all family squabbles, and never failed, whenever they talked those matters over in their evening gossippings, to lay all the blame on Dame Van Winkle. The children of the village, too, would shout with joy whenever he approached. He assisted at their sports, made their playthings, taught them to fly kites and shoot marbles, and told them long stories of ghosts, witches, and Indians. Whenever he went dodging about the village, he was surrounded by a troop of them, hanging on his skirts, clambering on his back, and playing a thousand tricks on him with impunity; and not a dog would bark at him throughout the neighbourhood.

The great error in Rip's composition was an insuperable aversion to all kinds of profitable labour. It could not be for the want of assiduity or perseverance; for he would sit on a wet rock, with a rod as long and heavy as a Tartar's[2] lance, and fish all day without a murmur, even though he should not be encouraged by a single nibble. He would carry a fowling piece on his shoulder, for hours together, trudging through woods and swamps, and up

8. Last governor of the Dutch province of New Netherlands (1592–1672); in 1655 (as mentioned in the next paragraph), his troops defeated Swedish colonists at Fort Christina, near what is now Wilmington, Delaware.
9. Archaic term for when a wife says no to her husband's sexual entreaties after the curtains around the four-poster bed have been drawn for the night.
1. Harsh-tempered; nagging.
2. Refers to medieval warriors of northern and central Asia.

hill and down dale, to shoot a few squirrels or wild pigeons. He would never even refuse to assist a neighbour in the roughest toil, and was a foremost man at all country frolicks for husking Indian corn, or building stone fences; the women of the village, too, used to employ him to run their errands, and to do such little odd jobs as their less obliging husbands would not do for them;— in a word, Rip was ready to attend to any body's business but his own; but as to doing family duty, and keeping his farm in order, it was impossible.

In fact, he declared it was no use to work on his farm; it was the most pestilent little piece of ground in the whole country; every thing about it went wrong, and would go wrong, in spite of him. His fences were continually falling to pieces; his cow would either go astray, or get among the cabbages; weeds were sure to grow quicker in his fields than any where else; the rain always made a point of setting in just as he had some out-door work to do. So that though his patrimonial estate had dwindled away under his management, acre by acre, until there was little more left than a mere patch of Indian corn and potatoes, yet it was the worst conditioned farm in the neighbourhood.

His children, too, were as ragged and wild as if they belonged to nobody. His son Rip, an urchin begotten in his own likeness, promised to inherit the habits, with the old clothes of his father. He was generally seen trooping like a colt at his mother's heels, equipped in a pair of his father's cast-off galligaskins,[3] which he had much ado to hold up with one hand, as a fine lady does her train in bad weather.

Rip Van Winkle, however, was one of those happy mortals, of foolish, well-oiled dispositions, who take the world easy, eat white bread or brown, which ever can be got with least thought or trouble, and would rather starve on a penny than work for a pound. If left to himself, he would have whistled life away, in perfect contentment; but his wife kept continually dinning in his ears about his idleness, his carelessness, and the ruin he was bringing on his family. Morning, noon, and night, her tongue was incessantly going, and every thing he said or did was sure to produce a torrent of household eloquence. Rip had but one way of replying to all lectures of the kind, and that, by frequent use, had grown into a habit. He shrugged his shoulders, shook his head, cast up his eyes, but said nothing. This, however, always provoked a fresh volley from his wife, so that he was fain to draw off his forces, and take to the outside of the house—the only side which, in truth, belongs to a henpecked husband.

Rip's sole domestic adherent was his dog Wolf, who was as much henpecked as his master; for Dame Van Winkle regarded them as companions in idleness, and even looked upon Wolf with an evil eye, as the cause of his master's so often going astray. True it is, in all points of spirit befitting an honourable dog, he was as courageous an animal as ever scoured the woods—but what courage can withstand the ever-during and all-besetting terrors of a woman's tongue? The moment Wolf entered the house, his crest fell, his tail drooped to the ground, or curled between his legs, he sneaked about with a gallows air, casting many a sidelong glance at Dame Van Winkle, and at the least flourish of a broomstick or ladle, would fly to the door with yelping precipitation.

3. Loose, wide trousers.

Times grew worse and worse with Rip Van Winkle as years of matrimony rolled on; a tart temper never mellows with age, and a sharp tongue is the only edge tool that grows keener by constant use. For a long while he used to console himself, when driven from home, by frequenting a kind of perpetual club of the sages, philosophers, and other idle personages of the village, that held its sessions on a bench before a small inn, designated by a rubicund portrait of his majesty George the Third.[4] Here they used to sit in the shade, of a long lazy summer's day, talk listlessly over village gossip, or tell endless sleepy stories about nothing. But it would have been worth any statesman's money to have heard the profound discussions that sometimes took place, when by chance an old newspaper fell into their hands, from some passing traveler. How solemnly they would listen to the contents, as drawled out by Derrick Van Bummel, the schoolmaster, a dapper learned little man, who was not to be daunted by the most gigantic word in the dictionary; and how sagely they would deliberate upon public events some months after they had taken place.

The opinions of this junto[5] were completely controlled by Nicholas Vedder, a patriarch of the village, and landlord of the inn, at the door of which he took his seat from morning till night, just moving sufficiently to avoid the sun, and keep in the shade of a large tree; so that the neighbours could tell the hour by his movements as accurately as by a sun dial. It is true, he was rarely heard to speak, but smoked his pipe incessantly. His adherents, however, (for every great man has his adherents,) perfectly understood him, and knew how to gather his opinions. When any thing that was read or related displeased him, he was observed to smoke his pipe vehemently, and send forth short, frequent, and angry puffs; but when pleased, he would inhale the smoke slowly and tranquilly, and emit it in light and placid clouds, and sometimes taking the pipe from his mouth, and letting the fragrant vapour curl about his nose, would gravely nod his head in token of perfect approbation.

From even this strong hold the unlucky Rip was at length routed by his termagant wife, who would suddenly break in upon the tranquillity of the assemblage, call the members all to nought, nor was that august personage, Nicholas Vedder himself, sacred from the daring tongue of this terrible virago, who charged him outright with encouraging her husband in habits of idleness.

Poor Rip was at last reduced almost to despair; and his only alternative to escape from the labour of the farm and the clamour of his wife, was to take gun in hand, and stroll away into the woods. Here he would sometimes seat himself at the foot of a tree, and share the contents of his wallet[6] with Wolf, with whom he sympathized as a fellow sufferer in persecution. "Poor Wolf," he would say, "thy mistress leads thee a dogs' life of it; but never mind, my lad, while I live thou shalt never want a friend to stand by thee!" Wolf would wag his tail, look wistfully in his master's face, and if dogs can feel pity, I verily believe he reciprocated the sentiment with all his heart.

In a long ramble of the kind on a fine autumnal day, Rip had unconsciously scrambled to one of the highest parts of the Kaatskill mountains.

4. King of Great Britain (1738–1820; reigned 1760–1820).

5. Ruling committee (Spanish).

6. Knapsack.

He was after his favourite sport of squirrel shooting, and the still solitudes had echoed and re-echoed with the reports of his gun. Panting and fatigued, he threw himself, late in the afternoon, on a green knoll, covered with mountain herbage, that crowned the brow of a precipice. From an opening between the trees, he could overlook all the lower country for many a mile of rich woodland. He saw at a distance the lordly Hudson, far, far below him, moving on its silent but majestic course, the reflection of a purple cloud, or the sail of a lagging bark, here and there sleeping on its glassy bosom, and at last losing itself in the blue highlands.

On the other side he looked down into a deep mountain glen, wild, lonely, and shagged, the bottom filled with fragments from the impending cliffs, and scarcely lighted by the reflected rays of the setting sun. For some time Rip lay musing on this scene, evening was gradually advancing, the mountains began to throw their long blue shadows over the valleys, he saw that it would be dark long before he could reach the village, and he heaved a heavy sigh when he thought of encountering the terrors of Dame Van Winkle.

As he was about to descend, he heard a voice from a distance, hallooing, "Rip Van Winkle! Rip Van Winkle!" He looked around, but could see nothing but a crow winging its solitary flight across the mountain. He thought his fancy must have deceived him, and turned again to descend, when he heard the same cry ring through the still evening air; "Rip Van Winkle! Rip Van Winkle!"—at the same time Wolf bristled up his back, and giving a low growl, skulked to his master's side, looking fearfully down into the glen. Rip now felt a vague apprehension stealing over him; he looked anxiously in the same direction, and perceived a strange figure slowly toiling up the rocks, and bending under the weight of something he carried on his back. He was surprised to see any human being in this lonely and unfrequented place, but supposing it to be some one of the neighbourhood in need of his assistance, he hastened down to yield it.

On nearer approach, he was still more surprised at the singularity of the stranger's appearance. He was a short square built old fellow, with thick bushy hair, and a grizzled beard. His dress was of the antique Dutch fashion—a cloth jerkin[7] strapped round the waist—several pair of breeches, the outer one of ample volume, decorated with rows of buttons down the sides, and bunches at the knees. He bore on his shoulder a stout keg, that seemed full of liquor, and made signs for Rip to approach and assist him with the load. Though rather shy and distrustful of this new acquaintance, Rip complied with his usual alacrity, and mutually relieving each other, they clambered up a narrow gully, apparently the dry bed of a mountain torrent. As they ascended, Rip every now and then heard long rolling peals, like distant thunder, that seemed to issue out of a deep ravine, or rather cleft between lofty rocks, toward which their rugged path conducted. He paused for an instant, but supposing it to be the muttering of one of those transient thunder showers which often take place in mountain heights, he proceeded. Passing through the ravine, they came to a hollow, like a small amphitheatre, surrounded by perpendicular precipices, over the brinks of which impending trees shot their branches, so that you only caught glimpses of the azure sky, and the bright evening cloud. During the whole time, Rip and his companion

7. Jacket fitted tightly at the waist.

had labored on in silence; for though the former marveled greatly what could be the object of carrying a keg of liquor up this wild mountain, yet there was something strange and incomprehensible about the unknown, that inspired awe, and checked familiarity.

On entering the amphitheatre, new objects of wonder presented themselves. On a level spot in the centre was a company of odd-looking personages playing at nine-pins. They were dressed in a quaint, outlandish fashion: some wore short doublets,[8] others jerkins, with long knives in their belts, and most had enormous breeches, of similar style with that of the guide's. Their visages, too, were peculiar: one had a large head, broad face, and small piggish eyes; the face of another seemed to consist entirely of nose, and was surmounted by a white sugarloaf hat, set off with a little red cockstail.[9] They all had beards, of various shapes and colours. There was one who seemed to be the commander. He was a stout old gentleman, with a weather-beaten countenance; he wore a laced doublet, broad belt and hanger,[1] high crowned hat and feather, red stockings, and high heeled shoes, with roses in them. The whole group reminded Rip of the figures in an old Flemish painting, in the parlour of Dominie[2] Van Schaick, the village parson, and which had been brought over from Holland at the time of the settlement.

What seemed particularly odd to Rip, was, that though these folks were evidently amusing themselves, yet they maintained the gravest faces, the most mysterious silence, and were, withal, the most melancholy party of pleasure he had ever witnessed. Nothing interrupted the stillness of the scene, but the noise of the balls, which, whenever they were rolled, echoed along the mountains like rumbling peals of thunder.

As Rip and his companion approached them, they suddenly desisted from their play, and stared at him with such fixed statue-like gaze, and such strange, uncouth, lack lustre countenances, that his heart turned within him, and his knees smote together. His companion now emptied the contents of the keg into large flagons, and made signs to him to wait upon the company. He obeyed with fear and trembling; they quaffed the liquor in profound silence, and then returned to their game.

By degrees, Rip's awe and apprehension subsided. He even ventured, when no eye was fixed upon him, to taste the beverage, which he found had much of the flavor of excellent Hollands.[3] He was naturally a thirsty soul, and was soon tempted to repeat the draught. One taste provoked another, and he reiterated his visits to the flagon so often, that at length his senses were overpowered, his eyes swam in his head, his head gradually declined, and he fell into a deep sleep.

On awaking, he found himself on the green knoll from whence he had first seen the old man of the glen. He rubbed his eyes—it was a bright sunny morning. The birds were hopping and twittering among the bushes, and the eagle was wheeling aloft, and breasting the pure mountain breeze. "Surely," thought Rip, "I have not slept here all night." He recalled the occurrences before he fell asleep. The strange man with the keg of liquor—the mountain ravine—the wild retreat among the rocks—the wo-begone party at nine

8. Male jackets covering from neck to upper thighs, where they hooked to hose.
9. Feather. "Sugarloaf": cone-shaped.

1. Short, curved sword.
2. Minister.
3. Gin made in Holland.

pins—the flagon—"Oh! that flagon! that wicked flagon!" thought Rip—"what excuse shall I make to Dame Van Winkle?"

He looked round for his gun, but in place of the clean well-oiled fowling-piece, he found an old firelock lying by him, the barrel encrusted with rust, the lock falling off, and the stock worm-eaten. He now suspected that the grave roysters[4] of the mountain had put a trick upon him, and having dosed him with liquor, had robbed him of his gun. Wolf, too, had disappeared, but he might have strayed away after a squirrel or partridge. He whistled after him, shouted his name, but all in vain; the echoes repeated his whistle and shout, but no dog was to be seen.

He determined to revisit the scene of the last evening's gambol,[5] and if he met with any of the party, to demand his dog and gun. As he arose to walk he found himself stiff in the joints, and wanting in his usual activity. "These mountain beds do not agree with me," thought Rip, "and if this frolick should lay me up with a fit of the rheumatism, I shall have a blessed time with Dame Van Winkle." With some difficulty he got down into the glen: he found the gully up which he and his companion had ascended the preceding evening, but to his astonishment a mountain stream was now foaming down it, leaping from rock to rock, and filling the glen with babbling murmurs. He, however, made shift to scramble up its sides, working his toilsome way through thickets of birch, sassafras, and witch hazle, and sometimes tripped up or entangled by the wild grape vines that twisted their coils and tendrils from tree to tree, and spread a kind of network in his path.

At length he reached to where the ravine had opened through the cliffs, to the amphitheatre; but no traces of such opening remained. The rocks presented a high impenetrable wall, over which the torrent came tumbling in a sheet of feathery foam, and fell into a broad deep basin, black from the shadows of the surrounding forest. Here, then, poor Rip was brought to a stand. He again called and whistled after his dog; he was only answered by the cawing of a flock of idle crows, sporting high in air about a dry tree that overhung a sunny precipice; and who, secure in their elevation, seemed to look down and scoff at the poor man's perplexities. What was to be done? the morning was passing away, and Rip felt famished for his breakfast. He grieved to give up his dog and gun; he dreaded to meet his wife; but it would not do to starve among the mountains. He shook his head, shouldered the rusty firelock, and, with a heart full of trouble and anxiety, turned his steps homeward.

As he approached the village, he met a number of people, but none that he knew, which somewhat surprised him, for he had thought himself acquainted with every one in the country round. Their dress, too, was of a different fashion from that to which he was accustomed. They all stared at him with equal marks of surprise, and whenever they cast eyes upon him, invariably stroked their chins. The constant recurrence of this gesture, induced Rip, involuntarily, to do the same, when, to his astonishment, he found his beard had grown a foot long!

He had now entered the skirts of the village. A troop of strange children ran at his heels, hooting after him, and pointing at his gray beard. The

4. Revelers.
5. Frolicking or cavorting.

dogs, too, not one of which he recognized for his old acquaintances, barked at him as he passed. The very village seemed altered: it was larger and more populous. There were rows of houses which he had never seen before, and those which had been his familiar haunts had disappeared. Strange names were over the doors—strange faces at the windows—every thing was strange. His mind now began to misgive him, that both he and the world around him were bewitched. Surely this was his native village, which he had left but the day before. There stood the Kaatskill mountains—there ran the silver Hudson at a distance—there was every hill and dale precisely as it had always been—Rip was sorely perplexed—"That flagon last night," thought he, "has addled my poor head sadly!"

It was with some difficulty he found the way to his own house, which he approached with silent awe, expecting every moment to hear the shrill voice of Dame Van Winkle. He found the house gone to decay—the roof fallen in, the windows shattered, and the doors off the hinges. A half starved dog, that looked like Wolf, was skulking about it. Rip called him by name, but the cur snarled, showed his teeth, and passed on. This was an unkind cut indeed—"My very dog," sighed poor Rip, "has forgotten me!"

He entered the house, which, to tell the truth, Dame Van Winkle had always kept in neat order. It was empty, forlorn, and apparently abandoned. This desolateness overcame all his connubial fears—he called loudly for his wife and children—the lonely chambers rung for a moment with his voice, and then all again was silence.

He now hurried forth, and hastened to his old resort, the little village inn—but it too was gone. A large rickety wooden building stood in its place, with great gaping windows, some of them broken, and mended with old hats and petticoats, and over the door was painted, "The Union Hotel, by Jonathan Doolittle." Instead of the great tree that used to shelter the quiet little Dutch inn of yore, there now was reared a tall naked pole, with something on top that looked like a red night cap,[6] and from it was fluttering a flag, on which was a singular assemblage of stars and stripes—all this was strange and incomprehensible. He recognised on the sign, however, the ruby face of King George, under which he had smoked so many a peaceful pipe, but even this was singularly metamorphosed. The red coat was changed for one of blue and buff,[7] a sword was stuck in the hand instead of a scepter, the head was decorated with a cocked hat, and underneath was painted in large characters, GENERAL WASHINGTON.

There was, as usual, a crowd of folk about the door, but none that Rip recollected. The very character of the people seemed changed. There was a busy, bustling, disputatious tone about it, instead of the accustomed phlegm and drowsy tranquillity. He looked in vain for the sage Nicholas Vedder, with his broad face, double chin, and fair long pipe, uttering clouds of tobacco smoke instead of idle speeches; or Van Bummel, the schoolmaster, doling forth the contents of an ancient newspaper. In place of these, a lean bilious looking fellow, with his pockets full of handbills, was haranguing vehemently about rights of citizens—election—members of congress—

6. Limp, close-fitting cap adopted during the French Revolution as a symbol of liberty (such caps were worn by freed slaves in ancient Rome).
The pole is a "liberty pole," a tall flagstaff topped by a liberty cap.
7. Colors of the Revolutionary uniform.

liberty—Bunker's hill—heroes of seventy-six—and other words, that were a perfect Babylonish jargon[8] to the bewildered Van Winkle.

The appearance of Rip, with his long grizzled beard, his rusty fowling piece, his uncouth dress, and the army of women and children that had gathered at his heels, soon attracted the attention of the tavern politicians. They crowded around him, eyeing him from head to foot, with great curiosity.[9] The orator bustled up to him, and drawing him partly aside, inquired "which side he voted?" Rip stared in vacant stupidity. Another short but busy little fellow pulled him by the arm, and raising on tiptoe, inquired in his ear, "whether he was Federal or Democrat."[1] Rip was equally at a loss to comprehend the question; when a knowing, self-important old gentleman, in a sharp cocked hat, made his way through the crowd, putting them to the right and left with his elbows as he passed, and planting himself before Van Winkle, with one arm akimbo, the other resting on his cane, his keen eyes and sharp hat penetrating, as it were, into his very soul, demanded, in an austere tone, "what brought him to the election with a gun on his shoulder, and a mob at his heels, and whether he meant to breed a riot in the village?" "Alas! gentlemen," cried Rip, somewhat dismayed, "I am a poor quiet man, a native of the place, and a loyal subject of the King, God bless him!"

Here a general shout burst from the bystanders—"A tory! a tory! a spy! a refugee! hustle him! away with him!" It was with great difficulty that the self-important man in the cocked hat restored order; and having assumed a tenfold austerity of brow, demanded again of the unknown culprit, what he came there for, and whom he was seeking. The poor man humbly assured them that he meant no harm; but merely came there in search of some of his neighbours, who used to keep about the tavern.

"Well—who are they?—name them."

Rip bethought himself a moment, and inquired, "where's Nicholas Vedder?"

There was a silence for a little while, when an old man replied, in a thin piping voice, "Nicholas Vedder? why he is dead and gone these eighteen years! There was a wooden tombstone in the church yard that used to tell all about him, but that's rotted and gone too."

"Where's Brom Dutcher?"

"Oh he went off to the army in the beginning of the war; some say he was killed at the battle of Stoney-Point—others say he was drowned in a squall, at the foot of Antony's Nose.[2] I don't know—he never came back again."

"Where's Van Bummel, the schoolmaster?"

"He went off to the wars too, was a great militia general, and is now in Congress."

Rip's heart died away, at hearing of these sad changes in his home and friends, and finding himself thus alone in the world. Every answer puzzled

8. Irving conflates the story of Babel (Genesis 11.1–9) with the Babylonian captivity of the Jewish people (see, e.g., the Book of Jeremiah). "Bunker's hill": i.e., Bunker Hill, site, in Boston, of an early battle in the American Revolution.
9. For a contemporary painting depicting Rip Van Winkle's appearance in his village, see John Quidor's *The Return of Rip Van Winkle* (1829).
1. Political parties that developed in the Wash-

ington administration (1789–97), with Secretary of the U.S. Treasury Alexander Hamilton (1755–1804) leading the Federalists and Secretary of State Thomas Jefferson (1743–1826) leading the Democrats.
2. I.e., Anthony's Nose, a mountain near West Point. "Stoney-Point": i.e., Stoney Point, site of Revolutionary-era British fort that was captured and briefly held by the Continental Army.

him, too, by treating of such enormous lapses of time, and of matters which he could not understand: war—congress—Stoney-Point;—he had no courage to ask after any more friends, but cried out in despair, "does nobody here know Rip Van Winkle?"

"Oh, Rip Van Winkle!" exclaimed two or three, "Oh, to be sure! that's Rip Van Winkle yonder, leaning against the tree."

Rip looked, and beheld a precise counterpart of himself, as he went up the mountain: apparently as lazy, and certainly as ragged. The poor fellow was now completely confounded. He doubted his own identity, and whether he was himself or another man. In the midst of his bewilderment, the man in the cocked hat demanded who he was, and what was his name?

"God knows," exclaimed he, at his wit's end; "I'm not myself—I'm somebody else—that's me yonder—no—that's somebody else, got into my shoes—I was myself last night, but I fell asleep on the mountain, and they've changed my gun, and every thing's changed, and I'm changed, and I can't tell what's my name, or who I am!"

The bystanders began now to look at each other, nod, wink significantly, and tap their fingers against their foreheads. There was a whisper, also, about securing the gun, and keeping the old fellow from doing mischief. At the very suggestion of which, the self-important man in the cocked hat retired with some precipitation. At this critical moment a fresh likely woman pressed through the throng to get a peep at the graybearded man. She had a chubby child in her arms, which, frightened at his looks, began to cry. "Hush, Rip," cried she, "hush, you little fool, the old man wont hurt you." The name of the child, the air of the mother, the tone of her voice, all awakened a train of recollections in his mind.

"What is your name, my good woman?" asked he.

"Judith Gardenier."

"And your father's name?"

"Ah, poor man, his name was Rip Van Winkle; it's twenty years since he went away from home with his gun, and never has been heard of since—his dog came home without him; but whether he shot himself, or was carried away by the Indians, nobody can tell. I was then but a little girl."

Rip had but one question more to ask; but he put it with a faltering voice: "Where's your mother?"

Oh, she too had died but a short time since; she broke a blood vessel in a fit of passion at a New-England pedlar.

There was a drop of comfort, at least, in this intelligence. The honest man could contain himself no longer.—He caught his daughter and her child in his arms.—"I am your father!" cried he—"Young Rip Van Winkle once—old Rip Van Winkle now!—Does nobody know poor Rip Van Winkle!"

All stood amazed, until an old woman, tottering out from among the crowd, put her hand to her brow, and peering under it in his face for a moment, exclaimed, "Sure enough! it is Rip Van Winkle—it is himself. Welcome home again, old neighbour—Why, where have you been these twenty long years?"

Rip's story was soon told, for the whole twenty years had been to him but as one night. The neighbours stared when they heard it; some were seen to wink at each other, and put their tongues in their cheeks; and the self-important man in the cocked hat, who, when the alarm was over, had

returned to the field, screwed down the corners of his mouth, and shook his head—upon which there was a general shaking of the head throughout the assemblage.

It was determined, however, to take the opinion of old Peter Vanderdonk, who was seen slowly advancing up the road. He was a descendant of the historian of that name, who wrote one of the earliest accounts of the province.[3] Peter was the most ancient inhabitant of the village, and well versed in all the wonderful events and traditions of the neighbourhood. He recollected Rip at once, and corroborated his story in the most satisfactory manner. He assured the company that it was a fact, handed down from his ancestor the historian, that the Kaatskill mountains had always been haunted by strange beings. That it was affirmed that the great Hendrick Hudson, the first discoverer of the river and country, kept a kind of vigil there every twenty years, with his crew of the Half-moon, being permitted in this way to revisit the scenes of his enterprize, and keep a guardian eye upon the river, and the great city called by his name.[4] That his father had once seen them in their old Dutch dresses playing at nine pins in a hollow of the mountain; and that he himself had heard, one summer afternoon, the sound of their balls, like long peals of thunder.

To make a long story short, the company broke up, and returned to the more important concerns of the election. Rip's daughter took him home to live with her; she had a snug, well-furnished house, and a stout cheery farmer for a husband, whom Rip recollected for one of the urchins that used to climb upon his back. As to Rip's son and heir, who was the ditto of himself, seen leaning against the tree, he was employed to work on the farm; but evinced an hereditary disposition to attend to any thing else but his business.

Rip now resumed his old walks and habits; he soon found many of his former cronies, though all rather the worse for the wear and tear of time; and preferred making friends among the rising generation, with whom he soon grew into great favour.

Having nothing to do at home, and being arrived at that happy age when a man can do nothing with impunity, he took his place once more on the bench, at the inn door, and was reverenced as one of the patriarchs of the village, and a chronicle of the old times "before the war." It was some time before he could get into the regular track of gossip, or could be made to comprehend the strange events that had taken place during his torpor. How that there had been a revolutionary war—that the country had thrown off the yoke of old England—and that, instead of being a subject of his Majesty George the Third, he was now a free citizen of the United States. Rip, in fact, was no politician; the changes of states and empires made but little impression on him. But there was one species of despotism under which he had long groaned, and that was—petticoat government. Happily, that was at an end; he had got his neck out of the yoke of matrimony, and could go in and out whenever he pleased, without dreading the tyranny of Dame Van Winkle. Whenever her name was mentioned, however, he shook his head, shrugged

3. The Dutch-born lawyer Adriaen Van der Donck (c. 1618–20–c. 1655), a landowner in New Netherlands, published his promotional history of the colony in 1655.

4. Actually, a small town on the east bank of the Hudson River. "Hendrick Hudson": see n. 2, p. 998.

his shoulders, and cast up his eyes; which might pass either for an expression of resignation to his fate, or joy at his deliverance.

He used to tell his story to every stranger that arrived at Mr. Doolittle's hotel. He was observed, at first, to vary on some points every time he told it, which was, doubtless, owing to his having so recently awaked. It at last settled down precisely to the tale I have related, and not a man, woman, or child in the neighbourhood, but knew it by heart. Some always pretended to doubt the reality of it, and insisted that Rip had been out of his head, and that this was one point on which he always remained flighty. The old Dutch inhabitants, however, almost universally gave it full credit. Even to this day they never hear a thunder storm of a summer afternoon, about the Kaatskill, but they say Hendrick Hudson and his crew are at their game of nine pins; and it is a common wish of all henpecked husbands in the neighbourhood, when life hangs heavy on their hands, that they might have a quieting draught out of Rip Van Winkle's flagon.

NOTE

The foregoing tale, one would suspect, had been suggested to Mr. Knickerbocker by a little German superstition about Charles V. and the Kypphauser mountain;[5] the subjoined note, however, which he had appended to the tale, shows that it is an absolute fact, narrated with his usual fidelity:

"The story of Rip Van Winkle may seem incredible to many, but nevertheless I give it my full belief, for I know the vicinity of our old Dutch settlements to have been very subject to marvellous events and appearances. Indeed, I have heard many stranger stories than this, in the villages along the Hudson; all of which were too well authenticated to admit of a doubt. I have even talked with Rip Van Winkle myself, who, when last I saw him, was a very venerable old man, and so perfectly rational and consistent on every other point, that I think no conscientious person could refuse to take this into the bargain; nay, I have seen a certificate on the subject taken before a country justice, and signed with a cross, in the justice's own hand writing. The story, therefore, is beyond the possibility of doubt. D.K."

1819

5. Irving later changed "Charles V." (Holy Roman emperor, 1519–56) to "The Emperor Frederick *der Rothbart*" (i.e., Frederick Barbarossa: Holy Roman emperor, 1152–90). ("Rothbart" and "Barbarossa" both mean "red-beard.") In either form, this allusion is to a source other than the actual one, the story "Peter Klaus" in the folktales of J. C. C. N. Otmar (1800).

Selected Bibliographies

Reference Works

The first volume of Sacvan Bercovitch's *The Cambridge History of American Literature* (1994) serves as a rich guide to the literature of this period. The first two volumes of *A History of the Book in America* (2000; 2010) recount the history of print culture through 1840. The journal *Early American Literature* publishes critical studies of the literature from this period.

The digital *Archive of Americana* has an immense variety of resources, including *Early American Imprints I and II*, which contains virtually every printed work from British North America and the early republic up to 1820. *Early American Imprints* is based on the work of Charles Evans in *American Bibliography: A Chronological Dictionary of All Books, Pamphlets and Periodical Publications Printed in the United States of America . . .* Volume 1: *1639–1729* (1903) for items issued in what became the United States, updated in Clifford K. Shipton and James E. Mooney's two-volume *National Index of American Imprints through 1800* (1969). For items issued elsewhere, consult Joseph Sabin and Wilberforce Eames's twenty-nine volume *Biblioteca Americana: A Dictionary of Books Relating to America* (1868–1936). William Matthews and Roy Harvey Pearce's *American Diaries: An Annotated Bibliography of American Diaries Written Prior to the Year 1861* (1945) lists over three hundred diaries from before 1700; Matthews's *American Diaries in Manuscript, 1580–1954: A Descriptive Bibliography* (1974) adds three dozen others. Harold S. Jantz's *The First Century of New England Verse* (1944) includes a full bibliography. A valuable collection is *Seventeenth-Century American Poetry* (1968), compiled by Harrison T. Meserole. William J. Scheick and JoElla Doggett edited *Seventeenth-Century American Poetry: A Reference Guide* (1977). In 2007 the Library of America published a volume of seventeenth- and eighteenth-century American poetry, edited by David S. Shields.

For background on writings in English, the basic resource is the three-volume *American Writers before 1800: A Biographical and Critical Dictionary* (1983), edited by James A. Levernier and Douglas R. Wilmes, supplemented by *American Prose to 1820: A Guide to Information Sources* (1979), edited by Donald Yannella and John H. Roch. Useful guidance on obscure figures can be found in Evert A. and George L. Duyckinck's two-volume *Cyclopedia of American Literature* (1855).

The texts, introductory materials, and notes in the following volumes of the *Original Narratives of Early American History* series remain useful for non-English (and in some cases English) writers: *Narratives of New Netherland, 1609–1664* (1909), edited by J. Franklin Jameson; *Journal of Jasper Danckaerts* (1913), edited by Jameson and Bartett Burleigh James; *Narratives of Early Pennsylvania, West New Jersey, and Delaware, 1630–1707* (1912), edited by Albert Cook Myers; *The Spanish Explorers in the Southern United States, 1528–1543* (1907), edited by Frederick W. Hodge;

Spanish Exploration in the Southwest, 1542–1706 (1916), edited by Herbert Eugene Bolton; and *Early Narratives of the Northwest, 1634–1699* (1917), edited by Louise P. Kellogg. Henry C. Murphy's *Anthology of New Netherland* (1865) remains the single best source of translated texts (with biographical sketches) of three seventeenth-century writers. John J. Stoudt's *Pennsylvania German Poetry, 1685–1830* (1955) surveys one form of expression in depth.

Histories

Given the involvement of much early American writing in the large-scale expansion of Europe in the first imperial age, considerable insight can be gained from histori-cal studies of that process. For North America, David Beers Quinn's thorough *North America from Earliest Discovery to First Settlements* (1977) and his *England and the Discovery of America, 1481–1620* (1973) give detailed narrative and analysis, as do Gary Nash's *Red, White, and Black: The People of Early America* (1974) and Colin G. Calloway's *New Worlds for All: Indians, Europeans, and the Re-making of Early America* (1997; 2nd ed., 2013). J. H. Elliott provides a comparative history of Span-ish and English colonization in *Empires of the Atlantic World: Britain and Spain in America 1492–1830* (2006), while Daniel K. Richter compares European and Native American histories in *Before the Revolution: America's Ancient Pasts* (2011).

The most comprehensive single-volume history of American religion is Sydney E. Ahlstrom's *A Religious History of the American People* (1972). The Great Awakening is covered in Alan Heimert's *Religion and the American Mind* (1966), Jon Butler's *Awash in a Sea of Faith* (1990), and Patricia U. Bonomi's *Under the Cope of Heaven: Religion, Society, and Politics in Colonial America* (1986; rev. ed. 2003). In *The Democratization of American Christianity* (1989), Nathan O. Hatch extends consid-eration of the relationship between religion and politics into the nineteenth century. David D. Hall explores the complexities of lived religious experience in *Worlds of Wonder, Days of Judgment: Popular Religious Belief in Early New England* (1989). The religious lives of women are addressed in Susan Juster's *Disorderly Women: Sexual Politics and Evangelicalism in Revolutionary New England* (1996) and Cathe-rine Brekus's *Strangers and Pilgrims: Female Preaching in America, 1740–1845* (1998). Albert J. Raboteau addresses the impact of Christianity on enslaved communities in *Slave Religion: The "Invisible Institution" in the Antebellum South* (1978). In *The Indian Great Awakening: Religion and the Shaping of Native Cultures in Early Amer-ica* (2012), Linford D. Fisher examines how religious transformation reshaped Native societies.

Russel B. Nye's *The Cultural Life of the New Nation* (1960), Neil Harris's *The Art-ist in American Society: The Formative Years* (1966), Kenneth Silverman's *A Cul-tural History of the American Revolution* (1976), and Michael Kammen's *A Season of Youth* (1978) offer useful overviews of literary and artistic culture in the early American republic. Henry F. May's *The American Enlightenment* (1976) provides a similar service for philosophical issues, while Bruce Kuklick connects religion to American philosophy in *Churchmen and Philosophers: From Jonathan Edwards to John Dewey* (1987). Foundational histories of American women include Mary Beth Norton's *Liberty's Daughters* (1980) and *Founding Mothers and Daughters* (1996) and Linda Kerber's *Women of the Republic* (1980). Gordon Wood's *The Creation of the American Republic* (1969) and *The Radicalism of the American Revolution* (1996) are the chief guides to revolutionary political history. Wood's *Empire of Liberty: A History of the Early Republic 1789–1815* (2009) and the first part of Sean Wilentz's *The Rise of American Democracy: Jefferson to Lincoln* (2005) provide alternative interpretations of the postrevolutionary United States.

Theory and Criticism

William Carlos Williams's *In the American Grain* (1925) offers evocative discussions of early American writings. Howard Mumford Jones places early American culture in the context of Renaissance Europe in *O Strange New World: American Culture, the Formative Years* (1964), as does Stephen Greenblatt's *Marvelous Possessions: The Wonder of the New World* (1991). Roy Harvey Pearce's *Savagism and Civilization: A Study of the Indian and the American Mind* (1953; 1988) serves as a starting point for a body of criticism exploring the literary impact of the idea of the Indian on "the American mind." This approach is further developed in Richard M. Slotkin's *Regeneration through Violence: The Mythology of the American Frontier, 1600–1860* (1973); Jared Gardner likewise makes race central in *Master Plots: Race and the Founding of an American Literature, 1787–1845* (1998). In *The Machine in the Garden: Technology and the Pastoral Ideal in America* (1964), Leo Marx offers insightful readings of some Renaissance texts (such as Shakespeare's *The Tempest*) that reflect on the sense of lands newly available to the Old World; responses to the New World (and a reading, again, of *The Tempest*) are considered in Eric Cheyfitz's *The Poetics of Imperialism: Translation and Colonization from "The Tempest" to "Tarzan"* (expanded ed., 1997). In *Eloquence Is Power: Oratory and Performance in Early America* (2000), Sandra M. Gustafson emphasizes the verbal art of oratory as a catalyst in the Atlantic world crucible of indigenous American, European, and African cultures. In *A New World of Words: Redefining Early American Literature (1994),* William C. Spengemann argues for the centrality of early American texts in the transformation of Western writing generally. Paul Giles has several major books that situate early American literature in a variety of transnational contexts.

Important reflections on Native literature appear in Arnold Krupat's *The Voice in the Margin: Native American Literature and the Canon* (1989) and Robert Dale Parker's *The Invention of Native American Literature* (2003). Hilary Wyss's *Writing Indians: Literacy, Christianity, and Native Community in Early America* (2000), Maureen Konkle's *Writing Indian Nations* (2004), and Phillip Round's *Removable Type: Histories of the Book in Indian Country, 1663–1880* (2010) are important studies of early Native writings. In *American Lazarus: Religion and the Rise of African and Native American Literatures* (2003), Joanna Brooks considers the impact of evangelical Protestantism on early African American and Native American writers. A good study of African American authors of the Atlantic Rim is Vincent Carretta and Philip Gould's edited *Genius in Bondage* (1996); Gould has also contributed *Barbaric Traffic: Commerce and Antislavery in the Eighteenth-Century Atlantic World* (2003). Henry Louis Gates Jr. establishes an African background in *The Signifying Monkey: A Theory of African American Literary Criticism* (1989). Dana D. Nelson's *The Word in Black and White: Reading "Race" in American Literature, 1638–1867* (1992) is an important early study; Katy Chiles offers a nuanced approach to race and representation in *Transformable Race: Surprising Metamorphoses in the Literature of Early America* (2014).

Wayne Franklin gives attention to sixteenth-century works in *Discoveries, Explorers, Settlers: The Diligent Writers of Early America* (1979), and Kathleen Donegan offers stylistic analysis of colonization narratives in *Seasons of Misery: Catastrophe and Colonial Settlement in Early America* (2014). A feminist perspective guides Annette Kolodny's *The Lay of the Land: Metaphor as Experience and History in American Life and Letters* (1975). Ralph Bauer considers Spanish and English colonial writings in *The Cultural Geography of Colonial American Literatures: Empire, Travel, Modernity* (2003). Gordon Sayre's *"Les Sauvages Américains": Representations of Native Americans in French and English Colonial Literature* (1997) offers fresh comparative readings of English and French texts and the codes they developed for depicting encounters with Native American peoples. In *A Harmony of the Spirits:*

Translation and the Language of Community in Early Pennsylvania (2013), Patrick E. Erben considers colonial German and English theories of language. Understandings of Asia are the focus of James F. Egan's *Oriental Shadows: The Presence of the East in Early American Literature* (2011).

Perry Miller's foundational studies of the Puritans include *The New England Mind: The Seventeenth Century* (1939) and *The New England Mind: From Colony to Province* (1953), while several important essays (notably "The Marrow of Puritan Divinity" and "From Edwards to Emerson") are collected in *Errand into the Wilderness* (1956). Important correctives to Miller appear in Philip F. Gura's *A Glimpse of Sion's Glory: Puritan Radicalism in New England, 1620–1660* (1986) and Janice Knight's *Orthodoxies in Massachusetts* (1994). Andrew Delbanco's *The Puritan Ordeal* (1989) and Michael J. Colacurcio's *Godly Letters: The Literature of the American Puritans* (2006) provide comprehensive analysis. Sacvan Bercovitch's influential works include *The Puritan Origins of the American Self* (1975). Patricia Caldwell discusses Puritan "relations" in *The Puritan Conversion Narrative* (1983); Teresa Toulouse analyzes the formal dimensions of Puritan sermons in *The Art of Prophesying: New England Sermons and the Shaping of Belief* (1987); and Ivy Schweitzer examines the poetics of gender in *The Work of Self-Representation: Lyric Poetry in Colonial New England* (1991). Lisa M. Gordis looks at Puritan hermeneutics in *Opening Scripture: Bible Reading and Interpretive Authority in Puritan New England* (2002). Puritan missions and their literature are considered in Kristina Bross's *Dry Bones and Indian Sermons: Praying Indians in Colonial America* (2004) and Laura Stevens's *The Poor Indians: British Missionaries, Native Americans, and Colonial Sensibility* (2004). Media-centered studies include Matthew P. Brown's *The Pilgrim and the Bee: Reading Rituals and Book Culture in Early New England* (2007); Matt Cohen's *The Networked Wilderness: Communicating in Early New England* (2009); and Meredith Neuman's *Jeremiah's Scribes: Creating Sermon Literature in Puritan New England* (2013). Sarah Rivett examines the intersections of early modern science and Reformed theology in *The Science of the Soul in Colonial New England* (2011), while Cristobal Silva considers understandings of disease in *Miraculous Plagues: An Epidemiology of Early New England Narrative* (2011). Nan Goodman treats Puritan legal culture in *Banished: Common Law and the Rhetoric of Social Exclusion in Early New England* (2012).

Revolutionary-era rhetoric and political writing are the focus of Emory Elliot's *Revolutionary Writers: Literature and Authority in the New Republic 1725–1810* (1982), Jay Fliegelman's *Prodigals and Pilgrims: The American Revolution Against Patriarchal Authority 1750–1800* (1982), and Robert A. Ferguson's *Reading the Early Republic* (2004). The cultural dynamics shaping political life and the public sphere in the Revolutionary and early national periods are central to Michael Warner's *Letters of the Republic* (1990), Paul Downes's *Democracy, Revolution and Monarchism in Early American Literature* (2002), and Eric Slauter's *The State as a Work of Art: The Cultural Origins of the Constitution* (2009). Stephen Shapiro highlights economic relations in *The Culture and Commerce of the Early American Novel: Reading the Atlantic World-System* (2007). Aesthetics are a leading concern in Christopher Looby's *Voicing America: Language, Literary Form, and the Origins of the United States* (1996) and Edward Cahill's *Liberty of the Imagination: Aesthetic Theory, Literary Form, and Politics in the Early United States* (2012).

David S. Shields's *Oracles of Empire: Poetry, Politics, and Commerce in British America* (1990) addresses transatlantic poetry, while his *Civil Tongues and Polite Letters in America* (1997) examines eighteenth-century club and manuscript culture. Max Cavitch discusses one major poetic form in *American Elegy: The Poetry of Mourning from the Puritans to Whitman* (2006); Christopher N. Phillips examines another in *Epic in American Culture: Settlement to Reconstruction* (2012). On the American novel, Cathy S. Davidson's *Revolution and the Word* (1986) is a foundational study. Shirley Samuels focuses on fiction and gender relations in *Romances of*

the Republic: Women, the Family, and Violence in the Literature of the Early American Nation (1996), while Julia Stern analyzes sentiment as a moral and philosophical category that informs the early American novel in *The Plight of Feeling* (1997). Elizabeth Maddock Dillon's *The Gender of Freedom: Fictions of Liberalism and the Literary Public Sphere* (2004) offers an approach anchored in political theory. Marion Rust presents the challenges facing women writers in *Prodigal Daughters: Susanna Rowson's Early American Women* (2008). Walter J. Meserve's *An Emerging Entertainment* (1977); Jeffrey H. Richards's *Theater Enough* (1991) and *Drama, Theatre, and Identity in the New Republic* (2005); Heather Nathans's *Early American Theatre from the Revolution to Thomas Jefferson* (2003) and *Slavery and Sentiment on the American Stage, 1787–1861* (2009); and Dillon's *New World Drama: The Performative Commons in the Atlantic World, 1649–1849* (2014) treat drama in a variety of contexts. In *Democratic Personality: Popular Voice and the Trial of American Authorship* (1998), Nancy Ruttenberg explores the performative and literary creation of "popular voice," spanning from the Salem witchcraft crisis of 1692, through the Great Awakening, to the antebellum era.

Naturalist writings are the focus of Susan Scott Parrish's *American Curiosity: Cultures of Natural History in the Colonial British Atlantic World* (2006) and Christopher P. Iannini's *Fatal Revolutions: Natural History, West Indian Slavery, and the Routes of American Literature* (2012), while Martin Brückner's *Geographic Revolution in Early America: Maps, Literacy, and National Identity* (2006) examines the place of geography in the broader literary culture. Studies of the environment include Timothy Sweet's *American Georgics: Economy and Environment in American Literature, 1580–1864* (2002); Thomas Hallock's *From the Fallen Tree: Frontier Narratives, Environmental Politics, and the Roots of a National Pastoral, 1749–1826* (2003); Monique Allewaert's *Ariel's Ecology: Plantations, Personhood, and Colonialism in the American Tropics* (2013); and Michael Ziser's *Environmental Practice and Early American Literature* (2013). Jennifer Jordan Baker explores economic themes in *Securing the Commonwealth: Debt, Speculation, and Writing in the Making of Early America* (2005), as does Ed White from a different perspective in *The Backcountry and the City: Colonization and Conflict in Early America* (2005). Two treatments of literature and risk are Eric Wertheimer's *Underwriting: The Poetics of Insurance in America, 1722–1872* (2006) and Joseph Fichtelberg's *Risk Culture: Performance and Danger in Early America* (2010).

Authors

John Adams and Abigail Adams
Lyman H. Butterfield has edited the authoritative *Adams Family Correspondence* (1963). There are numerous biographies of John and Abigail Adams, including Page Smith's two-volume *John Adams* (1962), David McCullough's *John Adams* (2001), and Woody Holton's *Abigail Adams* (2009). Joseph J. Ellis's *First Family: Abigail and John Adams* (2010) focuses on the couple's relationship.

William Bradford
Bradford awaits a new editor of his history and other works, including his poems. Douglas Anderson's *William Bradford's Books: Of Plimmoth Plantation and the Printed Word*

(2003) is a major study of Bradford's history. Michelle Burnham has a chapter on Bradford's economic context in *Folded Selves: Colonial New England Writing in the World System* (2007).

Anne Bradstreet
The standard edition is now Jeannine Hensley's *The Works of Anne Bradstreet* (1967), with an introduction by Adrienne Rich. Readers interested in textual variants will want to consult *The Complete Works* (1981), edited by J. R. McElrath Jr. and Allen P. Robb. Useful critical discussions may be found in Josephine K. Piercy's *Anne Bradstreet* (1965), Elizabeth W. White's *Anne Bradstreet: The Tenth*

Muse (1971), Ann Stanford's *Anne Bradstreet: The Worldly Puritan* (1974), Rosamond Rosenmeier's *Anne Bradstreet* (1991), and Jeffrey Hammond's *Sinful Self, Saintly Self* (1993). Tamara Harvey's *Figuring Modesty in Feminist Discourse Across the Americas, 1633–1700* (2008) includes discussions of both Bradstreet and Sor Juana Inés de la Cruz.

Charles Brockden Brown

The standard edition of Brown's works is from Kent State University Press (1977–87). Useful editions of Brown's novels *Wieland, Ormond, Arthur Mervyn*, and *Edgar Huntly* were edited by Steven Shapiro and Philip Barnard in 2006–09. *Wieland* is available in a Norton Critical Edition, edited by Bryan Waterman in 2010. There is no recent comprehensive biography of Brown. Harry R. Warfel's biography *Charles Brockden Brown: American Gothic Novelist* (1949) can be supplemented with David Lee Clark's *Charles Brockden Brown: Pioneer Voice of America* (1952). Good studies of Brown's complete works include Norman S. Grabo's *The Coincidental Art of Charles Brockden Brown* (1981), Bill Christophersen's *The Apparition in the Glass: Charles Brockden Brown's American Gothic* (1993), and Steven Watts's *The Romance of Real Life: Charles Brockden Brown and the Origins of American Culture* (1994). Thematic studies include Michael Cody's *Charles Brockden Brown and the Literary Magazine: Cultural Journalism in the Early American Republic* (2004), Bryan Waterman's *Republic of Intellect: The Friendly Club of New York City and the Making of American Literature* (2007), and Mark Kamrath's *The Historicism of Charles Brockden Brown: Radical History and the Early Republic* (2010), as well as chapters in Caleb Crain's *American Sympathy: Men, Friendship, and Literature in the New Nation* (2001) and David Kazanjian's *The Colonizing Trick: National Culture and Imperial Citizenship in Early America* (2003). Robert S. Levine includes a chapter on Brown in his *Dislocating Race and Nation: Episodes in Nineteenth-Century American Literary Nationalism* (2008); an opposing view is found in John Carlos Rowe's *Literary Culture and U.S. Imperialism: From the Revolution to World War II* (2000).

Álvar Núñez Cabeza de Vaca

The definitive three-volume edition is *Álvar Núñez Cabeza de Vaca: His Account, His Life, and the Expedition of Pánfilo de Narváez* (1999), edited by Rolena Adorno and Patrick Charles Pautz. *The Narrative of Cabeza de Vaca* (2003), edited by Adorno and Pautz, is available as a single volume. Studies of Cabeza de Vaca's itinerary include Cleve Hallenbeck, *Álvar Núñez Cabeza de Vaca: The Journey and Route of the First European to Cross the Continent of North America, 1534–1536* (1940; 1971) and Carl O. Sauer's *Sixteenth-Century North America* (1971). Morris Bishop's *The Odyssey of Cabeza de Vaca* (1933) treats the whole of the life, including the later South American episodes. Lisa B. Voigt has an important discussion of Cabeza de Vaca in *Writing Captivity in the Early Modern Atlantic: Circulations of Knowledge and Authority in the Iberian and English Imperial Worlds* (2009).

Bartolomé de las Casas

Casas's *General History of the Indies* was finished by 1561 but remained unpublished until the late nineteenth century. Agustín Millares Carlo's Spanish edition of 1951 is useful. An abridged translation by Andrée M. Collard (1971) makes part of it readily available in English. Casas's most influential text, the *Brevissima relación*, is well rendered in Herma Briffault's translation, *The Devastation of the Indies: A Brief Account* (1974; 1992). Stafford Poole has translated *In Defense of the Indians* (1992), a major manuscript treatise from the early 1550s. Studies of Casas include Lewis Hanke's *Bartolomé de las Casas: An Interpretation of His Life and Writings* (1951), Henry Raup Wagner and Helen Rand Parish's *The Life and Writings of Bartolomé de las Casas* (1967), and Daniel Castro's *Another Face of Empire: Bartolomé de las Casas, Indigenous Rights, and Ecclesiastical Imperialism* (2007).

Christopher Columbus

The best bilingual edition is Cecil Jane's *Select Documents Illustrating the Four Voyages of Columbus* (1930–33; 1988). Columbus's journal survives only in summaries and unreliable transcriptions by others. The best text is Oliver Dunn and James E. Kelley's bilingual *The Diario of Christopher Columbus's First Voyage to America, 1492–93* (1989); on the problems associated with this text (and others), see David Heninge's *In Search of Columbus: The Sources for the First Voyage* (1991). Biographies include Samuel Eliot Morison's now somewhat dated *Admiral of the Ocean Sea* (1942) and Kirkpatrick Sale's contentious *The Conquest of Paradise: Christopher Columbus and the Columbian Legacy* (1990). James Axtell's *After Columbus* (1988) and *Beyond 1492* (1992) are informative.

J. Hector St. John de Crèvecoeur

Dennis D. Moore has produced a new edition of *Letters from an American Farmer and Other Essays* (2013). The best biographies are by Thomas Philbrick (1970) and Gay Wilson Allen and Roger Asselineau (1987). Important treatments can be found in Ed White's *The*

Backcountry and the City (2005) and Wil Verhoeven's *Americomania and the French Revolution Debate in Britain, 1789–1802* (2013).

Jonathan Edwards
Yale University Press has published Edwards's complete works in twenty-six volumes (1957–2008). The best single-volume collection of Edwards's writings is *A Jonathan Edwards Reader* (1995), also from Yale. The best biographies are George Marsden's *Jonathan Edwards: A Life* (2003) and Philip F. Gura's *Jonathan Edwards: America's Evangelical* (2005). Daniel B. Shea Jr. includes a discussion of the *Personal Narrative* in his *Spiritual Autobiography in Early America* (1968). Sandra M. Gustafson highlights Sarah Pierpont Edwards in "Jonathan Edwards and the Reconstruction of 'Feminine' Speech" (*American Literary History*, 1994). Major essay collections are *Jonathan Edwards and the American Experience* (1988), edited by Nathan O. Hatch and Harry S. Stout, and *Jonathan Edwards's Writings* (1996), edited by Stephen J. Stein. See also M. X. Lesser's *Reading Jonathan Edwards: An Annotated Bibliography in Three Parts, 1729–2005* (2008).

Olaudah Equiano
Werner Sollors edited *The Interesting Narrative* in a 2001 Norton Critical Edition. Sidney Kaplan discusses the American publication of Equiano's *Narrative* in *The Black Presence in the Era of the American Revolution, 1770–1800* (1973). Vincent Carretta's *Equiano, the African: Biography of a Self-Made Man* (2005) is a major treatment of the life.

The Federalist
A very useful introduction to *The Federalist* papers is found in Benjamin Fletcher Wright's edition of 1961. On Alexander Hamilton, see Ron Chernow's *Alexander Hamilton* (2004); on James Madison, see Jack N. Rakove's *James Madison and the Creation of the American Republic* (1990); on John Jay, see Walter Stahr's *John Jay: Founding Father* (2005). Several of the works on the Revolutionary period listed in the theory and criticism section include readings of *The Federalist*. For a sustained reading, see Joseph Fichtelberg's "The Aesthetics of the Federalist" in *Early American Literature* (2014).

Hannah Foster
There is no full-scale modern biography of Foster, but see Cathy Davidson's introduction to *The Coquette* (1986) and her *Revolution and the Word* (1986). Helpful readings can be found in Julia Stern's *The Plight of Feeling* (1997) and Sharon M. Harris's *Redefining the Political Novel* (1995).

Benjamin Franklin
The Papers of Benjamin Franklin are being published by Yale University Press. The standard biography is J. A. Leo Lemay's three-volume *The Life of Benjamin Franklin* (2006). Stacy Schiff focuses on Franklin's French years in *A Great Improvisation: Franklin, France, and the Birth of America* (2006), while Carla J. Mulford situates Franklin in an imperial context in *Benjamin Franklin and the Ends of Empire* (2015). A good selection of Franklin's writings may be found in *Benjamin Franklin: Representative Selection* (1936), edited by F. L. Mott and C. L. Jorgensen. Nian-Sheng Huang surveys two hundred years of American response to Franklin in *Benjamin Franklin in America* (1994). Joyce E. Chaplin assembles D. H. Lawrence's famous attack on Franklin and several other major readings of the *Autobiography* in the 2012 Norton Critical Edition. Douglas Anderson analyzes text and context in *The Unfinished Life of Benjamin Franklin* (2012). Anderson's *The Radical Enlightenments of Benjamin Franklin* (1997) has a different emphasis. Mitchell Robert Breitwieser traces significant continuities in *Cotton Mather and Benjamin Franklin: The Price of Representative Personality* (1984).

Philip Freneau
The standard edition of Freneau's poetry is F. L. Pattee's three-volume *The Poems of Philip Freneau* (1902–07). Lewis Leary, who edited *The Last Poems of Philip Freneau* (1945), wrote the best biography, *That Rascal Freneau: A Study in Literary Failure* (1941). Harry H. Clark provides a useful introduction to Freneau in his edited volume *Poems of Freneau* (1929). Richard C. Vitzhum offers a study of Freneau's lyrics in *Land and Sea* (1978).

Washington Irving
The authoritative edition is *The Complete Works of Washington Irving* (1969–). The Library of America has published Irving's *History, Tales, and Sketches* (1983), along with two other volumes of his writings. Two recent biographies are Andrew Burstein's *The Original Knickerbocker: The Life of Washington Irving* (2007) and Brian Jay Jones's *Washington Irving: An American Original* (2008). For recent critical work, see David Dowling's *Literary Partnerships and the Marketplace* (2012) and Walter Hugo's *Sanctuaries in Washington Irving's The Sketch Book* (2014). A more complete bibliography appears in Volume B.

Thomas Jefferson
Princeton University Press is publishing the *Papers of Thomas Jefferson*. The most comprehensive biography is Dumas Malone's six-volume *Jefferson and His Time* (1948–81);

Malone's concise article on Jefferson in *The Dictionary of American Biography* (1933) is very helpful. Joseph J. Ellis's *American Sphinx: The Character of Thomas Jefferson* (1997) is an important recent biography. Annette Gordon-Reed examines Jefferson's relationship with Sally Hemings and her extended family in *The Hemingses of Monticello: An American Family* (2008). Frank Shuffelton produced two annotated bibliographies of work on Jefferson, extending from 1826 to 1990, as well as an edited collection of critical writings. Other major studies include Garry Wills's *Inventing America: Jefferson's Declaration of Independence* (1978), Jay Fliegelman's *Declaring Independence* (1993), Pauline Maier's *American Scripture* (1997), and Danielle Allen's *Our Declaration* (2014).

Cotton Mather

Kenneth Silverman's *The Life and Times of Cotton Mather* (1984) supersedes earlier biographies. The introduction to Kenneth B. Murdock's *Selections from Cotton Mather* (1926) is still useful, as are David Levin's *Cotton Mather: The Young Life of the Lord's Remembrancer* (1978) and Robert Middlekauff's *The Mathers: Three Generations of Puritan Intellectuals* (1971). Sacvan Bercovich has written about Mather in *Major Writers of Early American Literature* (1972), edited by E. H. Emerson, and in *The Puritan Origins of the American Self* (1975). Mitchell Robert Breitwieser takes a different approach in *Cotton Mather and Benjamin Franklin: The Price of Representative Personality* (1984).

Thomas Morton

The introduction to Charles Francis Adams's edition of *New English Canaan* (1883) answers a number of questions about the life of this enigmatic figure. The interested student will also want to read Donald F. Connors's *Thomas Morton* (1969) and Jack Dempsey's *Thomas Morton of Merrymount* (2000). Michelle Burnham discusses Morton's economic activities in *Folded Selves: Colonial New England Writing in the World System* (2007).

Judith Sargent Murray

The best biographical study is Sheila L. Skemp's *First Lady of Letters: Judith Sargent Murray and the Struggle for Female Independence* (2009). *Selected Writings* (1995), edited by Sharon M. Harris, offers useful commentary on Murray's work. A modern reprint of *The Gleaner* is available with an introduction by Nina Baym (1992).

Native American Oral Traditions

There is an extensive body of scholarship on Native American verbal arts originating in folklore and ethnography, with notable contributions including Dell Hymes's *"In Vain I Tried to Tell You": Essays in Native American Ethnopoetics* (1981) and Dennis Tedlock's *The Spoken Word and the Work of Interpretation* (1983). Barre Toelken's *The Dynamics of Folklore* (rev. ed., 1996) is an excellent survey of oral materials by someone specifically interested in Native American verbal arts. There is also a body of scholarship contrasting oral and written modes of expression, which needs to be approached carefully to avoid reductive characterizations. Walter Ong's *Orality and Literacy: The Technologizing of the Word* (1982) and Eric Havelock's *The Muse Learns to Write* (1986) should be supplemented with Brian V. Street's *Literacy in Theory and Practice* (1984). In *Eloquence Is Power* (2000), Sandra M. Gustafson emphasizes the symbolic dimensions of speech and text in the British colonial setting, with a focus on Native speech. Two recent analyses of the treaty literature are Andrew Newman's *On Records: Delaware Indians, Colonists, and the Media of History and Memory* (2012) and Jeffrey Glover's *Paper Sovereigns: Anglo-Native Treaties and the Law of Nations, 1604–1664* (2014).

Scholarship on the Iroquois and their creation story begins with Lewis Henry Morgan's *League of the Iroquois* (1972; orig. publ., 1851). Seneca ethnologist Arthur C. Parker's *Seneca Myths and Folk Tales* (1923) is also useful. Daniel K. Richter's *The Ordeal of the Longhouse: The Peoples of the Iroquois League in the Era of European Colonization* (1992) covers the basic elements of Iroquois language, culture, and history and begins with an overview of Iroquois cosmogonic myths. For David Cusick, see Susan Kalter's "Finding a Place for David Cusick in Native American Literary History" (2002) and Maureen Konkle, *Writing Indian Nations* (2004).

The earliest published version of the Navajo creation story is that of Washington Matthews, which appears in the first chapters of his *Navaho Legends* (1897; 2002). Other versions include Hasteen Klah's telling, which is recorded in Mary Wheelwright's *Navajo Creation Myth: The Story of the Emergence by Hasteen Klah* (1942); the version in anthropologist Aileen O'Bryan's *The Diné: Origin Myths of the Navaho Indians* (1956); and literary scholar Paul Zolbrod's account, with copious and detailed notes, in *Diné Bahané: The Navajo Creation Story* (1984). Gary Witherspoon's *Language and Art in the Navajo Universe* (1977) remains a good introduction to the subjects referenced in its title.

The only book-length treatment of Native American oral trickster tales is Franchot Ballinger's *Living Sideways: Tricksters in American*

Indian Oral Traditions (2004). Arnold Krupat revisits trickster tales in chapter 1 of *All That Remains* (2009). In his insightful *Trickster Makes This World: Mischief, Myth, and Art* (1998), Lewis Hyde deals with Native American tricksters, among others. Paul Radin's *The Trickster: A Study in American Indian Mythology* (1956, 1972), with commentaries by Karl Kerenyi and C. G. Jung, has achieved something of a classic status, although Radin's psychological interpretations have not worn well. Barbara Babcock-Abraham's "'A Tolerated Margin of Mess': The Trickster and His Tales Reconsidered," *Journal of the Folklore Institute* (1975), is still fresh.

Samson Occom
Joanna Brooks has edited The *Collected Writings of Samson Occom, Mohegan: Leadership and Literature in Eighteenth-Century Native America* (2006). Occom's "Short Narrative" was first published by Berndt Peyer in *The Elders Wrote: An Anthology of Early Prose by North American Indians, 1768–1931* (1982), and it is still worth consulting. Peyer's *The Tutor'd Mind: Indian Missionary-Writers in Antebellum America* (1997) continues to be useful as well. There are numerous readings of Occom's execution sermon, including a valuable one in Karen A. Weyler's *Empowering Words: Outsiders and Authorship in Early America* (2013).

Thomas Paine
Moncure D. Conway, who edited the four-volume *The Writings of Thomas Paine* (1894–96), wrote a valuable life of Paine (1892). More-recent biographies are by David F. Hawke (1974) and John Keane (1995). H. H. Clark's *Thomas Paine: Representative Selections* (1944) contains a helpful introduction. Eric Foner's *Tom Paine and Revolutionary America* (1976) puts Paine in context. Edward Larkin has written the major critical study *Thomas Paine and the Literature of Revolution* (2005) and edited a helpful critical edition of *Common Sense* (2004).

Mary Rowlandson
The introduction to Neal Salisbury's 1997 edition of the *Narrative* describes the major features of Rowlandson's life and world. Richard Slotkin's *Regeneration through Violence* (1973) contains an influential discussion of Rowlandson's captivity. Mitchell Robert Breitwieser focuses on affect in *American Puritanism and the Defense of Mourning: Religion, Grief, and Ethnology in Mary White Rowlandson's Captivity Narrative* (1990). The transatlantic significance of Rowlandson's narrative is central to Nancy Armstrong and Leonard Tennenhouse's *The Imaginary Puritan: Literature, Intellectual Labor, and the Origins of Personal Life* (1994). Christopher Castiglia explores issues of gender and captivity in *Bound and Determined: Captivity, Culture-Crossing, and White Womanhood from Mary Rowlandson to Patty Hearst* (1996), and, from a different perspective, so does Teresa Toulouse in *The Captive's Position: Female Narrative, Male Identify and Royal Authority in Colonial New England* (2007)

Samuel Sewall
The Diary of Samuel Sewall, 1674–1729 (1973), edited by M. Halsey Thomas, is the standard edition. Thomas's edition includes *The Selling of Joseph*, but the introduction and commentary in Sidney Kaplan's edition (1969) is valuable for what it tells us about slavery in New England. Ola E. Winslow has written a succinct biography (1964).

John Smith
Philip L. Barbour produced the definitive three-volume edition of Smith's writings, *The Complete Works of Captain John Smith* (1986). The Library of America has published a volume of his writings (2007). Critical treatments include Barbour's *The Three Worlds of Captain John Smith* (1964), Everett H. Emerson's *Captain John Smith* (1971), and J. A. Leo Lemay's *The American Dream of Captain John Smith* (1991). A useful descriptive bibliography can be found in *American Prose to 1820* (1979), edited by Donald Yanella and John H. Roche.

Annis Boudinot Stockton
Carla Mulford's *Only for the Eye of a Friend: The Poems of Annis Boudinot Stockton* (1995) collects all of Stockton's poems and provides a thorough introduction to her life and work. Susan M. Stabile, in *Memory's Daughters: The Culture of Remembrance in Eighteenth-Century America* (2004), treats the importance of women's poetry in that period. Stockton's literary network figures in *Milcah Martha Moore's Book: A Commonplace Book from Revolutionary America* (1997), edited by Karin Wulf and Catherine Blecki.

Edward Taylor
Donald E. Stanford's standard edition, *The Poems of Edward Taylor* (1960), can be supplemented with Daniel Patterson's *Edward Taylor's God Determinations and Preparatory Meditations: A Critical Edition* (2003). Francis Murphy edited Taylor's *Diary* (1964). The best critical biography (1961; rev. ed., 1988) is by Norman S. Grabo, who also edited Taylor's *Christographia* sermons (1962) and *Treatise Concerning the Lord's Supper* (1966). Thomas M. Davis and Virginia L. Davis edited *The Minor Poetry* (1981) with an informative

introduction. Thomas Davis also published *A Reading of Edward Taylor* (1992). Other critical studies include William J. Scheick's *The Will and the Word* (1974), Karen E. Rowe's *Saint and Singer* (1986), and Jeffrey Hammond's *Sinful Self, Saintly Self* (1993).

Royall Tyler

In *Early American Drama* (1997), Jeffrey Richards reprints *The Contrast* as well as several other plays that establish Tyler's context. Marius Peladeau collected *The Verse of Royall Tyler* (1968). Caleb Crain provides a valuable introduction in his edition of Tyler's novel *The Algerine Captive* (2002). The standard biography is G. Thomas Tanselle's *Royall Tyler* (1967).

Phillis Wheatley

Julian D. Mason produced the standard edition of Wheatley's poems (1966; rev. ed., 1989). William H. Robinson's *Phillis Wheatley: A Bio-Bibliography* (1981) establishes the background. Vincent Carretta has written the new standard biography, *Phillis Wheatley: Biography of a Genius in Bondage* (2014). John C. Shields provides critical treatments in *Phillis Wheatley's Poetics of Liberation: Backgrounds and Contexts* (2008) and *Phillis Wheatley and the Romantics* (2010). April Langley considers the African elements of Wheatley's poetry in *The Black Aesthetic Unbound: Theorizing the Dilemma of Eighteenth-Century African American Literature* (2008).

Michael Wigglesworth

Kenneth B. Murdock's edition of *The Day of Doom* (1929) includes a valuable introduction. Edmund S. Morgan edited Wigglesworth's *Diary* (1970). The standard life is Richard Crowder's *No Featherbed to Heaven* (1962). Critical treatments include Jeffrey Hammond's *Sinful Self, Saintly Self* (1993) and Amy Morris's *Popular Measures: Poetry and Church Order in Seventeenth-century Massachusetts* (2005).

Roger Williams

Major studies of Williams include Perry Miller's *Roger Williams: His Contribution to the American Tradition* (1953), Ola E. Winslow's *Roger Williams* (1957), Edmund S. Morgan's *Roger Williams: The Church and the State* (1967), and Henry Chupack's *Roger Williams* (1969). Perry Miller's introduction to *The Complete Writings of Roger Williams* (1963), Vol. 7, is also valuable. Important readings include Anne G. Myles's "Dissent and the Frontier of Translation: Roger Williams's *A Key into the Language of America*" in *Possible Pasts: Becoming Colonial in Early America* (2000) and Michelle Burnham's chapter on Williams's economic activities in *Folded Selves: Colonial New England Writing in the World System* (2007).

John Winthrop

The standard edition of *The Journal* was edited by Richard S. Dunn, James Savage, and Laetitia Yeandle (1996), with a valuable introduction by Dunn. Dunn and Yeandle previously prepared an abridged and modernized edition of *The Journal* (1966). *The Winthrop Papers, 1498–1654* (1929–) is in preparation under the auspices of the Massachusetts Historical Society, Boston. Dunn's *Puritans and Yankees: The Winthrop Dynasty of New England* (1962) and Edmund S. Morgan's *The Puritan Dilemma: The Story of John Winthrop* (1958) are among the best critical and biographical studies.

PERMISSIONS ACKNOWLEDGMENTS

IMAGE CREDITS

COLOR INSERT CREDITS

TEXT CREDITS

Publishing Division of the University. Reprinted with the permission of the University of Oklahoma Press via the Copyright Clearance Center.

Paul Radin: From "The Winnebago Trickster Cycle" from THE TRICKSTER: A STUDY IN AMERICAN INDIAN MYTHOLOGY by Paul Radin, copyright © 1956, published by Routledge & Kegan Paul Ltd. Reproduced with permission of Taylor & Francis Books UK.

Rebecca Samuel: From AMERICAN JEWRY: DOCUMENTS, EIGHTEENTH CENTURY, PRIMARILY HITHERTO UNPUBLISHED MANUSCRIPTS by Jacob Rader Marcus. Reproduced with permission of Hebrew Union College Press via the Copyright Clearance Center.

Edward Taylor: From THE POEMS OF EDWARD TAYLOR, ed. by Donald E. Stanford. Copyright © 1960, renewed 1988 by Donald E. Stanford. Published by University of North Carolina Press in 1989. Reprinted by permission of Don D. Stanford.

Phillis Wheatley: From THE POEMS OF PHILLIS WHEATLEY, ed. and with an introduction by Julian D. Mason, Jr. Copyright © 1966 by The University of North Carolina Press, renewed 1989. Used by permission of the publisher. www.uncpress.unc.edu.

John Winthrop: Reprinted by permission of the publisher from THE JOURNAL OF JOHN WINTHROP 1630–1649, Abridged Edition, ed. by Richard S. Dunn, James Savage, and Laetitia Yeandle. Cambridge, Mass.: The Belknap Press of Harvard University Press. Copyright © 1996 by the President and Fellows of Harvard College.

Index